Christian Dogmatics

Contributors

Carl E. Braaten is Professor of Systematic Theology at the Lutheran School of Theology at Chicago, Illinois.

Gerhard O. Forde is Professor of Systematic Theology at Luther Northwestern Theological Seminary in St. Paul, Minnesota.

Philip J. Hefner is Professor of Systematic Theology at the Lutheran School of Theology at Chicago.

Robert W. Jenson is Professor of Religion at St. Olaf College, Northfield, Minnesota.

Hans Schwarz is Professor of Protestant Theology at the University of Regensburg, Federal Republic of Germany.

Paul R. Sponheim is Professor of Systematic Theology at Luther Northwestern Theological Seminary in St. Paul, Minnesota.

CONTENTS

3. The Effect of Sin ... 409
   Sinner and Creature
   Bondage and Responsibility

4. Metaphysical and Natural Evil ... 433
   Finitude
   Suffering

5. The Work of God against Evil ... 447
   The Continuity of God
   The Decisiveness of God
   The Directivity of God

SIXTH LOCUS
The Person of Jesus Christ
by Carl E. Braaten
465

Introduction ... 469

1. The Nature and Method of Christology ... 473
   What Is Christology?
   History, Dogmatics, and Faith
   The Starting Point of Christology

2. The Historical Jesus and the Kingdom of God ... 483
   Jesus' Expectation of the Kingdom of God
   The Genesis of Christology in the New Testament

3. Classical Christology and Its Subsequent Criticism ... 497
   The Identification of Jesus with God
   Christological Heresies
   From the Creed of Chalcedon to the Formula of Concord
   Criticism of the Dogma

4. The True Humanity of Jesus Christ ... 517
   The Historicity of Jesus Christ
   The Humanity of Jesus Christ
   The Identity of the Earthly Jesus and the Risen Christ
   Jesus Christ as the Eschatological One

CONTENTS

5. The True Divinity of Jesus Christ — 527
   The Story of God Incarnate
   The Historicity of God
   The Divinity of Christ
   An Ontological Interpretation of the Incarnation

6. The Humiliation and Exaltation of Jesus Christ — 545
   The Preexistence of Christ
   The Virgin Birth
   The Crucifixion of Jesus
   Jesus' Descent into Hell
   The Resurrection
   The Ascension
   The Session at the Right Hand of God
   The Coming in Glory

7. The Uniqueness and Universality of Jesus Christ — 557
   The Heritage of Exclusiveness
   The Uniqueness of Jesus Christ
   The Universality of Jesus Christ

VOLUME 2

SEVENTH LOCUS
The Work of Christ
by Gerhard O. Forde

Introduction

1. The Shape of the Tradition
   The Scriptural Tradition
   Vicarious Satisfaction of Divine Justice
   The Triumph of Divine Love
   Victory over the Tyrants

2. Luther's Theology of the Cross
   The Debate over Luther's View
   The Reversal of Direction
   Critical Estimates

3. Reconciliation with God
   Cur Deus Homo?
   The Necessity for Atonement

4. Atonement as Actual Event
   Toward a New Understanding of Sacrifice
   The "Accident"

EIGHTH LOCUS
The Holy Spirit
by Robert W. Jenson

Introduction

1. The Spirit That Spoke by the Prophets
   The Hebrew Scriptures
   The New Testament
   The Creedal Tradition

CONTENTS

2. Pneumatological Soteriology
   The Doctrine of Grace
   Justification by Faith
   Predestination

3. Spirit-Discourse as the Church's Self-interpretation
   Ecclesial Christology
   The Spirit and God
   The Spirit and the Letter
   The Spirit and the Word
   The Spirit and History

4. Cosmic Spirit
   The Logic of Cosmic Pneumatology
   The Freedom of History
   The Spontaneity of Natural Process
   The Beauty of All Things

NINTH LOCUS
The Church
By Philip J. Hefner

Introduction

1. The Doctrine of the Church—Focus and Challenges
   The Trinitarian Context for the Doctrine of the Church
   Challenges Growing Out of the Church's Embodiment
   The Challenge to Correlate the Faith of the Church and Our Experience of the Church
   The Impossibility of Doctrinal Finality

2. The Being of the Church
   The Church's Own Testimony: One, Holy, Catholic, and Apostolic
   Significant Images from the Tradition: People of God and Body of Christ
   Models That Summarize the Theological Tradition: Institution, Mystical Communion, Sacrament, Herald, Servant
   The Being of the Church in Light of Its Origins

3. Basic Elements of the Church's Life
   Marks of the Church

Ministry
Liturgy and Sacraments
Preaching and Teaching
Community of Love and Care of Souls
Mission
Church Order or Organization
The Church's Concreteness as Source of Theological Truth
The Concept of Adiaphora

4. The Church and the Kingdom of God
   Possibilities for Relating Church and Kingdom of God
   The Church Transparent to the Kingdom

TENTH LOCUS
The Means of Grace
by Hans Schwarz and Robert W. Jenson

Introduction

Part One: The Word
by Hans Schwarz

1. The Biblical Understanding of the Word of God
   The Word as the Means of God's Self-Disclosure
   The History-Making Power of God's Word
   Jesus Christ as God's Final Word

2. The Dynamics of God's Word
   The Judging and Liberating Word: Law and Gospel
   The Word as Guidance: Third Use and Penance
   The Dialogical Word: Prayer and Liturgy
   The Empirical Word: Miracles

Part Two: The Sacraments
by Robert W. Jenson

3. Sacraments of the Word
   Commands
   Promises

CONTENTS

    Visible Words
    Fact and Meaning
    Actual Liturgy

4. Baptism
    The Command
    The Promises
    Regeneration
    The Integrity of Baptism
    The Uses of Baptism

5. The Supper
    The Command
    The Authenticity of the Supper
    The Promises
    Eucharist
    Ego Berengarius . . .

6. The Return to Baptism
    Rites of the Spirit
    Penance
    Ordination
    Healing
    Marriage

ELEVENTH LOCUS
Christian Life
by Gerhard O. Forde

Introduction

1. Justification
    Justification by Grace
    Justification by Faith
    Law, Gospel, and Conscience

2. Justification and Sanctification
    The Separation of Sanctification from Justification
    The Unity of Justification and Sanctification

3. Justification and This World
   Justification and the Law
   The Self as God's Creature
   This World as God's Creation

4. Justification Today
   The Question of Relevance
   Relevance: The Life of the Individual
   Relevance: The World Vision

TWELFTH LOCUS
Eschatology
by Hans Schwarz

Introduction

1. The Biblical View of the Future
   A Definition
   The Nascent Eschatology of the Old Testament
   The Eschatological Horizon of the New Testament

2. Continuing Tensions in the History of Eschatology
   The Gradual Transformation
   The Enthusiastic Fervor

3. Major Currents in Christian Eschatology
   The Tension between Promise and Fulfillment
   The Emphasis on the Individual Person
   The Emphasis on the Corporate Dimension
   The Cosmic Aspect of Eschatology

4. Secular Options
   Existentialism
   Marxist Communism
   Secular Humanism

5. The Content of Christian Hope
   The Starting Point of Christian Eschatology
   Death and Resurrection
   The Last Judgment
   Parousia and the Kingdom of God

Preface

The conception of this book took place in the late 1970s as the editors again remarked on the fact that almost all our usable dogmatics have been imported from Europe. In the decades since World War II we have used all or parts of the imposing volumes of the continental theologians—Emil Brunner, Karl Barth, Gustaf Aulén, Regin Prenter, and Paul Tillich. As teachers of dogmatic and systematic theology, we have had no textbooks that reflect the American context from the standpoint of the Lutheran tradition. We set out to rectify the situation by means of a team of authors.

Our intention in producing a complete dogmatics, with emphasis on information about the dogmatic tradition, is to serve two purposes above all: We hope our work will be a textbook in theological instruction and a resource for those who practice the arts of ministry. It lies in the nature of a work such as this to seek the widest possible churchly acceptance, since dogmatics speaks from the church to the church, by way of disciplined reflection on the sources of its faith and traditions. But theology at present is fragmented into an unusually large number of schools and movements. The fact of theological pluralism is inescapable. We have chosen to make a virtue out of a necessity by way of multiple authorship. A dogmatics by any one person would likely be received only as advocacy for the positions of that person's own school of thought, and thus fail to command the wide churchly use inherent in the notion of dogmatics. Hoping to avoid this fate, we offer this joint work of six authors.

Although all of us stand within the Lutheran tradition, the differences among us, and the consequent inconsistencies in the book, are considerable. Those who like to label theologians—"hope," "process," etc.—will by our calculations need seven or more labels for the six of us. The authors have different concentrations of historical knowledge; some refer most naturally to the fathers, others to the reformers, and still others to modern theologians. At some points the authors simply disagree, and this disagreement occasionally reaches the point of contradiction. We will leave it to the readers to discover the places where this occurs. Whether these differences and disagreements be taken as bane or blessing, they follow from the initial reason for multiple authorship.

PREFACE

Yet we do not think we are presenting a mere collection of essays. A draft of each *locus* has been read and criticized by the whole group. Perhaps more important, the likenesses among us as authors are as great as the differences. All of us understand ourselves by intention and calling to be churchly theologians; the goal of our work is primarily the liveliness and authenticity of the gospel, and only secondarily increased understanding of religion or metaphysical construction. All of us have written theological works of other kinds—exegetical, historical, apologetic, liturgical, homiletical, and so on—but here we are doing dogmatics in the classical tradition. All of us are of the same theological generation, and therefore influenced by the important theologians of the mid-twentieth century: Barth, Bultmann, Tillich, et al. We find it possible to disagree without either anathemas or relativism; the divergences between us are probably not greater than have always been usual in the theologically contentious Lutheran tradition from which we come. And we are indeed all Lutherans; this perhaps demands further comment.

It was an early decision to invite only Lutherans to write. At least so much commonality of tradition seemed essential if the book were not to be a mere collection and yet not be unified by common adherence to a current school of theology. At the same time, it is in the definition of Christian dogmatics that it aims at ecumenical validity and usefulness. None of us thinks of himself, either here or in his other works, as writing especially for Lutheran readers. The character of our Lutheranism will doubtless be detected in the book in many ways, such as a tendency to cite Luther himself when matters become earnest. But we believe that the true aim of the Lutheran movement has always been to serve the whole church, so that Lutheran commitment inherently bears an ecumenical orientation when it is true to its original nature.

The Lutheran movement has classically had two chief characteristics, as a look at the Augsburg Confession will reveal. The first is devoted affirmation of the catholic tradition. We think that our concurrence in this devotion can only make our work the more useful as a textbook, and also for those Protestants whose own relation to the catholic tradition is more distant. At some points in the history of Lutheranism, a full reception of the catholic dogmatic tradition has been hindered by an attempt of Lutheran confessionalism to deduce the whole of the church's life and teaching from the special principle of Lutheran theology—the article of justification by faith alone. Whenever this reductionistic error has been committed, it has produced a particularly inhumane form of Lutheran sectarianism. We trust that all participants in this project of dogmatics are free of it.

The second Lutheran concern is the specific Reformation proposal to the church: the doctrine of "justification by faith alone, apart from the works of the law." As will become clear at several points in the body of this work, the Reformation doctrine of justification is fundamentally a *critical* princi-

PREFACE

ple. It is the demand continuously to submit all preaching, liturgy, pastoral care, church administration, and so forth to this question: Does this particular act of ministry lead people to find their life's justification, their reason to be, in the fact that the crucified Jesus lives, or are people left on their own, to depend on themselves for the ultimate meaning of life? If a churchly word or practice in any way suggests the latter, it must, according to the doctrine of justification by faith, be reformed. We have tried to make this critical principle effective throughout this work for the ongoing reform of the church. And we will not conceal our opinion that the contemporary American church needs to be reformed by this criterion at least as much as that of the sixteenth century. We would only ask our readers: Is this critique not right and very much needed also in your part of the church? If readers can generally answer that it is, then adherence to this historically Lutheran specialty need not diminish the ecumenical scope and relevance of the dogmatics.

Finally, a word is in order about the organization of this work. The plan of multiple authorship suggested the usefulness of the older system of *loci*—literally, "locations." A *locus* in this sense is a point at which the historic teachings and theological investigations of the church are brought into focus. Each *locus* is developed on its own terms, without deduction from the others; and that is what mandates this more ancient method for us. Many of the traditional *loci* could be developed into entire systematic theologies. In a dogmatics organized as a set of such *loci*, some overlapping of topics is inevitable and desirable.

A sequence of *loci* is thus a set of pigeonholes intended to accommodate all the relevant and recurrent concerns of Christian dogmatics. We follow the traditional sequence of topics, arranging them in a kind of history-of-salvation order, roughly corresponding to the items in the three articles of the creed. But the set of *loci* is not derived from any particular theology of salvation-history or directly from the creeds. It reflects rather the actual history of the church to date; the *loci* mark the centers around which the church has in fact been compelled to gather its reflections. Any actual set of dogmatic *loci* is, of course, a proposal by the author or authors about the exact location of these centers. As far as we know, no previous work of Christian dogmatics has used the precise set and sequence of topics we have adopted here. This is most clearly evident in our inclusion of separate *loci* for "The Knowledge of God," "The Holy Spirit," and "The Christian Life." The extent to which this is an innovation indicates that in dogmatics, no less than in other theological disciplines, it is never a question of simply repristinating a previous achievement of the church.

CARL E. BRAATEN
ROBERT W. JENSON

Abbreviations in Volume 1

The abbreviations used in this volume, as given below, are with slight variations based on Siegfried Schwertner, *Internationales Abkürzungsverzeichnis für Theologie und Grenzgebiete* (Berlin and New York: Walter de Gruyter, 1974).

AnBib	*Analecta Biblica*
ANFa	*Ante-Nicene Fathers.* New York, 1926.
AThR	*Anglican Theological Review*
BC	*The Book of Concord: The Confessions of the Evangelical Lutheran Church.* Translated and edited by Theodore G. Tappert. Philadelphia: Fortress Press, 1959.
COD	*Conciliorum Oecumenicorum Decreta.* Basel, 1962.
CP	*Classical Philology*
CQR	*Church Quarterly Review*
CR	*Corpus reformatorum.* Berlin, 1934ff.
Crit.	Criterion
Denzinger	Heinrich Denzinger, ed. *The Sources of Catholic Dogma.* Translated by Roy J. Deferrari from the 13th edition of *Enchiridion Symbolorum.* St. Louis: B. Herder Book Co., 1957.
DThC	*Dictionnaire de théologie catholique.* Paris, 1903ff.
EnchP	*Enchiridion Patristicum.* Edited by Marie Joseph Rouët de Journel. Freiburg, 1911ff.
ER	*Ecumenical Review*
EvTH	*Evangelische Theologie*
Interp.	*Interpretation: A Journal of Bible and Theology*
JEH	*Journal of Ecclesiastical History*
JR	*Journal of Religion*
JThS	*Journal of Theological Studies*
KuD	*Kerygma und Dogma*
LCC	Library of Christian Classics
LuthQ	*Lutheran Quarterly*
LW	American Edition of *Luther's Works.* St. Louis: Concordia Publishing House; Philadelphia: Fortress Press, 1955– .

ABBREVIATIONS IN VOLUME 1

NSHE	*New Schaff-Herzog Encyclopedia of Religious Knowledge.* New York, 1908ff.
Pers.	*The Personalist: An International Review of Philosophy, Religion, and Literature*
PG	*Patrologiae cursus completus.* Series Graeca. Edited by Jacques-Paul Migne. Paris, 1857–66, 1928–36.
PhB	*Philosophische Bibliotek.* Leipzig, 1868ff.
PhQ	*Philosophical Quarterly*
PL	*Patrologicae cursus completus.* Series Latina. Edited by Jacques-Paul Migne. Paris, 1850–55, 1941–49.
RelSt	*Religious Studies*
RGG³	*Die Religion in Geschichte und Gegenwart.* 3d ed. Tübingen, 1956–65.
RMet	*Review of Metaphysics*
ScEc	*Sciences ecclésiastiques: Revue philosophique et théologique*
SM(E)	*Sacramentum Mundi: An Encyclopedia of Theology.* 6 vols. New York, 1968–70.
StNT	Studien zum Neuen Testament
TDNT	*Theological Dictionary of the New Testament.* 10 vols. Edited by Gerhard Kittel and Gerhard Friedrich. Grand Rapids, 1964ff.
ThTo	*Theology Today*
ThWNT	*Theologische Wörterbuch zum Neuen Testament.* Edited by Gerhard Kittel. Stuttgart, 1933ff.
TS	*Theological Studies*
USQR	*Union Seminary Quarterly Review*
VigChr	*Vigiliae Christianae*
VT	*Vetus Testamentum*
VT.S	*Vetus Testamentum*, Supplement
WA	*D. Martin Luthers Werke. Kritische Gesamtausgabe.* Weimar, 1883ff.
ZKG	*Zeitschrift für Kirchengeschichte*
ZThK	*Zeitschrift für Theologie und Kirche*

FIRST LOCUS

Prolegomena to Christian Dogmatics

CARL E. BRAATEN

PROLEGOMENA TO CHRISTIAN DOGMATICS

Introduction

1. Theology and Dogmatics
   What is Theology?
   The Task of Apologetics
   Method in Theology

2. The Heritage of Dogmatics
   The Discipline
   The Ancient Church
   The Middle Ages
   The Reformation
   Protestant Orthodoxy
   The Dissolution of Dogmatics in Pietism and the Enlightenment
   The Revival of Dogmatics in the Nineteenth Century
   The State of Dogmatics in the Twentieth Century

3. The Fundamentals of Dogmatics
   The Concept of Dogma
   The Confessional Principle
   The Fundamentals of Dogmatics

4. The Holy Scriptures
   The Authority of Scripture
   The Interpretation of Scripture
   The Problem of Scripture Today

Introduction

Dogmatics is one of the traditional disciplines of Christian theology. Its special task is the critical interpretation of the doctrines of the church's faith in light of our knowledge of Christian origins and the challenge of the contemporary situation. The term "dogmatics," however, is no longer in vogue in our schools of theology. In ordinary language the words "dogma" and "dogmatics" conjure up the worst possible associations. A "dogmatic" person is rigid and narrow-minded. "Dogmatism" recalls the period of the inquisition and its heresy-hunting. In the present situation dogmatic thinking seems to be the trademark of the more conservative groups of Christians. In pietistic circles dogmatic theology was held in great suspicion as the intellectualistic dry bones of a dead orthodoxy, in contrast to the warm, personal faith of true biblical Christianity. No wonder the term "dogmatics" has been largely replaced by "systematic theology" or "constructive theology."

As the title of our work makes clear, we believe it inadvisable to surrender the use of the term "dogmatics." We would emphasize that there is a doctrinal core of the faith of the church. Dogmatic theologians are not autonomous philosophers of religion creating their own system of ideas. Instead, they are interpreters of the living stream of the church's traditions of faith expressed in dogmas and doctrines. Dogmaticians function within the context of the church for the sake of its mission in the world. If theologians are writing dogmatics, odd as it may sound in the current theological situation, there can be no doubt that their calling is a service performed within the church and for the church.

The shift from the word "dogmatics" to more neutral terms has been accelerated by a steady secularization of theology and its transformation into the scientific study of religion. The question today is whether theology can be a meaningful discipline in the secular academic context. "Religious studies" have preempted the place of theology. They feature the history of religion, the sociology of religion, and the like, but never specifically a theology of religion. Why not? This situation may point to a twofold crisis in theology. The first is the fall of dogmatics into theology in general, and the second is the fall of theology itself into general religious studies, raising the critical question whether theology is possible at all in the modern secular context.

INTRODUCTION

The crisis in dogmatics reflects the larger crisis in theology as a whole, and the crisis in theology as such reflects itself in the dismal state of dogmatics.

Dogmatics is a part of theology, perhaps the heart but certainly not the whole of it. For this reason it is necessary to deal with theology in general and its method before defining the nature and task of Christian dogmatics in particular. This is not a novel procedure. It was good tradition in classical dogmatics to begin with a chapter on the general subject of theology and then to consider the articles of faith in the witness of Holy Scripture and the symbols of the church.

The retrieval of the discipline of dogmatics may help overcome the trend to dissolve Christian theology into religious studies. If there is a specifically Christian foundation for the study of religious phenomena, it is well to clarify the fundamental presuppositions of what makes theology Christian. These are explicitly dogmatic presuppositions:

The self-revelation of God in judgment and grace
The person of Jesus the Christ of God
The witness of Holy Scripture
The means of grace in word and sacraments
The one, holy, catholic, and apostolic church
The faith worked by the Holy Spirit

Suspending the methodological function of these central symbols of Christian dogmatics inevitably leads to the disintegration of the unity of theology into a multiplicity of positivistic-scientific approaches to the study of religious phenomena. The outcome is the current anarchy in the academic study of religion, generating results of little interest to the Christian faith and the church's mission. Scholars of religion study and teach more and more about things of less and less importance.

Dogmatics is like a thorn in the flesh of the purely academic study of religion. The claim on which dogmatics rests speaks for the absolute truth of the one God and the final meaning of all humanity and the whole world. This is the scandalous claim of the gospel about Jesus the Christ of God. Dogmatics is a believing response of the mind to this imperious and gracious claim. It is an echo of the gospel in the realm of ideas. Where there is no church to preach this gospel of God's self-revelation in the history of Jesus the Christ, there is no such thing as Christian dogmatics. This is the abiding truth we have learned from the great dialectical theologians of the preceding era, Karl Barth and Paul Tillich. They stressed that Christian theology is a function of the church. This churchly connection is a distinctive mark of dogmatic theology. Dogmatics exists for the sake of the identity and mission of the church. Of course, it has its own special way of serving, not by repeating the doctrines of the past, but by a critical interpretation of the received doctrines in light of our biblical knowledge and our present engagement with

INTRODUCTION

the modern world. This means that dogmatics is done not so much to defend the church as it is, but to criticize it. This criticism occurs in the interest of discriminating between true and false preaching, as well as between church-centered activism for its own sake and kingdom-oriented praxis for the good of the world.

1
Theology and Dogmatics

Theology deals with the knowledge of God, the *logos theou*. As ordinarily taught, theology covers a comprehensive agenda of beliefs and practices which the church requires for educating its ministry. In its apologetic form theology seeks to argue the claims for Christianity to those who do not yet believe. In its dogmatic form theology aims to clarify the contents of the Christian faith for those who already believe.

WHAT IS THEOLOGY?

It is appropriate for dogmatics to begin with a reflection on the subject of theology as a whole. What is theology? This question can be answered from two different standpoints, from that of a general philosophical theory of human knowledge or from that within a specific theological circle of Christian faith. The one places theology within the scope of natural reason; the other links it to the events of historical revelation. In classical dogmatics theology was defined as the knowledge of God and divine things, to be gained partly in a natural way by the use of reason, and partly in a supernatural way through special revelation. In new and varied proposals theology continues to define itself from two such perspectives, from the side of reason or from the standpoint of faith in special revelation, or perhaps a combination of both.

Beginning with the period of the eighteenth-century Enlightenment, theology gradually lost its confidence in natural reason and appealed more and more to special revelation. As theology failed to prove its case in the general academic setting, it became increasingly defined as an ecclesial science. This made it primarily a function of the practical requirement to produce a professional class of leaders for the church. The question which the history of modern theology has posed with inescapable urgency is this: Does theology belong exclusively within the province of the *ecclesia*, or does it also fit somehow within the framework of the universe of sciences in *academia*, where the faculty of theology can hold its own along with the faculties of law,

1 / PROLEGOMENA TO CHRISTIAN DOGMATICS

medicine, science, history, literature, and the arts? Does theology have a subject matter and a method that can be rationally defended, or is it merely a matter of professional skills which the practitioners of religion must acquire to be effective?

The church has no reason to claim to hold a monopoly on theology. The word "theology" was not originally an invention of the Christian faith. In ancient Greece the poets were the first to be called theologians. Homer and Hesiod narrated the stories about the gods in the special medium of myth; theirs was a mythic theology. Then came the philosophers Plato and Aristotle, who criticized and translated the mythic theology of the poets into the medium of the philosophical *logos*. These philosophers were the first demythologizers. In addition to the poetic and the philosophical, there was a political form of theology in ancient Greece.[1] Political theology dealt with the gods of state religion. Eventually, under Constantine, the political gods were Christianized, and the Christian God became the head of the political religion of the Roman Empire.

This tripartite theology—poetic, philosophical, and political—existed before the rise of Christianity. The apologists of the second century were the first to appropriate the Greek concept of theology into Christian discourse. Though not a biblical word, "theology" referred to the truth of God and God's word of revelation. In the early apologetic situation Christian theology was set forth as the true philosophy, a *philosophia Christiana*. Christian theology and Greek philosophy both dealt with the *logos theou*, except that Christianity had the advantage of knowing the *logos* in the flesh, making its grasp of universal truth humanly and historically concrete.

In the period of medieval scholasticism, theology was understood in two ways, first, in its literal sense as the doctrine of God (*logos theou*), but second, and more broadly, as the statement of the truth concerning all the sacred teachings of the church (*sacra doctrina*). Thus theology dealt with everything from the creation of the world and the sacraments of the church to the second coming of Christ. The *Summa Theologica* of Thomas Aquinas offers the most splendid example of this twofold meaning of theology. In this massive work, Thomas dealt with all things pertaining to the Christian faith. The system combined theology in general (natural theology) and dogmatics in particular (*sacra doctrina*). Natural theology forms a part of philosophy, subject to the faculty of human reason. Sacred doctrine is based on the supernatural knowledge of God, available through the special revelation of Scripture and passed on by church tradition.

If medieval scholasticism broadened the meaning of theology to include everything that could be known of God through reason *and* revelation, Martin Luther inaugurated a trend in Protestant theology to sharpen the distinction between theology and philosophy. The interest of Luther was to base Chris-

10

THEOLOGY AND DOGMATICS

tian theology exclusively on the Word of God. This Word was the subject of Scripture as a whole, manifest in the incarnation of Jesus Christ, and present today in the living voice of the gospel (*viva vox evangelii*). Luther's reduction of theology for the sake of the gospel was not upheld by the scholastic theologians of seventeenth-century Protestant orthodoxy. The great dogmaticians (John Gerhard, John William Baier, John Andrew Quenstedt, and David Hollaz) reverted to the pattern of medieval scholasticism, restoring the claim of natural theology to stand at the beginning of the dogmatic system, setting forth all that can be known about God by reason in general before specifying the pure doctrines of Christian faith (*sacra pura doctrina*).

The massive broadening of theology continued with the explosion of the new methods and results of historical-critical research in the eighteenth and nineteenth centuries. Theology as a whole became subdivided into various fields: Old and New Testament, church history, and the history of doctrine, dogmatics, and practical theology. The modern age of field specialization was dawning. At the beginning a theologian was liberated to specialize in one aspect of theology, using the new historical method, but this always presupposed the dogmatics of the church. Later a wedge was driven between the historical and dogmatic approaches to theology. Historical research opted for complete freedom from dogmatic controls, also in the theological seminary. The all-too-familiar anomaly developed whereby professors in the theological faculty could teach their specialty, whether in the biblical, historical, or practical field, without explicit reference to either the doctrine of the triune God or the christological faith of the church, and still be called theologians. This has led to the critical questions: What, then, is theology? And what is its proper method?

Friedrich Schleiermacher formulated a broad definition of theology to encompass the variety of studies pursued in the modern faculty of theology. In his *Brief Outline on the Study of Theology*, Schleiermacher stated: "Christian theology . . . is that assemblage of scientific and practical instruction without the possession and application of which a united leadership of the Christian Church, i.e., a government of the Church in the fullest sense, is not possible."[2]

This definition opened the door to the eventual expansion of the theological curriculum and the introduction of a host of new disciplines to supplement the traditional fourfold division of theology into its exegetical, historical, dogmatic, and practical fields. Whatever may contribute practically to the exercise of leadership in the church can be included in Schleiermacher's definition of theology. The question of truth need not arise, because theology deals descriptively with the theoretical ideas and practical rules which serve the professional and administrative needs of the church. The line from this definition to the present situation is direct. The place of dogmatics in the theological

1 / PROLEGOMENA TO CHRISTIAN DOGMATICS

curriculum began to shrink, making room for auxiliary studies that introduce new methods and results from the social and behavioral sciences, all of practical importance to the ordained leadership of the church. Steadily this specialization led to secularization. The new disciplines—the history and phenomenology of religion, the psychology and sociology of religion, and the like—became autonomous fields of study, each conspicuously remote from classical definitions of theology as the doctrine concerning God or as the interpretation of Christian faith. A palace revolution took place in which theology as the erstwhile "queen of the sciences" was taken hostage by the guards who had once been hired to serve. This represents the situation of crisis in which the study of theology now finds itself.

THE TASK OF APOLOGETICS

Friedrich Schleiermacher claimed that "apologetics is a theological discipline which needs to be refashioned for these present times."[3] There is evidence of a renewal of the apologetic tendency in contemporary theological thought. This is a response to the critical state of theology in general and of dogmatics in particular. Dogmatics presupposes the truth of the Christian faith as a whole and aims to make it explicit. It is the task of apologetics to establish the grounds on which the truth claims of Christianity can be understood and legitimated, in the face of questions raised by both outsiders and insiders. The apologist is a defense attorney for the meaning and truth of the Christian message in the modern world. Apologetics is the organ by which the case for Christianity can be made before the bar of human reason as such.

Classically, apologetics took the form of natural theology, enjoying a place of prominence at the head of the dogmatic system, preparing the way for the treatment of the gospel, a John the Baptist pointing toward the coming of Christ. The function of apologetics was to serve as an introduction to dogmatics, but in actuality dogmatics was the heart pumping life into the apologetic organs. Today, dogmatics and apologetics are generally not so closely linked. The *Systematic Theology* of Paul Tillich stands as the monumental exception. In his method of correlation the apologetic element is built into the structure of the theological system as the Christian answer to the questions put to it by the contemporary situation.[4]

Systematic theology is often used as an interchangeable term for dogmatics. Our terminology would be clearer if systematic theology were understood more inclusively than dogmatics, embracing apologetics, dogmatics, systematics, and ethics. "Apologetics" in Protestant theology would then mean the same thing as "fundamental theology" in Roman Catholic terminology. Their common task is to explain and substantiate the formal and fundamental conditions of the possibility of responding in human experience and understanding to the self-revelation of God. The purpose of dogmatics is to set forth the basis and contents of specifically biblical-Christian faith. Systematics goes beyond dogmatics in that it deals with the Christian doctrines in light of further questions. Systematics is more self-consciously aware of the most appropriate system of conceptualization, whether it be Platonic, Aristotelian, Cartesian, Kantian, Hegelian, Whiteheadian, or whatever the case may be. Ethics draws out the moral implications of the total Christian message in both personal and social spheres of existence. Such a comprehensive systematic theology is exceedingly rare at the present time. It is more common for apologetics and ethics to be treated separately from dogmatics, taking the form of independent monographs on special questions regarding the intellectual claims and moral praxis of Christianity.

The essence of the apologetic mode of procedure is to find common ground between Christian theology and the intellectual situation of its time. The apologist of the second century, Justin Martyr, combined the Stoic concept of the Logos with the biblical idea of the Word of God. The Alexandrian theologians, Clement and Origen, found common ground in Platonic philosophy, as did Augustine. Thomas Aquinas made use of Aristotle. Starting from common ground, the aim of the apologists was always to recommend the Christian truth to the outside pagan world, using all the evidences from history and human nature at their command. When Christianity became the majority religion of the empire, no longer a fighting minority in a pagan world, apologetics worked to clarify the reasonableness of Christian faith to those who already believed, arguing that it is perfectly reasonable to accept the biblical accounts of miracles and prophecies as proofs of the divine origin of Christianity. After the Reformation, apologetics became the defender of Christian orthodoxy against attacks from deism, rationalism, naturalism, materialism, and the like. At the same time, however, apologetics was placed on the defensive because of the findings of the natural and historical sciences. Apologetics discredited itself by looking for "God in the gaps" of our modern scientific and historical knowledge, steadily having to retreat from one outpost to another, until finally no significant ground was left to defend. There is no desire on the part of theologians to return to this self-defeating type of apologetics.

In twentieth-century theology the main apologetic way has been to latch on to the system of a leading secular philosopher and to show the "beauty" of the Christian faith in terms of its set of categories. Some biblical, kerygmatic, and confessional theologies have called for a complete separation of theology from philosophy, in the spirit of Tertullian's famous question: What does Jerusalem have to do with Athens? Careful analysis will show, however, that none of these theologies has successfully purged itself of all philosophical presuppositions and concepts, whether epistemological or metaphysical.

1 / PROLEGOMENA TO CHRISTIAN DOGMATICS

Today there are notable examples of the classical apologetic way in which theology makes use of philosophy as its handmaid. Existentialist theology has used the categories of Martin Heidegger's philosophy of existence to translate the kerygma into terms that modern people can understand. The need for translation is obvious: The kerygma is embedded in the mythical picture of the world. By demythologizing the New Testament, it is possible for Christianity to set forth a possibility of existence which philosophy also talks about. They share common ground in the understanding of human existence. Language-analysis theology has taken hold of Ludwig Wittgenstein's theory of "language games" to show that religious language has its own kind of logic. Christianity, accordingly, as every other religion, has its own rules which have to be learned to play the language game of faith. This approach has given religious language a reprieve in a secular age in which many intellectuals believed all talk about God to be literally non-sense. Process theology has adopted the metaphysics worked out by the process philosophers, most notably Alfred North Whitehead and Charles Hartshorne, in order to have the most adequate resources to express within the modern framework of the evolutionary world view what the Bible means by God and the world. The God of process metaphysics and the God of biblical revelation are supposedly one and the same. The apologetic intent is unmistakable; now it should be possible for theology and science to share the same frame of reference. A Christian can be at once explicitly theological and think scientifically without violating the canons of either side.

Contemporary apologetics has not only used twentieth-century philosophical thinkers, but has also reached back to appropriate in new ways some older nineteenth-century models. While Paul Tillich drew on the existentialist analysis of Heidegger, the influence of the absolute idealism of Friedrich Schelling was far more definitive throughout his theological system. The renaissance of G. W. F. Hegel's dialectical thought has also provided the undergirding for the universal-historical approach of Wolfhart Pannenberg. The role of Karl Marx and his concept of praxis has provided liberation theology with its main entree into the political realities of the modern world. Ernst Bloch's philosophy of hope gave eschatological theology a hermeneutical key for reading the Bible in light of the principle of hope. The transcendental Thomism of Roman Catholic thinkers, particularly Karl Rahner and Bernard Lonergan, has used the critical philosophy of Immanuel Kant and the existentialist anthropology of Heidegger as a bridge back to the Aristotelian metaphysics of Thomas Aquinas. Its direct apologetic relevance is clearly exhibited in the Thomist principle: Grace does not destroy but fulfills nature. Therefore, Christian revelation is bound to build on the natural knowledge of God and of the world.

With these examples we have barely skimmed the surface of the apologetic

THEOLOGY AND DOGMATICS

situation in the contemporary period. They are sufficient, however, to demonstrate the extent to which Christian theology has felt the need for an apologetic link between the Christian faith and the modern intellectual situation. In this way it is pursuing the classical line, repeating both its liabilities and assets.

It may be well for theological apologetics to proceed in a more eclectic fashion, refusing to bind itself to one particular philosophy. Kant, Hegel, Marx, Heidegger, Wittgenstein, Whitehead, and others may each have a different service to render to theology. At a minimum, we can cite three attainable goals of apologetics today. First, apologetics can thematize the ultimate questions concerning the meaning of human existence.[5] Apart from revelation, it cannot identify and name the reality of the One who is truly God. At best it can show that religious language and symbols do function in a meaningful way because they disclose dimensions of human existence which seek after the ultimate and the holy.

Second, apologetics can inquire into the formal conditions of the possibility of thought and speech about God.[6] The movement here is from human being to God, from anthropology to theology, starting from below in the human subject and leading to God as the ultimate term of human self-transcendence. Along this route it is not possible to know the will of God. But we can find traces of transcendence in the human spirit, which theology might link up with the Christian knowledge of the triune God.

Third, apologetics can relate theology to the human search for meaning in history.[7] Every particular science deals with only a part of reality. None can claim to know it all, to possess an omnicompetent method to deal with the totality of reality. Theology can be defined as that science which goes beyond partial meanings, seeking an answer to the question of the final and total meaning of all events in the history of nature and society. The human spirit, it can be shown, is inherently concerned about the totality of meaning, bent on transcending infinitely every partial embodiment of meaning, whether in secular or religious experience.

The discipline of theology can thus be justified within the framework of the hermeneutical inquiry into the conditions of possible meaning in history. There is some truth in the observation that modern hermeneutics from Schleiermacher to Gadamer is "a continuation of theology by other means."[8] Theology presses the question of the final meaning of things implied in the process of hermeneutical inquiry.

The type of apologetics we are briefly advocating seeks to raise the question of God within the philosophical framework of the general possibilities of human experience and knowledge. It may be called a "new style of natural theology."[9] It stops short of claiming to possess definitive knowledge of "God and divine things" on which human beings can base a life of faith, hope,

1 / PROLEGOMENA TO CHRISTIAN DOGMATICS

and love. But it does ground the meaning of the *idea* of God in the structures of common human experience. In this way we may claim a certain formal continuity with the twofold approach to the knowledge of God in classical dogmatics, through natural reason *and* through special revelation.

METHOD IN THEOLOGY

The method of theology must be adequate to its subject matter. It should be evident from the division of theology as a whole into exegetical, historical, systematic, and practical disciplines that the method appropriate to theology is bound to be complex. If we define Christian theology as the "science" which deals with the self-revelation of God in the history of Jesus Christ as confessed by the faith of the Christian church, we have reason to be open to every method that proves itself through trial and error to be capable of investigating the realities to which the elements of this comprehensive definition refer. There is no one absolute approach that can do everything theology requires. Despite the relativity of method, however, we can discuss various indispensable methodological principles that continue to prove their worth for theological work.

First, *Faith* is the methodological point of departure for every branch of real theology. We may call this the existential factor at work in all theological research and reflection, hidden or manifest. Anselm of Canterbury gave us the most succinct definition of theology as "faith in search of understanding" (*fides quaerens intellectum*). Luther called for a *theologia pectoralis*, saying that it is the heart that makes a theologian. Søren Kierkegaard, the father of modern existentialism, stated, "Subjectivity is truth," explaining that religious truth can be grasped only with infinite personal passionate interest. This captured the same point the pietists made earlier, insisting on a "theology of the regenerate," in contrast to the possibility of a "theology of the irregenerate," a notion some of the orthodox party had overzealously advanced to stress the objective character of truth. Paul Tillich claimed that the theologian, in distinction from a philosopher of religion, must stand within the "theological circle," for "the object of theology is what concerns us ultimately. Only those propositions are theological which deal with their object so far as it can become a matter of ultimate concern for us."[10] Similarly, Rudolf Bultmann stated that it only makes sense to speak of God from one's concrete existential situation, from a commitment of faith.

This idea that faith is the starting point of theology must be carefully distinguished from the error of nineteenth-century theological subjectivism, rooted in Schleiermacher's definition of religion as "feeling of absolute dependence." Faith would then be not merely the starting point but the source of theology, generating religious experiences that become objectified in the form of doctrinal statements. If faith is productive of its own basis and contents, the believer is caught in a vicious cycle of egocentric subjectivism. The great Erlangen theologian J. C. K. von Hofmann tried to improve on Schleiermacher's subjectivism of religious feeling by making the consciousness of the Christian person the object of theology. However, the danger of a solipsism of faith remains, as the gaze of the believer is radically turned inward.

Faith is not religious feeling or emotion in general, nor is it specifically Christian experience or consciousness as such. Faith in the biblical sense is not a human phenomenon that can be created by exercising at will a particular faculty of religious experience. The identifying mark of Christian faith is given by its object, so that faith is always faith in the living God whose self-identification is in the person of Jesus, God's Son and our Lord. Faith is not the source of theological knowledge; it does not produce the data of historical revelation; it is a state of radical receptivity. Faith receives what revelation gives. It is the receiving side of a relationship which the Spirit of God has created.

Second. The standpoint of existential faith does not diminish the fact that theology also claims to be an academic discipline with a reasonable method. For centuries theologians have debated whether theology is a *science*, and if so, of what kind. If theology is the "science of God," its claim to knowledge is not limited to the devotees of a believing sect, but has universal validity. The idea of God, by definition, is not merely a matter of private experience, but deals with the final power which determines the being and meaning of all reality. Any God who is less than this is no God at all. Yet it has been questioned whether theology can be seriously considered a "science," that is, a discipline dealing with some field of knowledge with an appropriate method.

It should be freely acknowledged that theology does not exhibit the ideal of science prevalent in the fields of mathematics and the natural sciences, but neither do any of the other humanistic disciplines—art, literature, history, politics, economics, and numerous others. Theology, like all these, must take great care in applying the most adequate procedures in dealing with its subject matter. It should also be admitted that theology is not a science in the usual sense that its object is potentially accessible to every rational human being. Reason alone is not sufficient; faith is an indispensable presupposition of theology. But if faith refers to an attitude of special interest in its object, theology is not alone in requiring such a passionate commitment in the process of inquiry. Art and music most obviously require a similar attitude. No doubt every science calls for a dimension of insight and interest in its specific field of inquiry as a condition for finding new truth.

The most serious difficulty in defending the "scientific" character of theology arises from the common claim that true science is limited to knowledge

1 / PROLEGOMENA TO CHRISTIAN DOGMATICS

about empirical objects in the world. There can, of course, be no empirical knowledge of God, because God is not an object at the disposal of our sensory perception. However, the concept of science need not be limited to an empiricist account of human knowledge. Should theology then abandon the claim to be a science in some sense, or work together with other humanistic disciplines to broaden the understanding of knowledge, and then render a reasonable account of its method appropriate to its own subject matter? Here we can only briefly outline the elements of a workable method in theology.

Theology is a human science. The mind at work in theology is the same mind called on to perform all other kinds of mental operations. The human mind is a dynamic structure of inquiry, moving forward in a ceaseless pattern of questioning beyond all known limits. This boundless propensity of the human mind to transcend every given answer represents a thrust toward the infinite mystery of being. The image of God in the human mind (the *imago dei*) may be interpreted as the orientation of human being toward ultimate reality, toward a complete set of answers to the most complete set of questions, embracing the universal, total, and final future of all things. Theology is ultimately concerned about a total understanding of all that can be understood, because its goal is the knowledge of God, the One who determines the meaning and being of everything that exists. The *logos* of theology has universal meaning.

In Christian faith the universal *logos* has become concrete. The method of theology is intended to bring to contemporary expression the ultimate meaning of what occurred in the concrete history of Jesus the Christ of God. In Jesus of Nazareth the eschatological kingdom of God became an incarnate reality, engendering hope in a future of universal fulfillment for all humanity. The test of the adequacy of theological method is whether it can thematize the significance of the Christ-event for one's theory of knowledge and view of the world, for epistemology and metaphysics. This means that faith as the methodological point of departure and reason as the instrument of understanding do not struggle against each other, but work together in a creative way. Thus, there is a two-way movement in theology, faith in search of understanding (*fides quaerens intellectum*) and understanding of faith (*intellectus quaerens fidem*). *Intellectus* without *fides* leads to rationalism; *fides* without *intellectus* falls into emotionalism.

The anthropological presupposition of theology is the presence of the image of God in human nature. This image is the root of the possibility of understanding the self-revelation of God. It is operative as the desire to know the "not yet" known, in quest of "the knowledge of things hoped for."[11] This leads theology to stress the function of the imagination and the role of myth in the knowledge of ultimate reality. The natural scientist and the rational philosopher do not possess the only ways to the knowledge of reality. The prophet and the poet, the storyteller and the myth-maker, have nourished a dimension of the human mind moved by the logic of anticipation, exhibiting its power in the medium of images, symbols, and myths that relate to the future of all reality. The human mind possesses a *sensus divinitatis*, the uncommon sense of people who divine the realm of "the true, the good, and the beautiful." Theology draws on this power of the imagination to mediate a critique of the present situation (prophetic judgment) and participation in the promise of the future (redemptive grace). The Old Testament speaks of "knowing" in this uncommon sense of sharing the secret mystery of things beyond their obvious meaning.

When the faculty of imagination is fully operative, it makes the human mind aware that there is another dimension of reality that does not yet exist. Method in theology must be guided by this dual dimension of the mind that corresponds to the nature of an unfinished and imperfect world. The method of theology must help us read the world in a realistic way, discerning the signs of contrast between the world as it is and the coming of the new. This power of the imagination to participate in the realm of the coming future is a structural part of the human mind potentially possessed by all, though many succeed in stifling their capacity to see beyond the end of their nose. Very often the knowledge of the realm of the future takes a negative form in the present, in the awareness of darkness, misery, and evil, and in protest against these negative forces. But the knowledge of the deficiency of things as they are may be coupled with the positive desire to transcend this negative state in the power of a more promising future. Otherwise despair is granted the last word. The knowledge of theological truth focuses not only on what already existing reality contains but also on what it fails to contain. Otherwise knowledge is one-sided, merely analytical and positivistic.

Thus the anticipatory dimension of knowledge must be given an adequate place in epistemology.[12] Anticipation is an integral element of the activity of knowing. The future of reality must be envisioned in the construction of a whole frame of reference within which all the fragments of knowledge can be given a meaningful place in relation to each other. The horizon of the future is an essential condition of the universal scope of a theological project of thought. A theological statement is a projection of the imagination that pictures God as the comprehensive unity of all things in their final state of being. Without this theological frame of reference, the unity of life's meaning falls apart into bits and pieces of experience, and the idea of truth as a whole is broken into fragments and segments of information. Theology can thus be called a "science" in the sense that it makes statements about God who is conceived to be the unifying power, universal meaning, and fulfilling destiny of all things. Without this reference to God, there can be no vision of the whole. Then human confidence in the worthwhileness of life and crea-

1 / PROLEGOMENA TO CHRISTIAN DOGMATICS

tion is threatened by a world of facts without values, movement without meaning, process without purpose, journey without goal, and future without promise beyond the prospect of nothingness and death.

(3) Third. The material content of theological statements about God derives from given texts and traditions of *history*. Inasmuch as Christian theology depends on historical sources, it is bound to use the critical methods of research common to historical science in general. The aim of the historical method is not only to establish facts, but also to search out their meanings in their original historical context. The latter is the primary aim of an historical hermeneutic. There are no naked facts as such that interpret themselves. Historical facts are always suspended in traditions of interpretation which keep them alive in the stream of a community's memories and hopes.

The historical criticism of the biblical texts and sacred traditions on which Christianity is based has been feared by conservative Christians as the destruction of the foundations of faith. Actually, however, the historical method is an indispensable ally of Christian theology. Paul Tillich said it well:

> The historical approach to Biblical literature is one of the great events in the history of Christianity and even of religion and human culture. It is one of the elements of which Protestantism can be proud. It was an expression of Protestant courage when theologians subjected the holy writings of their own church to a critical analysis through the historical method. It appears that no other religion in human history exercises such boldness and took upon itself the same risk.[13]

The historical-critical method is a tool which can be used by historians and believers from every school of thought. It is not essentially bound up with any particular set of presuppositions, nor do the results of its application favor any particular dogmatic position. Liberals and conservatives, naturalists and supernaturalists, use the findings of historical research to defend their own convictions. It is clear that the methods and results of critical scholarship are invoked by people on all sides of every conceivable issue. This highlights the fact that there is no such thing as a neutral appeal to the authority of modern historical science. Every historian is in fact coming from his or her own set of presuppositions, embedded in his or her own *Weltanschauung*, whether acknowledged or not. Many historians are blind to the role their own prior assumptions play in their scientific investigations. As a rule they need to have other critics open their eyes to the extent to which their own ideology controls their scholarly research. Usually scholars can see the ideological speck in the eyes of their critics more clearly than the beam of prejudice at work hidden in their own minds. The critical scholar, however, need not remain isolated, but works best within a community of scholars in a spirit of mutual criticism and freedom to pursue the path of truth wherever it might lead.

The first task of the historical method is research. Leopold von Ranke, the great German scholar, formulated the perennial ideal of the critical historian: to find out what actually happened. The historical method of research must be applied both to the texts of the Bible and to the traditions of the church. Criticism is necessary because numerous absurd beliefs claim for their support the witness of Scripture and Christian tradition. The clearing of the ground of mere opinion by discerning what really happened can help the ongoing process of reform in the church and the renewal of theology.

The second step of the historical method is interpretation. History is more than a reconstruction of naked facts of history. We always find the facts in a context of meaning, or we simply cannot grasp anything at all. In contemporary theology the task of interpretation is commonly referred to as hermeneutics. The texts and traditions of the Christian faith must be encountered for the sake of their meaning, first in terms of their original contexts and second in terms of the contemporary context of the interpreter. Without this process of interpretation in the historical method, we end up with a mere hodgepodge of names and dates and places and events. There is a living, dynamic, forward-moving history to be understood: the history of Israel among the nations, the history of Jesus and the apostolic community, the history of the life and doctrine of the Christian churches in the context of the general history of the world, right up to the present time. It is not possible to encounter the texts and traditions of all this history, from the past to the present, without taking a stand in some way, without daring to make judgments and decisions, without personal participation and self-involving encounter with the meaning of the texts and traditions of Christianity.

Traditionally, hermeneutics was defined in a narrow sense as the system of rules to be followed in biblical exegesis. In the modern discussion hermeneutics deals more broadly with all the conditions involved in the interpretation of history and historical documents.

Friedrich Schleiermacher is the father of modern hermeneutical theory. He realized that more is involved in biblical interpretation than the application of a set of principles. The gap between what a text meant in its own context and what it means now in a new context must be bridged somehow. Schleiermacher, and later Wilhelm Dilthey, proposed a psychological theory of hermeneutical understanding. The interpreter must somehow penetrate a text by an act of psychological imagination in order to reproduce the original creative moment of the author and his or her feeling for life.

Rudolf Bultmann revised Schleiermacher's hermeneutics, retaining its character as a theory of understanding at work in the interpretation of historical documents. Bultmann focused on the presupposition of all historical interpretation, the existential interest of the interpreter as one who puts a question to which the answer coming from the text will correspond. There is no

1 / PROLEGOMENA TO CHRISTIAN DOGMATICS

research without presuppositions, without some prior understanding of what a given text is all about, else one would not be motivated to inquire into its subject matter.

Fourth, Theology has frequently suffered from a fatal separation of the historical and the dogmatic methods. There has been a dualism consisting of two tracks, the facts of history going along one and the interpretations of faith along another. Theological hermeneutics seeks to unify the two approaches so that every new and serious interpretation is a creative synthesis of the results of historical research and the life situation of the present interpreter. Dogmatics enters into the hermeneutical process because theologians approach the text neither from a neutral point of view nor even from a merely existential standpoint. It is simply not the case, as Bultmann claims, that "the interpretation of biblical writings is not subject to conditions different from those applying to all other kinds of literature."[14] In their biblical interpretation theologians do bring a prior understanding of the Word of God conditioned by the life of faith and the worship of the church. General factors of philosophical and historical understanding retain their validity throughout, but in addition there is an ecclesiological dimension which acknowledges that God continues to speak to the church through the Scriptures.

Theology approaches the Bible as canon. This is a datum of prior understanding which cannot be derived from any philosophical theory or any result of historical research. What the Bible has meant as the canon in the tradition of the church and the life of believers, namely, the medium of the unique message of God's saving history, must be taken into account in a theological treatment of hermeneutics. Dogmatics is thus directly linked to the hermeneutical concern, because the interpretation of Scripture and dogmatic reflection are both carried on for the sake of the proclamation which creates and sustains the church. One of the main tasks of dogmatics is to facilitate the movement from the Bible to present-day preaching. This hermeneutical task of dogmatics is successfully carried out when the gulf is bridged from the written text of Scripture to the audible event of preaching.

The hermeneutical process does not take place by a leap from the Bible to a present-day sermon. The traditions of the church provide hermeneutical guidelines for biblical interpretation. The creeds and confessions of the church are important links in the hermeneutical chain that connects the biblical message with the contemporary church. Theologians who choose to interpret the Scriptures apart from the mainstream of the tradition tend to produce novel teachings out of touch with the church's life and mission. Especially Protestants have been so allergic to dogma that they try to reach back to the Bible for a kerygma that will leapfrog into the present without the intermediate developments of tradition. This widespread indifference to the significance

THEOLOGY AND DOGMATICS

of dogma accounts for the massive attenuation of Christian substance in the multiplicity of sects and denominations in Protestantism.

The dogma of the church does not automatically guarantee the faithful transmission of the biblical message into the contemporary situation. It is the Spirit who breathes life into the texts of Scripture and the words of tradition, so that the Christian community may be empowered by the hearing of the living Word. It is finally the Spirit who closes the hermeneutical gap between the biblical Word and the human world. It is the Spirit who fills the earthen vessels with heavenly treasures. The inner witness of the Holy Spirit within the community of faith and worship is an event that cannot be controlled by a rational hermeneutic or ecclesiastical magisterium. The Spirit blows where and when he wills.

The hermeneutical circle would not be complete without mention of the liturgy as the medium in which the church receives the living presence of the biblical Christ. The Spirit makes use of the liturgy to transmit the apostolic witness to Jesus Christ. In the liturgy the history of God with the world and God's chosen people is recited, remembered, and represented in a way that links the past to the eschatological future kingdom which the sacrament of Christ's body and blood makes really present.

Fifth. The Christian faith claims to represent the absolute, ultimate, unconditional, and everlasting *truth* of God in the once-for-all event of self-revelation in the person and history of Jesus Christ. It has always been difficult to delineate the conditions under which this claim to truth can be acknowledged. The New Testament clearly states that the final truth of faith will always meet the resistance of unbelief. What is wisdom to faith is foolishness to the world; the dynamics of agape infinitely surpass the reasonable demands of the law; and hope runs contrary to all appearances at hand.

Today the theological statement of truth is complicated by certain modern forms of consciousness. (1) Historical relativism deeply conditions our modern consciousness of truth. There is nothing in the world of human history exempt from the universal flux of things. Everything without exception is thus subject to historical analysis. There are no timeless ideals or values that exist above and beyond this one-dimensional history of humankind, no suprahistorical reality free from the laws and principles that govern all other events. In light of this radical historicism, all historical life becomes profane.

(2) The modern consciousness of truth is influenced by naturalistic reductionism. Human beings exist within a closed continuum of natural causes and effects. Without exception everything in history is explained in analogy with the phenomena of nature. What is un-natural or super-natural is *a priori* excluded from the realm of possibility. The ideal of science is to explain things in the most natural, simple, probable, predictable, and exact way. An awareness

1 / PROLEGOMENA TO CHRISTIAN DOGMATICS

of truth that confines itself to the limits of nature alone will be inherently skeptical of belief in providence or miracles. Everything going on in the real world is subject to the unbreakable laws of nature. And there can be no exception.

(3) The corollary of these two aspects of the modern concept of truth—historicism and naturalism—is an autonomous view of human reason. Reason is taken to be the measure of all truth. It would be a theological error to define faith in absolute contradiction to reason. It would be equally erroneous to require that the insights of faith be proved by the operations of reason. The history of the relations between faith and reason is full of variety and change. Faith has no special interest in defending irrationalism. There is a noetic element of faith, something to be known. It is not only a matter of feeling. A split between reason and faith is as intolerable as a reduction of faith to what reason will allow. If rationalism blunts faith, fideism throws the believer helplessly into a position of blind trust or the abyss of empty feeling. In the final analysis, faith is a gift of the Spirit, not the product of reason. Faith cannot be accounted for within the limits of reason alone. Rationalism invariably discounts the effect of the fall and sin on the capacity of reason to acknowledge the truth of God and his revelation.

(4) A fourth factor in determining the modern consciousness of truth is pragmatism. Pragmatism comes from the Greek word *prattein*, "to do." According to pragmatism, the criterion of truth is "what works." In France, Maurice Blondel's philosophy of action stressed that the center of philosophy must be shifted from intellection to action. The Blondelian shift in theory, as applied to theology, means that truth becomes present through choosing and doing, that the intellect alone is not the faculty of access to the real. Existentialism followed suit in stressing the moment of decision in human existence. The analytic philosophy of language, influenced by Wittgenstein, also emphasized that the meaning of language does not lie in its correspondence to an eternal world of ideas and objects, but is tied to its function within a particular "language game."

In contemporary theology the shift to the practical criterion of truth is taking place under the impact of the Marxist theory of praxis. From the left wing of the Hegelian school in the nineteenth century arose the call for philosophy to become practical in a revolutionary sense. Marx wrote in his "Theses on Feuerbach," "The philosophers have only interpreted the world in various ways; the point is to change it."[15] The attainment of objective truth, Marx said, is not a theoretical question but a practical question.

The Marxist theory of praxis has been appropriated by German political theology and Latin American liberation theology as a new criterion of truth. Jürgen Moltmann stated, "The new criterion of theology and of faith is to be found in praxis."¹⁶ This calls for a radically new model of truth quite unlike anything we can find in the classical Christian tradition. The heart of this novel proposal is the notion of the priority of practical activity to change the world. The Marxist idea of the priority of praxis cannot, however, be assumed into the Christian understanding of truth without utterly destroying the foundations on which it stands. In Marxist theory, the acting subject of transformative praxis is the human agent. In Christian theology the prius of fundamental change in history is the activity of God in establishing the right of divine rule. The divine indicative is prior to any human imperative. The idea of the priority of praxis has given rise to the substitution of an orthopraxis for an orthodoxy, leading to the legalization of the Christian faith.

The power to change the world in a fundamental way is not within human control. Transformative praxis can only be the historic working out of the reconciliation that the gospel has announced for the world through God's act in Christ. Within the structure of a Christian theology, the notion of the priority of Jesus' message of the kingdom of God is the prius of transformative praxis. Ethics stems from eschatology; the ground of the possibility of a truly liberating praxis lies in the eschatological event of God's kingdom in Christ. The criterion of the gospel comes first; praxis is always a second step.

These four modern post-Enlightenment forms of consciousness concerning truth—historicism, naturalism, rationalism, pragmatism—give expression to the common underlying premise of the autonomy of the human subject: "Man is the measure of all truth." The modern trend toward autonomy can be seen as a legitimate expression of the drive toward freedom and liberation from every heteronomous system of authority, ecclesiastical or secular. Christian theology cannot locate the final criterion of the truth it seeks on either side of the conflict between autonomy and heteronomy, although its own vision of absolute freedom will place it decidedly in sympathy with all who struggle to overthrow dehumanizing structures of domination, religious or political. The criterion of truth in Christian theology is grounded in the gospel of Jesus Christ, the authorized medium of the freedom which promises to set people free from *every* kind of bondage. True authority, as opposed to heteronomous authoritarianism, has its ultimate source in the power of freedom which God exercised in raising the crucified Jesus from the dead.

The task of dogmatics is to understand and interpret the authority of Jesus Christ and the apostolic witness in relation to the later history of Christianity and the faith of the church today. Without the authority of Jesus Christ and the derivative witness of Scripture and the tradition, Christian theology is unthinkable. This clearly implies a disclosure model of truth and revelation, which does not eliminate but invites the help of auxiliary disciplines such as historical criticism, phenomenological inquiry, sociological research, and

1 / PROLEGOMENA TO CHRISTIAN DOGMATICS

ontological reflection to interpret the connections and correlations between the texts and traditions of revelation and the conditions and experiences of human existence.

The authority of Jesus Christ in mediating the revelation of God to the generations of humankind is transmitted through Scripture and the symbols of tradition. The eschatological promise of the gospel in the history of Jesus is the basis of the unity of Scripture and the continuity of the Christian tradition. The history of doctrine, and particularly the ecumenical creeds and dogmas of the church, help transmit the message of God's saving presence in Jesus the Christ that transcends and relativizes that history itself. Nothing in the tradition of the church, not even its most crucial doctrines and offices, can be exempt from the criticism that emanates from the eschatological word of God in the person of Jesus Christ.

The final future of God is proleptically manifest in the christological foundation of the church. The church in history meets every new situation with reference to that transcendent future which has already been previewed in the coming of the crucified and risen Lord. The anticipation of this future reacts on the church's memory of the Word of Scripture and its traditional structures of faith and witness, putting the question whether they can still serve as instruments of the church's mission in the world. The fact that a structure can be traced back to the church fathers in the first five centuries, or some other period of church history, or even back to the Bible, is no sufficient reason to keep it. The authority of Scripture itself is based on what it conveys concerning Jesus Christ, not on its antiquity or sanction by church dogma. This is what it means to speak with Luther of *was Christum treibt* as the final criterion of truth in theology.

NOTES

1. Jürgen Moltmann, *The Experiment Hope*, trans. M. Douglas Meeks (Philadelphia: Fortress Press, 1975), p. 104.

2. Friedrich Schleiermacher, *Brief Outline on the Study of Theology*, trans. Terrence N. Tice (Richmond, Va.: John Knox Press, 1966), p. 20.

3. Friedrich Schleiermacher, *The Christian Faith*, ed. H. R. Mackintosh and J. S. Stewart (Edinburgh: T. & T. Clark, 1928), p. 4.

4. Paul Tillich, *Systematic Theology*, 3 vols. (Chicago: University of Chicago Press, 1951–63), 1:7.

5. An example is Langdon Gilkey's *Naming the Whirlwind: The Renewal of God-Language* (Indianapolis: Bobbs-Merrill, 1969).

6. See Karl Rahner's one-volume theology, *Foundations of Christian Faith*, trans. William V. Dych (New York: Seabury Press, 1978).

7. Wolfhart Pannenberg's program of theology as a whole is an apologetic answer

to the modern question of meaning. See esp. his *Theology and the Philosophy of Science*, trans. Francis McDonagh (Philadelphia: Westminster Press, 1976).

8. The observation is by Hans Albert, quoted by Pannenberg, *Theology and the Philosophy of Science*, p. 126.

9. I have adopted this term from John Macquarrie, *Principles of Christian Theology* (New York: Charles Scribner's Sons, 1966), p. 48, and first applied it in my own way in my *The Future of God* (New York: Harper & Row, 1969).

10. Tillich, *Systematic Theology*, 1:12.

11. See Robert W. Jenson, *The Knowledge of Things Hoped For* (New York and London: Oxford University Press, 1969).

12. This point is a major contribution of Pannenberg to theological epistemology in *Theology and the Philosophy of Science*.

13. Tillich, *Systematic Theology*, 2:107.

14. Rudolf Bultmann, "The Problem of Hermeneutics," in *Essays*, trans. James C. G. Greig (London: SCM Press, 1955), p. 238.

15. Quoted in Ernst Bloch, *On Karl Marx*, trans. John Maxwell (New York: Herder & Herder, 1971), p. 57.

16. Jürgen Moltmann, *Religion, Revolution, and the Future* (New York: Charles Scribner's Sons, 1969), p. 138.

2
The Heritage of Dogmatics

The history of dogmatics is a specialized field of theology. There are good reasons, however, to include an overview of the heritage of dogmatics in this introduction. The primary reason is didactic: Dogmatic reflection presupposes the concrete historical development of each of its themes. There is also a methodological reason: Every dogmatics begins within the context of a particular tradition and makes its inquiries into Scripture, gospel, dogma, philosophy, and culture from that standpoint.

THE DISCIPLINE

Dogmatics, as the term suggests, is a theological discipline that deals with the church's dogmas. It was first used in the seventeenth century by Lukas Reinhard in the title of his theological system, *Synopsis Theologiae Dogmaticae* (1659).[1] It was a synonym for other commonly used titles such as "Summa," "Loci," "Institutio," "Compendium," and "Medulla." These contain summaries and interpretations of the doctrinal decisions of the church covering all the chief articles of the Christian faith. In the nineteenth and twentieth centuries dogmatics became a highly specialized discipline in both Protestant and Roman Catholic circles, exemplified most eminently by Karl Barth's *Church Dogmatics* and Michael Schmaus's *Katholische Dogmatik*.

The term "dogmatics" may be of recent origin, but its substance is not. The heritage of dogmatics reaches back into the New Testament, where Paul speaks of preserving the "truth of the gospel" (Gal. 2:5, 14). The root of dogmatics is just such insight into the content of the gospel that its preaching might be true and every false doctrine, which inhibits a clear witness to the truth, might be decisively rejected. John too speaks much about the witness to the truth, who is Jesus Christ himself. The seeds of the dogmatic concern can be found in the apostolic testimony to the wisdom (*sophia*), the knowledge (*gnosis*), and witness (*marturia*) to the truth essential for communicating the gospel of salvation in the name of Jesus Christ.

1 / PROLEGOMENA TO CHRISTIAN DOGMATICS

Works on the history of dogma have been written by many scholars, most notably Adolf von Harnack,[2] but no one has yet written a history of dogmatics. Though no such thing can be attempted here, it may still prove useful to ground this introduction to dogmatics in a brief sketch of the main characteristics of dogmatics from earliest times to the present.[3] Instruction in dogmatics can be facilitated both by a systematic analysis of its fundamental elements as well as by an historical recapitulation of its development. Each topic in this outline of dogmatics is filled with references to historical materials from different periods of church history. This sketch can serve as a map to prepare the reader for the various excursions authors take below into the vast regions of classical dogmatics.

THE ANCIENT CHURCH

There is a notable difference between the dogmatic thinking of the Greek fathers of the East and the Latin fathers of the West. The Greek fathers tended toward speculative thought, delving into the deepest mysteries into which the mind can aspire. The Latin fathers were bound more to practical activity, concerned about legitimate authority and order in the church. The cast of their mind and interest was more juridical than speculative, oriented more to church *praxis* than mystical *gnosis*.

The earliest root of dogmatics can be seen in the apologies written by some of the Eastern fathers. The apologists wrote to defend the Christian faith to the outside pagan world. Their basic apologetic motive was to present Christianity as the fulfillment of the philosophical quest for truth and to affirm Greek philosophy as a preparation for the gospel. Justin Martyr used the concept of the *logos* as the chief term of comparison between Christianity and philosophy. This implied that philosophical concepts are capable of expressing the essence of Christianity. The apologists have been falsely accused of betraying the Christian gospel into the hands of pagan philosophy. They were committed to the belief that the meaning of Jesus Christ can be expressed in categories common to both the Bible and Greek philosophy.

In addition to the apologetic we can see the speculative root of dogmatics most clearly exhibited in the Alexandrian theologians Clement and Origen. These theologians took up the idea of *gnosis* to explain the Christian revelation. Gnosticism is thought to have existed as a pre-Christian mystery religion of Oriental origin, which Christianity encountered in a form transformed by Hellenistic philosophy. Gnosticism taught that mystical knowledge was the way of salvation. The soul aspires to salvation from its bondage to the body, which exists in a radically inferior, physical, fleshly, earth-bound form. Salvation is made possible by the descent of a redeemer from the highest eon to rescue the soul here below, giving it knowledge of the way back home. The gnostic drama of salvation was half mythological and half philosophical. The similarity to the biblical story of salvation was too striking to miss. Christian gnosticism is a fusion of biblical and gnostic symbols of salvation, the most serious heresy to threaten the gospel on Hellenistic soil. The concrete historicity and true humanity of Jesus Christ came to be of secondary importance. The church in the gnosticizing view comprised two levels of Christians: mere believers with nothing but faith (*pistis*) and the truly enlightened, those possessed of knowledge (*gnosis*).

The attempt of Christian gnosticism to transform Christianity into a mystery cult was defeated by church theologians like Clement and Origen. Ordinary believers (*pistikoi*) could grasp the same *logos* of God and his revelation through faith as the gnostics could through knowledge. Admittedly, however, gnosis was the higher form. Clement and Origen were confident that the best insights of philosophy and religion could be appropriated as preparations for the full system of Christian truth. Origen was the first to produce a dogmatics in the Greek language, *Peri Archōn* (*On First Principles*). Origen's significance for dogmatics lay in his fusing of the philosophical understanding of *logos* and *gnosis* with biblical interpretation and theological teaching. The great master was able to hold together biblical exegesis and ontological speculation, historical events and timeless ideas (Plato), faith and *gnosis*, *logos* and Jesus. But after Origen, dogmatics found itself at a crossroads: What Origen kept together split between right- and left-wing factions. Writings in dogmatics became embroiled in the struggle of the church to formulate a christology and a doctrine of the Trinity that would keep the preaching of the gospel continuous with the apostolic witness in opposition to various heresies of the time. The writings of Athanasius and the Cappadocian fathers provide examples of this type of dogmatics, but none of these produced a complete dogmatic system.

In Irenaeus we can see another root of dogmatics, the polemical concern for the truth of the gospel against the incursion of heresy inside the church. Irenaeus did not apologetically address the outside pagan world, as Justin did, nor did he speculatively accommodate Hellenistic wisdom, in the manner of Clement and Origen. Rather, he polemically attacked the gnostic heresy that had erupted inside the church itself. The power behind Irenaeus's dogmatic thrust came from the biblical history of salvation. What theology has recently referred to as "history of salvation" (*Heilsgeschichte*) is adumbrated in Irenaeus's idea of theology as a recapitulation of the economy of salvation in the Bible.

Dogmatics in the East reached its zenith in the orthodox theological system of John of Damascus, building on the chief dogmas of the church, Trinity and christology. Then the creative period of dogmatics in the Eastern church came virtually to an end. Since then the tendency in the dogmatics of Eastern

1 / PROLEGOMENA TO CHRISTIAN DOGMATICS

Orthodoxy has been to reproduce and preserve the traditions formulated by the ancient ecumenical councils.

The West built on the foundations of dogmatics laid in the East, but moved forward in a continual quest for a more precise system of concepts of practical relevance for the church. Tertullian was the first Western theologian to shape the Latin concepts used in later dogmatic thought. He was trained in jurisprudence and demonstrated the skills of a legal expert in choosing precise terminology, particularly in the areas of christology and anthropology. Cyprian, a follower of Tertullian and precursor of Augustine (all three of North Africa) left an indelible mark on the emerging Catholic doctrine of the church. But without doubt the greatest achievement in Western theology was reached by Augustine. Before embracing the orthodox dogmas of the church, Augustine's restless quest for saving truth led him to try the leading options of the day in Manichaean dualism, Ciceronian stoicism, and finally Neo-Platonism. Augustine's journey through the religio-philosophical systems of his epoch meant that as a theologian he would be challenged to answer their questions and to question their answers, and thus significantly broaden the heritage of Western dogmatic thought.

Augustine's dogmatic reflection on how he turned from Neo-Platonism to become a Christian placed a lasting stamp on the subsequent theology of grace in the medieval church and the Protestant Reformation. Augustine's passion was to know, as he said, "God and the soul, only God and the soul." Neo-Platonism taught him that the soul longs to make its way, through mystical contemplation, back to its origin in God. He became a Christian when he discovered the reverse movement of grace, that God in overpowering love comes, through the incarnation, down to the human soul. This is what happened in Jesus Christ, and this is what the church exists to communicate.

Once he became a Christian, Augustine found himself in a struggle against two movements within the church which seemed to threaten the meaning of grace. These movements, Donatism and Pelagianism, sought to restore the moral vigor of the church. Donatism, named after the schismatic bishop Donatus, aimed to purify the church by getting rid of clergy who had lapsed under persecution. This would make the efficacy of grace through Word and sacraments dependent on the moral worthiness of the priest and thereby spell the denial of God's unmerited grace. Pelagianism, named after the monk Pelagius, was declared a heresy because its notion of free will, coupled with the rejection of original sin, kept open the possibility of not sinning, thus denying the necessity of special grace. These movements represent the classical ecclesiological and soteriological heresies, which again and again have surfaced in church history under new guises, with the identical result of converting the gospel into law.

No other theologian in the West matched Augustine in contributing to the history of dogmatics. His teaching was so many-sided that both the reformers and the Roman theologians in the sixteenth century could appeal to Augustine for support, the reformers to his doctrine of sin and grace, law and gospel, letter and spirit, and the Romans, seemingly with equal right, to his concept of nature and grace, eros and agape, city of God and city of earth, and the hierarchical church as an institution dispensing sacraments of salvation.

Our review of dogmatics in the ancient church has given samples of different lines of development. They were the *apologetic* address to the outside pagan world, the *polemical* attack on heresies inside the church, and the *speculative* interest in building up a comprehensive system of Christian truth.

THE MIDDLE AGES

In the Middle Ages dogmatics reaped the harvest of the victory of the church in the Roman Empire. Culturally and politically paganism had given way to the Christian world. Two common prejudices need to be set aside. The first is the prejudice of the Enlightenment, which characterized this thousand-year period as the "Dark Ages" in contrast to the illumination of modern times. The second and opposite prejudice is that of romanticism, which idealized the organic unity and wholeness of religious and cultural life in the Middle Ages, in contrast to the fragmentation which Protestantism brought about. Modern scholarship has invalidated these stereotypes about the medieval period, bringing to light both the creativity and the diversity of the medieval contribution to Christian thought. It was neither as barren nor as monolithic as these distorted pictures would have us believe.

In this section we will list the most notable characteristics of medieval dogmatics, citing some of the classical works in which they were typically embodied.

1. The first is the *scholastic method.* The term "scholastic" refers to the method and doctrines taught by schoolmen in the medieval universities from the tenth to the fifteenth century. Regrettably it has come to mean pedantic quibbling about pointless issues, such as how many angels can dance on the point of a needle, or whether God, being omnipotent, can create a stone so large even God cannot move it. Actually, scholastic method was a dialectical treatment of the church's tradition, gathering opposing views and trying to harmonize the various decrees and doctrines through a process of "yes and no." Abelard's book, *Sic et Non* (Yes and No), set the pattern for all the later scholastics. This dialectical method aimed to reinforce the authority of the tradition by overcoming its apparent internal contradictions.

2. Scholastic theology presupposed the authority of the *tradition.* It proceeded by collecting the sentences of the fathers on the doctrines of faith and

1 / PROLEGOMENA TO CHRISTIAN DOGMATICS

then commenting on them. Peter Lombard's *Four Books of Sentences* became the manual of scholasticism and continued as a classic into the period of the Reformation and Protestant orthodoxy.

3. Scholasticism used *reason* to articulate faith and tradition. Anselm of Canterbury formulated the principle *"credo ut intelligam"* (I believe in order to understand). Faith and tradition are the prior givens; reason and theology are a second step, involving interpretation, even speculation. But not all scholastics agree with Anselm's way to harmonize faith and reason. There was the complementary model of Thomas Aquinas, in which supernatural faith supplements and completes the knowledge of God which reason can gain by natural means. In late scholasticism, the nominalist William of Ockham related faith and reason in an oppositional model. Faith becomes radically subject to authority, because reason is totally incapable of grasping the real ground and contents of faith.

4. There was, moreover, a core of *mysticism* in all of medieval theology, despite its formal allegiance to authority, tradition, and dialectics. Bernard of Clairvaux was the most eminent representative of Christian mysticism. The aim of Christian mysticism was to make the objective substance of Scripture and tradition a matter of subjective experience. Medieval mysticism was deeply nourished by the stream of Neo-Platonism in the Christian tradition, particularly as it was transmitted through the writings of Augustine and Pseudo-Dionysius. Theologically, Christian mysticism stressed the reality of God in the picture of Christ, and ethically the principle of following Jesus.

5. There was only one short step from Neo-Platonic mysticism to *pantheism*. In the early Middle Ages, Johannes Scotus Erigena wrote an outline of systematic theology, *De divisione naturae*, in which he poured the substance of Christian faith into the mystical ontological system of Neo-Platonism. Pantheistic ideas mingled with mystical piety in many of the great scholastics, including Anselm, Bonaventura, and Thomas Aquinas. In this pantheistic way of thinking, creation is conceived of as the actualization of the ideas in the divine mind; everything exists by virtue of participation in the divine being. This trend came to its fullest expression in German mysticism, particularly in the thought of Meister Eckhart.

6. Of utmost importance in the history of medieval scholasticism was the union of Augustine and Aristotle in the *Summa Theologica* of Thomas Aquinas. Thomas was undoubtedly the greatest of the dogmaticians since Augustine. He used the philosophy of Aristotle as an intellectual instrument to set forth the contents of the Christian revelation. Everything found a place in his system: faith and reason, nature and grace, the world and the church, intellectual thought and mystical piety, biblical exegesis and philosophical speculations. It is fitting that he should be called the Doctor of the Church

in Roman Catholicism, and not merely one of the church fathers, because his system is the purest expression of a Catholic vision of God and the world.

7. The introduction of Aristotle into the theological curriculum of the High Middle Ages (thirteenth century) meant that the classical conflicts in philosophy between Platonism and Aristotelianism would be renewed on theological soil. The Augustinians, steeped in Platonism, were not prepared to give way to the "modernism" (*via moderna*) of Thomas Aquinas, with his Aristotelian categories. This was a conflict between a more mystical experiential approach to theology and a more rational scientific approach. One form of this conflict became focused on the problem of universals. It is possible to refer to a whole set of individuals that belong to the same class by one word or name. What unites all the individuals is a universal. Medieval theologians battled over the ontological status of the universals. The Platonic line generally taught that the universals are the realities, existing independently and prior to their embodiment in individual entities. They exist, as it were, in the mind of God, and only thereafter become concepts in the human mind, while being actualized in the individuals of a particular class. Though this position is commonly called medieval realism, it resembles more closely what modern philosophy refers to as idealism. The extreme opposite position became known as nominalism, which holds that universals have no reality in themselves. There are only individual things that become grouped together under a common name or concept. Medieval theologians struggled with this problem of the ontological status of universals and individuals, with far-reaching repercussions in every area of dogmatics. The main schools of late medieval theology—Thomism, Scotism, and Ockhamism—were divided on the precise application of the philosophical problem of universals to theological doctrines.

Although the theologians of the High Middle Ages were receptive to philosophy, they kept it safely subordinate to the authority of the church, assigning to it at best the role of "handmaid" of theology. With confidence they developed the theory of a natural and a revealed theology, joined together in close harmony, the one as the preparation for the other.

THE REFORMATION

Martin Luther, the foremost leader of the Protestant Reformation, was not a dogmatician or systematic theologian. The starting point of Luther's reforming work was not dogma but gospel. His intention was to go deeper than dogma, down to the bedrock of gospel truth concerning how human beings really stand before God. Luther expressed his thoughts in exegetical works, such as his lectures on Romans and his commentary on Galatians, in sermons, and in an abundance of occasional and polemical writings. All this material

1 / PROLEGOMENA TO CHRISTIAN DOGMATICS

was pre-dogmatic, the stuff of which dogma might be constructed by the church. Luther's style was to think in terms of contrasts, for example, the antithesis of law and gospel, and not to systematize his ideas into a harmonious rational synthesis.

Philip Melanchthon's *Loci Communes* of 1521 was the first dogmatics of the Reformation period, winning the praise of both Luther and Calvin. In contrast to the massive *Summas* of medieval scholasticism, Melanchthon's work was merely an outline of dogmatics. "To know Christ is to know his benefits," said Melanchthon, and he followed this principle to reduce the stuff of dogmatics to the questions of soteriology. Melanchthon's little dogmatics underwent a series of editions and achieved its final form in 1559 under the title *Loci praecipui theologici*. Melanchthon's thought had evolved in the meantime. In the earlier work Luther's influence was dominant; the impact of the gospel produced new dogmatic insights into such basic questions as free will, sin, law, justification, faith, works, baptism, and the Lord's Supper. In his latest edition, Melanchthon began to restore certain doctrines of the scholastic tradition, without revising them in light of the new insights of the Reformation. Aristotle's methods and categories, which Luther had expelled, were brought back into the theological system. Thus the later work of Melanchthon formed a bridge to the subsequent dogmatics of Protestant scholasticism.

John Calvin was undoubtedly the most accomplished dogmatician of the Reformation era. His *Institutes of the Christian Religion*, like Melanchthon's *Loci*, gradually evolved through a series of editions until it reached its final form in 1559. It was marked by its biblical orientation and its Augustinian vision of grace, set against every form of Pelagianism in the doctrine of salvation. Although Calvin's intention was to carry forward the reforming work of Luther, it became his destiny to become the theological leader of the Reformed branch of Protestantism, in many ways the polar opposite of Lutheranism.

PROTESTANT ORTHODOXY

The Protestant Reformation, both in its Lutheran and Reformed branches, achieved a highly developed dogmatic form of orthodoxy. Orthodox dogmatics gave a place of prominence once again, as in the Middle Ages, to reason and natural law, cast in Aristotelian thought forms. Yet its chief concern was to frame the central article of the Reformation, justification through faith alone, and to use Scripture alone as the criterion of all true doctrine. These two points, *sola fide* and *sola scriptura*, have been called the material and formal principles of the Reformation.

THE HERITAGE OF DOGMATICS

When the church divided, dogmatics had to become confessional, reflecting either the Roman Catholic theology of the Council of Trent, or the Lutheran theology of the *Book of Concord*, or the Calvinist theology of the Synod of Dort (1618) and various other confessions, such as the Heidelberg Catechism (1563) and the Westminster Confession (1647). These various confessional theologies presupposed the unity of Christian truth and therefore contended with each other's competing claims for the sake of pure doctrine. None could conceive an apology for pluralism, since the loss of consensus in doctrine led directly to political strife and division. In this light it is understandable that the great scholastic systems of the seventeenth century were produced in the midst of the catastrophic religious wars of 1618–48. The central thrust of Lutheran dogmatics was on justifying faith and its realization apart from works of the law, whereas Reformed theology centered in predestinating grace and the unfolding of God's eternal decrees in history. These were not mutually exclusive positions, however, since the Lutherans also affirmed the doctrine of predestination and the Calvinists retained Luther's teaching on justification by faith alone.

Three phases in the development of Lutheran scholastic orthodoxy can be distinguished. First, early orthodoxy was dominated by the theological problems of the Formula of Concord (1577). The leading figure was Martin Chemnitz, whose lectures on Melanchthon's *Loci* were published posthumously as *Loci Theologici*, 1591. The second phase of high orthodoxy was productive of monumental works of doctrine, such as Leonhard Hutter's *Compendium locorum theologicorum* (1610) and Johann Gerhard's *Loci communes theologici* (1610–22). The third phase, that of late orthodoxy, witnessed a massive outpouring of multivolume systems: Abraham Calov's *Systema locorum theologicorum* (1665–77), John Andrew Quenstedt's *Theologia didactico-polemica* (1685), John William Baier's *Compendium theologiae positivae* (1686), and last, David Hollaz's *Examen theologicum acroamaticum* (1707), which marks the end of orthodoxy.

The orthodoxy of Reformed Christianity was far less clearly defined than that of Lutheranism. It possessed no common confession such as the Augsburg Confession (1530) and no book of confessional writings such as the Lutheran *Book of Concord* (1580). It was beset by various movements that challenged the heart of the Calvinist predestinarian system, such as Socinianism, Arminianism, and to some extent also Amyraldism. Finally, Reformed orthodoxy was from the beginning so pluralistic, having spread into so many different countries with such varied languages and cultures, that it remains difficult for historians to define exactly what it is, except that the doctrine of predestination was exalted to the position of dogma.

One of the most significant developments within Reformed Christianity

1 / PROLEGOMENA TO CHRISTIAN DOGMATICS

in the period of high orthodoxy was the "federal theology" of Johannes Coccejus, set forth in his *Summa doctrinae de foedere* (1648). This theology inaugurated the modern tendency to introduce the historical perspective into theology. Instead of thinking of predestination as an absolutely preordained decree which God is simply spelling out, predestination can be thought of as something God is working out in stages in the course of history. Here we find the seeds of the contemporary notion of the history of salvation (*Heilsgeschichte*). And here we find also an opening within orthodoxy to the modern historical interpretation of the Bible.

The achievement of Protestant orthodox dogmatics on the whole was considerable. It demonstrated that Aristotelian philosophy could be used as much in the service of Evangelical as of Roman Catholic theology. The great systems of Protestant scholasticism rivaled the greatest *Summas* of the medieval period. They shared many common features: the ideal of a complete system, natural theology, the *loci* method, propositional truth, the tradition of dogma, and an objective authority.

In the sphere of Roman Catholicism dogmatics was greatly stimulated by its ongoing polemical exchanges with the representatives of the Reformation. For example, the Jesuit Robert Bellarmine wrote his *Disputationes de controversiis Christianae fidei* (1586) as a challenge to Evangelical dogmatics, on the basis of the definitions of the Council of Trent (1545–63). Although the sharp differences between the leading medieval schools of theology continued in the post-Reformation period, Thomistic theology gained the upper hand in the sphere of dogma and church politics. However, it was chiefly the formulas of the system of Thomas, and not much of his spirit, that became the legacy. The Council of Trent defined the terms of Roman Catholic orthodoxy. It was not able to incorporate the leading ideas of the Protestant Reformers, but elevated the good and the bad, the wheat and the chaff, of late medieval theology to the status of ecclesiastical dogma. The shape and content of Roman Catholic dogmatics remained constant from the Council of Trent to the Second Vatican Council, where new winds of doctrine began to modify the monolithic orthodoxy of post-Tridentine Catholicism.

THE DISSOLUTION OF DOGMATICS IN PIETISM AND THE ENLIGHTENMENT

The objectivism of orthodoxy and its system of authority provoked the revolt of pietism and the Enlightenment. Pietism did not reject the objective truths of orthodox dogmatics as such, but reached back to the underlying faith—the subjective element—of Luther's reformation. Its interest was more in the *fides qua creditur* than the *fides quae creditur.* Orthodoxy had defined faith as *notitia, assensus,* and *fiducia. Notitia* (knowledge) involves the mind, *assensus* (assent) the will, and *fiducia* (trust) the heart. Pietism stressed faith as *fiducia,* as trust, and could appeal to what Luther said in his fight against scholastic theology, that it is the heart that makes the theologian. Pietism rightly saw that the inner power of the Reformation was its preaching of the Word, establishing a new personal relationship to God by the grace of forgiveness and not by the works of the law. Pietism produced no great works in the area of dogmatics. It was more concerned for practical religion and the Christian life, and even mistrusted the intellect at work in theology.

In the wake of pietism came the revolt of the Enlightenment against the supernaturalist dogmatics of orthodoxy. The goal of the Enlightenment was to reduce Christianity to what can be grasped by reason. Immanuel Kant wrote the religious manifesto for the Enlightenment, *Religion within the Limits of Reason Alone.* The theologians of the Enlightenment accepted the natural theology of orthodoxy, but overthrew its supernatural superstructure as beyond the principles of a reasonable religion. The specific elements of traditional dogmatics were subjected to rigorous criticism and finally dissolved into a rationalistic form of mysticism, metaphysics, and morality.

THE REVIVAL OF DOGMATICS IN THE NINETEENTH CENTURY

The task of the nineteenth century was to go beyond rationalism and place dogmatics on a new footing. At the same time, it could not simply repudiate the achievements of the Enlightenment, particularly the new methods of biblical criticism and the emerging world view of modern science. Nor was there much chance to repristinate the confessional dogmatics of Protestant orthodoxy, although the attempt was made.

The new beginnings in nineteenth-century dogmatics took up certain trends of the times, such as romanticism and idealism, that had overtaken the flatland of rationalistic thinking, yet without surrendering the critical spirit of the Enlightenment. Friedrich Schleiermacher made the initial breakthrough in his book, *Speeches on Religion to Its Cultured Despisers.* It is an apology for the category of religion as *sui generis,* distinct from rational knowledge and moral principle. The essence of religion is "the feeling of absolute dependence." Schleiermacher could also call it "God-consciousness." This general concept of religion became the starting point of Schleiermacher's new construction of dogmatics, which he called *Glaubenslehre,* the doctrine of faith. Dogmatics is to be the description of the faith that exists in the Christian community. Hence Schleiermacher could speak of dogmatics as a positive

1 / PROLEGOMENA TO CHRISTIAN DOGMATICS

science and subsume it under historical theology. The point of this descriptive task is to show how everything that is distinctively Christian is "related to the redemption accomplished by Jesus of Nazareth."[4] Therefore Schleiermacher's dogmatics was both grounded in the church and centered in Christ, characteristics which proved decisive in almost all later schools of theology.

In 1818 Georg Wilhelm Friedrich Hegel became Schleiermacher's colleague in Berlin, but he was far from collegial. Hegel inaugurated a trend in theology in polar contrast to Schleiermacher's. Hegel was a philosopher, perhaps in his own way a theologian, but certainly not a dogmatician. Yet he produced a universal system in which all the symbols of the Christian tradition were given a philosophical interpretation, and he thus became enormously influential on the most creative minds and trends in the nineteenth century. For Hegel, religion was not essentially subjective feeling, but the symbolic representation of the dialectical self-actualization of the absolute Spirit (*Geist*) in nature and history. Theology bearing Hegel's influence split into a left-wing and a right-wing school of interpretation. The issue on which the split occurred was whether the universal meaning of history can be tied to the particular historical events on which Christian faith is based, or whether these events are merely temporary exemplifications which can in principle be phased out or transcended in the further course of history. The significance of Hegel for dogmatics thus has to do with the interpretation of history. It opened the struggle for the truly historical character of Christian faith, a fight which is still going on with no end in sight.

The remainder of the nineteenth century lived in the shadow of the three towering philosophers of religion: Kant, Schleiermacher, and Hegel. The school of mediating theology (*Vermittlungstheologie*) combined features from both Schleiermacher and Hegel. The Erlangen school, epitomized by J. C. K. von Hofmann, developed the Christian interpretation of history known as *Heilsgeschichte*. Confessional theology worked to repristinate the pre-Enlightenment dogmatics of the church. Albrecht Ritschl and his school rediscovered the philosophy of Kant, as it was then interpreted by Hermann Lotze. Ritschl's dogmatics took a sharp turn away from Hegel, rejecting all metaphysics and choosing instead a moral foundation of religion. Ritschl claimed to follow Luther in his rejection of all scholastic speculation, focusing instead on justifying faith and its vocation in the world. Ritschl's influence dominated the teaching of dogmatics for decades, until it gave way at the turn of the century to new directions, some defined by Martin Kähler and Adolf Schlatter, and others by the history-of-religions school, which had a direct impact on theology through the works of Albert Schweitzer and Ernst Troeltsch.

THE STATE OF DOGMATICS
IN THE TWENTIETH CENTURY

The optimism of the post-Enlightenment view of human progress was shattered by World War I. The leading schools of modern Protestant dogmatics came to a crashing halt. The beginnings of a new theology emerged in the context of the parish. Karl Barth, Friedrich Gogarten, and Emil Brunner were all parish pastors, who read the "signs of the times" and asked the same question, "Do we have a Word of God for the crises of our time?" Thus there arose the school of dialectical theology, sometimes called theology of crisis, which was convinced that theology could no longer proceed along nineteenth-century lines. Rudolf Bultmann and Paul Tillich also agreed with Karl Barth about the need for a new beginning. All these theologians were united in their criticism of the theology of modern Protestantism. Once they began to sketch out their own proposals for a new dogmatics, however, the school of dialectical theology began to break up into various factions.

The early period of twentieth-century dogmatics, sandwiched between the two world wars, was a time of rediscovery. Karl Barth and Emil Brunner returned behind modern Protestantism and the Enlightenment to the christocentric theology of the Word of God in Luther and Calvin. Gustaf Aulén and Anders Nygren, co-leaders of Lundensian theology (Sweden), also returned to the theology of Luther, stressing the Reformation motifs of God's agape-love, Christ's dramatic victory over the tyrants, and the justification of sinners. At the same time, Oscar Cullmann and Gerhard von Rad developed the categories for a biblical theology of the history of salvation, aiming to supplant the traditional dogmatic concepts derived from Hellenistic metaphysics.

The second period covers the time from World War II to the new departures in theology in the early 1960s. "Hermeneutics" became the common word to express the concern for a meaningful interpretation of the Christian gospel in terms that modern people can understand. Rudolf Bultmann proposed his program of demythologizing the Bible in order to grasp its message in existential terms. Paul Tillich proposed the method of correlation. Like Bultmann he used the categories of existentialist philosophy to relate the biblical message to the modern situation. The difference between them was chiefly that Tillich went beyond existentialism and drew heavily on nineteenth-century German classical idealism (Schelling and Hegel) for his ontological interpretation of theology. The concern for a meaningful interpretation of the biblical message was then programmatically intensified in the hermeneutical theology of Gerhard Ebeling and Ernst Fuchs. They constructed a theory of language to explain the transition from the Word of God in Scrip-

1 / PROLEGOMENA TO CHRISTIAN DOGMATICS

ture to the event of faith in contemporary existence. In a parallel development, Friedrich Gogarten extended certain of Dietrich Bonhoeffer's prison insights in the direction of a secular interpretation of the gospel. The thesis in this line is that the gospel, rightly understood, promotes the process of secularization, and is no longer dependent on a prior religious category of experience. This trend took a radical turn in the American "Death of God" theology. In different ways the radical theologians Paul van Buren, William Hamilton, and Thomas J. J. Altizer speculated on the shape of a theology without God or belief in God. The phenomenon of Christian atheism quickly revealed itself as an absurdity and is now remembered as a curious wrinkle in the theology of modern times.

The Word-of-God theology of neo-orthodoxy operated without any positive correlation with philosophy in general or metaphysics in particular. During this time, Paul Tillich continued to stress that philosophy could serve in some way as the handmaid of theology. He coined the phrase "Philosophy asks the question, theology provides the answer." Others, too, worked to formulate an appropriate philosophical theology for use in the construction of a specifically Christian theology. This is a third significant phase in the development of contemporary theology. Process theologians like Schubert Ogden and John Cobb used the metaphysics of Alfred North Whitehead and Charles Hartshorne to make explicit the meaning of Christian faith. On another front theologians such as I. T. Ramsey used the philosophy of ordinary language of Ludwig Wittgenstein to clarify the logic of religious language. The Jesuit priest Pierre Teilhard de Chardin projected the outline of an evolutionary theology, bringing theology into a close correlation with the world view of the natural sciences. In Roman Catholic circles Karl Rahner and Bernard Lonergan, both Jesuits, placed traditional Thomist thought on the new foundations of post-Kantian critical philosophy. For this reason their thought is referred to as transcendental Thomism.

It is clear that no single philosophy is now universally acceptable among theologians as a partner for theological work. At the present time there is a new affirmation of the philosophy of G. W. F. Hegel and Karl Marx. The eschatological theologians—Wolfhart Pannenberg and Jürgen Moltmann—have launched their perspectives in conjunction with a creative appropriation of Hegelian insights. As eschatological theology sought to make itself relevant to the practical situation in the world today, it became fragmented into several schools of thought. Jürgen Moltmann together with Johann Baptist Metz developed a political interpretation of the gospel. Others, seeking to be more radical, called for a theology of revolution, drawing on eschatological messianism. At the present time the theology of liberation is the new key for a complete reinterpretation of the texts and traditions of Christian faith. It draws heavily on the revolutionary ideas of Karl Marx, seeking a practical

THE HERITAGE OF DOGMATICS

transformation of the world in accordance with the socialist vision of justice and peace.

It is no exaggeration to state that pluralism is the most fitting word to characterize the present situation in theology. There is no single reigning dogmatics for the church, no such thing as an ecumenical dogmatics that synthesizes the truths in all the bodies of Christendom. There are distinctly contradictory currents, some trying to restore old modes of orthodoxy, others reaching for equally tired ideas of liberalism, sometimes without enough knowledge of the tradition to know that some new proposals are not so new after all.

NOTES

1. Wolfgang Trillhaas, *Dogmatic* (Berlin: Alfred Töpelmann, 1962), pp. 15-16.
2. Adolf von Harnack, *History of Dogma*, trans. Neil Buchanan, 7 vols. (New York: Dover Publications, 1961).
3. The following works were consulted in this brief sketch of the history of dogmatics: Karl Barth, *Protestant Theology in the Nineteenth Century* (Valley Forge, Pa.: Judson Press, 1973); J. F. Bethune-Baker, *An Introduction to the Early History of Christian Doctrine* (Cambridge: At the University Press, 1902); Hans von Campenhausen, *The Fathers of the Greek Church*, trans. Stanley Godman (New York: Pantheon Books, 1959); Aloys Grillmeier, *Christ in Christian Tradition*, trans. J. S. Bowden (New York and London: Sheed & Ward, 1965); Gerhard Gloege, "Christliches Dogma," in RGG³, ed. Kurt Galling (Tübingen: J. C. B. Mohr [Paul Siebeck], 1958), cols. 221-25; Harnack, *History of Dogma*, vols. 1-7; Edward Caldwell Moore, *History of Christian Thought since Kant* (London: Gerald Duckworth & Co., 1912); J. L. Neve, *A History of Christian Thought* (Philadelphia: Fortress [Muhlenberg] Press, 1946); Jaroslav Pelikan, *The Christian Tradition: A History of the Development of Doctrine*, vol. 1, *The Emergence of the Catholic Tradition (100-600)* (Chicago: University of Chicago Press, 1971); Carl Heinz Ratschow, *Lutherische Dogmatik zwischen Reformation und Aufklärung* (Gütersloh: Gerd Mohn, 1964), part 1; Reinhold Seeberg, *History of Doctrines*, trans. Charles Hay (Grand Rapids: Baker Book House, 1954), vols. 1 & 2; Heinrich Schmid, *The Doctrinal Theology of the Evangelical Lutheran Church*, trans. Charles A. Hay and Henry E. Jacobs (Minneapolis: Augsburg Publishing House, 1899); Paul Tillich, *A History of Christian Thought*, ed. Carl E. Braaten (New York: Simon & Schuster, 1972); Henry A. Wolfson, *The Philosophy of the Church Fathers* (Cambridge, Mass.: Harvard University Press, 1956), vol 1.
4. Friedrich Schleiermacher, *The Christian Faith*, ed. H. R. Mackintosh and J. S. Stewart (Edinburgh: T. & T. Clark, 1928), p. 52.

3
The Fundamentals of Dogmatics

The aim of dogmatics is to contribute to the proper understanding of the gospel in the church. Dogmatic theology does not begin and end with an interpretation of dogma, but traces the meaning of dogma to its ground in the witness of Scripture and serves the missionary proclamation of the church. The main theme of dogmatics is the self-revelation of God in the history of God's people Israel, in Jesus Christ, and in the apostolic witness of faith.

THE CONCEPT OF DOGMA

There can be no doubt that the word "dogma" provokes an allergic reaction on the face of modern theological thought. "Dogma" conjures up a coercive teaching of an authoritarian church, a static and sterile statement of truth frozen in the manuals of ecclesiastical dogmatics. This allergic reaction can be seen throughout the Christian world today. Even at Vatican II the Roman Catholic church chose to promulgate no new dogma with a polemical bite, but only to issue teachings with a pastoral intent. No anathemas were pronounced! The age of dogmatism seemed to be over. Instead, there was growing recognition of pluralism and ecumenical openness. To many observers it seemed that Rome was going the way of Protestantism, implicitly acknowledging the thesis of Adolf von Harnack that the history of dogma has come to an end.

At the First Vatican Council dogma was defined as truth revealed by God, officially proclaimed by the teaching office of the church, and binding on all faithful Christians. The intention was clear even then that the church does not make up dogma on its own authority, but defines dogma from what is *given* in revelation.³ Dogma is therefore binding on the faithful not primarily because of the authority of the church but because of the divine revelation which dogma contains. Protestants have often mistakenly heard only the ring of ecclesiastical authoritarianism in the notion of dogma. In any case, the Second Vatican Council and leading Roman Catholic theologians today

1 / PROLEGOMENA TO CHRISTIAN DOGMATICS

teach that dogma is a witness to revelation,[2] a sign of the church's reception of revelation, whose truth is constant but whose formulation is subject to further development. What is permanent is the truth, but the statement of the truth is historically conditioned and open to change. Hence, a dogmatic statement points beyond itself to the mystery of God's self-communication in Jesus Christ. The dogma must make use of finite concepts to refer to what is inherently infinite and incomprehensible. The point is that the content and the meaning of the dogma must be distinguished, but not separated, from the linguistic and historical forms of expression which dogmatics utilizes at any given time.

The contemporary Roman Catholic concept of dogma makes allowance for the difference between the truth already known and the final truth yet to come. Dogma lives within the eschatological horizon of Christian faith and understanding. Walter Kasper has formulated this point very well:

> Both finality and provisionality belong to dogma. Dogma is one way in which the gospel of the eschatological coming of Christ expresses itself in the church. A dogma is the provisional occurrence of the eschatological final truth of Christ. By means of the word "provisional" the anticipatory character of the dogma should be expressed. It is not meant to be contradictory to "final." On the contrary, it is meant in the original meaning of the word as a provisional fore-conception of the eschaton, to which the church opens itself in light of the eschatological future. This means, then, that a dogma does not close history but keeps it open to the future.[3]

Dogma lives in the tension between the gospel of the kingdom which has already arrived in Jesus Christ and the final future of the promise which yet remains outstanding. The heart of dogma is Jesus Christ himself, to whom the Christian community can look back as its origin and to whom it can look forward as its destiny and goal in the future of God. This concentration of dogma on the Christ-event in current Roman Catholic teaching points to the primacy of Scripture over tradition, paving the way for possible rapprochement with the Reformation view of the relation between gospel and dogma.

The view of Adolf von Harnack that the history of dogma ended with the faith of Luther has nourished a widespread Protestant prejudice against dogmatic theology. But no one could have been more concerned than Luther for a faith clearly expressed in true doctrine. Against Erasmus, Luther cried: "Take away assertions, and you take away Christianity."[4] It is erroneous to picture Luther as placing faith on the side of feeling, opposed to pure doctrine. Luther was not opposed to the dogmas of the church as such, but only to a theology that derives dogma from the church rather than from the Word of God. The Apostles' Creed is true not because the church teaches it but because it is a true summary of the doctrine contained in Scripture. Hence,

THE FUNDAMENTALS OF DOGMATICS

also, Luther's words concerning the creeds and councils of the church in general had the effect of relativizing their authority, but always with respect to the prior authority of Scripture, not with respect to autonomous reason. Holy Scripture is a prior norm for reading the doctrines of the fathers and decrees of the councils. The dogmatic decisions of the councils do not stand on the authority of the church, but refer back to the prior authority of Scripture. Luther wrote:

> These then are the four principal Councils and the reasons they were held. The first, in Nicaea, defended the divinity of Christ against Arius; the second, in Constantinople, defended the divinity of the Holy Spirit against Macedonius; the third, in Ephesus, defended the one person of Christ against Nestorius; the fourth, in Chalcedon, defended the two natures in Christ against Eutyches. But no new articles of faith were thereby established, for these four doctrines are formulated far more abundantly and powerfully in St. John's gospel alone, even if the other evangelists and St. Paul and St. Peter had written nothing about it, although they, together with the prophets, also teach and bear convincing witness to all of that.[5]

As we compare Luther's view of the relation between dogma and Scripture to current Roman Catholic teaching, we find that both agree in referring the content of dogma to the revelation of Scripture. It was not Luther's intent to elevate *sola scriptura* at the expense of dogma, nor do Roman Catholic theologians today place dogma on a par with Scripture. In both cases, at least in principle, the priority of the Word of God is maintained over the creeds and councils of the church.

We enter another world of thought altogether with the rise of modern Protestant theology. The use of the critical historical method eroded the very concept of dogma as a binding statement of revealed truth. Adolf von Harnack drove a sharp wedge between the gospel and dogma. In his classic *History of Dogma* Harnack stated, "Dogma in its conception and development is a work of the Greek spirit on the soil of the Gospel."[6] Harnack's view that the gospel is not dogma, but is instead falsified by it, epitomizes the modern Protestant dream of an undogmatic Christianity, one that impinges on religious feeling or moral action and abandons the claim of doctrinal truth. For Harnack the hellenization of Christianity meant the conversion of the gospel into the static and timeless realm of intellectualistic ideas. Harnack did not object, of course, to the effort of the church to make the gospel intelligible in clear statements. He was even able to state, "Christianity without dogma, that is, without a clear expression of its content, is inconceivable."[7] He seems to contradict himself, but the contradiction is only apparent. Harnack actually maintained that it was inevitable for the church fathers to give systematic intellectual expression to the gospel, but the dogmas which resulted from their

1 / PROLEGOMENA TO CHRISTIAN DOGMATICS

effort are bound to the historical period in which they were produced and possess no binding validity for later times.

Harnack's work emphasized the historical relativity of dogma, but the generation of theologians that was to follow him did not accept his verdict at face value. Harnack's most famous pupil, Karl Barth, spent a lifetime writing dogmatics for the church and placed himself decidedly on the side of the classical dogmas. Barth, however, turned Harnack's relativization of dogma on its head. All doctrines of the church, emerging in history, are relativized primarily through their relation to the transcendent Word of God. The concrete dogmas of the church, though relativized by the revealed Word, Jesus Christ, do not lose their value as guides for our own dogmatic work.[8] They are not final and absolute, to be sure. Rather, they point beyond themselves to the *dogma* which is the perfect knowledge of the Word of God. This is never realized in the pilgrim church; it always remains an eschatological goal. Barth has not dissolved dogma in the relativities of history, like Harnack. But he has severely limited dogma in terms of the ongoing gap in time between faith and knowledge, human language and the Word of God, history and the eschatological goal. The *dogma* is a transcendent goal and model of the *dogmas*. Barth saw that the relation between the latter and the former is one of radical obedience to the Word of God revealed in Christ and Scripture and proclaimed by the church.

Emil Brunner, an early close associate of Karl Barth, defined truth in terms of encounter, appropriating Martin Buber's concept of the I-Thou relationship.[9] Brunner opposed this concept of truth to the notion of truth as a property of propositions, which fits into a subject-object scheme, an I-It relationship. Brunner argued that truth-as-encounter is the biblical concept of truth. It is difficult to fit dogma into this personalist theory of truth-as-encounter. Yet Brunner, admitting that dogma bears all the marks of legalism and is therefore alien to faith, does not wish to get rid of dogma altogether. The function of dogma or doctrine is to lead to the event of the personal encounter with God through the hearing of the Word. The purpose of dogma in the Christian faith is to lead to Jesus Christ, as the law to the gospel, as the letter to the spirit. In this way, Brunner follows Barth in subordinating church doctrine to the personal encounter with Jesus Christ. Doctrines are the setting for the jewel of the gospel.[10]

After World War II the journal *Kerygma und Dogma* was founded in Germany. It signaled a more positive turn to dogma and dogmatics. The nineteenth century, climaxing in Adolf von Harnack, rightly perceived the danger of dogma becoming a tool of an authoritarian church and a lifeless deposit of archaic beliefs. But the overreaction of Protestantism to the Catholic concept of dogma stood in need of correction. New Testament scholarship demonstrated clearly that the preaching of the kerygma in primitive Christianity was not the sole and all-sufficient medium of the knowledge of God's saving revelation in Jesus Christ.[11] Preaching was immediately accompanied by teaching (*didache*) and the transmission of tradition (*paradosis*). The New Testament does not record merely a series of existential encounters of an I-Thou type. It communicates a *subject matter* that claims the authority of God and of Jesus Christ. These are truths of revelation, meaningful events, that can be taught and learned and passed on by disciples who tell *what* they have seen and heard. New Testament Christianity is not simply concerned with personal encounters and existential relationships, let alone religious feelings; it contains the *dogmata* of the apostles which refer to the good news of salvation. There is a natural and continuous relationship between the *kerygma* which the apostles preached, the *didache* which they taught, and the *paradosis* which they passed on to their disciples. It is simply false to set these facets of early Christianity into an antagonistic relationship.[12]

Dogma is not an alienating move away from the gospel, but an intrinsic development of interpretation to a more advanced reflective level of consciousness within the Christian community. The gospel is not antidogmatic. Without dogma it would be inherently impossible to pronounce any anathema against heretical teachings which cut the nerve of the church's gospel. An undogmatic Christianity can no longer tell the difference between true and false preaching of the gospel. The point of dogma is to ensure the correct interpretation of the gospel, not to make faith legalistically dependent on church authority. As Luther put the matter:

> It is the promises of God that make the Church and not the Church that makes the promise of God. For the Word of God is incomparably superior to the Church, and in the Word the Church, being a creature, has nothing to decree, ordain, or make, but only to be decreed, ordained and made. For who begets his own parent? Who first brings forth his own maker?[13]

A dogma is not true because the church teaches it. It is true only if it brings to expression the true meaning of the gospel. Luther stated that only God's Word can establish an article of faith, no one else, not even an angel.[14] This leads to a critical, gospel-oriented notion of dogma and away from an ecclesiastical positivism which refers faith to whatever the church or its authorities happen to decree as revealed truth. The criterion to apply is whether dogma conveys the truth of the gospel, not whether it has been officially promulgated by the church. Whenever the church supports its dogmas by sheer appeal to its own authority, the hermeneutical link between dogma and gospel is weakened and the primacy of the gospel and its creative authority are surrendered.

The new affirmation of dogma as continuous with the kerygma can be found

1 / PROLEGOMENA TO CHRISTIAN DOGMATICS

in the dogmatics of major twentieth-century theologians. We need only refer to the works of Paul Althaus, Werner Elert, Regin Prenter, Gerhard Gloege, Edmund Schlink, and Wolfhart Pannenberg. Edmund Schlink made a notable contribution to the contemporary understanding of dogma in his article "The Structure of Dogmatic Statements as an Ecumenical Problem."[15] There is more than one form of human response to divine revelation. Schlink says, "Dogmatic scholarship is obliged to consider the rich diversity of Christian responses, whether in proclamation, in demanding, in thanksgiving, in assurance, in prayer, or in doxology."[16] Dogmas and creeds are among the forms of response which the Christian community makes in confessing its faith in God. The aim of a dogmatic statement is to make a clear and definitive expression of *what* God has revealed.

Wolfhart Pannenberg, once Schlink's pupil, integrated Schlink's positive assessment of dogma into his own systematic theology.[17] Pannenberg also moves dogma away from its traditional connection with the authoritarian claim of the church to its historical ground in the concrete history of Jesus Christ whose universal meaning the Scriptures declare. The function of a dogmatic statement is to bring to the level of knowledge the universal meaning of the historical particularity of the message of Jesus Christ. Church dogmas are true and refer to what really happened, but can never be more than provisional because our grasp of the universal meaning of Jesus is always partial. We should not absolutize dogma, because there is a real distinction between revelation and dogma. Dogma is the sum of the church's knowledge of revelation accessible to faith. But neither should we minimize the importance of dogma, because it intends to express nothing less than the apostolic witness to the truth of revelation in the actual history of Jesus. On the basis of history and the modern historical-critical method we have in Pannenberg's notion of dogma a new formulation of the Reformation principle of *sola scriptura*.

One of the chief motives for the Protestant flight from dogma can be removed by rejecting its authoritarian connections. What we retain is a clear picture of the essential place of dogma in the scheme of theological knowledge. Theology inevitably goes beyond telling the gospel story. It formulates its universal meaning for our consciousness of truth and for the whole of reality. Dogmatic statements do not merely repeat the events in historical sequence. They claim to speak of God as the Creator and Eschaton of history on the basis of the particular events witnessed in Scripture. They speak of the universality and totality of meaning, but always in a provisional and proleptic way, because history is still going on and the church is not yet at the end. "The church's dogma," says Pannenberg, "which is still on the way, cannot itself be the eschatological form of revealed truth."[18] The authority of a dogmatic statement must not pretend to straddle all history from the vantage point of the eschaton.

THE FUNDAMENTALS OF DOGMATICS

THE CONFESSIONAL PRINCIPLE

Within the tradition of the Reformation, the churches have developed their own confessional heritage beyond the classical dogmas of the ancient church. The attempt of some Protestants to profess "no creeds but Christ" has only produced a new confessional stance, even if not pronounced in so many words. A creedless, nonconfessional, undogmatic Christianity has proven itself incapable of reproducing vital forms of witness to the New Testament gospel.

Lutheran churches have stressed the confessional principle more than the Reformed and the Radical Protestant branches of the Reformation. Yet the confessional principle has been a constant source of controversy in world Lutheranism, not least in the United States. The right wing appeals to the confessional principle to exclude all new developments in modern theology. Committed to a theology of repristination, it lifts up the *Book of Concord*,[19] sometimes coupled with seventeenth-century scholasticism, as the golden age, the once-for-all model of what theology must be. Here doctrines become laws, creating a climate of doctrinal legalism in the church, snuffing out the freedom which is the church's birthright from the gospel.

The other extreme, the heritage of liberalism, strives to dissolve the confessional principle in theology. One form of this nonconfessional attitude goes behind the confessional writings of the church to the heroic faith of the young man Luther, making his image into an object of hero worship. Much of modern Luther research was inspired by the desire to undercut the authority of orthodox confessionalism, in the hope of salvaging Luther from Lutheranism, in order to gain leverage in the clash between liberalism and orthodoxy. Another form of the anticonfessional approach reaches back to the Bible, ironically turning the confessional principle of *sola scriptura* against itself, as a principle of self-dissolution. The pietistic heritage had a strong biblicist tendency, joined with a kind of antiintellectualism that looked upon dogmas and doctrines with suspicion. Each believer with Bible in hand had a right to his or her own private interpretation, pitting the Spirit against the collective consciousness of the community expressed in its confessional teachings.

The confessional principle can be maintained within a creative tension between the pole of continuity, which grounds dogmatics in the catholic substance of the faith, and the pole of contemporaneity, which keeps the church open to modern horizons of experience and understanding. The disregard of either principle leads to a polarization of theology between orthodox confessionalism and liberal modernism. Dogmatics can look for insights in the creeds and confessions of the church without being archaistic, and it can learn new ways of thinking without becoming modernistic.

The authority the confessions claim for themselves is limited. They always speak in the indicative rather than the imperative mood. They introduce their

1 / PROLEGOMENA TO CHRISTIAN DOGMATICS

statements with the phrase "We believe, confess, and teach," declaring not what must be believed in order to have true faith but what is already believed on the basis of faith in the gospel of Christ. They are not so much a legal requirement as an evangelical witness, not legally binding canonical norms, but human testimonies of faith in the Word of God. The confessions subordinate themselves to the Holy Scriptures of the Old and New Testaments. This means that no doctrinal dispute can be decided for the church merely by a legalistic appeal to the confessions. That would be a shortcut for a church that holds to the primacy of Scripture.

A confessional church stands for a concrete and specific witness to the truth of the gospel. Those who subscribed confessional writings in the sixteenth century were willing to stake their lives on the truth they believed and taught. They were convinced that their confession participated in the very truth of the gospel itself. The act of confessional subscription contains a risk, of course, because the church is fallible, councils can err, dogmas are provisional, and confessional statements are conditioned by the set of questions they address at a particular time of church history.

Today we may witness to the power of the confessions to liberate the church for a new hearing of the gospel. The confessions may become "emancipation proclamations" at a time when the church becomes captive to the spirit of the age. The Barmen Declaration was just such a confession, equipping the Confessing Church to withstand the heresy of the "German Christians." Nonconfessional churches were impotent in face of the Aryan heresy. The church at the time derived great strength and freedom from its confession of the one Lordship of Jesus Christ against all pretenders to the throne of absolute leadership. Under persecution and attack the Confessing Christians experienced the liberating effects of a church confession. As in the past, so in the contemporary period the church was bound to formulate a new confession in a special kairos to face a particular crisis.

The particular confessions of the Lutheran church, chiefly the Augsburg Confession and Luther's Small Catechism, claim to voice the truth of the gospel that concerns the whole church. The confessional principle intends to be ecumenical, not sectarian. If the particular confessions of the Lutheran church point to the gospel, and nothing else, and if other confessions point in their own way, in their own time and place, to the same gospel, we can expect a meeting of the confessions in their common reference to the same core and substance of faith. Article VII of the Augsburg Confession states that "for the true unity of the church it is enough to agree concerning the teaching of the Gospel and the administration of the sacraments" (*BC* 32). As the various communions strive to understand their own confessional heritage, they may converge on the same point which lies at the center of the faith they hold in common. It is erroneous to conceive of the rich diversity of Christian

52

confessions in history on the adversarial model. They may be more complementary than competitive. Each communion best serves the interest of the one, holy, catholic, and apostolic church when it remains true to the substance of its own confession and humbly calls on other communions to listen to its witness in a spirit of dialogue and mutual service.

It is the purpose of the confessional writings in the Lutheran *Book of Concord*, for example, to serve the catholic church by referring it to the unifying gospel of Christ. This gospel is summarized in terms of justification by grace alone, through faith alone, on account of Christ alone. This is a summary of the whole gospel. The stress on the word "alone" is not a denominational peculiarity, which other churches and sects may magnanimously allow to the Lutherans, while others are permitted to pursue and accent their own denominational specialty, be it papal infallibility, episcopal succession, presbyterian polity, congregational autonomy, liturgical legalism, or pentecostal spirituality. With the deletion of the *sola* the gospel itself is betrayed, not merely some Lutheran idiosyncrasy.

The crucial significance of the Reformation principle of *sola gratia/sola fide* has been confirmed by major contemporary Roman Catholic theologians, such as Karl Rahner, Hans Küng, Walter Kasper, and many others. In his *Foundations of Christian Faith*, Karl Rahner discusses the three famous "alone's" of the Reformation: grace alone, faith alone, and Scripture alone. He concludes his treatment by acknowledging that the core of the original Reformation and of Evangelical Christianity is identical with Catholic faith and doctrine. He writes, "We can and must, therefore, hold the doctrine 'by grace alone' with an ardour which is both Christian and Catholic."[20]

The chief dogma of the Reformation, justification through faith alone, is an hermeneutical proposal. It offers the key for the right interpretation of the Holy Scriptures. The decisive question to which the Scriptures provide an answer is how humanity stands before God in the ultimate dimension. If dogmaticians do not use this hermeneutical key in biblical exegesis, they will use some other one. There is no presuppositionless approach to the Scriptures. The purely scientific historian who imagines that the Scriptures can be read and understood without any presuppositions is a victim of naive positivism.

The confessions possess hermeneutical significance because they point to the central message of the Scriptures as a whole. They are like a map giving directions on how to find the way through the Scriptures. The absolute confessionalist is like one who studies the map but neglects to take the trip. The anticonfessionalist sets off on the trip with no map for guidance, and quickly gets lost on the way. The confessions are a means to an end, just that but not less than that.

The chief point of the church's creeds and confessions is not to guarantee

1 / PROLEGOMENA TO CHRISTIAN DOGMATICS

"true doctrine" but rather to set norms for the right preaching of the gospel. Preaching has a confessional content; it is also a confessing act. Every sound preacher is a public confessor of the faith of the church. Preaching is secularized if kerygmatic style is achieved at the expense of confessional content; this is the main temptation of modern Protestant Christianity. Conversely, preaching becomes sterile if the content is frozen in creedal propositions, lacking the existential dimension of the *credo*. This has been the tendency of orthodoxy in both its Protestant and Roman Catholic traditions. Christian preaching is not a mere report of what has been believed once upon a time; it is the announcement of what the living church believes today on the basis of the biblical witness to the gospel. Preaching thus reflects the truth of what the Samaritans said to the woman at the well: "It is no longer because of your words that we believe, for we have heard for ourselves, and we know that this is indeed the Savior of the world" (John 4:42).

The confessional life and understanding of the church need not be static. The church is free to take the risk of extending the confessional limits of her own tradition. The confessions are not the final formulation of the gospel. New confessions will need to be written and subscribed from time to time. The past creeds and confessions of the church must not be glorified, for the church is made of sinners on their pilgrim way, possessing at best imperfect and fragmentary knowledge. The church will watchfully live by faith and hope in the expectation of new light until at last she will see face to face in a state of eschatological glory. Meanwhile, the church is "at once just and sinner" (*simul iustus, simul peccator*). The eschatological perspective calls the church to repentance, in need of forgiveness also in its confessional life. Luther's distinction between a theology of the cross and a theology of glory is directly applicable to the way in which the church uses its creeds and confessions.

There is no *a priori* reason to oppose a new ecumenical council of all the churches in which a major confessional act might occasion the reunion of the divided churches. Jesus prayed to the Father that his followers might all be one. It is right that all Christians pray for the historical realization of his ecumenical prayer.

THE FUNDAMENTALS OF DOGMATICS

It is the task of dogmatics to present the truth of God's revelation as apprehended by the faith of the Christian church. Dogmatics deals with the knowledge of faith within the context of the church and the history of its traditions. There are no revealed dogmas which must be believed. The object of faith is always God, in and through the means of God's own self-revelation. "God and faith belong together," said Luther. But faith is not an empty response; it is no mere emotional reaction. When faith expresses what it has

THE FUNDAMENTALS OF DOGMATICS

received from God's saving revelation, it gives rise to the kind of truth and knowledge of which doctrines and dogmas are made.

The knowledge of faith is a subject of deep personal interest, but it is no private matter. God's revelation has created a community of believers and therefore a common faith which belongs to the one universal church as well as to each of its members. Dogmatics deals with the fundamental dogmatic decisions the church has formulated on the basis of the divine revelation which has created its common faith.

It is necessary for the Christian church to formulate dogmatics. No other community can do it. First, the church must formulate dogmatics to ground its own teachings in the truth which God's revelation has disclosed for the knowledge of faith. Dogmatics is concerned about the *identity* of the Christian faith. Second, the church must formulate dogmatics to criticize and renew itself with reference to the source and norm of its life and message. Dogmatics is concerned for the present *vitality* of the church's proclamation. Third, dogmatics is necessary to help the missionary church distinguish between the invariant essence of the gospel and the cultural forms in which it embodies itself from time to time. Dogmatics is concerned for the *integrity* of the Christian mission in the world. Fourth, dogmatics is indispensable to help the church remain faithful to its own interior meaning through the discontinuities of time. Dogmatics is concerned for the historical *continuity* of the faith. These principles of identity, vitality, integrity, and continuity are inherent in the classical Christian belief of the *una sancta catholica et apostolica*. When they are present in the right balance, the church will be doing rightly what it is called to do: preaching the gospel, teaching the faith, interpreting the word, evangelizing the nations, and liberating the captives.

The basic doctrinal decisions of the church provide a useful outline for the organization and development of the contents of dogmatics. Dogmatics today builds on what it has received from the past, on the creedal and confessional decisions of the classical Christian tradition. To be sure, the autobiography of the individual dogmaticians—their religious experience, their confessional tradition, their scholastic training, their field of specialization, their professional achievements, and so on—will be indirectly reflected in each of the topics. But there is a certain givenness about the dogmatic tradition which commends itself even today. There are fundamental principles of dogmatics, basic decisions of the church that are common to our tradition and whose order lends itself to such a cooperative venture in dogmatics as this one.

First, there is the canonical decision of the church which has established the preeminent position of the Holy Scriptures above all other witnesses to the revelation of God. They are the "norm that has no norm" (*norma normans non normata*). The methodological significance of this decision means that dogmatic theology must always in principle begin with biblical exegesis

55

1 / PROLEGOMENA TO CHRISTIAN DOGMATICS

and then exercise its critical and constructive function in correcting and interpreting the church's message to the world today. The chapter on Holy Scripture appears in this prolegomena because this canon is foundational; it is the fundament of all other witnesses in the life of the church. The canonical writings participate in the once-for-all events of revelation which founded the church and continue to perpetuate its life.

Second, the chief point of the canonical decision is to provide a framework, to set rules and limits, for the church to make the fundamental decision of its life, the theological one. This is the answer to the question Who is *theos*? Who is the God whose voice we hear within the words of Holy Scripture and through the witnesses of Christian tradition? The trinitarian dogmatic decision of the church answers that God is one being in three persons, whose names are Father, Son, and Holy Spirit, the Trinity in unity. In this decision the church decided against the gods of pagan polytheism and various forms of monotheism, religious, metaphysical, or political (Jewish, Greek, or Roman).

Third, the key to the trinitarian answer to the question of the nature and identity of God was the christological question: whether the Son incarnate as the person of Jesus of Nazareth is of the same essence as God the Father or is some subordinate intermediate being half-divine and half-human. In traditional dogmatics, the question arose as to what can be known of God apart from his special revelation in Jesus Christ and the history of salvation beginning with Israel. For this reason we include a *locus* on the knowledge of God, dealing with the significant differences between general and special revelation, or between natural and revealed theology. This issue of the knowledge of God is of particular importance today in the encounter between Christianity and the major non-Christian religions. The church has not rendered a dogmatic decision on this issue in any definitive way. It remains fluid and subject to lively controversy in the schools of theology.

Fourth, dogmatics respects the order of the creed, which in turn follows that of the Bible. Creation comes first, then the new creation. Belief in God the Creator precedes the confession of Jesus as Lord and Savior. Genesis is the first book of the Bible, and the Revelation to John is the last. The Old Testament begins with the statement "In the beginning God created the heavens and the earth." The New Testament lifts up the hope of a new creation in Christ, a new heaven and a new earth. The sequence of the law of creation prior to the gospel of redemption is a given of Scripture as well as of the nature of things.

Fifth, the doctrine of the goodness of creation is followed by the topic of sin and evil. Sin is a theological concept. It is rebellion against the Creator's will for the orders of creation. It is a contradiction of the image and likeness of God built into the created being of humanity. Evangelical dogmatics must define the confessional differences between the Reformation and the Roman

Catholic conceptions of sin. The problem of evil in Christianity has received no dogmatic solution. The Christian faith affirms the paradox that the creation is good, because God created it, and yet is radically distorted by evil for which God is not responsible. No theoretical explanation of evil has proved itself essential or crucial to the self-understanding of faith. The accent of the Christian faith is not on explaining sin and evil, but on narrating the gospel history of God's mighty acts in dealing with the conditions of a sinful and suffering world.

Sixth, the church's main christological decision was made to safeguard the mystery that we meet God in the person of Jesus Christ. At stake in the decision was the issue of what it takes to bring about a full salvation for humanity and the world. Two axioms were in control of the christological dogma: First, only God can save, no inferior half-divine figure; and second, what is not assumed cannot be saved. Therefore, Jesus Christ must unite in his very person the true meaning of being both divine and human, without one side being reduced or negated to make room for the other. To say that Jesus Christ is truly God and truly man (*vere deus et vere homo*) means that salvation does not occur the pagan way by turning humans into gods or making gods appear as humans. The incarnation represents the freedom to become truly human after the damage due to sin has been repaired.

Seventh, in addition to the "Person of Christ" dogmatic theology has dealt with christology also in a second topic, under the rubric "The Work of Christ." In the New Testament, of course, one can find no clear-cut distinction between Christ's person and work. There the emphasis is more on his function than on his being or essence. In the ancient church the reverse is true. It produced the dogma of the incarnation, defining who Jesus Christ *is* in terms of his one person and two natures. The church, however, never created a dogma of the atonement. In the history of Christian thought, there have been several distinctly different ways of interpreting the atoning death of Jesus. The early Christian communities used a host of symbols, most of them rooted in the Hebrew religion, especially the symbol of sacrifice. These symbols have given rise to the various "theories" of the atonement which Gustaf Aulén has delineated in his classic *Christus Victor*. The task of dogmatics today is to bring order out of the confusion that prevails in the teaching of contemporary Christianity on the reconciling work of God in Jesus Christ.

Eighth, the church has rendered a clear dogmatic decision on the personal being and meaning of the Holy Spirit. The first phase of this decision states that the Holy Spirit, like the Son himself, is truly God. The second phase occurred in the Western church centuries later with the statement that the Holy Spirit "proceeds from the Father *and the Son*" (*filioque*), an addition to the Nicene Creed which the Eastern church has rejected to this day. In Christian dogmatics the doctrine of the Holy Spirit is placed between Christ

1 / PROLEGOMENA TO CHRISTIAN DOGMATICS

and his church because he is the mediator of the saving benefits of Christ to the church and the world. The pneumatological dogma is in principle the answer to the question of how Jesus Christ and his benefits can be really present and appropriated through faith here and now.

Ninth, twentieth-century theology has produced more books and treatises on the church than any previous time in its history. This is a symptom of a profound struggle for a more adequate doctrine of the church. All churches confess their belief in the "one, holy, catholic, and apostolic church," but they do not share a common understanding of the elements of that formula. Contemporary Christianity has not received an ecclesiological dogma from the classical Christian tradition which can claim to be authoritative. The New Testament offers a plurality of images that point to the mystery of the church. The empirical history of the churches has generated competing, sometimes even mutually exclusive conceptions of the nature and mission of the church, each one critical of the others. Hence, there are many ecclesiologies. The question is whether they can be unified sufficiently to give expression to the essential unity of the church, manifest in the practice of their common faith.

Tenth, the doctrine of the means of grace asserts that the Holy Spirit uses the Word and sacraments to mediate the salvation which God has worked in Jesus Christ. God does not convey the grace of salvation immediately, apart from particular means. The Word is an audible sacrament, and the sacraments—baptism and the Lord's Supper—are visible words. They mediate the same salvation, only in different forms, the same Christ *in, with,* and *under* such things as words and water and bread and wine.

Eleventh, dogmatics in the tradition of the Protestant Reformation is based on the soteriological decision of its confessional writings, which has virtually the same value as any of the dogmas deriving from the ancient church, because it concerns "the article by which the church stands or falls" (*articulus stantis et cadentis ecclesiae*), "justification through faith alone." This article forms the existential basis of the life of the church in the world and all its individual members. The article on justification is the starting point for the Christian life, the freedom to live by faith before God apart from trust in the works of the law, and the possibility of living life to the hilt in one's secular vocation, in the service of one's fellow human beings and the world.

Twelfth, the tradition of dogmatics has ended with a chapter on "the last things." This dogmatic *locus* has dealt with biblical symbols such as the resurrection of the dead, the return of Christ, the final judgment, the end of the world, eternal condemnation and eternal life, heaven and hell, and so on. There is no such thing as an eschatological dogma in the history of Christianity. There are various strands of eschatological thinking in the New Testament, each of which has provided the confessional basis for a specific type of religious experience and church structure. There is the realized type of eschatology which stresses the present tense. The kingdom of God is already fully here and now, present somehow in the depths of present experience. There is the futuristic type of eschatology, which stresses the kingdom of God still to come in the future, and perhaps very soon but not yet now. Then there is the type of eschatology which places the kingdom of God and eternal life in another world above and beyond this one. In contemporary theology these various types are sometimes sharply juxtaposed in a diastatic way, sometimes coordinated in a multidimensional synthesis. Christian eschatology has received unparalleled attention in present-day theology because it has to do with the raw nerve of primitive Christian hope and at the same time offers a point of contact with the secular visions of modern ideologies.

The fundamental principles of dogmatics outlined here delineate a double tension in the history of God with the world. There is the tension that results from the distance between the original creation of the world and the new creation. Had there been no fall into sin, the original creation would still have enjoyed a history with God, pointing forward to something new. It would not have remained static. The new creation is no mere restoration of the old. The eschatological goal of the creation was originally something to be realized through God's involvement with the world. The second tension that runs through dogmatics is constituted by the difference between sin and grace, the sharp contrast between the righteousness of God and the sinfulness of humanity. Both kinds of tension find their resolution in Jesus Christ and the kingdom of God whose coming he signaled and embodied.

NOTES

1. See Dom Cuthbert Butler, *The Vatican Council, 1869-1870* (Westminster, Md.: Newman Press, 1962).

2. Two examples will suffice: Walter Kasper, *Dogma unter dem Wort Gottes* (Mainz: Matthias-Grünewald Verlag, 1965); and Michael Schmaus, *Dogma: God in Revelation* (New York and London: Sheed & Ward, 1968), vol. 1.

3. Kasper, *Dogma unter dem Wort Gottes*, p. 128.

4. Martin Luther, *The Bondage of the Will*, trans. J. I. Packer and O. R. Johnston (Westwood, N.J.: Fleming H. Revell Co., 1957), p. 67.

5. *LW* 41:121.

6. Adolf von Harnack, *History of Dogma*, trans. Neil Buchanan (New York: Dover Publications, 1961), 1:17.

7. Ibid., p. 22.

8. Karl Barth's views on dogma can be found in *Church Dogmatics*, vol. 1, part 1, *The Doctrine of the Word of God*, trans. G. T. Thomson (Edinburgh: T. & T. Clark, 1936), pp. 284-330.

9. Emil Brunner, *Truth as Encounter*, trans. Amandus W. Loos and David Cairns (Philadelphia: Westminster Press, 1964).

1 / PROLEGOMENA TO CHRISTIAN DOGMATICS

10. Brunner develops a more positive statement on dogma in his dogmatics, *The Christian Doctrine of God*, trans. Olive Wyon (Philadelphia: Westminster Press, 1950), 1:50–59.

11. Cf. Heinrich Schlier, reacting to a limited existentialist view of the relation between kerygma and dogma in the Bultmann school, in "Kerygma und Sophia: Zur neutestamentlichen Grundlegung des Dogmas," in *Die Zeit der Kirche* (Freiburg: Herder Verlag, 1958), pp. 206–32.

12. For a discussion of the contemporary controversy of dogma's relation to gospel, see F. W. Kantzenbach, *Evangelium und Dogma* (Stuttgart: Evangelisches Verlagswerk, 1959), pp. 293–98.

13. *LW* 36:107.

14. Quoted by Kasper, *Dogma unter dem Wort Gottes*, p. 15.

15. Edmund Schlink, "The Structure of Dogmatic Statements as an Ecumenical Problem," in *The Coming Christ and the Coming Church* (Edinburgh: Oliver & Boyd, 1967), pp. 16–84.

16. Ibid., p. 38.

17. Wolfhart Pannenberg, "What Is a Dogmatic Statement?" in *Basic Questions in Theology*, trans. George Kehm (Philadelphia: Fortress Press, 1970), 1:182–210.

18. Ibid., p. 210.

19. *The Book of Concord: The Confessions of the Evangelical Lutheran Church*, trans. and ed. Theodore G. Tappert (Philadelphia: Fortress Press, 1959).

20. Karl Rahner, *Foundations of Christian Faith*, trans. William V. Dych (New York: Seabury Press, 1978), p. 360.

4
The Holy Scriptures

The Holy Scriptures are the source and norm of the knowledge of God's revelation which concerns the Christian faith. The ultimate authority of Christian theology is not the biblical canon as such, but the gospel of Jesus Christ to which the Scriptures bear witness—the "canon within the canon." Jesus Christ himself is the Lord of the Scriptures, the source and scope of its authority.

THE AUTHORITY OF SCRIPTURE

The history of the church presents numerous examples of unhappy conflict between authority and freedom. The Gospels portray Jesus of Nazareth as a preacher of the kingdom of God in conflict with the keepers of the sacred traditions of Israel. "The Sabbath was made for man, and not man for the Sabbath." The apostle Paul defended the freedom of the gospel over against the "Judaizers" who would imprison it within a ritualistic legalism. The great Augustine of North Africa in the fifth century championed the freedom deriving from the grace of God against Pelagianism, on the one hand, which tied salvation to a moralistic system of good works, and Donatism, on the other hand, which based the validity of the church's ministry on the moral purity of the clergy. In the thirteenth century Thomas Aquinas was branded a "modernist" because he fought for the freedom to interpret the Christian faith to his contemporaries in the categories of Aristotle, which at that time attracted the leading minds of the universities. Church authorities attempted to curtail his efforts by condemning no less than twenty of his teachings.[1] Later the hierarchical authorities of Rome refused to respond to Luther's call to reform the church by the standard of the gospel of Jesus Christ. Still another sad chapter is how scientists had to suffer at the hands of orthodox inquisitors for the right to discover new truth. Galileo was silenced by the inquisition.

The theological question is whether we can grasp a concept of authority in the church that stands on the side of freedom. Is there an authority that releases rather than inhibits that power of the gospel which generates the

1 / PROLEGOMENA TO CHRISTIAN DOGMATICS

"freedom for which Christ has set us free" (Gal. 5:1)? An evangelical concept of authority calls for the freedom to renew and reform the church in accordance with the Word of God which "authored" the church in the first place. The foundational event of the church is Jesus Christ himself according to the original apostolic witness of faith. This event is no mere past-historical fact; it is the eschatological event which holds the key to the present meaning of the church and future destiny of the world. Because this event is the source of the church's faith, it is the norm of the church's doctrine. Creative authority occurs through a double movement of going "back to the sources" (*"resourcement"*) and bringing the church up-to-date (*"aggiornamento"*), as it was so well expressed by Vatican II. Every generation of believers must claim the freedom to go back to the original source of true authority as witnessed by the Holy Scriptures, open to its critical and constructive power and meaning.

The Reformation provides a paradigm case of the issue of authority and freedom in the church. What was the authority to which Martin Luther appealed against the highest authorities in the church and empire? Was it reason, conscience, religious experience, dogma, magisterium, or Scripture? The question of the ultimate authority, the final and absolutely reliable referee of matters of faith and life, is inescapable within the church. All Christians, of course, whether Protestant, Roman Catholic, or Eastern Orthodox, will begin by saying that the absolute authority can be none other than God. They will go further in agreeing that God is manifest and knowable in Jesus Christ, supremely, uniquely, and unsurpassably. Beyond this preliminary agreement, however, there are significant confessional differences, not to mention serious tensions, within each confessional position. How do we come to know the mind of Jesus Christ—God's Word of truth to us? Where do we have the trustworthy medium of God's self-communication? The answer to this question was given in the sixteenth century by the Reformation principle of *sola scriptura*. As the Epitome of the Formula of Concord tells us, "Holy Scripture remains the only judge, rule, and norm according to which as the only touchstone all doctrines should and must be understood and judged as good or evil, right or wrong." It further states that all other writings, no matter how classic and official, "are not judges like Holy Scripture, but merely witnesses and expositions of the faith, setting forth how at various times the Holy Scriptures were understood by contemporaries in the church of God with reference to controverted articles, and how contrary teachings were rejected and condemned."[2]

The Bible was the chief document of the Reformation. Luther's existential struggle to find a gracious God took place in the context of his encounter with the Bible. His ensuing call for the church to reform arose out of the gospel he discovered through his interpretation of Scripture. Luther was professor of biblical exegesis at the University of Wittenberg, not a systematic theologian like Melanchthon or Calvin. He came to possess a radical confidence in the word of Scripture for faith, proclamation, and theology.

The popular view of Luther rediscovering the Bible—or emancipating the Scriptures—is a misconception. There were many Bibles in Germany before Luther. His own Augustinian order encouraged a devout study of Holy Scripture. Thousands of copies of the Latin Bible (Jerome's translation) existed in Luther's time, mostly in churches, schools, and monasteries. There were also various translations into German in Luther's day. Humanistic scholars, like Reuchlin and Erasmus, were producing critical texts of the Bible in Hebrew and Greek, so that when Luther began to study the Bible in earnest he had access to the Bible in its original languages. Luther's unique contribution was a translation of the Bible into the language of the common people, peasants and villagers. The invention of printing made it possible to bring this popular version to the masses, so that the Reformation could be carried forward with a laity that knew the Scriptures. To advance the teachings of the Reformation, Luther provided prefaces for almost all the biblical books. Some of his sharpest and most memorable critical judgments on Scripture are found in these prefaces, for example, that he did not wish to have books like James and Revelation in the Bible.[3] Books that really belong in the canon of Scripture must clearly communicate the gospel. Books that fail to do that hold a lower rank in the canon.

Luther did not produce a new canon. He operated with the canon that had been in actual use in the church. However, he made fundamental distinctions between the books by applying *a christological canon of interpretation*: the gospel of free grace and justification through faith alone. This is the truly apostolic standard. It cannot be overemphasized that for Luther what counted was the *material* contents of the book and not its *formal* position within Scripture. Thus, although Luther retained the established canon of the ancient church, he discovered within it a canon by which all its parts could be judged. Luther says:

> And that is the true test by which to judge all books, when we see whether or not they inculcate Christ. For all the scriptures show us Christ, Romans 3:21; and St. Paul will know nothing but Christ, I Corinthians 2:2. Whatever does not teach Christ is not yet apostolic, even though St. Peter or St. Paul does the teaching. Again, whatever preaches Christ would be apostolic, even if Judas, Annas, Pilate or Herod were doing it.[4]

This "canon within the canon"[5] (Käsemann) is not something that Luther brought to the biblical text out of his subjective experience. Rather, it is to be found as the clear center of the main books of Scripture itself. In the New Testament the books that most clearly convey Christ are the Gospel and First

1 / PROLEGOMENA TO CHRISTIAN DOGMATICS

Letter of John, the epistles of Paul, especially Romans and Galatians, and 1 Peter. The Letter of James is inferior because it preaches the law instead of the gospel. As for the Revelation of John, Luther says he can find no evidence that it was written by the Holy Spirit.

The significant thing is not Luther's critical opinions on various parts of Scripture, but the fact that he applied criticism at all. In the following period of Lutheran orthodoxy, the beginnings of biblical criticism in Luther were virtually aborted. Whereas for Luther the canon was to be found in the Bible, for orthodoxy the canon came to be equated with the inspired text. Whereas for Luther the material principle of Scripture, justification through faith alone, was primary, for orthodoxy the formal principle of Scripture, namely, that it is verbatim the inspired Word of God, took precedence.

Yet even in the period of orthodoxy some dogmaticians continued to make a distinction between the canonical and the deuterocanonical (or apocryphal) books of the New Testament. Such a distinction had been consistently maintained by all the reformers with regard to the Old Testament. But now books like 2 Peter, 2 and 3 John, Hebrews, James, Jude, and Revelation were placed in a special class. In general it can be stated that the closer the dogmaticians stood to Luther, the more they preserved this distinction. Thus Martin Chemnitz insisted on the difference between the undoubtedly canonical books and those which had been marked with uncertainty by many in the ancient church as well as by Luther. By the time of David Hollaz, who represents orthodoxy in full bloom, the meaning of the distinction had been lost.[6] This undifferentiated view of the books of the Bible finally triumphed and today survives in Protestant fundamentalism. The canon which was open and flexible in Luther's thinking became closed and rigid in the circles that inherited the doctrine of Scripture in orthodoxy.

Luther and all his fellow reformers, Zwingli and Calvin, accepted the authority of Scripture, but in this respect they were not manifestly different from their opponents. The theology of the Middle Ages also affirmed the authority of Scripture and its full inspiration. Luther's departure consisted in deriving the authority of Scripture from its *gospel content*. The gospel is a promise; therefore the Bible is a book of promises that circulated first in the Word of preaching. The living Word of preaching is the basic form of the gospel. The Scriptures are the written form which became a necessary aid in the ongoing oral proclamation of the church. Luther stated: "The fact that it became necessary to write books reveals that great damage and injury had already been done to the Spirit. Books were thus written out of necessity and not because this is the nature of the New Testament."[7] Luther's decisive break with Medieval theology rests on this massive simplification of the manifold character of Scripture: The heart of Scripture is the promise of the gospel that is brought to expression in the Christ-event. Scripture's authority is not of a juridical kind; it is not essentially a book of legal doctrines, inerrant reports, or devotional materials. Scripture conveys the life-giving Word of salvation in Christ to those who accept it through faith. Authority in matters of faith rests on the gospel of Scripture, not on the creeds and councils of the church or on the hierarchical offices, papacy and episcopacy. The Word of Scripture alone (*sola scriptura*) is to be believed and accepted as finally valid with respect to the concerns of faith and salvation.

Luther's Scripture principle is articulated most clearly in the *Book of Concord* (1580), the final collection of Lutheran confessional writings. These confessions claim to be authoritative expositions of the truth of Scripture, always acknowledging the principle of the priority of Scripture over confession. Thus the Solid Declaration of the Formula of Concord states:

> We pledge ourselves to the prophetic and apostolic writings of the Old and New Testaments as the pure and clear fountain of Israel, which is the only true norm according to which all teachers and teachings are to be judged and evaluated. . . . The Word of God is and should remain the sole rule and norm of all doctrine, and no human being's writings dare be put on a par with it, but everything must be subjected to it.[8]

This same principle was even more clearly elaborated by Zwingli, Calvin, and the confessional documents of the Reformed churches. In none of the Lutheran confessions is there an article explicitly on the authority of Scripture; rather, it is presupposed and applied in implicit terms. But, in the Reformed confessions there are explicit articles on "the Word of God" or "the authority of the Scriptures." Thus, in the Genevan Confession of Faith (1536) the very first article deals with Scripture: "We desire to follow Scripture alone as a rule of faith and religion, without mixing it with any other thing which might be devised by the opinion of men, apart from the Word of God." The Scots Confession (1560) declares: "As we believe and confess the Scriptures of God sufficient to instruct and make the man of God perfect, so do we affirm and avow the authority of the same to be of God and neither to depend on men or angels. We affirm therefore that such as allege the Scripture to have no authority but that which it receives from the Church, to be blasphemous against God and injurious to the true Church." The Westminster Confession of Faith (1647) gives a much fuller account of Scripture, stating that the Old Testament in Hebrew and the New Testament in Greek are "immediately inspired by God, and by his singular care and providence kept pure in all ages."

These brief summaries of the early Lutheran and Reformed positions on Scripture indicate two things: first, that both agree completely on the authority of Scripture, and second, that the Reformed confessions express a more detailed

1 / PROLEGOMENA TO CHRISTIAN DOGMATICS

doctrine of Scripture. In the period of orthodoxy, however, the Lutheran dogmaticians show the same concern as the Reformed to have a complete doctrine of Scripture. This was due in part to external pressure from the Roman side, which could appeal to a full-fledged doctrine of papal authority, challenging the Protestants to produce one of equal force in the polemical situation. It was also due in part to an interior development, in which Luther's stress on the material content of Scripture—justification through faith alone—was relegated to the status of a true doctrinal proposition, along with others, which could be proved from Scripture. In this development the doctrine of the inspiration of Scripture enjoyed a great inflation in the works of the dogmaticians, both Lutheran and Reformed.

Thus in Protestant orthodoxy a shift away from Luther occurs in the account of Scripture's authority. For Luther, as we have seen, its authority resides in its gospel content. Scriptures are a means of grace. They are to be judged entirely in terms of Luther's famous formula *"was Christum treibt"* (what conveys Christ). For the seventeenth-century orthodox dogmaticians, Scriptures are authoritative because of their divine inspiration and inerrancy. Because this doctrine became the official teaching of almost all Lutheran and Reformed churches, and remains valid to this day, except where the historical-critical approach to Scripture has occasioned a new doctrine, it is well to consider some of the essential features of the doctrine of Scripture in Protestant orthodoxy.

According to this doctrine, the Scriptures are the written deposit of revelation which God communicated to the prophets and apostles by means of the inspiration of the Holy Spirit. God was the real author of Scripture; the human writers were the instruments God used to produce the Bible. The process of inspiration pertained to both the matter and the form of Scripture. God provided the correct ideas in the minds of the authors, the right words to use, as well as the stimulus to their wills to cause them to write. Hence it follows that, with the Holy Spirit in complete charge of the production of the Scriptures, they are totally free of all errors and imperfections. The final conclusion was that the difference between the Word of God and the Holy Scriptures, which Luther was able to assert, could be allowed to vanish. The activity of God in the writing of the Bible was so direct that it was likened to dictation. The Holy Spirit dictated in so many words, even the punctuation, everything to be written down. The prophets, evangelists, and apostles were but the inspired secretaries. David Hollaz writes, "All the words, without exception, contained in the Holy Manuscript, were dictated by the Holy Spirit to the pen of the prophets and apostles."[9] The ground of the authority of Scripture has been shifted from the gospel revelation to a verbal inspiration. A great fascination arises concerning the miraculous intervention of the Holy Spirit. It was even taught that everything the authors would normally know on their own had to be the subject matter of inspiration, in order to close every possible gap that might arise from human fallibility.[10]

The doctrine of inspiration continued to grow as the controversy with the Roman Catholics continued. All the weapons of Protestantism seemed to hang on this one doctrine—the absolutely inspired text of Scripture, down to the last syllable and punctuation mark. The result was the divinization of the biblical texts, the ascription of attributes which nearly rival the attributes of the Almighty. The faith and obedience which the New Testament refers to God, Christ, or the Gospel are now transferred to Scripture as the Word of God.

The authority the Scriptures possess in orthodoxy is of an authoritarian kind, commanding blind faith and obedience. This is so because it is affirmed that they are to be believed not because of *what* they say, but purely *because* they say it. The Scriptures are endowed with causative authority, so that in the language of orthodoxy it is said that the Scriptures create faith and obedience; the Scriptures create assent to the truths to be believed. This type of language indicates that the distinction between the Holy Spirit, who alone according to classical Christianity possesses such creative, regenerative, and illuminative power, and the Holy Scriptures has virtually collapsed.

Untiringly the orthodox dogmaticians drew up lists of the attributes of Scripture. They possess infallible truth and the power to interpret themselves correctly; the Hebrew and Greek texts are endowed by the providence of God with incorruptibility; and everything taught in the Bible is perfectly true. The Scriptures, in addition, have the attributes of perfection, perspicuity, and efficacy. The perfection of the Scriptures means that they are the solid Word of God and instruct us flawlessly in things that pertain to the salvation of humankind. In no way do they have to be supplemented by other sources with regard to the true knowledge of God's revelation. By the perspicuity of Scripture is meant that they are clear and plain for everyone to understand. No light outside of Scripture needs to be turned on to make its teachings explicit and meaningful. Thus Scripture has the quality of efficacy in itself, that is, "even apart from its use" (*etiam extra usum*).

In the theology of the Reformation we are thus faced with two doctrines of the authority of Scripture. For Luther and Melanchthon and their closest pupils the authority of Scripture is grounded in its witness to Christ. The Scripture is to be believed on account of Christ, its essential content. The other doctrine holds that Scripture is trustworthy because of the testimonies that prove its divine origin by means of inspiration. There are traces of this doctrine also in Luther and Melanchthon, which they inherited from a tradition going back to the early church and its Jewish antecedents. Likewise, within the Calvinist tradition the same two forms of the doctrine of Scripture exist side by side. For Calvin, Scripture's authority is communicated to believers by the internal testimony of the Holy Spirit (*testimonium Spiritus Sancti in-*

1 / PROLEGOMENA TO CHRISTIAN DOGMATICS

ternum); it is an immediate certainty of faith in response to hearing God's Word in Scripture. This is a certainty that only the Spirit can work, and cannot be built up inductively by rational proofs.

In later Calvinism a biblicism emerges which neglects Calvin's teaching and which petrifies the authority of the Bible in words mechanically dictated by the Holy Spirit. Testimonies in favor of Scripture, evidences of its divine origin, are enumerated, such as the miracles they report, the antiquity of the writings, the literal fulfillment of the prophecies, the moral superiority of its doctrine in comparison with the pagans, the joy of the martyrs, and so on.

This doctrine of testimonies for Scripture became the point at which the battleline was drawn between the orthodox defenders of Scripture and the critics of the Enlightenment who sought purely rational proofs for the contents of belief. The reasoning was simple: If the authority of Scripture was to be defended by rational evidences, it could be attacked on the same grounds. And so the Bible became the subject of a long, drawn-out controversy between the supernaturalism of the orthodox party and the naturalism of the biblical critics.

Luther's emphasis on the Bible as the living voice of the gospel enjoyed a revival in pietism. Pietism may be seen as a counteraction to orthodoxy, insofar as it was less concerned with having a systematic doctrine about Scripture than with reading it directly as a means of spiritual experience and growth in Christian living. This brought about an intensification of interest in the study of the Bible; here we find perhaps the origin of the modern existential exegesis of Scripture.

While Lutheran pietism recaptured the existential personal dimension of Scripture's message, the Calvinist "federal theology" of Johannes Coccejus (1669) read the Bible as a book of history and a series of interconnected covenants. This historical convenantal conception of the Bible had enormous influence on such thinkers as J. G. Herder, J. A. Bengel, J. T. Beck, and J. C. K. von Hofmann, all forerunners of the contemporary "history-of-salvation" theology. In this line the authority of the Bible rests on the meaning of the historical events which the Bible reports. The Bible itself bears witness to this meaning: All the events point to Christ as the midpoint of history. This christocentric view of the Bible again gathers up an emphasis central in the theology of Luther and Calvin.

The authority of the Bible was the basic presupposition which the Reformation held in common with the Middle Ages and with its Roman Catholic contemporaries. But already in the sixteenth century impulses of humanist criticism were beginning to be felt. These impulses increased until there was a flood tide of critical thought in the Enlightenment that applied the categories of "nature" and "reason" to wash away the foundations of biblical authority. The English deists, the French encyclopedists, and the German thinkers of the Enlightenment released such an avalanche of critical methods and insights that not only the orthodox theory of verbal inspiration was swept away, but the unique status of Scripture in theology and the church was also severely threatened. The result is that in modern theology the authority of the Bible no longer functions as an unquestioned presupposition, as it did in the theology of the reformers, but is treated precisely as that which has to be established.[11] The question of biblical authority stands or falls with the approach one takes; it has become a matter of interpretation. In the contemporary idiom it is an "hermeneutical" question.

THE INTERPRETATION OF SCRIPTURE

The church in history has always retained its identity by the ongoing activity of biblical interpretation. This essential appeal to Scripture has created a rich history of rediscovering ever-new means of grasping the biblical word. Luther's most revolutionary principle of interpretation was the insistence on the literal-historical and philological exposition of the Scriptures. Thereby he rejected the allegorical method of exegesis which had been practiced to excess since Origen. Allegorical exegesis could prove anything from Scripture. The effect was to rob Scripture of its own validity and to diminish its power to criticize the evolving traditions of the church. If Scripture was to regain its primacy in the church, the interpretation would have to be bound to the original sense as that appears in the Hebrew and Greek texts. So Luther said, "We shall not long preserve the Gospel without the languages. The languages are the sheath in which this sword of the Spirit is contained."[12] Against the spiritualists who sought hidden meanings behind the words of the text, Luther said, "The Holy Spirit is the plainest writer and speaker in heaven and earth, and therefore His words cannot have more than one, and that the very simplest, sense, which we call the literal, ordinary, natural sense."[13]

In addition to his insistence that the biblical expositor must search out the literal sense of Scripture, Luther maintained that every passage has only one authentic meaning. The allegorists had found sometimes as many as four meanings in a single verse: the physical, moral, spiritual, and mystical senses. Luther did away with this complicated apparatus, which filled medieval biblical commentaries with idle and sometimes dangerous speculations. The interpreter must not be the master and judge of Scripture, but must only bring to expression Scripture's own witness to itself. It is not the church which authorizes the meaning of Scripture; the Scripture authenticates itself. The church has only to listen and obey. "The gospel is not believed because the church confirms it, but because one recognizes that it is God's word."[14] To those who argued that at least the church determined the canon, Luther retorted that it is only the Word of God that determines what is canonical.

1 / PROLEGOMENA TO CHRISTIAN DOGMATICS

Luther stopped at this point. One searches in vain for a further answer to those who counter with the charge that this is circular reasoning, proving one unknown thing by appealing to another unknown thing.

A further step in Luther's hermeneutical position is the principle "the Scripture interprets itself." This means that the standard of interpretation cannot come from outside Scripture. "Scripture is therefore its own light. It is a grand thing when Scripture interprets itself."[15] This principle was applied polemically against both the Roman theologians and the Protestant enthusiasts. The Roman theologians controlled the interpretation of Scripture by the teaching office of the church; the enthusiasts read Scripture in light of their own spiritual experiences. In both cases some standard outside Scripture was used to determine what was relevant. Either way leads to the erection of an authority alongside Scripture or above it. Luther's position was that, to be sure, the Spirit of God enables the right interpretation of Scripture. The Spirit, however, does not operate apart from the scriptural word, but is mediated through it. Luther wanted nothing alien to Scripture to be permitted to determine the saving message it communicates.

Such an emphasis on the sovereignty of Scripture did not mean that the tradition of the church was rejected. This was not an exclusive biblicism, with no room for the classical creeds, dogmas, and traditions of the church. Martin Chemnitz observed that there are eight different meanings of tradition,[16] and almost all of them are positively affirmed by the Reformation theologians. First, there is the oral tradition of Christ and his apostles, written down by the evangelists. Here Scripture and tradition are identical. Second, there is the tradition of handing down the Scriptures from age to age on the part of the church. Third, there are apostolic doctrines referred to by the early fathers not written down in Scripture. Fourth, there is the exegetical tradition of expounding the Scriptures. Fifth, there is the tradition of doctrines built up by the church, taught in Scripture not in so many words but only by implication. Sixth, the term is applied to what is called the tradition of the fathers, the patristic consensus. Seventh, there is the ecclesiastical tradition of rites and customs that are very ancient. They may be observed on account of their antiquity, provided they do not conflict with the gospel. Eighth, there are traditions pertaining to faith and morals with no basis in Scripture, but which the Council of Trent commands to be revered with the "same reverence and pious affection" as Scripture itself. Only in this sense is tradition to be rejected.

The picture that emerges is one relatively conservative on tradition, calling for reform only at those points where tradition conflicts with the gospel. A wide range of freedom is permitted for new developments in church tradition, so long as the gospel message of Scripture remains clear and central.

For this reason the structures of the church and its forms of worship need not all derive from the New Testament, as some Protestants have tried to insist.

The hermeneutics of the orthodox period effected a systematization of the principles of interpretation that Luther applied. The basic premise was the clarity of Scripture; the Bible is not a dark and obscure book that only a few professors can understand. This does not mean that all the passages are clear, only that everything necessary for Christian faith and life is clearly revealed in Scripture. The rule was to clarify obscure passages by clear ones. The idea of the clarity of Scripture did not mean that unregenerate people can grasp the true meaning of Scripture. Without the aid of the Holy Spirit they can understand the words and syntax, but the real saving content of Scripture will elude them until their hearts are tuned into the Spirit. The true interpretation of Scripture is a gift of faith worked by the Holy Spirit. This was finally taken to mean the ability to hold fast to what Scripture says even if it means a break with reason and runs contrary to the evidence of the senses. It may, indeed, require a *sacrificium intellectus*.

With the full emergence of biblical criticism in the age of the Enlightenment, the pillars of orthodox hermeneutics were shattered. Yet the biblical critics, who applied the new methods of literary and historical analysis, conceived of their work as faithful to Luther's own pioneering critical insights. They could appeal to Luther's critical statements about certain books of the Bible. However, unlike Luther, they did not apply a canon of criticism from within Scripture itself, namely the free gift of justifying grace on account of Christ, but developed an autonomous scientific criticism of the biblical documents. The methods of historical-critical investigation which were applied to all ancient writings were now applied without hesitation to the biblical writings.

The history of the development and refinement of the historical-critical method covers the last two centuries and is very complex, so we can only highlight several of its main features. The first *premise* is that the orthodox doctrine of inspiration has no heuristic validity at all in the scholarly study of the Bible. The investigation must proceed without prejudice concerning the special authority of this book. The biblical writings are products of two thousand years of history and must be examined as are all other literary remains from antiquity. The startling *discovery* was that the ecclesiastical dogmas are not to be found in the Bible, but are products of a later time. In the age of Christendom, the dogmas of the Trinity and of Christ, as formulated in the Nicene and Athanasian creeds, were necessary to believe for salvation. Now the biblical critics could apply the Scripture-principle of Protestantism to show that these dogmas cannot be required for faith, since they lack solid biblical support. One of the main incentives in the history of criticism was in fact

1 / PROLEGOMENA TO CHRISTIAN DOGMATICS

to achieve freedom for scholarly research from the oppressive authority of the church and its dogmatic controls. If the dogmas could be undermined, no field of research could be declared off-limits. Three areas of research involving the interpretation of Scripture brought the new criticism into virulent conflict with traditional modes of understanding.

First, there arose the criticism of the Gospels, the main source documents of the birth, ministry, and death of Jesus of Nazareth. The overall result of Gospel criticism was shocking to those whose faith was dependent on the utter reliability of every word of Scripture, for the words and deeds of Jesus which the Gospels report were found to be intermingled with and modified by the beliefs of the early church. The question of who Jesus of Nazareth really was and what he accomplished became a matter of research and therefore in principle an open question always subject to continuing investigation. This research affected the christological dogma because it placed in question the traditional assertion of the divinity of Christ and the notion that a person's relation to God is determined by what is believed about Jesus of Nazareth.

Second, the unity of the New Testament was challenged on the grounds that there are different and rival theologies circulating in primitive Christianity. The theology of John is different from the theology of Luke, and Paul's theology is again very different from both. The upshot of this finding was to challenge the idea that the unity of the church could be founded on the unity of doctrine, since in the New Testament itself there is a plurality of theologies. This led to the relativizing of church dogma and the traditional demand for a *consensus doctrinae*.

Third, critics were eager to show that the biblical documents are not unique, but reflect the religious ideas of the environment in which they were written. The teachings of Jesus were traced back to various strands of Judaism; the Christianity of the Pauline and Johannine congregations was shown to be an expression of the religious syncretism of late antiquity.

In view of these critical results a question was bound to arise: What then is the ground and content of Christian faith? What is the essential core of the New Testament that defines the essence of Christianity for each succeeding generation? Is an objective answer to this question possible? A critical investigation of the history of biblical criticism indicates, as Albert Schweitzer documented so clearly in his *The Quest of the Historical Jesus*, that each epoch reads and interprets the Bible through the spectacles of its own milieu and world view. Eighteenth-century rationalism was able to portray Jesus as a teacher of moral enlightenment, espousing the eternal truths of rational religion. In the nineteenth century the Tübingen school of F. C. Baur interpreted the New Testament under the spell of Hegel's dialectical philosophy of history. Thus history is the dialectical unfolding of a religious idea; in the New Testament this idea clothes itself in the christological symbols of that day. In due time it is possible to dispense with the outer symbolic language in favor of the pure concept stated philosophically. David Friedrich Strauss shocked the Christian world with his *Life of Jesus*, in which he broke through the supernaturalism on the right and the rationalistic naturalism on the left and projected the mythological hypothesis. The New Testament can be interpreted only in terms of its mythical character. The point is not to argue whether the miracles happened or how they could be explained in natural terms, but to see that myth was the language of religion of that time. It is the nature of myth to speak of the otherworldly in terms of this world; therefore it is pointless to ask whether the myths convey historical facts.

Protestant liberalism in the nineteenth century provided numerous examples of a strange irony. On the one hand, the biblical critics were zealous in their commitment to scientific historical scholarship; on the other hand, their religious commitments and philosophical presuppositions shine through all their critical scholarship. In trying to be utterly historical they wound up reading the ideas of their own time into the biblical documents. The school of Albrecht Ritschl is a case in point. The Ritschlians were deeply influenced by the Kantian moral philosophy of religion. They looked for the ethical superiority of Christianity; they tended to interpret Jesus as a religious personality with a morally persuasive impact. Adolf von Harnack's bestseller *What Is Christianity?* portrayed Jesus as a religious personality who had the power to kindle a like religiosity in others. So he called theology away from the religion about Jesus, as we find in Paul, to the simple religion of Jesus, as he himself supposedly believed and taught it. Thus Harnack's famous assertion: "The Gospel, as Jesus proclaimed it, has to do with the Father only and not with the Son."[17] By the end of the nineteenth century the critical movement in theology had brought about a crisis in the Scripture-principle of modern Protestantism.

THE PROBLEM OF SCRIPTURE TODAY

In contemporary Protestantism the burning question continues to be how to unify the historical and hermeneutical approaches to the Bible. The purely historical interest can stifle the concern for the relevance of the biblical message today. The purely hermeneutical concern can force the Scripture into the mold of modern questions, so that the historical horizon of its own questions and answers is neglected. The attempt to take the message of the Bible on its own terms and make it speak prophetically to the current situation received a special impetus in the neo-Reformation theology of Karl Barth and Emil Brunner just after World War I. The appropriate name for this new movement is the "theology of the Word of God." These theologians took the Bible with a renewed seriousness, thinking of themselves as disciples of Luther and Calvin.

1 / PROLEGOMENA TO CHRISTIAN DOGMATICS

Owing to Karl Barth, biblical studies have played a vital role in recent dogmatic and systematic theology.

In Barth's theology the Word of God is the central concept. The Word of God comes to us in a threefold form: the preached Word, the written Word, and the revealed Word. The Word is by nature correspondingly speech, deed, and mystery, a threefoldness present in each form of the Word of God. This threeness-in-oneness and this oneness-in-threeness provide the only analogy to the doctrine of the Holy Trinity.

The Word of God is not a remote word of antiquity. It is the Word heard in the proclamation of the church today. This motif is a recurrence of Luther's stress on preaching from the Bible. The church preaches the Word which is witness to Christ, the revealed Word. This revealed Word proclaimed in the living language of the church is attested by the Word of Scripture. Thus the three forms, preaching, revelation, and Scripture, converge on the one name of Jesus Christ, in whom God is revealed as the Lord of humanity and the world. These themes of the Word of God are developed and repeated in the many volumes of Barth's *Church Dogmatics* and from there have found their way into many branches of the modern church, including Eastern Orthodoxy and Roman Catholicism.

The controversy over the Bible was not settled in the eighteenth and nineteenth centuries. An enormous gap has opened up within the Christian denominations regarding the interpretation of Scripture. In most denominations there is an attempt to recover the authority of the Bible in precisely the terms of seventeenth-century orthodoxy, before the rise of biblical criticism. Fundamentalist biblicism has not receded in vigor, even though it does not enjoy great prestige in the great theological schools. Masses of laity and clergy wish to possess an uncomplicated answer to the question of authority. Biblicism holds to an infallible Bible that can be the absolute authority in matters of belief and morals. The ancient doctrine of verbal inspiration survives. In some Christian groups the theory of inspiration is used to vouch for the absolute reliability of the Bible on all matters that relate to cosmology, biology, geography, chronology, and history. The Bible is used as a bulwark against the evolutionary hypothesis of modern natural science. The authority of Scripture for Luther and his followers was affirmed with respect to its chief purpose of declaring the gospel of Christ for faith and salvation. In modern Protestant fundamentalism, which ironically claims to bear the legacy of the Reformation, the authority of Scripture is extended to include infallible information on all kinds of subjects.

Fundamentalist biblicism is rejected by most theologians and is out of favor in most of the seminaries that train clergy for the parish ministry. They reject biblicism not merely because historical science has disclosed errors and contradictions in the biblical writings, but rather because the authority of the

Bible is elevated at the expense of the authority of Christ and his gospel. Nonfundamentalist Protestants also accept the Bible as the Word of God in some sense, but they point out that the concept of the Word of God, as Barth made clear, cannot be confined to the Bible. We cannot say that the Bible is the Word of God in a simplistic way, for the concept of the Word of God bears many diverse meanings in the classical Christian tradition.

Paul Tillich has observed that the "Word of God" has six meanings.[18] First, the "Word of God" refers classically to the second person of the Trinity, who was coeternal with the Father. Second, the Word of God was the active agent and medium of the creation of the world. Third, the Word of God was preached by the prophets in the Old Testament. Fourth, the Word of God became flesh in the person of Jesus of Nazareth. Fifth, the Word of God was proclaimed by the apostles of Jesus Christ in creating the church. Later it was written down by the apostles and their disciples. The Bible is the written Word of God in a derived way; it is the deposit of preaching of the early church. Sixth, the Word of God is the living voice of the gospel in every generation of Christians to follow. The Protestant fundamentalist doctrine of Scripture represents a reduction of the Word of God to only its written form.

A corollary of the revival of the Reformation theology of the Word of God has been the christological interpretation of Scripture. The christocentricity of Barth's theology has made an enormous impact on modern biblical theology. All the meanings of the Word of God have one center and norm: the appearance of Jesus Christ in history. For Christians following this line, the ultimate authority in matters of faith and life must be the Word of God made flesh, who died and rose again for the salvation of humanity. The honor of his name is mediated through Scripture and now lives through his Spirit in the Christian community today. The humanity of God in Christ is emphasized, as well as the historicity of all the means of his self-communication. The Word of God is not apart from humanity; rather, he uses human words and concepts, human hands and lips, human history in its glory and tragedy. The medium of his revelation is completely incarnational. Modern theology continues to show a marked preference for stressing the humanity of God in Christ, in the spirit of Luther who insisted that one can never draw God's Son too deeply into human flesh. The Scriptures, both Old and New Testaments, are Christ-centered; they point to the revelation of God in Jesus of Nazareth. Personal religious experience cannot add any stature to the magnitude of the Christ-event.

The uniqueness, the authority, and the value of the Bible, therefore, continue to be central for contemporary theological work. By means of Scripture, Christ is pictured and proclaimed as God's message and answer to the human predicament. Subsidiary to this central idea, the Bible is *also* treated as a collection of ancient documents which give us information about the

1 / PROLEGOMENA TO CHRISTIAN DOGMATICS

history of Israel and the beginnings of Christianity. The Bible is *also* appreciated as a library of great literature, ranking with the greatest literature of the ancient world from a humanist literary critical viewpoint. The Bible is *also* a source document for the imaginative construction of church doctrines; it provides fresh stimulus in every age to create new history in the realm of doctrine. The Bible is *also* a devotional book full of inspiring passages to cultivate the religious life. But beyond all these viewpoints, the Bible is the unique book of the church because of its original and intrinsic connection with the history of the promises of God and its astonishing climax in the career of Jesus the Christ. It is finally for the sake of Christ alone that the church continues to regard the Bible as a book without equal in the history of human literature. For this reason the churches that claim the heritage of Luther and the Reformation still affirm the Bible as the Word of God. This is not meant in the fundamentalistic sense that everything in the Bible stands directly as the Word of God. Nor is it meant in the sense that only some things in the Bible are the Word of God—the red-lettered passages in some versions of the New Testament or the most inspiring verses of anyone's choosing. The Bible is the Word of God as a whole, in its total import and impact, because it conveys the message of eschatological salvation.

This valuation of the Bible as the Word of God is asserted with greater difficulty today than in Luther's time and with greater awareness of the historical problems involved in biblical interpretation. First of all, the theological task is not so easily limited to the interpretation of the Bible, as it was for Luther. The God whom Scriptures attest is Creator and Lord of all, active in all spheres of life and human experience. Therefore, whatever theology asserts about God on the basis of Scripture must in some way be correlated with what can be learned about God's world in nature and history from other disciplines. Theology that attempts to be true to Scripture tries to relate all things to the God of the Bible, the God of history and of all humanity and of the entire world from the beginning to its future fulfillment. Modern theology is currently rediscovering and applying the universal perspective of the Bible, reasserting the implications of the monotheistic idea of God. It faces the challenge of overcoming the dichotomy between theology and the secular sciences, inasmuch as the world of life and history that the Bible talks about can hardly be totally other from the world that science explores with its different methods.

The role of the Bible in constructive theology is radically qualified today by historical consciousness. Luther believed that the literal meaning of Scripture is identical with its historical content; things happened exactly as they were written down. Today it is impossible to assume the literal historicity of all things recorded. What the biblical authors report is not accepted as a literal transcript of the factual course of events. Therefore, critical scholars inquire

THE HOLY SCRIPTURES

behind the text and attempt to reconstruct the real history that took place. In christology this has led to endless debates on the relation between the historical Jesus and the Christ of apostolic faith and preaching. This debate continues, and there seems to be no way to proceed except to make all christology an interpretation of the historical Jesus. Otherwise history and interpretation fall asunder, and theology ignores the wisdom of Kant's dictum that all concepts without percepts are empty and all percepts without concepts are blind.

Modern hermeneutics has expanded in scope and significance to come to grips with the historical problem of the distance between the historical events and written testimonies to those events. The Reformation principle that Scripture alone must interpret Scripture—*Scriptura est suipsius interpres*—is broadened to mean that the biblical texts can only be interpreted out of their historical contexts. Critical attention to the historical situation has magnified the sense of the distance between biblical and modern times. Its thought world, its symbols and myths, are felt to be utterly different from the modern ways of thinking. Therefore Bultmann's call to demythologize the biblical concepts is an attempt to interpret the biblical message in terms that moderns can understand, without taking offense at the alien modes of thought we encounter in the Bible.

Luther's principle of sticking to the single grammatical historical sense of each portion of Scripture is also applied in modern hermeneutics, but with a different result. Critical attention to what the texts actually say has exploded the notion that one orthodox dogmatics can be mined out of Scripture. There are different theological tendencies and teachings in the various texts. Ecumenically this has led to the practical conclusion that the traditional demand for a complete consensus of doctrine may be wrongheaded, if even the Scriptures fail to contain such a consensus. Perhaps the unity of the church can be realized without the kind of doctrinal uniformity demanded by the sixteenth-century theologians on both the Protestant and Catholic sides. In any case, the interpretation of the texts of Scripture can no longer be dominated by the history of dogma, so that the exegetes are compelled to produce nothing but proofs the dogmaticians require. Biblical theology and dogmatic theology are not reducible to each other. This awareness is a result of taking the historical development seriously. A deep gulf exists between the biblical world of thought and that of, say, Alexandria in the third century, Rome in the thirteenth century, Wittenberg in the sixteenth century, or New York in the twentieth century. It is the task of hermeneutics to make an intelligible transmission of meaning from the biblical text to the completely new situation here and now. This is a shared task. Theology plays a part, but so do preaching and worship, as well as the faith and the witness of the laity. For Christianity is not merely the ideas handed down from Scripture, but the

1 / PROLEGOMENA TO CHRISTIAN DOGMATICS

life and action of Christ's people in the world. The interpretation of Scripture is not successfully confined to the academic situation. The really creative insights come out of the crucible of missionary experience as the witnesses of Christ take on themselves the burdens of humanity and the pain of the world.

NOTES

1. Etienne Gilson, *History of Christian Philosophy in the Middle Ages* (New York: Random House, 1955), p. 728 n. 52.
2. The Epitome of the Formula of Concord, *BC* 465.
3. "Prefaces to the Books of the Bible," *LW* 35:225–411.
4. Ibid., p. 396.
5. Ernst Käsemann, "The Canon of the New Testament and the Unity of the Church," in *Essays on New Testament Themes*, trans. W. J. Mantague (London: SCM Press, 1964).
6. Heinrich Schmid, *The Doctrinal Theology of the Evangelical Lutheran Church*, trans. Charles A. Hay and Henry E. Jacobs (Minneapolis: Augsburg Publishing House, 1899), pp. 80–91.
7. Quoted by Paul Althaus, *The Theology of Martin Luther* (Philadelphia: Fortress Press, 1966), p. 73 n. 2.
8. *BC* 503–4, 505.
9. Schmid, *Doctrinal Theology*, p. 45.
10. Werner Elert refers to this exaggerated aspect of the doctrine of inspiration as an *Irrlehre* (wrong doctrine) in *Der Christliche Glaube* (Hamburg: Im Furche-Verlag, 1956), p. 171.
11. See Wolfhart Pannenberg, "The Crisis of the Scripture Principle," in *Basic Questions in Theology*, vol. 1 (Philadelphia: Fortress Press, 1970).
12. Martin Luther, "To the Councilmen of All Cities in Germany That They Establish and Maintain Christian Schools," *LW* 45:360.
13. Martin Luther, "Answer to the Hyperchristian, Hyperspiritual, and Hyperlearned Book by Goat Emser," *LW* 39:178.
14. Quoted by Althaus, *Theology of Martin Luther*, p. 75.
15. Ibid., p. 76.
16. Martin Chemnitz, *Examination of the Council of Trent*, part 1, trans. Fred Kraemer (St. Louis: Concordia Publishing House, 1971), pp. 220–307.
17. Adolf von Harnack, *What Is Christianity?* trans. T. B. Saunders (New York: Harper & Brothers, 1957), p. 144.
18. Paul Tillich, *Systematic Theology*, 3 vols. (Chicago: University of Chicago Press, 1951–63), 1:157–58.

SECOND LOCUS

The Triune God

ROBERT W. JENSON

THE TRIUNE GOD

Introduction

1. The Triune Name of God
   The Sense of "God"
   Israel's Identification of God
   Identifying God in the New Testament
   "Father, Son, and Holy Spirit" as Proper Name
   The Triune Name as Dogma

2. The Trinitarian Logic and Rhetoric
   The Trinitarian Logic
   The Hebrew Scriptures as the Root of Trinitarianism
   Primary Trinitarianism
   The Dogmatic Status of Primary Trinitarianism

3. The Nicene-Constantinopolitan Dogma
   The God of the Greeks
   The Initial Christianizing of Hellenism
   The Arian Crisis
   Nicaea and Constantinople

4. The One and the Three
   The Eastern Trinitarian Terminology
   The Three Hypostases
   The One Being
   The Western Version
   The Athanasian Creed
   Vicissitudes of Western Trinitarianism

5. The Being of God
   The Metaphysical Questions
   God as an Event
   God as Person

CONTENTS

    God as Spirit
    God as Discourse

6. The Attributes of God
    The Necessity of the Doctrine
    The Method of Derivation
    "Jesus Is Risen": Attributes for the Predicate
    "Jesus Is Risen": Attributes for the Subject

Introduction

The dogmatic *locus* about God is not and cannot be a description of God, though it often intends to state facts about God. Nor is the *locus* on God a piece of metaphysics, though it will raise and try to answer metaphysical questions. The dogmatic *locus* about God is a convenient gathering of certain questions that regularly arise in the Christian church, those that are most straightforwardly about God. These do, of course, turn out to have systematic relations to each other, and tracing these is a main task of dogmatics. But the specific set of questions that coalesce to make the *locus* "on God" is more the fruit of liturgical and catechetical history than of timeless logic.

The primary religious question is always about the identity of God: *Which* is God? Of history's putative or possible deities, which will sustain the claim? To whom may I—do I—pray?

Within biblical faith or within culture influenced by it, the question *whether* there is God can also acquire religious potency, for biblical faith poses the possibility of nihilism, of absolute distrust of reality, as not all religion does. And as long as it appears that there is only one plausible candidate for deity, that the biblical God's only competitors are such straw gods as "money" or "the belly," the awful issue between faith and nihilism is the first to claim attention. If we are sure who would be God if there were any, "Is there God?" heads our perplexity.

But history has already made clear that the "post-Christian era" will not be one of efficient and religionless secularity, but a combination of nihilist communal life, whether collectivist or chaotic, with a compensating efflorescence of non-Christian private religions. In the immediate future, Western streets will present a new divine claimant on every corner, as did those of the declining ancient world, and we will first have to make clear to ourselves which one we mean by "God" before we wager God's reality. In a religiously plural age, the question of God's identity reasserts its natural priority.

The question of *what* God is like cannot fruitfully be taken first. The big theological words—"salvific," "merciful," and so on—share a logical peculiarity: They are so determinedly analogous and open to interpretation that by themselves they mean almost nothing. "X redeems," for example, is not even an ordinary open sentence making a specific assertion about an unspecified

2 / THE TRIUNE GOD

subject, for until X is specified we do not know what "redeems" says about her/it/him. Only when "Baal," for example, replaces X does "redeems" acquire the operational value "sends rain." A theology of no-god-in-particular or of all gods at once would be, if not quite vacuous, wholly unhelpful. Prior to identification of God, all that can be said about it/him/her is "God is the object of ultimate concern" or "God is whatever you hang your heart on." The most that "X redeems" could mean is "X restores whatever state X defines as good." A doctrine that went no further would be of purely analytical use and no religious use.

We begin, therefore, and spend most of our space, with the *identity* of the gospel's God, and discuss the existence and nature of God afterward. That is, we begin with "the doctrine of the Trinity," for within Christian theology it is the identification of God which this body of teaching seeks to accomplish.[1] In following this order, we follow a minority tradition of dogmatics;[2] the minority, we claim, is right.

We must next note that the doctrine of the Trinity is no one teaching or homogeneous set of teachings, as is, for example, the doctrine of justification by faith alone. It is a complex of expressions of various forms and various relations to the identification of God. We distinguish four bodies of trinitarian discourse. Their classification makes the gross outline of the part of the following devoted to trinitarian doctrine (Chapters 1-4). Allotment of space among the four reflects relative complexity, not relative importance.

The doctrine of the Trinity is moribund in large sections of the church; indeed, it often serves as a prized example of useless theological hairsplitting. The book perhaps most frequently used in Protestant seminaries for instruction in systematic theology, Gustaf Aulén's *Faith of the Christian Church*, scarcely mentions the matter, and what it does say is inaccurate.[3] Other standard works are more informative, but little more helpful in seeing the point and vivacity of trinitarian language.[4] Such positive works as Leonard Hodgson's *The Doctrine of the Trinity*, Claude Welch's *In This Name*, or even Karl Rahner's pioneering *The Trinity* have not had the impact that might have been expected.[5] And when a "Trinity" is affirmed, it is often that of John Macquarrie or Paul Tillich, an interesting fruit of speculation but only distantly related to the church's trinitarianism here to be discussed. In general, such an enterprise as that of the present essay is a minority report in the present church.

It is to be feared that modern incomprehension of trinitarian discourse often expresses a morbidity of the faith itself; against this, dogmatics as such can do little. Error and incompleteness, both in the inherited body of trinitarian teaching and in current standard theological suppositions, play the chief role. We hope to make several contributions to overcoming these, but one suspects

INTRODUCTION

that the sheer bulk of inherited trinitarian discourse, of various functions and from various mostly distant times and places, also makes it hard simply to grasp what all this stuff is for. It is to the aid of this last perplexity that the organization of Chapters 1 through 4 was adopted, attempting to sort the mass of trinitarian language.

From discussion of God's triune identity, we must continue to the questions traditionally discussed as the doctrine of "the one God": what God is, whether God is, what God is like. The more clearly and dialectically specific our talk of God is, the more drastically—but perhaps also hopefully—it will in our time be challenged. The acids of modernity attack every aspect of belief. Is it even meaningful to talk of God? Is there any reason to affirm God's reality? Is it not rather evil or absurdity that is God, rather than fatherly goodness? And how do we find out what to think about God anyway? Would it not be better simply to adore God in silence or by meaningless speech?

It cannot be the task of dogmatics to complete faith's response to all challenges, but dogmatics can make a necessary contribution. In the course of theological history, three bodies of teaching have developed which seek to explicate the single reality of God. By no accident, each does in fact respond to an aspect of the modern perplexity. By no accident—for the questions just recited are historically faith's own questions, merely now reflected back in secularized form.

Doubt that talk about God makes sense is pervasive through the modern period. In the modern theological tradition, analysis of the logic of theological language has become an enterprise of its own. In response to this development, this book contains a separate *locus* on the knowledge of God, where direct discussion of the meaningfulness of God-language will be found. But the logical oddity of talk about God is not as such a modern discovery. Theology traditionally discussed it in the material mode and asked: What kind of "being" is God? How am I using "is" when I say "God is such-and-such"? These investigations have often led and may yet again lead to important material assertions about God and must therefore be pursued also in this *locus*, as Chapter 5.

The more or less biblical God of Western religion was long the only serious candidate among us. Just so, there has long been a standard topic: whether it is reasonable to think that God is. This question is often part of the present *locus*, but in this work it will be discussed in the next, epistemological, *locus* and is therefore omitted here.

Finally, since theologians must make sentences of the form "God is such-and-such," they must be concerned not only with the "is" but also with the such-and-such, with the predicate. What should we say about God? And why should we say one thing instead of another? Such questions make the prob-

2 / THE TRIUNE GOD

lem about what are traditionally called the attributes of God and are here discussed in Chapter 6.

NOTES

1. Karl Barth made this clear. Karl Barth, *Kirchliche Dogmatik* (Zürich: Zollikon, 1932–67), 1/1:313–20.
2. Most notably represented by Peter Lombard, Bonaventure, and Barth.
3. Gustaf Aulén, *The Faith of the Christian Church* (Philadelphia: Fortress Press, 1948), pp. 245–49.
4. E.g., Regin Prenter, *Creation and Redemption*, trans. Theodore I. Jensen (Philadelphia: Fortress Press, 1967); Helmut Thielicke, *The Evangelical Faith*, trans. G. W. Bromiley (Grand Rapids: Wm. B. Eerdmans, 1967), 2:124–83.
5. Leonard Hodgson, *The Doctrine of the Trinity* (New York: Charles Scribner's Sons, 1944); Claude Welch, *In This Name* (New York: Charles Scribner's Sons, 1952); Karl Rahner, *The Trinity*, trans. J. Donceel (New York: Herder & Herder, 1970).

1
The Triune Name of God

In functional continuity with biblical witness, "Father, Son, and Holy Spirit" is the proper name of the church's God. That God have a proper name is a demand of both the Hebrew Scriptures and the New Testament gospel. That God has *this* proper name is an immediate reflex of primary Christian experience.

THE SENSE OF "GOD"

What can be said prior to God's identification must, to be sure, be said. What do people use this word "God" for, that we ask so urgently to whom or what it is truly applied?

The horizon of life and its concerns is time, the inescapable already, no-more, still, and not-yet of all we know and will. Every human act moves from what was to what is to be; it is carried and filled by tradition but intends new creation. Just so our acts hang between past and future, to be in fact temporal, to be the self-transcendence, the inherent and inevitable adventure, that is the theme of all religion and philosophy. But also, our acts threaten to fall between past and future, to become boring or fantastic or both, and all life threatens to become an unplotted sequence of merely causally joined events that happen to befall an actually impersonal entity, "me."

Human life is possible—or, in recent jargon, meaningful—only if past and future are somehow bracketed, only if their disconnection is somehow transcended, only if our lives somehow cohere to make a story. Life in time is possible only if there is such a bracket, that is, if there is eternity. Thus in all we do we seek eternity. If our seeking becomes explicit, we practice "religion." If our religion perceives the bracket around time as in any way a particular something, as in any way the possible subject of verbs (as in, e.g., "The eternal speaks by the prophets"), we tend to say "God" instead of "eternity."

But already we are becoming intolerably indefinite, for manifestly there are many kinds of bracketing that can be posited around past and future,

2 / THE TRIUNE GOD

many possible eternities. There is, for example, the eternity of tribal ancestors who have become so old that nothing can surprise them any more and in whose continuing presence all the future's putative novelties are therefore mastered by traditional maxims. There is the eternity of nirvana, where a difference of past and future is just not permitted. There is the eternity of existentialism, in which decision brings time momentarily to a halt. So multiform is eternity that the mere assertion that it is, that there is some union of past and future, that life has some meaning, is for practice as good as the suspicion that there is none at all. Life is enabled not by a posit *that* life means but by a posit of *what* it means. The plot and energy of life are determined by which eternity we rely on, and the truth of any mode of life is determined by the reality of the eternity it posits. If we speak of "God," our life's substance is given by which God we worship, and our life's truth is given by whether this is the God that really is.

Meditating on the foundation of biblical faith, the exodus, Israel's first theologians made Moses' decisive question be: "If I come to the people of Israel and say to them, 'The God of your fathers has sent me to you,' and they ask me, 'What is his name?' what shall I say to them?" If Israel was to risk the future of this God, to leave secure nonexistence in Eygpt and venture on God's promises, Israel had first and fundamentally to know which future this was. The God answered, "Say this to the people of Israel, [Yahweh], the God of your fathers, the God of Abraham, the God of Isaac, and the God of Jacob, has sent me to you, this is my name for ever, and thus I am to be remembered throughout all generations" (Exod. 3:13-15).[1]

The answer provides a proper name, "Yahweh." It also provides what logicians now call an identifying description, a descriptive phrase or clause, or set of them, that fits just the one individual thing to be identified. Here the description is "the God whom Abraham and Isaac and Jacob worshiped." The more usual description is that found in a parallel account a few chapters later: God said to Moses, "Say . . . to the people of Israel, 'I am [Yahweh], and I will bring you out from under the burdens of the Egyptians . . . ; and you shall know that I am [Yahweh] your God, *who* has brought you out. . . . I am [Yahweh]'" (Exod. 6:2-7; emphasis added).

In general, proper names work only if such identifying descriptions are at hand. We may say, "Mary is coming to dinner," and be answered with, "Who is Mary?" Then we must be able to say, "Mary is the one who lives in apartment 2C, and is always so cheerful, and . . . ," continuing until the questioner says, "Oh, *that* one!" We may say, "Yahweh always forgives," and be answered with, "Do you mean the Inner Self?" Then we must be able to say, "No. We mean the one who rescued Israel from Eygpt, and. . . . "

Linguistic means of identification—proper names, identifying descriptions, or both—are a necessity of religion. Prayers, like other requests and praises,

THE TRIUNE NAME OF GOD

must be addressed. Thus the typical prayer-form of Western Christianity, the collect, usually begins with some identifying description such as, "O God, who didst give thine only-begotten Son to be. . . . " The moral will of God must be proclaimed as a particular will if we are to follow it. Paul set a pattern for Christian preaching when he wrote to the Philippians: "Have this mind among yourselves, which you have in Christ Jesus, who . . ." (Phil. 2:1–11). Eschatological promise must be specified. Proclamation of a final union of humankind is gospel because the gathering is to be around Jesus, but it would be quite something else were the gathering to be around Stalin. It was precisely the wrong address of praise in which Paul saw the perversion of heathendom (Rom. 1:24–25).

Trinitarian discourse is Christianity's effort to identify the God who has claimed us. The doctrine of the Trinity comprises both a proper name, "Father, Son, and Holy Spirit," in several grammatical variants, and an elaborate development and analysis of corresponding identifying descriptions.

We live in the present; that is a tautology. But the content of present life is memory and expectation, in some union. We speak of "God" to name that union. Or rather, we speak to and from God to invoke it. Just so, we need to know who God is, to know how our lives hang together. Trinitarian discourse is Christianity's answer to this need.

ISRAEL'S IDENTIFICATION OF GOD

What the word "Yahweh" may once have meant we do not know. Since historical Israel did not know either, the loss is not theologically great. "Yahweh" was for Israel a pure proper name which no doubt had once been applied on account of its sense but had survived the knowledge thereof.[2] Indeed, in the famous passage in which Moses asks for an explanation of the name, Yahweh is depicted as replying with a play on an ad hoc etymology precisely to reject such curiosity: "I am who I am" (Exod. 3:14).[3]

It is remarkable that "Yahweh," with its variants, was the *only* proper name in ordinary use for Israel's God. Other substantives, predominantly "Elohim," were used as common terms and appelatives. Other ancient peoples piled up divine names.[4] The comprehensiveness of a god's authority was achieved by blurring the god's particularity, by identification of initially distinct numina with one another, leading to a grandly vague deity-in-general. Israel made the opposite move. Israel's salvation depended precisely on unambiguous identification of its God over against the generality of the numinous. In the Yahwistic account of Yahweh's decisive self-revelation at Mount Sinai, the central passage is "And [Yahweh] descended . . . and proclaimed the name [Yahweh]. . . : '[Yahweh, Yahweh], a God merciful and gracious'" (Exod. 34:5–6), as gods in general could not be supposed to be. Therefore it was

2 / THE TRIUNE GOD

included in Israel's fundamental description of righteousness, the ten commandments, that Israel must not demean the name of Yahweh (Exod. 20:7).

A proper place for prayer, sacrifice, or consultation of the oracles was therefore one where the name Yahweh was known (Exod. 20:24). What happens at such a holy place can be compendiously described as "calling on the name [Yahweh]" (e.g., Gen. 12:8). Blessings are "applications" of the name Yahweh (e.g., Num. 6:27), and prayers are addressed by it (e.g., 1 Kings 18:24). The worshipers' use of "Yahweh" is their reason for confidence that their offering will be acceptable and their petitions heard (e.g., Ps. 20:1–3; 25:11), for those who know God's name are God's people, to whom God is committed. When God did not want to be grasped, he withheld his name (Gen. 32:30); the heathen are heathen just because they do not know it (Ps. 79:6).

To go with the name, Israel necessarily had identifying descriptions. At the very foundation of Israel's life, the introduction to the basic Torah of the ten commandments, the two are neatly side by side: "I am [Yahweh], your God, who brought you out of the land of Egypt" (Exod. 20:2). There were many descriptions that could be used to identify Yahweh, but this one, the narrative of Exodus, was that on which Israel's faith hung.[5] The exodus was the chief content of Israel's creed: "And you shall make response before [Yahweh] your God, 'A wandering Aramean was my father; and he went down into Egypt. . . . And the Egyptians treated us harshly and afflicted us. . . . Then we cried to [Yahweh] . . . , and [Yahweh] brought us out of Egypt with a mighty hand . . . and he brought us into this place and gave us this land'" (Deut. 26:5–9; see also Josh. 24:2ff.) The entire narrative of the Hebrew Scriptures is probably best understood as an expanded version of the creedal narrative just cited.[6] And the whole Torah was explication of the exodus' consequences: "You have seen what I did to the Egyptians, and how I . . . brought you to myself. Now therefore . . ." (Exod. 19:4ff.) To the question "Whom do you mean, 'God'?" Israel answered, "Whoever got us out of Egypt."

The act of calling God by name was in Israel so tremendous that, as the identification of the true God over against other claimants ceased to be a daily challenge, and use of the name therefore ceased to be a daily necessity, actual pronunciation of the name ceased, at least for all but the mightiest occasions.[7] This is reflected in the pointing of "YHWH" in our Hebrew text with the vowel points for "Adonai" (Lord) as a signal to speak this word instead, and in the Septuagint translation of "Yahweh" by Kyrios.

IDENTIFYING GOD
IN THE NEW TESTAMENT

The gospel of the New Testament is the provision of a new identifying description for this same God. The coming-to-apply of this new description is the

THE TRIUNE NAME OF GOD

event, witness to which is the whole point of the New Testament. God, in the gospel, is "whoever raised Jesus from the dead."⁸

Identification of God by the resurrection did not replace identification by the exodus; it is essential to the God who raised Jesus that he is the same one who freed Israel. But the new thing that is the content of the gospel is that God has now identified himself also as "him that raised from the dead Jesus our Lord" (Rom. 4:24). In the New Testament such phrases become the standard way of referring to God.⁹

To go with this new identifying description there are not so much new names as new kinds of naming. "Yahweh" does not reappear as a name in use. The habit of saying "Lord" instead has buried it too deeply under the appellative.¹⁰ But in the church's missionary situation, actual use of a proper name in speaking of God is again necessary in a variety of contexts. It is the naming of Jesus that occurs for all such functions. Exorcism, healing, and indeed good works generally are accomplished "in Jesus' name" (e.g., Mark 9:37ff., par.). Church discipline and quasi-discipline are carried out by sentences pronounced in Jesus' name (e.g., 1 Cor. 1:10), and forgiveness is pronounced in the same way (e.g., 1 John 2:12). Baptism is described as into Jesus' name (e.g., Acts 2:38), whether or not it was ever actually performed with this formula. Undergoing such baptism is equated with that calling on the name "Yahweh" by which, according to Joel 3:5, Israel is to be saved (Acts 2:21, 38). Above all, perhaps, prayer is "in Jesus' name" (e.g., John 14:13–14), in consequence of which the name can be posited as the very object of faith (e.g., John 1:12). Believers are those "who call on the name of our Lord Jesus Christ" (e.g. Acts 9:14).

So dominant was the use of the name "Jesus" in the religious life of the apostolic church that the whole mission can be described as proclamation "in his name" (Luke 24:47), "preaching good news about the kingdom of God and the name of Jesus Christ" (Acts 8:12), indeed, as "carrying" Jesus' name to the people (e.g., Acts 9:15). The gatherings of the congregations can be described as "giving thanks . . . in the name of our Lord Jesus Christ" (Eph. 5:20), indeed, simply as meetings in his name (Matt. 18:20). Where faith must be confessed over against the hostility of society, this is "confession of the name" (e.g., Mark 13:13). The theological conclusion was drawn in such praises as the hymn preserved in Philippians in which God's own eschatological triumph is evoked as cosmic obeisance to the name "Jesus" (Phil. 1:10), or in such formulas as that in Acts which makes Jesus' name the agent of salvation (Acts 4:12). However various groups in the primal church may have conceived Jesus' relation to God, "Jesus" was the way they all invoked God.

One other new naming appears in the New Testament, the triune name: "Father, Son, and Holy Spirit." Its appearance is undoubtedly dependent on naming God by naming Jesus, as just discussed, but the causal connections

2 / THE TRIUNE GOD

are no longer recoverable. It is of course toward this name that we have been steering. That the biblical God must have a proper name, we have seen in the Hebrew Scriptures. In the life of the primal church, God is named by uses that involve the name of Jesus. "Father, Son, and Spirit" is the naming of this sort that historically triumphed.

"FATHER, SON, AND HOLY SPIRIT" AS PROPER NAME

That "Father, Son, and Holy Spirit" in fact occupies in the church the place occupied in Israel by "Yahweh" or, later, "Lord" even hasty observation of the church's life must discover.[11] Why it came to be so is the matter of the next chapter; for now we register the fact. Our services begin and are punctuated with "In the name of the Father, Son, and Holy Spirit." Our prayers conclude, "In his name who with you and the Holy Spirit is. . . ." Above all, the act by which people are brought both into the fellowship of believers and into their fellowship with God is an initiation "into the name 'Father, Son, and Holy Spirit.'"

The habit of trinitarian naming is universal through the life of the church. How far back it goes, we cannot tell. It certainly goes further back than even the faintest traces of trinitarian reflection, and it appears to have been an immediate expression of believers' experience of God. It is in liturgy, when we talk not *about* God but to and for him, that we need and use God's name, and that is where the trinitarian formulas appear, both initially and to this day.[12] In the immediately postapostolic literature there is no use of a trinitarian formula as a piece of theology or in such fashion as to depend on antecedent development in theology, yet the formula is there. Its home is in the liturgy, in baptism and the eucharist. There its use was regularly seen as the heart of the matter.[13]

There are two New Testament occurrences of a trinitarian name-formula. The earliest is the closing benediction of Paul's second letter to Corinth (2 Cor. 13:14). The epistolary benedictions of the New Testament reflect epistolary custom, liturgy, and no doubt personal style. They occur in the opening salutations and at the closing. If we sort them out, there is a surprising result. The opening benedictions all name both "God the Father" and "the Lord Jesus Christ." The closing benedictions—with one exception—either name no one and are simple wishes of "grace," or name only the Lord Jesus. Moreover, the naming of the Lord Jesus occurs in all and only the authentic letters of Paul and is obviously Paul's idiosyncrasy. Then suddenly, in one Pauline letter (and that neither the earliest nor the latest) a trinitarian naming replaces the naming of the Lord Jesus only: "The grace of the Lord Jesus Christ and the love of God and the fellowship of the Holy Spirit be with you all."

THE TRIUNE NAME OF GOD

These circumstances prohibit all thought of development from one-membered to two-membered to three-membered formulas.¹⁴ As far as the texts let us see, all forms are equally immediate,¹⁵ the choice depending on epistolary custom. The particular trinitarian formula that ends 2 Corinthians looks very much like Paul's creation of the moment, apropos of nothing special in the letter and done only because it was natural to do. The purely christological benediction that was Paul's habit ("The grace of our Lord Jesus Christ be with you") expands in both directions by its own logic. Or if Paul did not create it here, he took it from liturgical use in the same unmotivated and obvious fashion.

The most important New Testament trinitarian naming is the Matthean baptismal commission (Matt. 28:19). Baptism is the church's chief sacrament, its rite of passage from old reality to new. Within such a rite, the new reality must be identified, for the neophytes must be directed into it. In baptism, as often elsewhere, this is done by naming the God whose reality it is. The name stipulated in the canonical rubric for baptismal liturgy is "Father, Son, and Holy Spirit."¹⁶

It is often supposed that the tripartite baptismal formula developed from unitary or bipartite formulas: "In Jesus' name" or "In the name of God and of the Lord Jesus." There is evidence from the second century of baptism with such formulas. But as to an origin of the trinitarian formula from these, there is no evidence.¹⁷ In any case, the tripartite formula was soon there, and it is the only one in the New Testament.

The trinitarian name did not fall from heaven. It was made by believers for the God with whom we have found ourselves involved. "Father" was Jesus' peculiar address to the particular transcendence over against whom he lived.¹⁸ Just by this address he qualified himself as "the Son," and in the memory of the primal church his acclamation as Son was the beginning of faith.¹⁹ "Spirit" was the term provided by the whole biblical theology for what comes of such a meeting between this God and a special human of his. It is involvement in this structure of Jesus' own event—prayer to the "Father" with "the Son" in the power of and for "the Spirit"—that is faith's knowledge of God. Thus "Father, Son, and Holy Spirit" summarizes faith's apprehension of God; this is the matter of the next chapter. But in the event so summarizable, "Father, Son, and Holy Spirit" came together also simply as a name for the one therein apprehended, and apparently did so before all analysis of its suitability.

One further matter must be discussed here: the masculinity of "Father." Emerging consciousness of the historic oppression of women rightly watches for expressions thereof also, or perhaps principally, in inherited interpretations of God. When such are found, Christianity has every reason to eliminate them. We will in fact find a decisive area where male sexism has shaped the

2 / THE TRIUNE GOD

structure of doctrine. Trinitarian Father-language cannot, however, be one such; and the widely spread supposition that it is reflects a breakdown of linguistic and doctrinal knowledge and judgment.

The church's trinitarian naming incorporates Jesus' filial address to God. That Jesus called God "Abba," which can only be translated "Father," must settle the matter for trinitarian naming, since it is Jesus' historical reality that created the name. But of course, that we may not substitute for "Father" in the triune name may only mean that the whole name is irremediably offensive. Nor can the use of "Father" within the trinitarian name be altogether separated from its more general use in Christian speech to and about God.

For filial address to God, the choice of words is limited, for us as for Jesus. "Parent" and its natural or artificial equivalents cannot be regular filial terms of address because they do not individuate. That leaves "mother" and "father." It is decisive for Israel's God that we are not of God's own substance, that God's role as our parent is not sexual, that God is not even metaphorically a fertility God.[20] The choice between "Mother" and "Father," as terms of filial address to God, was and must be made according to which term is more easily separable from the reproductive role.

Sexuality, as the union of sensuality and differentiated reproductive roles and apparatus, is the glory of our specific humanity. It is the way in which our directedness *to* each other, both among those now living and between generations—and that precisely by differences between us—is built into our bodies, into our sheer created givenness. Moreover, within the mutuality of male and female, the female is ontologically superior. She is the more ineradicably human, for while sensuality and reproduction can socially be ripped apart in the male, by alienating economic or political structures, not even abortion can do this to the female—short, of course, of the "brave new world" or of humankind's decision to die out. In societies that value members by especially inhuman standards, as in capitalist or technocratic-socialist societies that value only by contribution to the gross national product, the female's human superiority will indeed cause suffering, and many will understandably seek to be rid of it.

In religions where the direct religious analogy from human perfection to divine perfection is undisturbed, the female gender has therefore usually been religiously dominant, even in otherwise male-dominated societies. The whole of Christianity's soteriology can be summarized in the observation that in it this analogy is broken. Vice versa, it is just the ontological inferiority of the male that offers "Father" rather than "Mother" as the proper term of address to Israel's sexually transcendent God, when a filial term is needed.

That the biblical God is sexually transcendent does not, of course, mean that God is less than sexual, but rather that what we are by sexual differentiation God is without the various relations of more and less which sexual dif-

THE TRIUNE NAME OF GOD

ferentiation indeed involves. That Jesus, and we after him, have called God "Father" thus involves no valuing of masculinity above feminity. On the contrary, it is the only available way to satisfy the determination of Israel and the church to attribute neither to God. As for "Father and Mother," which incredibly has actually been used in services wishing to be Christian, it is most objectionable of all since by insisting on both it makes the attribution of sexual roles entirely inescapable and repristinates the deepest fertility myth, that of divine androgyny. The biblical God is not both our begetter and our bearer; he is neither.

In general, the assumption that it is a deprivation not to address God in one's very own gender is a case of humankind's general religious assumption of direct analogy from human perfections to divine qualities. In the faith of the Bible, this direct line is, for our salvation, broken. All speech about God is of course, in a commonsensical way, by analogy. But the gospel is free to take its analogies sometimes from human perfections and sometimes from human imperfections, depending on theological need. Sometimes it takes them from death and sin. If we must, irrelevantly, worry about whether calling God "Father" is praise or dispraise of earthly fathers, the answer, in the structure of Christian language-use, must be that it will be in some contexts the one and in some contexts the other.

THE TRIUNE NAME AS DOGMA

So far we have merely noted an historically contingent fact about the church's discourse. Now we must note that it is a fact with authority, for in view of the function of canonical sacramental mandates, the biblical stipulation of a triune formula for baptism must be regarded as dogma.[21] Moreover, the impact of this dogma extends far beyond the baptismal rite itself.[22] The function of naming God in initiation, in baptism as elsewhere, is to address the initiate to new reality, to grant new access to God. In the community of the baptized, therefore, the divine name spoken in baptism is established as that by which the community has its particular address to God.[23]

It has in fact worked out so in the church, both liturgically and theologically. In the church's life of prayer and blessing, threefold invocation is established at every decisive point. And in the theological history we will trace in a following chapter, we will find the role of the baptismal formula so predominant that there would be reason to call "Go . . . baptizing in the name of the Father and of the Son and of the Holy Spirit" the founding dogma of the faith.

This dogma is not about something we are to think but about something we are to do. When we pray or give thanks or otherwise invoke God, it is by this formula that we may most precisely address our utterance. There are other such orthopractic dogmas. The very stipulation of washing in God's name

2 / THE TRIUNE GOD

as the church's initiation is one. So is the stipulation of a meal of bread and cup, with christological thanksgiving, as the church's chief gathered occasion. So, for that matter, is the stipulation that final authority in the church is to function by our reading of the Bible.

From time to time, various concerns lead to proposed replacements of the trinitarian name, for example, "In the name of God: Creator, Redeemer, and Sanctifier" or "In the name of God the Ground and God the Logos and God the Spirit." All such parodies disrupt the faith's self-identity at the level of its primal and least-reflected historicity.

Such attempts presuppose that we first know about a triune God and then look about for a form of words to address that God, when in fact it is the other way around. Moreover, "Creator, Redeemer, and Sanctifier," for example, is, like other such phrases, not a name at all. It is rather an assemblage of after-the-fact theological abstractions, useful in their place but not here. Such assemblages cannot even be made into names, for they do not identify. Every putative deity must claim, for example, somehow to "create," "redeem" and "sanctify." There are also, to be sure, numerous candidates to be Father or Spirit, but within the trinitarian name, "the Father" is not primarily *our* Father, but the Father of the immediately next-named Son, that is, of Jesus. The "Holy Spirit," within the name, is not any spirit claiming to be holy, but the communal spirit of the just-named Jesus and his Father. By these relations inside the phrase, "Father, Son, and Holy Spirit" is historically specific and can be what liturgy and devotion—and, at its base, all theology—must have, a proper name of God.[24]

These last remarks again claim that "Father, Son, and Holy Spirit" is not an arbitrary label, like "Robert" for the author of these pages. A proper name is proper just insofar as it is used independently of aptitude to the one named, but it need not therefore lack such aptitude. "Father, Son, and Holy Spirit" is appropriate for naming the gospel's God because the phrase immediately summarizes the primal Christian interpretation of God. It is this second level of trinitarianism to which we must now continue.

NOTES

1. Brackets around "Yahweh" (Hebrew: YHWH or JHWH) are used throughout this *locus* in quotations from the Revised Standard Version of the Bible. The RSV follows the Jewish custom of avoiding the proper name of God and substituting "the Lord," but in this *locus* we are speaking precisely of God's proper name and thus use the name "Yahweh."

2. Gerhard von Rad, *Old Testament Theology*, trans. D. M. G. Stalker, 2 vols. (New York: Harper & Row, 1962–65), 1:10–11.

THE TRIUNE NAME OF GOD

3. On the exegesis, Walther Zimmerli, *Old Testament Theology in Outline*, trans. D. E. Green (Atlanta: John Knox Press, 1978), pp. 19–20.
4. Von Rad, *Old Testament Theology*, 2:180ff.
5. E.g., Zimmerli, *Old Testament Theology*, pp. 21–27.
6. Von Rad, *Old Testament Theology*, 1:121ff.
7. From the third century B.C. *RGG*³, s.v. "Namenglaube," by K. Baltzer.
8. The most convenient recent marshaling of the evidence is by Peter Stuhlmacher, "Das Bekenntnis zur Auferweckung Jesu von den Toten und die biblische Theologie," *ZThK* 70 (1973): 377ff., 389ff.
9. Cf. Rom. 4:24 with Rom. 8:11; 1 Cor. 15:15; 2 Cor. 1:9; 4:14; Gal. 1:1; Col. 2:12; 1 Pet. 1:21.
10. As a name, *Kyrios* appears only in Scripture references, e.g., Matt. 4:10; 22:37. Otherwise, referring to God, it is only an alternate to *theos*.
11. For less hasty observation, see Josef A. Jungmann, *The Place of Christ in Christian Liturgical Prayer*, trans. A. Peeler (New York: Alba House, 1965).
12. Ignatius, *To the Magnesians*, xiii,1,2; Clement, *To the Corinthians*, xlii,3; xlvi,6; lviii,2; *2 Clement*, xx,5; *Martyrdom of Polycarp*, xiv,3.
13. Georg Kretschmar, *Studien zur frühchristlichen Trinitätstheologie* (Tübingen: J. C. B. Mohr [Paul Siebeck], 1956), pp. 182–216.
14. As posited by Henry A. Wolfson, *The Philosophy of the Church Fathers* (Cambridge, Mass.: Harvard University Press, 1956), 1:147–54. See also Hans von Campenhausen, "Taufen auf den Namen Jesu," *VigChr* 25 (1971): 1–16.
15. So also J. N. D. Kelly, *Early Christian Creeds* (New York and London: Longmans, Green & Co., 1950), pp. 23ff.
16. For the second and third centuries, Kretschmar, *Studien*, pp. 196–216.
17. The passages in Acts that describe baptism "in Jesus' name" (2:38; 8:16; 10:48; 19:15) are all theological descriptions, not rubrics.
18. E.g., Günther Bornkamm, *Jesus of Nazareth*, trans. I. and F. McLuskey (New York: Harper & Row, 1960), pp. 124–29.
19. Martin Hengel, *The Son of God*, trans. J. Bowden (Philadelphia: Fortress Press, 1976).
20. Von Rad, *Old Testament Theology*, 1:24ff., 62ff.
21. Robert W. Jenson, *Visible Words* (Philadelphia: Fortress Press, 1978), pp. 6–11.
22. For an account of the spread of the baptismal formula into the rest of the primal church's worship, see Kretschmar, *Studien*, pp. 182–216.
23. The ancient church laid great stress on this point. See Basil the Great, *On the Holy Spirit*, 26, in *PG* 32:67–218: "For if baptism was the beginning of life for me . . . , clearly the address spoken to me in the grace of my adoption is for me the foremost of utterances." According to Gregory of Nyssa, *Refutation of Eunomius' Confession*, in his *Opera*, ed. W. Jaeger (Leiden: E. J. Brill, 1952), 2:313: "For we have learned once for all from the Lord to whom we must attend . . . : to 'the Father and the Son and the Holy Spirit.' Therefore we say that it is a fearful and evil thing, to contemn . . . these divine sounds."
24. This is not only our after-the-fact interpretation. The ancient trinitarian theologians who created the developed doctrine worked out this logic explicitly; e.g., Gregory of Nyssa, *Refutation*, pp. 314–15.

2

The Trinitarian Logic and Rhetoric

"Father, Son, and Holy Spirit" is a slogan for the temporal structure of the church's apprehension of God and for the proper logic of its proclamation and liturgy. Within the Hebrew Scriptures' interpretation of God, trinitarian discourse remains unproblematic and so generates new language and images but not analysis.

THE TRINITARIAN LOGIC

"Father, Son, and Holy Spirit" became the church's name for its God because it packs into one phrase the content and logic of this God's identifying descriptions. These in turn embody the church's primal experience of God. In turning from the trinitarian name to the history and logic by which it became the name, we therefore also move out from the church's specific life of praise and petition, in which a name is most needed, to the wider whole of the church's life and reflection.

The gospel identifies its God thus: God is the one who raised Israel's Jesus from the dead. The whole task of theology can be described as the unpacking of this sentence in various ways. One of these produces the church's trinitarian language and thought.

If for any reason we attend to the temporality of "God is whoever raised Jesus," we note certain temporal features, which have been noticed at least liturgically, from the church's very beginning. God is here identified by a narrative that uses the tense-structure of ordinary language, whereas divine identification is more ordinarily done by time-neutral characters, as in "God is whoever is omnipotent to bolster my weakness" or "God is whatever is immune to the time which takes my life." Nor is this narrative mythic, so that the tenses would not be used in their ordinary way, for its power to identify depends on mention of an historical individual and so, in turn, on the historical narrative by which that individual—as any such individual—must be identified. Such a procedure is religiously peculiar, as has often been noticed, for while religions often mention some historical event (a "revelation") as

2 / THE TRIUNE GOD

epistemologically necessary for their knowledge about God, they do not normally identify the subject of this knowledge by that event.

To identify the gospel's God, we must identify Jesus. In this sense we may first say that God "is" Jesus. Every reality is somehow identifiable, and we cannot identify this God without simultaneously identifying Jesus. This also displays why religions do not normally pin their identifications of God to the identity of an historical event, for drastic restrictions are imposed on the ways in which we can go on to talk of a God so identified. If God, in any sense, is Jesus—or were Abraham Lincoln or the British Empire—we cannot rightly talk of this God in any way that would make the temporal sequences, the stuff of narration, unessential to his being, and that, of course, is just how religions normally want to talk of God. Indeed, the posit of one to whom tenses are insignificant and in whom, therefore, time may be evaded is the whole usual point of their enterprise.

God, we may therefore identify, is what happens with Jesus. But if we said only that, we would show no reason why it should be *God* that happens with Jesus and not merely, perhaps, an important religious epoch. Moreover, it is not as if we in any case knew about God, and then for some reason decided to "identify" God by reference to Jesus. It is what in particular happens with Jesus that compels us to use the word "God" of *this* Father in the first place.

Following much of the New Testament, let us use "love" as a slogan for what humanly happened with the historical Jesus. Then we may say that Jesus was a lover who went to death rather than qualify his self-giving to others; the love which was the plot of his life is an unconditional love. Of this person it is said that he nevertheless lives, that he is risen. Said of this particular person, such an assertion—whether true or not—is at least appropriate, for love means an unconditional self-giving, an acceptance of death; and a successful love would be an acceptance of death that resulted not in the lover's absence from the beloved but in his or her presence. Love *means* death and resurrection. For this particular man, resurrection, if it happened, was therefore but the proper outcome of his life.

Moreover, if this lover's resurrection happened, then there also now lives an unconditional lover with death—the limit of love—already behind him, so that his love must finally triumph altogether, must embrace all people and all circumstances of their lives. If he is risen, the human enterprise has a conclusion: a human communion constituted in its commonality by one man's unconditional self-dedication to his fellow creatures and thus embracing each individual and communal freedom established in the history so fulfilled.

Thus, if Jesus is risen, his personal love will be the last outcome of the human enterprise. If he died, his self-definition has been written to its end, as each of ours will be, but if he also yet lives, just this life so defined is not thereby a dead item of the past, but an item of living, surprising time, an item of

THE TRINITARIAN LOGIC AND RHETORIC

the future and indeed of the last future. Only of a person whose life had been defined as this particular man defined his would these propositions be appropriate. And it is because they are appropriate, and in that they are made, that "God" is an appropriate word for the reality identifiable as what happened with Jesus. A God is always some sort of eternity, some sort of embrace around time, within which time's sequences can be coherent, and if Jesus is risen he is to be both remembered and awaited.

Conversely, we may identify God so, now a second time: God is what will come of Jesus and us, together. In our original proposition, "God is whoever raised Jesus," the event by which God is identified, Jesus' resurrection, is the event in which Jesus is future to himself and to us.

In the Bible generally, the "Spirit" is God as the power of the future to overturn what already is, and just so fulfill it. The Spirit is indeed a present reality. But *what* is present is that there is a goal, and that we therein are free from all bondage to what is. The Spirit is the power of the eschaton now to be at once goal and negation of what is. In the New Testament, this Spirit is identified as Jesus' spirit, as every human being has spirit. That Jesus' particular spirit is the very power of the last future is the "spirit"-form of the identification of God by Jesus from which trinitarian language begins. Therefore the biblical "Spirit" is the inevitable word for this second identification of God, although developed trinitarian doctrines, since they respond to postbiblical problems, need by no means be bound exclusively to this name.

Finally, this particular embrace around time must be universal, for it is the embrace of an unconditional love. It must grant a universal destiny. Therefore this God may also be identified so: God is the will in which all things have Jesus' love as their destiny. Jesus, we saw, "is" God only *as* God's identifiability. In our original identifying proposition, "God is whoever raised Jesus," "Jesus" is the object of an active verb. God is—a third time—identified as the one who does Jesus' resurrection, as a given active transcendence to all that Jesus is and does. As what happens with Jesus is its own and our end, so also it is its own and our given.

In the New Testament, "Father" is Jesus' address to the transcendence *given to* his acts and sufferings, the transcendence *over against* whom he lives and to whom he is responsible—addressed in trust. For Jesus' disciples, therefore, "the Father" is God as the transcendent givenness of Jesus' love, the one in whom we may trust for that love.

Thus we have a temporally three-point identification of the gospel's God. If we think of an identification as a pointing operation (as in "Which one?" "That one"), we must point with all three of time's arrows in order to point out this God: to the Father as Given, to the Lord Jesus as the present possibility of God's reality for us, and to the Spirit as the outcome of Jesus' work. The identification is triple—rather than, say, double or quintuple—because time

2 / THE TRIUNE GOD

does have three arrows. The past, present, and future of all that is, is doubtless a peculiar sort of fact, but it is also the most inescapable.

That the gospel's identification of God is threefold rests, therefore, on the way the gospel modulates a generally inescapable metaphysical fact. What is peculiar about the gospel's identification of God is not the number three but rather that it follows the three arrows of time without mitigating their difference. It is the very purpose of most discourse about gods to mitigate the threatening difference of past, present, and future. Among us Greeks, this is ordinarily accomplished by a doctrine of God's being as a timeless persistence in which past, present, and future are "really" all the same. The gospel's theology cannot produce such a doctrine, for thereby it would saw off the limb of narrative identification on which all its talk of God sits. But if such a doctrine is not produced, we are left with the three peculiar identifications of God just described and with their even more peculiar mutual relation.

The God of the gospel is the hope at the beginning of all things, in which we and all things are open to our fulfillment; this God is the love which will be that fulfillment; and this God is the faithfulness of Jesus the Israelite, which within time's sequences reconciles this beginning and this end. All else being equal, no more need be said. The rhetorical and soteriological space opened here is vast and permissive. Ignatius of Antioch was once moved to say, "We are drawn up [to God the Father] by Jesus Christ's crane—the cross—suspended by the rope that is the Holy Spirit" (*To the Ephesians* ix,1).

The temporal structure we have analyzed is the unreflected open and free temporal horizon of the church's life and proclamation. Trinitarian discourse becomes problematic, and the difficult metaphysical dialectics we first think of as "the doctrine of the Trinity" become necessary, only when mitigation of time becomes tempting, that is, only in confrontation with more normal identifications of God. The confrontation of that sort which historically occurred is the matter of the next chapter.

THE HEBREW SCRIPTURES AS THE ROOT OF TRINITARIANISM

There is a famous saying of an anonymous first-century preacher that we must "think about Jesus Christ as we do about God."[1] The dictum formulated a principle that was immediate and self-understood through the apostolic and immediately postapostolic time,[2] for to think of God in the way this chapter has so far analyzed is to think of Christ "as of" God.[3]

Whether such thinking remains immediate and obvious or is difficult and problematic, and so also whether we just *do* such thinking or also reflect on what we do, depends on how one does in fact antecedently think about God.

THE TRINITARIAN LOGIC AND RHETORIC

As the Hebrew Scriptures, and so the earliest church, think of God, there is no problem, and none was felt. As the religion and philosophy of the Greeks and ourselves think of God, there are many great problems, which will be the matter of the next two chapters.

To be sure, superficial reflection supposes the opposite. It is commonly thought that trinitarian language about God marks Christianity's discontinuity with the Hebrew Scriptures. Increasingly Hellenist Christians were supposedly led by their devotion to Jesus to "divinize" him and so to mitigate God's uniqueness. This common supposition is false.

It is true—as we will see in the next chapter—that from about A.D. 150 Christianity's confrontation with Hellenism led to formulations which initially smacked of divinization. But—as we will also see—the whole developed doctrine of the Trinity was the church's effort to resist this temptation. And at the level of immediate trinitarian witness and experience which we are now discussing, and during the period before massive confrontation with Hellenic theology, there was not even incipient conflict between trinitarian and Hebrew interpretations of God. On the contrary, this immediate trinitarianism was the only possible fulfillment of the Hebrew Scriptures.

Israel's interpretation of God was undoubtedly the historical result of a multitude of factors, many now untraceable. But systematically and at least in part historically, Israel's theology can all be derived from the identification of God by the exodus. If God is, more than trivially, *the one who* rescued Israel from Egypt, the main characteristics of this God are immediately evident.[4]

First, Yahweh is *not on the side of established order*. The usual God, whose eternity is the persistence of the beginning, has as his very honor among us that in him we are secure against the threats of the future. Ancient imperial peoples poignantly experienced the fragility of their achievement: The situation in which seedtime and harvest return each year had barely been secured, and the barbarian destroyer was each year at the door. The gods of the ancient civilizations simply *were* the certainty of return, the guarantee of continuance. Marduk, for example, was *the one who* back at the beginning divided the Mesopotamian swamps into irrigated land and channeled water, and in that he was always still there the people could transcend the ever-renewed threat of relapse into precreation disorder. The damnation against which Yahweh fought for Israel was the precise opposite.

Israel understood itself not by an established order but by rescue from oppression under the archtypically standing order, that of Egypt. Throughout its history, Israel longed to become an established state "like all the nations" (1 Sam. 8:4–5). But God always saw to it that Israel would fail, and the prophets regularly denounced the very attempt (see 1 Sam. 8:7–9). Indeed, and most uncanny of all, Yahweh remained free to undo the standing order of

103

2 / THE TRIUNE GOD

his own people: "For, behold, [Yahweh, Yahweh] of hosts, is taking away from Jerusalem and from Judah stay and staff, the whole stay of bread, and the whole stay of water; the mighty man and the soldier, the judge and the prophet, the diviner and the elder" (Isa. 3:1-2).

Second, Yahweh's will is not identical with natural necessity—that is, Yahweh's will is indeed what we mean by "will." In great ancient myths, the beginning of the people's worship of God is in each case identical with the absolute beginning of all things. Therein lay assurance: nothing can overthrow the people's basis, since outside it there is nothing. Israel, on the other hand, knew very well of a history, including a history of Israel's own ancestors, that preceded the exodus. The great myths of other peoples tell of a primeval event which set the pattern of time and is therefore above time, which never really ceases to happen—as Marduk's primeval separation of water and land recurred at each yearly inundation and draining. Israel's story told of an event which, for all repeated cultic celebration, had happened only once, in time rather than above it.

Israel, of course, could and did attribute general creation to its God. But Yahweh's creation of the world and of Israel were two acts, not one. Israel knew that created reality did not necessarily include it, that Israel might not have been. Since Israel did nevertheless exist, by an act of Yahweh, that act was just so understood as a choice:[5] "You have seen what I did to the Egyptians, and how I . . . brought you to myself. Now therefore . . . , you shall be my own possession among all peoples" (Exod. 19:4-5).

Third, since there was history before there was Israel, and yet the God of Israel ruled that history, this question must be asked: How was Yahweh the God of Israel before there was Israel? The developed form of Israel's tradition had an answer: Between creation-times and the exodus was the time of the fathers, of Abraham, Isaac, and Jacob. But how were these Israel? The solution of the ancient narrators was that patriarchal Israel was Israel by the promise of a land and a land's possibility of nationhood.[6] Abraham and the other fathers had lived in response to the promise that their descendants would be a great people. Having as yet no established order, the fathers had lived by the word that promised one.

Thus Israel knew itself as created by God's word, in the exact sense in which we until recently spoke of "a gentleman's word." Yahweh made a promise and kept it, and so Israel came to be. From the start, salvation for Israel is given by promise of what is not yet, of the future that is real only in the word that opens it. What other nations could say of a visible and tangible presence of God in holy images and places, Israel could say only of God's utterance: "The grass withers, the flower fades, but the word of our God will stand for ever" (Isa. 40:7-8). Moreover, Israel knew of a time when Israel had been Israel only by this word, without security, when Israel's whole existence had been hope. There remains only to note that with the exile of 587 B.C., when all secure national existence was (at least until A.D. 1948) taken away, historical Israel was put in exactly the position posited for the fathers.⁷

Thus the identity of Israel's God, his difference from other gods, is precisely that Israel's God is not eternal in the way the other gods are, not God in the same way. That the past guarantees the future is exactly the deity of the gods, but Yahweh always challenges the past and everything guaranteed by it, from a future that is freedom. The key steps of the trinitarian logic described in the previous section are the very specificity of the Hebrew Scriptures' interpretation of God.

As to how, positively, Yahweh is eternal, Israel's interpretation is that he is faithful. Where other ancient religions said that God is beyond time, Israel said: "For ever, [Yahweh], thy word is firmly fixed in the heavens. Thy faithfulness endures to all generations; thou hast established the earth, and it stands fast" (Ps. 119: 89–90). *Emunah* (faithfulness) is the reliability of a promise; thus the Revised Standard Version often translates it "truth" (e.g., Prov. 12:17; Hos. 5:9), and a promise which is verified by events is "made *emun*" (e.g., 1 Kings 8:26). If God continues to bless Israel in spite of everything, it is because he "is keeping the oath which he swore" to the fathers, "because [Yahweh] is the *faithful* God who keeps covenant" (Deut. 7:8–9). And when the fulfillment comes, when "kings shall see and arise," it will be "because of [Yahweh], who is faithful" (Isa. 49:7).

In one famous passage, the interpretation of God's eternity as faithfulness approaches a metaphysical definition. Within the tradition of the covenant with David, the most beautiful statement of Israel's hope proclaims: "I will make with you an everlasting covenant, my steadfast, sure love for David" (Isa. 55:3).

Unlike the normal gods, Yahweh does not transcend time by immunity to it. The continuity of Yahweh's being is not that of a defined entity, some of whose defining characteristics persist from beginning to end. It is rather the sort of continuity we have come to call "personal." It is established in Yahweh's words and commitments, by the faithfulness of later acts to the promises made in Yahweh's earlier acts. The continuity of Yahweh's being is eternity, transcends time, in that Yahweh keeps all promises, in that time cannot take any commitments away. It is just this interpretation of God's eternity that we introduced as the logical necessity—given the resurrection and the resultant necessity to identify God by Jesus—of trinitarian identification of God.

PRIMARY TRINITARIANISM

Therefore, so long as Christian interpretation of God was in unshaken continuity with that of the Hebrew Scriptures, Christian discourse and reflection

2 / THE TRIUNE GOD

shaped themselves naturally and unproblematically to the triune logical and rhetorical space. This can be seen in the New Testament and so long thereafter[8] as the communities were not strongly confronted with Hellenic interpretation of God.

That "God" and God's "Spirit" form a rhetorical and conceptual pair for proclamation of God's work and interpretation of our life is entirely unproblematic in the New Testament. The use was imposed by the experience of Pentecost and needed no conceptual or linguistic innovation over against the Hebrew Scriptures. Also that "Christ" and the "Spirit" form such a pair in that the Spirit is *Christ's* Spirit was direct and historically legitimate interpretation of the Hebrew Scriptures, asserting merely the fulfillment of certain expectations in fact contained therein and involving no conceptual or linguistic innovation. These matters are analyzed in detail in another *locus* of this work.

That "God the Father" and "Jesus Christ his Son" form a similar pair is more complicated. It was of course the immediate consequence of that identification of God by Jesus' resurrection which is the whole import of the New Testament. But although the identification of God by historical events is fundamental in the Hebrew Scriptures, that the conclusively identifying events turn out to be the life of an individual person requires language beyond that of the Hebrew Scriptures, though in the New Testament itself never incongruous therewith. We cannot avoid a quick survey of these developments, though in detail they too belong to another *locus*.

The emergence of a semantic pattern in which the uses of "God" and "Jesus Christ" are mutually determining is fundamental. That pattern is firmly established before the earliest Pauline writings,[9] for example, the formula quoted by Paul "If you confess with your lips that Jesus is Lord and believe in your heart that God raised him from the dead, you will be saved" (Rom. 10:9). The pattern is the logical backbone of all Paul's own discourse about God.[10] In Paul the standard Hebrew theological predicates take either God or Jesus as subject, or both at once;[11] for example, "grace" is interchangeably "of God" (Rom. 5:15) or "of Christ" (Rom. 16:20) or bestowed "from God our Father and the Lord Jesus Christ" (Rom. 1:7). Parallel constructions have "God" in one part and "Christ" in the other.[12] "So we are ambassadors for Christ, God making his appeal through us" (2 Cor. 5:20). For Paul, *God* will rule the kingdom, Jesus is *Lord*, and these two circumstances are one fact only: "For the kingdom of God [means] righteousness and peace . . . ; he who thus serves Christ is acceptable" (Rom. 14:17–18, e.g.). Christ simply is "the power of God and the wisdom of God" (1 Cor. 1:24), the manifestation of that "righteousness" in which Judaism summed up the godliness of God (Rom. 3:21–22). Yet "God" and "Christ" are not simply identified; thus prayer and thanksgiving are always directed to God, through Christ or "in his name."[13]

THE TRINITARIAN LOGIC AND RHETORIC

This semantic pattern best displays the relation between the Father and Jesus, "the Son," as the apostolic church experienced it. The titles and images by which various groups more directly attempted to grasp the relation are for our present concern of secondary importance. We need only note primal Christianity's eclecticism in the drafting of such conceptions, and their general concord with the Hebrew Scriptures. Such mythic christology as appears, for example, in Philippians 2 or the Book of Hebrews or John's Gospel, where Christ is a "pre-" or "postexistent" heavenly being of unstipulated relation to God, displays a kind of thinking fully shared by contemporary Judaism[14] and well grounded in the Old Testament.[15] The various "christological titles" by which the risen Lord was addressed and proclaimed are without exception functional in their import. They do not say what sort of "being" Christ has, but merely what role he has. Most typical in its logic is "Lord."[16] Initially merely Jesus' disciples' term of address to their master, it was naturally resumed for their risen Lord after the resurrection. But now this Lord is enthroned in God's own power and directs their mission by a Spirit that is God's own. In these circumstances, the Hebrew Scriptures' use of "Lord" for God cannot help but resonate the in-itself still purely human title. With the experience of the ancient church in our inheritance, *we* cannot but ask what sort of being ("divine," "human," or what) this title and the others used by the primal church attribute to Jesus. It is vital to understand that they raised no such question for the primal church itself, that the analysis, for example, just given of "Lord" completely describes what it did or could do for the apostolic users.

The resurrection compelled the apostolic church to find new language. Only for us does this language raise questions over against the Hebrew Scriptures. The language once available, and given the logic of the Hebrew Scriptures' talk of God, Christian invocation, exhortation, and explanation seem to have taken triune form merely by following the path of least difficulty and quite without need for explicit reflection on the pattern itself. We will best assure ourselves of this by means of samples cited at near random from different strands of the New Testament: "But you, beloved . . . , pray in the Holy Spirit; keep yourselves in the love of God; wait for the mercy of our Lord Jesus Christ" (Jude 20–21); "But it is God who establishes us with you in Christ . . . ; he has . . . given us his Spirit in our hearts as a guarantee" (2 Cor. 1:21–22);[17] "For through him [Christ] we both have access in one Spirit to the Father" (Eph. 2:18).[18] Nor is this merely a matter of stock phrases; the essential temporal logic appears in triune formulas lacking one or another of the standard titles, for example, "I charge you in the presence of *God*, and of *Christ Jesus* who is to judge the living and the dead, and by *his appearing and his kingdom*" (2 Tim. 4:1).[19] Again, "May the *God of hope* fill you with all joy and peace in *believing*, so that by the power of the *Holy Spirit* . . ." (Rom. 15:13).

2 / THE TRIUNE GOD

The initial place in life of such language is doubtless displayed by the writer of Ephesians at 5:18–20: "But be filled with the Spirit, addressing one another in psalms and hymns and spiritual songs, singing and making melody to the Lord . . . giving thanks in the name of our Lord Jesus Christ to God the Father." The essential Christian experience was of assemblies gripped by the dynamism of a particular future—"his appearing and his kingdom"—which dynamism the Scriptures taught them to call "the Spirit" and in which grip all prayer and praise was to "God the Father" and in the name of the one under whose lordship we are indeed God's children and share his Spirit. Given this sort of liturgical experience, it was utterly natural for the work of salvation to be compendiously described simply by reversing the order and going through the same sequence starting with God, as does the same writer to the Ephesians: "In him according to the purpose of him who accomplishes all things . . . , we who first hoped in Christ have been destined . . . to live for the praise of his glory. In him you also, who . . . have believed in him, were sealed with the promised Holy Spirit, which is the guarantee of our inheritance" (Eph. 1:11–14). Just so this writer obtains a complete framework for theology and can describe the entire Christian reality in the coordinates of "God's grace," "the mystery of Christ," and revelation "by the Spirit" (e.g. Eph. 3:2–6).

The most remarkable trinitarian passage in the New Testament, amounting to an entire theological system, is Romans 8. Its conceptual and argumentative heart is verse 11: "If the Spirit of him who raised Jesus from the dead dwells in you, he who raised Christ Jesus from the dead will give life to your mortal bodies also through his Spirit which dwells in you." The subject phrase displays in the uttermost conceptual compression the precise structure we have called "the trinitarian logic": the *Spirit* is "*of* him *who* raised *Jesus*." And from the prepositional structure of this phrase, Paul then develops a rhetoric and argument which sweeps justification and the work of Christ and prayer and eschatology and ethics and predestination into one coherent understanding. With somewhat less dialectical and rhetorical complexity than Romans 8, many other passages display what can only be called a standard Pauline trinitarian conceptuality. "God" is named as the agent of salvation, which is accomplished in an act described by such phrases as "in Christ Jesus," the purpose of which act, both eschatologically and penultimately, is a "sending" of the Spirit with "gifts" (e.g., 1 Cor. 1:4–8; Gal. 4:4).

The new thing that appears in the immediate postapostolic church is the attempt to *grasp*—mostly in mythic images—the constitution of God by Christ and the Spirit, that is, not merely to speak in a trinitarian fashion but to speak about the Trinity. What we have here to examine is the trinitarianism of what Daniélou somewhat misleadingly called "Jewish Christianity,"[20] that is, all Christianity up to the direct challenge of Hellenic thought around A.D. 150, and thereafter the Christianity of those areas not heavily so challenged.

THE TRINITARIAN LOGIC AND RHETORIC

The principle of all this trinitarianism is classically stated by the epexegetical continuation of the saying of Clement earlier cited: "as of God, *as of the judge of the living and the dead.*"²¹ The equation of Christ—and the Spirit—with God is in all this thinking an attribution of *function* inseparable from God.

There were many "Jewish" Trinity-images.²² The most important evoked the Son and the Spirit as "angels." In the most ancient postapostolic church there was undoubtedly an angel christology immediately dependent on apocalyptic Judaism's angel speculation, but there was an angel pneumatology too, on the same basis.²³ And so the full trinitarian experience of God found expression, as in the apocalyptic vision of Isaiah: "And I saw him [Christ] ascend into the seventh heaven, and all the saints and angels praised him. And I saw him sit down on the right hand of the Glory. . . . And the Angel of the Holy Spirit I saw sitting on the left hand."²⁴ This vision of God and two great angels seems to have had great continuing importance for the later development of trinitarianism: Origen, creator of the first great trinitarian theology, repeatedly proof-texts with Isa. 6:1-3, interpreting the two great seraphim of that passage as allegories of the Son and the Spirit and explicitly attributing this interpretation to a Jewish teacher.²⁵

We now find this angel christology and angel trinitarianism alarming. It seems to create a large class of demigods and to locate Christ and the Spirit among them, surely a case of "divinization," and halfhearted at that. But this happens only because we anachronistically project our question about kinds of being back on this essentially Semitic discourse, and are then disappointed²⁶ to find Christ and the Spirit not fully divine, and Christ not fully human either. But in this thinking itself, an "angel" is simply one to whom God gives a mission and whose own reality is constituted by this mission. *Nothing* is thereby suggested about what sort of being is possessed by either God or this manifestation.²⁷ It can well be that the mission is in fact God's own mission. If it is, this will simply appear in descriptions of what the angel does—judges all people, forgives sin, or whatever.²⁸ And that Christ and the Spirit are transcendent over "other" angels appears iconographically, as in Hermas, where Christ is bigger than the other archangels and is a seventh, when all know the full number of archangels is six, or as in the *Ascension of Isaiah* where God and the two great angels are together worshiped by the other angels.²⁹

The kinds of trinitarian discourse developed in the New Testament and in the immediately subsequent period have continued through the history of the church. With use of the triune name, they are the substance of living trinitarian apprehension of God. Christians bespeak God in a triune coordinate system; they speak *to* the Father, *with* the Son, *in* the Spirit, and only so bespeak *God*. Indeed, they *live in* a sort of temporal space defined by these coordinates, and just and only so live "in God." And they represent the God

2 / THE TRIUNE GOD

with whom they have thus to do in iconography and metaphor that is functional in its attribution of deity. Where, as in the medieval and modern Western church, these modes lose some of their power to shape actual proclamation and prayer, an alienation of the church must be suspected.

Pastors often believe that the Trinity is too complicated to explain to the laity. Nothing could be more misguided. Believers *know how* to pray to the Father, daring to call him "Father" because they pray with Jesus, God's Son, and so enter into the future these two have for them, that is, praying in the Spirit. Those who know how to do this, and who realize that just in the space defined by these coordinates they have to do with God, do understand the Trinity. All the intellectual complexities we must shortly embark on are a secondary phenomenon, whose proper location is the back of teachers' and preachers' minds, determining the way they guide and, when necessary, explain, this relation to this God.

THE DOGMATIC STATUS OF PRIMARY TRINITARIANISM

The structures of language and experience analyzed in the previous two sections are not merely in fact present in the life of the church. They are daily and explicitly acknowledged and proclaimed as fundamental by the worshiping assemblies of all Christendom, being embodied in the great liturgical creeds of the apostles, and of Nicaea. The three-article creeds are the daily education and public self-definition of the Christian community in all its branches, recited at baptism and often at the Supper or other main services. And they are acknowledged such by Eastern, Roman Catholic, and Reformation bodies alike—as, for example, in the Lutheran *Book of Concord*, where they are set in first place and aptly called "the ecumenical" creeds.

Creedal formulations are as old as the gospel.[30] For our immediate purposes, two forms are important. First, the initial preachers and catechists and their successors used and passed on narrative summaries of the chief claims and facts about Jesus (see 1 Cor. 15:1–7).[31] Second, there is the rubric that baptism is to be "in the name of the Father and of the Son and of the Holy Spirit." We do not know what liturgical form this naming initially took, or even if it took the same form in all communities. But by the time ancient baptismal practice emerges into clear view,[32] in the writings of Hippolytus at the turn of the second and third centuries, the naming is an interrogation of trinitarian confession: "Let the baptizer . . . say, 'Do you believe in God, the Father Almighty? Do you believe in Christ Jesus, the Son of God . . . ?' [etc.]."[33] There are signs that such interrogation may have been the—or an—original way of baptismal "naming"; in any case, the primal church did de-

THE TRINITARIAN LOGIC AND RHETORIC

mand confession of faith at baptism,[34] and this confession was shaped by the triune pattern of baptismal naming, however the latter was done.

The sort of declaratory creeds we know and use, such as the Apostles' Creed or the creeds used as bases by the councils of Nicaea and Constantinople, developed from the fusion of these two forms: the baptismal questions with their canonically stipulated triune pattern, and the summaries of christological narrative.[35] It seems likely that the location of this development was catechetical discipline, which had both to prepare for baptism and to reinforce the main items of christological missionary preaching. The shift to declaratory form from interrogatory form—which was retained at baptism itself—was probably occasioned by the demand that catechumens, before baptism, report to the congregation their participation in the faith into which the congregation had been baptized: "I believe—as do you—in. . . ." It also seems likely that the earliest stable product of this development was the forerunner of the Apostles' Creed, the old creed of the church of Rome, fixed sometime toward the end of the second century. This old Roman creed was created by addition of the christological kerygma "who was conceived by" to a trinitarian baptismal interrogation about "God the Father Almighty, and . . . Christ Jesus, his only Son, our Lord, and the Holy Spirit, the holy church, the resurrection of the flesh."[36]

What is dogmatized by the classical three-article creeds is thus not only or even primarily any one list of kerygmatically vital christological events or necessary theological items. There has never, in fact, been any one universally accepted creedal list of either. Even now, when we have reduced the creeds in practical use to two, they do not present quite the same list. What is first of all dogmatized are the kerygmatically narrated history itself, the triple-name structure, and the union of the two. Moreover, the popular impression is precisely wrong, that first there is a three-step history of God's works—the "three articles"—and that then the triune name is a sort of summary and the trinitarian logic a kind of explanation thereof. The reverse is the case.

The Apostles' Creed and those like it were created by the catechetical and liturgical affinity, and the logical fit, between the triune baptismal name of God and the evangelical history narrated in the gospel. That is, it is exactly the logic analyzed in this chapter which the creeds declare to be the true and necessary logic of the gospel.

NOTES

1. See *2 Clement*, i,1–2.
2. Thus Ignatius, who has the Greek diction, a Logos concept, and treats the ascription of deity and temporality to one subject as a paradox, nevertheless refers to Jesus

2 / THE TRIUNE GOD

simply as God, quite without noting a problem: *To the Ephesians*, viii,2; *To the Smyrneans*, i,1; *To the Romans*, viii,2; *Ephesians*, xix,2; xvii,2.

3. Thus "Clement" does exegesis on his own dictum in *2 Clement*, i,1-2: ". . . as about the Judge of the living and the dead."

4. On the following about Israel, see Walther Zimmerli, *Old Testament Theology in Outline*, trans. D. E. Green (Atlanta: John Knox Press, 1978), pp. 21-32. On the general pattern of ancient religion, see Mircea Eliade, *Cosmos and History*, trans. W. R. Trask (New York: Harper & Row, 1959), the classic study.

5. Zimmerli, *Old Testament Theology*, pp. 43ff.

6. Ibid., pp. 27-32, 64-65.

7. Walther Zimmerli, "Die Bedeutung der grossen Schriftprophetie für das alttestamentliche Reden von Gott," *VT.S*, 1972, pp. 63-64.

8. I.e., in what Jean Daniélou, *The Theology of Jewish Christianity*, trans. J. A. Baker (Chicago: Henry Regnery Co.; London: Darton, Longman & Todd, 1964), somewhat misleadingly calls "Jewish Christianity."

9. Klaus Wengst, *Christologische Formeln und Lieder des Urchristentums*, StNT 7 (Gütersloh: Gerd Mohn, 1972).

10. See Wolfgang Schrage, "Theologie und Christologie bei Paulus und Jesus," *EvTh* 36 (1976): 123-35.

11. Ibid., pp. 124-25.

12. Ibid., p. 125.

13. Ibid., pp. 127-28.

14. Wilhelm Bousset, *Die Religion des Judentums*, ed. Hugo Gressman, 3d ed. (Tübingen: J. C. B. Mohr [Paul Siebeck], 1966), pp. 302-57; Robert L. Wilken, ed., *Aspects of Wisdom in Judaism and Early Christianity* (Notre Dame, Ind.: Notre Dame University Press, 1975), pp. 1-31, 103-41; Martin Hengel, *Judaism and Christianity*, trans. J. Bowden (London: SCM Press, 1974), 1:153-75.

15. From the "angel of the Lord" in the patriarchal narratives (e.g., Gen. 22:9-19) to the great eschatological figure of Dan. 7:13-14.

16. E.g., Ferdinand Hahn, *The Titles of Jesus in Christology*, trans. H. Knight and G. Ogg (Cleveland: World Publishing, 1969), s.v. "Lord."

17. In Paul the list of such uses is long, e.g., Rom. 14:17-18; 15:30; 1 Cor. 2:2-5; 12:4-6; 2 Cor. 3:3; Phil. 3:3; 1 Thess. 5:18-20.

18. Elsewhere in this literature: Eph. 1:11-14; 1:17; 2:18-22; 3:2-7, 14-17; 4:4-6; 5:18-20; Col. 1:6-8; Titus 3:4-6.

19. It is regularly "Spirit" that is omitted as a word but present in substance; e.g., 1 Pet. 1:3.

20. Daniélou, *Theology*. Cf. n. 8, above.

21. *2 Clement*, i,2.

22. On these images, see Daniélou, *Theology*, pp. 146-66; Aloys Grillmeier, *Christ in Christian Tradition*, trans. J. S. Bowden (New York: Sheed & Ward, 1965), 2:41-53; Jaroslav Pelikan, *The Christian Tradition: A History of the Development of Doctrine*, vol. 1, *The Emergence of the Catholic Tradition (100-600)* (Chicago: University of Chicago Press, 1971), pp. 176ff., 184ff.; Georg Kretschmar, *Studien zur frühchristlichen Trinitätstheologie* (Tübingen: J. C. B. Mohr [Paul Siebeck], 1956), pp. 20-22.

23. Daniélou, *Theology*, pp. 117–47, esp. pp. 128ff.; Johannes Barbel, *Christos Angelos* (Bonn: Hauslein, 1941), pp. 181–311; Martin Werner, *The Formation of Christian Doctrine* (New York: Harper & Row, 1957), pp. 120–61; Grillmeier, *Christ*, pp. 46ff.

24. *Ascension of Isaiah*, xi,32–35. For other documentation, Kretschmar, *Studien*, pp. 71–124.

25. E.g., Origen, *Commentary on Isaiah*, 1,2; 15; 41; *Commentary on Ezekiel*, 14,2; *On First Principles*, i,3,4; iv,3,14. See Kretschmar, *Studien*, pp. 220–23.

26. Or we may be gleeful if we oppose the later doctrines of true godhead and believe ourselves now to discover that the earliest church contradicted them. This is Martin Werner's blunder, which invalidates all the arguments of his otherwise admirable investigations.

27. Daniélou, *Theology*, pp. 117ff.

28. E.g., Hermas, *Similitudes*, viii,1–2.

29. Ibid., ix,12,7–8; *Ascension of Isaiah*, viii,16–18.

30. The standard presentation is by J. N. D. Kelly, *Early Christian Creeds* (New York and London: Longmans, Green & Co., 1950), pp. 6–29.

31. Ibid., pp. 17ff.

32. See ibid., pp. 40–49.

33. Hippolytus, *Apostolic Tradition*, 21.

34. Kelly, *Creeds*, pp. 40ff.

35. Ibid., pp. 30–130.

36. Ibid., 119ff.

3
The Nicene-Constantinopolitan Dogma

Over against the Hellenic identification of God, the church's discourse about God was and still is tempted to alienation from its proper trinitarian logic. The dogma of Nicaea and Constantinople was a decisive victory over this temptation.

THE GOD OF THE GREEKS

In much of this chapter we have a story to tell. The gospel mission did in fact meet with another and fundamentally incompatible identification of God, that of the Greeks, which could not be ignored. Christianity as we know it, and especially our inherited body of developed trinitarian dogma and analysis, is the result.

If the gospel had not met the challenge to its strange identification of God in the form of the Greek interpretation, it would have met it in some other— and indeed it did and does in those branches of the mission that lead into great culture areas other than that in which our narrative is set. Moreover, the clash will always be at the same point: religion's normal reluctance to take time seriously for God. Thus any possible great non-Western theology must contain some functional equivalent for the developed trinitarianism on which we are about to embark. But such possibilities are beyond the scope of this work.

From its beginning, Hellenic theology was an exact antagonist of biblical faith.[1] Israel's interpretation of God was determined by the rescue of wandering tribes from oppression under an established civilization, Greece's by an established civilization's overthrow by just such tribes.[2] The flourishing religious and material world of Mycenaean Greece was swept away by the flood of Dorian tribes from the north. But in certain areas the memory and traditions of lost glory survived. When Greek civilization began to revive in the ninth century, it was these surviving Ionians that led the way. Thus the historical memory of Greece began with catastrophe, with a national experience of sheer irrational contingency and power, and of death and destruction

2 / THE TRIUNE GOD

brought by it. Greek religion and reflection were tragic from their root. They were a sustained attempt to deal with the experience that we must "not reckon any mortal blessed . . . until he has reached the end of his life without suffering disaster."³ Greek religion and reflection were thereby imprinted with five characters important for our purpose.

First, their driving question was: "Can it be that *all* things pass away?" The assurance they needed, as formulated by Aristotle, had to be: "Being as such neither comes to be nor perishes."⁴ In the myth of Chronos, "Father Time" who devoured all his children, the Greeks stated their experience of time and its surprises. Their religion was the determination that "Time" not be supreme, that he be overthrown by a true "Father of gods and men." Greek religion was the quest for a rock of ages, resistant to the flow of time, a place or part or aspect of reality immune to change. The gods' one defining character was therefore immortality, immunity to destruction. Whereas Yahweh was eternal by his faithfulness *through* time, the Greek gods' eternity was their abstraction *from* time. Yahweh's eternity is thus intrinsically a relation to his creatures—supposing there are any—whereas the Greek gods' eternity is the negation of such relation.

Second, Greek religion and reflection were an act of human self-defense against mysterious power and inexplicable contingency, that is, against just what humankind has mostly called "God." The Ionian survivors willed that history have a humanly comprehensible pattern, of such a kind that its events be in principle predictable and plannable. If superhuman (i.e., immortal) actors were needed to explain some events and so vindicate their sense, these too had to be understandable and predictable in their motivations and reasons. Such were the Olympian gods, the Ionian Homer's rationalized versions of various inherited nature and clan deities, whose singular lack of holiness and mystery scholars have always noted. The Ionians rescued themselves from chaos by enlightenment, by explanation of time's seeming mysteries.

Homer's successors, as religious thinkers, were the Ionian philosophers.⁵ With them the reduction of all godly characteristics to one, immortality, and the inclusion also of the gods within one comprehensible scheme of events, led (and this is the third character on our list) to the concept of "the divine," a unitary abstraction of godly explanatory power in and behind the plural gods of daily religion; for example, Aristotle reports, "The Unbounded has no beginning . . . , but seems rather to be the Beginning of all other realities, and to envelope and control them. . . . This is the Divine. So the opinion of Anaximander and most of the natural philosophers."⁶ For the educated class of Greece's classic period, this abstraction, often called "Zeus," was the true religious object: timelessness simply as such. So also the word "God" is understood as an adjective, applicable to various manifestations in various degrees.

THE NICENE-CONSTANTINOPOLITAN DOGMA

Fourth, the quest for timeless reality is never satisfied by anything directly presented in our experience. All the world we see, hear, and touch does indeed pass away. If there is the divine, it must therefore be above or behind or beneath or within the experienced world. It must be the bed of time's river, the foundation of the world's otherwise unstable structure, the track of heaven's hastening lights. Greek religion and reflection, by their inner function, were metaphysical, a quest for the timeless ground of temporal being that just so is a different sort of being than we ever immediately encounter.

And fifth, Greek religion and reflection were precisely the quest we have been calling them, for since the timeless ground is never directly presented in experience, it has to be searched for. A whole complex of motifs that will be centrally important for our story is involved here. Greek apprehension of God is accomplished by penetrating through the temporal experienced world to its atemporal ground. This theology is therefore essentially negative: The true predicates of deity are negations of predicates that pertain to experienced reality by virtue of its temporality. God is "invisible," "intangible," "impassible" (i.e., unaffected by external events), "indescribable." This theology is essentially analogical, for while it consists in negations of predicates that apply to the temporal world, it cannot dispense with such predicates. The pattern is always "Deity is F, only not as other, temporal reality is F." This theology necessarily raises the question of true deity, of the characteristics marking the final and so real ground, for if deity must be searched out, we have to be able to recognize it when we find it. And finally, all this penetration is accomplished by "mind" (*nous*), that is, not by discursive analysis or argument but by instantaneous intellectual intuition, by a sort of interior mirroring, for what is to be grasped is precisely a timeless pattern.

So far the essentials of Greek interpretation of God, in practiced religion and in the philosophy to which it gave birth. Before returning to the main line of our narrative, we must note one great event in the history of this religion.

The posit of timelessness was initially a sustaining posit: Deity was the reliable meaning and foundation of the human world. But only a sort of blink was needed for the value signs to reverse themselves. Timeless and temporal reality were posited as different kinds of being, defined by mutual negation. All meaning and value were located in timeless being. If we are given a metaphysical shock, we may suddenly see the line between time and eternity as a barrier, shutting us out from meaning, for we are temporal. Without attempting to assign a cause, it is enough for our purpose to note that in the transition from the local communities of classic Greece to cosmopolitan Hellenism exactly this reversal of values occurred.

Thus the dominant religious apprehension of late antiquity was of deity's distance, created by the very characteristics that made it deity. We are in time and God is not, and just so our situation is desperate. Therefore the religion

117

2 / THE TRIUNE GOD

of late antiquity was a frenzied search for "mediators," for beings of a third ontological kind between time and timelessness, to bridge the gap.¹⁰ Already Socrates had posited such a third kind, Eros, the child of Fullness and Want, and perceived that the language appropriate to speak of this realm is myth, that is, stories about divine beings, speech about eternities as if they were in time.¹¹ Discourse about deity was in any case understood to be analogical; "god" is basically adjectival and thus applicable in various grades to deity itself and to any mediators one or more steps down. In cosmopolitan Hellenism, such interpretation was put into practice. All the vast heritage of the world's savior-gods, demigods, reified abstractions, and mid-beings generally were pressed into mediatorial service. It was inevitable that when the gospel appeared on this scene, Christ would be too.

THE INITIAL CHRISTIANIZING OF HELLENISM

When the gospel mission confronts the Hellenic interpretation of God, it cannot and could not simply reject it. Israel proclaimed Yahweh as God for all peoples. In confrontation with Hellenism, this had to mean the claim that Israel's is the real God posited by Hellas' philosophers.¹² Moreover, Hellenism's interpretation of God both caused and expressed late antiquity's chief religious problem, the distance of God; the gospel had to address the problem. It was at the middle of the second century that Christian thinkers first posed the Hellenic analytic tasks to themselves as explicit matter for reflection. It is there we begin our narrative.

However the confrontation might have begun, it was in fact begun thus: Both bodies of discourse about God, the biblical and the Hellenic, were simply set alongside each other and more or less well carpentered together, depending on skill. On the one side this meant that Christians took over the procedure of penetrating to the "real" God by abstracting from time with negative analogies.¹³ Accordingly, Christians also adopted the negative predicates by which Hellenism had qualified true deity, and made one composite list with items from biblical language.

Already Ignatius, in A.D. 125, adopted the central and least biblical concept of late Hellenic theology: God is "impassible," immune to being acted upon (*To the Ephesians*, vii,2). This concept was to be the clearest and most troubling mark of Hellenic interpretation within Christian theology.¹⁴ Justin Martyr, the most influential second-century theologian, defined God as the eternally self-caused and changeless cause of the being of all other beings, (e.g., *Dialogue with Trypho*, 3), to the satisfaction of believers and unbelievers alike. For Justin and his fellows, God is therefore "unoriginated," "unutter-

THE NICENE-CONSTANTINOPOLITAN DOGMA

able," "immovable," "impassible," "inexpressible," "invisible," "unchangeable," "unplaceable," "immaterial," "unnameable."[15]

Yet the same theologians could also speak of God in incisively and even creatively biblical fashion. So Justin again: God is concerned with us; God is the "just overseer" of our lives (*Apology*, ii,12); God is compassionate and patient (the flat contradiction of "impassible") (*Dialogue*, 108); God's omnipotence is exercised above all in Jesus' resurrection (*Apology*, i,19); God actively intervenes to reward and punish (*Apology*, i,12); God's course of action is determined by regard for us (*Apology*, i,28). The true God, indeed, is to be identified as the one who led Israel from Egypt (*Apology*, i,11).[16] Such language is not mediated with the negative theology; the two conceptions of God are not so much synthesized as merely added together.[17] It is this additive tactic that has, from the apologists to the present, remained standard in theology. The notion of divine timelessness, once thus given room in Christian interpretation, then promptly attacks liturgical and proclamatory immediate trinitarianism.

The immediate question of every Hellenist, hearing the gospel's talk of God the beginning and God who is our fellow Jesus and God the fulfillment, must be But what is the timelessly self-identical something that is all these three? What is the time-immune continuity that must be the being of the real God? If we are not firm enough to challenge the question, there are only two possible answers: It is a fourth, of which the three are only temporal manifestations, or it is one of the three (which must then be the Father, since the other two are "from" him), of which the other two are only temporal manifestations. Historians label the first move "modalism," the second "subordinationism." Together, they comprise the whole list of ancient trinitarian heresies. They are heresies because they speak of God in just the way that saws off our narrative limb. They are precisely as common and contrary to the gospel now as in the second and third centuries. In history, they had to be worked through to be found out.

Modalism is the teaching that God is above time and the distinctions of Father, Son, and Spirit, but appears successively in these roles to create, redeem, and sanctify.[18] From its first recorded appearance in Rome, around A.D. 190, it was the standard theory of the congregations, as it still is. It was, indeed, a direct attempt to systematize congregational piety on the assumption of the timeless God. It keeps Father, Son, and Spirit in the same row and so stays close to liturgical use of the triune name and to the linear past, present, and future of baptismal and eucharistic life. But it was nevertheless as much a compromise with Hellenic deity as subordinationism. Indeed, it was and is the more complete submission, since the whole biblical talk of God is deprived of reference to God. None of the three is God. This is not noticed

119

2 / THE TRIUNE GOD

in immediate liturgical and proclamatory experience, but it is immediately noticed upon reflection. At the levels of learned or dogmatic theology, therefore, modalism has always been rejected promptly on its appearance.[19] We hear of only two actual modalist theologians in the ancient church, Paul of Samosata and Sabellius. Of the details of their thought we know next to nothing; only their names survived, as the ancient church's labels for modalism.

Subordinationism appears able to identify at least the biblical "Father" with God. Moreover, it had the missionary advantage that it answered directly to late Hellenism's religious need. Since it puts the Father on top, and ranks the Son below the Father—in vertical order, so to speak—it makes the Son just such a middle being between God's eternity and our time as late antiquity longed for.

Whenever Christ is grasped as a halfway entity between the supposedly timeless God and the temporal world, the subordinationist scheme is established. This can be, was, and is done strictly mythologically, with a demi-God descending and ascending.[20] But it is the sophisticated subordinationism inaugurated around A.D. 150 by the so-called apologists, the famous Logos christology, which we must describe, since it created the theological system within and against which developed trinitarianism was to be worked out. Christ, said the apologists, is—almost—God in that "the Logos" is incarnate in him.

However Justin, Theophilus, and the rest derived or invented their Logos concept, what they meant by it is plain. In the Greek philosophical tradition,[21] "logos" is at once discourse and the meaningful order which discourse discloses. If then the universe has such order, this is a divine Logos which is both deity's self-revelatory discourse and the reasonable order of the cosmos. Just so the apologists spoke of "the Logos." Moreover, as the divine reason *in* our world, the Logos could become the mediator of deity *to* our world, a "second God," and with the intensifying religious anxiety of late antiquity that is just what happened.[22] With or without dependence on this extra-Christian development, the apologists paralleled it and made "the Logos" the name of a typical personalized mediator-entity of second-century religiosity, "the next power after the Father of all, a Son. . . ."[23] Right or wrong, they thought that in all this they were but continuing John's testimony to the Logos who "was in the beginning with God," "illumined every man," and came in flesh to make God known (John 1:1–14).

In that the apologists shared the interpretation of God as the one who grounds all being by negating time, they shared also late antiquity's great problem, this God's distance. If we are to be saved, God must somehow dwell in our world, all agreed. And in the Old Testament, Christians possessed a narrative of God's activity here. But God has been defined just by his elevation above temporal action. It cannot have been God himself who walked

THE NICENE-CONSTANTINOPOLITAN DOGMA

in Adam's garden or shut the door of Noah's ark or talked to Abraham and Moses, for—as Justin asked—how should he "speak to anyone or be seen by anyone or appear in a particular part of the earth. . . . ? Neither Abraham nor Isaac nor Jacob nor any other human saw the Father, the unutterable Lord . . . , but rather they saw that other, who by his will is his Son and the messenger ("angel") to serve his purpose." An "other God," one step down the hierarchy of being, is needed to bridge the chasm between God and time.[24]

This "other God" is the Logos, the self-manifesting God, "the angel of the Lord" of the Hebrew Scriptures. Subordination is explicit. The Logos is "called" God, but over against "the creator of all things, above whom there is no other God," this predication is not literal. The Logos has "come into being," unlike the Father; he is "from" the unnameable and unoriginated Father, and just so is worshiped "after him."[25]

Since God is rational, the Logos is eternally in himself, as his own rationality. Then when God moves to create, that is, to be related to a reality other than himself, his Logos becomes external to him, as the rationality of artisans is manifest in their creations, and so also as God's relation to creation, that is, as revelation. Thus the Logos is the "first originated being" or even simply "first creature,"[26] over against the Father, who has no beginning. No distinction is yet made between different ways of deriving from God, so the difference between the Logos and the world is stated by adjectives like "first." It is this divine bridge to time that is then present in Jesus,[27] thus anchoring the bridge more securely at our end. For the second God's derivation from the Father, "Son" suggests "born" and "Logos" suggests "uttered"; both appear and combine in the neutral "gone forth."[28] He is numerically distinct from the Father, yet not set off from him.[29]

Not much has been said of the Spirit, which leads us to a vital point. The Logos theology is *not* the origin of developed trinitarianism. In itself, it is not in fact trinitarian at all.[30] The primal trinitarian naming and liturgical pattern make a temporal structure horizontal to time and inherently triple as time is. The God/Mediator/World scheme is timelessly vertical to time and of itself would posit either a deity of God and God's one mediator, or of God and infinitely *many* mediators. The space between God and the temporal world may be thought of either as one space or as indefinitely divisible, but there is no reason to think of two subspaces. In fact, the status of the Spirit was ambiguous in the whole apologetic theology. Since God "*is* Spirit" according to John (4:24), Spirit can be the name of the divine in Christ.[31] But how then is "the" Spirit a third? In the trinitarian pattern itself, on the other hand, there is no problem. On the contrary, we have seen that it is precisely in the self-posit of Spirit that triune Godhead is established. It was the Spirit's lack of place within the world view to which subordinationism was an adaptation that prevented the assimilation of all three items of the baptismal faith

121

2 / THE TRIUNE GOD

into the subordinationist scheme and preserved the three-article formulas of baptism as the chief counterinstance against it.

Insofar as the apologists were nevertheless trinitarian, sometimes they tried to stack all three vertically to time, with little conceptual success, and sometimes they assigned the Spirit his biblical role outside their mediator scheme altogether.³² What kept them trinitarian in intention was the presence of factors outside their system: the continuing trinitarian life of the church; the developing three-article creedal structure, based on baptismal confession as just noted;³³ perhaps the continuing availability and influence of a picture by which to imagine God in accord with this creed, the "Jewish-Christian" picture of the Father and the two great angelic advocates; and churchly critique of the religious and metaphysical basis of subordinationism.³⁴

In the interplay of all these factors, apologetic theology reached its historical fulfillment in two great figures of the early third century. In the West, Tertullian taught a more creedal and terminological trinitarianism; in the East, Origen taught a more speculative trinitarianism. Each set the style of his region for centuries to come.

For Tertullian, Logos theology was not so much the solution of his own religious problems as part of the now available intellectual repertoire for use on quite a different problem: the Trinity itself, the proper explication of the Christian interpretation of God.³⁵ For him, the trinitarian rule of faith was already a given (*Against Praxeas*, ii,1–2). Tertullian was moved to trinitarian analysis by a propagandizing explanation of the rule, the modalism urged in Rome by one Praxeas, around A.D. 190. He rightly thought this explanation explained the creed away, and set out to refute it and offer a better. As it turned out, he set the terminology of all subsequent Western analysis: There are in God "three persons" (*personae*) who are "of one substance" (*unius substantiae*).

Tertullian's chief trinitarian concern was to show how God's "monarchy" and "economy" could be simultaneously preserved (ibid., vii,7). "Monarchy" was his opponents' slogan for the abstract oneness of God as such, which Tertullian made mean instead the uniqueness and self-consistency of God's rule, of his divine work.³⁶ Tertullian himself adapted "economy" to be a term of trinitarian analysis from Irenaeus, for whom it meant the historical unfolding of God's saving work; Tertullian uses it for God's own inner self-disposition to this saving history.³⁷ It is "the economy . . . which disposes the unity into trinity" (ibid., ii,4). Plainly, it is theological interpretation of the three-step creed that is Tertullian's task. *Both* the one and three are those of God's reality in saving history.

For the three, Tertullian used *personae*, establishing the word for all subsequent Western theology. *Persona*³⁸ had been first the actor's mask, through which the actor spoke, then the role the actor thus played, and by Tertullian's

THE NICENE-CONSTANTINOPOLITAN DOGMA

time was the everyday term for the human individual, established in individuality by social role, by speaking and responding. The immediate background of the word's trinitarian use was an established exegetical use. The Logos was considered by ancient theology as the agent of all revelation; therefore when Scripture attributes speech to the Father or the Spirit, this was said to be the Son speaking "in the person" (*ex persona*) of the Father or the Spirit. Exegetically, Tertullian was thus accustomed to the three, in their distinction from one another, being called "persons." The step to use in trinitarian analysis was apparently taken before Tertullian; it was in any case a short one.

Tertullian's assertion of three *personae* in God is thus the assertion against modalism that the role distinctions, the relations of address and response, found in Scripture between the Father and Jesus and the Spirit, establish reality in God, just as such relations do among human individuals.[39] Tertullian's cases of the distinction of "persons" all come down to the distinction of Father, Jesus, and Spirit in scriptural narrative (ibid., xxiff.). They are three in that they speak to and about one another (ibid., xi,9-10) in such scriptural incidents as Jesus' baptism. They are three because they have three mutually recognized proper names (ibid., iv,4). Also the inner-trinitarian eternal roles are defined by the roles in saving history; when God said, "Let us make man," "he spoke, in the unity of the trinity, with the Son, who was to put on man, and with the Spirit, who was to sanctify man, as if with ministers and councillors" (ibid., xii,3).

In his use of *substantia* for the unity of God, Tertullian followed his own philosophical tradition. This was not adhered to by later Western theology, so that "one substance" came simply to mean somehow one thing[40] and then to be interpreted within whatever philosophy was in vogue.

The resultant terminology was useful both for good and for bad. It gave the Western church language with which to get on with its daily proclamatory and disciplinary business, 175 years before this urgent necessity was filled in the East. But in its conceptual blandness, it also served to cover the very real religious and intellectual problems posed by the Christian identification of God. These were to be faced in the East.

That event was prepared by the first truly great thinker and scholar of Christian history, Origen of Alexandria, who carried subordinationist trinitarianism to its unstable perfection and created a way of thinking that dominated the Eastern church for the remainder of its theologically creative history. Though he was a far greater theologian than Tertullian, his role in our special story is so much that of the fulfiller of already-described tendencies that our treatment can be brief. One great aspect of his work may be simply noted here, for future reference: He was the creator of hermeneutically self-conscious biblical exegesis.

2 / THE TRIUNE GOD

Origen's God the Father is Hellenic deity in purest form: sheer mind, utterly removed from the temporal material world, utterly undifferentiated, and just so unknowable (*On First Principles*, i,1,5–6). The unknowability of God is identical with the difference between the temporal and the timeless (*Fragments to John*, i,xiii). God is knowable only as ground of his works, by the intuition of *nous* (*On First Principles*, i,1,6; iv,3,15).

Accordingly, Origen's entire soteriological concern is for mediation of the knowledge of God. He succeeded in creating a consistently subordinationist system to mediate this deity that had place for the Spirit and so did not obviously clash with the trinitarian creeds and liturgies. He created a grandiose version of late antiquity's vision of a hierarchy of being—the Christian pair to Plotinus's—descending in successive mediations from God, like the rays from the sun, down finally to the material universe.[41] The "birth" of mediating deity from God is an eternal event: God just is self-mediating (ibid., i,2; i,9; Iv,5). Also, the Spirit is eternal, given from God without beginning (ibid., i,3,4).

The problem of the place of the Spirit is ingeniously solved. The Spirit's work is sanctification; its sphere is the church; Origen includes the church's special reality in the mediation system. He conceives the work of Father, Son, and Spirit as three concentric circles, along the line of mediation between God and us, as an inverted, stepped cone. The Father gives being to all beings; the Son gives the knowledge of God to all beings capable of knowledge; the Spirit gives the holiness in which such knowledge is fulfilled to those among rational beings who are to be saved. Both the downward mediation of being and the upward mediation of fulfillment are thus essentially triple—if dubiously triune (ibid., i,3,5; i,3,8).

THE ARIAN CRISIS

The Origenist system was unstable, since the initial mere compromise between biblical and Hellenic interpretation of God still lay at its heart. In historical particular, it could not stand the question "Well, which *is* the Logos, Creator or creature?" The secret of subordinationist trinitarianism, perfected by Origen, was the posit of an unbroken continuity of being from the great God, through the Logos, the Spirit, and other "spiritual" beings, down to temporal beings. Across this beautiful spectrum the biblical radical distinction of Creator from creature could only make an ugly slash somewhere. But the intense and open study of Scripture which was the other great achievement of Origenism itself had sooner or later to pose the Creator-creature difference.

The intellectual and religious instability of Origenism was also a confessional instability of the Eastern church. At the turn of the third and fourth

THE NICENE-CONSTANTINOPOLITAN DOGMA

centuries, the great bishoprics and professorships of the East were almost all occupied by Origenists of one shade or another, from a left wing of those most drawn by Origen's intellectual respectability, to a right wing most drawn by his christological passion.[42]

Subordinationism's inevitable breakdown was triggered by the students and other disciples of Lucian of Antioch.[43] Lucian's theology is not well known. In the last decades of the third century and the first of the fourth, he was a great teacher in the style of Origen, a martyr, and the founder of Antioch's scholarly fame. His students learned a methodical exegesis of Scripture more devoted to the literal sense than Origen's, and therefore more likely to intrude the dangerous Creator-creature distinction. They also learned a more coolly analytical—Aristotelian—Platonism, amenable to such commonsensicalities as that each thing is itself and not another. This made Origen's spectrum of being look more like a set of steps than a glissando, and so emphasized its subordinationism. If the Logos is a distinct entity only a very, very little bit different from God, then he is, said the Lucianists, in fact different.[44]

The struggle began among the Egyptian clergy. The priest of an Alexandrian parish, a second-rate Lucianist named Arius, attacked the Origenist right wing's tendency to attribute full divine eternity to the Son.[45] Since the attack touched the bishop, Alexander, a synod of Egyptian bishops deposed Arius and a few sympathizers from office.

Thereupon Arius appealed to the old-school tie. Leaving Egypt, he and his fellow rebels sought and found place with the most notable of the Lucianists, Bishop Eusebius of Nicomedia. Eusebius launched a correspondence campaign among the Eastern bishops to have Arius restored to office. Alexander responded, and a general uproar ensued which can only be explained by the theological development being ripe for it.

What Arius and his friends were concerned about is explicit and clear in the first document of the conflict, Arius's appeal to Eusebius of Nicomedia. As Arius understands it, those who attribute to the Son coeternity with the Father must either regard the Son as some sort of emergent from within the Father's being or as a parallel unoriginated being. Both are termed "blasphemies."[46]

For Arius, and for the whole Lucianist group to which he appealed, and indeed for all the more left-wing disciples of Origen, there were only two identifying characteristics of God. First, God is "unoriginated." As we have seen, the theology deriving from the apologists did not differentiate between possible different ways of having an origin; left-wing Origenism made the catchall negative definitive of deity.[47] Second, God is altogether devoid of internal differentiation. For Arius, therefore, to say that the Son is "co-unoriginated," or anything of the sort, posits two "co-gods,"[48] while to say that the Son is an emergent from within the Father introduces differentia-

2 / THE TRIUNE GOD

tion into even the Father, that is, denies that there is any real God at all.⁴⁹ Arius therefore teaches: "The Son is not unoriginated, nor is he in any way a part of the Unoriginated."⁵⁰

It is plain that what moves Arius is the late-Hellenic need to escape time, become utterly dominant. If we are to be saved, there must be some reality entirely uninvolved with time, which has no origin of any sort and whose continuity is undifferentiated and uninterrupted. Just so, it is because Christ is involved with time that he will not do as really God: "How can the Logos be God, who sleeps like a man and weeps and suffers?"⁵¹ It had long been decided, against the modalists, that the longed-for absolute timeless and impassible One cannot be a divine essence other than Father, Son, and Spirit. Then it must be the Father. Very early, the Arians put their whole case in two sentences: "As the monad, and the Source of all things, God is before all things. Therefore he is also before the Son."⁵² All other considerations must be sacrificed to this logic and the religious need behind it.

It was around the converse that the controversy was to be conducted. Arius had to say, "There was once when he [the Logos] was not,"⁵³ that is, the Logos is a creature. In the direction of the transcendence from which we come and into which we are to return, the way, according to the Arians, leads beyond what happens in time with Christ, to a God who is not yet the Father of the Son, who is a sheer unoriginate, above all differentiation and relation. As we climb back up the ladder of being, the Logos, so long as he is above us, is God *for us* but is not God in himself.⁵⁴ The great thinker of later Arianism (350–380), Eunomius, was finally to draw the religious conclusion: the last goal is precisely to transcend the revealer and see God as does he.⁵⁵

In the long term of the conflict, the opposition to Arius was to be carried above all by Athanasius, Alexander's adviser and then his successor as bishop. He attacked precisely the Arian vision of God as not that of the gospel. If God is not intrinsically Father of the Son, he is not intrinsically Father, for "father" is relational (*Discourse II against the Arians*). But being fatherly defines the God Christians worship. Therefore he can no more be God without the Son than light can be without shining (*Epistle on the Decree of Nicaea*, 2;12). It is Origen's doctrine of the eternal generation of the Son—that the origin of the Son from the Father is not *in* time at all—that is here adapted. The very being of the Father would be unfinished without the Son; God's goodness is that God is Father; God's truth is the Son (*Discourse I against the Arians*, 14,28;20); and the Son cannot be a creature willed by the Father because the Son *is* the Father's will (*Discourse III*, 68). It is not too much to say that, for Athanasius, *what* the Son reveals about God is exactly that God is his Father.

Since relation to us, as the Father of our Lord, is internal to God's being, there is no need for bridge-beings between God and us. The great religious need of late antiquity is not filled by the gospel; it is abolished. Then Athanasius is free to label the adjectival and graded use of "God" as what it is: "polytheism, for since they [the Arians] call [the Son] God, because it is so written, but do not call him proper to the Father's being, they introduce a plurality of . . . forms of divine being" (*Discourse* III, 15). Assimilating created beings to God is the very principle of the non-Christian religion: "This is the characteristic of the Greeks, to introduce a creature into the Trinity" (*Discourse* III, 18). The middle realm is gone altogether: "If Son, not creature; if creature, not Son" (*Nicaea,* 13).

NICAEA AND CONSTANTINOPLE

Therefore, driven by equal and opposite ultimate concerns, the churchmen of the eastern Empire fell on one another when Arius said, "when he was not." Just at this point the first Christian emperor assumed power. Constantine came as an agent of universal peace, dreaming of the *pax Romana* restored by the new religion of love, and he found the very bishops in a brawl, the most learned in the front. After initial efforts to restore peace failed, he commanded a general council of the bishops of the eastern Empire, to meet at Nicaea in 325 in succession of an earlier Egyptian council.

Those who attended found themselves at the first great meeting of ecumenical Christianity, in a world suddenly turned from persecution to supplication. Understandably, they were in no more mood for disturbers of unity than was Constantine. They confirmed the condemnation of Arius and deposed his more intransigent supporters. And they produced a rule for talk about Christ which excluded Arius and his immediate followers but which all others, even Eusebius of Nicomedia, contrived to sign. Into a typical three-article liturgical creed, they inserted four theological explications: Christ, they said, is "out of the being of the Father," "true God of true God," "begotten not created," and *homoousios* (of one being) with the father."[56] This is the dogma of Nicaea, the first deliberately created dogma and a main object of this whole *locus*.

"Out of the being of the Father" affirms just that origin of Christ within God's own self that Arius most feared. The phrase says that the Son is not an entity originated outside God by God's externally directed choice, that he is not in any sense a creature. And it says there *is* differentiation within God, that the relation to the Son is an internal relation in the Father, a relation necessary to his being God the Father. *To be God is to be related.* With that the fathers contradicted the main principle of Hellenic theology.

"Born, not created . . ." makes exactly that distinction between two ways of being originated from God, the lack of which enabled the subordinationist glissando from God himself, who is unoriginated, to us, who are originated,

127

2 / THE TRIUNE GOD

through the Son, who is a bit of each. On the contrary, we are "created," the Son is "begotten," and these are just two different things. Nobody claimed to know exactly what "begotten" meant in this connection. Yet a tremendous assertion is made: There is a way of being begun, of receiving one's being, which is proper to godhead itself. To be God is not only to give being, it is also to receive being. And there went the rest of Plato.

"True God of true God" prohibits all use of the analogy principle in calling Jesus "God." He is plain God, not qualified God. What the clause prohibits is the whole Greek use of "God" as an adjective applicable in various degrees.

Finally there is the famous and fateful "*homoousios* with the Father." The history of the word *homoousios* was checkered.[57] Its first theological use was by gnostics, for the mythic emergences of their sundry divine entities. Origen used the word, but rarely, to say that the Son had all the same essential characters as the Father, but on another ontological level.[58]

We do not know how or why this came to be Nicaea's big word. Perhaps it was introduced precisely by Arius's negative use simply to contradict him. Arius had said, "The Son . . . is not *homoousios* with [the Father]" to reject Western-type trinitarianism or any notion of Father and Son being two by division of one substance.[59]

The bishops seemingly did not have any one meaning in mind when they used *homoousios*. Constantine's Western advisers at Nicaea, thinking in Latin, no doubt took *homoousios* as a simple translation of Tertullian's "of one substance" and had no further problem. For those who thought in Greek it was not so simple. Did *homoousios* mean the same as it did in Origen? The most ardent anti-Arians, such as Athanasius, suspected it might, and might therefore be a poor guard against subordinationism; they were for a time wary in their use of it. Did it mean that Father and Son both had all the characteristics of godhead, whatever these are? Then are there not two (or three) Gods? Or did it, in more Aristotelian fashion, mean that Father and Son were numerically one actual entity? But how then could modalism be avoided? The Lucianists feared modalism could not be avoided, and when one of the chief Nicene anti-Arians, Marcellus of Ancyra, turned out in fact to be a modalist, they had a horror example ever after.[60]

Yet so much was clear: *homoousios* meant that Arius was a heretic. Affirmatively, there is only one divine being, and both Father and Son have it. Whatever it means to be God, pure and simple, Christ is. And that suffices to make the needed and revolutionary point: Christ is not at all the sort of halfway entity that normal religion needs and provides to mediate time and eternity. He is not a divine teacher or example, a personal savior, a mediator of grace, or any of the beloved semigods of standard religion. He is constitutive

THE NICENE-CONSTANTINOPOLITAN DOGMA

of God, not merely revelatory—or if one develops a whole theology of revelation, then being revealed in Christ is itself constitutive of God.

Abrupt and almost instinctive though they were, the Nicene phrases make the decisive differentiation between Christian and other interpretations of God, then and now. Proclamation of a God or salvation that do not fit cannot be the gospel, however otherwise religious or beneficial. The Arian incident was the decisive crisis to date, and the Nicene Creed the decisive victory to date, in Christianity's self-identification. The gospel—Nicaea finally said unequivocally—provides no mediator of our ascent to a timeless and therefore distant God. It rather proclaims a God whose own deity is not separable from a figure of our temporal history and who therefore is not and never has been timeless and distant from us.

The bishops were not clearly aware of what they had said with this creed, except that Arius had gone too far. When they went home, they slowly became aware. Then the real fight began, to last for sixty years. In some ways, it still continues.

Subordinationist trinitarianism had not yet undone itself from within; it had only been renounced in a crude version. A variety of moves could seemingly yet be tried to combine the glissando of being with the difference between Creator and creature. In the next forty years each such move would produce a new creedal proposal and a new alignment against Athanasius. Moreover, the Nicene dogma was incomplete; what about the Spirit? So soon as the matter was noted—in Egypt again—a whole new spectrum of disputes displayed itself.

The Lucianists began the new struggle, refusing to take Nicaea as the last word and working for possession of the bishoprics and for ecumenical acceptance of a more moderate creed.[61] The lineup shifted with each new theological attempt. At one end of the spectrum were two groups: Athanasius with his followers, and the Western bishops, who stuck to Tertullian's formula, never quite understood the Easterners' problems, and supported Athanasius when they dared. It took some daring, for after Nicaea the anti-Nicene reaction usually contrived to look like the peace-loving middle of the road, and so to secure imperial support. At the other end were actual Arians, some willing to be called that and others not, sporadically recruited from the Origenist middle. In between were the majority of Eastern churchmen, whose common purpose was to preserve the traditional Origenist theology of the East. But, once the challenge of the *homoousios* was there, their ground proved slippery, and the left wing constantly slid into practically Arian positions.

After initial hesitation Athanasius made *homoousios* his slogan, to mean that the Father and the Son—and the Spirit—together make the one reality of God: It is the Trinity as such that is God.[62] Whatever sundry bishops at

2 / THE TRIUNE GOD

Nicaea meant by *homoousios*, it is with this point that the word enters dogmatic history. The various anti-Nicene coalitions took the Father *by himself* as really God, and the Son, next down on the spectrum of being, as very closely—perhaps even altogether—assimilated to God. Confused as the terminologies were, the issue was and is clear and vital to faith. The issue is not so much about the status of Jesus as about who and what is God himself.

Anti-*homoousian* slogans waxed and waned.[63] None quite worked; then a new one would be tried. The final result of the anti-Nicene movement was the discrediting of subordinationism, by the destruction of the confessional unity of the Eastern church. For example, in Antioch just before 360 there was a complete denominational system: a congregation of out-and-out Arians, a congregation of sophisticated Arians, the official church with a Eusebian bishop, a pro-Nicene group that had submitted to the bishop but held their own meetings, and a separate congregation of intransigent Nicaeans.[64]

As the weary creed-making went on, many not originally of Athanasius's party began to see that the vision of God evoked by *homoousios*—as used by Athanasius—was theirs too.[65] What was needed for the East was an explanation of how this could work, of how one might indeed say that Father and Son are one God, and that this is not a matter of levels, without thereby falling into modalism, that is, how one could hold to Origen's decisive insight that Father, Son, and Spirit are indeed three in God, otherwise than by ranking them ontologically.

Such a theory was finally provided in the 370s by a brilliant new generation of teachers and bishops, again schooled by Origen but using his dialectic to overcome his subordinationism. The most powerful thinkers among these were the Cappadocians: Basil, primate of Cappadocia, his brother, Gregory of Nyssa, and his protégé, Gregory of Nazianzus. Analysis of their thought belongs to the next chapter. Here a rough characterization will suffice. The Cappadocians took Origen's three hypostases and his real distinctions among them, in Origen a ladder reaching vertically from God to time, and tipped it on its side, to make a structure horizontal to time and reaching from point to point in God. Just such a stroke of dialectic was what was needed to enable general acceptance of Nicaea's dogma.

Emperor Theodosius I, determined like his predecessors to reunite the church, summoned yet another council at Constantinople in 381.[66] It was a council of Basil's followers, and it succeeded where all before had failed. It proclaimed the Nicene confession as the official confession of the East by adopting another regional baptismal creed that in Nicene use had been enriched with the Nicene phrases. And it added an affirmation of the full deity of the Spirit, with insertions into the third article: ". . . the Lord, the Giver of life, proceeding from the Father, worshiped and glorified with the Father and

THE NICENE-CONSTANTINOPOLITAN DOGMA

the Son. . . ." In this article, the word *homoousios* was itself avoided, so as not to start the struggle about terminology again.

The article on the Spirit completed the trinitarian dogma. Since the Spirit was, on the subordinationist hierarchy, one more step from God than the Logos, affirmation of the full godhead of the Spirit marked final rejection of the whole subordinationist principle. On this affirmation the middle of the road sorted itself into those who entered the reconstituted ecumenical church and those who continued in waning opposition or sectarianism.[67]

One step remains in the story of the Nicene dogma. In 451, long after these battles were over, the Council of Chalcedon formally proclaimed both the creed of Nicaea and the creed of Constantinople as dogma for the whole church, East and West.[68] Since then, the Constantinopolitan creed—incorrectly called the Nicene Creed—has come to dominate liturgical use, since it contains the phrases for the Spirit. Both creeds together are the dogmatic documents. It has since been an ecumenical rule of all talk in the Christian church: In all three temporal directions of our relation to Jesus Christ, we have unsurpassably to do with God, and just by this circumstance our God differs from the culture-God of Western civilization, even in his christianized versions.

NOTES

1. The following depends on the standard histories: Jane Ellen Harrison, *Prolegomena to the Study of Greek Religion* (Cambridge: At the University Press, 1903), chaps. 1, 6, 7; Martin P. Nilsson, *A History of Greek Religion*, trans. F. J. Fielden (Oxford: At the Clarendon Press, 1925); Martin P. Nilsson, "Die Griechen," in *Lehrbuch der Dogmengeschichte*, ed. Chantepie de la Saussaye (Tübingen: J. C. B. Mohr [Paul Siebeck], 1925), 2:281–417; Ulrich von Wilamowitz-Moellendorf, *Der Glaube der Hellenen* (Berlin: Weidmann, 1932). The interpretation is heavily influenced by Ulrich Mann, *Vorspiel des Heils* (Stuttgart: Klett, 1962).

2. Mann, *Vorspiel*, pp. 62ff.

3. Sophocles, *Oedipus the King*, ii,1528–30.

4. Aristotle, *Metaphysics*, 1051b,29–30.

5. Werner Jaeger, *The Theology of the Early Greek Philosophers* (Oxford: At the Clarendon Press, 1947).

6. Aristotle, *Physics*, 4,203b7.

7. See Eberhard Jüngel, *Zum Ursprung der Analogie bei Parmenides und Heraklit* (Berlin: Walter de Gruyter, 1964).

8. K. von Fritz, "The Function of *Nous*," *CP* 38 (1943): 79–93; 40 (1945): 223–42; 41 (1946): 12–34; Werner Marx, *The Meaning of Aristotle's "Ontology"* (The Hague: Nijhoff, 1954), pp. 8–29.

9. See Hans Jonas, *Gnosis und spätantiker Geist* (Göttingen: Vandenhoeck &

2 / THE TRIUNE GOD

Ruprecht, 1954); Hans Jonas, "Gnosis und Moderner Nihilismus," *KuD*, 1960, pp. 155-71. On the *Corpus Hermeticum*, which preserves the best witness of the crisis, see André M. J. Festugière, *La Révélation de l'Hermes Trismégiste* (Paris: Lecattre, 1944-54), vol. 4.

10. E.g., Hal Koch, *Pronoia und Paideusis* (Berlin: Walter de Gruyter, 1932), pp. 180-314; Nilsson, "Die Griechen," pp. 394-417.

11. Plato, *Symposium*, 101A-212B.

12. See Wolfhart Pannenberg, "Die Aufnahme des philosophischen Gottesbegriffs als dogmatisches Problem der frühchristlichen Theologie," *ZKG* 70 (1959): 1-45; Yehoshua Amir, "Die Begegnung des biblischen und des philosophischen Monotheismus," *EvTh* 38 (1978): 2-19.

13. E.g., Theophilus of Antioch, *Apology to Autolycus*, i,2,5; Melito of Sardis, *Address to Antonius Caesar*, 6-8.

14. Jaroslav Pelikan, *The Christian Tradition*, vol. 1, *The Emergence of the Catholic Tradition (100-600)* (Chicago: University of Chicago Press, 1971), pp. 52ff.; René Braun, *Deus Christianorum: Recherches sur le vocabulaire doctrinal de Tertullian* (Paris: Presses Universitaires, 1962), pp. 62ff.

15. Justin Martyr, *Apology*, i,12, 13, 25; Melito of Sardis, *Address to Antonius Caesar*, 2; Theophilus of Antioch, *Apology to Autolycus*, i,3; Athenagoras, *Supplication for the Christians*, 10. On the standard middle-Platonist theology of Justin, see L. W. Barnard, *Justin Martyr: His Life and Thought* (Cambridge: At the University Press, 1967), pp. 79ff.

16. Barnard, *Justin Martyr*, pp. 77ff.; Braun, *Deus Christianorum*, p. 74.

17. On the failure of creative synthesis, see Pannenberg, "Die Aufnahme," pp. 312-46.

18. Pelikan, *Emergence*, pp. 136-82; RGG³, s.v. "Trinität," by F. H. Kettler.

19. The first great antimodalist work was Tertullian's *Against Praxeas*, shortly after A.D. 207. At the theoretical level, another had never been needed.

20. Aloys Grillmeier, *Christ in Christian Tradition*, trans. J. S. Bowden (New York: Sheed & Ward, 1965), 1:190-206.

21. See *TDNT*, s.v. "Word," by H. Kleinknecht.

22. E.g., *Theologia Graeca*, 16; "Hermes is the Logos, whom the gods sent to us from heaven, to make man rational (*logikos*) . . . but even more to save us."

23. Justin Martyr, *Apology*, i,32.

24. Ibid., 13, 62-63; see also Justin Martyr, *Dialogue with Trypho*, 10, 126-28; Theophilus of Antioch, *Apology*, ii,22.

25. Justin Martyr, *Dialogue*, 55-62; *Apology*, ii,6,13.

26. E.g., Athenagoras, *Supplication*, 10; Theophilus, *Apology*, ii,22; Justin Martyr, *Dialogue*, 61.

27. E.g., Justin Martyr, *Apology*, i,5.

28. See Braun, *Deus Christianorum*, pp. 287-91.

29. Justin Martyr, *Dialogue*, 62,128.

30. Georg Kretschmar, *Studien zur frühchristlichen Trinitätstheologie* (Tübingen: J. C. B. Mohr [Paul Siebeck], 1956), pp. 1-15.

31. E.g., Tatian, *Address to the Greeks*, 7. See Kretschmar, *Studien*, pp. 40-61; Pelikan, *Emergence*, pp. 185-86.

32. On the first, see Justin Martyr, *Apology*, i,13; on the second, see J. Armitage Robinson, ed., "Introduction," in Irenaeus, *The Demonstration of the Apostolic Preaching* (London: SPCK, 1920).

33. Novatian, *On the Trinity*, is entirely concerned for the Logos' mediatorial function but appends a piece on the Spirit (xxx-xxxi) because, he says, "the authority of the baptismal confession reminds us . . . that we also believe in the Spirit" (xxix).

34. E.g., Irenaeus, *Against All Heresies*, ii,i-ii; ii,vi; ii,xvii,3; ii,vii,6; ii,xiii,4-6.

35. On this and the following, see Braun, *Deus Christianorum*.

36. Ibid., pp. 71-72.

37. Ibid., pp. 158-67.

38. On the following, see ibid., pp. 207-32.

39. Ibid., pp. 228-32. On the following, see ibid., pp. 235-36.

40. Ibid., pp. 173-94.

41. On Origen, see Robert W. Jenson, *The Knowledge of Things Hoped For* (New York: Oxford University Press, 1969), pp. 26ff.; there further bibliography.

42. The most typical representation of the left was Eusebius of Caesarea, *Demonstration of the Gospel*, iv, v. For the right, we may name the young Athanasius, *Discourse on the Incarnation of the Word*.

43. On Lucian and the Lucianists, see Gustave Bardy, *Recherches sur Saint Lucien d'Antioch et son École* (Paris: Gabriel Beauchesne, 1936); here the remaining Lucianist texts are collected. On the following theological history, see Louis Duchesne, *Early History of the Christian Church* (New York and London: Longmans, Green & Co., 1912), 2:98ff.; Grillmeier, *Christ*, 218ff.; J. N. D. Kelly, *Early Christian Doctrines* (New York: Harper & Row, 1960), pp. 223-71.

44. See, e.g., Kelly, *Doctrines*, p. 231.

45. Arius, *To Eusebius*, in Bardy, *Recherches*, p. 227: "We do not agree with those who daily cry, 'always God, always Son.'"

46. Ibid., p. 227.

47. Asterius the Sophist, chief publicist for the Arians in the ensuing controversy, formulated the principle: "ageneton . . . to me poiethen . . ." (frag. vii, in Bardy, *Recherches*). The great leader of later Arianism, Aetius, made the whole doctrine of God a mere abstract dialectic on *agennetos/gennetos*; *Syntagmata*, in *PG* 42:533-45.

48. Arius, *Thalia*, in Bardy, *Recherches*, p. 286: ". . . he monas en, he duas de ouk en prin hyparxe."

49. Arius, *To Alexander*, in Bardy, *Recherches*, pp. 236-37.

50. Arius, *To Eusebius*, in ibid., p. 228.

51. Arius, cited by Athanasius, *Discourse against the Arians* (in *PG* 26:321-407), iii,28.

52. Arius, *To Alexander*, in Bardy, *Recherches*, p. 237.

53. Arius, *Thalia*, in ibid., p. 261.

54. Ibid., 267: "Nor is the Logos true God. He is, to be sure, called 'God' . . . , but by participation granted by grace."

55. Eunomius, cited by Gregory of Nyssa, *Against Eunomius*, in his *Opera*, vols. 1-2, ed. W. Jaeger (Leiden: E. J. Brill, 1960), iii/viii,14.

56. The text of the relevant part of the second article and of the appended anathemas: "And in one Lord, Jesus Christ, the Son of God; born of the Father (*ek tou patros*)

2 / THE TRIUNE GOD

uniquely, i.e., out of the being of the Father (*ek tes ousias tou patros*); God of God; light of light; true God of true God; born, not made; of one being with the Father (*homoousion to patri*). . . ." "The catholic church condemns those who say, 'There was when he was not' and 'Before he was born he was not' and 'He originated from what is not,' calling him either 'of another hypostasis' or 'of another being' (*ousia*), so that he would be a changeable and mutable 'Son of God.' "

57. Heinz Kraft, "OMOOUSIOS," *ZKG* 66 (1954-55): 1-24; Adolf M. Ritter, *Das Konzil von Konstantinopel und sein Symbol* (Göttingen: Vandenhoeck & Ruprecht, 1965), pp. 270-93.

58. Origen, fragment 540, as collected by M. J. Rouët de Journal, *EnchP*, 1965.

59. Arius, *Thalia*, in Bardy, *Recherches*, p. 256.

60. If Marcellus was not a modalist (as Grillmeier, *Christ*, pp. 275-96, labors to show), he fooled everyone at the time.

61. See Duchesne, *Early History*, pp. 125-200, 218ff. For the best brief account of the theology, see Michel Meslin, *Les Ariens d'Occident* (Paris: Servil, 1967), pp. 253-99.

62. Athanasius, *Discourse I against the Arians*, 18. Athanasius explains that *homoousios* is the logical product of "possessed of identical characteristics (*homoiousios*)" and "from the being (*ek tes physeos*)" (*Epistle on the Councils of Ariminum and Seleucia*, 41-42).

63. See Ritter, *Konzil*, pp. 64-85.

64. Duchesne, *Early History*, pp. 276-77.

65. Ritter, *Konzil*, pp. 68-85.

66. On this paragraph, see ibid., pp. 21-40, 132-204, 293-307.

67. Meslin, *Ariens*, pp. 325-435; Ritter, *Konzil*, pp. 68-85.

68. Ritter, *Konzil*, pp. 133-51, 172-75, 204-8.

4

The One and the Three

Developed trinitarian dialectics, such as the proposition that God is "three persons of one substance," are metaphysical analysis of the gospel's triune identification of God, and especially of its difference from the Hellenic interpretation of God. The need for such analysis has not passed; indeed, at present it is more urgent than since antiquity.

THE EASTERN TRINITARIAN TERMINOLOGY

Two centuries of passionate reflection brought the Eastern church back to the rule of faith with which it began. But now there is an agreed conceptuality, provided by the Cappadocians: "one being (*ousia*) of God in three hypostases (*hypostaseis*)." The conceptuality was derived from expressions of Origen[1] and at a second session of Theodosius' council, in 382, was taken into approved ecclesiastical use.[2] In elucidating it, we will both explicate the Cappadocian analysis and continue to some analysis of our own.

At a first level, "one being in three hypostases" was merely a sort of linguistic settlement, stipulating terminology for a perceived need that somehow we be able to refer both to one reality of God and to three realities of God. In most theological use, *ousia* and *hypostasis* had previously been handled as rough equivalents. The decree of Nicaea used both indiscriminately in the singular in asserting the oneness of the triune reality, as did Athanasius all his life.[3] The entire Origenist spectrum used both in the plural in asserting that there really are three somehow different realities in the Trinity.[4] The new terminological regulation, finding two words for "what is real" in trinitarian use, split the difference and took one for the one and the other for the three.

Thereby the East was provided with a trinitarian terminology extensionally equivalent to the West's "one substance (*substantia*) in three persons (*personae*)." But it is vital to understand that the two terminologies are not intentionally equivalent: If a proposition in the one is simply set into the other,

2 / THE TRIUNE GOD

its meaning is not necessarily preserved. Failure to observe this has been and is the cause of a great deal of confusion. "Substance" and "person" had never been interchangeable. Just so, their distinction evoked no new insight. Nor did they carry any history of trinitarian controversy.[5]

Ousia and *hypostasis* both came into theology from the philosophical tradition.[6] There they were used almost interchangeably, for *what is*—conformably to Hellenic apprehension, for what is by possession of some specific complex of permanent characteristics. Just so, they are also used for the "being" so possessed, that is, for both this complex of characteristics and for the stability through time their possession bestows.

Between *ousia* and *hypostasis* there were nevertheless slight nuances of difference. *Ousia* tended to be used for the reality that real things have and so to evoke, for example, the humanity Socrates has, but not so much the marks by which he as human differs from other beings, while *hypostasis* sounded more strongly the notes of distinguishability and identifiability. When trinitarian use divided the terms, the division was made along the line of these nuances. *Hypostasis* now meant simply that which can be identified, while *ousia* meant *what* such an identifiable *is*.[7] This necessarily dropped *hypostasis* to the level of individuals and located *ousia* at the level of the being any one kind of individuals are in common—except that *hypostasis* brought with it an aura of metaphysical dignity that previous terms for the individual lacked.

Just this is the starting position of the Cappadocian analysis: Father, Son, and Spirit, they say, are three individuals who share Godhead, as Peter, Paul, and Barnabas are three individuals who share humanity.[8] The one being of God is common to the three hypostases, which are distinguished by the individually identifying characteristics of "being unbegotten," "being begotten," and "proceeding."[9] Clearly this lays them open to this question: "As Peter, Paul, and Barnabas are three men, why are Father, Son, and Spirit not *three gods*?"[10] The Cappadocians' metaphysical creativity appears in their answer to this challenge.

THE THREE HYPOSTASES

The Cappadocians reworked the concepts *ousia* and *hypostasis*. We will consider *hypostasis* first. The plural individuals that share humanity differ from one another by characteristics adventitious to—indeed, in the usual Hellenic view, privative of—the humanity they have in common: by brown hair, moderate intelligence, Athenian ancestry, or whatever. Just so, they are plural humans. But, said the Cappadocians, Godhead can receive no such adventitious or privative characteristics. Therefore there is no way for a plurality of divine hypostases, if their plurality is somehow established, to make a

THE ONE AND THE THREE

plurality of Gods.¹¹ Their argument, it should be noted, holds only if the graded adjectival use of "God" has become utterly inconceivable, which is just what Christian theological self-consciousness had achieved.

And there is indeed a way, without characteristics adventitious to or privative of Godhead, for the three to be individually identified. Their individually identifying characteristics are the *relations* they have to each other, precisely with respect to their joint possession of deity. God is the Father as the source of the Son's and the Spirit's Godhead; God is the Son as the recipient of the Father's Godhead; and God is the Spirit as the spirit of the Son's possession of the Father's Godhead.¹² The different way in which each is the one God, for and from the others, is the only difference between them.¹³

We have arrived at a certain completion of the dialectic. We have also arrived at a point where some more than historical interpretation and reflection is needed. There are two matters to consider.

First, we must remind ourselves what all these word games are about. The "hypostases" are Jesus, and the transcendent will he called Father, and the Spirit of their future for us. Just as vital to remember, the hypostases' "relations" are Jesus' historical obedience to and dependence on his Father and the coming of their future into the believing community. "Begetting," "being begotten," "proceeding," and their variants are biblical terms for temporal structures of evangelical history, which theology then uses to evoke relations constitutive of God's life. What happens between Jesus and his Father and our future happens in God—that is the point.

It was the achievement of the Cappadocians to find a conceptualized way to say this, by arranging Origen's hypostases and their *homoousia* horizontally to time rather than vertically to time, making the hypostases' mutual relations structures of the one God's life, rather than steps from God down to us.¹⁴ Then the Trinity as such is the Creator, over against the creature, and the three in God and their relations become the evangelical history's reality on the Creator side of the great biblical divide. Across the Creator/creature distinction, no *mediator* is needed;¹⁵ "Creator"/"creature" names an absolute difference, but no distance at all, for to be the Creator is merely as such to be actively related to the creature. Each of the inner-trinitarian relations is then an affirmation that as God works creatively among us, so he is in himself.

It was time, we said, to remind ourselves of these things. The Nicene dogma and the Cappadocian analysis were victories in the confrontation between the gospel's and Hellenism's interpretations of God. But the confrontation is by no means concluded. One continuous post-Nicene threat has been the temptation to interpret the Trinity as a whole by the Hellenic negative theology, so that the Trinity in its turn disappears into the old distant timelessness, carrying its internal reflection of evangelical history right with it. Already in the Cappadocians there is a danger signal: their tendency to take refuge in

137

2 / THE TRIUNE GOD

mystery when asked what "begetting" and "proceeding" *mean*.¹⁶ Why should there be a problem? There is none about what these words mean as slogans for saving historical events. No more should there be about their trinitarian meanings—unless the understanding of the triune life itself is infiltrated with impassibility, immobility, and so on, with reference to which a word like "proceeding" cannot indeed mean much.

Once the temporal reference of trinitarian language is reaffirmed, we can turn again to the conceptual problem of the three hypostases. As a piece of trinitarian language, *hypostasis* is merely an item of linguistic debris knocked from Hellenic philosophy by collision with Yahweh. Present understanding would be advanced if we replaced it with a word now philosophically active. Readers will not be surprised that we propose "identity," for as is apparent from the history of the adaptation of *hypostasis* to trinitarian use, it is exactly the ontological function now marked by "identity" that the trinitarian *hypostasis*, in its separation from *ousia*, invoked. We explicate this function in two steps.

First, something's identity is the possibility of picking it out from the maelstrom of actuality so as to talk about it. The enumerability of the world, whereby we can say "this, and this, and then this," is one of the world's deepest metaphysical characters. This character, taken of any one such "this," is an identity.

We identify in various ways. We point and say "this." But often we cannot point. Then we have two linguistic resources: proper names and identifying descriptions, as discussed earlier.

Accordingly, that there are three identities in God means that there are three discrete sets of names and descriptions, each sufficient to specify uniquely, yet all identifying the same reality. Among them that which says "God is what happens with Jesus" has the epistemological priority of the present tense, so that in each of the other two, terms will appear which, if interpretation is required, can only be interpreted by reference to Jesus' story. For example, if we say "God is the hope at the beginning of all things" and then are asked "Hope for what?" we must answer, "Hope for Jesus' triumph."

The three identifications can otherwise be performed independently. But the predicates we use of the one identified in any of the three ways can be made unambiguous—should ambiguity threaten—only by running them across all three identities. For example, "God is good in the way that a giver is good; and God is good in the way that a gift is good; and God is good in the way that the outcome of a gift is good."

Second, "identity" is now regularly used to interpret personal existence, as we may say that someone is "seeking identity." This sense is connected to the first; it names the mode of identifiability proper to certain entities,

# THE ONE AND THE THREE

those we currently call "personal" in a sense very different from the trinitarian "person." As person, in this modern sense, I am what I am only in that I remember what I have been and hope for what I will be. If Jones is a person, in this modern sense, the "is" in "Jones is lazy" is not quite a normal copula; It is more like a transitive verb, modifiable by adverbs. It is the word for a specific act of positing oneself in and through time. Existentialist thought has invented words like "existence" or *Dasein* for this act. *Hypostasis* in its pretrinitarian and prechristological uses did not have this sense, but in the often tortured ways in which the theological tradition has used *hypostasis*, just this sense for the peculiar identity of person-realities struggled for expression already in the Cappadocians.

Accordingly, that there is even one identity in God means that God is personal, that he *is* God in that he *does* Godhead, in that he chooses himself as God. That there are three identities in God means that this God's deed of being the one God is three times repeated,[17] and so that each repetition is a being of God; and so that only in this precise self-repetition is God the particular God that he in fact is. God does God, and over again, and yet over again—and only so does the event and decision that is this God occur.

THE ONE BEING

Back to the Cappadocians. They needed also a correlated analysis of the divine *ousia* to show how it could be the being of three individuals without these being three instances of God. They had a variety of arguments; we will follow one by Gregory of Nyssa.

Since there is only one Godhead, the Trinity is somehow individual and must therefore be identifiable if real. And Gregory indeed provides an identifying description of the one *ousia* of God—but this is precisely that God's being is infinite.[18] We can identify God's one being as and only as life that knows no boundary and that therefore will always go on to surpass each—even true—identifying description.[19] This need not mean we cannot at all identify God affirmatively: God is "the one who raised Jesus," but then we are with the three rather than with the one.

Gregory is fully aware of the break he is making with philosophical tradition. He states the view "of the many," which he rejects. According to that view, "God" is, like "human" or "rock," "an unmetaphorical name by nature," "predicated to identify by the nature of the thing" (*To Ablabius*, 121). Such a word evokes some entity's entire set of essential characters all at once, insofar as these make an organic complex so that each character is itself only together with the others. Just so, such a word uniquely displays "the underlying individual subject" (ibid.), that which in any real thing *has* all the

139

2 / THE TRIUNE GOD

characters by which that thing is what it is, and is itself established as the possible possessor of these characters and no others. For God, says Gregory, there is no such word (ibid.).

Thus—and we are finally to the point—Gregory's answer to the question why three individuals sharing God's *ousia* do not make three gods is that "God" and all its equivalents are not predicated of the divine *ousia* at all, singly or trebly. "God" is a predicate, and how many gods are asserted depends on how many logical subjects it is attached to. A plurality of instances of the divine *ousia* is not a plurality of *gods,* for the *ousia* is not the logical subject of "God" to begin with, and neither then are the *ousia*'s instances; how many individuals are instances of God's *ousia* is irrelevant to how many gods there are.

What then *is* "God" predicated of? Gregory's revolutionary answer: of the divine *activity* toward us (ibid., 124). And since all divine action is the structuredly mutual work of Father, Son, Spirit, their divine activity is but one logical subject of "God": "All action which comes upon the creature from God . . . begins from the Father and is present through the Son and is perfected in the Holy Spirit. Therefore the name of the action ("God") is not divided among the plurality of the actors" (ibid., 127). Gregory of Nazianzus once revised an old trinitarian illustration in an astonishing way. Instead of comparing Father, Son, and Spirit to the sun and its beams, he compared them to three suns, so focused as to make but one beam: The beam is God (*Oration XXXI*, 14).

The divine *ousia* does not drop out of the picture, for the inner-trinitarian relations, by which there are three to begin with, are defined in terms of it. It is precisely deity as infinity which the Father gives, the Son receives, and the Spirit communicates; by their relations, the action of each is temporally unlimited, to be *God's* action. But it is the *work*, the creative event, done through Jesus' life, death, resurrection, and future advent, done by his Father for their Spirit, that is the one God.

Surely this tendency is biblically right, at least by that understanding of the biblical witness sketched above. Stipulating an event as the subject of "God" imposes a task of ontological revision, to which we must eventually turn, as did Gregory. But leaving that for the moment, and recalling the discussion of "identity," we obtain the following formula: There is one event, God, of three identities. Therewith this essay's proposed basic trinitarian analysis.

THE WESTERN VERSION

The struggle and creation we have narrated in this and the previous chapter took place in the Eastern church. Its results were assimilated into the West from the late fourth century on. The circumstances of the assimilation have been decisive for the thought and life of the Western church. Without attempting to judge relative importance, we may list three such circumstances.

First, the doctrine of the Trinity came to the West as a finished product. Thus it was more something to be explained, than itself an explanation.

Second, in conducting trinitarian analysis and speculation in Latin, the Greek results were pressed into a terminology previously established in the Latin tradition: There is one "substance" of God (or "essence" or "nature"), in three "persons." But these terms had been through none of the Eastern conceptual wars; and when it came to the creative thrusts of such Easterners as Gregory of Nyssa, Western readers invariably missed the point. Augustine himself confessed incomprehension of the key Greek distinction: "I do not know what difference they intend between *ousia* and *hypostasis*"[20]

Third, the work of synthesis between Eastern thought and Western language and need was almost entirely the work of one man, Augustine, one of history's few history-shaping geniuses. Augustine's personal spiritual and intellectual experiences impressed themselves on Western theology in a way unparalleled in Christian history. In much of theology, this has been a blessing, but it has blighted our trinitarianism, for Augustine's particular religious experience led him to understand the triune character of God as one thing, the history of salvation as quite another. Thus the trinitarian formulas completely lost their original function.[21]

All these circumstances promoted a sort of reversion to pre-Nicene thinking. Hellenic interpretation of God had never been fully overcome in the general theology of the Eastern fathers, only within the trinitarian dogma and analyses themselves, and there by subtle and easily lost distinctions. The way thus remained open for Western theology to repristinate the old apologists' additive tactic in a new form. And that is what happened over the long history of Western theology. The inheritance of Hellenic interpretation was received as what the scholastics would come to call "natural" theology, a body of truth about God shared with the heathen and so taken to be resultant, at least in principle, from the merely created circumstances of life and the merely created religious and intellectual capacities of the soul. Such of the biblical discourse about God as was not shared by the heathen was therefore thought not to be thus generally available; it was received as a higher supernatural body of truth about God, given only by revelation. But when the matter is put so, the natural knowledge of God becomes the foundation of the supernatural; Homer and Parmenides get to write the first chapter in the *locus* on God. Consequently, the supposed timelessness and impassibility of God inevitably determine all that follows, including the trinitarian discourse.[22]

Augustine laid down this axiomatic status of divine timelessness for all subsequent Western theology: "Speak of the changes of things, and you find 'was'

2 / THE TRIUNE GOD

and 'will be'; think God, and you find 'is' where 'was' and 'will be' cannot enter."[23] God not only does not change, he cannot; just so, "he is rightly said to be" (*On the Trinity*, v,2).

This uncritical repristination of Greek assumptions had two consequences directly relevant to our interest. One was the doctrine of divine "simplicity," which became a key technical device of all consequent Western trinitarian analysis. Since it is by having "accidents," that is, characteristics that can come and go, that ordinary realities give hostages to time, God, it was agreed, has none such (ibid., v,3). As Thomas Aquinas argued it, accidents are the mark of potentiality, of capacity for becoming other than one is; this is absent from God (*Summa Theologica*, i,3,6). But so long as there is a real difference between the thing and its characteristics, it must be possible for the substance to remain while at least some characteristics come and go, that is, some must be accidents. Therefore in God there is no such difference; as Augustine puts it: "God is not great by a greatness other than himself . . . ; he is great by that greatness . . . he himself is" (*On the Trinity*, v,11). "God is called 'simple' because he *is* what he *has*" (*City of God*, 1,xi,10,1).

The second consequence was the reintrusion into the heart of trinitarianism of the old late-antique worry about the relation of a supposedly timeless God to his temporal creation, with evil results. Augustinianism forbade any assertion about God's relation to time that could suggest change in God himself. That there is a difficulty here, Augustine himself acknowledged: "To see how God . . . creates temporal things and events without any temporal movement of his substance . . . is hard" (*On the Trinity*, i,3). Nevertheless, he lays down the rule: When we speak of God being "our Lord," which he could not be before we existed, or of God's "becoming our Father at baptism," or of all the like, we must understand that "nothing is added to God, but only to that to which God is said to take up a relation." Thus, for example, "God begins to be our Father when we are reborn. . . . Our substance is changed for the better when we become his children; therewith he also begins to be our Father, but without any such change" (ibid., v,17).

The single most disastrous trinitarian result of this rule is that Western teaching, rigorously sorting out usages that had in the East been beneficially vague, makes the trinitarian "processions" in God (i.e., "begetting" and "breathing") and the divine persons' "missions" in time (i.e., the Son's Incarnation and the Spirit's entry into the church; i.e., again, the whole triune reality as Tertullian or Athanasius evoked it) be two simply different and metaphysically separated things: "'mission' and 'sending' . . . are predicated only temporally, 'generation' and 'breathing' only eternally."[24] That the Son, for example, is "begotten" by the Father, and that he is "sent" to redeem humanity, are now thought of as distinct events, one in eternity and the other in time: "The Son is said to be sent, not . . . in that he is born of the Father, but either in that he appears in this world as the Word made flesh . . . , or in that he is inwardly apprehended by a temporal mind."[25] Indeed, Aquinas' argument why there must be exactly the two processions is that the Son emerges by an act of the Father's mind and the Spirit by an act of his will, and that thinking and willing are the only two personal movements that do not necessarily emerge from the agent, that is, here, from God to a temporal object (*Summa Theologica*, i,27,5). In this theology, there are in effect two distinct sets of trinitarian relations, one constituting an "immanent" Trinity, the triune God himself, and the other the "economic" Trinity, the triune pattern of God's work.

The final consequence of these developments is that the trinitarian language of "persons" and "relations" in God loses its original meaning and indeed threatens to lose all meaning of any sort. That God is "one and three" becomes the sheer mystification Western churchgoers accept—or reject—it as: something we assert because we are supposed to, not knowing even what we are asserting. Augustine provided Western theology with a neat formula to sum up the decades of Eastern trinitarian reflection: The Father is God, and the Son is God, and the Spirit is God; and the Father and the Son and the Spirit are not the same one; and the three are but one God.[26] But the formula no longer represents an activity of analysis to help to understand God. It is instead a paradox formula: Since God is infinite, so that addition and substration do not apply, "one is as much as three are together." (*On the Trinity*, vi,12). And with his invariable clarity Augustine sees very well what then happens to the trinitarian language. He explicitly stipulates that when we say one "substance" or three "persons" we communicate nothing whatever, using the words only to say "somehow one" and "somehow three" and using these particular words only because they are traditional (ibid., v,10; vii,7–11). Later theology then makes pious mystery-mongering of the vacuity; for example, it is standard from Lombard on that the Son's "being begotten" differs from the Spirit's "proceeding" only by a difference that cannot be "known in this life" (*Sentences*, i,13).

That the saving works of God, the "works *ad extra*," are works of the whole Trinity no longer can mean that each work is the joint work of Father, Son, and Spirit, in which each identity plays a distinct role,[27] but that the saving works are *indifferently* the work of each person and all; the "inseparability" of God's works is now identified with a mathematically equal abstract divinity of the triune persons. Creation is undifferentiably the work of the Trinity as one God. And the "sender" of each divine mission is the Trinity, or any of the persons, including the one sent.[28]

So also there is no longer any necessary connection of the trinitarian persons to roles and structures of saving history. According to Augustine, the theophanies of the Hebrew Scriptures could have been appearances of any

2 / THE TRIUNE GOD

trinitarian person, or of the Trinity as such; only exegesis decides for each instance, and no theological difference is made by the result (*On the Trinity*, ii; iii,3). Finally, with Lombard it becomes standard for all scholasticism that "just as the Son was made man, so the Father or the Holy Spirit *could* have been and can be now" (*Sentences*, iii,i,3). With this last proposition, the bankruptcy of trinitarian meaning is complete. "The Son" or "the Logos" were originally titles for Jesus in respect of his role in God's saving reality; now they name a pure metaphysical entity, not necessarily related to Jesus at all and—equally with the other divine persons—available for whatever divine duty comes along.

The original meaning of "Father," "Son," "begets," "gift," and so on, as words for the reality of saving history in God, having evaporated, Western theology was compelled to find other ways of sustaining the trinitarian terminology's meaningfulness—unless, of course, the whole doctrine was to be abandoned, which was not thinkable before the sixteenth century. Since the relation between the creature and God is now back to the old Hellenic stand-off between temporality and its abstract negation, also the Hellenic way of giving meaning to talk of timeless deity was inevitably adopted: "Persons" and "relations" are taken to be reality in God describable by *analogy* from temporal reality.[29] The whole pattern of Western theology is already set in the sequence of Augustine's *On the Trinity*. The first seven books analyze inherited trinitarian formulas by the axiom of divine simplicity and end with their reduction to vacuity. This result demands the search for created analogues of triunity that occupies the remaining books.[30] And the chosen created reality is the human soul, where from Socrates on the "image" of timeless deity had been chiefly sought.[31] In that God is triune, and in that temporal being is ontologically dependent on inner analogy to timeless being, and in that for the intrinsically self-conscious soul the grasp of this analogy is its own active reality, we can meaningfully say "Father, Son, and Spirit" about God[32]— according to Augustine and his followers. Therewith the whole relation of God to his work in time reverted to the pre-Nicene conception of the temporal imaging of timeless reality. Arius was the winner after all.

All temporal being, according to Augustine and his Platonist teachers, is dependent on God in respect of its being, of its intelligibility, and of its activity. The triune image of God in the soul is the realization of these dependences in the mode appropriate to consciousness:[33] "We *are*, we *know* that we are, and we *love* this being and this knowing" (*City of God*, xi,26,7-9). And since this self-consciousness is necessarily also God-consciousness (e.g., *On the Trinity*, viii,3-6), the triple structure of consciousness is an image of divine triplicity: "This . . . trinity of the mind is not the image of God only because the mind remembers itself and knows itself and loves itself, but

144

because it can also remember and know and love the one by whom it is created" (ibid., xiv,12).

All Augustine's trinitarian analogies, the stock-in-trade of subsequent Western reflection, are but variant descriptions of this structure of simultaneous self- and God-consciousness. The triple dependence is most directly reflected in this formula: being/knowledge/love.[34] Since in the soul's dependence its being is love, this formula can turn into: the soul as lover/the soul as object of its own love, that is, as known to itself/the soul as love (ibid., viii,ix,1–3). The love trinity in its turn, translated into a description of the soul as a substance, becomes: mind/knowledge/love (ibid., ix,3–4). And translating yet again, to a more functional analysis, we get memory/knowledge/will (ibid., x), for the mind as consciousness is identical with itself as being in that it is memory, and love is the action of will.

Our discussion of Western trinitarianism must alternate between lamentation and admiration of the virtues of its defects. We must now note the first such virtue. In turning to the soul for a meaning-giving analogue of divine triunity, Augustine necessarily exposed his introspection to some pressure from inherited trinitarian language. Thus he discovered the dialectical complexity of the soul's own reality. That the soul is complex, all antiquity knew. But that the complexity is living and dialectical, that in it each factor is what it is only by and for the other factors, Augustine was first to note. "The soul would not seek to know itself . . . , if it did not in some fashion love itself, with a love which again depends on the knowledge given in memory."[35] In effect, Augustine, looking for analogues of triune deity, discovered the ontological difference of conscious from unconscious being, the great theme of all subsequent Western philosophy.[36] And then Augustine does, however grudgingly, reflect all this back again on God: "Or are we indeed to suppose that the consciousness that God is, knows other things and does not know itself . . . ? Behold therefore the Trinity: consciousness, and knowledge of self, and love of self" (ibid., xv,10). Several steps removed from authentic trinitarian insight though this interpretation of God is, it is a great intellectual achievement in itself, and one made under the pressure of Scripture. That God is personal is a deeply Christian notion and an abiding contribution of Western theology.

The second virtue of Western trinitarianism is that precisely the ultimately hopeless task of thinking the plurality of persons within the notion of a temporally undifferentiable God, and within so abstract a notion of God's unity as represented by the simplicity axiom, compelled Western theology to work out the abstract dialectics of tri-identicality to perfection.[37] Lombard, following Augustine, laid down the dialectical boundary conditions: "The Father is not greater than the Son nor the Father or the Son than the Holy Spirit;

145

2 / THE TRIUNE GOD

nor are two persons together any greater something than one, nor three than two; nor is the divine essence greater in three persons than in two, nor in two than in one." In consequence, "the Father is in the Son and the Son in the Father and the Spirit in both, and each is in each and all" (*Sentences*, i, vix,4–5). The rule acquired conciliar status: "The three persons are one . . . substance, one essence, one nature, one divinity, one immensity, one eternity; all divine reality is one where an opposition of relation does not prevent it."[38]

Distinctions in God are posited by inner divine "processions," of which there are two: the "begetting" of the Son and the "breathing" of the Spirit.[39] A "procession" is a "movement to an other"; the other of generation and spiration in God is God himself; therefore the divine simplicity is supposed not to be violated.[40] Therefore also, since every procession establishes relations, there are relations in God. Moreover, these are "real" relations, that is, not merely external as between two coins possessed by one owner, each of which is the same as if not so related. For since *both* terms of each such relation are God, the relation cannot be external to its terms.[41]

This immediately gives a list of four relations: The Father "begets," the Son "is begotten," the Father and the Son "breathe," and the Spirit "is breathed."[42] And then we have five "notions" applicable to the inner-divine distinctions, the four relations plus "unbegotten" or "unoriginated" of the Father, marking his position as the starting point of all the processions, who himself does not proceed.[43] If now we seek identifying properties for each of the persons, "unoriginated" drops out, since it applies also to the Trinity as such, and so does "breathes," since it applies both to the Father and the Son. Thus, by the sheer geometry of the relational structure, we arrive at exactly three "properties" or "personal notions": "begets," "is begotten," "is breathed."[44] It surely must be said that the mere aesthetic rightness of this analysis somehow commends it. Figure 1 shows a flow chart of deity.

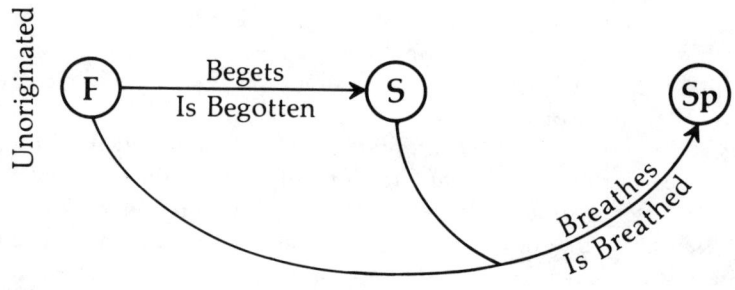

FIGURE 1

THE ONE AND THE THREE

Then come the great metaphysical assertions. First, the relations, and so the personal properties, are each identical with the one divine substance, "with respect to the entity," that is, as we would say, "objectively," for "paternity" and "breathing forth" are in themselves divine attributes, and by the simplicity axiom each divine attribute is "with respect to the entity" the divine substance. The relations-properties differ from the divine substance only "with respect to the way we know them," except that "only" is misleading, since this necessity of our knowing is itself founded somehow in the divine reality. The relations and the essence are really the same, but the distinction we cannot help making is necessitated by that one reality.[45]

But if the relations are not merely real in God, but real insofar as and only insofar as they are identical with the divine substance, then they are real in God in the same way the divine substance is real. Thus they "subsist," that is, they are possessors of attributes (here the divine attributes) and doers of deeds (here the divine deeds). That is, again, they are proper "persons" in the regular Latin sense of the word.[46] And now, conversely, we can say what the "persons" truly are: " 'Divine person' . . . means a relation as a subsistent."[47]

Within the metaphysical tradition, the notion of a subsistent relation is of course sheer nonsense. The scholastics labored mightily to mitigate the offense of their definition to what they accepted as natural truth. But so radical a doctrine of the reality of relations cannot be contained by Plato or Aristotle. That some relations, such as paternity, are founded in the related terms, inherited wisdom can accept. But this doctrine identifies the substantiality of the related terms with the internality of the relations between them. Even the classification of the personal properties to which the scholastics are driven—that they are *both* "relative" and yet "eternal and immutable"[48]—is a defiance of all Hellenic common sense.

This assertion of the substantiality of relations, that is, of their ontological independence and possible priority over against the related terms, is the main place at which the metaphysically revolutionary power of the gospel breaks out in Western theology. In the lead of the Greeks, our inherited ways of thinking suppose that there must first be *things* that in the second place may be variously related. But there is nothing intrinsically obvious about it; in fact, by biblical insight, it is the other way around. The general consequences of this reversal of interpretation have long appeared in Western philosophy, most explicitly in some aspects of German idealism, as Hegel's definition of spirit as the relation between self and not-self, which just so is the being of the self.[49] The task of drawing out the more specifically theological consequences has lagged, as it must until the Augustinian doctrine of divine simplicity is discarded. That, indeed, is one purpose of this study, to which we have made various approaches and to which we will return.

147

2 / THE TRIUNE GOD

THE ATHANASIAN CREED

The extent to which Augustinian trinitarian teaching can be taken as official doctrine of the Western church depends on the extent to which the so-called Athanasian Creed[50] establishes such doctrine. The long first section of this composition is a rhetorically splendid and theologically astute brief statement of Western trinitarian language-rules. The basic principle is that we "are neither to confuse the persons nor divide the substance."

The unity of substance will be preserved if we are careful to attribute all divine attributes equally to each person, but never so as to posit three logical subjects: "Uncreated is the Father, uncreated the Son, uncreated the Holy Spirit . . . ; and yet there are . . . not three Uncreateds . . . but one Uncreated. . . ." Etc. This is hammered home in rolling repetitive periods, choosing just those attributes of God that were decisive over against the Arians: "uncreated," "immense," "eternal," "omnipotent," "infinite." In the straight line from Athanasius, the posit of three kinds of deity is rejected as polytheistic: "For just as we are compelled by Christian truth to confess that each person singly is God and Lord, so we are forbidden by the catholic religion to say that there are three gods or lords."

The distinction of persons is to be achieved by the language of relations, though this technical term does not appear. "The Father is from no one, not made nor created nor begotten. The Son is from the Father only, not made nor created but begotten. The Holy Spirit is from the Father and the Son, not made nor created nor begotten but proceeding." It should be registered that the most unfortunate features of Western analysis do not explicitly appear.

The Athanasian Creed seems to have originated around the turn of the fifth and sixth centuries in Spain or southern France. It became the text for trinitarian instruction in the Carolingian theological institutions, and enjoyed great prestige through the Middle Ages. From the eighth century on, it was sung as a canticle, usually at the first Sunday office. Most Reformation compendiums of official doctrine included it. It does indeed state the unproblematic part of the Western church's trinitarian inheritance.

Yet the text of the Athanasian Creed was never adopted by an ecumenical gathering in the style of Chalcedon. In the modern period, many committed to its doctrine have nevertheless had great difficulty in affirming it, especially in using it liturgically. The problem has been, generally, the creed's identification of "the catholic faith" with a particular theological analysis, and specifically the opening anathema: "which if anyone does not preserve integral and inviolate, he will without doubt perish eternally." That one should be damned for bad, or even merely out-of-date, theology has seemed a bit hard.

Perhaps the difficulty will at least appear in a different light if indeed, as now seems proven,[51] the text was written and initially used neither as a liturgical or personal confession but as a memory piece for seminary instruction. It is one thing for future preachers to understand that salvation hangs on their preaching and that they are to preach thus and so. It is quite another thing for a congregation publicly to proclaim curses on the theologically maladroit or anachronistic. At any rate, the retreat of the Athanasian Creed back into the classroom may be regarded as a return to the proper locus of its authority. There, however, it surely deserves the highest respect.

VICISSITUDES OF WESTERN TRINITARIANISM

The danger of the West's abstract trinitarian analysis is not only that it is false, but also that it is likely to reflect negatively on the fundamental liturgical and proclamatory levels of trinitarian discourse. It seems plain that this has in fact happened, though tracing the history is beyond the scope of this work. One need only think of such phenomena as popular Catholicism's replacement of the triune structure for prayer with one or another piety of the "Jesus-Mary-Joseph" type, or of denominational Lutheranism's centuries-long affection for forms of prayer and praise with only second-article remembrance-content and no invocation of the Spirit, or of Calvinism's concentration of fear and hope on a pretemporal deity resembling nothing so much as Eunomius' "Unoriginate."

From Augustine on, the doctrine of the Trinity tended to become increasingly a "revealed mystery," taught in the proper place of theological systematics because it was supposed to have been supernaturally revealed that God was in fact triune, but having less and less interpretive force for the actual concerns of believers. As such, it was a setup for destructive critique. The critique has come from both the church and the world.

The doctrine has not easily been seen as functional within religious life. Thus one sort of critique, from within the heart of the church, has been benign neglect. The first Reformation system of theology, Melanchthon's *Loci Communes* of 1521, omitted the developed doctrine altogether, on the grounds that "to know God is to know his benefits," thus clearly supposing that trinitarian discourse is not about God's benefits. Pietists in all branches of the church have regularly taken the same attitude,[52] as did John Locke[53] and other forerunners of the Enlightenment. Another sort of churchly critique has been more explicit. Western Christians have in effect found themselves, so far as experience is concerned, in a pre-Nicene situation. Many, liberated by historical or philosophical critique from affirming inherited doctrine just because it is inherited, have recapitulated pre-Nicene theological history, reinventing apologetic subordinationism and Arianism. It is this phenomenon

149

2 / THE TRIUNE GOD

which appears in such "unitarian" movements as have been explicitly Christian: Servetus, the Socinians,[54] or the English and American Unitarians.[55] It appears again in the "neologians," who in Germany mediated the first impact of the Enlightenment.[56] Since we have been over all that ground once, we need not here investigate any of these theologies, only note their existence and influence.

Such critique has not abated in our century. Currently influential are the arguments of Cyril C. Richardson that inherited trinitarianism is the result of the use of inappropriate biblical and Hellenic language to state necessary theological insight into God's transcendence and immanence,[57] of G. W. H. Lampe, that we need more "personal" language and that the metaphysical problems generated by traditional language are insoluble,[58] and of C. F. D. Moule, that a "binity" would make sense but that there is no need to make a "person" of the Spirit.[59] In general, current objections are not very different from those of the eighteenth and nineteenth centuries and like them are based on the assumption that standard Western teaching is "the doctrine" of the Trinity.

The full Enlightenment, of course, rejected trinitarianism from quite another side.[60] The tradition itself posited two bodies of knowledge of God, "natural" and "supernatural," and stipulated the first as that accessible to "reason" and the second as obtained only by bowing to the authority of some agency of revelation. The Enlightenment was a declaration of reason's freedom over against authority; just so it countenanced only the "natural" part of theology. Thus the Enlightenment affirmed Aristotle's God in its purity, untouched even by such biblical contaminants as maintained by Augustine. Insofar as the Enlightenment was simply unchurchly, as in France, its unitarianism is outside our story. But insofar as it remained inside the church, as often in England or Germany or the United States, it mingled with such currents as described just before, to promote sundry modalisms and subordinationisms, as well as gentlemanly silent compacts to let sleeping "dogmatic" dogs lie. Under all these sorts of critique, the inherited doctrine of the Trinity was by the opening of the nineteenth century nearly defunct in all those parts of the church open to modernity.

The history of nineteenth-century spirituality and theology, at least in such parts of the church, was a series of attempts to overcome the Enlightenment with respect to its evacuation of religious substance, without returning to reliance on supernatural authority. Two great figures dominate the effort: Friedrich Schleiermacher and G. W. F. Hegel. Both are in fact important for current trinitarian thought. Schleiermacher typifies and largely inaugurated the dominant pattern of the nineteenth and twentieth centuries, which continues to get along without much trinitarianism. Hegel deliberately "renewed" the doctrine as a speculative insight, providing the pattern of other such at-

150

THE ONE AND THE THREE

tempts thereafter and much of the impetus and conceptual style for the more churchly twentieth-century renewal by Karl Barth.

Schleiermacher put his exceedingly brief section on the Trinity at the end of his systematics, as a sort of summary. There it cannot function to identify or interpret the God spoken of in the body of the work. Rather, having expounded what is effectively the contents of a three-article creed, Schleiermacher then takes such a creed's "Father . . . , Son . . . , Spirit" as a concluding memory device suggested by tradition. At the level of the immediate expression and critique of piety—which according to Schleiermacher is the only legitimate level for dogmatics—the doctrine's necessary function, he says, is to insist "that nothing less than the divine being was in Christ and inhabits the Christian church as its communal spirit, and that we do not take these expressions in any weakened sense . . . and intend to know nothing of . . . subordinate divinities" (*The Christian Faith*, 170,1).[61] To that we must say, so far so good.

As a doctrine about the "divine being" itself, however, the doctrine of the Trinity is, according to Schleiermacher, a bungle. Such doctrine first results from "eternalizing the distinction between the being of God for itself and the being of God for the unification [with Jesus and the church]" (ibid., 170,3). But just that move is disastrous. Schleiermacher's difficulty, it is vital to note, is precisely Augustine's: uncritical acceptance of the Greek dogma that divinity equals timelessness (ibid., 171,52) and can therefore be spoken of only in analogies. "The divine causality [Schleiermacher's interpretation of God's reality] . . . must be conceived as utterly timeless. This is achieved through expressions which name temporal reality, and is therefore achieved by pictures; . . . one equates the temporal opposites before-and-after, earlier-and-later, and so suspends them" (ibid., 171,1).

But where Augustine struggled to maintain some sense for the inherited trinitarian propositions, Schleiermacher just drops them. He is free to do this because of the new historical situation, but also because, according to him, specifically Christian apprehension does not reach to the basic understanding of God at all; this is borrowed (his word) from universally valid philosophical analysis (*Brief Description of Theological Study*, 43–53). In fact, despite what is usually said of him, Schleiermacher maintains a particularly simpleminded form of the disastrous old distinction of natural from revealed theology.

If, for reasons of purely intellectual harmonization, we still want a doctrine of triunity, Schleiermacher has two recommendations. First, the doctrine should be "Sabellian," a description of successive temporal manifestations of a divine reality itself unaffected thereby. Second, we should take "the Father" as a name for this divine reality, and "the Son" and "the Spirit" as names for the manifestations (*The Christian Faith*, 172,3). Thus Schleiermacher's recommendation is exactly and compendiously Arian after all.

151

2 / THE TRIUNE GOD

We need not decide whether Schleiermacher's version of the Trinity has greatly influenced nineteenth- and twentieth-century ordinary Christianity, or only marvelously exemplifies it. It is enough to note that most Protestant readers will recognize in the last paragraphs a description of what they gleaned from the catechetics and preaching of the main-line denominations.

Hegel deliberately set out to reinvigorate the inherited doctrine of the Trinity, by releasing its metaphysically revolutionary implications.[62] He made the Augustinian-Western version of the doctrine the center of his philosophy, the West's last universal and perhaps last great system of thought. Augustine, we have insisted, failed to describe a genuinely tri-identical God. But in the attempt he did perceive new truth; he perceived an in the modern sense *personal* God, whose being is constituted in the inner dialectics of consciousness, in the play of—now we will use the language of Hegel's time—immediate self-consciousness ("memory"), objective knowledge of self, and will that unites them. Hegel abandoned Augustine's hesitations, made this interpretation a universal concept of personal being, and then made all reality personal.

It was Hegel's goal to make a true synthesis of the two clashing streams of western thought: the Greek will rationally to grasp reality's sense, and the Bible's grasp of reality as history, with all its contingencies and contradictions. This can be done, said Hegel, if we see that history makes its own kind of sense, which is the sense not of the merely beholding and sense-describing mind, but of the living and sense-creating spirit. The spirited rationality of poets and great statesmen—and of authentic philosophers like Plato—does not abstract from contingency and contradictions, only so to achieve itself; it posits them, to overcome and encompass them and so achieve an expanding, *living* meaning. Napoleon does not abhor enemies; he seeks them, to create a larger European order in the struggle. Goethe does not banish irrationality and conflict from his plots; he invents them, to achieve the meaning of drama rather than of mere chronicle. Abstractly stated: The rational subject posits the object, that which is not itself, not sheer transparent meaning. Then the rational subject achieves itself as the *process*, the *act*, of rediscovering itself in the object, that is, of finding meaning in what is not merely as such meaningful. This reconciliation of reason-as-subject with object-made-reasonable, is living reason, spirit.

Since reality is historical, it is the sort of sense just described that reality has: the eternal creating and overcoming of contradiction in higher harmony. Since reality has this sort of sense, true reason is the mind that fulfills itself as just described, that works out its own reason precisely in contingent and contradiction-laden objective reality. The great metaphysical claim follows of itself: Reality-as-history makes sense only as the object of a Subject that finds itself therein, and so is itself Spirit. God is the Mind that has the world for object; he is the world insofar as Mind indeed finds sense, and so Itself, in the world; and he is the free Spirit that occurs as this event. God is the absolute Poet-Statesman-Philosopher. God is just what Augustine said: Mind and Knowledge and Love that joins them.

Hegel believed Western thought fulfilled itself with him; at least so far as its trinitarianism is concerned, he was right. Augustine's insight can be taken no further. Neither can Augustine's failure: this trinitarianism's distance from the saving history that necessitated it in the first place. In Hegel, Augustine's trinitarianism fulfills its constant tendency by finally explicitly taking the world as God's object, rather than Jesus the Son. From Hegel on, there has been a continuous tradition in which the trinitarian dialectics are exploited for their speculative possibilities, without much direction of the speculation by the dialectics' original object. The most notable recent exponents of this tradition are John Macquarrie and Paul Tillich.[63] From the point of view of this work, such efforts merely perfect ancient error.

In our century, the decisive step in repairing the great flaw of Augustinian-Hegelian trinitarianism has been taken. Karl Barth has reachieved an authentic doctrine of triunity, by what amounts to a christological inversion of Hegel's.[64] Only make *Jesus* God's object in which he finds himself, instead of Hegel's "world" or Augustine's merely metaphysical "Logos," and you have the doctrine of Barth's *Church Dogmatics*, Volume 1 I/1—which observation takes nothing from the extraordinary ingenuity of Barth's move.[65]

Barth perceives the difference between the Hellenic quest for God (he says "natural theology") and the gospel's proclamation that Jesus is God's quest for us (he says "revelation") more rigorously than any but Luther before him and uses this insight as the sole motor of trinitarian discourse. The entire doctrine of the Trinity, he says, is but the specification of which God it is that can so reveal himself as God is in fact revealed in Christ.[66]

The biblical claim of revelation, Barth says, poses three questions: Who is revealed? What does he do to reveal himself? What does revelation accomplish? The answer to each must be God, without qualification.[67] "*God* reveals himself. He reveals himself *through himself*. He reveals *himself*."[68] And apart from each of these three sentences, the other two remain ambiguous.[69]

The key point is why the answer to all three questions must be simply God. Summarizing drastically, we may state Barth's answer: All three questions must be answered just "God," in order to negate our religious quest conceptually as revelation in Jesus' death and resurrection in fact negates it.[70] If the revelation, Jesus, or the achievement of revelation, the divine presence among us, were not simply God himself, we would by them merely be launched on a religious quest for God himself. But what the cross and resurrection reveal

2 / THE TRIUNE GOD

is exactly that such a quest, denying the sufficiency of the word of the gospel, is unbelief. Yet the God who so reveals himself does not thereby become merely identical with historical revelation and accomplished presence; that God is never thus grasped by us is, again, what the cross reveals. Also the one revealed is God utterly. Finally, having thus prevented subordinationism, Barth excludes modalism by the very same considerations. The necessity of giving the same answer to all three of revelation's questions does not amalgamate the questions themselves into one, for then again the real God would remain behind revelation and we would be back on our quest.

Since it is Barth who taught twentieth-century theology—or the living parts of it—the importance and point of trinitarian discourse, his influence has been pervasive through this entire study. That must here be explicitly acknowledged. But his contribution to required new trinitarian analysis is not so great as might be expected. Nor does he carry us to full liberation from a past-determined interpretation of God.

Trinitarian analysis is by no means complete, nor will it be until the struggle between the gospel's and Hellenism's identifications of God is over. It is time to state such of our own proposals as are not yet explicit.

The first step is to free trinitarian doctrine from captivity to antecedent interpretation of deity as timelessness.[71] In part that is already done in this work—as in Barth and some other post-Hegelian treatments—by the mere sequence of topics and by the christological concentration we, again like Barth, have insisted on at every step. In part it must be accomplished in the next chapter, where we will attempt an evangelical concept of deity, the basis of which is already laid throughout the previous chapters.

Within the trinitarian dialectics themselves it is the relation of the "immanent" and "economic" Trinities that must in this connection be reconsidered. The most important contemporary Catholic trinitarian theorist and the most important Protestant, Karl Rahner and Eberhard Jüngel, agree on a rule for the contemporary task: "The 'economic' Trinity *is* the 'immanent' Trinity, and vice versa."[72]

The legitimate theological reason for the "immanent"/"economic" distinction is the freedom of God. It must be that God "in himself" could have been the same God he is, and so triune, had there been no creature, or no saving of fallen creation, and so also not the trinitarian history there has in fact been. Here is a second rule (which is perhaps too little observed by both Rahner and Jüngel). Reconciling it with the other just stated has always been the problem. The two rules are compatible, we propose, only if the identity of the "economic" and "immanent" Trinity is eschatological.

Within theology's captivity to the timelessness axiom, the eternity of Jesus could be conceived only as a reality that always was in God. Thus was posited

154

THE ONE AND THE THREE

the "Logos *asarkos*," the "not [yet] incarnate Word," Jesus' metaphysical double, who always was in God and then *became* the one sent in flesh to us. The Logos' relation to the Father was described as a Father-Son relation, and rightly, since it is Jesus' relation to his Father that is to be interpreted. But the begetting and being-begotten of *this* Father and Son had to be timeless; thus this "procession" could not in fact be the same as the temporal relation of Jesus to his Father, that is, as the "mission." The Greek fathers mostly ignored the difficulty, thus permitting authentic trinitarian discourse in which the processions and missions occur together. But when more rigid thinkers came along, the difficulty proved fatal. This whole pattern must be exactly reversed.

Instead of interpreting Christ's deity as a separate entity that always *was*—and proceeding analogously with the Spirit—we should interpret it as a final outcome, and just so as eternal, just so as the bracket around all beginnings and endings. Jesus' historical life was a sending by the Father, the filial relation between this man and the transcendence to whom he turned temporally occurred; and this man is risen from the dead, so that his mission must triumph, so that his filial relation to his Father is unimpeachable. Thus Jesus' obedience to the Father, and their love for us which therein occurs, will prove an unsurpassable event, that is, are a God-event, a "procession" in God. Jesus' Aramaic or Hebrew prayer, and his prophetic apprehension of God's Word, will be the Father's final self-expression, by which he establishes his identity for us and for himself. And the Spirit that is the breath of this future will blow all things before himself into new life. The saving events, whose plot is stated by the doctrine of trinitarian relations, are, in their eschatological finality, God's transcendence of time, God's eternity. Thus we need posit no timelessly antecedent extra entities—Logos *asarkos* or not-yet-given Spirit—to assert the unmitigated eternity of Son and Spirit.

Within trinitarian thought's captivity to an alien definition of deity, we have been unable to say simply that Jesus *is* "the eternal Son," that what happens between the human Jesus and his father and the believing community *is* eternity. Instead, we have had to say that Jesus is the dwelling and manifestation of his own preexistent double—and with that, all the impossibilities we have trudged through are there. It is the need for the "pre-" that causes them; that is, it is the interpretation of eternity as persistence of the first past that causes them. If instead we follow Scripture in understanding eternity as faithfulness to the last future, *these* problems merely disappear.

Truly, the Trinity is simply the Father and the man Jesus and their Spirit as the Spirit of the believing community. This "economic" Trinity is *eschatologically* God "himself," an "immanent" Trinity. And that assertion is no problem, for God *is* himself only eschatologically, since he is Spirit.

155

2 / THE TRIUNE GOD

As for God's freedom, only our proposal fully asserts it. The immanent Trinity of previous Western interpretation had but the spurious freedom of unaffectedness. Genuine freedom is the reality of possibility, is openness to the future. Genuine freedom is Spirit. And it is only in that we interpret God's eternity as the certainty of his triumph that we are able without qualification to say that God is Spirit. If we so understand God's freedom, we are indeed unable to describe *how* God could have been the selfsame triune God other than as the Trinity now in fact given. But neither have we any call to, so long as God's utter freedom, as Spirit, is acknowledged. In that acknowledgment we are equally commanded to say *that* God could be otherwise God and forbidden to say *how*.

Therewith we are at the next required amendment of inherited teaching. On a traditional diagram of trinitarian relations, the procession of divine being is all one way, from the Father. Son and Spirit derive their deity from the Father, but Father and Son do not derive deity from the Spirit; in Augustine's formula, "The Father is the principle and source of the whole of deity" (*On the Trinity*, iv,29). The places for relations whose arrows would point *to* the Father are vacant.

Pre-Nicene subordinationism had two closely related roots. One was the need for mediation of time and eternity. The other was the apprehension of God as fundamentally located at the beginning rather than the end, so that the trinitarian relations, even when rightly set parallel to time, had as active relations to point only *with* time's arrow. It corresponded to this apprehension that to command, beget, give, and so on, were felt as more appropriate to deity than to be given, obey, and so on.[73] Of these roots of subordinationism, only the first was pulled up by the Cappadocians. Thus it became a fixed axiom that the Father's begetting marked a sole primacy in deity,[74] that the transcendence to whom Jesus looked back was actively deity, while the Spirit he gave to the future was only passively so.

The asymmetry of the trinitarian relations is the more remarkable in that the Bible clearly presses candidates for the missing parts of the diagram. We propose to fill them in. Which biblical language we choose for the future-to-past active relations is at present of secondary importance. Using "witnesses" for the Spirit and "frees" for the Spirit with the Son, we may say the following. The Spirit's witness to the Son is equally God-constituting with the traditional relations. And so is the Son's and the Spirit's joint reality as the openness into which the Father is freed from mere persistence in his pretemporal transcendence. Moreover, since the only biblical approach to a definition of deity is "God is Spirit," the Spirit must at least be recognized as differently but equally "principle and source" with the Father; let us mark this with a "notion," and let that be "unsurpassed." Thus we obtain a new diagram, shown in Figure 2.

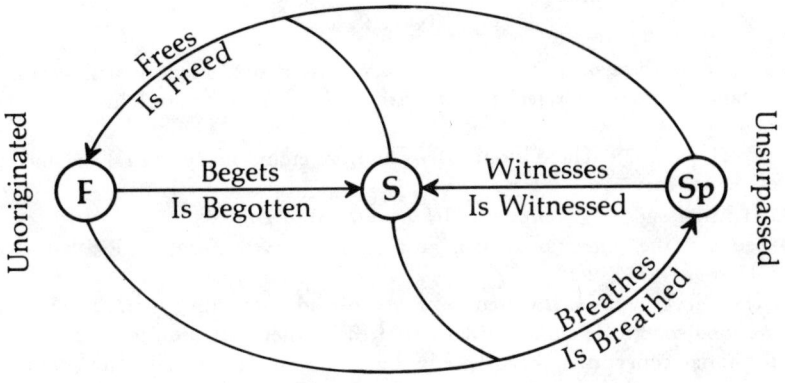

FIGURE 2

The tradition could say how sending and obedience, giving and being given, are realities not merely between God and us, but in God—and so final goods. But it could not say how freeing and being freed, witnessing and being witnessed to, are equally realities in God. Thus the tradition could show that—to use Reformation language—God's *law* is his own true self-expression. But it could not show that the *gospel* is similarly anchored in his being. We do not suggest that the church so persistently slides into legalism because of gaps in a diagram; we do suggest that it does so because of a conception of God accurately represented by the traditional diagram, by which God is indeed God of the law but not of the gospel, defined in his deity as the Father but not as the Spirit. We wish to amend the conception.

This is perhaps also the place where the traditional doctrine of God does indeed reflect male dominance. Whether or not dominance is biologically a male characteristic, it has been culturally. The traditional trinitarian relations, unsupplemented by those we propose, display command as constitutive of deity but not obedience, assertion but not reception. Indeed, the very definition of deity as assertion against time and its chances, which lies behind the asymmetry of relations and against which we have been arguing, bears the same value preference. It has been convincingly argued that these characteristics of traditional trinitarianism are the last outpost of the ancient world's dominance of male solar and sky gods over female earth and lunar gods.[13] Teaching a symmetry of trinitarian relations is not, of course, intended to balance female characteristics with male characteristics, and certainly not to posit obedience or receptivity as inherently female. The point is rather to eliminate altogether the influence of antiquity's sex-role doctrines.

2 / THE TRIUNE GOD

NOTES

1. Origen, *Commentary of Romans*, in *EnchP*, 1965, 502:7, 13: "naturam Trinitatis et substantiam unam." Origen, *Commentary on John*, 2,10,75: "treis hypostaseis . . . tyganein."

2. *COD*, 1973, 28: There is one "deity and power and being (*ousia*) . . . in three perfect hypostases."

3. In Athanasius, e.g., *Discourse III against the Arians*, 65.

4. See, e.g., the "Creed of Lucian," in *Creeds of Christendom*, ed. P. Schaff (New York: Harper, 1889), 2:27.

5. The Greeks occasionally used *prosopon* instead of or with *hypostasis*. *Prosopon* and *persona* should be close translations of each other. But *prosopon* was never of any trinitarian conceptual importance in the East. And the Latins did not adopt *persona* as its translation, but for its own sake. See René Braun, *Deus Christianorum: Recherches sur le vocabulaire doctrinal de Tertullian* (Paris: Presses Universitaires, 1962), pp. 240–47.

6. On *ousia*: Joseph Ownes, *The Doctrine of Being in the Aristotelian Metaphysics* (Toronto: Pontifical Institute, 1951); Werner Marx, *The Meaning of Aristotle's "Ontology"* (The Hague: Nijhoff, 1954). On *hypostasis*: *ThWNT*, s.v. "Hypostasis," by H. Koester.

7. Basil the Great, *Letters*, ccxiv,4: "As a common noun is related to a proper name, so is the *ousia* related to the *hypostasis*."

8. Ibid.

9. E.g., Gregory of Nazianzus, *Oration XXXI*, in *The Five Theological Orations*, ed. A. J. Mason (1899), 9; Gregory of Nyssa, *Against Eunomius*, in his *Opera*, vols. 1–2, ed. W. Jaeger (Leiden: E. J. Brill, 1960), 1:278–80.

10. Posed by Gregory of Nyssa, *To Abablius: That There Are Not Three Gods*, in his *Opera*, vol. 2/1, ed. F. Mueller (Leiden: E. J. Brill, 1958), p. 117.

11. E.g., Gregory of Nazianzus, *Oration XXXI*, 15–16.

12. E.g., Basil the Great, *Against Eunomius*, ii,22; Gregory of Nazianzus, *Oration XXXIV*, 10.

13. According to Gregory of Nyssa, *To Ablabius*, 135, there are three ontological questions: "Whether [it] is," "What [it] is," "How [it] is." The distinction of the three hypostases is relative to the third question only.

14. E.g., Gregory of Nazianzus, *Oration XXIX*, 11: "If it is a great thing for the Father to have no source, it is no less great for the Son to have the Father as source."

15. Or alternatively, the incarnation and not the Logos as such is the mediation. So Gregory of Nyssa, *Refutation of Eunomius' Second Book*, in his *Opera*, 2:144.

16. E.g., Gregory of Nazianzus, *Oration XXXI*, 8.

17. This is Karl Barth's language.

18. This is now so thoroughly researched that there is no point in passage-listing here; Ekkehard Muehlenberg, *Die Unendlichkeit Gottes bei Gregor von Nyssa* (Göttingen: Vandenhoeck & Ruprecht, 1966). For earlier theological use of "infinite," see Werner Elert, *Der Ausgang der altkirchlichen Christologie* (Berlin: Lutherisches Verlagshaus, 1957), pp. 118–32.

THE ONE AND THE THREE

19. This too is now thoroughly analyzed; Jean Daniélou, *L'Être et des Temps chez Grégoire de Nysse* (Leiden: E. J. Brill, 1970).
20. Augustine, *On the Trinity*, v,10.
21. So much at least is proven by Olivier du Roy, *L'intelligence de la Foi en la Trinité selon Saint Augustine* (Paris: Études Augustiniennes, 1966); his conclusions are summarized on pp. 413–14, 435–56.
22. Thus in Aquinas, *Summa Theologica*, i,2–26, the existence, simplicity, perfection, goodness, infinity, etc., of God are all discussed before there is any reference to his triunity. And note which of these comes first.
23. Augustine, *Commentary on John*, 38,10.
24. Aquinas, *Summa Theologica*, i,43,2. On Augustine himself, see Alfred Schindler, *Wort und Analogie in Augustin's Trinitätslehre* (Tübingen: J. C. B. Mohr [Paul Siebeck], 1965), pp. 160–62; Jean-Louis Maier, *Les Missions Divines selon Saint Augustin* (Freiburg: Presses Universitaires, 1960), pp. 7–98. Lombard, at the foundation of medieval discussion, develops the distinction at great length in *Sentences*, i,14–16.
25. Augustine, *On the Trinity*, iv,28.
26. Michael Schmaus, *Die psychologische Trinitätslehre des heiligen Augustinus* (Münster, 1927), pp. 125–26, lists the texts.
27. As, e.g., again in Athanasius, *Letter to Serapion*, iv, 3.
28. Augustine, *On the Trinity*, i,12–15; iv,30; i,7–10.
29. Schindler, *Wort*, lays all this out; there is a summary on p. 233.
30. Ibid., e.g., p. 180.
31. Augustine, *On the Trinity*, iv,1: "Let the reader strive to use those things which are made, to know him by whom they are made; so we will arrive at that image that man himself is, in that . . . which is called 'mind' or 'soul.'"
32. Du Roy, *L'intelligence*, esp. pp. 420–28, 447–50. In *On the Trinity*, it is the argument of book 8 that makes this pivot.
33. Ibid., pp. 447ff.; there abundant citations.
34. Pervasive in *City of God*.
35. Maier, *Missions*, p. 187.
36. If we line up Augustine's main soul-analogies in columns, so:

being	knowledge	will
lover	loved	love
mind	knowledge	love
memory	knowledge	will

The posited equivalence of the terms in the first column gives the proposition: the being of mind as subject is immediate self-consciousness. Therewith the whole of Western philosophy to come.

37. On the following technical history, *DThC*, s.v. "Trinité" and "Relations Divines," by A. Michel.
38. Council of Florence, "Decree for the Copts," *COD*, 1973, pp. 57–58.
39. Aquinas, *Summa Theologica*, i,27–28; Bonaventura, *Sentences*, xiii,1.
40. Aquinas, *Summa Theologica*, i,27,1.
41. E.g., ibid., i,28,1.
42. In all these formalities, I will follow Aquinas' version; here, ibid., i,28,4.

2 / THE TRIUNE GOD

43. Ibid., i,32,3.
44. Ibid., i,40.
45. Ibid., i,28,2–4; Bonaventura, *Sentences,* xix/ii,1,2. This is the main medieval line; *DThC,* s.v. "Relations Divine," 2147ff. It was denied by a line of thinkers from Gilbert de la Porrée to Joachim of Flores; see ibid., 2145ff.; *DThC,* s.v. "Trinité," 1715–32.
46. E.g., Bonaventura, *Sentences,* xxiii,1,1; 1,2; xxv,1,1–2.
47. Aquinas, *Summa Theologica,* i,29,4.
48. Lombard, *Sentences,* i,xxvi,2–3.
49. E.g., Georg W. F. Hegel, *Phänomenologie des Geistes,* 1952, ed. in *PhB,* pp. 313ff.
50. The critical text is in J. N. D. Kelly, *The Athanasian Creed* (New York and London: Longmans, Green & Co., 1964), pp. 76ff., which see also on the following.
51. Ibid., pp. 53–69, 109–14.
52. Emanuel Hirsch, *Geschichte der neuern evangelischen Theologie* (Gütersloh: Bertelsmann, 1951), 2:114–20, 186–93.
53. John Locke, *The Reasonableness of Christianity as Delivered in the Scriptures,* 1695.
54. *RGG*[3], s.v. "Servet," by H. Bornkamm; and "Sozinianer," by H. R. Guggisberg.
55. Ibid., s.v. "Unitarier," by M. Schmidt.
56. Hirsch, *Geschichte,* 4:1–119.
57. Cyril C. Richardson, *The Doctrine of the Trinity* (Nashville: Abingdon Press, 1958).
58. G. W. H. Lampe, *God as Spirit* (New York and London: Oxford University Press, 1977).
59. C. F. D. Moule, *The Holy Spirit* (Oxford: Mowbray, 1978), pp. 43–51.
60. The classical document of Enlightenment religion is Immanuel Kant's *Religion within the Limits of Reason Alone* (1783). On this, see Hirsch, *Geschichte,* 4:271–76, 320–29.
61. Quotations from Friedrich Schleiermacher's *The Christian Faith* are from the 7th edition (Berlin: Walter De Gruyter, 1960).
62. Hegel, *Phänomenologie* iv,A; vii,C; Georg W. F. Hegel, *Vorlesung über die Philosophie der Religion,* Intro.; pts. 1, 3; *Encyclopädie der philosophischen Wissenschaften,* 1840 ed., vol. 6; Hirsch, *Geschichte,* 5:231–68; Robert W. Jenson, *God after God* (Indianapolis: Bobbs-Merrill, 1969), pp. 33–35.
63. John Macquarrie, *Principles of Christian Theology* (New York: Charles Scribner's Sons, 1966), pp. 94–110, 174–93; Paul Tillich, *Systematic Theology,* 3 vols. (Chicago: University of Chicago Press, 1951–63), 3:283–94.
64. On Barth's trinitarianism, see Eberhard Jüngel, *The Doctrine of the Trinity* (Grand Rapids: Wm. B. Eerdmans, 1976); Colin Gunton, *Becoming and Being* (New York and London: Oxford University Press, 1978), pp. 117–85.
65. For fuller analysis, and on the following, see Jenson, *God after God,* pp. 95–156.
66. Karl Barth, *Church Dogmatics,* vol. 1/1, trans. G. T. Thomson (Edinburgh: T. & T. Clark, 1936), pp. 32, 329.
67. Ibid., pp. 311–52.
68. Ibid., p. 312.

69. Ibid., pp. 321–22.
70. On this and the following, see ibid., pp. 101–8; there also citations.
71. Eberhard Jüngel, "Das Verhältnis von 'ökonomischer' und 'immanenter' Trinität," *ZThK* 72 (1975): 363: "The concept of the divine essence can no longer be thought in abstraction from the event of God's triune existence." This demand, nearly universal in contemporary theology, is variously met, most ambitiously by Karl Barth and "process theology."
72. Karl Rahner, *The Trinity*, trans. J. Donceel (New York: Herder & Herder, 1970), pp. 21–22; Jüngel, "Verhältnis."
73. Bluntly stated, e.g., by Tertullian, *Against Praxeas*, ix,2–3.
74. E.g., Bonaventura, *Sentences*, vii,1,ii.
75. Franz K. Mayr, "Trinitätstheologie und theologische Anthropologie," *ZThK* 68 (1971): 427–77.

5
The Being of God

Specification of the kind of being God is must follow the trinitarian identification. When it does, we will specify God's being as event, person, spirit, and discourse.

THE METAPHYSICAL QUESTIONS

All the creeds begin "I believe in God, the. . . ." It is dogma that God *is*. There can be no such thing as a Christian atheist, except in very special senses of "atheist."[1] But in what sense "is" God? Is God as an idea is? Or as a tree is? Or how? The question needs only to be asked to become desperately puzzling. The question of the being of God is thus dogmatically imposed on the theological enterprise and has in fact been at all times vigorously investigated. With it, we land decisively on the far side of a border we have been crossing through the previous two chapters. We land in the middle of metaphysics.

Metaphysics asks two great questions. First, What sort of being has . . . ? Second, Whatever sorts of being there are, how are they all sorts of "being"? That is, What is being? These are not esoteric questions. We will instantly see that the first is not, if we insert "I" in the blank: What sort of being have I? The sort that vanishes with time? The sort that transcends time? Or some other? That there are several kinds of being is at a common-sense level obvious; there are things, events, ideas, numbers, consciousnesses, and who knows what else. It is against the threat of time that the plurality of being's kinds becomes portentous, as our expansion of the question in the first person assumed. Thus the Greeks' reflection about kinds of being was driven by the fear that all "things" may pass away. Ordinary things clearly are subject to time, they saw; ideas clearly are not; how about consciousnesses?[2] And if the first metaphysical question is lively, so—at one further remove—the second must be.

Theology has asked the first metaphysical question also about God: What kind of being has God? This is clearly a grammatically possible instance of the question, but it is a logically odd one, for the word "God," as we have seen, means "eternal reality." Therefore any actual religion which identifies its God and so specifies how God is eternal thereby answers the metaphysical

2 / THE TRIUNE GOD

question in advance. Adherents of an actual religion have no direct need to ask what sort of being God has. For them, the questioning runs the other way around. And it is of course only the adherents of some religion who use the word "God," in such questions or otherwise. Thus, "What kind of being has God?" can be a lively question only *between* religions, as the effort of one religion to understand itself over against another.

In fact, it is in the long confrontation of biblical and Hellenic religion, to which we have already devoted so much attention, that Christianity has necessarily and rightly asked about the being of God. The special character of these two religions has made the confrontation uniquely creative metaphysically, but it has also given the confrontation a treacherous twist. Since Greece needed criteria by which to recognize "real" deity when its quest should reach it, its religious reflection involved an embryonic form of the metaphysical question about God: What are the marks of true timelessness? Because Christian Hellenists had to deal with the demand that Jesus' Father be displayable as *really* God, and so had to deal with the demand for criteria of true deity, it was all too easy for them to be led to pose the question of God's being in a way that begged the question to their own betrayal: What are the other metaphysical characteristics of God, besides timelessness?[3] It is in this very form that we have already encountered the question in Augustine. Insofar as the fathers thus entangled themselves, Christianity was set in the pattern we have been trying to overcome: that Christianity's interpretation of God, properly become metaphysical in discussion with Greece, assumes an initial definition of deity that aborts the discussion and merely recites Hellenic principles.

Method, therefore, is decisive. A doctrine of any putative God's being is a certain abstraction from the reflectively developed form of that God's identification: if, for example, "God is the one who raised Jesus," we have already referred to him as a person, by speaking of him as "the one who" followed by a transitive verb. Thus theology's habit of treating God's being first and his triunity thereafter is a disaster, for if the trinitarian identification of God is not made the basis of the doctrine of God's being, some other identification will too easily be unwittingly presupposed. The right question, which we will try to answer in the following, is: What sort of being must God have, since he is triune?

The second metaphysical question "What is being?" has no special theological form, since it is itself a theological question. Thus Aristotle himself sometimes defined his "first philosophy" as the investigation of deity[4] and sometimes as the investigation of *ousia*,[5] for if there is God—and the denial that there is, is also a theological position—then to be is either to be God or to be dependent on her/him/it to be whatever else. In a religious reflection, therefore, it is the "either . . . or" of the previous sentence that is the

THE BEING OF GOD

key to the question of being. The question will be answered by finding a determinant that can be switched to display the difference between God and other reality and then stating it indifferently to this switch. For example, the standard such move in scholastic Christian thought is: God is the explanation; creatures are that-which-needs-explanation; and therefore to be is to be intelligible—*ens est veritas*.

Our tradition has a standard answer to the first metaphysical-theological question: God has persistent being. And to the second: God is persistent, all else is temporary, and therefore to be is to have a past. We need not here again attack these answers. The entire story of the last two chapters told of Christianity's struggle with them; our rejection is already stated. It is the task of this chapter to display the faith's alternative. We will make four specifications of God's being: that God is event, person, spirit, and discourse.

Since the great confrontation began with the capture of biblical faith by its rival and interlocutor, faith's alternative has always appeared as breakthrough, as Christian thinkers' wrenching disaccord with what they too suppose is obviously true. The full story of the long breakthrough would be a complete history of theology; we will here proceed more systematically, referring at random to a few great figures of the tradition. In what ways our own contribution is also a wrench with deep assumptions of our thinking, we cannot say; others will have to do that.

We will not explicitly investigate the second metaphysical question. That would carry us too far beyond the limits of dogmatics. But an answer to that question will at once guide and emerge from our consideration of God's being. It will be well to state that answer here, that readers may know it as they read: God anticipates; creatures recoil; therefore to be is to have a future.

GOD AS AN EVENT

The entire exposition of God's triunity demands our first proposition: God is an event. The kind of reality God has is like that of a kiss or an automobile accident. The argument for this proposition is the previous three chapters.

In the dominating tradition, God's being has been specified by the notion of "substance," whether understood more according to Plato or more according to Aristotle: for example, John Gerhard, "God is a spiritual substance: utterly simple, infinite. . . ."[6] A substance[7] is *what is* something, maintaining itself in being by possessing some definite complex of attributes answering to "something"; or substance is the reality possessed by and as those attributes; and the word in use shimmers between the two and derives much of its metaphysical power from the ambiguity. A substance is, for example, what is "legged," "with a seat," and so on, so as to *be* a chair, and persists in being as long as it retains possession of "leggedness" and "seatingness."

2 / THE TRIUNE GOD

Thus the metaphysics of substance realize a cluster of existentially-laden notions: of persistence, independence, and possession. To be substantial is to endure, by having reality as "attributes," that is, independently of other substances. It is plain that no immediately experienced reality quite fulfills this vision. All are subject to action by other realities, and thus from time to time gain and lose attributes: The two-legged animal, Jones, may in fact lose a leg. Thus all give hostages to time, and may endure long but not forever: The bipedal, vertebrate Jones may survive the loss of bipedality but not of vertebration. "God" is then posited as the one *true* substance,[8] all of whose attributes are securely possessed, so that times' chances are nothing to him. God has no "accidental" attributes which come and go, and so gives no hostage to time or other realities. God is the *perfect* substance. All the attributes we attribute to God—"simplicity," "infinity," "omnipotence," or whatever— merely explicate God's perfection.

That Christians cannot approve this metaphysics should have been apparent: "For whoever would save his life will lose it" (Matt. 16:25). We have seen how the greatest trinitarians were driven by the dialectics of the trinitarian identification of God to deny that there is any complex of attributes by possessing which God is, and so had to make the subject of "is God" be not a substance at all but an act, an event. We have also seen how thoroughly most theology subsequently relapsed from that insight.

Rejection of the dominant tradition just at this point is endemic in contemporary theology. We may illustrate almost at random. So the Roman Catholic radical Leslie Dewart: We must "de-hellenize" the faith by overcoming the ideals of immortality, stability, and impassibility.[9] But so also the conservative Lutheran Peter Brunner: "In view of God's . . . self-determination to us, we must . . . abandon all pictures of God that with the help of antiquity's mode of thought read into God a fixed, unmovable, and abstract perfection, so that . . . talk of new judgments, new reactions, new deeds, and new words in God . . . appears to be naive anthropomorphism." [10]

But while the demand is general, the fulfilling thereof is less frequent. One great project of twentieth-century theology was devoted to it, Karl Barth's *Church Dogmatics*:[11] "God's deity consists, into its farthest depths, therein—or at least *also* therein—that it is event." Moreover, God's being is not eventhood, or something of the sort, but a particular event, "that event of God's activity in which we are involved in his revelation," [12] the active relation of the triune persons.[13] Barth's doctrine of God's being as love and freedom is then the explication of this being-as-event.[14] To the extent that theology currently tends to ignore the main parts of Barth's work (and in English-speaking territories has never grasped them), it has cut itself off from the only fully-realized attempt thus far to fulfill modern theology's own constant demand.

One other ponderable and very influential contemporary theological project

THE BEING OF GOD

is often thought to specify God's being as event, but in fact does not. Just so, we must devote some attention to "process theology." We will here not denote by this phrase every theology that has learned from Alfred North Whitehead or Charles Hartshorne (that would be almost all English-language theology) but only those theologies that find in their thought "the right philosophy" and so maintain the key doctrines of their interpretation of God.[15] Thus our own analysis will be of Hartshorne himself.[16]

It is true that "process" metaphysics understands all reality as concretely consisting in events, and so also God as so consisting. What there most concretely is, is in no case a substance (e.g., "this man") but the momentary events of the man's life. The enduring human is a series of the events, established as a series by certain kinds of likeness and relation between the events. "This man" is the fact that a unity can be abstracted from some particular sequential events that is more than their mere aggregate.[17]

Thus no enduring entity is, in this metaphysics, an event, but rather an abstraction from some set of events. But whereas each human, or each galaxy or indeed each other enduring entity than God, is an abstraction from its own specifiable set of events—so that it makes sense to say that this human *is* such-and-such events—the events that God concretely is are simply all the events that are the history of the world.[18] Therefore, if our discourse remains at the concrete level, the word "God" has no import of its own; we cannot with it denote any identifiable reality. Concretely (i.e., as *event*) there is only the world. There is God as *God*, as more than the world, only in God's "*abstract* character," in that sort of his reality that is grasped by our abstractions from concrete reality, that is, there is God, not as event but only as an in itself timelessly given structure of relations between all events. Process metaphysics contribute greatly to our understanding of the general character of reality. But they do not expound the assertion "God is an event," since they do not in fact make the assertion. Process metaphysics ontologically demote the notion of substance. But once we do come to speak of the enduring entities to which the notion was traditionally applied—whether "Jones" or "God"—they also apply it, and then do not really modify it at all.

We wish to say that God is an event. We see two necessary explanations.

First, traditional metaphysics are insofar commonsensically right, that an event must happen *to* some enduring entity. What does not follow and what we have denied is that the enduring entity is therefore ontologically prior to the event. What God happens to is Jesus and the world. God is the event of the world's final transformation by Jesus' love. That "all manner of things will be well" and that it is now true that all manner of things will be well is the reality of God. Thus God is not an event in time, nor even an event extended through all time. God is rather the event by which the world has a future, to *be* a world of time. Were there no eschaton, were the world as

167

2 / THE TRIUNE GOD

a whole not thus open to a future, the world would not occur within that unstoppable oncoming of uncertainty which we call time. God is the temporalizing of the world.

But what if no such thing happened to the world, if it were not temporalized? Then *this* world would be no-thing at all. Instead of the world that actually is, there might be another world, of which the great mythic vision of circling time were true, in which all things always returned to their beginning. And for this world there might be its appropriate God, Brahman-Atman. But that is another matter altogether. As to whether the real God could have been God without any world, we can only answer as before: The analysis of God as free event, as spirit, equally compels us to say that he would have been and forbids us to say how.

Second, God, if real, must be a logical subject. It must be possible to make sentences with a verb and "God" as the subject. And if the God is the one we have been speaking of, it must be possible for the verb to be active, indeed transitive. With events in time, it is precisely the awkwardness of making an event a logical subject, especially of active verbs, that has led to the doctrine of the priority of substances to what happens to them. How can an *occurrence* be said, for example, to "speak by the prophets" or to "sustain the universe?"

A logical subject must be not only identifiable but also reidentifiable, as when one calls the service station and says, "This is the man who brought (note the tense) in the Horizon for tuning." For if I say, "John is angry," and you say, "Who is John?" I cannot merely respond with "the one who is angry." A logical subject must indeed be an enduring entity in some sense or other.[19] It is just this point that has traditionally disqualified events as logical subjects: an event happens, and then where is it?

It is, we suggest, in that God is the *triune* event, that God is not over after God happens. It is the tri-identicality of the divine action that makes it a logical subject. What happens to the world with Christ has plural identifiabilities bracketing time and just so reaching through time. Nor are these disconnected, leaving, as it were, gaps of time between them, for their plurality is the same as their relations with each other. Thus we may say that what happens with Christ has a self-repeating identifiability, which we may plausibly treat as the continuing identifiability of a logical subject, without this being the sort of reidentifiability the tradition has taken for the only sort: the persistence of some one set of identifying characteristics, the temporal extension of a "substance."

We will pick up one last suggestion from Gregory of Nyssa. The divine *ousia*, "deity," is, according to him, sheer temporal infinity.[20] For Gregory, the word no longer stands for something that is God; it denotes sheerly the infinity of the act that is God. It is this *ousia* that the three hypostases derive from and with each other, that is, the acts of the Father or the Son or the Spirit, within their joint act that is God, are indeed *within* that act, are *divine* acts, in that they are subject to no temporal limits. The distinction and relation of three identities are a structure of pure triumphant possibility-as-such. They are the structure of the temporally plural ways in which the action that is God overcomes all conditions. The Cappadocians' "one *ousia*" means that whether the conditions that might be imposed on what happens with Christ are the burdens of the past (imposed on the Father, were only he God) or the risks of the future (imposed on the Spirit, were only he God) or the statistics of the present (imposed on the Son, were only he God), they are no hindrance to the action that in fact is God, which just in this utter unhinderedness can be only *one* action.

GOD AS PERSON

The concept of personhood as a particular kind of being seems to be modern and, moreover, a result of Christian theology's influence on Western life and reflection.[20] But once the concept is there, it is obvious that all the Bible's talk about God in fact speaks of him as what we now call personal.[21] Indeed, most practiced religion treats deity as personal, since it addresses deity in hope of response. Yet the personhood of God is also regularly attacked religiously. Thus all actual Vedic religion assumes the personhood of deity, and nearly all sophisticated Vedic reflection denies it.[22] In the history of Christian theology, discomfort with the notion of God's personhood or, prior to the emergence of the notion, with those biblical descriptions of God which we now comprise therein, has greatly depended on the Hellenic interpretation of deity. In that this deity is the timeless ground of temporal reality and can therefore be simultaneously and successively manifested by many different persons, it is natural for Hellenic interpretation to conceive deity itself as impersonal.

There is a problem here that cannot be obviated merely by decrying Hellenic religion. As soon as the confrontation with Hellenism awakens metaphysical reflection in the church, whether in antiquity or now, it becomes clear that it will not do to call God "a person," without qualification. For "a" person is individualized by difference from other persons, and in the case of God who would they be? But if God is not "a person," can it be meaningful to call him "personal"? The problem is not esoteric. Every believer faces it, and it is safe to say that most merely take their choice and either think vaguely of God as rather like electricity or picture God entirely mythically as a mighty but invisible woman or man.

The tendency of our analysis is given in advance. In view of the clear language of the Bible we will maintain God's personhood until driven from it. We have already entered Christianity's deep stream of insight into God's

2 / THE TRIUNE GOD

personhood, as represented by Augustine and Hegel, and will not leave it willingly.

Johann Gottlieb Fichte may pose the problem. He imprinted the turn of the eighteenth and nineteenth centuries in Germany with the "atheism controversy" occasioned by his views.[23] A conscious being, said Fichte, with all the thought of his time, and rightly, establishes its individual being by *self-consciousness*. But it is not possible for there to be an object of consciousness that has no boundary distinguishing it from the rest of reality. Therefore the self of self-consciousness must be a bounded, finite self; and therefore, said Fichte, God cannot be a conscious being, since God is infinite and so cannot know himself as finite. And therefore again, God cannot be personal, since "unconscious personhood" is a contradiction.

There are two possible replies to Fichte's sort of worry. One is argument that God can be personal without being *a* person. The other is argument that there can be an infinite person, meeting Fichte head-on. We will pursue the latter.

The object as which God knows himself is Jesus. Thus God's self-consciousness is indeed consciousness of a bounded, particular individual, so that this requirement of personhood is fulfilled. But the decisive question is just *how* the reality of this individual is bounded. The reality of each created person is defined by the event sequence, the plot, of his life, as this sequence is made into a determinate whole, into indeed a plot, by his death. So with Jesus. He is defined by his particular life and particular death as "love," as a life for all other lives. He is the crucified one, whose life was lived in the promise he brought his fellows and who finally gave up his self wholly to that promise. That he is risen does not mean that this death is canceled so that this life is again undefined. It means that *this one*, this defined one, is future and present reality and not merely past, so that he can be the objective self of the living God. But if God's self-consciousness is consciousness of *this* present, bounded individual, God is conscious of his self as the person for all persons, as a particular defined love, and so is not shut in by this bounded self-consciousness, but freed.[24]

It all depends on what sort of infinity, what sort of freedom from limitation, we have in mind when we attribute infinity to God. If we think of simple absence of definition, an infinite being cannot indeed be self-conscious. But if we think of God's infinity as trinitarianism (e.g., Gregory of Nyssa) should teach us to think of it, as freedom to transcend each new definition while never lacking one, or as the Hebrew Scriptures should teach us to think of it, as unconquerable faithfulness, then that the bounded individual Jesus is God's object-self does not hinder God's infinity, it constitutes it.

The "a person" that God is, is the human person Jesus, the Son. The triune event that God is, is by its triunity a person, this one. We need not, therefore,

170

think of the other identities, of the Father or the Spirit, as, with respect to their distinction from one another, individual personal beings in the modern sense. If the Father and the Son were singular persons, they would be metaphysical somethings in the very style of the "Logos *asarkos*" we have just eliminated, about whom we might well have Fichte's qualms. Instead, we will press the scholastic interpretation of the triune identities as "subsisting relations." We will say, All there is to being God the Father is being addressed as "Father" by the Son, Jesus; all there is to being God the Spirit is being the spirit of this exchange.

In that Jesus cries "Father if it be possible . . . ," and in that he will give up his rule at the last, and in that he is not disappointed in these relations, there is the Father. In that Jesus gives his spirit, and in that he will gather all to himself in that spirit, and in that this movement is final, there is the Spirit. This does not mean that the Father and the Spirit are created by Jesus. The relations necessarily posit some individual terms, but this does not mean they are secondary to them. And finally, in that all this is true, Jesus *is* the Son (not: *there is* the Son!). About the Father and the Spirit, Fichte and those who have argued as he did were right. The sort of being possessed by them, and so by the triune God each of them is, *relatively to* each of them, is not that of a something, personal or otherwise. But that is not the entire account. God is not an individual person. But there *is* an individual person who is God. And therefore the Augustinian-Hegelian dialectics of consciousness, which define the very notion of personhood in the modern sense, can indeed in their trinitarian application to God establish the personhood of God.

We now can deal with a difficulty that may bother readers: Can it make any sense to speak of an event as a person, even in the sense just described? We respond: *Only* an event can be a person.

The life of any of us is an event, but it is also made up of many events. To grasp my life as an event, I must therefore grasp the dramatic connection, the faithfulness, of each of its constituent events to all the others. But I, as a creature, do not have this faithfulness in myself. The days of my life do not cohere in anything visible in them but only in the promises of God. And I, as a fallen creature, do not hearken to Gods' promises. My days therefore threaten to fall apart, to become an incoherent sequence that could just as well have members other than those it does, to become "absurd." Yet so long as God does not punish my unbelief by indeed loosing my identity into the flux of events, I cannot avoid recognizing some events as *my* deeds and sufferings and others as not. Thus I am driven either to faith in God or to suppose a mysterious something other than my life and its intrinsic coherence, "whose" life my life is, "whose" deeds and sufferings the events of my life are. And so arises the myth of the "person" I am as something other than the event that I am.

2 / THE TRIUNE GOD

In our fallenness, we may in fact be unable to deal with ourselves without the myth just described. But there is no reason to apply it to God. God is neither creature nor fallen. God is speaker and hearer of the Word by which he lives. And he believes his Word. With God, "person" and "event" are therefore only alternative insights into one reality.

Now we can also deal with the difficulty raised by the Bible's drastically personal language about God: that God changes his mind, reacts to earthly events, and the like.[25] Or rather, we can see that there is no difficulty.

Over against and in the time established and embraced by the occurrence of God, God is an enduring entity by virtue of his triunity. And this enduring entity's objective self, the criterion of its self-identity, is Jesus of Nazareth, in his openness to his fellows. Therefore, that over against time God listens and considers and truly responds is but faithfulness to himself. God's action and reaction over against us through time, in that it is faithful to his self that is Jesus and so is an indefatigable wooing and rescuing, does not compromise God's eternal self-identity, it constitutes it.

That God answers prayer, that God makes threats and "repents" of them when the evil is past, that God makes promises and fulfills them by new and unexpected promises—all this is not "anthropomorphic" or "symbolic" statement. It is the strictest descriptive propositional truth. It is when *we* are said to initiate something new, to be surprising and faithful at once, that language must be stretched a bit. God has no problem here at all. "From eternity the Father sees us in the Son . . . , as determined for fellowship with him. . . . In that God in the totality of his being and from eternity thus enters the covenant of relation he has willed, saving history as real history is possible also for God."[26]

It is in the determinations of God's being as event and person that the main problems arise. "God is spirit" and "God is discourse," to which we now turn, can therefore be more briefly discussed. Nevertheless, they are the religiously decisive determinants.

GOD AS SPIRIT

Western understanding of personhood as a kind of being has classically found two great essential movements of and within personal being: mind and will. Thus Thomas Aquinas, following Aristotle, lists five powers of "the soul," but gives only two theological significance: the "intellectual" and the "appetitive."[27] Schleiermacher based the necessity of religion on the necessity for unity in our life of "thinking" and "acting."[28] Or again, all Kant's thought can be read as an analysis of personhood; his great work was in three volumes, one on knowing, one on willing, and a third on how they work together.[29]

As the examples of Schleiermacher and Kant suggest, the great analytical problem about personhood has been how mind and will are joined. Is the person a mind steering appetites, as Socrates and all his followers have taught (e.g., Plato, *Phaedrus*)? Or is the person a will, using reasoning to think through how to get his way, as Arthur Schopenhauer taught most bluntly?[30] Or are they joined in some other way? We are here not concerned with this problem as a problem about human persons.[31] But in that we see God as person, we see also God as mind and will. Augustinian-Hegelian trinitarianism defines God as consciousness established in knowledge of self—the Son, and love of self—the Spirit. And so the problem is posed also about God.

The great scholastics argued the problem in a particularly sophisticated form. Since God is Creator, what God knows and what God wills are the same. And since God is good, what God wills is the good. So the question: Does God know what is good, and therefore will it; or is the good good because God wills it? Thomas Aquinas was the great proponent of the first option, Duns Scotus and the later nominalists of the second.[32]

The matter at issue is vital for faith, despite its esoteric appearance. We may think of an absolute event and person, and yet not think of *God*—or anyway of the God of the Bible. The God whose primary reality is unmovedly to know us and all things, as what we are, in order then perhaps to make plans for us accordingly, is simply not the one of whom the Bible speaks. The God of the Bible is a storm, blowing us like leaves from what we are to what we will be and only knowing us in this motion. The great Mind's Eye is doubtless a noble conception and may even subsist, but he is much too harmless to be God by an Ezekiel's lights. Yet neither is the Bible's God a sheerly arbitrary force. We must somehow learn to think God as *faithful* will.

One work, from all the history of theology, can be the reality test. Martin Luther's *On the Bondage of the Will*[33] is intemperate, prolix, and sometimes misguided; it is also the book after the Bible that is most inescapably about God. God is the one who "works life, death, and all in all" (*Bondage*, p. 685), who indeed cannot not work all in all (ibid., pp. 709, 712). We know this about God not because of philosophical speculation but because of the gospel. Only in confessing that God is responsible for all that happens are we so humbled before him as to need the gospel. And only in that God rules absolutely can he make unconditional promises, that is, can the gospel be true (ibid., pp. 614, 619, 632). But just so God is hidden, and exactly in his reality as God of the gospel, for the "all" that he works is at best morally ambiguous by the gospel's own lights: "This is . . . faith, to believe that he is merciful who saves so few and condemns so many . . . , so that he seems . . . to delight in the tortures of the wretched and to be more worthy of hate than of love" (ibid., p. 633). Our only hope is to flee from God in this undefined power and naked majesty, to God as he has defined himself in Christ, as redeeming love (ibid., pp. 684–85). Yet this self-definition is not a *mitiga-*

2 / THE TRIUNE GOD

tion of God's unchecked will and majesty, nor therefore our flight to it a flight to a mitigated God, as nearly all other theology understands it. For God's self-definition as love occurs as the crucifixion, as yet another hiding, yet deeper than the first in the world's ambiguity (ibid., pp. 689–90), and so as the final event of that powerful hiddenness which, we have just seen, *is* God's majesty. With this touchstone, we may not define God either as mere mind or mere will. We must make will the more central to our reflection, but we must posit a will that just *is* also mind. That is, we will think of God as spirit.

Were God the Father God by himself (which is contrary not merely to fact but to logic), there would indeed obtain about him precisely the scholastics' problem: Does he choose what he chooses because he knows what is good, or is what is good good because it is what he chooses? And the problem would be insoluble, given in the very conception of such a "naked majesty."

As it is, God is God the Father and God the Son, and just so God the Spirit. Therefore if we first think of the Father as *mind*, so that he has his self-identity in self-knowing, then the self as which he knows himself is Jesus, and so is a particular love and particular hope, a particular good thing *willed* by the Creator, that is, by God himself. Or if we first think of the Father as *will*, so that he has his self-identity in self-choice, then the self he chooses for himself is Jesus, who as a created person is always determined in his choices by others, that is, by his *knowledge* of them, including of the Father. Thus as God in fact is, the abstract and finally impotent dialectics of mind versus will cannot describe him. His reality is complex and alive; mind and will are given in him only in original structured unity.

That is, God is freedom. God is neither mind using will nor will using mind; God is creativity that is both. God is transforming and faithful liveliness. God is *spirit*.

We must hasten to prevent misunderstanding. The word "spirit" is often now used in a way that has little to do with its use in Scripture or here. That God is spirit does *not* mean that God is disembodied, a "pure spirit" in the vulgar sense. On the contrary, he has a body,[34] and did he not, would in fact not be spirit. That God has a body means, first, that[35] there is an *object* of our intention that is he, and that this same reality is the object of God's own intention of himself. And second, that there is an enduring entity by which God can be identified and by which he identifies himself. This enduring object that is God's body is the Jesus that walked in Palestine and was raised into present eternal life. Had God no body, he could not be spirit, for we have just seen how the freedom and complex temporal urgency of God is given in his having Jesus as his objective self.

The common religious conception of "pure spirit," meaning disembodied personhood, has no application to the triune God, even though nearly the whole theological tradition has tried to apply it, led by confusion between

THE BEING OF GOD

the biblical opposition of "spirit"/"flesh" and the Hellenic opposition of "mind"/"body," and by too hasty identification of "body" with "mass in space." The suppositious mere "God the Father" of three paragraphs back would be such an entity, and just so neither free nor temporally potent. A "pure" spirit would be either an impotent mind or an aimless will. To our salvation, the real God is neither. He is the living union of the Father and the Son. He has a body and therefore can be free creative spirit, the power of the last future.

GOD AS DISCOURSE

"In the beginning was the Word, and the Word was with God, and the Word was God" (John 1:1). It was the first deliberate dogma of Christianity, by which the faith forever defined its difference from other religions, that with Christianity's God there is *no* "silence of eternity," that we do *not* lose our voice and ears as we approach him, that he not only has a word for us—which is eccentric enough in the world of religion—but *is* his word for us: The Word is "of one being with the Father."

God is event, person, and spirit. The three propositions achieve their synthesis, and therewith their final clarity, in the proposition that God is word. Or perhaps we should say that Christianity first knew that God is word and has been engaged in working out the other three determinants.

It is religiously offensive to say that God is word. To be sure, all religions acknowledge that God must initially reveal itself/himself/herself to us if we are to know her/him/it, for if God were simply there for our inspection, she/he/it would not be God. A communication of some sort, a "word" in some kind of sign system, must begin the relation. But then, by normal religious apprehension, we must move on to a deeper or higher grasp of God. And as we move toward God we move beyond the initial communication, for God as such is silence. The God of normal religion is not personally present in address to us; God addresses us only to call us into the distance where God truly dwells.[36]

The word is the medium of life in time. It is because the world is not merely present to us, but present as *interpreted* in signs and symbols of indefinitely many sorts, that time can be the horizon of our life. For the world experienced in and by interpretation is just so the world that could be experienced as interpreted otherwise than it is; and thus *potentiality* is present in our world. Since the word is the medium of life in time, normal gods eschew the word except as a temporary measure.

The word is the medium of our life's commonality. It is in speech about the world, in whatever kinds of signs, that we inhabit a world that is not my world only or yours only but precisely *ours*, so that we can come together

2 / THE TRIUNE GOD

in it. Since the word is the medium of mutual determination, normal gods are in themselves silent.

That the Bible's God is different in this respect became so soon apparent that there is on this point no continuing history of theological alienation such as we have traced on other points. The temptation has worked mostly in the mystical tradition, and in the tradition of piety, in hymnody and prayer. Thus an anonymous English mystic counseled: "Forsake as well good thoughts as evil thoughts, and pray not with thy mouth."[37] And we have a considerable number of vehemently anti-Christian poems that by virtue of their pious sound and associated sentimental tunes are favorites of the congregations. We cite only the most brazen: the communion between Jesus and the Father is "the silence of eternity, interpreted by love," to share in which we are exhorted to "let sense be dumb, let flesh retire."[52]

Not only does the *triune* God speak to initiate relation to us, but the initiated relation eternally remains speech, remains communication. This God's eternity is his unconquerable futurity, and it is in the word that the future is present. This God *is* fellowship with us, and it is in the word that we are there for one another. The Christian vision of the end is not of a great silence but of a great liturgy, of preaching and our eternal response of praise and acclamation (Rev. 4—5).

Nor is the triune God speech only over against *us*. The second identity is "the Word," is God's address to us. The third identity is the Spirit of this address, the Word's power to open us to the last future. It is precisely the relation between these three in which God lives. God *is* each of the identities, so he *is* the Word. And by the triune reality of whatever God is, the word that God is is an exchange, not a lecture. Thus the final characterization of God's reality must be: God is a conversation. Or choosing a more dignified word: God is discourse.

The conversation that is God is not a conversation in heaven—at least, if heaven is some other *place* than earth. The conversation that is God is the proclamation of the law and the gospel. Where human discourse occurs which opens human life to the last future, there is the occurrence of God. It is precisely as the exalted Lord, as what trinitarian theology has come to call the second hypostasis of God, that Matthew quotes Jesus: "Where two or three are gathered in my name, there am I in the midst of them" (Matt. 18:20). And it is as God-*present* that the second identity *is* God. God is indeed present to every quark or every galaxy, but he is present to all things at and from the verbal event of the law and the gospel.

Thus the body of God, the object that is God and by virtue of which he indeed has a location, is "the body of Christ," the body-side of the law-and-gospel event. Every communication event has a body-side, an object-reality, as which those who address each other are there for each other.[58] If the

THE BEING OF GOD

preaching of the gospel is indeed the occurrence of God's word, then the body-side of the preaching of the gospel—the sights and sounds, the bread, the cup, the bath, the gestures of fellow believers—is the body-side of God's presence. Christ, we said earlier, is the body of God. It is into the embodiment of the gospel, that is, into the objective life of the church, that Christ is bodily risen. It is the embodiment of the gospel that is the "body of Christ" and so the body of God.

This matter has some dogmatic significance. We confess in the Lord's Prayer that God the Father is in "heaven," and in the three-article creeds that Christ is risen as a body and is at the Father's "right hand" there. But where is that?

The location of heaven, or rather the nature of heaven as a location for God, became confessionally divisive between Calvinists and Lutherans. Calvinists have maintained that heaven is a metaphysical *part* of creation, created by God as his own place within creation, so that it makes sense to speak of going and coming between heaven and the rest of creation, and of Christ's risen body being located there and therefore not located elsewhere in creation, for example, in the assemblies for the Supper. This tradition is still maintained by Karl Barth. Lutherans have, with some waverings, followed Luther's own view: that God has no *particular* space within creation, and that just so his place in creation, that is, his object-presence for us, is wherever the gospel sounds, to let us apprehend him there. Heaven is the "space" of the Word and the sacraments, the space of the Supper and baptism and however many other such events there are.[40] Readers will perceive this work's adherence to the Lutheran position, indeed, the determining force of that decision for the whole understanding of God. At the same time, we will hardly now wish to judge any continuing division on the matter itself as legitimately church-divisive.

NOTES

1. As in Altizer's use; Thomas J. J. Altizer, *The Gospel of Christian Atheism* (Philadelphia: Westminster Press, 1966).
2. E.g., Plato, *Phaedo*.
3. Wolfhart Pannenberg, "Die Aufnahme des philosophischen Gottesbegriffs als dogmatisches Problem der frühchristlichen Theologie," *ZThK* 70 (1959): 1–45.
4. E.g., Aristotle, *Metaphysics*, 1028a,13–15.
5. E.g., ibid., 1026a,15–19.
6. John Gerhard, *Loci communes theologici*, ii,93. Aquinas, *Summa Theologica*, i,3,3. Since Boethius, *essentia* was the standard theological equivalent for *ousia*, instead of *substantia*, which is more natural and used elsewhere. To compound confusion, translating *essentia*, where it stands for *ousia*, into English, we are compelled to revert to the anglicization of *substantia*.

2 / THE TRIUNE GOD

7. See, e.g., Werner Marx, *The Meaning of Aristotle's "Ontology"* (The Hague: Nijhoff, 1954).
8. In Aristotle, see *Metaphysics*, bk. lambda.
9. Leslie Dewart, *The Future of Belief* (New York: Herder & Herder, 1966), pp. 134-43.
10. Peter Brunner, "Die Freiheit des Menschen in Gottes Heilsgeschichte," in *Pro Ecclesia*, vol. 1 (Berlin: Lutherisches Verlagshaus, 1962), p. 110.
11. Karl Barth, *Kirchliche Dogmatik* (Zürich: Zollikon, 1932-69), 2/1:288-305.
12. Ibid., p. 284.
13. Ibid., p. 300.
14. Ibid., pp. 306-61. On this, see Colin Gunton, *Becoming and Being* (New York and London: Oxford University Press, 1978), pp. 17-214; Robert W. Jenson, *God after God* (Indianapolis: Bobbs-Merrill, 1969).
15. E.g., John Cobb, *A Christian Natural Theology* (Philadelphia: Westminster Press; London: Lutterworth Press, 1965); Ralph E. James, *The Concrete God* (Indianapolis: Bobbs-Merrill, 1967); Schubert Ogden, *The Reality of God* (New York: Harper & Row, 1966).
16. I will be heavily dependent on Gunton, *Becoming and Being*, pp. 11-114.
17. E.g., Charles Hartshorne, *The Logic of Perfection* (LaSalle, Ill.: Open Court Publishing Co., 1962), pp. 216ff.
18. On this paragraph, see, e.g., Charles Hartshorne, *A Natural Theology for Our Time* (LaSalle, Ill.: Open Court Publishing Co., 1967), pp. 6-28; Charles Hartshorne, *The Divine Relativity: A Social Conception of God* (New Haven: Yale University Press, 1948), pp. 30-47, 67-75, 88-94.
19. P. F. Strawson, *Individuals: An Essay in Descriptive Metaphysics* (Garden City, N.Y.: Doubleday & Co.; London: Methuen, 1959).
20. *RGG*[3], s.v. "Person," by Wolfhart Pannenberg.
21. *RGG*[3], s.v. "Gott," by E. Würthwein.
22. Sten Konow, "Die Inder," in *Lehrbuch der Religionsgeschichte*, ed. Chantepie de la Saussaye (Tübingen: J. C. B. Mohr [Paul Siebeck], 1925), 2:1-88; Radakrishnan, *Indian Philosophy* (New York: Macmillan Co., 1923-27), 1:63-267; and vol. 2.
23. On the following, Emanuel Hirsch, *Geschichte der neuern evangelischen Theologie* (Gütersloh: Bertelsmann, 1949-54), 4:345-75. Also *RGG*[3], s.v. "Person," 232.
24. It is worth noting that this is the same dialectic by which Paul Tillich argued Jesus' qualification to be "final revelation": *Systematic Theology*, 3 vols. (Chicago: University of Chicago Press, 1951-63), 2:135-37.
25. For a change of reference, Johannes Pedersen, *Israel*, trans. A. J. Fausboll (London: Oxford University Press, 1926-40), 2:611-69.
26. Brunner, "Freiheit," pp. 109-10. This article is the best single investigation of the matter here at issue.
27. Aquinas, *Summa Theologica*, i,78,introd.
28. Friedrich Schleiermacher, *Speeches on Religion to Its Cultured Despisers*, ii.
29. *Critique of Pure Reason* (1781), *Critique of Practical Reason* (1788), *Critique of Judgment* (1790).
30. Arthur Schopenhauer, *The World as Will and Idea*, ii,19.
31. The first Protestant systematic theologian, Philip Melanchthon, built his entire

systematics around the disconnection of mind and will in the fallen creature; *Loci communes* (1521), (T. Koldeed, 1890), pp. 68ff.

32. Neatly summarized in RGG³, s.v. "Voluntarismus," by H. Blankhertz.

33. Martin Luther, *On the Bondage of the Will* (1525), hereafter cited in the text by pagination of *WA* 18. See Gerhard Forde, "Bound to Be Free: Luther on the Gospel and Human Freedom," *Bulletin of the Lutheran Theological Seminary, Gettysburg* 57 (Winter 1977): 3–16; Eberhard Jüngel, "Quae supra nos, nihil ad nos," *EvTh* 32 (1972): 197–240.

34. For more extensive analysis, especially on soteriological import, see Robert W. Jenson, *Visible Words* (Philadelphia: Fortress Press, 1978), pp. 120–39.

35. Ibid., pp. 34ff.

36. On this paragraph, see, e.g., G. van der Leeuw, *Religion in Essence and Manifestation*, trans. J. E. Turner (London: George Allen & Unwin, 1938), p. 21.

37. Cited from Evelyn Underhill, *Mysticism* (1910: New York: Noonday, 1955), p. 320.

38. For further analysis, see Jenson, *Visible Words*.

39. Read Martin Luther's *Confession Concerning Christ's Supper* (1528), *LW* 37:151–372.

40. Ibid. One great Lutheran thinker, Johannes Brenz, developed a profound speculative understanding of space from this position of Luther; e.g., *Von der Mayestet unsers lieben Herrn und einigen Heilands Jesu Christi* (1562).

6
The Attributes of God

Since God is, we can make factual statements about God. The method of obtaining such statements is decisive for their truth. True attributions to God are then forms of the gospel.

THE NECESSITY OF THE DOCTRINE

If there is God, it must be possible to form subject-attribute sentences (such as "God is loving" or "God is a nuisance") that are and can be judged to be true or false. The traditional doctrine of God's attributes is the attempt to make a list of the important true attributes and to work out the method of their derivation. Given the initial meaning of the word "God," and given a previous specification of God's sort of being (so that we are not concerned, e.g., with whether God is liquid), the words in question as predicates will be those that name some value.

The attempt now easily assumes a comic air. There was no problem so long as certain assumptions of classical philosophy could be made: that there just are a definite number of desirable attributes, each in any given natural language with its appropriate word. But we now tend to think of language as a creative activity, and so of the good as a pie that can be divided by words indefinitely many ways. Thus the possible number of value words is infinite. On these assumptions, it is absurd to ask What are God's (six? seven? or one hundred?) perfections? Shall we put "gentle" on the list? Or hold the slot for "humorous"?

What can be retained from the traditional doctrine is the attempt to state the method of deriving predicates for use with "God" and the discussion of a sampling of cases. But so much must be retained, for if we cannot say, for example, "God is loving" and know that we speak truth, God is not real. It is dogma in the three-article creeds that God is in fact Father, Almighty, Creator, Lord, Judge, and Giver of life, and so also that such statements can be factual. It will probably also be desirable to take our cases mostly from the traditional lists since these have shaped the language of the church.

2 / THE TRIUNE GOD

THE METHOD OF DERIVATION

Our first concern is method. Unfortunately we have a quarrel also with the traditional method of derivation. It is an immediate consequence of everything in the previous chapters, that Martin Luther was correct when in 1518 he presented the thesis "The true theologian is not the one who comes to see the invisible things of God by thinking about what is created; the true theologian is the one who thinks about the visible and hinder parts of God, having seen them in sufferings and the cross."[1] The key to the thesis is the chiasmus on "see" and "think about," which readers should note before proceeding.

Luther's first clause exactly captures the standard method,[2] at least since Augustine. God, in his timeless glory, is "invisible." Our initial object is therefore the created, "visible," world. About this world, thought reveals that it contains within itself no sufficient reason for its own existence or character. Unless the world is reasonless—an unthinkable possibility until recently, and perhaps in fact not capable of consistent assertion—there must be a reason of the world that is not part of the world.

This reason can be reached only by the method of negative analogy. To the world's reason can be attributed those characters which it must have to *be* the world's reason. But all our words for causation and purpose are modeled on causes and outcomes that belong to the created world. We can fit them to the world's reason only by striking their reference to the world: so, for example, "God is a loving Father—only not as created fathers love, unreliably . . . [etc.]." And we will perform this operation only on such of our words as, in their worldly use, name what is good in creation, for it is the reason, the value, of the world for which we are reaching. The end of this path cannot be thought in the normal sense; the logic of our words has been disrupted on the way by the striking of temporal reference. The end is rather a vision, a seeing with the mind's eye[3] "of the invisible things of God." It should also be noted that there is no fundamental difference of method here between "natural" and "revealed" knowledge. The revelation in Christ simply adds special items to the total of the effects in the world from which God's character as its reason in intuited.

Luther's second clause proposes a very different method. The starting point is not our reflection on the world but particular events *in* the world, summed up as "the cross." These are directly presented to our experience, our "seeing." Nor do these exemplify the perfections of the world; they are rather "sufferings." The vision of God is then not the end of our cognitive path; it is the same act as this—cognitively normal—experience of the cross, and so the beginning. The events summarized "cross" simply *are* God insofar as God becomes our object, what we can see. This does not mean that there

THE ATTRIBUTES OF GOD

is no mystery in our experience of God, but the mystery is not the mystic shimmer of distance; it is that God presents himself in sufferings. What we see as God is correspondingly God's "visible" and inglorious reality, God's participation in sin and death and ignominy. And the work of the theologian is now to think hard about all this, in itself a normal rational exercise rather than a seeing at great distance. Just so, the world by no means drops out as an object of theological reflection. On the contrary, it is in at the beginning *and* at the end.

One step must be added to Luther's description, a step he either assumed or perhaps inadequately noted. That on the cross we see God is not our arbitrary choice. It is the crucified one's resurrection, which presents him and his sufferings as God-for-us, in which alone, indeed, he *is* God-for-us.[4] Whether we thereby quite follow Luther or not, we must say that the worldly object as which we have God for our object is the historic Jesus *as* the body of the risen Lord.

With the foregoing demands in mind, we propose a method of attribution to God, which can be summarized: Every true proposition of the form, "God is . . ." is a *slogan* either for the gospel's pivotal claim or for some true version of actual gospel proclamation. In this summary, "the gospel's pivotal claim" denotes one pole of all actual gospel proclamation: the assertion that "Jesus is risen," where "Jesus" can at need be backed up by such descriptions as "the one who preached the kingdom's imminence and was crucified for it." The other pole is the hopes and fears by which those of a time and place have a future, for example, hope for freedom or heaven or food. "Actual gospel proclamation" occurs as the mutual interpretation of these poles.

We should give an example of this interpretation. Large areas of the world are now swept by the hope of "liberation," of escape from conditions of institutionalized economic and political exploitation. The claim of Jesus' resurrection can interpret this hope and interpret itself by it. In the one direction, the interpretation gives an eschatological vision: Jesus, whose life and death defined him as life for others, lives in spite of the death such selflessness had to bring, so that there is now one human who need not exploit others, and so that his relation to others must finally shape all their lives. Therefore, we *will* be liberated. In the other direction, the interpretation gives ethics: Our hope for liberation is a realistic hope in that it is finally hope for Jesus' triumph; and therefore also we need not become ourselves exploiters in order to pursue it. "God liberates" is a slogan for this entire gospel interpretation.[5]

There are, we have proposed, two classes of divine attributes: slogans for the gospel's claim merely as such, and slogans for actual versions of gospel proclamation. In this dualism, we follow the tradition, in which the habit of bipartite classification is universal and deeply rooted. Thus John Gerhard lists nine possible classification systems, all bipartite (*Loci communes*

183

2 / THE TRIUNE GOD

theologici, ii,105). This dualistic propensity is doubtless finally rooted in the dualism of God and creature and the correlated dualism (following Luther's scheme) of God in his naked majesty and God in his defined majesty.

But while we may approve the deep reason for bipartite classification, we cannot approve the particular bipartite classification that in fact dominates the tradition. Continuing with Gerhard: "Some [attributes] are predicated of God *absolutely*, i.e., without any relation to creatures, as when God is called 'eternal' or 'immense'; and some are predicated *relatively*, as when God is called 'creator,' 'being,' or 'judge' " (ibid.). This division betrays all too clearly the definition of God himself by abstraction from his relations, against which we have been struggling. We therefore have proposed a different classification, to serve the legitimate part of the same purpose.

Some true subject-attribute sentences about God are slogans simply for "Someone (Jesus) is *risen*." They stipulate, over against some religious concern, what is involved in saying that he is "risen." Thus, for example, over against the question whether Jesus, this figure of historic antiquity, can mean anything to us in our so very different world, we may reply that since he is risen, his life is not in fact distant in time but brackets our time, defining all our possibilities. As a slogan: "God [always the *triune* God, of whom Jesus is the second identity] is eternal."

Other true subject-attribute sentences about God are slogans for actual proclamations of the gospel, for what is said when "Jesus is risen" and some community's or individual's penultimate hopes and fears so interpret one another as to give eschatological vision and founded ethics. We have already given an example, and will give others later. Such slogans are intrinsically historic in their validity. For the hopes and fears of humankind are not constant; their change and succession are indeed the very substance of history. Thus that because Jesus lives we will yet be free of exploitation would not have been a gospel-proclamation to, say, Paul's Corinth, and "God liberates" therefore would not have been a meaningful predication to God. Herein these attributes differ from those of the first class, which always have point.

The true God occurs as Jesus' resurrection. With some oversimplification, we may say that the two classes of God's attributes are those posited in saying that anyone is risen, and those posited in saying that it is Jesus who is risen. Had Nero risen instead of Christ, there would still be an eternal something, but it would be an eternal malignity. That there is instead an eternal benignity is what is said by attributions of the second class. And it is the actual content of Jesus' human life that interprets penultimate hopes and fears to give such content to eschatological vision. That Jesus' humanity and ours interpret each other at all depends on his resurrection, but the matter of the interpretation depends on the specificity of his humanity.

THE ATTRIBUTES OF GOD

"JESUS IS RISEN": ATTRIBUTES FOR THE PREDICATE

The first class of attributes, then, are those that explicate the notion of resurrection, bearing always in mind that this notion is itself derived not from general considerations but from the apostles' attempts to describe a particular event that happened to them and Jesus the Nazarene after his death. That stipulated, we may say that the first class of attributes are those which explicate the notion of deity as such, that deity which Father, Son, and Spirit have together in that they derive it from each other. We already have our primary explication of this deity, and so our first attribute: *temporal infinity*.

God is *infinite*. That is, God can be limited by no temporal conditions. Rules of the form "If X happens/has happened, Y must/cannot therefore happen" do not apply to God. God can accept and approve not only the godly but also the ungodly. He can use in his final fulfillment not only the virtues and successes of history, but also its sins and disasters. God can give life not merely to the not-yet born but also to the already dead. He is not predictable by the probabilities. God transcends what has happened and now is, creating what cannot but must yet be. Allowing for the skew introduced by the majority tradition's presumption of divine timelessness, we thus state the legitimate content of a traditionally listed attribute of the "absolute" class, *eternity*.[6]

Since this infinity occurs as the resurrection of Jesus, God's creative transcending is not arbitrary. It has a character: faithfulness to the historical Jesus. A second attribute: God is *faithful*. With this, we replace a second traditional "absolute" attribute, changelessness,[7] and we replace it with a fundamental apprehension of the Hebrew Scriptures. God's continuity as an enduring entity is that of a successful personal life, the very truth of which is to unite unpredictability and reliability. Aristotle defined a successful drama as one in which each event is a surprise when it happens, but makes us afterward say it was just what had to happen.[8] It is this sort of continuity that we attribute to God's temporal infinity by calling him *faithful*.

Following the lead of the traditional listing of "absolute" attributes, we next come to *omnipresence*, or as the Protestant scholastics were accustomed to say, "immensity." Here we have less quarrel with the tradition. According to Aquinas,[9] God "is everywhere by essence, presence and power" (*Summa Theologica*, i,8,3). He is everywhere "by essence," that is, in his own selfhood, in that he is the creator, the giver of being. Both any place and what is located in it exist only by the direct action of God, who just so is at that place (ibid., i,8,2). God is everywhere "by presence" as anyone is present to those things that are in the scope of his intention, that he "sees" (ibid., i,4,3, resp.). God

185

2 / THE TRIUNE GOD

is everywhere "by power," as a ruler is present to all those subject to him (ibid.). It will be seen how, partly in spite of the language, this concept of omnipresence is that of a *personal presence* to all creation: God is present to the world as I am to one I meet and effectively and creatively address.

In the Christian tradition, there has been a long rethinking of the notion of space—beginning decisively with the Greek fathers,[10] and achieving a fulfillment in the work of the seventeenth-century Lutheran metaphysicians—that has moved from the notion of a universal container to the notion of a coordinate system for mutual presence. Thus later scholastics distinguished three modes of spatial presence: an entity may be somewhere "locally," in that the entity has spatial boundaries; an entity may be somewhere "definitively," in that a bounded space can be indicated as the entity's location, even though the entity has itself no spatial boundaries, as a thought is in the brain; or an entity may be somewhere "repletively," by "containing" the space. Only in the third mode is God anywhere, and in it he is everywhere: "God, contained in no space, contains all spaces by the immensity of his being."[11]

We have only one amendment to this general tradition, but that is sizable. The traditional doctrine, subtly and distinctively Christian though it is, assumes the essential disembodiment of God. Against this (but continuing in the scholastic terminology) we will want to assert the "definitive" presence of God at certain places in created space. Just so, Martin Luther made "definitive" presence the mode of Christ's presence in the Eucharist.[12] God, he argues, is "repletively" present everywhere, and so therefore is Christ, "at his right hand." But if God in Christ is to be present *for us* as conscious beings, we must be able to direct ourselves toward him, to *intend* him. Though this is not Luther's language, God's subjective "repletive" omnipresence must have an objective side, constituted by his "definitive" presence at certain places to which his word calls us. If we direct ourselves to the space occupied by, for example, the eucharistic loaf, we thereby are spatially related to God, even though God has no spatial boundaries.

God's infinity, in our view, is basically his temporal infinity, the unhinderedness of his transcendence through time. God's *spatial* infinity is merely an expression thereof. He "contains" all spaces not by being a larger space but by temporally bracketing the spatial world. The subtly interrelated meanings of the word "present" are no accident and may guide our thinking. Space, the horizon of presence, is simply the experienced reality of the temporal present. God's spatial infinity is his ability to be *now there* for, to be present to, every creature. God's spatial infinity is the present tense of his faithfulness: God is wherever Jesus' self-giving reaches.

We could continue indefinitely with such absolute attributes, but perhaps infinity, faithfulness, and omnipresence are enough and sufficiently basic cases. Taking Gerhard's list as typical of the tradition, he had also spiritual, uncor-

THE ATTRIBUTES OF GOD

poreal, invisible, simple, immortal;[13] all these have in fact been considered at some place in this *locus*. We turn to the second class of attributes.

"JESUS IS RISEN": ATTRIBUTES FOR THE SUBJECT

The second class of attributes are those that state what it means that it is *Jesus* who is risen. They explicate what it means that it is the particular event that happens between *him* and *his* Father and *their* Spirit, and not some other, to which "deity"—temporal infinity—pertains. Despite the skew of which we constantly complain in this part of traditional doctrine, this logic can easily be seen also in the traditional lists. Thus Gerhard had as his second class: omnipotence, goodness, mercy, justice, omniscience, freedom of will, and truth, all of which explicate the gospel. The assertion of God's attributes of this sort, for example, "God is good," is therefore itself a mode of gospel proclamation.

It must be admitted that some traditional relative attributes seem but distantly related to the gospel, for example, omnipotence and omniscience. Yet why must God be, for example, omnipotent? Many putative Gods are not, and it would even seem possible to speak of someone as risen and yet not attribute omnipotence to that being. It is the specific character of the promises to be made because *Jesus* is the risen one that requires believers in those promises to think of God as omnipotent. These are promises of the triumph of the *unconditionally* loving one and therefore of a good so encompassing as to be realizable only by a will that encompasses all events, and so contrary to probability as to be expectable only from a will that recognizes no other mode of impossibility than self-contradiction. It must be admitted that in many scholarly deductions of God's omnipotence this evangelical derivation is not very apparent; yet even in the most abstract it can be detected in the warrants and biases of the argument. Luther goes straight to principle: "It is the one and highest *consolation* of Christians in all their adversities, to know that God . . . does all things immutably, that his will cannot be resisted nor yet changed or impeded."[14]

We will therefore not be surprised that also the creedal "almighty" had its matrix of a particular era's hopes and anxieties.[15] The great fear of late antiquity was meaninglessness: that the gap between this temporal world and eternity might be unbridgeable, or, expressed in terms of the divine, that the God who is fully divine, who is unqualifiedly eternal, may not function as God of this world. That would mean that no divine being was all-ruling. To those so tormented, the gospel speakers said: Jesus' Father and ours is in spite of everything *all*-ruler, Lord both of this world and the next.

Once current in the church's language (and in this case even taken into

2 / THE TRIUNE GOD

the creed) a word like "almighty" tends to acquire a life of its own. "God is almighty" becomes a theological axiom, from which can be deduced soteriology for situations very different from that in which it had its own soteriological meaning. And the word itself lies in the language, ready for life when the gospel again meets fear of debility at the heart of being, as decidedly in our present time. Both these continuing histories can go well or badly for the gospel.

We continue to a second attribute of this sort, this one untraditional. If we adhere to Luther's methodological rule and then examine traditional lists of attributes, we find them radically incomplete. All the traditional "relative" attributes are characteristics that are good also in this world. That we see God in sufferings and the cross would never be guessed from them. Of possible attributes that are *not* good in this world, we will discuss the most offensive and decisive: God is mortal. God has in fact suffered death and therefore is somehow or other qualified and qualifiable by dying.

Jesus died, indeed, was executed. According to trinitarian apprehension of God, he is an identity of God. What he does and suffers, God does and suffers. Nor can his significance for us be abstracted from his death. The crucifixion cannot be made an incident irrelevant to Jesus' being as God for us, however our otherwise derived suppositions about God may make us wish it could: "but we preach Christ crucified, a stumbling block to Jews and folly to Gentiles" (1 Cor. 1:23). It is therefore an unavoidable item of Christian proclamation and reflection: "God the Son died." And such language was from the first deeply anchored in the liturgy and piety; so, for example, Melito of Sardis: "The Invisible is seen . . . , the Impassible suffers . . . , the Deathless dies. . . . God was killed."[16]

Despite the proposition's obvious gospel-necessity, it has been resisted through the whole history of the church. Arianism was at heart one long attempt to evade it: The Logos could not be God straight out precisely because he is one person with Jesus and so a sufferer of death. Indeed, the whole agony of trinitarian development was, as we have seen, occasioned by second-century acceptance of the impassibility axiom, of which "God died" is the extreme contradiction.

In the christological controversies leading to and following the Council of Chalcedon, the continuing attempt by those most committed to the impassibility axiom to evade attributing death and suffering to the Logos, and the insistence by those most committed to the biblical image of Christ that this must *somehow* be done, was perhaps the chief problem.[17] These controversies generally belong in another *locus*, but we must here note the "theopaschite" controversy at the turn of the fifth and sixth centuries, where the matter was put explicitly to the test.[18] In the first phase of the controversy,

THE ATTRIBUTES OF GOD

liturgical enthusiasm and theological scruples clashed directly. A new and instantly beloved version of the *Trisagion* "Holy God, Holy Almighty, Holy Immortal," enriched with "who were crucified for us," was suppressed by church authorities committed to standard theology, lest the Trinity be taken for the subject of suffering. In the second, a compromise explanation of such liturgy was proposed, phrased to make clear that the Trinity as such was not crucified: "*One of* the Trinity suffered in the flesh." But even this was resisted, by the pope among others, despite its manifest biblical authenticity and perfect agreement with orthodox tradition. It took the Emperor Justinian, whose motives were mixed, to compel official churchly acceptance, sealed at a general council in 553.[19] And even though theopaschite language has thereafter had dogmatic status, it has continued to be rare in systematic theology and has remained unreckoned with in standard lists of divine attributes.

The understanding of God's mortality must indeed be trinitarian. "One of the Trinity" died; and when patripassionists have extended the suffering of Jesus' death to the Father, this has rightly promptly been rejected.[20] Let us set up the dialectics by posing a naive but inescapable question: What about the time between Jesus' death and his resurrection? If the second identity died on Friday and rose on Sunday, was God meanwhile a binity?

If we have grasped the point of trinitarianism, the question answers itself. Jesus' death was not an interruption of his deity; as the conclusion of his obedience to the Father, as part of what the Father intends in intending Jesus as his self, Jesus' death is *constitutive* for his relation to the Father and so for both his deity and the Father's. Jesus is not God despite his death; he is God in that he died.

This answer will still seem puzzling if we continue to understand being as persistence, if we think that something really *is* whatever it was and persists in being. Then the three days of death must be an interruption of Jesus' being and so of his godhood. But just that understanding of being is what Christian interpretation of God contradicts. Something really *is* what it will be and now is open to being.

Jesus' death is part of his eventful relation to the Father and the Spirit. In that he is risen, this relation is future and present reality. And just this event is God's eternity, in which Jesus is always God. Jesus' death and resurrection are the way the particular Christian God goes about to be eternal, to be temporally infinite. For it is what happens between the identities, of which event Jesus' death is a main constituent, that *is* the eternal God.

Participation in our finitude, alienation, and consequent disaster thus belongs to the event that in fact God is. Exegeting "belongs"; it essentially characterizes the true God that, *if* there are creatures and fallen creatures, he is able and apt so to participate in their life. It is appropriate to what it

2 / THE TRIUNE GOD

means to be this God that in his second identity he died with and for us. God is not subject *to* death, but he conquers death only by undergoing it. In this way God is indeed mortal.

Finally, one other of the traditional attributes must be discussed: *goodness*.[21] Given the creeds and the liturgy, it is dogma that God is good. It is the simplest and most encompassing interpretation of the resurrection: History will have a good outcome; goodness is the heart of events.

Yet there are two traps in the notion of divine goodness. The first is that "God is good" is construable as gospel-proclamation in any and all situations, and just so tends to become general and then empty. Second, since the traditional derivation of divine attributes by analogy from features of creation necessarily used the "*good*" features of creation, it has been easy to confuse the divine goodness proclaimed by the gospel with an abstractly necessary character of the prime reason, and so again to empty it of its gospel import. Either way, the outcome is the familiar conception of "the good God," whose goodness is unquestionable and mostly irrelevant.

"God is good" is a Christian sentence only insofar as it is used precisely equivalently for "Jesus of Nazareth will triumph." The difference between the two sentences is only that between rhetorical or metaphysical contexts in which one or the other is more convenient: One sentence is in the present tense, the other in the future.

There is no way to round off our discussion of the attributes of the second class, since in principle we can invent new ones forever. We will instead round off our entire *locus* on God by harking far back. God is the universally transforming event between Jesus the Israelite, and the transcendence he called to as "Father," and their Spirit among us. Given who Jesus is, this event is good. So we conclude the doctrine of God.

NOTES

1. Martin Luther, *Theses for the Heidelberg Disputation*, WA 1:350-74, theses 19-20. English translations of these theses have not successfully dealt with the ingenious chiasmus of *conspicere* and *intelligere* and therefore miss most of the point.

2. The following is modeled on Aquinas, on whom see Ralph McInerny, *The Logic of Analogy* (The Hague: Nijhoff, 1961); George P. Klubertanz, *St. Thomas Aquinas on Analogy* (Chicago: Loyola University Press, 1960); Robert W. Jenson, *The Knowledge of Things Hoped For* (New York: Oxford University Press, 1969), pp. 67-85. That classic Protestantism followed the same general method can be seen from, e.g., John William Baier, *Compendium theologiae positivae* (1686-94), i,i,4ff.

3. This "intellectual perception," *nous*, is the deepest and most original ideal of Greek theology; here it dominates the methodology of theology as elsewhere it

dominates the matter. See Werner Marx, *The Meaning of Aristotle's "Ontology"* (The Hague: Nijhoff, 1954), pp. 11–16.

4. Behind this amendment lies that broad methodological movement in recent theology that can be represented in one of its aspects by Wolfhart Pannenberg, ed., *Revelation as History*, trans. D. Granskou (New York: Macmillan Co., 1968); and in another by Jenson, *Knowledge*.

5. For the intellectually most vigorous instance of this interpretation, see the work of James Cone, e.g., *A Black Theology of Liberation* (Philadelphia: J. B. Lippincott Co., 1970).

6. Aquinas, *Summa Theologica*, x; John Gerhard, *Loci communes theologici*, i,137; and for an example from the Calvinist tradition, the textbook of colonial American theology, William Ames, *The Marrow of Theology*, i,iv.

7. Aquinas, *Summa Theologica*, ix; Gerhard, *Loci communes theologici*, ii,150; Ames, *Marrow of Theology*, i,iv.

8. Aristotle, *On Poesy*, 1452a,1–11; 1554a,33–36.

9. Standard Protestantism is materially identical; e.g., Gerhard, *Loci communes theologici*, ii,171ff.

10. Pioneeringly analyzed by Thomas F. Torrance, *Time, Space, and Incarnation* (New York and London: Oxford University Press, 1969).

11. Gerhard, *Loci communes theologici*, ii,172.

12. Martin Luther, *Confession Concerning Christ's Supper* (1528), *WA* 26:327ff.

13. Gerhard, *Loci communes theologici*, ii,113.

14. *On the Bondage of the Will*, *WA* 18:619.

15. On this paragraph, J. N. D. Kelly, *Early Christian Creeds* (New York and London: Longmans, Green & Co., 1950), pp. 136ff.

16. Melito of Sardis, fragments xxxi, xvi.

17. On this, see Werner Elert, *Der Ausgang der altkirchlichen Christologie* (Berlin: Lutherisches Verlagshaus, 1957), pp. 71–169.

18. Ibid., pp. 105–9.

19. Ibid., pp. 165ff. The council's decree reads: "If someone does not confess that the one crucified in the flesh, the Lord Jesus Christ, is the true God and the Lord of Glory, and one of the Holy Trinity, let him be condemned" (*Sacrorum conciliorum nova et amplissima collectio*, ed. J. D. Mansi [Firenze, 1759–1827], 9:375).

20. Jaroslav Pelikan, *The Emergence of the Catholic Tradition* (Chicago: University of Chicago Press, 1971), pp. 176–82.

21. Aquinas, *Summa Theologica*, vi; Gerhard, *Loci communes theologici*, ii, 208–15.

THIRD LOCUS

The Knowledge of God

PAUL R. SPONHEIM

THE KNOWLEDGE OF GOD

Introduction

1. The Reality and Revelation of God
   The Self-Revelation of God
   God as the World's Ground and Goal
   The Legitimation and Limitation of the Knowledge of God

2. The Reception and Recognition of Revelation
   The Experience of World, Self, and God
   Knowledge as Paradigm, Parable, and Prophecy

3. God's Call and the Human Question about the Ground of Life
   The Divine Incognito: The Real, the Beautiful, and the Good
   Human Awareness: Argument and Adoration

4. The Human Quest and God's Free Answer
   Human Intentionality and Historical Ambiguity
   Teleological Religion and Divine Decisiveness
   God's Justification and Human Responsibility

Introduction

One who in the late twentieth century sets about to write dogmatically of the knowledge of God faces two kinds of difficulties. The first difficulty is *textual*. What will the text be? The church has not produced a clear dogmatic statement on this matter. Yet the teaching of the church does entail a claim that God is known. Moreover, there is an ample body of Christian reflection concerning the knowledge of God. That body is characterized by a bewildering diversity; it is ample in range as well as in extent. Hence the difficulty: A dogmatic statement calls for some clear and definitive formal teaching, but we look for such in vain, finding instead a buzzing multiplicity of individual Christian opinion.

The second difficulty is *contextual*. To speak convincingly of knowing God now seems too hard, or too hard to be worth the effort. It is difficult, for example, to speak of knowing a present ontological ground for the universe, when such unlikely colleagues as the rule of law (even statistical law) and respect for raw historical particularity combine to resist such speech. The battle for explanatory control seems to be between these two: my stubborn sense of subjectivity and the ineluctable web of objective causality which natural and social scientists monitor. That standoff hardly hints at a "wholly other" explanatory principle. On the contrary, the Christian is regularly offered explanations of the thinking and speaking that were once supposed to be about God. It is no easier today to enter the realm of historical contingency in order to elevate a single instance to the status of the norm by which I am to be judged and from which I am to take my bearings in life. That seems against the grain, if we are dealing with something that is, after all, precisely a part of an historical series.

Is it worth the effort to attempt such speech concerning the knowledge of God? Why bother to stake out intelligibly in the public arena such knowledge claims regarding God, if the splendor of private ecstasies is available? These difficulties must be addressed if Christian faith in God is to be clearly distinguished from mystical union with who-knows-what. The stakes are high. If God is not known, our claims elsewhere in these volumes are altered in devastating fashion. If God is known but we know not how, at least we can be asked to say how we understand our possession of and confidence in such knowledge.

3 / THE KNOWLEDGE OF GOD

There seems to be a sort of reciprocal dependence in these matters. We have just stressed the importance of our task for the content-claims that occur elsewhere in this dogmatics. Yet the Christian understanding of that and how we know God cannot be developed adequately in purely formal terms. Some attention must be given to *what* is claimed to be known about God, as the reference to a ground and a goal for the world suggests. We shall draw on that content as it bears on the questions concerned with the knowledge of God. We shall also need to consider the reflective significance for this topic of other *loci*, such as those on sin and the person of Christ. Thus the textual problem will be addressed, as the faith's claims about God can and must be probed to speak of how God is known.

To speak of the knowledge of God is to speak of aspects of the relationship between God and humankind. Thus this *locus* cannot be comprehended without clarity about how human beings come to know accurately and then to speak clearly about that which they know. To speak of human beings in their knowledge of God is to speak of them widely. In that breadth of speech the occasion is given for responding to the contextual difficulties.

Indeed, breadth is needed materially as well as formally. We shall argue that to speak of the knowledge of God is to speak of much more than religion. Without trying to argue that Christianity is not a religion, or that there is no truth in any other religion, one may well contend that God is not to be known merely in matters religious—Christian or otherwise. It is, after all, God of whom we speak in this matter. God is not merely the beneficiary of our ritual, but the benefactor who is ceaselessly at work to bless in all that is real. But may God, *is* God, to be known that widely? That question and the others put so far drive us to the *locus* itself.

1
The Reality and Revelation of God

God is known because in creation and in redemption God's will and action to bless reveal God to humankind as the world's ground and goal. In the mission of Jesus, what God intended and intends in creation is firm and therefore clear, though it is grasped as the word of promise to a pilgrim whose question and quest can only be answered by one who is qualitatively other.

THE SELF-REVELATION OF GOD

Christians understand their claim to know God to be dependent on the will and action of the one who is known. While our knowledge of God is emphatically human in its condition, its origin lies in the revelation of God.

Three further claims are involved in this assertion. The first is of the reality of God. While, for the believer, faith and God may belong together, the believer is clear that faith does not create God and does not elect God. While theologians like Paul Tillich may doubt that it is appropriate to formulate the reality of God in terms of existence, that doubt does not hint at unreality, but is rooted precisely in the conviction of God's superiority. It may seem offensively obvious to begin thus with a repudiation of all fictionalist understandings, but popular appeals to the power of positive thinking and scholarly references to religion as the "entertaining" of a story make it necessary.[1]

The second claim is of the categorical supremacy of God. Charles Hartshorne makes the point well:

> God is a name for the uniquely good, admirable, great, worship-eliciting being. Worship, moreover, is not just an unusually high degree of respect or admiration; and the excellence of deity is not just an unusually high degree of merit. There is a difference in kind. God is "Perfect," and between the perfect and anything as little imperfect as you please is no merely finite, but an infinite step. The superiority of deity to all others cannot (in accordance with established word usage) be expressed by indefinite descriptions, such as "immensely good," "very

3 / THE KNOWLEDGE OF GOD

powerful," or even "best" or "most powerful," but must be a superiority of principle, a definite conceptual divergence from every other being, actual or so much as possible. We may call this divergence "categorical supremacy."[2]

It is this truth that leads some theologians to suggest that "existence" is inappropriately applied to God. I disagree, as I shall try to make clear later. It is this truth, moreover, which has (unfortunately, I believe) encouraged many theologians—particularly when the lure of Platonism was strong—to distinguish God's reality from God's actions in the world of time and space. Many contemporary theologians, from otherwise differing perspectives, insist that the categorical transcendence of God is to be found and so known not apart from but precisely in the divine action in history.[3]

The third claim is of the initiative of God. God is not merely *there*—even eminently there—as an object to be known. It is God who acts to reveal. We know God because of God, who is categorically superior. Both God's action generally and God's revelation specifically are marked by the decisiveness available to a will that is fully free. Thus the writer to the Ephesians speaks of God blessing us "in the heavenly places," choosing us "before the foundation of the world." Action that is so emphatic leads toward revelation that is sure: "For he has made known to us in all wisdom and insight the mystery of his will, according to his purpose which he set forth in Christ as a plan for the fulness of time, to unite all things in him, things in heaven and things on earth." (Eph. 1:9–10).

Revelation by God and so knowledge of God occur because God's living will is for relationship. The Christian teaching about the Trinity reminds us that to speak of God's relatedness is to speak first about God. But faith also confesses that God wills to relate to that which is not God. Again we speak of all of God: the works of the Trinity may be *internally* divisible, but when we are related to God we are related to all of God, to the only God. This God wills to relate to that which is not God. So do Christians speak of God's will in terms of creation, of covenant, of presence.[4]

God wills, then, to reveal. That is the basis for Christian confidence in claiming the knowledge of God. But what does the reality of the God known suggest about the nature of the knowing? Let it first be said that it does not undercut the reality and reliability of the knowledge. Christians find their clearest access to the knowledge of God in the gospel concerning what God has done in the person and work of Jesus for the salvation of all. Knowledge is claimed emphatically, as when Lutherans and Catholics in dialogue agree:

> This gospel (a) was proclaimed by witnesses—apostles and others in the early Church; (b) was recorded in the New Testament Scriptures, which have a "normative role for the entire later tradition of the Church"; (c) has been made living in the hearts of believers by the Holy Spirit; (d) has been reflected in the "rule

THE REALITY AND REVELATION OF GOD

of faith" (*regula fidei*) and in the forms and exercise of church leadership; (e) has been served by Ministers.[5]

Clearly there is here a claim to content and to confidence. The categorical uniqueness of God undergirds rather than undercuts that claim. That which is known here is the sure will of God. The testimony of the Scriptures is clear: "Do not be deceived, my beloved brethren. Every good endowment and every perfect gift is from above, coming down from the Father of lights with whom there is no variation or shadow due to change. Of his own will he brought us forth by the word of truth that we should be a kind of first fruits of his creatures" (James 1:16–18). And "If we are faithless, he remains faithful—for he cannot deny himself." (2 Tim. 2:13). May we not say that Paul is sure that "nothing can separate" from the love of God in Christ Jesus not merely because there is no adequate external threat, but also because there is no internal challenge at all? It is God's role to justify, Paul knows. He is confident that God will not turn against what none other than God has done in Christ.

What God has so surely done can be stated intelligibly. It can be communicated to those who do not share the faith; it is not a word whose meaning can be understood only by initiates. Moreover, the one who believes does not fall prey to blind credulity, precisely because there is in this relationship clear content which can be possessed competently and with integrity. Wolfhart Pannenberg has made this point forcefully: "Every act of trust reaches backwards (or forwards) to a ground of trustworthiness in the object being relied on. . . . Knowledge of the content of faith (*notitia* with *assensus*) remains the logical presupposition of the trust which is based upon it."[6] It also follows that the content of the faith can be formulated, that faith may seek understanding. Clarity can be sought in the statement of the gospel and in the formulation of its implications, because the word here is that the one who is categorically supreme has willed to bless. Toward that end light is given, and so sermons are preached and dogmatics are written.

But perhaps we have made things too easy for ourselves. Søren Kierkegaard appropriately reminds us that as soon as we speak of revelation everything becomes dialectical.[7] It is after all *God* of whom we speak: the categorically supreme one who is radically unlike us. This God is the one who creates out of nothing and whose revelation seems discontinuous with what precedes it. So Paul can claim that he did not receive the gospel from some human source, "nor was I taught it, but it came through a revelation of Jesus Christ. . . . When he who had set me apart before I was born, and had called me through his grace, was pleased to reveal his Son to me . . . I did not confer with flesh and blood" (Gal. 1:12, 15–16). Moreover, even when God is revealed, that revelation hardly makes perfect sense. We are told that God's revelation is always in the form of the opposite, indeed, that God remains hidden even in self-revelation.[8]

3 / THE KNOWLEDGE OF GOD

This dialectical emphasis does not contradict what we have said of the sure will of the God who reveals. It is will and life with which we deal here. God is not a principle or a mechanism droning on through the ages. When we speak of a personal will, we speak of that which has newness about it. The freshness and spontaneity of living will may so surprise the knower as to yield cognitive dissonance. Nor should we underestimate the distortions due to finitude and sinfulness in our reading of God's acts.

Similarly, the categorical supremacy of God complicates any attempt to respond simply to the question. "Is God's revelation direct *or* indirect?" Revelation is indirect in the sense that God works through means: persons, words, water, bread, and wine. While mysticism will require attention, Christian knowledge must be distinguished from unmediated knowledge. Even the clearest revelation of God is "dialectical," if the humanity of Jesus is not to be denied. Yet we need also to say that it is God's own self who is at work in and through these means. God is not off in some more interesting corner of the universe; the one who works here is none other than God. Again, the categorical supremacy of God is such that the one who brings reality into being is able to be potently at work in that being, directly but mediately. It is thus fitting that the church has steadfastly insisted that the content of revelation includes both a *who* and a *what*, a someone as well as a something. Through God's work and word we do in fact know God.

GOD AS THE WORLD'S GROUND AND GOAL

The God whom Christians know is "maker of heaven and earth." The categorical supremacy of God cannot be stated simply in moral terms. Indeed, in moral terms it may be that the more than moral superiority of God is that the will of God grounds the meaning of "the good" and "the right," even if one goes on to affirm that God's will is so sure and clear that the good can be known apart from God. Thus Christian thinkers have been drawn to ponder the connection between moral and metaphysical supremacy, as when Kierkegaard develops the theme that purity of heart is to will one thing. Anyway, it is clear that Christian faith attributes to God a metaphysical or ontological uniqueness. At times this uniqueness seems even to threaten the moral character of God, as when Second Isaiah writes: "I form light and create darkness, I make weal and create woe, I am the Lord, who do all these things" (Isa. 45:7).

A prevailing traditional dogmatic focus for this ontological supremacy is the doctrine of creation *ex nihilo* (from nothing). The focus has usually been formulated in terms of the absolute temporal origin of all that is not God, as expressed in the notion of original creation. That formulation is currently the subject of considerable debate on both exegetical and contextual grounds. The matter is of intrinsic importance and is directly discussed in the *locus* on creation. It is not necessary here to enter that debate, since the bearing of the *ex nihilo* doctrine on the subject of the knowledge of God can be discussed independently. In such a way Langdon Gilkey, for example, affirms the formula "from nothing" as an apt statement of God's present relationship to us; in that relationship God is "the deep, transcendent, and yet immanent ground of our passage; the power that gives us our past and preserves it, that creates and recreates our freedom, and that lures and calls us with new possibilities." [9] Even those who affirm a distinction between original creation and continuing creation or preservation claim also under the latter categories such a special ontological role for God as Gilkey has described.

It seems helpful to gather these associations together in the metaphor of God as the world's *ground*, letting logical and ontological priority mingle in this metaphor. Without following Tillich at every point, one may well speak with him of God as the originating, sustaining, and directing ground of the world.[10]

The church has steadily affirmed that it is possible for human beings to know that they are so grounded. Indeed, it may be that those Christian thinkers are right who have spoken of human being as precisely freedom that asks even about its own basis, that asks the question of God. Is life sound and fury only, signifying nothing, or is there a ground, a purpose, on which freedom can build, a call to which freedom can respond? Humankind naturally—precisely *naturally* as created by God—asks this question of the ground and can find an answer that is affirmative. Perhaps that is why atheism did not become a major problem before the modern period. It is only the fool who supposes there is no God. If the question is disallowed or distorted, can the answer be expected to fare any better? It is not our task at this point to ask what is different about the modern context. Here we seek only to clarify what it means to speak of God as foundation for *knowledge.*

It is striking that perhaps the major motif carrying this meaning, the *logos* tradition, links *life* and *light* so intimately (John 1). It would be a mistake completely to identify these themes, since God's *creative* work is the more encompassing. Yet the word that orders does reveal. Thus the church does speak of God as there to be known, whether by appeal to an original creation or to a more present grounding.

Even the least optimistic of the church's voices affirm such a "natural" knowledge of God. Thus Luther spoke of a "general knowledge" of God to be had in reflection on creation, reason and philosophy, and conscience.[11] John Calvin affirmed a universal "sense of divinity." [12] Even Tertullian spoke of a "natural knowledge" of God deriving from the order and beauty of the visible cosmos and from the immediate testimony of the soul, though he found

3 / THE KNOWLEDGE OF GOD

that philosophy confuses this knowledge (*Apologeticus*, 17.6). Christians agree that God may be known as the ground for the project that is the world, for the venture that is humankind.

Christians also agree that to know God as the world's ground is not sufficient. To know the world's ground is not yet to know the world's goal, the *telos* of the striving that is human life. On the reading of matters represented by the faith, to ask about the goal is to ask about God. The God who is alpha will be omega as well. Where does the world go? It goes to God. Humankind particularly is not merely made *by* God—as is everything that is; we are made *for* God. Perhaps we ask the question of God as ground precisely because we are in quest of God as goal. To know God as the world's ground is to know that life is well begun. But humankind is haunted by its dream of a goal out ahead. The dream is not of the last item in a series, so that the world ends in stultifying sameness, but of a new reality of unending life and light. Christians call it "heaven" and believe that then we shall know God "face to face."

Meanwhile, we do not know so. It is, after all, a venture of freedom upon which we are embarked. Freedom as we now know it is characterized by risk, by contingency. It is a good and noble thing to know God as the ground of life, for in knowing that one knows the gift of freedom and its concomitant, responsibility. Thus one may speak of knowing God, the world's ground, not only as *logos*, but as *nomos* as well. So Clement spoke of philosophy as the "torah" of the Greeks, and Tertullian explained the good elements in pagan philosophy on the basis of natural law.[13] The law is given for life; God acts here to bless.[14]

Can one know anything about God as goal in one's knowledge of God as ground? God's claim as ground does call toward God as goal. It suggests that the meaning of life is somehow to be found in the relationship to God. But it does not reveal what that meaning is. Inference might well lead to an association of God with the moral good—we shall ponder that process of inference later. But this would not seem to yield any decisive resolution to the multifarious project which any human life— and a fortiori all human life—represents. Just as the good of being called by God does not yield the goal of sure consummation, so these indicators in the area of knowledge remain indecisive. Such ambiguity may well be the epistemic correlate to the ontological reality of freedom.[15]

Moreover, given the reality of sin and our sense of sin, it is not strange at all that the knowledge of God as *logos* and *nomos* would in fact terrify. This is the particular contribution of Luther's understanding. Regin Prenter points out that the God of creation's purpose is blessing and life. But this purpose is hidden to the sinner, because sin's curse opposes God's work and hides its purpose.[16] The wisdom the law brings thus accuses and kills. One does not blame the law for this, as Luther says in the twenty-fourth Heidelberg thesis:

THE REALITY AND REVELATION OF GOD

"Nevertheless, this wisdom is not bad nor is the law to be fled. But without a theology of the cross man misuses the best things in the worst way."

But of course the Christian need not be without a theology of the cross, for the world is not in fact without a cross. It is not the task of this *locus* to develop a soteriology, to ponder what was wrought in Jesus. Christians have spoken differently about Jesus, but it is he about whom they all speak when they reflect on God as the world's goal. Pannenberg says: "God's revelation in Jesus Christ is indeed only an anticipation of the final event, which will be the actual revelatory event. And yet, we have the well-founded confidence that the final event will not bring anything decisively new that was not already anticipated in the resurrection of Jesus." [17] Thus Luther, pondering the God hidden in predestination, can appeal to the way in which the light of grace resolves the questions of the light of nature to sustain the hope that the light of glory "will one day reveal God, to whom alone belongs a judgment whose justice is incomprehensible, as God whose justice is most righteous and evident." [18]

This Jesus is kairotic for the *reality* of the relationship between God and humankind. That point is developed elsewhere in this dogmatic. Here we merely note that the church's recognition of Jesus also has kairotic significance for the *knowledge* of God. The author of the prologue to John's Gospel, that poet of the Word of God active as the light to bless in all that has life, declares: "For the law was given through Moses; grace and truth came through Jesus Christ. No one has ever seen God; the only Son who is in the bosom of the Father, he has made him known" (John 1:17–18).

So, then, God is known as ground and goal, as *logos* (*nomos*) and in *kairos* (*eschatos*). God acts to reveal. How shall the relationship between the two be formulated? Two major tendencies are apparent in the history of Christian thought. The first thinks that the kairotic, the special, supplements and fulfills the natural or general knowledge available through God as *logos*. This view has been developed in strikingly different ways. In general it may be said that special and general knowledge of God are here regarded as logically comparable and materially congruent. One way in which this is done is to say that the philosophers have systematized the natural knowledge of God and then call Christianity a philosophy as well. That early Christian thinkers such as Justin Martyr and Clement of Alexandria tended so to speak may not surprise if one recalls that the philosophies of the early Christian era were highly religious and were, as opposed to the cults, monotheistic.[19]

In the writings of the theologians of the golden age of scholasticism, especially Bonaventura and Aquinas, there is the confidence that philosophy, if rightly understood, is on the side of theology and that reason is in fundamental harmony with revelation. Bonaventura, following Augustine's epistemology, traces an ascent from finding God's vestiges in the visible world, through seek-

3 / THE KNOWLEDGE OF GOD

ing his image in our soul, to mystical knowledge of God. Aquinas, reflecting a more Aristotelian epistemology, argues to God from features of the existence of the sensible world, applying the *via negativa*, analogy, and eminence and then adds truths to be known only through revelation. Thus reason can show that God created the world, but revelation informs us that God willed it in time rather than in eternity.[20]

The relationship of supplementation in Aquinas is not a simple one. Many things which can be known naturally can also be known by scriptural revelation. Indeed, all knowledge necessary for salvation has been specially revealed. Moreover, reason is not excluded from the realm of faith, for revealed doctrines can be shown to have a certain fit with reason. Yet the two spheres do not simply converge. The closest classical Christian thought comes to an argument for complete convergence may be Anselm, whose "faith seeking understanding" led him to try to prove the necessity of the Trinity and the incarnation.[21] We exclude here those thinkers, such as the extreme deists, who really did not think of two realities that converge, but spoke instead simply of the gospel as the "republication of the religion of nature."[22] Insofar as theological liberalism stopped short of such identification, it represents the position of supplementation, as when Friedrich Schleiermacher located the decisiveness of Jesus' redemption in the strengthening of a universally present consciousness of absolute dependence on God.[23]

If the tendency in this first group of thinkers is synthesis, diastasis prevails in the second tendency. The general and the special, the natural and the revealed, do not come together but are driven apart.

The opposition may be thought of as a logical opposition. John Duns Scotus declined to be troubled by logical contradiction, when the subject at hand is the action of infinite will. Clearly nothing that can be derived philosophically can bind the operation of an absolutely free will. The best that philosophers can muster is the notion *that* there is an infinite will. William of Ockham carried this tendency further. While Scotus spoke of God choosing the essences to be created, Ockham suppressed universals altogether and stressed instead the ultimate reality of singulars. No intrinsically necessary relation of causality can be recognized between singulars, and—a fortiori—between the realm of the finite and the infinite. To speak of a conflict between faith and reason is really beside the point. Nicholas of Cusa made the point still more emphatically, speaking of the infinite as the absolute and perfect coincidence of contraries, thus rejecting Aristotelian reliance on the principle of contradiction.[24]

The opposition between *logos* and *kairos* can be cast in more existential terms. Tertullian represents this emphasis. Athens and Jerusalem do not converge, not because there is no accurate natural knowledge of God, but because only Jerusalem heeds the call of true religion to obey the supreme and active

THE REALITY AND REVELATION OF GOD

will of God known in the rule of faith.²⁵ More clearly still, Luther and Calvin denied that natural revelation can be a foundation for the proper knowledge of God. In Calvin, natural revelation serves to leave the human person without excuse. In Luther it condemns and terrifies. This view prevailed in the mid-twentieth century's so-called neo-Reformation or neo-orthodox reaction to theological liberalism's custodial distribution of the heritage of the Enlightenment. At times the reaction seemed so sharp as to say that natural knowledge of God does not avail because it does not exist.

Since dogma does not decide between these tendencies, how may the contemporary Christian understand the church's voices as a common witness to the knowledge of God? The range of opinion reflected in these tendencies may be integrated into the argument begun earlier—and so that argument may be advanced—in two summary comments:

1. The Christian faith confesses the epistemic priority of the kairotic event of Jesus for the knowledge of God. The faith utters a resounding "yes" to Kierkegaard's questions: "Is an historical point of departure possible for an eternal consciousness; . . . is it possible to base an eternal happiness upon historical knowledge?"²⁶ Here the human person knows what beings questing after the *telos* of life need to know, for here the word of justification is spoken. This knowledge is distinctive and decisive because God who is living will has acted decisively toward the world in Jesus.

2. Yet the authority of this kairotic word depends on its being the word of the one who is maker of heaven and earth. It is precisely the *logos* that becomes flesh in this *kairos*. Thus continuity must be affirmed. The faith understands that the continuity is the constancy of the personal will of God who is active for us also in creation. Thus some measure of continuity also in knowledge is to be affirmed. In some measure this is an inverted continuity. Thus Calvin can speak of how the regenerate again see God in the world.²⁷ Or one may speak of how the *nomos* is sharpened in the ministry of Jesus.²⁸ But the continuity is not altogether inverse. Perhaps that is the point to the law-gospel dialectic's order. It is the question about God that gives rise to the quest for God. However sinful we may be, it remains true, as Luther said, that God did not make heaven for geese.²⁹

THE LEGITIMATION AND LIMITATION OF THE KNOWLEDGE OF GOD

We have spoken of God's active will to reveal himself. This is the foundation for Christian claims to know God. God's activity does in principle legitimate such human claims. The genitive in the phrase "the knowledge of God" is objective; it is human beings who know God. Therefore Christian talk on this theme should avoid such easy disjunctions as "divine disclosure, not

3 / THE KNOWLEDGE OF GOD

human discovery." Rather, is it the case that because God discloses, humans do discover.

This understanding of the situation of knowing is appropriate to the content claimed to be known concerning a categorically supreme will seeking a relationship of trust and obedience with finite freedom. We have spoken of God as the world's ground and the world's goal, as the one answering the human question and the human quest. Those metaphors do just that: they answer. What Christians say about God represents a response to human reality, a word that supports and receives human striving. In turn it is fitting that when Christians reflect on *how* it is *that* they know *what* they know, an affirmation of the human is heard. Revelation, address, word—and so knowledge—fit a God who creates and woos freedom.

In this understanding, knowledge is affirmed but is not absolutized. Along with legitimation there is limitation. Once again the order of knowing reflects the order of being. We are speaking of the being and becoming, of the relationship between God and the human person. Let us begin with ourselves and ask the counterquestion: What view of the human would undercut the assertion of a revelation by God to humankind? Abraham Heschel has pointed out that two anthropological conceptions have militated against the notion of revelation: "One maintained that man was too great to be in need of divine guidance, and the other maintained that man was too small to be worthy of divine guidance. The first conception came from social science, and the second from natural science."[30] The human person, on the Christian view, is one for whom revelation is "right."

The conception of God and of humankind also qualifies the conception of revelation/knowledge which it has introduced. We have already spoken of certain limits to human knowledge of God which divine revelation entails. Some of those limits derive from human finitude over against the categorically supreme. In this relationship the persons are not ontological equals.[31] We have sought to cast this divine transcendence in dynamic and relational terms. God is one; we are not. God's will is sure; our wills are not. God's becoming is not subject to contingency in the way that ours is. Christian thinkers have struggled to express the notion of transcendence in relationship.[32]

To finitude must be added sin and its effect on the human capacity to know God. We have already argued that faith in the categorically supreme God entails the confidence that God can accomplish revelation. This applies to both *logos* and *kairos*, in differing measure perhaps. Nonetheless, the sin which turns us in on ourselves does impede God's revelation. Perhaps it cannot destroy revelation, but it does seem to distort it. Here it would be difficult to disentangle the factors. How are ignorance and defiance related? When is ignorance culpable?

One of the ways in which human sin may distort divine revelation is precisely

THE REALITY AND REVELATION OF GOD

in reading the relationship between the knowledge of God given in *logos* and the knowledge of God given in *kairos*. In what sense is God hidden? One may think of God as hidden apart from the kairotic word. But one may also think of God as hidden *in* the kairotic word, which speaks of God's "opposite," of suffering and death. While both sin and finitude may contribute to a certain element of distortion euphemistically hiding under "hiddenness," it is particularly instructive to consider the relationship between the two kinds. Thus one may well suppose that an original misreading of *logos* contributed to the identification of suffering as "opposite" to God. Conversely, appropriate confidence in the kairotic word may mistakenly lead one to diminish God's revelation as *logos*, classifying it simply as ignorance. Perhaps Luther's thought runs this risk. Or, worse yet, one may suppose that kairotic advance can be won only at the price of actual opposition between *kairos* and *logos*. Brian Gerrish worries about this tendency in Calvin: "Perhaps Calvin went further than Luther toward a resolution of the theoretical problem of the 'two wills,' although at the fearful cost of reducing the universal benevolence of the revealed will to a mere appearance."[33]

It seems better to follow Luther's insistence that predestination is intended as gospel for the anguished conscience. That God is for us already as *logos* is not to deny that in the mystery of freedom sin can be against God and as such real for God. A will is a living reality that can be sure and yet know struggle and advance. In *kairos*, God's rule also over sin is shown. That kairotic word does not merely confirm the creative logos. Yet part of its decisive advance may precisely be to correct our distorted reading of *logos*.

How, then, is our knowledge of God here both legitimated and limited? For the most part Christians have legitimated faith's content, the "faith that is believed," but have not sought to claim a direct relationship for faith's passion, the "faith that believes." In faith, God's will and work are known, but God is not possessed. Claims for infallible teaching seem to stretch this legitimation beyond the breaking point; though it is encouraging to note the economy that characterizes the identification of such infallible pronouncements.[34]

But what may be said of the act of knowing that takes place in faith, of the "faith that believes"? Clearly here the limitation applies. This was made clear when the church rejected the gnostic heresy that makes gnosis itself perfect redemption.[35] This limitation corresponds with the fact that knowledge is not the height of the human condition, since it merely though significantly "raises the bid." So pagans also know of God, Luther noted, and Kierkegaard reluctantly raised his voice against Socrates, since sin lies not in the understanding but in the will.[36]

Yet legitimation applies as well. Just as some knowledge of God is given in the call of God to salvation, so there is knowing of God in the relationship

3 / THE KNOWLEDGE OF GOD

of faith. The distortions represented by gnosticism and mysticism do not invalidate this truth.

What, then, of the condition of knowing, however limited the significance? In what sense is the finite "capable" of the infinite, or even the infinite of the finite? What account may be given of the condition of knowing God? How far is an epistemology of the knowledge of God possible? We must next consider what may be legitimately said of this matter.

NOTES

1. I have in mind that awesome spectrum running from Hans Vaihinger, *The Philosophy of "As If," a System of the Theoretical, Practical, and Religious Fictions of Mankind* (London: Routledge & Kegan Paul, 1965), through R. B. Braithwaite, *An Empiricist's View of the Nature of Religious Belief* (Cambridge: At the University Press, 1965), to the "positive thinking seminars" held in sports stadiums.

2. Charles Hartshorne and William L. Reese, eds., *Philosophers Speak of God* (Chicago: University of Chicago Press, 1953), p. 7.

3. That insistence may be found in Barth's handling of the doctrine of the Trinity in the terms of revealer, revelation, and revealedness, in Pannenberg's theme of the prolepsis in Jesus of the absolute future, and in process thought's attempt to understand God within the metaphysics of creativity. It is not, however, universal; a prominent exception would be Tillich's preference for "being-itself" as a term descriptive of God, despite the dynamic aspects present in his own analysis of the ontological polarities.

4. Cf. Walther Eichrodt, *Theology of the Old Testament*, trans. J. A. Baker, 2 vols. (Philadelphia: Westminster Press, 1961–67); Samuel Terrien, *The Elusive Presence: Toward a New Biblical Theology* (New York: Harper & Row, 1978).

5. Paul C. Empie, T. Austin Murphy, and Joseph A. Burgess, eds., *Teaching Authority and Infallibility in the Church: Lutherans and Catholics in Dialogue VI*, "Common Statement" (Minneapolis: Augsburg Publishing House, 1980), p. 15.

6. Wolfhart Pannenberg, *Basic Questions in Theology*, vol. 2, trans. George H. Kehm (Philadelphia: Fortress Press, 1971), p. 30.

7. Perhaps Kierkegaard's most thoroughgoing statement of this point is *The Concluding Unscientific Postscript to the Philosophical Fragments*, trans. David F. Swenson and Walter Lowrie (Princeton: Princeton University Press, 1944), where the dialectical is discerned in appeals to the Holy Scriptures, the church, and "the proof of the centuries."

8. One thinks of Luther's theses for the Heidelberg Disputation. See B. A. Gerrish, "To the Unknown God: Luther and Calvin on the Hiddenness of God," *JR* 53 (July 1973): 263–93.

9. Langdon Gilkey, *Message and Existence: An Introduction to Christian Theology* (New York: Seabury Press, 1979), p. 84. For a fuller discussion see his *Maker of Heaven and Earth* (Garden City, N.Y.: Doubleday & Co., 1959).

10. Paul Tillich, *Systematic Theology*, 3 vols. (Chicago: University of Chicago Press, 1951–63), 1:252–71.

11. See B. A. Gerrish, *Grace and Reason* (Oxford: At the Clarendon Press, 1962); and Roland Zimany, "Enduring Values of Luther's Approach to Knowing God," *LuthQ* 27 (Fall 1975): 6–26.

12. Edward A. Dowey, Jr., *The Knowledge of God in Calvin's Theology* (New York: Columbia University Press, 1952), pp. 50–56, distinguishes this sense from a special organ or faculty of soul, from the formality of a "religious a priori," and from the products of ratiocination (as Calvin grants in his notion of *semen divinitatis*). He speaks of it as an "intensely numinous awareness" and links it with the universality of religion, the servile fear of God, and the troubled conscience.

13. See John Ferguson, "The Achievement of Clement of Alexandria," *RelSt* 12 (1976): 59–80. Jaroslav Pelikan in *The Emergence of the Catholic Tradition (100–600)* (Chicago: University of Chicago Press, 1971), p. 32, notes: "Tertullian's explanation of the presence of noble and good elements in paganism employed the idea of natural law rather than that of seminal Logos. For him these elements included knowledge of the existence, the goodness, and the justice of God, but especially the moral precepts flowing from that knowledge."

14. Claus Westermann, *Creation*, trans. John J. Scullion (Philadelphia: Fortress Press, 1974), pp. 90–91, relates and distinguishes taboo (prepersonal), command (personal), and law (postpersonal). But the intent of command would seem to apply here: "The command therefore opens up the possibility of a relationship to him who commands. . . . Something is entrusted to man in the command. The command introduces him to freedom. . . ."

15. Cf. John Hick, *Evil and the God of Love* (New York: Harper & Row; London: Macmillan & Co., 1966), p. 317, on "epistemic distance."

16. Regin Prenter, *Creation and Redemption*, trans. Theodore I. Jensen (Philadelphia: Fortress Press, 1967), p. 207.

17. Pannenberg, *Basic Questions*, 2:44.

18. Quoting John Dillenberger's edition of *The Bondage of the Will*, in *Martin Luther: Selections from His Writings* (Garden City, N.Y.: Doubleday & Co., 1961), p. 202.

19. See A. D. Nock, *Conversion* (Oxford: At the Clarendon Press, 1933), chap. 11.

20. E. Gilson, *History of Christian Philosophy in the Middle Ages* (New York: Random House, 1955), pp. 325–79.

21. Ibid., p. 129.

22. I take this phrase from the subtitle of Matthew Tindal's *Christianity as Old as Creation* (London, 1732). Other such authors are John Toland and Thomas Chubb.

23. Friedrich Schleiermacher, *The Christian Faith*, trans. and ed. H. R. Mackintosh and J. S. Stewart (New York: Harper & Row, Harper Torchbooks, 1963), par. 100. For a general discussion of these tendencies in recent thought, see my *Contemporary Forms of Faith* (Minneapolis: Augsburg Publishing House, 1967), chaps. 4, 5.

24. Gilson, *History*, pp. 454–539.

25. R. A. Norris, Jr., *God and World in Early Christian Theology* (New York: Seabury Press, 1965), chap. 4.

3 / THE KNOWLEDGE OF GOD

26. The sources in Kierkegaard are *Philosophical Fragments* and the *Postscript*. It is this theme in Kierkegaard that Gordon Kaufman takes as the key for his *Systematic Theology: A Historicist Perspective* (New York: Charles Scribner's Sons, 1968).

27. François Wendel, *Calvin: The Origins and Development of His Religious Thought*, trans. Philip Mairet (New York: Harper & Row, 1950), p. 165.

28. Gustaf Wingren, *Creation and Law*, trans. Ross Mackenzie (Philadelphia: Fortress [Muhlenberg] Press, 1961), pp. 42–43.

29. Luther, *Bondage of the Will*, Dillenberger ed., p. 188.

30. Abraham J. Heschel, *God in Search of Man: A Philosophy of Judaism* (New York: Farrar, Straus & Cudahy, 1955), p. 169.

31. Michael Polanyi even broadens this question to ask of the nature of scientific knowledge in particular in *Personal Knowledge: Towards a Post-Critical Philosophy* (Chicago: University of Chicago Press, 1958).

32. G. L. Prestige, *God in Patristic Thought* (London: SPCK, 1964), pp. 25, 57.

33. Gerrish, "To the Unknown God," p. 285.

34. Thus "Roman Catholic Reflections," in *Lutherans and Catholics in Dialogue VI*, p. 52, note three undoubted instances in which infallibility has been invoked: the conciliar dogma of papal infallibility itself (1870) and the two papal dogmas of the Immaculate Conception (1854) and the Assumption (1950).

35. R. M. Grant, *Gnosticism and Early Christianity*, 2d ed. (New York: Columbia University Press, 1966).

36. Walther von Loewenich, *Luther's Theology of the Cross*, trans. H. Bouman (Minneapolis: Augsburg Publishing House, 1976), p. 48, argues against T. Harnack and Seeberg that Luther's theology of the cross is the native soil of his concept of the hidden God. For an anthropological limitation, see Kierkegaard's *The Sickness unto Death*, trans. W. Lowrie (Princeton: Princeton University Press, 1941).

2

The Reception and Recognition of Revelation

Human beings know the categorically supreme God in the purposive receiving of the world as the self is created and claimed. In knowing God as ground and goal, it is the one will for human good that is known. While the human experience of this knowing varies significantly, there is given here the reality and commonality needed for intelligible speech about God.

THE EXPERIENCE OF WORLD, SELF, AND GOD

The concern of this chapter is to discuss the state of knowing God. Wherever God is known, *how* is he known? Our task is confessional: it is to overhear, albeit somewhat analytically, Christians speaking of their knowledge of God. It is not essentially apologetic. We are not trying to persuade non-Christians that they can or do know God.

If knowing God is truly a human act, the accounts of it will likely reflect the diversity that characterizes us. We may begin with a famous passage from Paul Tillich in which he points to one such apparently basic difference:

> One can distinguish two ways of approaching God: the way of overcoming estrangement and the way of meeting a stranger. In the first way man discovers *himself* when he discovers God; he discovers something that is identical with himself although it transcends him infinitely, something from which he is estranged, but from which he never has been and never can be separated. In the second way man meets a *stranger* when he meets God. The meeting is accidental. Essentially they do not belong to each other. They may become friends on a tentative and conjectural basis. But there is no certainty about the stranger man has met. He may disappear, and only *probable* statements can be made about his nature.[1]

It is clear, in this instance at least, that when one overhears Christians speaking about knowing God, one hears talk of the God whom they know. That is

3 / THE KNOWLEDGE OF GOD

fortunate, and it would be a mistake to try to develop the discussion in this chapter apart from content claimed to be known about God. Again our work is shown to be reflective. But when one attends to the difference to which Tillich points, one suspects that it is human diversity with which one is occupied. Or at least it is clear that a Christian is called to consider how varying human accounts of knowing God, as they develop within the church catholic, may in truth speak of the same God.

In any case the difference is there. The names of Augustine and Aquinas leap to mind as one reads Tillich's sentences. Tillich set his stage in the thirteenth century, when the roles were well defined. Let us examine first the second and less favored of Tillich's options: the cosmological approach. Thomas Aquinas, as Tillich says, rejected claims to immediate knowledge of God. We do not know God as one with the knowing self, for in knowing a human concept or a human drive, we do not yet have God. Moreover the ideal reality of concepts must not be confused with extraideal reality. Statements about extraideal reality must be derived from sense-experience. Here the Aristotelian heritage is clear.[2] But given divine effects, we can reason to God.

Bonaventura, on the other hand, held that "God is most truly present to the very soul and immediately knowable; He is knowable in Himself without media as the one which is common to all. For He is the principle of knowledge, the first truth, in the light of which everything else is known."[3] God's image in our soul is the midpoint in the ascent from the visible world to the mystical knowledge of God. In this ontological approach one does sense a kinship to Plato's sustaining unity of being in which, even though the natural mind does not possess vision, a sudden illumination may overwhelm the self from its own depth. Just as the sun, supremely visible in its own right, renders other things visible to the eye, so the Good, supremely intelligible in itself, renders the other forms intelligible to the mind. This analogy had a long future ahead of it.[4]

So there does seem to be a difference between the two traditions to which Tillich points, the empiricist and the illuminationist. Leaving aside for the moment the matter of the knowledge of God available in special revelation, it becomes clear that we must move with care in describing this difference. One familiar characterization employs the contrast between faith and reason, as far as priority in knowing is concerned. If we use the word "reason" to refer to reflection on a publicly accessible reality, then the Thomistic approach stresses reason, to be sure. On the other hand, what could be more public than the bare logic of the notion of perfection, which the ontologically superior being authorizes in the Anselmian version of the Augustinian tradition? We seem in either case to say that knowledge of God is readily available, though the means are different.

THE RECEPTION AND RECOGNITION OF REVELATION

One wonders how dominant even this difference is, once one considers the actual history of theological reflection. Can the data be organized by the familiar appeal to Plato versus Aristotle? It is true that in both the *Summa Theologica* and the *Contra Gentiles*, Thomas places great stress on the Aristotelian "prime mover," which provides an unchangeable "pure act." But Thomas knows that Aristotle's prime mover is not the *efficient* cause of anything (*Metaphysics*, xii,1072,a and b). Aquinas in fact appeals to other arguments, indeed to other sources. Thus he argues from degrees of being to a highest being, as Anselm does, and appeals with John of Damascus to the governance of the world.[5] Moreover, his empiricism is checked otherwise by an aprioristic element, in that knowledge occurs as principles present in the intellect are applied to the data of experience. When Thomas repeatedly says, "And this all understand to be God," the point is that the arguments help us find the God we already have.[6]

It is not far to the appeal to supernatural truths of faith which step into place of the natural principles of knowledge (*Summa Theologica*, i,12,5). So too the Augustinian-Anselmian tradition appeals to both faith and reason. While Augustine is not prepared to begin otherwise than with faith, the most significant ground for that insistence is not the reality of the inner self's quest, but the historical actuality of the divine response in the raw particularity of Jesus. Moreover, there is movement here toward intelligibility precisely as the things of God become clearer through the employment of human knowledge and experience. Augustine is no fideist; understanding is affirmed. The human hearing of the word occurs by the mind, not by the body (*City of God*, xi,2). Thus, true to their master, the Augustinians always resented the Thomistic notion of the soul as the form of the body, because it entailed an empirical intellectualism, eliminating the illumining supplement which was to be affirmed even in natural cognition. Nevertheless, similitudes drawn from human experience are helpful to the mind, as is clearly illustrated by Augustine's sustained evocation of the several trinities of the human soul as intelligible likenesses of the triune God.

Thus we find significant unity in classic Christian accounts of the knowledge of God. In both streams which Tillich identifies, there is a strong sense that the God known is—knowledge notwithstanding—transcendent. Hence both traditions emphasize negation, if not estrangement, in the knowing of God. The *via negativa* is suggested early, in the works of Clement of Alexandria and Origen. The issue is first focused directly, however, in the controversy between the Cappadocians and Eunomius. To Eunomius' assertion, "I know God as God knows himself," the Cappadocians replied that God is fundamentally incomprehensible and that all human knowledge of God is remotely analogical. In the East this led to the development of a highly apophatic

3 / THE KNOWLEDGE OF GOD

theology, which served a Christianized Plotinean mysticism. In the West Aquinas also used Plotinus' threefold method of negation, analogy, and eminence—but with more pronounced noetic concerns.[7]

Perhaps, then, Gilson is right in arguing that the East and the West do not differ because the East was more Platonic but because the West from Augustine on was concerned for the relationship of nature to grace, while the East was concerned for the relationship of the image of God to the process of deification.[8] In turn this theological difference yields, on the Western side, a still deeper epistemological divide, when we introduce the distinctive emphases of Reformation thought. In the theocentric stress of the Reformation, there is a tendency to juxtapose faith either to experience as universally accessible as one's own self or to the shared experience of a world. Given human obduracy, the knowledge of God must be God's doing. Writing in this tradition, Helmut Thielicke says:

> God's true presence, then, is to be sought in the incarnate Word, in the manifestation of Jesus Christ. Here is the mirror of the fatherly heart (Luther) and hence the Father himself. Even under the cover of the cross, even in the alien form of the suffering, death, and lowliness of the Son of God, even under apparent concealment, God is present in the directness of his form as the Word. For the lowliness of this manifestation is the form of his self-emptying love. This is his very nature. It is God himself.[9]

Is this really a *third* view? Is faith—or even God—to take its place alongside world and self in our sketch? Is fideism to be placed in a list of epistemological options? It is apparent that any answer cannot be an unqualified one. Just as the other two views intermingle historically and conceptually, the Reformation emphasis retains some of their elements. One might well argue that its strong emphasis on the historical revelation in Jesus is more Aristotelian than Platonic, at least in the sense that when one is looking outside the self one is facing in the right direction. Similarly, Luther placed great stress on those "visible words," the sacraments. Indeed an argument has been made that Luther follows Aquinas' course of correction of Aristotle, by which revealed truths both check any simple empiricism and replace Platonic apriorism.[10]

Yet sharp differences remain between Luther and Aquinas. For Luther, the knowledge of God given in Jesus is not a particular item of doctrine, which supplements a general knowledge of God, but is the beginning of all true knowledge. This is fundamentally a theological difference. It is linked with a philosophical difference in that Luther represents the nominalist rejection of realism's structure of necessary essences.

Nominalism's purpose was to show the deficiencies of the natural knowledge of God.[11] The notion of will came to be crucial. Nothing that depends on the free decision of an absolutely free God is philosophically deducible. Both the Thomistic *analogia entis* and the Anselmian *necessitas* are eliminated. Reason is reduced to probabilities, not simply in the encounter with empirical reality—as Thomas would readily grant—but in the process of inference from such particulars.

When God cannot reliably be known metaphysically, revelation takes on crucial importance. Nominalism lifted up the historical particularity affirmed also in the other traditions. There seems to be the more reason for this in Luther; and the reason is theological, even anthropological, rather than merely metaphysical. After all, on issues of nature and grace Luther stood even further from nominalism than he did from Thomism. Thomas, at least, granted that no person could turn to God unless God turned to that person first and offered assisting grace. In nominalist thought, on the other hand, a person without God's aid can perform works worthy of merit.[12] Luther reached back behind both realism and nominalism to the anti-Pelagian side of Augustine.

We are in effect asking what epistemological theory is to be associated with the view that opposes *logos* and *kairos*. Both the empiricist and the illuminationist traditions can be viewed as translations into epistemology of the view that *logos* and *kairos* supplement each other. Does Luther have a distinct epistemology, derived from the stress on historical revelation?[13] One can argue that on epistemological issues, as often otherwise, the reformers stand with Augustine. John Smith has written of the appeal to experience in the work of Luther and Calvin:

> The appeal to experience meant a *trying out*, an actual attempt to live through the cycle of contrition and penance, so that each could truthfully say, "the traditional way of understanding justification before God has been *tried* and found wanting." The important point is that, while all experience must remain subject to the interpreting word, it nevertheless exercises a *critical* function, since the individual makes a discovery for himself.[14]

Thus Luther could declare that "only experience makes a theologian," and Calvin made a determined appeal to the inner witness of the Holy Spirit, both in service of the revelation in history.[15]

Yet it must be said that Augustine's sense for the unity of being—which remains in restless tension with his writing on sin and grace and which informs *his* appeal to experience—is missing in the reformers. Thus in them the explicit theological stress on history stands out the more. While there may be in the reformers an appeal to experience as against late medieval Aristotelianism's analytical detachment, there is not a developed cosmological or metaphysical position that could prevent Protestantism from being regarded as, and indeed from becoming, merely "subjective." When that danger threatened in "enthusiasm," the mainstream figures became understandably restive. The opposite danger then threatened: new scholasticism. This

3 / THE KNOWLEDGE OF GOD

epistemological vacillation seems to suggest that the striking directness of the historical appeal requires some fuller conceptual framework if its gains are not to be lost.

Christian thought has faced many of the same pressures in the modern period. Would Christianity be best linked with the line from Descartes through Leibniz and Spinoza, with its emphasis on the self and the *a priori* knowledge available to the self? Or would empiricism in the British tradition be a resource with which the faith could make alliance? How shall one identify and appraise such influential appeals as that made by Schleiermacher to the consciousness of absolute dependence, or by Kant to moral experience? These appeals do seem reminiscent of the Platonic turn within, and suggest the difficulty facing any attempt to reclaim a shared world of experience once reductionistic empiricism has swept it clean of spirits, divine or human. But is there a genuine third way? Is God to be known apart from self and world?

We shall address some of these issues when the context of the knowledge of God is discussed. Our contention will be that we must claim a knowledge of God "in, with, and under" the knowledge of self and world. Regrettably, contemporary thought seems to represent the dynamic of diastasis, by which the realities of the self and the world are so pulled apart in perception that one is nearly persuaded that God can slip through the chasm unscathed and indeed unclothed. We need to think of self and world together in such a way that the God who is truly other than either can be understood to be known without requiring the repudiation of self and/or world, as if their presence and service in the knowing of God were a threat.

In Chapter 1, speaking of God as the world's ground, we spoke of the giving of the past, the creating of freedom, the lure to the future. Without relationships a person is not a self. As the temporal passage is gathered into the focus of the self, a world is given to the self. God is at work in that. As the reality of a world is gathered to be given, a self comes to be, a fresh synthesis of necessity and possibility held together in freedom.[16] And God is at work in that.

We can transgress no further on the anthropological *loci*; but it does seem that, having said only this much, it is already apparent how the differences chronicled in this section come about. Some Christians attend particularly to the giving of the world, others to the fresh coming-to-be of selfhood. As the categorically superior one, God is at work in precisely their connection. Both the empiricist and the illuminationist emphases have a place, it would seem. Also, the more specific approaches can be understood to develop aspects of God's reality as ground. The gift of the world, a cosmological association, is received as bearing purpose, a teleological association. God does act; God does will. That purpose bears in on the self with its claim, a moral association. The differences are fitting, and the commonality is no less so, for the God who does all this is eminently one.

THE RECEPTION AND RECOGNITION OF REVELATION

And the "ontological" approach? Perhaps it not only suggests the creation of selfhood, but the reality of categorical supremacy which underlies all the approaches. In a sense, then, it does abstract from specific associations, as if it were indeed an argument or approach from concept alone. But if matters are as we have portrayed them, it is not strange that this most rationalistic of approaches at the same time keeps company with mysticism. Perhaps Tillich is right, after all, that "*Deus est esse*, and the certainty of God is identical with the certainty of Being itself: God is the presupposition of the question of God."¹⁷ This is, it must be affirmed, an existential presupposition and not merely an activity alluring to people with a penchant for abstractions.

The kairotic knowledge of *telos*, while bearing priority, does fit within this framework. I have argued that how we know depends on what we know. Inasmuch as this Jesus reveals to us none other than God, the ground and goal of the world, our knowing that fact must at least cohere with the patterns applying in the knowledge of God as Logos. Our discussion has distinguished strands stressing world and self. The claim to know God in this Jesus does essentially involve that which is neither God nor the self; but in this knowing the self understands its world and indeed itself in a way that is decisively new. One must come to hear from without the story of this one from Galilee. In that sense at least it is a "worldly" story. But one may well say more. A God who wills so to be known will be at work within the hearer to make the occasioning word an enabling word, even an efficacious one. It is to be hoped that the theologians who have worked so hard to make clear the decisive newness of the historical word of revelation will apply themselves to showing how that word becomes concretely decisive by being known in relation to self and world.

We turn now to a specific part of that task. If what has been said in this section is true, then we must face the question of the cognitive status of our knowledge. If God is known, then the intelligibility and truthfulness of the claims made about God need to be discussed and even defended. However much it may be God who reveals, it is we who know; and we must give account of what it is so to know as to speak as we do.

KNOWLEDGE AS PARADIGM, PARABLE, AND PROPHECY

Our task is to reflect on the cognitive claims involved in the knowledge of God. The question is not what they are but of what sort they are. How is language being used when Christians speak of God? We ask about *Christian* speech; therefore again in this section our discussion must be conducted precisely in the light of what the faith says of God. If God is as the faith declares, how does language work in this instance? But, of course, it is *our*

3 / THE KNOWLEDGE OF GOD

language and *our* meaning and speaking, so we need to ask as well how such God-talk finds a place within the range of human speech-acts. How is it like and how is it unlike other uses of language?

Obviously the discussion of this topic in our time will reflect the concerns raised by the philosophers of language. We cannot avoid the familiar issues raised about the meaningfulness of religious language by the likes of Alfred Jules Ayer and Anthony Flew. A brief review may be in order. Crucial in this regard was insistence on the criterion of verifiability to test the genuineness of apparent statements of fact. In Ayer's words, "We say that a sentence is factually significant to any given person, if, and only if, he knows how to verify the proposition which it purports to express—that is, if he knows what observations would lead him, under certain conditions, to accept the proposition as being true, or reject it as being false."[18] Metaphysical statements were found by this criterion to be "pseudo-propositions," since one could not conceive of an observation which would verify or falsify such statements. Claims about the existence of a transcendent god or an immortal soul were stripped of literal significance because of their metaphysical involvement. Flew shifted the issue to that of falsifiability, and voiced his skepticism in these terms: "Now it often seems to people who are not religious as if there was no conceivable event or series of events the occurrence of which would be admitted by sophisticated religious people to be a sufficient reason for conceding 'there wasn't a God after all' or 'God does not really love us then. . . . '"[19] He went on to speak of religious assertions' death "by a thousand qualifications."

How shall one respond to this challenge? On balance, if offered a multiple-choice question concerning the nature of their statements, Christians would have to pass by "analytic or definitional" and "emotive" and select "synthetic" or "empirical" in *some* sense. While Christians make statements of different logical types, the game is up unless among those types is speech about real states of affairs. We have just been speaking of the *experience* of revelation in world, self, and God. "God is the world's ground and goal" belongs with "There is a tiger in this room" (to take a notorious example), more than with mathematical formulae or moans and groans.

Is the Christian then subjected to the tyranny of the verification principle? Already at the early stage of the discussion two points were clear: that it would not do to say that Christian claims were empirical yet nonfalsifiable in principle, and yet that the standards of verification/falsification by sense perception left Christian theologians puzzled about how even to formulate the conditions for meeting the challenge. Of course it soon became evident that those standards tended to undercut the verification principle itself, as Ayer seemed to acknowledge already in the second edition of *Language, Truth, and Logic*. Christian theologians were then tempted to take comfort in the afflictions of the enemy, and to mask their own difficulties by appealing to faith, as when Basil Mitchell wrote: "So the theologian *does* recognize the fact of pain as counting against Christian doctrine. But it is true that he will not allow it—or anything—to count decisively against it; for he is committed by his faith to trust in God."[20] Such papering over the problem could not settle the matter for long.

There followed the enthusiastic discovery of the later Wittgenstein with his fine sense for the concreteness and specificity of particular language usages. One may even wonder whether the theologians did not invent rather than discover the master, for the alacrity and even abandon with which apologists pleaded the distinctiveness of the religious "language game" was impressive. At the very least, insufficient attention was given to formulating the distinctive rules (but rules nonetheless) which were to be understood to apply in this game—not to mention engaging in discussion of how this game was related to other games, why anyone would want to play this game, and the like.

Where is the discussion now? A major movement attaches itself to the category of "paradigm," rejecting the positivist model of scientific understanding. We are thinking of such writers as Thomas Kuhn, N. R. Hanson, and Stephen Toulmin. Briefly, this movement has argued that there are large-scale models, assumed in every era of science, and that these are never able to be verified because it is in terms of them that verification is carried out. The practice of science refutes the positivist model of scientific thinking. Moreover, the history of science shows that there is a class of propositions which are not capable of verification but are clearly meaningful—and meaningful in a nontrivial and nonpathological sense.[21]

It is understandable that this view has won many adherents. Yet the points cited in its favor actually count against it, not least because they reveal that the view does not accommodate the historical reality of the Christian religion. The view seems to take us beyond the verification/falsification disputes; issues of theodicy become mere methodological anomalies.[22] Commitment can be described as inheritance. But the history of the Christian church contains arguments *for* God, not merely from God. Christians and adherents of other religions do in fact converse with each other and change their views. True, we speak of "conversion" in such a case, but the change does not take place without attending to the data. Formal criteria—simplicity, scope, coherence, and the like—are not sufficient in such matters. Christians claim something about the world, about the self—indeed, about God.

There is the rub: the Christian faith is about God. The solution in terms of "paradigms" suggests that religious statements be treated not as statements about particulars but as statements functioning at the level of theoretical entities in complex, multileveled systems. Patrick Sherry puts the point in these terms:

3 / THE KNOWLEDGE OF GOD

Now the comparison between theology and theoretical concepts or explanations in science is trying to meet these problems, by suggesting that a system of religious belief is like a scientific theory in that it only needs to "touch down" at some points in our experience (though unlike it in that we do not seek to test religious beliefs through experiments).[23]

But surely it is crucial that the faith touches down by reference to alleged states of affairs in reality in such a way that control is exercised in the process of stating the faith. While difficulties abound in identifying those states, the debate is about the data, not merely about how best to organize the data conceptually. Data and theory must be held together. Christians speak their language not because, or not merely because, it serves well to organize the state of affairs in which they find themselves, but because they consider it to be the truest account of what is there to be confronted by any inquirer. They might well find themselves more naturally linked with those philosophers of science who suggest that while all data are theory-laden, rival theories are not incommensurable as if walled off from each other. Such contend that while comprehensive theories are highly resistant to falsification, observation does exert control over theory construction and maintenance.[24]

The faith, then, would seem to suggest that in principle questions of verification and falsification are appropriate to it. Obviously recent understanding of how to proceed in arbitrating these questions coheres more easily with the empiricist tradition of theology than with the illuminationist. Perhaps that understanding works better with certain types of statements. One might, for example, specify with Sherry three categories of statements: first, those about the unique (miracles, prophets and their statements, events in the lives of believers), second, those about the recurrent (the beauty of nature, love and holiness, stages of human life), and third, those about the world as a whole (the universe as such, being as such).[25] Sherry suggests that Christian speech's difficulties are with the first and the third categories of statement and the relationships between them.

Comment is possible, even with the so far minimal sketch of content. To start with the last point, Christians do speak about the whole. But it is important to note that what is said is not that God is the whole, but that God works in the whole, that God is the ground and goal of the whole. That is, Christian talk is discriminate talk about the whole: the world is not God, though it is *by*—and for—God; we are not God, though we are *for*—and by—God; most emphatically, sin is not God's doing, though it is *against* God. Everything has to do with God; we do talk of the whole in that sense.

Clearly Christians talk as well about a unique person and event, and assign epistemic priority to that talk. Speech about the unique is difficult enough, but here we are called on to speak of this one precisely in relation to the whole. This is *kairos*, but it is the *kairos* of the *logos*. Perhaps we may catch up this connection with the term "parable." In such a way Austin Farrer says: "If Christ is called Word or Logos, it is not meant that he is the lucid instance of general ideas, but that he is the self-enacted human parable of Godhead."[26] Above all we must recall that in a unique and normative way we are linking this particular one with the one who is categorically supreme. *That* is the infamous "scandal of particularity." That is what lies behind appeals to an analogy of proportionality which includes negation—"As a father pities his children, so the Lord pities those who fear him" (Ps. 103:13).[27] Perhaps this is why some Christians speak of the *kairos* "sub contrario" as reflecting back even on the cognitive status of statements made about God.[28] Such talk does seem very fuzzy and soft—almost in principle, as it were. But there is a cognitive claim here. As Robert King puts it, "The story of Jesus has become for Christians the master-image by which God's action is identified. This master-image functions in at least two ways: it focuses the action of God in relation to man, and it particularizes God's intention for man."[29] King's statement is helpful, though it may still understate the reality of the new in the historical particularity of Jesus.

We have at best barely managed to hold the cry for verification at bay. What may we say of this? It may be possible by the art of imaginative generalization to formulate meaningful propositions about the whole, which have a significant empirical anchorage.[30] Of course, if the one at work in the whole is categorically supreme, if God works precisely in giving a world that is creative of self, then ordinary ostensive reference will fail. There will be an indirectness, a "parabolic" character to the data which can be introduced.

We have neglected to mention another major impediment facing an attempt to respond to the verification challenge. How shall one verify empirical claims about the *whole*, given the "open texture" character of reality? How shall we know about the truth of such claims, *in medias res*? Does this make the matter of verification an essentially eschatological matter, as people as different as John Hick and Wolfhart Pannenberg have suggested?[31] We think not, though we have of course already alluded to the Christian recognition that only "then" will we see "face to face."

We appropriate the multisignificance of the word "prophecy" to address this issue. The prophets were at once "forth-tellers" and "fore-tellers"; that point is not really in dispute. What we underline, however, is that they could be both precisely because of the character of the God whose word came to them. It is precisely the prophets with whom we associate a so-called "moral" interpretation of holiness, as distinguished from a ritualistic view. It is clear what God will do, because it is clear what God is doing. In the parable of God we have the prophecy of God. Christians can attend to the developing reality of the whole in the light of the parable of God.

This is why Christians speak of the *living* character of the word of God.

3 / THE KNOWLEDGE OF GOD

Luther, for example, spoke of the church as a "mouth house," rather than a "book house," and the Reformation tradition speaks of how the Scriptures *function*, of what they *do* to the hearer. This seems to fit with such approaches to language as Wittgenstein's emphasis on *use* and Austin's stress on the performative character of speech. If this faith claim is true, if the whole is a developing reality, it is not strange that such a fundamental matter as language reveals that characteristic.

Where, then, does that leave us, in the unfriendly present, in understanding the cognitive status of the statements we make concerning God? We list a series of points.

First. We should claim no more than what fits the relationship between two free and personal wills. Philosophers have worked hard—perhaps too hard, reflecting excessively dualistic premises—to explain how we know that other minds exist. Some ambiguity is appropriate and perhaps even inevitable in such a matter. We are in contact, sharing a common world; but we do not inhabit each other as centered selves. As we join together in common cause, we seem to know the other more significantly as we know the other's will. But significant clarity is possible for the message's intention without commitment in advance. Obviously there may be nuances in a lived relationship of trust which are not available apart from the relationship.[32]

Second. The faith declares that the will and activity of God are essentially clear. Moreover, they are true, for reality will come to correspond to them. The prophetic word will prove true. It *is* proving true. The kingdom grows now, albeit secretly.

Third. Given the emphasis on time and the developing reality of God's intention, it is helpful to speak in terms of the "story" character of reality, and our language may appropriately reflect that character. This, of course, does not compromise the truth claims involved. In particular, it does not diminish the importance of affirmation of, and critical study into, the historical event which created the story the Scriptures tell.

Fourth. Given the constancy of God, the Christian is not a Lone Ranger on some frontier of spirituality. We find ourselves together in the faith; we write confessions and subscribe to them, though we may hesitate when infallibility is claimed for such statements.[33]

Fifth. The direction in which God is working is clear. God is *for* us; and the promise is that what God intends in creation and has made sure and clear in Jesus will come to pass.

Sixth. Given the continuity of God's creative-redemptive intention for us, faith fulfills the structure of human personhood, while transcending it; it does not destroy it.[34] While it is notoriously difficult to attach specific empirical reference to such a phrase as "true personhood," it is clear that plastic smiles do not adorn the altar of God.

THE RECEPTION AND RECOGNITION OF REVELATION

So we claim to know God in the giving of world creative of self. We claim to have more than a paradigm; we confess a parable and claim a prophecy. It remains to be seen how wisely and how well such knowing may be said to occur in the reality of the human context.

NOTES

1. Paul Tillich, *Theology of Culture*, ed. Robert C. Kimball (New York: Oxford University Press, 1959), p. 10. (Italics his.)
2. Gustave Weigel and Arthur Madden in *Religion and the Knowledge of God* (Englewood Cliffs, N.J.: Prentice-Hall, 1961), pp. 123-24, apply this position in Aquinas' rejection in *Contra Gentiles* of Anselm's argument for the immediate knowledge of the existence of God: "Even if we wish to define God as the being than which nothing greater can be conceived, we are confronted by a double possibility: either that we have conceived a merely ideal reality which does not necessarily imply extra-mental existence or we are supposing without guarantee that there is a being than which nothing greater can be conceived."
3. Tillich, *Theology of Culture*, p. 13. For a recent influential statement in this tradition, see John Baillie, *The Sense of the Presence of God* (New York: Charles Scribner's Sons, 1962). In these Gifford lectures Baillie notes of such Christian "God-talk" as eternal, unchanging, omniscient, holy: "It is quite impossible to believe that such characters as these are suggested to us by anything we find in ourselves or elsewhere in the created world. To say that we gain the conception of perfect being by arranging our feeble human approaches towards perfection in an ascending series, and then imagining the indefinite prolongation of this series, is to forget that such an arrangement could not have been made by us save by the aid of a standard of perfection already present to our minds. . . . What is false is the assumption that the comparison moves from man to God instead of from God to man" (pp. 116-17).
4. A. H. Armstrong and R. A. Markus, *Christian Faith and Greek Philosophy* (London: Darton, Longman & Todd, 1960), pp. 59-77, note particularly that the Platonic understanding includes the dependence of the forms on the Good not only in the order of knowledge, but also in that of being. Wolfhart Pannenberg, *Basic Questions in Theology*, vol. 2, trans. George H. Kehm (Philadelphia: Fortress Press, 1971), pp. 119-83, provides a useful account of that history, noting, e.g., of Origen that even though the Platonic doctrine of illumination presupposed divine assistance for knowledge of God, Origen argued that this doctrine was independently available in Hosea and John.
5. *Contra Gentiles*, i,13. Weigel and Madden, *Religion and the Knowledge of God*, pp. 126-27, suggest that the argument from the degrees of being is already insinuated in Augustine in *City of God*, viii,6; *Of True Religion*, xviii,35-36; and *Confessions*, vii,11,17.
6. Weigel and Madden, *Religion and the Knowledge of God*, p. 128.
7. For a discussion of "the Eunomian problem," see John Murray, *The Problem of God* (New Haven: Yale University Press, 1964), pp. 53-62. On the uniqueness of the Byzantine form of this theology, see John Meyendorff, *Byzantine Theology:*

225

3 / THE KNOWLEDGE OF GOD

Historical Trends and Doctrinal Themes (New York: Fordham University Press, 1974), pp. 11ff. Jaroslav Pelikan, *The Spirit of Eastern Christendom* (Chicago: University of Chicago Press, 1974), p. 34, comments: "It was the consensus of the theologians that God was not to be worshipped on the basis of his essence, which is supremely unknowable, but on the basis of his procession 'outward,' that is, his providence and foreknowledge."

8. E. Gilson, *History of Christian Philosophy in the Middle Ages* (New York: Random House, 1955), p. 94. Gilson is arguing that Plato heavily influenced *both* East and West.

9. Helmut Thielicke, *The Evangelical Faith*, 2 vols., trans. and ed. G. W. Bromiley (Grand Rapids: Wm. B. Eerdmans, 1967), 2:13.

10. Pannenberg, *Basic Questions*, 2:56–57, expanding on the works of Bernard Lohse, *Ratio und Fides: Eine Untersuchung über die ratio in der Theologie Luthers* (Göttingen, 1958).

11. Heiko Oberman, "Headwaters of the Reformation," in *Luther and the Dawn of the Modern Era* (Leipzig: E. J. Brill, 1974), p. 57. In his *The Harvest of Medieval Theology: Gabriel Biel and Late Medieval Nominalism* (Cambridge, Mass.: Harvard University Press, 1963), p. 41, Oberman notes that the nominalist epistemology granted experimental, intuitive, and indirect knowledge of the world but not of God.

12. B. A. Gerrish, *Grace and Reason* (Oxford: At the Clarendon Press, 1962), pp. 68–69. Cf. my discussion of this point in the *locus* on sin.

13. See Pannenberg, *Basic Questions*, 2:63–64, on the difference that remains between faith and reason even when reason is itself conceived historically: "Faith is directed to this future which constitutes reality as a whole and thereby brings everything individual to its essential perfection. However, because this future is not alien to reason, but is rather its origin from which it implicitly always derives, faith cannot stand in opposition to reason. Much more does it remind reason of its own absolute presupposition by speaking about the eschatological future and its pre-appearance in the history of the resurrection of Jesus, from which faith derives."

14. John E. Smith, *The Analogy of Experience: An Approach to Understanding Religious Truth* (New York: Harper & Row, 1973), p. 28. (Italics his.)

15. In *The Bondage of the Will* (in *Martin Luther: Selections from his Writings*, ed. John Dillenberger [Garden City, N.Y.: Doubleday & Co., 1961], p. 171), Luther makes a very specific statement of this sort: "The Holy Spirit is no Sceptic, and the things He has written in our hearts are not doubts or opinions, but assertions—surer and more certain than sense and life itself." François Wendel in *Calvin: The Origins and Development of His Religious Thought*, trans. Philip Mairet (New York: Harper & Row, 1950), p. 157, summarizes Calvin's emphasis: "The Spirit inspired the authors of the books of Scripture, and it is he also who inspires us when we read their writings so that we may have tangible proof of the identity of that inspiration.... For Calvin, the interior witness of the Holy Spirit is the supreme criterion upon which the authority of the Scriptures is founded."

16. While I do not believe this formulation is particularly idiosyncratic, I take it from Kierkegaard's *Sickness unto Death* (Princeton: Princeton University Press, 1941).

17. Tillich, *Theology of Culture*, pp. 15–16.

THE RECEPTION AND RECOGNITION OF REVELATION

18. Alfred Jules Ayer, *Language, Truth, and Logic*, 2d ed. (New York: Dover Publications, 1946), p. 35.

19. Anthony Flew and Alisdair MacIntyre, eds., *New Essays in Philosophical Theology* (London: SCM Press, 1955), p. 98.

20. Basil Mitchell, in ibid., p. 104.

21. Thomas Kuhn, *The Structure of Scientific Revolutions*, 2d ed. (Chicago: University of Chicago Press, 1970); cf. his "Second Thoughts on Paradigms," in *The Structure of Scientific Theories*, ed. Frederick Suppe (Champaign: University of Illinois Press, 1973). N. R. Hanson, *Patterns of Discovery* (Cambridge: At the University Press, 1958); and Stephen Toulmin, *Foresight and Understanding* (New York: Harper & Row, 1961).

22. L. Hughes Cox, "Why Not Drop the Theological-Falsification Issue Altogether?" *Pers.* 58, no. 1 (January 1977): 18–27.

23. Patrick Sherry, *Religion, Truth, and Language Games* (New York: Barnes & Noble, 1977), p. 108.

24. Ian Barbour, *Myths, Models, and Paradigms* (New York: Harper & Row, 1974).

25. Sherry, *Religion, Truth, and Language Games*, pp. 71–73.

26. Austin Farrer, "Revelation," in *Faith and Logic*, ed. Basil Mitchell (Boston: Beacon Press, 1957), p. 98.

27. For a defense of Aquinas' use of the analogy of proportionality, see Henri Bouillard's *The Knowledge of God*, trans. Samuel D. Femiano (New York: Herder & Herder, 1968). According to Bouillard, the attack is from Karl Barth, who "supposes that there is a supreme concept . . . embracing at the same time God and his creature. . . ." Bouillard contends that "when Barth reproaches the 'Thomistic *analogia entis*' for placing God and creature under the common denominator of being, it is not St. Thomas himself whom he is thinking of, but the theologians who claim to take their inspiration from Thomas. . . . Several of the theologians in question seem to have let the Thomistic notion of analogy slip away from the order of judgment toward that of concept (as representation). In doing so they have followed the interpretation of Cajetan, or sometimes that of Suarez. In their writings, analogy seems to us to designate the *partial resemblance* of the creature to the Creator, or the imperfect representation of God in human speech, rather than the *mode* in which one affirms the first and validates the second. The process of negation is less radical than in St. Thomas" (italics his). The suggestion made in Chapter 1 that divine transcendence be formulated in qualitative and relational terms may caution against casting the debate in the terms of negation, though distinction is essential.

28. Gerhard O. Forde, "Infallibility Language and the Early Lutheran Tradition," in *Teaching Authority and Infallibility in the Church: Lutherans and Catholics in Dialogue VI*, ed. Paul C. Empie, T. Austin Murphy, and Joseph A. Burgess (Minneapolis: Augsburg Publishing House, 1980), pp. 120–37.

29. Robert H. King, *The Meaning of God* (Philadelphia: Fortress Press, 1973), p. 112.

30. A related case may be metaphysical propositions formulated by such a method; see Alfred North Whitehead's *Process and Reality*, ed. David Ray Griffin and Donald W. Sherburne (New York: Free Press, 1978), chap. 1.

31. John Hick, *Faith and Knowledge* (Ithaca, N.Y.: Cornell University Press, 1957); Pannenberg, *Basic Questions*, 2:27, e.g.: "Since the emergence of historical con-

3 / THE KNOWLEDGE OF GOD

sciousness, the unity of all reality is conceivable only as a history. The unity of truth is still possible only as a historical process, and can be known only from the end of this process."

32. See Alvin Plantinga, *God and Other Minds* (Ithaca, N.Y.: Cornell University Press, 1967). Plantinga's "tentative conclusion" is: "If my belief in other minds is rational, so is my belief in God. But obviously the former is rational; so, therefore, is the latter" (p. 271). On the critique of dualistic tendencies in this regard, see P. F. Strawson, *Individuals: An Essay in Descriptive Metaphysics* (Garden City, N.Y.: Doubleday & Co.; London: Methuen, 1959).

33. Thus in *Lutherans and Catholics in Dialogue VI*, pp. 13–14, Lutherans worry about usurpation of what is conferred on Jesus Christ alone.

34. Paul Tillich, *Systematic Theology*, 3 vols. (Chicago: University of Chicago Press, 1951–63), 1:111–15.

3

God's Call and the Human Question about the Ground of Life

As Logos, God blesses by calling into life. In varying degrees and forms that life asks of and knows its ground is both its gift and its task. The call is sure as the response is not, so that the question of life may seem to be most certainly answered apart from life.

THE DIVINE INCOGNITO: THE REAL, THE BEAUTIFUL, AND THE GOOD

This *locus* is about the knowledge of God. We began in Chapter 1 by asking *why* God is known and found the answer in God's will and action to reveal. We continued in Chapter 2 by asking *how* God is known, and spoke of the human condition of knowing and speaking of God. Taking a leaf from Aristotle, we might say that Chapter 1 treated the efficient cause and Chapter 2 the material cause of the knowledge of God. In this chapter and the next we shall ask how widely God is known. Perhaps this chapter is about Aristotle's formal cause, the forms or structures in and through which God is known. *Where* is God known? That is our theme.

How well is God known? That question is also our concern in these chapters. We have two matters in mind: First: With what degree of awareness is God known? One may perhaps "know" without recognizing the true identity or full significance of what one knows. Does one know that one knows *God*? Second: What is the effect of this knowing? Is the knowledge of God received as the answer that it is to the human question?

These matters are, of course, more than we can manage. To address these questions is to risk both offense and ridicule, quite apart from the answers one offers. I make no claim to command the phenomenological amplitude of data, as would be necessary if one were to somehow evoke the categorial scheme from the context. It is, after all, still context. That is, it is still a theological inquiry which I conduct. Thus it is the theological understanding of God as ground which identifies what we are looking for in this chapter,

3 / THE KNOWLEDGE OF GOD

though it is to be hoped that orientation does not tell us what we see. Context, then, is not trivialized. We do look about, albeit selectively and with text in mind.

That text speaks of God as the world's ground. If human beings ask about their ground, what form(s) will the question take? The question will be *about* us, that frail synthesis of necessity and possibility thrown ahead in freedom.[1] It will be about how a world is given, how a self created, how that self is claimed. The question will be *after* a word that fits us, that grounds us. Such a word must be sure and it must be universally applicable. Life is and life intends. It knows the dialectic of being and becoming; it is gift and task. As such, life finds its ground in order to move toward its goal. Ground may support life's movement toward goal by directing in bestowing. God calls into life and calls in life—toward the goal. It is that kind of word for which we are looking. How widely and how well is it heard?

We begin with words like "the real," "the beautiful," "the true." These words are good words, but not clearly God-words. Precisely so! They are not *clearly* God-words. But here humankind asks about and knows of God as the world's ground. Bernard Lonergan speaks about such asking:

> The question of God is epistemological, when we ask how the universe can be intelligible. It is philosophic when we ask why we should bow to the principle of sufficient reason, when there is no sufficient reason for the existence of contingent things. It is moral when we ask whether the universe has a moral ground and so a moral goal. It finally is religious when we ask whether there is anyone for us to love with all our heart and all our soul and all our mind and all our strength.[2]

The faith assures us that God is the world's *present* ground, for that is a matter of God's action. God wills to be known and can be known. It remains to look about to see how widely and how well question and ground fit each other.

One may ask how we are called into life, by asking what is most fundamental in reality. *Metaphysics*, in identifying indispensable explanatory principles, seems to provide a word that is sure and universal. We seek the pervasive and primitive in reality. The real, so understood, becomes God's incognito. Perhaps it was this incognito that prevailed in the ancient world. Werner Jaeger has argued so about the pre-Socratics, saying that we meet here not rudimentary natural science, but rather natural theology bent on identifying the God who does not depend on convention.[3] It is clear that the Socratic-Platonic literature contains occasional explicitly religious references alongside the quest for wisdom deriving from knowledge of the most real. But it is in Aristotle that metaphysics and divinity come together most clearly. He is looking for "a cause which will move things and bring them together" (*Metaphysics*, i.4.984b30),

GOD'S CALL AND THE HUMAN QUESTION ABOUT THE GROUND OF LIFE

and reasons that "if there is an immovable substance, the science of this must be prior and must be first philosophy, and universal in this way, because it is first" (ibid., vi.1.1026a23–30). Thus Aristotle reaches the first mover which "exists by necessity" (ibid., xii.7.1072b10–29) and "produces motion by being loved, whereas all other things move by being moved" (ibid., xii.7.1072b1–4).

With Aristotle, we do seem to be on the ground of religion, but it may be doubted that the project of life is well grounded in his answers to the metaphysical question. How does one whose categorical supremacy lies precisely in being unmoved sustain the striving that is life? One can understand the suspicion with which such God-talk will be greeted by those who are dedicated to affirmation of the human venture. Aristotle pulls ethics back into metaphysics; the good life is the life that comes closest to the divine life in self-sufficiency. Philosophic wisdom is the higher virtue (*Nicomachean Ethics*, x.7.1177a24), for its pleasures are pure and enduring and the philosopher needs no one besides himself to exercise his virtue. A just man, on the other hand, needs others to be just.

There is clearly something right about the metaphysical question about God. We should not be troubled by the emphasis on reality in incognito, or by the certainty claimed here. It is not strange that Christians like Clement of Alexandria speak of philosophy as having a divine origin and of Christianity as the true philosophy. Yet the fit here is not as fine as one might wish. The fundamental difficulty is not the specific one examined in the previous paragraph, that the Greek tradition happens to regard what is unmoved as having a higher reality than what is moved. It would hardly remove the difficulty if we were to make no such distinction. It is precisely a distinction between God and all else that is needed; and reality merely as such hardly seems supple enough to yield it. We need to state God's ontological superiority, but the sense of reality merely as such is too blunt an instrument to convey that superiority. The identification of God's incognito requires some specificity; God's creature is not only called into life, but called in life. That is hard to come by in an appeal to "the real," particularly in the modern situation, where distinctions between degrees of being lack persuasive power.

But perhaps the *beautiful* can serve as God's incognito. After all, is there not here a combination of givenness and specificity?

Clearly a kind of transcendence is claimed in art. At least that is the testimony of many who write about art. John Dewey argued that in aesthetic experience the factors determining any experience "are lifted high above the threshold of perception and are made manifest for their own sake."[4] R. G. Collingwood makes apparently salvific claims for the healing power of art. What is healed?

Consciousness can never attend to more than a part of the total sensuous-

231

3 / THE KNOWLEDGE OF GOD

emotional field; but either it may recognize this as belonging to itself, or it may refuse so to recognize it. In the latter case, certain feelings are not ignored, they are disowned; the conscious self disclaims responsibility for them, and thus tries to escape being dominated by them without the trouble of dominating them. This is the "corrupt conciousness" which is the source of what psychologists call repression.[5]

If art is to be more than entertainment, and yet not heal by magic,

> It must be prophetic. . . . But what he has to utter is not, as the individualistic theory of art would have us think, his own secrets. As spokesman of his community, the secrets he must utter are theirs. The reason why they need him is that no community altogether knows its own heart. . . .[6]

There is a kind of revelatory completeness about the clarity art bestows; it is a joy to experience it. But if the disease is more than ignorance, what then? Does art offer any sense of the efficacy of the new? Or perhaps art is exercised precisely to call us back to the beginning? Schiller puts it well:

> It is neither charm, nor is it dignity, which speaks from the glorious face of Juno Ludovici; it is neither of these, for it is both at once. While the female god challenges our veneration, the godlike woman at the same time kindles our love. But while in ecstasy we give ourselves up to the heavenly beauty, the heavenly self-repose awes us back. *The whole form rests and dwells in itself—a fully complete creation in itself*—and as if she were out of space, without advance or resistance; it shows no force contending with force, *no opening through which time could break in*.[7]

No wonder, then, that we find ourselves "in the state of greatest repose." Things were (are) clearer at the beginning—a beginning in which creativity has reached its end. Matthew Arnold, stricken with skepticism and despair, reaches for that kind of salvation in his "Memorial Verses" on the death of Wordsworth. This long passage is not too long to repeat:

> He too upon a wintry clime
> Had fallen—on this iron time
> Of doubts, disputes, distractions, fears.
> He found us when the age had bound
> our souls in its benumbing round;
> He spoke, and loosed our heart in tears
> He laid us *as we lay at birth*
> on the cool flowery lap of earth,
> Smiles broke from us and we had ease;
> The hills were round us, and the breeze
> Went o'er the sun-lit fields again;
> Our foreheads felt the wind and rain,

GOD'S CALL AND THE HUMAN QUESTION ABOUT THE GROUND OF LIFE

> Our youth return'd; for there was shed
> On spirits that had long been dead,
> Spirits dried up and closely furl'd
> *The freshness of the early world.*[8]

How can one achieve a salvation that is other than romantic reverie or ironic perception? Or, short of salvation, how can we understand the ground sensed in art as one which supports and informs human striving, and so points toward a goal which is not simply the "freshness of the early world"? Hegel sought to do so by linking art with the movement of the "idea," by which movement the sensuous is spiritualized in the "concrete universal." But this emphasis on concreteness is still linked with stress on the independence of the object of art, so that the interest of art is purged of desire.[9] Indeed, this difficulty about human freedom may reveal that art in this reading still suffers from the more general deficiency in specificity noted above in the Greek metaphysical vision. How may the gift of beauty preserve its independence and universality and yet engage the task of the individual life?

Kant may provide a transition. Here there is no attempt to make understanding of the efficacy of art dependent on acceptance of a metaphysical vision, for such visions always reach beyond what our senses can tell us. *The Critique of Judgment* opens in art a kind of spiritual vista closed to empirical reason, by identifying an objective purposefulness in nature. Here there is the ecstasy of self-discovery, which is yet purged of particularity through the universality of aesthetic judgment.[10]

Yet on Kant's view we must proceed cautiously in speaking of transcendence. If God is known here as ground, it is certainly through an incognito: *"Beauty is the form of the purposiveness of an object, so far as this is perceived in it without any representation of a purpose."*[11] Kant does try to muster a kind of religious passion for his "philosophy of as-if," despite the subjectivity of all purpose-language:

> We can regard it as a favor which nature has felt for us that, in addition to what is useful, it has so profusely dispensed beauty and charm, and we can therefore love it, as well as regard it with respect on account of its immensity, and feel ennobled ourselves by such regard, just as if nature had established and adorned its splendid theatre precisely with this view.[12]

This is followed by explicit rejection of any religious inference:

> If then we introduce into the context of natural science the concept of God, in order to explain the purposiveness in nature, and subsequently use this purposiveness to prove that there is a God, there is no internal consistency in either science [i.e., either in natural science or theology]; and a delusive circle brings them both into uncertainty, because they have allowed their boundaries to overlap.[13]

3 / THE KNOWLEDGE OF GOD

Kant's reading of art attempts to link the ground with freedom, by way of the category of purposiveness. The self is engaged here in relation to the world outside the self. Nature is extolled, as is evident in the view that art is to copy nature. Yet Kant's skepticism prevents him from making any direct connection with religious talk at this point. What "physico-theology" (the endeavor of reason to infer the supreme cause of nature from the purposes of nature) *does* appropriately do is to open another door, in that "it discloses to us an outlook over nature by which perhaps we may be able to determine more closely the otherwise so unfruitful concept of an Original Being."[14] Aesthetic judgment has brought us across the great divide separating the barren world of pure reason from the richer fields of moral reason. While Kant's distinctions may be tidier than we would like, it is clear that in pointing to *moral* reason he directs us to another pseudonymous witness to the reality of God as ground. Perhaps "the good, the right" may represent an incognito which may convey the sense of personal will missing in metaphysical and aesthetic approaches.

We delay further consideration of Kant to the next section, where we attend to explicit appeals to God. The incognito may be vanishing there. But people do make moral claims without such a theological appeal. We are not thinking of people who make such claims precisely *against* religious appeals (as Kai Nielsen from a Wittgensteinian perspective and S. DeBeauvoir from an existentialist perspective).[15] Rather, we are thinking of the way in which Erich Fromm could commend "the art of loving," or of how Walter Kaufmann can argue that "humbition" (the synthesis of humility and ambition, of course) is "intrinsically admirable."[16] Such people seem to hear a word that is universal and sure. Moreover, that word is specific and instructive; these people hear a call in life. Do they have a sense for the ground of that call?

If ancient Greek wisdom seemed a good place to sample the *metaphysical* incognito, and the idealistic-romantic writers served such a function for the *aesthetic* approach to the question about the ground, is there some such natural locus also in the moral good? We ask, "How does one get an ought from an is?" and the contemporary Anglo-Saxon discussion invites attention. Granting the presence of moral claims, how are we to understand their origin and justification? Hume and others in the empiricist tradition caution against arguing for the empirical character of ethical claims. A matter's "oughtness" does not seem to reside in its "isness." The theologian who insists on the full reality of evil would seem to agree. But then what ground(s) may be found for moral claims?

John Searle's famous article, boldly entitled "How to Derive Ought from Is," exploits a form of language—the performative, e.g., "I promise"—which is neither descriptive nor evaluative. But it seems clear that Searle's derivation

GOD'S CALL AND THE HUMAN QUESTION ABOUT THE GROUND OF LIFE

is dependent on existing "institutions," that is, public standards or systems of rules within which obligations are defined, and on commitment to those institutions. Here we seem at best to have hypothetical imperatives, for he gives us no convincing reason for uttering the performative.[17]

It would seem more promising if we could identify some form of discourse or activity which every rational person engages in, and then show that this requires a certain presupposition. Thus R. S. Peters argues that public discourse presupposes that one ought to consider the interests of others, and Alan Gewirth claims that the very concept of action entails the securing of respect for the freedom and well-being of all agents.[18] Here we do seem to have sufficient scope to ground human life as such. One finds oneself asking, however, "What do the presuppositions this transcendental approach uncovers themselves presuppose?"

As one follows out that question, one encounters a large group of writers who appeal not to logical presuppositions but to particular aspects of the human condition. We are, of course, near the natural law argument. At the level of argument, the incognito is being removed. But the approach can be quite restrained, as when H. L. A. Hart develops a limited concept of teleology (e.g., survival) and appeals to some broad constants of human nature (e.g., vulnerability). Similarly, Karl Rahner seeks to find not a moral law-code, but simply a constant reference point, the creative self, from which to interrogate experience.[19] This is not an appeal to prudence, or if it is, it is a very fundamental prudence indeed. One is saying that injustice, immorality, and amorality destroy or obliterate a dimension of reality in the self.

This last group of moral theorists hints at something very fundamental in the human condition. Can human reality stand alone and still provide a sense of its own ground? The Anglo-Saxon discussion seeks to provide an affirmative answer, since it disavows any metaphysical or theological consideration. But this does leave the discussion rather circular. One wants to ask, May something itself ground this (only apparently) self-authenticating spiritual dimension of human existence?

In all these visions—metaphysical, moral, and aesthetic—there is talk that sounds like faith's speech about *logos* and *nomos*, albeit in an altered tongue. Faith will be interested in the task of translation. Faith may find an ally in that task, for explicit God-talk is clearly not exclusively Christian property. Having followed the putting and answering of the question of a ground, in what do seem to be divine incognitos—the real, the beautiful, the good—we turn to consider this question in explicit connection with the notion of *God*. If human beings ask of and know God this widely without knowing well what they are about, may we not be hopeful in turning to human speaking of God, even outside the Christian community?

3 / THE KNOWLEDGE OF GOD

HUMAN AWARENESS: ARGUMENT AND ADORATION

We consider here human speech that makes explicit reference to the notion of a God. One large body of such thought is the attempted "proofs"—we shall make clear that it seems better to consider them "arguments"—for the existence of God. Specifically, we are asking: How is the God declared in the Christian faith known in these arguments? How widely and how well? I take "How widely?" to ask "How accessibly?" I understand "How well?" to mean "How certainly?" "How accurately?" "How completely?" From within the dogmatic orientation, two preliminary observations direct our discussion. In arguing for the *existence* of God, the "proofs" are "about" an appropriate subject: the reality of the God who does intend and does act. And the focus for our discussion will be the understanding of God as the world's ground, though the notion of God as the world's goal will be in view as well.

We have suggested that if we are looking for a ground for the world, we are looking for a word that is sure and universal, for something that will not be found inapplicable because of internal discord or external limitation. If it is certainty that we seek, it would seem that it would be the ontological argument which would interest us most strongly. Here, after all, is an argument which proceeds *a priori* from analysis of a concept, so that we are not nervously collecting instances while watching over our shoulders for falsifying counterinstances. Moreover, if the argument is from a concept only, it ought to be accessible to anyone who can think. It is accordingly not surprising that the ontological argument has been and is the object of a great deal of interest.

The historically most influential form of the argument is that presented by Anselm in *Proslogion* II. Here is offered the famous definition of God as "that than which nothing greater can be thought." Does this concept, which even the atheist can entertain, exist only in the mind, or does it also exist in external reality? If it existed only in the mind, it would be lesser than that which existed in the external reality as well. Therefore it must exist in external reality as well.[20]

Does the argument work? Kant has a great deal of company in contending that "existence is not a predicate" that can form part of the concept of perfection, but something that must always be asserted (or denied) on synthetic grounds. Does it help to offer a "second form" of the argument depending on the notion of *necessary* existence, the existence of something which is such that it cannot be thought not to exist?

Can, on the contrary, God's nonexistence be shown to be necessary? Is the notion of God self-contradictory? Charles Hartshorne has argued that a classical concept of divine perfection which effectively denied the divine relativity would be self-contradictory. But if the perfect God is defined as the "self-surpassing

GOD'S CALL AND THE HUMAN QUESTION ABOUT THE GROUND OF LIFE

surpasser of all," self-contradiction is avoided and the necessity of existence for the divine essence is shown. Other philosophers continue to grumble that Hartshorne has reached his conclusion by sleight of hand, moving equivocally from logical necessity to factual or ontological necessity.[21]

The difficulties and dissent cited suggest that the "ontological" proof functions as an argument rather than a proof. Apart from the issue of the validity of the argument, how accurately is God known in this approach? We find here the theme of God's aseity, an important element in Christian tradition. John Hick elaborates what is at stake:

> From God's *aseity* his eternity, indestructibility and incorruptibility can be seen to follow. A self-existent being must be eternal, i.e., without temporal limitation. For if he had begun to exist or should cease to exist, he must have been caused to exist or to go out of existence by some power other than himself; and this would be inconsistent with his *aseity*. By the same token, he must be indestructible, for to say that he exists in total independence is to say that there is and could be no reality able to constitute or to destroy him; and likewise he must be incorruptible, for otherwise his *aseity* would be qualified as regards its duration.[22]

The difficulty, however, is that once again a God so conceived hardly seems to ground human freedom. Spinoza, following out the logic of the notion of aseity, must finally simply locate within God the reality of everything. Ground and goal, as different as they are for us, coincide in God's "total independence." What is expressed in this approach is what we have earlier called the categorical supremacy of God. But if God is to be known as the authorizing ground of human freedom, God's supremacy must be stated in such a way that it relates to what is not God. By definition the ontological argument declines to do that.

Perhaps we may group the cosmological and the teleological arguments together in that both try to think of God's superiority in "worldly" terms. Indeed, unlike the ontological argument, both depend on empirical premises, which might roughly be identified as causality and design (adaptation toward an end) respectively. As such, they will inevitably offer less certainty, since they remain forever open to empirical counterattack, as David Hume so remorselessly observes.[23] Yet presumably most people will grant such empirical premises.

In the famous Thomistic presentation of the cosmological argument (*Summa Theologica* Ia,2,3), those premises were motion, causation, and contingent existence. What will suffice as a reason explaining those premises? Perhaps the second form is most representative:

> In the world of sensible things we find there is an order of efficient causes. There is no case known (neither is it, indeed, possible) in which a thing is found to

3 / THE KNOWLEDGE OF GOD

be the efficient cause of itself; for so it would be prior to itself, which is impossible. Now in efficient causes it is not possible to go on to infinity, because in all efficient causes following in order, the first is the cause of the intermediate cause, and the intermediate is the cause of the ultimate cause, whether the intermediate cause be several, or one only. Now to take away the cause is to take away the effect. Therefore, if there be no first cause among efficient causes, there will be no ultimate, nor any intermediate, cause. But if in efficient causes it is possible to go on to infinity, there will be no first efficient cause, neither will there be any ultimate effect, nor any intermediate efficient causes; all of which is plainly false. Therefore it is necessary to admit a first efficient cause, to which everyone gives the name of God.[24]

It may be possible to restate this argument in terms of logical, not temporal, priority. That might make the argument more attractive to many moderns, who find the notion of an infinite temporal regress more plausible than the idea of an absolute beginning. Is the complex *present* hierarchy of causes infinite, or is there a higher cause which does not itself depend on the existence of another cause? If some are inclined to appeal to the existence of the universe as no less arbitrary than the existence of God, they will be rejecting the priority of mind over matter as an explanatory principle. John Hick writes of that priority:

> We can readily conceive of superior minds to ourselves; but not of kinds of reality superior to mind. Thus there is for us an explanatory ultimacy about mind which we do not find in the existence or the laws of matter. As minds we do not ask why there should be any such thing as mind, although we do ask why there should be any such thing as matter obeying the particular laws which we find matter to obey.[25]

Here the cosmological argument's link with the teleological appeal to design becomes apparent. The latter provided the last of Aquinas' five ways, but was most prominently displayed in the seventeenth and eighteenth centuries. Once again one explains what is experienced, now order in nature, by tracing it back to something mental, divine purpose in the creator. As with the cosmological argument, contemporary restatements are available, such as Alfred North Whitehead's appeal to a single "primordial" decision responsible for the novel yet relevant order characterizing the beginning of *every* particular actual occasion of reality.[26]

How well is God known here? How accurately? How certainly? In each case the argument's reach seems to exceed its grasp, though something valuable is indeed possessed. The difficulties are particularly apparent in the unqualified forms of the argument that proceed on large scale, appealing to the origin and design of the cosmos as a whole, and command much popular attention.

GOD'S CALL AND THE HUMAN QUESTION ABOUT THE GROUND OF LIFE

I have mentioned the matter of an infinite regress. Similarly, the logic of design hardly reaches to creation "from nothing"—a destination which is further troubled by the apparent presence in the universe of considerable disorder. In both instances philosophers may well hesitate over what seems to be a probability argument for an absolutely unique case.[27] In the revised forms of the arguments available in current discussion, the reach is reduced so that the grasp seems surer if not larger. Perhaps we no longer find ourselves brought to shudder under what Tillich called the shock of nonbeing. Rather we find ourselves pondering at best why there is *such* a world as there is. Why this? Why that?

But in putting that question and in answering it, these arguments have something valuable in hand. They do not speak convincingly of an absolute beginning or of an invincible purpose, but they speak appropriately of a being who does intend and who does act. They invite us to broaden talk about a first time to talk about every time. Moreover, that talk will be undertaken by faith in relationship to action and purpose which is not God's. The reality of evil (which was, so to speak, lying in wait for the ontological argument—how good can a perfect God be in this world?) points to the nondivine, as the sense of human agency and responsibility already does. The hesitancy about the principle of sufficient reason ("Why can't the world be self-regulating, self-generating?" "Why does a fact—*especially* the fact of freedom—need an explanation?" "Is God *as fact* any different from, any more explanatory than, other facts as facts?") does so as well. That is, here the categorical supremacy of God is expressed in gift and claim, so that the venture of human freedom can be supported.

Of course not every kind of supremacy is available within relationship, as Hume's Cleanthes knew:

> I scruple not to allow, said Cleanthes, that I have been apt to suspect the frequent repetition of the word *infinite*, which we meet with in all theological writers, to savour more of panegyric than of philosophy, and that any purposes of reasoning, and even of religion, would be better served were we to rest contented with more accurate and more moderate expressions. The terms, *admirable, excellent, superlatively great, wise,* and *holy*—these sufficiently fill out the imaginations of men. . . . If we preserve human analogy, we must forever find it impossible to reconcile any mixture of evil in the universe with infinite attributes; much less can we ever prove the latter from the former. But supposing the Author of nature to be finitely perfect, though far exceeding mankind, a satisfactory account may then be given of natural and moral evil. . . .[28]

It seems unwise to ask a philosopher limited to empirical reason to give us any fuller statement of God as the world's ground.

3 / THE KNOWLEDGE OF GOD

What, finally, may be said of the moral argument for the existence of God? Can we take any comfort from the fact that Kant, who was so critical of the other arguments, actually offered this one, almost as if in their place? For us, I suspect, the moral argument will seem more like the cosmological-teleological argument than it did to Kant. That is, this argument also appeals to an empirical premise, the moral sense.

The argument in the *Critique of Practical Reason* proceeds by pleading that "ought" implies "can" and that "can" requires the postulate of a God who can bring about the coincidence of moral virtue and happiness. Other forms of the moral argument contend that if there were no God, the moral "ought" could not even be known. The "ought" can be known because it can be justified, by appeal to the will of God. As one justifies the "ought," one reaches for its ground in God.

How certainly does this argument begin? Does the world, as we know it, offer the enabling premise? A moral sense, formally considered at least, does seem a remarkably stubborn survivor. The formulation of this argument's premise will today emphasize more the quantitative extension than the qualitative sureness of the moral sense. Those philosophers who argue eloquently for the widespread existence of moral conviction without association with religion should not be permitted suddenly to withdraw the data at this point. Furthermore, there are those, such as anthropologist Clyde Kluckhohn, who will argue for a remarkable cross-cultural material unity in that moral sense.[29] Of course, the argument remains empirical, and in its modern setting it is particularly vulnerable to the open-textured character of an empirical approach. One wishes to avoid trying to persuade individuals and/or cultures that *really* deep down they too have a moral sense.

Also, the movement from the premise may not be wholly untroubled. Is "God" needed to sustain commitment to the moral ideal, if that ideal is of a will devoid of (self?) interest and as such presumably indifferent to result or reward? Perhaps for many moral moderns the notion of God is simply not readily available as a "regulative idea" functioning in the unifying work of pure reason's realm, and thus will not be appropriated as easily by them as by Kant.

Nonetheless also this argument does grasp something essential in the Christian understanding of God as the world's ground. In the giving of the world, as the self is created the self is claimed, for the right and good of humankind. For the Christian the "ought" is from God—that is what the moral argument sees clearly. But it is also for us and indeed for our good. That is what nontheistic ethicists see so clearly. They see less clearly, though, when they go on to argue that a claim that is *for* us cannot be *from* someone who is other than us. Simone de Beauvoir seems to fall into that disjunction:

240

GOD'S CALL AND THE HUMAN QUESTION ABOUT THE GROUND OF LIFE

> When a man projects into an ideal heaven that impossible synthesis he wishes the regard of this existing Being to change his existence into being; but if he agrees not to be in order to exist genuinely, he will abandon the dream of an inhuman objectivity. He will understand that it is not a matter of being right in the eyes of a God, but of being right in his own eyes.[30]

That the claim is for us humans is no embarrassment to the faith. That nontheists, non-Christians, can know what is right and, so far as any of us can judge, give their energy to that right is no objection to faith in God.[31] Rather, the Christian finds here precisely the grounding and directing of the human venture of freedom. It is God's good pleasure to make the claim known, and God's will is sure. God's will *will* be known, even if its origin and its issue remain in doubt. That is why a humanistic ethic does not collapse into absurdity and values do not collapse into tastes. The Christian faith does not contradict human convergence and competence at this point, but precisely comprehends them. It takes them within a more inclusive and far-reaching perspective which roots the human good in the one sure divine will for all. God is the world's ground. The argument will "click" for those who seek such comprehensiveness. But the Christian will have a moral commonality also with those who choose instead to cling to the integrity which seems imperiled by a theistic grounding.

What we have been examining thus far in this chapter may not be "proofs," as if their recital could lock in the mind's assent by logical entailment. But they are arguments, for they do appeal to something that may be had in common, and seek to guide us from there toward an understanding of reality in which the notion of God is essential. How well that journey will go will depend on one's material reading of the other components of reality, one's methodological judgment concerning what kind of perspective is desirable, and one's existential judgment as to whether the theistic conclusion supports or undermines the human locale of the starting point(s). Christians will recognize the arguments as approaches to God, the world's *ground*.

God is the world's *goal* as well—so the faith confesses. Is anything known about that in these arguments? Not very much. The ontological argument might suggest certainty of destination, *if* it could more easily accommodate a significant divine mission in the world. The cosmological argument does suggest that the theme of consequence rhymes with talk of God, but a contemporary setting stressing action with and in the world does not yield a sense of an ultimate goal. The sense of a goal is in the teleological argument's stress on purpose, but only of a goal *sought*. That is true of the moral argument as well, particularly if our contemporary sense for the ineluctability of human failure seems to challenge the Kantian postulate, "I ought . . . therefore I can."[32]

3 / THE KNOWLEDGE OF GOD

Thus, without being ungrateful for the knowledge of the ground, there is reason to look for more. That will be particularly true if God is, as faith declares, personal and active will. Will can instruct, but it can respond as well; it can judge. Whatever God may be formally or metaphysically, what has God decided about us? What is God's heart, so far as we are concerned? Is the universe and its churning course related to a personal will? Does life not only come from something, as a "ground," but matter to someone? The moral and teleological arguments move in this direction, but there may be less abstract materials to consider in this connection. I refer, of course, to religion. What may be known of God there?

When human people act to adore, what do they know? My response to this question occurs within a Christian dogmatics. It does not claim to be disinterested and notes that such claims to objectivity are made today less often and less loudly than in the burgeoning early years of the history of religions. In making this response we are grateful that there are available expository and analytical accounts of the religions. The competence of those accounts does not depend on disinterested objectivity.[33]

We have already argued in Chapter 1 that God as the world's ground can be—indeed *is*—known, apart from the specific Christian *kairos*. It was, after all, the apostle Paul who spoke about the natural knowledge of God's "invisible nature, namely, his eternal power and deity" and of the law written on the heart (Rom. 1 and 2). We continue to ask "how widely and how well" is God known, now applying that question to the dizzying plentitude of things religious. Thus the Christian faith itself prepares us to consider other faiths with the expectation that there is knowledge of God in those faiths. Moreover, since the Christian faith dwells in human houses and hearts, the Christian needs to be self-critical about the Christian religion. One way of doing that is to try to hear the word that comes from other faiths. One still hears the word as a Christian, of course, though one also does so as a human being to whom the faith may seem a restless guest. As a human being, however "secular," when one faces the reality of religion, one is struck by the power, the intensity, the persistence of what is there. Something real is at work. Is not God, the world's ground, known here? Knowledge may not be joined by trust and true worship, as Paul says in Romans 1 and 2. That is a more advanced question. Our question is: Can the Christian recognize in the other religions knowledge of God?

Very apparently the venture of living is caught up in the religious. Some call is heard here; life is engaged. Perhaps no religion illustrates this as well as Islam, which for its adherents is clearly not part of life but a way of life, steadfastly resisting any cordoning off in "religion." "Islam" is "submission," and not just in literal translation; for the orthopraxy of the five pillars orders all existence. And what of the many faiths not sharing Islam's formal similarities

GOD'S CALL AND THE HUMAN QUESTION ABOUT THE GROUND OF LIFE

with Christianity? Hinduism has not the same emphasis on the moral, but the self is claimed for meditation, while the caste system continues to order life. Indeed, the tolerance stressed in Hinduism itself doubles back to affect life: The individual must choose his or her God.

Life is engaged here, but is it grounded? Is life's Other known? Again, one could make things easy for oneself by referring to Islam, for the Quran makes the point directly in regarding Adam as Allah's vice-regent. As Annemarie Schimmel puts it: "When the Quran says 'He taught Adam the names' (2/31) it means that he gave him power over the things, since to know the name of something means to possess power over it."[34] But there appear to be nontheistic religions, Hinayana Buddhism and some forms of Zen, for example. It will not do to ask simply about a specific notion of God. Is life engaged in relationship to a reality which is categorically supreme, whose call can be sure?

Clearly, the religious person has a sense of something absolute, something ultimate. On this the records agree.[35] In some instances this sense is stated theistically. I have argued that if God's call is to be sure, it cannot be subject to internal division. Islam has such monotheistic sureness in spades. First against Arabic pagan polytheism, then against the Christian doctrine of the Trinity, Sura 112, the logical end of the Quran, proclaims: "Say: He is Allah, the One; Allah, the Eternal; He brought not forth nor hath He been brought forth; Co-equal with Him there hath never been anyone." But matters are not as clear elsewhere. Hinduism is notoriously polytheistic. The Confucianist absolute, "heaven," is probably best conceived as impersonal, though subordinate gods are recognized.

How, then, does the absolute or ultimate known in religion engage life? It is in that connection that the notion of God as ground roots. There seem to be dynamics at work in religion which divert or distort the sense of grounding. It may be useful to list those dynamics:

First, an emphasis on the magical, whether by direct divine action or through human intermediaries, seems to compromise the clarity of the ground's authorization of the human venture. This emphasis is not found only in primitive religions. One thinks of the incantations of the early Hindu Atharvaveda and of the Tantras from the fifth century A.D. One may think as well of magical tendencies elsewhere, not the least within Christian history.

Second, at times the categorically supreme One seems to be the only actor. Schimmel identifies such a tendency within Islam:

> God has created the world once from nothing and does not cease creating it every moment—this idea of atomism was developed in ash'arite circles: secondary causes are eliminated, and whatever happens happens through the direct action of God: fire does not burn by its inherent quality but because it is God's

243

3 / THE KNOWLEDGE OF GOD

custom to connect burning with fire. This *sumnat Allah*, "God's custom" is visible both in nature and in the course of history. . . .[36]

This emphasis does not seem actually to cancel the place of human effort, but such striving is set within a fatalistic perspective, as the phenomena of Christian religion also reveal.

Third, the sense of efficacy toward the new which seems essential to the reality of freedom may be compromised if the ultimate truth about reality is cast in terms of being rather than becoming. The idea of harmony can be stated in such terms, as may be suggested in the statement by J. R. Fox concerning "the essence of the religions of the aboriginal Americans":

> Harmony between nature, Man and the supernatural, means fertility of men and crops, and success in hunting, war and personal achievement. Disharmony—often caused by witchcraft—leads to tribal, personal and even cosmic disaster. Ritual therefore is a means of either maintaining or restoring this basic harmony.[37]

But one need not speak only of the aboriginal, if one recalls the Taoist emphasis on the balance between the Ying and the Yang, or the Confucianist casting of this theme in the metaphysical basis for ethics, Ch'eng.[38] While dynamic balance as in stable advance would seem possible, the religious employment of this theme seems regularly to draw this theme back into the association of rest and original order.

Fourth, in Buddhism the ultimate is so understood as to yield precisely an escape from the world of striving. Obviously the point must be delicately put; after all, we do seem called toward, we even *desire*, escape into nirvana. Yet here we seem near the core of the Buddhist understanding, as Alex Wayman recounts:

> When ancient Buddhism divided into eighteen sects, naturally there arose discussion of what the basic Buddhist doctrinal position is, upon which all sects can agree, however disagreeing on other points. The solution to this problem came to be called the four "aphorisms" or "seals" of the Doctrine: (1) All constructed things are impermanent; (2) All constructed things are suffering; (3) All natures are devoid of self; (4) Nirvana is calm.[39]

Perhaps we may break off this tally of trends to risk a more general question: Does religion tend to answer the question of God by referring the questioner to a realm more real than and competitive with the sphere in which human beings struggle to survive and create? This seems to be Mircea Eliade's understanding of preliterary religion.[40] Moreover, many literary religions find a "golden age" in the past and can speak of creation as merely the "sport" of a self-sufficient deity. R. N. Dandekar speaks thus of Hinduism:

GOD'S CALL AND THE HUMAN QUESTION ABOUT THE GROUND OF LIFE

> The theory which seems to have been found generally acceptable by various schools of thought is that the world-process is but the sport—*lila*—of God. This *lila*, which provides an outlet for the exuberant spirit of God, is to be thought of just as play for the sake of play. . . . Actually to impute any motive to god's activity would mean denying his very god-head.[41]

Eric Voegelin offers comparisons at this point:

> In the culture of Hinduism, historical consciousness is muted by the dominance of late-cosmological speculations on the cosmos as a "thing" that is born and reborn in infinite sequence. The hypostasis of the cosmos, and the fallacious infinite of cosmological speculation, can be identified as the stratum in the Hinduist experience of reality that has not been broken by epochal events comparable to the noetic and pneumatic theophanies in Hellas and Israel.[42]

One may find in these dynamics something like what was noted in discussing the divine incognitos: The call is back to the "freshness of the early world." Perhaps that attraction is not hard to comprehend. On Christian faith's account, God's call is sure, but the response is not. Are we not constantly tempted to find the answer to the question of life apart from life? Then a call is still heard, but its content calms us by suggesting that the beginning is what really matters—now in the middle and at the end. It does seem to be so in the world of religion, and Christian religion may at times illustrate the same dynamic. Of course, one must make the point carefully.[43]

At least it seems clear that there is also life and striving in the world of the religious. Religion may at times identify the categorically supreme in such a way that the venture of life is undercut, but that threat of formal contradiction does not seem much to bother the submissive devotee of Islam or the capitalistic Calvinist. At its best, religion does affirm the significance of the human venture in responsible freedom. The adherent of Islam with its high doctrine of God does stand with father Abraham looking toward the future. Human deeds do matter; the Muslim will not fast beyond the month of Ramadan lest the body be weakened. Even Hinduism, in which the Vedic sacrifice establishes a magical rapport with cosmic order, adapts and shows itself in fact to be a "growing" religion. As Radhakrishnan points out: "Hinduism is a movement, not a position; a process, not a result; a growing tradition, not a fixed revelation."[44] In its practice, if not as clearly in its theory, religion asks after and knows about the ground for life, for living.

Perhaps the difficulties noted here remind us that more is needed for life than a ground. That may be clearly seen precisely where the ground's connection with life seems clearest: the moral, ground as *nomos*. That God wills something for the world honors temporality in that it does not call us back from the project of existence. To give my life to the case of God *is* deeply

3 / THE KNOWLEDGE OF GOD

meaningful. But what of the end? Even if matters were to go well, and especially as they go quite other than well, humankind quests after God as the goal.

NOTES

1. Søren Kierkegaard, *The Sickness unto Death*, trans. W. Lowrie (Princeton: Princeton University Press, 1941).
2. Bernard Lonergan, *Philosophy of God and Theology* (London: Darton, Longman & Todd, 1973), pp. 54–55.
3. Werner Jaeger, *The Theology of the Early Greek Philosophers* (Oxford: At the Clarendon Press, 1947), pp. 2ff.
4. John Dewey, *Art as Experience* (New York: G. P. Putnam's Sons, Capricorn Books, 1958), p. 57. Dewey is notable for his emphasis on imaginative purpose in art: "Art has been the means of keeping alive the sense of purposes that outrun evidence and of meanings that transcend indurated habit" (ibid., p. 348).
5. R. G. Collingwood, *The Principles of Art* (New York: Oxford University Press, Galaxy Books, 1958), p. 224.
6. Ibid., p. 335.
7. F. Schiller, "Letters on the Aesthetic Education of Man," in *Modern Continental Literary Criticism*, ed. O. B. Hardison, Jr. (New York: Appleton-Century-Crofts, 1962), p. 38. (Emphasis added.)
8. "Memorial Verses," April 1850, from *Poetry and Criticism of Matthew Arnold*, ed. A. Dwight Culler (Boston: Houghton Mifflin, 1961). (Emphasis added.)
9. Consider this passage as one which catches up these themes: "Thus, the element of art distinguishes itself from the practical interest of desire by the fact that it permits its object to subsist freely and in independence, while desire utilizes it in its own service by its destruction. On the other hand, artistic contemplation differs from theoretical consideration by the scientific intelligence, in cherishing interest for the object as an individual existence and not setting to work to transmute it into its universal thought and notion." Georg W. F. Hegel, *On Art, Religion, and Philosophy*, ed. J. Glen Gray (New York: Harper Torchbook, 1970), p. 66.
10. Immanuel Kant, *The Critique of Judgment*, trans. J. H. Bernard (New York: Hafner Publishing Co., 1968), p. 28.
11. Ibid., p. 73. (Emphasis added.)
12. Ibid., p. 227.
13. Ibid., p. 228.
14. Ibid., p. 287. Again: "For if the contemplation of the world only afforded a representation of things without any final purpose, no worth could accrue to its being from the mere fact that it is known; we must presuppose for it a final purpose, in reference to which its contemplation itself has worth. . . . That is, a good will is that whereby alone his being can have an absolute worth and in reference to which the being of the world can have a final purpose" (p. 293).
15. Kai Nielsen, *Contemporary Critiques of Religion* (New York: Macmillan Co., 1971), chap. 6; Simone de Beauvoir, *The Ethics of Ambiguity*, trans. Bernard Frechtman (New York: Philosophical Library, 1948).

16. Erich Fromm, *The Art of Loving* (New York: Harper & Row, 1956); Walter Kaufmann, *Without Guilt and Justice* (New York: Dell Publishing Co., 1973).

17. John R. Searle, "How to Derive 'Ought' from 'Is,'" in *Theories of Ethics*, ed. Philippa Foot (New York and London: Oxford University Press, 1967), pp. 101-14. In a footnote (p. 113n) Searle argues as follows from—or beyond—the concept of institution: "Standing on the back of some institutions one can tinker with constitutive rules and even throw some other institutions overboard. But could one throw all institutions overboard (in order perhaps to avoid ever having to derive an 'ought' from an 'is')? One could not and still engage in those forms of behaviour we consider characteristically human."

18. Alan Gewirth, *Reason and Morality* (Chicago: University of Chicago Press, 1978). See the discussion by E. M. Adams in *RMet* (March 1980): 579-92. A. J. Watt, "Transcendental Arguments and Moral Principles," *PhQ* 25 (January 1975): 40-57, contains a helpful discussion of R. S. Peter's argument that public discourse presupposes that one ought to consider the interests of others.

19. H. L. A. Hart, *The Concept of Law* (Oxford: At the Clarendon Press, 1961). D. J. O'Connor, *Aquinas and Natural Law* (New York: Macmillan Co., 1967), offers a contemporary attack, stressing the variability of natural law faced with a society changed by education and technology. James F. Bresnahan, "Rahner's Ethics: Critical Natural Law in Relation to Contemporary Ethical Methodology," *JR* 56 (January 1976): 36-60, notes that Rahner's approach is grounded in an ontology of freedom which requires a critical response to an instrumentalist view of human activity.

20. In addition to Anselm's treatment, see Descartes, *Meditations*, v, and Spinoza's *Ethics*, pt.1, props. 7-11. For Kant's famous criticism, see *Critique of Pure Reason: Transcendental Dialectic*: II, chap. iii, sec. 4.

21. Charles Hartshorne, *The Divine Relativity: A Social Conception of God* (New Haven: Yale University Press, 1948), pp. 20-21. For a good sample of the debate, see John Hick and Arthur C. McGill, *The Many-Faced Argument: Recent Studies on the Ontological Argument for the Existence of God* (New York: Macmillan Co., 1967).

22. John Hick, *Arguments for the Existence of God* (New York: Herder & Herder, 1971), pp. 86-87. (Italics his.)

23. David Hume, *Dialogues Concerning Natural Religion*, ed. with intro. by Henry D. Aiken (New York: Hafner Publishing Co., 1948).

24. I am quoting the translation in Anton C. Pegis, *Basic Writings of Saint Thomas Aquinas*, 2 vols. (New York: Random House, 1945), 1:22.

25. Hick, *Arguments for the Existence of God*, pp. 49-50. (Hick moderates the discussion between such contemporary defenders as Eric Mascall, *He Who Is* (New York and London: Longmans, Green & Co., 1948), and critics as Anthony Kenny, *The Five Ways* (London: Routledge & Kegan Paul, 1969).

26. See Alfred North Whitehead, *Process and Reality*, ed. David Ray Griffin and Donald W. Sherburne (New York: Free Press, 1978), pp. 32-33. Cf. Lewis S. Ford, "Process Philosophy and Our Knowledge of God," in *Traces of God in a Secular Culture*, ed. G. F. McLean (New York: Alba House, 1973), pp. 85-115, esp. pp. 108ff.

27. F. R. Tennant's *Philosophical Theology*, 2 vols. (Cambridge: At the University Press, 1935-37), 2:245ff., provides a statement of the probability argument. See John Hick's *Arguments for the Existence of God*, pp. 28-33, for a discussion of the objections.

3 / THE KNOWLEDGE OF GOD

28. Hume, *Dialogues*, p. 71. (Italics his.)
29. David Little cites numerous publications of Kluckhohn (and others) in constructing his argument in "Calvin and the Prospects for a Christian Theory of Natural Law," in *Norm and Context in Christian Ethics*, ed. Gene Outka and Paul Ramsey (New York: Charles Scribner's Sons, 1968), pp. 175–98.
30. De Beauvoir, *Ethics of Ambiguity*, p. 14.
31. Kai Nielsen has argued against theism by pointing out the devastating consequences that follow on any attempt to deny independence of access to ethical judgment. See his *Ethics without God* (Buffalo, N.Y.: Prometheus Books, 1973).
32. It should be noted that Kant did deal specifically with the "propensity to evil in human nature" in *Religion within the Limits of Reason Alone*, trans. Theodore M. Greene and Hoyt H. Hudson (New York: Harper & Row, 1960), pp. 23–40.
33. For a bibliographic survey at this point, see Hans H. Penner, "Fall and Rise of Methodology," *Religious Studies Review* 2 (January 1976): 11–16. In "Method in the History of Religions," *ThTo* 32 (January 1976): 382–94, Paul Ingram contrasts a Whiteheadian model with a Cartesian model in such studies. Robert Baird, *Category Formation and the History of Religions* (The Hague: Mouton, 1971), asserts the possibility of objective historical knowledge, and accepts the qualification that such historical statements can only be very probable at best (pp. 38, 51).
34. Annemarie Schimmel, "Islam," in *Historia Religionum*, ed. C. Jouco Bleeker and G. Widengren, 2 vols. (Leiden: E. J. Brill, 1969, 1971), 2:179.
35. See the survey by Reinhard Pummer, "Recent Publications on the Methodology of the Science of Religion," *Numen* 22 (December 1975): 161–82.
36. Schimmel, "Islam," p. 144.
37. J. R. Fox, "Religions of Illiterate People: North America," in *Historia Religionum*, 2:593.
38. Hans Steininger, "Religions of China," in *Historia Religionum*, 2:488.
39. Alex Wayman, "Buddhism," in *Historia Religionum*, 2:420.
40. E. g., consider Mircea Eliade's discussion of the "abolition of time" in *Cosmos and History*, trans. W. R. Trask (New York: Harper & Row, 1959), pp. 49–92. As an instance of the Jungian psychology (and ontology) presupposed here, see Eliade's *Rites and Symbols of Initiation: The Mysteries of Birth and Rebirth*, trans. W. R. Trask (New York: Harper & Row, 1965), p. 128, where "modern man" is in view: "The imaginative activity and the dream experiences of modern man continue to be pervaded by religious symbols, figures, themes. As some psychologists delight in repeating, the unconscious is religious. From one point of view it could be said that in the man of desacralized societies, religion has become 'unconscious'; it lies buried in the deepest strata of his being; but this by no means implies that it does not continue to perform an essential function in the economy of the psyche."
41. R. N. Dandekar, "Hinduism," in *Historia Religionum*, 2:298. (Italics his.)
42. Eric Voegelin, *The Ecumenic Age*, vol. 4 of his *Order and History* (Baton Rouge: Louisiana State University Press, 1974), p. 321.
43. Ibid., p. 327.
44. Dandekar, "Hinduism," p. 341.

4

The Human Quest and God's Free Answer

Human life is so grounded that it is intended toward a goal. In varying degrees and forms, human life seeks that goal and so knows that it is made for God. In the *kairos* of Jesus, God has acted freely to answer the quest of all by giving a sure word about the end which honors and intensifies life.

HUMAN INTENTIONALITY AND HISTORICAL AMBIGUITY

Human beings sense that their reality is tied up with their eventuality. In what will the events of life eventuate—finally? The question cannot be answered abstractly, as if life did not exist. It is not a question about the presuppositions for life and thus a question about something intelligible apart from life. In this way, the question about the goal is logically asymmetrical with the question about the ground. Indeed, perhaps it is better not to speak of this matter as a question. What we speak of here is the human quest for God as the one in whom life can well end.

What is required if life is to end well? Three elements cluster together in the notion of a goal: First, life must end here; that is, all of life must be caught up in this reality. Universality is needed. Second, life must end here; that is, the end must comprehend, cohere with, fit, receive that which here ends. Affirmation is needed. Third, life must end here; that is, the end must be sure, not subject to overturning. Finality is needed. That God is the world's goal in these senses we have already claimed in Chapter 1. Does the world know about this? Does the world know its goal?

It is clear that human beings know that the meaning and worth of life must be won within life, and that the odds often seem to be against us. While it is to be won within life, the goal is recognized to be not simply another state of life—a piece of the process arrogantly reified and absolutized.[1]

The quest for the goal seems to be against great odds. That is true already analytically in that the very certainty and finality we seek seem incompatible

3 / THE KNOWLEDGE OF GOD

with the contingency essential to the quest that we are. One can well understand Sartre's sentiment that the human project is a useless passion. It is more than analytically true in that the diagnosis of the human venture materially may speak of something much darker than the mere incompleteness of our progress. With such odds at hand it is not strange that one witnesses a tendency to isolate the quest from the goal.

That tendency may be found in the many-splendored wonder of "humanism." At work in such thinkers as Bertrand Russell, the early Sartre, and Camus in the *Myth of Sisyphus* is an affirmation of the human venture for efficacy, together with a strong suspicion of any more-than-human appeals. Still, the quest itself seems in jeopardy, and not because of any appeal to a goal. At one point the problem may appear to be that of incompleteness due to the inexorable reality of the death of the individual. Classical humanism could handle this difficulty easily enough, as George Steiner notes:

> The thrust of will which engenders art and disinterested thought, the engaged response which alone can ensure its transmission to other human beings, to the future, are rooted in a gamble on transcendence. The writer or thinker means the words of the poem, the sinews of the argument, the personae of the drama, to outlast his own life, to take on the mystery of autonomous presence and presentness. The sculptor commits to the stone the vitalities against and across time which will soon drain from his own living hand.[2]

But now the difficulty within the quest comes to be seen as more qualitative and hence as more far-reaching. Again Steiner:

> The time-death copula of a classic structure of personal and philosophic values is, in many respects, syntactic, and is inherent to a fabric of life in which language holds a sovereign, almost magically validated role. Diminish that role, subvert that eminence, and you will have begun to demolish the hierarchies and transcendence-values of a classic civilization. Even death can be made mute.[3]

If faith in the humanities' core curriculum is beset by failing vision in the future and failed health in the present, to what may the humanistic quest repair? We have each other, one might reply—and then hurry to try to make that good news. Thus on the matter of meaning in history Karl Popper insists,

> We should refuse to speak of the meaning of history in the sense of something concealed in it, or of a moral hidden in the divine tragedy of history, or in the sense of some other meaning which might perhaps be discovered by some great historian or philosopher or religious leader.[4]

Yet he insists that we can give meanings to history that are "feasible for and worthy of human beings." The appeal is to the free competition of thought,

THE HUMAN QUEST AND GOD'S FREE ANSWER

not a singular scientific method but precisely the public testing of ideas. That process is to make possible a piecemeal social engineering.

There is a quest here, but it seems to amount to "keeping on keeping on." One finds the same sense of resignation to historical destiny cast in aesthetic terms in George Steiner:

> We cannot turn back. We cannot choose the dreams of unknowing. We shall, I expect, open the last door in the castle even if it leads, perhaps *because* it leads, onto realities which are beyond the reach of human comprehension and control. We shall do so with that desolate clairvoyance, so miraculously rendered in Bartok's music, because opening doors is the tragic merit of our identity.[5]

This sort of appeal is deliberately antitheistic, as a kindred statement by novelist Brigid Brophy makes clear:

> I suspect the correct answer to "What have we put in the place of religion?" is "What have we put in the place of belief in fairies?"—not by way of a rhetorical debating point but because, if you anatomize the answer, it indicates what we *ought* to put in the place of belief in God. One branch of the answer implies that we have used our scientific imaginations. . . . The other branch of the answer refers to the other branch of our imagination, with its faculty for lending aesthetic belief. . . . Shakespeare's poetry bears witness to more and to something of greater constancy than literal-minded belief. It performs the psychological, non-supernatural miracle of creating in us poetic faith. We have replaced belief in fairies by A Midsummer Night's Dream.[6]

More than that, it gives up any appeal to a more than human agency and an other than historical destiny. For all that such thinkers acknowledge difficulty (Popper even dedicates *The Poverty of Historicism* to those who "fell victim to the fascist and communist belief in Inexorable Laws of a Historical Destiny"), or perhaps precisely because of the difficulties they can only "acknowledge," these humanists seem almost romantically optimistic. It remains to consider a casting of human hope which seems to speak of something other than more of the same, while still stopping short of theism.

The vision of Karl Marx qualifies. Here something is known about the quest for the goal of human life. Human essence is human quest, as surely as that essence "is not abstraction inhering in each single individual [but is] in its actuality . . . the ensemble of social relationships."[7] With this social understanding the individual is called to and constituted in relationships. Of course not every relationship is appropriate. Marx attacked religion as the externalizing of the self-consciousness: "And indeed religion is the self-consciousness and self-regard of man who has either not yet found or has already lost himself. But *man* is not an abstract being squatting outside the world."[8] But while

3 / THE KNOWLEDGE OF GOD

the criticism of religion may be the premise of all criticism, religion is the *sigh* of the oppressed before it is their opiate. To address the conditions which cause human suffering human effort is needed, of course. The scope of Marx's vision is impressive. He looks as well to the emergence of the proletariat, the class that is not a class and which can redeem itself only "through the total redemption of humanity."[9]

Marx's vision was historical. How do matters stand now? What do his visionary disciples see? In a figure like Georg Lukacs one still senses the grasp for totality and the commitment to historical dialectic. But the vision seems to be fossilizing. Even if one successfully resists the tendency toward positivism and its predictive laws of the evolution of human society, one may still let the dialectic lose its genuine historical expectancy. It seems to have become a matter of a standpoint or perspective:

> The task of orthodox Marxism, its victory over Revisionism and Utopianism can never mean the defeat, once and for all, of false tendencies. It is an ever-renewed struggle against the insidious effects of bourgeois ideology on the thought of the proletariat. Marxist orthodoxy is no guardian of traditions, it is the eternally vigilant prophet proclaiming the relation between the tasks of the immediate present and the totality of the historical process.[10]

In other Marxists reactions to this *via media* may be found. Adorno's negative dialectics retains the struggle, though it is not as clear that we may here speak of quest:

> Negation or negativity did not designate a spiritual haven or retreat but rather the scene of an incessant struggle or hand-to-hand combat between thought and reality—a struggle which ultimately was an outgrowth of man's involvement in nature and his concrete sufferings as an embodied creature.[11]

On the other hand in the statements of Antonio Negri, of the Italian Communist party, the eschatological vision does seem within reach; though one may struggle to find here the affirmation (goal) of all life:

> I immediately feel the warmth of the worker-proletarian community every time I pull the ski mask over my face.
>
> Our sabotage organizes the proletarian assault on heaven so that finally that damned heaven may be no more.[12]

Maurice Merleau-Ponty has argued that the essential task of Marxism is to find a violence which recedes with the approach of the human future. But he recognizes the difficulties at this point:

> Marxism does not offer us a Utopia, a future known ahead of time, nor any philosophy of history. However, it deciphers events, discovers in them a common

THE HUMAN QUEST AND GOD'S FREE ANSWER

meaning and thereby grasps a leading thread which, without dispensing us from fresh analysis at every stage, allows us to orient ourselves toward events. Marxism is as foreign to a dogmatic philosophy of history which seeks to impose by fire and sword a visionary future of mankind as it is to a terrorism lacking all perspective. It seeks, rather, to offer men a perception of history which would continuously clarify the lines of force and vectors of the present.[13]

The obvious difficulty is that one is left without any sure brake against terrorism when the contingency in history seems to prevail over the rationality.

Faced with this difficulty, one may of course simply renounce closure and affirm the essential and radical incompleteness of the human quest, as Sartre's rendition of the Marxist vision suggests.[14] Or one might settle for an aesthetic resolution of the dilemma, as Georg Lukacs seems to do:

> This principle [of art] is the creation of a concrete totality that springs from a conception of form oriented toward the concrete content of its material substratum. In this view form is therefore able to demolish the "contingent" relation of the parts to the whole and to resolve the merely apparent opposition between chance and necessity.[15]

But we have already suggested (in Chapter 3) that an aesthetic reading of transcendence hardly seems to honor the reality of the human quest. Some clear expression of transcendence as goal seems needed, something that so speaks of the end as to yield the clear and sure resolution sought. Marx had that in principle in the notion of the proletariat. But as the proletariat fails to develop, the Marxist movement threatens to come apart, yielding the disparate versions we have briefly sampled.

In the instances just cited we do find an authentic human sense for life's intentionality. There is a recognition of the significance of history, that a goal lies ahead of humankind. But there appears no clear and convincing word about the shape of that goal. There seems to be an erosion of hope occurring within the movement itself. That history will end, or at least that life is always ending, that at the end and the endings it will matter what we have made of life, all this is clear. But the clarity still seems formal and pales before the material ambiguity of history. Is more known? Perhaps the best place to look may be to the stuff of explicit appeal to transcendence, the religious quest of humankind.

TELEOLOGICAL RELIGION
AND DIVINE DECISIVENESS

In *The Christian Faith*, Friedrich Schleiermacher argued that the widest diversity between forms of piety is that which exists, with respect to the religious affections, between those forms which subordinate the natural in human con-

3 / THE KNOWLEDGE OF GOD

ditions to the moral and those which, on the contrary, subordinate the moral to the natural.[16] In the former class, which he designates "teleological,"

> the passive states (whether pleasant or unpleasant, whether occasioned by external Nature or by social relationships) only arouse the feeling of absolute dependence in so far as they are referred to the spontaneous activity, i.e. in so far as we know that some particular thing (just because we stand in that relation to the totality of existence which is expressed in our passive state) has to be done by us, so that the action which depends on and proceeds from that state has thus precisely this God-consciousness as its impulse.[17]

The notion of absolute dependence is not the most felicitous formulation of our relationship to the One who is categorically supreme. God's honor is secured by robbing human reality. But what is striking about Schleiermacher's work at this point is that despite the strong pressure toward passivity which the notion of absolute dependence exerts, he appraises teleological religion, rather than "aesthetic," as the higher form. Schleiermacher thus identifies a concept of religion, if not a clear concept of deity, which supports the human venture with its concern for efficacy.

Teleological religion does exist, or at least teleological elements are to be found within the world of the religious. It is apparent that the religious self may know not only that its mission is from God but also that it is for God and to God, that, as Schleiermacher puts it, "the action which is pre-figured in the religious emotion is a practical contribution to the advancement of the Kingdom of God." We are concerned in this section to ascertain "how widely and how well" this knowledge may be at hand, and we have a particular interest in how the concept of God functions in this connection.

Schleiermacher classifies Islam with Christianity and Judaism as teleological religions. There is indeed a very direct teleology in the notion of Allah, who will punish those who treat their slaves badly and do not care for orphans, widows, and the poor, and will reward those who do good. But there are teleological elements also elsewhere. These elements bear witness to the human sense for God as the world's goal, but they seem subject to distortion in their respective contexts. Thus Hans Steininger finds such elements even in the East, as in Taoism:

> In contrast to Buddhism which sees life as suffering and demands that, when he attains the ideal stage of ultimate reality, man ought to be "dead" to the things of this world, Taoism holds that life is valuable and ought to be enjoyed in the right way, and prolonged. The World and the individual's Ego are not illusions but are very agreeable realities. He who has understood the teaching of *Yang* and *Ying* and their interaction in the Five Elements and in the all-embracing (Taoist) *Tao*, is able to procure for himself a glorified body so that he may enjoy immortality or at least longevity. . . .[18]

THE HUMAN QUEST AND GOD'S FREE ANSWER

"Immortality or at least longevity"—precisely so! One finds conceptions of the next life that are so much like this one as to constitute a merely quantitative supplement. In a sense the Hindu teaching about *karma* represents this, since a person's doings in the course of one life inexorably govern the nature and conditions of that person's next life. Any religious formula by which God functions as a direct instrument of judgment would seem to do so as well. Tellingly, deliverance (*moksa*) entails freedom from involvement in this chain of causality, precisely by realization of one's essential identity with the one absolute reality.[19]

Eric Voegelin has stressed the linkages between the questions human beings ask when they act religiously. He identifies six structures that raise questions:

1. The existence of the cosmos
2. The hierarchy and diversification of being
3. The experience of questioning as the constituent of humanity
4. The leap in existential truth through noetic and pneumatic illuminations of consciousness
5. The process of history in which the differentiations of questioning consciousness and the leaps in truth occur
6. The eschatological movement in the process beyond its structure

Despite his concern to find continuity in the questioning, Voegelin acknowledges that "the questions concerning the existence of the cosmos and the essence of its order (1 and 2) differentiate earlier than the questions concerning the process of consciousness (5 and 6)."[20] If the process of life does not get "beyond the structure," we do precisely have immortality as longevity, or resurrection as immortality, one might even say. Here the given hardly seems to hold a hint of anything qualitatively other, unless by opposition.

Is there any way out of this bind? Can the categorical supremacy characterizing God as goal be so cast as to get humankind surely beyond a "more of the same" future, while yet receiving the efficacy of the historically contingent present? Such a goal would warrant precisely the preposition "beyond," rather than "before," "with," or even "against" to formulate the relationship between that God and us. If there were such a God, could we know about that? Do we?

There is and we do. At least that is the claim of the Christian faith: God *has acted* decisively within time and because of that a sure word is clear about the end. The Christian understanding of "the work of Christ" is that the God who is at the end has acted decisively in the chaotic middle and that this can be surely known. This decisive action does not undercut human efficacy. But it does make clear that we do not need to be in doubt about the will and work of the categorically supreme one who is the world's goal.

Christians claim to know this. Is knowledge like this claimed elsewhere?

3 / THE KNOWLEDGE OF GOD

Here we must proceed carefully. One would like to avoid adding to the list of those who have claimed unique doctrines for Christianity only to suffer the embarrassment of encountering empirical disconfirmation. Thus the idea of a God of love is hardly the private property of Christians. For example, Dandekar writes of Hinduism:

> Divine grace is a frequently occurring religious motif. God is said to have assumed finite forms for the sake of love for his worshippers and in order to free them from the shackles of this worldly existence. . . . Ramanuja, who seeks to give a philosophical foundation to the theistic ideology, has to encounter the problem of the coordination of the two concepts, namely, the grace of god and the law of Karma. . . . God is the source and substratum of both grace and law of Karma. There is, therefore, no question of one of these two being subservient to the other. God often employs the law of Karma as a kind of testing exercise for one to whom grace is to be ultimately shown.[21]

Similarly, the notion of incarnation has not been successfully patented by Christianity. Moreover, this notion is present precisely in linkage with human freedom, as when the Hindu *avataras* are understood to present a person with a norm for orienting that person's spiritual quest. God comes to us that we might come to God.[22]

Here we have human responsibility, human hope, divine initiative—all familiar themes. What may not be present is a conception of incarnation which entails a free and sure resolution of the human quest for a goal. There is some sense for the sure: the incarnation of the Hindu *avataras* is held to be unmistakable, and in Islam the person of the prophet is considered the expression of God's greatest mercy since in the exemplary pilgrimage Allah's will is *finally* revealed. There is as well some sense in the world of the religious for the divine freedom. Confucianism, for example, resists classification as moralistic, because the believer here knows that good conduct cannot force Heaven to be benevolent and distribute blessings and benefits. Islam's variegated history includes a debate between those who held that God, comprehending all qualities of possibility and impossibility, can do anything whatsoever and those who held that God's justice was such that God must bring the pious to paradise and condemn the sinner to hell.[23]

What Christian faith does is draw these dynamics together into a center that deserves to be designated kairotic on formal terms, if for no other reason. Christian faith claims that the sure word about the end is now known in the free action of God in history in Jesus. Because of this one, "nothing can separate" and none can condemn. Here the free and the sure come together in the good. This good is not unrelated to the good of the call into life and the call in life; *kairos* does come in the context of *logos* and *nomos*. But this good is not won out of nothing; it is won against something. In this *kairos* God proves to be Lord even over sin. God does this precisely by accepting what is human. The one who took human flesh into his person takes human sin into his mission.

Here we do not speak as does the Hindu of Kalki, who is yet to come at the end of ages when he will put an end to all evil powers and reestablish moral order. We speak of the goal as present, not of the ground as future. Christian faith does not share Islam's appeal to the unicity of God, which although it permits Jesus a special place in the Quran does not allow him a special place in God. The God of the Christian knows relationships within— and without. Thus Christians do not share the Quran's denial of Jesus' crucifixion; their Jesus was not replaced by someone "made in his likeness" and taken up immediately into heaven to return shortly before doomsday (43/61).[24] For the Christians' Jesus, humankind seems to have been looking; the elements are there. They come together in the confession of the decisive act of God in Jesus, so that Christians find themselves saying to others, "This one we declare to you."

Just how scandalous is this particularity? We have risked analytical comparisons lest it be supposed that one may settle the status of "the religions" without looking at them. More—much more—of that needs to be done by Christians. But at the same time it is important to render some judgment which reflects the faith centered in this particular. Thus we make five responses:

First. All *life* is grounded in the gracious will and activity of God, the world's ground. Humankind can hear and respond to the call of God in life, quite apart from the kairotic word.

Second. What God has done decisively in Jesus, God has done *for all*. When the time was full, God acted once for all time; that is the scope of the divine decisiveness. Jesus, then, does not belong to the Christians in his efficacy; he is the Son of the One in whom all life is grounded.

Third. The knowledge of this kairos does matter, so surely as it is we in our knowing and willing who are to be saved. It makes a difference to us, to what and whom we can become, that we know of this kairos. The God who acted decisively in Jesus is a God who cares that humankind know this good news and rejoice in it. There is joy in heaven over every sinner who repents.

Fourth. Our knowledge of this *kairos* is particular and confessional. We know a gospel which tells of this divine decisiveness and which has claimed us in the telling. We are instructed by this word that comes to us from beyond ourselves. We do not deduce it analytically; we do not derive it experientially; we confess it because we have been told of it.[25] This gospel does win us; we do believe it; the *logos* in this *kairos* is one that we can recognize. But there

3 / THE KNOWLEDGE OF GOD

remains a certain stubborn idiosyncrasy about the particularity. We would not have guessed the ending, much less the name. We are glad to know now and to tell.

Fifth. We do not know as surely about others who do not know of the *kairos*. That fits the particularity of our knowledge. We do know that God is their goal and that God is surely for them. Whatever the next life is for them, it will be *their* life. Who they are as they come to God will depend on what is given to them and on what the given has come to be in their lives.

In these last remarks stress has been placed on the time between *kairos*—and knowledge of *kairos*—and *eschatos*. The word about the end of the quest is not *at* the end. We are to continue. Without the "in-between" ground and goal coincide. They do not in the Christian reading of reality. So we must speak of how the knowledge of the *kairos* honors and even intensifies the reality of human life.

GOD'S JUSTIFICATION AND HUMAN RESPONSIBILITY

The Christian knows a God whose act in Jesus for all humankind is so sure and free and good that it answers the world's quest for a goal. Nothing beyond this one is asked or expected. In the bargaining logic of the marketplace, to reveal the goal so surely might be to encourage slackness, even embezzlement, in the use of the gift given. But that logic does not apply. It is not merely that the goal is known only "in principle" in this *kairos*, that this one must still come again "in glory." Such a tactical delay would not suffice to nerve our effort, so long as the end was already clear. Rather, it is intrinsically the case that to know this God as ground and goal is to have one's life honored and even intensified.

This follows from the specific nature of God's act in Jesus. What has been made firm and clear in Jesus is God's will to love, even in the teeth of our sin. Thus Kierkegaard writes;

> Seriousness lies precisely in this: that loving and being loved is God's passion, almost as if—infinite love—he were himself bound in this passion, in the power of the passion so that he could not cease loving, almost as if it were a weakness, while it is indeed his strength, his omnipotent love, in such a degree is his love not subject to change.[26]

God has acted for our justification in Jesus, and this justification is not a ledger entry but a living commitment, which works toward and in the beloved. Love creates freedom and responsibility. This does not undo what God has done; it empowers and directs our doing.

In effect I have pointed out in the preceding paragraph that our "continu-

THE HUMAN QUEST AND GOD'S FREE ANSWER

ance" is called for *from God*. That call takes effect *in us*. That God's justifying *kairos* is a living will to love us, no matter what, "changes the values" in our own situation. To know of this is to be unable to go on unchanged. Knowing this may not create response, but it clearly entails responsibility. In the rhythm of Kierkegaard, we might speak of the bid, which is human life, being raised:

> But what an infinite accent falls upon the self by getting God as a measure! The measure for the self always is that in the face of which it is a self; . . . so each thing is qualitatively that by which it is measured; and that which is qualitatively its measure is ethically its goal. . . . And now for Christianity! Christianity teaches that this particular individual, and so every individual, whatever in other respects this individual may be . . . this individual exists *before* God, . . . can talk with God any moment he will, sure to be heard by Him; in short, this man is invited to live on the most intimate terms with God! Furthermore, for this man's sake God came to the world, let himself be born, suffers and dies; and this suffering God almost begs and entreats this man to accept the help which is offered to him! Verily, if there is anything that would make a man lose his understanding, it is surely this!

The Christian understands this and knows life to be intensified!

One might add that life is intensified by the knowledge that it is *for God*. The Christian knows a goal which is not an unmoved mover, but a loving will, not merely something we can desire, but someone who can desire and receive, and so honor and intensify, our life. That our lives matter so calls us, precisely as justified, to continue.

The task of these final pages is not to write of the Christian life in general, but to speak of the Christian life with respect to what follows specifically from and for our knowing God. In doing so, we add the "final" cause to our earlier discussion of "efficient," "material," and "formal" causes in the knowing of God. In a sense, of course, we need give no final cause for the knowledge of God. Why know God? Know God to worship God—simply that is the final cause, after all. But in knowing and trusting God we are caught up in a relationship which carries us into a number of activities. The joy of God and the service of God come together as one continues in these activities. As we consider them we shall find the *logos/kairos* relationship and distinction serviceable again. And one last time we may enumerate.

First. We continue as we respond to the task of dogmatics. Our knowledge of God makes us responsible to do this. In every age the church is called to state faithfully and winsomely what it knows. There is a gracious familiarity about this task because the "old, old story of Jesus and his love" does not change. It is this story and its telling which have given birth to the church, again and again; and the church neither dares nor desires to give it up.

3 / THE KNOWLEDGE OF GOD

But the telling is ours and so emphatically human. It is a story about which we must think, for it speaks of a world, of persons, of time. Understandings of such matters do change, and have changed dramatically since the classic statements of Christendom were cast. Thus two Christian groups who agree in valuing tradition, Catholics and Lutherans, also appropriately agree that "as cultures evolve, new emphases in the proclamation of the gospel may be needed, new conceptualizations may take shape, new formulations may become urgent."[27] So the church struggles to find the best categories, the most illuminating perspective in which to tell the story. Christians who so struggle know that the reality they study to develop these conceptual tools is in fact grounded in the God of their salvation, as surely as it was the *logos* who came to be flesh in this *kairos*. So too in their thinking, Christians may find the understanding of the *kairos* revealed freshly to them in their probing of the *logos*, of the order or structure of reality.

Thus responsible continuance in the statement of the faith calls for both continuity and novelty. Just so, the church has reached dogmatic consensus on some points of doctrine, but not on others.

Second. We continue as we respond to the task of the mission. To know and trust this story is to be responsible to tell it. We have tried to consider how God may be known in the other religions. That consideration is appropriate precisely on Christian grounds, given the recognition that God is known beyond the boundaries of the Christian church. How well and how widely, are empirical questions. The Christian will find those questions answered in specific contact with persons of other faiths. In that contact the Christian aims to tell the story. Thus the Christian is not open in that contact, if to be open is to be without an identity. But in order to tell the story the Christian need not believe that the person of the other faith knows nothing of God.

The Christian knows that this precious *kairos* is held in earthen vessels. Indeed, the very specificity of the *kairos* makes it especially vulnerable to cultural accommodation as one seeks to make it bear flesh freshly in each time. To know Jesus is not necessarily to know what it means to do everything in the name of the Lord Jesus. Moreover, this *kairos* is only to be understood within the structure of the *logos* in whom all things hold together, even now. Surely that has some application to something as powerful and pervasive as a religion! So one comes to the contact with persons of other faiths pledged to tell, expecting to teach, prepared to learn.

Third. We continue as we respond to the task of apologetics. Since we know God, we are prepared to give a reason for the hope that is in us (1 Pet. 3:15). In the apologetic task we respond to the questions, the concerns, indeed the objections, of those who are outside the household of faith. In doing that we render a responsible service to God who wills to be known by all. God may need no defense, but our formulations and understandings surely do. Indeed, such a defense may itself provoke revisions—so human is our grasp of the truth and thus so fundamental is the apologetic task.

Again our knowledge of God as *logos* and in *kairos* informs us. To one who knows God as *logos*, all convincing statements about reality are pertinent, even if they seem to undergird objections to the faith. The Christian accepts God-questions generated by those understandings of reality, for the Christian recognizes that what is at stake in these exchanges serves the specific kairotic confession of Jesus. What the faithful apologist may do is plead for the richest understanding of reality, as those convincing nontheistic statements about reality are indeed comprehended within a perspective in which reality is grounded in God and claimed by God. Moreover, the apologist may find that knowledge of the *kairos* serves to focus and direct what is otherwise quite properly known in particular terms.

Fourth. We continue to the task of ethics. In this *locus*, of course, our reference is not so much to our doing as to the thinking we must do for that doing. Here the Christian happily makes common cause with all those who respond to the call of God in the good and the right. Their insights are honored, as the world's Ground is known as *nomos*. But the ethical call is also intensified, and so Christian ethicists come to speak of an "accentuation, newness, and heightening" of the law, as the Christian is "filled with a new willingness to suffer for the good of the neighbor and to do so with joy."[28] One may speak here of specific motivations, such as a sense of dependence, gratitude, repentance, obligation, and possibility.[29] Beneath them all is the recognition that God is the world's goal in the sense that what we do does go to God, does matter to God. Thus Wolfhart Pannenberg can draw such an allegedly abstract doctrine as the Trinity into ethical relevance. As Jesus refers us to the Father, so we serve in the Spirit:

> Thus the doctrine of the Trinity is the seal of the pure futurity of God, which does not harden into an impotent diastasis, a mere beyond contrasting with man's present, but which instead draws it into itself and through enduring the pain of the negative reconciles it with itself.[30]

Again one detects the relationship between *logos* and *kairos*. The Logos may well teach that relatedness is given with creatureliness, but it hardly reveals sacrifice and suffering as that to which we are called. But the Logos may well help one to understand that the kairotic call is not to masochism, so that self-sacrifice becomes the means to the end of neighbor-regard rather than an end in itself.[31] Or again, the Logos teaches well enough about the eventful character of life, but the Kairos focuses that character materially. Thus Kierkegaard writes, "a man's eternal worth lies precisely in this, that he can

3 / THE KNOWLEDGE OF GOD

get a history; the divine in him lies in this, that he himself, if he will, can give that history continuity."[32] So wrote Kierkegaard as a philosophical ethicist; but Kierkegaard the Christian also knew of a "second ethics":

> The new science then begins with dogmatics, in the same sense that the immanent science begins with metaphysics. . . . The first ethic foundered upon the sinfulness of the individual . . . for the fact that the sin of the individual widens out and becomes the sin of the whole race. At this juncture came dogmatics and helped by the doctrine of original sin. The new ethics presupposes dogmatics and along with that original sin, and by this it now explains the sin of the individual, while at the same time it presents ideality as a task, not however by a movement from above down, but from below up.[33]

So, knowing God, we continue in dogmatics, missions, apologetics, and ethics. We know of our Ground and of our Goal. Our knowledge is of one who justifies us, who honors our life by undergoing it, and intensifies it by calling us freshly into the mission for which we were created. We know this and so we continue, but there is much we do not know. We believe this continuance will itself come to an end and then all ambiguity and error will cease in the most blessed vision of God:

> For now we see in a mirror dimly, but then face to face. Now I know in part; then I shall understand fully, even as I have been fully understood (1 Cor. 13:12).

NOTES

1. Wolfhart Pannenberg, *What Is Man?* trans. Duane A. Priebe (Philadelphia: Fortress Press, 1970), p. 8.
2. George Steiner, *In Bluebeard's Castle* (New Haven: Yale University Press, 1971), p. 89.
3. Ibid., p. 114.
4. Karl Popper, "Emancipation through Knowledge," in *The Humanist Outlook*, ed. A. J. Ayer (London: Pemberton Publishing Co., 1968), p. 283.
5. Steiner, *In Bluebeard's Castle*, p. 140. (Italics his.)
6. Brigid Brophy, "Faith Lost—Imagination Enriched," in *The Humanist Outlook*, p. 197.
7. Karl Marx, "Theses on Feuerbach," in *Writings of the Young Marx on Philosophy and Society*, ed. and trans. Loyd D. Easton and Kurt H. Guddat (Garden City, N.Y.: Doubleday & Co., 1967), p. 402.
8. Karl Marx, "Toward the Critique of Hegel's Philosophy of Law: Introduction," in *Writings of the Young Marx*, p. 250. (Italics his.)
9. Ibid., p. 263.
10. George Lukacs, *History and Class Consciousness: Studies in Marxist Dialectics*, trans. Rodney Livingstone (Cambridge, Mass.: M.I.T. Press, 1971), p. 24.

11. This summary is by Fred R. Dallmayr in "Phenomenology and Critical Theory: Adorno," *Cultural Hermeneutics* (July 1976): 393.

12. I have these quotes of Negri's by way of Thomas Sheehan, "Italy: Behind the Ski Mask," *New York Review of Books*, August 16, 1979, p. 26. The first is from Negri's *Domination and Sabotage: On the Marxist Method of Social Transformation*; the second is not documented.

13. Maurice Merleau-Ponty, *Humanism and Terror, an Essay on the Communist Problem*, trans. John O'Neill (Boston: Beacon Press, 1969), pp. 98 and xviii.

14. In "Sartre's Constriction of the Marxist Dialectic," *RMet* 33 (September 1979). George Allan provides a useful summary (p. 87): "Jean Paul Sartre, in the *Critique de la raison dialectique*, develops a theory of praxis which extends the anthropology of *L'être et le néant*, while simultaneously claiming to correct and complete Marxism. Central to Sartre's argument are two assertions: (1) that dialectic is fundamental to human action, and (2) that all historical development is rooted in the *praxis* of individual persons. These twin assertions, by insisting upon the existential element in social change, do not merely correct Marxism. They fundamentally alter it. In affirming the dialectical structure of *praxis*, Sartrean Marxism is compelled to deny a dialectic of history. It modifies the Marxian dialectic by radically constricting its scope, denying a becoming of the dialectic by insisting upon a dialectic of becoming."

15. Lukacs, *History and Class Consciousness*, p. 137. Agnes Heller makes the juxtaposition even more explicit in "The Philosophy of the Late Lukacs," *Philosophy and Social Criticism* (Summer 1979): 161: "Works of art—as unities of the individual and the species—have always represented the immanence of humankind, and are in fact objectivations of this immanence. Myths and religions, because they are expressions of transcendence, have always been enemies of art, even in times when art made use of mythical and religious subjects. Only in a free world, a world without myths and religions, will art be 'homebound' again, returning to the everyday life of man. Lukacs still insists on his absolute, but this absolute is no longer identical with a movement, a class, or a party. The absolute is simply the proclamation of Karl Marx—since that proclamation the world of freedom is open to us. . . . The philosophy of history inherent in this aesthetics is conceived in the spirit of hope, in the sense of a *guaranteed* hope." (Italics hers.)

16. Friedrich Schleiermacher, *The Christian Faith*, trans. and ed. H. R. Mackintosh and J. S. Stewart (New York: Harper & Row, Harper Torchbooks, 1963), 1:39–40.

17. Ibid., p. 41.

18. Hans Steininger, "Religions of China," in *Historia Religionum*, ed. C. Jouco Bleeker and G. Widengren, 2 vols. (Leiden: E. J. Brill, 1969, 1971), 2:497. (Italics his.)

19. R. N. Dandekar, "Hinduism," in *Historia Religionum*, 2:241.

20. Eric Voegelin, *The Ecumenic Age*, vol. 4 of his *Order and History* (Baton Rouge: Louisiana State University Press, 1974), pp. 326–27.

21. Dandekar, "Hinduism," pp. 307–8.

22. Ibid., p. 303.

23. Annemarie Schimmel, "Islam," in *Historia Religionum*, 2:143, 145.

24. Ibid., p. 175.

25. One might find this emphasis reflected in Paul Ricoeur's shift to language as

3 / THE KNOWLEDGE OF GOD

the encompassing category (rather than the voluntary/involuntary) for understanding the human. Gary B. Madison has stated one view of the consequences: "If systematic metaphysics is something more or something other than poetry, something more than the pure imaginative use of metaphorical language, as Ricoeur wants to say, it would seem that it would have to be the *abuse* of metaphor, in which case it would be a form of myth, and the truths of metaphysics would be believed-in dead metaphors." "Reflections on Paul Ricoeur's Philosophy of Metaphor," *Philosophy Today* 21 (supp) (Winter 1977): 429. For responses see Mary Gerhart, "The Extent and Limits of Metaphor: Reply to Gary Madison," ibid., pp. 431–36; and David Pellauer, "A Response to Gary Madison's 'Reflections on Paul Ricoeur's Philosophy of Metaphor,' " ibid., pp. 437–45.

26. Søren Kierkegaard, *Papirer*, ed. P. A. Heiberg and Victor Kuhr, 11 vols. (Copenhagen: Gyldendals, 1909–48), XI 2 A 54 (translation mine). The quotation which follows on page 259 is from Kierkegaard's *The Sickness Unto Death*, trans. W. Lowrie (Princeton: Princeton University Press, 1941), pp. 210, 216. (Italics his.)

27. Paul C. Empie, T. Austin Murphy, and Joseph A. Burgess, eds., *Teaching Authority and Infallibility in the Church: Lutherans and Catholics in Dialogue VI*, "Common Statement" (Minneapolis: Augsburg Publishing House, 1980), p. 24.

28. Gustaf Wingren, *Gospel and Church*, trans. Ross Mackenzie (Edinburgh: Oliver & Boyd, 1964), p. 181.

29. James Gustafson, *Can Ethics Be Christian?* (Chicago: University of Chicago Press, 1975), pp. 92–93.

30. Wolfhart Pannenberg, *Basic Questions in Theology*, vol. 2, trans. George H. Kehm (Philadelphia: Fortress Press, 1971), p. 249.

31. Gene Outka in *Agape: An Ethical Analysis* (New Haven: Yale University Press, 1972), pp. 276–78, points out how self-sacrifice leads to self-contradictory circumstances if everyone were so to act, and that this theme can at best be incorporated as a subordinate feature in neighbor-regarding considerations.

32. Søren Kierkegaard, *Either/Or*, trans. David F. Swenson, Lillian M. Swenson, and Walter Lowrie, 2 vols (Princeton: Princeton University Press, 1944), 2:209–10.

33. Søren Kierkegaard, *The Concept of Dread*, trans. Walter Lowrie (Princeton: Princeton University Press, 1944), pp. 18–19.

FOURTH LOCUS

The Creation

PHILIP J. HEFNER

THE CREATION

Introduction

1. The Biblical Witness to Creation
   The Form of the Biblical Witness
   The Substance of the Biblical Witness: The Old Testament
   The Substance of the Biblical Witness: The New Testament

2. The Creation of the World
   The Nature of the Claim
   God and the World: Issues for Creation Arising from God's Nature
   Creation Out of Nothing ("*ex nihilo*")
   Contemporary Challenges and Contributions to the Doctrine

3. The Human Being
   The Question of Human Destiny
   The Human Being as Created Co-Creator
   The Primeval Condition ("*status integritatis*")
   The Imago Dei
   Spirit and Matter in the Human Creature
   The Fall and Original Sin ("*status corruptionis*")
   Restoration
   Challenges to Christian Anthropology

4. The Continuing Work of Creation
   Historical Survey
   Perennial Concerns of the Doctrine of Providence

5. Challenges to the Ongoing Doctrinal Task
   Credible Doctrine in Every Situation
   Creation and the Concept of Evolution
   Evil and the Reliability of the Created Processes

Introduction

In asserting the doctrine of creation, the Christian community affirms a relationship between God and the world. In spelling out what the doctrine involves, the community gives conceptuality to the relationship and thinks through its meaning. When we grasp fully what the affirmation and the concept of creation are about, we understand at the same time the scope of the doctrine. We understand its significance and the challenges it faces.

As our reflection on creation will make clear, even though our understanding and affirmation of creation does not precede the doctrines of grace and redemption, the creation doctrine does decisively affect the framework in which those latter beliefs occur. Langdon Gilkey's statement is still true:

> Thus without the idea of God's creation of the world, of history, and of man, the Gospel of redemption of man's life from sin becomes meaningless, self-contradictory, and vain. The idea of creation expresses that fundamental relation between God and the world within which the Gospel of redemption is both important and viable, and so this conception provides the indispensable framework within which the Christian faith speaks its message of love.[1]

Several examples reinforce the sense that the doctrine of creation is decisive for other doctrines. Our conception of creation is correlated directly to our concept of the way God encounters us. If, for example, we consider the creation activity of God to be of a piece with the evolutionary process of the world's development and of life within that world, our "natural" development itself becomes the arena for meeting God. But, on the contrary, a kind of sovereignty over the processes of nature may be ascribed to the creation work of God, such that they are made to appear so inferior as to be only indirectly related to God's action. It would then appear blasphemous to assert that any particularities of our natural constitution are correlated with the mighty acts of God.

Neither of these views separates God from the created world. Nor does either deny the divine freedom and sovereignty over God's creation. But one will veer more toward God's immanence, while the other will move toward God's transcendence. There is a substantial difference between these two positions for our understanding of the way God encounters us. The creation concept

4 / THE CREATION

is not less immediately relevant than issues about redemption and revelation, because unless those issues are correlated consistently with creation, they will appear absurd or incredible.

As the doctrine of creation conceives the relationship of God and the world, it also lays the groundwork for understanding the relationship of faith and the community of faith to the world. This may be illustrated by referring to four sets of faith/world polarities: reason and revelation, nature and grace, world and church, creation and redemption. A firm understanding of God's action as Creator out of nothing of all that is builds bridges between the two terms in each set. As such, this understanding makes a decisive difference in how one understands the pairs.

If, for example, the creative power of God is the source and continuing ground of reason, Christian faith need not struggle to discover a basis or occasion for relating revelation and reason. Rather, faith can proceed directly to the task of setting forth the benefits that accrue if reason and revelation take each other seriously. Or, if God has created the world according to plan, then the church, as a community within the world, need not wrestle with the questions whether it ought to address the world, or whether it is possible for it to address the world. On the contrary, as a coexistent with the world in the larger framework of creation, it can speak immediately to the world about the life both share. It can speak also about the meaning of the church's gospel for the world. The church can proceed as Paul did in his letter to the Romans: "Ever since the creation of the world . . . [God's] eternal power and deity have been clearly perceived in the things that have been made" (Rom. 1:20). From there Paul went on to state the implications of Christ's gospel.

As the doctrine of creation unfolds, it will be clear that one very fundamental challenge faces it. This challenge raises the question whether any of the foregoing is meaningful. Philosopher Ronald Hepburn has written correctly:

> The doctrine of creation is remarkably rich in the evaluative and evocative overtones characteristic of religious doctrines. If God, as Christianity conceives him, is the author and sustainer of the world, then the world is a planned and purposed enterprise. It will not do to speak of life as "absurd," as the atheist existentialists do. It will make sense to ask "Why am I here? What is the purpose God has for my life?" The questions may not be readily answerable, but they will at least be meaningful and proper.[2]

The challenge that confronts faith today is the widespread skepticism whether the world is a "planned and purposed enterprise." This challenge may take a number of forms. The scientist, who will certainly not wish to cast doubt on the orderliness of the world, will nevertheless often feel uneasy at the Christian's talk about plan and purpose. The absurdist—to whom Hepburn refers—

and the Marxist will reject plan and purpose. The absurdist rejects these categories altogether, while the Marxist insists that the only plan and purpose that exist are those that enlightened human agents themselves conceive and actualize.

Behind the dilemma the Christian faces is the fundamental implication of the creation doctrine: not only that the world is "a planned and purposed enterprise," but also that its processes are so reliable and trustworthy that we can say the created world is a home for humans and other forms of life, rather than an uncaring or even hostile environment.

The ultimate sources of the challenge must be noted. One criterion for judging the adequacy of a doctrine of creation will be its ability to hold its own in the face of these counterproposals. Science is a source of the challenge to the extent that it propounds a view of nature's laws proceeding inexorably, impersonally, and by chance. Some hold, for example, that the evolutionary development of stars is inexorable and by chance, and further that our own sun's evolution will take it to the stage of a "red giant," during which phase it will expand in size and engulf planet earth in its fiery mass. If such claims are accepted, it becomes difficult to assert the postulate of creation: that the world is planned, purposeful, and a congenial home for life. Even if the possible hostility of nature is dealt with, the challenge is not disposed of. The breathtaking new vision of what nature is, both physical and human nature, challenges Christian theological reflection on creation. The challenge calls for a religious vision that is both intelligible and persuasive when facing current views of the created world.

The appearance of evil in all its forms is a source of challenge to the doctrine of creation. "The theologian must admit to the thoughtful inquirer that the existence of evil poses no such intellectual problems for other points of view as it does for the Christian faith." This statement is Gilkey's, and he has shown how such secular philosophies as the dualisms, monisms, and naturalisms seem to be confirmed by the presence of evil.[3] As our subsequent discussion will elaborate, the presence of evil is baffling for those who affirm that the good God has created the world out of nothing, and that therefore all unfolding of the world and all purpose are dependent on God.

Neither the facts of science nor the appearances of evil can be ignored or gainsaid by Christian theologians. The doctrine of creation may be understood and interpreted, however, in the light of these realities. When it is, it will naturally assume a form that seeks to take such realities into account and speak to them. Just how the doctrine of creation is to be explicated in the face of these challenging forces today is a matter of much attention and some controversy. Still, the outlook is not altogether bleak for theological reconstruction that takes the challenges seriously.

The present situation in theology has been made difficult for our

4 / THE CREATION

understanding of the doctrine of creation by the response of theologians to science over the past two centuries. When it became clear, under Immanuel Kant's sharp gaze, that religion could not validate its concerns and its truths in the same manner that science did, many theologians followed Kant's lead into a "special realm" in which religion could be free. Religion and theology were restricted to the realm of values, separated sharply from the realm of everyday life and of the physical world. These were the realms where scientists carried out their work and dazzled populations with their insights and technical accomplishments.

The consequence of this restriction was a short-term benefit: that faith gained a "storm-free area," where it could speak its word in peace. The long-term cost of such a restriction is, however, now clear to us. Theology is cut off from the world of "facts," the world at issue in the developments of science and technology and in the ecological crisis. Theology is alienated from our efforts to alter radically the pathological relationships that have developed between the human species and the environing world.

Since Kant's "fact" versus "value" distinction is now widely accepted, the Christian finds great difficulty in affirming the doctrine of creation. That doctrine, after all, involves the repossession of the physical world and the physical aspect of human existence for theological discourse. When we wish to emphasize the doctrine of creation, we find that we must overcome a considerable intellectual tradition at least two centuries old, one asserted by some very prestigious figures in modern Western thought.[4]

The doctrine of creation not only serves as an essential framework on which the soteriological statements of faith depend for their credibility and meaning. It is also one of the chief resources for overcoming what has come to be known, perhaps exaggeratedly, as the "unitarianism of the second article." The object of concern in this phrase is a reduction of Christian theology to soteriology, which falsifies the Christian faith because it cuts off the larger connectedness between redemption in Christ and the panorama of God's intentions and actions from creation to consummation. Such a reduction also thereby cuts the link between redemption and the physical world, society, and world history. If theology does not overcome this tendency, it finds it difficult to relate the faith to such issues as ecological concerns, our vocation in society, and the manifestations of God's Spirit in the world's history.

We take as the scope of the doctrine of creation those matters that pertain: (1) to the constitution of the world and the picture that has emerged in the Christian faith of God as the Creator of the world; (2) to God's provision of modalities of grace within the created world and the relations of those modes to the creation; (3) to the creation of humankind in particular.

These themes are prefaced by a discussion of the biblical understanding

INTRODUCTION

of creation, since that understanding has figured so prominently in the Christian doctrinal tradition.

NOTES

1. Langdon Gilkey, *Maker of Heaven and Earth* (Garden City, N.Y.: Doubleday & Co., 1959), p. 17.
2. Ronald Hepburn, "Creation, Religious Doctrine of," in *The Encyclopedia of Philosophy*, ed. Paul Edwards (New York: Macmillan Co., 1967), 2:252.
3. Gilkey, *Maker of Heaven and Earth*, pp. 178–82.
4. Gustaf Wingren, *Creation and Gospel*, trans. Henry Vander Goot (New York and Toronto: Edwin Mellen Press, 1979), pp. 57ff. See Ole Jensen, *Theologie zwischen Illusion und Restriktion* (Munich: Chr. Kaiser, 1975), pp. 267–77.

1
The Biblical Witness to Creation

Christians confess their faith when they praise God as Creator, who has made the world and human beings. God has created humans in the divine image, thereby giving them a special place in that world and special responsibility for it. The creation has taken place through Christ. God's work as Creator is originating, continuing, and consummating. Human beings are the recipients of this creative power of God, not only in their origination but also in the availability of God's creative power to redeem them, to make them "new creatures," to make them participants in the reality of Christ, and thereby to enable them to work God's will in a transforming manner in the world.

THE FORM OF THE BIBLICAL WITNESS

Two aspects of the biblical witness to creation make it significant for our theological understanding. Both the *content* of its witness and what its *form* tells us about the style or method of Christian testimony to creation are important. We will first consider method.

John Reumann writes: "More than fifteen different 'creation theologies' in the Old and New Testaments can be identified, to say nothing of variations which appear in the literature of the Intertestamental Period outside the usual canon."[1] This statement may be an exaggeration, but it does pose a problem for those who insist that theology should be able to propound "*the* biblical doctrine of creation." The diversity of the biblical materials does not, however, destroy the unity of witness to creation. Rather, it points to the wide range of situations in which the creation witness was forged and to the impressive flexibility and versatility with which biblical traditions responded to those situations. The biblical witness to creation, like the witness to many other themes of faith, did not appear full-blown. On the contrary, it emerged from the testimony of believers in different situations.

4 / THE CREATION

No fixed way of presenting the belief in creation can be found in the Bible. Instead, "a number of different presentations, which have arisen at different times and with different philosophical presuppositions, have been allowed to stand side by side."² This is particularly evident in the traditions concerning the creation of man and woman, as we shall note in more detail. The fundamental affirmations in the creation traditions remain remarkably unified, however.

Most commonly, the biblical understanding of creation is identified with the first three chapters of Genesis. This is unfortunate and even misleading on several counts. For one, chapters 1–3 do not convey fully what the Yahwistic and Priestly traditions intended to say about origins. Genesis 4 is essential, in order to assert that the fall includes crime against fellow humans as well as disobedience toward God. The subsequent chapters in Genesis are essential if we are to understand that creation includes culture and civilization as well as nature (Gen. 4:17–22) and that the growth and development of culture, including the diversification of labor, are part of the creation account of origins. Chapters 6–9 in Genesis are parallel to the first chapters and relate the motifs of destruction and creative preservation to primeval creation. As God has created life in the world, so God can also destroy it—but God has promised to sustain creation (Gen. 9:8–17).

Beyond Genesis, however, we find that other parts of the Old Testament are rich in creation traditions. The period after the exile was especially rich in such traditions. We refer to the Psalms (e.g., 8, 19, 24, 46, 74, 77, 89, 93, 97, 99, 104), First Isaiah (27, 30, 17, 34), Second Isaiah (40–55), and Third Isaiah (65–66). Further, there are Habakkuk 3; Ezekiel 29; Nahum 1; Jeremiah 4, Amos 4, 5, and 9; Hosea 8; Malachi 2; Proverbs 3 and 8; Ecclesiastes 3 and 12; and Job 3, 22, 37, and 38.

Theologians have often suggested that the Hebrew Scriptures should be read from the viewpoint of the New Testament. Such a starting point radically challenges the view that Genesis 1–3 constitutes the essential creation testimony. Emil Brunner speaks so forcefully for this position that we cite him at length:

> Unfortunately the uniqueness of this Christian doctrine of Creation and the Creator is continually being obscured by the fact that theologians are so reluctant to begin their work with the New Testament; when they want to deal with the Creation they tend to begin with the Old Testament, although they never do this when they are speaking of the Redeemer. The emphasis on the story of Creation at the beginning of the Bible has constantly led theologians to forsake the rule which they would otherwise follow, namely, that the basis of *all* Christian articles of faith is the Incarnate Word, Jesus Christ. So when we begin to study the subject of Creation in the Bible we ought to start with the first chapter of the Gospel of John, and some other passages of the *New* Testament, and not

THE BIBLICAL WITNESS TO CREATION

with the first chapter of Genesis. If we can make up our minds to stick to this rule, we shall be saved from many difficulties, which will inevitably occur if we begin with the story of Creation in the Old Testament.[3]

Brunner's position raises a host of questions. In his insistence on the priority of the New Testament, is he suggesting that the Old Testament is so alien to the Christian faith that if one began theological reflection in the former, that reflection would not be consonant with Christian faith? Does Brunner's position blend into Marcion's, that the God of creation in the Old Testament is another God from the Redeemer-Father of the New Testament?

The Christian confidence in God's providence lets us accept Old Testament traditions as reliable, yet also affirm the New Testament as the fulfillment of Israel's religious pilgrimage. Such a position grows out of our faith as much as our reasoned scholarship.

More often, theologians who agree with Brunner's essential thrust use a christological interpretation of the Old Testament to make their point. Karl Barth's discussion in the third volume of his *Church Dogmatics* is one such approach. Our approach shall be a dialectical one, in which the faith and affirmations of Israel are accepted as our own faith, as well as that of Jesus, but in which that faith will finally be interpreted christologically.

The most nearly adequate way to handle the diversity of creation witnesses in the Bible is to incorporate, within our Christ-centered faith, the traditions-history approach so prominent among biblical scholars. Such an approach puts the biblical testimonies in the sequence in which they emerged, to the extent that such a sequence can be established. "The biblical doctrine thus becomes a series of statements of faith in differing situations over the centuries, about which we must make decisions concerning what is normative and what is useful today."[4] John Reumann has produced two traditions-history studies of the biblical doctrine of creation that serve as models of such presentation.[5] In the discussion of biblical content that follows in the next section, we shall follow Reumann's organization of the traditions.

The relations between the biblical witnesses to creation and the various cultural situations from which they emerged is a much discussed, disputed, and thorny issue. Scholarly opinions have tended to insist on the distinctiveness of the biblical traditions, even though the past two centuries have seen a growing appreciation of their borrowing from other cultures.

Studies of the history and structure of world religions shows their universal concern for creation. These studies remind us that, although biblical reflections on creation may be distinctive, there is nothing distinctive about their preoccupation with the issue.

A number of scholars have classified the myths of creation in the world's religions. Charles Long, for example, has provided five different categories

4 / THE CREATION

of such myths: emergence myths, world-parent myths, myths of creation from chaos and from the cosmic egg, creation from nothing, and earth-diver myths.[6] Within the creation-from-nothing classification, he gathers the following: the Australian myth of the Great Father, Hesiod, Rig Veda, the ancient Maya myth from the Popol Vuh, and myths from Polynesia, the Maori, the Tuamotua, the Egyptians, and the Zuni—in addition to the Hebrew myth from Genesis.

Although there is no suggestion that all the myths are related or that they exerted influence on one another, it is instructive to place the Hebrew/Christian primal myth of creation within the context of the universal human mythic reflection upon origins. We find that all the creation-from-nothing myths share four characteristics:

> First of all, the Creator deity is all-powerful. He does not share his power with any other deity or structure of reality. Secondly, . . . the deity exists by himself, alone, in a void, or space. There is no material or reality prior to him in time or power. . . . Thirdly, the mode of ceation is conscious, ordered, and deliberate; it reveals a plan of action. Finally, the Creator is free since he is not bound by the inertia of a prior reality.[7]

It is important to keep such universal characteristics in mind, so that we can understand more adequately just what our own traditions share with humanity and where they differ. Each of these four shared characteristics has at one time or another been mistakenly heralded by theologians as unique to Judaism and Christianity. As we shall see, however, there are other genuinely distinctive marks of our creation traditions. They have mainly to do with the elevation of history as the medium of revelation and creation.

Claus Westermann has properly said that it is misleading to dwell exclusively on the distinctiveness of biblical creation traditions. Since we now know that the various myths have arisen independently over the whole of the earth and its history, "the conclusion is unavoidable that mankind possessed something common in the stories about primeval time."[8]

This broad common basis of thought and understanding suggests to Westermann that the Old Testament traditions were first of all part of this universal human reflection. He finds that whatever is distinctive in the traditions can thus be seen as a contribution to the larger human quest for understanding. Among the shared motifs, Westermann counts the creation of man out of clay, the flood, the first offense, the origins of death, of civilization, of fratricide, and the building of a tower.

Westermann distinguishes four types of creation myths: creation through making, through generation or birth, through conflict, and through the word. He finds all four of these types reflected in Genesis, not discounting that the Hebrews interpreted the shared material in their own way.[9] The motif of making is seen clearly in the creation of man from clay and of woman from Adam's rib (Gen. 2); generation is the motif of the seven days of creation, which form a segment of the *toledot* ("generations"); conflict is not accepted as a motif in the Old Testament view of creation, but it echoes in Isa. 51:9–10, where the myth of Rahab the dragon is recalled, and in Gen. 1:2, where the word for "deep" is a "distant reminder" of Tiamat (the dragon in the Babylonian epic *Enuma Elish*), conquered in battle at the time of creation.

Westermann has made another significant contribution to our understanding of the Old Testament traditions' relationship to the larger human quest for understanding of origins. He notes four basic stages "in the reflection on Creation in the overall history" of humankind: the primitive stage, the stage of great religious cosmogonies, the philosophical-theological stage, and the scientific stage.[10] The primitive and the religious cosmogonic eras are marked by the fact that only in reflecting on the world's coming into being could humans grasp the world as a whole. Philosophical-theological reflection moved into an abstract manner of reflection, away from personal categories to those of causality. Or, in the case of Christian theology, they combined the personal and the philosophical concepts of causality. The final era, the mathematical-scientific, is marked by the empirical approach to the whole of the world, with experiment and calculation as its hallmarks.

Westermann's point is that the Old Testament traditions fall in the middle of these periods, toward the end of the religious cosmogonic era. Since the first two periods are much longer than the latter two, the Old Testament actually represents a huge segment of human reflection. It absorbed essential elements of early humankind's reflection on creation and preserved them for our benefit today. This is the great significance of the obvious Babylonian, Egyptian, and other influences on the Old Testament accounts of creation. The distinctiveness of the Old Testament must be viewed in this greater context of the history of human reflection. Furthermore, the advances made in the New Testament and in later Christian theology are to be understood as proceeding out of this grand historical sweep, of which the Old Testament is a part.

THE SUBSTANCE OF
BIBLICAL WITNESS: THE OLD TESTAMENT

Given the diversity of the biblical witness and its complex relation to the cultural settings in which it emerged and developed, let us survey what has been bequeathed to us in the many-layered repository of biblical tradition. What follows illustrates how the traditions-history method may bear fruit in uncovering scriptural materials. It is also a brief compendium of the essential, primal testimony to the creation affirmation to which Christians hold themselves accountable. What we encounter in this primal testimony is itself

4 / THE CREATION

rich, complex, and intellectually challenging. It grew, after all, out of a wide variety of circumstances in which it was necessary, first for the Hebrew community and then later for the Christians, to raise their witness to the creator God and the work of that God.

We will devote much of our discussion to the biblical materials—there is so much there! Perhaps more than any other doctrine, creation is central to much of the biblical witness. It is not only central, but so richly developed that theological reflection can preoccupy itself with Scripture and become engrossed with the themes, complexities, and ramifications of the biblical legacy. It is not enough to be so preoccupied, but one finds a great deal in the ancient sources that is immediately relevant for theological reflection.

Certainly no theological presentation can be thought adequate if it overlooks Scripture and the five basic biblical propositions outlined at the end of this section. What follows should be considered the irreducible minimum to be retrieved from the biblical witnesses for the current theological exposition of the creation affirmation.

We have already discussed the first chapters of Genesis, commonly thought to be not only normative but also exhaustive of the biblical witness. Scholars are nearly unanimous that Genesis 1–11 is put together from several literary accounts. The one called "J" (designated by the Germans "Jahwist"—English spelling, "Yahwist"—from its habit of calling God "Jahweh") begins with Gen. 2:4 and continues off and on through chapter 11. The other called "P" (from "Priestly" writing) begins with the first chapter. J emerged in the tenth or ninth century B.C., probably under the reign of King Solomon, while P is from the fifth century B.C., as Israel was trying to reestablish Jerusalem after its destruction and the exile in Babylon. We shall not have occasion to discuss Genesis 1–11 as a whole; in accord with the traditions-history method, we will divide its parts, noting each in the context of its period.

It is not surprising that Israel should begin in a major way to put its traditions into more permanent and ordered form during the time of its first great king. We keep in mind that a multitude of traditions—stories, hymns, cultic materials, brief historical sketches, and the like—existed before the ordering process. The process of reflection, writing down, editing, and creative rewriting required a certain sophistication. It required education and leisure for reflecting and learning. The process had to await the right conditions. It became possible only when the society had achieved the affluence and "high" civilization that emerged with the Israelites' monarchy. Israelite kings moved to Jerusalem, a Jebusite city. There began the trend toward centralization of all aspects of life. This was a genuinely new phenomenon for Israel, and much had to be borrowed or created from scratch, including the characteristics of a temple religion and a cult—all largely borrowed from existing forms. The collecting of traditions and the putting together of a sacred tradition and a "theology" in a usable form were part of this new phase of the community's life.

Some scholars have suggested that "Yahweh" itself is a name that refers to the Creator, while others have said that the new Jerusalem priesthood (Jebusites) of David applied the creator name to Yahweh, in accordance with Canaanite usage. In any event, the significant development is that this rising monarchy and high civilization sought to relate the God of the cosmos, of creation, and of the very foundations of the world to its own particular history. The Israelite people and their exodus from Egypt, their wilderness journey and their conquest of the land, their nation-building phase and their burgeoning monarchy—all this was to be brought into relationship with the God of the cosmos. All was to be given the kind of affirmation and reinforcement that such a linkage could bring. Here we see the process that Jaroslav Pelikan has described: "The story or stories of creation in Genesis are not chiefly cosmogony but the preface to the history that begins with the calling of Abraham." [11] It was important for the monarchy of David to make this connection. Gen. 14:19, 22 is probably the earliest reference to God as Creator in the Old Testament.

The formation of the creation traditions, in the context we have just described, is part of what the scholars call the development of a "Zion theology." It aimed at legitimizing the monarchy and the whole culture centralized in David's city. Creation themes were important in this theology (see Psalms 24, 74, 77, 89, 93, 97, 99). Psalm 89 is particularly revealing of this theological tendency; verses 5–13 set forth the power and glory of the creator God, while the succeeding verses 19–37 relate that God to the reign of David. These psalms speak of creation as originating the world, but also as continuing to sustain the world and to redeem it. As Helmer Ringgren writes,

> The doctrine of creation is not primarily a theoretical statement about the origin of the world, about something that has happened long ago. It is rather a proclamation of a present reality; creation means that the evil powers are defeated, and that the order of the world is established for ever. . . . Creation, therefore, is also a redemptive act. . . .[12]

The Zion theology borrowed from the traditions of other cultures, as we see in Psalm 104, with its reworking of Egyptian sources. Developments of the time were shaping an alternative interpretation of Israel's identity, an alternative to the almost exclusive emphasis on the exodus. Israel's identity was now said to be rooted not only in God's mighty acts in history but also in the very origins of the cosmos itself. The witness from this source is almost exclusively from the cultic life of the people—hymns and prayers as found in the Psalms.

Turning to the preexilic prophets, we find scanty evidence of creation-

4 / THE CREATION

themes, and what we do find has been inserted in places to underscore the prophets' judgments. For example, Amos (4:13; 5:8-9; 9:5-6), in contrast to the "Zion theology," invokes the creator God against the immorality and injustice of his society. First Isaiah appears to invoke the creator God against the nations (Isa. 17:12-14; 27:1; 34:11). As we read these sections, it is easy to understand why some scholars argue that they could be insertions from a later period when creation theology was more in vogue. A verse like Jer. 4:23, with its view of the "world without form and void," makes us wonder whether the prophet borrowed from earlier traditions that later became Genesis 1, or whether later writers were influenced by the prophet.

Some of the grandest expressions of the creation witness come from the wisdom traditions. This material is not distinctive to Israel; it is part of an international movement. Generally, these traditions speak in universal human terms, with fewer references to Israel's particular history. Proverbs (3:19-20; 8:22-31) and Ecclesiastes (3:11; 12:1, 7) invoke creation themes to reinforce their ethical reflections. This amounts to the assertion that human patterns of living are rooted in the foundations of the created world itself, and that they are of concern to the Creator.

Job intensifies this affirmation in what may be the most stunning witness to creation in the entire Bible (Job 3:1-10; 22:12-14; 37; 38:22—39:30). These passages also imply what Christians later called creation "out of nothing." He relates the life of the individual directly to the creator God, with virtually no references to Israel and its history with God. The individual stands naked before God with no mediator whatsoever. In this position, Job reflects on the grandeur of God:

> Hearken to the thunder of [God's] voice and the rumbling that comes from his mouth. Under the whole heaven he lets it go, and his lightning to the corners of the earth. . . . God thunders wondrously with his voice; he does great things which we cannot comprehend. For to the snow he says, "Fall on the earth"; and to the shower and the rain, "Be strong."

This meditation on grandeur turns to amazement at God's ways, and then to perplexity and resentment. The creator God is the God who speaks from the whirlwind: "Where were you when I laid the foundation of the earth?" The man is reduced to silence; adoration and awe are the only appropriate responses before the creator God; God's ways are beyond understanding and not to be questioned. Nevertheless, the implication is that this God will redeem humanity, not destroy it. This literature is a profound reflection on the relationship between human affairs and the God of creation. A holy agnosticism as to God's plans is encouraged, with an undertone of confidence in the final outcome as one that will be a blessing for the world.

THE BIBLICAL WITNESS TO CREATION

Genesis 2—4:26 is considered to be part of the Yahwist's history of Israel, designated by scholars as the "J" document. Written between 950 and 900 B.C., during the movement of "Solomonic humanism," the J document was an attempt to show that God has indeed worked through history from the time of creation through David's reign. J might be considered a counterpoint to the Zion theology of the same period. The Yahwist seems to have been a layperson, in contrast to the cultic, priestly setting of the authors of the Zion theology. The centralizing developments that we discussed earlier did indeed bring together a "critical mass" of educated, capable people committed to the cultural enterprises of the Davidic monarchy. At the same time, the age was marked by several contrasting trends of considerable moment.

There was an enormous amount of borrowing from other cultural sources, for example, the new capital city, Jerusalem, the Jebusite priesthood, and a new cultus. There was an incredible attempt to bridge the disjunctions between the nomadic-tribal social and religious traditions that emerged from the exodus period and the subsequent generations of wandering, of conquering Canaan, and of settling the land, on the one hand, and the new, highly civilized society centered in Jerusalem, on the other. There was also a secularizing thrust brought about by the combination of two dynamic elements. One was a group of highly gifted people capable of thinking for themselves quite apart from the ancient traditions. The other was the influx of much cultural borrowing not readily assimilated into older Israelite patterns of thought and action.

In this situation, it is not surprising that a crisis of meaning developed in some quarters. In the midst of great change, where was God to be found? Where was God at work? The Zion theology gave one response, the Yahwist another. The Yahwist was a product of the Solomonic humanism that emerged in the new cultural context. He sought to show how Yahweh had worked in Israelite history up to his own time. He did so by recasting older traditions, by relating Yahweh to the everyday life of his age, by utilizing traditions borrowed from other peoples (like the creation out of clay) or which (like other creation motifs) were previously not much used, and by trying to cut through the jargon and cult which was losing its credibility in some quarters.

The achievement of J, when seen in the light of the times, is very attractive. J's story of creation is not stylized or abstract, as is the Genesis 1 account. Rather, it is a bit irreverent, earthy, vivid, perhaps even tongue in cheek. The account is rich with provocative meanings. Humans are totally dependent on God for their life—their very breath comes from God. The man at first was given the animals for companionship but could be at peace only with a companion that was free and personal like himself. The fact that woman

4 / THE CREATION

came from Adam's rib could mean that she is his subordinate, but it could also mean that she is the only one who is "like" man so as to be a genuine companion, a genuine mate.

Evil is not a cosmic, ontological phenomenon so much as it is the product of human will and disobedience. If we read Genesis 3 as if it were an eyewitness account, written on the very day of the fall, it is misleading, because then it seems that humans were from the very beginning sinful. But when we keep in mind that the account is put together in the tenth century B.C. as an explanation of how God works in history, then it becomes not an etiology or even a protology but rather a way of expressing far greater optimism, of saying that evil is not written in the very law of things, but is located discretely in human will. As such it can be dealt with and guarded against. The writer is saying, "Humans are like this. If you keep this in mind, it is possible to deal with sin and evil constructively."

In light of the Canaanite fertility and nature-religion of the Yahwist's time, both the creation account in Genesis 2 and the story of the fall in Genesis 3 may be viewed as polemics against those who would encourage the Israelites to ape their neighbors. Yahweh is Lord over nature. Sinning is not a cosmic principle inherent in the structure of the world. God is able and willing to work the divine will and forgiveness through ordinary history.

We have surveyed the three chief traditions that witness to the creation affirmation in Israel before the exile—Zion theology, Wisdom, and the Yahwist. That they are relatively scanty reminds us that creation was not a dominant motif in Israel's self-understanding prior to the exile. Exodus, Sinai and the law, and the patriarchs figured more prominently than creation in the traditions and beliefs of Israel. Nevertheless, the witness to creation is clear and significant. Both the Yahwist and the Zion theology make creation the prologue to the more extensively elaborated historical narratives. Israel's history, particularly as it reaches a climax in the Jerusalem monarchy, is rooted in the very foundations of the cosmos, in God's activity as Creator. The Creator is all-powerful; the creation is essentially good; there is ground for hope.

We follow the scholars who put the Wisdom literature, including chapters 38 and 39 of Job, into the period before the sixth century B.C. These Wisdom pieces contain an internationally widespread type of reflection which Israel accepted and harmonized with other traditions. Even though it could equally well be placed after the exile, this literature, too, may have its origins in the Solomonic court of the tenth century; its appeal is a universal human one, with little reference to the particularity of Israel. It makes a statement that is of a piece with the other traditions, namely, that human existence transpires in the hand of the creator God. Beyond this, however, the testimonies to that God are grander than those found in the Yahwistic account in Genesis 2—4

THE BIBLICAL WITNESS TO CREATION

and at the same time less overtly confident of God's mercy than either the Zion theology or the Yahwist.

After 586 B.C. we find a much more developed witness to creation. Although it is only speculation, we can imagine why the emphasis on creation emerges more extensively at this time. Perhaps the invocation of the historical traditions—of exodus, Sinai, and the patriarchs—was no longer persuasive precisely because that strand of historical development had been interrupted. Interrupted, the promise lost credibility, because it had been one of fulfillment and blessing, not of devastation, dispersion, and exile. Something beyond those historical traditions was needed. Furthermore, in the dispersion in Babylon, the Hebrews were brought into intimate contact with a people who interpreted themselves by means of a powerful creation theology—the theology of Marduk, the victor in the struggle with the chaos monster at creation, and the annual representation of this battle at the New Year festival.

Chapters 40–55 of Isaiah (Second Isaiah) present to us the work of a prophet who dramatically recast Israel's story, in an attempt to renew his people's sense of identity and purpose and to restore that people's *esprit de corps*. No element of his effort is more striking than his extensive use of creation themes. He introduces creation as a sign of God's power and merciful plan, as well as an image for God's future work. A typical example is chapter 42, where, in the context of an oracle about the servant of Yahweh, we find this:

Thus says God, the Lord,
  who created the heavens and stretched them out,
  who spread forth the earth and what comes from it,
who gives breath to the people upon it
  and spirit to those who walk in it:
"I am the Lord, I have called you in righteousness,
  I have taken you by the hand and kept you;
I have given you as a covenant to the people,
  a light to the nations,
  to open the eyes that are blind,
to bring out the prisoners from the dungeon,
  from the prison those who sit in darkness."

The juxtaposition of creation images and redemptive—for the Christian, messianic—motifs makes clear why one scholar has termed this Isaiah's "creative redemption" or "redemptive creation."[13] The point is that God's creation work is continuing now and will constitute the future as well. Chapter 40 concludes with this exalted imagery after a long affirmation of God as the Creator, almost reminiscent of Job:

4 / THE CREATION

> The Lord is the everlasting God,
>   the Creator of the ends of the earth.
> He does not faint or grow weary. . . .
> He gives power to the faint. . . .
> They who wait for the Lord shall renew their strength,
>   they shall mount up with wings like eagles. . . .

Whether this prophet borrowed heavily from the Babylonians is finally not certain (even though plausible), but his development of a vision of Israel that incorporated creation motifs in a central fashion is unmistakable. He has not forgotten the preexilic ways of telling Israel's story, but he has recast the story in a dramatic new way. He has taken creation from protology—in which he is not much interested—to continuing creation and new creation.

It will seem strange to many that "the" basic text for the doctrine of creation, Genesis 1, is discussed late in this survey of biblical traditions. As with all the bodies of tradition, this one contains very early material, but the Genesis 1 account was put in its present form rather late, in the sixth or fifth centuries B.C., by the person or group known as the Priestly writer. P is a long segment of historical narrative, stretching throughout Genesis, Exodus, Leviticus, and Deuteronomy. Since this compilation contains a great deal of cultic material, including most of the liturgical rubrics of the book of Leviticus, it has been said that it was politically motivated to legitimate the postexilic cult. Others have said that it was theologically intended, to affirm that God is present in the postexilic community of the chosen people, and that the inclusion of cultic and other detailed materials are part of this intention to speak of God's concrete presence.

Whatever the circumstances of P's composition, P has taken in a wide range of sources, including ancient Near Eastern ones. It has purified them of pagan notions and woven them into the powerful, stylized account that Jews and Christians look on as normative. A detailed exegesis of the first chapter of Genesis is not essential here, but it should be noted that this witness to creation is a doxology whose intention is to praise God and honor the mystery of creation, not to "explain" the world's origins in a modern sense. At the same time, the account is not a stumbling block to those who want to relate creation to modern ways of thinking.

Whether there is a creation out of nothing implied in the first verses is debatable; some interpreters even use those verses to substantiate a view of preexistent chaos on which God worked as a demiurge. It is probably safer to rest the *ex nihilo* on other texts. The progressive unfolding of God's work of creation in Genesis 1 renders it congenial to modern notions of evolution or development. The creation of humans is given special emphasis, with the introduction of the concept of the "image of God." This term will occupy us at some length at another point, but its mention in this creation account is the basis for the church's preoccupation with it. The conjunction of being created in God's image with multiplying and filling the earth, with subduing the earth and having dominion over it, has been at the root of much later thought and practice, even as it has been the source of much difficulty in recent decades. Genesis 1 places the creation work of God in a large, symmetrical framework; its conclusion is the sabbath, the perfect wholeness of God's work.

The prophet responsible for Isaiah 56—66 (so-called "Third Isaiah") introduces a new element into the creation witness—that of the "new heavens and a new earth" (Isa. 65:17; 66:22). This writer lived in the restored Jerusalem of the Second Temple of Zerubbabel. The times were hard and disappointing for those who had expectations of a grand rebuilding of Jerusalem and a restoration of former glories. Some scholars interpret Third Isaiah as a harbinger of apocalypticism. This writer does not look for the continuation of previous grand historical developments that hark back to the exodus and to David. Nor does he simply affirm that God has led the people to their present state. He does not take the stance of the Priestly writer (who wrote at the same time), that God's hand is discernible in the times. Rather, Third Isaiah speaks in tones that are desperate in one sense, that are not corollary to the experience of this world, but are in radical contrast to it.

The oracle in 65:17-25 bears this out. The new heavens and the new earth will include a Jerusalem in which there is no weeping or crying; the wolf and the lamb will feed together, the lion will eat straw like the ox. There is a definite intent to glorify the "new Israel," a sort of eschatological Zion theology, but the dimensions of universality are also present in 66:23—"all flesh shall come to worship before me, says the Lord." The same creative work of God is lifted up at this point, but the arena of that work is different from what was spoken of in earlier traditions. God's creative work is not to legitimate Zion-Jerusalem, nor is it to sustain human existence, as in Job. It does not even point to a future restoration of Jerusalem. Rather, God's creative work builds a new world that is related to this world only in the sense that earthly metaphors are used to describe it in a most un-earthly fashion.

From this survey, it is clear that the Old Testament traditions of the Hebrews possessed a deep conviction in God as Creator and ruler of all things. As several scholars have suggested, creation was not really a creedal matter with the Hebrews; rather it was a presupposition that the Hebrews would not think even of questioning. This they shared with their Near Eastern neighbors. From very early times, they demonstrated the desire to forge links between their earthly existence and the power and purpose of the creator God. They were distinctive among their neighbors in that they did not forge these links through

4 / THE CREATION

the immediacy of the nature and fertility cults, but rather rooted them in their concrete historical pilgrimage. In so doing, they inevitably spoke of creation in three nuances: originating, continuing/sustaining, and consummating. The creator God thus, in the creating activity, was redeemer and final perfecter.

THE SUBSTANCE OF
THE BIBLICAL WITNESS: THE NEW TESTAMENT

The New Testament stands in continuity with the Old Testament traditions in that Christians believed that their existence was just as surely linked to the creator God as Israel's had been. They were convinced that the God of the Hebrew traditions was the God who had drawn near to them in Jesus Christ. When once we understand these twin affirmations—which are really one—as the basis of continuity between the two Testaments on the theme of creation, the New Testament materials take on naturally their role as the extension of Israel's belief for Christians.

The traditions of the synoptic Gospels do not include reference to the doctrine of creation as such. At the same time, it is clear that the intimate relationship they describe between Jesus and the Father implies an affirmation of the creation-belief. Jesus is pictured as a person "in touch" with the creator God and God's activity. As such he is himself an agent of the Creator's power. The nature miracles portray this vividly. Jesus stills the storm in a quiet and matter-of-fact manner; the swine serve his purposes with the demoniac; he knows where the fish are to be found even when the master fishermen are confounded. "The so-called 'nature miracles,' whatever their exact background, are really creation stories reflecting Jesus' basic trust in the creator."[14] Matthew 6:26–34 is another example of Jesus being portrayed as one who was close to the basic rhythms of nature and to their purposes—hence also to their Creator.

If we view Jesus through the apocalyptic traditions, as we surely must, the creation-motifs are also implied. It was of the essence of the apocalyptic vision that the dramatic events of judgment and messianic redemption which it proclaimed were the work of the cosmic God, who was Creator of the world and Lord over history. The apocalyptic world view was preoccupied with history, it is true, but history is guided by the God who controls all things, including cosmic realities. The very power of the apocalyptic interpretation of history lies in the assumption that all cosmic powers are focused in the historical unfolding that the apocalyptist describes. Consequently, there is an irresistible character to the movement of history that is analogous to the movements of the cosmos.[15] Therefore, the widely attested apocalyptic background of the synoptic presentation of Jesus assumes for its credibility that this man is the agent of the cosmic God who is Creator of the world and the controller of its

THE BIBLICAL WITNESS TO CREATION

history. In the events of history in which the messianic agent figures, "God will create a new world, a new heaven will appear, and the whole creation will be renewed."[16]

One of the most striking and significant contributions of the New Testament to the creation-affirmation is the effort of Paul and other writers to place Christ in the position of preexistent agent of creation. 1 Cor. 8:6, Heb. 1:2–3, Phil. 2:6–11, Col. 1:15–20, and John 1:1ff. are the passages that deal with this theme. First Corinthians 8:6 is perhaps the most significant: "Yet for us there is one God, the Father, from whom are all things and for whom we exist, and one Lord, Jesus Christ, through whom are all things and through whom we exist." This creedal statement, complex and polished in its literary form, dates from not later than A.D. 50, finding its way into Paul's letter by the year 54 or 55. To find a passage such as this at such an early time is impressive: a creed in a polished form, whose substance is such "high" christology, so metaphysically demanding, no later than twenty-five years after Jesus' earthly ministry. The complexity must be noted. The four lines contain high Hebrew-Jewish tradition ("One God, the Father"), Stoic borrowing ("from whom are all things and for whom we exist"), allusion to the wisdom tradition ("through whom are all things and through whom we exist"—this could also be Stoic), and a breathtaking leap of creative imagination in placing Jesus Christ in this context. Christ is explicitly paralleled to Yahweh, "the One God," as well as to the Jewish Wisdom (cf. Prov. 8:22ff.).

When we consider how early this piece is, that it is in the letter of a writer who is thoroughly Jewish in upbringing, and that it has a history of creedal use before Paul appropriated it, we are impressed by the audacity with which the early Christians "upped the ante" of belief claims for their contemporaries and for us. The passage poses nearly insuperable difficulties for those theories that hold that Christian belief evolved from the simpler to the complex, from low christology to high, and that the apostolic generation was blissfully unburdened by developed beliefs in contrast to later generations of theologians who allegedly dogmatized the simpler beginnings.

Theologically, two items must be considered. On the one hand, we see in this affirmation of Christ as agent of creation a profound intensification of the Old Testament effort to link present historical and personal experience to the creator God, thereby providing legitimation for such experience. The Christian affirmation is that not only is the apostolic experience rooted in the creator God, it is the experience *of* that God in a form that is very nearly univocally related to the Creator. Hebrews 1:2 (which dates from the generation after 1 Corinthians, A.D. 80–90) accentuates this: "In these last days he has spoken to us by a Son, whom he appointed the heir of all things, through whom also he created the world." We see here another way in which the *skandalon* of Christianity to the Jews may be stated, that Yahweh-Creator is iden-

4 / THE CREATION

tified with Jesus. Some scholars have observed that, in the New Testament, Jesus' person replaces the Jewish temple; Jesus' presence is the successor to Zion. If this be so, then we might suggest that we have in the passages from 1 Corinthians and Hebrews a radically recast "Zion theology."

Also to be noted, however, is the great difficulty these New Testament affirmations pose to *us*. It simply staggers the mind to attempt to explain conceptually how Jesus Christ could be declared to be the agent of creation, "through whom are all things and through whom we exist." One is finally moved to recognize that only a very nearly full-blown trinitarian theology can explain these affirmations which date from the late 40s and early 80s A.D. Such a conclusion is not popular, nor is it one that settles easily on the theologian, because it seems to impose too much on an early time of Christian faith. The conclusion brings with it intellectual and historical difficulties, but it appears to be inescapable. J. N. D. Kelly provides us some support when he writes, in the context of his discussion of 1 Cor. 8:6 and other binitarian creedal statements that occur in the New Testament:

> A host of other passages stamped with the same lineaments might be quoted. In all of them there is no trace of fixity so far as their wording is concerned, and none of them constitutes a creed in any ordinary sense of the term. Nevertheless the Trinitarian ground-plan obtrudes itself obstinately throughout, and its presence is all the more striking because more often than not there is nothing in the context to necessitate it. The impression inevitably conveyed is that the conception of the threefold manifestation of the Godhead was embedded deeply in Christian thinking from the start, and provided a ready-to-hand mould in which the ideas of the apostolic writers took shape. If Trinitarian creeds are rare, the Trinitarian pattern which was to dominate all later creeds was already part and parcel of the Christian tradition of doctrine.[17]

It has been said that these hymnic pieces, including the sections from Philippians, Colossians, and John, are expressions of the early Christian's immediate experience of redemption through Christ, not of ontological claims. There is no doubt much truth in such a claim. At the same time, it is difficult to believe that the apostolic generation was unaware of the implications of bringing the creation-motifs into conjunction with their affirmations about Jesus, particularly in light of Judaism's long tradition of such motifs. In any case, the substantial thrust of this Christian contribution to the creation-belief stands: What transpired in the life and work of Jesus Christ is a direct expression of the Creator; what Jesus did and said points to the underlying meaning and purpose of the creation.

Paul's writings are immensely significant for at least two reasons. He laid the foundations for relating Christ to the Old Testament as well as to intertestamental and Hellenistic reflection upon creation. And he also developed the concept of new creation to the point where it becomes a prime source for thinking about God's providential work in the world as an extension of the creation-work.

Paul's reflection on Christ as the Second Adam is a substantial contribution to the creation-affirmation (1 Cor. 15:45–49; Rom. 5:14, 4:17), because he is one of the few biblical writers, and the most important, to pick up the themes of Genesis 1—3 and develop their meaning. The Second or New Adam reflection is a way of saying that what was done at creation is Christ-shaped and fulfilled in Christ. Geoffrey Lampe has written:

> The Pauline parallel between Christ and Adam implies that God's design for Adam has been effectively realized in Christ. Adam was intended to be son of God; he was created in the image of God. Christ is God's Son; he is the image of God; he is "in the form of God"; he is truly Adam, which means that he is truly and completely human. The sonship to God which was fully realized in Christ belongs to the nature of all men; it characterizes humanity as the Creator intends it to be.[18]

When Lampe's comments have added to them the nuance that Christ is not only affirmed to be the true Adam but also is the one who was the agent of Adam's creation, then the richness and complexity of the New Testament propositions about Christ and creation begin to unveil themselves. Conceptually, nothing less than a doctrine of the Trinity could give coherence to such a proposition. In Rom. 4:17, Paul gives the earliest New Testament witness to creation out of nothing. This term originated in 2 Macc. 7:28 and also appears in Heb. 11:3. It is worth noting that in this passage Paul parallels the resurrection of Jesus with the creation out of nothing: "the God in whom [Abraham] believed, who gives life to the dead and calls into existence the things that do not exist." The Second Adam discourse in 1 Corinthians 15 also parallels that creation-motif to the resurrection.

Such insights lead naturally to Paul's thought about the new creation. Romans 5—8, as well as Gal. 6:15 and 2 Cor. 5:17, show this motif. In the Romans passages, we see Paul moving from the parallelism of 4:17 between resurrection and creation out of nothing to the discussion in chapter 5 of Christ as the Second Adam overcoming sin and restoring the original creation of humans. There follows the reflection on baptism as dying with Christ, so that we might rise with him. This new life is related to the law/grace duality, culminating in chapter 8 with commentary on our redemption as the new creation which liberates the rest of creation (8:19), "the creation waits with eager longing for the revealing of the sons of God." This redemption is our participation in God's predestination (8:20), which leads to the final victory, in which neither death, life, angels, heights, depths, "nor anything else in all creation will be able to separate us from the love of God in Christ Jesus our Lord."

4 / THE CREATION

Paul here rises to unrivaled heights of intensity as he pictures our redemption as a participation in God's ongoing creation work. When this motif is added to those discussed earlier, of Christ as Creator, Second Adam, whose resurrection parallels creation out of nothing, then it becomes clearer how fully Paul has integrated his christology with the creation affirmation. This is a concept of new creation that differs from the Old Testament concepts, in that the desired outcome is in no sense tied to the self-interest of the religious community and its reestablishment and vindication. Rather, the end that is sought is participation in God's work for its own sake. Paul interprets his own individual experience as "new creation" (Gal. 6:15), and he attaches the image to the life of all Christians. "New creation" is a description of what happens when we are united with Christ, and it is the goal of such union. "Therefore, if any one is in Christ, he is a new creation; the old has passed away, behold, the new has come" (2 Cor. 5:17).

Ephesians 1 and Colossians 1 have in recent decades been lifted up, particularly by Teilhard de Chardin, Allan Galloway, and Joseph Sittler, to set Christ clearly at the center of God's creator-activity and of the whole created world which Christ redeems.[19] Some exegetes have now sought to discredit such an emphasis, on several grounds. Even allowing for their objections, the cosmic christology of these passages is significant. It amounts to the assertion of Christ's preexistence; ". . . even as he chose us in him before the foundation of the world" (Eph. 1:3–4). It joins together our history with Christ and God's eternal creative will; "For he has made known to us in all wisdom and insight the mystery of his will, according to his purpose which he set forth in Christ, as a plan for the fulness of time, to unite all things in him, things in heaven and things on earth" (Eph. 1:9–10). In light of our survey of the biblical literature, these affirmations appear to be fully consistent with what the Old Testament and the other New Testament traditions set out to do.

Revelation 21 and 2 Pet. 3:13 speak of God's "new heaven and a new earth." The content of Revelation 21, as well as the language, is reminiscent of Third Isaiah. The intent is to encourage persecuted Christians with visions of hope. The New Testament image of the New Jerusalem, however, is a heavenly city "from above," rather than the earthly restoration of Zion. Second Peter puts apocalyptic creation imagery in the service of a just city where the righteous can live in peace.

As we observed at the outset, this lengthy survey of the biblical materials was undertaken not so much because theology must in every time reiterate the Bible, but because the Bible has such a rich and complex witness to creation. Even if subsequent history had contributed nothing, theology would be fully occupied with elaborating and seeking to understand more fully what the Bible has bequeathed to us. The following summary statements may serve as the transition to the next part of our theological reflection.

THE BIBLICAL WITNESS TO CREATION

First. The scriptural witness evidences a basic assumption that God is creator of all that is. This is, even when it is doubted (as in some Wisdom sections), so basic an assumption that it may be termed preconceptual and predecisional. To recall Ronald Hepburn's phrase, the biblical witnesses seem scarcely ever to have doubted that God "is the author and sustainer of the world" and that consequently "the world is a planned and purposed enterprise."

Second. Despite this nearly unanimous affirmation, there is genuine and ineradicable diversity in the biblical witness. The Zion theology of David's and Solomon's court is not the same as the Yahwist's humanism or the Wisdom reflection of Job. And none of these is the same as Third Isaiah's eschatological vision. Paul's profound, sometimes involuted, probings are still different. This diversity has produced richness, which in turn provides for us an almost illimitable resource for speculation and edification. The diversity stems largely from the fact that creation was affirmed by groups and individuals with integrity in the situation in which they found themselves, with admirable freedom from simply reiterating what previous generations said. Note, for example, how little explicit reverberation Genesis 1 and 2 make in subsequent sections of Scripture.

Third. There is a persistent effort in each biblical witness to forge links between the situation of the witnesses and the activity of the creator God. This has often been explained as a subsuming of the interest in origins under existential need or soteriology. No doubt the judgment is profoundly true, but it also runs the danger of making the creation-witness seem to be an afterthought, whose legitimation must be sought in a sort of perennial ritual. It may be preferable to say that for most people the current existential situation does not make full sense unless it is related to origins and to the power of creation. Many peoples forged links between their present and their origins through nature and fertility cults. Israel (both old and new) eschewed such a strategy. The linkage for our biblical and Christian traditions has been made by relating to the creator God through our history, as well as through our reflective capacities (as in Job), our wills, and our introspection, rather than through "natural unification," such as might come through liaison with ritual prostitutes, worship of the seasons, and the like.

Fourth. When the links are forged between the present and the original creation and its God, creation becomes as much a present and a future reality as a present one. From this circumstance it develops that creation becomes what Paul Tillich has called originating, sustaining, and directing creativity.[20] The tradition has called these protology, continuing creation, and new creation or Providence. From our survey, it should be very clear that such terms grow quite naturally from the biblical witnesses; they are not "new creations" of the theologians.

Fifth. It is unmistakably clear that the Christian traditions in the apostolic

4 / THE CREATION

period placed Christ in a revelational and ontological center position with respect to the creation affirmation. They did not work out the conceptual details of this position, but they left us no option but to confess Christ's centrality as the agent of creation, the goal of creation, and the power of creation's fulfillment in the new creation. This central position is intimately tied to the later doctrine of the Trinity.

Each of these five elements becomes a given for subsequent theological reflection, including our own theological efforts. How they are spelled out shapes the task of the next chapters of this locus.

NOTES

1. John Reumann, *Creation and New Creation* (Minneapolis: Augsburg Publishing House, 1973), p. 20.
2. Claus Westermann, *Creation*, trans. John J. Scullion (Philadelphia: Fortress Press, 1974), p. 48.
3. Emil Brunner, *The Christian Doctrine of Creation and Redemption*, trans. Olive Wyon (Philadelphia: Westminster Press, 1952), p. 6.
4. Reumann, *Creation and New Creation*, p. 21.
5. The more scholarly study is John Reumann, "Creatio, Continua et Nova," in *The Gospel as History*, ed. Vilmos Vajta (Philadelphia: Fortress Press, 1975), pp. 79–110. *Creation and New Creation* is longer and more popular. Neither, as Reumann points out, is a complete treatment.
6. Charles H. Long, *Alpha, the Myths of Creation* (New York: George Braziller, 1963).
7. Ibid., p. 149.
8. Westermann, *Creation*, p. 10.
9. Ibid., pp. 39–41.
10. Ibid., pp. 36–39.
11. Jaroslav Pelikan, "Creation and Causality in the History of Christian Thought," in *Issues in Evolution*, ed. Sol Tax (Chicago: University of Chicago Press, 1960), p. 31.
12. Helmer Ringgren, *The Faith of the Psalmists* (Philadelphia: Fortress Press, 1963), p. 96.
13. Carroll Stuhlmueller, "Creative Redemption in Deutero-Isaiah," *AnBib* 43 (1970): 9, 233.
14. Reumann, "Creatio, Continua et Nova," p. 91.
15. Walter Schmithals, *The Apocalyptic Movement*, trans. John E. Steely (Nashville: Abingdon Press, 1973), chaps. 1–2.
16. Ibid., p. 22.
17. J. N. D. Kelly, *Early Christian Creeds* (New York and London: Longmans, Green & Co., 1960), p. 23. See also G. B. Caird, "The Development of the Doctrine of Christ in the New Testament," in *Christ for Us Today*, ed. Norman Pittenger (London: SCM Press, 1968), pp. 4–80.
18. Geoffrey Lampe, *God as Spirit* (New York and London: Oxford University Press, 1977), p. 178.

19. See Joseph Sittler, "Called to Unity," *ER* 14 (1961–62): 177–87; Joseph Sittler, "The Scope of Christological Reflection," *Inter.* 26 (1972): 328–37; Allan Galloway, *The Cosmic Christ* (New York: Harper & Brothers, 1951); Pierre Teilhard de Chardin, *Science and Christ*, trans. Rene Hague (New York: Harper & Row, 1969), pp. 37–86, 151–73.

20. Paul Tillich, *Systematic Theology*, 3 vols. (Chicago: University of Chicago Press, 1951–63), 1:252–70.

2

The Creation of the World

The Christian doctrine of creation is above all a statement of how Christians regard the world in a manner commensurate with what they believe about God. This linkage between God and the world must be respected if we are to comprehend this Christian doctrine fully and adequately. The idea of creation "out of nothing" is integral to the doctrine, because it is a powerful way of asserting the total dependence of the world on its Creator. Elaborating how this dependence is to be conceived is at the heart of theological reflection.

THE NATURE OF THE CLAIM

To begin with, we must be clear about what sort of statement the Christian affirmation of creation is. Arguments about this point are endless, and probably no other theological issue has caused more misunderstanding. In a notable dialogue entitled "Creation," Donald MacKinnon and Antony Flew point out that most of the laity believe the doctrine of creation deals with the beginning of the world and its details. As such, the creation-doctrine is a matter for preaching, but also one to which "the latest news from the science front" is also relevant.[1] The average theologian, on the contrary, insists on quite a different understanding of the doctrine, one to which scientific discoveries are simply irrelevant, because the doctrine intends to affirm something that science is not competent to assess. Such a division of the church according to theological expertise cannot go without close scrutiny. The issue is all the more pressing for Americans because of the "creationist" challenge, which insists on understanding the doctrine of creation as a parallel to scientific cosmology. The problem strikes modern Christians with particular force, since before the rise of modern science and secularization, nearly all Christians, including sophisticated theologians, took for granted that the doctrine of creation addresses both the question of the world's origins and other theological questions.

The doctrine of creation is thoroughly and completely a religious-theological affirmation. We must probe more deeply just what this means before we can

4 / THE CREATION

go on to clarify the relationship between the doctrine and modern knowledge about the world and its origins. The affirmation of creation is the form in which the community of faith sets forth its understanding of the world. As it does so, its goal is to permit its understanding of the world to be fully congruous with its belief in God. This point must be appreciated in depth. Theology, when it speaks of creation, does not seek to obfuscate or avoid certain embarrassing questions, or stake out an esoteric realm beyond common language where only the initiated can enter. Rather, it insists that Christian belief in God has consequences, consequences to which we are accountable and consequences that must be observed if the coherence of Christian faith is to be respected. "Creation" is a word that refers to the whole of the world when viewed as belonging to God, and the doctrine of creation is an elaboration of how we understand the world when we permit our understanding of God to permeate and dominate our thinking.

The doctrine of creation is from the outset, therefore, shaped by powerful presuppositions, the most important of which concern God. It presupposes a conviction both that God is related to the world and that this relationship makes a difference that is determinative of all else. Because it does rest on such presuppositions, the affirmation of creation is an article of faith.[2] It is not the case that our affirmation of creation rests partly on our belief in God and partly on our natural knowledge. On the contrary, no matter what role natural knowledge plays in our affirmation, the belief in God plays the decisive role. It is belief in God that makes our statements about the world a doctrine of creation, rather than cosmology plain and simple. Our affirmation of creation is consequently not "more or less" influenced by our belief in God; it is decisively influenced by such a belief or else it is not an affirmation of *creation*.

From such considerations, the following axiom derives: There is a correlation between the nature of the world and the nature of its source or creator. In this axiom is to be found the power and the unsettling pointedness of the Christian affirmation of creation. When the Christian faith takes this axiom seriously, its proclamation of the creation-witness becomes a vital advocacy that allows neither the church nor the world to treat it as if it were a bland utterance of thoughtless piety. It demands attention, even if that attention is hostile, because what it says about the world does make a difference.

GOD AND THE WORLD: ISSUES FOR CREATION ARISING FROM GOD'S NATURE

The creation-affirmation requires a relationship between God and the world that is complex, difficult to conceptualize, and sometimes more significant for what it hints at or denies than for what it explicitly asserts. We may say of the Christian view of the God/world relationship what Langdon Gilkey has said of the Christian concept of God's transcendence, that it "is a baffling mixture of ontology and religious faith."[3] We may summarize the issues here as they pertain, first, to the way in which the creation came into being and, second, to the way in which God and the creation coexist after God's creative work.

There are two basic Christian doctrinal assertions about the beginning. The world came into being as a result of a free act of God. And God *created* the world, as opposed to generating it, or putting its parts together as a carpenter might, or being the origin of the world as the source of its emanations.

That God creates freely, by God's own volition, is a universal theological assertion in the Christian tradition. The assertion is put in a representative way by Irenaeus:

> I . . . begin with God the Creator, who made the heaven and the earth, and all things that are therein . . . and demonstrate that there is nothing either above him or after him; nor that, influenced by any one, but of his own free will, he created all things, since he is the only God, the only Lord, the only creator, the only Father.[4]

Irenaeus instructively places the assertion of God's freedom in the context of a recital of God's greatness and uniqueness. The assertion of God's freedom is not an attempt to preserve God's right to be arbitrary or God's distance from the creation. Rather, if God did not create freely, God would not be God. If God created by some necessity, it would imply some antecedent, determining power.[5] It is sometimes asserted that insistence on power and uniqueness is rooted in archaic notions of imperial power or place God beyond meaningful relationship with the created world.[6] While such arguments are not without grounds, they miss the point: creation by an entity that does not have the character of genuine deity is religiously and theologically unsatisfying.

There has been much debate over the centuries concerning the nuances of the words "create," "make," "generate," and the like when applied to God's activity. Athanasius and Arius debated this point at length during the fourth century. Athanasius' argument was that the verb carries overtones as to whether the outcome of the activity was like God, identical, equal, or dissimilar to God. In the Arian controversy, he insisted on a verb that expressed the unity and equality of Father and Son, so he argued that "beget" was the proper word, whereas Arius, with contrary interests, argued for "make."[7] There is a comparable problem with respect to describing God's creative activity. Thomistic theology has recognized the parallels between the persons of the Trinity emerging from one another (*processio*) and the emergence of the creation from God (*emanatio*).[8] The chief difference between the two kinds of

299

4 / THE CREATION

emergence is that the inner-trinitarian process is necessary and results in co-equal entities, whereas the process of creation is a freely willed action of God's, and it produces an entity that is qualitatively different from God the Creator.

The narratives of Genesis 1—3 were able to use a term for "create" (*bara*) that was used exclusively for God's activity. It is not so simple for us. "Emanate" and "generate" may seem to be satisfying concepts for describing God's creating activity because they point to the intimacy between God and the world. We may even be influenced by the fact that Thomas Aquinas used the term *emanatio* to designate creation activity. These terms are to be rejected, however, because they suggest that the world is "of the same substance" with the Creator. Such terms suggest the bizarre notion that the created world is a "piece" of God, a child of God, or even God's body. Such suggestions are manifestations of the age-old option of pantheism or extreme monism, which the theological tradition has repudiated time and again. An example of pantheism is found in the Hindu Upanishads: "That which is the finest essence—this whole world has that as its soul. That is Reality. That is Atman."[9] Besides Hinduism, other Eastern religions could be called pantheistic. So can Neo-Platonism, Stoicism, and Spinozism. Pantheists hold that the world is a tightly unified whole whose parts perfectly intertwine and that this system is divine, made of the same substance as God. The power of pantheism lies in its ability to speak of the intimate relationship between God and the world and to give high value to the created order. It also provides the basis for a thoroughly ordered and reliable world.

Pantheism, while it does make certain appealing affirmations, violates what Christians deeply believe about God and God's relationship to the world. Christians have opposed pantheism because they perceive that it takes away God's freedom, so essential to the Christian concept of deity. For the world to be of the same substance with the Creator bespeaks a process whereby creation has "oozed" from God or broken off from God in some sort of mitosis. The Christian understanding of creation rests on a conviction that the world is the product of God's intentional activity; it did not just happen, nor is it a "natural" process. This free intentionality is essential to the Christian understanding of God. Gordon Kaufman has put it accurately: pantheism "maintains in its own way that the world is not God's deliberate creation, the purposive and meaningful expression of his will."[10]

The carpentering image of God's activity is also unsatisfactory from a Christian point of view. This image is essentially that of Plato's Demiurge, who found preexistent material at hand and imposed order upon it, thereby creating the world. Such an image is once again being proposed by some theologians as fully consonant with Christian faith.[11] The difficulty with the Demiurge image of the creator is that it violates the Christian conception of God as the originator of *all* that is. Preexistent material suggests a pre-God source.

Demiurge theories often are employed to provide a source for evil other than God. God is absolved of responsibility for evil, because, after all, God is not responsible for the tendencies to be found in the preexistent material before God began to work on it. Often these tendencies are those associated with chaos.[12] This sets up a dualism that not only deprives God of being the Creator of all things but also resolves the problem of evil by introducing material thrusts beyond God's power to control. This would postulate a source and process of evil that God cannot overcome. Such an image of God is foreign to the biblical traditions we have observed in Job ("Where were you when I laid the foundation of the earth?") or in the Psalms (e.g., Ps. 104) or in Second Isaiah. It is not in accord with the christological contributions the New Testament makes to our understanding of creation. These traditions bespeak a God who is the origin of all that is.

The nature of God, in the Christian conception, also makes demands on our concept of how God and the creation coexist after creation has come into existence. On this point the basic Christian affirmations are that the world is qualitatively different from God, that God maintains a caring concern for the world, that the world is totally dependent on its Creator from whom it has received order and unity, purpose, and goodness, and that the world has its own freedom and value. These elements are not readily brought into conceptual harmony. One might argue that they have never been adequately conceptualized, despite vigorous effort today to do so.

Emil Brunner has stated the qualitative difference between God and creation correctly:

> As the One who alone is Creator, God stands "over against" His creation, because it does not participate in his Being as Creator—the "Wholly Other." The fact that God is the Wholly Other refers to that which distinguishes Him as Creator from the creature. He alone is Lord, He alone is the Source of all life; He alone is the giver of every good and perfect gift. He alone is "*a se, non ab alio.*" Thus there is no "way" between the creaturely and the divine; between both there lies the absolute gulf: that outside of God there is only that which has been created, outside Him who is "*a se,*" only that which is "*ab alio*"; thus outside the One who is entirely independent, there is only dependent being, the creature. This difference is greater than all other differences of any kind; this is the absolute transcendence of essence of Him who alone is God.[13]

This is the famous "wholly other," the *totaliter aliter* of the so-called "neo-orthodox" theology of the mid-twentieth century. Whatever the ramifications of this school of thought, it is important to see that the quality of "wholly

4 / THE CREATION

otherness" in this citation is focused on one point: the distinction between Creator and created, source and sourced. This is not a statement about distance, uncaring, or otherness as such; rather, it is an assertion about the infinite qualitative difference between source of all that is and that which is sourced, which receives its being from the source of all being.

Conjoined with the assertion of God's freedom in creation, the assertion of God's otherness is not made to distance God from the world, nor is it an attempt to preserve for God some glory or status that protects God from the world's contamination. Rather the affirmation is this: This world is the creation of a God who created the world freely and who is the source of all that is. The governing considerations are that God can in no way be considered a created being and that God's creating activity is not coerced. There are no limits on our conceptions of the closeness, reciprocity, or intimacy between God and the world, so long as these essential elements are preserved intact. On the contrary, we are pressed to probe deeply the nature and quality of the intimacy that exists between God and the world. Theologically and religiously, however, we cannot be satisfied until our concepts take into account that such relationships are really with as the God whom Christians have worshiped in Jesus Christ. If this genuine godhood of God is not maintained in our theological concepts, then the closeness between God and the world that may be illumined will prove meaningless and intolerable.

Emphasis on the nature of God as free and qualitatively different from the world, in that God is its source, should not inhibit our reflection on the closeness of God and the world. The character of this closeness or intimacy is best described as *caring*. The Lutheran tradition has emphasized this caring quality of God vis-à-vis the creation by referring to the Creator as "Father." In his Large Catechism, Luther conveys the intimacy of God's caring both in the form and in the content of his explanation of the creed:

> The Creed is nothing else than a response and confession of Christians based on the First Commandment. If you were to ask a young child, "My boy, what kind of God have you? What do you know about him?" he could say, "First, my God is the Father, who made heaven and earth. Apart from him alone I have no other God, for there is no one else who could create heaven and earth."[14]

And when we turn to Luther's explanation of the first commandment, we find:

> A god is that to which we look for all good and in which we find refuge in every time of need. To have a god is nothing else than to trust and believe him with our whole heart. . . . The purpose of this commandment, therefore, is to require true faith and confidence of the heart. . . . The meaning is: "Whatever good thing you lack, look to me for it and seek it from me, and whenever you suffer misfortune and distress, come and cling to me. I am the one who will satisfy you and help you out of every need."[15]

THE CREATION OF THE WORLD

The caring motif is elaborated at great length in the theological concepts of continuing creation (*creatio continua*) and providence (*conservatio, concursus,* and *gubernatio*), which receive extended discussion below. A number of recent theologians have insisted that this caring dimension of the creator God may be rendered more vivid if we keep in mind Christ's role in creation. Brunner suggests that the purpose of the creation is the will of God, and God's will is love. God's will is the "sufficient reason" (*ratio sufficiens*), whereas the love of God is the "final cause" (*causa finalis*) of creation. "In Jesus Christ this ideal reason for the Creation is revealed."[16] Gustaf Aulén and his successor as the Lundensian dogmatician, Gustaf Wingren, assert strongly what has come to be a hallmark of contemporary Swedish interpretations of creation:

> The doctrine of creation implies that God's loving and sovereign will is the matrix of creation. The purpose of creation is that God's will should rule and control all things. In other words, God's loving will is the law of creation. . . . It must be strongly emphasized again that this law of love which Christ has revealed and fulfilled is in principle nothing else than the law of creation.[17]

The Danish theologian, Regin Prenter, varies this general emphasis by suggesting that creation is proclaimed both as law and gospel; the caring emphasis is asserted under "The Gospel of Creation."[18]

The coexistence of the creator God and creation is characterized by the world's utter dependence on the Creator and yet also by its genuine freedom and autonomy. Dependence on God is an inescapable consequence of the qualitative difference we have mentioned. God alone is source, and therefore everything that is must be dependent on God in the most significant way: It has received its being from God. Thomas Aquinas asserted this point in scholastic terms: "Therefore all beings other than God are not their own being, but are beings by participation . . . caused by one First Being, who possesses being most perfectly."[19] The psalmist uses poetry in Psalm 104:

> When thou hidest thy face, they are dismayed;
> when thou takest away their breath, they die
> and return to their dust.
> When thou sendest forth thy Spirit, they are created;
> and thou renewest the face of the ground.

Dependence on God is the chief thrust of the idea of creation "out of nothing." All that is is contingent on a cause, a source, a creator.[20] Again, this is not an insistence on coercive or imperial power for God, but rather an acknowledgment that the source of all that is exercises the power appropriate to being that source, namely, the activity of sourcing, on which all else depends. Friedrich Schleiermacher, in his dogmatic work *The Christian Faith*,

4 / THE CREATION

which first appeared in 1821, made dependence the heart of Christian faith. His dogmatic theses concerning creation and preservation are worth repeating here.

In Thesis 36, Schleiermacher states the issue: "The original expression of this relation, i.e., that the world exists only in absolute dependence upon God, is divided in Church doctrine into the two propositions—that the world was created by God, and that God sustains the world."[21] Of creation, he wrote: "The religious consciousness which is here our basis contradicts every representation of the origin of the world which excludes anything whatever from origination by God."[22] Of preservation: "The religious self-consciousness, by means of which we place all that affects or influences us in absolute dependence on God, coincides entirely with the view that all such things are conditioned and determined by the interdependence of Nature."[23] The assertion of dependence as made by Aquinas—and as discussed by such contemporary theologians as Robert Neville, Thomas Torrance, and Wolfhart Pannenberg—is an ontological statement, whereas Schleiermacher is reporting on what the religious self-consciousness perceives in its experience. While it is impossible to move from the consciousness of experience to ontological statements, the combined testimony of an Aquinas and a Schleiermacher expresses what the Christian tradition has asserted.

The affirmation of the world's total dependence on the Creator as its source provides an opportunity to reflect on the inadequacy of all dualistic modes of relating God and the world. Dualism holds a special significance for Christian faith, because in the first two and a half centuries, the church was threatened both within and without by a dualism of massive proportions: gnosticism. The onslaught lasted over a century and involved church government, liturgy, and the understanding of Christ and his redemption, as well as the interpretation of the obedient life and doctrine. In the early centuries, the church faced other dualisms besides gnosticism, such as Manicheism. One can hardly overemphasize the importance of the fact that the church, out of this turmoil, came down decisively against dualism.

For our purposes, it is enough to characterize gnosticism as positing the essential inferiority and evil of the world, separating the God of creation (in the Old Testament) from the God of redemption (in the New Testament), and as exhorting people to flee the earthly and bodily realm. Tertullian and Irenaeus stand as the formative and normative theologians in responding to the gnostics. Irenaeus deserves preeminent consideration because of his nonlegalistic, creative theological responses. Tertullian, although he defended the church's authority against the gnostics, was himself prone to dualisms; hence his eventual submission to Montanism.

In their elaborate theosophical systems, the gnostics saw the origin of the created world in a liaison between a feminine divine figure (an "Aeon") with a nondivine male figure. The result is that, in their terminology, the world is "the fruit of a defect." With the inferiority of the earthly realm thus ontologically grounded, the earth-renouncing of gnosticism came "naturally." The "spiritual" realm and the more "spiritual" persons took preeminence over "physical" counterparts. The goal was to free the spirit from its prisonhouse of matter. This might lead to world-renouncing through asceticism or through scornful antinomianism. The bifurcation of the Old and New Testaments was initiated by Marcion, the gifted mid-second-century schismatic and heterodox organizer. With it came the corresponding separation of the God of creation, the God of law, purported to be cruel and arbitrary, from the God of redemption, the God of love.

The church's struggle with the gnostics should not be construed as a case of "orthodoxy" confronting and successfully vanquishing "heresy." The issue was more ambiguous than that. Even though the gnostics were part of a larger intellectual and religious movement existing also outside the church, the struggle was between two groups within the church, each of whom could claim some "orthodox" antecedents. Orthodoxy was defined in the conflict. The definition included the formation of a canon of Scripture that included both Old and New Testaments, and a creed that affirmed one Creator and Redeemer God, an affirmation of the goodness of the created world and a confession of God's intentions to bring it to consummation. Irenaeus developed his celebrated christology of "recapitulation" (*anakephalaiosis*), which spoke of the created world as being incomplete in the beginning but possessing the capacity to grow into its fullness. Christ was affirmed by Irenaeus as the prototype of what creation should become. Christ recapitulated, incorporated all things and their destiny in himself. To be created in the image of God meant to be created in Christ's image and to grow into the Christ-destiny for which God has prepared creation.

Irenaeus thus effectively counters the view that would set God against the world, that would put a part of the created world outside God's sphere of responsibility, and that would abandon a part of the world to remain outside God's redemption. These two elements, pitting God against the world (or a part of it), and removing a part of the world from both God's creating and consummating activity—these are at the core of dualism, ontologically speaking. Irenaeus repudiated both these core elements by insisting that the world was created in Christ, that Christ is the prototype of its development or growth, and that at the end it will grow into its Christ-perfection. We have already observed the roots of creation-through-Christ in early traditions. *Apokatastasis*, or "universalism," as it is sometimes called (often tendentiously), has been affirmed by theologians from Origen to Barth as a way of asserting that there is no evil that God cannot overcome, that God is intent on bringing the whole of creation to its perfection at the end.

4 / THE CREATION

Irenaeus' specific resolutions of the problems posed by dualism are distinctive and not reiterated universally throughout the tradition. Nevertheless, the points he made have become the Christian faith's perennial response to dualisms that threaten the fundamental assertion that God is the God on whom all creation is dependent for its being.

This discussion of dualism has focused on its ontological aspect. Moral dualism is a different matter; this aspect has been prominent in Christian faith. Paul Tillich has said that Christian faith grants evil only moral, not ontological, foundation.[24] The Christian recognizes that the struggle between good and evil is an inescapable characteristic of earthly existence, but that it is not written into the very nature of things. It is not at the foundation of the creation. Tillich thereby laid bare the limits to the Christian faith's tolerance of dualism.

Christians are sensitive to the ongoing conflict within each person's existence and within history between good and evil in many different forms. Precisely, however, because they believe that evil has no ontological foundation, Christians can believe in the redemption of existence and history. As we shall discuss in detail later, this firm belief is rooted in the character of the creator God and God's creation activity.

Thus far, we have noted only the general dependence of the created world on the Creator for its being. This being is specified in Christian belief to include the order and unity, purposiveness, and goodness of creation. These characteristics of the created world derive from the character of God. The nature of God as one and good, together with the conviction that God has created the world intentionally and freely, leads inescapably to the assertion that the created world is a unity, that it is good, and that it has a purpose and meaning. These characteristics are reinforced by the assertion of Christ's role in the creation.

We have observed the intimate relation between the biblical assertion of Christ's role in creating and the doctrine of the Trinity. In recognizing Christ as the second person or hypostasis of the triune Godhead, the Christian faith emphasized his position as Logos and Wisdom, as *ordo intellegendi*. In locating Christ so, the theologians demonstrated their dependence both on stoic and Platonist philosophy and on the Hebrew wisdom tradition. They also demonstrated the creative imagination that put together a new intellectual and religious synthesis the exact like of which had not been seen before.

So to place Christ and to link him with the agency and the goal of creation is to put meaning and purpose "deep-down in things," precisely because the second person of the Trinity *is* meaning and purpose, thematized within the Godhead and revealed in all reality. The same must be said about goodness.

THE CREATION OF THE WORLD

God the Creator is good, and that goodness is revealed, actualized, and incarnate in Christ.

Finally, in recounting the manner in which the Christian understanding of God influences our understanding of the God/world relationship, we turn to the question of the world's independent reality, its autonomous worthwhileness. God gives creation a genuine reality, not a docetic pseudoreality. As Gilkey writes, "Christians believed that the finite world was the product of the will as well as of the divine wisdom. Nature was, therefore, a creature and not an appearance of God, a distinct and relatively independent reality posited into being by God's will."[25] Erich Frank has made a similar point:

> The concept of creation . . . acknowledges both the rational and irrational elements in the world. For creation means that free individual beings are brought forth, or, from the point of view of the creator, it signifies that he has infused his own being into another thing which thereby has taken on an independent existence of its own and may later on itself become productive. Thus the idea of creation, although transcending human experience, serves to explain the world as it really is in its twofold character of individual autonomy and universal dependence.[26]

This concept of a certain autonomy belonging to the created order has been judged by historians to be distinctive of the Judeo-Christian tradition. There is no concept of "nature" in the Bible, writes the Dutch historian, R. Hooykaas, but only the concept of creatures. "Nature" had the ring of a deified order that was of the same substance as God, whereas the biblical view of nature is "de-deified."[27] Not only the nature and fertility cults of Canaan, which surrounded the Israelites, but also the views of Plato, Aristotle, and the other Greek philosophers, bestowed a divinity on nature, though the philosophers' reasoning was different from that of the Near Eastern religions.

Among the consequences of this view of creation was an antipathy to pantheism in any form. Earlier we observed that pantheistic views violate the basic concept of how God was originally related to the world. It contravenes the assertion of God's free creative act. Pantheism also violates the integrity of the created order. This requires some spelling out.

We might think that pantheism would not downgrade the earthly order but rather would glorify it, since this monistic world view asserts that at its most essential all matter is divine. However, pantheism has always resulted in a depreciation of matter—as in the cases of the Neo-Platonists, the stoics, Indian pantheisms, and the like. The clue to this depreciation lies in the essential idea "that the reality and value of finite things consist in the degree to which they are identical to or united with God. What is not God, then, is neither real nor good."[28] Finite things, insofar as they are finite, possessing the characteristics of materiality, partialness, changeableness, relativity,

4 / THE CREATION

limitedness, and the like, are certainly not God. What results is a degradation of the material order. Matter becomes illusory; docetism enters in. The claim is that "at the core" or "in their essence," finite things are divine, so what is required is a strategy of sloughing off all that is not of the essence or at the core. This poses at least two problems for the Christian. In the first place, we are impressed that the quantity of what must be sloughed off is rather great, including a good deal that we consider central to our humanity. Further, we know that at the core we are sinners, capable of considerable evil.

A strong argument could be made that what must be sloughed off as unessential is so central to the earthly realm that without this "unessential" element there would be no identifiable material realm left. For people, such "unessentials" would include changeable emotions, physicality, and dependence upon others. We could also argue that the reality of evil in the heart of every person, with the enormous harm that those evil hearts can accomplish, is a testimony not to the unreal, illusory quality of finite selves but on the contrary to the very much undeniable, concrete reality of those same selves.

The distinctive Christian affirmation of the independent reality of the created order has had other important consequences. Chief among them is the influence this affirmation may have had on the emergence of modern science and on the development of secularization. A substantial number of historians argue that in both cases—science and secularization—Christianity's de-deification of nature has triggered significant historical trends.[29] The change from a deification of nature to the assessment that nature is creation brought with it an interest in nature for its own sake, as well as an affirmative attitude free from inordinate fear of nature. The conviction that God had bestowed orderliness, intelligibility, and unity upon creation (especially strong among the medieval theologians) encouraged confidence that scientific study of nature would produce results. If the Christian theological tradition as a whole contributed significantly to the intellectual foundations of the rising science, the "Protestant ethic," particularly the zeal of English Puritans in the seventeenth century, provided practical energy and (through the rise of capitalism) a financial base for science.

Secularization is the development of the attitude that nature is its own realm, that it does not need to be decoded like a cipher in order to be understood. Weather can be understood by terrestrial principles, without consulting oracles and divinities. So can illness, nutrition, sexuality, and warfare, to mention just a few aspects of life affected in important ways by secularizing trends. Some theologians—Friedrich Gogarten, Schubert Ogden, J. A. T. Robinson—would distinguish between "secularization" and "secularism." The former is the wholesome recognition that nature, including human and social nature, is not divine, that it has its own rationale and orderliness. Secularism, in contrast, is a destructive elevation of this insight of secularization into an all-encompassing philosophical position. Secularization recognizes that the natural world is not itself a system of reality that is ontologically self-sufficient, and as such is reconcilable with the Christian view of God and creation. Secularism denies both God and creation, and as such is antithetical to the Christian faith.

CREATION OUT OF NOTHING ("EX NIHILO")

Although we have scarcely mentioned it explicitly, we have been skirting the classical doctrine of *creatio ex nihilo*, creation out of nothing. Because of linguistic difficulties with the formulation, which may lead to confusion, we have deliberately made our way to the doctrine through these other reflections, so that it might be clear just what kinds of considerations the *ex nihilo* tries to comprehend. Augustine, in his *Confessions*, gives us one of the most vivid formulations of the doctrine:

> But *how* didst thou make the heaven and the earth, and what was the tool of such a mighty work as thine? For it was not like a human worker fashioning body from body, according to the fancy of his mind, able somehow or other to impose on it a form which the mind perceived in itself by its inner eye (yet how should even he be able to do this, if thou hadst not made that mind?). He imposes the form on something already existing and having some sort of being, such as clay, or stone or wood or gold or such like (and where would these things come from if thou hadst not furnished them?). . . . But how didst thou make them? How, O God, didst thou make the heaven and earth? For truly, neither in heaven nor on earth didst thou make heaven and earth—nor in the air nor in the waters, since all of these also belong to the heaven and the earth. Nowhere in the whole world didst thou make the whole world, because there was no place where it could be made before it was made. And thou didst not hold anything in thy hand from which to fashion the heaven and the earth, for where couldst thou have gotten what thou hadst not made in order to make something with it? Is there, indeed, anything at all except because thou art? Thus thou didst speak and they were made, and by thy Word thou didst make them all. But how didst thou speak? . . . Whatever it was out of which such a voice was made simply did not exist at all until it was made by thee."[30]

Augustine wrote his *Confessions* between A.D. 395 and 398. He was by no means the first to assert *creatio ex nihilo*. There is some question among scholars as to whether already the Old Testament asserts this proposition. A recent "process" theologian, David Griffin, has argued that Plato's theory of creation out of chaos, with God as Demiurge, is consistent with Genesis 1 and is philosophically preferable to the *ex nihilo*.[31] The contention of our discussion has been that the traditions in Job, Second Isaiah, and the Psalms

4 / THE CREATION

do indeed imply the *ex nihilo* and that the New Testament traditions, particularly in their christocentric dimension, are consistent only with the *ex nihilo*. The first explicit reference to the idea as such is in Macc. 7:28 (which dates from the period between 100 B.C. and A.D. 70), which in the Vulgate is translated *"ex nihilo fecit illa Deus"* (God made them out of nothing). Romans 4:17 and Heb. 11:3 express the idea. In the mid-second century A.D., the term is found in Hermas, *Visio*, 1,1,6, and in the latter half of the century, it is argued by a number of theologians, including Clement of Alexandria, Theophilus of Antioch, Tertullian, and Irenaeus.

We have already rehearsed the principal contents of the doctrine of creation out-of-nothing. We do not properly understand the doctrine, however, unless we recognize that it is not only a material assertion. The *ex nihilo* is just as importantly a proposition of method or strategy. In this respect, it teaches: Unless the formula "out of nothing" is emphasized, the basic affirmations Christians want to make about God the Creator and God's relationship to the world cannot be maintained. This recognition prompted Paul Tillich to observe: "The formula *creatio ex nihilo* is not the title of a story. It is the classical formula which expresses the relation between God and the world."[32] The doctrine does not assert that God created all things out of the prior reality called "nothing," "nonbeing," the Greek *ouk ōn*. It is rather insisting that everything that is depends for its being on God the Creator. *Creatio ex nihilo* is first and foremost a statement about who God is and what kind of a God that God is. It is because of their experience of God that the Hebrews, the Jews, and the Christians have asserted the Creator of the *creatio ex nihilo*. Writers as diverse as Augustine and Schleiermacher have described the existential correlate of the doctrine, namely, the sense that one's existence is totally dependent, that it is itself a created entity. Philosophers have also expended great effort to make intellectual and conceptual sense of the assertion.[33]

It is only through this assertion of the total dependence of all things on the creator God that the axiom can be maintained that there is a correlation between the nature of the world and the nature of the God who created the world. This correlation is essential for genuinely religious and theological statements; without the axiom, it is not possible for Christians to state what difference their understanding of God makes for their understanding of the world. On this ground the theologian is bound to say that beyond the historical witnesses to the *ex nihilo* in Scripture and in the tradition, there is a theological rationale which renders the concept necessary for Christian faith. As we have already discussed, the affirmations about the goodness of the created order, its unity, and its meaningfulness are all consistent with the axiom of the correlation between the nature of the Creator and that of the world. Conversely, the rejection of dualisms, pantheism, and monisms also follows from the

THE CREATION OF THE WORLD

axiom. These affirmations and rejections would be compromised without the "out of nothing." In this sense, we can speak of the Christian proclamation of the good news about nothingness. Every religion and philosophy of life requires the axiom of correlation, but not every one of them requires the *ex nihilo* in order to sustain the axiom. For this reason, we conclude that the *ex nihilo* formula is essential to Christian belief.

There are several objections to the *ex nihilo* in current theological thought.

First. The *ex nihilo* diverts attention away from creation as a statement about the dependence of the world on God.[34] This point of view argues that theologians have allowed themselves to be preoccupied by the arguments of the Hellenistic philosophers who opposed Christianity. It argues that, in defense of the faith, they fell into the trap of arguing that creation has to do with *origins* rather than *dependence*. Aquinas is criticized in particular, because he allowed dependence to be a matter of public debate by reason, whereas *ex nihilo* was a matter of faith in his system, discernible only with the help of revelation.

Our discussion to this point should have demonstrated that the *ex nihilo* is a statement about dependence as much as it is about origins. The wisdom of the "out-of-nothing" formula holds that dependence cannot otherwise be persuasively set forth. This fact tells us something about the interrelationship of the concern for origins with the more existentially vivid themes associated with the creation-affirmation. The question of origins is a matter of logic and speculation, rather than of existential consolation. Augustine's reflections demonstrate, however, that the existential raises the logical/speculative considerations and that it cannot be at peace unless it finds an existentially satisfying and reasonable speculative resolution of its concerns. Furthermore, it is clear that in this matter not all speculative resolutions are equally adequate. Our discussion has insisted that the criterion of satisfaction and adequacy is the concept of God. The *ex nihilo* is the only explanation of origins that meets the criterion of consistency with the Christian concept of God.

Second. The *ex nihilo* renders it difficult, if not impossible to deal with the problem of evil. In his history of Christian theology, Jaroslav Pelikan writes that the second century theologians accepted the *ex nihilo* "in spite of the difficulties [it] raised for any attempts to cope with the problem of evil."[35] What was apparent in the second century has proved true ever since. If we could say earlier that its effective grounding of the basic Christian affirmations about God's relationship to the world makes the *ex nihilo* formula our good news about nothingness, we are forced now to say that the problems it raises for Christian reflection on evil very nearly turn it into bad news.

The problem is that the "out-of-nothing" idea makes God responsible for everything, including evil. Christian theology seems to be faced with the alternatives of asserting that God is ultimately responsible for evil or that there

4 / THE CREATION

are some things over which God has no control, one of which is evil and the matrix out of which it comes. The *ex nihilo* doctrine disposes the theologian to the first of these alternatives. There is scarcely a more offensive idea for the Christian than one that holds God in some way responsible for evil. Perhaps the only idea more repugnant is the alternative we mentioned—that God is limited in power over anything, including evil. We face here, in an inescapable manner, the limitations of human thought.

We realize that the *ex nihilo* doctrine is itself a speculation that is always a matter of faith, not of observation and demonstration. As such it leaves origins in a secondary position. A comparable statement must be made about evil: its origins are a matter of speculation. The primary affirmation in the creation-doctrine is that we are dependent on the Creator for our being; the primary affirmation with respect to evil is that we are dependent on God for victory over evil, whatever form that victory takes.

We should, however, not consider that the *ex nihilo* concept is without value for the discussion of evil. If the concept renders evil a particular bafflement because it seems to root the ultimate ground of evil in God, it also provides a source of high motivation for engaging in the struggle against evil. And it adds hope that the struggle will finally succeed.

The rationale of the creation-affirmation's support for this motivation and hope is a bit involved, but it should be grasped clearly. The hope for victory over evil stems ultimately from the conviction that God is directly responsible for the creation, "out of nothing." The essential goodness and purposiveness of the world, assertions that are rooted in the *ex nihilo*, give hope that evil cannot ultimately hold out against God's creative purpose.

The ground for motivation to enter the struggle against evil lies in the basic Christian notion that humans live in a realm that includes nothing else but this created order and the will and power of God who has created the world and whose intention is to bring it to consummation. The historian of religions G. van der Leeuw has written about the Hebrew understanding of creation: "The God who sustains the world is not a static source, but one who is active from *olam* to *olam*. The source is nothingness; *God's act of creation is the only reality*. God is not contingent on the world; the world is only and always contingent on God. This is expressed in the *theologoumenon* of *creatio ex nihilo*."[36] "God's act of creation is the only reality"—in these words, van der Leeuw has rightly emphasized the important matter. Contrary to most of the world's other myths of creation, the Hebrew creation-traditions give no more than a hint at any significant events in primordial time. There are no stories of gods and goddesses whose behavior in heaven influences what happens on earth, as, for example, in Virgil's *Aeneid*, where Aeneas' fortunes hang on the events taking place "in heaven above." There is no Hebrew hint at such heavenly history, whether before the world began or contemporaneous with world history. Consequently, Christians and Jews have not looked for an escape hatch out of history and nature. Rather, they look for their hope in the future of the created continuum, its consummation at the hands of the creator God. This being the case, the Christian has a vested interest in the betterment and perfection of this created world, regardless of how Christians at any given time and place have defined the terms "betterment" and "perfection." Since evil is a definite obstacle to the purposes of God and God's will to consummate the world, the Christian should be mightily motivated to participate in God's struggle against evil.

The emphasis on God's act of creation as the only reality and on the historical character of this reality that moves toward consummation has received renewed interest in the "eschatological" theologies, as well as in the "liberation" theologies of Latin America. Jürgen Moltmann, an exponent of eschatological theology, calls for an "eschatological understanding of creation," to replace a predominant "protological understanding of creation." The latter view sees redemption as "nothing other than the restoration of original creation. . . . History . . . is primarily the history of the Fall. It cannot bring anything new."[37] Such a "protological" understanding betrays what van der Leeuw rightly lifts up as the distinctive heart of the Christian view of creation. This view is also emphasized at many points in the tradition, beginning with the growth and development-oriented theology of Irenaeus. "Liberation" theology makes the same point as, for example, when Juan Luis Segundo links creation and Providence, with the power of God directed to the remaking of history.[38] Paul Tillich emphasized Christianity's distinctive interpretation of history, one which opposes the "nonhistorical" interpretations of Chinese, Indian, and Greek philosophies. At one point he underscores the biblical roots of this historical interpretation and contrasts the biblical-traditional view of creation with the Greek concept of the Demiurge, who does not create, but rather "fashions." Tillich writes:

> The *demiourgos* has shaped the world by forming and ordering the matter according to the picture of the idea of the good. In doing so, he elevates the matter which is controlled by necessity to the greatest possible similarity with the idea. But he can succeed only in a limited way. He cannot overcome the evils which are rooted in the resistance of matter. The Septuagint and the New Testament use the word *ktizein* for the creative activity of God, emphasizing the idea of a new foundation and dropping entirely the connotation of something "given" by the idea of a creation out of nothing. The world is *ktisis*, it is created, not shaped; therefore it is good in itself; the evil has no ontological, but only moral, foundation, *and thus a history of salvation is possible.*[39]

Elsewhere Tillich suggests that the *ex nihilo* formula has two truths inherent in it: that tragedy is possible in the created order, but that it is not rooted in the essence of that order.[40]

4 / THE CREATION

CONTEMPORARY CHALLENGES AND CONTRIBUTIONS TO THE DOCTRINE

For many Americans the most energetic discussions of creation may arise from the efforts of "creationists" to revise public school textbooks. Parallel to scientific accounts of the world, its origin, and its development, they seek a presentation of divine special creation as set forth—in their opinion—in Genesis 1—3. This creationist effort is earnestly intended to reshape the teaching of natural science in the schools. After a creationist victory in California in 1972, the prestigious National Academy of Sciences passed a resolution taking note of the California controversy and closing with the strong plea "that textbooks of the sciences utilized in the public schools of the nation be limited to the exposition of scientific matters."[41]

The substance of the creationist position seems to consist of the following tenets. First, the biblical accounts of creation in Genesis 1—3 and other biblical statements about the natural world are factual accounts. "We insist that God is communicating history to us here."[42] Second, evolution-based views of the world's origins and processes are antithetical to a belief in God and to the Bible. A "theistic evolutionism" is unacceptable, because it is a contradiction in terms. Third, the essence of the biblical position on creation is belief in God's special creation, involving catastrophic interventions at times, belief that God has created everything with a purpose and that this purposiveness continues up until the present, and belief that God's continuing creation is efficacious today. Fourth, evolutionary theory is not able to explain all that science has discovered about the world. The scientific establishment imposes evolutionary theory ideologically, until it has attained the status of a de facto religious belief-system.

Creationism can be applauded for its opposition to *scientism*—the improper elevation of certain hypotheses to ideologically oppressive positions. Similarly, creationists are not to be faulted for calling attention to the biblical witness as a relevant body of tradition for contemporary people, a witness that contains an intellectual challenge for current culture, as well as a religious and a moral challenge. Beyond this, however, there are few points where we can agree with them or join forces with them. We mention three chief areas of critique.

First. The creationists misuse the biblical literature by setting it over against scientific treatises, as if there were a one-to-one correlation between them. It is asserted, for example, that there is "absolute Bible accuracy on the subject of plant physiology," among the proofs for which is that Deut. 33:14 ("Precious fruits brought forth by the sun" [KJV]) correctly "indicates that sunlight plays a role in plant food synthesis."[43] Our studies show, however, that the Old Testament combines many types of literature, most of which is doxological in one way or another, and that much of it is poetic, symbolic, often borrowed from other cultures, and certainly not intended as "science" or "history" in our sense of those terms. Furthermore, and very significant, creationists utilize only a small portion of the biblical witness to creation.

Second. The creationist position is so simplistic in relating the Bible to scientific discoveries and so unwilling to accept dynamic change in natural processes through natural development that it actually betrays the Christian affirmation that God relates to the world as it is, in all its plural forms. The creationists do not relate the biblical affirmations to contemporary science or to our contemporary experience of the world. Rather, they relate contemporary scientific understandings to the understandings of the world that prevailed in biblical times, then proceed further to insist that such a matching of epochs is what is required for faith. To believe in God the Creator is supposedly to relate photosynthesis to biblical statements about the sun and plants, and then to affirm that God has created it all, and so marvelously! The result is that the classical creation witness is proclaimed with little relevance to the world that people today actually experience.

Third. The creationist strategy does not relate biblical faith to the ongoing activity of scientific research and discovery; it only tries to verify biblical statements about the natural world. The task for the creationist scientist is to lift out hypotheses from Scripture and show that they fit the facts. When this is done, "it is conceivable that theoretical frameworks in this whole discipline can be brought back to reality while being brought back to God the Creator."[44] There is no two-way traffic between faith and science. The creationist, from the descriptions that proceed from creationists themselves, is not interested in contributing to scientific discovery so much as in verifying the Bible with scientific means. If this is an accurate picture, they do not enter vigorously into the pursuit of knowledge as scientists.

The greatest harm done by the creationists is certainly their energetic pressing of a simplistic understanding of the creation-affirmation and its significance. They thereby deprive both their adherents and the secular society of a forceful presentation of the power and the problematic of the claim that this world is dependent on God the Creator for its being, with all that entails.

No school of twentieth-century theology has devoted more attention to the themes of which this essay is comprised than the so-called "process theology," the theologians who have taken the metaphysical constructions of Alfred North Whitehead and Charles Hartshorne as their basis for theological work. This school is so substantial and extensive in its achievement that it cannot be discussed in detail here. However, precisely because of its importance, some mention must be made of the significant and problematic contributions it has made to the understanding of creation.

4 / THE CREATION

Succinctly put, process theologians deny the *ex nihilo* doctrine and challenge the interpretation of evil associated with it. However, before any response can be given to their challenge, some analysis must be made of how their position came to be what it is.

Proceeding as it does from the base of Whitehead's philosophy, process theology restricts itself to the realm of "actual entities," to what we would popularly call *this world*. Whitehead called this a "descriptive" metaphysics, and he intended that it should interpret "every element of our experience . . . everything of which we are conscious."[45] As such, Whitehead stands in the long tradition of philosophers who do not presume to discuss ultimate origins or endings. In this, Whitehead stands in the same position as the whole body of natural, physical, and social sciences to which he intentionally conformed his philosophy. We do not fully comprehend the process theological opposition to the *ex nihilo* if we do not understand this methodological feature of restriction to the interpretation of experience, a restriction which is the result of a conscious intention on Whitehead's part and on the part of those who follow him.[46]

Beyond this important methodological characteristic, which proceeds from their starting point, process theologians tend to limit their discussions of the natural world to the area in which theology and philosophy share perspectives. In this they resemble Thomas Aquinas, who distinguished clearly between knowledge gained by reason and knowledge gained by revelation. The former knowledge constituted the area in which theology did not go beyond philosophy, whereas in the latter area it left philosophy behind. Process theologians do not actually leave philosophy behind when they discuss items of Christian belief that plainly exceed the natural realm—for example, christology—but they do follow a strategy similar to Aquinas in the area of the natural world.[47] One such theologian terms the *ex nihilo* "exceptional talk," which should not be appealed to when theology is in the same arena of conversation as philosophy.[48] This might be viewed as an apologetic strategy.

The most important aspect of the process theological restriction is its effect on the concept of God. The process theologians, by and large, present the concept of a God who does not *create* in the *ex nihilo* sense. A passage from a leading process theologian, John Cobb, illustrates this point:

> In Whitehead's analysis, God's role in creation centers in the provision to each actual occasion of its initial aim. This role is of such importance that Whitehead on occasion acknowledges that God may properly be conceived in his philosophy as the creator of all temporal entities. Yet, more frequently, he opposes the various connotations of the term "creator," as applied to God, and prefers to speak of *God and the temporal world as jointly qualifying or conditioning creativity*, which then seems to play the ultimate role in creation.[49]

Cobb testifies clearly that "Whitehead envisions no beginning of the world, hence no first temporal creation out of nothing."[50]

This concept of God is clearly not the same as the one that we have elaborated in our survey of biblical and later traditional sources. We have portrayed a God who is Creator *ex nihilo*, a God on whom all things depend for their being, as well as for meaning and purpose, goodness, and order. Process theologians object that such a picture of God is autocratic, "imperial," and conceptually impossible, since a being who has the power to control and determine other beings is not even thinkable to our minds. Our discussion has put the matter in such a way as to suggest that the process-theological objection is not precisely on target. The Christian concept of God intends to break away from an autocratic God and an imperial image of deity. It wishes to speak of the freedom and self-determination that the entities of this world possess. It insists, however, that all this must be done without overlooking or dismissing the fact that God is Creator and source, while the entities of this world are created and sourced by God.

What sorts of relationship of reciprocity, interaction, and the like are possible between source and sourced? And how can they be conceptualized so as to maintain the source/sourced distinction, yet be faithful to the insistence that God is loving Father, good shepherd, as tender and sensitive as Hosea depicts? The process theological concept of God has tended to dismiss one side of this bifocal view of God, the source/sourced, to focus only on the caring, sensitive, intimate side. This is understandable in light of their restriction to the realm of actual entities and their experience, since the *ex nihilo* is an item not of experience but of faith. Schleiermacher came as close as possible to the experience of the *ex nihilo*, namely, the experience of being *fully caused* in certain areas of life. But that is still not truly an experience of the "creation out of nothing."

The challenge *to* process theology must focus on its concept of God. Philosophical alternatives have been suggested,[51] perhaps the most important of which is a form of Hegelianism, which builds upon the datum of christology. The challenge *of* process theology is its insistence that its conceptualities are more adequate to contemporary experience, as described and analyzed in the give-and-take of public discussion, providing corrections to the traditional ways of conceiving of God and the world.

It will not do, in the final analysis, simply to rule against process theology because its God is not the God of the tradition, although that is an important point too seldom argued clearly. Rather, one must ask whether the process-theological concept of a God who creates jointly with the cooperation of the rest of the world is a more adequate interpretation of our experience of creativity.

4 / THE CREATION

On the question of evil, one must ask whether the process-theological view that evil is rooted in the primordial chaos, which God was confronted with and put into some sort of order, but over which God had no control, is more consonant with what we experience. These questions cannot be argued here. One can suggest, however, that our experience does include the never-satisfied quest to discover the ultimate beginning, the beginning-point for both the Demiurge and the preexistent chaos on which he worked. This raises the question whether the process-theological position has yet truly found the God to which the Hebrew-Christian tradition witnesses. This question cuts through to the process-theodicy, as well. If there is a defect in the concept of God, then the theodicy based on that concept must be reworked too.

The most adequate conclusion to be drawn at this point is that the dialogue between process theology and the classical Christian tradition is not yet finished. The continuation of the dialogue is an item high on the Christian theological agenda; until it is carried out with thoroughness, dogmatics today has not finished its work.

The challenges and contributions of *modern science* to our theme of creation are enormous. Since these challenges are relevant to subsequent sections as well, the examination of science will be placed later in the discussion. It is useful, however, to keep in mind the specific areas of challenge posed by science.

Scientific discovery in the past 150 years has opened up breathtaking vistas for a new understanding of nature (physical, biological, and social). The concepts of the creator God and of creation must be related to this new understanding of nature if they are to be credible. Scientific concepts provide the most persuasive interpretations of the natural world for the majority of people today. Those interpretations, however, cannot undergird the Christian affirmations that the world is dependent on God for its being and that it is a purposive order. But neither do scientific concepts, properly understood, disprove the ideas of dependency and purpose. Nevertheless, considerable effort is required to relate the Christian affirmations to the scientifically described earthly realm.

NOTES

1. Antony Flew and Donald M. MacKinnon, "Creation," in *New Essays in Philosophical Theology*, ed. Antony Flew and Alisdair MacIntyre (London: SCM Press, 1963), p. 174.

2. Emil Brunner, *The Christian Doctrine of Creation and Redemption*, trans. Olive Wyon (Philadelphia: Westminster Press, 1952), pp. 7–9. Karl Barth, *Church Dogmatics*, vol. 3/1, trans. G. T. Thomson (Edinburgh: T. & T. Clark, 1936), pp. 3–4.

3. Langdon Gilkey, *Maker of Heaven and Earth* (Garden City, N.Y.: Doubleday & Co., 1959), p. 94.

4. Irenaeus, *Against Heresies*, ii,1,1, *ANFa* 1.
5. See Robert Neville, *God the Creator* (Chicago: University of Chicago Press, 1968), pp. 80–81.
6. Such charges are made by some of the process theologians. See Schubert Ogden, *The Reality of God* (New York: Harper & Row, 1966), pp. 16–18; Bernard Loomer, "Two Kinds of Power," *Crit.* 15 (Winter 1976): 11–29. The source of this tendency may be found in Alfred North Whitehead, *Process and Reality* (New York: Free Press, 1978), p. 520.
7. See Athanasius' *Discourses against the Arians*.
8. *Summa Theologica*, qu. 45. See also the discussion in Johannes Brinktrine, *Die Lehre von der Schöpfung* (Paderborn: Ferdinand Schoeningh, 1956), pp. 16–19.
9. From the Chandogya Upanishad, in R. E. Hume, *The Thirteen Principal Upanishads* (London: Oxford University Press, 1949), p. 246.
10. Gordon Kaufman, *Systematic Theology: A Historicist Perspective* (New York: Charles Scribner's Sons, 1968), p. 293.
11. David Griffin, *God, Power, and Evil: A Process Theodicy* (Philadelphia: Westminster Press, 1976), p. 39.
12. Ibid., pp. 286–91. Pierre Teilhard de Chardin, "Reflections on Original Sin," in his *Christianity and Evolution*, trans. René Hague (New York: Harcourt Brace Jovanovich, 1969), pp. 187–98.
13. Emil Brunner, *The Christian Doctrine of God*, trans. Olive Wyon (Philadelphia: Westminster Press, 1950), p. 176.
14. *BC* 412.
15. Ibid., p. 365.
16. Brunner, *Christian Doctrine of Creation and Redemption*, p. 13.
17. Gustaf Aulén, *The Faith of the Christian Church*, 2d ed., trans. Eric. E. Wahlstrom and G. Everett Arden (Philadelphia: Fortress Press, 1960), pp. 162–66. Gustaf Wingren, *Creation and Law*, trans. Ross Mackenzie (Philadelphia: Fortress [Muhlenberg] Press, 1961), pp. 42–45.
18. Regin Prenter, *Creation and Redemption*, trans. Theodore I. Jensen (Philadelphia: Fortress Press, 1967), chaps. 16, 17.
19. *Summa Theologica*, qu. 44, 1st art.
20. See three important recent discussions of contingency and creation: Neville, *God the Creator*; Wolfhart Pannenberg, "Theological Questions to Scientists," in *The Sciences and Theology in the 20th Century*, ed. Arthur Peacocke (London: Routledge & Kegan Paul, 1981); Thomas F. Torrance, "God and the Contingent World," in ibid.
21. Friedrich Schleiermacher, *The Christian Faith*, trans. H. R. MacKintosh and J. S. Stewart (Edinburgh: T. & T. Clark, 1928), thesis 36.
22. Ibid., thesis 39.
23. Ibid., thesis 46.
24. Paul Tillich, *The Protestant Era* (Chicago: University of Chicago Press, 1948), p. 2.
25. Gilkey, *Maker of Heaven and Earth*, p. 117.
26. Erich Frank, *Philosophical Understanding and Religious Truth* (London: Oxford University Press, 1956), p. 62.

4 / THE CREATION

27. R. Hooykaas, *Religion and the Rise of Modern Science* (Edinburgh: Scottish Academic Press, 1977), pp. 1-28.
28. Gilkey, *Maker of Heaven and Earth*, p. 60.
29. See Friederich Gogarten, *Verhängnis und Hoffnung der Neuzeit, die Säkularisierung als theologisches Problem* (Stuttgart: Friedrich Vorweg, 1958); Hooykaas, *Religion and the Rise of Modern Science*; H. van Leeuwen, *Christianity in World History*, trans. H. H. Hoskins (London: Edinburgh House, 1964); Michael Foster, "The Christian Doctrine of Creation and the Rise of Modern Natural Science," *Mind* 43 (1934): 446-68; Herbert Butterfield, *The Origins of Modern Science*, rev. ed. (New York: Free Press, 1965). For a brief summary, Ian Barbour, *Issues in Science and Religion* (Englewood Cliffs, N.J.: Prentice-Hall, 1966), pp. 44-50.
30. *Confessions*, bk. 11, chaps 5, 6.
31. Griffin, *God, Power, and Evil*, p. 39.
32. Paul Tillich, *Systematic Theology*, 3 vols. (Chicago: University of Chicago Press, 1951-63), 1:254.
33. Neville, *God the Creator*, pp. 64-81.
34. Pelikan, "Creation and Causality." Also L. Charles Birch, *Nature and God* (Philadelphia: Westminster Press, 1965), pp. 85-90.
34. Jaroslav Pelikan, *The Christian Tradition: A History of the Development of Doctrine*, vol. 1, *The Emergence of the Catholic Tradition (100-600)* (Chicago: University of Chicago Press, 1971), p. 36.
35. G. van der Leeuw, "Primordial Time and Final Time," in *Man and Time*, ed. J. Campbell, vol. 3 of *Papers from the Eranos Yearbooks* (New York: Pantheon Books, 1957), p. 346.
37. Jürgen Moltmann, "Creation as an Open System," in his *The Future of Creation*, trans. Margaret Kohl (Philadelphia: Fortress Press, 1979), p. 116.
38. Juan Luis Segundo, *Our Idea of God* (Maryknoll, N.Y.: Orbis Books, 1974), pp. 196-99.
39. Tillich, *Protestant Era*, p. 29. Emphasis added.
40. Tillich, *Systematic Theology*, 1:253-54. This is basically the position of the Lutheran tradition, as enunciated in Article I of the Formula of Concord.
41. October 1972. Quoted in Arthur Peacocke, *Creation and the World of Science* (Oxford: At the Clarendon Press, 1979), p. 2.
42. John W. Klotz, "Creationist Viewpoints," in Henry Morris et al., *A Symposium on Creation* (Grand Rapids: Baker Book House, 1968), p. 49.
43. George F. Howe, "Creationist Botany Today: A Progress Report," in *Symposium on Creation IV*, ed. Donald Patten (Grand Rapids: Baker Book House, 1972), p. 62.
44. Ibid., p. 79.
45. Whitehead, *Process and Reality*, p. 4.
46. See Robert Neville, *Creativity and God: A Challenge to Process Theology* (New York: Seabury Press, 1980), p. 139.
47. See important hints in Paul Sponheim, *Faith and Process* (Minneapolis: Augsburg Publishing House, 1980), pp. 47, 261.
48. Ibid., p. 47.
49. John Cobb, *A Christian Natural Theology* (Philadelphia: Westminster Press,

1965), pp. 203–4 (emphasis added). See also Charles Hartshorne and William L. Reese, *Philosophers Speak of God* (Chicago: University of Chicago Press, 1953), pp. 23, 270–71, 274.

50. Cobb, *Christian Natural Theology*, p. 205. See also Griffin, *God, Power, and Evil*, pp. 37, 50. Also John Cobb and David Griffin, *Process Theology: An Introductory Exposition* (Philadelphia: Westminster Press, 1977), chap. 4.

51. See the comments of Richard Swinburne, *The Coherence of Theism* (Oxford: At the Clarendon Press, 1977), chap. 8, p. 139, for a philosophical view that is not inhibited in its talk about the *ex nihilo*. See also Neville, *Creativity and God*, pp. 139–40, for a trenchant statement of how the denial of the *ex nihilo* weakens the process-theological case.

3
The Human Being

The important thing to say about human being, from a Christian perspective, is that it is created with a destiny, the unfolding of which comprises the human adventure. This understanding must now be cast in new terms if it is to convey Christian faith adequately. We choose the term "created co-creator" to articulate what humanity under God's will is about. This term speaks of dependence, of God-given power and authority, and of freedom within finitude.

THE QUESTION OF HUMAN DESTINY

Nathan Scott ended his 1965 essay on the Christian understanding of the human being with these words:

> So now we have come full circle: created in the "image of God"; "fallen"; restored to God by Christ's reconciling work, for life in the Blessed Community of *diakonia*, of "deputyship," of service "for others"—this, in short, is the story that Christianity tells about humankind. And though it is a story that on one ground or another may be rejected by a generation eager to congratulate itself on having arrived at the threshold of what is trippingly spoken of in the Sunday supplements as our "post-Christian" age, there is at least one ground on which it is gloriously secure against all attack. For, amidst all the isms and ologies of our time which willy-nilly have worked to impugn or to reduce the fullness of man's human stature, at least it cannot be said of the Christian faith that it is in any way *against* man.[1]

Scott strikes the appropriate note in considering the human factor within the framework of the doctrine of creation. He calls attention to a drama of the human: created in the image of God, fallen, restored to God in Christ for service to others. This drama will occupy us in what follows. Scott also points correctly to the intention of the Christian story of humankind: to tell us who the human being really is and to remind us that the whole creation and God the Creator support human beings in their efforts to become more fully what they are created to be. Christian anthropology sets forth a distinct understanding of who and what the human is. The force of its interpretation of the human experiment is definitely for humans, not against them.

4 / THE CREATION

In the present context, our purpose in discussing the human being is to set forth the created roots and the created destiny of humankind. This is Christian anthropology in its broadest sense. Since there are other *loci* on sin and evil and the Christian life, a good deal of Christian anthropology is left for discussion in those places.

The human being is created with a destiny. We use the term "destiny" to include the connotations of "vocation" or "calling" as well as to point to an intrinsic character that is a dimension of the human's created "nature." Therefore, "destiny" has the nuances of gift, determinism, purpose, and goal. The first task of the distinctively Christian view of the human being is to make this clear: that *Homo sapiens* has a destiny, and a high one at that. One need not subscribe to Nicolas Berdyaev's philosophical presuppositions to affirm his statement of this essential point: "Christian anthropology should unfold the conception of man as a creator who bears the image and likeness of the Creator of the world. . . . Man has sprung from God and the dust."[2] Christian anthropology does not isolate itself from any other source of knowledge about the human being—from the sciences, experience of all sorts, literature, or art. What the Christian view has to say about human being is in the context of the knowledge gleaned from these other sources.

Nevertheless, no knowledge from other sources can be allowed to hide or weaken this fundamental assertion of Christian faith: As people created by God, we are beings whose origin and destiny are linked with that God. Everything that was said earlier about the implications of the doctrine of creation *ex nihilo* applies here, to be sure: that human being is caused, not self-generating, and is *creature*, not *creator*. Despite the truth in the often-repeated assertion that humans are proud creatures whose arrogance is their undoing, the affirmation of God-given destiny takes priority over all other elements in Christian anthropology. The basis for this priority is simply stated: Unless we perceive the human being's divinely ordained destiny, we have failed, from the outset, to comprehend who and what *Homo sapiens* is. It is not even possible to assert human pride, sin, or fallenness, if we overlook human destiny. Without a sense for that destiny, it would be as meaningless to describe humans as "sinners" and "evil" as it would be to describe a pet dog in such terms. Only the presupposition of high destiny gives point to the discernment of sin and evil in humans.

The theological tradition has spoken of this destiny in two important sets of symbols: paradise or the Garden of Eden, and creation in the image of God. As we survey these two sets of symbolic statements, we shall note that they are difficult to accept at several points because of a present cultural awareness that shies away from the concept of "destiny." On the one hand, the idea of "human destiny" seems too grandiose for the contemporary spirit to comprehend. Despite many opinions to the effect that humans suffer from the disease of pride, a hubris that presses them on to storm the gates of heaven and make themselves equal with the gods, we find impressive contrary voices that point to the contemporary human loss of nerve.

Preston Roberts's analysis of the contemporary human situation as one of all-encompassing pathos has an accurate ring.[3] The pathetic hero, or antihero, of contemporary drama epitomizes this contemporary loss of morale. The antihero is not an Oedipus engaged in an Olympian struggle with his fate. Nor is he a Macbeth, consumed with a primal power of greed. Rather, today's man or woman is like Camus's nameless stranger, who is sentenced to die in a trial he does not understand, because he has committed a crime of absurdity that he does not recognize. Or, perhaps even more vividly, as Arthur Miller portrays in *Death of a Salesman*, our current hero is a nondescript traveling salesman, sitting in a cheap hotel room, depressed and sentimental at the same time, contemplating his inability to buy love on the road and his unwillingness to cultivate love in his home.

To speak to a pathetic antihero about human "destiny," about an origin that links this earthly species with the foundations of the universe, is to lay on a burden which pathos simply has not the strength to carry. We cannot go into a detailed discussion here of the historical and cultural roots of this condition of pathos. We must note, however, that even though the Christian view of human being as founded in a high destiny is essentially a message that is *for* humanity, it comes across to the condition of pathos as a hard word of obligation. Because it portrays what is perceived in the current malaise as an impossibility, it appears as a threatening pronouncement of a law that can be neither obeyed nor escaped.

It is not clear just how this condition of pathos is related to a second element of the current cultural condition. This is the element that finds anthropocentrism and the thought of human superiority over other species so repugnant that it forecloses the possibility of intelligible speech about humanity's obvious distinctiveness and preeminence within its earthly ecosystem.[4] We shall have occasion to note how such a concern can, when subjected to the pathetic modulation, become antihuman in itself, and thus destructive of life's wholeness within creation.

THE HUMAN BEING AS CREATED CO-CREATOR

The motif by which we gather together the various affirmations of the Christian tradition about the human creature, and that expresses their meaning, is that of _created co-creator_. This motif is novel in its formulation. We are driven to novelty at this point because of a basic characteristic of the Christian view of human being. The primary dramatic description of the human adventure—that we are created in the image of God, fallen, and restored for

4 / THE CREATION

service—is universally asserted as a formal framework, but it allows for a number of material elaborations. Formally, human destiny is to bring to fulfillment the position the human was given at creation—placed by God the Creator in the preeminent position in the ecosystem. The material elaborations of this formal status of the human species have included rather rapacious anthropocentric justifications of human manipulations of the world about us. But they have also included sensitive interpretations of how humans are the responsible stewards of the "garden" in which they are placed.

The human species is clearly distinguished from all other species, even as it is intimately related to the rest of creation. This relation is in part external; *Homo sapiens* is dependent on all the other elements in the ecosystem, just as the species contributes reciprocally to the same ecosystem. But it is internal as well. The elements of the world, focusing in that "primordial soup" from which all living creatures emerged, are the elements of the human; every atom in the human body has been elsewhere in the universe before it came to rest in *Homo sapiens*; the evolution of hydrogen and DNA—for just two examples—has reached the point where it shapes the human's internal constitution.

Homo sapiens is distinctive in terms of six important characteristics: consciousness, self-consciousness, the ability to make assessments, the ability to make decisions on the basis of those assessments, the ability to act freely on those decisions, and the ability to take responsibility for such action. Such self-aware, free action becomes a kind of creating activity, a co-creating, with God. Humans can claim no arrogant credit for being co-creators; they *were created co-creators*. Even put in materialistic terms, humans did not evolve themselves; the evolutionary process—under God's rule, we would argue—*evolved them as co-creators*.

To be co-creator means that *Homo sapiens* shares self-consciously and responsibly in the formation of the world and its unfolding toward its final consummation under God. Teilhard de Chardin has put this evocatively in his maxim that "man is evolution become aware of itself."⁵ Whatever range we give to human creative activity, the destiny of that activity is to participate in and perfect the substance and goal of God's creative activity. God's creating is the norm for human co-creating, not in the sense that *Homo sapiens* is to equate its activity with God's, but rather in the sense that human activity is perverse if it does not finally qualify as participation in and extension of God's primordial will of creation. Put in this way, the created status of the human is thoroughly eschatological; that is, it is an *unleashing*, not a full-blown given that has simply to be reiterated and replicated throughout time. The primordial *humanum* that emerges from God's creation is constituted by the calling (destiny) and the capacity to participate as an ordained co-creator in the creative thrust of God. That thrust consists of sharing as a free, self-aware creature in shaping the passage forward toward God's own *telos* of the consummation and perfection of the creation.

Thus construed, the motif of created co-creator points clearly to the distinctiveness of humans as creatures with a high destiny, a destiny that is essential to the world if it is to bear the mark of its creator God. The characteristics of being co-creator are in continuity, within the evolutionary scheme, with previous forms of life, but at the same time unique in their precise and highly sophisticated configuration in the human species. We suggest that this co-creatorhood is what it means to be "in the *image of God*." The characteristics of being able to make self-aware, self-critical decisions, to act on those decisions, and to take responsibility for them—these are the characteristics which comprise the image of God in us. However, it is not just these characteristics that comprise this image. In addition, the human reflection on its unique abilities unveils a deep mystery that, if profoundly probed, clarifies to the human creature the sense in which they are grounded in a basic relationship to God. Without such grounding, the abilities themselves would mean little.

When humans ponder their co-creator status, they recognize that it includes the freedom to conceive of actions and to carry them out. This is a pleasant, even delicious, freedom; it undergirds human aggressiveness as *homo faber*, even to the large-scale technological results now around us. Beyond this freedom, however, lies the freedom in which the human agent must take responsibility for judging whether the conceived action is desirable. Then there is the responsibility for living with the consequences of the action, even if they prove undesirable.

Human agents always seek to determine whether their plans and actions are good or bad, desirable or undesirable. The tendency is to seek legitimation for carrying out the intended action or for prohibiting it, and to rest content if either the carrying out or the prohibiting conform to persuasive laws or motives.

Thus, for example, we ask whether we should in fact proceed with the capabilities we possess for production of nuclear energy, and we tend to take comfort in mandates or motives that count either for or against. The tendency to take such comfort is, however, a retreat from our real freedom as co-creators.

That freedom presses us to the point where we recognize that finally it is neither an absolute mandate nor pure motivation that legitimates the action, but rather only our own free decision. Furthermore, to be co-creator means that we must continue to live with the decision and exercise our responsible co-creatorhood, whether the decision proves to be desirable or undesirable or, as is more likely, to have both undesirable and desirable consequences.

When we ponder our co-creatorhood at this depth, we discover our likeness to God and our origin and destiny in God, but we also come face to face with our own finitude, with our createdness. We do so when we recognize

4 / THE CREATION

that, even though there is no legitimation for our action beyond our own free and responsible decision, such free and responsible decision is limited. We cannot foresee adequately the outcomes of our most important actions, nor can we mitigate all the undesirable consequences of our free but finite decisions and actions. In the exercise of the *imago dei*, in carrying out our cocreatorhood, we come hard upon the fact of our createdness. This is the fact that our mandate to co-create has come to us as creatures, at the behest of the creator God *ex nihilo*, and not from our own self-generating will.

Furthermore, when we ponder such considerations, we come to know that our sin is both our understandable unwillingness to accept our status as cocreator—even our fear of that status—and our faulty execution of our cocreatorhood, once we are forced to accept it. This sin is both original and actual. With this contemporary motif in mind, we proceed to unfold the traditional materials that inform all thinking on Christian anthropology.

THE PRIMEVAL CONDITION ("STATUS INTEGRITATIS")

It is now almost universally held among theologians that the stories and concepts we have of Adam and Eve in paradise are legends and myths. The idea of humans living in a blessed primeval stage before the fall is looked on as poetical speculation, not history. It is sometimes argued that faithfulness requires our belief in a primeval condition of blessedness. Such an argument confuses faithfulness with the imposition of a mythical speculation on a modern historical outlook on human life. To hold to the primeval condition in Eden as a matter of history would be an intellectual impossibility and to misunderstand faith. Emil Brunner states the problem for theology:

> Thus we are confronted by the very difficult theological task of formulating the distinction between the nature of man in accordance with Creation and as sinner, and the idea which this involves of the Fall of Man, *without using the thoughtform of an historical "Adam in Paradise" and of the Primitive State*.[6]

Having said this about the myths of primeval conditions in Paradise, we must immediately add that these myths tell us a great deal that is essential to Christian anthropology. No one has probed the meaning of these myths more profoundly than Paul Tillich. His thesis is that these myths of the primeval time point to the *essential rootage* of human existence. He shares with Nicolas Berdyaev the insight that "the fall" speaks not so much of the degradation of the human as it does of the glory of the human, that it could fall so low.[7] Only a creature of very great stature would be described as "fallen." As Tillich says:

THE HUMAN BEING

The possibility of the Fall is dependent on all the qualities of human freedom taken in their unity. Symbolically speaking, it is the image of God in man which gives the possibility of the Fall. Only he who is the image of God has the power of separating himself from God. His greatness and his weakness are identical. Even God could not remove the one without removing the other. And if man had not received this possibility, he would have been a thing among other things, unable to serve the divine glory, either in salvation or in condemnation.[8]

In short, the myths of our primeval conditions are important affirmations of the ultimate destiny of the human being, which is grounded in the origins of the human in ultimacy. Another citation from Tillich lays out the argument:

> We must have an image of the state of essential being in which the motifs [of the primeval myths] are working. The difficulty is that the state of essential [i.e., primeval] being is not an actual stage of human development which can be known directly or indirectly. The essential nature of man is present in all stages of his development, although in existential distortion. In myth and dogma man's essential nature has been projected into the past as a history before history, symbolized as a golden age or paradise.[9]

What we have called the "ultimate destiny" of the human being is what Tillich calls the "essential nature." This essential or primeval nature and destiny are attested to by the myths of creation and the image of God. Gregory of Nyssa (fourth century) was one of the most brilliant and influential theologians in Christian history. His treatise *On the Making of Man* is a pivotal document for our theme. He underscores the exalted origins of the human being by describing the beauty of the prehuman creation—the stars, the sea, the air, and the earth: "The gentle motion of the waves vied in beauty with the meadows, rippling delicately with light and harmless breezes that skimmed the surface; and all the wealth of creation by land and sea was ready, and *none was there to share it*."[10] When all this natural beauty was fashioned, then and only then was it appropriate for the human being to enter on the scene. Gregory proceeds immediately to say:

> For not as yet had that great and precious thing, man, come into the world of being; it was not to be looked for that the ruler should appear before the subjects of his rule; but when his dominion was prepared, the next step was that the king should be manifested. When, then, the Maker of all had prepared beforehand, as it were, a royal lodging for the future king, . . . and when all kinds of wealth had been stored in this palace, . . . he thus manifests man in the world. . . . For this reason man was brought into the world last after the creation, not being rejected to the last as worthless, but as one whom it behoved to be king over his subjects at his very birth.[11]

4 / THE CREATION

We observed above the difficulties that such talk poses for our cultural condition of pathos today. It is not popular nowadays to speak of "man, the crown of creation," because it seems to invite a manipulation of the created world by humans, a manipulation deemed dangerous today. These concerns are certainly laudable and not to be ignored, but they do not exhaust the meaning of the Christian emphasis on the high calling of the human being. This emphasis, far from intending to insulate humans in their superiority, is much more concerned with reminding them of their lofty origins. The conclusion to be drawn is that they are gifted with a noble destiny, even as they are charged with great responsibility.

THE "IMAGO DEI"

Genesis 1:27 has provided one of the key building blocks for Christian anthropology since the first century: "So God created man in his own image, in the image of God he created him; male and female he created them." The image of God (*imago dei*) presents a fundamental image of human being as being-with-a-destiny. "The image of God" has been one of the most discussed and ambiguous phrases in the history of Christian theological reflection. It has been used to mean a number of different things over the centuries and within each century. Some theologians have even suggested that the term be excised from the theological vocabulary, so frustrating is its interpretation. Accordingly, we provide here a brief survey of the concept; given the historical ambiguities, we shall be content with a few hints as to its possible meaning for us today.

The exegesis of Genesis is itself the battleground of varying interpretations of the *imago dei*. As Claus Westermann indicates in his own survey of the exegesis of Gen. 1:27, even though the topic has been of enormous interest in the history of theology, it played little role in the Old Testament itself, and the discussion among specialists in Old Testament studies did not really begin until the end of the nineteenth century.[12] He lists the following groups of opinions in the history of interpretation: (1) those who distinguish between natural and supernatural likeness to God; (2) those who define the likeness in spiritual capacities or abilities; (3) those who interpret it as external form; (4) those who differ sharply with 3; (5) those who interpret the term as denoting that the human being is God's *counterpart*, one who corresponds to God; (6) those who interpret the *imago* as the human's status as representative of God on earth.[13]

Although Westermann himself favors the fifth option, he is quite skeptical about the history of exegesis: "One is deeply convinced that Biblical exegesis is very time-conditioned."[14] The Old Testament, one must conclude, asserts that the human is indeed created in God's image, without much specification of what that means. Nevertheless, representing God, exercising dominion over the earth and other living things, and being God's "co-responding creature" seem to be the chief contenders as interpretations of the term. New Testament exegetes have done very little on the term, but the chief conclusion is that *Christ* is the image of God (*eikon tou theou*) and therefore the image into which humans are formed.[15]

In the history of the concept, James Childs suggests four categories: (1) the *imago* as ideal humanity (Gregory of Nyssa, Aquinas, Schleiermacher); (2) dualistic interpretations (Irenaeus, Aquinas); (3) ontological monism, that is, the *imago* indicates an "ontological communion between God and man that is constitutive of man's being"[16] (Augustine, Tillich, Reinhold Niebuhr); and (4) theological monism, that is, a relationship of the total human person to God, described in theological terms (Luther, Calvin, Barth, Brunner).[17]

These categories are useful, but for the purposes of a brief survey, it may be just as well to speak of two categories: those interpretations of the *imago dei* which speak of it in terms of specific human attributes, and those which speak of it as a fundamental relationship between God and the human. In the first group, which is by far the largest, we can place the second-century apologists, who identified the *imago* with freedom of the will, capacity for goodness, moral responsibility, and reason. Basil the Great also fits in this group, defining the *imago* as human dominion over the earth.[18] Gregory of Nyssa writes:

> I would have you understand that our Maker also, painting the portrait to resemble his own beauty, by the addition of virtues, as it were with colours, shows in us his own sovereignty: and manifold and varied are the tints, so to say, by which his true form is portrayed . . . *purity, freedom from passion, blessedness, alienation from all evil*, and all those attributes of the like kind which help to form in men the likeness of God.[19]

He goes on to say that the *imago* includes love as Christ has loved us, wisdom, and possession of the word.

The second group of interpreters consider the image of God to refer to the fact of relationship to God, of co-responding to God, of being God's counterpart, as Westermann says. Augustine is the monumental representative of this position. To be created in God's image brings with it the capacity to know God and, more profound, a human nature correlative to God's, so that within the human self the knowledge of God is to be found. Augustine points to the trinitarian character of human psychic life as a great *analogy* (*analogia entis*) *of God's* triune life; and the exposition of this triune psychic life forms his great treatise, *On the Trinity*. In his *Confessions*, he pursues the same line of thinking, linking the *imago dei* to the transformation of the human spirit into God's likeness, quoting Rom. 12:2, "Do not be conformed to this

4 / THE CREATION

world but be transformed by the renewal of your mind." The human was not, like the other animals, "created after their kind," but rather created in the image and likeness of God.

> Therefore thou didst not say, "Let man be made," but rather, "Let us make man." And Thou didst not say, "After his kind," but after "our image" and "likeness." Indeed, it is only when man has been renewed in his mind, and comes to behold and apprehend thy truth, that he does not need another man as his director, to show him how to imitate human examples. Instead, by thy guidance, he proves what is thy good and acceptable and perfect will.... Man is thus transformed in the knowledge of God, according to the image of Him who created him. And now, having been made spiritual, he judges all things—that is, all things that are appropriate to be judged—and he himself is judged of no man.[20]

Luther, too, emphasizes the relationship between God and the human as the *imago*, although he is critical of Augustine's way of speculating.[21] In his lectures on Genesis, Luther describes the image of God in Adam thus:

> ... that Adam had it [the image] in his being and that he not only knew God and believed that He was good, but that he also lived a life that was wholly godly; that is, he was without fear of death or of any other danger, and was content with God's favor. In this form it reveals itself in the instance of Eve, who speaks with the serpent without any fear.[22]

This statement is striking in that it is a direct corollary to Luther's understanding of original sin, as stated in Article II of the Augsburg Confession, that "since the fall of Adam all men who are propagated according to nature are born in sin. That is to say, they are without fear of God, are without trust in God, and are concupiscent." Fear and trust in God are the criteria of the *imago dei* by their presence, and of original sin by their absence.

Luther is critical of Augustine and other early theologians because their descriptions of the image of God foster "works." Westermann is critical of much of the tradition because it speaks of attributes or qualities of human nature as the *imago* rather than of the relationship with God. Such criticisms do indeed point to some real differences in interpreting the image of God in humans. Aquinas, for example, included in the *imago* the "superadded gift" (*donum superadditum*) granted to humans before the fall so that they could achieve the good. This gift was lost in the fall and therefore needs to be infused by grace after the fall. For Aquinas, the *imago* functions at both levels: It is the superadded gift that enables the attainment of the good, and it is also the constant (pre- and post-fall) human nature that enables us to know and love God. Such speculations lose the point that Luther and Gregory and Westermann wish to make, that the image of God refers to a total orientation of the human toward God, a total relationship. As such it cannot be divided or parceled out, as Aquinas was wont to do. On the other hand, Westermann's polemic against equating the image of God with attributes may be misguided, since the attributes generally associated with the *imago* are so profound that they are not separable from the human's basic orientation to God.

SPIRIT AND MATTER IN THE HUMAN CREATURE

The composition of the human being has been a matter of great concern for the Christian theological tradition. This tradition of thought has been closely tied to secular philosophical and scientific understandings of the human creature, no doubt because of the deep-seated conviction that even though human being possessed marvelous spiritual capabilities, it emerged from the earth (Gen. 2). Gregory of Nyssa expresses the thought of many early theologians in speaking of the human as a middle factor between the earthy, animal realm and the spiritual realm of God. In every age, the theologians have been alert to what secular knowledge could say about the physical structure of *Homo sapiens*.

Consequently, the elements of "body," "soul," and "spirit" have figured prominently in Christian anthropology over the centuries. These concepts serve to make the theological view of the human quite complicated and at times beyond easy interpretation. The terms grow out of Greek thought, particularly the body-soul dualism of Plato and the revision of that dualism by Aristotle, called "hylomorphism," whereby he insisted that the human is indivisible.

We can summarize a voluminous body of historical material by saying that "spirit" (*pneuma, ruach*) refers generally to life itself, in distinction from "body," whereas "soul" (*psyche, nephesh*) refers to life as it occurs in a particular, concrete organism, the organism being the medium of the soul's action. All human bodies possess spirit, and the spirit manifests itself within the soul of the individual. "Spirit is the condition, soul the manifestation, of life."[23] The soul includes the spirit within itself, but it is the spirit that enables the soul and the body to be integrated into a *personal* existence and to be oriented on God.

We speak of a "trichotomous" view when we speak of body, soul, and spirit, whereas a "dichotomous" view knows only body and soul. The dichotomous view has been more prevalent in Christian theology for two reasons. First, it recognizes that the spirit is a reality that has caught up the entire person, body and psyche, and it does not exist as a third entity alongside physical (somatic) and psychical aspects of the human. Further, the dichotomous interpretation is not so susceptible to the Platonizing, dualistic tendency to speak of the spirit as a detachable part of human being that can have a special rela-

4 / THE CREATION

tionship to God, just as gnosticizing views such as Origen's considered that souls could leave the body to join God, apart from the body.

Since the soul is such a precious dimension of human existence, that aspect of human being that orients it to God and makes it possible to know about the destiny and origin of the human, it was important for earlier theologians to explain how humans receive their souls. "Traducianism" is the theory, held, for example, by Tertullian and the reformers, that the soul comes into being with the normal generative process, through sexual intercourse. "Creationism" (not to be confused with the cosmological theory of fundamentalist Christians), holds that God creates each person's soul in a special act. This view is affirmed by Arnobius, Lactantius, and the Thomist tradition. "Preexistence"—a minority Platonizing tradition, represented by Origen—holds that souls come into this world from some preexistent soul-material.

There is a serious question whether any of these categories is useful or even intelligible to us today. Luther, for example, already challenged them because he believed that the human creature was a unitary being before God, a person wholly the creation of God, wholly sinful, and wholly redeemed. In the phrase, "*simul justus ac peccator*" (justified and sinner at the same time), the creature is *wholly* "*justus*" and *wholly* "*peccator*." As Emil Brunner puts it, for Luther, "man's relationship to God is not something added to his human nature; it is the core and the ground of his *humanitas*."[24]

In addition to this theological consideration, contemporary understanding of the human being and the human personality structure do not allow of either a dichotomous or a trichotomous view, except metaphorically. A modern evolutionary perspective is called for. Within this perspective, there is still considerable ambiguity, uncertainty, and disagreement about the relationship between body and spirit or mind. There is not even total agreement on how the mind should be described. Nevertheless, spirit or mind and body or matter are seen to be part of the same process, rather than separate entities. The unification of the human organization into a centered self, governed by spirit or mind, is a process in which the organizing spirit is understood as matter, but matter that has become complex enough to become an ordering force. Put physiologically, the spirit is a function of the brain that is neither immaterial nor nonmaterial but that is matter in the form that can become spirit, that can conceive of God and one's personal relationship to God, that can write poetry, conceive of and build a space ship, compose music, organize and govern a city, and engage in altruistic love for others.

Robert Francoeur has pursued this contemporary thrust with respect to the doctrine of the human being more thoroughly than most theologians. He describes it as a sort of "evolutionary monism."[25] This term may be objectionable, but it does point up the problem of all types of dualistic thought that seek to avoid evolutionary modes of thought. He writes:

334

Instead of picturing man as the fixed, though active unity of prime matter and substantial form, of body and soul, would it not be more appropriate to our modern understanding to look at man as a whole, an inner consciousness or spiritual (personal) aspect emerging out of our materiality, our outer aspect seen in the relationships and dependence on persons and things outside which form the background of being for our emerging selfhood. . . . As Teilhard noted so emphatically, the two aspects of man, personality and materiality, are dynamically and *genetically* related in a life-long process. Thus, man's personality gradually emerges from the universe in which he is conceived, from our necessary dependence on others, on the structured complexity of human society and the world in general.[26]

For theologians in the Reformation tradition, the contemporary categories of thought are liberating, because they allow lucid expression of a unitary perspective on the human creature. The human is one creature, a creature of nature, created with a special relationship to God the Creator, and with the capacity to perceive that relationship and to live a life of responsiveness to God. The human is one unitary creature in terms of origin and destiny, in terms of sin and error, and in terms of redemption.

THE FALL AND ORIGINAL SIN
("STATUS CORRUPTIONIS")

According to the myth of the fall, the *imago dei* is partially intact but grievously damaged, so that restoration is necessary. Here we wish simply to indicate how these realities fit into the general Christian anthropological scheme. The Christian traditions are not at one on these issues. The Eastern churches were inclined to put greater emphasis on the grace inherent in creation, to speak less stringently about original sin. Thus they conceived of Christ's restoration differently. These conflicts in viewpoint were central to the controversies between Augustine and Pelagius. Although Pelagius has in the West been considered unambiguously defective and in error, the East never did canonize Augustine and did not accept his theology. Robert Evans has termed Pelagius "one of the most maligned figures in the history of Christianity."[27] Some important Eastern traditions, such as those of the Syriac church, considered sin a cause of the fall, not its consequence. Arthur Vööbus has written of these traditions,

> Sin cannot be located inherently in nature. Therefore one cannot say that human nature has been fundamentally affected by sin or transformed into evil. . . . Man's moral power and ethical strength may have received a blow from Adam's example; in themselves, however, they have not been seriously endangered. The reason is that man's freedom has not been affected.[28]

4 / THE CREATION

Such views are strange to the Western tradition and to Reformation theology in particular. These views do not violate the formal structure of the Christian drama concerning the human adventure, but they do place an uncomfortable material content into the phases of that drama.

These Eastern views remind us, however, that the basic Christian insight into the human wishes to preserve the integrity of humanity over against sin. Sin and evil are not to be equated with humanity, even after the fall. For Lutherans, this is stated in the first article of the Formula of Concord:

> We believe, teach, and confess that there is a distinction between man's nature and original sin, not only in the beginning when God created man pure and holy and without sin, but also as we now have our nature after the Fall. Even after the fall, our nature is and remains a creature of God. The distinction between our nature and original sin is as great as the difference between God's work and the devil's work.[29]

John Gerhard, in dealing with the *imago dei*, listed five ways in which the *imago* might be said to be lost in the fall.[30] He judged that in four of these ways, the image was *not* lost, namely, insofar as the *imago* (1) refers to the very essence of the human soul; (2) refers to the general similarities to divinity, intelligence, etc.; (3) refers to human dominion over other creatures; and (4) refers to some moral principles. It is in the fifth sense, when the *imago* refers to righteousness and holiness, that the image of God is lost in the fall. Our very need for regeneration proves that the *imago* in this last sense is lost.

It is exceedingly difficult to conceptualize persuasively the sinfulness of human beings and their actions while at the same time asserting the goodness of human nature as such, since that nature is "a creature of God." However, it is a perennial trait of the Christian theological and homiletical tradition that it has attempted to do so.

RESTORATION

God, in Jesus Christ, has restored humanity to reconciliation with its Creator. This has been said in many ways, but it is the climactic assertion of Christian faith. The recovery of the dimension of eschatology in the Christian faith, which has taken place since 1900, has reminded us that the restoration of humanity is not a return to Eden. It is not a return to the primeval state. Much of the tradition is defective in this respect: It has viewed the reinstitution of the primeval *status integritatis* as the goal and consequence of God's restorative work. Such a view fundamentally contradicts the basic understanding of the human as participating in the divine work of bringing the creation to its consummation, a work that is always eschatological.

Jürgen Moltmann has called for a view of "creation as an open system,"

336

which calls for a revision of the understanding of creation as a *restitutio in integrum*. He argues that only in this way can we envision creation as a process of God's genuine creativity, rather than a spelling out of the fall, endlessly.[31]

CHALLENGES TO CHRISTIAN ANTHROPOLOGY

The Christian view of the human is beset on all sides. One of the most perverse and potentially devastating challenges comes from the widespread inability to accept the high view of *human destiny* as Christian theology sets it forth. We mention here two sources of this challenge: emerging scientific knowledge and the view that evil is intrinsic to human nature.

In its most straightforward manifestation, each scientific discipline threatens our view of human destiny, because it tends to perform one type of reductionism or another on the human being. Life of all sorts is reduced to processes that operate by pure chance. Or, it is reduced to genetic processes, or to psychosocial trends, or to unfathomable psychic or physical drives, depending on the discipline in question. All these reductionisms do indeed *reduce* the human to something much less than is set forth in the myths of creation in the image of God, as co-responding, co-creating creature of God who shares in the dynamic unfolding of the universe.

There is an even more devastating threat from scientific knowledge, one that is more subtle than the reductionisms. Our emerging knowledge of ourselves challenges our ability to accept ourselves as creatures in the *imago dei*. Traditionally, certain attributes of the human were clear testimonies to the *imago*. We think of Gregory of Nyssa's descriptions: purity, freedom from passion, love, intellect. Can human beings look at themselves today and read the image of God off the script of these attributes? Our knowledge of love, for example, now includes deep insights into its physical and psychic components, how it serves our sexuality, how it is intermingled with lust, self-interest, masochism, and the like. How does one go about sorting out these elements and pointing to the purity of love in oneself that is genuinely the *imago dei*? Of course, we are no more sensitive to this dilemma than the great Christians of the past—Paul, Augustine, Luther, Ignatius. But we are undoubtedly much more keenly aware of how all our actions, even at their purest, serve our needs, whether physical, sexual, or emotional.

To say, with the Lutherans and with Westermann, that an introspective look into ourselves will never reveal *imago* attributes, that we must instead look to our total relationship to God as co-responding creatures, depending on God and yet rebelling against the dependence—this is not much help in our dilemma either. We are only too aware of the ways in which our total stance toward the world and our fellow humans is shot through with the same com-

4 / THE CREATION

plex set of survival demands. So long as we see ourselves in all our complexity serving proximate mechanisms of survival, at several levels, it will not be possible to see ourselves as created in the *imago dei*. That is, it will not be possible unless we can reconceive our self's dynamic processes or unless we can bring all those processes, survival-oriented as they are, under God's providential will. This challenge will occupy our theological efforts, because we know the centrality of the Christian affirmation of high human destiny at God's hands.

Many critics have charged Christianity with an essential *ecological* irresponsibility, whether with respect to the natural and physical ecosystem or with respect to the intrapersonal network of relationships. Christian anthropology has been charged with anthropocentrism, with a concern to dominate ("Have dominion over the fish of the sea and over the birds of the air and over every living thing that moves upon the earth"), and with a sense that nothing has value outside the human.

Efforts are well under way to recast certain aspects of the Christian view in the direction of ecological responsibility, toward the physical world and the world of humans around us. This ecological understanding of anthropology will be incomplete, however, until it also fully recognizes how the ecosystem has made us what we are and continues to do so. The challenge is clear, whether we think of the Feuerbachian *"Der Mensch ist, was er isst"* (Man is what he eats), of more complex interrelationships between our selves and the entire evolutionary process, or of complex social and cultural interactions—language, for example—that have "created us." On the one hand, we dare not separate ourselves from the ecosystems in which we live and move and have our being. On the other hand, we have the task of re-forming our vision of how God creates us in, with, and under these ecosystem processes. For many Christians, it is not an easy thing to retain God's glory as Creator, while at the same time giving credit to the proximate processes of creation. We shall deal with this question at greater length in the next section.

One of the sorriest thickets in the Christian tradition of thought is that of *sexuality* and the relationships between the sexes. There is little question that too often sexuality and the man/woman relation are described in ways demeaning of the body, the physical element of human life, and of woman. Gregory of Nyssa wrote that, since Paul tells us that in Christ there is no male or female, original creation must not have included sexual differentiation. Since the prototype of the human, Christ, did not allow of sexuality, sexual differentiation must be subsequent to the fall, along with sexual propagation. Gregory was a rigorous ascetic, Augustine was less so, yet Augustine fell into similar errors. He writes that sexuality existed in Eden, but was governed by will, not by desire or passion. Sexual desire in marriage was not sin, but it was the transmitter of sin. Martin Chemnitz paraphrases Augustine in the following passage, and accepts Augustine's ideas as normative: "In matrimony

338

there are two things which are good and of divine ordination and institution, but *there is also a desire in marriage* without which there is no propagation, and *because of that desire infants are born in sin.*"³² We have other ways of explaining sin's transmission, but much work remains to develop a theological understanding of sexuality that can be a persuasive substitute for such a discussion as Chemnitz's.

The problems our tradition has had in interpreting men/women relationships are well known. Luther's lectures on Genesis are humorous and painful reminders of how even Luther's basically wholesome understanding of marriage and of the earthy aspects of life was not unambiguously clear about the worth of women and could not separate women from their role as objects of masculine sexual desire. Over and above the development of genuinely humane theological interpretations of sexuality and women in their relationship to men, there is the question of how our increasing insight into the male/female character of all people and of all aspects of personhood can be translated into our anthropology. This task awaits a great deal more work.³³

The sexual dimension of life raises, more generally, the appreciation of the material, earthy aspect of human creaturehood. As our discussion has suggested, the human was created material, and this material has evolved spirit. To denigrate the earthy is to undercut the material foundations of spirit. This insight is yet to be incorporated in a lucid manner which can enable Christian doctrine to conceive the spirit-matter unity of creation.

NOTES

1. Nathan A. Scott, Jr., "The Christian Understanding of Man," in *Conflicting Images of Man*, ed. William Nicholls (New York: Seabury Press, 1966), pp. 7–30.

2. Nicholas Berdyaev, *The Destiny of Man* (London: Geoffrey Bles, 1948), pp. 49, 54.

3. Preston Roberts, "A Christian Theory of Dramatic Tragedy," *JR* 31 (1951): 1–20.

4. See the classic essay by Lynn White, "The Historical Roots of Our Ecologic Crisis," in *The Subversive Science: Essays Toward an Ecology of Man*, ed. Paul Shepard and Daniel McKinley (Boston: Houghton Mifflin, 1969), pp. 341–50.

5. Pierre Teilhard de Chardin, *The Phenomenon of Man*, 2d ed., trans. Bernard Wall (New York: Harper & Row, 1965).

6. Emil Brunner, *The Christian Doctrine of Creation and Redemption*, trans. Olive Wyon (Philadelphia: Westminster Press, 1952), p. 52. Emphasis added.

7. Berdyaev, *Destiny of Man*, chaps. 2, 3.

8. Paul Tillich, *Systematic Theology*, 3 vols. (Chicago: University of Chicago Press, 1951–63), 1:32–33.

9. Ibid., p. 33.

10. Gregory of Nyssa, *On the Making of Man*, i,5, *Nicene and Post-Nicene Fathers*, vol. 5 (Grand Rapids: Wm. B. Eerdmans, 1954), pp. 389–90.

11. Ibid., ii,1,2.

4 / THE CREATION

12. Claus Westermann, *Genesis*, vol. 1, Biblischer Kommentar, Altes Testament (Neukirchen: Neukirchener Verlag, 1980), pp. 204-5.
13. Ibid., pp. 205-14.
14. Ibid., p. 57.
15. See the discussion by James M. Childs, "The *Imago dei* and Eschatology" (Th.D. diss., Lutheran School of Theology, 1974), esp. pp. 253ff.
16. Ibid., p. 66.
17. Ibid., chap. 3.
18. Basil, *The Hexaemeron*, ix,5.
19. Gregory, *On the Making of Man*, v,1. Emphasis added.
20. *Confessions,* book XIII, chap. xxii, 32.
21. *LW* 1:60.
22. Ibid., pp. 26-32.
23. *NSHE* 11:12.
24. Emil Brunner, *Man in Revolt*, trans. Olive Wyon (Philadelphia: Westminster Press, 1947), p. 94.
25. Robert Francoeur, *Evolving World, Converging Man* (Englewood Cliffs, N.J.: Prentice-Hall, 1970), p. 101.
26. Ibid.
27. Robert Evans, *Pelagius: Inquiries and Reappraisals* (New York: Seabury Press, 1968).
28. Arthus Vööbus, "Human Nature in Ancient Syrian Traditions," in *The Scope of Grace*, ed. Philip Hefner (Philadelphia: Fortress Press, 1964), p. 109.
29. *BC*, p. 466.
30. John Gerhard, *Loci Theologici*, Locus IV, 9, in *The Doctrine of Man in Classical Lutheran Theology*, ed. Herman Preus and Edmund Smits (Minneapolis: Augsburg Publishing House, 1962), pp. 61ff.
31. Jürgen Moltmann, *The Future of Creation*, trans. Margaret Kohl (Philadelphia: Fortress Press, 1979), pp. 119-20.
32. Chemnitz, *Loci Theologici*, Locus VII in *Doctrine of Man*, p. 171. Emphasis added.
33. For new and relevant insights to many items discussed in this chapter, from a position that is open to feminist views, see Phyllis Trible, *God and the Rhetoric of Sexuality* (Philadelphia: Fortress Press, 1978).

4

The Continuing Work of Creation

The creation-affirmation has never been solely a statement of protology, of how things were at the beginning. It has also confessed God's active presence throughout history, leading to divine consummation of the world at the end. That the term "creation" or "new creation" is used to describe this presence is an important witness to the Christian sense that the One God deals with the world in a manner that is consistent with God's original creative and beneficent intention. We ordinarily use the term "providence" to express this confession. The great challenge to faith and theology today is to comprehend how this world's history can be said to be unfolding within God's will and guidance.

HISTORICAL SURVEY

The creation is in its very essence historical; that is, it is always *in transit*. It develops, unfolds, builds cumulatively on the past, and yet begets novelty throughout its course. Consequently, the question of God's ongoing relation to the creation is a perennial concern for religious traditions in general and for Christian faith in particular. There is no theme in the Christian tradition that has received more attention than this one, unless it is that of the saving work of Jesus Christ.

A rich and complex vocabulary has grown up in the theological tradition to express what Christians have believed and hoped for in God's work in the world. Much of this vocabulary has been developed to link God's ongoing work to the original creating work. This vocabulary has, furthermore, developed in the dual attempt to describe the ongoingness of the created world and to testify to the character of God, as God relates to the world. "Redemption" and "new creation" are two of the most obvious terms that relate to God's continuing work. They certainly are not unrelated to creation.

Johannes Brinktrine, the contemporary Thomist, writes that the creation-act of God is "the foundation and the necessary presupposition, the *condicio*

341

4 / THE CREATION

sine qua non of all God's redemptive works,"[1] and as such it is the transitional doctrine between our teachings about God and about redemption. Redemption, however, receives fuller treatment in other sections of this work, and therefore we let it pass unmentioned. "New creation" has figured prominently in our discussion of the biblical traditions about creation. As we observed, the biblical writers, in both the Old Testament and the New, used the terminology "new" or "renewed" creation to describe God's continuing presence in the lives of individuals and in the life of the nation and the church. They also used such terminology to refer to what God would do at the end of history to bless humanity. These issues are also given detailed attention elsewhere in this work. They cannot, however, be far out of mind when we reflect on creation if we remember the forceful presentations of such theologians as Gustaf Aulén and Karl Barth. Aulén's emphasis we have already noted, in his statement that the *lex creationis* (law of creation) is finally identical with God's loving will, the *lex redemptionis* (law of redemption). Barth puts the point even more strikingly: "The ordaining of salvation for man and of man for salvation is the original and basic will of God, the ground and purpose of His will as Creator."[2]

Traditionally, however, a substantial body of reflection has developed that speaks of God's involvement with creation in terms other than of redemption as such. This reflection has spoken of "continuing creation" (*creatio continua*), "preservation," and "providence." In the Middle Ages, in the Reformation, and in Protestant orthodoxy, these terms became quite complex, with many adjunct phrases that related them to Aristotelian philosophy.

Much has been written about the biblical breakthrough in understanding nature and history in linear, temporal terms. As a consequence, the Old Testament vision perceived both the created order as dynamic and unfolding teleologically and God as the One who called this dynamic movement into being and guided it. At times this sensibility related to nature, as dependent on the processes of God's own free direction of creation. At other times and more often, it focused on human history, with varying perspectives that ranged from the confidence that God was building the Hebrew nation in specific regimes (e.g., David and Solomon), to a hope for a new and reformed existence (Amos, Hosea), and to brilliantly eschatological and apocalyptic visions (Second Isaiah, Third Isaiah, Revelation). This understanding conceives of God *guiding* the course of the world and also being *involved in it*. God's guidance furnishes confidence and hope in history, whereas God's involvement gives rise to central, pivotal events, which provide structure and meaning.[3]

Although the Bible focuses upon the history of human beings in its witness to God's providential guidance of creation, the natural order also figures. Furthermore, there is no perceived conflict between nature and history, in respect to their both being under God's guidance. Some theologians of our time sug-

THE CONTINUING WORK OF CREATION

gest that nature and history are discontinuous, that they are two different orders of existence. Our contemporary understanding of nature, however, shows it to be a dynamic, unfolding constellation of processes, marked by the same contingency, relativity, and event-character as history, so that history appears to be in nature in one sense, while nature is also one of history's substrates.[4] Collingwood has suggested that the concept of nature that proceeds from modern science draws on analogies from the historical continuum, so that a thorough reflection upon the idea of nature leads directly to the idea of history.[5] This is quite in line with our growing awareness of the interrelatedness of spirit and matter, *psyche* and *soma*. From the evolutionary perspective, God created history through the instrumentality of a nature that is itself a process, one that becomes increasingly complex until it reaches the sphere of human being.[6] In the light of this realization, we must comprehend both physical and social "nature" under the concepts of creation and providence.

Origen (185–254) and Augustine (354–430) provided the two most important and influential discussions of providence in the ancient church. Both of them related providence directly to God's activity as Creator. Origen's work stands in the context of Hellenistic philosophy, which spoke forcefully of fate, *pronoia*. Pelikan describes the situation of Origen's predecessors:

> In the period of the empire, this consciousness of fate grew even more dominant, as the Stoic doctrine of necessity coincided with the incursion of the Chaldean astrologers. . . . Stoicism identified fate with divine will, but in the process had to surrender the freedom of the human will. . . . In the conflict of Christian theology with classicism it was chiefly this sense of fate and necessity that impressed itself upon the interpreters of the gospel as the alternative to their message.[7]

Origen shared this context of philosophical pressure toward fate as determinism, and he considered it to be antithetical to the Christian teaching. He did not reject destiny or providence, but he linked it to free human will, which emphasized the need for humans to take responsibility under God. For Origen, the central theme of Christianity was "the idea of the pedagogy of free rational beings through Providence."[8] Origen painted a broad picture of this "pedagogy" of God's, through creation, Judaism, the Logos, the church, and future fulfillment. He acknowledged the universal immanent Logos of the philosophers, but protested that it had not succeeded in carrying out the proper pedagogy that would bring humankind from sin into blessedness. It was only in the incarnation of the Logos in Jesus Christ that a change occurred; only Christ the Logos can be teacher and leader of all.

Augustine, in his *Confessions* and in his *City of God*, gives us a grand vision of both creation and providence. In the former work, he relates providence to his own individual life, his pilgrimage from unbelief among the pagans

4 / THE CREATION

to Christian faith. The latter work relates God's guidance to universal history. In book 5, chapter 11, he writes:

> Therefore God supreme and true, with His Word and Holy Spirit (which three are one), one God, omnipotent, creator and maker of every soul and of every body; . . . who made man a rational animal consisting of soul and body, who when he sinned, neither permitted him to go unpunished, nor left him without mercy; . . . who has not left, not to speak of heaven and earth, angels and men, but not even the entrails of the smallest and most contemptible animal, or the feather of a bird, or the little flower of a plant, or the leaf of a tree, without an harmony . . .—that God can never be believed to have left the kingdoms of men, their dominations and servitudes, outside of the laws of His Providence.[9]

Augustine preserved the emphasis on human freedom, just as Origen had done, within the framework of God's providence. His *City of God* literally moves from the original creation to his own time and beyond, showing how God has raised up the church, even as the Roman Empire collapses.

The Lutheran tradition has taken on a complex set of categories to speak of continuing creation and providence, categories which it received from the medieval tradition. Thomas Aquinas had spoken of Providence and of its constituent actions: preservation (*conservatio*), divine cooperation (*concursus*), and divine control (*gubernatio*).[10]

Luther himself had a vivid sense of God's continuing creative work. In his study of Luther's theology of creation, David Löfgren believes that he has found the key to the Reformer's entire thought.[11] *Creatio continua* encompasses all of human life for Luther:

> For Luther, the world is not a ship which is built in order to sail by itself; the "nihil" of the world from which it has come, therefore, does not lie somewhere in the past but is that from which each new creature, each new person appears at his birth; in fact, every moment and every hour are constantly newly created by God.[12]

Luther apparently held to a view that emphasized God's continual interventions for the sustaining of creation, even though created things participate and cooperate in their conservation. God's personal relationship to the world, not its own immanent powers, sustains creation. This sense of God's creative presence made it difficult for Luther to hold much stock in miracles, because God is so much at work in creation that it is difficult to distinguish between what is natural and what is supernatural.

The dogmatic development of post-Reformation Lutheranism used the medieval scholastic terms to speak of this closeness of Creator and creation. The vigor of Luther's sensibility was thereby dampened, but the emphasis on the closeness of God and the role of continuing creation is still expressed.

THE CONTINUING WORK OF CREATION

Technically, *creatio continua* was included under "preservation" (*conservatio*), which Hollaz describes as "the act of Divine Providence whereby God sustains all things created by Him, so that they continue in being with the properties implanted in their nature and the powers received in creation." The dogmaticians believed that without God's sustaining activity created things could not maintain themselves. Gerhard wrote, "God the Creator of all, did not desert the work which He framed; but, by His omnipotence, up to the present time preserves it."¹³

Concursus, or divine cooperation with the processes of creation, is defined by Hollaz as the activity "whereby God, by a general and immediate influence, proportioned to the need and capacity of every creature, graciously takes part with second causes in their actions and effects."¹⁴ This introduces us to the concepts of "first and second creation" or "matter" (*creatio* or *materia prima* and *secunda*), as well as "first and second causes" (*causa prima* and *causa secunda*). The broad consensus of the earlier theologians, which Aquinas and Luther shared, was that *ex nihilo* God created *prima materia*, an as yet shapeless matter. In his lectures on Genesis, Luther calls it "crude and formless masses. . . . This primary matter, so to speak, for His later work God, according to the plain words of the Decalog (Exod. 20:11), did not create outside the six days but at the beginning of the first day."¹⁵ This primary matter, the result of the *creatio prima*, was directly dependent on the *causa prima*, God the Creator. Subsequent to this, however, God undertook the *creatio secunda*, in which secondary matter, that is, specific, determinate things, was created. These determinate things possessed their own *causae secunda*; that is, species could continue to propagate themselves. They are dependent on God, but not at first hand. As the First Cause, he moves the secondary causes.¹⁶ In both the medieval and Reformation theologies, this concept of *concursus* bespeaks God's intimate involvement in the created processes. The concept lent itself to many fine distinctions. John Andrew Quenstedt conveys the general tone in this passage:

> With second causes, God concurs according to the need and requirement of each, i.e., when, as often as, and in the manner that, the cause, according to the condition of its nature, demands this concurrence. For God does not change the nature of the agents or the manner and order of their action, but He permits natural agents to act naturally, free agents to act freely.¹⁷

This intimacy of relationship and divine cooperation is set forth meticulously. One could argue that it is no more intimately conceived than the conception of the court theologian in David's and Solomon's times, who saw the hand of God working in the details of political intrigue and nation-building. It is this notion of *concursus* which enables us to give scholastic foundation to the possibility of God working in and through the evolutionary process—

345

4 / THE CREATION

whether it be biological evolution or the psychosocial evolution we call *history*.

Abraham Calov described God's "government" (*gubernatio*) as "the act of divine providence by which God most excellently orders, regulates, and directs the affairs and actions of creatures according to His own wisdom, justice, and goodness, for the glory of His name and the welfare of men."[18] Whereas *conservatio* pertains to the continuation of created things, *gubernatio* speaks of the divine ordering of those actions which creatures carry out. As Heinrich Schmid puts it, "God inclines and leads them according to His will so as to accomplish His designs."[19] Further specifications are possible, partially in order to preserve freedom of the creation, such as "permitting," "hindering," "directing," and "determining" providence.

The so-called "orders of creation" terminology was originated in the nineteenth century, probably by Adolf von Harless, but it does carry on a genuine interest of the Reformation. These are structures within the creation, structures that provide order and governance for human life. The orders consist of *status politicus*, *status ecclesiasticus*, and *status economicus*—corresponding, in some renditions, to heads of state, clergy, and all other people, whereas others say that every person, in Luther's view, exists in all three orders.[20]

Regin Prenter separates the orders of creation from providence under the rubrics "The Law of Creation" and "The Gospel of Creation" respectively. His argument is that the historical orders are the covenants of creation, in which "the Creator forces his law of creation into external realization, this law being known in the world of man as the commandment of love to God and the neighbor. Through a struggle against death and damnation God thus promotes among men the life and blessing of creation."[21] However, this divine "forcing" also brings human rebellion, and to this rebellion, the divine action seems to be wrath. Prenter is surely correct in this insight. The most oppressive law, as Tillich rightly observes, is the law of our own being, the law formed by the shape of what we are created to be.[22] "The Gospel of Creation" is the proclamation that through God's grace creation is indeed "working for good," that is, that it is governed by providence. Prenter writes:

> But the gospel of creation proclaims that all tribulation, suffering, and anxiety which God allows to come upon man, serve to restore man and to impart life to him. Tribulation can destroy only the old Adam, without whose death man cannot arise to eternal life. When this gospel is heard, the will rejoices and thankfully accepts even suffering, because it clings to the hope for resurrection. ... *All* things work for the good of those who love God. It is therefore impossible for anyone who believes the gospel of creation to hold life in contempt.[23]

The purpose and value of this concept of the "orders" can be readily appreciated. It has come under critique for its possible distortions, the chief of which is that the dynamic and change of "orders" may be overlooked. This can have the result that the societal structures of a given time are elevated to normativeness. Or the orders may be defined according to the vested interests of the one who is defining, and thus be made oppressive.

What has just been said of the "orders of creation" could be said about all the scholastic categories as well, categories that have become a part of theological reflection on providence. They bear a general evangelical thrust that can scarcely be faulted. But when taken with philosophical overtones that may or may not have been intended, they may lead to perversions. For example, the "primary/secondary causes" scheme may be helpful in speaking about how God works in this world without violating the inherent laws and energies of the orders that God created. As Brunner suggests, however, if one were to take the laws of causality with precise seriousness, the question arises whether it is not a perversion to subject God to those laws. Or, even if one may do so, can one do so intelligibly?

The concern for providence has continued strong to our day. The traditions of pietism emphasized the doctrine, personalizing it with great force. The nineteenth-century liberal theologians, Friedrich Schleiermacher and Albrecht Ritschl, made significant contributions. Schleiermacher collapsed the distinction between creation and preservation; thus providence became the whole of creation. So conceived, providence becomes progressive. It works immanently to perfect human potentiality in the processes triggered by Jesus Christ's God-consciousness. Those processes manifest the efficacy of Jesus' consciousness in subsequent history. Ritschl was of great importance, because he introduced in a significant manner the concept of the kingdom of God. He believed that the kingdom was a this-worldly, social reality. It was a kingdom of ends, in which God worked to bring about a harmony between the *summum bonum* of humans, for which they strove, and God's own *telos* for the creation. This too resulted in a progressivist concept. Ritschl's ethicized kingdom of God now appears somewhat out of touch with biblical witness, but he made a salutary contribution because he brought the concept into the center of theological reflection.

Twentieth-century theology, under the aegis of Barth, Brunner, and Bultmann, corrected Schleiermacher and Ritschl. They elevated the kingdom of God and other categories of providence, but they also took them out of the realm of concrete history into that of salvation history (*Heilsgeschichte*). Barth emphasized providence as intensively as did the Protestant orthodox theologians. He outlines a "radically contingent, relativized and transient history preserved and ruled by God's will."[24] The providential will of God serves the covenant community above all, which idea is the source of Barth's celebrated notion that creation is the "external basis" for the covenant, whereas the covenant is the "internal basis" for creation.[25]

The early Paul Tillich[26] and the so-called "eschatological" and "liberation"

4 / THE CREATION

theologians have introduced a new and constructive element into the discussion of providence. They are thoroughly eschatological, which means that they preserve the forward-looking emphasis which the generation of Barth and Bultmann lost. For these older theologians, "eschatological" had tended to mean "eternal," whereas for the newer group it refers to the horizontal unfolding of God's final goal for history. The final end of God's creation is what determines every moment of the preceding continuum. Further, these newer theologians tend to see definite social and political consequences emerging from the providential activity of God. These consequences lie in the realm of universal history; they do not restrict themselves to the history of the covenant community. Providence is in the public realm, where it can be discussed, debated, and demonstrated. As such, it enters into dialogue with other, non-Christian proposals for interpreting human history.

The liberation theologians of Latin America have provided indications that they may make a decisive new contribution to theology precisely on the ground of the doctrine of providence. The Latin Americans have fashioned their thought in reflection on their sociocultural situation and the relation of God's work of creation and redemption to that situation. Their thinking is therefore thoroughly social from the very beginning.

It has been observed that these thinkers are constructing a natural theology that takes into account and criticizes the exclusively revelational theologies of the mid-twentieth-century neo-orthodox period. This new natural theology takes as its reference point, however, not so much the realm of physical nature as that of social nature and history.[27] Obviously, even though the term may not appear explicitly throughout their works, if this interpretation of the liberation theologians is correct, theirs is inherently a theology of providence.

From this perspective, it is understandable why a concept such as that of *liberation* surfaces as central, since in a context of sociocultural bondage God's providential work may well be described as liberation. Providence is distinguished from pure human passivity, however, since it incorporates human effort to share in the liberating and building up of the creation. These assertions have been hotly debated by European and North American critics, but it is fair to say that the measure of the Latin American proposals has not yet been taken.[28]

Two citations may give the flavor of the Latin American theologians' contribution to this doctrine. Hugo Assmann writes: "The Kingdom of God does not ever identify itself with the structures of the world, but it inserts itself into and unfolds itself in them as a process. The notion of process is perhaps one of the categories to introduce into the theological vocabulary in order to talk about the Kingdom of God."[29] From Juan Luis Segundo:

> We can see that the *divine providence*, in the Christian view, is not and cannot

THE CONTINUING WORK OF CREATION

be a doctrine, propounding some sort of divine interference that dislocates man's affairs and efforts. Nor can it be the inaccessible start of a world that goes on from there to operate under its own laws. In the concrete, temporal history of his love for us, God gives us a world that functions in accord with its own proper laws. But he does not give it to us as some sort of alien and inert material. He fashions this world into a system of signs and revelation which culminates with his total insertion of himself into this world. Thus he leads us to shoulder the task of freeing all its dimensions for the service of love and the construction of the world.

In its definitive form, this world will be not only the *new earth* of man, but also the new heaven of God. "Providentialism" and "passivity," which were so often tied together in customary usage, are in reality contradictory.[30]

PERENNIAL CONCERNS OF THE DOCTRINE OF PROVIDENCE

In a recent study of providence, Langdon Gilkey summarizes the classical concept as it has developed and persisted over the centuries:

(1) Representing the sovereignty of God over history, the activity of God's providence was controlled, directed and defined by God's eschatological goal. (2) The work of providence concerned itself with the external realm of "objective" events, both natural and historical, cosmological and social, amidst which men and women lived in time. (3) Because of providence there was no fate in historical experience; rather, the purpose of providence, and so the ultimate goal of history, was the establishment and so the freeing of freedom—the transformation for all men and women of fate into destiny. (4) God does not work in history as an external cause but in and through the creaturely forces and dynamic factors of history. (5) Thus providence works through, not against, human freedom; it is, therefore, not contradicted by man's sin but made necessary because of sin— if the eschatological goal is to be reached.[31]

Gilkey's statement corresponds to the brief survey we have presented here.

The doctrine of providence has been set within the context of the doctrine of creation by the theological tradition, and that setting is instructive for us as we look at the perennial concerns and problems of the doctrine. First, it presses to our attention that creation and redemption cannot ultimately be separated. God's work is the expression of God's will, wherever it takes place. As the Swedish theologians remind us, God's redemptive love is the rationale of whatever God does, whether in original creation, in the governance of history, or in redemption. What occurs under the rubric "creation," however— whether it be originating, sustaining-continuing, or guiding-governing—is not appropriated as redemptive grace except in faith, because unless one has accepted the action of God as grace, set forth in Christ, the activities of crea-

4 / THE CREATION

tion come across with the force of demand, of law, as imperative rather than indicative.

It is part of the dialectic of creation that since the fall, and perhaps even before it, we have not yet become what we were created to be. We must heed the dictum of Goethe's *"Werde was du bist!"* (Become what you are). Under grace, the created order and its processes do not alter outwardly, but are perceived as friendly, fulfilling, under God's eschatological activity. These are processes to which we are reconciled in grace, rather than being oppressive demands to which we can never live up. Ritschl was correct in observing that the gift of grace did not change the world-system of nature and history, except at two points: It enabled people to see the rationale of that system as God's system rather than as an inexporable, natural, cause-and-effect machine, and it revealed the proper human response within that system.

Two errors are of great concern in this context. On the one hand, the oppressive appearance of the created order apart from grace must not lead us to separate creation from redemption, as if creation could never be subsumed under redemption or as if redemption would lead us out of creation rather than into it. On the other hand, creation and redemption must not be collapsed into equivalence, as if redemption has nothing to add to creation. Redemption, properly perceived, is the fulfillment of creation. It is indeed true that "grace does not destroy nature, but perfects it" (Aquinas).

Thus, the necessity for creation to be linked with faith is even more vividly brought home to us when we consider providence. Only faith could look on this world and call it "creation." Similarly, only such a faithful reflection could look on the ongoing processes of nature and history and call them *"creatio continua, concursus, gubernatio*—providence." The issues raised by this set of insights lead us to a consideration of the great problem facing the doctrine of creation in all its manifestations—original, continuing, and eschatological.

This great problem stems from the fact that the affirmation of creation, original and continuing, is an affirmation that the processes of nature and history are basically friend and not foe, ultimately fulfilling under God and not destructive. To perceive the world as creation is to understand that its processes are finally reliable and trustworthy, because they do proceed from our God, *ex nihilo*. This judgment about the world of nature and history is precisely what is called into question, particularly in our own time.

This calling into question of basic assumptions underlying the Christian doctrine of providence brings us to what Gilkey and others term the foremost challenge of the contemporary world to that doctrine: modern historical consciousness. As Gilkey analyzes it, this consciousness includes several basic elements: the relativity of historical life, a new insight into the role of human creativity and freedom in history (note our emphasis on "created co-creator"), the temporalizing of all being, and a new sense of progress in history. Gilkey is certainly correct in his assessment that the concept of providence must take these issues into account if it is to be credible in our time.

In one form, this challenge is another instance of the problem of evil, and it is because evil manifests itself in this context that theodicy is often discussed within the doctrines of creation and providence. Creation affirms that the processes of this world are God's instrumentalities for initiating, maintaining, and perfecting God's handiwork, creation itself. Evil appears on every hand, because those processes of nature and history seem to disrupt, pervert, and ultimately to destroy that divine handiwork, specifically the human sector but in general all nature. Consequently, one cannot accept the affirmation of creation in any of its forms unless one has come to terms with evil.

Furthermore, the logic of this set of insights underscores that creation, faith, and evil cannot be considered for long apart from the action of redemption from and over evil. The Christ who is the Logos of creation is the Christ who redeems. His creative work illumines the meaning and scope of his redemptive work, as his redemptive work clarifies the purposes and the underlying principles governing his creative work. The perennial concern of the doctrine of creation in all its forms is to lift up with crystal clarity this Christian affirmation: Despite all appearances, in the face of all apparent signals to the contrary, this world of nature and history *is* creation!

NOTES

1. Johannes Brinktrine, *Die Lehre von der Schöpfung* (Paderborn: Ferdinand Schoeningh, 1956), p. 16.

2. Karl Barth, *Church Dogmatics*, vol. 4/1, trans. G. T. Thomson (Edinburgh: T. & T. Clark, 1936), p. 9.

3. Karl Löwith, *Meaning in History* (Chicago: University of Chicago Press, 1957), pp. 182ff. R. G. Collingwood, *The Idea of History* (New York: Oxford University Press, 1957), pp. 49ff.

4. See C. F. von Weizsäcker, *The History of Nature*, trans. Fred D. Wieck (Chicago: University of Chicago Press, 1947); S. C. Alexander, "The Historicity of Things," in *Philosophy and History*, ed. R. Klibansky and H. J. Paton (Oxford: At the Clarendon Press, 1936).

5. R. G. Collingwood, *The Idea of Nature* (New Haven: Yale University Press, 1945), pt. 3, esp. pp. 174–77.

6. It was Teilhard's significance to have emphasized and explained this fact with great detail and force. See his *Phenomenon of Man*, 2d ed., trans. Bernard Wall (New York: Harper & Row, 1965). See also Charles E. Raven, *Natural Religion and Christian Theology* (Cambridge: At the University Press, 1953).

7. Jaroslav Pelikan, *The Emergence of the Catholic Tradition (100-600)* (Chicago: University of Chicago Press, 1971), p. 281.

8. Hal Koch, *Pronoia und Paideusis* (Berlin: Walter de Gruyter, 1932), p. 159.

4 / THE CREATION

9. *Nicene and Post-Nicene Fathers*, vol. 2 (Grand Rapids: Wm. B. Eerdmans, 1956), p. 93.
10. *Summa Theologica* i, qu. 97, 103–19; i–ii, qu. 109–14. *Summa contra Gentiles*, bk. iii, chaps. 64–113.
11. David Löfgren, *Die Theologie der Schöpfung bei Luther* (Göttingen: Vandenhoeck & Ruprecht, 1960), p. 7.
12. Ibid., p. 25.
13. Hollaz and Gerhard quoted in Heinrich Schmid, *The Doctrinal Theology of the Evangelical Lutheran Church*, trans. Charles A. Hay and Henry E. Jacobs, 3d ed. rev. (Minneapolis: Augsburg Publishing House, 1875), pp. 170–71.
14. Quoted in ibid., pp. 171–72.
15. *LW* 1:6.
16. Brinktrine, *Die Lehre von der Schöpfung*, pp. 76–84.
17. See the selections in Schmid, *The Doctrinal Theology of the Evangelical Lutheran Church*, p. 185.
18. Ibid., p. 172.
19. Ibid.
20. Werner Elert, *The Christian Ethos*, trans. Carl S. Schindler (Philadelphia: Fortress [Muhlenberg] Press, 1957), pp. 77–81.
21. Regin Prenter, *Creation and Redemption*, trans. Theodore I. Jensen (Philadelphia: Fortress Press, 1967), p. 202; see also pp. 202–16.
22. Paul Tillich, *Morality and Beyond* (New York: Harper & Row, 1963), chap. 1.
23. Prenter, *Creation and Redemption*, p. 211.
24. Langdon Gilkey, *Reaping the Whirlwind: A Christian Interpretation of History* (New York: Seabury Press, 1976), pp. 219–20.
25. Barth, *Church Dogmatics*, 3/1:231.
26. See esp. Paul Tillich, *Systematic Theology*, 3 vols. (Chicago: University of Chicago Press, 1951–63), vol. 3, pt. 5.
27. This insight is elaborated by Vitor Westhelle, in his "Representation and Method: The Element of *Vorstellung* in the Hegelian-Marxist Tradition and the Locus of Theology" (Th.D. diss., Lutheran School of Theology, 1984).
28. E.g., Gustavo Gutierrez, *A Theology of Liberation*, trans. Sister Caridad Inda and John Eagelson (Maryknoll, N.Y.: Orbis Books, 1973), pp. 154, 159–60.
29. Hugo Assmann, *Teología desde la praxis de la liberación: Ensayo teológico desde la América dependente*, 2d ed. (Salamanca: Sgueme, 1976), p. 154.
30. Juan Luis Segundo, "Intelecto y salvación," in G. Gutierrez, J. L. Segundo, et al., *Salvación y Construcción del Mundo* (Santiago/Barcelona: Dilapsa-Nova Terra, 1968), pp. 163–64.
31. Gilkey, *Reaping the Whirlwind*, p. 240.

5
Challenges to the Ongoing Doctrinal Task

We turn to a recapitulation of some challenges that face anyone intending to carry theological thinking forward, so as to render it relevant to new situations and epochs. Some of these challenges have already been discussed; others appear briefly here for the first time. In this catalog of challenges lies the ongoing excitement of theology. Even though the theologian may bring reflection to an end before these challenges are thoroughly dispatched, there can be no final satisfaction that the task has been completed until such issues as we shall here face have been confronted.

CREDIBLE DOCTRINE IN EVERY SITUATION

The mandate for theological reflection on creation was clear from the survey of biblical materials—a deep attachment to the creation-affirmation was evident at the same time we noted a refreshing freedom to let that affirmation take whatever form the situation demanded. The ground of this freedom lies in the overriding concern that doctrine be *credible* in whatever circumstance it finds itself. Since the creation-affirmation stands in an especially intimate interface with the ordinary, secular, nontheologically conceived realities of life, the demand for credibility impinges on it with particular poignancy.

The various themes in which the discussion here has been divided indicate the points at which the nontheological conceptions engage the reflection on creation: beginnings of the world and life; the process of history; the nature of the human being and the processes underlying human development; endings, whether that be thought of as extinction of the species, the death of the planet and the universe, or individual death; and the question of final perfection whether in this life or in some other. The information and conceptualities rush in on the theologian when the attention is turned to any of these issues, and a doctrine of creation fails of credibility to whatever extent it ignores these data or fails to deal with them adequately. When one con-

4 / THE CREATION

siders that each of these interfaces represents an area on the forefront of scientific discovery and interpretation, and at the same time an area in which common experience is undergoing great change, the task that faces the theologian becomes almost overpowering.

We can recite only a few of the pertinent questions raised in scientific study and common experience: Did the universe have a beginning, or is it without beginning or end, the so-called "Big Bang" being only an episode in its oscillation? How can a *telos* be ascribed to history when its processes appear to be free and blind? What sort of divine fulfillment can we conceive in light of the seemingly assured demise of our planet in two and a half billion years by the evolution of our sun into a huge fireball (a so-called "red giant") that will burn the earth to a cinder?[1]

CREATION AND THE CONCEPT OF EVOLUTION

The Christian church and its theologians have found the concept of evolution difficult to handle, especially since Charles Darwin elaborated it in 1859. Consequently, some Christians have rejected it altogether. Even among those who have accepted the concept, there has been relatively little done toward a thoroughly reformulated doctrine commensurate with evolutionary theory yet faithful to the tradition. A summary of the key issues may help to set the agenda.

According to R. G. Collingwood, the concept of nature is a changing one, and our own epoch is one that has moved from a relatively static view of nature, which compared nature and its elements to a machine and its parts, to a dynamic view, which operates with the analogy of history for interpreting nature. The sciences, ranging from physics and astronomy to biology and psychology, have opened for us a view that recognizes change, mystery, and unexpected potential in nature. That the marvelous creature we call human being could evolve in its entirety from the explosion of the Big Bang or, more immediately, from the "primordial soup" of perhaps three billion years ago, suggests vividly that this "nature" that could traverse the space and time those billions of years encompass is in its own right marvelous.

The first chapter of Genesis speaks of creation as a process of six days. Reflection on those days, whether twenty-four hours in length or simply symbols denoting indeterminate periods, has proliferated over the centuries. The enormous time-scale of evolutionary thinking has seldom been carefully considered, however. A few simple observations will make the point. The universe may have come into existence through the Big Bang some 18 billion years ago; the earth's crust congealed 4 billion years ago; dinosaurs flourished 180 million to 63 million years ago; *Homo erectus*, an important ancestor of our species, flourished 600,000 to 350,000 years ago.

If we were to put the history of planet earth on a calendar division, with one "day" equaling 14 million years and one "hour" equaling a half million years, the facts just recounted would appear thus: The earth's crust congealed on January 1; dinosaurs appeared on December 21; Neanderthal man, after 11:50 P.M. on New Year's Eve. If we change the time equivalence to one "day" equaling 6,000 years, Neanderthal appears in mid-November, agriculture begins during the evening of December 29, Greece flourished in the afternoon of December 31, and Columbus discovered America shortly after 10 P.M. on New Year's Eve.

Human creatures, whom we consider to be created in the image of God and whose history is the arena of divine providence, fill a very small portion of the history of the universe. This does not detract from the marvel that attaches to human being or from the significance of history, but it does add an important dimension of mystery and complexity to our consideration of the creation of human beings and the providential guiding of human history. Why was *Homo sapiens* created in this manner? What is the significance of the eons of nonhuman history? Why did God do it this way?

It is impossible today to conceptualize how God might have control over every item and event in nature and history. The best of current scientific thought also renders inadequate the picture of the evolutionary process proceeding by pure chance, as Jacques Monod forcefully insisted some years ago in his celebrated book, *Chance and Necessity*. It now appears that chance plays a role in evolution at its most primitive condition, but order and patterning also play a role alongside chance. The interrelation of the two factors is complex and beyond our scope here. Arthur Peacocke has suggested that the most adequate picture of the creator God is that of the composer of intricate fugues, who builds on original elements while employing an almost infinite number of variations of those elements.[2] Others have suggested the Hindu God of the dance, Shiva. In any case, it appears that the transcendence of God the Creator may now be conceived more adequately as being "in there," in the very stuff and possibility of creation, rather than "out there."

The most recent advances in biological evolutionary theory point to the complex and unexpectedly rich role played by genes. Genetic materials can no longer be thought of as only "crass material" in the customary sense of the term. Some basic and refined human values, such as altruism, honesty, mother-love, truthfulness, and curiosity, are understood to be correlated to genetic bases, even though that base is too complex to identify precisely. What does such an insight do to the traditional assertion that God's revelation presents the purest form of love and other such values? Or that Christ is the

Logos of all truth? We might suggest that such scientific insights into the relative autonomy of genetic evolution need not be considered antithetical to Christian faith. Is the place of Christ, the promulgator and embodiment of sacrificial love, as Logos of all truth, not enhanced when that truth is seen to be written into the genetic structure of life itself?[23]

Our new appreciation for the complexity of matter and the versatility of the evolutionary processes points to the possibility that spirit and matter may have the same point of origin and that it may indeed be true to say that the terms "matter" and "spirit" refer to two configurations of the same reality, not to two different realities.

Traditional doctrine has predicated that humans were perfect in paradise, that they possessed the maximum of their abilities and their goodness at the beginning of their career on this earth. Evolutionary theory suggests that humans were primitive at their origins, particularly if those origins include humanoid forms prior to *Homo sapiens*. Consequently, the career of the human being is an ascent toward fulfillment rather than a descent from greatness. For this reason, we have emphasized the concept of "destiny," namely, that human being was created with a high destiny, toward which it is tending. The reinterpretation of the fall and original sin as universally valid myth enables this line of thought.

EVIL AND THE RELIABILITY OF THE CREATED PROCESSES

As we conclude this essay, it is appropriate once again to describe what is surely the most serious challenge to the doctrine of creation and the issue that provokes our deepest reflection. We are confronted with the question whether this world intends us good or ill. We ask about participation in the processes of creation, whether those processes be within us or external to us (the evolution of DNA illustrating the former; the progress of our technology, the latter). We ask whether participation will bring us to fulfillment, to destruction, or to a natural end that deserves to be thought of as neutral, neither a fulfillment nor a destruction, not a bang but a whimper. This is the setting in which the God-question engages us today, perhaps with more force than in any other realm. The question of evil enters here dramatically because it is the force that appears to destroy whatever reliability the world processes have, that appears to undercut our sense of the trustworthiness of the creation and to devastate our thought of fulfillment.

The creation-doctrine is an item of faith, because in the absence of any final demonstration or disproof, faith affirms that the created world, including ourselves, *is* God's creation—that it is finally friend, not foe; cosmos, not chaos; consummation, not dissolution. If this is the doctrine's character, the recogni-

CHALLENGES TO THE ONGOING DOCTRINAL TASK

tion of that fact illuminates both the substance and the task of proclamation, namely, to make actual in our time the sense that we are creation and that we live in a creation that will ultimately unite us with the creator God.

NOTES

1. Robert Jastrow, *God and the Astronomers* (New York: Warner Books, 1978).
2. Arthur Peacocke, *Creation and the World of Science* (Oxford: At the Clarendon Press, 1979), chap. 3.
3. For suggestive hypotheses that give a lead to further theological thinking, see Ralph Wendell Burhoe, "Religion's Role in Human Evolution: The Missing Link between Ape-man's Selfish Genes and Civilized Altruism," *Zygon: Journal of Religion and Science* 14 (1979): 135-62. Also Donald T. Campbell, "On the Conflicts between Biological and Social Evolution and between Psychology and Moral Tradition," *Zygon* 11 (1976): 167-208.

FIFTH LOCUS

Sin and Evil

PAUL R. SPONHEIM

SIN AND EVIL

Introduction

1. The Nature of Sin
   The Object of Sin
   The Agent of Sin
   The Efficacy of Sin

2. The Origin of Sin
   Creation and Fall
   The Goodness and Integrity of Creation
   The Possibility and Actuality of Sin

3. The Effect of Sin
   Sinner and Creature
   Bondage and Responsibility

4. Metaphysical and Natural Evil
   Finitude
   Suffering

5. The Work of God against Evil
   The Continuity of God
   The Decisiveness of God
   The Directivity of God

Introduction

Christian dogmatics has no independent interest in sin and evil, for it seeks to follow the order of faith which claims and confesses God, who is Lord whether there is evil or not. But the reality of sin and evil is in fact of crucial importance to dogmatics, for faith clings to a God who forgives sin and delivers from evil. The Christian theologian will find reason to speak of sin and evil in connection with nearly every rubric of the faith. Thus all three articles of the Apostles' Creed raise questions for one who knows sin: Does sin or evil undercut the meaningfulness of Christian claims about creation? How is God's work in Jesus of Nazareth to be understood in relation to sin and evil? What hope may the Christian have that sin and evil may be combated and indeed overcome?

Talk about sin and evil does not stand at the same level as talk about God; it is derivative. Yet the reality embodied in these words is so thoroughgoing in extent and so critical in quality that the Christian's talk of God is in fact always in the face of that which stands against God.[1] While the concept of God can be adequately defined in principle apart from any reference to sin, the converse is not true. Sin is, precisely, "before God." More explicitly, sin is a person's volition, action, or condition which is against the will of God. In speaking so of sin, the emphasis is on personal activity or on a condition issuing from and sustained by such personal activity. "Evil," on the other hand, is not so much action as passion; it is the undergoing or suffering of something. We may link the two theologically by speaking of both sin and evil as being against the will of God. Thus we may speak of sin as moral evil, issuing from volition and issuing in experience that is against God, as distinguished from metaphysical evil which seems to follow from the very structure of existence, or natural evil that comes from subpersonal causes.

The action of sin against God may not require that the sinner be conscious of God. Clearly the sensing of an experience as evil does not require explicit reference to God. Rather, evil may be experienced and described simply as that which thwarts such purposes as seem intrinsic to the human condition. The Christian accepts such an account as formally appropriate, but seeks to transcend purely subjective material definitions of human nature by reference to a doctrine of creation. We cannot assume that the knowledge of that for

5 / SIN AND EVIL

which we were made is consciously intact in us. Yet the criteria needed to mark and measure evil lie in our creaturehood.

While the experience of evil may not include conscious reference to God, it does provide a large part of the basis for a formidable contemporary case against belief in God. In the face of evil the goodness of an omnipotent creator and/or the sovereignty of a suffering divine victim are in jeopardy. In a time when the experience of evil is indisputable but the sense for God flickers faintly, Christian attention to this rubric must accept an apologetic as well as a dogmatic agenda. While the issue of theodicy, "the justification of God," conventionally ranges broadly through the experience of evil, from the indiscriminate destructiveness of the tornado to the obscene selectivity of terminal illness in children, the reality of sin already serves in its own right to focus the issue of the goodness and power of God.

Even the mere task of *stating* the Christian understanding of God intelligibly faces considerable difficulties today. How will the category "against God" be clear if the meaning of God is muddled? If there is no sense for God, sin-talk will have to settle down uncomfortably in psychological and sociological categories. If God stands more for a principle than for a person, the framework will be intrinsically juristic, potentially legalistic. Or the difficulty may be precisely in what we think of the nondivine self; our view may be too high or too low to let speech about the sin of such a self make sense. Sin is only possible for a self set in the ambiguous "middle distance" constituted by God's gift and task of freedom with responsibility. Finally, Christian speech about sin reaches for some understanding of the connectedness of human selves, for some notion of involvement in a being-against-God which goes well beyond individual volition. Such speech is problematic in a time when atomistic or episodic accounts of reality prevail, at least to the extent that responsibility does not reach beyond individual agents. Even if there were no problem about the meaning of "God," how shall talk of sin make sense without will, without self, without race, without Satan? How shall we proceed?

First, the *scope* of our work must be rather broad, because sin is not an eternal reality that can generate its own tidy dogmatic discussion regardless of what history may bring. This is so also because sin, while derivative, is so experientially and systematically pervasive that an extraordinarily rich set of resources exists for our work. Neither the control of personal speculation nor the clarity of determinative dogmatic subordination is available here. Both authoritative word and experiential world call for attention in this locus in a more complete way than can be said to be a commonplace in dogmatics.

Second, crucial to the direction of the argument is the matter of the *order* in which the several facets of our topic are to be considered. The Christian faith entails an essentially historical perspective as the key to find the invariant structure of what is real. Accordingly, our consideration begins with moral

INTRODUCTION

evil, rather than with metaphysical or natural evil. The interest in concreteness characterizing an historical approach further suggests that we begin our consideration of moral evil by confronting its nature, rather than by inquiring after its cause. Starting with moral evil suggests that we focus on God's action in Jesus of Nazareth. Christian faith may appropriately be said to be clearer about the remedy than the disease. Of course, one cannot fully possess the confession *that* in Jesus God has decisively addressed the human predicament, if one cannot state *what* that predicament was/is. But one can let that which is more clear guide one in probing what is less clear. Thus it may be appropriate for the faith to permit clear convictions concerning the "second Adam" to lend firmness to the shadowy figure of the first Adam. That process would be inappropriate only if it violated the sense of what, apart from Christ, commends itself as true about either the specific reality of evil or the broader drama in which God and humankind are involved.

Third, the *status* of what we seek is a "second-order" understanding of the "first-order" reality of confession and faith. We do not seek to replace faith with understanding, but to serve it. For example, with respect to sin, two distortions of this relationship must be resisted. The first-order must not rule out the second-order, as when the fact that we cannot understand *why* we sin is taken to mean that we cannot describe whence sin comes and whither it goes, or even locate that which is inexplicable in relation to that which is explicable.[3] And the second-order must not rule out the first-order, as when one supposes that the dogmatician's act of identifying the world of sin somehow discharges the sinner's responsibility for the confession and the commission of sin.

NOTES

1. This point has been made recently and emphatically by Douglas John Hall in *Lighten Our Darkness* (Philadelphia: Westminster Press, 1976).
2. See, e.g., Karl Menninger, *Whatever Became of Sin?* (New York: Hawthorn Books, 1973).
3. Another form of this error suggests that reflection about sin is impossible because sin has cast the reason into darkness. This claim seems at once to overestimate the connection of reason and will (dismissing clear-eyed defiance, for example) and—granting *some* connection between reason and will—underestimate the illumination available within the Christian community. Presumably the call to sanctification somehow includes the reason as well as the will. One wonders, then, if it is not the power of piety which seems to suppose that to understand the depth of one's predicament is somehow to resolve that predicament—in which case, understanding must be resisted as arrogance.

1

The Nature of Sin

Sin is an act and state of personal will against God and the will of God. Sin arises from the total person rooted in and related to that which is beyond the person, expresses itself in the complexity of the person's strength and weakness, and issues in distortion in all the person's relationships.

THE OBJECT OF SIN

Sin has to do with God; it is against God. Were there no God and no relationship to God, there could be no sin. The biblical writings come together to make this point. While there are traces in the Old Testament of a dynamistic system of thought, in which the objectivity of the offense is so extreme that an unwitting ritual offense involves punishable guilt, the main development of thought is otherwise.[1] The ritual gives way to the moral. Assessment in moral terms points toward the God who stands behind the commandment. One may still speak of law, but no longer in a purely formal or juristic sense. By a sheerly objective understanding the emphasis is placed on factual failure in performance, and so on an equivalent reparation. The moral understanding anchors the appeal to the law in the unconditional authority of the covenant God, from whom in principle no sphere of life can be isolated.[2]

The sense of the presence of God as personal transcendent will lay behind the constant struggle of the prophets to resist the erosion of the concept of sin in dynamistic and moralistic understandings. Similarly, in the New Testament sin is understood as against the kingdom of God, against Christ (Matt. 10:33; 11:20, 24; 12:28–32; John 15:18, 23–25) and against the Holy Spirit (Mark 3:28–29). Most fundamentally sin is *asebia*: the sinner acts and wills as though there were no God. Sin as sin "against God" is not a simple unity; it encompasses a great diversity of human dynamics. Sin may be described as denying God the fear and trust God deserves.[3] Thus Paul describes both the root of sin and its flowering in Rom. 14:23: "Whatever does not proceed from faith is sin."

The sinner is against God, but what is the sinner *for*? In turning from God the sinner turns toward something. That something may be something out-

367

5 / SIN AND EVIL

side the self, yielding the phenomenon of idolatry, which receives the condemnation of both Testaments. Indeed, Gerhard von Rad finds in Israel's "awareness of the barrier which men erect between themselves and God by means of images" nothing other than "Israel's greatest achievement."[4] This dynamic can also be described as adultery (Hosea); it means seizing something tangible as directly representing God. That must be diagnosed as sin, despite the elements of world affirmation in the biblical witness. To affirm the world as created and therefore good is not to divinize it, despite the temptation of the nature-religions.[5] Perhaps that temptation is especially difficult to resist because it sets the sinner's quest for security within the control of the self. While the natural object possesses a kind of illusory transcendence in its externality, the self can largely manipulate the relationship to that object.[6]

Or one may speak of the sinner turning from God so as to turn more directly toward the sinner's own self. This is what Reinhold Niebuhr means by sin as pride.[7] Paul Tillich prefers the term "hubris," which is universally human and can appear in acts of humility as well as pride.[8] Hubris amounts to an attempt to deny the limits of finitude. Thus in the Genesis account the temptation to sin is the temptation to claim "knowledge of all things and the mastery over all things and secrets, for here good and evil is not to be understood one-sidedly in a moral sense, but as meaning 'all things.'"[9]

A self seeking to be without limits is a concupiscent self, one that would draw the whole of reality into itself.[10] But such self-expansion does not create self-fulfillment. Sin against God, whose commandment is "for life," becomes sin against the self as well.[11] Nor can the reality of sin be isolated within a God-self relationship insulated from the rest of humankind. The decalogue invokes God in forbidding sins against the neighbor, and the prophets' denunciation of injustice must not be forgotten. The claim on the self is at once a claim for God and neighbor. Sin is lawlessness.[12] Nathan's word from the Lord to the murderous David links these two: ". . . because you have despised me, and have taken the wife of Uriah the Hittite to be your wife" (2 Sam. 12:10).

The persistent tendency to lose this linkage and so to spiritualize sin—which, of course, is precisely to misunderstand the extent of the disrelationship between self and God in sin—has recently called forth a sharp protest from the theologians of liberation. In their view the interior, personal dimension of sin derives from its social and historical character.[13] These theologians certainly identify an important component in emphasizing what José Maria Gonzalez Ruiz has called the "Hamartiosphere," referring to objective oppressive structures which transcend individual agency. We discuss this component in Chapter 3, relating agency and efficacy in the continuity of sin. At this point we are describing the nature of the agency, and on this point

THE NATURE OF SIN

a derivative status for the personal is not the clear testimony of Christian theology. But that the social and the historical dimension requires treatment in any adequate understanding of sin has been made indisputably clear by the theologians of liberation.

Sin is *against* God and the will of God. It is, accordingly, not *from* God. Whence does it come? To that question we must turn, but we pause to draw two inferences from this opening discussion. First, Christian faith is incompatible with *monism*; sin is against God and thus not from God. To speak of sin—as already to speak of creation—is to speak of a relationship or disrelationship between God and an other.[14] In the next chapter, in articulating the bearing of the theme of creation on our topic, we shall grant that in wishing to resist eternal or metaphysical dualisms, Christian reflection may acknowledge or even insist that God bears some responsibility for the origin and issue of all that is real. But such reflection should not lose sight of this: that sin, while emphatically real, is against God and not from God.

Second, Christian faith is incompatible with *moralism*. Sin is against *God*. The objection here is not to the necessary attempt to include other humans in the God-self relationship, but rather to all views that exclude God in the conception of sin. Both friends and foes of Christianity represent this misunderstanding.[15] Indeed, the very tendency to objectify matters in such a way that the Lord is lost in the commandment becomes the target of the Pauline critique of any justification by the works of the law.[16]

In all this it is assumed that humankind, the sinner, knows God. The knowledge of God is discussed elsewhere in this dogmatics, but the understanding of sin as being against God has a contribution to make to that discussion. Briefly, we may note the following components of that contribution.

The biblical materials, classically represented in Paul's indictments in Romans 1—3, do assume sufficient universal knowledge of God to sustain an appeal to responsibility. Yet the problem of cognitive atheism warrants serious consideration in its own terms, without simple reduction to volitional atheism. The will is not to be reduced to the reason, nor fully isolated from it. That sin may take the form of self-deception in culpable ignorance (*agnoema*) does not require us to deny the ambiguity of claims for God. Such ambiguity in the relationship of knowledge may appropriately reflect the character of the participants in the relationship as the epistemological correlate to the ontological character of both divine and human freedom. Accordingly, a simplistically moralistic assessment of cognitive atheism must be resisted. Clearly "the bid is raised," when we consider the revelation of God in Jesus of Nazareth, though the dialectical cautions mentioned above may reappear, if Pascal's sense of the "divine incognito" did not overstate matters too strongly when he wrote, "God is hidden more decisively in the incarnation than in the creation."[17]

5 / SIN AND EVIL

THE AGENT OF SIN

To recognize that sin rises up against God *from an other* is to distinguish Christian reflection from certain historically influential interpretations. Thus we cannot say that sin is nonbeing or privation, since we are not prepared to say the person is unreal. Any confidence in divine victory which so underestimates evil is purchased with inflated currency.

How shall one account for the prevalence of the privation theme? It seems best to view this tradition as entailing an understandable confusion between the formal and the material analysis of sin. As surely as God deserves worship and trust, sin may be described as having the *form* of "missing" (Gk., *hamartia*) or "twisting" (Heb., *awon*). One may even say, though less satisfactorily, that the *material* effect of sin is disruptive, destructive. The negative reference of those adjectives begs for a positive definition of the truly human good. Surely in our time, when the formal notion of varying degrees of being seems counterintuitive and when the holocaust is our mentor materially, it should not be difficult for the reality of sin to warn us against the seductive assurances of the interpretation of sin as privation.

A more subtle form of the same error might be to accede to an anthropological dualism by which the reality of sin is ostensibly acknowledged, but promptly relegated to something less than the essential center of the person. We need to reclaim the biblical meaning of *sarx* as referring to the *whole* earthly person: "We all once lived in the passions of our flesh, following the desires of body and mind" (Eph. 2:3).[18] Perhaps to hold the two together a third is needed: will. That was the point of Kierkegaard's attack on the "Socratic" position of sin as ignorance.[19] Kierkegaard saw this point very clearly—and it needs to be seen, for the gnostic virus in the religious body does not die easily. Yet ironically Kierkegaard may have been so preoccupied with the relationship between reason and will that his own anthropology may lack balance. He aligned the notion of will so closely with that of consciousness that his own notion of a sinful alternative to sinful defiance is somewhat underdeveloped.[20] We shall want to examine that option in a moment. But his desire to locate sin in the self's very center faithfully seeks to resist any tendency toward an anthropological dualism. Our task here is not to develop a full-scale anthropology, though in this and the next chapter we sketch a view that is much in debt to Kierkegaard's voluntarism. What is required of any Christian theologian is to indicate that the entire person is involved in the reality of sin. Such scope is suggested by the biblical emphasis on the unity of the person.[21] An adequate doctrine of sin will, then, be no less complex than a truly descriptive anthropology.

In fact, the biblical writings not only incorporate many different shades of meaning in their portrayal of sin; they also offer an explicit awareness of

THE NATURE OF SIN

these differences and their relationships, as in Job 34:37: "For he adds rebellion (*pesha*) to his sin (*hatta'th*)."[22] Cutting across the richly nuanced understanding of sin in the tradition is a fundamental distinction between what we may call—following Kierkegaard—sins of "weakness" and sins of "strength."

By sins of "strength" we have in mind the classic action of unmitigated conscious defiance. It is clear-eyed rebellion of which we speak—*pesha* or *asebia*. Here the self is assertive with a fist clenched in the face of God. It was this of which Luther wrote, "Man cannot of his nature desire that God should be God; on the contrary, he desires that he himself might be God and that God might not be God."[23] In such sin there is an element of consciousness; the next short step is direct knowledge, and then direct defiance. If one *knows* God, does one not know (have) what it takes to *be* God? Thus in his theses for the Heidelberg Disputation Luther warns that the wisdom which beholds "the invisible things of God as perceived from works—puffs up, blinds, and hardens man altogether."[24] Paul Ricoeur warns against premature syntheses, violent totalizations as the birth of "idols, substituted for the 'Name,' who should remain faceless."[25] While one may demur if the suggestion is made that conscious knowledge of God *entails* conscious defiance, it may be granted that such knowledge seems at least a condition for what Reinhold Niebuhr analyzes as pride or what Tillich describes as "hubris."

This is the understanding of sin that stands out most starkly in Western Christendom. That is not strange, for here the positive "being" of sin, or perhaps even more clearly its "becoming," is most sharply displayed. Indeed, the power of sin in this dynamic has been so dramatically apparent in Western history that sin easily comes to be seen as involving something more and other than the self. There arises a tendency toward a *theological* dualism in which the sinner is no longer personally responsible but is seen rather as the helpless victim of an alien power. Thus the Kittel article on sin in the New Testament traces the development of sin as an individual act through sin as a determination of human nature to sin as a personal power, as in Rom. 7:14–20:

> We know that the law is spiritual; but I am carnal, sold under sin. I do not understand my actions. For I do not do what I want, but I do the very thing I hate. Now if I do what I do not want, I agree that the law is good. So then it is no longer I that do it, but sin which dwells in me. For I know that nothing good dwells within me, that is, in my flesh. I can will what is right, but I cannot do it. For I do not do the good I want, but the evil I do not want is what I do. Now if I do what I do not want, it is no longer I that do it, but sin which dwells within me.[26]

Clearly some account of the bondage of sin is required of us. It will not do to regard such talk as a fanciful extension of the self's capacity to objectify itself.[27] Fuller consideration of the demonic in itself will be deferred to a discus-

5 / SIN AND EVIL

sion of the origin of sin. Here we are concerned with the demonic in relation to the human experience of sin. In this context the demonic must be considered as far as the temptation to sin and the results of sin are concerned. The agency intervening between temptation and result is our immediate topic in this subsection; here the consensus of Christian reflection resists any reference to the demonic that would compromise the reality of human responsibility. Even the bondage of which we must speak below must be understood to affirm human responsibility.

Hans Conzelmann has collected the "hints" regarding the satanic as the tempter (as 1 Thess. 3:5), the seducer (Acts 5:3), the hinderer (2 Thess. 2:18), the unleasher of persecution (1 Pet. 5:8-9), as the one who has the power of death (Heb. 2:14), who holds the kingdoms of this world (Luke 4:5-6), and who can change himself into an angel of light (2 Cor. 11:14). He concludes:

> There is no question of reconstructing a "New Testament doctrine of Satan" from these hints. They are simply fragments. For example, the devil acts in the passion, but his work there has no significance for theological understanding. No account is taken of him in the description of God's rule. Paul outlines man's position before God, the nature of sin, judgment and salvation, without using the idea of Satan (Rom. 5; cf. on the other hand the account in the Wisdom of Solomon). In the New Testament, Satan is not a being with whom one can explain, e.g., sin and death. He is the evil one against whom precautions must be taken, and who is driven away by the confession of faith.[28]

Whatever we shall make of the tempter's role in the origin of sin, in the primeval account the human pair come to bear the consequences of their own deeds. At best one might speak of the demonic and the human as conjunctive causes in the evil that comes into God's good world. The Lutheran confessions, for example, use such a construction, as when Article XI of the Epitome of the Formula of Concord speaks of the source of sin as "the devil and man's wicked and perverse will."

In any case, Christian reflection concerning the demonic does not challenge, but rather supports and strengthens, our understanding of sin as will against will. It is will *against* God, as Article XI of the Formula puts it: "Everything which prepares and fits man for damnation emanates from the devil and man through sin, and in no way from God" (*BC* 629). And it is *created* will against the Creator. The Fourth Lateran Council (1215) put the point in these terms in confessing that the true God is one alone and eternal: "For the devil and other demons were created by God good in nature, but they themselves through themselves have become wicked."[29]

Of course, human freedom is not without its social, historical, and natural roots. Freedom could not be efficacious if it were not related precisely to that which is other than itself. But in this very rootedness, in this relatedness, resides the possibility of temptation of the self by that which is outside the self.[30] This can be put very strongly in some Christian circles, as when the explanation to the second article in Luther's Large Catechism says: "When we were created by God the Father, and had received from him all kinds of good things, the devil came and led us into disobedience, sin, death, and all evil" (*BC* 414). Yet the explanation continues by immediately claiming that it is *we* who accordingly "lay under God's wrath and displeasure, doomed to eternal damnation, as we had deserved." Human responsibility is here intact. Human sin occurs through external temptation, but not through external coercion.

The sheer reality of defiant human will is such a challenge to understanding that it is not strange that the "clearer" position of an eternal dualism seems attractive, as in the rabbinic speculation on Gen. 6:5, which excuses humankind because of the evil imagination implanted in human hearts after the "sons of God" took to themselves "the daughters of man."[31] But Paul Ricoeur seems right in contending that Christian symbolism of evil represents a choice of the Adamic myth, though it may incorporate "tragic" elements. Regin Prenter summarizes the dynamic that drives Christian thought to such incorporation of the tragic: "Because sin, understood as man's rebellion against creation, is the absolutely unexplainable reality, it is without any presupposition (original sin). Original sin, understood as the unexplainable and all embracing reality, is itself the indispensable presupposition for the Christian message concerning creation and redemption."[32]

We agree: the very experience of our "actual" sin requires that we repair to the topic of original sin; that movement is no heteronomous dogmatism. It is the logic of this chapter which leads to the next chapter's discussion of original sin. But it may be questioned whether our description of that experience of actual sin is not incomplete even in its own terms as yet. That is, the difficulty with the notion of sin as defiant will, as the sin of strength, may not be so much its conceptual dissonance as its empirical deficiency. Who sins so, after all? Apart from the brooding existentialist in the dark garret, who musters so mighty a charge on the gates of heaven? One may suspect the answer is that *we* do, we *all* do. The stress on defiance is not unempirical. Yet much of our failing seems less flamboyant. We need to recognize what may be called sins of weakness.

The largest amount of biblical material referring to sin does not support a strict identification with consciously willed defiance. The most frequently used words are the Hebrew *hatta'th* and the Greek *harmartia*, with which the Septuagint usually translates *hatta'th*. Of *hatta'th* Gottfried Quell writes: "This word conveyed a clear objective picture to the mind, with no reference to the inner quality of sinful behavior."[33] Eichrodt has noted that in the preprophetic period "the Israelite concept of sin was primarily concerned with establishing an objective offence. . . . *All the emphasis falls on the objective*

5 / SIN AND EVIL

offence, while the sinful will of the person involved manifestly plays no part." [34] Eichrodt seems to devalue this material in speaking in this connection of "the after-effects of a dynamistic system of thought," but he does not dispute its presence and prevalence. Ricoeur takes these materials more seriously in noting "the decisive fact that those archaic modes of behavior were *resumed* after the ethical stage represented by propheticism":

> It seems to me that this resumption, this resurgence of a postethical ritualism, so to speak, cannot be understood unless we take as our point of departure the project of a consistent and voluntary heteronomy. The esotericism of the rite bears witness to conscience that conscience is not the source of the Law, since the Law is not transparent to conscience. [35]

May it be that this Old Testament material, despite its tendency toward prepersonal tragic defilement talk, is not so recessive, formal, and pictorial after all?

The New Testament material may shift the emphasis, if Gustav Stählin is right that it follows the Septuagint usage of *hamartia*, where the term "first came to have the moral and religious quality which it lacked, both in the rapidly changing Greek of common speech and in the 'tragic' language of Aristotle, and to indicate guilt as the outcome of an evil will, an evil purpose, i.e., of a conscious rebellion against God and contradiction of him (equals *adikia*)." [36] Yet Stählin notes that aside from John and Paul the word is always used in the plural and that the emphasis is on single acts, and he cites considerable Johannine material which seems more like the synoptic stress on *sins* than on the Pauline understanding of sin as a positive force alienating from God. Such usage does not readily suggest the unified inwardness of defiance. Must this biblical material be understood simply as the underdeveloped raw material of the prophetic and Pauline emphasis on consciously defiant will, or does it deserve consideration as an alternative dynamic within the complex reality of sin?

Kierkegaard's discussion of "sins of weakness" depends on his notion of the self as a synthesis of necessity and possibility that relates itself to itself in freedom. God's will for that self is not only that God be trusted, as if that could be done almost impersonally and passively, but that "by relating itself to its own self and by willing to be itself the self is grounded transparently in the Power which posited it." [37] Thus it becomes possible to discern a twofold structure to sin. As Wanda Warren Berry has put it, "One can lose the relationship either by negating God in defiant 'strength' or by negating the self in weakly refusing to constitute a gathered will." [38]

This latter notion seems to fit the conventional idea of sins of omission, just as defiant strength is a matter of commission. Moreover, this category seems helpful in evaluating the contemporary human predicament. Omission will be a particularly crucial category in a time when a more static conception of reality and of God's claim within reality gives way to a recognition of the thoroughly temporal character of life. Without endorsing every rebellion or designating every development divine, one may in such a time be more sensitive to the sinfulness of clinging to past formulations of thought and life.[39] The crucial determiners of contemporary life seem beyond the control of any individual. One's sin in such a state seems to be collaboration in anonymous injustice, as the theologians of liberation have not failed to point out.[40]

Even in an apparently impersonal age the sense of innocent helplessness may depend on a capacity for self-deception. But the self's very exercise of that self-deception seems to yield a weakened self.[41] This is the sin of weakness. This may make some sense of the interpretation of sin as privation or nonbeing, beyond the formal sense of nonconformity, of which we spoke earlier.

There is will in such sin. But if God's call is to become a particular synthesis of givenness and possibility, to acquire continuity by "making a decision and renewing it," [42] then the will to decline God's call will manifest itself in the diffuse swamp of immediacy of which we have been speaking. The synoptic emphasis on the plurality of sins fits this category. The self does not gather itself, even defiantly. One might even consider the biblical emphasis on lack of consciousness, even on unwitting defilement—which seems both post- and preprophetic—as fitting the decision to decline the call to a particular synthesis. There is motion here, but not gathered movement toward that to which God calls.[43]

Indeed, perhaps the will that acts in such weakness and the will more starkly on display in defiance are not unrelated to each other. Clinical psychoanalysis suggests that pride and self-contempt are often mutually fortifying companions.[44] At least they are together in being the pathological agency that is sin.

THE EFFICACY OF SIN

Whither, then, sin? As a "positive" act of will, as something totally other than "nonbeing," sin is "effective"; it brings about effects. It is against God, and it affects God. Here the categories of guilt and wrath apply. The psalmist finds the one blessed "unto whom the Lord imputes not iniquity" and the Pauline speech about God's judgment of human guilt echoes the psalmist's cry (Ps. 32:1-4; 51:1-4; Rom. 1:20, 2:2, 3:19-20). Guilt belongs to humankind; indeed, it belongs to the individual sinner, for here the symbolism of evil reaches a deeply personal level. But this is no mere subjective intrapsychic reality to be banished by the analyst's wand—though such there surely are.[45] The sinner is guilty before God, and God is wrathful toward the sinner. Yahweh refuses to go in the midst of Israel because they are a stiff-necked people who

5 / SIN AND EVIL

would be consumed at once (Exod. 33:3–5). When God shines the light of the divine presence on hidden human faults, sinners are consumed in God's anger (Ps. 90:7–8).

Is this biblical reference to the wrath of God to be set aside as a hopelessly anthropomorphic category, because God is purely and simply Love? That God's love is pure is central to Christian faith, but it does not follow that it is a simple thing to love sinners. Sin does create something in God: wrath.[46] But sin does not create God; it cannot make God over in its own image. Indeed, perhaps it is best to think of God's wrath as letting sin be precisely what it is. The act of sin in its reality and so its efficaciousness produces a destiny. Particularly in the Old Testament this sense of correspondence between crime and punishment plays a role, though not an unchallenged one.[47] This sense of nemesis in history, of divine judgment active in life, depends on the theme of God's continuing activity in the world. Our task here is to recognize that the biblical witness calls for such a notion in understanding God's reaction to sin. As the persistent Pauline theme has it: "For the wrath of God is revealed from heaven against all ungodliness and wickedness of men. . . . Therefore God gave them up in the lusts of their hearts to impurity . . . to dishonorable passions . . . to a base mind and to improper conduct" (Rom. 1:18–32). Two statements seem required here: sin produces its own effect, *and* that producing passes not only into God but through God back into the world.[48]

But God's reaction to sin is not to be likened to the mechanical functioning of a pipeline for sin's self-destructive tendencies. The fuller biblical witness speaks of God's action in freedom toward what God receives from the world. Thus Hosea:

> How can I give you up, O Ephraim! . . .
> My heart recoils within me,
>   my compassion grows warm and tender,
> I will not execute my fierce anger,
>   I will not again destroy Ephraim;
> for I am God and not man,
>   the Holy One in your midst,
>   and I will not come to destroy.
>
> (Hos. 11:8–9)

Judgments following disobedience are no mechanical system. Gerhard von Rad makes that clear:

Certainly, the Old Testament tells of many judgments which overtook the disobedient nation. But who was their author? Was it the Law? It was God himself acting on Israel, and not a legal system of salvation which worked out according to a prearranged plan. In particular, it was God himself who always remained

Lord even over Israel's sin, and whose judgments even the pre-exilic prophets—and their successors even more clearly than they—represented as being at the same time evidence of his faithfulness to his chosen people.[49]

That God is Lord even over sin does indeed anticipate the witness in the New Testament to the decisive divine response to the human predicament.

Whatever one may say soteriologically regarding God's lordship over sin, it cannot be denied that sin is efficacious. One might even say that through sin a world is made. We have been speaking of how sin yields effects in the sinner. A completely episodic account of this reality is manifestly inadequate. At least the cumulative character of action must be recognized. In the words of John: "Every one who commits sin is a slave to sin" (John 8:34). Kierkegaard can hardly be charged with ignoring the event-character of human existence but he recognizes that precisely the positive character of the act of sin yields something more:

> Is not sin precisely the discontinuous? Lo, here we have again the notion that sin is merely a negation to which one can acquire no title, as one can acquire no title to stolen property, a negation, an impotent attempt to give itself consistency, which nevertheless, suffering as it does from the torture of impotence in the defiance of despair, it is not able to do. Yes, so it is speculatively; but Christianly . . . sin is a position which out of itself develops a more and more positive continuity. And the law for the growth of this continuity is moreover different from the law which applies to a debt or to a negation. For a debt does not grow because it is not paid, it grows every time it is added to. But sin grows every instant one does not get out of it.[50]

Our contemporary sense for the particularity of events may be so keen that it is difficult for us to grasp the coming-to-be of a state or a condition. Yet this is what is required of us to locate rightly the depth of sin. Perhaps one might say that in the case of sins of strength the state grows precisely because it does yield defiant acts, while in the case of sins of weakness the state grows because the call of God to becoming a self is not heeded. In neither case does the will to commit or to omit sin begin with a clean slate. In any case the biblical writers do recognize a "continuity in sin," particularly in Paul, whose advance on the synoptic stress on individual sins and even on the Johannine stress on the condition of sin yields a personification of sin as a power, as Gustav Stählin notes:

> Thus, dwelling in man (Rom. 7:17, 20) and bringing forth passions (7:5) and lust (7:8), sin obtains mastery over him, as a demonic power. Man is under sin (Rom. 3:9; Gal. 3:22; cf. Rom. 11:32), as a slave (Rom. 6:16, 20; John 8:34; cf. Gal. 2:17), sold to it (Rom. 7:14), in bondage to it (Rom. 6:6), under its law (7:23, 25; 8:3), presenting parts of his body to it as instruments of unrighteousness (6:13).[51]

5 / SIN AND EVIL

The sinful act of will yields cumulatively a sinful state of willing; sin yields sin which yields sins. Sin, then, makes a world *in* the *sinner.* But surely sin also makes a world *for* the *creature.* The effects of sin do not rest tidily with their individual makers. Selves do not exist in insulated tubes of becoming; they exist in relationships, and it is those relationships which make up the world. Whither sin? The sin and sins of selves enter the world to yield a solidarity in sin. No self begins with a clean slate; it is born into this world with its racism, sexism, profit-oriented economy, consumerism, and so forth.

But the biblical authors seem to speak of solidarity in sin in a still stronger sense. Eichrodt notes:

> [The prophets] bring not only their own contemporaries before God's judgment, and denounce them for their rebellion, but also see them linked with all previous generations in a unitary entity, for which the sins of the fathers are also the sins of those now alive, and will be required of them, while at the same time the fact that the sinful condition of the present generation has resulted from the perverted direction of an earlier one in no sense does away with the responsibility of the former group.[52]

Here we seem to move through a solidarity of effect to a solidarity of agency. The "whither" of sin seems to yield a "whence" for sin. In Chapter 3 we will discuss more fully the very considerable reflections of the church on the subject of such connectedness in agency. Obviously there we must consider the relationship between "original sin originated and original sin originating" and varying theories as to how humankind stands together before God in sin. But even in this chapter in considering "actual" sin as act and state, we come to issues which drive us to anticipate that later discussion. Beyond what has already been discussed, two points may be mentioned: the universality of actual sin and the inevitability of actual sin.

A familiar biblical refrain is "There is no man who does not sin" (1 Kings 8:46; 2 Chron. 6:36), "None is righteous, no, not one" (Rom. 3:10). Even those who may be said to be righteous (as Noah and Job) are such not because they are without sin but because they are in relationship with God. This judgment of universality seems more than a striking statistical consensus. The sense of inevitability builds in the prophetic materials of the Old Testament. Thus von Rad points out that Ezekiel is concerned to demonstrate the "total dominion" of sin: "It is not a matter of separate transgressions, nor simply of the failure of one generation, but of a deepseated inability to obey, indeed of a resistance to God which made itself manifest on the very day that Israel came into being."[53] At times this inevitability seems to be associated with active willing, which we have spoken of as sins of strength.

Yet there may be a sense in which those reformers who minimized the role of active will were right in their view of original sin. Without our consent,

THE NATURE OF SIN

sin ineluctably separates us from God.⁵⁴ Still, the "I" is other than an innocent victim in some mechanical march of sin. One may exorcise the will too readily, particularly if will does not entail contingency. Perhaps the will at work in what we have called the sin of weakness may help us approach the notion of truly personal yet noncontingent will. In any case, in speaking of inevitability Christians do not intend to give up responsibility, as Reinhold Niebuhr makes clear.⁵⁵ Hans Conzelmann finds that concern to be faithful to the theology of the New Testament: "I am not relieved of responsibility for myself through the *servitude* of my *arbitrium*. I may be subjected to an alien power and incapable of freeing myself, but the seat of my actions is still myself. It is I who bring about the compulsion of sin."⁵⁶

What we have brought together here is clearly an unstable mixture. We seem to have arrived at something like Augustine's "I had willingly come to be what I unwillingly found myself to be"—though even that formulation may permit an easing of the tension through a temporal parceling out of the dynamics.⁵⁷ While we may not be able to resolve the tension, clearly more must be said. Paul Ricoeur is right in claiming that the concept of the servile will is not directly accessible and depends on other symbolism for the filling out of its content.⁵⁸

Niebuhr found the clue to responsibility-despite-inevitability in the situation of the creature as finite freedom.⁵⁹ We turn in the next chapter to the discussion of the absolute origin of sin, the first sin, in order to isolate the essential components and dynamics in the coming-to-be of sin over against that which is not sin. But for us sin does not come to be as an interruption of a course well begun. Indeed, many of the biblical references and much of the church's reflection concerning the inevitability of sin refer to some kind of givenness at birth: "that which is born of the flesh is flesh" (John 3:6; cf., of course, Ps. 51:7).

Where does sin end? Christian faith wishes to say that it ends in the broken and risen body of our Lord. This is hardly the place to develop this point, but it needs to be sounded, however abruptly. We do not speak here of the *whence* of sin. While sin ends in the Christ, it does not begin there. It ends well, there—at least that is the confidence of the blessed who cry out on Easter Eve: "O happy crime which merited such and so great a redeemer." But in this saying one's temporal location does matter. Sin does not begin well, for its being is against God. But in our "second-order" reflection about sin, we may indeed take our bearings by the decisive divine response to sin. This is true most fundamentally of the act of God in Christ in its emphatic quality and universality of scope. It is true as well of such subordinate "divine response" themes as the virgin birth and infant baptism which have assumed a kind of primacy in the life of Christian people.⁶⁰

It is not strange that sin should be understood most clearly through the

5 / SIN AND EVIL

remedy made available by divine faithfulness. This is not a challenge to the anti-monistic emphasis which has prevailed in this chapter's discussion of the nature of sin. Sin is *against* God. But it turns out that *God is against sin* and has contrived to deal with it. Sin is most clearly understood when viewed from the perspective the divine response provides.

NOTES

1. Walther Eichrodt, *Theology of the Old Testament*, trans. J. A. Baker, 2 vols. (Philadelphia: Westminster Press, 1961–67), 2:382. Cf. Paul Ricoeur, *The Symbolism of Evil*, trans. Emerson Buchanan (Boston: Beacon Press, 1967), p. 48.
2. Eichrodt, *Theology of the O. T.*, 2:383.
3. Article II, The Augsburg Confession. Cf. Luther's famous explanation of the first commandment in his Large Catechism.
4. Gerhard von Rad, *Old Testament Theology*, trans. D. M. G. Stalker, 2 vols. (New York: Harper & Row, 1962–65), 2:340.
5. Ibid., p. 339.
6. Wolfhart Pannenberg, *What Is Man?* trans. Duane A. Priebe (Philadelphia: Fortress Press, 1970), p. 35.
7. Reinhold Niebuhr, *The Nature and Destiny of Man*, 2 vols. (New York: Charles Scribner's Sons, 1941–43).
8. Paul Tillich, *Systematic Theology*, 3 vols. (Chicago: University of Chicago Press, 1951–63), 2:50. Luther also emphasized the sins of the pious. See Albrecht Peters, *Glaube und Werk: Luthers Rechtfertigungslehre im Lichte der Heiligen Schrift* (Berlin: Lutherisches Verlagshaus, 1962), pp. 147–51.
9. Von Rad, *Old Testament Theology*, 1:155. Cf. Dietrich Bonhoeffer's reference to the prohibition showing Adam his limit in his creatureliness, *Creation and Fall*, trans. John Fletcher (New York: Macmillan Co.; London: SCM Press, 1959), p. 52. In *Images of Good and Evil*, trans. Michael Bullock (London: Routledge & Kegan Paul, 1952), pp. 17–19, Martin Buber criticizes this "favorite" interpretation (and others) and settles for this: " 'Knowledge of good and evil' means nothing else than cognizance of the opposites which the early literature of mankind designated . . . the opposites latent in creation."
10. Tillich, *Systematic Theology*, 2:52.
11. Rudolf Bultmann, *Theology of the New Testament*, trans. Kendrick Grobel, 2 vols. (New York: Charles Scribner's Sons, 1954–55), 1:232.
12. For a development of this Johannine theme (1 John 3:4), see Werner Elert, *The Structure of Lutheranism*, trans. W. A. Hansen 2 vols. (St. Louis: Concordia Publishing House, 1962), 1:33.
13. Gustavo Gutierrez, *A Theology of Liberation*, trans. and ed. Sister Caridad Inda and John Eagelson (Maryknoll, N.Y.: Orbis Books, 1973), p. 175. Cf. Dorothee Soelle, *Political Theology*, trans. John Shelley (Philadelphia: Fortress Press, 1974), p. 90.
14. Ricoeur, *Symbolism of Evil*, p. 143.

15. Søren Kierkegaard, *The Sickness unto Death*, trans. W. Lowrie (Princeton: Princeton University Press, 1941; Anchor Books), p. 213 (emphasis his). Cf. Ricoeur, *Symbolism of Evil*, p. 52.

16. Ricoeur, *Symbolism of Evil*, p. 143: ". . . that in it [scrupulousness] which had not been felt as fault, becomes fault; the attempt to reduce sin by observance becomes sin. That is the real meaning of the curse of the law."

17. Kierkegaard cites Pascal to this effect in *Papirer*, ed. P. A. Heiberg and Victor Kuhr, 11 vols. (Copenhagen: Gyldendals, 1909-48), X 3 A 626, and adds his own development of the theme.

18. See Werner Georg Kümmel in *Man in the New Testament*, trans. John J. Vincent (London: Epworth Press, 1963), p. 84. Bultmann (*Theology of the N. T.*, 1:209) has argued against any attempt to split up the self by appeal to the various Greek terms Paul uses.

19. Kierkegaard, *Sickness unto Death*, pp. 220-21.

20. Ibid., p. 162: "Generally speaking, consciousness, i.e., consciousness of self, is the decisive criterion of the self. The more consciousness, the more self; the more consciousness, the more will, and the more will, the more self." For a correction of this tendency from within Kierkegaard, see Wanda Warren Berry, "Images of Sin and Salvation in Feminist Theology," *AThR* 60 (January 1978): 25-54.

21. As Eichrodt, *Theology of the O. T.*, 2:147.

22. Cf. Jer. 33:8; Lev. 16:21.

23. *Disputatio contra scholasticam* (1517), *WA* 1:225. See also Gerhard Ebeling, *Luther*, trans. R. A. Wilson (Philadelphia: Fortress Press, 1970), chap. 13; and Peters, *Glaube und Werk*, pp. 142, 146.

24. Heidelberg Thesis 22. See also theses 19 and 21.

25. Paul Ricoeur, "Guilt, Ethics, and Religion," in *Talk of God*, Royal Institute of Philosophy Lectures (London: Macmillan & Co., 1969), vol. 2 (1967-68), pp. 115-16. Ricoeur is developing Kant's critique (in *Religion within the Limits of Reason Alone* [New York: Harper & Row, 1960]) of the reconciliation of virtue and happiness.

26. Walter Grundmann, "Sin in the New Testament," in Gerhard Kittel, *Sin*, in *Bible Key Words*, trans. and ed. J. R. Coates (New York: Harper & Brothers, 1951), pp. 64-87.

27. As Bultmann does, *Theology of the N. T.*, 1:195.

28. Hans Conzelmann, *An Outline of the Theology of the New Testament*, trans. John Bowden (New York: Harper & Row, 1969), p. 18.

29. Cf. Denzinger, 427, 237. See also C. K. Barrett, *From First Adam to Last* (New York: Charles Scribner's Sons, 1962), pp. 12-13.

30. Gordon Kaufman, *Systematic Theology: A Historicist Perspective* (New York: Charles Scribner's Sons, 1968), pp. 355-56.

31. N. P. Williams, *The Ideas of the Fall and of Original Sin* (New York and London: Longmans, Green & Co., 1927), chap. 2.

32. Regin Prenter, *Creation and Redemption*, trans. Theodore I. Jensen (Philadelphia: Fortress Press, 1967), p. 284. For Ricoeur's distinction, see *Symbolism of Evil*, chap. 5.

33. Gottfried Quell, "Sin in the Old Testament," in Kittel, *Sin*, pp. 1-32.

5 / SIN AND EVIL

34. Eichrodt, *Theology of the O. T.*, 2:381 (emphasis his). Cf. von Rad's discussion of subjectively guiltless sin in *Old Testament Theology*, 1:267.

35. Ricoeur, *Symbolism of Evil*, p. 135. Cf. in *Talk of God*, p. 104: "Stain was still external contagion, sin already the rupture of a relation; but this rupture exists even if I do not know it; sin is a real condition, an objective situation."

36. Gustav Stählin, "Greek Usage," in Kittel, *Sin*, pp. 46-52.

37. Kierkegaard, *Sickness unto Death*, pp. 146-47.

38. Berry, "Images of Sin and Salvation," p. 46.

39. Bernard Häring, *Sin in the Secular Age* (Garden City, N.Y.: Doubleday & Co., 1974), p. 18.

40. Soelle, *Political Theology*, p. 89.

41. Berry, "Images of Sin and Salvation," p. 46.

42. This formulation is from Kierkegaard's *Concluding Unscientific Postscript to the Philosophical Fragments*, trans. David F. Swenson and Walter Lowrie (Princeton: Princeton University Press, 1944), p. 277, although the theme is already suggested in his earlier work, *Repetition*.

43. See F. R. Tennant, *The Concept of Sin* (Cambridge: At the University Press, 1912), chaps. 5 and 6; and Friedrich Schleiermacher, *The Christian Faith*, trans. H. R. Mackintosh and J. S. Stewart (New York: Harper & Row, Harper Torchbooks, 1963), pp. 291-304.

44. See, e.g., Karen Horney, *Neurosis and Human Growth* (New York: W. W. Norton & Co., 1950), p. 341.

45. See Ricoeur's masterful discussion of guilt, *Symbolism of Evil*, chap. 3, in which Greek, Judaic, and Christian conceptions are distinguished and related. Cf. Grundmann, "Sin in the N. T.," p. 79.

46. Jürgen Moltmann, *The Crucified God*, trans. R. A. Wilson and John Bowden (London: SCM Press, 1974), p. 272, drawing on the thought of Abraham Heschel, writes: "His wrath is injured love and therefore a mode of his reaction to men. Love is the source and basis of the possibility of the wrath of God. . . . As injured love, the wrath of God is not something that is inflicted, but a divine suffering of evil. It is a sorrow which goes through his opened heart."

47. Von Rad, *Old Testament Theology*, 2:73-74. For a discussion of this theme from a more systematic standpoint, see Langdon Gilkey's *Reaping the Whirlwind: A Christian Interpretation of History* (New York: Seabury Press, 1976), pp. 253-65. Cf. Klaus Koch, "Gibt es ein Vergeltungsdogma in Alten Testament?" *ZThK* 3 (1955): 1-42. For a brief discussion of Koch's view, see W. Sibley Towner, *How God Deals with Evil* (Philadelphia: Westminster Press, 1976), pp. 48-50.

48. There is also the sense in which divine wrath not only reveals sin as what it is but makes it more what it is—the hatred of God. For this strand in Luther's thought, see Peters, *Glaube und Werk*, p. 154.

49. Von Rad, *Old Testament Theology*, 2:405-6. Thus the Priestly writer has God giving Noah and his sons a new blessing (Gen. 9:1ff.) and the Yahwist suggests a divine resolution of grief (6:5ff.) in mercy (8:21-22).

50. Kierkegaard, *Sickness unto Death*, pp. 236-37.

51. Stählin, "Greek Usage," p. 51.

52. Eichrodt, *Theology of the O. T.*, 2:407. See A. M. Dubarle, *The Biblical Doctrine of Original Sin*, trans. E. M. Stewart (London: Geoffrey Chapman, 1964), pp. 34ff., for an application of connectedness to contemporaries.

53. Von Rad, *Old Testament Theology*, 2:229. Cf. Eichrodt, *Theology of the O. T.*, 2:394.

54. Holsten Fagerberg, *A New Look at the Lutheran Confessions*, trans. Gene J. Lund (St. Louis: Concordia Publishing House, 1972), p. 143: "According to Catholic theologians sin was not sin unless carried out with the consent of the will. To speak meaningfully of sin requires that man can be held responsible for his actions. . . . The reformers, on the other hand, saw in sin something which ineluctably separates man from God. . . . To speak of will and the freedom of the will in this context is evidently meaningless."

55. Niebuhr, *Nature and Destiny of Man*, 1:255–60.

56. Conzelmann, *Outline of the Theology of the N. T.*, p. 255 (emphasis his). Elert, *Structure of Lutheranism*, pp. 34–35, traces suggestions of the "tragic synthesis of destiny and guilt" "even in Kant and Schiller."

57. *Confessions*, bk. 8, chap. 5.

58. Ricoeur, *Symbolism of Evil*, p. 151.

59. Niebuhr, *Nature and Destiny of Man*, p. 251.

60. Jaroslav Pelikan, *The Emergence of the Catholic Tradition (100–600)* (Chicago: University of Chicago Press, 1971), p. 286, and Denzinger, 102 (Carthage, 418) on virgin birth and infant baptism; L. Sabourin, "Original Sin Reappraised," *Biblical Theology Bulletin* 3 (1973): 51–81, and Fagerberg, *A New Look*, p. 143, on redemption/justification.

2

The Origin of Sin

The nature of sin points to the origin of sin in a fall, a human reality disrupting the integral goodness of the creature. As the object of God's special creative endowment, the creature is good; as one called in finite freedom to God's special intention, the creature is not yet perfect, but able to be tempted and able to sin; and in the mystery of freedom, the creature originates sin.

CREATION AND FALL

The Christian struggle to diagnose, if not understand, the nature of sin has led the faithful to speak of the origin of sin. There are two steps in such speech: (1) the absolute origin of sin in the "fall"; (2) the proximate origin of sin in the connectedness of humankind. Thus one speaks of the distinction between "original sin originating" and "original sin originated." Or less abstractly, both themes are held together in single sentences, as when the fathers at the Council of Carthage in 418 reject the opponents of infant baptism who suppose that infants "draw nothing of the original sin from Adam" and the confessors at Augsburg teach that "since the fall of Adam all men who are born according to the course of nature are conceived and born in sin."[1] Or more concretely still, in the *locus classicus* of Rom. 5:12 Paul writes: "Therefore as sin came into the world through one man and death through sin, and so death spread to all men because all men sinned."

Sin comes into the world . . . death spreads . . . all sin. In this chapter we pose the question of the absolute origin of sin. Why must Christians raise this question? Sin is so pervasive a reality that the issue of origin, though latent in this as in any phenomenon, might be set aside. To ask, "Why sin?" seems almost like asking, "Why anything at all?" Why not recognize that sin presents its credentials simply by its omnipresence and then get on with the warfare against sin? It is because of God that Christians must speak of the origin of sin.

Faith in God yields the distinction between creation and fall. The intentionality of the distinction represents a choice of what Paul Ricoeur has called the Adamic myth that roots sin in human freedom over against the tragic

5 / SIN AND EVIL

myth that roots sin in divine decree and the theogonic myth that roots sin in an eternal dualism.² We shall follow out this intentionality in three respects: (1) the distinction between creation and *falling* with respect to the *reality* of evil, (2) the distinction between creation and *fallenness* with respect to the *continuity* of evil, and (3) the distinction between creation and the *fall* with respect to the *negativity* of evil.

The intention of Christian faith in God requires us to move fully through this series of distinctions—though the three are not on the same level of immediacy. The commitment of the Christian tradition is clear on this point. It is also clear that this commitment is an exceedingly difficult one for modern people to make, since it seems to fly in the face of much of what contemporary science tells us of the history of the race. Since the contemporary Christian can hardly relinquish either the contemporary pole or the Christian pole, reflection on this matter is mandatory if we are not to be split in two by appeal to a double truth theory. Here we turn to the tradition to analyze the intentionality of the three distinctions showing *why* in each case the distinction matters and *that* it drives us toward an absolute origin of evil in "the fall." Next we will show *how* the distinctions can be stated intelligibly for the contemporary sensibility without sacrificing the concerns of the tradition.

Faith in God leads the Christian to the distinction between creation and fall. Christians claim superiority for this God, not superiority to other gods, there being none, but to other life, there being some. God is not only other than we and all else that is not God, but God is superior. It is not moral superiority to which we refer. To compare God to us by appeal to a moral standard is to insult God. Charles Hartshorne has seen the point clearly:

> The superiority of deity to all others cannot (in accordance with established word usage) be expressed by indefinite descriptions, such as "immensely good," "very powerful," or even "best" or "most powerful," but must be a superiority of principle, a definite conceptual divergence from every other being, actual or so much as possible. We may call this divergence "categorical supremacy." ³

One of the ways in which Christians appeal to such categorical supremacy is in speaking of God as Creator. Because of God, Christians refuse any ultimate dualism, even if that refusal drives them to such awkward abstractions as *creatio ex nihilo*. Nothing at all comes into being without God. Christian reflection assigns as *ontological* superiority to God, the Creator.

This theme is essential, but an obvious question interrupts the hymn to the Creator. If God is the maker of heaven and earth, how can anything as real as sin slip past God's creative hand? Must not this too come from God? Yet two considerations weigh heavily against such a conclusion: The superiority of God is sensed as carrying *moral* as well as ontological meaning. Faith cries out: "Give thanks unto the Lord, for he is *good*; his steadfast love endures for ever" (Ps. 107:1). This does not imply that there is some eternal principle of goodness to which both God and humankind are subservient. But while it is God's creative will that determines what "good" means materially for God's creatures, this God does work for that good. God is for us, but sin is not. Moreover, sin is against God, not just indirectly by being against the creatures God loves, but with violent directness. Sin is an assault on the goodness of God. Perhaps that character is most clear to faith in what sin does to the Anointed One of God and in what God does to sin through that One.

Somehow, thus, a distinction is required of faith. God is Creator, but clearly sin is not from God, but against God and the creatures of God. One must grant that the tradition does not always make this distinction. Even the soteriological center in which the distinction seems so clear does not always control the work of theologians. Thus one may find that a more dualistic tendency in atonement thinking and a more monistic one in matters of theodicy exist side by side.[4] As to theodicy, it is as if the fathers of the church followed the attractive note of God's ontological superiority and, somehow swallowing all the objections welling up within, appealed to none other than God as the ultimate author of what we call evil. Thus for the writer of Isa. 45:7 the God who can say, "I am the Lord and there is no other, besides me there is no God" is the God who has to say: "I form the light and create darkness, I make weal and create woe, I am the Lord, who do all these things."[5]

There is more than one way in which this can be done. One can opt for monism stridently with Augustine and Calvin by arguing for a doctrine of double predestination, a move which the Second Council of Orange (529) rebuffs in violent terms: "We not only do not believe that some have been truly predestined to evil by divine power, but also with every execration we pronounce anathema upon those, if there are any such, who wish to believe so great an evil."[6] Perhaps a subtler form of this same dynamic can be seen in a theological concept of the human person, such that sin—whether or not it is to be regarded as particularly grievous—*must* occur sooner or later. Or one may try for a more obscure connection with God by linking sin with Satan, who not only tempts but seduces humankind but who must himself be none other than "God's devil."[7] Of Satan there must indeed be speech in this discussion, but it is clear already from Chapter 1 that such speech is of one who is against God.

Despite the presence of this monistic strand which would collapse the distinction between creation and fall, faith remembers the two themes just mentioned: the moral superiority of God who is for us, as sin is not, and the against-Godness of sin. Faith knows a third thing as well. Sin is against

5 / SIN AND EVIL

me, but it is also *by me*. The stubborn sense of responsibility points the way toward some kind of free-will defense. God's love for human creatures entails the risks the gift of creaturely freedom bears. This, in turn, permits the quest for a cause for sin to appeal to the free "falling" of creatures, if not to *a* race-shackling fall. In this appeal the distinction between sin and God's good work of creation is intact, as Langdon Gilkey makes clear:

> Because sin is an estrangement of our essential structure, an alienation from our nature, a misuse of freedom in which freedom is itself bound, it is not possible to describe it in ontological terms—for ontology knows only structure and not its misuse. Among the most important things a Christian interpretation says of history is that that which is fated or evil in experience, while an undoubted part of the concrete reality of history, is not the result of its ontological and so its necessitating structure. Rather, this strange, "fallen" aspect of concreteness is the creation of sin, of a warped human freedom, and not of God, of time, of the structure of our finitude or of inexorable natural and social forces.[8]

Could one leave it at that, saying simply that "each of us is the Adam of his or her own soul"?[9] After all, whatever we say must not defy the reality of personal will which we know to be sin's nature. Whatever we say of Paul's Adam (original sin originating) and of the psalmist's (Ps. 51) mother (original sin originated), it will not do to put either "outside the race," so that they no longer relate to that which I know as my personal will to sin.[10]

It is the nature of sin itself which brings faith to say more of sin's origin. We have already referred to the empirical and confessional witness to the universality of sin. This is a remarkable and troubling coincidence. But an episodic account of this universality fails on another score as well. We refer to the experience of the *continuity* of sin. Sin represents a state or condition in the individual. This state carries a sense of the ineluctability, the inevitability of sin. We find ourselves not just falling freely but *already fallen*, and so falling. Heinrich Ott has tried to describe this by appealing to the Kantian notion of a "transcendental act":

> The fall, the primal guilt, the turning away from God, the loss of freedom, is no doubt an act; but it is not an act which, historically or biographically demonstrable, has taken place once for all (when in fact could it have taken place?), but an act which has always already taken place, in short, a "transcendental act." . . . For each sinful deed takes place in a state of bondage because the sinner has already and always lost his freedom; and that is so, not through one particular action which initiates the series of all other acts of effective sin, but through one transcendental act which lies behind and governs the whole series of particular acts, and which does not take place at some time or other but which always takes place, or rather, which has always already taken place.[11]

THE ORIGIN OF SIN

We are always already fallen. We seem to be saying here that sin is the sort of thing that simply goes with being human. Paul Tillich does that, for example, when he speaks of the tragic-universal character of existence as the motif of the myth of the transcendent fall: "The meaning of the myth is that the very constitution of existence implies the transition from essence to existence."[12]

But if we are speaking of "the very constitution of existence," we would seem to be back to speaking of the work of the Creator. If sin is something that is given with existence, is not its giver God? That seems to be the logic which controls the tortuous history of Gen. 6:5's reference to the evil imagination of humankind.[13] While the immediate context might suggest a dualistic origin in the marriages of the "sons of God" to the "daughters of men," the evil imagination has also been regarded as something implanted in the person, presumably then a matter for which the ultimate responsibility is to be assigned to the Creator. Thus in Gen. 8:21 the presence in humankind of an evil imagination "from youth" brings God to promise never again to curse the ground.

The sense of the fallenness of human existence does tend to lead reflection away from the theme of individual responsibility. It can lead faith toward the "tragic" assignment of responsibility for evil to God. It can lead as well toward the theogonic myth where evil roots in an eternal dualism. The heritage of paganism and the persistence of dualism might well have inclined early Christians to a simplistic distortion of the Johannine "You are of your father the devil, and your will is to do your father's desires" (John 8:44).[14] But the dualistic lure was resisted. Even those biblical passages where the demonic is stressed stop short of metaphysical dualism. It is in the postcanonical writings that we detect the movement toward a complete absolutizing of Satan over against God.[15] John's dualism, while it may exceed Paul's, still remains an ethical dualism, and so stops short of gnosticism. Similarly, Reformation and neo-Reformation critiques of optimism have not been made by appeal to the pessimism of dualism, though that continues to attract occasional representatives.[16]

Christian faith is called back from the tragic and the theogonic by the sense that fallenness somehow must derive from falling. While Satan may be goodness fallen par excellence, that figure explains human fallenness only by illustration and not by causation. Temptation is not coercion. But it is difficult to resist the tragic lure, given the universal sense of fallenness, for is it not precisely the universals of life, including death, which we wish to assign to God? Again, further reflection is required of faith.

The continuity of sin reveals itself to be temporal, an organic continuity. Sin spreads not only within but between people. We refer to this aspect of

5 / SIN AND EVIL

the nature of sin to indicate how Christian faith follows the distinction between creation and fall into a third range to speak of the *negativity* of evil. Kant suggests that the "already fallen" cannot be limited to the individual:

> Since, therefore, we are unable to derive this disposition, or rather its ultimate ground, from any original act of the will in time, we call it a property of the will which belongs to it by nature (although actually the disposition is grounded in freedom). Further, the man of whom we say "He is by nature good or evil" is to be understood not as the single individual (for then one man could be considered good, by nature, another as evil), but as the entire race.[17]

Yet Kant's application of fallenness to the race seems more a summary statement of individual findings than a recognition that the continuity of sin points to something at work not merely within all individuals but *between* and therefore within them. Such a recognition would support the sense of the inevitability of sin. But this recognition seems once again to acquit human beings and convict God, for what would fall under God's continuing creation and preservation if not care for the continuities of life? Of course one can extend the free-will defense to include the point that in the gift of freedom God gives freedom such efficacy that its misuse results in the spreading of sin remorselessly through the structures that sustain human life. Freedom even in its misuse has access to those very structures. Ultimately, then, responsibility and bondage are not discrete themes to be kept on parallel tracks. Rather, I am responsible in my bondage, and humankind is responsible for its bondage.

Still the question troubles: Whence this falling and this fallenness? If sin is granted reality and continuity, does it not compete with God on fully equal terms? Presumably the point that sin is against and so not from God has been made by now. But is it not eternally against God, given its reality and its continuity? If sin comes from freedom, and yet freedom-become-sin is no work of God, is freedom perhaps not so much given by an ontologically superior God as given *for* God, so that it is some kind of eternal other as the theogonic myth supposes? If it is not so, then one must be able to distinguish freedom and sin temporally. Paul Ricoeur does recognize the temporal echo in the Adamic myth's emphasis on contingency:

> In telling of the fall as an event, springing up from an unknown source, it furnishes anthropology with a key concept: the *contingency* of that radical evil which the penitent is always on the point of calling his evil nature. Thereby the myth proclaims the purely "historical" character of that radical evil; it prevents it from being regarded as primordial evil. Sin may be "older" than sins, but innocence is still "older."[18]

What is at stake here is making clear the *negativity* of sin. Faith confesses the ontological ultimacy of God and exposes the nullity of sin's claims. The fall shows that sin has no fair title to the lordship it claims. It is a usurper, real and efficacious, but an intruder and pretender for all that. Were it not so, humankind would elect "God" and evil's bid to be good would become a matter for determination by popular mandate. Faith resists this not because it supposes evil to be unreal or inefficacious. Evil is neither, but it is parasitic. Moreover, the claim that God's creativity is *ex nihilo* is not merely retrospective. Here faith finds the ontological conditions required for God to act decisively with respect to sin within what we now know as time and beyond it as well.

Clearly it is a difficult task to think of the fall. Thus Ricoeur for all his phenomenological "distance" grumbles that "the myth puts in succession that which is contemporaneous and cannot not be contemporaneous," though he acknowledges that this "is how it attains its depth." Similarly Tillich assigns to "biblical literalism" any who cannot join him in the indentification of actualized creation and estranged existence. Several difficulties may be distinguished. We may prove too much, so that what begins with the first fall has a mechanistic efficacy that denies the responsibility of later individuals. Or we may wonder how the structure of life can serve the spread of sin so efficaciously without God being implicated or evacuated from the universe. Our present difficulties concern the matter of absolute origin itself: they are, as it were, ontological and epistemological. The ontological: How shall one conceive of an absolute beginning to sin? How may that be supposed to occur? Is God implicated? The epistemological: How shall one recover the vanishing moment? Or, if that is not to be expected, can one intelligently speak of the history of humankind as such that a "fall" could have occurred?

THE GOODNESS AND INTEGRITY OF CREATION

What, then, may be said of the human creature apart from—before—sin? What do the sources of our faith lead us to say? We speak of the existence in relationship of one who in finite freedom is the object of God's special endowment, relationship, and intention.

The human creature is finite: limited and dependent. This one is not God. This one is of the earth and belongs to the earth. Despite occasional diversions, such as with Origen's notion of a premundane fall of souls into the earthly realm, Christian faith has insisted that the fact that humans are physical, earthly beings who belong to nature is due to the creative work of God, not to sin against God. Any discontinuity with nature in the coming-to-be of the human is within continuity—though there is reason to talk of such discontinuity. Given that continuity, if an evolutionary account of origins is convincing in general, that account will also have its contribution to make

5 / SIN AND EVIL

to Christian anthropology. It may be that the Lutheran traducianist position expresses the continuity more consistently and more emphatically than the Calvinist and Roman Catholic preference for the "creationist" view by which a special act of God is posited to account for the human soul. But no Christian theologian claims that our finite participation in the web of physical nature is in itself alien to our identity as God's creatures.[19]

Yet we must speak of discontinuity in such continuity. Even nontheistic writers have rightly observed that the human person stands out from nature, although such writers tend to speak of this as a "fall upward."[20] Christian faith welcomes the comment of the descriptive sciences on the differences that seem to mark the emergence of the human: walking upright, social organization, the use of tools, the development of language and of religion.[21] Teilhard de Chardin links the whole spectrum with "the threshold of reflection":

> In man, considered as a zoological group, everything is extended simultaneously—sexual attraction, with the laws of reproduction; the inclination to struggle for survival with the competitions it involves; the need for nourishment, with the accompanying taste for seizing and devouring; curiosity, to see, with its delight in investigation; the attraction of joining others to live in society. Each of these fibres traverses each one of us . . . and each one of them has its story to tell of the whole course of evolution—evolution of love, evolution of war, evolution of research, evolution of the social sense. But each one, just because it is evolutionary, undergoes a metamorphosis as it crosses the threshold of reflection.[22]

Chardin emphasizes that in the augmentation of consciousness there is the enrichment of new possibilities. The movement from external dependence to inner autonomy may be traced in the movement from stimuli to signals to symbols.[23]

If our physical nature confirms our finitude and dependence, does reason—that novel level of consciousness reached, as Chardin suggests, when some further calories were added to the anthropoid already mentally at the "boiling point"—promise freedom? At the least one might speak with Paul Tillich of reason as "the structure of freedom" in that in the movement from "environment" to "world" one reaches what Pannenberg has called "openness to the world." Here at least is qualitatively distinct possibility, if not yet freedom. Possibility waits on will to become realized freedom.

The distinctively human, then, is a dynamic reality. Any unique possession is but a presupposition for purpose, function, and becoming. One can make that case concerning human existence apart from the issue of origin. As Pannenberg writes: "Openness to the world must mean that man is completely directed into the open. He is always open further, beyond every experience and beyond every given situation."[24] But the dynamic character of human existence is rooted in God's cosmic creative work of origin, as in Genesis the Priestly writer incorporates creation into a great genealogical framework, the plan of *Toledoth* (Gen. 2:4).[25]

What is to be made of these dynamic elements of human existence? That which gives meaning to the functional forward thrust of human being is the reality of relationships. Moreover, this relatedness is not to be regarded as merely the raw material for a solitary advance into autonomy. Rather, freedom itself, the dynamic core of selfhood, is to be construed in relational terms. Thus Dietrich Bonhoeffer has caught the biblical sense of freedom well:

> In the language of the Bible, freedom is not something man has for himself but something he has for others. No man is free "as such," that is, in a vacuum, in the way that he may be musical, intelligent or blind as such. Freedom is not a quality of man, nor is it an ability, a capacity, a kind of being that somehow flares up in him. . . . Why? because freedom is not a quality which can be revealed—it is not a possession, a presence, an object, nor is it a form for existence—but a relationship and nothing else.[26]

Perhaps this is the point in the contrast Brunner stresses: that other creatures come to be *through* the word, but humankind comes to be only *in* the word, and thus summoned to responsibility.[27] Clearly something was meant to come from the human: The divine blessing yields imperatives: "Be fruitful . . . multiply . . . fill the earth . . . subdue it . . . have dominion." Something is supposed to happen in response to God who visits and holds converse with the human creature (Ps. 8:4).

We have been speaking of God's work of creation, seeking to disassociate that work from the evil associated with the fall. It is God's verdict that creation is good. What would good mean in this dynamic context? Westermann writes:

> "Good" in this context does not mean some sort of objective judgement, a judgement given according to already fixed and objective standards. It is rather this: it is good or suited for the purpose for which it is being prepared; it corresponds to its goal. But for what or for whom can creation be good? . . . The Creation story with its goal as the rest on the seventh day shows that Creation introduces a self-contained history—history in the broadest sense that can be given to the word—a history of the cosmos and in the midst of it a history of the human race which, as it has grown out of God's Creation, will also have a goal, which has been set for it by God. Looking then at the history both of the cosmos and of mankind, "All is very good."[28]

That, then, is the context for speaking of the goodness of the human creature. This creature can respond to the word heard; this creature is "able not to sin." Many voices in the tradition have not stopped with this strong

5 / SIN AND EVIL

but simple statement, but have gone on to speak of an "original righteousness" by which Adam is the more emphatically separated from us as each excellence is added. Ambrose is a representative of the strong theme in the fathers in speaking of Adam's life before the fall as "heavenly," "most blessed," and "like the angels." [29]

For Thomas Aquinas the original *rectitudo* entailed that a right relationship to God was formed on the basis of a person's inner harmony. Perhaps the reformers placed the emphasis on the relationship rather than on the internal psychological harmony, but the Apology resists too simple a distinction at this point:

> But what is righteousness? Here the scholastics quibble about philosophical questions and do not explain what original righteousness is. In the Scriptures righteousness contains not merely the second table of the Decalogue, but also the first, commanding fear of God, faith and love toward him. So original righteousness was intended to involve not only a balanced physical constitution, but these gifts as well: a surer knowledge of God, fear of God, trust in God, or at least the inclination and power to do these things.[30]

Indeed, the German variant can claim for Adam "perfect health and, in all respects, pure blood, unimpaired powers of the body."

Difficulties abound. Descriptive claims are here made which fly in the face of contemporary scientific opinion concerning the earliest stages of human life. Prescriptive claims are so extravagant that writers so dissimilar as Schleiermacher and Kierkegaard must agree that a "fall" for such beings becomes inconceivable.[31] One may respond to that difficulty by collapsing the distinction between creation and fall either in an evolutionary (Schleiermacher) perspective or an existentialist (Kierkegaard) perspective.

But are not those alternatives chosen too readily? For the reasons identified in the first section of this chapter, Christian faith has much at stake in the assertion of the ontological and temporal priority of God's good creative work in the coming-to-be of the human. Let us follow the suggestion implicit in the stress on the dynamic and functional character of the human creature. This will prevent us from supposing that the human creature was perfect in the sense of being complete. With Adam, God's adventure with humankind was not perfected, but begun and well begun.

Unfallen humanity was not perfect, then. Perhaps the first step in constructing a rehabilitated notion of the state of integrity is to remove the descriptive extravagances, which tend to draw attention away from what matters: the relationship to God. While still drawn to the idealistic notion of "complete consciousness," C. S. Lewis points the way:

> Judged by his artefacts, or perhaps even by his language, this blessed creature

was, no doubt, a savage. All that experience and practice can teach he had still to learn. We do not know how many of these creatures God made, nor how long they continued in the Paradisal state. But sooner or later they fell.³²

Such a correction of the description is not a product of intimidation by the scientific community. Attention to our own story suggests no evidence of an exceptionally developed original knowledge or culture. These creatures could name animals and appreciate one another. They may be supposed to have had a kind of confidence and mutual esteem—"naked and not ashamed," despite the fact that otherwise nakedness suggests the loss of human and social dignity. They were, in Westermann's word, "adequate" for that to which they were called.³³

But what of the relationship to the One who calls prescriptively? The distinction between creation and fall requires that we begin with a negative determination: as created the human is not fallen. Adam is indeed innocent. But surely this relationship is not perfected either. In such a case God's call would be merely an echo in Eden. It seems better to speak of a kind of childlike innocence which provides the necessary presupposition for will. Thus Augustine writes:

> No one is so foolish as to call an infant foolish, though it would be even more absurd to call it wise. An infant can be called neither foolish nor wise though it is already a human being. So it appears that human nature receives an intermediate condition which cannot be rightly called either folly or wisdom. . . . There is a transitional state between sleeping and waking as between folly and wisdom. But there is this difference. In the former case there is no intervention of will; in the latter the transition never takes place except by the action of the will. That is why the consequence is just retribution.³⁴

Thus it seems important to draw the notion of original righteousness toward the theme of integrity rather than that of perfection. Integrity is to be understood in dynamic and relational terms. In this creature of God there is together what is needed for what God seeks with this being. Adam is able not to sin. But will becomes real through alternatives, and clearly Adam is also able to sin. What does this require regarding the creature's relationship to God, not as goal but as given? That depends on how we conceive the relationship between will and reason. John Hick draws the two close together:

> In creating finite persons to love and be loved by Him God must endow them with a certain relative autonomy over against Himself. But how can a finite creature, dependent upon the infinite Creator for its very existence and for every power and quality of its being, possess any significant autonomy in relation to that Creator? The only way we can conceive is that suggested by our actual situation. God must set man at a distance from Himself, from which he can then voluntarily come to God. But how can anything be set at a distance from One

5 / SIN AND EVIL

who is infinite and omnipresent? Clearly spatial distance means nothing in this case. The kind of distance between God and man that would make room for a degree of human autonomy is epistemic distance. In other words, the reality and presence of God must not be borne in upon man in the coercive way in which their natural environment forces itself upon their attention. The world must be to men, to some extent at least, etsi deus non daretur, "as if there were no God." God must be a hidden deity, veiled by his creation. He must be knowable, but only by a mode of knowledge that involves free response on man's part, this response consisting in an uncompelled interpretive activity whereby we experience the world as mediating the divine presence.[35]

In some ways this is an attractive speculation, though one may wonder whether Hick underestimates the present experience of conscious defiance and extrapolates too much from our experience of sin as weakness. Different Christian anthropological emphasis will yield parallel differences in what it takes to have sin as a real possibility.

We have studiously avoided introducing the concept of the creation of humankind in the image of God. We have wanted to stay closer to the particulars, before they come to be assembled in such a concept. But the biblical witness and the massive historical tradition at this point cry out for some attention which may provide an occasion to collect and summarize the discussion in this section.

In identifying the "image" the sources of our faith hardly speak with a single voice. The notions emerging from the tradition seem to be strict alternatives, yet their negations may not be strictly tied to their affirmations. That is, without being hopelessly eclectic, it seems possible and desirable to fashion a formulation which encompasses most of the traditional themes—albeit in a different conceptual environment. Our lead sentence for this chapter speaks of the human creature as the object of God's special endowment, relationship, and intention. The "image of God" (*imago dei*) concept draws on the relational and functional emphases already offered in this section in order to speak of endowment in and for relationship as serving the divine intention.

Emil Brunner argues that to speak of the image of God in the human person is to speak at once of a gift and a task, and it may be helpful to follow Brunner in speaking of the gift as formal and the task as material. Such a distinction permits us to accommodate both the Old Testament sense for the human universality of the image (*tselem* and *demuth*) and the New Testament sense for the Christian specificity of the image (as Rom. 8:29). Unfruitful efforts to distinguish between image and likeness should not obscure a valid distinction by which each term refers distinctively to the full unified person.[36] The Western church has tended to stress the divine endowment, and the East the divine intention. The notion of relationship, set in a dynamic, functional context, permits us to hold the two emphases together. The relationship is both gift and task. What is needed for the task is given, given for the task.

What, then, is this given in the human person? Whatever we say at this point dogmatically must not put asunder the almost complete consensus of biblical scholars concerning the unity of the human person.[37] Such putting asunder of the consensus and, more important, of the person has tended to deny any place for the physical. Thus the medieval church tended to identify the *imago* (*tselem*) with human reason to which the supernatural likeness of the *similitudo* (*demuth*) had been added. Or one may hear the same tendency in Tillich's linking human *logos* with divine Logos.[38] But Gerhard von Rad helpfully responds that if one must accept the physical versus spiritual set of alternatives as the terms for the discussion, "we should have to decide in favour of a predominantly physical likeness," although he declines to speculate on God's form or corporeality.[39] Moreover, one's bodiliness may be said to be the primary vehicle through which one responds to the divine call to relate to other creatures as God's representative. As surely as our bodies bear the traffic of our becoming through and in each other, so surely does a wholly non-physical image concept contribute to an individualistic piety.

In turn, mind may be understood as the custodian of possibility, of planning by which direction is given to the human person's physically anchored stewardship. So Irenaeus alternately identifies reason and body as the image.[40] Neither body nor mind moves from given to goal effectively without the agency of will. We stress again that in speaking of "body," "mind," and "will," we distinguish conceptually what is always together existentially, although in particular instances there will be variety in the manifestation of this unity.

We are suggesting that an adequate understanding of the *imago dei* concept requires incorporation of both the Roman Catholic anthropological emphasis and the Reformation theological emphasis. With the former we need to speak of a togetherness—even a balance—of the constituent elements in the human person, but without deferring the God-relationship to a separate superadded gift. With the latter we need to stress the relationship to God, but ward off any spiritualizing tendency to deny anthropological, even psychological, participation in this relationship.[41] It seems important not to freeze this understanding in some momentarily fashionable anthropology. Perhaps Augustine's thought recognizes this dialectic, even if he did not offer a unified synthesizing formulation. On the one hand, Augustine sought for a trinity immanent in the human individual, of self-memory, self-knowledge, and self-love; on the other hand, he prayed: "Thou hast made us for Thyself and our hearts are restless until they find their rest in Thee."[42]

The endowment of which the *imago* concept speaks is, then, precisely the relationship to God. As Westermann remarks: "The creation of man in God's image is directed to something happening between God and man. The Creator

5 / SIN AND EVIL

created a creature that corresponds to him, to whom he can speak, and who can hear him."[43] The Eastern church has tended to cast this dynamic relationship in mystical terms. One is human only as one "participates" in God. Indeed, that is already the human's particular privilege as created in God's image. But one is to *grow* toward the divine likeness. The Western church draws back from the idea of divinization, responding to the fact that of the two creation stories the *imago dei* concept is to be found in P with its emphasis on divine transcendence. Following this line, one will preserve the distinction in the relationship and stress that as made in the divine image the human creature is *for* God.

The one made in God's image acts for God toward the world; "have dominion" immediately follows "let us make." This one acts for God toward the human other as well: "In the image of God created he them, male and female he created them." If the sexual relationship symbolizes the relatedness which is the goal for humankind—both a parable and an earnest of the relation of the church to God in Christ—it is also a primordial gift in which the self is created in relationship. As such it does mirror the God who is eternally in relationship within God and who creates and makes covenant in order to be in relationship with that which as free is fully other than God's self. The one made in God's image is made for God; gift and goal are to serve God's purpose, ultimately to share and reflect the divine glory (Rom. 5:2; 1 Pet. 5:4), to bring God delight. The purpose clauses continue to carry the note of contingency needed for the free-will defense. If one is to fault God for the human freedom by which sin springs up, one must deny God love for the creature—a love meant to be a joy to both parties in the relationship.[44]

Our discussion of the distinction between image as formal endowment and material goal has itself been quite formal, especially with respect to that goal. May something more be said of that? One may at least suggest that the indicative and the imperative are to be held together. As surely as God's creation praises God by being what it is made to be—witness Job's hymn of praise sung by the creatures and the psalmist's reference to the praise rendered by sun and moon and the shining stars—so must the human goal be rooted in the human given. One has dominion over the earth only by listening to, even obeying, the earth of which one is, after all, a part.[45] Perhaps, too, one seeks so to relate to other creatures as to serve and prosper what is in them. So act, one might say, as to maximize the other's harmonious participation in the structures of creation.[46] These structures are corruptible in the sense that they may also carry the efficacy of sin. Similarly, one's response to God is rooted in what God is, the being truly worthy of worship, but sin may reject God precisely for what God is.

Our discussion of the *imago* has spoken only of creation and not of fall.

How much shall we claim for creation apart from and before the fall? Again we seek to hold together the formal and the material. There is given here what is needed to move toward the goal. There is here such endowment in relationship as is needed to move toward the destiny God has intended. That much must be claimed, though no more, if Adam was created good but not perfect. Was that movement toward destiny also begun? Was there a focusing of endowment in will to respond to the divine call? To speak of that would be to speak of human will, not of divine will, to speak of creaturely life, not of divine creating. Our distinction between creation and fall does not require such a claim, although it permits it.

We said that we would seek to show how the distinction between creation and fall could be stated intelligibly for the contemporary sensibility without sacrificing the concerns of the tradition. Our immediate task has been to respond to questions we termed ontological: to suggest a conception of the human person such that an absolute beginning to sin, a "fall," is conceivable. The issue really is the intelligibility of our link with that creature of God who originates sin absolutely. We can imagine creatures who do not sin, but they have no link with us, for they cannot sin, and we, it seems, cannot not sin. Can we see ourselves linked with a creature in whom sin makes a contingent but absolute start? The issue here has not been sin's continuance. But can we, who continue to sin, identify with one in whom sin begins absolutely? By definition the point of identification cannot be that sin *continues* in this one, for it is sin's *start* of which we are asking. We have spoken here of what is not (yet) sin, arguing that even in this respect we can somehow identify with this one, for even we are not simply sin. Moreover, this creature is such that sin can start with this one. Such a start of sin is a fall, though we are eager to insist that the *degree* of the fall is reduced for one for whom perfection represents only a goal and not a given.

THE POSSIBILITY AND ACTUALITY OF SIN

What is required if the fall is to be into that very condition of sin in which we can recognize our bondage? What cannot be required is that the fall is itself bound to happen before it happens. Were that the case, we would no longer be speaking of a start of sin, but of how sin presupposes itself endlessly. That surely would reflect against God's good and efficacious work in creation.

If sin roots in freedom, it cannot be finally explained. This is true if the task of explanation is to identify conditioning factors, causal connections, and the accumulation of ingredients out of which the act naturally emerges. Such

5 / SIN AND EVIL

an understanding may serve us fairly well in many circumstances—as in the chemistry laboratory—but it will fail before the origin of sin. The Adamic myth, with its emphasis on human responsibility, pleads that all such explanatory talk regarding the origin of sin is necessary but not sufficient. Such talk is relevant. It does explain *that* and *how* sin is *possible*. Yet finally one must say that the actual fall occurs in freedom. The *start* of sin is that emphatic. But the theologians of the church have been restless with this idea.

Some would find the cause of sin to reside in the imperfection which necessarily characterizes a creature made for a freely chosen relationship with God. Irenaeus seems to stop just short of saying this:

> For it was necessary, that at first, that nature should be exhibited; then, after that, that what was mortal should be conquered and swallowed up by immortality, and the corruptible by incorruptibility, and that man should be made after the image and likeness of God, having received the knowledge of good and evil. (*Against Heresies*, iv,38,4)

Much depends on whether one takes "mortality" and "the receiving of the knowledge of good and evil" as consistent with the human creature's status as good though not perfect. But it is clear that Irenaeus has been the inspiration to others who more resolutely draw the cause of sin back into the immaturity of humankind. This may be done in various ways. One may speak of one's abiding immaturity, or traces of it, as representing that which impedes intended human development, that is, of immaturity as itself sin. Thus Williams writes of the "arrested development of the herd instinct" and Schleiermacher of the "head-start" by which the sensuous consciousness hinders the development of the God-consciousness.[47] In this handling of the immaturity theme the guilty component is usually regarded as human physicality. Thus Clement of Alexandria writes:

> The first man, when in Paradise, sported free, because he was the child of God; but when he succumbed to pleasure (for the serpent allegorically signifies pleasure crawling on its belly, earthly wickedness nourished for fuel to the flames), was as a child seduced by lusts, and grew old in disobedience by disobeying his Father, dishonoured God. Such was the influence of pleasure, man, that had been free by reason of simplicity, was found fettered to sin. (*Protrept.*, xi)

Or, more broadly and more starkly, one may identify human immaturity as sin by speaking of the inevitability of both positive and negative factors in evolution, appealing to entropy and the proclivity of the human person to settle for simple syntheses against the evolutionary call to complexity.[48] Perhaps one may find something here that is analogous to the manifestation of the sin of weakness.

THE ORIGIN OF SIN

On the other hand, one may more brazenly identify human incompleteness with human immaturity. To move ahead from this "given" is to "fall."[49] All that is needed is to regard sin as that which emerges naturally from the unstable synthesis. Development becomes defiance. What, after all, is more natural than the acquisition of knowledge? Does the prohibition concerning the tree of knowledge invite, perhaps even require, this interpretation by which one can remain innocent only by remaining ignorant? How could such an interpretation be aligned with other biblical materials, as, for example, the emphasis in the Wisdom literature on the human person "summoned and wooed by the mystery of the world itself and responding to that wooing with an intellectual love"?[50]

Claus Westermann gives an alternative interpretation of the prohibition which does not violate the boundaries of the "good, not perfect" theme. Of the temptation to be like God, he writes:

> This is a temptation not because the drive towards knowledge, towards all-embracing knowledge, was of itself opposed to God; it is not, because man is created with it. But the possibility is there of a disturbance and a destruction of the proper relationship between God and man, when man in his drive after knowledge oversteps or tries to overstep his limits.[51]

To grow in knowledge is indeed God's intention for the human creature, but that is to occur in relationship with God. The growth intended is for a self who is in its development to come to trust God the more fully. Bonhoeffer has caught well this intended combination of dependence and development:

> In the prohibition Adam is addressed in his freedom and in his creatureliness, and by the prohibition his being is confirmed in its kind. . . . *Man's limit is in the middle of his existence*, not on the edge. The limit which we look for on the edge is the limit of his condition, of his technology, of his possibilities. The limit in the middle is the limit of his reality, of his true existence. Adam knows that. . . . The limit is grace because it is the basis of creatureliness and freedom; the limit is the middle. . . . The prohibition of paradise is *grace* of the Creator towards the creature. God tempts no man.[52]

To resist identifying the cause of sin as human immaturity in either of these senses is not to deny the relevance of such immaturity for the understanding of the origin of sin. To reject a physicalist understanding of sin is not to opt for a disembodied will, as most dramatically represented by Origen's speculation concerning a premundane fall of souls.[53] As immature we are able to sin—formally. But more than that, the very stuff through which sin comes to be draws on the volatile mixture underlying the immature self. That which is given in creation is not merely the abstract possibility of sin, but sin's real

5 / SIN AND EVIL

potential as well. But while in our created givenness we must, in Kierkegaard's image, be dizzy, that is not yet to fall.

What of the fact that the given is there only as given toward a goal? As immature the human person is called to become. Indeed, this being has the peculiarity that only by becoming can it continue to be. In speaking of the gift of freedom, we recognize again that sin is more than abstract possibility; rather, the possibility attaches itself to the dynamism that centers the person. Thus Kierkegaard speaks of the dreadful sense of "being able" which the prohibition awakens:

> What it is he is able to do, of that he has no conception; to suppose that he had some conception is to presuppose, as commonly is done, what came later, the distinction between good and evil. There is only the possibility of being able, as a higher form of ignorance, as a heightened expression of dread.[54]

Similarly, the Genesis story underlines the momentousness of freedom with the sense of consequence: "Thou shalt surely die."

Yet this development is still dread, not sin. It resides in the sphere of creation, not the fall. To move from "being able" to the act itself is not in principle sin. Thus to stress that sinning will be more than the "given," more than the body (sin does not lie in the instincts), and more than the mind (sin does not lie in the acquisition of knowledge) is not to suggest that freedom in its very mutability must sin. Perhaps in this "more" there is a kind of *ex nihilo* quality to will, but that does not entail holding that the nonderivable choice must be to sin. Thus Christians reject the privation view in which the cause of freedom's incompleteness issuing in sin is sought precisely in the *nihil* out of which the human person is created. That which starts—from nothing even—need not be sin. But in rejecting such an easy explanation, they deny themselves as well the confidence which would seem to follow for the future. To be able to sin is not yet to sin. But in the more that is needed lies the fuller possibility of ultimate defiance.

The various forms of the sin/immaturity correlation all amount to placing sin within the divine creative work and thus either compromise the goodness of God or the radicality of sin—and commonly do both. The other non-Adamic option has been to move toward some kind of eternal dualism. This option is incompatible with Christian faith. The most vigorous proponents of dualism within Christianity have recognized this and proceeded to a counterproposal: an angel created good but fallen in freedom does not in principle violate the monotheistic character of the faith. Indeed, one might argue that this notion simply advances the free-will defense to its ultimate level. In this instance there is no mitigating tempter whom the fallen can cite as at least an accessory before the fact.

THE ORIGIN OF SIN

Yet the unrestrained development of this dualistic theme compromises the responsibility of the human creature for sin. Some compromise may indeed be required of faith. The figure of Satan speaks powerfully of such realities as the clarity (Kierkegaard), the ineluctability (Ricoeur), and the perversity (Kant) of the evil will. But one still struggles to retain the reality of human responsibility.

The argument of this chapter has been that Christian faith, following the distinction between creation, the good work from God's hand, and sin, that which is against God, locates the absolute origin of sin in a fall from created goodness. Yet ironically this third section in which the actual agency of the fall formed our topic has been the briefest part of the chapter. Perhaps that must be so, if we speak of a "free fall." True origin by hypothesis is the nonderivable, and Kierkegaard applies the point to the origin of sin:

> That human nature must be such that it makes sin possible, is, psychologically speaking, perfectly true; but to want to let this possibility of sin become its reality is shocking to ethics and sounds to dogmatics like blasphemy; for freedom is never possible; as soon as it is, it is actual. . . .[55]

"Sin presupposes itself" when we say glibly that a good Adam fell into sin because of pride, of wanting to be like God. Just when we may think we are halfway to an explanation, we discover we have slipped in an appeal to sin in speaking of the path to sin.

Have we by some sleight of hand banished what we earlier called the epistemological question? Need we no longer seek to recover the moment of the fall in our store of the memory of the race? If freedom is as we have described it, perhaps the act of the fall itself does not itself reside somewhere to be unearthed with the other relics in a cave. It is not only that despite the scientific consensus that humankind roots in a single stem (monophyletism), the scale on which science works requires one to say with Chardin that "man came silently into the world" and also fell as silently.[56] In order to have a start, sin must come from the center of the person, and that defies the most avid paleontologist. But what of the effects? While our appeal to the fall is by way of consistency with the tradition and coherence with the requirements of the doctrine of creation, we accept the point that one must be able to speak intelligibly of the history of humankind as being such that the "fall" could have occurred. We have tried to show that a creature with whom we sense some linkage apart from sin could bring sin to start. That start becomes fully *the* fall as sin proves itself to continue in those after Adam. How certainly, how massively, how at all does sin continue? It is to those questions we now must turn.

5 / SIN AND EVIL

NOTES

1. Denzinger, 102; Augsburg Confession, Article II, *BC* 29.
2. Paul Ricoeur, *The Symbolism of Evil*, trans. Emerson Buchanan (Boston: Beacon Press, 1967), pp. 171–74.
3. Charles Hartshorne and William L. Reese, eds., *Philosophers Speak of God* (Chicago: University of Chicago Press, 1953), p. 7.
4. Frances Young, "Insight or Incoherence? The Greek Fathers on God and Evil," *JEH* 24 (1973): 113–26.
5. Cf. Deut. 32:39; 1 Sam. 2:6; Amos 3:6; and Job 2:10.
6. Denzinger, 200.
7. See Karl Heim, *Jesus the Lord*, trans. D. H. van Daalen (Edinburgh: Oliver & Boyd, 1959), pp. 99–102. Cf. a "softer" tension in Walther Eichrodt's *Theology of the Old Testament*, trans. J. A. Baker, 2 vols. (Philadelphia: Westminster Press, 1961–67), 2:406, where "two essential statements" are: "Evil does not come from God, and it is subject to God's power."
8. Langdon Gilkey, *Reaping the Whirlwind: A Christian Interpretation of History* (New York: Seabury Press, 1976), p. 256.
9. As Martin J. Heinecken, *Christian Teachings* (Philadelphia: Fortress Press, 1967), p. 88.
10. Søren Kierkegaard, *The Concept of Dread*, trans. Walter Lowrie (Princeton: Princeton University Press, 1944), chap. 1.
11. Heinrich Ott, *Theology and Preaching*, trans. Harold Knight (Philadelphia: Westminster Press, 1965), p. 104.
12. Paul Tillich, *Systematic Theology*, 3 vols. (Chicago: University of Chicago Press, 1951–63), 2:38.
13. N. P. Williams, *The Ideas of the Fall and of Original Sin* (New York and London: Longmans, Green & Co., 1927), chap. 2. Cf. J. Daniélou, *The Theology of Jewish Christianity*, trans. J. A. Baker (Chicago: Henry Regnery, Co.; London: Darton, Longman & Todd, 1964).
14. In his *A History of the Christian Church* (New York: Charles Scribner's Sons, 1959), p. 39, Williston Walker suggests that since it was hard for ex-pagans to deny the existence of the old gods, those gods persisted for them as demons. On the struggle with dualistic gnosticism, see R. M. Grant, *Gnosticism and Early Christianity*, 2d ed. (New York: Columbia University Press, 1966), pp. 174–75. Grant sums up the rejection of gnosticism (against Harnack's thesis that the gnostics were the first Christian theologians) in these terms: "The triumph of orthodoxy meant the triumph of the created world over the aeons, of collective experience over individual freedom, of history over the freely creative imagination, of objectivity over subjectivity. Something was lost. . . . Yet something was certainly gained. The rule of God over history and nature could be asserted by the Church as by no Gnostic group. The goodness, actual and potential, of the creation and of human existence could be affirmed. The reality and meaningfulness of historical events could be proclaimed. In other words, orthodox Christians could hold, as Gnostics could not, that this world is neither heaven nor hell."
15. The Kittel article on *diabolos* makes this clear (*Theological Dictionary of the Bible*, ed. Gerhard Kittel, trans. G. W. Bromiley [Grand Rapids: Wm. B. Eerdmans,

1964]). Gerhard von Rad, *Wisdom in Israel*, trans. James D. Martin (Nashville: Abingdon Press, 1972), p. 305, argues that no dualism is to be found, even in Job, until the appearance of the Wisdom of Solomon.

16. For Reformation writers the favored formulation is a conjunctive one in which sin is caused by "the will of the devil and of all ungodly men" (Augsburg Confession, Art. XIX, *BC* 41), though subjection to the devil may be spoken of in connection with the *consequences* of sin (as in the Smalcald Articles, I, 1). More recent writers inclining toward dualism are Edwin Lewis, *The Creator and the Adversary* (New York: Abingdon-Cokesbury, 1948); and Kenneth Cauthen, *Science, Secularization, and God* (Nashville: Abingdon Press, 1969). On the role of nature as a "third" in the relationship between God and humankind, see Gordon Kaufman, *Systematic Theology: A Historicist Perspective* (New York: Charles Scribner's Sons, 1968), p. 355.

17. Immanuel Kant, *Religion within the Limits of Reason Alone*, trans. Theodore M. Greene and Hoyt H. Hudson (New York: Harper & Row, 1960), p.21.

18. Ricoeur, *Symbolism of Evil*, p. 251. (Emphasis his.)

19. For a Lutheran statement of the traducianist view, see Heinrich Schmid, *The Doctrinal Theology of the Evangelical Lutheran Church*, ed., trans. Charles A. Hay and Henry E. Jacobs (Minneapolis: Augsburg Publishing House, 1875), pp. 166, 248. For a Calvinist statement of the creationist position, see G. C. Berkouwer, *Man: The Image of God*, trans. Dirk W. Jellema (Grand Rapids: Wm. B. Eerdmans, 1962), pp. 279-309.

20. Erich Fromm, *Man for Himself* (New York: Holt, Rinehart & Winston, 1947), pp. 47ff.

21. See, e.g., C. Loring Brace and Ashley Montagu, *Human Evolution: An Introduction to Biological Anthropology*, 2d. ed. (New York: Macmillan Co., 1977).

22. Pierre Teilhard de Chardin, *The Phenomenon of Man*, trans. Bernard Wall (New York: Harper & Row, 1959), p. 179.

23. John B. Cobb, Jr., *The Structure of Christian Existence* (Philadelphia: Westminster Press, 1967), pp. 36-40.

24. Wolfhart Pannenberg, *What Is Man?* trans. Duane A. Priebe (Philadelphia: Fortress Press, 1970), pp. 3-8. Tillich, *Systematic Theology*, 1:71-105.

25. Gerhard von Rad, *Old Testament Theology*, trans. D. M. G. Stalker, 2 vols. (New York: Harper & Row, 1962-65), 1:139. It is not surprising that the Yahwist's account is not as clear at this point if Humbert is right in finding a struggle here between a creation myth (2:4b-7, 9a, 18-24; 3:20-21, 23; and 4:1) and a paradise and fall myth (2:8, 9b, 16-17, 25; 3:1-19, 22, 24).

26. Dietrich Bonhoeffer, *Creation and Fall*, trans. John C. Fletcher (New York: Macmillan Co.; London: SCM Press, 1959), p. 37.

27. Emil Brunner, *Man in Revolt*, trans. Olive Wyon (Philadelphia: Westminster Press, 1947), pp. 96-99.

28. Claus Westermann, *Creation*, trans. John J. Scullion (Philadelphia: Fortress Press, 1974), p. 61.

29. See Ambrose's sermons on the Psalms, *PL* 15:1422.

30. Apology of the Augsburg Confession, Article II, 15-17, in *BC* 102.

31. Friedrich Schleiermacher, *The Christian Faith*, trans. and ed. H. R. Mackintosh

5 / SIN AND EVIL

and J. S. Stewart (New York: Harper & Row, Harper Torchbooks, 1963), par. 72. Kierkegaard, *The Concept of Dread*, chap. 1.

32. C. S. Lewis, *The Problem of Pain* (New York: Macmillan Co., 1948), p. 65.

33. Westermann, *Creation*, p. 72.

34. Augustine, *On Free Will*, iii, 71, 73; translated by John H. S. Burleigh (*Augustine: Earlier Writings*, LCC [Philadelphia: Westminster Press, 1953]).

35. John Hick, *Evil and the God of Love* (New York: Harper & Row; London: Macmillan & Co., 1966), p. 317.

36. Brunner, *Man in Revolt*, p. 98. See David Cairns, *The Image of God in Man* (London: SCM Press, 1953). It is this distinction Barth employs in drawing on the ambiguity of the German *Bestimmung* to speak of the image as "determination" and as "destiny."

37. See Gerhard von Rad, *Genesis*, trans. John Marks (Philadelphia: Westminster Press, 1961), p. 58; and W. D. Davies, *Paul and Rabbinic Judaism* (London: SPCK, 1948), p. 54.

38. Tillich, *Systematic Theology*, 1:156–59.

39. Gerhard von Rad, "The Divine Likeness in the Old Testament," in *Theological Dictionary of the Bible*, 2:391.

40. Cairns, *Image of God in Man*, p. 76.

41. Robert C. Schultz, "Original Sin: Accident or Substance: The Paradoxical Significance of F.C.I., 53–62 in Historical Context," in *Discord, Dialogue, and Concord*, ed. Lewis W. Spitz and Wenzel Lohff (Philadelphia: Fortress Press, 1977), pp. 38–57, seems to stress the distinction: "Luther could describe both sin and salvation in terms of people's relationship to God without needing to describe the interior structure of human personality" (p. 44).

42. For the grounding of this Augustinian theme, see *On the Trinity*, xiv,8.

43. Westermann, *Creation*, p. 56.

44. See Karl Barth, *Church Dogmatics*, 5 vols. in 14 (Edinburgh: T. & T. Clark, 1936–77), 3/1. Cf. John Meyendorff, *Byzantine Theology: Historical Trends and Doctrinal Themes* (New York: Fordham University Press, 1974), pp. 139ff.

45. H. Paul Santmire, *Brother Earth* (Toronto: Thomas Nelson, 1970).

46. Tillich, *Systematic Theology*, 1:156–59.

47. N. P. Williams, *The Ideas of the Fall and of Original Sin* (New York and London: Longmans, Green & Co., 1927), pp. 477–88; Schleiermacher, *The Christian Faith*, pars. 67, 68.

48. F. R. Tennant, *The Concept of Sin* (Cambridge: At the University Press, 1912), p. 122; Juan Luis Segundo, *Evolution and Guilt* (Maryknoll, N. Y.: Orbis Books, 1974), p. 129.

49. Reinhold Niebuhr's notion of the instability of the human synthesis of the finite and the infinite (*The Nature and Destiny of Man*, 2 vols. [New York: Charles Scribner's Sons, 1941–43]), Paul Ricoeur's finding that synthesis to constitute a "fault" cutting across the human terrain (*Fallible Man*, trans. Charles Kegley [Chicago: Henry Regnery Co., 1965]), and Ernst Becker's rooting evil in the temptation to Titanism (*The Denial of Death* [New York: Macmillan Co., 1973]) all permit such an interpretation.

50. Gerhard von Rad, *Wisdom in Israel,* trans. J. D. Martin (Nashville: Abingdon Press, 1972), p. 309.
51. Westermann, *Creation*, p. 93; cf. p. 106.
52. Bonhoeffer, *Creation and Fall*, pp. 52–53 (emphasis his). Cf. von Rad, *Old Testament Theology*, 1:155, on the knowledge of all things suggesting the mastery of all things.
53. Origen, *On First Principles*, I, v, vi, vii; II, viii, 3; III, v, 4.
54. Kierkegaard, *Concept of Dread*, p. 40.
55. Ibid., p. 20.
56. Teilhard de Chardin, *Phenomenon of Man*, p. 185.

3

The Effect of Sin

The effect of sin is to work against the Creator within creation. Sin works against the Creator by misappropriating the endowment, distorting the relationship, and frustrating the intention, though the person still remains the creature of God. Sin works within creation by spreading inexorably through the structure of reality represented by the responsible self in tragic relationship.

SINNER AND CREATURE

When we spoke in Chapter 1 of the "whither" of sin, we briefly described a "continuity" in sin which seems to make acts of sin inevitable. We now return to address that topic in the light of Chapter 2's discussion of creation and fall. Here we are asking two questions. First, What does sin effect in the one who is God's special creature? Here the question is not Chapter 1's more abstract question regarding any and all effects, but rather that of what effects previous sin has on the individual at any present state of existence. And second, How do such effects of past sins come to bear on the present?

We are pursuing these questions in the light of the distinction between creation and fall, following our contention in Chapter 2 that the fall must not be identified with creation logically or even temporally. Yet these questions must be faced also by those who grant no temporal distinction between creation and fall. All Christian theologians make the logical or theological distinction and so accept the terms of our first question. This question presses, since no Christian theologian asserts that the individual starts from scratch, with respect to sin or otherwise. What then, in the individual's legacy, derives from God's creativity and what from sin? Similarly, our second question of the "how" of the continuity of effect does not depend on arguing for the notion of an absolute beginning for sin. Even if one does not wish to speak of original sin "originating" somewhere, some*time*, it is clear that it is *originated*, though the difference in the degree of continuity granted indicates that there is no clear consensus about how and whether to speak of "sin" in this human connectedness. In any case, what we seek to understand is how the sin that is before me comes to yield so surely the sin that is in me.

5 / SIN AND EVIL

As Christian faith probes these questions, it is aware of others as well, touching the "God and self" structure that underlies Christian experience and understanding. If faith must ask "*What* does the sin of one creature create in others?" must we not wonder if a fulsome answer will usurp God's role in the coming-to-be of these creatures? We speak to that in the first section. Perhaps some distinction can still be managed in what is given, but what of the giv*ing*? If faith asks *how* the continuity in sin is constituted, must we not wonder whether God will be implicated in the answer? Of course these questions are such that the answers we intend to give seem to cancel each other out. Can God still be significantly Creator for one thoroughly in sin without assigning to God responsibility for the sin itself? In addressing both questions we remain concerned to show that the responsibility of the individual is not lost. Here the threat is not only from God. Perhaps God can somehow show omnipotence precisely by creating freedom.[1] But will not sin's power to originate effects in and then through the individual proportionately reduce that individual's responsibility for sin?

We begin with the reflection of the church. It is clear that the biblical witness claims that sin is efficacious. In the Genesis material one may see how, in Ricoeur's words, sin "pervades all the registers of human life"—naming, communication, the relationship to nature, procreation, death.[2] The Pauline litany of effects in Romans 1 may lie behind the pondering of the principle of connection in Romans 5. It seems best to begin with the church's very considerable and very developed reflection and let the material lead us back to and through the biblical understanding, and then on to the interpretation of our contemporary experience.

Rhythms may be detected in the historical material. An overarching issue deals with the degree of gravity assigned to the ongoing consequences of sin. Frederick Tennent says that the earliest patristic thought on this subject falls far short of Augustine's dark appraisal of the human condition. His argument is helped because it is set in terms of the role of "absolute origin," of the effects of Adam's sin on his descendants. While we accept that setting, we should not ignore the negative appraisals which do not appeal to an absolutely original fall as cause. In any case, Tennant surveys the material:

> Polycarp speaks of the universality of sin, but not of the cause thereof. Ignatius, after S. John, conceives of the world as lying in wickedness, in the might of Satan and under the rule of death, or in a state of *phthora*, but this state is not ascribed to the fall of mankind in its first parent. . . . Justin speaks strongly of the universality of sin, and of our need of grace; and he alludes to an evil inclination which is in the nature of every man. These things, however, are not deduced from, or connected with, the Fall.[3]

Putting the issue in these terms, linking "original sin originating" and "original sin originated" so strictly, Tennant may be right in stressing the gap between Augustine and the earlier fathers. It does seem that the corruption traced to Adam was at first largely limited to our mortality. Moreover, even leaving aside the issue of the link with the absolute origin, the earliest fathers do not anticipate Augustine's pessimism.

Jaroslav Pelikan stresses the effects of the context: the church provided what is needed in the polemical situation. What was needed?

> While both responsibility and inevitability had been prominent in the classical understanding of man, [it was] chiefly this sense of fate and necessity that impressed itself upon the interpreters of the gospel as the alternative to their message, rather than, for example the Socratic teaching that with proper knowledge and adequate motivation a man could, by the exercise of his free will, overcome the tendency of his appetites toward sin.

Moreover: "Not only the Greco-Roman critics of the faith, but also its heretical opponents seemed to err chiefly on the side of emphasizing the inevitability of sin at the expense of the responsibility for sin." Pelikan is alluding to the way in which "the theories of cosmic redemption in the gnostic systems were based on an understanding of the human predicament in which humanity's inability to avoid sin or to evade destiny was fundamental."[4]

Perhaps one might qualify this optimistic pattern in the pre-Augustinian fathers by appeal to Irenaeus and Origen. Irenaeus, after all, does develop a recapitulation soteriology and so needs to appeal to some kind of unity of condition brought about by the first Adam. Yet Irenaeus not only places the emphasis on unity in mortality—not in sin—but seems to qualify even this by suggesting that the "likeness" was present only in a germinal way before sin (*Against Heresies*, iv,38,1). While the "likeness" may be lost, the "image" remains with its reality of freedom:

> And to as many as continue in their love towards God does He grant communion with Him. But communion with God is life and light, and the enjoyment of all the benefits which He has in store. But on as many as, according *to their own choice*, depart from God, He inflicts that separation from Himself which they have chosen of *their own accord*. But separation from God is death, and separation from light is darkness; and separation from God consists in the loss of all the benefits which He has in store.[5]

Origen represents a more significant qualification of the prevailing optimism. While his earlier writings place a strong emphasis on human freedom, two later elements change this emphasis. The one is the infamous appeal to premundane fall, which Origen develops in dependence on Platonic sources. Yet this theme is still cast in individualistic terms, where concupiscence is not regarded as sin until voluntary consent has carried the natural desire into

5 / SIN AND EVIL

action (*On First Principles*, iii,2,2–3). More significant is Origen's appeal to a "stain of sin," which he makes after coming in contact with the practice of infant baptism in Caesarea. In this appeal the physical (mortality) and the moral (guilt) merge, without great precision, but we do seem significantly on the way to Augustine.

But the way is not any sort of broad path. Thus the Antiochenes stress free will more than Origen, insisting that sin is always personal sin, though mortality can be inherited. The Cappadocians resemble Origen, in appealing to a fall from a celestial, though not premundane, paradise to account for the division of the sexes, and for mortality, desire, and darkened understanding. But they insist that the image of God remains, so that free will may be exercised in progress toward the likeness of God. This is the position that wins out in the East in the person of Maximus the Confessor.

One pattern, then, that suggests itself is relatively optimistic. We shall see this reasserting itself, after Augustine, in the work of medieval theologians and after the Reformation, in the Tridentine formulations. It is helpful to understand this pattern in the light of the contextual elements Pelikan identifies. Yet the context calls forth what is in the faith already, as other responses to such contextual elements, including other readings of the context, were indeed possible. This relatively optimistic reading of the human condition does retain something essential to Christian faith: the sense of human responsibility. Moreover, even in doing that this pattern does not fail to make a significant judgment against unqualified optimism. Even later, when this pattern casts itself in only negative terms, without positing a continuity in a positive potency to sin, it is still significant that to speak thus of the privation of the human is to speak of a genuine existential loss, not merely of the logic of negation.

But the church did come to speak more strongly of sin's continuity in effect. Augustine represents the classical foundation for such speech, but we may do well to begin with his antecedents in Tertullian and Ambrose. Tertullian represents an important third-century parallel in the West to Origen's anticipation in the East of Augustinian thought. In *On the Soul*, 41, he writes:

> There is, then, besides the evil which supervenes on the soul from the intervention of the evil spirit, an antecedent and in a certain sense natural, evil, which arises from its corrupt origin. For, as we have said before, the corruption of our nature is another nature having god and father of its own, namely the author of that corruption.

Clearly we are dealing here with an active sinfulness, not merely with a negative effect.

Tertullian's most famous contribution to the doctrine of original sin is no doubt his traducianist theory of the derivation of the soul's reality from the parents and ultimately from Adam's soul. That theory bears most directly on the concerns of the next section, where we ask how the effects of the sins of the past reach us. But it is worth noting here that the traducianist theory supports the emphasis on active sinfulness and may even have functioned to suggest that theme to Tertullian. Tennant has presented Tertullian in that light, with the additional speculation that the notion of a corrupted nature, once that action has been so derived, continues to have a life of its own, cut off from its foundation in a theory of traducianism.[6] While there may be something to Tennant's scenario, we would argue that the notion of a corrupted nature has a more direct empirical source in Christian experience.

In any case, Augustine seems to have been more directly influenced by Ambrose. Ambrose speaks of the fall as involving the loss of the divine image and is cited by Augustine as an upholder of the doctrine of hereditary corruption. Clearly sin for Ambrose is fully a state, not merely individual acts. Yet he appears to stop short of regarding concupiscence as itself sin. As with Tertullian, his most significant contribution may be to the issue of the "how" of our connectedness in sin, for Ambrose was the first to draw a definite connection between Christ's sinlessness and his virginal conception. While we have argued that the issue of the "how" of continuity in effect is not only separable from but also secondary to the issue of the "what," it does seem probable that at times in the church's reflection formative influence also flowed in the other direction.

Several threads of Christian reflection on original sin are woven together by Augustine in a complex pattern that puts these materials at the church's disposal in a distinctively new way. His defenders and detractors agree that matters were not the same after Augustine. The originality of his synthesizing work should not be minimized. He draws on Cyprian's connection between infant baptism and original sin, though Tertullian had affirmed original sin but not infant baptism. Indeed, whereas Cyprian had taught that the sins remitted in the baptism of infants are not properly their own sins, Augustine draws from original sin the strict conclusion that unbaptized infants are condemned. He drew on Ambrose's connection between Christ's sinlessness and his virginal conception. This led him toward a conclusion regarding the mode of transmission—the topic of our next section in this chapter—though he did not embrace Tertullian's traducianism as the foundation for that conception. We have been taught that he reacted to Pelagius, but Augustine's originality is suggested by the fact that his main positions on this matter were developed well before the Pelagian controversy.

What were those positions? What is the human condition "after Adam"? Augustine argues that our condition is one of guilt (*reatus*) and corruption (*vitium*). We defer the topic of guilt to the next section and consider here only corruption. To speak of this with Augustine is to deal with his elusive

5 / SIN AND EVIL

concept of "concupiscence," which stands for everything that makes us turn from God to find satisfaction in material things. While Augustine's emphasis at times seems to be on unbridled sexual passion, this concept of concupiscence is broad enough to include pride (*cupiditas*). Concupiscence is both a consequence and a cause of sin. Most basic of all distinctions bearing on this concept is that between liberty (*libertas*) and free will (*liberum arbitrium*). While we retain psychological free will, we have no actual liberty. There is in fact a "cruel necessity of sinning" upon us, for the race is after Adam "a universal mass of perdition."[7]

Original sin, then, is in Augustine's view clearly something more positive, more virulent than a mere privation. No informed reader will charge him with optimism about the human condition. As if to leave no doubt about that, Augustine placed this doctrine of original sin in the framework of absolute predestination, reading the "all" of 1 Tim. 2:4 as "all the predestined." This teaching—together with Augustine's attack on human liberty after Adam—provoked the criticism of a number of churchmen (Prosper of Aquitaine, Hilary, John Cassian) who have been identified since the seventeenth century as "semi-Pelagians." While the Council of Orange (529) reaffirmed the emphasis of the Council of Carthage (418) on original sin inherited from Adam and present as a taint of sin in every person, it did specifically drop the predestinarian casting of the doctrine.[8]

Can Augustine's thought be accommodated within the dialectic suggested by this section's title, "Sinner and Creature"? That each person after Adam is sinner is surely clear to him, but is each one still God's special creature? In some ways against the grain of his thought, Augustine clings to this theme:

> For man has such excellence even after the fall in comparison with the brute that what is a fault in man is nature in the brute. Still man's nature is not changed into the nature of the brute. God, therefore, condemns man because of the fault by which his nature is disgraced, not because of his nature, which is not abolished through its fault. (*On Original Sin*, 40, 46).[9]

Similarly, even in his late writing on predestination Augustine distinguishes the "grace by which we are distinguished from cattle" as a natural endowment from that grace "which pertains to a holy life." Thus he writes: "The capacity to have faith, as the capacity to have love, belongs to man's nature; but to have faith, even as to have love, belongs to the grace of believers" (*On the Predestination of the Saints*, 5, 10).

The affirmation of the Augustinian theology at Carthage and Orange and the explicit condemnation of Pelagianism at Ephesus (431) would seem clear. But development in the church's thinking on original sin does not stop at this point. Jaroslav Pelikan finds the seeds of such continuing development in the resolution of Orange itself:

The official Augustinianism of Gregory also contained the possibility for subtle shifts from the doctrine of the sovereignty and necessity of grace, to a reintroduction of the notions of merit and human initiative; on the other hand, the thought of Augustine always contained the possibility for a shift back in the direction of predestinarianism.[10]

In an historical tracing of the oscillating "footnotes to Augustine" the first direction to be noted would be toward a weakening of Augustine's emphasis on the positive character of concupiscence as sin. Medieval reflection on the human condition after Adam has in common this more optimistic view, though nuances abound. In the earlier scholastics a comparison of Anselm and Abelard at the turn of the twelfth century can serve to make this point. Anselm defines sin negatively as the privation or absence of "owed justice," through the loss of a special gift of a right directedness of the human will. Yet Anselm's realism yields a concept of race that retains a more active conception of original sin. Thus the sin of infants is not personal, but it is voluntary, carrying with it condemnation, albeit the lightest sort. Abelard concurs in Anselm's judgment, but he lacks the philosophical realism needed to support it. Since the sin of infants does not pass the criterion of a free and voluntary act of an incommunicable person, Abelard's vague appeal to "carnal concupiscence" finally settles for saying: God's justice is not our justice.[11]

Thomas Aquinas appears to offer a synthesis of Augustine and Anselm, for he speaks of concupiscence as the matter and privation of original justice as the form of original sin. But this places the matter within the form of a disorder of human nature—rather than, say, the defiance of personal will in relationship to God. Adam's rebellion brings the loss of God's sanctifying grace, so that the interior harmony of human nature is lost and natural drives are no longer under the control of reasoned will. Accordingly, despite the reference to "material" concupiscence, Aquinas seems to regard the human condition less gravely than even Anselm does and *a fortiori* than Augustine—at least that may be suggested by the fact that he assigns unbaptized infants who die to a state of natural bliss. Moreover, despite the loss involved in original sin, the natural human inclination to virtue is in no way diminished by sin, though without special grace it will fall short of its goal. Human nature, though wounded, remains intact.[12]

In Anselm and Aquinas, Irenaeus' distinction between "image" and "likeness" returns, but now cut off from the view that Adam was created immature. "Likeness" becomes "superadded gifts" which can be lost without a radical corruption of human nature itself, made in God's image. In Scotus and the Franciscans this affirmation of human nature is the more emphatic and once again is aligned with the notion of human immaturity. If Adam had preserved the "supernatural gift," he would have acquired a confirmation in grace. The same rule would have applied to every other human being.

5 / SIN AND EVIL

In the fallen state concupiscence is seen as fully natural, as the necessary reaction of the sensitive part of the soul to intrinsically desirable objects. Though weakened by the loss of the supernatural harmony, we are not in sin. Yet we are in guilt, for we participate forensically in the debt represented in the lost original righteousness. While Scotus himself could still stretch toward this unity in guilt by appeal to philosophical realism, more nominalistic later Franciscans settled for a bare appeal to the independence from criticism of the truths of faith. In any case the creature after Adam, though weakened, remains free both psychologically and metaphysically. As Heiko Oberman puts it:

> Man after the fall is prone to all evil, through an error of judgment; the will, weak in its fights against the lower powers, is tempted to disobey the command of reason; spirit and flesh are in constant struggle, and the will is unstable and weak because of the physical impact of original sin. . . . All these obstacles, due partly to man's created condition, partly to the consequences of his initial disobedience, do not, however, diminish the liberty of the will to choose freely between good and evil; they only diminish the ease with which the good acts are elicited.[13]

Good can, then, be done and done efficaciously. God is obligated to infuse divine grace in all people who have done their very best ("facere quod in se est").

This way of conceiving the human person "after Adam" is essentially optimistic. That is not so obvious in Aquinas, who insists that no person can turn to God unless God turns to that person first and throughout offers "assisting grace." But there is a place for merit in his thought, as Brian Gerrish points out:

> Justification is not enough, not even when interpreted as itself a "making righteous." It is merely the first step towards ultimate salvation, and eternal life is only to be obtained by the justified man who goes on, in the power of habitual grace, to perform meritorious works . . . and from this it follows of necessity that salvation is given as a reward, indeed a reward "de condigno."[14]

Gerrish's reference becomes clearer when set over against nominalist theology with its still more optimistic slant:

> First, acting upon his own native powers a man may perform acts worthy of merit "de congruo." Now, strictly speaking, God is not obliged to reward such imperfect merit; God is not thereby made a debtor. . . . Still, provided only that a man has done his best ("quod in se est"), it is at least fitting ("decet") that God, being both just and good, should crown human endeavor with divine grace. Thereupon, the second stage in man's attainment of eternal life begins: equipped with the inpouring of divine charity, he is enabled to perform works meritorious

in the strictest sense, that is "de condigno." God now becomes, quite precisely, a debtor, and He is obliged ("cogitur") to grant eternal life as a well-earned reward.[15]

These summaries serve to set the stage for the Reformation corrective to this optimism, whether in its more subtle form or its more blatant form. This seems the more important context in which to regard Luther's attack against optimism—rather than, say, that of his argument with Erasmus. Long before the dispute with Erasmus, Luther had been asserting the bondage of the will. Thus in the Heidelberg Theses (13) of 1518 he asserts: " 'Free Will' after the fall is nothing but a word, as long as it is doing what is within it, it is committing deadly sin." Here the foundation is already laid for his response in 1525 to Erasmus: "Hence it follows that free choice without the grace of God is not free at all, but immutably the captive and slave of evil, since it cannot of itself turn to the good."[16] John Calvin also defines himself directly over against the medieval Catholic optimism:

> Those who have defined original sin as a lack of original justice which ought to be in men, although in these words they have comprehended all the substance, still they have not sufficiently expressed the force of it. For our nature is not merely empty and destitute, but it is so fecund of every kind of evil that it cannot be inactive. (*Institutes*, ii,1,9)

Here Luther and Calvin must be distinguished from the so-called "radical" reformers, whose more individualistic concept of sin yielded the Anabaptist refusal to baptize children, since Christ took away original sin from the whole world.[17]

Can this pessimism about the human condition speak of the person as still God's special creature? Luther's inclination is to identify the image of God so strongly with the "material image" that he will not be apt to speak of the continuing creaturely status in terms of the "image." Yet we can find a trace of a "relic" theory, evident in our continuing dominion over the animals.[18] In any case, Luther continues to recognize human competence in reason and morals regarding "the things that are below us." Gerrish argues for a threefold distinction in Luther's understanding and evaluation of reason:

> (1) natural reason, ruling within its proper domain (the Earthly Kingdom); (2) arrogant reason, trespassing upon the domain of faith (the Heavenly Kingdom); (3) regenerate reason, serving humbly in the household of faith, but always subject to the Word of God. Within the first context, reason is an excellent gift of God; within the second, it is Frau Hulda, the Devil's Whore; within the third, it is the handmaiden of faith.[19]

But what of the relationship to God? Has this endowment been so misappropriated that the relationship no longer exists? Is it necessary to assert a

5 / SIN AND EVIL

complete loss of relationship to God in order to correct the medieval optimism? It is not, for Luther's critique asserts that humankind is against, but not without, God.[20] Indeed, *The Bondage of the Will* (ix) seems to suggest that only one who is especially meant for God can truly sin against God, and that the later point does not eliminate the former:

> But if the power of free choice were said to mean that by which a man is capable of being taken hold of by the Spirit and imbued with the grace of God, as a being created for eternal life or death, no objection could be taken. For this power or aptitude, or as the Sophists say, this disposing quality or passive aptitude, we also admit; and who does not know that it is not found in trees or animals? For heaven, as the saying is, was not made for geese.

Calvin follows Luther in these matters. The "natural gifts" bestowed on the human creature have undergone a loss in efficacy but have not been wholly obliterated. Even in the God-relationship sin means that we are deprived not of will but of a healthy will. Calvin cites Bernard as follows: "Simply to will, is human; to will the bad belongs to corrupted nature; to will the good is of grace" (*Institutes*, ii,3,5). This leads him to a formulation reminiscent of Luther's distinction between necessity and constraint:

> We must observe this distinction: that man, after having been corrupted by the Fall, sins voluntarily, not against his heart nor by constraint; that he sins, I say, by liking and strong inclination, not by constraint or violence; . . . and nevertheless that his nature is so perverse that he cannot be moved, driven or led except to evil. (Ibid.)

In Calvin's assertion that "every part of man, from the understanding to the will, from the soul to the flesh, is defiled and altogether filled with that concupiscence"[21] we hear a hint of the anthropological interest which dominated medieval discussion of this topic. On the Lutheran side this interest is represented by Melanchthon. At least in his *Loci Communes* of 1543 (if not earlier) he implies a distinction and cooperation between the Holy Spirit, who effects and generates new spiritual affections through the reading or hearing of the word of God, and the human will that follows the affections, namely, the love of God and the knowledge of God's mercy. Ekkehard Muehlenberg comments:

> Human will does not materially add anything to the process, because object and objective are given in reason's knowledge and the movement or locomotion in the affection. Nevertheless, human will has to turn to the new affection and has to follow it against other affections in man.[22]

In the debate between Strigel and Flacius that led to the Formula of Concord's decisions, Strigel wanted to defend the Lutheran doctrine of original sin against the Catholic assertion that it denied the goodness of creation by making the created human appetite the cause of sin. Strigel argued that God indeed creates the appetites, but whether they fasten on good or bad ways of fulfillment is contingent. Thereby Strigel returned to the basic medieval frame of reference. It was to precisely this that Flacius objected. But he too did not fully escape the medieval frame, and so was trapped into describing sin as the substance of human nature.[23]

The Formula of Concord, leaning to Flacius' insight but not accepting his conclusion, stated the issue, but hardly resolved it. What we seek to understand is how "that which is accident and not substance" can be

> inexpressible impairment and such a corruption of human nature that nothing pure nor good has remained in itself and in all its internal and external powers, but that it is altogether corrupted, so that through original sin man is in God's sight spiritually lifeless and with all his powers dead indeed to that which is good. (BC 519)

What is it to say that the fallen person retains the capacity for salvation, though this is not an active capacity but a passive one? Muehlenberg argues that the Formula impales itself by arguing on the one hand that the unregenerated person is "a stone, a block, or a lump of clay," "a wild unbroken animal" and on the other hand that "the Lord God draws the person whom he wills to convert, and draws him in such a way that man's darkened reason becomes an enlightened one and his resisting will becomes an obedient will." Muehlenberg comments:

> Either the Holy Spirit effects and accomplishes an initial turn and change of sinful man against the thoroughly sinful will of man, or unregenerated man is capable of responding to the offer of grace. . . . The Formula of Concord wants it both ways, that is, it rejects forceful conversion but does not admit the Philippist alternative either.[24]

Is this the self-contradiction Muehlenberg finds it to be? An adequate response to that question forces us to focus the dialectic of this section (sinner/creature) in that of the next: tragic/Adamic. But before doing that we need to close the historical discussion pertinent to this section and offer some assessment of the historical development from a constructive theological vantage point.

The rival currents of optimism and pessimism may be identified once again as we complete our sampling of the reflection the church has made available for contemporary faith. For a post-Reformation Roman Catholic response, the decree promulgated on June 17, 1546, at the fifth session of the Council of Trent is the most important document. The ambiguity in the formulation probably reflects the fact that the participants were split between Augustin-

5 / SIN AND EVIL

ian, Anselmian, and Thomistic emphases. But the ambiguity does not obscure a clear weakening of the gravity of the effects of original sin, when these formulations are measured against those of Orange.

Thus the Tridentine decree on original sin specifies that Adam "lost his holiness and the justice in which he had been established" and proceeds to cite Orange to the effect "that through that offense of prevarication the entire Adam was transformed in body and soul for the worse" (Denzinger, 788). What is more striking is that the formulation at Orange adds that the freedom of the soul does not remain uninjured. This is omitted at Trent, despite the fact that a preliminary text of this canon did have a weakened version of the formulation at Orange. Consistently, Trent's decree on justification makes the point explicitly that the free will "was not extinguished in them, however weakened and debased in its powers" (Denzinger, 793). Other canons speak more directly to the questions we defer to later: How do the effects reach us, and how may they be overcome? But one may say that in none of them is the more optimistic "privation" emphasis significantly challenged.

On the other hand, a challenge to this optimism may be heard in the formulations found in the Thirty-Nine Articles of the Church of England (1571) and the Westminster Confession of Faith (1647). The text of the ninth article of the former hardly requires comment:

> Man is very far gone from original righteousness, and is of his own nature inclined to evil, so that the flesh lusteth always contrary to the spirit; and therefore in every person born into this world, it deserveth God's wrath and damnation . . . the Apostle doth confess, that concupiscence and lust hath of itself the nature of sin.

Accordingly, the tenth article ("Of Free Will") stresses that "we have no power to do good works pleasant and acceptable to God without the grace of God" and the thirteenth article ("Of Works before Justification") adds:

> Works done before the grace of Christ . . . are not pleasant to God, forasmuch as they spring not of faith in Jesus Christ; neither do they make men meet to receive grace, or (as the School-authors say) deserve grace of congruity . . . we doubt not but they have the nature of sin.

The Westminster Confession also rejects any human preparation for salvation and speaks of our share in the "original corruption" by which we are "dead in sin, and wholly defiled in all the faculties and parts of soul and body" (Westminster Confession of Faith, VI, II).

The most interesting differences in the formulations concern not the human condition after Adam, but God's role in all of this. The Thirty-Nine Articles affirm simply selective "predestination to life," while the Westminster Confession has God permitting the sin of "our first parents," "having purposed to order it to his own glory," and among those hearing the word specifies an "effectual calling" only to the predestined, who can never fall from the state of justification. Of the others, it is said:

> The rest of mankind God was pleased, according to the unsearchable counsel of his own will, whereby he extendeth or withholdeth mercy as he pleaseth, for the glory of his sovereign power over his creatures, to pass by, and to ordain them to dishonour and wrath for their sin, to the praise of his glorious justice. (Ibid., III, VII.)

We mention these differences not because we intend to treat them as they bear on the issues of earlier chapters (the agency in sin) or of later ones (the remedy for sin). We do so because it is apparent that a doctrine of God may in effect bracket one of two apparently essentially identical formulations of original sin and so significantly qualify any comparative assessment of its optimism or pessimism. Nonetheless, both formulations—each in its distinctive systematic context—still stand as challenges to optimism in the church's teaching on original sin.

From this brief discussion of the massive material that represents the church's reflection on the effects of original sin, we draw a few statements in relation to considerations that are other than historical:

First, despite Luther and Calvin, it will not do to speak of the image of God as being entirely lost. Already the Priestly writer of the Pentateuch has God blessing humankind after the flood of judgment in nearly the same terms as the initial blessing and making specific appeal to the image of God (Gen. 9:1–2). Ernst Käsemann's statement is simply too strong: "Adam is a different person before and after the fall. The apostle therefore does not adhere to the Jewish view which . . . maintained a divine likeness still remained. For him, only Christ has an *imago dei*, an image which is only given back to us with faith."[25] Emil Brunner serves both empirical and biblical sense better—and grants the status the reformers' own statements about the "non-brutish" character of the human creature after Adam seem to require.

> We make a distinction of category; formally the image is not infringed upon even in the least degree—whether he sins or not, man is a subject, and responsible. Materially, the image is completely lost, man is a sinner through and through, and there is nothing in him which is not stained by sin.[26]

The strain of optimism in the tradition appropriately raises the question whether Brunner's complete pessimism concerning the material is warranted. What material reality, if any, is given in order to retain formal responsibility?

Second, biblical faith and contemporary experience witness to the universality and inevitability of sin. The "positive pessimism" strand within the tradition accords with this witness better than the privational understanding does.

421

5 / SIN AND EVIL

Third, the unity of the human person is such that the affirmation and the critique of that person after Adam cannot be isolated from each other. Edmund Schlink makes this point well in commenting on the Lutheran Confessions: "There is no doubt that the same features of man recur whether we view him in his creatureliness *or* in his corruption. No part of man is mentioned which, subtracting corruption from his creatureliness, could remain as a positive residue."[27]

Fourth, the unity of the human person, together with the recognition that that person is fully a sinner and fully a creature, suggests that Luther's distinction between freedom toward that which is "below us" and bondage toward that which is "above us" is too facile. At this point fresh constructive work is needed. Perhaps the recognition in Lutheran circles that "civil righteousness" is possible can point the way, if one asks how such righteousness matters to God without displacing the more direct relationship to God.

Fifth, the unity of the person in sin and creatureliness forbids only the isolation of elements, not the empirical description of this dialectic. Against Schlink's characteristically Lutheran claim that "it is evident that this is merely a conceptual distinction, in no case an empirical one,"[28] the Augustinian, medieval, and Melanchthonian anthropological interest is to be affirmed.

How is all this to be held together? While one may appropriately distrust simplicity and finality about a topic over which Christians have differed so strenuously, some further word of orientation within the maelstrom of opinion is clearly desirable. We attempt that now by asking about the "how" of this "what" of sin that reaches us after Adam.

BONDAGE AND RESPONSIBILITY

Let us look back to see where the momentum of our argument may be tending. In the Christian view of things the human project is not what it should be, given the divine intention denoted by the "image of God." This is not a matter of some few depraved or deprived types. Christian witness and human experience come together to speak of the universal human predicament. For Christians the chief (though not the only) word to describe this state is "sin." We shall speak later of other forms of evil. What matters now is to ponder further the Christian conviction that all come to be sinners—all, save one, at least. There is essential Christian agreement on the universality of sin, despite the disagreements reported in the previous section. But what shall one make of this universality? If all come to sin, are all bound to sin? Many Christians will grant that the sin they know in themselves has the quality of inevitability to it. But *how* does it begin with us? Surely in some sense what we come to be is rooted in how we begin to be, in what we are as we begin.

THE EFFECT OF SIN

Thus sin's quantity and sin's quality drive Christian reflection to ask of the beginning of each of us, to ask how it is that we are such when we begin that we all come to be sinners. Do we all end bound in sin because we are bound to sin as we begin? It clearly makes sense to relate the sad tale of what we come to be to the ominous suggestion that there is something radically wrong with us even as we begin to be.

Yet we wish whatever we say of how we are bound at the beginning to be coherent with what we said in earlier chapters about the Adamic character of the agency at work in sin. Both Christian witness and human experience bring us to speak of human responsibility for the human predicament. To speak of human responsibility may well be to speak of more than individual responsibility, but it is surely not to speak of less. When we speak of what is given as we begin, we speak of the "bound." But we must ask as well how that which is given for us can become fully and responsibly our own. This suggests that we should speak of guilt only as and after we speak of sin. Sin is that *in* me which constitutes something *about* me: guilt. Thus juridical understandings which assign guilt without recognizing sin are inadequate. The formulations of fathers like Ambrose, who declined to speak of concupiscence as sin but who spoke of guilt through our involvement with Adam, or of Augustine, who spoke occasionally of concupiscence as the punishment for Adam's sin, depend on some clarification of a more than legal or forensic relationship to Adam. Just ahead we turn to that. Further ahead, in the next chapter, we attempt to state how the dying which inevitably comes on us is related to this chief reality of sin.

At times human connectedness in sin has been thought of as a kind of mystical unity. Thus Nygren can comment on Rom. 5:12, "Adam is significant as the head of the 'old' humanity, as the head of the present aeon. That which happened to the head involves the body also."[29] Old Testament scholars speak of the reality of a common spiritual world, by which the prophets can condemn later generations for the sins of earlier ones, for the later generations are still responsible.[30] Perhaps this is more a rejection of the question of "how" it is that we are bound than it is an answer to it. Yet at times this conception is clarified by appeal to definite conceptual structures, as when theologians appeal to what H. Wheeler Robinson has called the notion of "corporate personality" in ancient Israel. Robinson identified four aspects to this notion: the "vertical" extension into past and future, the "realism" by which the concept is distinguished from fictitious or poetic personifications, the "oscillation" between more individual and more group reference, and the persistence of the concept despite developing emphasis on the individual.[31]

Does this concept adequately clarify how we are bound but still responsible? A sense of corporate responsibility cut off from the reality of some kind

5 / SIN AND EVIL

of psychical unity will be hard put to sustain itself. Thus in 1 Samuel 14 the people suffer the consequences of Jonathan's sin but are not responsible for the sin itself. An individual's responsibility for his or her sins is not denied, but one does need to recognize that an individual affects others to the point, as it were, of possessing or defiling them.[32]

What, then, of psychical unity? Robinson's appeal to Levy-Bruhl's hypotheses about the primitive mind has been weakened by the work and writing of field anthropologists.[33] The effect of these responses to Robinson is not to deny a sense of corporateness but to cast doubt on a supraindividual agency at work within the individual. Even without such specific responses, the theme of corporate personality may be said to have been in considerable difficulty in its implicit appeal to philosophical realism in a pervasively pluralistic context.

But perhaps "corporate personality" is a premature speculative synthesis of elements which require further attention. I refer particularly to the realism and extension into past and future of which Robinson speaks. These, taken together with the symbols of defilement, may suggest a way forward. Paul Ricoeur may be right that the symbolism of defilement resists reflection, because it is pre-ethical and quasi-material.[34] Yet it should be noted that the notion of defilement does accept the event structure sustaining individuals as the context in which the human predicament spreads. It is thus implicitly closer to our experience (which surely includes being acted upon) than the notion of a psychical unity which somehow acts in us. Perhaps some clue to the universality of sin can be found by attending to the structures through which sin spreads. After all, that structure at once sustains and binds the self. That structure applies both in the beginning-to-be and the coming-to-be of the self. As that structure reaches back behind the self, it may well carry the deeper continuity of sin to the self.

The sense for this more empirical connectedness has been prominent in the church's reflection. Such connectedness is not a matter of choice. Thus it was seen to be clearly inadequate to speak merely of sin spreading by the force of example, as did Pelagius, who held that sin "is carried on by imitation, committed by the will, denounced by the reason, manifested by the law, punished by justice."[35] To this the church was moved to insist that sin is carried "not by imitation, but by propagation" at Carthage in 418 and at Trent in 1546, for example.[36] Here the church's teacher has been Augustine, whose conviction was that it is "by the begetting of the flesh . . . that sin is contracted which is original."[37] This biological emphasis may have been first suggested by Ambrosiaster and was brought to bear on Augustine through Ambrose's linking the sinlessness of Jesus and his virginal conception. The passage in Ps. 51:5 ("Behold, I was brought forth in iniquity, and in sin did my mother conceive me") seemed to point this way. And Augustine's Latin

Bible translated Rom. 5:12: "Sin came into the world, and death through sin, and so death spread to all men, through one man, in whom [*in quo*] all sinned."

This formulation of the "how" of connectedness faces insuperable difficulties. Exegetically there are compelling arguments to translate Rom. 5:12 "because all men sinned," at least weakening the note of presence in Adam. More significant, this view seems to attribute too great and too negative a role to our biological givenness. Tertullian's traducianism—while not clearly held by Augustine—is the logical basis for this understanding of original sin. Drawing on Stoic sources, Tertullian wrote: "Everything that is, is body." He drew what seemed to be the necessary conclusion for our theme:

> Our first parent contained within himself the undeveloped germ of all mankind, and his soul was the fountain-head of all souls: all varieties of individual human nature are but different modifications of that one spiritual substance. Therefore the whole of nature became corrupt in the original father of the race, and sinfulness is propagated together with souls.[38]

The difficulty here is that what is claimed is claimed on an insufficiently ample basis: Biological connection lacks the tensile strength to support such a prison house of personal bondage. The way ahead is not to appeal to a "creationist" theory of God's special role in the coming-to-be of souls, for that—apart from its inherent conceptual two-world difficulties—threatens to make sin trivial or God evil. Nor is it helpful to pull back to a vague mystical connectedness or to settle for a clear but shallow individualism, which in compromising the corporateness must always puzzle over the universality of sin. Rather, it seems better to recognize that the alternatives "imitation or propagation" are too simple. A growing stream of reflection about sin draws on material in the middle distance between the logical extremes of propagation and imitation. That others inevitably play a constitutive role in relation to our very selfhood is increasingly recognized, even by someone as attracted to individualism as J. P. Sartre, who closes his autobiography with these words: "What remains? A whole man, composed of all men and as good as all of them and no better than any."[39] To move in this direction is not to jettison talk of corporateness but to extend the move implied in the shift from mystical identity to biological propagation. By that shift such talk is placed in the context of empirical, temporal connectedness.

Piet Schoonenberg has shown that this doctrine of "social heredity" can speak of far more than bad example. Writing of "the sin of the world" he speaks of how certain values may be totally obscured for a child, so that freedom cannot realize itself in that sphere.[40] Rosemary Ruether has made the same claim on a broader scale:

5 / SIN AND EVIL

The breakup of the communal life of earlier tribal society coincided historically with the patriarchal systems of the formative period of Western civilization. Psychologically, this means that the emerging individual ego did not have its negative projections challenged by the independent self-definition of the "other." Therefore the ego became fixated in immature adjustments, habitually dealing with threats to its rule through strategies of separation, denial, devaluation, and oppressive domination.[41]

Perhaps it may be objected that this way of speaking seems to claim too much, that it fits better with the privation theme than with the view of original sin as positive concupiscence. No act of individual will seems needed to sustain the human predicament. It may be difficult to see how guilt could be claimed in this situation, unless one says with some current Roman Catholic thought that original sin, as the historical privation of that to which the self is transcendentally oriented, is a condition of guilt because it exists in contradiction to that to which we are called.[42]

But perhaps the sociality of our existence can illumine also the positive character of our predicament after Adam. Schoonenberg tries to cling to both the individual and the sociality of existence for that individual: "As a free person, I cannot be deprived of my freedom by the free decisions of others, but they may well place me in a situation which may determine me inwardly even in my freedom. Another can, for instance, disclose a value which makes an appeal to my freedom."[43]

Let us pause to assess the argument. There is will in this conditioning by social heredity. It does pass through the center of my person. There is, to be sure, a givenness here which seems not to possess the sense of contingency we normally require for will. But must personhood and personal will be linked with contingency?

The possible responses to the last question are not many. If one responds in the affirmative, one may then emphasize the sense in which no contingent act of will is required for sin to emerge.[44] Or if one holds that sin must be "personal," one may then decline to speak of this condition itself as sin, bearing guilt, though one may still grant that out of it does culpable sin invariably proceed.[45] In this view, linking the person so strongly with contingency, the reality of sin's universality proves puzzling. Perhaps this position need not collapse before the question just when a freely personal will to sin joins the difficulties given at the self's beginning; for that question is not harder than the broader one about when the freely personal will can be said to be "there." But one would need to ask *how* the one yields the other. That which is free cannot derive necessarily from that which is unfree. Here, then, we seem near affirming responsibility so simply that the sense in which we are bound is lost.

If, on the other hand, we grant that personal will may be present without contingency, we will likely call this condition at the beginning personal sin.[46]

THE EFFECT OF SIN

Where there is sin without contingency there can surely be guilt of the same sort. But if sin begins in a free fall, must it not somehow continue still in freedom and so with responsibility? Otherwise I join Adam only as victim and not as co-perpetrator after all. But when and how does individual responsibility come to be associated with sin—through contingency or otherwise? Here we seem near affirming bondage so simply that the sense in which we are responsible is lost. These difficulties drive a Catholic theologian like Charles Baumgartner to say: "This state, antecedent in choice, is real but analogous guilt, thus lying midway between personal guilt and natural defect."[47] Perhaps such Catholic anthropological ambiguity states in simpler fashion the principled ambiguity characterizing many Protestant theologians in the existentialist tradition. Kierkegaard stressed that sin roots in individual will, but he could add: "and this corruption of the will goes well beyond the consciousness of the individual. This is a perfectly consistent declaration, for otherwise the question how sin began must arise with respect to each individual."[48]

While such Protestant writers may not share the anthropological interest in specific distinctions which characterize the Catholic approach to hamartiology, they too seem to recognize that it is difficult to know where to locate the self so that its responsibility can be properly assessed. The problem is not merely postcanonical. Consider Paul's plight in Romans 7. To say with Conzelmann that I am necessarily concerned for the good and necessarily fail, or with Bultmann that "man has always already missed the existence that at heart he seeks, his intent is basically perverse, evil," is in principle to share the difficulty afflicting the Catholic discussions.[49]

Perhaps current reflection concerning the nature of human selfhood, which recognizes the plenitude of competing centers of organization within the self, can provide an empirical context for the discussion of these difficulties. Similarly, the contemporary sense for the temporality of the self might help us understand that what is given is given for a self freshly constituting itself precisely in the terms of what is given to it. While in many respects the given poses more possibilities, there are in principle always some nonnegotiable realities *there* for the self. Part of what is there is the structure, given by God, which leads the self to seek someone to worship, to trust, to seek some God. Thus Augustine could say that the health in us expresses itself in our desire to relate by using and enjoying, but that our disease twists the relationships so that we enjoy things and use people. *How* do we do so? Faith is only prepared to say that we do so as persons bound but still responsible. Thus one can well say that Paul in Romans attempts no explanation of the physical or historical relations between Adam's sin and those who followed and "became sinners." Can one simply leave it at that?

There is an agenda here for constructive theology— precisely this dialectical dogmatic conviction that in sin we are bound, but responsible still. That

5 / SIN AND EVIL

claim can be responsibly made on material grounds. We have argued that it fits faithfully the witness of the tradition. It is anchored as well in our own experience. Blaise Pascal makes the point well:

> Nothing, to be sure, is more of a shock to us than such a doctrine, and yet without this mystery, which is the most incomprehensible of all, we should be incomprehensible to ourselves. The tangled knot of our condition acquired its twists and turns in that abyss; so that man is more inconceivable without the mystery than the mystery to man.[50]

We cannot let the formal criterion of coherence intimidate such material testimonies. Yet we accept that criterion, but recognize the direction in which further progress may be sought: the empirical connectedness of selves. This difficulty would only become intolerable if it were to immobilize Christian thought and life. We have at least indicated a direction in which to think.

NOTES

1. Søren Kierkegaard, *Christian Discourses,* trans. Walter Lowrie (London: Oxford University Press, 1939), pp. 132–33.

2. Paul Ricoeur, *The Symbolism of Evil,* trans. Emerson Buchanan (Boston: Beacon Press, 1967), pp. 246–47.

3. F. R. Tennant, *The Sources of the Doctrines of the Fall and Original Sin* (Cambridge: At the University Press, 1903), p. 275.

4. Jaroslav Pelikan, *The Emergence of the Catholic Tradition (100-600)* (Chicago: University of Chicago Press, 1971), pp. 281–83.

5. *Against Heresies,* v,27,2 (emphasis added). See Adolf von Harnack, *History of Dogma,* trans. Neil Buchanan, 7 vols. (Boston: Little, Brown & Co., 1961), 2:270–71; and John Hick, *Evil and the God of Love* (New York: Harper & Row; London: Macmillan & Co., 1966), chap. 9. For such an emphasis in contemporary work, see Alfred Vanneste, *The Dogma of Original Sin* (Brussels: Vander, 1975); and Maurizio Flick and Zoltan Alszeghy, *Il peccato originale* (Brescia: Queriniana, 1972). See also Brian O. McDermott, "The Theology of Original Sin: Recent Developments," *TS* 38 (September 1977): 478–512.

6. Tennant, *Sources,* pp. 332–36.

7. See J. N. D. Kelly, *Early Christian Doctrines* (New York: Harper & Brothers, 1958), pp. 365–66.

8. Ibid., pp. 369–72. Cf. Pelikan, *Emergence,* pp. 318–29.

9. Cf. Kelly, *Early Christian Doctrines,* p. 364: "Augustine does not inculcate a doctrine of 'total depravity,' according to which the image of God has been utterly obliterated in us. Even though grievously altered, fallen man remains noble, 'the spark, as it were, of reason in virtue of which he was made in God's likeness has not been completely extinguished.' "

10. Pelikan, *Emergence*, p. 330.
11. See G. Vandervelde, *Original Sin: Two Major Trends in Contemporary Roman Catholic Interpretation* (Amsterdam: Rodopi N.V., 1975), pp. 26–28; and Henri Rondet, *Original Sin: The Patristic and Theological Background*, trans. Cajetan Finegan (New York: Alba House, 1969), pp. 143–45.
12. Vandervelde, *Original Sin*, pp. 28–32.
13. Heiko Oberman, *The Harvest of Medieval Theology* (Cambridge, Mass.: Harvard University Press, 1963), p. 49.
14. Brian A. Gerrish, *Grace and Reason* (Oxford: At the Clarendon Press, 1962), p. 132.
15. Ibid., p. 122.
16. This passage and the one cited below on p. 417 are taken from Luther's *The Bondage of the Will*; see *Luther and Erasmus: Free Will and Salvation*, trans. Philip S. Watson, LCC 17 (Philadelphia: Westminster Press, 1969), p. 141, for both passages.
17. George Hunston Williams, *The Radical Reformation* (Philadelphia: Westminster Press, 1962), p. 799.
18. As in Luther's comment on Gen. 1:26 ("Let them have dominion over the fish of the sea. . . .") in his lectures on Genesis.
19. Gerrish, *Grace and Reason*, p. 26.
20. Robert C. Schultz puts the point nicely in "Original Sin: Accident or Substance: The Paradoxical Significance of F.C. I, 53–62 in Historical Context," *in Discord, Dialogue, and Concord*, ed. Lewis W. Spitz and Wenzel Lohff (Philadelphia: Fortress Press, 1977), p. 44: "Unbelief—not fearing, not loving, not trusting God—does not mean that relationship has been lost. The personal relationship to God remains, but it has been converted into its opposite. Mistrust is not the absence of trust but an active relationship which not only results in the commission of sins but is the essence of sin itself."
21. *Institutes* ii,1,8. See also François Wendel, *Calvin: The Origins and Development of His Religious Thought*, trans. Philip Mairet (New York: Harper & Row, 1950), pp. 188ff.
22. Ekkehard Muehlenberg, "Synergia and Justification by Faith," in *Discord, Dialogue, and Concord*, p. 34.
23. Schultz, "Original Sin," pp. 47–50.
24. Muehlenberg, "Synergia and Justification by Faith," pp. 21–23.
25. Ernst Käsemann, *Perspectives on Paul*, trans. Margaret Kohl (Philadelphia: Fortress Press, 1971), pp. 58–59.
26. This passage is from Emil Brunner's *Natural Theology* (1935), trans. Peter Fraenkel (London: Geoffrey Bles, 1946). For a discussion of this widespread emphasis in Brunner, see David Cairns, *The Image of God in Man* (London: SCM Press, 1953), pp. 146–63.
27. Edmund Schlink, *Theology of the Lutheran Confessions*, trans. Paul F. Koehneke and Herbert J. A. Bouman (Philadelphia: Fortress [Muhlenberg] Press, 1961), p. 45.
28. Ibid., p. 46.
29. Anders Nygren, *Commentary on Romans*, trans. Carl C. Rasmussen (Philadelphia: Fortress [Muhlenberg] Press, 1949), p. 312.

5 / SIN AND EVIL

30. Walther Eichrodt, *Theology of the Old Testament,* trans. J. A. Baker, 2 vols. (Philadelphia: Westminster Press, 1961–67), 2:407.

31. H. Wheeler Robinson, *Corporate Personality in Ancient Israel* (Philadelphia: Fortress Press, 1964).

32. Cf. J. R. Porter, "The Legal Aspects of the Concept of Corporate Personality in the Old Testament," VT 25 (1965): 379: "The Hebrew realized as well as we do that, if a particular person commits a crime, he is responsible and guilty for it, in a way that even those closest to him, his wife and his son, really cannot be. But his basic recognition is qualified, as far as the operation of the law was concerned, not so much by ideas of 'corporate personality' as by the notion that a man can possess persons in much the same way that he possesses property and by early religious beliefs about the contagious nature of blood, holiness, sin, and uncleanness."

33. J. W. Rodgerson, "The Hebrew Conception of Corporate Personality: A Re-examination," *JThS* 21 (April 1970): 1–16.

34. Ricoeur, *Symbolism of Evil,* pp. 25–28.

35. Pelikan, *Emergence of the Catholic Tradition,* p. 315.

36. At Carthage the formulation stresses baptism for infants "so that that which they have contracted from generation may be cleansed in them by regeneration." (Denzinger, 102). For Trent, see Denzinger, 790.

37. Pelikan, *Emergence of the Catholic Tradition,* p. 300.

38. This is the paraphrase of Augustus Neander in *General History of the Christian Religion and Church,* vol.2, trans. Joseph Torrey (London: Henry G. Bohn, 1851), pp. 346–47.

39. Jean-Paul Sartre, *The Words,* trans. Bernard Frechtman (New York: George Braziller, 1964), p. 255.

40. Piet Schoonenberg, *Man and Sin,* trans. Joseph Donceel (Notre Dame, Ind.: University of Notre Dame Press, 1965), pp. 115–18.

41. Rosemary Radford Ruether, *Liberation Theology* (New York: Paulist Press, 1972), as paraphrased by Wanda Warren Berry, "Images of Sin and Salvation in Feminist Theology," *AThR* 60 (January 1978): 25–54.

42. For a full statement of this theme drawn from Karl Rahner, see K. H. Weger, *Theologie der Erbsünde* (Freiburg: Herder Verlag, 1970).

43. Piet Schoonenberg, "Sin," *SM(E)* 6, p. 90.

44. Holsten Fagerberg, *A New Look at the Lutheran Confessions,* trans. Gene J. Lund (St. Louis: Concordia Publishing House, 1972), p. 143, with special reference to Apology II.

45. See Brian O. McDermott, "The Theology of Original Sin: Recent Developments," *TS* 38 (September 1977): 478–512, for a summary of such thinking in Alfred Vanneste and Domiciano Fernandez.

46. Ernst Kinder, *Die Erbsünde* (Stuttgart: Schwabenverlag, 1959).

47. I have the paraphrase from McDermott, "Theology of Original Sin," p. 485. Cf. Ricoeur, *Symbolism of Evil,* p. 100.

48. Søren Kierkegaard, *Sickness unto Death,* trans. W. Lowrie (Princeton: Princeton University Press, 1941), p. 226.

49. Hans Conzelmann, *An Outline of the Theology of the New Testament,* trans. John Bowden (New York: Harper & Row, 1969), p. 234; Rudolf Bultmann, *Theology of the New Testament*, trans. Kendrick Grobel, 2 vols. (New York: Charles Scribner's Sons, 1954–55), 1:227.

50. Blaise Pascal, *Pensées* (New York: E. P. Dutton, 1958), p. 121, no. 434.

4
Metaphysical and Natural Evil

As finite freedom the creature suffers. The creature is called to a life which transcends this life but depends on it, is set within a structure impartially bestowing connection and consequence, and undergoes the distortion—objectively and subjectively—of that structure due to sin.

FINITUDE

After three chapters devoted to the treatment of moral evil, we turn to consideration of metaphysical and natural evil. We have found ourselves speaking of the universality of sin; we begin here with another universal: finitude. That we are finite in understanding, in ability to communicate, above all in span of years, is this not evil? Christians have not agreed about this matter, and we shall have to chronicle that division. But we can begin by identifying two convictions that are held in common and that bear on this issue.

The first is the conviction that God is categorically supreme. In Chapter 2 we considered this theme in speaking of God as Creator. Now it becomes the basis for constructing a perspective on finitude, especially on death. First, God's supremacy strips death of the sacral or numinous qualities so commonly associated with it. Death possesses no independent power, as if to rival the sovereignty of Yahweh. Second, somehow God must be related to death, if God is the Creator, if there are not two Gods.

But how is God related to death? Close at hand lies the inference that part of God's categorical supremacy is that God alone is infinite, so that our finitude, our death, is given with creation as a "natural" state. Yet this reflection must face the second common Christian conviction in this matter: that our death, our dying, is evil. The Scriptures do not deny the hideousness of death.[1]

How shall these two convictions—God's supremacy, death's evilness—be held together? At times the sense of the evil character of death seems to get its very content from its relationship to the categorically supreme God. Von Rad comments on Psalm 88: "The dead were cut off from praising Jahweh and from hearing him proclaimed, and above all, they were cut off from him

5 / SIN AND EVIL

himself."² But what follows from this for our understanding of the cause of death? Perhaps the clearest line in Christian reflection moves back from the universality of death to the universality of sin, with the connecting link being provided by the experience of death as evil. God's supremacy, then, finds expression in the notion that death is the fruit of sin. Perhaps Paul is often too simply identified with this view, which fits Romans 5 better than it does 1 Corinthians 15.³ In any case, by the time of the Council of Carthage (418) it was clear to the church that

> whoever says that Adam, the first man, was made mortal, so that, whether he sinned or whether he did not sin, he would die in body, that is he would go out of the body not because of the merit of sin but by reason of the necessity of nature, let him be anathema. (Denzinger, 101)

This understanding prevailed at the Council of Orange as well and has been the most prominent view in the teaching of the church to our day.

This position can recognize the implication of God's categorical supremacy. To be sure, one might say, only God is naturally immortal, but the possibility of indefinite life in dependence on the living God is given as promise until sin severs the connection with God, rendering death effective.⁴ What shall be said of God's role in this? While the simplest view is to see the deed of sin as bringing its own destiny, there is a persistent biblical witness to God's own involvement in human death. It is possible, of course, to conceive of that involvement as direct and particular causation, entailing specific, albeit apparently universal, intervention. The problems concerning such divine involvement are part of more general difficulties afflicting this view.

While this view does coherently combine the two orienting convictions, two objections occur: First, there is the ecological or evolutionary point, as made by R. Troisfontaines:

> Evolution as an incontrovertible fact . . . is unthinkable without death, for immortality would by its very nature undo evolution because of a surplus of people. Indeed, life—and certainly its progressive development—is unthinkable, unless by the grace of the death of individuals. Hence human nature must be necessarily mortal in its very essence.⁵

This objection is strengthened the more we grant humankind's membership in the animal kingdom, where death presumably occurred well before the advent of sin with humankind. We may seem here to be on too secular ground. But the second major objection to an absolute causal link between sin and death is an exegetical one. Claus Westermann puts the point directly enough: "Man, just because he has been created, carries within him limitation by death as an essential element of the human state."⁶ The curse applies until we die; we die because we were created out of dust and shall return to dust. On the edge of death one knows this: "I am about to go the way of all the earth" (Josh. 23:14; 1 Kings 2:2).

The force of these objections has led nearly all contemporary theologians to regard physical death as something given with creation.[7] It does not follow from this that such natural death would have been simply a peaceful transition, "the highest, definitive, personal self-consummation," in the words of one of the more enthusiastic exponents of this view.[8] Rather, Barth seems more right in speaking of this death, though natural, as yet belonging to the "shadowside of creation."[9] That fits with the recognition that humankind was created "good, not perfect" and that if the human creature's relationship to God knew the tension of "epistemic distance," surely the reality of death would not be unaffected.

Perhaps this contemporary emphasis is not without some continuity with the church's traditional reflection. Canon 1 of the Council of Carthage, which we have cited above, was not specifically approved by Pope Zosimus in the letter he addressed to the whole church on the subject of original sin. The Council of Trent did not reproduce this canon, and a draft condemnation which said, "If anyone says that Adam was bound to die in any way, even if he had not sinned, let him be anathema," was left in the archives.[10] Within the Lutheran tradition, similarly, there has been a recognition that the *most* one could claim for the creature was "a freedom from the proximate power of dying and the natural tendency to death," not an absolute freedom from death which belongs only to God.[11]

More important, the contemporary understanding surely agrees with the traditional view that there is a connection between sin and death, though it does not conceive that connection in simple and absolute causality. In sin death is exacerbated. It is changed objectively. Thus von Rad notes that Israel's wisdom teachers spoke of "having to die" and by this meant "the premature death which the fool, the lascivious and the lazy bring upon themselves" by ignoring the proper limits involved in the relationships of created goodness.[12] Death is also changed subjectively—it takes on a new quality. Bonhoeffer writes:

> Death as transitoriness is not the death that comes from God. What does "to be dead" mean? It does not mean the abolition of created being; it means no longer being able to live—and yet having to live—in the presence of God . . . outlawed, lost and damned, but not nonexisting . . . to have life not as a gift but as a commandment.[13]

Thus death is not exhausted in the physical process of dying. In the qualitative experience of dying one knows the distortion of the relationship to God. While at the immediate level of causality it may seem sensible to follow an organic rather than a juridical link between sin and death,[14] it re-

5 / SIN AND EVIL

mains doubly true that our dying cannot be fully separated from God. Helmut Thielicke writes of Luther's understanding:

> The terrifying quality of man's death consists thus not merely in his loss of physical life, but in his forfeit of the living fellowship with God . . . death is not merely a quantitative boundary, but the imposition of qualitative limits; it is a fateful event in the personal relationship between God and man . . . death still carries the poison of wrath and thus remains a living reality focused on us, a power holding us spellbound.[15]

While reflection will resist substituting such theological considerations for the organic connections by which sin hurries us toward our death quantitatively, the sinner's qualitative experience of dying does include the painful awareness of that which is terribly wrong in the relationship with God. Even abstracting from sin to the death given with creatureliness, one must say that God does not stand related to the death-bearing organism of life merely deistically, but as living will. The "wrath of God" refers to something real within the sinner, within God, and between God and the sinner. Our dying is also caught up in the reality. Also, God has acted in Christ to show that God is Lord over sin, Lord even over God's own wrath.

Given these quantitative and qualitative links between sin and death, perhaps the contemporary emphasis can even find itself in significant continuity with conciliar statements which seem to take the other tack. Pelagius said that Adam would have died even if he had not sinned, and the church rejected his assertion. But Pelagius was speaking of the only death he and we in fact know: death as punishment for sin.[16]

Perhaps contemporary reflection can also understand itself in continuity with that tradition in the Eastern church which stresses that after the sin of Adam we "fell sick of corruption" and that "by becoming mortal, we acquired greater urge to sin." [17] Ernest Becker has argued persuasively that one of the things that follows from death is a will to deny it. The denial of death yields many aberrations, including the sacrifice of the lives of others, whether literally or through scapegoating: "The death fear of the ego is lessened by the killing, the sacrifice of the other; through the death of the other, one buys oneself free from the penalty of dying, of being killed." [18]

God's faithful have managed to live with death, because they lived with God. In the Old Testament fear of death is overcome, not by appeal to the particularity of another life but by calm reliance on the One whose faithfulness cannot be destroyed.[19] Later the believer's confidence became more specific:

> What you sow does not come to life unless it dies. And what you sow is not the body which is to be, but a bare kernel, perhaps of wheat or of some other grain. . . . So is it with the resurrection of the dead. What is sown is perishable,

METAPHYSICAL AND NATURAL EVIL

what is raised is imperishable. . . . The first man was from the earth, a man of dust; the second man is from heaven. . . . Just as we have borne the image of the man of dust, we shall also bear the image of the man of heaven (1 Cor. 15:36–37, 42, 47, 49).

Again we return to the theme of the divine intention in creation. Humankind is meant for God and is given what is needed to that end. Freedom is such a gift, and a precious one, though from that gift comes the reality of moral evil. But trust does not mature without risk. Moral perfection cannot be created "from nothing," if mature trust is intrinsic to the conception itself. Now Paul seems to suggest that while we are meant for unending life, that too cannot be given as inherent possession but only as something to which one passes trusting the promise of God. Just as sin can disrupt the gift of freedom, so it can sorely trouble the passage from finitude.

There is as well a third face of evil which troubles the human pilgrimage and we must now turn to that reality, suffering, and its relationship to our status as creatures and sinners.

SUFFERING

How does a child dying of inoperable cancer of the brain serve humankind? Must not the Creator who establishes the criteria by which such an event could count as service be regarded as simply evil? With a God like that who needs a devil? Perhaps it is in face of the stark reality of suffering that the issue of the justification of God comes before us most unavoidably. Perhaps moral evil (sin) and metaphysical evil (finitude, death) do not pronounce the verdict of guilty with unambiguous finality, though the indictments are hardly silenced. But before the face of suffering, will one not respond with Dostoevski's Ivan?

> Too high a price is asked for harmony; it is beyond our means to pay so much. And so I give back my entrance ticket, and if I am an honest man I give it back as soon as possible. And that I am doing. It's not God that I don't accept, Alyosha, only I most repectfully return the ticket to Him.[20]

Alyosha's response, "That's rebellion," and his appeal to the One who, having given "His innocent blood for all and everything," has a right to forgive and does forgive does not satisfy us. That response fits better the context Dostoevski has chosen: the suffering we inflict on each other in sin. We have commented on that by speaking of God's commitment to the venture of human freedom. But what, now, of that suffering which comes on us from sources that are not human? What of that evil we call "natural"? How can human freedom intercept the verdict against God in this case? If God has

5 / SIN AND EVIL

made us such that this suffering serves us, is not such a God to be rejected? Some familiar responses must be resisted.

It will not do to say that suffering does not exist. Although there may be a basis for distinguishing between the physiology of pain and the psychology of suffering,[21] and although we can create suffering subjectively which has no basis in reality outside ourselves, the sheer reality of pain and suffering still stands out as precisely that violence against our being which comes on us against our will and without our receptivity.

Nor may we say that suffering serves us by its sheer testimony to the splendor of existence. This way of thinking, loosely called the principle of plenitude, amounts to the sheer evocation of existence; what could be, should be—suffering included. Christian theology has at times drunk from this metaphysical wisdom, as when Augustine writes: "From things earthly to things heavenly, from the visible to the invisible, there are some things better than others; and for this purpose are they unequal, in order that they might all exist." (*City of God*, xi,22). But to argue so is finally to reduce goodness to being, which is to solve our difficulty by giving up what we are seeking to defend, that the Creator of being is not marred by the evil which is so real in the world of creatures.

We must also deny that suffering serves by introducing contrast into the universe. This response can be put in an aesthetic and static way, as when one argues that one would not appreciate the good without the experience of its opposite. Or it can be cast in an ethical and active way, as when one argues that suffering is needed as challenge to the human project. Both responses seem to cling still to the distinction between good and evil, and thus do not represent a simple appeal to some self-justifying transcendence of aesthetic contrast. Against both responses arguments converge from two sides. The inner life of the Trinity does not depend on contrast or challenge for its goodness. Why must we, made in God's image, need such? The argument is in difficulty on theological grounds. And in any case, there is far too much suffering for these purposes, and it is far too unevenly distributed. The argument fails on empirical grounds.

We have given cursory treatment to these historically influential responses because they do not represent genuinely theological responses. They are metaphysical, aesthetic, or at best moral arguments. But there are as well three theological responses which are commonly made but which need to be emphatically resisted.

First, whatever God does is right, and thus suffering is to be accepted without complaint. This response has something right: that no independent standard exists to which God's conduct must be held accountable. To grant the existence of such a standard would be to jettison the moral absoluteness of God. But it has at least two things badly muddled. God is committed to a venture with creation. Indeed, in the covenant and in Christ God has willed that all the peoples of the earth will be blessed. God's own intention, then, does become a basis on which the faithful accept the question of the justice of God, as that question is put outside and inside the walls of the sanctuary. Nor does mere acceptance of suffering follow from the claim that whatever God does is right, unless it can be shown either that God does all things or that God does the particular things that cause suffering. God's responsibility must be assessed with respect to the framework, its creation and preservation, within which specific events occur, but this is vastly different from contending that God "does" the specific events.

A second inadequate theological response argues that the devil causes the specific events of suffering. We have already repelled an appeal to the devil as the direct explanation for sin, for two reasons. One of these reasons, that stressing human responsibility, would seem by definition not to apply in speaking of natural evil. Perhaps it is not surprising, then, that theologians should seem to move the demonic into the vacuum.[22] We have accepted Paul Ricoeur's suggestion that the demonic be incorporated into the Adamic myth as a complicating factor, because such a move is suggested by the logic of temptation, the experience of the pervasiveness of evil, and the biblical witness particularly to the liberating work of Jesus. Here too there may well be a subordinate place for such incorporation. But that is all. The second reason holds also for natural evil. What is at stake is responsibility for the framework in creation by which natural evil comes upon us. Any simple appeal to the devil as an explanatory factor would once again jettison the absoluteness of God—in this case saving God's goodness at the expense of sacrificing God's power.

A third inadequate theological response suggests that specific sufferings are "sent" by God to particular individuals for specific purposes: punishment, education, and the like. Again, this view raises the issue of how God acts in the world. In raising this issue the view moves near the difficult territory of prayer for the sick and gratitude for those who recover. That God wills health and is at work against the forces of destruction in an ultimate sense is something we strongly affirm. But our attempt to recognize death as given within human finitude should give us pause even in our grateful praise. More pointed still, the excruciating differentiations ("Why me, O Lord?") baffle, if we are assuming that God sends specific sufferings directly. What is needed is a retreat to the general framework in order to ask the basic question of how God can be said to be good inasmuch as God made a world which is turning out no better than this one.

We have been saying that God willed human freedom as a necessary means toward a greater end. We believe the best approach—and it is surely none too splendid—is to seek to understand natural evil within what is required for a metaphysics of freedom. The structure of reality, whence natural evil

5 / SIN AND EVIL

comes, is made by God in the service of human freedom. Let us take the argument apart.

God gives what freedom needs to be freedom, and part of what is needed is consequence. In saying this we do not rush ahead to the commonsense truth that we must suffer the consequences of our folly or to the tragic one that in our defiance we bind ourselves. It is natural evil of which we would speak. C. S. Lewis makes the point that human beings need nature, if human freedom is to have consequence:

> What we need for human society is exactly what we have—a neutral something, neither you nor I, which we can both manipulate so as to make signs to each other. I can talk to you because we can both set up sound-waves in the common air between us. Matter, which keeps souls apart, also brings them together.[23]

Lewis's idealism shows through in his ghostly view of human identity, but he is quite right about the human necessity for that which is not human. Moreover, he is right about the required stability of that which sustains the human:

> But if matter is to serve as a neutral field it must have a fixed nature of its own.... If you were introduced into a world which thus varied at my every whim, you would be quite unable to act in it and would thus lose the exercise of your free will.[24]

Given the needed neutrality of the natural field, this reality can oppress and destroy us as well as serve us. As Frederick Tennant puts it:

> If water is to have the various properties in virtue of which it plays its beneficial part in the economy of the physical world and the life of mankind, it cannot at the same time lack its obnoxious capacity to drown us. The specific gravity of water is as much a necessary outcome of its ultimate constitution as its freezing point, or its thirst-quenching and cleansing functions.[25]

This seems particularly the case if it is the identical capacity within a natural system which in one instance blesses and in another destroys. Would we trade such a system for a world of instant miracle in which the deity would act to intercept the deleterious consequences of a natural system before they could occur? Two responses are possible:

We might say that the possibility of suffering—even its actuality—is not too high a price to pay for the moral benefits of stability of structure. Thus Tennant writes: "Without such regularity in physical phenomena there could be no probability to guide us: no prediction, no prudence, no accumulation of ordered experience, no pursuit of premediated ends, no formation of habit, no possibility of character or of culture."[26] It seems important to note that

METAPHYSICAL AND NATURAL EVIL

this does not claim that suffering is directly useful, as providing a stimulus to the development of certain human virtues. That tack seems to amount to one or the other of the errors we have said should be avoided. But it is not always avoided. Thus John Hick writes of what is required for human love:

> It is, in particular, difficult to see how it could ever grow to any extent in a paradise that excluded all suffering. For such love presupposes a "real life" in which there are obstacles to be overcome, tasks to be performed, goals to be achieved, setbacks to be endured, problems to be solved, dangers to be met.[27]

It seems better not to be so optimistic about actual suffering, though at least Hick stops short of sanctifying specific sufferings as sent by God.

Or we might say that God's commitment to human freedom, including as it does what freedom needs to be freedom, is so complete that God cannot intervene to prevent suffering. We seem prepared to say this about the direct exercise of freedom yielding consequence: What is sown shall be reaped. Again C. S. Lewis put it well:

> His omnipotence means power to do all that is intrinsically possible, not to do the intrinsically impossible. You may attribute miracles to Him, but not nonsense. This is no limit to His power. If you choose to say "God can give a creature free-will and at the same time withhold free-will from it" you have not succeeded in saying *anything* about God: meaningless combinations of words do not suddenly acquire meaning simply because we prefix to them the two other words "God can."[28]

Lewis seems to have understood that freedom's reality is in its efficacy. Now should we not say as much of the natural structure which is required in God's gift of freedom? God's commitment to freedom is so absolute that God cannot intervene in the workings of the world where freedom flourishes and flounders.

We hasten to add that this is not to say that God does not work *within* the structure; a limited God is not a deistic God. Nor is what we have said to suggest that God does not have in store for this world a reality which is qualitatively other than this, one where every tear of suffering too shall be wiped away.

Before hastening to a summary, two important though secondary matters must at least be mentioned. First, that suffering oppresses as well as serves us is surely due in large part to sin. That has not been our emphasis in these remarks, because we find the common correlation between suffering and sin to be sorely incomplete. But we do bring suffering on others and ourselves, objectively, in our sin, and we do experience suffering more intensely subjectively because of our unfaith. Here too the exacerbating and perduring character of the demonic is apparent.

5 / SIN AND EVIL

Second, we have not spoken of pain and suffering below the human level in the evolutionary cycle. While humankind must be held responsible for a great amount of such suffering, clearly we did not cause such suffering before we came into being, and presumably we do not cause all of it even now. Two responses seem to be appropriate: (1) Suffering below the human realm is to be understood in relation to the structure needed for human freedom. That structure out of which human nature evolved and which now oppresses as well as serves possesses in its very neutrality the same dialectical capacities in relation to all life. (2) God intends a new heaven and a new *earth*. Whether or not there is something analogous to human freedom in the "lower" levels of life, the suffering as oppression experienced at those levels constitutes a groaning in travail to which God will not fail to respond.

To what, then, have we come? We have tried to understand suffering within the creative intention of God, since the connection between suffering and sin seems inadequate in scope and in principle. In this area we do not have available the kind of gathered dogmatic resolution to which we have been able to refer in our consideration of moral evil and, to a lesser extent, of metaphysical evil. Lacking that, we have tried to offer a line of argument which is congruent with what we take the faith to have asserted dogmatically regarding the relationship between God and humankind in creation. But we are conscious that in doing this we appear to move against a strand of piety which would place at least much greater emphasis on suffering as directly willed by God. Some brief recognition of this strand and response to it are needed.

One way in which the direct connection between suffering and God is made is to interpose the reality of sin. One could do this softly by simply tracing suffering back to sin, while recognizing that whether we suffer as victims or as perpetrators, God can heal.[29]

Or, one may take a harder stand and introduce a notion of retribution, a theme that has probably prevailed in the thinking of many of the faithful who have undergone suffering of an unusual degree or kind. W. Sibley Towner has shown that the biblical writings do have a cycle of retribution in such materials as the Wisdom psalms, where God rewards the righteous and destroys the wicked. But he notes too the softening of this theme within the very texts themselves, appealing to the relative late date of the suzerainty treaty pattern of curse and blessing, for example. Or he looks at the vehicle that carries the texts:

> Finally, the very literary form of the book of Deuteronomy seemed to me suggestive of a way of giving a softening nuance to the obvious retributional understanding of history contained in the book. Israel is left at the brink of the Jordan not yet foresworn to a course that will lead to certain disaster. . . . The people wait eternally at the bank of the Jordan. In the open-ended literary struc-

ture of the book, the people still have the option to obey. In its form and in its hortatory style, the book emerges as an evangelical appeal to obedience rather than an announcement of doom.[30]

Towner then proceeds to a second cycle:

> Over against the lex talionis and Deuteronomy . . . the J creation story in Genesis. In contrast to the prophetic oracles of judgment . . . the prophetic promise. Job and Ecclesiastes countered the language of the Psalms of the Two Ways. Christological materials and parables of the Kingdom . . . as alternatives to the apocalyptic world judgment by God and the Son of Man.[31]

Among the conclusions emerging within this second cycle is what Towner calls the affirmation of the place and the integrity of the secular world: "There are events in the world which happen by chance or because some chain of causes made them inevitable, and over which God exercises sovereignty only in the remote sense of allowing them to take place within his created world."[32]

Some Christian theology has linked God with specific suffering without interposing talk of sin, consequence, retribution, and the like, by speaking of God's testing or trying the believer. The book of Job would seem to be the *locus classicus* for this theme. What shall one make of the conclusion of Job in which the power of the Creator seems to strip humankind of all significance? Dorothee Soelle states what may seem to be God's case against Job: "What is man, compared to oceans and galaxies, to impressive meteorological displays, to the permanency of nature! A nonentity, a grain of sand, a being that simply because of his insignificance, his cosmic triviality, has no rights whatsoever."[33] She then vents the reaction that wells up within us:

> This God is a nature demon, who bears no relation to the God of the exodus and of the prophets. What once revealed God to the prophets was not the depths of the sea but justice which flows like water. . . . That Job at the conclusion of the book submits himself to this power-being who dwells beyond good and evil, is incredible because it is intolerable.

Soelle goes on to point to the interpretation of the atheist Ernst Bloch, who focuses on Job's quest for an advocate (19:25, 16:18–19):

> This helper, this true friend, goes beyond all the roles for God offered in the book of Job. He is neither the arbitrary tester, nor the avenger who establishes his absolute purity by dirtying his own hands with blood, nor the Lord of stars, seas and clouds, "the mere *Tremendum* of nature."

Bloch finds Job appealing to the God who led the chosen people out of suf-

5 / SIN AND EVIL

fering in Egypt, while the God Job encounters seems merely another pharaoh. So Bloch must conclude: "Job is pious precisely because he does *not* believe." Soelle's conclusion, in turn, is:

> But then Job's call for the advocate, the redeemer, the blood-avenger and blood-satisfier is to be understood only as the unanswered cry of the pre-Christian world which finds its answer in Christ. Job is stronger than the old God. Not the one who causes suffering but only the one who suffers can answer Job.

Soelle's simplicity is misleading but instructive. It is misleading because it grants too easily the severity of Bloch's judgment about Job, and especially because it ignores so much else in the "pre-Christian" world, such as the steel in Hosea's eloquence about a God who will not come to destroy. But her simplicity is also instructive. Though God did not come to destroy, God did come. It is time to turn to the divine response to evil—whether moral, metaphysical, or natural—and to the subject of how we are to live in the light of that response.

NOTES

1. On the first conviction, see Hans Walter Wolff, *Anthropology of the Old Testament*, trans. Margaret Kohl (Philadelphia: Fortress Press, 1974), p. 107; and Gerhard von Rad, *Old Testament Theology*, trans. D. M. G. Stalker, 2 vols. (New York: Harper & Row, 1962–65), 2:349. On the second conviction, see Wolff, p. 102.

2. Von Rad, *Old Testament Theology*, 2:349.

3. Robin Scroggs, *The Last Adam* (Philadelphia: Fortress Press, 1966), p. 73; Rudolf Bultmann, *Theology of the New Testament*, trans. Kendrick Grobel, 2 vols. (New York: Charles Scribner's Sons, 1954–55), 1:246–49.

4. As Robert Martin-Achard, *From Death to Life*, trans. John Penny Smith (Edinburgh: Oliver & Boyd, 1960), p. 19: "Before the Fall, between Adam and death, which is part of his natural lot as an element in his human heritage, there stands the Living God; His presence is sufficient to ward death off, to conceal it. . . . But when God withdraws, nothing is left to Adam, but the presence of death. . . . Man, then is born mortal, but by his sin he renders death effective; it enters as a reality into his existence."

5. As paraphrased by S. Trooster, *Evolution and the Doctrine of Original Sin*, trans. John A. Ter Haar (New York: Newman Press, 1968), p. 22.

6. Claus Westermann, *Creation*, trans. John J. Scullion (Philadelphia: Fortress Press, 1974), p. 22.

7. E.g., John Macquarrie, *Principles of Christian Theology*, 2d ed. (New York: Charles Scribner's Sons, 1977), p. 264: "Apart altogether from sin, death belongs to finitude." For a statement of the consensus in recent theology on this point, see H. Paul Santmire, *Brother Earth* (Toronto: Thomas Nelson, 1970), chap. 6.

8. Trooster, *Evolution and the Doctrine of Original Sin*, p. 23.

9. Karl Barth, *Church Dogmatics*, 5 vols. in 14 (Edinburgh: T. & T. Clark, 1936–77), 3/3: 296.

10. W. J. Rewak, "Adam, Immortality, and Human Death," *ScEc* 19 (1967): 67–79.

11. Heinrich Schmid, *The Doctrinal Theology of the Evangelical Lutheran Church*, trans. from the 5th ed. by Charles A. Hay and Henry E. Jacobs (Philadelphia: Lutheran Bookstore, 1876), p. 249.

12. Gerhard von Rad, *Wisdom in Israel*, trans. James D. Martin (Nashville: Abingdon Press, 1972), pp. 304–5. Cf. Santmire, *Brother Earth*, pp. 125–26.

13. Dietrich Bonhoeffer, *Creation and Fall*, trans. John Fletcher (New York: Macmillan Co.; London: SCM Press, 1959), p. 55; cf. p. 86.

14. Hans Conzelmann, *An Outline of the Theology of the New Testament*, trans. John Bowden (New York: Harper & Row, 1969), p. 197. Paul Ricoeur, *The Symbolism of Evil*, trans. Emerson Buchanan (Boston: Beacon Press, 1967), pp. 141–42. Bultmann, *Theology of the N.T.*, 1:246.

15. Helmut Thielicke, *Death and Life*, trans. Edward H. Schroeder (Philadelphia: Fortress Press, 1970), p. 153. Cf. Walther Eichrodt, *Theology of the Old Testament*, trans. J. A. Baker, 2 vols. (Philadelphia: Westminster Press, 1961–67), 2:406.

16. Rewak, "Adam, Immortality, and Human Death," p. 78.

17. John Meyendorff, *Byzantine Theology: Historical Trends and Doctrinal Themes* (New York: Fordham University Press, 1974), p. 145: "There is indeed a consensus in Greek patristic and Byzantine traditions in identifying the inheritance of the Fall as one essentially of mortality rather than sinfulness, sinfulness being merely a consequence of mortality."

18. Ernest Becker, *Escape from Evil* (New York: Free Press, 1975), p. 108, quoting Otto Rank.

19. E.g., Wolff, *Anthropology of the O.T.*, pp. 108–9.

20. Feodor Dostoevski, *The Brothers Karamazov*, trans. Constance Garnett (New York: New American Library, 1957), p. 226.

21. John Hick, *Evil and the God of Love*, rev. ed. (New York: Harper & Row; London: Macmillan & Co., 1975), pp. 328–30.

22. See, e.g., Arthur C. McGill, *Suffering: A Test of Theological Method* (Philadelphia: Geneva Press, 1968), pp. 41ff.

23. C. S. Lewis, *The Problem of Pain* (New York: Macmillan Co., 1948), p. 19. Cf. F. R. Tennant, *Philosophical Theology*, 2 vols. (Cambridge: At the University Press, 1935–37), 2:199.

24. Lewis, *Problem of Pain*, p. 19.

25. Tennant, *Philosophical Theology*, p. 201.

26. Ibid., pp. 199–200.

27. Hick, *Evil and the God of Love*, p. 362.

28. Lewis, *Problem of Pain*, p. 16. (Emphasis his.)

29. Von Rad, *Old Testament Theology*, 1:274–75: On the theology of the hexateuch: "all serious illnesses were subject to a . . . sacral assessment. . . . Such disturbances of the vital basis of human existence brought a man into a *status confessionis*. Only God could heal. . . . It was of course from Jahweh that bodily sickness came . . . there was a very close connection between sin and physical disease."

5 / SIN AND EVIL

30. W. Sibley Towner, *How God Deals with Evil* (Philadelphia: Westminster Press, 1976), p. 145.
31. Ibid., p. 147.
32. Ibid., p. 149.
33. This and the following quotations are from Dorothee Soelle, *Suffering*, trans. Everett R. Kalin (Philadelphia: Fortress Press, 1975), pp. 117-19.

5
The Work of God Against Evil

God continues to work for life and order through people and institutions with and without the knowledge of God. God responds decisively to sin in Jesus and the sacramental life of the church, and God draws human beings to faith, obedience, and hope in a kingdom which is beyond Eden.

THE CONTINUITY OF GOD

In the beginning we emphasized that our topic was a derivative one, logically and theologically. Throughout we have argued for a distinction between creation and fall, between finitude and sin. Our focus has been on sin and fall. Now, in this last chapter, we reenter the broader dogmatic terrain, for we look here at what has been done, what is being done, and what is to be done—in the light of evil. It is the work of God of which we write. While it may have been right in principle to claim that the concept of God can be adequately defined apart from any reference to sin, the Christian claim is that the work of God, in actuality, is against evil—moral, metaphysical, and natural. God works against sin. God leads us through suffering. God summons us beyond death.

Sin is not so strong that it can overrule the creative intention of God. While Western Christendom—particularly in its Pauline-Augustinian-Lutheran form—has done its theology in the form of a drama in the three acts of creation/fall/redemption, this theology should not be read as denying a unity of the entire plot, or action beyond the third act. Of course those theologians who tend not to distinguish chronologically between creation and fall will be able to speak more emphatically of unity, of continuity, in the divine intention and action. Continuity then would be found simply in this: that our talk of God's work, even of the work of creation, is always in the face of evil.[1]

This is correct as far as the situation of the speaker is concerned. But we have argued that the threatened human being is best served by a faith in a God whose categorical supremacy is such that even a chronological distinc-

5 / SIN AND EVIL

tion between creation and fall is to be affirmed. For such a position, ironically, both creation and fall in their distinctness assume heightened significance. Yet the "new" act of the fall is not so significant that the curtain must be rung down on what God was about in creation. Despite sin, God continues to will and to work in continuity with the divine creative intention. Perhaps one will be more inclined to speak of this as "preservation," distinguishing it from both creation and redemption. There are differences between the three. God acts to constitute and preserve the human project, despite the difficulties due to sin; and God acts to redeem that project even in the defiance that is sin. But underlying the differences, there is the unity of the divine will.[2]

Despite the abstractness of our prose, it is biblical faith of which we speak. Moreover it is not merely the highly theological faith of Paul's Epistle to the Romans. Von Rad notes that the priestly writer in Genesis holds that when sin broke in the earth was corrupted in God's sight and filled with violence (Gen. 6:11, 13), so that "all that Jahweh had 'separated out' at creation was falling together in collapse. . . . The natural relationships between created beings are in desperate disorder." To check the *hatta'th*, the violence,

> Jahweh promulgated certain dispositions. He allowed the killing and slaughter of animals. But the life of man he put under his own absolute protection—though he did so in terms of putting the onus of avenging murder on men themselves. Jahweh even guaranteed the preservation of the continued physical existence of the universe by the making of a covenant (Gen. 9:8ff.). It is within the stability thus established by the grace of Jahweh that the saving history is in due time to operate.[3]

What is it that God does in the face of sin? The Yahwist's Adam names his wife Eve (a variant of the word for "living") *again* (Gen. 3:20; cf. 2:23). His faith is that God will still bless. Perhaps we can still make something of that, saying that in sexuality humankind is creative even in the midst of destruction.[4] What is to be resisted is a reductionist reading of this "order of creation," which makes human identity essentially a matter of biology. Without propagation there is no real life, to be sure, but real life is far more than biological life. In the recognition that despite sin God is still the God of the living, one may hear a call to development, for the human being is created with a vocation—something we have suggested throughout in our evocation of the "good, not perfect" theme. We were not perfected in creation, but called ahead. We are clearly not perfect in our fallenness, but we are to be perfected. We are still called ahead.

It is in this dynamic sense that the notion of "orders" is to be understood. Gustav Wingren warns against a view in which creation is

> assigned to some past time, and the ordinances regarded as a surviving product

of the past act of Creation. In such a case, however, we lose all idea of God's continuing Creation and reforming of the world. And since we have completely lost the "dynamic aspect" of Creation, we also lose *the* dynamic aspect which is the transformation by the Gospel of human life in the attitude to one's neighbor.[5]

Certainly marriage, work, and the economy suggest this dynamic sense easily, though they do remain vulnerable to a rigidifying interpretation. Government, though, seems to retain its developmental character only with the greatest difficulty. Here particularly there is need to stress the possibility of abuse, of forfeiting the mandate, lest the faith become an ideological accessory to oppression.

The "orders," then, are there for life, for the living. Life does require ordering. Even that metaphysical student of novelty, Alfred North Whitehead, wrote, "Novelty may promote or destroy order; it may be good or bad."[6] Order is needed not to balance life but to serve it, indeed to constitute it qualitatively. We are created for relationship; in the gift of life there is the call to the sociality of being. The qualitative value of human order is anticipated in the aesthetic reality of interrelationships and the biological imperative against inbreeding.[7] But on the human level, qualitative life through order is a particularly temporal reality. Thus James Gustafson writes: "To be human is to have a vocation, a calling; that is it is to become what we now are not; it calls for a surpassing of what we are; . . . apart from a telos, a vision . . . we will flounder and die."[8]

The call ahead is a call through the structures of creaturely life, rather than a call to withdraw from those under the inspiration of redemption, although the distinction is often muddled. That distinction seems to be the sense of the Augsburg Confession's rebuff to those who teach that "Christian perfection requires the forsaking of house and home":

> Actually true perfection consists alone of proper fear of God and real faith in God, for the Gospel does not teach an outward and temporal but an inward and eternal mode of existence and righteousness of the heart. The Gospel does not overthrow civil authority, the state, and marriage but requires that all these be kept as true orders of God and that everyone, each according to his own calling, manifest Christian love and genuine good works in his station of life. (Augsburg Confession, XVI, *BC* 37–38)

Moreover, one might suggest that this positive endorsement of civil orders is certainly not required by the emphasis on the spiritual character of the life rooted in God's redemption. Rather, it seems to derive from an implied doctrine of creation which attributes independent value to such social order. Of course such social order may also possess an instrumental value in the service of the gospel.

5 / SIN AND EVIL

It should be emphasized that the work of God for ordered life, for living order, does not depend on any conscious awareness in human agents of that work. Indeed, human will may even be at cross-purposes with divine will. Yet it should also be said that despite sin humankind can know the creative will of God for the world. Nor does such knowledge depend on some peculiarly spiritual revelation. At least that is true in the biblical writings. The Old Testament Wisdom literature carries this message strongly, as von Rad notes:

> For Israel there was only one world of experience and . . . this was apperceived by means of a perceptive apparatus in which rational perceptions and religious perceptions were not differentiated. Nor was this any different in the case of the prophets. . . . The experiences of the world were for her [Israel] always divine experiences as well and the experiences of God were for her experiences of the world.[9]

Moving across centuries and literary genera with some abandon, we note the same stress on concreteness in Paul's anthropology.[10]

Biblical faith and human experience come together to suggest that human beings can not only know God's creative will but also can perform it. Again this is open to alternative theological formulations. We have noted the strain of optimism in the medieval interpretation of the human condition after Adam. But even the Lutheran protest against this strain did not fail to grant that "civil righteousness" was possible, despite the bondage of the will toward that which is above humankind. We have wondered whether that concession would not lead to a broader range of significance for the human pole in the relationship to God.

Does this warrant a fundamental optimism about the human project?[11] Optimism seems to depend on an understanding of evil as privation and on a context in which evil's positively defiant character is obscured; such a view is not acceptable to us. We have stressed the efficacy of sin: within God, within humankind, and between God and humankind. As helpful as the theme of the continuity of divine action may be, it does not adequately address the human predicament. Given the extensiveness and efficacy of evil, we need precisely a divine response which is somehow more than the basis upon which we can try and fail again. In a sense we find ourselves with the book of Genesis, where the story of the Tower of Babel concludes without any note of grace. Von Rad comments:

> The whole primeval history, therefore, seems to break off in shrill dissonance, and the question . . . arises even more urgently: Is God's relationship to the nations now finally broken? That is the burdensome question which no thoughtful reader of ch. 11 can avoid; indeed, one can say that our narrator intended by means of the whole plan of his primeval history to raise precisely this question

and to pose it in all its severity. Only then is the reader properly prepared to take up the strangely new thing that now follows the comfortless story about the building of the tower: the election and blessing of Abraham.[12]

We do not now leave behind the continuity of the work of God, but we do advance to a new theme: the decisiveness of God.

THE DECISIVENESS OF GOD

We write here of what was done in Jesus. But our purpose is not to attempt an analysis of the various soteriological theories which have been put forward, or to offer our own. We wish only to speak of the intersection between hamartiology and soteriology in order to show how the analysis of evil with which we have been concerned reenters the dogmatic system. The connection can be suggested by a single phrase: God's decisive response.

The Christian faith understands the work of Christ as a response to the human predicament. While this is not obvious in the Scotist emphasis that Christ would have come even had there been no sin, even in this understanding a significant element of response is recognized. Whatever the formulation, what is done with Jesus carries a heightened sense of newness in comparison with what we have spoken of as God's continuing work of preservation. A new word is needed; the continuing work of preservation will not suffice.[13]

The gravity and efficacy of evil threaten to trivialize the continuing work of God, unless some decisive resolution can be managed. God continues to work, but so does sin, after all. Who is to say that all this does not add up to a cosmic standoff? Or perhaps sin will even wear down the divine determination itself. There is needed something that indicates—more clearly than the "more of the same" of God's preserving work—what the disposition of evil is or is to be, as far as God is concerned.

The church has claimed that a divine response to evil is at hand and that it is so decisive, so clear in its message, that the predicament itself is only first fully understood in light of this response. The shadowy first Adam and we who are of him become clear against the sharper focus of the Second Adam. The decisiveness is not merely an epistemological matter. Repeatedly Paul drives home the point: "For if many died through one man's trespass, *much more* have the grace of God and the free gift in the grace of that one man Jesus Christ abounded for many" (Rom. 5:15; cf. 5:17). "Where sin increased, grace abounded *all the more*" (Rom. 5:20). We have used strong words about sin: inevitable, bound, and the like. Paul and the basic Christian intuition of the normative particularity of Jesus will not let us use weaker ones of the divine response.

5 / SIN AND EVIL

One might argue that the alternative formulations concerning this Jesus are so disparate that the sense of decisiveness is altogether eroded. Perhaps one must grant that no single material insight prevails in the welter of soteriological theories. But it is most significant that widely differing theories come together to affirm the decisiveness of Jesus, and then—appropriately, one might argue—specify that decisiveness variously, depending on what humankind, on each view, needs.

Thus even the so-called "subjective" theories of atonement, in which the newness of the response is drawn very far back into God's continuing work, still reach for such decisiveness as is needed to meet the human predicament understood as weakness or ignorance. Thus Schleiermacher's reading of the need as residing in a weak or obscured God-consciousness specified the decisiveness of the Christ to be not that of an example (*Vorbild*), but that of the generative archetype (*Urbild*) from whom redeeming impulses irresistibly arise. Indeed, one might quietly respond to criticisms of the "small Christ" of figures like Schleiermacher and Tillich by noting that even if the soteriological categories employed seem merely epistemological ("realize," "consciousness," "revelation"), they do yield a universal salvation.[14]

If such soteriologies are to be faulted, it must be because they have underestimated the gravity of the human predicament, so that the apparently decisive Christ they provide in fact fails to resolve what we know to be in us. That would be the direction of our own criticism. Ironically, one may purchase one's optimism by selling the reality of humankind too cheaply. One may then understate the gravity of the venture with freedom in which God is engaged. If one fails to recognize the full reality of the nondivine will, one may fail to reckon with our efficacy for ourselves and for God. If we cannot "be" for God (Schleiermacher declines to call God "Lord," inasmuch as that implies too much over-againstness for God), God can hardly be wrathful toward us. If God has not let us out of the divine hand in freedom, we can hardly bind ourselves. It should not then surprise us that God can bring the project to completion without resorting to radically novel means, for God remains clearly in control.

Other main directions in soteriological thinking also cling to the fact that it is God who is at work in the decisive Christ, but formulate the need differently—reflecting a self and a race granted more aweful freedom. We spoke in Chapter 1 of the wrath of God as a category supported by the understanding of the divine will and human sin. Perhaps the "objective" soteriological theory—purporting to understand none other than God to be the object of the work of Jesus—permits the most emphatic resolution at this point. Our problem is out of our hands, for it is within God: Our guilt calls forth God's wrath. God must somehow deal with divine wrath, and this God does in the one called Jesus. Thus in Romans, Paul begins his statement of

the gospel of which he is "not ashamed" by referring to the "wrath of God
... revealed from heaven against all ungodliness and wickedness" (Rom. 1:18).
He aims to make clear that since we are justified by Christ's blood, we shall
"be saved by him from the wrath of God" (Rom. 5:9).

It is no doubt often the case that in theological formulations of this theme
it is no longer God who is in control, but some juridical or ritual dynamic.
Paul Ricoeur sees the interplay of purification and pardon themes as a hazardous process, but one that ultimately yields rich results:

> It is because the foreign vegetation of ceremonial expiation grew like an excrescence on the tree of "repentance" and "pardon" that the symbolism of expiation could, in return, enrich that of "pardon," and so one sees God invoked in the Psalms as the subject of expiation (78:38; 65:3; 79:9). To say that God "expiates" is to say that he "pardons." The symbolism of expiation, then, gives back to the symbolism of pardon what the latter had lent it.[15]

God is in charge of deciding who will be pardoned; this theory can provide
a decisive response precisely because it places the response within God.

The church's belief in the incarnation contends that God takes the venture
with human freedom so seriously that this act of pardoning cannot occur
"above our heads." Only in God's complete identification with human flesh
and human sin can sin find its decisive disposition in God. If wrath is injured
love, then surely the resolution will be through suffering.[16] Perhaps love finally
does refuse to let its suffering be a passive matter to be undergone. Ricoeur
anticipates the merger in one person of what appear to be two quite distinct
lines:

> On the one hand, the evil that is *committed* leads to a just exile; that is what the figure of Adam represents. On the other hand, the evil that is *suffered* leads to an unjust deprivation; that is what the figure of Job represents. The first figure calls for the second; the second corrects the first. Only a third figure could announce the transcending of the contradiction, and that would be the figure of the "suffering Servant," who would make of suffering, of the evil that is undergone, an *action* capable of redeeming the evil that is committed. This enigmatic figure is the one celebrated by the Second Isaiah in the four "songs of the Servant of Yahweh" (Isa. 42:1–10, 49:1–6; 50:4–11; 52:13—53:12), and it opens up a perspective radically different from that of "wisdom." It is not contemplation of creation and its immense measure that consoles; it is suffering itself. Suffering has become a gift that expiates the sins of the people.[17]

The logic of Christian faith requires that all of God be involved in this suffering, though this does not require the confusions represented by the patripassianist heresy.[18]

We have not made a gathered statement of the objective tendency in

5 / SIN AND EVIL

soteriological thought. We have simply remarked that the very objectivity of the theory—its "within-God-ness"—permits a singularly unconditional decisiveness for the work of Christ, though that work must pass through the realm of sin and guilt which is "for God." Since sin is paradigmatically against God, it is God's response to sin which ultimately matters as far as the question of sin's efficacy is concerned. If God is such that a decisive response is available (as we have argued), that is what matters. As Paul says, "It is God who judges." Yet inasmuch as sin is at least as much ours as wrath is God's, there remains open here the issue of the future of human sin. We seek to comment on that in the final section of this chapter, but note even now that some formulations draw such comment back into the very decisiveness of the work of Christ itself. At least that seems to be what is claimed in the "Christus Victor" theory.

In this view sin is seen as an objective power standing behind humankind, and the atonement is seen as the triumph of God over sin, death, and the devil. There is admittedly a dualistic tendency in this view, but Aulén defends the view despite the difficulties:

> The work of Atonement is accomplished by God Himself in Christ, yet at the same time the passive form also is used: God is reconciled with the world. The alternation is not accidental: He is reconciled only because He Himself reconciles the world with Himself and Himself with the world. The safeguard of the continuity of God's operation is the dualistic outlook, the Divine warfare against the evil that holds mankind in bondage and the triumph of Christ.[19]

Again we attempt no full analysis, but we do wish to show that the content of Christ's work and the degree of decisiveness available for that work is directly correlated to the perception of the human predicament. While the "victory" theory overlaps somewhat with the "objective" tendency in what Aulén calls the "Latin" form (cf. the appeal to the law and the wrath of God as enemies), the emphasis in understanding the predicament of humanity shifts somewhat from the Adamic toward the theogonic. Just as in the "objective" view the unity of God and the particularity of Jesus permit a truly decisive disposition to sin in the resolution of wrath, so here the added unity of sin, as an "objective" power, permits an apparently emphatic victory.

Here too, however, there remains the question of the future of *my* sinning, if the Adamic emphasis on responsibility is not to be rejected altogether. Indeed, that question seems to press the more painfully in this understanding, since the formulation of God's decisiveness is cast directly in relation to the occurrence of sin itself, not in relation to the significance of the occurrence to and in God. Yet the more we seem in our sin to be victims before we are perpetrators, even if victims only of our own identity in the race, so much the more does vindication seem to meet our need more truly than forgiveness.

THE WORK OF GOD AGAINST EVIL

That has been Krister Stendahl's reading of Paul against the distortion represented in the Lutheran "introspective conscience of the West":

> Paul's thoughts about justification were triggered by the issues of divisions and identities in a pluralistic and torn world, not primarily by the inner tensions of individual souls and consciences. His searching eyes focused on the unity and the God-willed diversity of humankind, yes of the whole creation.[20]

The scope of Stendahl's reading of the solution reveals the narrowness of our traditional focus. In this chapter also we have still been focusing mainly on moral evil, on sin. Does the work of God in Jesus represent a response to metaphysical and natural evil as well? The category of "response" seems less appropriate if suffering and death are given with creation rather than being the result of sin. Of course the benefits Christ brings will respond to the exacerbating detriment sin adds to our experience of suffering and dying. But in relation to metaphysical and natural evil there will be greater stress on the coming and activity of Jesus in *continuity with* the creative intention of God. Here Jesus—and in Jesus, God—will be perceived as partners in the pilgrimage of suffering toward perfection. Perhaps Jürgen Moltmann has caught that note in recording the insistence that God must suffer along with the Jews in the holocaust: "To speak of a God who could not suffer would make God a demon. To speak here of an absolute God would make God an annihilating nothingness. To speak here of an indifferent God, would condemn men to indifference."[21] If this is right about that suffering that issues from the sin that is against God, it is *a fortiori* so regarding the suffering that comes through the conditions that are from the Creator's hand.

The resurrection of Christ surely "responds to" our experience of dying. Paul's focus on the link with sin is familiar: If Christ is not raised, we are still in our sins (1 Cor. 15:17). A God who cannot do anything about death provides only a futile basis for any faith in forgiveness. But what of death itself? If one regards death as given with finitude, one will still find in the resurrection a powerful witness to what lies in store for humankind, and indeed for all creation. As Karl Schmitz-Moormann puts it:

> Christ's redemption affects the universe, not just the human race, and it affects the universe at a level deeper and wider than that of factual sin. For the deepest threat to evolution is death—death which is not the fruit of "Adam's" sin but is natural to creation as much as it is a threat to it. Christ's death and resurrection answers the question, does evolution have an issue? Is extinction the ultimate fruit of the human hunger for unconditional meaning? The paschal mystery tells us that all creatures have a definite, consummating goal, thanks to God's creative union in Christ with his developing world. Physical death of the universe through the victory of entropy, and spiritual death through the victory of sin, are both overcome in the identification of Omega with the Lord.[22]

5 / SIN AND EVIL

We are again pressed to return to the issue of God's creative intention, in order to ask how it goes with and in that human partner to whom God is committed. God continues to work for life and order and God responds decisively to sin. But what of the future of my sin and of my sinning? The way to Christian reflection on this troublesome matter leads through the sacramental life of the church, with particular attention to the sacrament of baptism.

The sacrament of baptism represents the decisive response of God to the human predicament of sin. This is clearest in infant baptism. While the practice of infant baptism was not always linked with the teaching of original sin by its supporters or by its opponents, there was an increasing tendency to move in that direction. That baptism is not the act of the baptized is not in doubt in infant baptism, despite occasional attempts to speak of infant faith. Since it is God's act, the faith and character of the officiant are not required for the validity of baptism, as the church decided during the Donatist controversy in the fourth century. Indeed, by the time of the Council of Trent in the sixteenth century, the objectivity of the efficacy of baptism could be put in still stronger terms: rightly administered, baptism is always valid, for it takes effect not as a mere sign of faith, but *ex opere operato*.[23] Many Christians who reject this Roman Catholic formulation still place a strong objective emphasis in their understanding of baptism. Thus, for example, Lutherans stress that it is the Word of God active in baptism which secures its validity. In the words of Luther's Large Catechism, God is bound to the water of baptism by the saving Word, which "contains and conveys all the fullness of God."

Whether one tends toward a Roman substantial emphasis or toward a Protestant dynamic emphasis, baptism is understood as decisive. What God does here need not to be repeated: we do not rebaptize those who fall away and return or who come to us from other Christian flocks. Thus the sacrament of baptism seems to represent the objective decisiveness of God's response to the human predicament in a way quite like the objectivity of God's work in Christ. Indeed, one may sense a certain superfluity here, as did the Anabaptists who refused to baptize their children on the grounds that Christ in effect had already done so.[24] But if God's decisiveness is not completed act but sure and living will, then that will renews itself in the reality of baptism, as God relates the divine self freshly to the one who is baptized. What God has resolved in Christ is now renewed for us.

In saying this we are moving the locus of God's decisiveness into a slightly more relational field. Thus Lutherans argue that baptism is efficacious not merely because it was instituted by Christ in his historical decisiveness, but also because there is attached to baptism the word of promise. The promise is for this one, the one now baptized. The promise thus becomes effective as it is received in faith. If one declines to say this, one seems to exempt baptism from the general truth that in God's will to bless humankind God creates freedom. Roman Catholics agree that response matters, distinguishing between objective validity and a fruitfulness which depends on right dispositions in the baptized. This matter of human response to the divine decisiveness lies ahead of us in the final section. It can surely be overrated, as for example in the tendency in the ancient church to delay baptism until just before death, lest sin after baptism destroy its benefits. Here it will suffice to note that baptism represents the divine decisiveness, but that it calls for the response of faith and obedience.

What, then, are the blessings of God's decisive act in baptism? Just as "justification" seemed most clearly to state the decisiveness of Jesus' works, so the forgiveness of the guilt of original sin stands out as common Christian teaching concerning the benefits of baptism. The Council of Carthage in 418 could assert, "Infants fresh from their mothers' wombs . . . are indeed baptized unto the remission of sins." Original sin is specified in these words: "Even infants, who in themselves thus far have not been able to commit any sin, are therefore truly baptized unto the remission of sins, so that that which they have contracted from generation may be cleansed in them by regeneration" (Denzinger, 102).

This theme is strengthened in later Catholic teaching, as when the Tridentine decree on original sin specifically adds that such baptism is needed for newly born infants "even though they be born of baptized parents" (Denzinger, 791). This strong stand on the forgiveness of the guilt of original sin may rest a little uneasily with those Roman Catholic figures who are not inclined to speak of the infant's condition as truly sin, but it links Roman Christendom with Reformation Christendom in the doctrine of baptism. Reformation Christians may in turn move closer to their Roman colleagues in declining to follow Augustine's robust logic: that unbaptized infants who die are condemned. The sense of baptism as promise suggests not a magical transformation, but a gracious adoption by which God calls the developing person to God. Hence the emphasis on incorporation into a living community of faith.

A harder question is whether a second decisive soteriological theme—that of liberation or healing—is to be found in baptism. With striking differences of degree, Christians of many stripes wish to incorporate this theme. A very ambitious formulation is that of the Council of Orange (529): "Freedom of will weakened in the first man cannot be repaired except through the grace of Baptism" (Denzinger, 186). Of course at issue in this is how to regard the infant before baptism. Liberation will be rather easily purchased if our reading of the human condition sets the price low enough. On the other hand, someone like Luther, with a very strong claim for the sinfulness of concupiscence, will not be inclined to speak as readily of liberation. Despite the new birth in baptism, "our human flesh and blood have not lost their old skin" (Large

5 / SIN AND EVIL

Catechism, *BC* 449). Thus the Christian is ever *simul justus et peccator.* Over against this the Council of Trent follows Pope Leo X who had condemned Luther's thesis, "To deny that sin remains in a child after baptism is to despise both Paul and Christ alike."[25] Thus Trent's decree reads:

> But his holy Synod confesses and perceives that there remains in the baptized concupiscence of an inclination, although this is left to be wrestled with, it cannot harm those who do not consent, but manfully resist by the grace of Jesus Christ.... This concupiscence, which at times the Apostle calls *sin* (Rom. 6:12ff.) the holy Synod declares that the Catholic Church has never understood to be called sin, as truly and properly sin in those born again, but because it is from sin and inclined to sin. (Denzinger, 792)

Here the more optimistic and more pessimistic strains of our historical survey in Chapter 3 return. Trent is following Thomas, but whether Trent or Luther is nearer Augustine is not clear.[26] But even Lutherans have wished to stress that baptism is to aid the Christian in the struggle against sin, death, and the devil. Perhaps, then, it is best to continue this discussion in the context toward which we have been tending: the Christian's response to the continuing and decisive work of God.

THE DIRECTIVITY OF GOD

Christians are to work against evil. God is committed to a covenant venture with humankind. In the face of evil, God still works for ordered life. God has responded decisively to human sin in the person of Jesus. In baptism God graciously brings human beings directly into the covenant community. God did not do all of this that we might remain in evil. There is not only the sacrament of initiation, there is the supper of continuance. God blesses people through means of grace, that they might move toward the calling God intended even before the cosmic seas were brought into being. The Scripture builds an imperative on the divine indicative: "Work out your own salvation with fear and trembling; for God is at work in you, both to will and to work for his good pleasure" (Phil. 2:12–13). While this dogmatics has an entire locus on "the Christian life," in this final section we need to indicate briefly how the locus on sin and evil reenters the broader system also at this point. If stylistic inelegance be permitted, we may gather our remarks around the theme, the directivity of God.

The struggle against sin is a struggle to believe, to have faith. In that sense the struggle is directed *to* God, for God is the object of faith. In Chapter 1 we spoke of how the opposite of sin is not virtue but faith. While there may be some sense in which one simply does not, indeed cannot, *choose* to believe, one can choose to live out one's life in a way congruent with trust and praise of God. In that sense one is called to discipleship, indeed to obedience.

In this matter we wish to stress the Christian's continuity with God's creative intention and the continuing work of God, as discussed in the first section of this chapter. In Chapter 2 we indicated that to say that humankind is made in the image of God is to say that we are made incomplete. We are directed toward a destiny. That we might reach that destiny, directions are given. This is the point of "Torah," however much this gift of God may be twisted. For the Christian those directions still apply. That is, we have been graciously restored to the pilgrimage toward our destiny, and we stand in need of directions. I am speaking of what Paul Althaus has called the divine *Gebot,* or command, following Article VI of the Formula of Concord. William Lazareth provides a succinct statement:

> As the "command" of the Creator to all creatures in his holy image, it is ultimately love. It is the reverse side of God's *Angebot*—the offer with which the eternal love of God originally encounters persons. God's *Gebot* of love corresponds to man's original righteousness. It is supralapsarian, depicting the proper relation between the Creator and his human creatures before their fall into sin. It is the human's ethical expression of the image of God.[27]

Althaus is pleading that this wholistic sense of God's "command" be distinguished from the "law," the Mosaic and Judaic laws by which God punishes crime and reveals sin. While as sinners Christians still need the "law," in their new life they are called to obey the "command" of God. This seems a useful way to lead beyond the strife-torn debates about the "third use" of the law. Moreover, it brings us to a matter of ecumenical consensus: that we are called to obedience.

What, if anything, is the distinctive Christian contribution to this obedience? Does the Christian have a new insight into the command of God? Both the witness of experience and that of faith would seem to deny this. In the first section of this chapter we argued that the human being is able to know the requirements of God. Indeed, we even claimed that as human we are able to perform in some measure what God requires for life on this planet. Yet is there not some kind of ethical "gain" within the Christian community? Gustaf Wingren ponders this matter:

> The connection and the distinction between natural law and the commandment of Jesus is from one point of view a reflection of another connection and another distinction. . . . Redemption gives more than creation when it restores creation. We are dealing here with a connection and distinction between natural and Christian, and both are reflected on the level of law or commandment. . . . This is what is meant by the accentuation, newness, and heightening of the law. The Christian attitude is that of a natural love for the neighbor which is thoroughly

5 / SIN AND EVIL

"of this world" and conveyed in the rough forms of man's daily vocations, but it is filled with a new willingness to *suffer* for the good of the neighbor and to do so with *joy*.[28]

Perhaps there is some sharpening of insight here, as suffering and death—though quite natural—are not easily seen as imperatives. Similarly, with respect to the doing of what is seen to be good, the Christian faith can provide a direction for ethical life, and with that such "reasons" or motivations as a sense of dependence, gratitude, repentance, obligation, and possibility.[29] There are, after all, some things that do distinguish the Christian. The Christian knows of God's continuing work and of God's decisive response. This knowledge will make a difference in one's life. To mention only one point here: Christian prayer is directed to and through God against the reality of evil in all its forms.

Our topic happily does not require us to argue for the ethical superiority of Christians. But it does require us to recognize that Christian growth is to be sought in the struggle against evil. That is the word of the Scriptures which should not be relativized by appeal to the idea of an "interim" ethic.[30] Even the Paul of Romans, who can hardly be accused of underestimating sin, could exhort: "Let not sin therefore reign in your mortal bodies. . . . For sin will have no dominion over you, since you are not under law but under grace" (Rom 6:12, 14). It is this kind of Pauline material which suggests that the "righteousness of God" is more than a subjective genitive, for God's gift is with power.[31]

Does the Lutheran Christian have to see in this the specter of Christian perfection? While we should perhaps not worry over much about that, we do need to understand what is involved in Luther's and Calvin's insistence that never in this life do we get beyond sin. We are called in the new life to a direction other than the "curved-in-ness" of sin. But the cumulative power of the past and the complexity of the self's life argue against any expectation of a score of 100 on the quantitative scale of opportunity. Even for John Wesley perfection was seen to be compatible with "involuntary transgression."[32]

That vexing adjective "involuntary" raises the issue of Chapter 3: How fully must contingency be in place in order to speak of personal responsibility for sin? This is still not clear. What is clear is that we are called to a direction other than that of sin. Thus the author of 1 John knows that "if we say we have no sin, we deceive ourselves" (1:8), but knows as well that "no one born of God commits sin; for God's nature abides in him, and he cannot sin because he is born of God" (3:9). The verb in the latter passage is the Greek imperfect: No one born of God keeps on sinning, that is, no one born of God makes sin the direction of life. Or in Paul's language, sin may be present, but it is not to reign, not to have dominion. Christians are called to work against evil. Thus at Ephesus (431) the church condemns anyone who says: "that the grace of God, by which we are justified through Jesus Christ our Lord, has power only for the remission of sins which have already been committed, and not also for help, that they may not be committed" (Denzinger, 136). Similarly, the Formula of Concord (I) rejects the Flacian position as Manichaean: It would deny the scriptural teaching on sanctification and in effect baptize original sin.

To reject the call to sanctification is to open the church to the criticism that ideological diversion is at work here. To accept the call is not to claim the possibility of perfection. Thus Dorothee Soelle notes that a "political theology" need only assume that by making specific changes in social structures "the number of forces compelling us to sin today can be decreased."[33] In this struggle against evil there will be suffering for the Christian. This was seen with particular keenness in the tradition represented by Thomas Münzer, who offers a sharp critique of the "honey-sweet Christ": "This faith, 'that suffering is put on Christ alone, as though we are not permitted to suffer,' corresponds politically to the two kingdoms doctrine, ecclesiastically to infant baptism."[34] We should want to claim that Münzer is right in what he affirms but mistaken in his negative inferences. Baptism admits us to the fellowship of Christ's sufferings and intensifies the suffering to which we are called already as God's creatures. Soelle is right that it is a false faith which would escape suffering, for it represents "a narcissistic desire of the ego to settle down in God, immortal and almighty." In rebuffing this thirst for immediacy, one will recognize that "if it is true that a person's riches consist in the riches of his human relationships, then the pain that grows out of these relationships belongs necessarily to our riches. The more we love . . . the more likely it is that we . . . experience pain."[35]

If natural evil (suffering) and moral evil (sin) persist despite our struggle, what of that third face of evil: death? That this abides seems the most clear of all. But within the struggle the Christian lives in hope for another reality even beyond that third evil, death. It has always been so that God's people have lived in hope. Von Rad writes: "In one way or another (the specific tradition determines the way) Israel was always placed in the vacuum between an election made manifest in her history, and which had a definite promise attached to it, and a fulfillment of this promise which was looked for in the future."[36] For the Christian this becomes confidence, anchored in the resurrection of Jesus, in life beyond the grave. Only then and there will the struggle against evil end.

How does it end? Of that we will say only three things: First, it will be a time of consequence; the direction of our pilgrimage will reach its consum-

5 / SIN AND EVIL

mation in a new ontological state in which identity will no longer be linked with contingency. God's faithful will be clearly beyond Eden, for they will be "not able to sin."

Second, in the main Christians have held that God does indeed will that all be saved and come to the knowledge of the truth. Does our confidence in the continuing, decisive, and directing work of God lead us to believe that God's will will prevail? It requires us so to hope, that is clear. It provides us with suggestions that in that life all ambiguity will be removed, so that final clarity will lead all to acknowledge that Jesus Christ is Lord to the glory of God the Father (Phil. 2:11). But the question remains whether God's commitment to creaturely freedom does not leave the possibility that the tongue, the knee, the will—now stripped of any rational basis for resistance—may move only grudgingly, even defiantly.

Third, that new life perfects the pilgrimage which is our present life. But it does not destroy it. Too often static conceptions of heaven have represented a virtual destruction of what we know to be human life in its activity, in its becoming. Surely that new condition will entail an intensification of life, of living. But all that hinders us in our relationship to God will not remain. Ford Madox Ford wrote a poem "to V. H. who asked for a working Heaven." In our life against evil it is as much as we need

> . . . in this beloved place,
> There shall be never a grief but passes; no, not any;
> There shall be such bright light and no blindness;
> There shall be so little awe and so much loving-kindness;
> There shall be a little longing and enough care,
> There shall be a little labour and enough of toil
> To bring back the lost flavour of our human coil;
> Not enough to stain it;
> And all that we desire shall prove as fair as we can paint it.
> For, though that may be the very hardest trick of all
> God set Himself, who fashioned this goodly hall.
> Thus He has made Heaven;
> Even Heaven.

NOTES

1. Claus Westermann, *Creation*, trans. John J. Scullion (Philadelphia: Fortress Press, 1974), p.11, writes that the Old Testament reflection on creation "was the reflection of threatened man in a threatened world. The creation myths then had the function of preserving the world and of giving security to life."

2. Dietrich Bonhoeffer, *Creation and Fall*, trans. John Fletcher (New York: Macmillan Co.; London: SCM Press, 1959), p. 88.

3. Gerhard von Rad, *Old Testament Theology*, trans. D. M. G. Stalker, 2 vols. (New York: Harper & Row, 1962–65), 1:157.

4. Westermann, *Creation*, p. 46: "The act of creation, by directing itself to the living being, includes the capacity to propagate one's kind. That is the basic meaning of the word *bless*: the power to be fertile. The life of the living being, whether man or beast, clearly includes the capacity to propagate." (Emphasis his.) Cf. Bonhoeffer, *Creation and Fall*, p. 78, on the situation in destruction.

5. Gustaf Wingren, *Creation and Law*, trans. Ross Mackenzie (Philadelphia: Fortress [Muhlenberg] Press, 1961), p. 125.

6. Alfred North Whitehead, *Process and Reality*, ed. David Ray Griffin and Donald W. Sherburne (New York: Free Press, 1978), p. 187.

7. William Gallagher, "Whitehead's Theory of the Human Person" (Ph.D. diss., New School for Social Research, 1974), p. 45: "Inbreeding reduces the effectiveness of exploratory behavior, appetitive and aversive learning, and motility. Thus a decline in appetitive initiative on the reproduction level has a 'snowball' effect, which might be described as follows: the second generation suffers from decreased ability to face a novel environment, a low tolerance for challenging situations, a low level of adventuring on several levels."

8. James Gustafson, *Theology and Christian Ethics* (Philadelphia: United Church Press, 1974), p. 244.

9. Gerhard von Rad, *Wisdom in Israel*, trans. James D. Martin (Nashville: Abingdon Press, 1972), p. 61.

10. Cf. Hans Conzelmann, *An Outline of the Theology of the New Testament*, trans. John Bowden (New York: Harper & Row, 1969), pp. 182ff., on Paul's understanding of conscience.

11. F. R. Tennant, *Philosophical Theology*, 2 vols. (Cambridge: At the University Press, 1935–37), 2:194.

12. Gerhard von Rad, *Genesis*, trans. John Marks (Philadelphia: Westminster Press, 1961), p. 149.

13. Langdon Gilkey, *Reaping the Whirlwind: A Christian Interpretation of History* (New York: Seabury Press, 1976), p. 276.

14. Paul Tillich, *Systematic Theology*, 3 vols. (Chicago: University of Chicago Press, 1951–63), 1:147; Friedrich Schleiermacher, *The Christian Faith*, ed. H. R. Mackintosh and J. S. Stewart, 2 vols. (New York: Harper & Row, Harper Torchbooks, 1963), 2:425–38, 720–22.

15. Paul Ricoeur, *The Symbolism of Evil*, trans. Emerson Buchanan (Boston: Beacon Press, 1967), p. 98.

16. Abraham Heschel, *The Prophets* (New York: Harper & Row, 1962), p. 277. Cf. Jürgen Moltmann, *The Crucified God*, trans. R. A. Wilson and John Bowden (London: SCM Press, 1974), p. 272.

17. Ricoeur, *Symbolism of Evil*, p. 324. (Emphasis his.)

18. Moltmann, *The Crucified God*, p. 243.

19. Gustaf Aulén, *Christus Victor*, trans. A. G. Hebert (New York: Macmillan Co., 1931), pp. 162–63.

5 / SIN AND EVIL

20. Krister Stendahl, *Paul among Jews and Gentiles* (Philadelphia: Fortress Press, 1976), p. 40.

21. Moltmann, *The Crucified God*, p. 274, drawing on Elie Wiesel's *Night*.

22. Karl Schmitz-Moormann, *Die Erbsünde: Überholte Vorstellung-Bleibender Glaube* (Freiberg: Walter, 1969), as paraphrased by Brian O. McDermott, "The Theology of Original Sin: Recent Developments," *TS* 38 (September 1977): 497–98.

23. So Burkhard Neunheuser, "The Sacrament of Baptism," in *Encyclopedia of Theology*, ed. Karl Rahner (New York: Seabury Press, 1975), p. 72: "Rightly administered in accordance with the intention of the Church, baptism is always valid; it is not a mere sign of faith but takes effect *ex opere operato*, that is, by the power of God that is at work in the sacrament. . . ."

24. George Hunston Williams, *The Radical Reformation* (Philadelphia: Westminster Press, 1962), p. 799.

25. See G. Vandervelde, *Original Sin: Two Major Trends in Contemporary Roman Catholic Interpretation* (Amsterdam: Rodopi N. V., 1975), p. 39.

26. Ibid., pp. 37–42; Holsten Fagerberg, *A New Look at the Lutheran Confessions*, trans. Gene J. Lund (St. Louis: Concordia Publishing House, 1972), pp. 139–43.

27. William H. Lazareth, "Love and Law in Christian Life," *The Seminary Bulletin* (Lutheran Theological Seminary) 12 (Summer 1978): 32.

28. Gustaf Wingren, *Gospel and Church*, trans. Ross Mackenzie (Edinburgh: Oliver & Boyd, 1964), pp. 180–81. (Emphasis his.)

29. James Gustafson, *Can Ethics Be Christian?* (Chicago: University of Chicago Press, 1975), pp. 92–93.

30. Conzelmann, *Outline of the Theology of the N.T.*, p. 125: "The content of the demand—loving one's enemy, etc., is not derived from the nearness of the kingdom of God, nor is its validity restricted to a last, brief period. On the contrary, in ethics, as in the doctrine of God, there is no limit to the duration of the world. Jesus believes that the demand of God is understandable and possible in itself, not only by way of apocalyptic expectation."

31. Ernst Käsemann, *Perspectives on Paul*, trans. Margaret Kohl (Philadelphia: Fortress Press, 1971), p. 77.

32. Van A. Harvey, *A Handbook of Theological Terms* (New York: Macmillan Co., 1964), p. 178.

33. Dorothee Soelle, *Political Theology*, trans. John Shelley (Philadelphia: Fortress Press, 1974), p. 84.

34. This is Dorothee Soelle's paraphrase of Münzer's critique in *Suffering*, trans. Everett R. Kalin (Philadelphia: Fortress Press, 1975), p. 129.

35. Ibid., p. 165.

36. Von Rad, *Old Testament Theology*, 2:414.

SIXTH LOCUS

The Person of Jesus Christ

CARL E. BRAATEN

THE PERSON OF JESUS CHRIST

Introduction

1. The Nature and Method of Christology
   What Is Christology?
   History, Dogmatics, and Faith
   The Starting Point of Christology

2. The Historical Jesus and the Kingdom of God
   Jesus' Expectation of the Kingdom of God
   The Genesis of Christology in the New Testament

3. Classical Christology and Its Subsequent Criticism
   The Identification of Jesus with God
   Christological Heresies
   From the Creed of Chalcedon to the Formula of Concord
   Criticism of the Dogma

4. The True Humanity of Jesus Christ
   The Historicity of Jesus Christ
   The Humanity of Jesus Christ
   The Identity of the Earthly Jesus and the Risen Christ
   Jesus Christ as the Eschatological One

5. The True Divinity of Jesus Christ
   The Story of God Incarnate
   The Historicity of God
   The Divinity of Christ
   An Ontological Interpretation of the Incarnation

6. The Humiliation and Exaltation of Jesus Christ
   The Preexistence of Christ
   The Virgin Birth
   The Crucifixion of Jesus

CONTENTS

    Jesus' Descent into Hell
    The Resurrection
    The Ascension
    The Session at the Right Hand of God
    The Coming in Glory

7. The Uniqueness and Universality of Jesus Christ
    The Heritage of Exclusiveness
    The Uniqueness of Jesus Christ
    The Universality of Jesus Christ

Introduction

Christology is the church's doctrine of the person of Jesus as the Christ. It is always central in a system of dogmatics that claims to be Christian. Every attempt to remove christology from its place of centrality threatens the heart of Christian faith. The christocentric principle of theology does not compete with a theocentric point of view. Whoever looks to Jesus the Christ from the New Testament perspective will inevitably stand within a theocentric frame of reference. The more deeply theology probes the meaning of Jesus as the Christ of God, the more directly is it drawn to the very God of Christ. Jesus' way was to point not to himself but to his Father who sent him. He did not preach his own identity as such. Rather, he announced the coming of God's kingdom; he lived and died to make the kingdom a reality "on earth, as it is in heaven." The entire ministry of Jesus was radically theocentric.

Christian dogmatics is christocentric insofar as no doctrine can be called Christian at all if it bears no significant connection with the definitive revelation of God in the person of Jesus the Christ. The centrality of Christ is not limited to a particular part of theology, for example, the doctrine of the church or the sacraments. Christ is central both in the order of creation and in the realm of redemption. He is central in a Christian theological interpretation of nature, history, and existence. Even our knowledge of God is finally determined by the way in which God is revealed in the person of Jesus. No matter what may be known about God apart from christological revelation, a subject that still remains in controversy, Christian faith looks to the apostolic witness to Jesus the Christ as the final criterion of the truth concerning the nature and identity of God.

In recent times the principle of christocentricity in theology has come under attack. Speaking of Karl Barth's theology, H. Richard Niebuhr coined the phrase "unitarianism of the second article." [1] Others have described Barth's position as christomonist or mono-christological.[2] Christocentricity is allegedly incompatible with the "radical monotheism" of biblical faith. It makes of Christ a "second God" alongside the One God of Israel, thus falsely putting him into the place of Yahweh as the sole object of faith and worship. Theologians who debunk christocentricity maintain that the status of Christ in Christian faith scarcely warrants a central role for christology in shaping

6 / THE PERSON OF JESUS CHRIST

and ordering all other doctrines.[3] The christocentric pattern in modern Protestant theology from Friedrich Schleiermacher and Albrecht Ritschl in the nineteenth century to Karl Barth and Paul Tillich in the twentieth century is regarded by the critics of christocentricity as a mark of failure. The mandate to view all theological doctrines in the light of Christ is no longer binding. In dramatic fashion, John Hick has called for a "Copernican revolution in theology."[4] This revolution would place *God* at the center of the universe of all the religions, thus dislodging Christ from the central position he has held in the old "Ptolemaic" scheme of things. The traditional claim of seeing all things *sub specie Christi* and of viewing Christ as the source of our knowledge of God as well as the ultimate standard by which all teachings are to be judged, as the focal point of faith itself, can thus presumably be explained as a habit of mind that could thrive in that age of Christendom when Christianity regarded itself as the one and only saving religion in the world. But now Christendom is dying, and along with it the narrow parochialism which it bred. Christocentricity allegedly becomes anachronistic in an age characterized by ecumenical openness, theological pluralism, and interreligious dialogue.[5]

What is at stake in the principle of christocentricity? The type of christocentricity that accompanied the "death of God" theology has proved to be false.[6] Here Jesus of Nazareth as a figure of history was treated as a substitute for the God who allegedly died with the rise of secular and scientific consciousness and with the demise of myth and metaphysics. For Christian theology the principle of christocentricity is not a mechanism of compensation for loss of belief or lack of meaning in the idea of God. Jesus is no substitute for God! Rather, the principle of christocentricity underscores the identity of the God who is really God. It aims to answer the question: Which God? Gods are a dime a dozen in the history of religions. Which God are we talking about in Christian dogmatics? In light of the christocentric principle our answer is: This God is not the simple, solitary, and self-sufficient unit of radical monotheism. That would be the God of classical deism and unitarianism. The God of classical Christianity, in contrast, is the self-structuring reality of trinitarian faith, the One who antecedently differentiates the divine self as Father, Son, and Holy Spirit and is revealed as such in the economy of history and salvation.

Originally, the *doctrine* of the Trinity came about as a product of theological reflection on the revelation of God in the person of Jesus the Christ. At the heart of this development of the trinitarian dogma was the primitive Christian kerygma of God's identification with the death and resurrection of Jesus. Where faith in Jesus as the bringer of absolute salvation is set aside, there also trinitarian theology loses the fertile soil from which it has grown into its more fully developed dogmatic and liturgical forms. The doctrine of the

INTRODUCTION

Trinity and the principle of christocentricity are mutually implicative. One reinforces the other. It is not by chance that the most christocentric of modern theologians, namely, Karl Barth, has also produced the most thoroughly trinitarian theology of them all.

Christianity is universally categorized as a monotheistic form of belief. This does not mean, however, that its doctrine of the Trinity and its confession of Christ arise subsequently at a lower level of symbolic meaning. There have been various forms of mystical, metaphysical, political, and moralistic monotheism which have relegated both the doctrine of the Trinity and belief in the uniqueness of Christ to secondary importance, making them appear dispensable.[7] In a dogmatic system of trinitarian monotheism the principle of christocentricity, far from being a function of subjective faith and traditional piety, operates as a criticism of every type of monotheism that would loosen the links between the identity of God and the person of Jesus the Christ.

NOTES

1. H. Richard Niebuhr discussed the idea of a unitarianism of the second person of the Trinity in "The Doctrine of the Trinity and the Unity of the Church," *Theology Today* 3 (1946): 371–84.

2. Cf. H. Urs von Balthasar, *Karl Barth: Darstellung und Deutung seiner Theologie*, 2d ed. (Cologne, 1962).

3. Eugene Te Selle, *Christ in Context* (Philadelphia: Fortress Press, 1975).

4. John Hick, *God and the Universe of Faiths* (New York: Macmillan Co., 1973).

5. Paul Knitter has provided an extensive critique of Protestant christocentricity in *Towards a Protestant Theology of Religions: A Case Study of Paul Althaus and Contemporary Attitudes* (Marburg: N. G. Elwert Verlag, 1974).

6. This form of pseudo-christocentricity was represented by William Hamilton, *The New Essence of Christianity* (New York: Association Press, 1961); Paul van Buren, *The Secular Meaning of the Gospel* (New York: Macmillan Co., 1963); Thomas J. J. Altizer, *The Gospel of Christian Atheism* (Philadelphia: Westminster Press, 1966).

7. Cf. Erik Peterson, "Der Monotheismus als politisches Problem," in *Theologische Traktate* (Munich, 1950), pp. 45–147; Eberhard Jüngel, *The Doctrine of the Trinity* (Grand Rapids: Wm. B. Eerdmans, 1976).

1
The Nature and Method of Christology

Christology is the church's reflection on the basic assertion that Jesus is the Christ of God. Its aim is to construct a comprehensive interpretation of the identity and meaning of the person of Jesus as the Christ, under the condition of contemporary knowledge and experience.

WHAT IS CHRISTOLOGY?

Christology is the interpretation of Jesus of Nazareth as the Christ of God from the standpoint of the faith of the Christian church. The word "christology" means literally the *logos* about *Christos*, thought and speech about Christ. Christ is a title, and not the second name of Jesus. The title expresses the identity of Jesus of Nazareth, according to the apostolic witness and the catholic tradition. The question of Jesus' true identity was raised already in his own lifetime, as recorded in the Gospel of Mark (8:27–29). Jesus is reported to have asked his disciples on the way to Caesarea Philippi, "Who do men say that I am?" They replied, in effect, that people could not make up their minds about him. Some said he was John the Baptist, others Elijah, still others that he was one of the prophets. Then, turning to his disciples, Jesus asked, "But who do you say that I am?" Peter answered him, "You are the Christ." Peter's statement was a confession of his own personal faith. Other contemporaries of Jesus reached an opposite conclusion about who he really was. They said he was the Son of Satan!

Christology is not a scientific discipline which can be appropriately pursued apart from the discipleship of faith. Faith signifies an existential interest in the contemporary meaning of Jesus as the Christ of God. The experience of faith in Jesus as the living Christ means that christology is more than critical reflection on who Jesus was in his earthly existence. Jesus Christ can be the object of faith because he is not merely Jesus of Nazareth, an historical figure who lived and died once upon a time, but also the risen and living Christ who is presently embodied in the community of believers. Christology reflects

6 / THE PERSON OF JESUS CHRIST

on the meaning of Jesus the Christ now in the present encounters of Christian faith and action in the world.

Without the confession of faith in Jesus as the Christ, christology would be reducible to Jesuology. Faith is not a mere human performance, a work of the intellect, the will, or the emotions. No one can call Jesus the Christ purely as a result of historical scientific research. Traditional dogmatics has rightly stressed that faith is brought about through the inward witness of the Holy Spirit (*testimonium spiritus sancti internum*). This means that there is a dimension of mystery in the process of christological reflection. A fact-finding committee of scientifically trained historians could not prove that Jesus is the Christ. They could only show that this was the unanimous witness of believers in the early church, for which the New Testament stands as primary documentary evidence. The witness is clear. But was that witness true? The question of truth places every person before an either-or that cannot be decided without the power of faith and the witness of the Spirit.

The affirmation of the contemporaneity of Christ means that the Holy Spirit actualizes Christ's presence through faith, the receiving side of a real personal relationship. The Holy Spirit is the power to bring personal faith and Jesus who is the living Christ together now. This happens where and when it happens (*ubi et quando visum est deo*) by the power of the Holy Spirit, not when an investigating committee of historians issues the final report of their factual findings. It is the Spirit who raises the historical Jesus out of the remoteness of past history and situates him as the living Christ in the existential context of the present moment. The Holy Spirit does not, however, work in a direct, unmediated way. The Spirit is the inner power of the living voice of the gospel (the *viva vox evangelii*) which can be heard in, with, and under the preaching of the church. Christology would suffer from sterile historicism if its reflections were not nourished in a matrix of inquiry involving a complexity of vital factors including faith and the Spirit as well as preaching and the church.

The church as a community of believers is the appropriate context of responsible christological reflection. Faith in the living Christ is not a private mystical exercise between "Jesus and me." Apart from the gathered assembly (the *ecclesia*) of those who worship God in Jesus' name, there is no proclamation which has the power to awaken faith in Jesus as the living Christ of God. There are many forms of interest in Jesus of Nazareth which are powerless to mediate faith. Modern biographical and psychological speculations about the external and internal developments in the life of Jesus are the most notable examples of such faith-less interest.[1] The picture of Jesus the Christ which animates the preaching of the church is framed not by such arbitrary constructions of the imagination but by the christological creeds and confessions of the church. The purpose of the christological dogma of classical Christianity is to guide the church in faithfully representing the apostolic picture of Jesus as the Christ of God, so that its contemporary witness to the living Christ will not be a mirror in which the church idealizes itself or ideologizes its position in society. The christological dogma points beyond the church, ensuring that its Lord is the living Christ embodied in Jesus of Nazareth, and not an ahistorical myth, a metaphysical principle, a religious personality, or a moral virtuoso.

The authentic picture of the living Christ is given in the Bible; everything else is at best some kind of reproduction. Thus it will always be necessary for the church to test its christological interpretations by referring to the biblical picture of Jesus the Christ. The biblical picture of Christ, however, is not like a single snapshot. It is more like a montage of portraits sketched by several artists, from various angles and at different times and places. For this reason scholars now speak of a multiplicity of christologies in the New Testament. Nevertheless, all of them stem from the earliest witness of the apostles to Jesus of Nazareth, his life and teachings, and particularly his suffering, death, and resurrection.

We have shown that christology by its very nature moves between the poles of the contemporaneity of the Christ and the historicity of Jesus. If christology moves toward the pole of contemporaneity in a one-sided way, it veers off into subjectivism and modernism. We may speak of this in traditional terms as docetism: denial of the historicity of the Christ who is Jesus. If christology moves toward the pole of historicity in a one-sided way, it tends to fall back into either positivistic historicism or biblicistic fundamentalism. We may speak of these errors as ebionitism: denial of the presence of the living Jesus who is the Christ in the ongoing history of the church's proclamation of the word.

HISTORY, DOGMATICS, AND FAITH

The historian, the dogmatician, and the believer have their own ways of approaching the historical Jesus. Since the Enlightenment, Jesus of Nazareth has become the object of strictly historical scientific inquiry. Historical science first had to emancipate itself from dogmatic controls in order even to raise the question of the historical Jesus. Today scarcely anyone doubts the right of historians to inquire into the biblical sources for the most reliable information concerning the man Jesus as a figure of past history. But many scholars are skeptical of the possibility of uncovering the real Jesus of history behind the blanket of interpretations which the earliest believers laid on him. Theology has been posed a dilemma by the application of the historical-critical method to the Gospel sources. What is the dogmatic significance of the ongoing quest of the historical Jesus? By the "historical Jesus" we mean Jesus of Nazareth insofar as he can be made the object of historical-critical research. What is

6 / THE PERSON OF JESUS CHRIST

the relevance of the results of such research? Are they crucial for faith? Do they provide data for preaching? Or are they merely matters of endless debate among scholars, whose statements about history can never be advanced beyond a shadow of doubt? It is important to keep the boundary lines straight between historical science, dogmatics, and faith.

The critical historian can use the New Testament writings as source documents for the history of primitive Christianity. From these sources historians can reconstruct the beliefs and activities of the early church. Can they also penetrate these sources and reach back to the underlying facts concerning Jesus himself? The historian faces two kinds of difficulty. First, the Gospels present the history of Jesus as the Christ in forms of tradition that were written and transmitted under the impact of the resurrection faith. It has proved impossible to disengage naked facts of history from the interpretations in which they were embedded. Second, the modern historian can never approach the past without some kind of presuppositions. Some prior understanding about the nature of human existence and the meaning of religion will qualify all the statements a historian can make about the identity of Jesus of Nazareth. There is a philosophical or theological dimension of understanding implied in every use of the historical method to establish "what really happened." As historians proceed to a profound level of interpretation, it will become evident whether the results of their research are framed by the world view of a personalistic theist, a rationalistic deist, an immanentalist pantheist, a Marxist atheist, or whatever. There is no such thing as presuppositionless research.

In turning to the Gospel traditions concerning Jesus of Nazareth, the historical method of research can serve to raise the question of faith. All these traditions represent Jesus as the Christ of God. This is the irreducible minimum of the earliest apostolic witness. Either historians share the perspective of this witness to Jesus or they do not. There is no neutral ground. Historians who are believers, who confess Jesus as the Christ, the Savior of humankind, and the Lord of the world, are bound to read the Gospels differently from people who regard Jesus of Nazareth as an historical personality on the same level with all other human beings. The work of historical research can renew the age-old question: "Who do men say that I am?" The offense aroused by Jesus in his lifetime and the scandal of the apostles' preaching can be described by the historian in such a way as to renew the question of the true identity of Jesus. The answer to the question, however, is itself never purely a product of historical research. It involves a decision of faith.

Faith in Jesus as the Christ is not based on the results of historical-critical scholarship. Some dogmaticians have opposed the use of the historical method in biblical interpretation because they fear that faith will be made dependent on the shifting results of scientific research. This is the result of a misunderstanding. The results of historical inquiry do not form the basis and contents of Christian faith. It is the task of dogmatics to serve as the "defense attorney" for believers in face of the heteronomous claim of science to provide the contents or legitimate the basis of faith. The saving knowledge of Jesus as the Christ is passed on "from faith unto faith," not by publishing the latest results of historians or exegetes. An essential dependence of faith on the results of historical research would force believers to deliver their faith in trust to the authority of historical critics, as once it had to exist in bondage to an authoritarian church, a magisterial dogmatics, or an infallible Bible.

What then is the theological relevance of historical science, if faith is free of dependence on its most recently assured results? It is important to observe a distinction between dogmatics and faith. What is relevant for the constructive reflections of the theologian is not necessarily essential to the being or even the well-being of faith. Faith can exist very well without being caught up on the latest research, but dogmatics cannot ignore the ongoing process and results of historical-critical scholarship. Faith lives from the witness to Christ in the preaching of the church and the message of the Scriptures. Dogmatics is critical reflection that goes on in the church for the sake of a more mature understanding of faith, its foundations and contents. To this end dogmatics will help itself to every available means of acquiring knowledge about the historical events and interpretations which make up the living tradition that generates and sustains faith. The highly developed skills of historical research provide us with the best tools we have to ascertain what really happened in the past.

THE STARTING POINT OF CHRISTOLOGY

One of the points at issue in contemporary theology concerns the right starting point of christology. Traditionally christology was done "from above," starting with the christological dogma of the ancient church. Both the medieval scholastic and the Protestant orthodox dogmaticians modeled their systems on Peter Lombard's *Four Books of Sentences*, beginning with the classical dogma of the two natures of Christ, divine and human. This christological dogma presupposed the dogma of the Trinity and the incarnation of the Son of God. Christology proceeded deductively from the eternal deity of Christ above to his human nature here below.

For a long time it seemed reasonable to begin christology with the dogma of the incarnation. It was the revealed doctrine of the church and the norm by which every heresy was to be anathematized. But once the dogma lost its status as the principle of authority in modern theology, it could no longer function as the starting point.[2] The christological dogma had to be justified

6 / THE PERSON OF JESUS CHRIST

as a legitimate interpretation of the New Testament picture of Jesus the Christ in the categories of the Hellenistic world of thought.

When the christological dogma was placed on the defensive by its modern critics, the attempt was made to salvage its meaning by concentrating on the kerygmatic Christ. This is a contemporary way of doing christology from above. It begins christology not with the traditional dogma of the two natures but with the kerygmatic picture of the Christ in apostolic Christianity. Christology then goes in search of the existential meaning of kerygmatic symbols, rather than the dogmatic truth of metaphysical concepts. We acknowledge a sympathy with this point of view, for two reasons. First, the actuality of faith in the living Christ is the condition of the possibility of doing christology today. Faith is the medium of christological reflection, even though history and not faith is the primal source of its data. Second, the New Testament is a collection of Easter stories that presuppose the faith of the apostolic community. Without that faith not a single story of Jesus would have been preserved for posterity. Yet we cannot be satisfied to assume the kerygmatic Christ as the starting point of dogmatic construction. The type of question put to the christological dogma can be transposed to the christological kerygma. What is its legitimating ground? What is the historical basis and content of the kerygma? The dogma does not rest on itself; neither does the kerygma.

There is now virtual consensus among theologians that christology must start from below. Here lies the deepest significance of the new quest of the historical Jesus. Scholars who participate in the new quest use various methods and reach different results, but most agree that it is historically possible and theologically necessary to penetrate behind the New Testament kerygma to traditions that convey some reliable knowledge about Jesus of Nazareth. Neither the dogma nor the kerygma is sufficient of itself to provide the basis and content of faith. Granted, there are no naked facts of history that can be shelled free of their husks of interpretation. That would be like looking for a nut inside an onion. Granted also that faith is not based on the results of any new quest of the historical Jesus. Faith is based rather on the preaching of the Easter kerygma, and certainly not on a modern scholarly reconstruction of the historical Jesus. Yet there is good reason to require that christology begin from below. This makes clear that both the christological dogma and the kerygmatic christology refer back to Jesus of Nazareth as the historical object of christology. Christology is based on the Christ to whom apostolic faith witnesses, and this Christ is none other than Jesus of Nazareth.

The dogma of the divine-human Christ and the kerygma of the risen Lord have to do with the history of Jesus. Christology seeks to understand the meaning and the connections between history, kerygma, and dogma. Kerygmatic and dogmatic interpretations are empty without grounding in the historical reality of Jesus. The other side of the dialectic is that historical facts are blind

THE NATURE AND METHOD OF CHRISTOLOGY

without the interpretative sequences in the kerygmatic and dogmatic formulations of the church.

The danger in starting christology from below is that it might end in a "low christology" of no use to the Christian faith. We define a "low christology" as an interpretation of Jesus which treats him as a mere man.[3] It converts the classical christological category of the "truly human" (*vere homo*) into the "merely human." This is a modernistic version of the ancient ebionitic heresy which taught that Jesus was only a man (*psilos anthropos*) and not the truly divine Son of God. On the other hand, starting christology from below with the historical Jesus need not preclude the development of a "high christology." A high christology treats the resurrection of Jesus and his unity with God as predicates belonging to the personal identity of Jesus the Christ, and not only as value judgments imposed on him from the arbitrary perspective of religious experience.[4]

Despite the current preference for doing christology from below, starting with what can be known about the historical Jesus, christological reflection is a hermeneutical process in which the movements "from above" and "from below" are not so much mutually exclusive as dialectically related in a comprehensive understanding of the identity and meaning of the person of Jesus the Christ. The process of interpretation extends from the contemporary act of faith in the believing community to the past-historical fact of Jesus interpreted by the apostolic kerygma as the Christ. This process of interpretation can be called a hermeneutical "circle" or "arc." The circular nature of this interpretation relativizes the distinction between starting "from above" or "from below." It is essential to acknowledge that the question of Jesus' identity cannot be separated from the engagement of faith and the Spirit. "No one can say 'Jesus is Lord' except by the Holy Spirit" (1 Cor. 12:3). The attempt to bracket out faith and proceed by reason alone is just as problematic as excluding reason and appealing to faith alone. The modern quest of the historical Jesus is eminently the work of historical reason. In abstraction from the total system of hermeneutical operations involved in christological thought, it cannot be regarded as the starting point. Within the horizon of an adequate hermeneutics, however, christology can begin with the question of how Jesus of Nazareth came to be called the Christ of God in the early church. Perspectives from the New Testament kerygma and the history of dogma may generate insight in the process of trying to understand how the historical Jesus can be the object of faith without violating the first commandment, "Thou shalt have no other gods before me."

For apologetic reasons christology today may choose to start with the appearance of the man Jesus and then lead up to the knowledge of his divinity through his death and resurrection. The divinity of Christ, it can be argued, no longer functions as a self-evident presupposition. Instead, modern historical

6 / THE PERSON OF JESUS CHRIST

consciousness looks on such a statement as a hypothesis that demands some sort of historical legitimation. But we should not allow our apologetic concerns to cross the boundaries of what can be seriously defended. The transition from the historical Jesus to the risen Christ of the apostolic kerygma or the divine Son of God of the ecclesiastical dogma cannot be explained and legitimated purely by historical argumentation. The effort to do so accounts for the trend in conservative New Testament scholarship to derive all the high christology of the later church from the lips of the historical Jesus. This means that the New Testament scholar must find all the seeds of later christological development in the teachings of Jesus. Failure to achieve this would mean that christology loses its origins in the real Jesus of history, shifting the basis and beginnings of christology to the creative developments in the early church.

If today dogmatics is to build on historical foundations, it will have to take the question of the origins of christology into consideration. Within the total hermeneutical framework, what do we understand to be the central datum of christology? Where is it to be found? How far back can we trace historically the rise of christology? How did it happen that the man Jesus who preached the coming of God's kingdom soon became the Lord of the kingdom in the kerygma of the church? Faith does not need an answer to these questions, but dogmatics will seek to understand the historical roots and ramifications of christology from its earliest origins to the present time.

First, some scholars locate the root of christology in the self-manifestation of Jesus himself. The christological predicates and titles in the apostolic kerygma are to be traced back to some aspect of the historical Jesus, whether his messianic self-consciousness, his claim to possess authority to forgive sins, his message of the coming kingdom, or his way with others. Scholars hold different opinions, but many agree that the roots of christology can be found in the historical person of Jesus.

Second, another group of scholars locate the central datum of christology in the historical event of Jesus' resurrection. The resurrection is something that really happened to the crucified Jesus. He was raised to a new mode of being beyond the fate of death. This Easter event is the presupposition for the primitive Christian proclamation of Jesus as the Christ of God. It is the key, finally, to the knowledge of Jesus' unity with God.

Third, there are those who ground christological faith neither in the earthly Jesus nor in his resurrection, but only in the kerygma of the early church. The resurrection is interpreted as the rise of faith in the disciples; the Easter kerygma is viewed as an interpretation of an otherwise unmessianic Jesus. The kerygma alone is the central datum of christology. Every attempt to inquire behind the kerygma to the underlying events of Jesus' life, death, and resurrection is ruled out as trying to establish proofs of faith.

There is no need for dogmatics to play off one of these lines of interpretation against the others. In our christological synthesis the person of Jesus Christ himself is not limited to the historical Jesus. The concept of the personal identity of Jesus Christ includes his earthly existence as well as his resurrected state of being. And the history of the interpretation of Jesus has a trajectory through the kerygmatic proclamations of the early church, the multiplicity of christologies assuming their embryonic form in the New Testament, and the creedal and dogmatic definitions of christology in church tradition. The historical Jesus, the kerygmatic Christ, and the christological dogma—these three are the stuff of which christology is made. The elimination of a single one of these factors deals a crippling blow to a christology that aims to serve the church in its preaching, life, and mission.

NOTES

1. This was the main point of Martin Kähler's attack on the "life of Jesus movement" of modern scholarship in *The So-Called Historical Jesus and the Historic Biblical Christ*, trans. Carl E. Braaten (Philadelphia: Fortress Press, 1964).

2. Cf. Wolfhart Pannenberg, *Jesus—God and Man*, trans. Lewis Wilkins and Duane Priebe (Philadelphia: Westminster Press, 1968), pp. 21ff.

3. As an example of this tendency, see *The Myth of God Incarnate*, ed. John Hick (Philadelphia: Westminster Press, 1977).

4. Pannenberg's *Jesus—God and Man* is an example of such a "high christology."

2

The Historical Jesus and the Kingdom of God

The point of departure of the New Testament as a whole is the appearance of Jesus and his message of the kingdom of God. The explicit christology of the early church is founded on the historical and material transition from Jesus' preaching of the kingdom of God to the early church's Easter proclamation of Jesus as the Christ and the risen Lord.

JESUS' EXPECTATION OF THE KINGDOM OF GOD

The "kingdom of God" was the central theme in the entire message of Jesus. All three synoptic Gospels picture Jesus as an itinerant preacher from Galilee announcing the good news of the kingdom of God (Mark 1:15; Matt. 4:23; Luke 4:43). Rudolf Bultmann states, "The dominant concept of Jesus' message is the Reign of God,"[1] expressing a consensus among New Testament scholars. But the reign or kingdom of God was more than a concept in the mind of Jesus set forth in speech. It was the driving force of his whole career. It penetrated his sermons and sayings and motivated all his acts and miracles. Whatever Jesus performed in word and deed was depicted as a "sign" of the inbreaking rule of God. This is at once the most certain result of modern historical exegesis and the starting point for our constructive christological interpretation.

The consensus among scholars, however, breaks up the moment they begin to describe the meaning of the kingdom of God. In nineteenth-century Protestant theology, the kingdom of God was interpreted predominantly in moral terms, either personal or social. From Friedrich Schleiermacher to Albrecht Ritschl, the kingdom of God was conceived as an inner spiritual or an outward social moral force. The kingdom of God exists wherever people live according to the moral principles which Jesus taught, summarized especially in the Sermon on the Mount. This morality reached its zenith when Jesus exhibited the love of God by dying on the cross. Such a morality reveals the true essence of being human. Rightly understood, being a true Christian and an authentic person are one and the same thing.

This moral interpretation of the kingdom of God was shattered when in separate studies Johannes Weiss[2] and Albert Schweitzer[3] proved that the kingdom of God in Jesus' preaching was mainly an eschatological concept. The kingdom of God will not come as the cumulative result of human good works and historical progress. Rather, it is a miracle of God's power breaking in from beyond the realm of human potentiality. The research of Weiss and Schweitzer showed that the kingdom of God which Jesus expected in the near future was more like an apocalyptic end to the world than a paradise on earth gradually wrought by human means. Weiss dropped a bombshell in late-nineteenth-century Protestant theology, ruled at that time by the school of Albrecht Ritschl, when he wrote, "As Jesus conceived it, the Kingdom of God is a radically superworldly entity which stands in diametric opposition to this world. This is to say that there *can* be no talk of an *innerworldly* development of the kingdom of God in the mind of Jesus!"[4]

Neither Weiss nor Schweitzer did anything to make his own discoveries fruitful for Christian faith and theology. Neither could salvage Jesus from the wreckage of his apocalyptic-eschatological world view. What could such a view have to do with the evolutionary and progressive view of modern times? Better to cling to the modernized ethical construction of Jesus' message—although it rests on a misunderstanding—than try to retain his antiquated eschatological ideas. It is to the lasting credit of the dialectical theologians, Karl Barth, Rudolf Bultmann, Emil Brunner, Friedrich Gogarten, and others, that they sought to take seriously the eschatological hypothesis of Weiss and Schweitzer. In the name of eschatology they fought against the reduction of Christianity to a moralistic ideology.

In dialectical theology, however, eschatology took on a questionable meaning when it was transcendentally emptied of all concrete historical facts and temporal contacts, becoming instead a principle of radical otherness—the otherness of God standing against the world, of faith against reason, and of Christ against culture. The eschatological event comes like a sharp blade cutting into the present moment. Such an event can call one's life into question, cause a deep vibration in the soul, or generate a new self-understanding, but it tends to narrow the promises of the Bible that engender hope for changes in the real world of people and nations and the material conditions of their common life.

There is no way around the eschatological message of Jesus for any contemporary interpretation of his significance. The "new quest of the historical Jesus,"[5] pursued with such scholarly vigor in recent years, has slammed the door on any merely ethical appropriation of Jesus' relevance for modern times. But it was the "theology of hope"[6] that set in motion a new attempt to make good the aborted exegetical discoveries of Weiss and Schweitzer. At the same time, this movement has overcome the purely transcendental view of eschatology that dominated the dialectical and existentialist models of systematic theology. The result is that Jesus' proclamation of the kingdom of God is now placed at the very beginning of a historical reconstruction of the christology of primitive Christianity, and at the center of a systematic treatment of his significance in contemporary theology. Not so long ago it was thought that our chief problem in christology was that we know virtually nothing concerning the historical Jesus.[7] Now the problem is more that a massive amount of research has focused on Jesus' message of the coming kingdom, leaving us still unsure of how to interpret it. The problem has shifted from history to hermeneutics.

How can we follow Jesus in thinking of the *basileia* of God as an otherworldly reality of cosmic magnitude about to break in at any time? We moderns go on with our plans as though the world were to last forever, buying life insurance against that day when our own personal lives will come to an end. At best, people have an eschatological attitude as individuals, living as though each day were their last. Jesus related the coming of the kingdom to the world, as power to overthrow the dominion of Satan and to create a new world of lasting righteousness and happiness. He expected God to establish the power and glory of his rule in the *immediate* future. Instead the world has gone on without any real fulfillment for two thousand years. Was not Jesus' expectation of the coming kingdom proved wrong by the ongoing course of history? Is this not an error that touches the heart of his message, and not mere details of marginal significance? No wonder Adolf von Harnack gained a following when he separated an ethical kernel from the eschatological husk of Jesus' preaching.[8] According to Harnack the ethical teachings of Jesus are still valid, whereas his eschatological ideas are strange to modern time. If such a separation of Jesus' ethics from his eschatology is no longer tenable, how can we make the historical Jesus *cum* eschatology the point of departure for christological interpretation today?

The place to begin is with the question of what Jesus really meant by the kingdom of God. When Jesus spoke of the kingdom, he did not have in mind a realm in space and time. The word refers not to a spatial realm but to the dynamic rule of God. The kingdom is the kingly rule of God, God's unequaled power and sovereign authority. Perhaps we should say quite simply that the coming of the kingdom means the coming of God. The kingdom comes when God actually comes, when God seizes power and establishes dominion over all things. To expect the kingdom is to be open for *the coming of God*, nothing less.[9] But this has universal meaning, for when God comes in power, the world must change. Things cannot remain as they are. God's coming is the power to destroy all resistance to God's rule and freely to grant God's gracious kingdom to those in need of a new beginning—poor people,

6 / THE PERSON OF JESUS CHRIST

publicans, and prostitutes. God is not an idle sovereign sitting on a throne. God will act when he comes, both in works of judgment and in works of grace. The kingdom is not a condition of this world that can be brought about by human means. It is not a predicate of this world. As the rule of God it is inseparable from the actual being of God. The eschatological being and the historical acts of God are the inner and outer aspects of the same ultimate reality.

The kingdom of God becomes manifest in the ministry of Jesus through sign-events. A great reversal in the order of things is about to take place. According to Luke 6:20–21, the poor will become happy, the hungry will be satisfied, and those who weep will laugh. Only the coming of God's kingdom can generate the power to produce such a miraculous turnabout in the human world. But the purpose of such sign-events is to point to the coming of God and God's rule, not to focus on a new social order as an ultimate good in itself. The history of the kingdom of God in the West has made it practically synonymous with utopia. Utopias, however, are people-centered schemes, born of human imagination and run by human effort. Hence the Marxist humanist Ernst Bloch speaks paradoxically of a kingdom of God without God, for the true essence of the kingdom, he says, is nothing more than human fulfillment.[10]

This idea reduces the kingdom of God to anthropology. In Jesus' message *God* is the subject of ultimate concern when God comes with the kingdom. *God* is the essential condition of a radically new order. The kingdom of God is no longer the same thing when converted into a kingdom with humankind at the center. The cash value of the kingdom of God will be lost when exchanged for phrases like "realm of freedom" or "kingdom of peace." There is a surplus of meaning in the mystery of God that prevents God's kingdom from becoming a predicate of humankind or the world.

The kingdom of God never ceases to be mystery in Jesus' message. He never offered a definition or a straightforward description. He spoke in riddles and parables; he left hints and clues; his miracles and deeds could be taken several ways. The mystery lies hidden in the words he preached, the parables he told, and the miracles he did as signs of the rapidly approaching kingdom of God. Others—Pharisees and Zealots—were trying to bring in the kingdom of God, either through religious and moral good works or through revolutionary praxis. But Jesus, dismissing both techniques as human presumption, offered no direct formula for translating the kingdom into an earthly state of affairs. To be sure, Jesus did present ethical teachings—the ethics of the kingdom—but they could be comprehended only within the eschatological frame of his message as a whole. Nowhere did he teach common-sense moral principles that could be practiced by morally sensitive people in this kind of world. The ethics of Jesus are laden with eschatological presuppositions;[11] they make sense

THE HISTORICAL JESUS AND THE KINGDOM OF GOD

as a morality prefiguring the new reality of God's approaching kingdom. When Jesus' ethics are put to work in an earthly context, they are intended to function as signs of the coming kingdom. They were finally contradicted by the world in the violent language of the cross. The cross was the world's reply to the uncompromising love which Jesus poured into all his words and deeds. This means that the praxis of the kingdom invariably ends in the shape of a cross.

Jesus proclaimed the coming kingdom as an urgent appeal to his hearers. His point was not to pass on information about the kingdom, as other apocalyptic visionaries had done in colorful detail. It was rather to convince his audience that it was high time to get ready for the coming of God. His call to "repent and believe" was issued as if for the last time, as if soon it would be too late. He issued an invitation to be open to the mystery not of the being of God attained by mysticism and ecstaticism, as in Hellenistic religion, but of the coming of God which calls for repentance and faith in line with the Hebraic tradition.

One of the most heated debates in modern New Testament research has been whether Jesus expected the arrival of the kingdom in the very near future, or whether it was already being fulfilled in the present. There are passages that point in both directions.[12] Most scholars agree, however, that by far the majority of the passages which can be ascribed to the historical Jesus picture the kingdom of God as having drawn so near as to have a present impact. The kingdom is not yet fulfilled, but its coming is imminent and its initial impact is already being felt, at least so far as the present becomes a time to get ready and watch for signs of its actual arrival.

Why has it been so difficult for scholars to determine the exact nature of Jesus' expectation of the kingdom? The reason is that in producing the Gospels the early church mixed its own eschatological ideas into its picture of Jesus as the Christ. Shortly after Easter the church developed an eschatology balanced between two poles. The first pole was determined by the past appearance of Jesus as the Christ, the second by his future return on the day of judgment. Meanwhile the early church was enjoying life in the afterglow of Jesus' resurrection and filled by the outpouring of the Spirit. On this side of Easter and Pentecost the early church looked back to the time of Jesus as the source of the salvation it was experiencing in the present. Features of fulfillment due to Easter were written into the story of Jesus' own time. If Jesus looked ahead for salvation from the coming kingdom, the early church looked back to him as the Christ who had already made the kingdom present. Despite this orientation to the past, the early church also strained forward in expectation of a future fulfillment. Even some of these ideas of cosmic eschatology were read back into the message of Jesus (e.g. Mark 13). We are thus faced with at least three layers: first, Jesus' own expectation of the coming kingdom; second, the early church's conviction that the time of Jesus was pregnant with fulfillment; and third, its belief that Christ would return at the close of the age. New Testament scholarship has shown how these three layers of tradition were commingled after Easter and put back into the mouth of the historical Jesus. Apparently the early church sought historical legitimation for its dogmatic beliefs by grounding its own post-Easter eschatology in the earthly Jesus.

It now appears to be a firmly established result of critical Gospel research that Jesus of Nazareth did not think of the kingdom of God as already fulfilled in his ministry. Had he done so, that would have had the effect of drastically narrowing the meaning of the kingdom and rendering it impotent. Then its presence would have been so hidden in the world as to have had no power to change it. Then the meaning of fulfillment would have been so spiritualized as to be relegated to a supraworldly realm. But with Jesus it was different. His healing miracles and demon exorcisms were advance signs of the coming kingdom. His beatitudes and woes prove that he was fully aware that this world was still enthralled by evil powers. Obviously God's kingdom had not yet been established here and now. Now there are poor and hungry people. When the kingdom comes their misery will be lifted. Now they are suffering; soon they will rejoice. Jesus did not accept their fate as an everlasting condition. He put all the weight of God's kingdom into his promise to change it.

Those who teach that the kingdom of God has already been realized in the time of Jesus make a farce of his love for the poor, the oppressed, the hungry, the bereaved, the sick, the overburdened, the alienated, the ostracized, the imprisoned, the accursed, and the sinful. To all these people, Jesus promised that the kingdom would soon come to change their lot. Moreover, there are no preconditions, qualifications, or moral requirements of any kind. It is enough that they are defenseless; they are prime candidates for the friendship of God. This message was good news to poor sinners, but a slap in the face of the righteous. It does not seem fair to people who have made a profession of "full-time service for the Lord." But Jesus was operating with an eschatological transvaluation of moral values. Joachim Jeremias says that this was the unique thing in Jesus' message, the very thing that provoked the Pharisees to protest.[13]

But if Jesus promised the kingdom to the poor and the oppressed first, why did he do nothing to improve their condition? To be sure, he healed a few of them, but thousands became sick and died without his help. Most of the people in Palestine were left in their misery at the very time Jesus was preaching the kingdom, telling stories, and doing miracles. Some Christians, wanting to follow Jesus, have shared his vision but not his method. They have proposed the revolutionary method of putting the poor in office and the rich in jail. Even the sword and the guillotine have been consecrated for the service of the coming kingdom. Others of more liberal persuasion have created welfare programs and medical clinics to help the poor and the sick. But Jesus was neither a political revolutionary nor a social liberal.

Nor was Jesus a quietist, offering cheap consolation to those whose situation he deplored but did nothing about. There are Christians who want to take up the cross and follow Jesus, but have no hope to alter the conditions that create poverty and oppression. Enjoining patient suffering in this world, they promise a heavenly reward in the world to come. But Jesus was not a do-nothing quietist, directing all the traffic of the coming kingdom to a heavenly realm outside this world. Jesus used his leverage to bring the power of God's rule down to earth. His parables and miracles were concrete samples of the comprehensive salvation which the rule of God was about to establish for the world in general.

This brief sketch of Jesus' message of the kingdom of God does not enter into all its details. We are rather trying to catch that thread of his teaching about the kingdom that links up with the christology of the New Testament as a whole. The decisive question is not whether historians can reconstruct all aspects of Jesus' teaching, but what role he actually played in bringing about the kingdom he preached. The question is whether the beginning of christology as the New Testament sets it forth in a plurality of expressions reaches back to the central theme of Jesus' message—the kingdom of God. Or does christology spring *de novo* from the early church, with no material continuity with the historical Jesus?

THE GENESIS OF CHRISTOLOGY IN THE NEW TESTAMENT

Christology cannot ignore the most heated debates going on in New Testament scholarship. Neither can it settle questions that still remain open in the field of critical historical research: Did Jesus understand himself as the Messiah? Did he identify himself with the coming Son of Man, taken in the eschatological sense? The wide-ranging difference between scholars on such questions can be easily detected by contrasting the methods and results of C. F. D. Moule's *The Origin of Christology*[14] with Willi Marxsen's *The Beginnings of Christology: A Study in Its Problems.*[15] They reach exactly opposite conclusions about whether Jesus believed he was the Messiah and the coming Son of Man, or whether these are titles which the early church transferred to him. The same contrast is visible with respect to other honorific titles applied to Jesus, such as Son of God and Lord. Dogmatics has no method of its own by which to resolve the strictly historical problems of New Testament research. But neither is it paralyzed by the failure of biblical scholars to reach a consensus on all the critical issues.

If Jesus did not explicitly refer to himself by any of the major christological

6 / THE PERSON OF JESUS CHRIST

titles, how could the early church do so? How may we understand the genesis and development of christology that makes a real difference to Christian faith, so that what the early Christians said about Jesus does not flatly contradict Jesus' own estimate of himself? If we take seriously Jesus' preaching of the kingdom of God, then the question of how christology began is not first which titles Jesus used about himself but whether he played a crucial role in bringing in the divine kingdom he proclaimed with such finality. The forerunner of Jesus, John the Baptist, also preached the message of the coming kingdom, announcing impending judgment and time for repentance. But Jesus was different. He was not the last prophet of the coming kingdom; he was the medium of its arrival in beginning and in power. The realities of the kingdom were already beginning to stir within history through the impact of Jesus' ministry.

The root of christology in the ministry of Jesus is not located in a particular title of honor he claimed for himself. What is important is that Jesus was not only the proclaimer but also the bringer of the kingdom at the point of its eruption. So Jesus could say, "But if it is by the finger of God that I cast out demons, then the kingdom of God has come upon you" (Luke 11:20). Even Rudolf Bultmann and members of his school who find no explicit christology in Jesus' teaching strongly emphasize his authoritative claim as the present mediator of the oncoming kingdom. In the words of Willi Marxsen, "the eschatological element is the primal datum of Christology." [16] Thus, the genesis of christology lies in the fact that a person becomes related to the coming kingdom by his or her decision for or against Jesus, as the occasion of its inbreaking in time. This eschatological role of Jesus is the basis for speaking, with Bultmann and others, of an "implicit christology" in Jesus' message.[17]

Whether Jesus was the Messiah, the Son of Man, the Son of God, or the Lord depends not on finding these terms as self-designations on the lips of Jesus but on whether the primitive community had good reason to apply these titles to him as confessions of faith. What happened to bring the first believers to such an awareness, if they did not simply read their christology from the very words of Jesus?

Jesus was crucified and he was raised from the dead. His message had aroused hope that God was coming soon in power and glory to put an end to misery, poverty, and oppression, but instead Jesus got caught up in the power struggles of passion week that led to the cross. So where was the fulfillment of Jesus' keen expectation of the coming kingdom? It was shattered on the cross. The fulfillment did not come to pass as expected. Instead, the death of Jesus by crucifixion took place, a gory substitute for the glory of the kingdom. This means that either the kingdom of God emptied into the cross, using it as a strange instrument of its way to fulfillment, or the kingdom finds

THE HISTORICAL JESUS AND THE KINGDOM OF GOD

its fulfillment elsewhere, with no structural connection with the crucifixion of Jesus.

Many schools of theology do not look for the fulfillment of Jesus' expectation in the double ending of his life: cross and resurrection. Instead, quite different types of interpretation are offered, each in its own way avoiding the cross and its link to the coming kingdom. One type holds that the kingdom of God has not yet appeared; it is still future and otherworldly, not of this world. A second position views the kingdom as a call to decision here and now in the encounter with the message of Jesus; it is already present in every moment of existential decision. A third view sees the kingdom of God as something that lies in the historical future, coming by means of social and political transformations, either gradually and progressively or by means of revolutionary praxis. In none of these views is the crucifixion of Jesus integral to the arrival of the kingdom in history. Thus, they fail to connect Jesus' eschatological preaching of the kingdom to the early church's proclamation of Jesus as the crucified Christ in a fundamental way.

Jesus began his public ministry by announcing the coming kingdom with great expectation. He ended it by his death on the cross. The Gospel writers interpreted the death and resurrection of Jesus as the fulfillment of the kingdom whose coming he expected in the nearest possible future. But it was a fulfillment hidden under the sign of the cross, and therefore not manifest in all the power and glory that Jesus had expected. The one who had announced the coming of God with power to put an end to sin, death, and the power of the devil was condemned to die on the cross. This assassination could have been taken to mean that Jesus, self-deceived or betrayed by God, was simply proved wrong in his expectation of the kingdom. Instead, a great reversal of the disappointment on Good Friday took place. On the road to Emmaus the disciples had sighed, "But we had hoped that he was the one to redeem Israel" (Luke 24:21). But on the third day stories began to circulate that the crucified Jesus had appeared to some of his friends and disciples. These appearances of the living Jesus were interpreted by the first witnesses as evidence that God had raised Jesus from the dead and that this event was of an eschatological order, the beginning of the eschaton in the middle of history, a real fulfillment *in* Jesus of the expectation aroused *by* his message.

In the crucifixion and resurrection of Jesus the early church found the proof that Jesus was the expected Messiah, and further that he was the king of the kingdom he preached, crowned with a crown of thorns and enthroned on a cross, then granted a victory over the powers of evil in his resurrection from the dead. Here the Christ of faith and the Jesus of history prove to be one and the same Lord Jesus Christ. The primitive Christian community preached the kerygma of the crucified and risen Christ as the eschatological event that at least partially fulfilled the future eschatological kingdom which Jesus an-

6 / THE PERSON OF JESUS CHRIST

ticipated in all his preaching and activity. When the Catholic modernist Alfred Loisy said, "Jesus foretold the kingdom, and it was the church that came,"[18] many Christians felt a crisis of contradiction between the preaching *of* Jesus and the early church's preaching *about* Jesus. Adolf von Harnack provided the classic statement of this supposed contradiction when he sharply contrasted the religion *of* Jesus with the religion *about* Jesus.[19] Ever since the time of the Enlightenment there has been the fear that a critical penetration of the sources will drive a wedge between Jesus and the church, separating the claims of apostolic faith in Christ from their roots in the Jesus of history. In fact, however, there is no such contradiction. The fear of sheer discontinuity between the historical Jesus and the kerygmatic Christ need not be nourished by a critical study of the Gospel sources. The basic claim of the gospel is that the identity of Jesus is revealed and the kingdom of God is fulfilled in the history of his death and resurrection. The validity of this claim explains how the early church could collect a plurality of christological titles from many quarters and transfer them to the historical Jesus in telling the whole story of his birth, life, death, and resurrection.

Faced with the events of Jesus' crucifixion and his Easter appearances, the early Christians began the history of christological interpretation that has now run for nearly two thousand years. But where has the church found its dominant symbols of interpretation? What has it used as a norm against an uncritical adoption of all novel interpretations? What has been the church's hermeneutical key to open the traditions of the past, to find new meanings in the present, and to gain new directions for the future? The earliest interpreters searched the Hebrew Scriptures, the Old Testament, and used its symbols and stories to point ahead to the events of "these last days" (Heb. 1:2) in which the promises of Yahweh were being fulfilled in the Son. The hermeneutics of promise and fulfillment can be traced in all the traditions of the New Testament, even in those most subject to Hellenistic influence. Thus, the cross of Jesus was interpreted as a sacrifice for sin in light of the Old Testament idea of atonement. The resurrection was interpreted as the dawning of a new era, the initial breakthrough of the new things prophesied in Isaiah 65—66. In reaching back to the Old Testament, however, the controlling norm was the apostles' belief that Jesus' message of the kingdom reached its apex in his death and resurrection, revealing that he was in person the Christ of God.

If the early church witnessed to the resurrection of Jesus as a fulfillment in line with Jesus' own kingdom expectation, this had a retroactive effect on its interpretation of the history of Jesus and the history of Israel as well. What the church came to believe about Jesus as the Christ was retrojected into the beginnings and then narrated as a story that unfolded according to a plot that was there all along. The story starts at the beginning and proceeds to the end. But in fact, hermeneutically speaking, the end of the story—the cross and resurrection of Jesus—was there from the beginning and guided the community in shaping the Gospel traditions. No wonder that the presence of the kingdom, experienced by the Christian community on account of the Easter fulfillment, could be traced back to the ministry of Jesus prior to Easter. Features from the Christ of Easter and the Jesus of history are interwoven in the Gospel narratives, since the church put them to use in its own kerygmatic and missionary career.

The church's interest was to concentrate on the person of Jesus as the Christ of God, for in him it had experienced eschatological salvation. Because this salvation was hidden in the crucified Christ and present through the Spirit in the risen Lord, faith was required from the beginning to acknowledge its reality. Faith is the only mode of access to the salvation which the coming of God with the kingdom works in the person of the crucified and risen Jesus. The coming of the kingdom in the cross keeps the kingdom hidden in history and can be seen only with the eyes of faith. If we leave faith aside and look to history with ordinary eyes, we find no convincing evidence that the kingdom of God has already come. The rabbis of Judaism taught that when the Messiah comes the world ought to look different.[20] And did not Jesus himself promise that when the kingdom comes there would be an end to suffering, oppression, poverty, hunger, and death? But history shows that these bitter realities continue; they have not diminished in even the slightest degree. Hence, if the early church's faith is true, its truth cannot be read off the open face of history, but lies hidden in the person of Jesus Christ and can be grasped through faith alone.

The primitive Christian faith kept two truths in tension. According to the truth of faith the kingdom of God has *already* arrived in Christ. This stands in tension with the truth about history that the kingdom has *not yet* come. Despite all the enthusiasm generated by Easter, the early Christians came to see that the kingdom of God was overlapping with the kingdom of this world, and that they had to live hopefully and realistically at the same time, citizens of two realms or ages still in conflict. The full reality of the kingdom of God was thus split into an *already* and a *not yet.* Easter is the sign of the already. But there is more to the story of the kingdom than Easter. Easter is only the first fruits. There is still the *parousia* to come, the final advent of Jesus to judge the living and the dead, the oncoming power of God's future in glory until God is all in all.

If the fulfillment of Easter were all there is to the coming of God's kingdom, there would not be much hope for the real world in which people live. The kingdom would be so spiritualized as to lose touch with the human struggles of life and death and of sin and suffering. There was perhaps from the beginning the temptation for Christians to allow their Easter faith to carry them

6 / THE PERSON OF JESUS CHRIST

into a gnostic type of spiritualized fulfillment, collapsing the two-dimensional kingdom of the *already* and the *not yet* into a one-dimensional present, beyond this world of nature and history. Some of the early Christians even tended to believe that their new life in Christ would place them beyond the pale of suffering and death. But soon they had to learn that the truth of the cross overlaps the fulfillment of the resurrection, as a sign that the struggles of history continue and hopes must be rekindled for a future fulfillment of the whole creation. When God comes with the kingdom, God comes to establish rule not only in the personal sphere of faith but also in the public realm in which the powers and principalities hold sway. Thus christology becomes related to eschatology as a down payment on a purchase to be paid in full only when the rule of God completely annihilates all the negativities of this life—the powers of sin, death, and the devil. Meanwhile, the lordship of Christ is hidden under the cross, guaranteed by the resurrection, alive in the Spirit, attested by faith, and at work through the church in contesting the powers that still rage against God in this world. But what is now hidden in history will be unveiled in glory when the world at last reaches its fulfillment in the final future of God's coming kingdom.

NOTES

1. Rudolf Bultmann, *Theology of the New Testament*, vol. 1, trans. Kendrick Grobel, (New York: Charles Scribner's Sons, 1954-55), p. 4.
2. Johannes Weiss, *Jesus' Proclamation of the Kingdom of God*, trans. R. H. Hiers and D. L. Holland (Philadelphia: Fortress Press, 1971).
3. Albert Schweitzer, *The Quest of the Historical Jesus*, trans. N. Montgomery (London: A. & C. Black, 1910).
4. Weiss, *Jesus' Proclamation*, p. 114.
5. Cf. James M. Robinson, *A New Quest of the Historical Jesus* (London: SCM Press, 1959).
6. Cf. Jürgen Moltmann, *Theology of Hope*, trans. James W. Leitch (New York: Harper & Row, 1967).
7. Rudolf Bultmann wrote in *Jesus and the Word*, trans. L. P. Smith and E. H. Lantero (New York: Charles Scribner's Sons, 1958): "I do indeed think that we can know almost nothing concerning the life and personality of Jesus, since the early Christian sources show no interest in either, are moreover fragmentary and often legendary; and other sources about Jesus do not exist" (p. 8).
8. Adolf von Harnack, *What Is Christianity?* trans. T. B. Saunders (New York: Harper & Brothers, 1957), pp. 55, 180.
9. Joachim Jeremias, *New Testament Theology*, trans. John Bowden (New York: Charles Scribner's Sons, 1971), 1:103.
10. Ernst Bloch, *Man on His Own*, trans. E. B. Ashton (New York: Herder & Herder, 1970). Building on Ludwig Feuerbach's idea that man is God to man (*homo hominis*

Deus), Bloch speaks of "God as the utopianly hypostasized and unknown human idea" (p. 208).

11. On the relation between eschatology and ethics in the teachings of Jesus, see Richard H. Hiers, *Jesus and Ethics* (Philadelphia: Westminster Press, 1968); Carl E. Braaten, *Eschatology and Ethics* (Minneapolis: Augsburg Publishing House, 1974); James M. Childs, *Christian Anthropology and Ethics* (Philadelphia: Fortress Press, 1978).

12. Werner G. Kümmel, *Promise and Fulfillment*, trans. Dorothea M. Barton (London: SCM Press, 1957).

13. Jeremias, *New Testament Theology*, 1:118–21.

14. C. F. D. Moule, *The Origin of Christology* (Cambridge: At the University Press, 1977).

15. Willi Marxsen, *The Beginnings of Christology: A Study in Its Problems*, trans. Paul Achtemeier (Philadelphia: Fortress Press, 1969).

16. Ibid., p. 33.

17. Cf. Rudolf Bultmann, "The Primitive Christian Kerygma and the Historical Jesus," in *The Historical Jesus and the Kerygmatic Christ*, ed. Carl E. Braaten and Roy A. Harrisville (Nashville: Abingdon Press, 1964), pp. 15–42.

18. Alfred Loisy, *The Gospel and the Church*, trans. Christopher Home (Philadelphia: Fortress Press, 1976), p. 166.

19. Adolf von Harnack's famous statement affirms: "The Gospel, as Jesus proclaimed it, has to do with the Father only and not with the Son." *What is Christianity?* p. 144.

20. Dorothee Soelle, *Christ the Representative*, trans. David Lewis (Philadelphia: Fortress Press, 1967), p. 108.

3
Classical Christology and Its Subsequent Criticism

The christological dogma of the church succeeded in steering a middle course between heretical extremes to the right and the left, between the denial of the union of God and humanity in the person of Jesus and the denial of the duality of their respective natures. The formula "one person in two natures" preserved the central biblical message in the church that salvation comes from meeting the true God in the man Jesus Christ.

THE IDENTIFICATION OF JESUS WITH GOD

There is a wide gulf between the messianic kerygma of the apostolic period and the trinitarian dogma of the ancient church. Most studies of New Testament theology do not even discuss the Trinity, the central doctrine of the patristic era. They proceed as if the New Testament were on the side of unitarianism. How is it possible, then, to move from the kingdom of God, the central datum of Jesus' message, to the dogma of the Trinity, which identifies the person of Jesus Christ with God? The motive for the transition is to be found in the Easter kerygma of the primitive Christian community.

The early church believed that the coming of God's kingdom took place in the crucifixion and resurrection of Jesus of Nazareth. For this reason Jesus was confessed as the King of the coming kingdom that he announced in the name of God. The early church faced a crucial theological problem. Was the death of Jesus a sign of failure or of fulfillment? The resurrection event made it possible to glimpse a hidden fulfillment of the kingdom in Jesus' own death on the cross. This belief in the hidden presence of eschatological fulfillment became the root cause of the early church's identification of Jesus with God. Without the resurrection there could have arisen no belief in the divinity of Jesus. But if God really came to establish the kingdom in Jesus' cross and resurrection, and if these events were actually a fulfillment of eschatological expectation, then God was truly identified with Jesus of Nazareth.

6 / THE PERSON OF JESUS CHRIST

The coming of God and the coming of Jesus are thus unified in the experience of eschatological salvation. The logic of salvation demanded the identification of Jesus with God. The experience of Jesus' cross and resurrection as the definitive event of salvation generated a faith, centering on the person of Jesus Christ, that traditionally belonged only to God if idolatry were to be avoided. If salvation had really arrived through the person of Jesus, he must also have been God, because God and God alone is the power of salvation.

The transition from Jesus' message of the kingdom to the apostolic preaching of him as the Christ—from the proclaimer to the proclaimed (Bultmann)—is grounded in the faith-claim of the *ecclesia* that God has established the reality of the kingdom in the person of Jesus Christ through his death and resurrection. If for Jesus the kingdom was near, for the church it was already here—*in Christ.* The kingdom became history, bringing the power of God deep into the flesh and blood of Jesus the man. The preaching of Christ became the primary means of access to the mystery of the kingdom. The coming of the kingdom in Christ came to grips with the major powers that oppress humanity and the world in their depths.

In the cross of Christ, God was dealing victoriously with the *sin* of the world. In his resurrection, *death* was conquered and new life was made to last. In his ministry Jesus had challenged the rule of *Satan* by casting out demons. God had gained a victory in the encounter of Christ with sin, death, and the devil, precisely the kind of victory God was expected to win in the establishment of divine rule. These perspectives made clear why the early church could concentrate all its faith, hope, and love in the person of Jesus Christ and identify his coming with the advent of God's eschatological rule, in both judgment and grace.

The identification of Jesus with God was not at first the result of a dogmatic development. When Clement of Rome wrote early in the second century, "We must think of Jesus Christ as of God" (2 Clement 1:1), he was not passing on a dogmatic decree of a church council. He was, rather, summarizing in a few words what the primitive community had been expressing from the beginning in confessional, kerygmatic, and liturgical formulas.

The confession that "Jesus is Lord" (Rom. 10:9; 1 Cor. 12:3; Phil. 2:11) was not the product of a later hellenization of Christianity. This formula appeared already in the worship of the Palestinian community, placing Jesus on the line with God. Even though the title "Lord" was also frequently used at that time as a polite form of address, as in the expression "My Lord," its use in early Christian worship exalted the name of Jesus above every name (Phil. 2:9), because it was nothing less than the name of God. *Kyrios* was the Greek translation of the Hebrew *Adonai,* the favorite name for God among the Jews. Its application to Jesus in the context of worship could not be mistaken by

CLASSICAL CHRISTOLOGY AND ITS CRITICISM

people familiar with the rules of reverence due God's name in a Hebrew setting.

On the basis of faith in Jesus and the worship of him, the early church not only acknowledged Jesus as Lord but also transferred all the high divine titles and attributes to him. The exalted Lord Jesus Christ rules the world as only God can do. The Lordship of Jesus Christ is universal in scope, reaching beyond history and the church, encompassing nature and the creation, including all visible and invisible beings in heaven, on earth, and below the earth. The presupposition of the universal rule of Christ from his resurrection to the parousia is his identity with God in a preincarnate state and his role as the agent and medium of all creation (Col. 1:16ff.; Heb. 1:2). The dominion of Christ is not limited to the realm of redemption and the new creation. The New Testament concentrates the Lordship of Christ in soteriology, but actually the presupposition of his soteriological dignity is the role of Christ as mediator of all life in the original order of creation.

CHRISTOLOGICAL HERESIES[1]

The identification of Jesus with God did not take place without grave danger to the faith of the Christian church. The danger in stressing the divinity of Christ was that faith might lose sight of the real humanity of the man Jesus. Even in the New Testament period, and increasingly throughout the second century, there developed a tendency to see Jesus one-sidedly in terms of divinity. This one-sided view produced the heresy known as *docetism,* the perennial heresy of the "right wing" in christology. Docetism is the name of a christological teaching, circulating mostly in gnostic circles, that Jesus Christ only *appeared* to have a human body and only *appeared* to suffer and die. Docetism comes from the Greek word *dokein*, meaning "to seem." Marcion, the second-century heretic, was the most prominent theologian to popularize a docetic christology.[2] The gnostic influence, emanating in general from Oriental spirituality, regarded matter as evil and the flesh as unreal. Therefore, when God became man and the Word became flesh in the person of Jesus the Christ, this was only apparently so. For docetism the divinity of Christ posed no problem; it could hardly be emphasized enough. In its view, however, the Son of God could not really become human. The human life of Jesus evaporated into a cloud of divinity.

At the opposite pole there was *ebionitism,* the perennial heresy of the "left wing" in christology. "Ebionitism" is the name of a widespread christological teaching in the second century that presented Jesus as a mere man, denying his divinity altogether. We know of the Ebionites, as well as of the Docetists, not from their own writings but only through the polemics of their orthodox critics. Ebionitism was not named after a heretic called Ebion. The word comes

6 / THE PERSON OF JESUS CHRIST

from the Hebrew word *ebionim,* meaning "poor." The Ebionites stemmed mainly from Jewish circles, in contrast to the Hellenistic orientation of the Docetists. For the Ebionites, Jesus was certainly the Messiah, the Christ, but he was only a man. He could not be God. Impossible! They also denied the virgin birth. Jesus was born the natural son of an earthly father and mother, Joseph and Mary.

These christological heresies to the right and to the left seemed to be poles apart from each other. The one side enthusiastically affirmed the divinity of Christ, the other side denied it. The one side denied the real humanity of Jesus, the other side affirmed it. But these extremes were reverse sides of the same christological coin: a rejection of a real incarnation of God in the man Jesus.

The Docetists were bound to a Hellenistic concept of God as a timeless absolute who could not really change. Therefore, God's involvement in history, the realm of flux, could only be apparent. Because God is God, God is immutable. Thus there could be no real incarnation, no real change in an ontological sense, only an apparent one. The God of Greek metaphysics was completely in charge of the docetic christology.

The Ebionites were committed to a Jewish concept of God as totally other in transcendence and holiness. God is God and humanity is humanity; the infinite is not capable of entering the finite. The ontological separation makes a real incarnation of God unthinkable, even blasphemous. The God of Jewish monotheism was the controlling force behind the ebionitic christology.

These early docetic and ebionitic trends continued to develop in the ancient church and to generate more complex types of christological expression. The docetic line to the right can be seen in modalistic monarchianism, a third-century teaching advanced by Sabellius, bishop of Rome. The modalists were not docetists of the old style, for they acknowledged Jesus Christ to be a real man. However, the old spirit of docetism crept into the teaching of Sabellius. He taught that the One God (the divine monarchy) appeared as the Father in the Old Testament, as the Son in the life of Jesus, and finally as the Spirit in the church.[3] But these distinctions between Father, Son, and Spirit were more apparent than real. The human life of Jesus was a temporary mask of the One God in whom no differentiations could exist. The identity of Jesus as the Son of God was unmasked by Sabellius as the second mode of the divine self-manifestation, a temporary theophany, which in turn gave way to a third. This new type of docetism also made a real incarnation impossible, since that would violate the metaphysics of monotheism underlying the modalistic christology.

There was also in the third century a continuation of the ebionitic line to the left, in dynamistic monarchianism, represented by Paul of Samosata,

CLASSICAL CHRISTOLOGY AND ITS CRITICISM

bishop of Antioch. Adoptionism is the more common name for this type of christology.[4] It was not a repetition of the crass ebionitism which taught that Jesus was a mere man (*psilos anthropos*). In fact, the adoptionists could attack the ebionitic denial of the divinity of Christ. Christ was indeed divine; he was filled with the dynamism of the Spirit and uniquely was adopted by the Father as his only beloved Son. This was not an appearance of God from above as in modalistic monarchianism. On the contrary, in the adoptionist model Jesus Christ became divine from below by the indwelling of the Spirit and by his growth in godlike holiness. Adoptionist christology could not accept a real incarnation of God, a movement of the divine descending deep into the human. The movement went in the opposite direction, the human ascending by spiritual and moral development to the level of godlikeness.

The road to Chalcedon continued to bend now to the right and now to the left on the way to a definition of christology in which two truths could be affirmed at once: (1) the identification of Jesus as God in the interest of Christian worship and (2) the differentiation of the real humanity of Jesus from his divinity in fidelity to his Gospel picture. Christology to the right, with its stress on the divinity of Christ, was driven by the logic of the Christian liturgy in which Jesus Christ was exalted as God. Christology to the left, upholding the humanity of Jesus, was guided by the historical picture of Jesus in the synoptic Gospels. In general, theologians influenced by the great school of Antioch used a more historical-exegetical approach to the Bible and usually leaned to the left in christology. Theologians of the rival school of Alexandria applied a more speculative metaphysical method which postulated the divinity of Christ as the necessary condition of salvation, veering to the right in christology. These trends were typically illustrated in certain christological developments in the fourth and fifth centuries.[5]

At the time that Constantine became Pontifex Maximus (A.D. 321), Christianity was threatened by a serious attack from the left on the Christian confession of God's real presence in Jesus. The attack was led by Arius, who was influenced by the adoptionist theologians Lucian of Antioch and Paul of Samosata. Arianism, however, was a more complex denial of the divinity of Christ than we find in either ebionitism or adoptionism.[6] For Arius, Christ was more than a human being and more than the adopted Son of God. He was the Logos, the Son of God, who existed before God the Father created the world. But he was not God; he did not share the divine essence. The Logos was not eternal. The Arians chanted in a hymn, "There was when he was not." In the beginning there was God alone (the principle of monarchianism); then the Logos was created to assist God in the creation of the world. Because the Logos was a creature, he did not share God's metaphysical attributes of being immutable, impassible, and infinitely removed from time and history.

6 / THE PERSON OF JESUS CHRIST

So the Logos could change, enter into history, unite himself with human flesh in the person of Jesus, even suffer and die. Thus the incarnation of the Logos was inferior to a real incarnation of the true essence of God.

Athanasius, the fierce opponent of Arius argued that Arianism was heresy because it called into question the whole reality of salvation.[7] If the Logos as the redeemer is ontologically inferior to God, as a creature is to the Creator, there can be no real salvation, for such a system places the burden of salvation on a creature. Athanasius asked how a being lower than God could raise human beings to the level of God. How could the mediator between God and humanity be less than fully divine and fully human? Is the gospel a story about a holy person ascending to God, or is it about a loving God condescending to humanity in a human way? Who mediates salvation? God, or some creature?

The fathers at the Council of Nicaea, A.D. 325, inserted an old word of gnostic origin, *homoousios*,[8] to expose the deficiency in the Arian christology. The *homoousios* affirmed the oneness of substance of the Son and the Father. This meant that the person of Jesus Christ would henceforth be confessed as "eternally begotten of the Father . . . true God from true God." Only on this basis could the worship of Christ make sense and the reality of the salvation of humanity and the world be secured.

The Nicene Creed became the fundamental statement of the church in the interpretation of the incarnation. It became the starting point for all who subsequently joined the christological debates on how the eternal Son of God, of the same substance as the Father, could become flesh in the person of Jesus Christ. The development of orthodox christology was accompanied by anathemas of precisely defined heresies. Our brief sketch of this development cannot enter into the labyrinth of historical questions that modern critical scholarship raises in connection with each of the ancient christological controversies. We cannot deal, for example, with the historical question whether the important leaders who lent their names to the classical heresies were in fact guilty as charged by their orthodox critics. When we speak of these heresies, we shall deal with them as "isms," following Friedrich Schleiermacher's suggestion that this is the appropriate way for dogmatics: "But these names are here intended only to denote universal forms which we are here going to unfold, and the definitions of which they are intended to remind us proceed from the general nature of the situation, even if, e.g., Pelagius himself should not be a Pelagian in our sense."[9]

Christology proceeded from its trinitarian connection to establish the relation between the divine Christ and the human Jesus. Apollinarianism, named after Apollinarius, bishop of Laodicea, began by affirming the high christology of the Nicene Creed.[10] As a friend of Athanasius, Apollinarius was thoroughly orthodox on the doctrine of the Trinity. He held that the Son is distinctly other than the Father (against Sabellianism) but eternally shares the one substance of the Father (against Arianism). But being right on the Trinity by the standard of orthodoxy did not determine how a theologian might interpret the incarnation. Apollinarius moved in the direction of docetism when he taught that the humanity of Christ assumed in the incarnation was incomplete.[11] Surely the Logos in Christ was truly God; but in the incarnation he did not become wholly human. The Logos took upon himself the body and soul of the man Jesus, but took the place of his human spirit. Apollinarius' interest was to solve the problem of the unity of the person who was both divine and human. How can two beings unite into one? Apollinarius believed that a genuine union is possible only when the Logos, as the active principle of self-consciousness and self-determination, substitutes himself for the human spirit. The result is a truncated view of the human reality in Jesus Christ. The union in Christ was a union of the perfect Logos with an incomplete human nature. Apollinarius believed he had secured what was essential for salvation, an integral divine-human person, a real God-Man, not just a godly man.

Why was Apollinarianism condemned as heretical? The Council of Constantinople in A.D. 381 affirmed the completeness of Christ's human nature and refused to accept any abbreviation of its faculties. The same logic which called for the *homoousios* with the Father was at work to demand a comparable *homoousios* with humanity. It was the logic of salvation. The operative principle was this: What was not assumed cannot be saved. If Christ was not fully human, then the whole human person cannot be saved. The spirit in fact constitutes the true essence of human being in the trichotomous scheme of Platonism—body, soul, and spirit—within which Apollinarius worked. If the human spirit is displaced by the divine Logos, the deepest spiritual dimension of human beings, enslaved by Satan, corrupted by sin, and condemned to death, lies beyond the scope of salvation. The first church council to decide against Apollinarianism declared, "If therefore the whole man was lost, it was necessary that that which was lost should be saved" (Council of Rome, A.D. 374–376). The church had struck one more blow against the heresy of docetism.

The reaction to the docetic tendencies of Apollinarianism came swiftly from the theologians of the Antiochian school, championed by Nestorius, patriarch of Constantinople.[12] In earlier days the school of Antioch had been identified with ebionitic or adoptionistic tendencies. The new school of Antioch accepted the Nicene doctrine of the Trinity, namely, that Christ was fully God. But the leaders of this school—Diodore of Tarsus, Theodore of Mopsuestia, and Nestorius—retained the traditional Antiochian emphasis on the humanity of Jesus. Jesus Christ was completely human, in body, soul, and spirit. One of Nestorius' priests attacked the cultic term *theotokos* for Mary, meaning that Mary was the "mother of God." The term seemed to detract from the human nature of Jesus, confusing it with the divine. For Nestorius, Jesus Christ was both fully God and fully man, but the divine and human natures must be kept distinct and unabbreviated in the incarnation. There must be two of everything—two natures, two substances, two wills, two sets of attributes— and therefore also two persons (*prosōpa*). If there were two natures in Christ, there had to be two persons. Nestorius could not imagine a nature without a person. Nature is what a thing essentially is and person (*prosopon*) is how it appears.

This doctrine of two persons joined in Christ became the defining mark of Nestorianism as a heresy. Here again we must remind the reader that we cannot deal with the modern historical question whether Nestorius was a Nestorian.[13] No matter what modern research may conclude about Nestorius' own teachings, Nestorianism denotes one of those "universal forms" to which Schleiermacher referred, which can contradict true Christian doctrine. The essential problem with Nestorianism is simple: It could not affirm a real incarnation. Its scheme was dualistic, stressing the divine and the human in their complete difference, thus failing to achieve a real incarnational union of God and humanity in the one person of Jesus Christ. The only type of unity which Nestorianism could allow was that of conjunction (*synapheia*), or a close communion of two persons enjoying a relation of mutual give and take.

The theologians of the school of Alexandria regarded Nestorianism as typical of the Antiochene tendency to teach that Jesus was a mere human being. The Nestorians offered a union of two persons living side by side in a fellowship of love and moral freedom. The Alexandrians insisted on a deeper ontological unity of God with the man Jesus. For Eutyches, patriarch of Constantinople, and Dioscuros, bishop of Alexandria, the most significant thing about Christ was his divine nature, not his humanity. The human nature was not denied so much as absorbed into the higher power of the divine nature, with the result that from the moment of the incarnation there remained only one nature. Hence this heresy is fittingly called *monophysitism,* meaning "one nature," and sometimes also Eutycheanism, after its one proponent.[14] The monophysites sacrificed the integrity of Jesus' humanity for the sake of his divinity. They missed the whole point of the incarnation: God's involvement deep in human history so that human beings might encounter God on a human plane and not have to search for salvation in the remoteness of God's heavenly being.

In the fifth century the church struggled between the Scylla of a divine Christ who was not really human (monophysitism) and the Charybdis of a human Jesus who was not really one with God (Nestorianism). At Nicaea (A.D. 325) the church condemned the Arian heresy for denying the full deity of Christ. At Constantinople (A.D. 381) the church rejected Apollinarianism for

CLASSICAL CHRISTOLOGY AND ITS CRITICISM

denying the complete humanity of Jesus. The emerging orthodox confession henceforth was to be that Jesus Christ was fully God and fully human. But how are the two related? This question preoccupied the church in the fifth century, as theologians struggled to integrate the diametrically opposed tendencies of Nestorius and Eutyches. Finally, at Chalcedon (A.D. 451) the council fathers formulated the christological dogma of two natures, divine and human, in the one person of Jesus Christ. Thus the church chose a middle course between the Nestorian and the Eutychean alternatives. Both extremes impaired the doctrine of the incarnation.

The final verdict pronounced by the Creed of Chalcedon reads:

> Following, then, the holy Fathers, we all with one voice teach that it should be confessed that our Lord Jesus Christ is one and the same Son, the Same perfect in Godhead, the Same perfect in manhood, truly God and truly man, the Same (consisting) of a rational soul and a body; *homoousios* with the Father as to his Godhead, and the Same *homoousios* with us as to his manhood; in all things like unto us, sin only excepted; begotten of the Father before ages as to his Godhead, and in the last days, the Same, for us and for our salvation, of Mary the Virgin *Theotokos* as to his manhood;
>
> One and the same Christ, Son, Lord, Only Begotten, made known in two natures (which exist) without confusion, without change, without division, without separation; the difference of the natures having been in no wise taken away by reason of the union, but rather the properties of each being preserved, and (both) concurring into one Person (*prosōpon*) and one *hypostasis*—not parted or divided into two persons (*prosōpa*), but one and the same Son and Only-begotten, the divine Logos, the Lord Jesus Christ; even as the prophets from of old (have spoken) concerning him, and as the Lord Jesus Christ himself has taught us, and as the Symbol of the Fathers has delivered to us.[15]

This is the famous Chalcedonian definition of the personal identity of Jesus Christ. We must first understand what the Chalcedonian Creed accomplished in its own time, before we examine it from the perspective of its modern critics. The main point of the creed was to affirm a true incarnation, not to explain its mystery. People who tried to explain the mystery, whether from the left (Nestorianism) or from the right (Eutycheanism), were anathematized. The Nestorian picture of a double personality and the monophysitic annulment of the human were both alike condemned. Against Nestorianism the creed asserted that between the two natures there was no division or separation, and against Eutycheanism that the two natures were not confused or changed one into the other. The two natures, though remaining distinct, were united in the one person of Christ. The creed did not, however, explain how two complete natures could be united in one person. It safeguarded the unity of the person as against Nestorianism and the completeness of the two natures as against Eutycheanism. It can be safely concluded that the council accomplished the negative purpose of condemning heresy, for a time building a protective fence around the mystery of the person of Jesus Christ. On the positive side it certainly left room for further development.

FROM THE CREED OF CHALCEDON TO THE FORMULA OF CONCORD

Christological controversy did not end at Chalcedon. The pressures from the right and the left wings continued for more than a millennium, until in the sixteenth century the Lutheran and the Calvinist confessions placed their own characteristic and conflicting interpretations on the christological dogma. At the fifth ecumenical council in Constantinople (A.D. 553) an inference from Chalcedon was drawn, proposed by Leontius of Byzantium, affirming the "impersonal" humanity of Christ.[16] This is known as the doctrine of the *anhypostasia* and *enhypostasia*. Today it sounds strange to learn that orthodox christology entails the denial that Jesus was an individual human person. Docetism seems to have been thrown out by one council only to reappear in the next. The Council of Constantinople denied that Jesus had a human hypostasis, something that belongs to every other human being. Did this not conflict with the confession of Chalcedon that Jesus Christ was "*homoousios* with us as to his manhood; in all things like unto us"? Did not the doctrine of the anhypostatic nature of Christ rob him of something essential to every person: human personality and self-consciousness? This is the common view. Some critics have angrily dismissed this doctrine as the "beheading" of Christ; others have alleged that it represents the victory of monophysitism. Consider the sharp attack by Paul Althaus: "One cannot separate the nature from the person. Human personality is an essential constituent of human nature. Hence 'anhypostasia' abolishes the true humanity of Jesus, his believing and praying human ego, the truth of his being tempted."[17]

The decision for or against the doctrine of the *anhypostasia* depends on what it does to the truly human nature of Jesus Christ. Does this doctrine really violate the integrity of Jesus' complete humanity? Countering Althaus's criticism is Karl Barth's strong defense. Barth observes that *anhypostasia* as a negation must be linked with *enhypostasia* as an affirmation.[18] On the basis of the incarnation of the Word of God in the man Jesus Christ, what *anhypostasia* denies is that the human nature of Jesus existed or exists by itself outside the Word, and *enhypostasia* affirms that Jesus had personal existence but only in and through the Word. The humanity is not abolished or truncated but elevated and fulfilled in union with the person, the *hypostasis*, of the Word of God. Whether one sides with Althaus or Barth, it is clear that the council intended to draw a line once more against ebionitism, adoptionism,

CLASSICAL CHRISTOLOGY AND ITS CRITICISM

and Nestorianism, all of which viewed Jesus as an independent personality who lived a life of close spiritual fellowship with the Father.

In the seventh century, fear arose that christology had veered too far to the right in the direction of monophysitism. Insisting on *two* natures in line with Chalcedon, the dyophysites were confronted by a new edition of monophysitism in the teaching that only one "will" or one "energy" was operative in Christ. Hence this new style monophysitism was referred to as monenergism or monotheletism. At the sixth ecumenical council in Constantinople (A.D. 681) monothelitism was condemned, along with Pope Honorius I, who put down the whole controversy as a mere dispute about words.

The millennium between the six ecumenical councils of the ancient church and the christological controversies in the period of the Reformation was one of comparative barrenness. John of Damascus produced a scholastic synthesis in the tenth century that became normative for the future of Eastern Orthodoxy. It aimed to combine the various decisions of the ancient ecumenical councils. In the West there was scarcely any noteworthy development through the Middle Ages, except for a resurgence of adoptionism in eighth-century Spain. In this view Jesus, in his humanity, was the adopted Son by the grace of God (*adoptivus homo*). This teaching was condemned in various synods as a revival of the Nestorian impiety of dividing Christ into two sons, the eternal Son of God and the adopted Son of Man. In general, medieval scholasticism remained within the approved categories of Chalcedonian christology and turned its more creative energies from the doctrine of the person to the work of Christ.

The christological problem was raised again in the heated controversies between Lutherans and Calvinists on the doctrine of the communication of attributes (*communicatio idiomatum*).[19] Both sides claimed to stand on the basis of Chalcedon, which had taught that the attributes of the two natures were preserved in the personal union. Luther taught that at the Lord's Supper the whole Christ was really present, including his human nature, and therefore also his body and blood. Zwingli responded with his theory of *alloeosis*, which explains faith's language about the real presence as a figure of speech. Such verbal predications, Zwingli taught, strictly apply only to Christ's divine nature. The human Christ cannot be really present in the Lord's Supper, since he is finite and so can be present only one place at a time. Luther countered Zwingli's argument with his doctrine of ubiquity. Ubiquity or omnipresence is essentially an attribute of the divine nature, but is communicated to the human nature because of the incarnational union. Starting with the Lord's Supper, the controversy on the communication of attributes exploded into a full-scale war on christology between the Lutherans and the Reformed.

Lutherans and Calvinists both inherited standard Chalcedonianism from

6 / THE PERSON OF JESUS CHRIST

medieval scholasticism.[20] They agreed: (1) that in Christ there was one person in two natures, fully divine and fully human; (2) that there was a close intercommunion of the natures in a personal union; (3) that these natures kept their identities and were not commingled (against Eutycheanism) and yet did not exist separately in two different persons (against Nestorianism); (4) that the attributes of the natures were preserved, the divine being infinite and the human finite, the divine impassible and the human passible, etc.; (5) that nevertheless on account of the hypostatic union there was a communication of attributes to the person of Christ, so that he possessed and used both divine and human powers. But just at this point there arose a difference. The Lutherans, taking a cue from Luther's doctrine of ubiquity in the Lord's Supper controversy, proposed a novel extension of the traditional understanding. Not only were the attributes of both natures communicated to the one person (acceptable to the Calvinists), but also the majestic powers of the divine nature were communicated to the human.

The Formula of Concord and later Lutheran dogmatics systematized the doctrine of the exchange of attributes in three genera, which the Lutheran fathers believed were supported by Scripture. First, there is the "idiomatic" genus: qualities of either nature may be ascribed to the entire person. Second, there is the "apotelesmatic" genus: actions of the one person may be ascribed to one or the other of the two natures. Third, there is the "majestatic" genus: divine qualities such as omnipotence and omnipresence are attributed to the human nature. This third type of communication of attributes, the *genus majestaticum,* [21] became the distinctive feature of Lutheran christology. The Calvinists remained loyal to the traditional limits of Chalcedon.

The ancient trends in christology were at work in the Reformed-Lutheran controversy.[22] The Reformed position was branded the child of Nestorianism, bearing a family resemblance to the ancient school of Antioch, and the Lutheran position the child of Eutycheanism, going back to the lineage of Alexandria. The Lutherans were eager to stress the *unity* of the divine-human person, running the monophysitic risk of mixing the natures. Their battle formula was *"finitum est capax infiniti,"* the finite is capable of the infinite. The human nature of Jesus Christ was capable of using the infinite powers of God, acting truly omnipresent, omnipotent, and omniscient at will. Did this picture of Christ remain within the classic limits of Chalcedon? The Reformed said "No!" They maintained a clear distinction between the two natures, so their counterslogan became *"finitum non capax infiniti,"* the finite is not capable of the infinite. Because the human nature of Christ was finite, it was not capable of being both at the right hand of the Father in heaven and present on earth in the bread and wine of holy communion.

The Calvinist zeal for the distinction of the natures was backed by the old-fashioned Nestorian logic. If the Logos is divine, then it could not limit itself to the flesh of Jesus. Accordingly, the Calvinists taught that the Logos, being infinite, must exist *extra carnem* (outside the flesh) and not be limited by its union with the flesh. The Heidelberg Catechism states: "Because the divinity is everywhere present, it must follow that it is indeed ouside its adopted humanity and yet none the less also in the same and remaineth in personal union with it." Among Lutherans this doctrine was dubbed the *extra-Calvinisticum*. It implied a very loose linkage between the Logos and the man Jesus of Nazareth and led to a theology of glory, opening the door to exalted language about the Logos apart from its enfleshment. The Lutherans countered with a theology of the cross, holding that the Logos can be known only in the flesh. So they coined the phrase *"totus intra carnem* and *numquam extra carnem"* (wholly in the flesh and never outside the flesh).

The christological issue that divided Lutherans and Calvinists, producing two confessional groups, erupted very early also within the Lutheran camp, creating two rival schools. Article VIII of the Formula of Concord (A.D. 1580) aimed at reconciling differences between the school of John Brenz (the Swabians) and the school of Martin Chemnitz (the Lower Saxons). Philip Melanchthon had written in his *Loci Communes* (1521) that "to know Christ is to know his benefits." He said that the mystery of divinity is more to be adored than investigated and complained of the *rabies theologorum* (the fury of theologians), which turned hairsplitting distinctions into polemical weapons. Melanchthon had little patience for analyzing the chemistry of the incarnation, determining how much divinity and how much humanity were operative in Christ and how their respective attributes were related to each other. But other Lutherans made these investigations their specialty.

The Formula of Concord tried to find balanced language to settle the disputes among Lutherans, but with little success. It looked for middle ground, but waffled on the issue of the divine attributes during the earthly life of Jesus. Did the Formula teach a doctrine of *"krypsis"* or *"kenosis"*? *Krypsis* means that the divine attributes were "hidden" in the incarnation, *kenosis* that they had been "laid aside." The combinations of these two alternatives were endless. Did the Formula teach that the person of Christ enjoyed full possession of the attributes but used them secretly? Or did it teach full possession and voluntary abstinence from use? Or did it teach full possession and partial arbitrary use? Or did it teach partial possession and partial use? Or partial possession and abstinence from use? And in the event of partial possession, with some degree of *kenosis*, which attributes were retained and which left behind in the incarnation?

The Formula of Concord did not achieve its aim of settling christological disputes. Instead the battle raged into the seventeenth century between the Lutheran dogmaticians of Giessen and of Tübingen. If the human nature of Jesus became ubiquitous, undergirding the real presence of the whole Christ in the Lord's Supper, was he also universal in an absolute sense in the whole world and in all creatures? Having started with a theology of the cross, stressing the grace of God in the concrete existence of the man Jesus, the Lutherans were drawn into a theology of glory by divinizing the flesh of Jesus, by glorifying the human with qualities of divinity. The Giessen theologians wanted to stress the state of humiliation (*status exinanitionis*), limiting the use of divine attributes in the earthly Jesus. The Tübingen theologians would tolerate no limitation of the divine in the human Jesus, but allowed that the powers were exercised in secret. They affirmed the doctrine of *krypsis* but no *kenosis*. Lutheran theology was threatened by an overdose of docetism. A settlement was reached, called the Saxon decision, which set limits to the Tübingen school and came out in favor of the partial kenotic theory of the Giessen theologians.

The christological problem lingered within confessional Lutheranism without finding a satisfactory solution. Only in the nineteenth century did some confessional Lutherans attempt a radically new point of departure, using the idea of *kenosis*, suggested by Phil. 2:6–7: "Who, though he was in the form of God, did not count equality with God a thing to be grasped, but emptied himself, taking the form of a servant, being born in the likeness of men." The kenotic christology of the nineteenth century was an attempt to remain faithful to the old Lutheran doctrine of the *communicatio idiomatum*. It occurred to Gottfried Thomasius that a fourth *genus* could be added to the *communicatio idiomatum*.[23] If the divine attributes were communicated to the human nature, why could not the reverse happen, with the human attributes being communicated to the divine nature? If the *finitum capax infiniti* is true, the reverse may also be true, the *infinitum capax finiti*. The infinite God may submit to the finite in the incarnation; the Logos may empty himself and take on a limited human form. To express this idea, Thomasius improvised the term *genus tapeinoticum*, from *tapeinos*, meaning "humble" and "lowly."

This kenotic christology affirmed that in becoming man the divine logos limited itself. According to Thomasius, the Son of God in becoming man abandoned those divine attributes which had to do with his cosmological or metaphysical role: omnipotence, omnipresence, and omniscience. He retained those personal moral attributes which identify him as God: truth, love, and holiness. His divine freedom and love made it possible to set aside his divine power and majesty during the days of his humiliation in the earthly Jesus.

Other kenotic theologians radicalized the notion of *kenosis*. H. R. von Frank spoke of a depotentiation of the consciousness of the Son in the person of Jesus. Gradually, he thought, the human consciousness of Jesus evolved into his self-consciousness as God. Wolfgang F. Gess went even further, completely abandoning the ancient idea of the immutability of God. Thus he paved the way for saying that the Son of God left behind all traces of his divinity in the incarnation. This raised the problem: If the Son of God became kenotically incarnate in Jesus in such a way that no traces of divinity were left, in what sense was Jesus really anything more than a mere man? How is a totally kenotic divinity different from no divinity at all? This could be tantamount to saying that in Jesus Christ, God had to become absent in order to be incarnate. In kenotic christology the content of the *vere deus* seemed to disappear to the vanishing point.

CRITICISM OF THE DOGMA

A widespread revolt against the classical dogma of the incarnation began in the period of the Enlightenment and continues virtually unabated in contemporary works on christology. Albert Schweitzer's indictment against the doctrine of the two natures was typical of many others: The life of Jesus was trapped in a dogma.

> When at Chalcedon the West overcame the East, its doctrine of the two natures dissolved the unity of the Person, and thereby cut off the last possibility of a return to the historical Jesus. . . . The formula kept the life prisoner and prevented the leading spirits of the Reformation from grasping the idea of a return to the historical Jesus. This dogma had first to be shattered before men could once more go out in quest of the historical Jesus, before they could even grasp the thought of His existence. That the historic Jesus is something different from the Jesus Christ of the doctrine of the Two Natures seems to us now self-evident.[24]

Oscar Cullmann, too, states that the Creed of Chalcedon shifted the categories of the New Testament from the function of Christ to a metaphysical problem about the two natures of his person.

> There is thus a difference between the way in which the first Christians and the later Church understood the Christological problem. . . . The Church fathers subordinated the interpretation of the person and work of Christ to the question of the "natures." . . . Their emphases were misplaced. . . . The discussion of "natures" is ultimately a Greek, not a Jewish or biblical problem.[25]

The attacks on the classical christology cover a wide range. To the extreme left there is the type of rationalistic criticism which wants to get rid of the Christ of the creeds in order to return to a historical Jesus whose moral principles, it is thought, would be directly relevant to modern times. The biography of Jesus is proposed as a fitting substitute for the christological dogma.[26] A more moderate approach argues that the philosophical language of the ancient christology is obsolete; whatever truth it contains must be translated into categories of modern thought. Schleiermacher shared this latter sentiment. He took the traditional formula that in Jesus Christ we have divine

6 / THE PERSON OF JESUS CHRIST

and human natures combined into one person to express the truth that Jesus was conscious of God in a perfectly complete way. He spoke of an "absolute potency of God-consciousness in Christ."[27] The term "divine nature," he argued, had been borrowed from pagan philosophy and was therefore ill-adapted to express the being of God in Christ. Further, the word "person" can only mean a life-unity, but this real unity is incompatible with the assertion of two natures, since every nature must have a will. There is another terminological difficulty in that the word "person" in the christological formulation does not harmonize with the way the same word had been used in the trinitarian language, where three persons were united in one essence or substance. If the individuality of Christ is one of the three persons in the Trinity, we are left with a tritheistic concept of God, or else the personality of Christ becomes unreal, yielding inevitably a docetic interpretation. Thus, for Schleiermacher the "two natures in one person" formula led to such contradictory statements in dogmatics that it finally proved to be of little service to the church.[28]

Adolf von Harnack expanded Schleiermacher's notion that the categories of classical christology stemmed from pagan philosophy. The dogmas were the product of the "hellenization" of Christianity.[29] They exhibit the acute intellectualization of faith in the New Testament sense. Harnack was aware that it could not have happened otherwise on Greek soil, especially if Christianity was to make good its claim to be a universal religion and to extend its mission into the world of Hellenistic culture. The corollary of this concession was, however, that modern dogmatics must undo the process of hellenization and recapture the essence of Jesus' message in terms relevant for today. The Trinity and the incarnation were the first dogmas to be sacrificed, being the most eminent examples of the transformation of Christianity into a system of intellectual doctrines.

In recent systematic theology, Paul Tillich developed a dialectical critique of the classical christological formulas.[30] He was able to say "yes" and "no" to them. This dialectical approach interpreted the creeds of classical Christianity in a more positive way. The church used the concepts of Greek philosophy and Hellenistic mysticism to interpret and defend the Christian message, not to substitute the concepts for the message itself. The message is Jesus Christ as the paradoxical appearance of essential God-manhood in existence. When this message was attacked by heresies, the church had to defend it, and in defending, had to define it in whatever language it found most adequate. It proved itself free to use nonbiblical philosophical terms to articulate a living message. The Council of Chalcedon was successful in defending the message, but it was bound to fail if forced to define the message for all generations to come. It could not have succeeded for all time, because the Greek concepts were culture-bound and not timelessly valid. Yet the church at Chalcedon was right in rejecting the heretical formulations of Eutycheanism and Nestorianism, as well as of Arianism and Apollinarianism. But its own "two natures—one person" formula is open to serious question as a positive statement. It gives rational form to an impossible myth which says that a divine person coming from heaven unites himself with an earthly person. For Tillich the essence of the incarnation is not this myth, but rather the paradox of the appearance of essential God-manhood. The potential eternal relationship of God and humanity appeared in Christ under the conditions of existence and history. Here Tillich is reaching back to Hegel's type of christology, which aimed to penetrate the external data of dogma, myth, and history to their inner meaning: the essential unity of God and humanity.

There is truth in each of the types of criticism we have summarized. Schweitzer was right; the dogma did tend to obstruct the view of the real historical life of Jesus. And every historian would agree with Cullmann's point about a shift of categories from the New Testament to the ecclesiastical creeds. Schleiermacher correctly pointed out terminological ambiguities in the trinitarian-incarnational complex of thought that have never been successfully cleared up. Harnack's slogan about the hellenization of Christianity may have been an exaggeration in its time, but it eloquently underscored how Christianity evolved into an intellectualized system of dogmas in the encounter with gnosticism. Finally, Tillich made several cogent points: first, the dogma is not the message, so to speak of faith in dogma would be a contradiction in terms, and second, the dogma combines elements of the myth of the incarnation in a seemingly rational way that is certainly open to question.

The criticism of the dogma of the incarnation is voluminous and unending. Yet when all the modern criticisms have been heard and measured, the church today still has good reason to retain continuity with the core of classical christology.[31] What is at stake is not the questionable philosophical terms and categories of Chalcedon, but quite simply the Christian confession that the person of Jesus Christ unites the reality of God with humanity in a way sufficient for salvation. The confession allows plenty of room for speculative analysis, but no room at all for finding in Jesus Christ something less than a real union of the true identity of God and the final definition of humanity. It is not necessary to know the precise philosophical meaning of such Greek terms as *homoousios, hypostasis, ousia, physis, prosōpon*, and *idiotes* to perceive even today in a totally different cultural setting that Chalcedon aimed to demarcate the boundaries beyond which the preaching of Christ cannot stray if it wishes to remain faithful to the apostolic kerygma of salvation. The issue today is not *whether* the classical christology is to be criticized, but *why*? Do the critics share the underlying faith that Chalcedon sought to defend, or do their quarrels with the ambiguous philosophical terms of the creed disguise their alienation from its fundamental content?

The dogma of the incarnation continues to warn the church against every

6 / THE PERSON OF JESUS CHRIST

solution of the christological paradox that stems from the ebionitic-adoptionistic left or from the docetic-monophysitic right. In predicating divine and human natures, as well as divine and human attributes, of the one Lord Jesus Christ, we are giving expression to the knowledge of faith that God has entered history as the power of final salvation of humanity and the cosmos. The dogma can help the church discern the difference between heresies to the right and to the left, past and present. It also positively aligns the church with the true preaching of Jesus Christ from the apostles to the present, making it possible to retrace the footsteps of orthodoxy. Hermeneutically, orthodoxy is always a sort of ex post facto construction. Only the future was able to tell whether the many christological proposals swimming in the sea of Nicaea or Chalcedon would be hooked on heresy or drawn into the nets of orthodox definition. Similarly, the multiplicity of modern christologies which have arisen in the nineteenth and twentieth centuries are being submitted to the test whether they "teach Christ aright" and prepare the way for the true preaching of the Word. The church will continue to use the Creed of Chalcedon in this process of testing, rejecting every view that tears God and human existence apart in the person of Jesus Christ and every view that separates the salvation of humankind from the person of Christ.

NOTES

1. For more extensive information about the christological developments treated in this section, consult the following works: Aloys Grillmeier, *Christ in Christian Tradition*, trans. J. S. Bowden (New York: Sheed & Ward, 1965), vol. 1; J. N. D. Kelly, *Early Christian Creeds* (1950; London: A. & C. Black, 1972); R. V. Sellers, *Two Ancient Christologies* (London: SPCK, 1940); H. A. Wolfson, *The Philosophy of the Church Fathers* (Cambridge, Mass.: Harvard University Press, 1956), vol. 1.

2. Adolf von Harnack, *History of Dogma,* 7 vols., trans. Neil Buchanan (New York: Dover Publications, 1961), 1:267–86.

3. It is customary to distinguish between the "economic Trinity" and the "immanent Trinity." Immanent Trinity means that the names of the Father, the Son, and the Spirit refer to real distinctions within God. Hence we also speak of the essential or ontological Trinity. Economic Trinity means that the distinctions arise from the three ways in which the one God has been manifested in the history of revelation (the divine economy). Ever since Friedrich Schleiermacher reopened the debate on Sabellius, scholars have questioned whether Sabellius actually taught that Father, Son, and Spirit refer merely to temporary and successive manifestations of God in relation to the world. (Friedrich Schleiermacher, "On the Discrepancy between the Sabellian and Athanasian Method of Representing the Doctrine of the Trinity," trans. with notes by Moses Stuart, *The Biblical Repository and Quarterly Observer* 6 [July 1835]: 1–116).

4. J. N. D. Kelly, *Early Christian Doctrines* (New York: Harper & Brothers, 1958), pp. 115–19.

5. See esp. Sellers, *Two Ancient Christologies.*

6. Kelly, *Early Christian Doctrines,* pp. 226–27.

7. Ibid., pp. 240ff.
8. Grillmeier, *Christ*, p. 269.
9. Friedrich Schleiermacher, *The Christian Faith*, ed. H.R. Mackintosh and J. S. Stewart (Edinburgh: T. & T. Clark, 1928), p. 97.
10. Charles E. Raven, *Apollinarianism* (Cambridge: At the University Press, 1923).
11. Wolfson, *Philosophy*, p. 599.
12. Friedrich Loofs, *Nestorius and His Place in the History of Christian Doctrine* (Cambridge: At the University Press, 1914).
13. On the modern debate whether Nestorius was a Nestorian, touched off by the discovery of a book Nestorius wrote in exile, *The Bazaar of Heracleides*, see Carl E. Braaten, "Modern Interpretations of Nestorius," *Church History* 32 (September 1963): 251–67.
14. Wolfson, *Philosophy*, p. 444.
15. This English version of the Creed of Chalcedon is quoted from R. V. Sellers, *The Council of Chalcedon* (London: SPCK, 1953), pp. 210–11.
16. Wolfson, *Philosophy*, pp. 409–15.
17. Paul Althaus, *Die Christliche Wahrheit* (Gütersloh: Bertelsmann, 1948), 2:225.
18. Karl Barth, *Church Dogmatics*, vol. 4/2, trans. J. W. Bromiley (Edinburgh: T. & T. Clark, 1958), pp. 49–50, 91–92.
19. Ian D. Kingston Siggins, *Martin Luther's Doctrine of Christ* (New Haven: Yale University Press, 1970).
20. Heinrich Schmid, *The Doctrinal Theology of the Evangelical Lutheran Church*, trans, Charles A. Hay and Henry E. Jacobs (Minneapolis: Augsburg Publishing House, 1875).
21. The *genus majestaticum*, the issue in the Lutheran-Reformed controversy, owes its name to the notion that the Son of God in the incarnation communicated his divine majesty to his assumed human nature.
22. Barth, *Church Dogmatics*, 4/2:73ff.
23. *God and Incarnation in Mid-Nineteenth-Century German Theology: Thomasius, Dorner, Biedermann*, ed. Claude Welch (New York: Oxford University Press, 1965).
24. Albert Schweitzer, *The Quest of the Historical Jesus*, trans. N. Montgomery (London: A. & C. Black, 1910), pp. 3–4.
25. Oscar Cullman, *The Christology of the New Testament*, trans. Shirley Guthrie and Charles Hall (Philadelphia: Westminster Press, 1959), p. 4.
26. Martin Kähler, *The So-Called Historical Jesus and the Historic Biblical Christ*, trans. Carl E. Braaten (Philadelphia: Fortress Press, 1964).
27. Friedrich Schleiermacher, *The Christian Faith*, ed. H. R. Mackintosh and J. S. Stewart (Edinburgh: T. & T. Clark, 1928), p. 385.
28. Ibid., pp. 391ff.
29. Harnack, *History of Dogma*, 4:219ff.
30. Paul Tillich, *Systematic Theology*, 3 vols. (Chicago: University of Chicago Press, 1951–63), 2:145ff.
31. See Karl Rahner's important essay "Chalcedon—Ende oder Anfang?" in *Das Konzil von Chalcedon*, ed. Aloys Grillmeier and H. Bacht, vol. 3 (Würzburg, 1954), pp. 3–49. In this essay Rahner argues that the Chalcedonian formula must be regarded more as a beginning than as an end.

4
The True Humanity of Jesus Christ

Christian faith has an interest in the historicity of Jesus Christ that cannot be surrendered. The quest of the historical Jesus is a mark of taking seriously the full humanity of Jesus. The humanity of Jesus cannot be confined to his earthly state of existence, but is continuous with the postresurrection reality of Jesus Christ as the eschatological One.

THE HISTORICITY OF JESUS CHRIST

Two factors divide classical and contemporary christology: first, modern criticism of the metaphysics of the traditional trinitarian and incarnational dogmas, and second, the historical quest of the life of Jesus. In this chapter we will deal with the latter issue under the heading "The Historicity of Jesus Christ" and in the next chapter with the former as "The Historicity of God."

The critical study of the life of Jesus began in the Enlightenment with the application of the historical method of research as a tool of christological thinking. Hermann Samuel Reimarus was the first critical historian to attempt to portray the historical Jesus as he "really" was before the embellishments of faith and preaching exalted him to the level of divinity. For some of the more skeptical scholars, such as David Friedrich Strauss and Bruno Bauer, the historical Jesus exercised a negative function in theology. They probed the sources to discover a residual core of factual history, in order to prove their religious indifference to it. What mattered was the idea of the incarnation, the truth of the essential union of God and humanity, not its embodiment in the individual personality of Jesus. For more moderate scholars, such as Friedrich Schleiermacher and Alexander Schweizer, the historical Jesus had positive meaning, both as the source of faith and as the substance of christology. The historicity of Jesus Christ was basic to the Christian faith, not only as its starting point, but also as part of its essential content. The question of the *historicity* of Jesus Christ became the modern form of the debate over the classical assertion of his true humanity (the *vere homo*).

6 / THE PERSON OF JESUS CHRIST

Just as classical christology had to steer its way between the Scylla of ebionitism and the Charybdis of docetism, so also in the nineteenth century these same two options reappeared as a challenge under the new conditions of the historical-critical approach to the Bible and Christian origins. The classical rivalry between the schools of Antioch and Alexandria was replayed on the ground of nineteenth-century theology. This rivalry is no less fierce in the twentieth century. The ebionitic left is exhibited in the modern attempt to replace the christological dogma with a biographical treatment of the life of Jesus. As the christological undercurrent of the main stream of the "Life of Jesus" movement, ebionitism was especially strong in eighteenth-century rationalism and in the later line of psychological analysis influenced by Schleiermacher. The aim of this approach was to describe the moral and religious consciousness of the man Jesus, and then to commend it as an exemplary model for human emulation. Scholars tried to discover timeless moral and spiritual values in Jesus, with great relevance for modern humanity. In fact, however, the substitution of the modern biography of Jesus for the classical dogma of the incarnation proved to be a deception. In pretending to be interested in history, rationalism reflected itself in the mirror of the past. It interpreted Jesus in the light of its own morality, not its morality in the light of Jesus. Albert Schweitzer was right in calling the bulk of these biographies totally unhistorical.

The docetic right flourished in the christologies influenced by the philosophical thought of the German idealists—Immanuel Kant, G. W. F. Hegel, Johann Gottlieb Fichte, and Friedrich Schelling. The christological dogma was not dissolved into a biography of the Jesus of history, but was translated into the Christ of faith as an abstract idea. Docetism became explicit in idealistic indifference to the historical Jesus as the basis and content of faith, substituting instead the idea of an essential unity of God and humanity related not to a specific individual but to generic humanity as a whole. This speculative metaphysical approach poured its own preferred ideas into the mold of christology and thus, like the rationalism before it, merited Schweitzer's verdict of a sovereign indifference to the real Jesus of history.

On the whole, however, the reinterpretation of christology in the nineteenth century was not dominated by the two extremes we have characterized as ebionitic (the more empirical psychological approach) and docetic (the more speculative metaphysical approach). Most biblical and systematic theologians took a mediating approach. Here the quest of the historical Jesus was assumed into the framework of a dogmatic christology. The conservative wing in Hegelian theology fought against its own school's docetic tendency to separate the universal idea of Christ from the historical facticity of Jesus. Similarly, many who wrote biographical and psychological treatments of the historical Jesus attempted to overcome the implicit ebionitism of the "Life of Jesus" movement, claiming that their project was the modern equivalent of taking the humanity of Jesus seriously. How could their scholarly interest in the Jesus of history be opposed to the intent of the christological dogma, since it too affirmed the true humanity (*vere homo*) of Jesus Christ? The quest of the historical Jesus was certainly legitimate as a venture of historical criticism; it was also theologically necessary as a motive of Christian faith. The mediating theologians were moderates. They worked both to establish points of contact between the quest of the historical Jesus and the classical dogma of the church and to minimize the areas of conflict that arose. Hence the historicity of Jesus Christ was an object of historical-critical research as well as a subject of faith and dogmatics.

It has become common to view the eighteenth- and nineteenth-century quest of the historical Jesus in a negative way. Albert Schweitzer's history of the movement testified to its failure, Martin Kähler's critique called it a dead end, and Karl Barth's renewal of classical dogmatics dubbed it a heresy of modern Protestantism. A more positive assessment is now possible. The quest for the historical Jesus was and continues to be christologically significant as an expression of faith's interest in the historicity of Jesus Christ.

THE HUMANITY OF JESUS CHRIST

The confession of the true humanity of Jesus was first elaborated in the writings of the antignostic fathers, Irenaeus, Hippolytus, and Tertullian, in the second century A.D. Their confession was not the result of the critical study of the life of Jesus, but rather the datum of a living faith handed down in the traditions of liturgy and preaching and firmly anchored in the Gospel narratives. In later orthodoxy, however, this confession became an ossified formula of ecclesiastical dogmatics. It is no wonder that many modern Christians were prepared to welcome the historical view of the life of Jesus as a liberation from christology's conceptual bondage to an abstract dogmatism. Hoskyns and Davey exclaimed in their *Riddle of the New Testament*, "Whatever else Jesus may be, He is a man."[1] The full humanity of Jesus has become as important to modern believers as it was to earlier Christians who struggled against gnosticism and its variant docetic derivations.

The contemporary emphasis on the historicity of Jesus Christ has renewed the meaning of the ancient phrases of Chalcedon, "perfect in manhood . . . truly man . . . of a rational soul and a body . . . *homoousios* with us as to his manhood . . . in all things like unto us." It has reinforced Luther's statement that Jesus came as "one of the hoi polloi"[2] or that he was "bone of our bone, flesh of our flesh." The soteriological thrust of these assertions is unmistakable.

But what about the "sinlessness" of Jesus? The ancient creeds, echoing the

6 / THE PERSON OF JESUS CHRIST

New Testament witness, claimed Jesus to be in all respects as we are, "except without sin." He "committed no sin" (1 Pet. 2:22), and he was tempted, "yet without sin" (Heb. 4:15).

The sinlessness of Jesus has been called into question by theologians who believe that sinning is implied in the full humanity of Jesus.[3] They regard the idea of sinlessness as a docetic cancer spreading into the earliest attempts to picture the life of Jesus. The "Life of Jesus" movement as a whole found the idea bothersome, because it calls into question the principle of analogy underlying every attempt to write a biography or to psychoanalyze Jesus. Here the principle of analogy allows our modern knowledge of the stages of human development and forms of human behavior to be applied in reconstructing the life of Jesus from the Gospel sources. But if Jesus was sinless, he was unique. How could we hope to explain the unique development of this man in terms of principles that apply to common human experience? In writing against the biographical and psychoanalytic "Lives of Jesus," Martin Kähler stated the problem clearly:

> Is this method justified in writing about Jesus? Will anyone who has had the impression of being encountered by that unique sinless person, that unique Son of Adam endowed with a vigorous consciousness of God, still venture to use the principle of analogy here once he has thoroughly assessed the situation? We must not think that we can solve the problem with a pantograph, reproducing the general outlines of our own nature but with larger dimensions. The distinction between Jesus Christ and ourselves is not one of degree but of kind. . . . Sinlessness is not merely a negative concept. The inner development of a sinless person is as inconceivable to us as life on the Sandwich Islands is to a Laplander.[4]

The ambiguity is clear. If Jesus was like us in all respects, the principle of analogy would seem to apply in his case as much as in the study of other great personalities of the past. But if he was sinless, the method of analogy is seriously limited, if not altogether invalid.

What, then, is the logic of asserting the sinless humanity of Jesus? Is it a result of research or a presupposition of faith? How do we know that Jesus was sinless? Does Jesus' sinlessness really contradict the assumption that he was entirely human? Some scholars have recently exploited every imaginable hypothesis in taking seriously the humanity of Jesus. They have speculated about his sexuality, his marital status, and his psychological hang-ups.[5] Since the Gospel sources contain no such data, the imagination must run riot and generate its phantasies *ex nihilo*. But to what end? Some defend these speculations as taking the humanity of Jesus seriously and getting rid of the last vestiges of docetism. A less than fully human Jesus would be of no value to us. The ring of the ancient logic of salvation can be heard. Jesus must have been wholly what we are.[6] But here the logic turns against itself. If he was entirely like us, *with no difference*, he would have been in the same predicament as everyone else, with no power to save. How could a common sinner be the savior of humankind? The ancient logic of salvation was two-dimensional. Jesus Christ must be wholly what we are, so that we may become wholly what he is. In sharing our human lot, he is not reduced to its sinful condition. This statement is not the result of historical research, but the vivid impression of the total impact of Jesus' person on his followers' memory injected in the stream of apostolic interpretation. Every layer of tradition in the New Testament witnesses to the confession of Jesus' sinless humanity. This is an historical judgment, but whether or not a person or the church today assents to its truth is a matter of faith and dogmatic interpretation.

The sinlessness of Christ does not diminish his solidarity with the fallen condition of human existence. Classical dogmatics became the victim of a deductive type of logic, concluding to the sinlessness of Christ from the hypostatic union. With seemingly flawless logic it was reasoned that if Christ was the Logos, the divine Son of God, he must have been sinless. Even the possibility of sin (*posse peccare*) must be excluded, because God is opposed to the nature of sin, and God cannot be self-contradictory. The modern impact of the historical picture of Jesus has done much to blunt the force of such logic from above. Starting with the story of Christ's temptation, it has been inferred that Christ must have been able to sin. To be human is to be tempted, and real temptation presupposes the possibility of sin. Here the logic of inferential reasoning proceeds from below, arguing from the humanity of Christ to the reality of temptation and the ability to sin. Whether coming from above or from below, however, this type of logical reasoning contributes little to christological insight.

It is better not to indulge in a logical overkill. The biblical story of Christ's temptation is presented in terms of a real struggle. According to the principle of analogy, which we, along with Kähler, have already called into question, our common human experience of real conflict in temptation is invariably associated with a sense of standing at the crossroads and the possibility of taking the wrong turn, of sinning. If these connections hold for us, they must logically hold for Christ. But by what kind of logic? It is the psycho-logical law of experience under the conditions of our fallen human nature. Does it apply to Christ in the same way? Schleiermacher pronounced an emphatic "no," but paid the price of eliminating the element of conflict from Christ's perfectly God-conscious and sinless life.

Docetism hangs like a dark cloud over such a reading of the temptation stories. The temptations involved real conflict. They were profoundly experienced by Jesus as a pull away from the Father's will. We are not dealt a psychological card with which to trump the story and take away its existential seriousness. We are given no theory about whether he could have sinned or could not have sinned. He was tempted and he did not sin. He prayed in

6 / THE PERSON OF JESUS CHRIST

the crisis of temptation. He fled for strength to his Father and put Satan behind him. His sinlessness lay in doing the Father's will, in taking up the cross of the kingdom.

We can say this much: Jesus could not have sinned and really been the One he was revealed to be in his cross and resurrection. This is not a logical inference from the hypostatic union or the preexistent Logos. It is a retroactive type of judgment based on the role of Christ in the mission of God's approaching kingdom. There is a dimension of mystery in the life of Christ, seen on this side of Easter. The proposition of the great tradition that he could not have sinned (*non posse peccare*) was an unfortunate explanation of this mystery. It converted the mystery of Christ's person into a metaphysics of his nature. The New Testament points to this dimension of mystery in the wilderness temptations, speaking symbolically of Christ being filled with the Holy Spirit and of his self-consciousness as the Son of God. Could he have sinned? The question cannot be answered from above by a metaphysics of the incarnation or from below from the psychology of common human experience. The story is written to point to the mystery of Christ in the special context of his messianic identity and mission.

A related question has occupied the minds of theologians: Did Jesus' consanguinity with the human race mean that he shared the nature of humanity before the fall or that he inherited the fallen nature along with all others? In late medieval theology, Jesus' birth of the Virgin Mary settled the issue. Sin was transmitted by the male sperm in the sexual act; therefore, Jesus was exempt, having been born of a virgin and conceived by the Holy Ghost. This explanation is another pseudotheological example of deductive reasoning, not to mention outdated biology. The confession that Jesus was not a sinful man does not place him in a kind of existential demilitarized zone beyond the limits of our fallen human existence.

Jesus shared the existential condition of our fallen human nature. Perhaps few have stressed the human experience of Jesus more dramatically than Luther. Luther said, "He ate, drank, slept, worked, suffered, and died like any other human being." He added, "He had eyes, ears, mouth, nose, chest, stomach, hands, and feet, just like you and I have. He took the breast; his mother nursed him as any child is nursed."[7] It is impossible to exaggerate Jesus' solidarity with our common human experience—with this single exception, that he did not fall into sin. He knew the feelings of hunger, fatigue, fear, anger, grief, and sadness. Luther stressed the agony of the suffering and dying man forsaken by God and all his friends. Of course, this emphasis on the humanity of Christ was pointless to Luther, unless the Christ who was so utterly human was at the same time qualitatively different from all others. The humanity by itself was not able to accomplish anything, apart from the power of divinity that came through it. Jesus became our brother that God might become our Father; he condescended to assume our flesh and bone, our body and soul, this "poor bag of worms," in order that God might have mercy on all the wretched people of this world. The homiletical force of this vision of Christ makes sense only on the christological premise that Jesus is at once "very God and very man."

THE IDENTITY OF THE EARTHLY JESUS AND THE RISEN CHRIST

There is a type of interest in the historical Jesus that possesses no fundamental meaning for Christian faith. The apostle Paul referred to it as a knowledge of Christ "from a human point of view" (*kata sarka*) (2 Cor. 5:16). We adopt such a point of view whenever we seek to learn about Jesus as merely Jesus, abstracting him from the total evangelical picture as the risen Christ. The naked facts about Jesus do not speak for themselves. They require a framework of meaning to be grasped. The preaching of Jesus as the risen Christ influenced the shape of the history that was narrated in the Gospels. The Gospels give us a character sketch of Jesus, depicting him as a real historical person and as human in the fullest sense.

If we take the New Testament message as our criterion, we cannot reduce the historicity of Jesus to the narrow limits of positivistic historicism, nor his humanity to the limits of naturalistic humanism. The history of Jesus and his humanity cannot be interpreted within the limits of an historical empiricism. The historiographical goal of discovering the empirical truth about the Jesus of history by means of a presuppositionless research has been doomed in modern hermeneutics but still hangs on in some historical circles. The empirical truth does not exhaust what we mean by the historical truth.

The historical truth about the reality of Jesus cannot be separated from the living impression he made on those who gave us the only sketch we possess of his being and meaning. To look for his historicity apart from his meaning is like trying to locate the Kantian *Ding an sich*. The meaning of a person is the key to understanding whatever is true and real about him or her. So it is with Jesus of Nazareth. Jesus means Christ; Jesus means Savior; Jesus means Lord; Jesus means Son of God; and so forth. The point is that apostolic interpretation of the meaning of Christ is the transparent medium of the historical truth and reality of Jesus—if we are no longer to regard him *kata sarka*.

The resurrection of Jesus is an essential element of his total picture. It belongs to his history; it has a factual side. Otherwise, it disappears into the quicksand of arbitrary interpretation. After his death by crucifixion Jesus appeared to some of his friends, and they spread the news about what they had witnessed in two words: Jesus lives! They did not say merely that his cause

6 / THE PERSON OF JESUS CHRIST

lives on. Theirs was not a mere belief in the immortality of Jesus' influence. The resurrection of Jesus was not a postulate of faith, nor an expression of the hidden meaning of his life, nor an existential interpretation of his death on the cross. Faith was not the basis of the resurrection; the resurrection was the basis of faith. The event of Jesus' resurrection, then, explains the transition from Jesus as the announcer of the kingdom to Jesus as the announcement itself.

The earthly Jesus and the risen Christ are one and the same person. The personal identity of Jesus Christ includes both his earthly existence and the exalted mode of his being and acting. It is not the case that Jesus is fact and all the rest myth, legend, or fiction. That would spell the end of Christian faith. Yet the personal equation of the earthly Jesus and the risen Lord is not open to a process of verification which suspends the factors of faith, worship, prayer, and preaching. There are no proofs of the Easter event. We have only the testimonies of witnesses, all of whom were believers. They are no longer available for cross-examination. The experience of being grasped by faith and the power of the Spirit, however, can liberate the mind to be receptive to the evidences of the resurrection—eyewitness accounts of the appearance of the risen Christ and the empty tomb—and to make a judgment in their favor. Faith and reason work together in the act of confessing that the risen Lord encountered in faith is identical with the earthly Jesus nailed to the cross.

JESUS CHRIST AS THE ESCHATOLOGICAL ONE

The event of the resurrection made Jesus God's eschatological representative for the whole of humankind. The resurrection of Jesus belongs to his humanity. It cannot be subtracted from his history without cutting him off from the future which God granted him on "the third day." In raising Jesus from the dead, God incorporated the dimension of eschatological fulfillment into the definition of human being. The resurrection is a symbol of hope for a fulfilling future of life beyond the annihilating power of death. The message of the resurrection makes sense only within the horizon of our own most certain existential destiny, of having to die. Other religions offer different solutions to the problem of death. Christianity proclaims the resurrection of Jesus as God's answer to the human question whether death is the eschaton of life.

The resurrection is a unique event; it is the only event in human history in which the power of death has been challenged and its claim to finality discredited. The resurrection of Jesus was the "first fruits," to be followed in the end by a universal resurrection. The destiny of Jesus in the resurrection reveals a future for humanity that carries the promise of fulfillment beyond death.

THE TRUE HUMANITY OF JESUS CHRIST

We have underscored the historicity of the true humanity of Jesus Christ. We now stress that the resurrection expands the definition of his humanity to include an eschatological destiny beyond death. The new life of Christ beyond death is an element of the image of God (*imago dei*) which he represented perfectly—without sin.

Much of the Christian tradition has taught that Jesus Christ restored the image of God in humanity to its state of integrity before the fall. The damage caused by the fall of the first Adam has been undone by Jesus as the second Adam, by his obedience, by his sinlessness, and by his victory over death. Irenaeus used the idea of *recapitulation* to speak of Jesus going over the ground covered by Adam, "so that what we had lost in Adam—namely, to be according to the image and likeness of God—that we might recover in Christ Jesus."[8] But Irenaeus' idea of recapitulation did not entail a mere restoration of the broken image to its state before the fall. Something *new* happened in Jesus.[9] He did, of course, bring about a renewal of the image, but at the same time actualized a fulfillment to the highest possible state of perfection. Irenaeus taught that Adam's innocence before the fall was enjoyed in a state of immaturity. He was "unfinished man."[10] He was like a child who had yet to become a mature person. Christ was the new Adam. He was all that Adam failed to become, on account of the fall. Adam was not created perfect all at once. His completion was something to be realized in the future of humanity. Jesus Christ has been revealed as that new human being of the future, as the final measure of the nature and destiny of humankind.

Irenaeus located the event of the recovery of the image of God in the incarnation rather than in the resurrection. He said,

> Man is created for the Son, and he attains his perfection in the Son. His destiny was realized only when the image of God took human life in the Incarnation and took up into himself the man who had been created in the image of God. The Incarnation and its benefits had no reality when man was first created; man, therefore, is a child, son, whose goal and objective is full growth.[11]

It is doubtful, however, that Irenaeus recaptured Paul's way of picturing Jesus Christ as the image of God. For Paul, the newness in Christ was an eschatological reality that occurred in the resurrection and became representatively valid on that basis for the whole of humanity.

The risen Christ is the future destiny of all humankind. The goal of human development is to become mature in the perfect image of God as it became realized in the exalted and resurrected humanity of Jesus Christ. We can point to its incarnational presence in the life of Jesus only because of prior knowledge of eschatological fulfillment in the resurrection victory of Christ over death. If death had been the end of Christ, if the resurrection had not put an end to death, the New Testament could not have begun to speak of the incarnation of the image of God in the man Jesus. Death would have swallowed up the life of Jesus forever. Instead, he became the person embodying the good news of a fulfilling future beyond the fate of personal and cosmic death.

NOTES

1. Edwyn Hoskyns and Noel Davey, *The Riddle of the New Testament* (London: Faber & Faber, 1936), p. 209.

2. Quoted in Ian D. Kingston Siggins, *Martin Luther's Doctrine of Christ* (New Haven: Yale University Press, 1970), p. 36.

3. See G. C. Berkouwer, "The Sinlessness of Christ," in his *The Person of Christ* (Grand Rapids: Wm. B. Eerdmans, 1954), pp. 239-304.

4. Martin Kähler, *The So-Called Historical Jesus and the Historic Biblical Christ*, trans. Carl E. Braaten (Philadelphia: Fortress Press, 1964), p. 53.

5. E.g., William A. Phipps, *Was Jesus Married?* (New York: Harper & Row, 1970); Tom Driver, "Sexuality and Jesus," *USQR* 20 (March 1965): 235–46.

6. The classic axiom in traditional christology affirms: *Quod non est assumptum non est sanatum*. This means: "What has not been assumed [in the incarnation] is not saved."

7. Siggins, *Martin Luther's Doctrine of Christ*, p. 199.

8. Quoted in James M. Childs, *Christian Anthropology and Ethics* (Philadelphia: Fortress Press, 1978), p. 20, n. 9.

9. See Gustav Wingren's definitive study on Irenaeus, *Man and the Incarnation*, trans. Ross Mackenzie (Philadelphia: Fortress [Muhlenberg] Press, 1959).

10. Ray Hart, *Unfinished Man and the Imagination* (New York: Herder & Herder, 1968).

11. Quoted in Childs, *Christian Anthropology and Ethics*, p. 95.

5
The True Divinity of Jesus Christ

The truth of the incarnation is that God took on a truly human reality, so that in Jesus Christ he stands on both sides of the boundary separating the Creator from the creation. The confession that Jesus in his person is truly God means that God's decisive and final word for the world has been communicated once for all in his Word made flesh.

THE STORY OF GOD INCARNATE

The doctrine of the incarnation was the pillar of orthodox christology from the Council of Chalcedon to the age of the Enlightenment. This pillar has been shattered by the blows of modern criticism. Nineteenth-century studies in the history of dogma (Adolf von Harnack) linked the christology of the ancient church to the process of hellenization. In the twentieth century, form-critical analysis of the Gospel traditions has shown that the incarnation was not part of the earliest preaching of the apostles. In the beginning was the Easter kerygma; the motif of the incarnation entered at a subsequent stage of development. Finally, the history and phenomenology of religions have called our attention to the mythic character of the incarnation. The notion of the preexistent Son of God becoming a human being in the womb of a virgin and then returning to his heavenly home is bound up with a mythological picture of the world that clashes with our modern scientific world view.

There are two opposite reactions to the discovery of the mythic character of the incarnation. The conservative reaction is to reject the discovery in defense of traditional faith. In its simplest form, this view argues that the Bible contains truth, not myth.[1] The incarnation was a real event of history. The Son of God really became human in the person of Jesus. Calling the incarnation a myth detracts from its truly historical character. Would that not turn the incarnation into a universal truth equally applicable to all human experience and likely to be enshrined in all the great religions? Myth abhors being tied to a concrete historical event or to a unique historical person. Myth deals with

6 / THE PERSON OF JESUS CHRIST

recurrent patterns and archetypal notions valid wherever they may be found. But the incarnation is bound to what happened at one point in space and time—the concrete life of the historical Jesus. Therefore myth is an inappropriate category to apply to the incarnation of the Son of God.

The liberal reaction is to acknowledge the discovery of the mythic character of the incarnation, and then to demythologize the Christian faith to make it relevant to the contemporary world. In this view the story of the incarnation is not essential to the Christian faith. The myth can be eliminated and other concepts more compatible with the modern mind can be found to express the significance of Jesus Christ for us.

Arguments in favor of demythologizing the story of Christ are numerous. Let us summarize some of the most common. (1) The very concept of an incarnate person being both divine and human is not really intelligible. (2) It is intellectually impossible to accept the incarnation as literally true and to equate Jesus ontologically with God. (3) The incarnation was a bad myth to begin with. Such mythical speculations draw attention away from the real Jesus of history, his role and agency in representing God for us. (4) The essence of the myth can be stated in nonincarnational terms; for example, in Jesus we encounter God's claim on us, or in Jesus the meaning of God for our lives has been disclosed in an existentially significant way. We moderns can more easily use existential and ethical categories in formulating the meaning of Christ for life in our time.

Neither the conservative denial of myth in the New Testament nor the liberal approach of demythologizing has proven adequate for constructive Christian theology. A third approach is possible:[2] an interpretation of the myth as story, without taking its symbolic elements literally but also without eliminating its historical aspects. Rudolf Bultmann was right in his observation that the New Testament kerygma was proclaimed within the framework of mythology. There were three levels in the mythical picture of the world: heaven above, hell below, and earth between. There were beings—angelic beings, demonic beings, and human beings—passing from one level to the other. God was in heaven, humankind on earth, and the demons in the underworld. Divine and demonic forces were engaged in a cosmic struggle, producing effects in the inner life of human beings and the outer world of nature.

The story of the incarnation took place within the structure of such a mythological universe. The preexistent Son of God came down from heaven, entered earthly existence by means of virgin birth, worked miracles on nature, sacrificed himself for the sins of the world, overcame the power of demons by his resurrection, descended into hell to preach his victory, ascended to heaven to sit at the right hand of God the Father, and finally promised to come again in a blaze of glory to judge the world. The main statements of the Apostles' Creed are so bound up with its mythological form that to get rid of the myth would destroy the creed *in toto*. Can modern people still be expected to accept the creed, with its mythological elements? We know that in the scientific picture of the world, the categories "above" and "below" do not make sense. Therefore the story of the descent of the Son of God to earth and his ascent into heaven cannot be taken literally. The question is whether the meaning of the myth of the incarnation can be saved without taking it literally, yet without getting rid of its mythic structure. Can it be interpreted in a way that both grasps the essence of the Christian message and does not misplace the scandal of the gospel?

Bultmann proposed the method of existentialist interpretation to salvage the kerygma in the myth, so that modern men and women will not take offense at outdated myth and miss the saving message. The truth of the myth, he said, lies in its existential meaning for each individual.[3] The New Testament message of Christ is overlaid by mythical elements from Jewish apocalyptic eschatology and gnostic dualistic cosmology. Bultmann challenged theology to demythologize the New Testament, in order to lay bare the existential meaning of the kerygma enshrined in the myth. The story of Christ in the Gospels is a mixture of historical events and mythological symbols. The purpose of the myth is to interpret the significance of the events. Today we must search the myth for the existential meaning of the events, and not take the myth at face value. We must ask about the existential significance of the myth of the preexistent Christ and of his cross and resurrection. To accept these as objective descriptions of a supernatural realm of happenings is to miss the point of the myth: to relate the apostolic kerygma to human existence.

Bultmann's project of existentialist interpretation was too narrowly conceived to sustain itself in the field of biblical hermeneutics. The sole purpose of the myth cannot be to interpret the *existential* significance of the events on which the kerygma is based. The kerygma speaks of the *act of God* in Christ. God cannot be reduced to a term of human existence. Theology cannot be translated into anthropology without remainder. To speak of God acting in history is at the barest minimum a piece of symbolic mythology. There is no way to demythologize the New Testament kerygma by means of existentialist interpretation without losing its transcendent reference to God. The kerygma does not only speak of the possibilities of human existence; it speaks first and foremost of the history of the acts of God, not literally but in symbolic terms.

Myth and its symbols are indispensable to express the reality of God in the person of Jesus. Myth is an appropriate form of language for expressing the events and meanings of God's revelation in history. Even Bultmann's definition of myth makes this clear. He defines myth as "the use of imagery to express the otherworldy in terms of this world and the divine in terms of human life, the other side in terms of this side."[4] The story of the incarnation offers a perfect illustration; it speaks of God entering time and space in the person

6 / THE PERSON OF JESUS CHRIST

of Jesus. God was in Christ. This points to a real event that affected the inner life of the divine Trinity. Although this is a symbolic way of speaking, it counters a subjectivist interpretation of the myth which sees the incarnation either as the revelation of a hidden potential of common human experience or as the objectification of humanity's longing to be reconciled with God. The very truth and word of God, God's own grace and love, entered the history of humankind and the world with the appearance of Jesus Christ. The myth of the incarnation is, therefore, not reducible to its existential core of meaning. When an existential criterion of meaning is strictly applied, elements of the myth which are not considered to be existentially relevant are eliminated, such as the preexistence of Christ or the story of the virgin birth. We would be well advised not to allow the existentialist—or any reductionist—mode of interpretation to acquire a monopoly on the categories used in christology.

THE HISTORICITY OF GOD

The story of the incarnation is a mixture of mythical and historical categories. Because the incarnation affirms that the *Son of God* is Jesus, mythical language is essential; because it claims that *Jesus* is the Son of God, historical categories must be used. The early church did not simply repeat the story of Christ in the two languages of myth and history. Already in the second century the church borrowed ontological categories from Greek philosophy to interpret the myth of God becoming human, of the Logos becoming flesh. Terms like *ousia, hypostasis, physis, prosōpon,* and *idioma* are nonbiblical categories coming from the Greek philosophers. The bridge from the mythological language of the Gospels to the ontological statements of the creeds could be found, the church fathers believed, in the New Testament itself. When John's Gospel says that "the Logos became flesh," the church fathers exegeted this statement in ontological terms. In ontologizing the incarnation, they may have had the purest intention of remaining biblical, but they introduced an ontology into their christology that was alien to its fundamental meaning. If the myth of the incarnation must be set forth in ontological speech, the question becomes: What kind of ontology? What ontological assumptions about the nature of God, humanity, and the world should be applied in the interpretation of the reality and truth of the incarnation of Jesus Christ?

There is a sharp contrast between the idea of God in Greek ontology and the picture of God reflected in the biblical story of the incarnation. The God of the Greek philosophers was not a dynamic, living, acting, self-communicating subject who became freely involved in the world of space and time, of physical matter and human flesh. There could be no coming or becoming, no motion or emotion, no pain or plurality in the God of Greek metaphysics. How could the static transcendence of an immutable and impassible deity be correlated with christology without contradicting the gospel of God's *coming* and of the Logos *becoming* flesh in the person of Jesus? The church fathers worked with the only ontology they had at their disposal, transforming it to fit their biblical faith. They were by no means uncritical in assimilating ideas from Greek metaphysics.[5] They stressed the biblical motifs of the living power and gracious freedom of God in their doctrines of creation and providence, involving God deeply in the world of matter and the flux of history. They stressed these in sharp contrast to the Greek concept of an absolutely unaffected and eternally remote God. It would therefore be erroneous to charge the church fathers with having made the Christian faith captive to the principles of Greek philosophy. The use of Greek ontology was the *aggiornamento* of the church's theology in that time.

In retrospect, however, it is possible to see that the theological transformation of Greek ontology was not carried through radically enough. The problem of using the Greek philosophical concept of God came to a head in the formation of christological doctrine. The absolute God of Greek metaphysics was heartless, graceless, and faceless. That God could not suffer, because suffering meant lack, and God does not lack anything. God must be beyond the pale of human suffering. God must be impassible, apathetic, and without compassion. The picture of Christ in the New Testament, by contrast, is full of suffering. Jesus Christ suffered what every human being suffers: hunger and thirst, fatigue and loneliness, disappointment and betrayal, and finally death. There was suffering in body, soul, and spirit. This was not, however, merely the suffering of the man Jesus or of the human nature of Christ, far removed from the being and life of God. In the New Testament, passages abound which involve the Son of God, and indirectly therefore also the Father, in the destiny of Christ's suffering. "God sent forth his Son, born of woman, born under the law" (Gal. 4:4). First Corinthians 2:8 claims that the rulers of this age "crucified the Lord of glory," and Acts 3:15 that they killed "the Author of life." The classical passage is Phil. 2:6–8: "Who, though he was in the form of God, did not count equality with God a thing to be grasped, but emptied himself, taking the form of a servant, being born in the likeness of men. And being found in human form he humbled himself and became obedient unto death, even death on a cross."

Against the background of Greek metaphysics the idea of God would have to be kept far removed from involvement in the suffering of Christ. A God who suffers cannot really be God. There were two heretical ways of relating God to the problem of the suffering of Christ. The one way was that of the ebionites and the adoptionists: affirm the suffering of Christ but then make sure he was only a human. The sufferings could be accepted as real because Christ was merely human. The reality of his sufferings proves that he was not truly God, because God cannot suffer. The underlying axiom came not from

6 / THE PERSON OF JESUS CHRIST

the Bible but from the Greek ontological concept of God. The other way was that of the docetists and the monophysites: affirm the divinity of Christ but then make sure the sufferings were not real. Christ was God beyond doubt. This proves that the sufferings referred to in the Gospels were only apparent. Christ did not really suffer, because he was truly God, and God cannot suffer. Again, the underlying axiom was the impassible God of Greek metaphysics, not the living God of the Bible.

The God of Israel, the Father of Jesus Christ, was no apathetic being, an anonymous essence infinitely removed from the pain and suffering of creation. The Father suffered along with the Son. God was not bound to suffer as an essential predicate of his being. Rather, God was free to suffer as a function of divine love. Suffering cannot be predicated of God as a metaphysical attribute implied by God's immanence in the world process, nor as an ontological limitation of God's own being and nature, out of the need to be fulfilled. The Greeks were right; there is no deficit in God. But they wrongly concluded that for this reason there can be no pain in God.[6] The Father of Jesus Christ suffered, not from any lack in being but from the abundance of love. "For God so loved the world that he gave his only Son" (John 3:16).

Orthodox christology denied that the Father suffered when it rejected patri-passianism as a heresy in the Sabellian controversy. Sabellianism claimed that the Father suffered because it collapsed any real personal distinction between the Father and the Son. Orthodoxy reacted to this modalistic view by attributing suffering only to the Son. Only one of the Trinity suffered. We today are not threatened by the Sabellian problem; we are thus able to reach a different conclusion about the suffering of God. The Father did not personally suffer through some ontological lack, but rather through the compassion that the Father had for a Son who took the destiny of humankind into his own life. Even on orthodox grounds it does not make sense to divorce the suffering of Christ from the Father. Christ suffered in his person, and this person (*hypostasis*) is God the Son, of one being (*homoousios*) with the Father. If God was in Christ, then suffering became a part of the experience of God. "For in him the whole fulness of deity dwells bodily" (Col. 2:9). The incarnation would not be real if the Father's heart were not open to the suffering of his beloved Son. The distinction between the Father and the Son can be maintained without denying the Father a share in the incarnate fate of his Son Jesus Christ. If the dispassionate God of Greek metaphysics is supplanted by the compassionate God of Israel, the Father of Jesus Christ, a major barrier has been removed to a constructive interpretation of the myth of the incarnate Son of God. The myth does not need to be denied. It calls for interpretation with the help of an ontology different from that of Greek metaphysics. Only a suffering God can be harmonized with the picture of Christ in the Gospels. The suffering of Christ was a shaft deeply driven into the heart of God. The revelation of God, therefore, includes the negativities of Christ's human experience in this world from birth unto death.

The Greek idea of the impassibility of God made a real incarnation of the Son of God intellectually offensive; the immutability of God made it impossible. The Creed of Chalcedon called Mary the Mother of God, "*theotokos*." The term provoked heated opposition from the side of the Nestorians, who argued that Mary was only the Mother of Christ, "*Christotokos*." The advantage of the *theotokos* formula is that it underscored that the subject of the incarnation was actually God—God the Son. If the Son of God was not born of Mary, he could not truly be the One who lived, suffered, and died. Then only Jesus, a mere human, carried the full burden of salvation, contradicting our two initial christological statements: *God* was in Christ and the *Logos* became flesh.

The gospel narrative of God becoming one with humanity in Jesus the Christ conflicts sharply with an ontology of divine immutability in which God simply is what he is in static identity. An absolutely immutable God is not able to become the subject of incarnational predicates, making the history of human existence his own history and assuming the reality of the world's becoming into his own reality as the Logos of God. An ontology constructed in the light of faith in the gospel will speak not of the utter impassibility and immutability of God but rather of the historicity of God and God's coming-to-be in the humanity of Jesus the Christ.

The classical doctrine of the exchange of divine and human attributes (*communicatio idiomatum*) in the one person of Jesus Christ represented in principle a break with the Greek metaphysical doctrine of God. The absolute of Greek metaphysics was ontologically incapable of acting in a state of humiliation, in the flux of history, and under the conditions of finitude. The christology of the ancient church, however, did not succeed in drawing out all the consequences of its own conciliar decisions at Nicaea, Constantinople, and Chalcedon for its concept of God and the incarnation.[7] The categories of ancient metaphysics found their way into the theology of the church fathers and to a large extent replaced the biblical categories of historical and eschatological thinking.

It was Martin Luther who made the most complete break with the hybrid system which the Christian tradition had developed out of Greek metaphysics and biblical faith. His theology of the cross (*theologia crucis*) meant that the philosophical idea of God would have to be radically transformed in light of the cross. He said that a theologian worthy of the name is one who perceives the mystery of God through the suffering and cross of Christ, and not by speculating on the essence of God from the way things are. Luther struck the first blow against the medieval doctrine of the analogy of being (*analogia entis*), which lay at the heart of medieval natural theology. For Luther, the hidden God is revealed in the cross. In the light of the crucified Christ we understand the true being of God and of humankind. God's self-revelation was *sub contrario*, in terms that seem contrary to God's nature as such. In drawing out the implications of the exchange of attributes between the two natures in Christ, Luther began the construction of a new christology, which is still in the process of being developed. The living God did not exclude but embraced the opposite in a process of exchanging qualities of nature and destiny. In exchange for death God gave life, in exchange for foolishness God gave wisdom, in exchange for bondage God gave freedom, in exchange for sin God gave righteousness, in exchange for weakness God gave power, and so on. Consequently, in exchange for God's own glory, God assumed humility; in exchange for eternity, God entered time; in exchange for God's love, God absorbed hatred.

In an eloquent passage Luther said:

> What does it mean that the Son of God should be my servant, and so utterly debase Himself that He should take the burden of my misery and sin—Yes, the whole world's sin and death? He says to me, "You are no longer a sinner, but I am. I step into your place—you have not sinned, but I have. The whole world is in sin, but you are not in sin—I am. All your sins are to lie on Me and not on you."[8]

Luther's interest in what he called the "happy exchange" (*fröhliche Wechsel*) between God and God's people in Christ was not primarily speculative but soteriological. His emphasis on the humanity of God in Jesus was for the sake of humanity. This accounts for such realistic language as "Mary makes broth for God." "Mary suckles God with her breasts, bathes God, rocks and carries Him; moreover, Pilate and Herod crucified and killed God." His concern was for the integrity of the worship of Christ as God in the flesh and for the presence of God in Christ "for us men and for our salvation."[9]

THE DIVINITY OF CHRIST

The starting point for a new ontological interpretation of the identity of Jesus Christ lies in the worship of the Christian church from earliest times until now. The early church responded to the apostolic proclamation of God's redemptive act in Christ in the language of prayer, praise, and thanksgiving. This language customarily refers not only to the *acts* of God in history but also to the *being* of God who is eternally free in power and love. The original language of faith points to the eternal glory, holiness, wisdom, love, and power of God. This is the primary language of faith and confession. Its supreme form is doxology, the sheer praise of God for being God. As a sec-

THE TRUE DIVINITY OF JESUS CHRIST

ond step the church appropriated ontological concepts to help explicate the doxological utterances about the being, nature, and attributes of God. The dogmatic statements of the ancient church, its trinitarian and christological definitions, represent a grand interweaving of doxological and ontological terms.[10]

Although these doxological-ontological statements refer ultimately to the being of God, they are rooted in the soil of redemptive historical events. They cannot be uprooted and taken as abstract speculative theses about the essence of God. Doxology has its basis in the message of God's activity and presence in the history of Jesus. The ontological interpretations similarly intend to serve the church's worship of the mystery of God.

The tendency in modern christology, from Ritschl and Harnack to Cullman and Bultmann, to eliminate the ontological in favor of functional statements in christology failed to observe the doxological source of ontological thinking. Not even in the New Testament can we reduce christology to purely functional historical categories. There is no full-blown ontology, to be sure, but there are statements that clearly imply an ontological understanding of the status of Jesus as the Son of God, even as actually *God*. Ernst Käsemann, master exegete of the New Testament, wrote in his commentary on Romans, "A metaphysical sense of the divine Sonship of Jesus is clearly presupposed by the whole of the New Testament."[11]

Ontological christology is most evident in the Fourth Gospel. The mission of Jesus is obediently to carry out his ontological divine Sonship, to reveal the being of God in him and with him. There is no divorce here between his being and his mission; ontological and functional statements are united in the mission of Jesus to set forth the Father's love in history.

The total impact of the New Testament leads to the conclusion that Jesus Christ is not only the Son of God in some subordinate sense, but is actually God. At the center is the Easter confession that Jesus is *kyrios*, the Greek translation of the Old Testament name of God, *Adonai*. The confession of Jesus as God is rooted in the liturgy of the early church. Jesus as the Christ "reflects the glory of God and bears the very stamp of his nature" (Heb. 1:3). Nothing less than an ontological equation of Jesus with God is implied in all these New Testament descriptions of Jesus' relation to the Father and of his saving function. His being and his mission are mutually implicative. His function as Savior without his being as God would be powerless and baseless; his being as God without his saving mission would be abstract and empty. Ontological-doxological statements belong together with functional-historical statements in a comprehensive christology.

It has been recently suggested that the classical christology of the two natures of Christ in the Creed of Chalcedon was not about two natures at all. Rather, says R. A. Norris, the creed is about two languages. "The *Definition* is not

6 / THE PERSON OF JESUS CHRIST

talking about Jesus; it is talking about Christian language about Jesus."[12] In line with this statement is an earlier one by P. T. Forsyth, "The mighty thing in Christ is His grace and not His constitution,"[13] here echoing unmistakably Philipp Melanchthon's famous saying that to know Christ is simply to know his benefits.[14] These are examples of the modern inclination to play off the functional significance of Christ against his ontological status. We believe this is an understandable but mistaken tendency.

The best way to overcome the bad effects of Greek metaphysics on classical christology is to find a better one, not to opt for none at all. When existentialist christology speaks of Christ as a possibility of existence or when the approach of linguistic analysis explains christology as a descriptive grammar of the language of faith, both fail to formulate the ontological relation of Jesus to God, of the Son to the Father. The language of Chalcedon about two natures and two sets of attributes in Christ is not merely offering rules for the language of faith and preaching. That would beg the question of why such rules should be binding for the church in all ages. The creeds of Nicaea and Chalcedon make definite assertions concerning two dimensions of reality in Christ because there *are* two dimensions. It is not enough for the language of faith to be logically correct. There is an ontological dimension which is the condition of the truth and meaning of the language of faith.

Christology is free to use modern categories from existentialism, language-analysis philosophy and the philosophy of history to explain the duality implied in the two-natures doctrine of the Chalcedonian definition. Nothing is to be gained by forever binding the church's christology to the ontological concepts of Platonic and Aristotelian philosophy. We wish to say the same thing in reworking christology into a new system of concepts. We certainly do not want to say anything less. If we say there are two natures in Christ, a divine *physis* and a human *physis*, this is language that has to be explained. What is meant is not nature as natural physical substance, but nature as the essence of what something is. The expression "the divine nature" of Christ means that whatever it is that makes God God and not something else is really present in the person of Jesus Christ. "Human nature" means that whatever it is that makes humans essentially human is fully actual in them. The quest for an adequate definition of what it is that makes God and humans what they are will continue in the history of philosophy. These definitions will, in turn, continue to be tested and transformed in light of Jesus Christ who represents God to humanity and humanity to God in his own person.

In the nineteenth century, Protestant theologians tried every new metaphysical and epistemological approach to explain the Christian confession that Jesus Christ is "very God and very man." Schleiermacher certainly intended to affirm the uniqueness of the Redeemer and to assert that in some sense we can speak of a "real existence of God" in Christ. The philosophies

THE TRUE DIVINITY OF JESUS CHRIST

of Immanuel Kant, Friedrich Schelling, and G. W. F. Hegel[15] triggered numerous attempts to rethink the old christological formula on the new ground of modern critical thought. In the twentieth century, too, the thought of every major philosopher has been exploited for the sake of new christological construction. Martin Heidegger in Germany, Ludwig Wittgenstein in England, and Alfred North Whitehead in the United States are three of the most noteworthy philosophers whose methods and concepts have been used in the revision of christology. Currently attempts are being made to go back to some earlier philosophers to rediscover old ideas with new significance, such as Thomas Aquinas in Roman Catholic theology, Karl Marx in Latin American liberation theology, and G. W. F. Hegel in Protestant eschatological theology.

Not all philosophies are equally successful in expressing what the church meant to confess in its formula "very God and very man." In principle they have not had so much difficulty providing categories to explicate the true humanity of Jesus, although even here they have tended to idealize, moralize, or romanticize the picture of the man. Trouble surfaces when they turn to the confession of the true divinity of Christ. Karl Barth once contrasted Wilhelm Herrmann's christology with orthodox christology in this fashion: "Orthodox christology is a glacial torrent rushing straight down from a height of three thousand meters; it makes accomplishment possible. Herrmann's christology, as it stands, is the hopeless attempt to raise a stagnant pool to that same height by means of a hand pump; nothing can be accomplished with it."[16]

Thomas's confession of Jesus Christ, "My Lord and my God!" is an immediate analytic judgment of faith that one either makes or does not make. If one prefers to call it a judgment of reason, it is in any case a reason emancipated by the power of the Spirit and faith. This is not a retreat to subjectivism. In confessing the divinity of Jesus Christ, we do not attribute to him a notion of deity which we have derived beforehand from our own philosophical speculations. We do not look at Jesus and call him God because he conforms so remarkably to our preconceived idea of what a God must be. Jesus is not the fulfillment of our prior notion of God. He *is* God for us. We apprehend the final meaning of God in Jesus, and nowhere else. The whole spectrum of reality in Jesus Christ, his life, death, and resurrection, is the locus of God's self-definition. Christian faith looks to Jesus Christ and confesses, "There is no other God."

We do not approach the biblical picture of Christ armed with a sufficient idea of God derived from an autonomous metaphysics, laying our own mantle of divinity on him, as it were; but neither do we call Jesus God as an inference derived from our own religious experiences. To borrow Barth's metaphor, that would be like trying to raise the level of Lake Michigan with a hand pump. This approach has led to the idealizing and deifying of Jesus as a great man.

6 / THE PERSON OF JESUS CHRIST

But God is not humanity raised to the *n*th degree. Making Jesus into the hero of a Christian cult does not warrant calling him God. Neither the metaphysical approach from above nor the experiential approach from below escapes the charge of arbitrary subjectivism. If our confession of the divinity of Jesus is based on a prior conception we hold of God or on the fact of our religious experience, we are confronted with a Jesuology thinly disguised by superlatives of our own making. The alternative is to discover the divine and human dimensions of reality in the one person of Jesus Christ in the act of his self-manifestation.

Faith is brought to the confession of God in Christ, not on the strength of reason (philosophy) or religion (experience), but solely by the power of the Holy Spirit. "No one can say 'Jesus is Lord' except by the Holy Spirit" (1 Cor. 12:3). The Holy Spirit mediates the relation of faith to the person of Christ and generates the understanding that Jesus is not merely Jesus; he is the Christ in whom *God* is present and active. The divine-human reality of Jesus Christ becomes a living presence to faith through the preaching of the Word. This Word is a representation of the Christ who reveals himself through the Scriptures. When preaching is faithful to the Scriptures, Jesus is proclaimed as the Christ, the Savior, the Lord, the Logos who was with God, who was God, and who became flesh (John 1:1, 14).

It is well and good that the confession of the true humanity of Jesus has come into its own in contemporary christology, perhaps more persistently than at any time in the history of theology. But all this would amount to nothing in the cause of the world's salvation if the divine Sonship of Jesus were not the power to back it up. In confessing the true divinity of Jesus Christ, we are saying that in Jesus God is revealed as the finally valid answer to all our ultimate questions about the meaning of existence and the future of life. As the exclusive medium of God's final word of judgment and hope, Jesus is the one through whom the knowledge of ultimate salvation enters history. He represents the final hope of each individual and the future of the cosmos. There is simply no need for another revelation of God, because Jesus is God's unsurpassable self-revelation. The world still awaits, however, the realization of what has been revealed—fulfillment of life's potential in the eschatological kingdom of God.

Jesus can be our God because the power of God's absolute future—*basileia*—was shown to be effectually present in his person and ministry. Whoever is united with Jesus in faith is assured, therefore, of an everlasting future with God. This presence of the power of God's future eschatological kingdom in the person, miracles, parables, sayings, and above all in the death and resurrection of Jesus constitutes the meaning of the confession that God is one with Jesus and that Jesus is very God for us. The essential unity of God with Jesus of Nazareth is manifest in Jesus' unlimited love for God and his absolute devotion in representing God's unconditional love for the world. The heart of the final and future kingdom of God is the unrestricted freedom to have life in the plenitude of love. The classical confession of the *homoousios* of Jesus as God's Son with the Almighty Father is rooted in this agapeic union of God and Jesus.

AN ONTOLOGICAL INTERPRETATION OF THE INCARNATION

The special task of an ontological interpretation of the incarnation is to explicate the relationship between God and Jesus, between divinity and humanity in the one person of Jesus. Its task is to characterize the kind of unity effected in the life of Jesus between divinity and humanity, to analyze the *locus divinitatis* in him. How does this unity between Jesus and his Father differ in principle from the unity between God and humanity in general, expressed in the notion that God created humankind in the divine likeness and image (*similitudo et imago dei*)? Is the incarnation here the actualization of a potential human union with God, or is it a miraculous transcendent act from beyond the immanent potentialities of nature and history? All these considerations aim to illuminate the confessional answer to the question: Who is Jesus Christ?

In trying to understand the unity of the divine and the human in the one person of Jesus, we can approach the matter from two sides, from above or from below. From below means from the human side, and from above means from the divine side. Both sides are manifest in the personal history of Jesus of Nazareth. From below, from the human side, we can say that Jesus' unity with the Father represents a perfect realization of the humanity of humankind. The original unity between God and humanity lost in the fall is restored in the perfect actualization of Jesus' humanity in union with the Father. The incarnation seen from below reveals the truth that humanity realizes the true essence of human being only by becoming one with the Father. Seen from below, that is, from the perspective of the Gospel story, "Jesus increased in wisdom and in stature, and in favor with God and man" (Luke 2:52). Throughout life he maintained a perfect union with the Father, showing no trace of sin and unbelief, but only perfect love to God and obedience to God's will. The more human he showed himself to be, the more radically did his unity with the Father become manifest.

From the divine side we can do no better than say that the eternal love which flows freely between Father, Son, and Spirit overflows the circle of divine being, positing a world in which God can communicate divine love in a human way. The classical doctrine of the hypostatic union means that Jesus is the unique event of God's loving self-communication.

6 / THE PERSON OF JESUS CHRIST

In this section we shall propose a historical revision of ontology in light of the biblical understanding of the eschatological future kingdom of God appearing in the history of the person of Jesus the Christ. The metaphysical ontology of the Greek philosophers not only hindered the understanding of the incarnation but also blocked an eschatological interpretation of historical events. In an eschatological interpretation of historical reality the truth belongs to the whole. Only from the end does it appear what the whole truth of reality is. The final meaning of history can be disclosed only from its future end. Jesus the Christ as a figure of history is presented in the New Testament as the true revelation of the future end of all reality. The total biblical picture of Jesus as the Christ is a fusion of two sets of symbols. Both incarnational and eschatological symbols are interwoven in the ealiest traditions which tell of the identity and meaning of Jesus the Christ. Eschatology and incarnation join in the interpretation of the history of Jesus as the locus of divine presence and activity.

Paul Tillich once suggested that the ancient discussions of the unity of two natures and two wills in Christ must be transformed in our present situation into the problem of the interpretation of history and its relation to the kingdom of God. The ontological dimension in christology retains its validity, but it must be an ontology broken open by eschatology and history, and no longer determined by the Greek spatial myth of origin and its metaphysics of substance. It must become an ontology revised in light of the historical-eschatological framework of the Bible.[17]

The union of two histories, the history of *God's* coming within the personal history of *Jesus* of Nazareth, is an event which calls for an ontological interpretation. Paul Tillich reached back to the categories of German idealism, particularly to Schelling and Hegel, to discover conceptual tools that might facilitate an ontological interpretation of the incarnation. The modern opposition to Hegel—partly because of his own later development, partly because of his left-wing disciples, Strauss, Feuerbach, and Marx—has been so vehement that his potential contribution to a new historically determined ontology has been overlooked until very recently. Karl Barth, in his history of theology in the nineteenth century, closed his chapter on Hegel with this enigmatic valediction: "We must therefore be content to understand him as the man he was: as a great problem and a great disappointment, but perhaps also a great promise."[18] It is the promise of Hegel that interests theology today.[19] The promise lies in a new interpretation of the Trinity and of the incarnation in light of an historical revision of ontological thought, thus overcoming the ahistorical metaphysics of Greek philosophy. For Hegel the absolute was not unmoved substance but acting subject, which expresses itself in a dynamic way through what is other than itself. For him it was not metaphysical nonsense but dialectical truth that Being Itself would mediate itself through its op-

THE TRUE DIVINITY OF JESUS CHRIST

posite: life through death, love through wrath, fulfillment through negativity, and the divine through the human. The Infinite is capable of embracing itself and the finite in a dialectical unity of opposites. How do we know? Because it has happened. This is not a matter of *a priori* speculative knowledge which the philosopher can derive from the logic of reality in general. Rather, it is *a posteriori* theological reflection based on the event of the incarnation and its transparent structure in the biblical picture of Jesus the Christ.

Our knowledge of God has been mediated through the Christ-event. How can we express the self-revelation and self-manifestation of God in the person of Jesus? How can we best understand the identity of Jesus Christ in ontological terms? Taking a clue from Hegel, we have said that it belongs to the nature of ultimate reality to express itself dialectically through what is other than itself, expressing identity in difference. This is an abstract interpretation of the Johannine statement: God is love. If there is only one, in static identity, the occurrence of love cannot take place. It is the nature of love to unite two who can be differentiated, to overcome the difference, to reconcile through self-emptying. This vision of God as love is projected from the concrete history of Jesus Christ, his relation to his Father, and his death on the cross.

What happened in Jesus Christ, through his human experience of suffering love and sacrificial death, was nothing less than the coming and history of God. The truth of the incarnation is that God is identified with this one man, communicating the divine Word through this man's particularity and the deepest love in the event of the cross. God who does not need to change to be fully divine has become someone utterly human out of the fullness of love and freedom, not out of any lack in God's being or fatal necessity. Birth, death, change, history, and negation no longer happen only on the human side of the ontological abyss between God and the world.

The incarnation of love in the history of Jesus Christ is thus an ontological event. For the love God has communicated in the history of Jesus Christ is the love which is the very nature of God's own being. God *is* love. The ontological meaning of this statement has been explained in the doctrine of the Trinity. The inner relations between the members of the triune God are characterized by the eternal dynamics of love. The good news of the incarnation is that this love has come to be in the person of Jesus, reconciling the world and humanity to their eternal source in God. God's coming in Christ has taken human history and the world's becoming into the divine life. God entered the world of time and space, reestablishing the whole creation as the realm of God's rule. The incarnation is God's self-emptying of everything that separated the Creator from the creation, to embrace the entire cosmos as an acceptable part of the kingdom of God. In the act of *kenosis*, self-emptying, we see the self-surrender of God to others in order to win them back. God was able to do this because of the freedom of divine love. The power of love

6 / THE PERSON OF JESUS CHRIST

by which God created the world in the first place is the same power by which God showed freedom for self-emptying and self-humiliation in Jesus Christ, entering the conditions of human existence, and thus claiming the history of humanity and of the world as the means of divine self-communication.

NOTES

1. See *The Truth of God Incarnate*, ed. Michael Green (Grand Rapids: Wm. B. Eerdmans, 1977), which was an instant response to *The Myth of God Incarnate*, ed. John Hick (Philadelphia: Westminster Press, 1977).

2. See Paul Tillich, "The Meaning and Justification of Religious Symbols," in *Religious Experience and Truth*, ed. Sidney Hook (New York: New York University Press, 1961), pp. 3–11.

3. Rudolf Bultmann, *Jesus Christ and Mythology* (New York: Charles Scribner's Sons, 1958).

4. Rudolf Bultmann, "New Testament and Mythology," in his *Kerygma and Myth*, ed. Hans W. Bartsch, trans. R. H. Fuller (London: SPCK, 1954), p. 10.

5. Wolfhart Pannenberg, "The Appropriation of the Philosophical Concept of God as a Dogmatic Problem of Early Christian Theology," in his *Basic Questions in Theology*, vol. 2, trans. George H. Kehm (Philadelphia: Fortress Press, 1971), pp. 119–83.

6. See Kazoh Kitamori, *Theology of the Pain of God* (Richmond: John Knox Press, 1965).

7. See Werner Elert, *Der Ausgang der altkirchlichen Christologie* (Berlin: Lutherisches Verlagshaus, 1957).

8. Ian D. Kingston Siggins, *Martin Luther's Doctrine of Christ* (New Haven: Yale University Press, 1970), p. 241.

9. Ibid., p. 232.

10. See Edmund Schlink, "The Christology of Chalcedon in Ecumenical Discussion," in *The Coming Christ and the Coming Church* (Edinburgh: Oliver & Boyd, 1967), pp. 87–95.

11. Ernst Käsemann, *An die Römer* (Tübingen: J. C. B. Mohr [Paul Siebeck], 1973), p. 3.

12. R. A. Norris, "Toward a Contemporary Interpretation of the Chalcedonian Definition," in *Lux in Lumine: Essays to Honor W. Norman Pittenger*, ed. R. A. Norris (New York: Seabury Press, 1966), p. 78.

13. P. T. Forsyth, *The Person and Place of Jesus Christ* (London: Independent Press, 1909), p. 10.

14. "Hoc est Christum cognoscere, beneficia eius cognoscere." Philipp Melanchthon, *Loci Communes*, CR 21:85.

15. See James Yerkes, *The Christology of Hegel* (Missoula, Mont.: Scholars Press, 1978).

16. Karl Barth, *Theology and Church*, trans. Louise Pettibone Smith (New York: Harper & Row, 1962), p. 265.

17. See Paul Tillich, "A Reinterpretation of the Doctrine of the Incarnation," *CQR*

147 (January 1949): 113-148; also, *The Interpretation of History* (New York: Charles Scribner's Sons, 1936).

18. Karl Barth, *Protestant Thought: From Rousseau to Ritschl*, trans. Brian Cozens (New York: Harper & Row, 1959), p. 305.

19. See Hans Küng, *Menschwerdung Gottes, Eine Einführung in Hegels Theologisches Denken als Prolegomena zu einer Künftigen Christologie* (Freiburg: Herder Verlag, 1970).

6

The Humiliation and Exaltation of Jesus Christ

The story of the incarnation of Christ is told in images and symbols as a passage back and forth between two states of being, the state of exaltation and the state of humiliation. The essence of the story is the participation of God in the human condition for the salvation of humanity and the fulfillment of the world.

THE PREEXISTENCE OF CHRIST

The preexistence of Christ is an integral part of the myth of the incarnation. References to the preexistence of Christ (or the Logos or the Son of God) can be found in the epistles of Paul and the Gospel of John.[1] Their intention is to be understood soteriologically. They say that Jesus is the eternal Son of God because the salvation he delivered to humankind has its origin in God. If the One who lived, suffered, and died for our salvation is not eternally from God, there is no real and certain salvation. Jesus and Yahweh must share the same eternal ground if the salvation Jesus has wrought for us is to count as equally valid for God. God sent the Son into the world in human form. The mythological structure may be transparent on its surface, but its essential meaning is basic to the gospel. The implicit argument is soteriological. Jesus is the acknowledged Savior of humankind. But only the eternal God can grant salvation. Therefore the ultimate identity of Jesus must derive from the eternal life of God.

Arianism was rejected as heresy because it left a gap between Jesus and Yahweh of an ontological order, thereby undermining the basis of salvation. For this reason Luther referred to Arius as Narrius,[2] "Narr" being the German for "fool." It would be foolish for Christians to reopen a gap between Jesus and Yahweh if they are in earnest about the salvation they claim to have received through Jesus himself. Jesus must have always been one with God if the salvation he brought is divinely authorized. The idea of preexistence means that Jesus never was an individual person apart from the event of the incarnation of the Son of God. If Jesus truly represented God for us, there never was when he was not divine. He was not an afterthought in the divine plan for the world. He was the eternally begotten Son of God, not only the historically born son of Mary.

THE VIRGIN BIRTH

In the Apostles' Creed we confess that Jesus was conceived by the Holy Spirit and born of the Virgin Mary. Since the Enlightenment, this has become one of the most disputed doctrines. In contemporary theology Emil Brunner denied the virgin birth of Christ in his book *The Mediator*. He called it a "biological curiosity"[3] and saw a possible connection with docetism because it made the Holy Spirit usurp the function of the human father. How could Jesus be like us *in all respects* if he did not actually have a human father? Karl Barth dismissed Brunner's arguments as "a bad business."[4] Wolfhart Pannenberg sides with Brunner and asks whether Barth's arguments for the virgin birth do not put him "on the path of Roman Mariolatry?"[5] For Pannenberg, "the story of the virgin birth bears all the marks of a legend."[6] He concludes: "Theology cannot maintain the idea of Jesus' virgin birth as a miraculous fact to be postulated at the origin of his earthly life. To that extent it is problematic that the virgin birth found entry into the Apostles' Creed."[7]

The primary interest of dogmatics is to interpret the virgin birth as a symbol and not as a freakish intervention in the course of nature. Scientific inquiries into the frequency of parthenogenesis in the world of nature are beside the point. They contribute nothing to deeper insight into the revelatory reality to which the story of Jesus' birth points. It is possible to hold to the virgin birth as a biological fact and miss its point. It is also possible to make the same point without reference to the virgin birth, as the writings of Paul and John prove by not mentioning it. It is important, then, not to let the story get bogged down in biology, but to read it as a symbol witnessing to the truth of the kerygma. The truth of the conception by the Holy Spirit is that God was the author of salvation through Christ from the beginning, not first in his resurrection, nor on the cross, nor at the baptism, but from the moment of his conception by Mary. The story reinforces the idea of the preexistence of Christ and serves the same purpose of grounding the history of salvation in the eschatological reality that is prior to the world itself. The story works against an adoptionistic christology by engaging the power of the Spirit in the birth of Jesus prior to anything he might have done to merit adoption. The story vindicates a theology of grace alone by attacking the root of works-righteousness at the base of christology itself.

The exclusion of a human father in the birth of Jesus has become more problematic to modern Christians than it was in ancient times. Originally the confession of Jesus' birth from the Virgin Mary was a sign of his real humanity, pointing away from the docetic denial of his solidarity with the human race.⁸ The fact that Jesus was born of a woman like every other child was proof that he was a real human being. The point of the story was to work against docetism. Unfortunately, the symbol of the virgin birth no longer has a clear antidocetic ring for modern ears. We cannot imagine how the story could concretize the interest of faith in the real humanity of the Savior. Why should the absence of human paternity make the truth of God's presence in the incarnation more apparent? Is God the Father in competition with the role of our human father? Did not God create fatherhood and look upon it as "very good"? Why then should human fatherhood be eliminated in the work of salvation? If we grasp the original intention of the story to witness to the real humanity of Jesus, we must not allow a shift in the situation from ancient times to the present to play a trick on us, which it would do if we were to use the story apologetically to prove the divinity of Christ or to explain the sinlessness of Jesus. The story has become increasingly ambiguous because our natural tendency is to take it to mean the opposite of what it originally intended.

THE CRUCIFIXION OF JESUS

The descent of the Son of God into the womb of Mary and his birth in history as a Hebrew baby have been theologically discussed as the transition from glory to a state of humiliation. It forms the heart of the notion of *kenosis*—self-emptying. The descent into the human depths of humiliation continued in the ministry of Jesus and came to a climax in his suffering and death. The crucifixion of Jesus was an historical event, the outcome of a political trial in which all the powers of the establishment conspired to put an innocent man to death. The crucifixion, however, was more than an event of past history with ripple effects on the subsequent course of world history. The historicity of the cross of Jesus must be maintained against every possible tendency to dissolve its once-for-allness in an existentialist interpretation that stresses its timeless quality as an ever-present possibility of self-understanding. Such an interpretation would stand closer to gnosticism than to the gospel.

Before the cross can be seen in its relation to existential experience, it must be grasped as an event of past history. Otherwise it has nothing to do with the cross of Jesus Christ. The crucifixion of Jesus happened only once and will never happen again. Nevertheless, the meaning of the historical cross was transmitted in the suprahistorical language of mythological symbolism. The cross is not a fact of history that interprets itself. The New Testament writers used a rich variety of symbols taken from the world of ancient Jewish and gnostic mythology to interpret the meaning of the cross. When the cross is viewed mythologically, and not simply as one historical event alongside others,

6 / THE PERSON OF JESUS CHRIST

it receives redemptive significance of cosmic proportions. It is the task of the doctrine of the atonement to explicate the dogmatic meaning of the cross. Here we need only include it as one further stage in the kenotic self-abasing movement of the Son of God from the heights of glory to the depths of humiliation in a death by crucifixion under Pontius Pilate, a death whose universal redemptive significance has been interpreted according to Jewish ideas of atonement (sacrifice and satisfaction) and the gnostic myth of redemption (death and resurrection).

JESUS' DESCENT INTO HELL

The downward curve of the incarnational line reached its lowest point in Jesus' descent into hell. In the seventeenth century, Lutheran and Reformed dogmaticians debated whether Jesus' descent into hell was the extreme limit of his humiliation or the initial step toward triumph and exaltation. We are including it under the state of humiliation, because the descent into hell is a symbol which conveys the truth that Jesus' victory over the enemies of man (sin, death, and the devil) was attained by first suffering the negation they introduced into the world.

The phrase in the Apostles' Creed "He descended into hell" unites two different ideas. Hell is a translation of the Greek word "hades," designating the abode of the dead. Later in church usage, hell was equated with the place of the damned. The verse in 1 Pet. 3:19 states that after his death Jesus "went and preached to the spirits in prison," and verse 4:6 makes clear that on this trip "the gospel was preached even to the dead." Originally it was thought that when people died they went to hades, a waiting room for the dead until the last judgment. A shift in meaning occurred in later theology, so that when people died they went directly to heaven or hell, except for those who went to purgatory to be cleansed of their impurities. The transition from a descent to hades to a descent into hell is easy to explain. Hell is the sphere of Satan's dominion. If Christ is to free also those who have died, he must declare his victory in the stronghold of Satan himself.

The theological significance of Christ's descent into hell/hades is twofold. First, insofar as we emphasize that Christ descended into hell—the place of the damned—we are stressing the depth-dimension of his suffering and humiliation for our sakes. At one and the same time he suffered and overcame through his suffering the torment of hell as separation from God. Jesus did not only suffer the wrath of God in his conscience, not only anxiety about his calling, not only temptation to compromise his loyalty to the kingdom; he also suffered the deepest distress of humanity all the way to the cross, subjecting himself to the alienating powers of death, Satan, and hell. The meaning of this symbol is that the deepest humiliation of Christ happened so that as the Lord of hell he might vanquish once for all the existential power that hell holds over our future. Second, insofar as we confess Christ's descent to hades as the realm of the dead, we are claiming that his work of salvation is universal and reaches beyond the limits of those who preach and hear the gospel in this life. Nations and generations of people who lived before the coming of Christ and who have never been confronted with the preaching of salvation in his name are not eternally lost. Christ goes even to the dead, so that he might be acclaimed the Lord of the living and the dead.

THE RESURRECTION

Three days after his death Jesus appeared again to a small circle of friends. The crucified Jesus revealed himself as the living, risen, exalted Lord who had triumphed over death and the devil. The raising of Jesus was an act by which God put an end to his humiliation and exalted him above all the enemies of humankind, and without it our faith is in vain (1 Cor. 15:14). Mythological symbolism contributed to the interpretation of the event of the resurrection. The question has become acute in modern theology whether in the resurrection we are dealing only with a myth or with a truly historical event.

Some theologians dismiss the resurrection as of little importance. Consider this statement by a "process" theologian: "Christian faith (as I understand it) is possible apart from belief in Jesus' resurrection in particular and life beyond bodily death in general, and because of the widespread skepticism regarding these traditional beliefs, they should be presented as optional."[9] Other theologians are doubtful about the possibility of verifying the resurrection as a specific, historically definable event, but would still wish to speak about it as a way of interpreting the real significance of the cross. So Bultmann writes: "Belief in the resurrection is simply and exactly the same as belief in the cross as 'salvation event!' "[10] The cross is the historical fact, the resurrection its symbolic meaning. On the other side, there are theologians who share Wolfhart Pannenberg's view that the resurrection of Jesus was an historical event and that it must so be proved by historical reason. He writes:

> There is no justification for affirming Jesus' resurrection as an event that really happened, if it is not to be affirmed as a historical event as such. Whether or not a particular event happened two thousand years ago is not made certain by faith but only by historical research, to the extent that certainty can be attained at all about questions of this kind.[11]

Paul Althaus split the difference between Bultmann and Pannenberg, arguing with Pannenberg that the resurrection was truly an event of history, empty tomb and all, but agreeing with Bultmann that it cannot be verified by the critical methods of the historian. Althaus wrote in his dogmatics *Die*

6 / THE PERSON OF JESUS CHRIST

Christliche Wahrheit: "That Jesus was raised from the dead and appeared to his disciples as the Risen One is something we can only know for sure by faith under the impact of all the witnesses to Jesus, his life and message and death, as well as his resurrection."[12]

All the modern scholarly differences on the historical problem of the resurrection should not overshadow the prevailing exegetical consensus that from the point of view of the whole New Testament the resurrection of Jesus was an event that really happened in time and space, that eyewitnesses were prepared to vouch for it, and that the earliest Christians believed it to be a firmly established truth. Unfortunately scholars are in much greater agreement on what the resurrection *meant* in the New Testament than on what it *means* to Christian faith today. The degree of consensus that exists at the historical level does not prevail in systematic theology. Other factors intervene, such as the nature of an historical event, the meaning of history, the relation of faith to facts, and the relevance of believing in life beyond death.

An historian's presuppositions may determine for him or her that the resurrection did not really happen because such a thing could not happen. But who knows beforehand the limits of what is historically possible? If what is "humanly possible" is the measure of what is historically possible, the resurrection of Jesus must be regarded as impossible. In the biblical view, what is historically possible is always weighed within the horizon of a world that is ever open to the activity of the living God. Nature and history are not closed in on their own inherent possibilities. In face of *a priori* denials of the resurrection of Jesus, it is necessary for theology to become critical of criticism, to free the mind and prepare the way for an unprejudiced hearing of the witnesses.

However, no matter how positive the results of historical research may ever be in verifying the earliest testimonies to the resurrection of Jesus, we can never dispense with the role of faith in responding to the message of Easter. The preaching of the risen Christ goes on in the context of the church's celebration of his real presence. This preaching and the faith it generates cannot take the place of historical-critical examination of the texts. On the other hand, no historian can convert historical statements with their higher or lower degrees of probability into a personal decision of faith in Jesus as the living Lord. The judgment of historians is likely to lean in favor of the historical reliability of the resurrection reports only if they already approach the reports with the bias of belief that Christ is risen indeed. They need not be apologetic about their faith. Would it not be absurd to argue that lack of faith enhances the skills of an historian in cross-examining the witnesses with a critical eye?

Faith does not close the eyes of reason; it may open them to see things that seem to contradict all analogies from ordinary human experience. The report that a dead man has been raised from his grave and lives a new life beyond the reach of death is without analogy in history. It is *sui generis*—so far the only event of its kind. There is therefore no conflict here with natural science, as often presumed. Conflict with natural science arises only if the resurrection entails suspension of the so-called laws of nature. But this is not the case, since such laws function in the natural world all the way to death. Jesus' death was no exception. Whether beyond death there is another kind of story to tell in the language of myth and symbol or legend and metaphor does not lie within the purview of the natural sciences to prove or disprove.

We cannot summarize here the exegetical results of modern scholarship regarding the Easter traditions. Suffice it to recall that the gospel of Easter was conveyed through two strands of early tradition, the older one dealing with the appearances of the risen Lord, the other with the discovery of the empty tomb. In both traditions the irreducible minimum was the conviction that Jesus is no longer dead but alive. We can call the resurrection an historical event because it happened in a particular place, in Palestine, and at a definite time, a few days after his death and prior to Pentecost. The knowledge of this event depends on witnesses who passed on the reports of what they heard and saw. On the other hand, the nature of the reality that appeared to the witnesses was more than historical. It was an eschatological event. The witnesses reported that they had seen Jesus alive and the tomb empty. Immediately they interpreted this event as the first instance of the widely anticipated eschatological event of resurrection from the dead. The New Testament refers to the resurrection of Jesus as the "first fruits" of the new world that dawns with the coming of God's kingdom. This dual character of the resurrection— that it is at once an event within the horizon of history and an eschatological event—accounts for the fact that some theologians are willing, others unwilling, to call the resurrection an historical event. The event and the reports which transmit the knowledge of the event occurred within the framework of history, but when we turn to the meaning of this event, we see clearly what it means to speak of the resurrection as an eschatological event.

Christianity is based on the gospel of the resurrection of Jesus of Nazareth, because in this event God vindicated the claim of Jesus to be the prime representative of his coming kingdom. Christianity could not have had a beginning if the crucifixion had been the absolute end of Jesus. The cause of Jesus would have perished with him.

In raising Jesus from the dead, God raised the cause for which he lived and died to the highest power in the history of salvation. By ratifying Jesus' claim to be the authoritative mediator of God's kingdom, the cause of the kingdom itself gained a promising future in world history. The church of Jesus Christ entered at this point as a creation of the Spirit to announce the eschatological breakthrough in the new and deathless form of life which Jesus' inherited through the resurrection.

6 / THE PERSON OF JESUS CHRIST

THE ASCENSION

The exaltation of Jesus Christ moves from his resurrection on the third day through the forty days of his self-manifestation to the day of his "ascension." The mythical features of this trajectory of exaltation are obvious the moment we ask where Jesus went when he ascended to heaven. Christian art has depicted the ascension as a visible movement of Jesus' body through the clouds, with the disciples standing by, looking up and watching him disappear. In some realistic paintings all one can see is the feet, the rest of the body having been enveloped by clouds. The need to demythologize the story should not, however, weaken our sense for the message it contains.

The story of the ascension is preceded by a period of forty days after the resurrection. The symbolic significance of the number forty was already firmly established in the biblical history of salvation. We can recall Moses' forty days and forty nights on top of the mountain (Exod. 24:18), or Elijah's sojourn on Mount Horeb forty days and forty nights (1 Kings 19:8), or Israel's wandering in the wilderness forty years, or Jesus' fasting and temptations in the wilderness forty days. The forty days between the resurrection and the ascension was a time in which the risen, exalted Christ revealed himself to those who still had to live and preach the message under the old conditions of this world of transiency and death. It was eminently a time qualified by the self-revealing presence of Jesus on his way from humiliation to exaltation.

The ascension of Jesus came at the end of the forty days. It signified the end of the time in which Jesus himself was the revealing subject of revelation and the beginning of the time in which the Spirit through the Word and the sacraments conveys him as the revealed subject matter of revelation. The ascension prepared the way for the time of the church which takes place between the ascension of Christ and his return at the end of time. Not only Rudolf Bultmann but before him Martin Luther ridiculed the literalistic images of the ascension common in popular piety as childish ideas. If we ask, "Where did Jesus go?" we can only answer, "He went to the Father." Even the scholastic theologians did not interpret the ascension in a purely spatial way. To be sure, they took the myth literally, visualizing Jesus going up into the clouds of heaven. But this was only an outer sign of an invisible ascension to the throne of God which is not located in a particular place but represents the omnipresent rule of God. Karl Barth similarly referred to the ascension of Jesus as the homecoming of the Son who had wandered into a far country, a homecoming to the Father's house.

In one respect the content of Easter and the ascension are one and the same. They both mean that God exalted Jesus. In the earliest Christian preaching the resurrection of Jesus from the dead was itself interpreted as an act of exaltation (Acts 2:33; 5:30–31; Phil. 2:9). Yet there are good reasons for

THE HUMILIATION AND EXALTATION OF JESUS CHRIST

distinguishing the two events in the church year, separated by forty days, even though dogmatics would be hard pressed to justify these distinctions with sound historical arguments. The end of Jesus' time on earth is like the beginning. It is a mystery clothed in the language of myth and symbol. History does not give us a key to unlock it.

The ascension marked the beginning of something new in history. John quotes Jesus as saying, "It is to your advantage that I go away" (John 16:7). The absence of Christ according to the flesh (*kata sarka*) opened the possibility of a new form of presence according to the Spirit (*kata pneuma*).

At first it seems that the ascension draws the Christian faith into the vortex of the myth of eternal recurrence, in denial of the historical structure of the gospel as a message of events that never repeat themselves. It seems that the Son ascends to exactly the same place from which he descended. Origen enunciated the formula "The end is always like the beginning." This was an axiom taken from Neo-Platonic philosophy and applied as an hermeneutical key to open the mysteries of biblical revelation. But actually the ascension was an advance, not a return to the *status quo ante*, to the previous place of the Son with the Father. It was an advance to a new epoch of history, to the sending of the Spirit and the mission of the church in world history.

THE SESSION AT THE RIGHT HAND OF GOD

Jesus was exalted to the right hand of the Father. The "right hand" was a symbol in the ancient East for a position of power exercised in the name of the ruler. The Christian confession that Jesus was exalted to the place of power at the right hand of God was an adaptation of a statement in Ps. 110:1: "The Lord says to my lord: 'Sit at my right hand, till I make your enemies your footstool.'" Originally this saying was God speaking to the king of Jerusalem. When, in the early church, Jesus was called "Lord," the saying was interpreted as God speaking to Jesus. Between the time of Jesus' earthly ministry and his return at the end of time to judge the world, Jesus rules now as the Lord of history and the church.

The confession that Jesus is sitting at God's right hand is not to be taken in a literal sense as referring to a definite place. This became a topic of major dispute in Luther's controversy with Zwingli on the Lord's Supper. Zwingli argued that since Christ ascended and sits at the right hand of God in heaven, he cannot at the same time be really present at every altar on earth. Luther argued that this is precisely the point of the phrase "at the right hand of God." The right hand of God refers to God's power to fill heaven and earth; it refers to royal omnipotence and majesty; it is the efficacious dominion by which God is everywhere governing, controlling, and administering all things.

6 / THE PERSON OF JESUS CHRIST

Therefore, when Christ sits at God's right hand, it means that he participates in the divine power, glory, and dominion over all things in heaven and on earth. It is a statement acknowledging the present Lordship of Jesus Christ.

The older dogmaticians (Martin Chemnitz, John Andrew Quenstedt, John Gerhard, David Hollaz) interpreted the "right hand of God" in a broad sense to refer to the Lordship of Christ in terms of three ways in which he rules in the world. First there is the "rule of grace" (*regnum gratiae*). Jesus participates now in the power of God's Spirit to rule in the hearts of humankind. Because Jesus sits now at the right hand of God, he is no longer bound to the limits of his earthly ministry. He shares in a suprahistorical freedom to be universally present to all generations everywhere and at all times. For this reason he can be the Lord of the one ecumenical church dispersed among the nations. Because he sits at the right hand of God, he can keep his final promise: "Lo, I am with you always, to the close of the age" (Matt. 28:20).

Jesus exercises his rule of grace by means of the church's ongoing witness to his earthly life and ministry according to the Gospels. The living Christ who sits at the right hand of God does not create faith by a direct "I-Thou" kind of mystical relationship apart from the mediation of the Word and the sacraments. Individuals who claim to have mystical visions of the living Christ do not thereby acquire new knowledge of revelation on which the church as a whole can act.

The Lordship of Christ in the New Testament is not limited in scope to his rule of grace in and through the church. The center of gravity, to be sure, is Christ's Lordship of the church. This is clear from the idea that the church is the body of Christ and that Christ is the head of the church. As the body of Christ, the church plays a special role in the rule of Christ. The church is where the Lordship of Jesus Christ is acknowledged. But the Lordship of Christ is not restricted to the church. It is universal in scope, extending beyond his spiritual rule in the hearts of believers, beyond his rule in the church through Word and sacraments, and reaching the outer circumference of creation, including everything that lives and moves in nature and history. All powers—political, economic, social, national, and international—have been in principle submitted to the Lordship of Christ, who exercises his dominion at the right hand of God. The older dogmaticians referred to this as the "rule of power" (*regnum potentiae*). Nineteenth-century German theology, with some twentieth-century Lutheran theologians, have said that this aspect of the Lordship of Christ is exercised from the "left hand of God." They defend it on the basis of Luther's doctrine of the two kingdoms. But this notion of the "left hand of God" is not a concept that can be found in the New Testament. The "left hand" is not a biblical symbol for the way that God relates to the world of history and nature. Instead, God's political rule of power as well as God's reconciling rule of grace are functions of the dominion of Christ who sits at the "right hand" of God. The theology of "the left hand of God" produced a dichotomous nonchristological approach to contemporary social and political ethics and should be replaced, on the basis of the New Testament, by a christocentric theology of the session of Jesus Christ at God's right hand.

The church fathers—Ignatius, Justin, Irenaeus, and Origen—carried forward the New Testament witness to the cosmic Lordship of Christ. All things were created through Christ, and for him and in him all things cohere and have their meaning (Col. 1:16–17). The church fathers taught that invisible powers are working behind the back of all the visible powers on earth. There are powers, principalities, angels, thrones, dominions, authorities, and eons that are the real rulers of history. The church fathers declared, on the basis of the cosmic christology of the New Testament, that all these hierarchies in heaven and on earth have had to succumb to the superior dominion of Christ. The victory of Christ counts against all the invisible superpowers which are the directing forces behind the earthly powers: the nations, the world rulers, the empire, and so on. The *regnum potentiae* of Christ at the right hand of God is one of the foundation stones of a Christian political ethic.

The third aspect of the Lordship of Christ at God's right hand was referred to by the old dogmaticians as the "rule of glory" (*regnum gloriae*). It is the eschatological dimension which can be more clearly dealt with in connection with the expectation of the return of Christ as the future judge of the world.

THE COMING IN GLORY

The Lordship of Christ has an eschatological dimension which makes clear that the world is still struggling in a state of separation from its promised future fulfillment. The glory of Christ and the misery of the world stand in sharpest contrast to each other. The hope that was born at Easter for the world has not yet been realized in history. The hope for the new humanity and the new world still awaits a future in which the victory of Christ over his enemies—sin, death, and the devil—will be established beyond doubt. Primitive Christianity expressed this hope for final victory in the symbol of the coming again of the risen Lord to fulfill the rule of God which Jesus had proclaimed in his earthly ministry. The picture of Jesus returning in the clouds of heaven through which he left the earth in his ascension cannot be taken literally. What it points to, however, is that the world faces an ultimate judgment and that the earthly Jesus is the revelation of the ultimate standard by which the world will be judged. Nobody will escape being judged by the standard of life which Jesus inaugurated in his own ministry. The expectation of the return of Christ in glory is a sober reminder that this life is moving toward ultimate accountability. Jesus is the Lord who will exercise judgment by the authority

6 / THE PERSON OF JESUS CHRIST

of God. Yet Christians face this judgment with hope for themselves and the world, for the eschatological judge is none other than Jesus, who revealed the absolute love and mercy of God. If we ask why Jesus should be the judge in the end, the answer is that Jesus is the essence of what it means to be fully human. Humans will not be judged by a heteronomous law alien to their very being. Jesus is the final revelation of the essence and future of humanity. The return of Christ in glory is awaited as the future realization of the humanity of humankind and the fulfillment of the world, passing through judgment to an eternity in which God will be all in all.

NOTES

1. See the study of the idea of preexistence in the New Testament by R. G. Hamerton-Kelly, *Pre-Existence, Wisdom, and the Son of Man* (Cambridge: At the University Press, 1973).

2. Ian D. Kingston Siggins, *Martin Luther's Doctrine of Christ* (New Haven: Yale University Press, 1970), pp. 194–95.

3. Emil Brunner, *The Mediator*, trans. Olive Wyon (Philadelphia: Westminster Press, 1947), p. 326.

4. Karl Barth, *Church Dogmatics*, vol. 1/2 (Edinburgh: T. & T. Clark, 1936–77), p. 184.

5. Wolfhart Pannenberg, *Jesus—God and Man*, trans. Lewis Wilkins and Duane Priebe (Philadelphia: Westminster Press, 1968), p. 149.

6. Ibid.

7. Ibid.

8. See the most comprehensive study on the virginal birth of Jesus in the primitive Christian traditions by Raymond E. Brown, *The Birth of the Messiah* (New York: Doubleday & Co., 1977).

9. David Griffin, *Process Christology* (Philadelphia: Westminster Press, 1973), p. 12.

10. Rudolf Bultmann, "New Testament and Mythology," in his *Kerygma and Myth*, ed. Hans W. Bartsch (London: SPCK, 1954), p. 41.

11. Pannenberg, *Jesus—God and Man*, p. 99.

12. Paul Althaus, *Die Christliche Wahrheit* (Gütersloh: Bertelsmann, 1948), p. 269. (Translation mine.)

7

The Uniqueness and Universality of Jesus Christ

God has been revealed in the particular history of Jesus Christ, to embrace the universal future of the church and the world. The claim of the gospel is that the uniqueness of Jesus lies in his universal meaning, that this concrete person in history holds in himself the key to the universal fulfillment which God intends for all.

THE HERITAGE OF EXCLUSIVENESS

The true identity of Jesus Christ has been mediated to us in texts and traditions which unanimously confess that he is the exclusive medium of eschatological salvation. Acts 4:12 is the classical locus of this christological exclusiveness: "And there is salvation in no one else, for there is no other name under heaven given among men by which we must be saved." Christian exclusiveness has found several ways of manifesting itself. Traditionally, the Catholic type of exclusivism has focused on the church. "Outside the church there is no salvation." The statement first appeared in one of Cyprian's letters in the third century. It was reiterated in the papal bull *Unam Sanctam* of Boniface VIII in 1302: "We believe that there is one holy catholic and apostolic church . . . outside of which there is no salvation. . . . We declare that it is necessary for salvation for every human creature to be subject to the Roman Pontiff."[1] Traditionally, the Protestant type has felt uncomfortable with the ecclesiocentric form of exclusivism. It has focused instead on faith, quoting passages like John 3:18: "He who believes in him is not condemned; he who does not believe is condemned already, because he has not believed in the name of the only Son of God." Also Rom. 10:17: "So faith comes from what is heard, and what is heard comes by the preaching of Christ."

The heritage of Christian exclusiveness runs deep into the New Testament and dominates the tradition from earliest times to the present. But from the beginning the same tradition has created loopholes to provide people outside the Christian circle with the chance of salvation. Catholics of the most exclusive type conceded that people outside the church can be saved through

6 / THE PERSON OF JESUS CHRIST

the loopholes of "invincible ignorance" or "baptism by desire." Protestants in the older line of dogmatics appealed to 1 Pet. 3:19, which states that Christ preached to the spirits in prison, as proof that people who did not encounter Christ and believe in this life would be given a "second chance" on the threshold of the future life. Sometimes they also talked about the invisible church whose limits are unknown, and thus presumably might also include some "noble pagans." The judgment that reservations will be taken in heaven only for Christians, only for those who accept Christ by faith in this life or belong to his church, has seemed too harsh to be taken in a strictly literal sense.

Currently there are voices raised against every sort of Christian exclusivism, including all the loopholes which continue to reinforce the underlying premise. The question is now whether there is full and equal salvation through the non-Christian religions. The loopholes only provided an exceptional way of salvation. What is said to be needed now is a full acknowledgment of the other major religions as valid ways of salvation. We are living in one world with a plurality of cultures, religions, and ideologies. Either we acknowledge the legitimacy of this pluralism, or we threaten the possibility of living together in a peaceful world. We expect governments, corporations, and other agencies to do their part to cooperate in establishing conditions that drive toward the unity of the human world without diminishing the plurality of its forms. Why should not the religions of the world do their part? Christianity has begun to open up channels of dialogue with people of other religions. But many feel that the exclusivistic premise which it brings to the dialogue clogs the channels and makes a real exchange impossible.

Professor John Hick of Birmingham, England, has taken the lead among Protestants in calling for a "Copernican revolution"[2] which aims to overturn the christological dogma at the bottom of all Christian exclusivism. It is not enough to broaden the way of Christian salvation by speaking with Tillich of a "latent church" or with Rahner of "anonymous Christianity." Those are the convenient modern loopholes. He calls them "epicycles." So Hick goes deeper and lays the axe at the christological roots of exclusivism. He says, "For understood literally the Son of God, God the Son, God-incarnate language implies that God can be adequately known and responded to *only* through Jesus; and the whole religious life of mankind, beyond the stream of Judaic-Christian faith is thus by implication excluded as lying outside the sphere of salvation."[3] Pluralism is compatible with the unity of all humankind if we acknowledge that the various streams of religion in the world carry the same waters of salvation leading to eternal life with God. God is at the center of the universe of faiths; Jesus is only one of the many ways—the Christian way—that leads to God. He is not the one and only Son of God, Lord of the world, and Savior of humankind. Each religion has its own and does the job in its own way. In this way John Hick has rooted out the last vestige of exclusivism.

On the Catholic side the leftwing of Rahner's school has also abandoned the Christian claim that Jesus Christ is "different," "decisive," "unique," "normative," or "final," toppling the pillar on which the traditional claims to exclusiveness lean. For surely it makes no sense to argue that believing in Jesus Christ or belonging to his church are essential for salvation, if he is ultimately only one among many founders pointing the way to God. Paul Knitter has made the clearest case among Catholics for a revision of the traditional claim that Jesus Christ is the one and only Savior of humankind, that he is the once-for-all revelation of God's eschatological salvation in store for the whole world. In "A Critique of Hans Küng's *On Being a Christian*,"[4] Knitter like Hick lays his axe at the roots not only of the christological dogma but also of the apostolic kerygma. His motive is the same: to pave the way for dialogue with other religions that won't be "hamstrung"[5] by the exclusivist mindset. He writes, "Intellectually and psychologically is it not possible to give oneself over wholly to the meaning and message of Jesus and at the same time recognize the possibility that other 'saviors' have carried out the same function for other people?"[6] He answers "yes" and argues "that the claim for Jesus' exclusive uniqueness does not form part of the central assertions of Christian texts."[7] The claim that salvation takes place only in Jesus can be chalked up to "the historically conditioned world view and thought-patterns of the time."[8] Knitter concludes that there is no exclusive claim that belongs to the core of the Christian message. He would agree with Harnack that the exclusive element is not part of the kernel, but only the husk of the gospel.

Far to the right of this antiexclusivist position, we find a new affirmation of the heritage of exclusiveness among the neoevangelicals, who are conducting a vigorous campaign against every form of universalism. The idea that there is salvation in the non-Christian religions is denied point-blank. At Lausanne the evangelicals declared dogmatically that "it is impossible to be a biblical Christian and a universalist simultaneously."[9] They now teach as dogmatic truth and as a criterion of faithfulness to the gospel of Jesus Christ that all those who die or who have died without conscious faith in Jesus Christ are damned to eternal hell. If people have never heard the gospel and have never had a chance to believe, they are lost anyway. The logic of this position is that children who die in infancy are lost, the mentally retarded are lost, all those who have never heard of Christ are lost. Nevertheless, evangelicals cling to this view as the heart of the gospel and the incentive to mission.

THE UNIQUENESS OF JESUS CHRIST

The texts and traditions that tell us about Jesus of Nazareth represent him as the expected Messiah of Israel, God's only Son, the Lord of creation, and

6 / THE PERSON OF JESUS CHRIST

the Savior of all humanity. We have no nonchristological picture of the historical Jesus. Every recollection of his identity is penetrated by an identification that raises his significance to the highest possible power. If one should subtract all the special titles of identification, one would not be left with the identity of Jesus who is really Jesus. One is rather left with the question whether Jesus of Nazareth ever existed or with an empty assertion of his naked historicity. But what of his meaning? What about his true identity?

When John the Baptist wondered about the true identity of Jesus, he asked, "Are you he who is to come, or shall we look for another?" (Matt. 11:3; Luke 7:19). The answer of the early church was clear: Jesus is the One who was to come. He is the Messiah. Similarly, when Jesus asked his disciples on the way to Caesarea Philippi, "Who do men say that I am?", Peter answered, "You are the Christ, the Son of the living God" (Mark 8:27; Matt. 16:16). The New Testament abounds with titles that serve to identify the uniqueness of Jesus. The historical Jesus probably did not designate his true identity by such titles of honor as Christ, Son of God, Lord, Savior, Logos, and so on, but the early church did without any shadow of doubt. These titles were conferred on Jesus in the light of faith in the risen presence of Jesus. They are titles which in the same writings are bestowed on God. Both God and Jesus are spoken of as Savior. Both God and Jesus are spoken of as Lord. Jesus is the Savior because he will save his people from their sins. Jesus is the Lord because God has raised and exalted him above all others. Jesus is the subject of names that are above all other names, because they are the names of God. They speak eloquently of the uniqueness of Jesus.

New Testament theologians argue whether these titles of honor go back to the historical Jesus himself, or whether they have been written back into the Gospel texts from the post-Easter situation of faith. In one sense it does not matter, for both sides must agree that the Jesus of history is represented to us in texts and traditions which describe his uniqueness. He is depicted not as a son of God but as *the* only begotten Son of God, not as *a* savior but as *the* Savior, not as *a* lord but as *the* Lord, and so on. These designations of Jesus as Lord and Savior identify him as the foundation of divine salvation. They are not name tags loosely attached to the personal reality to which they refer. There is no nominalism intended in the transference of high titles of honor to Jesus of Nazareth.

If we strip away the names that are above all the names which generally apply to other human beings, we have no way to speak of the meaning of Jesus. We can speak of him in the symbols of the texts and traditions, or we cannot speak of him at all, unless we fabricate our own image of Jesus and arbitrarily call him what we will. Nothing is clearer in the New Testament and the Christian tradition than the uniqueness of Jesus in whose name alone

THE UNIQUENESS AND UNIVERSALITY OF JESUS CHRIST

there is salvation, before whom every knee should bow and every tongue confess that he is Lord to the glory of God the Father (Phil. 2:10–11).

One of the earliest symbols of Christianity was the fish. In Greek the letters that spelled fish—ΙΧΘΥΣ—represented an ancient christological confession: Jesus Christ Son of God Savior. By what other names can Jesus be known? These are symbols that participate in the reality to which they refer, to use Tillich's definition of a symbol. Christian faith has no knowledge or interest in Jesus as Jesus, minus the names which symbolize his unique meaning. These symbols have a prehistory in the religions of that time, but when transferred to Jesus they crown him with a significance that underscores his uniqueness. They do not mean that Jesus is unique as every individual is unique. Although he is truly human, these titles place him in a class by himself. He is the one and only Christ, or he is not the Christ at all. He is the one and only Son of God, or he is not God's Son at all. He is the one and only Savior, or he is no Savior at all. The exclusive claim is not a footnote to the gospel; it is the gospel itself. Not part of the husk, it is the kernel itself. The answer of the gospel to John the Baptist's question "Are you he who is to come?" is "Yes, and we shall not look for another" (Matt. 11:3).

All the christological titles of the texts and traditions of historic biblical and catholic Christianity intend to lift up the uniqueness of Jesus as the living Christ, the risen Lord, and the eschatological Savior of the world. They alone can legitimate the role that Jesus came to assume as the cultic center in primitive Christian worship. Without these titles that acclaim the exclusive uniqueness of Jesus, he loses the vehicles of interpretation by which he is no mere dead hero of the past, buried in the ruins of his own time and place, but the living presence of God in the flesh. These titles—and they alone—tell us what the earliest believers in Jesus thought he was all about. They reveal the true identity of Jesus; at the core of this revelation is the exclusive uniqueness of Jesus in relation to God and his coming kingdom, in relation to the church, and in relation to the entire world of history and nature. If we do not use these christological titles as our linguistic access to the knowledge of Jesus' identity and meaning, then we shall have to find some other way of speaking about him, unless we are to remain silent. Who would we then say that he is, if he is not the one whom the earliest texts and traditions identify as the only true embodiment of God's Word in history?

What is the essence of the uniqueness of Jesus? It does not lie in the fact that he was an historical individual who lived once upon a time in Palestine. Every one of us is a unique individual in the sense that none of us has a duplicate. But the uniqueness of Jesus is *sui generis*. He died as a unique historical individual at one time and place, under Pontius Pilate just outside the gate, but he was raised to be the living presence of God in every new

6 / THE PERSON OF JESUS CHRIST

age and every strange place. The issue of Jesus' uniqueness finally has to do with the resurrection. "God raised him up, having loosed the pangs of death" (Acts 2:24).

When we confess the uniqueness of Jesus, we do not mean merely that he was a concrete individual human being, which he was. We mean that he is the concrete embodiment of universal meaning. The true identity of Jesus was revealed to his disciples only after the resurrection, or at least only then could they begin to understand what he had been disclosing step by step along the way. If we could turn back the reel of history to the days before Easter, if we could find some tapes or pictures of the man Jesus, if we could read the obituaries that appeared in the *Galilean Gazette*, we would hardly gain a deeper insight into the true identity of Jesus. The true identity of Jesus is something which in the last analysis "flesh and blood" cannot reveal to us. More historical information will not solve the riddle of Jesus' personal identity. If people look into the abundant texts and traditions of the Christian past and conclude that Jesus is not the one he is said to be, they may invent other names and labels to transfer to Jesus, but in doing so they are not adding to the fund of our knowledge about the historical Jesus, but only telling the world where they personally stand in relation to him. For the christological titles which the apostles applied to Jesus were not projected on an objective screen of history. They were born in the struggles of following Jesus, of preaching the kerygma of his cross and resurrection and taking the gospel to the gentiles. A christological title is a dialectical statement that lives in the polar tension between subject and object. It says something about Jesus, but also about the person making the confession. No one can call Jesus Lord unless he or she has been grasped by the Holy Spirit (1 Cor. 12:3). The statement is not a product of objectifying analysis. Peter's confession "You are the Christ, the Son of the living God" was an ecstatic statement, a miracle of the mind (Tillich).

The true identity of Jesus can be acknowledged only by faith in him as the risen Lord and the living Christ. We do not expect that anyone will confess the uniqueness of Jesus, in the special sense implied by the sum of the christological titles, by means of a reconstruction of the historical Jesus. That Jesus is dead and buried and will always remain sealed in the tomb to people who do not believe that he now lives freely beyond the limits of his own earthly fate.

THE UNIVERSALITY OF JESUS CHRIST

The uniqueness of Jesus belongs to the core of the Christian gospel. What is unique about Jesus, however, is precisely his universal meaning. This par-

THE UNIQUENESS AND UNIVERSALITY OF JESUS CHRIST

ticular and concrete man, Jesus of Nazareth, is unique because of his universal significance. His uniqueness lies in his universality. If Jesus is the Savior, he is the universal Savior. I cannot confine him to being my personal Savior, merely the focus of my own experience of God.

We are back to the beginning. If Jesus is the unique and universal Savior, how can there be a dialogue with other religions? Are not Christians bound to say that theirs is the only way of salvation, that non-Christians will be saved either by being evangelized here and now or by some loophole or other? We seem to be confronted with a dilemma. If Jesus is the unique and universal Savior, there is no salvation in the non-Christian religions. If there is salvation in the non-Christian religions, then Jesus is not the unique and universal Savior. Theology is facing this dilemma.

Christians should not be afraid of dialogue with other religions. The religions are part of the universal context in which the true identity of Jesus must find new expression. The christological titles did not descend on Jesus all at once and ready-made. There was a development in which new titles were discovered for Jesus in the hermeneutical process of transmitting the traditional texts within the horizon of new contexts. Every christological title had to be born again in history, in the process of encountering the story of Jesus in a new religious context. We do not yet fully know how we shall confess Jesus in the future of dialogue with other religions. We shall continue to confess him in the language of our familiar texts and traditions. But the universality of Jesus means that he will live in the medium of symbols which may still seem strange to us. Churches and theologians are calling us to a new dialogue with the world religions. It is therefore urgent that we know what we mean by the uniqueness and universality of Jesus Christ.

We have spoken about the uniqueness of Jesus, guided by the import of the major christological titles applied to him after Easter. But how shall we understand the universality of Jesus?

Christians believe in the universality of salvation in Jesus' name. It is God's will that all people shall be saved and come to the knowledge of the truth (2 Tim. 2:4). Evangelicals generally accept universal salvation in this sense, as valid in principle for all people. But they restrict salvation in the end to those who actually hear the gospel and put their faith in Christ.[10] Under this restriction the rift that has been opened up in the world through sin will widen to an eternal chasm, splitting the one world of God's creation into two unreconcilable halves, only God's half will be much smaller than the devil's, in fact, only a remnant of the whole. There is not much for the angels to sing about, if the evangelicals get what they expect—a heaven sparsely filled with only card-carrying Christians.

Biblical universalism transcends the particularist eschatology of the evangelicals. There are stern warnings in the New Testament threatening eternal

6 / THE PERSON OF JESUS CHRIST

perdition. There are reservations; there are qualifications of the universal hope. But these are addressed more to those inside with apparently the right credentials than to those outside. "This people honors me with their lips, but their heart is far from me" (Matt. 15.8; Mark 7:6). "Not every one who says to me, 'Lord, Lord,' shall enter the kingdom of heaven" (Matt. 7:21). The New Testament warns of the spiritual danger of using the right evangelical words and ecclesiastical doctrines as the basis of trust and hope. There is spiritual danger in reducing the power and future of the universal Christ to the pinhole size of the believer's faith or the church's confession here and now.

New Testament universalism, however, is always a predicate of the uniqueness of Jesus Christ, not a metaphysical attribute of the world in process (as in the Origenistic doctrine of *apokatastasis ton panton*), nor of a saving potential inherent in the world religions, nor of an existential possibility universally available to every person in a moment of decision. The uniqueness Christians claim for Jesus as World-Savior lies in the revelation of his eschatological identity, constituted by his resurrection victory over death as the "last enemy" of humankind. The uniqueness of Jesus is not a function of our Christian *blik*. It belongs to him by virtue of his enthronement as the Lord of the coming kingdom. A particularist eschatology can be constructed only by picking particular passages and choosing to ignore others.

What about the universalist thrust in the Pauline theology? As in Adam all men die, so also in Christ shall all be made alive" (1 Cor. 15:22). "For in him [Christ] all the fulness of God was pleased to dwell, and through him to reconcile to himself all things, whether on earth or in heaven, making peace by the blood of his cross" (Col. 1:19-20). "For he has made known to us in all wisdom and insight the mystery of his will, according to his purpose which he set forth in Christ as a plan for the fulness of time, to unite all things in him, things in heaven and things in earth" (Eph. 1:9-10). "That at the name of Jesus every knee should bow, in heaven and on earth and under the earth, and every tongue confess that Jesus Christ is Lord, to the glory of God the Father" (Phil. 2:10-11). "When all things are subjected to him, then the Son himself will also be subjected to him who put all things under him, that God may be everything to every one" (1 Cor. 15:28). "And he is the expiation for our sins, and not for ours only but also for the sins of the whole world" (1 John 2:2). These verses create a total impression of the universalizing tendencies in the New Testament.

Christian theologians are debating the question whether there is salvation in other religions and taking sides on the issue, without first making clear the model of salvation they have in mind. What is the salvation theologians expect to find or not to find in other religions? Vastly different things are meant by salvation. If salvation is whatever you call it, there is no reason for a Christian to deny that there is salvation in other religions. We may speak of salvation on two levels, phenomenologically and theologically. On a purely phenomenological level, there are numerous models of salvation and there are ways of delivering each of the models and making them work. When the nomads needed a land for their salvation, they were promised a land by their God, and they got it, and have suffered ever since. When the slaves in Egypt needed deliverance from oppression for their salvation, God called Moses to lead the exodus out of Egypt. When the wandering people of God needed food for their salvation from hunger, God supplied them with daily manna from above. And the history of salvation went on, creating different models for its expression, but always pointing forward to new dimensions generated by the experience of fundamental lack. Land is needed, but it is not enough. Freedom is needed, but it is not enough. Food is needed, but it is not enough.

If we are told there is salvation in the other religions, there is no *a priori* reason to deny the claim. It depends on what is meant by salvation. If salvation is the experience of illumination, then the Buddha can save. If salvation is the experience of union with God, then Hinduism can save. If salvation is being true to the ancestors, then Shintoism can save. If salvation is revolution against the overlords and equality for the people, then Maoism can save. If salvation is liberation from poverty and oppression, then Marxism can save. If salvation is psychological health, there is salvation not only outside the church but outside the religions as well. If salvation is striving for humanization, for development, for wholeness, for justice, for peace, for freedom, for the whole earth, for whatnot, there is salvation in the other religions, in the quasi-religions and in the secular ideologies. The reason Christians are confused and have appeared so smug about salvation is that they imagined they held a monopoly on salvation. Then when they have discovered virtues and values that match or excel what they find among Christians, they are prepared to accept the doctrine of salvation in non-Christian religions, perhaps even to the point of surrendering every version of the *solus Christus*.

On a theological level, salvation is not whatever you want to call it, the fulfillment of every need or the compensation for every lack. We do not deny that we may also speak of salvation in this extended phenomenological sense, with the warning that it has generated much of the confusion in which our topic languishes. Salvation in the Bible is a promise that God offers the world on the horizon of our expectation of personal and universal death. The gospel is the power of God unto salvation because it promises to break open the vicious cycle of death. Death is the power that draws every living thing into its circle. Here we cannot enter into the mystery of death. But if anyone denies the reality of death and its power to insinuate itself as the eschaton of all life, which threatens the very conditions of the possibility of meaningful existence, we should take a patient "wait and see" attitude. It is just a question of time before death will punctuate everybody's personal story with its own

6 / THE PERSON OF JESUS CHRIST

annihilating force. We cannot derive a final meaning for life on this side of death. We can gain the partial salvations we are willing to pay for, but no techniques of salvation can succeed in buying off death.

Salvation in the New Testament is what God has done to death in the resurrection of Jesus. Salvation is what happens to you and me and the whole world in spite of death, if only the resurrection of Jesus means what the apostolic kerygma and the catholic dogma have interpreted it to mean. The story of salvation is a drama of death and resurrection, whatever other human personal and social problems the word might trade on. The gospel is the announcement that in one man's history death is no longer the eschaton, but was only the second-to-last thing. It has now become past history. Death lies behind Jesus, qualifying him to lead the procession from death to new life. Since death is what separates humankind from God in the end, only that power which transcends death can liberate humanity for eternal life with God. This is the meaning of salvation in the biblical Christian sense. It is eschatological salvation, because the God who raised Jesus from the dead has overcome death as the final eschaton of life. Our final salvation lies in the eschatological future when our own death will be put behind us. This does not mean that there is no salvation in the present, no realized aspect of salvation. It means that the salvation we enjoy now is like borrowing from the future, living now as though our future could already be practiced in the present, because of our union with the risen Christ through faith and hope.

Theologians who speak of salvation in the non-Christian religions should tell us if this is the same salvation which God has promised the world by raising Jesus from the dead. The resurrection gospel is the criterion of the meaning of salvation in the New Testament sense. When Chistians enter into dialogue with people of other religions, they must do their utmost to communicate what they mean by the assertion that Jesus lives, and explain how this gospel intersects the hopes and fears of every person whose fate is to anticipate death as the final eschaton. If the dialogue should show that other religions are not much moved by the problem of death, that the problem of death is limited to a particular way of viewing the human predicament, we would have to say that the encounter with Christianity itself becomes the occasion for everyone to see that the problem of death arises out of the structure of existence itself. The gospel falls on the human situation and illuminates the universal existential problem. This is the hypothesis that Christians bring into interreligious dialogue.

The new challenge to christology is to speak of the identity of Jesus Christ in the context of the world religions and secular culture. In the past, theology has dealt with the religions from afar, giving us a Christian interpretation of the non-Christian religions from a ready-made theological point of view.

THE UNIQUENESS AND UNIVERSALITY OF JESUS CHRIST

In a sense this is all we can do prior to the event of dialogue. But if we really believe that the uniqueness of Jesus lies in his universality, that his identity is always being mediated through the concrete events of history, then we should be open to exploring what the non-Christian religions can contribute to our understanding of the universal identity of Jesus Christ. The history of the religions once contributed all the christological titles to the interpretation of the Jesus-event. Some of them were rooted in the ancient Hebrew traditions, others not, but all of them were transformed in the process of being assimilated to the traditions about Jesus. That process is still going on in the openness of world history, engendered by the universal missionary witness to Jesus as the Christ, the Lord and Savior of the world.

The identity of Jesus cannot be limited to the particular contexts of our past. Christology is not static. New contexts have made it possible for new meanings to blossom on old texts. They relate to the concrete struggles of people for life, health, wholeness, fulfillment, salvation. In India, Jesus is pictured by some as the Avatar. To us this means practically nothing, but in India it may mean a great deal. In many parts of the Third World, Jesus is the liberator. Liberation has become the focal image of a whole new christology. To us it may also mean something, but not exactly the same as to people suffering the conditions of poverty, exploitation, and oppression. In the patristic era Jesus was called the Logos, and that carried a metaphysical meaning quite different from the same word in the Gospel of John. In Nazi Germany, Martin Niemöller preached about Jesus as the true *Führer*. In the context of Western atheism and the trend to depersonalization in technological society, Dorothy Soelle has animated the theme of Jesus as the "representative." Similar titles such as "advocate," "delegate," and "deputy" have been used to speak of the meaning of Jesus for modern people, and perhaps soon, if not already, someone in the Far East will suggest "chairman." Every culture has to ask of Jesus in its own way, "Are you the One who is to come, or do we look for another?" Every people will have to answer, "Who do you say that I am?" in a language they can understand. The crucifix of Jesus as a tortured Peruvian Indian on the cover of Gustavo Gutierrez's *Theology of Liberation* could not have been sculpted in our part of the world.

The point we have been making is that the exclusive uniqueness of Jesus, mediated by the texts and traditions that announce his resurrection as the living Lord, drives us to discover his universal significance, not in another world after this one but in the real contexts of ongoing history. His true identity is still being disclosed in the encounter of the gospel with the world religions. The gospel does not meet the world religions on a one-way street, giving them the traditional symbols of christology and receiving nothing back. The dialogue will be a two-way street, in which the condition of openness to the other

6 / THE PERSON OF JESUS CHRIST

religions will be motivated by knowledge that they also somehow speak of Jesus Christ. The Old Testament is the paradigm case of how one religion of another time and place can speak of Jesus Christ in a proleptic way. If the apostles and the church fathers could find anticipations of Christ in the Old Testament, we have a right to expect a similar thing in the texts and traditions of other religions. For God is not without witnesses in these religions.

We have steered a course between the Scylla of an evangelicalism without the universality of Jesus Christ and the Charybdis of a universalism without the uniqueness of Jesus Christ. But ours is not essentially a middle position that combines elements at random from the right and the left. Rather, the right and the left are splinters of a holistic vision of the eschatological Christ whose uniqueness lies in his concrete universality. This universality is being worked out in the world mission of the church. The ultimate horizon of this historically mediated universality is hope for an eternal restitution of all things in God. We have a universal *hope* in Christ, not a universal gnosis. It is a hope that engenders the actions of witness and mission in history, not a knowledge that pretends to know the final outcome of things in advance. It is a hope that the Lord of the church will finally rule as the Lord of the world, inclusive of its religions. Meanwhile, we can witness and work as though God is at work behind the backs of the plurality of world religions, pushing them forward into a final unity that has become proleptically incarnate for all in Jesus Christ. There are not two ways of salvation.[11] There is one salvation and one way of salvation. That is the eschatological salvation valid for all through the One who came that all might find life, who died that the world might be reconciled, who was raised that hope might live for the victory of God and the restitution of all things in God.

NOTES

1. Quoted in Robert L. Wilken, "The Making of a Phrase," *Dialog* 12 (Summer 1973): 174.
2. John Hick, *God and the Universe of Faiths* (New York: Macmillan Co., 1973), pp. 121ff.
3. John Hick, "Jesus and the World Religions," in *The Myth of God Incarnate*, ed. John Hick (Philadelphia: Westminster Press, 1977), p. 179.
4. Paul F. Knitter, "A Critique of Hans Küng's *On Being a Christian*," *Horizons* 5/2 (1978): 151–64.
5. Ibid., p. 156.
6. Ibid., p. 153.
7. Ibid.
8. Ibid., p. 154.

9. *Let the Earth Hear His Voice,* ed. J. D. Douglas (Minneapolis: World Wide Publications, 1975), p. 76.

10. See Harold Lindsell, "Universalism," in *Let the Earth Hear His Voice,* pp. 1206–13.

11. The notion of two ways of salvation has been clearly proposed by H. R. Schlette, *Colloquium salutis—Christen und Nichtchristen heute* (Cologne, 1965); also "Einige Thesen zum Selbstverständnis der Theologie angesichts der Religionen," *Gott in Welt II,* ed. J. B. Metz (Frieburg: Herder Verlag, 1964), pp. 306–16.

Christian Dogmatics

Contributors

Carl E. Braaten is Professor of Systematic Theology at the Lutheran School of Theology at Chicago, Illinois.

Gerhard O. Forde is Professor of Systematic Theology at Luther Northwestern Theological Seminary in St. Paul, Minnesota.

Philip J. Hefner is Professor of Systematic Theology at the Lutheran School of Theology at Chicago.

Robert W. Jenson is Professor of Religion at St. Olaf College, Northfield, Minnesota.

Hans Schwarz is Professor of Protestant Theology at the University of Regensburg, Federal Republic of Germany.

Paul R. Sponheim is Professor of Systematic Theology at Luther Northwestern Theological Seminary in St. Paul, Minnesota.

VOLUME 2

Christian Dogmatics

Carl E. Braaten, *editor*
Gerhard O. Forde
Philip J. Hefner

Robert W. Jenson, *editor*
Hans Schwarz
Paul R. Sponheim

FORTRESS PRESS   PHILADELPHIA

Biblical quotations, unless otherwise noted, are from the Revised Standard Version of the Bible, copyright 1946, 1952, © 1971, 1973 by the Division of Christian Education of the National Council of the Churches of Christ in the U.S.A. and are used by permission.

COPYRIGHT © 1984 BY FORTRESS PRESS

All rights reserved. No part of this publication may be reproduced, stored in a retrieval system, or transmitted in any form or by any means, electronic, mechanical, photocopying, recording, or otherwise, without the prior permission of the copyright owner.

Library of Congress Cataloging in Publication Data
Main entry under title:
Christian dogmatics.

Includes index.
1. Theology, Doctrinal. 2. Lutheran Church—Doctrines. I. Braaten, Carl E., 1929– II. Jenson, Robert W.
BT75.2.C48 1984   230'.41   83-48007
ISBN 0-8006-0712-0 (set)
ISBN 0-8006-0703-1 (v. 1)
ISBN 0-8006-0704-X (v. 2)

Printed in the United States of America   1-704

94 93 92 91 90   4 5 6 7 8 9 10

Contents

VOLUME 1

Preface by the Editors

FIRST LOCUS
Prolegomena to Christian Dogmatics
by Carl E. Braaten

Introduction

1. Theology and Dogmatics
   What is Theology?
   The Task of Apologetics
   Method in Theology

2. The Heritage of Dogmatics
   The Discipline
   The Ancient Church
   The Middle Ages
   The Reformation
   Protestant Orthodoxy
   The Dissolution of Dogmatics in Pietism and the Enlightenment
   The Revival of Dogmatics in the Nineteenth Century
   The State of Dogmatics in the Twentieth Century

3. The Fundamentals of Dogmatics
   The Concept of Dogma
   The Confessional Principle
   The Fundamentals of Dogmatics

4. The Holy Scriptures
   The Authority of Scripture
   The Interpretation of Scripture
   The Problem of Scripture Today

CONTENTS

SECOND LOCUS
The Triune God
by Robert W. Jenson

Introduction

1. The Triune Name of God
   The Sense of "God"
   Israel's Identification of God
   Identifying God in the New Testament
   "Father, Son, and Holy Spirit" as Proper Name
   The Triune Name as Dogma

2. The Trinitarian Logic and Rhetoric
   The Trinitarian Logic
   The Hebrew Scriptures as the Root of Trinitarianism
   Primary Trinitarianism
   The Dogmatic Status of Primary Trinitarianism

3. The Nicene-Constantinopolitan Dogma
   The God of the Greeks
   The Initial Christianizing of Hellenism
   The Arian Crisis
   Nicaea and Constantinople

4. The One and the Three
   The Eastern Trinitarian Terminology
   The Three Hypostases
   The One Being
   The Western Version
   The Athanasian Creed
   Vicissitudes of Western Trinitarianism

5. The Being of God
   The Metaphysical Questions
   God as an Event
   God as Person
   God as Spirit
   God as Discourse

6. The Attributes of God
   The Necessity of the Doctrine

The Method of Derivation
"Jesus Is Risen": Attributes for the Predicate
"Jesus Is Risen": Attributes for the Subject

THIRD LOCUS
The Knowledge of God
by Paul R. Sponheim

Introduction

1. The Reality and Revelation of God
   The Self-Revelation of God
   God as the World's Ground and Goal
   The Legitimation and Limitation of the Knowledge of God

2. The Reception and Recognition of Revelation
   The Experience of World, Self, and God
   Knowledge as Paradigm, Parable, and Prophecy

3. God's Call and the Human Question about the Ground of Life
   The Divine Incognito: The Real, the Beautiful, and the Good
   Human Awareness: Argument and Adoration

4. The Human Quest and God's Free Answer
   Human Intentionality and Historical Ambiguity
   Teleological Religion and Divine Decisiveness
   God's Justification and Human Responsibility

FOURTH LOCUS
The Creation
by Philip J. Hefner

Introduction

1. The Biblical Witness to Creation
   The Form of the Biblical Witness
   The Substance of the Biblical Witness: The Old Testament
   The Substance of the Biblical Witness: The New Testament

CONTENTS

2. The Creation of the World
   The Nature of the Claim
   God and the World: Issues for Creation Arising from God's Nature
   Creation Out of Nothing ("*ex nihilo*")
   Contemporary Challenges and Contributions to the Doctrine

3. The Human Being
   The Question of Human Destiny
   The Human Being as Created Co-Creator
   The Primeval Condition ("*status integritatis*")
   The Imago Dei
   Spirit and Matter in the Human Creature
   The Fall and Original Sin ("*status corruptionis*")
   Restoration
   Challenges to Christian Anthropology

4. The Continuing Work of Creation
   Historical Survey
   Perennial Concerns of the Doctrine of Providence

5. Challenges to the Ongoing Doctrinal Task
   Credible Doctrine in Every Situation
   Creation and the Concept of Evolution
   Evil and the Reliability of the Created Processes

FIFTH LOCUS
Sin and Evil
by Paul R. Sponheim

Introduction

1. The Nature of Sin
   The Object of Sin
   The Agent of Sin
   The Efficacy of Sin

2. The Origin of Sin
   Creation and Fall
   The Goodness and Integrity of Creation
   The Possibility and Actuality of Sin

CONTENTS

3. The Effect of Sin
   Sinner and Creature
   Bondage and Responsibility

4. Metaphysical and Natural Evil
   Finitude
   Suffering

5. The Work of God against Evil
   The Continuity of God
   The Decisiveness of God
   The Directivity of God

SIXTH LOCUS
The Person of Jesus Christ
by Carl E. Braaten

Introduction

1. The Nature and Method of Christology
   What Is Christology?
   History, Dogmatics, and Faith
   The Starting Point of Christology

2. The Historical Jesus and the Kingdom of God
   Jesus' Expectation of the Kingdom of God
   The Genesis of Christology in the New Testament

3. Classical Christology and Its Subsequent Criticism
   The Identification of Jesus with God
   Christological Heresies
   From the Creed of Chalcedon to the Formula of Concord
   Criticism of the Dogma

4. The True Humanity of Jesus Christ
   The Historicity of Jesus Christ
   The Humanity of Jesus Christ
   The Identity of the Earthly Jesus and the Risen Christ
   Jesus Christ as the Eschatological One

CONTENTS

5. The True Divinity of Jesus Christ
   The Story of God Incarnate
   The Historicity of God
   The Divinity of Christ
   An Ontological Interpretation of the Incarnation

6. The Humiliation and Exaltation of Jesus Christ
   The Preexistence of Christ
   The Virgin Birth
   The Crucifixion of Jesus
   Jesus' Descent into Hell
   The Resurrection
   The Ascension
   The Session at the Right Hand of God
   The Coming in Glory

7. The Uniqueness and Universality of Jesus Christ
   The Heritage of Exclusiveness
   The Uniqueness of Jesus Christ
   The Universality of Jesus Christ

VOLUME 2

SEVENTH LOCUS
The Work of Christ
by Gerhard O. Forde
1

Introduction	5
1. The Shape of the Tradition	11
The Scriptural Tradition	
Vicarious Satisfaction of Divine Justice	
The Triumph of Divine Love	
Victory over the Tyrants	
2. Luther's Theology of the Cross	47
The Debate over Luther's View	
The Reversal of Direction	
Critical Estimates	
3. Reconciliation with God	65
Cur Deus Homo?	
The Necessity for Atonement	
4. Atonement as Actual Event	79
Toward a New Understanding of Sacrifice	
The "Accident"	

EIGHTH LOCUS
The Holy Spirit
by Robert W. Jenson
101

Introduction	105
1. The Spirit That Spoke by the Prophets	109
The Hebrew Scriptures	
The New Testament	
The Creedal Tradition	

CONTENTS

2. Pneumatological Soteriology   125
   The Doctrine of Grace
   Justification by Faith
   Predestination

3. Spirit-Discourse as the Church's Self-interpretation   143
   Ecclesial Christology
   The Spirit and God
   The Spirit and the Letter
   The Spirit and the Word
   The Spirit and History

4. Cosmic Spirit   165
   The Logic of Cosmic Pneumatology
   The Freedom of History
   The Spontaneity of Natural Process
   The Beauty of All Things

NINTH LOCUS
The Church
By Philip J. Hefner
179

Introduction   183

1. The Doctrine of the Church—Focus and Challenges   187
   The Trinitarian Context for the Doctrine of the Church
   Challenges Growing Out of the Church's Embodiment
   The Challenge to Correlate the Faith of the Church and Our
      Experience of the Church
   The Impossibility of Doctrinal Finality

2. The Being of the Church   203
   The Church's Own Testimony: One, Holy, Catholic, and Apostolic
   Significant Images from the Tradition: People of God and Body of Christ
   Models That Summarize the Theological Tradition: Institution,
      Mystical Communion, Sacrament, Herald, Servant
   The Being of the Church in Light of Its Origins

3. Basic Elements of the Church's Life   223
   Marks of the Church

    Ministry
    Liturgy and Sacraments
    Preaching and Teaching
    Community of Love and Care of Souls
    Mission
    Church Order or Organization
    The Church's Concreteness as Source of Theological Truth
    The Concept of Adiaphora

4. The Church and the Kingdom of God   243
    Possibilities for Relating Church and Kingdom of God
    The Church Transparent to the Kingdom

TENTH LOCUS
The Means of Grace
by Hans Schwarz and Robert W. Jenson
249

Introduction   253

Part One: The Word
by Hans Schwarz
255

1. The Biblical Understanding of the Word of God   257
    The Word as the Means of God's Self-Disclosure
    The History-Making Power of God's Word
    Jesus Christ as God's Final Word

2. The Dynamics of God's Word   269
    The Judging and Liberating Word: Law and Gospel
    The Word as Guidance: "Third Use" and Penance
    The Dialogical Word: Prayer and Liturgy
    The Empirical Word: Miracles

Part Two: The Sacraments
by Robert W. Jenson
289

3. Sacraments of the Word   291
    Commands
    Promises

CONTENTS

    Visible Words
    Fact and Meaning
    Actual Liturgy

4. Baptism   315
    The Command
    The Promises
    Regeneration
    The Integrity of Baptism
    The Uses of Baptism

5. The Supper   337
    The Command
    The Authenticity of the Supper
    The Promises
    Eucharist
    Ego Berengarius . . .

6. The Return to Baptism   367
    Rites of the Spirit
    Penance
    Ordination
    Healing
    Marriage

ELEVENTH LOCUS
Christian Life
by Gerhard O. Forde
391

Introduction   395

1. Justification   399
    Justification by Grace
    Justification by Faith
    Law, Gospel, and Conscience

2. Justification and Sanctification   425
    The Separation of Sanctification from Justification
    The Unity of Justification and Sanctification

3. Justification and This World 445
   Justification and the Law
   The Self as God's Creature
   This World as God's Creation

4. Justification Today 461
   The Question of Relevance
   Relevance: The Life of the Individual
   Relevance: The World Vision

TWELFTH LOCUS
Eschatology
by Hans Schwarz
471

Introduction 475

1. The Biblical View of the Future 481
   A Definition
   The Nascent Eschatology of the Old Testament
   The Eschatological Horizon of the New Testament

2. Continuing Tensions in the History of Eschatology 501
   The Gradual Transformation
   The Enthusiastic Fervor

3. Major Currents in Christian Eschatology 513
   The Tension between Promise and Fulfillment
   The Emphasis on the Individual Person
   The Emphasis on the Corporate Dimension
   The Cosmic Aspect of Eschatology

4. Secular Options 541
   Existentialism
   Marxist Communism
   Secular Humanism

5. The Content of Christian Hope 555
   The Starting Point of Christian Eschatology
   Death and Resurrection
   The Last Judgment
   Parousia and the Kingdom of God

CONTENTS

Indexes 589
   Index of Names
   Index of Subjects

Abbreviations in Volume 2

The abbreviations used in this volume, as given below, are with slight variations based on Siegfried Schwertner, *Internationales Abkürzungsverzeichnis für Theologie und Grenzgebiete* (Berlin and New York: Walter de Gruyter, 1974).

AASF	Annales academia scientiarum Fennicae
AGTL	Arbeiten zur Geschichte und Theologie des Luthertums
AHC	*Annuarium historiae conciliorum.* Amsterdam, 1969ff.
BC	*The Book of Concord: The Confessions of the Evangelical Lutheran Church.* Translated and edited by Theodore G. Tappert. Philadelphia: Fortress Press, 1959.
BHH	*Biblisch-historisches Handwörterbuch.* 3 vols. Ed. Bo Reicke and Leonhard Rost. Göttingen, 1962–66.
CR	*Corpus reformatorum.* Berlin, 1834ff.
CTM	*Concordia Theological Monthly*
EvTh	*Evangelische Theologie*
FL	Fontana Library
HDG	*Handbuch der Dogmengeschichte.* Freiburg, 1956ff.
Interp.	*Interpretation: A Journal of Bible and Theology*
KuD	*Kerygma und Dogma*
LW	American Edition of *Luther's Works.* St. Louis: Concordia Publishing House; Philadelphia: Fortress Press, 1955–
NPNF	*A Select Library of the Nicene and Post-Nicene Fathers of the Christian Church.* Oxford, 1887ff.
RGG³	*Die Religion in Geschichte und Gegenwart.* 3d ed. Tübingen, 1956–65.
TDNT	*Theological Dictionary of the New Testament.* 10 vols. Edited by Gerhard Kittel and Gerhard Friedrich. Grand Rapids, 1964ff.
THAT	*Theologisches Handwörterbuch zum Alten Testament.* Edited by Ernst Jenni and Claus Westermann. Munich, 1971ff.
ThLz	*Theologische Literaturzeitung*
TS	*Theological Studies*

ABBREVIATIONS IN VOLUME 2

TU	*Texte und Untersuchungen zur Geschichte der altchristlichen Literatur.* Berlin, 1882ff.
UUA	Uppsala universtets arsskrift
UnSa	Unam Sanctam
VigChr	*Vigiliae Christianae*
WA	*D. Martin Luthers Werke.* Kritische Gesamtausgabe. Weimar, 1883ff.
WA Br	*D. Martin Luthers Werke.* Briefwechsel. Weimar, 1930ff.
WA DB	*D. Martin Luthers Werke.* Deutsche Bible. Weimar, 1906ff.
ZKTh	*Zeitschrift für katholische Theologie*
ZThK	*Zeitschrift für Theologie und Kirche*
ZNW	*Zeitschrift für die neutestamentliche Wissenschaft*

SEVENTH LOCUS

The Work of Christ

GERHARD O. FORDE

THE WORK OF CHRIST

Introduction

1. The Shape of the Tradition
   The Scriptural Tradition
   Vicarious Satisfaction of Divine Justice
   The Triumph of Divine Love
   Victory over the Tyrants

2. Luther's Theology of the Cross
   The Debate over Luther's View
   The Reversal of Direction
   Critical Estimates

3. Reconciliation with God
   Cur Deus Homo?
   The Necessity for Atonement

4. Atonement as Actual Event
   Toward a New Understanding of Sacrifice
   The "Accident"

Introduction

> Therefore, if any one is in Christ, he is a new creation; the old has passed away, behold, the new has come. All this is from God, who through Christ reconciled us to himself and gave us the ministry of reconciliation; that is, in Christ God was reconciling the world to himself, not counting their trespasses against them, and entrusting to us the message of reconciliation. So we are ambassadors for Christ, God making his appeal through us. We beseech you on behalf of Christ, be reconciled to God. For our sake he made him to be sin who knew no sin, so that in him we might become the righteousness of God. (2 Cor. 5:17–21)

So reads a central New Testament passage on the work of Christ which can stand as a theme for this *locus*. We are concerned here with what God did in Jesus Christ, with the *work* rather than the person of Christ. The distinction cannot be made absolutely. In the broadest sense, Christ is what he does and does what he is. Dogmatic convention has made the distinction, however, and it is useful to continue it, if for no other reason than that so much curiosity and effort are invested usually in the dogma of Christ's person that his work would be shunted off into a few remarks and footnotes were the two doctrines treated together. So with the caveat that person and work should not and cannot ultimately be separated, we treat here that part of the dogmatic tradition which has dealt with the work of Christ.

There is no official dogma of the work of Christ—not in the sense in which one could speak of the dogmas of the Trinity, of the person of Christ, or even of justification in the churches of the Reformation. At best, one can speak of certain dominant doctrines, views, or motifs in different epochs. Yet the tradition bears witness to the tenacity with which the church has accorded a central place to Christ's work. The churches of the Reformation, for instance, have looked on that work as the "chief article" on which everything rests,[1] no doubt because of its importance for the doctrine of justification. To the Augsburg Confession, Christ "was crucified, died and was buried in order to be a sacrifice not only for original sin but also for all other sins and to propitiate God's wrath."[2]

The statement from the Augsburg Confession points to the major question for this *locus*: *Cur deus homo?* Why did God become a human person in the particular way manifest in the actual story of Jesus? What is accomplished

7 / THE WORK OF CHRIST

thereby? What does Jesus do? We are concerned about the action and the passion of Jesus and what results from them, as distinguished from his being. Why must he be crucified and raised? If it is a doing, a work of Christ, and not just a being with which we are concerned, then it must have some result, some effect. What is that effect, and why is there just this form of doing to achieve it?

Central throughout the discussion is the question of God's relation to the doing. Does God in Jesus do it for us, or does Jesus do it for God on our behalf? Is God propitiated, satisfied, or in some way altered by the event? Is God wrathful? Does God "need" Christ's work to become merciful? Or does God act on us through the event, changing us or the situation in which we find ourselves? Does God need the cross, or do we? Who is the real obstacle to reconciliation? God? Humans? Or some others—demons, perhaps?

The dogmatic tradition of the church has attempted to answer the question posed by Christ's work by means of various "theories," "pictures," "models," or "motifs" of atonement. The very proliferation of such patterns of thought has itself become a problem for dogmatics and poses a second question for this *locus*: What is or should be the relationship between these patterns and the thing itself, the actual story of Jesus? It seems fair to say that considerable confusion reigns. Since the time of Anselm the dominant theory in the West has been some version of "vicarious satisfaction"—the so-called objective view, also called the "Latin," or "penal" view. Christ satisfies what is demanded for salvation instead of us, thus "objectively" changing God. Yet such a view enjoys at best an uneasy dominance. Whenever it is propounded, opponents protest. Anselm had Abelard. Protestant orthodoxy had Socinus. Revivalism and biblicism in the nineteenth century had liberal theology. Opponents press the central question already stated: Does God have to be satisfied? Is God not always a God of love and mercy?

For at least a century and a half there has been a sustained polemic against vicarious satisfaction. Yet also the various subjective theories usually fail to convince. Termed "subjective" because they propose that we, the subjects, are changed rather than God, such theories are usually charged with failure to take divine judgment and human sin seriously, so that they succumb to mere moralism. The God of mercy and love sends Christ to teach by his example, inspiring us to follow in the way of love. "A God without wrath brought men without sin into a kingdom without judgment through the ministrations of a Christ without a cross"—so H. Richard Niebuhr characterized popular nineteenth-century liberalism.[3]

When the objective and subjective views were fighting to a standoff, Gustaf Aulén's *Christus Victor* (1931) seemed to offer an alternative.[4] Aulén broadened the question by maintaining that neither theory was part of the classic Christian faith, both being later rationalizations. The classic view was rather that

INTRODUCTION

of "victory" over sin, death, and demonic forces through Christ. Christ's work brings not a change in God or merely in God's subjects, but a changed *situation*. In many ways, *Christus Victor* was epoch-making, especially in Scandinavia and the English-speaking world, because it raised the level of argument to a new plane. Yet it too was not able to satisfy everyone. Proponents of the objective view charge it with slighting the problem of guilt, justice, and divine holiness.[5] Subjectivists find the idea of victory over demonic forces too mythological and archaic to carry much weight.

The argument over theories and motifs, while stimulating and broadening, seems to have brought more rather than less confusion. Multiplying theories, models, and pictures seems to have become a theological hobby. The inability to settle the dispute among them leads to the attempt to make a virtue of the vice, under the auspices of the platitude that no one view or theory can do justice to the profound mystery of Christ's work. Each theory is supposed to convey an aspect of the truth. J. W. C. Wand, for instance, counts as many as seven different pictures and likens atonement to "a precious jewel, which is so large that you can only see properly one facet at a time." One has to turn it around in one's hand to see each facet in turn.[6] Almost every writer on atonement now appears obligated to play this game.

In spite of the broadening of perspective that development of such facets may bring, there is something profoundly unsatisfactory about the underlying presupposition and thus about the eventual outcome of the approach. We refer to this here as the problem of the relationship between the dogmatic construction and "the thing itself." Carved up into so many bits and pieces, the work of Christ becomes the plaything of human need. One is confronted with a cafeteria of ideas about Christ to which one pays lip service, but one's own taste then settles the matter. Left to one's own devices, one usually opts for the least offensive view, or at least that which supposedly meets what we consider to be our needs. Indeed, Wand betrays this when he says, "Our conception of the Atonement is likely to prove the more complete and satisfying the more it is able to meet all the manifold needs of the human personality."[7] Theologians seem to have forgotten that the work of Christ in atonement is one event and not several different ones. The Roman Catholic scholar Hans Kessler makes the same observation in reviewing Catholic dogmatic textbooks.

> They explain the—by them assumed—decisive meaning of the death of Jesus by a collection of categories—satisfaction, sacrifice, merit, redemption, etc., which they more or less throw together paratactically and at best bring into external order by means of conceptual analysis. But thereby it is neither clear what material connection there is among the categories nor is it apparent whether they have a common internal intent. Much rather one gets the impression it is as though one unified living process were split into an impenetrable multiplicity of concepts and the intended phenomenon lost at the outset.[8]

7 / THE WORK OF CHRIST

The multiplicity of more or less unrelated views in the tradition is itself a problem for dogmatics. There seems to be a kind of "embarrassment at the center" when we come to the work of Christ. The doctrine seems to falter, as though, to use Barth's words, it were tripping over some invisible object. We need to ask why. Is it because, as the platitude has it, dogmatics is not completely adequate to the task? That our subject is a mystery or paradox too elusive for us? Or is language inherently too limited to convey transcendent truth? Must we content ourselves with partial, pictorial, parabolic or symbolic utterances and try to overcome the limitation as best we can by sheer multiplication? But that is just the linguistic justification for pluralism and relativism.

Dogmatics has, in various ways, always been aware of its limitations, and will, one hopes, remain so. But we must press the question: Does that general caveat cover the embarrassment here? Can we in this case invoke such modesty to mask our ineptitude? Could it not be that the difficulty is of quite a different order? Martin Hengel concludes his recent study of crucifixion in the world of Jesus' time with these words:

> The theological reasoning of our time shows very clearly that the particular form of the death of Jesus, the man and the Messiah, represents a scandal which people like to blunt, remove, or domesticate in any way possible. We shall have to guarantee the truth of our theological thinking at this point.[9]

Indeed. We shall have to ask whether dogmatics itself is immune from this particular error: not that the blaze of transcendent truth dazzles, but that we are unwilling to face what stands quite clearly before our eyes.

> Who has believed what we have heard?
>   And to whom has the arm of the Lord been revealed?
> For he grew up before him like a young plant,
>   and like a root out of dry ground;
> he had no form or comeliness that we should look at him
>   and no beauty that we should desire him.
> He was despised and rejected by men;
>   a man of sorrows, and acquainted with grief;
> and as one from whom men hide their faces
>   he was despised, and we esteemed him not.
>   (Isa. 53:1-3)

The question we face in considering the work of Christ is whether and to what extent our very attempts to find meaning for ourselves in the tragedy and horror of Golgotha are attempts to insulate against the offense. H. J. Iwand says:

> We have made the bitterness of the cross, the revelation of God in the cross of Jesus Christ, tolerable to ourselves by learning to understand it as a necessity

INTRODUCTION

for the process of salvation. . . . As a result the cross loses its contingent and incomprehensible character.[10]

We have surrounded the scandal of the cross with roses. We have made a theory of salvation out of it. But that is not the cross. That is not the bleakness inherent in it, placed in it by God.[11]

The question is whether our very attempts to understand the cross in our conventional ways may not simply put roses on the cross, and just so blunt the actual work of Christ on us through his cross and resurrection. The question is whether this itself may not be the secret reason for the failure of all our theories. For theories do not reconcile. If dogmatics covers the offense with its theories, it cannot serve a proclamation that actually *is* a ministry of reconciliation.

The questions we have put set for us the procedure to follow: first, investigation and evaluation of the tradition; second, an attempt at reconstruction which seeks to avoid the hazards and to state the work of Christ in a form true to Scripture and viable today. Obviously we cannot rehearse the whole tradition. Our purpose is dogmatic and not historical. Dogmatic rather than historical considerations govern, for the most part, the selection of representatives from the tradition. After a preliminary consideration of the New Testament materials, Chapter 1 deals with central figures representing the major theories: objective, subjective, and classic. Chapter 2 is a transitional piece preparatory to attempted reconstruction in Chapters 3 and 4.

NOTES

1. Smalcald Articles, Part II, Article I, *BC* 292.
2. Augsburg Confession, Article III, *BC* 29–30.
3. H. Richard Niebuhr, *The Kingdom of God in America* (New York: Willett, Clark & Co., 1937), p. 193.
4. Gustaf Aulén, *Christus Victor*, trans. A. G. Hebert (New York: Macmillan Co., 1931).
5. See Osmo Tiililä, *Das Strafleiden Christi*, AASF 48 (Helsinki, 1941).
6. J. W. C. Wand, *The Atonement* (London: SPCK, 1963), p. 1.
7. Ibid., p. 9.
8. Hans Kessler, *Die theologische Bedeutung des Todes Jesu,* Themen und Thesen der Theologie (Düsseldorf: Patmos Verlag, 1970), p. 16.
9. Martin Hengel, *Crucifixion in the Ancient World and the Folly of the Message of the Cross* (Philadelphia: Fortress Press, 1977), p. 90.
10. From Iwand's unpublished *Christologievorlesung*, cited in Jürgen Moltmann, *The Crucified God*, trans. R. A. Wilson and John Bowden (New York: Harper & Row, 1974), p. 41.
11. Ibid., p. 36.

1

The Shape of the Tradition

The dogmatic tradition strives to understand and present Jesus' work in his life and death in a way that stresses his historical act for us rather than his being as such. The various theories of the atonement have this aim. Insofar, however, as they attempt to capture the significance of the event in theories, they tend to defeat their own purpose and obscure the offense with roses.

THE SCRIPTURAL TRADITION

The basic material relevant to the work of Christ is simply the biblical story as it culminates in the cross and resurrection of Jesus, and some ad hoc attempts to interpret the significance of that story for its first hearers.

The story is simple enough and well known. Jesus, the carpenter's son from Nazareth, came declaring the imminent coming of the kingdom of God in connection with his own person and ministry, preaching repentance, forgiving sins, and performing signs and wonders. Those whom he encountered were confronted with a finality, with an ultimate judgment that could not be avoided. He opened a new vision of God for those who accepted him, a vision of the God whom he called his Father. In Jesus' being for them, this God was there for them. He brought new life and freedom. He did not demand, he gave; he did not crush, he raised up; he did not judge, he removed burdens and let people breathe freely. He broke and transcended the bounds of convention and tradition and advocated the poor, the downtrodden, the outcast, the oppressed. He gave hope. Jesus manifested the love of God.

But he was not accepted. Perhaps he could not be—here. One cannot forgive sins here. It destroys all account books. One cannot run roughshod over the laws and traditions that keep earthly life and community in shape. The radical and unconditional love of God the Father could not go unchallenged—not when there is important business to attend to. He had to go. He was handed over to the Roman authorities and crucified, apparently as a messianic pretender. His life ended in an agonizing cacophony of voices.

7 / THE WORK OF CHRIST

> "Shall I crucify your King?" "We have no king but Caesar" (John 19:15).
>
> "Do not weep for me, but weep for yourselves and for your children" (Luke 23:28).
>
> And the inscription of the charge against him read, "The King of the Jews" (Mark 15:26).
>
> "Aha! You who would destroy the temple and build it in three days, save yourself, and come down from the cross!" . . . "He saved others; he cannot save himself. Let the Christ, the King of Israel, come down now from the cross, that we may see and believe" (Mark 15:29–32).
>
> "My God, my God, why hast thou forsaken me?" (Mark 15:34).

His death was not pretty. It is easy to forget that, when centuries of worship and art have made of the cross a beautiful cult symbol. Martin Hengel's *Crucifixion in the Ancient World* reminds us not only that the cross was excruciatingly painful, humiliating, and degrading—a death reserved for the public humiliation of slaves and political outcasts to deter further crime—but also that precisely that kind of death is the culmination of the story, an ineradicable part of the historical deposit with which the theology itself must grapple.[1] The very folly and offense of it is the stuff from which the theology must start.

But the story does not end with the cross. There are other voices that write the end—and a new beginning!—to the story:

> He has risen, he is not here (Mark 16:6).
> Why do you seek the living among the dead? (Luke 24:5).

God raised Jesus from the dead. God vindicated the one rejected by all. God put the stamp of approval on the one humiliated and degraded. God ratified the action of the one who had the audacity to forgive sins here.

Such, in brief, is the story. What does it tell us about the work of Christ? What does this Jesus and his story do? It is amazing, when one takes the New Testament as a whole, how little is explicitly said which gives what could be called a dogmatic explanation of the work of Christ—at least of the sort that has become so dominant in the tradition. The earliest layers of the New Testament Gospel sources, the sayings sources such as Q, indicate no particular reflection on or view of Jesus' work or his fate. Jesus' death was no doubt a mighty shock, but it seems mostly to have been understood in terms of the usual fate of God's prophets: they were rejected and came to a bad end. Such rejection, of course, unmasks the unrepentant, unbelieving, and guilty stance of God's people. This early view of the life and death of Jesus is reflected also in some of the speeches in Acts, such as Peter's speech in Acts 2, and even in some of Paul's earlier writings (see, e.g., 1 Thess. 2:14ff.). Jesus himself, though he might have and quite possibly did reckon with a violent death

THE SHAPE OF THE TRADITION

at the hands of his adversaries, seems not to have understood or interpreted his own death as a sacrifice for others or ransom for sin. Such interpretation apparently came as the result of later reflection.[2] Even in their final redaction the synoptic Gospels contain little direct or explicit interpretation of Jesus' work. Mark 10:45 has Jesus say that the Son of Man came to give his life "as a ransom for many," and the accounts of the Last Supper speak of Jesus' blood as his "blood of the covenant, which is poured out for many" (Mark 14:24) and "my blood of the covenant, which is poured out for many for the forgiveness of sins" (Matt. 26:28). Such passages, in their present form at least, are usually regarded as having come not from Jesus himself but from later interpretative traditions. The same is true of the instances where Jesus predicts his own death and resurrection, such as Mark 8:31ff. and 9:31, and parallels in the other Synoptics. They are interpretations attributed to Jesus after the fact. But aside from such scanty references, the Synoptics even in their final form afford little explicit interpretation of Jesus' work.

There is, however, a great deal of interpretation implicit in the presentation of Jesus' life and death. This is no doubt more important than the few explicit passages. The passion predictions placed on Jesus' lips show that already in the earliest days there was an attempt to come to grips with the terrible tragedy and offense of his death by seeing it as part of the divine will. Jesus' death was not the result of mere human caprice; it happened "according to the Scriptures," just as the Scriptures reveal—especially in the psalms of lament and suffering. The drama is played out according to the apocalyptic timetable. The ultimate reason for it lies in the hidden counsel of God which is now being revealed. The interpretation given Jesus' life could also be extended to his death: It was part of the apocalyptic drama.

The apocalyptic setting leads almost naturally to a second and deeper level of interpretation also implicit in the Gospels: Jesus' life and death have eschatological import. They are an end-time event—above all one through which final judgment is exercised. It means judgment pronounced over the old ways, over godlessness, over holding on to the old cultic rituals and laws as ways of salvation. The apocalyptic judgment is anticipated. The Son of Man, rejected by humans, is revealed paradoxically as the hidden judge of all. This understanding is especially evident in the many controversies between Jesus and his adversaries.

The concept of judgment also brings with it a new element: Jesus' life and death have soteriological significance. He brings salvation. The night is past, the light shines. God has drawn near to all people. In the earliest layers of the tradition, there was apparently no special emphasis put on his death as the saving event. Jesus as a whole brought salvation. Mark, in the first Gospel, apparently took this kind of material and interpreted the whole in the light of the crucifixion as its *telos* and climax. Thus, following Mark, the Gospels

7 / THE WORK OF CHRIST

in their present form are predominantly passion narratives, with the other material organized to lead inexorably to the cross. The cross assumes a paramount position for interpreting the work of Jesus, the risen Christ.

But how can a humiliating and offensive death on a cross be of soteriological significance? This is the question with which the entire Christian tradition has wrestled ever since. The materials in the New Testament indicate that beyond the kind of interpretation given in the synoptic Gospels there was from the earliest days, most probably in circles influenced by Hellenistic Judaism, a tradition that interpreted Jesus' death as in some sense an atonement or expiation for sin. Just exactly what that sense is seems to be a matter for debate among current scholars. At any rate, this tradition drew on cultic materials, the concept of sacrifice, covenant sacrifice, Passover, the concept of the suffering servant (Isaiah 53), and so forth, to interpret the significance of Jesus' life and death. Although this tradition seems to have intruded only quite late into the synoptic materials (Mark 10:45 and pars. plus 14:24 and pars. being the only instances), it was apparently a very early tradition. It is generally held that Paul in Romans 3:25-26 and also in 4:25 is drawing on this earlier tradition, quoting hymnic and confessional material from Hellenistic Jewish-Christian circles. But this indicates that the tradition is already well established before Paul's writing. Romans 3:25-26 speaks of Christ as one "whom God put forward as an expiation by his blood . . . to show God's righteousness, because in his divine forbearance he had passed over former sins." Romans 4:25 speaks of Jesus as "put to death for our trespasses and raised for our justification"—perhaps part of an early Jewish-Christian confessional statement. Echoes of this tradition interpreting Jesus' death as in some sense a sacrifice or expiation for sin are to be found quite regularly in the writings related to or dependent on Paul (though not so much in Paul himself) and in the Johannine literature (see, e.g., John 1:29; 6:51; 1 John 1:7; 2:2; 3:5-6; 4:10; Rev. 5:8-9; 7:14; 12:11). Such a view comes to most sustained expression in the Epistle to the Hebrews, where Jesus' sacrifice is interpreted against the background of the rite for the Day of Atonement. Jesus' sacrifice is better and more perfect, fulfilling and thus ending "once and for all" the need for cultic sacrifices. He has opened up a "new and living way" through his flesh, accomplishing in actuality what the old rite could only foreshadow.

But what is the import of this tradition? The history of interpretation shows that it has been easy to move from this kind of material to an understanding of Christ's work as a vicarious satisfaction of divine honor (justice, wrath, etc.) akin to that usually associated with Anselm. Put in its most crass form, this view would hold that Jesus' death is a sacrifice in which he is a substitute for us who pays the divine justice what is due for human sin and/or appeases the divine wrath. As we shall see, there is a long tradition, especially among

Western conservative Christians, which has taken this line. There seems to be a virtual consensus among contemporary biblical scholars, however, that this tradition finds little support in the Scriptures, either in the Old or New Testament. Scripture never speaks of God as one who has to be satisfied or propitiated before being merciful or forgiving. God is always the *subject* of the action, not the object.

Yet even if Jesus' death is not to be thought of as propitiating God, the New Testament quite clearly insists that it was substitutionary, or at least representative. The many "for you," "for us," "for our sins," "for many" formulas certify that. What the "for our sins" or "for us" formulas mean exactly, however, has been and continues to be a subject of debate. Some, following more traditional lines, would insist that such formulas mean *substitution*: "For us" means "instead of us." Those following this line usually like to insist that the idea of one person's sacrificial death having propitiatory or expiatory efficacy for others belongs to a firm biblical and Jewish tradition current and well known in Jesus' time. Such interpretation draws on various strands of the Old Testament materials, the sacrificial cult, and especially the suffering servant motif of Isaiah 53, as well as later accounts of the vicarious efficacy of the sufferings of the "just man" and the martyrs of the Maccabean era.[3] In light of this material, it has been common among New Testament scholars until quite recently to hold that the idea of a death having vicarious or even atoning significance was a firmly held biblical and Jewish view. Some (most notably Oscar Cullmann) have asserted that Jesus quite probably understood his own life and coming fate in this fashion, combining the "Son of Man" concept with the "suffering servant" of Isaiah.

Recent scholarship, however, has begun to cast doubt on these "received" positions. The most telling argument is that there simply seems to be no literary evidence that such interpretation was present in Jewish circles in Jesus' time. There seems to be no concept of a death having vicarious significance in Jewish circles in the sense given it by later Christian interpretation.[4] Even though such passages as Isaiah 53 seem most explicitly to point in that direction, it is apparent that no Jewish tradition of the time of Jesus (prior to A.D. 70) understood it as indicating a vicarious death. Furthermore, there seems to be no evidence that "Son of Man" or "suffering servant" materials were current or combined in the fashion suggested by scholars like Oscar Cullmann.[5] The literary evidence, therefore, just does not seem to support what has been a widely held view among New Testament exegetes. The idea of a death having vicarious significance was not a commonly held tradition. Persuasive arguments can be made that the idea came not from Jewish but from Christian sources, Christians "thoroughly at home in the Greek-Hellenistic thought world."[6] Even the interpretation of the death of the martyrs in 4 Maccabees is most likely quite late and influenced by the same sort of thought.

7 / THE WORK OF CHRIST

Such recent scholarship casts considerable doubt on the right of the "vicarious death" strand to claim preeminence in interpreting the death of Christ and the "for us." At the least one could not claim that it is *the* biblical and Jewish tradition which could pretend once and for all to settle the metaphysics of the matter. At the most it could claim to be only one of the ways the early Christians sought to come to terms with Jesus' death.

The line of interpretation that draws on the cultic materials, the idea of sacrifice, and the suffering servant is no doubt an attempt to deal with the stark offensiveness of the cross with the biblical materials themselves: Where Jewish thought had almost insurmountable difficulties, one used Jewish means to try to overcome them (the Epistle to the Hebrews is a prime example of that). But it is doubtful that one could press these materials into a hard-and-fast theory of atonement, as was later done. In essence, perhaps little more is being said through such materials than was said in the synoptic Gospels: In Jesus' life and death, God turns toward the lost, the sinners, the outcast, and accepts them. Jesus' death is what it cost God to do that. But we shall have to say more about that in the reconstructive part of our *locus*.

For now, the point is that the "for us," while it does certainly mean a sacrificial death on our behalf, cannot be systematized into a hard-and-fast theory. The "for us" formulas should be interpreted more in the sense of "on our behalf," "for our good," or "for our benefit," rather than "instead of us." Indeed, one could argue that the "instead of us" runs the danger of missing the point altogether, for then it seems primarily the *hindrances* to salvation that necessitate the death. The act is oriented solely toward the past. But Jesus' work "for us" in the New Testament is oriented also toward the future. He died not only to repair past damage but to open a new future "for us."

If one interprets the "for us" in the sense of also opening a new future, it is more possible to combine—as the New Testament repeatedly does—an understanding of Jesus' death as atonement with the concept of example. Many of the central New Testament passages on atonement do this very thing. First Peter 2:21–24 is an excellent illustration:

> For to this you have been called, because Christ also suffered for you, leaving you an example, that you should follow in his steps. He committed no sin; no guile was found on his lips. When he was reviled, he did not revile in return; when he suffered, he did not threaten; but he trusted to him who judges justly. He himself bore our sins in his body on the tree, that we might die to sin and live to righteousness. By his wounds you have been healed.

Even the only two passages in the New Testament which speak directly of Jesus' sacrifice as offered "to God," Eph. 5:2 and Heb. 9:14, seem more concerned with the exemplary nature of that sacrifice than with any sort of propitiatory machinery. In the Ephesians passage we are exhorted to be "imitators of God,

THE SHAPE OF THE TRADITION

as beloved children. And walk in love, as Christ loved us and gave himself up for us, a fragrant offering and sacrifice to God." The Hebrews passage makes a similar point. The cultic sacrifice is limited, purifying only the "flesh," that is, effecting only a ritual purification. Jesus' sacrifice, however, "without blemish to God" should "much more" purify the conscience from dead works to serve the living God. The cultic type of sacrifice, that is, is directed toward the past, dealing with the ritual impurities incurred by past actions. Jesus' sacrifice "for all," "for us," opens up a new future: One might serve the living God from the heart, no longer concerned about "dead works"! If one interprets the "for you" as opening that new future, one no longer has to tear apart what so often has been sundered in the tradition: the atoning work and the example.

But it is to the writings of Paul that one must look for the most concentrated and sustained exposition of the significance of the cross and the resurrection of Jesus. Paul's writings are gripped by a sense for the utter folly and offense of the cruelty and humiliation of the crucifixion and the startling nature of the reversal in the resurrection. He holds this tirelessly before his hearers and readers. Paul was well aware of the reality of it all and found this to be of the essence. Martin Hengel has put it well:

> When Paul speaks of the "folly" of the message of the crucified Jesus, he is therefore not speaking in riddles or using an abstract cipher. He is expressing the harsh experience of his missionary preaching and the offence that it caused, in particular the experience of his preaching among non-Jews, with whom his apostolate was particularly concerned. The reason why in his letters he talks about the cross above all in a polemical context is that he deliberately wants to provoke his opponents, who are attempting to water down the offence caused by the cross. Thus in a way the "word of the cross" is the spearhead of his message. And because Paul still understands the cross as the real, cruel instrument of execution, as the instrument of the bloody execution of Jesus, it is impossible to dissociate talk of the atoning death of Jesus or the blood of Jesus from this "word of the cross." The spearhead cannot be broken off the spear. Rather, the complex of the death of Jesus is a single entity for the apostle, in which he never forgets the fact that Jesus did not die a gentle death like Socrates, with his cup of hemlock, much less passing on "old and full of years" like the Patriarchs of the Old Testament. Rather he died like a slave or a common criminal, in torment, on the tree of shame. Paul's Jesus did not die just any death; he was "given up for us all" on the cross, in a cruel and a contemptible way.[7]

For Paul the proclamation of the cross is crisis, the eschatological crisis, the absolute end and the new beginning. In his own constructions Paul does not seem to speak so much of Jesus' death as a sacrifice for sin or a ransom. Nor does he dwell on the concept of guilt and forgiveness coming from the cross. As already noted, he quotes the already existing traditions with apparent ap-

7 / THE WORK OF CHRIST

proval in this regard, but does not pursue it in his own thinking. Rather, for him the cross is total crisis, the end of the old, the breaking of the demonic powers and the opening of something new, the life of love and freedom. The "for us" means "on our behalf," the new life "in Christ," "in the Spirit." It has to do with the future, the new age.

Paul is thus adamantly opposed to every attempt to avoid, stop short of, leap over, or detour around the cross in its reality and offensiveness. When he is dealing with a Jewish-Christian legalism that stops short of the cross (Galatians), he will preach the gospel of the utter freedom the cross brings, the cross as the end of the law. Jesus has borne the curse of the law in his own accursed death—actually. Now all that is over; faith has come; all distinctions are abolished and freedom is given.

If in another instance Paul is confronted with perfectionism or arrogant enthusiasm that thinks it has surpassed or leaped over the cross to a resurrected life already in the present (1 Corinthians), Paul will preach the utter folly of "Christ and him crucified" to judge and destroy all such premature presumption. Christians cannot be better than their crucified Lord. One cannot leap over the cross. Jesus indeed brings the new, but through the cross, not around it. The perfection is not yet, and the world is in travail until the eschatological fulfillment.

Or if, still further, there are those who want to look on the earthly Jesus as a kind of "divine man" of Greek provenance, a charismatic hero and wonder-worker whose charismatic power one can possess and use to one's own advantage and glory (2 Corinthians), Paul will again preach the lowly and despised Christ and speak of a power manifest in weakness and folly.

No avoidance, no detour, no leaping over the cross to premature fulfillment is possible. The cross is ultimate judgment and grace. The new comes through it, not around it. To be a beneficiary, an heir, of the work of Christ is to be "in Christ," by faith, to be "baptized into his death," in order to share the hope of his resurrection.

When Paul wants, therefore, to describe the new flowing from the work of Christ, he can simply say that faith has come, faith born out of the shame, offense, and weakness of the cross, where the love of God for all is hidden from the wise of this age, but revealed to those who believe. It is perhaps not inaccurate to say that Paul sees Christ as placing humans in the same eschatological crisis manifest in the Gospel accounts, but that (at least in the extant letters of Paul) the crisis comes predominantly in the cross, not so much in the life of the historical Jesus as such. Paul apparently could not escape the shock of the cross and its offense. He could not easily write off the fact that this crucified one was the one approved and vindicated by God. The willingness and capacity of theology or of the Christian life to be transformed by the "*logos* of the cross" is the test of its viability. The shattering fact, for

THE SHAPE OF THE TRADITION

Paul, was that all God's history with Israel had led to the hill of Golgotha. The "custodian" (Gal. 3:24) had led them to that awful place. It was the end—and the possibility of a new beginning.

In summary, we can safely say that the New Testament materials give evidence of several strands of interpretation. One strand, perhaps the earliest (as evidenced by the sayings sources), interprets Jesus' work much as that of a prophet or teacher who met the same fate as all genuine prophets among God's people: he was rejected and killed. Already implicit in that, however, is the element of judgment on the people who refuse to accept him. The judges are judged in Jesus. This forms the basis for what could be called the next strand, or layer, of the tradition: Jesus' life and death have apocalyptic or eschatological significance. The resurrection makes that evident. His death is not just historical accident, it is a part of the apocalyptic drama of the end-times: In him and in his message the ultimate judgment has been revealed. This would mean also that his life and death have soteriological significance: Those who accept him will be able to stand in the day of judgment. A third strand of the tradition speaks of Jesus' work more directly in sacrificial terms. Jesus' death is a sacrifice, an expiation, a ransom, "for us," "for our sins." This strand no doubt attempts to overcome the almost insurmountable antipathy to the shame and offense of the cross by drawing on traditional biblical material (the cultic ritual, the suffering servant, the Psalms, and so on) to show that Jesus died "according to the Scriptures." He fulfilled and ended "once for all" the sacrificial rite. It is this strand that has enjoyed most extensive development in the subsequent dogmatic tradition. Fourth, we must point to the Pauline "*logos* of the cross." In the weakness, folly, shame, and offense of the painful and humiliating death of Jesus on the cross, God has reached the end and ultimate judgment on humanity, the world, the demons, the "elemental spirits," the entire creation. Those who die with Jesus and receive him in his hiddenness, humiliation, and weakness shall be raised in him to newness of life. The way lies through the cross to the resurrection in him. He is ultimate judgment and grace. Such, in brief summary, are the New Testament materials. Now we turn to see what the subsequent dogmatic tradition has done with them.

VICARIOUS SATISFACTION OF DIVINE JUSTICE

The closest thing to a dogma of the atonement through the years in the West has been the doctrine of vicarious satisfaction. First worked out by Anselm of Canterbury (1033–1109), and refined through the years, it became standard for the great systems of medieval scholasticism and Protestant orthodoxy and has remained so for most of conservative Christianity. Its "inner solidity"

7 / THE WORK OF CHRIST

has made it the "seed of crystallization" for atonement thinking;[8] it seems presupposed both by Reformation confessional documents and by the Council of Trent, and it was almost raised to the level of formal dogma by Vatican I.[9]

Prior to Anselm soteriology was defined mostly in terms of knowledge: Christ gives true knowledge of the "eternal *logos*" in contrast to the false knowledge and speculation of the gnostics. Knowledge, however, proves to be an inadequate model for taking account of the actual historical life and fate of Jesus. One can too easily develop a split vision in which the history becomes a mere allegory or appearance of the transcendent gnosis. The actual history, the offense of the cross, can become an embarrassment. The gnostics, of course, spiritualized altogether—some, such as Basilides, holding that the "gnostic redeemer" departed from Jesus, leaving only "the man" to be crucified.

Christian theologians were concerned to press beyond gnosticism and give the actual history theological import. The knowledge model, however, caused difficulties. Three possibilities seemed to suggest themselves. The first was to make the historical life a "pattern" or "way." If one conforms to the pattern, especially to the extent of martyrdom, one will see God as the martyr Stephen saw God. Early martyr theology, the apologists, and to some extent later Antiochene theology were influenced by this option. A second tendency was to substantialize the model and see the incarnation as the joining of the "eternal *logos*" and the historical flesh, so that by participating sacramentally in the "God-man," we receive "the medicine of immortality." A third possibility was to read a kind of inner logical order out of—or into!—the historical facts themselves, so as to arrive at the "true gnosis." Here we think of Irenaeus.

The problem with all these attempts to give significance to the history itself is that the split vision is not cured. One still sees through the history to the ideal. The emphasis tends to shift from the action, the history, to the being of the God-man, the "union of the two natures." Even in Irenaeus and the theology of recapitulation—Jesus repeats the stages of human growth, overcoming where Adam succumbed to the tempter—the history is seen through. All events mean the same thing.[10] When one systematizes the history, one sees through the scandal of the cross, and history is in fact transcended by gnosis.[11]

There were also the various pictures of atonement, such as that of ransom paid to the devil or reconciliation through sacrifice. But these received no solid dogmatic treatment and did not explain the necessity for the work of Christ.[12] Origen, for instance, fecund source of many such ideas, regarded them more as instructive pictures for the simple than as doctrine for the accomplished gnostic.[13]

Anselm was the first to pose the question about the necessity for the actual event of the cross, and thus the first to pose the soteriological question as a specific theme in itself. His question is "Why?" *Cur deus homo* (why the God-man?), his major treatise on the atonement, relentlessly pursues the question of necessity—not just the *a posteriori* necessity of previous pictures, but a rationally deduced *a priori* necessity.[14] He claims to demonstrate both the absolute reasons for the necessity of a God-man and the necessity for salvation to take place in exactly the way it did.[15] He wants to demonstrate that atonement had to take place the way it did.[16]

Anselm dismisses both the theory of recapitulation and the idea of a ransom paid to the devil as insufficient (though not wrong). A recapitulation theology, working with contrapuntal pictures, has aesthetic appeal but does not give substantial reasons for the cross. It is like painting "on clouds or in water" (*Cur deus homo*, i,4). Talk about the deception and defeat of Satan is equally insufficient, because it does not explain why the Almighty had to go to such trouble to defeat enemies. Could not God simply have crushed Satan and released the captives by divine decree (ibid., i,1, 5, 6, 7)?

The answer to the question "Why?" must therefore lie in God, in a necessity laid on God in relation to the fallen creation. The basic contours of Anselm's argument are simple enough. No doubt the simplicity has commended it to dogmatics through the years. The rational creature owes God the Creator the debt of total response. Sin is a withholding of this response and thus a dishonoring of God, a disruption of the order of creation. Furthermore, since total obedience is owed, a simple return to obedience will not be able to pay for past sins. Restitution can be made to the divine honor only by giving back more than the total obedience owed.[17] The situation seems hopeless.

But what of God? Can God not simply forgive? If that were so, there would be no necessity for the God-man. Hence Anselm insists that it is not possible or fitting for God simply to forgive. Such mercy would cancel justice and order by its arbitrariness; sin and justice would be on the same level, and chaos would result. To protect the divine honor and created order, some other way must be found.[18]

Thus Anselm arrives at his great either-or: "*aut poena aut satisfactio*" (either punishment or satisfaction). God could, of course, punish the sinner. But punishment would mean destruction and thus frustrate God's hope for creation—there would be no one left to replace the fallen angels in paradise. So if the creature is not to be punished, satisfaction must be rendered to the divine honor.[19] The creature must do this but cannot; God could do it but must not; hence the only solution is the God-man. Only one who is sinless can render to God a satisfaction more than the sinner is obligated to give. It is a necessity.

The necessity is met by Jesus Christ. As sinless God-man it is not incumbent on him to die. Since he voluntarily gives himself up to death, he gives more than was required. His death is worth more than anything that is not

7 / THE WORK OF CHRIST

God. So great a sacrifice deserves a reward. But as God-man he needs no reward. Therefore he can give it to those for whom he became incarnate. Those who receive his merits shall be saved.

Such is the vicarious satisfaction of the divine honor. The major question bequeathed to the subsequent dogmatic tradition by Anselm's construction—and one should bear in mind that Anselm was perfectly aware of it, since it is repeatedly pressed by the interlocutor, Boso—is the question of mercy. If God is satisfied, how is it mercy? Before going on to press the question, we must let Anselm have the word. He concludes by telling Boso:

> Now we have found the compassion of God which appeared lost to you when we were considering God's holiness and man's sin; we have found it, I say, so great and so consistent with his holiness, as to be incomparably above anything that can be conceived. For what compassion can excel these words of the Father, addressed to the sinner doomed to eternal torments and having no way of escape: "Take my only begotten Son and make him an offering for yourself"; or these words of the Son: "Take me and ransom your souls." For these are the voices they utter, when inviting and leading us to faith in the gospel.[20]

Note how Anselm's words reflect the sacrifice of the mass.

Anselm's doctrine represents an acute juridicizing of Christ's work—some call it a Latinizing.[21] To give the actual history rational necessity, Anselm is driven to call on ideas from the realm of law and justice.[22] The relationship between God and God's creatures comes to be understood in terms of legal order, a *iustitia commutativa*.[23] Sin is not so much a personal matter as it is an objective and legal matter. God's relation to it is not so much wrath—Anselm never speaks of God's wrath—as one determined by the logic of order. So the possibility of atonement comes to hinge on making equivalent restitution; the payment must equal the debt. "The order permeated by the *iustitia commutativa* becomes in this fashion a merciless law, in which—without the satisfier furnished by God—no remedy appears possible."[24]

Does Anselm successfully answer the why of the terrible event of the historical cross? Can the necessity be demonstrated in this fashion? It is possible, of course, to point to holes in Anselm's logic.[25] How could Christ's death be necessary and at the same time a free and voluntary sacrifice? Anselm sputters and seems never quite able to put the question to rest. How can the equivalence between Christ's death and the demand of the divine honor be demonstrated? Anselm tries to argue that because the evil of destroying the Son of God is greater than the evil of allowing the whole human race to be destroyed, his life is an incomparably greater good than the mass of all human sin and evil and can hence be offered as an equivalent satisfaction.[26] But the logic will not work. It is like the attempt to prove the worth of something by asking how great an evil it would be to destroy it; one assumes the worth to begin with. Equivalence cannot be demonstrated in that fashion.

Logical problems in Anselm's doctrine led later theology to surrender his insistence on an absolute or *a priori* necessity for atonement and to speak rather of a relative necessity. God could have done it differently, but the way God actually did it was most appropriate to give an example and awaken our hope.[27] It is dangerous, however, to retain the idea of vicarious satisfaction without Anselm's argument for its necessity. The cruel death of Jesus is a costly example. The protest Anselm puts in the mouth of Boso comes back to haunt: "that the Most High should stoop to things so lowly, that the Almighty should do a thing with such toil."[28] Anselm may have ventured too far, but he was at least correct in his attempt to insist that the history, the concrete life and death of Christ, was more than a mere picture or example of truths already known. Anselm was right in insisting that something vital happened to the God-creature relationship in the death of Jesus.

The more serious problems with Anselm's doctrine are theo-logical rather than logical. The most persistent one is the question of justice versus mercy and its consequences for the doctrine of God. The attempt to prove the necessity of satisfaction leads to the idea that mercy can be exercised only when the demands of justice have been fulfilled. But if God has to be paid and has been paid, how is God merciful? Why cannot God, the almighty, simply forgive? Indeed, we are enjoined to forgive our debtors; why cannot God? Anselm is aware of the questions, since Boso constantly nags about them. Anselm's answer is basically that God cannot use divine freedom in a manner that is unfitting. Just as it is unfitting for God to lie, it is also unfitting to let sin go unpunished.[29] But the reasoning is questionable. To lie is indeed wrong and would be unfitting for God. But is it wrong to have mercy? Mercy is of a different order from lying. The result of the attempt to prove necessity is inevitably the elevation of justice over mercy. The question remains: If God has been satisfied, where is God's mercy?

It was Abelard (1079–1142) who sensed the vulnerable spots in Anselm's argument and gained the historical reputation of being Anselm's great antagonist, even though he did not work out a complete or consistent alternative. Abelard does not see why justice must be satisfied before God can be merciful. Did not Jesus forgive before his death? Does not the cruel death on the cross increase human sin rather than compensate for it? What can possibly atone for the murder of Christ? Is it not cruel and unjust that anyone should demand innocent blood as a ransom or be in any way delighted with the death of the innocent, that God should find the death of the Son so acceptable that through it God should be reconciled to the world?[30]

Abelard shows clearly how the vicarious satisfaction doctrine recoils on God.

7 / THE WORK OF CHRIST

It restricts the freedom of God and leads to a gruesome and forbidding picture of the deity. This remarkable outcome of the dogmatic enterprise must be noted carefully. The very attempt to construct a neat theory about reconciliation to God leads to the exact opposite: It alienates from God by creating a forbidding picture of God.

Abelard's attack was picked up and broadened by the Socinians at the time of the Reformation and after. Divine freedom and love were raised above justice. "For God can, especially since He is Lord of all, abandon as much of His rights as He pleases."[31] Satisfaction is superfluous, indeed, senseless. Why should God pay God? Furthermore, the account does not balance. How can the suffering of one man outweigh the punishment due the whole race? The sufferings of Jesus are finite, not eternal. What was demanded was eternal death, but Jesus was dead only three days. And so on. The theory does not deliver what it promises: the necessity for just this life and death.

The Socinians also exposed what even staunch contemporary advocates of the doctrine admit is its Achilles' heel: the idea of substitution.[32] The transfer of someone else's sin to the innocent is absurd and improper, just as in reverse the transfer of someone else's righteousness to the unrighteous.[33]

A final fault, common to both sides, is the neglect of the resurrection. Anselm hardly mentions it and can develop his entire doctrine virtually without it. For the Socinians, too, resurrection does not really function except as a kind of promotion of Jesus as teacher-revealer to divine worthiness and power.

The doctrine of vicarious satisfaction, or more accurately, of vicarious punishment, acquired its final shape in the great systems of seventeenth-century Protestant orthodoxy. While the Reformation itself did not need to pay specific attention to the question of atonement, since the doctrine was not explicitly controversial, the theologians of the late sixteenth and the seventeenth centuries had to work out the implications of the doctrine of justification and contend with the Socinians. This led to a final shaping of the doctrine begun by Anselm.

The development of the doctrine of justification as a forensic decree drove to a juridicizing of the atonement even more stringent than Anselm's. The concept of law as a fixed, eternal way of salvation takes the place of the more aesthetically tinged Augustinian concept of order. Law is understood as an objective schema of commands and prohibitions, a checklist of what must be done and not done to be saved.[34]

Once this occurs it is easier to make the logic of substitution work: someone might fulfill the checklist for someone else. Christ as the substitute fulfills the law instead of us. This takes place "objectively," entirely and exclusively outside of us, and thus is the presupposition for forensic justification. Jesus satisfies the demands of the divine law, the wrath and justice of God, the utterly strict judge.[35] This construction also enabled these theologians to insist even more adamantly than Anselm on the absolute necessity for the satisfaction and thus confute the Socinians. Since God threatened Adam and Eve with death in the garden, he would have lied had he not carried out this sentence.[36] God, many insisted, could not forgive without satisfaction. His love and mercy are not "absolute" but "ordinate," that is, possible only within the bounds established by Christ's satisfaction.

> God indeed loved already from all eternity the whole human race, yet not absolutely and unconditionally, but ordinately; namely, in His beloved Son. . . . Therefore, this ordinate affection or love of God necessarily presupposes His wrath, so that this love in God could not have a place, unless, likewise from all eternity, satisfaction had been made to this divine wrath or justice through the Son, who from eternity, offered Himself as mediator between God and man.[37]

God is the most just judge who requires, "according to the rigor of his infinite justice," an infinite price of satisfaction.[38]

Orthodox Protestantism also went beyond Anselm in surrendering the distinction between satisfaction and punishment. Christ suffers the punishment due us under divine wrath. Punishment and satisfaction are more or less equated. Here too the Anselmian view is legalized, simplified, and made more penal in character—at the same time it is deepened. These theologians do not need Anselm's idea of satisfaction by means of the voluntary sacrifice of something more than the sinner is obligated to give, and are not so troubled about the contradiction between the voluntary versus the necessary in the sacrifice.[39] They can simply say that Jesus suffers the punishment due and that since he is also divine, his suffering is of infinite worth.[40]

Nothing new is said, however, about the problems of substitution: how the suffering and obedience of one can be transferred to another. They simply content themselves with the biblical witness that it was "for us." Substitution remained the Achilles' heel of the doctrine.

The most original contribution of Protestant orthodox teaching was the distinction between the passive and the active suffering and obedience of Christ. Christ's work was not only a passive suffering under the law and wrath, but also an active doing of the law for us in his life.[41] While this was a step in the right direction, since it was an attempt to give soteriological significance to Jesus' life as well as to his death, it had the unfortunate effect of legalizing his life as well.

The full-blown soteriology of Protestant orthodoxy was finally codified in the doctrine of the threefold office of Christ: Prophet, High Priest, and King. This doctrine became the common property of virtually all Protestant and Roman Catholic dogmatics, though Catholics usually spoke of Shepherd rather than King. As Prophet, Christ proclaims salvation; as Priest, he offers himself and intercedes eternally; as King, he governs, preserves, and rules all things.

7 / THE WORK OF CHRIST

The doctrine of the threefold office shows also an attempt to extend soteriology beyond the death of Christ. Yet the main emphasis remained on the priestly office, and it is doubtful that the doctrine is ultimately of much help.[42]

THE TRIUMPH OF DIVINE LOVE

The doctrine of vicarious satisfaction or punishment has always been vigorously resisted in the tradition, in the name of divine love and mercy. Yet the protest always has difficulty assuming convincing positive shape. If God can forgive before the death of Jesus, what is the point of it? The difficulty is to avoid reducing the Christ-event to a mere example, an illustration of a generally known truth. When Jesus becomes just another teacher, no matter how impressive, there is nothing new about the New Testament. Jesus does not do anything someone else could not do. The criticism of vicarious satisfaction can just as well recoil on this view: God must be particularly heartless to go to such lengths just to provide an example, especially when everyone already knows what is being taught.

The earliest attempts at this so-called "moral influence" theory of atonement already suffer from this difficulty. Abelard spoke of Christ as one who persevered unto death in instructing in the way of love, binding us to himself in the way of love so we too should fear nothing in the exercise of love. God is not changed; we are.[43]

The Socinians did not take matters much further. Christ is the confirmation of the will of God to save. His life manifests the will of God to forgive, and his death certifies what is promised under the New Covenant. He is the prophet, the divine legate, who proclaims the gospel in God's name and in God's stead, the Logos who reveals the will of the Father. The resurrection shows how God delivers those who trust in God, and Christ is elevated to virtual divine dignity and power even though he remains a man. Faith is obedience to and imitation of Christ in the hope of eternal life as a reward.[44]

Such reconstructions involve a complete moralization of Christ's work. The basic structure remains a legal one. The ironic fact is that, for all their opposition, the antagonists in this great debate are usually brothers and sisters under the skin. For both sides the basic scheme is law and reward. The only argument is about human ability to fulfill what is demanded. For the conservative, the fallen creature cannot do it and so needs a substitute. For the liberal or "moral influence" theologian, the creature needs only guidance and encouragement. The argument is a standoff. A new departure is needed.

The great nineteenth-century theologians such as Friedrich Schleiermacher and Albrecht Ritschl tried to provide a new departure by describing Christ's work as the establishment of a new historical community in which the redeeming influence of Christ could be experienced, raising us above the fate of merely natural and empirical life. Schleiermacher sought a mean between the kind of theology represented by vicarious satisfaction and that of the moral-influence type.[45] This could be done, he thought, by seeing the redeeming activity of Christ as establishing a new life common to us and to him—original in him, new and derived in us. The historical activity of Jesus is not mere example, it is the establishment of a new corporate life in an actual historical community.

To avoid both moralism and vicarious satisfaction, Schleiermacher depends on a view of religion based on something other than legal or moral categories: the religion of "the feeling of absolute dependence" and the idea of God-consciousness. Sin is that which arrests the free development of God-consciousness, the proper relationship between self, world, and God. Sin is the arresting of the power of the spirit by the flesh. In the new historical community, redemption is effected by the communication of Jesus' sinless perfection. This is not to mean that Jesus is recognized, in Kantian fashion, as a person of exceptional moral excellence by those who already have the moral ideal within them. The communication of sinless perfection is Jesus' own work. He communicates it. It is perfection, not mere moral improvement. He works on his followers in such a way that they are drawn into the sphere of his sinless perfection. This faith is passed on through history from him under the power of his personal influence. In ordinary circumstances the power and influence of historical figures diminish with time. Not so here. Christian faith depends on the communication of the absolutely potent God-consciousness in Christ as something inward yet derived from without in history.[46] The sinless perfection of Jesus, the absolutely potent God-consciousness radiating from his historical life, is the *Urbild*, the productive ideal, manifest in time, creating something new. Jesus does not merely enhance the moral impulses we already have. The perfection radiating from him convicts of sin at the same time it draws under his influence. "Grace" is received only in the community.

What does Jesus do? It seems fair to say that Jesus' significance does not lie in anything particular that he does. Rather, everything he does serves to illustrate one thing: his sinless perfection and potent God-consciousness. Somewhat in the fashion of Irenaeus, Christ succeeds at every point where fallen beings fail. The acts point to the peculiar character of his being.

Schleiermacher's masterful work shows the difficulty of steering between the Scylla of vicarious satisfaction and the Charybdis of moral influence. The idea of the new historical community (the kingdom of God) is a fruitful one, and in this Schleiermacher is a founder of the age to come in theology. But the interpretation of Christ's work in terms of feeling, God-consciousness, and sinless perfection results in a Jesus who is a religious virtuoso, the hero-artist romantics admired so much. In spite of Schleiermacher's passion for a Christ who communicates himself to us in an historical, human, and non-docetic fashion, it is difficult not to suspect at least a tinge of docetism. Jesus

7 / THE WORK OF CHRIST

dies a protected death. He manifests the power and constancy of his God-consciousness to the end, maintaining his divine dignity. The cry of dereliction from the cross cannot be real. The death does not establish anything new, it merely illustrates the truth of the system. Even here the orthodox system and its antagonists are brothers and sisters under the skin. The orthodox speak of a divine nature that guarantees the infinite worth of Jesus' sacrifice. Jesus "offers" his sacrifice knowing the "system." He dies knowing why, and does not need to ask. He is protected from the terror and disaster of his own death by the system. The cross is covered with roses. Schleiermacher may reject talk of a divine "nature" and prefer "God-consciousness" and "divine dignity," but the result is the same. Jesus does not really die; he demonstrates his God-consciousness. This too is to put roses on the cross. Just as in the orthodox system, a resurrection is superfluous.

Albrecht Ritschl, the most influential of those who tried to redefine the work of Christ in terms of the new historical community, represents a synthesis between the kind of thinking found in Schleiermacher and the emerging *heilsgeschichtliche* theology of the later nineteenth century. He approved of the emphasis on the historical community (the kingdom of God) but rejected the religion of absolute dependence and its abstract monotheism as being too metaphysical and impersonal. The kingdom, for Ritschl, must be understood in more biblical, historical, actual, and practical terms. To get at this, Ritschl tried a variety of distinctions to set off the kingdom from false alternatives. Most prominent for our purposes was the Kantian distinction between the theoretical and the practical. Theology has to do with the practical knowledge of God gained in the historical community and the manner in which this relates one to the world, not with "theoretical," "scientific," "abstract," "objective," or "disinterested" knowledge. Practical knowledge is "religious," "ethical," and "moral," a knowledge that involves the whole person and one's way of life.[47]

Religion is concerned with rising above mere "nature" to "spirit," above subjection to the sway of death, the "flesh," the "world," time, and decay, to the position of *dominion*.[48] In Jesus, God takes the last, decisive, and concrete historical step with humankind in establishing the kingdom, God's true dominion. Everything flows from the practical influence of Jesus as an historical person. Jesus reveals God as Father, the God of love to whom we can draw near with confidence. Wrath is replaced by love; wrath pertains only to life outside the kingdom. Christ draws people into this community of confidence and trust in the God of love who in creation and redemption has set the true *telos* for human existence: a kingdom where all are united to God in love in spite of all hindrances of a natural, physical, or metaphysical sort. One is saved from false conceptions of God by being drawn into the community of love by Jesus.[49]

What then does Jesus *do*? Vicarious satisfaction must be rejected as a prime example of the way natural theology intrudes into and distorts theology.[50] At the same time, Ritschl attacks the idea that Jesus is a mere teacher or example. The forgiveness he brings is not a matter of course, nor can it be a simple deduction from the love of God. If so, then the new community would be a school, not a church, and one would not get beyond theoretical knowledge. Forgiveness and reconciliation must be dependent on and flow from Jesus' actual work, his life, suffering, and death, the practical effect of the historical person.

The point is similar to Schleiermacher's. Sin—resistance to God's sovereign and moral rule—forms a kingdom of evil opposition. Because of sin, humans feel guilt and experience the world and God as hostile, interpreting natural vicissitudes as the result of guilt. The approach to God is therefore distorted, a confusion of nature and spirit. Outside the kingdom, humans are unreconciled to God. Jesus enters this world and suffers all the antagonisms to God's rule operative in the unreconciled. He is true to his calling to the end. He suffers and dies without giving in and thus triumphs over all that stands against God's true rule and *telos*.

The key idea is Jesus' "faithfulness to his calling" (*Berufstreue*). In his faithfulness Jesus rises above all natural, national, and political limitations, even those of the Old Testament, transcending the expectation of mere material well-being, and introduces a new religion "by advancing its significance for mankind to a spiritual and ethical union, which at once corresponds to the spirituality of God and denotes the supramundane end of spiritual creatures."[51] In his faithfulness to his calling, Jesus exercises a double role. He is the revealer of God in taking up a position that "corresponds to the idea of the one God and to the worth of God's spiritual Kingdom."[52] He also reveals true man in being one who according to this knowledge of God worships and serves God to the end without giving in to the opposition of the world.

Jesus' sacrifice is thus not vicarious in the traditional sense, but it is a death in faithfulness to his calling.

> It is not the mere fate of dying that determines the values of Christ's death as a sacrifice; what renders this issue of His life significant for others is His willing acceptance of the death inflicted on Him by his adversaries as a dispensation of God, and the highest proof of faithfulness to his vocation. Thus it is impossible to accept an interpretation of Christ's sacrificial death, which, under the head of satisfaction, combines in a superficial manner His death and His active life, while at bottom it ascribes to the death of Christ quite a different meaning, namely, that of substitutionary punishment.[53]

By his faithfulness, Jesus establishes a community of communion with God in spite of human sin and feelings of guilt. Indeed, in this new relationship

7 / THE WORK OF CHRIST

we first come really to recognize our sin—our ignorance of God and God's true dominion. The sense of guilt is not simply removed but is rather intensified. But the power of sin and guilt to separate us from God is overcome in the Jesus who reveals the Father as love and draws us into communion with God. Since it is only in the actual historical community that this relationship is realized, it must be seen as rooted and grounded in the action of Christ as founder of that community. In his faithfulness, Jesus Christ is the perfect revealer, the founder of a new and perfect religion, the triumph of the spirit of love over nature and the world. He secures life even against the power of death.[54]

Ritschl, more conservative biblically than many liberals, does not seem to brush aside the resurrection or to have any problems with its miraculous nature. At the same time, his insistence on the "spiritual" and "ethical" nature of Jesus' "religion" prohibits giving too much theological importance to such miracles. The resurrection appearances have only the function of freeing the disciples from the "erroneous first impression" that he was subject to the fate of death. Resurrection does not bring anything new to light; it only reinforces the idea of spirit's victory over nature and receives little treatment or mention in Ritschl's development of the work of Christ.[55]

What is to be said of Ritschl's treatment? On the positive side, it represents the recovery of many important biblical themes: the centrality of the kingdom, the rejection of juridical hegemony in understanding divine righteousness, the passion for the actual rather than the theoretical in considering reconciliation. Ritschl did recover much that had been sacrificed to the gods of metaphysics. Negatively, however, his reconstruction is plagued by much the same problems as Schleiermacher's. The concern for the actual and the practical leads him to interpret atonement in terms of the religion of "practical reason" and "ethical religion" gleaned largely from Immanuel Kant and Hermann Lotze. The result is a Jesus who turns out to be the hero of this religion, whose influence is communicated through the subjective experience of the community.

Several consequences then follow. Since Jesus dies in "faithfulness to his calling," he must be different from all others in that for him no vacillation, no profound disruption or temptation, no *Anfechtung*, is possible. He must die a hero's death, the hero of religion. The cry from the cross does not represent a serious disturbance. Subtle exegesis can put it aside. The lament of the psalmist, from which it is taken, is only of a hypothetical sort, the psalmist is not to be taken as actually suffering the wrath of God, since at the same time the psalmist cries to God for deliverance. The same is true of Jesus. Whoever calls on God as "my God" is not far from God and certainly not subject to God's wrath.[56] So the hero does not really die, but carries out a vocation. The roses remain on the cross.

THE SHAPE OF THE TRADITION

Further, there is no way to deal with the wrath of God. Wrath must be banished by the system, not by the cross and resurrection. Ritschl's theology thus becomes just another that attempts to remove wrath by theological erasure. He removes it from *the system* and thus conducts the battle against natural theology and metaphysics on the wrong front. The love of God threatens to turn into a mere banality.

All this is the result of Ritschl's attempt to solve the problems of justification and reconciliation by equating Luther's *"pro me"* (for me) with Kantian practical religion.[57] The "I" of the Reformation *pro me* is not the "I" of Kant's practical reason. It is rather the "I" of the divine election which encounters me "from without" in the proclamation. The *pro me* does not belong in the *fides qua creditur* (the faith which believes) but rather in the *fides quae creditur* (the faith which is believed). Any *pro me* apart from the radical *extra nos* (outside us) is mistaken and a fatal methodological error. All christological assertions are indeed *pro me* assertions, but also all *pro me* assertions must be christologically interpreted.[58]

Schleiermacher's and Ritschl's attempts at reconstruction are highly instructive for dogmatics. The attempt to grasp Christ's work as the *historical* triumph of divine love is important in its stress on concreteness and actuality. But it will fail if we simply accommodate such love to *religious* possibilities immanent in this age. The eschatological dimension is lost, and Jesus becomes the hero of religion. The bleakness and disaster of the cross are covered by all the theological roses. Jesus is rescued from death by *theology*, so any further resurrection is largely superfluous.

Theologians who appreciated the liberals' stress on the love of God and the critique of vicarious satisfaction, but still found that view wanting, often took the tack of deepening the idea of love to include divine holiness. The love of God, they insisted, is not banal sentimentality; it is *holy* love, a love shaped by morality and justice, a revulsion against sin. God's wrath cannot simply be erased from the system. The necessity for the cross cannot be based only in the divine will to love; it must also be based in the need to meet the demands of divine holiness.

P. T. Forsyth's thought is a good example of this move. Inheritor, on the one hand, of the vast British literature on the atonement (no group of theologians has been so concerned with the atonement as the British through the eighteenth, nineteenth, and twentieth centuries)[59] and, on the other hand, a student of Ritschl, Forsyth set out to combat the sentimentalizing and aestheticizing he detected in his liberal teachers. He repeatedly makes a sharp distinction between the "liberal Jesus" and the "real theological Christ."[60] To realize his program, Forsyth proposed what he called the "moralization" of dogma. He apparently saw this as a remedy to both the abstract metaphysicalizing complained of by Ritschl and the aestheticizing or sentimen-

7 / THE WORK OF CHRIST

talizing of the liberals themselves. What is needed, he insisted, was not mere criticism of ancient dogma but recasting it in a new form to recapture its moral seriousness and depth. The juridical element in older doctrines of atonement had been lost due to rejection, in many ways legitimate, of vicarious satisfaction. The baby had been thrown out with the bath water. To carry out the program of "moralization," Forsyth employed the concept of the divine holiness: God's personal self-identity and unchangeable faithfulness to the divine self as the Holy One. Everything depends on this. "We have to stir the interest of our congregations," he says, "as much with the holiness of God as the church was stirred—first with the justice and then latterly with the love of God."[61]

Even the omnipotence of God is limited by God's holiness: God's love cannot negate that holiness.[62] The holiness of God dictates the character of theology and finds its echo in the moral order of the universe and the conscience of humans. "The incarnation, being for a moral and not a metaphysical purpose, must be in its nature moral. . . . It is the moral experience alone which can and must dictate the shape of theology. What Christ does is to bring about a new moral creation, a new creation of the moral soul."[63] The unity of the human race (an important idea for Forsyth) is a moral unity, a unity of conscience. "What makes the world God's world is the action and unity of God's moral order of which our conscience speaks."[64] The changeless order of the moral world, manifest in conscience, makes humankind universal.

The "moralization of dogma" leads Forsyth to cast the work of Christ as a work of *redemptive holiness* and to reintroduce the juristic dimension lost in liberalism.[65] But this cannot mean a simple return to ideas about vicarious or equivalent payment and punishment. God is not paid off. Grace is not procured. There can be no transfer of guilt or suffering or punishment.[66] What is needed, for Forsyth, is a reconstruction that retains the moral seriousness of the older views but purges them of commercialism.

In summary, Forsyth's view is as follows. Vital is the Pauline passage "God was in Christ reconciling the world unto himself." What occurs in Christ is the justification of God's holiness. Christ, though sinless, enters into the world of sin, and in solidarity with it renders perfect obedience to and confession of divine holiness. God, as holy, is bound to his own personal will, which he cannot change or relax. But since he is also love, God desires reconciliation. This can be accomplished only in such a way that divine holiness be perfectly maintained, confessed, and satisfied. Christ, by his own consent and obedience, is "made to be sin for us" so that the treatment due sin actually falls on him. Being found among sinners, he accepts the judgment, and in going to his death he bears witness to and confesses the divine holiness in the world of sin. The event of the cross therefore actually establishes and reveals in this world the holiness of God as a *redeeming* holiness, a holy love, because it is revealed in such a way that it can have a sanctifying effect. The cross gives holiness its due, and when humans see this they are made new creatures, drawn into the actual kingdom of holiness in Christ.

In effect, the structure of Forsyth's argument is much the same as Ritschl's. The difference is that holiness tends to replace love as the decisive factor, so that "the moral" replaces sentiment. Christ's sacrifice is obedience unto death in identification with human sin, so as to render compelling confession to the holiness of God and draw the world into this confession. What is of atoning value in Jesus' death is not vicarious suffering as such, but his obedience as the summation of his life, or, as Ritschl would have said, his "faithfulness to his calling" to the end.[67] But what Jesus is obedient to is not love but the vision of the holiness of God which must be confessed among humankind. In this sense, Christ's death can even be said to "satisfy" God. God is satisfied when God's holiness is confessed. Indeed, God must be satisfied. "For an unsatisfied God, a dissatisfied God, would be no God."[68] What makes satisfaction also love is that *God* does it. God sends Jesus to do this for us and for the world and to reconcile us to himself.

The problem of substitution, the Achilles' heel of the older views, is handled by Forsyth through his concept of the "solidary" character of Christ's work, as he likes to call it. Christ's work is not a vicarious substitution in the sense that he was a third party in an individualistically conceived relationship. Indeed, the Gospels show that God can forgive repentant individuals on the basis of divine freedom and mercy without the cross. But such repentance is insecure as long as it does not rest on something of more universal scope. What Christ must do is reconcile the world to God universally, bring the world to its knees before God to be forgiven. Christ's work is solidary in that it has to do with the pardon of the world, with solidary sin. The cross alone can effect that.[69] The necessity for an atonement of an objective sort rests in Forsyth's conception of the moral order of the world. Something must be done to repair and change that moral order and bring the world to confess its solidary sin.[70]

Christ's work is therefore not that of a substitute for individuals, but is representative, creative of a new order.[71] Even the idea of "representation" is too weak. "Surety" is more accurate for Forsyth; Christ is surety for the fallen race, creating the holiness that is lacking.[72] The moral foundation of the world is altered by his act; and as one is *in him*—not just taught *by* him—one is made part of the new moral order in which God's holy love is confessed. Christ's work means a new stage in the history of creation.[73]

A remarkable passage sums up Forsyth's view:

> The work of Christ was thus in the same act triumphant over evil, satisfying to the heart of God, and creative to the conscience of man by virtue of his soli-

7 / THE WORK OF CHRIST

> darity with God on the one side, and on the other with the race. He subdued Satan, rejoiced the Father, and set up in humanity the kingdom—all in one supreme and consummate act of his one person. He destroyed the kingdom of evil, not by way of preparation for the kingdom of God, but by actually establishing God's kingdom in the heart of it. And he rejoiced, filled, and satisfied the heart of God, not by a statutory obedience, or by one private to himself, which spectacle disposed God to bless and sanctify man; but by presenting in the compendious compass of his own person a humanity presanctified by the irresistible power of his own creative and timeless work.[74]

Forsyth explicitly saw Christ's work as bringing together all the aspects later separated by the various theories. The atoning work of Christ is "objective" since it is creative of the new kingdom of holiness. It is "victorious" because this kingdom is the conquest of evil on a cosmic scale. It is also "subjective" in creating in us the sanctity pleasing to God. In Christ the God who is always love sanctifies us by creative holiness so we can be treated differently.[75]

In many ways Forsyth's work is a remarkable achievement—reasserting essential dimensions of Christ's work without resorting to the more objectionable features of the older views. His insistence that Christ's work must be creative of a *new* order, that something must actually be done in and for the "race," is a helpful advance. The creation of a new order also helps bring together the various dimensions of atonement: the "objective," the "victory," and the "subjective."

Yet for all that, there is something disconcerting about Forsyth's reconstruction. No doubt it lies in the nature of the program itself: the moralization of dogma. This leads to employing holiness as a moral category that qualifies love. It is difficult to escape suspicion that the long shadow of the "great and sublime Kant" still broods over the enterprise. Can holiness be thus moralized? Rudolf Otto taught us to look with suspicion on such a move.[76] Moralization always involves a narrowing and perhaps trivialization of "the Holy."[77] Further, when the love of God is qualified by moralized holiness there is a pronounced loss of New Testament eschatology. Forsyth does not seem able to make much of the fact that Christ is the end of the law to those who believe, or of the idea that love conquers wrath. The result is a "new order" that still tends to look like Kant's moral kingdom, blurring the distinction between the eschatological kingdom and a this-worldly kingdom of law and morality. In this regard, Forsyth was more captive to liberalism than he would like to admit. The relatively minor role played by the resurrection indicates this. Forsyth does not fail to speak of the resurrection and give it more prominence than his predecessors did. Nevertheless, he can explain the work of Christ largely without it. As in other systems, *theology* rescues Jesus from death. Christ dies in obedience, quite conscious of the system. The cry of dereliction is not what it seems: not the anguished cry of a dying man but the concrete

THE SHAPE OF THE TRADITION

confession of the holy God's repulsion of sin. It is doubtful that the New Testament would sustain such an interpretation. Jesus dies too much like a good Kantian. There are still too many roses on the cross.

Emil Brunner, in his classic work *The Mediator*, affords another example of the attempt to qualify love by holiness.[78] Like Forsyth, Brunner rejects the idea that God is changed by an "equivalent payment." Yet Brunner too insists that atonement has indispensable juristic and forensic aspects. God's love cannot be mere sentimentality. Hence the insistence on holy love. The points at which traditional ideas of vicarious satisfaction went astray are that they were too much fettered by primitive religious conceptions that see God as the object rather than the subject of atonement, and that atonement thinking has been taken captive to general revelation rather than special revelation.[79] This latter point is Brunner's most significant contribution to the argument. Aspects of the truth have been obscured or lost, he says, because we have transformed them into "general religious or moral truth." The problem with penal aspects in atonement thinking is not that they are not true but rather that, taken as general truth, they are never the truth.[80] Taken as special revelation, however, they find their true place.

Brunner's construction differs from Forsyth's in that it comes after the full impact of the rediscovery of biblical eschatology and of the consequent neo-orthodox vision of God. The need for atonement roots not in God's need to be paid but rather in the need for a *special* revelation, a special act of deliverance on the part of the God who is holy love. We cannot be saved by general truth. God's wrathful holiness stands and cannot be mitigated or synthesized with love. Love must conquer wrath concretely in the cross *for us*. Brunner's view is therefore more dialectical than Forsyth's. The moral law indeed stands: "The law is the backbone, the skeleton, the granite foundation of the world of thought."[81] But it is "natural knowledge" and as such can never become fully personal. The dialectical counterpart is the special revelation, the act of love in which God claims us as his own. The necessity for atonement, for the cross, rests for Brunner in the need for a revelation that actually changes the situation. God comes, in Christ, into an alien reality, that of sin under divine wrath, and reveals God in such a way that we perceive that both God's holiness and God's love are infinite. But everything depends on the actual coming of God to us. It cannot be just an idea. If ideas could help, we would not be so badly off. The wrath of God is overcome only to faith in the special revelation. The cross is therefore the event in which wrath is broken through; it is the "expiatory" and "penal" sacrifice of the Son of God because he enters under wrath and suffers to reveal God as holy love. In God's nearness his distance is revealed; in God's holiness his mercy is revealed; in God's grace his judgment is revealed; and so on.

Thus Brunner can conclude that special revelation and atonement are in-

7 / THE WORK OF CHRIST

timately associated—"indeed, rightly understood, they are one."[82] Apart from the actual event of the cross, God is wrath. In the cross God is revealed as holy love to faith.

Like Forsyth, Brunner is right in insisting on the place of biblical concepts such as judgment, condemnation, expiation, and so on, which had been shunted aside by liberalism. Yet one wonders again whether the whole has not been too stringently moralized. Strangely absent once again is reference to the resurrection in connection with atonement and death. Of course, Brunner talks about it at length elsewhere; but his system of atonement seems to work without it. The emphasis on special revelation is a step in the right direction, but it alone cannot carry the burden and is distorted when made to do so. A theological distinction is once again made to do the work of the eschatology itself and threatens therefore even to displace the cross and resurrection. One fears once again that the construction reconciles more to the moral order and holiness of God than it leads to the proclamation of the love of God which really brings a new creation.

VICTORY OVER THE TYRANTS

In 1930 the Swedish theologian Gustaf Aulén published *Den kristna forsoningstanken* (English translation: *Christus Victor*, 1931).[83] This book became a theological event, especially in Scandinavian and English-speaking circles. By claiming that the idea of victory over demonic forces was the classic Christian view of atonement, it had the effect of breaking the deadlock between "objective" and "subjective" views. What had been considered merely a crude pictorial and imaginative curiosity was raised to the level of dogmatic respectability. The victory motif seemed to offer a fresh alternative.

Aulén did not claim to set forth a new theory (only vicarious satisfaction and moral influence, for him, are theories), but simply to bring to light a motif which had governed the thinking and liturgical practice of the church in the early centuries and which was revived by Luther. The motif is that of a dramatic and cosmic battle rather than a logical argument: "Christus Victor" triumphs over the powers of evil in a dramatic battle and releases enslaved humankind. In this victory, God reconciles the world to himself by winning it back, not by being "satisfied." Aulén insists that this is a doctrine of atonement, against nineteenth-century interpreters who often referred to it rather as a doctrine of redemption or salvation, of release from captivity rather than expiation for sin.[84] God is reconciled in the very act in which God reconciles the world.

The background is dualistic and the action is dramatic: God in Christ does battle against the demonic forces. The dualism is not absolute and metaphysical, however, but rather of the sort found in Scripture: radical opposition between the forces of evil and the creator God, even though evil does not have eternal existence.[85] The scriptural roots of the motif are the synoptic picture of Jesus' battle with the demons and tyrants.

The proof that the victory motif is a discreet doctrine that cannot be reduced to other views is provided by a series of contrasts. In vicarious satisfaction God's action is discontinuous: God sends Christ, but then must be satisfied by the act of the God-man. In the victory motif the action is continuous: God sends Christ and works through and in him to defeat the demonic powers. The contrast with the subjective view is also evident. There is not simply a change in the subject. There is rather a complete change of cosmic scope, in the *situation*, and a change in the *relation* between God and the world, including a change in God's own attitude. The classic view, Aulén insists, is if anything more objective than the so-called objective view, because it deals not only with individuals but with the whole world.

The essential features of this view are to be found in Irenaeus' theology of "recapitulation." Christ recapitulates human history by overcoming at every step where Adam succumbed to demonic temptation. The work of Christ is battle and victory over powers that hold humans in bondage: sin, death, and the devil. The victory creates a new situation, bringing the rule of hostile forces to an end, setting humans free. There is no cleavage between incarnation and atonement. It is God who accomplishes the work throughout.

Aulén considers the double-sidedness of the view to be one of its characteristic features: God is both reconciler and reconciled; God both gives and receives the sacrifice. Aulén, far from being worried about this duplicity, seems to find it an advantage, a mark of the dramatic nature of the view that defies enclosure in a rational scheme.

The victory motif leads to an emphasis on the resurrection conspicuously absent from other views. The resurrection is the manifestation of the decisive victory over the powers of evil and death, the starting point for the new dispensation, the new "situation," the gift of the Spirit.

Aulén insists that the classic view was the dominant and basic view in the church for a thousand years, in both East and West, until Anselm's Latin view intruded in the West. It was also, for Aulén, the basic view of the New Testament. Only with the development of the idea of penance in Tertullian and later thinkers did the Latin view gain prominence. Luther revived the victory motif, adding the law and the wrath of God as principal among the tyrants to be defeated. Argument about Luther's views on atonement will concern us later.

The troublesome dogmatic question for the victory motif is the one we have been encountering all along: wherein lies the necessity for Christ's death and

7 / THE WORK OF CHRIST

resurrection? Anselm, we recall, put the basic question: If defeat of demonic powers is all that is necessary, why could not the almighty God have done it some other way? Why subject the Son to such torture?

As Aulén points out, the Greek fathers did wrestle with just this question. Generally they seem to say that God's true nature, God's righteousness and love, and so on, would not have come to light if God had just used force. Sometimes there is the suggestion that the devil has gained rights over fallen creatures and God must respect them to show the divine righteousness.[86] Most frequently, however, the deepest reason cited is the inner necessity of the divine love. God shows love most clearly by coming and taking the suffering of our bondage on the divine self.[87] Gregory of Nyssa takes this thought even further by saying that divine power and invincibility is not shown by acts of force, by the vastness of the heavens, the orderliness of the universe, and so on, but precisely by condescension to the weakness of human nature, there to do battle and overcome.[88] The early fathers were striving to say something vital in all this, but for the moment their ideas seem to lack coherent persuasive power. At least they were not, apparently, persuasive enough to stave off the logical demands of Anselm and his followers.

The dogmatic tentativeness is also evident in the treatment of the devil and his "rights." The fathers could not agree. They believed that the devil had been rightly and reasonably overcome, but they were uncertain as to whether the devil had gained rights over fallen creatures or was simply a usurper. The idea that the devil had gained rights and deserved proper ransom seems most common.[89] The religious motive behind such language, Aulén insists, is to assert the guilt of humankind and the judgment of God on human sin.[90] One might say that the stress is not so much on the rights of the devil, but that since the "wages of sin is death," the devil has the job, the "right," to execute the sinner, thus carrying out God's judgment. At the same time, however, it can be said that the devil is a deceiver since his dominion of death is contrary to God's ultimate will for humankind. The devil receives the ransom price to which he has a right. To this point the inner logic is virtually the same as with vicarious satisfaction; the difference is who is paid. Not all could accept the logic, however. Gregory of Nazianzus denied the idea of the devil's rights, insisting he was a usurper who gained power by deception and thus deserved only to be despoiled and forced to surrender.[91]

The argument about the devil's rights indicates the difficulty in answering the question of necessity, in consistent fashion, for the victory motif. Perhaps the reason is that just as with vicarious satisfaction the logic tends to falter. A law that cannot give life takes the center of the stage. The devil may have the power to inflict death, but the devil cannot give life—just as the law cannot. The devil cannot release the captives and give freedom. No doubt that is why the idea of the rights of the devil had to be augmented by the thought

THE SHAPE OF THE TRADITION

that the devil exceeded his rights in the case of Christ and thus was deceived and despoiled. By attacking the innocent one the devil lost his rights and his dominion.[92] Instead of saying the devil is satisfied, one has to say he is defeated. The point is that something new has to be brought to light in the death and resurrection of Christ.

Thus there is a proliferation of pictures having to do with the *deception* of the devil. The basic idea is that Christ appears incognito among humans; the devil, thinking him an easy prey, attacks, and is defeated by the divinity hidden in the flesh. The image of the devil being deceived like a fish taking the worm but not seeing the hook becomes a favorite.[93]

All this, however, does not answer Anselm's question about necessity very clearly. The logic repeatedly leads one into blind alleys in which God and the devil threaten to change places, in a sort of dizzying tail-chase. If one says the cross was necessary to pay the devil, one risks making the devil a god with rights to the creation. Thus the protest: the devil is a usurper. If, on the other hand, one presses the idea of the deception of the devil, one makes God a deceiver—precisely the devil's art. Thus the insistence that God acts righteously even with the devil.

Aulén contents himself with the assertion that the view is not a rational theory but a dramatic picture defying systematization. But even he is constrained to give some orderly account of what the pictures are supposed to convey and to insist that we penetrate beneath the surface to the "religious values" that lie concealed there. They are, Aulén says, as follows. First, God does not use force but enters into the drama to gain his purpose by giving himself. Second, the idea of rights expresses God's fair play even in dealing with evil powers. Third, the alternation between the devil as one with rights, carrying out the divine judgment, and as a usurper serves to convey both the dualistic outlook and the limitations of dualism. The devil is the embodiment of evil, the dark protagonist, but even so the devil is not equal to God and can derive power only from God. This is a way of asserting both the responsibility of the creature for sin and the justice of the judgment. Fourth, the idea of the deception of the devil means that evil ultimately overreaches itself when it comes into conflict with good and loses the battle at the moment it seems most victorious. The ultimate evil act, the cross, is the victory.[94]

The double-sidedness of the view must stand, in Aulén's opinion. "For theology lives and has its being in these combinations of seemingly incompatible opposites."[95] The very incompatibility of the opposites, Aulén says, stood in the early days as a barrier against transforming theology into speculative metaphysics. The drama is of the essence.

How shall one assess the victory motif? One cannot deny its positive importance for dogmatics. Aulén has succeeded in isolating a distinct view of atonement, which had gotten lost through the years. Historians may com-

7 / THE WORK OF CHRIST

plain that he has oversimplified or misrepresented the history of the matter, but that does not detract from its dogmatic importance. The single most important advance is the manner in which the resurrection regains its proper place in atonement doctrine. The dramatic-dualistic background facilitates understanding the breaking in of a new age through the death and resurrection of Christ and forestalls any return to moralism. This is an advance of great significance and must be developed further.

But it is questionable whether the motif in its mythological form can make sustained appeal to the modern mind. The "cosmic-dualistic battle" tends to appear extraneous to us and lends itself easily to a kind of triumphalism that says nothing to the despairing, the losers of the world. A way must be found to assert the reality of the victory that retains its cosmic scope and still makes it concrete and viable existentially.

Perhaps this is the reason for the persistent criticism that the victory motif tends to overlook sin and guilt and to shift the emphasis to mortality, finitude, and death. Aulén struggles to overcome this criticism, but it sticks nevertheless.[96] When the basic presupposition is that the major obstacle to salvation is finitude and death, one is not far from gnosticism. Sin recedes into the background as a prehistoric miscarriage in the emanation of the cosmos. Then also it is difficult to maintain the necessity for the cruel death on the cross. Simply to save us from *death*, the redeemer could impart life in some other way. The gnostic teacher liberated from death by imparting knowledge. Irenaeus' Christ "recapitulates" human history: the power of immortal life wins over temptation at every step, and the cross, though the supreme instance of victory, is relativized. One event is as important as another. The point is always the same: the victory of immortality over mortality. The imagery of ransom paid to the devil demonstrates the confusion. Since the one who is to die is immortal, the devil is deceived. The one who is to die could not die. One comes perilously close to the gnostic idea that the cross was a "seeming" to die—the gnostic redeemer escapes before the crucifixion. If the redeemer's death is a deception of the devil, how much is there to choose between the two?

In sum, the dramatic-dualistic imagery can also misdirect our attention away from the Jesus who was crucified for us under Pontius Pilate to a mythic figure who was paying a ransom to the devil and deceiving the devil at the same time. Why the cross? Could the redeemer not just as well have died in bed after a full and saintly life, or perhaps even in battle leading a Zealot crusade or a popular revolution? Or would it not have been better, after having won the victory at every step where Adam succumbed, to turn the tables on death by not dying at all? The "victorious" Jesus can all too easily be portrayed as one who does not finally die. The roses still obscure the truth.

THE SHAPE OF THE TRADITION

Before moving on, we must assess the importance of the victory motif for dogmatics. It must be seen in context. It arose and gained credence in an age when old optimisms and structures were being destroyed by dark tyrannical forces. Its revival in Reformation times and in our day can also be seen as a protest against any legalistic rationalization that oversimplifies the human problem and ends with a God who is either a vindictive bookkeeper or an overindulgent lover. The dramatic imagery interjects a note of desperate conflict that is more true to actual experience. There is danger and darkness, and God is not uninvolved in or even untainted by the darkness. The demonic forces execute his judgment on sin. Yet once unleashed, they threaten to exceed their prerogatives and usurp those of divinity. It is God who must deal with the problem properly. The victory imagery is helpful in that it restores drama, action, and life where there had been only legalistic bookkeeping.

Yet we must question whether revival of the victory motif has been entirely fortunate for dogmatics. While it rightfully challenged the hegemony of previous views, the alternative it suggests does not seem equal to the task. Aulén himself speaks of it as a series of images with glaring contrasts, and intimates that any attempt to put it into consistent rational shape would rob it of its depth and frustrate the purpose of theology. There may be some truth in this, but it is not clearly specified enough to be convincing.

The inconclusive outcome of the debate has had a relativizing effect. Where one motif becomes "just an image" or "picture," *all* tend to become so, each representing some aspect of the truth. Atonement becomes a theory, a projection in thought, and one can easily lose confidence that anything meaningful is being said at all about *God* and *God's* activity. No doubt it is necessary for dogmatics to go through this crisis in confidence; after all, it had exceeded its proper limits. But merely to relativize a collection of such excessive images is hardly an advance. The cross loses its overagainstness. The roses are not removed; one only changes them now and then. Willy-nilly the cross becomes even more the object of our speculation, something we look at and assign meaning with our images, models, and theories. The relativization leads to the platitude that no one view does justice to the profound mystery of the atonement.[97] Theologians can then revel in the art of multiplying theories and models—apparently on the assumption that the more one discovers the more truth one will uncover. Thus we arrive at the view quoted above, likening atonement to a precious jewel with many facets which one turns around in one's hand because one can only see one facet at a time. The analogy is itself a damaging one. Imagine looking at the terrible event at Golgotha as though it were a precious jewel one examines at leisure to discern its facets. Instead of judging us, the cross becomes the object of our curiosity, our search for "religious values." We continue the search for roses.

7 / THE WORK OF CHRIST

NOTES

1. Martin Hengel, *Crucifixion in the Ancient World and the Folly of the Message of the Cross* (Philadelphia: Fortress Press, 1977).
2. See the discussions in Hans Kessler, *Die theologische Bedeutung des Todes Jesu,* Themen und Thesen der Theologie (Düsseldorf: Patmos Verlag, 1970), pp. 227ff.; and Sam K. Williams, *Jesus' Death as Saving Event: The Background and Origin of a Concept,* Harvard Dissertations in Religion 2 (Missoula, Mont.: Scholars Press, 1975), pp. 203ff.
3. See Williams, *Jesus' Death,* esp. pp. 59–135, 165–202, for an account of the use of this material.
4. Ibid., passim.
5. See Morna Hooker, *Jesus and the Servant* (London: SPCK, 1959).
6. Williams, *Jesus' Death,* p. 230.
7. Hengel, *Crucifixion,* pp. 89–90.
8. Friedrich R. Hasse, *Anselm von Canterbury,* vol. 2 (Leipzig: Verlag von W. Engelmann, 1852), pp. 608–9. Cited in Kessler, *Die theologische Bedeutung des Todes Jesu,* p. 84.
9. Kessler, *Die theologische Bedeutung des Todes Jesu,* p. 84.
10. Ibid., p. 35.
11. Ibid., p. 55.
12. See below, and Kessler, *Die theologische Bedeutung des Todes Jesu,* p. 75.
13. Ibid., pp. 75ff.
14. Ibid., pp. 139ff.
15. Anselm, *Cur Deus Homo,* preface.
16. Kessler, *Die theologische Bedeutung des Todes Jesu,* p. 145.
17. Anselm, *Cur Deus Homo,* i,11.
18. Ibid., i,12.
19. Ibid., i,13.
20. Ibid., ii,20.
21. Kessler, *Die theologische Bedeutung des Todes Jesu,* p. 63.
22. One should not drive this too far, since Anselm did work with the more aesthetically tinged Augustinian concept of *order* rather than strict justice and law. The fact remains, however, that Anselm did make the concept of justice determinative for his entire soteriology and that one can therefore speak of a juridicizing of the Augustinian *ordo.* See ibid., pp. 130, 136.
23. Ibid., pp. 130ff.
24. Ibid., p. 134. Cf. Anselm, *Cur Deus Homo,* i,24.
25. See John McIntyre, *St. Anselm and His Critics* (Edinburgh: Oliver & Boyd, 1954).
26. *Cur Deus Homo,* ii,14.
27. Kessler, *Die theologische Bedeutung des Todes Jesu,* p. 168. Also W. Kasper, *Jesus the Christ* (New York: Paulist Press, 1976), p. 220.
28. *Cur Deus Homo,* i,8. This remains a standard—and the best—refutation of exemplarist theories. Protestant orthodoxy later turned it against the Socinians. It would be absurd for God to go to such lengths merely to provide an example of what everyone knew already. See Hans Emil Weber, *Reformation, Orthodoxie und Rationalismus,*

part 2, "Der Geist der Orthodoxie" (Gütersloh: Gerd Mohn, 1951), p. 190, n. 5.

29. *Cur Deus Homo*, i,12; cf. i,24.

30. See R. S. Franks, *The Work of Christ* (New York: Thomas Nelson & Sons, 1962), p. 145; and Kessler, *Die theologische Bedeutung des Todes Jesu*, p. 167.

31. Cited in Franks, *Work of Christ*, p. 365. Usually the emphasis on the freedom of God in Socinus and followers is attributed to the influence of Duns Scotus.

32. Osmo Tiililä, *Das Strafleiden Christi*, AASF 48 (Helsinki, 1941), pp. 67–68.

33. Weber, *Reformation, Orthodoxie und Rationalismus*, p. 185.

34. See Lauri Haikola, *Studien zu Luther und zum Luthertum*, UUA 2 (Uppsala: Lundequistska Bokhandeln, 1958), pp. 9, 106.

35. Weber, *Reformation, Orthodoxie und Rationalismus*, p. 198; also Heinrich Schmid, *The Doctrinal Theology of the Evangelical Lutheran Church*, 3d ed., trans. Charles A. Hay and Henry E. Jacobs (Minneapolis: Augsburg Publishing House, 1899), p. 347.

36. Schmid, *Doctrinal Theology*, p. 347.

37. Leonard Hutter, *Loci communes theologici*, 415, cited in ibid., p. 348.

38. John Andrew Quenstedt, *Theologica didactico-polemica*, iii,227, cited in ibid., p. 348.

39. In this regard they were following Luther, who also dispensed with the distinction between satisfaction and punishment. For Luther it was quite pointless, since as we shall see he reversed the direction. If Anselm feared punishment because it would mean destruction, Luther said that is just what happens. Jesus is "destroyed" *for us* and yet conquers. Orthodoxy, however, legalized the punishment and tended to miss Luther's point.

40. Schmid, *Doctrinal Theology*, p. 359.

41. John Gerhard, cited in ibid., p. 356.

42. Ibid., pp. 340ff. The doctrine of the threefold office, though quite prominent in the older dogmatics—even among liberals (who, however, generally reinterpreted it to fit their particular scheme)—is not treated kindly by contemporary dogmaticians. It did have the advantage of stressing that Christ was carrying out a mandate from God through the office and not doing something randomly from mere human caprice. Also, it attempted to encompass the whole of Christ's life and death in one convenient scheme. Nevertheless, it seems to be an artificial scheme that does not contribute essentially to the understanding of Christ's work. It can even distort when the abstractions begin to crowd out the actualities of his life by speculations about whether and when he used his kingly powers while on earth, and so on. Werner Elert's criticism exposes the problems. He sees the idea of the threefold office to be a classic misapplication of the promise-fulfillment scheme. The fulfillment is taken captive by the expectation. Jesus tends to get "imprisoned" in the Old Testament offices. What is new and better in Christ is precisely what distinguishes him from the offices, not what he has in common with them. (*Der Christliche Glaube*, 2d ed. [Berlin: Im Furche-Verlag, 1941], pp. 405ff.) As Prophet he did not merely speak the word; he *was* the Word. As Priest he did not offer selected "spotless lambs" in a temple ritual; he was killed himself "outside the camp." As King he was not a despot in a theocratic dynasty; he came to serve, to suffer, to die. There is something of a cruel irony in decking Jesus

7 / THE WORK OF CHRIST

out in the offices which he resisted and which eventually destroyed him. He was not any of those. The law and the prophets were until John, "grace and truth came through Jesus Christ" (John 1:17). Thus it does not seem useful for dogmatics to continue using this scheme. For this reason we pay little attention to it in subsequent treatment.

43. Franks, *Work of Christ*, p. 145.
44. Ibid., pp. 370ff.; Weber, *Reformation, Orthodoxie, und Rationalismus*, pp. 186ff.
45. Friedrich Schleiermacher, *The Christian Faith*, ed. H. R. Mackintosh and J. S. Stewart (Edinburgh: T. & T. Clark, 1928), pp. 431-38.
46. Ibid., pp. 425-31.
47. Albrecht Ritschl, *The Christian Doctrine of Justification and Reconciliation*, ed. H. R. Mackintosh and A. B. Macaulay (Edinburgh: T. & T. Clark, 1902); cf. intro. pp. 1ff. See also Albrecht Ritschl, *Theologie und Metaphysik* (Bonn: Adolph Marcus, 1881). Later in life Ritschl used the idea of independent value judgments to characterize the peculiarity of religious perceptions (*Justification and Reconciliation*, pp. 204-5).
48. *Justification and Reconciliation*, IV,27, pp. 193ff.
49. R. Schäfer, *Ritschl* (Tübingen: J. C. B. Mohr [Paul Siebeck], 1968), pp. 112ff.
50. Ritschl, *Justification and Reconciliation*, pp. 477ff.
51. Ibid., p. 455.
52. Ibid., pp. 455-56.
53. Ibid., p. 477.
54. Ibid., p. 457.
55. Schäfer, *Ritschl*, pp. 59-62.
56. Ibid., p. 63.
57. H. J. Iwand, "Wider den Missbrauch des pro me als methodisches Prinzip in der Theologie," *ThLz*, 7/8 (1954): 454-58.
58. Ibid., p. 455.
59. The list is seemingly endless: J. McLeod Campbell, R. C. Moberly, Robert Dale, James Denney, Hastings Rashdall, Robert Franks, to name but a few. For a good survey of the arguments, see Robert S. Paul, *The Atonement and the Sacraments* (Nashville: Abingdon Press, 1960), pp. 162-281.
60. See, e.g., P. T. Forsyth, *The Person and Place of Jesus Christ* (London: Hodder & Stoughton, 1909), pp. 7-8.
61. P. T. Forsyth, *The Work of Christ*, FL (London: William Collins Sons, 1965), p. 85.
62. Ibid., p. 107: "He could will nothing against his holy nature. . . . Nothing in the compass of the divine nature could enable him to abolish a moral law, the law of holiness. . . . If God's love were not essentially holy love, in the course of time mankind would cease to respect it, and consequently to trust it. . . . What love wants is not simply love in response, but respect and confidence. . . . God's holy law is his own holy nature. His love is under the condition of eternal respect. It is quite unchangeable."
63. Forsyth, *Person and Place of Jesus Christ*, p. 222.
64. Forsyth, *Work of Christ*, pp. 113, 114.
65. Ibid., p. 181.
66. P. T. Forsyth, *The Cruciality of the Cross* (London: Independent Press, 1948), p. 41.

67. In the idea of the "confessional obedience of Christ" to the divine holiness, Forsyth modified currents in British thinking on atonement. McLeod Campbell had suggested that the atoning work be understood as a perfect and vicarious confession of sin before God. R. C. Moberly had suggested the idea of vicarious penitence offered to God. The criticism of both was that neither confession of sin nor penitence can be offered vicariously for another, nor could a sinless Christ do either. Forsyth modified these suggestions by saying that Christ as the sinless one neither confesses sin nor does vicarious penitence, but precisely as the sinless one in solidarity with the world of sin and in his obedience confesses the divine holiness in his death. He "who knew no sin" was "made to be sin" and in obedience confesses the rectitude of divine judgment on sin. Only the sinless one could do that.

68. Forsyth, *Work of Christ*, p. 165.
69. Ibid., p. 155. Emphasis added.
70. Ibid., pp. 107-9.
71. Ibid., p. 168.
72. Ibid., p. 170.
73. Ibid., p. 173.
74. Ibid., p. 178.
75. Ibid., pp. 162ff. Forsyth was already conscious of the different aspects (as he called them) of Christ's atoning work (the triumphant, the satisfactionary, and the regenerative) and of the need to draw them together into a unity. The first, the triumphant, must be seen as the condition of the second, the satisfactionary, and the second of the third, the regenerative, so that they all condition one another in a "living interaction." "This one action of the holy Saviour's total person was, on its various sides, the destruction of evil, the satisfaction of God, and the sanctification of men. And it is in this moral medium of holiness (if I may so say) that these three effects pass and play into each other with a spiritual interpenetration." (*Work of Christ*, p. 163.)

76. Rudolf Otto, *The Idea of the Holy* (London: Oxford University Press, 1923).

77. John H. Rodgers argues that Forsyth does not intend to moralize holiness and that he understands it rather as a total claim on human existence, embracing all one is, thinks, feels, and does. The response to divine holiness is not morality but the obedience of faith which thereafter affects one's conduct. No doubt that is true. But would not Schleiermacher and Ritschl have said just the same? The question is whether one can really repair the damage of liberal theology in this fashion. Even Rodgers has to admit that Forsyth himself is not consistent and repeatedly complicates matters by identifying the moral with the holy. John H. Rodgers, *The Theology of P. T. Forsyth* (London: Independent Press, 1965), pp. 35ff.

78. Emil Brunner, *The Mediator*, trans. Olive Wyon (Philadelphia: Westminster Press, 1947).
79. Ibid., pp. 470, 456.
80. Ibid., p. 456.
81. Ibid., p. 458.
82. Ibid., p. 488.
83. Gustav Aulén, *Christus Victor*, trans. A. G. Hebert (New York: Macmillan Co., 1931).

7 / THE WORK OF CHRIST

84. Ibid., p. 5.
85. Ibid., pp. 4–5, n. 1.
86. John of Damascus, *Against the Arians*, ii,68, cited in ibid., p. 45.
87. Aulén, *Christus Victor*, p. 45.
88. Ibid., p. 46.
89. Ibid., p. 48.
90. Ibid., p. 48.
91. Ibid., pp. 49–50.
92. Ibid., p. 51. The same idea is found in Augustine and in Luther, as Aulén notes. In Luther it is most often the law which overreaches itself in condemning Christ and loses its tyrannical power.
93. Gregory of Nyssa, *Great Catechism*, chap. 24; cited in ibid., p. 52.
94. Aulén, *Christus Victor*, p. 129.
95. Ibid., p. 155. Emphasis added.
96. Tiililä, *Das Strafleiden Christi*, p. 65 and passim.
97. Some interpreters find this move a fortunate one. Robert S. Paul, for instance, says: "Aulén not only revived the note of victory in the ancient images, but he liberated theology from the categories of logic and unimaginative rationality in which the doctrine of the Atonement had often been incarcerated and showed that the Church has been most reasonable and most logical when it has expressed the drama of the work of Christ in the pictures and images of the drama itself. He re-emphasized . . . that the fact of the Atonement is ultimate and that our theories about it are relative" (*Atonement and Sacraments*, p. 257).

2
Luther's Theology of the Cross

A theology of the cross provides material for reconstruction by positing a reversal in direction: God comes to us; we do not mount up to God. Atonement occurs when God succeeds in getting through to us who live under wrath and law. God is satisfied, placated, when his move toward us issues in faith. A "happy exchange" takes place: Jesus takes our sinful nature and gives us his righteous and immortal life.

THE DEBATE OVER LUTHER'S VIEW

About the time Aulén's *Christus Victor* appeared, Luther's theology of the cross was rediscovered.[1] Both events have contributed to a ferment in reflection on the atonement which makes consideration of Luther's views an important transition to contemporary reconstruction. Aulén's attempt to claim Luther for the "classic" motif sparked a lively debate, which has continued to the present and sheds new light on the contribution of Luther and the Reformation to atonement thinking. Rediscovery of a theology of the cross likewise furnishes new direction for a post-Reformation restatement.

One can say with justification that the views considered so far are all essentially pre-Reformation in structure, or at least have their roots in pre-Reformation formulations of the problems. The "classic" view is a return to a patristic age; the "Latin" view goes back to Anselm's medieval understanding. Even the "subjective" view, which could lay claim to being the most modern, is usually credited to Anselm's medieval contemporary Abelard. The basic structure of the views, however disparate, remains the same. The aim is to escape, to ascend toward God, whether by law and moral improvement or by victory over the tyrants who chain us to our mortality and finitude. Atonement occurs when the ascent to God succeeds. The discussions about Luther's theology raise fundamental questions about the propriety of such views for a truly post-Reformation understanding.

7 / THE WORK OF CHRIST

So to the debate. Aulén's claim that Luther espoused the classic view was based on solid evidence.[2] Luther's writings abound in the imagery characteristic of the view, and he had a special love for those most disliked by its opponents. He repeatedly uses the picture of the devil taking the bait of the incarnate Christ and getting caught on the unseen hook of the divinity.[3] The vocabulary he prefers when speaking of Christ's work against human sin is almost invariably that of strife, conquest, destruction, killing, and devouring, rather than satisfaction, payment, sacrifice, and propitiation.

Interpreters had noted Luther's love for the classic imagery before, but mostly they had treated it as linguistic or poetic embroidery, or perhaps a hangover from medieval folklore. The basic dogmatic structure of Luther's thought, it was maintained, remained that of vicarious satisfaction. Aulén disputed that, claiming that Luther's thought manifests the classic pattern: there is a continuity in the divine action throughout; atonement is closely connected with incarnation; and there is no thought of an offering made to God from the side of the human. It is God who overcomes the tyrants by divine omnipotence; there is a stupendous, dramatic conflict, a *mirabile duellum*, in which Christ prevails over sin, the law, death, wrath, and the devil.[4]

Aulén maintains, moreover, that the patristic view not only returns in Luther but is deepened on several counts. Luther sees more clearly that the law is one of the tyrants over fallen humanity. The law demands not merely obedience to external commands but also the spontaneous obedience and love of the heart. This makes the legalistic way impossible and turns the law into a tyrant. Likewise, Luther sees more clearly how this places fallen humanity under the wrath of God. Without spontaneous obedience, the love of the heart, one stands under the wrath of God. No mere payment in an abstract legalistic sense will do. The wrath of God will be stilled only when the love is there. The wrath therefore cannot be bought off at a particular point in time. A battle is fought in which the love of God *breaks through* the wrath. A victory must be won which is effective *in the present* for the believer.[5]

The Latin view dies hard, however. Several interpreters disagree that the basic structure of Luther's view is "classic," or at least that Luther can be claimed for that view without qualification or remainder. Paul Althaus is a prominent example.[6] Althaus maintains that Aulén does not see clearly enough that the powers Christ defeats have a just place as executors of the righteous wrath of God and that Luther constantly emphasizes the *right* of such powers. The connecting link between the victory motif and a more juridical view for Luther comes in the idea that the devil is the accuser of sinners. His accusation has force only because it exposes actual transgression of divine law, our failure to meet the demands of the divine righteousness. Thus, "The satisfaction which God's righteousness demands constitutes the primary and decisive significance of Christ's work and particularly of his death. Everything else depends on this satisfaction, including the destruction of the might and the authority of the demonic powers."[7]

Althaus resists all attempts to put aside this juridical element and its priority. It will not do, he says, to claim that the victory motif expresses Luther's own view and that he uses the juridical terminology only as a concession to traditional formulations. For Luther, he insists, we must be freed first and foremost from the wrath of the righteous God. The satisfaction made by Christ's death accomplishes this, and all other victory over the demonic powers is a consequence. "God," Althaus insists, "cannot simply forget about his wrath and show his mercy to sinners if his righteousness is not satisfied."[8]

It is not difficult to find quotations from all periods of Luther's career which at least appear to substantiate the claim made by Althaus and like-minded critics of Aulén, even though they may not be so numerous as those of the classic sort.[9] Yet even such critics have to admit the picture is by no means unambiguous, for Luther often and explicitly attacks the idea of satisfaction as at best too weak and at worst an abomination and the source of all error.

> Even if one wants to retain the word satisfaction and say thereby that Christ has made satisfaction for our sins, nevertheless it is too weak and says too little about the grace of Christ and does not sufficiently honor Christ's suffering. One must give them higher honor because he did not only make satisfaction for sin but also redeemed us from death, the devil, and the power of hell, and guarantees us an eternal kingdom of grace as well as the daily forgiveness of subsequent sins, and so becomes for us (as St. Paul, 1 Cor. 1:1 says) an eternal redemption and sanctification.[10]

Satisfaction is not only too weak a term for Luther, but it is also spoken of as the "beginning, origin, door and entrance to all the abominations" of the medieval system.[11] Usually such discussion comes in the context of an attack on the medieval penitential system, in which penance is understood as satisfaction for sin. Luther was keen enough to see that the whole medieval edifice with its doctrine of atonement grew out of and drew its strength from the ideas of penance, which had begun as early as Tertullian.

THE REVERSAL OF DIRECTION

How is one to account for this confusing state of affairs? Is Luther simply inconsistent or, to put a better construction on it, too rich and varied in his thought and expression to be pressed into a unified scheme? There have been many attempts to explain or resolve the matter. But the arguments are largely sterile, because they end only by claiming Luther for previously existing views.[12] If Luther can be claimed merely as a representative of one or another of the pre-Reformation theories already expounded, he has no particular significance

7 / THE WORK OF CHRIST

for dogmatics. If, however, in his own thinking he had somehow transcended the differences so as to point the way to something quite different, enabling him freely to use the various terms without contradiction, that would be significant and might point in new directions for restatement of the doctrine. This is the perspective from which dogmatics should investigate his teaching on atonement. When this is done, it becomes clear that to understand Luther's utterances one must begin quite differently than the debate has done. Luther sought to be "a theologian of the cross." This involves a great reversal. A theologian of glory, he said, calls the bad good and the good bad. A theologian of the cross says what a thing is. To be a theologian of the cross, one has to learn to see things as they are.[13]

Who are the enemies? What is the wrath under which we suffer? It is the alienation, the guilt, the lostness, the antipathy toward the gods, which we actually feel and experience. The voice of the law which we hear is not an abstract ideal but the terror of the darkness, the demand arising from anything and everything that we do something to fulfill our being and secure our destiny in the face of death. In such a strait, atonement theories do little good. Their explanations do not placate the actual wrath under which we live. They do not end it. They do not end it because there is no reversal of direction. Their assumption is still that payment must be made to God or "the gods" or even to "the demons." But who can ever see or know that payment has in fact taken place, or that it is sufficient? Even if it is, I am left with the task of mustering up the ability really to believe it, on pain of death. How can I do that? I am still under wrath, actual wrath.

Luther saw that it makes little difference for the lost creature whether one says that payment is made to God or says it is made to the devil. So long as the basic structure is payment of a debt on pain of death, nothing new breaks in. Wrath remains. If nothing new happens, one is still under the law. When that is the case, God and the devil are virtually interchangeable and merge into one confusing picture.

For atonement and reconciliation to occur, there must be a reversal of direction. Something must happen, something quite new and different, to end the wrath and defeat the enemies in actuality. If one thinks in terms of an actual end to wrath, an actual stop to the accusing voice of the law, then satisfaction and victory mean the same thing. If the God from whom we are alienated could actually put an end to the separation, then the wrath under which we live would be ended. If we could actually receive this God and trust this God's self-giving, then the divine wrath would be satisfied, and God would win the victory. The key lies in the reversal: not that something is given to God, but that God gives something to us.

This is Luther's concern in speaking of atonement. Atonement occurs when

God gives himself in such fashion as to create a people pleasing to God, a people no longer under law or wrath, a people who love and trust God. When God succeeds in that, God is "satisfied." Atonement occurs, that is to say, exactly in that God was in Christ reconciling the world unto himself. The question for atonement is whether God can succeed in doing this. The question is not whether there is blood precious enough to pay God, or even the devil, but whether God has acted decisively to win us. The question is whether God can actually give himself in such a way as to save us. For God is not the problem, we are. Can God actually deliver us from wrath, save us from sin and embittered hostility and bring something new? What Luther has to say centers around the question of *the way things are*. Can wrath be ended? But that is a question of what God gives and not what God gets, for it is, one should not forget, *God's* wrath, and only God can end it.

The reversal is responsible for our puzzlement over Luther's statements about satisfaction or placation of God's wrath. That God's wrath must be placated if we are to be saved is self-evident when dealing with actuality. It is a tautology. But wrath cannot be placated in the abstract by heavenly transactions between Jesus and God. Nothing is accomplished for us by that. God's wrath against us is placated only when God's self-giving makes us his own, when God succeeds in creating faith, love, and hope. Thus the following remarkable statement (concerning the Lord's Supper):

> God's majesty is greater than the blood of the whole world and the merits of all the angels are able to placate. The Body of Christ *is given* and his blood *is shed* and just so is it placated. Indeed it is given and shed *for you*, just as it is said, "for us." Why "for us" except to placate the wrath of God which threatens our sins? Moreover, *the wrath of God is placated when sins are forgiven*. That is, as it is said, "Given and shed for the remission of sins." *For unless it is given and poured out the wrath will be retained.* So you see that the work of satisfaction or sacrificial placation are *worth nothing except by faith alone.*[14]

When one is dealing with the way things are, wrath cannot be placated in the abstract—say at the moment of Christ's death when payment is supposedly made. Wrath is placated when the body and blood are given *to us* and are received in faith. It is in the giving and the receiving that wrath is placated.

Statements about satisfaction made in criticism of penance indicate the same reversal of direction. The following is a good example, in which Luther says that a distinction should have been made in using the concept:

> ... namely, that it should be done to humans but not to God, as Christ shows in Matt. 7 and 18 and also St. Peter did ..., *otherwise Christ would have stayed with his entire satisfaction for us in heaven.* Then all the traffic to God in memorials and cloisters and indulgences would not have happened and the great

7 / THE WORK OF CHRIST

> god belly be so well served. But it was all mixed up and finally sent up to God alone. . . . For this error is the most ancient from the beginning of the world and will remain also the latest until the end of the world.[15]

If God were the object of satisfaction, there would be no need for incarnation or the cross.

The question for Luther's doctrine of atonement is thus not that of abstract payment to God but rather how God can succeed in giving himself to us so as actually to take away our sin, to destroy the barrier between us and God. This is the reason for the prominence in Luther's thought of "the happy exchange." Christ, through his actual coming, his cross and resurrection, takes away our sinful and lost nature and gives us his sinless and righteous nature. This cannot be an abstract metaphysical transaction. We must, through the cross of Christ, his terrible suffering and death, be actually purchased and won, indeed, killed and made alive. If it is to be a "happy" exchange, our hearts must be captured by it.

The exchange can take place, therefore, only if Christ actually takes our place, takes our sinful nature, "has and bears" our sins. He cannot just take human nature; he must take sinful human nature and come under the curse of the wrath of God. To give us his life he must take our death. Satisfaction cannot be, as for Anselm, a substitution for punishment. Christ suffers the punishment and destruction of death in our place, our nature, in order to give us his. He must take our sins and destroy them, devour them.

This is made explicit in what is perhaps the classic statement of Luther's doctrine of atonement in his commentary on Gal. 3:13 ("Christ redeemed us from the curse of the law, having become a curse for us—for it is written, 'Cursed be every one who hangs on a tree' " [in the 1535 Galatians commentary, *LW* 26: 276ff.]). The type of thinking—in this case, of the medieval scholastics—that posits payment to God cannot, Luther says, abide this kind of passage: "They strive anxiously with what they think is godly zeal not to permit the insult of being called a curse or an execration to come to Christ" (*LW* 26: 176). Such thinking would rather have, no doubt, an unambiguously spotless Lamb, a sinless Christ to offer God as a substitutionary payment. But Luther will have none of that. Christ must be one who has and bears our sins; he must actually become a curse for us to set us free from the curse of the law. If not, Christ merely becomes an example of purity or of patience in suffering to be imitated. That simply puts roses on the cross and turns Christ into a new law. The "sophists" deprive us of the most "delightful comfort"

> when they segregate Christ from sins and from sinners and set him forth to us only as an example to be imitated. In this way they make Christ not only useless to us but also a judge and a tyrant who is angry because of our sins and who

damns sinners. But just as Christ is wrapped up in our flesh and blood, so we must wrap him and know him to be wrapped up in our sins, our curse, our death and everything evil (ibid., 278).

If we are to deny that Christ is a sinner and a curse, we should also deny that he suffered, was crucified, and was buried (ibid., 278). A Christ who is unwrapped from our sins and offered to God as payment and who all the while is privy to this celestial machinery does not die any more than the gnostic redeemer died. In Luther's view, if there is to be redemption, Christ must become, as Paul says, a curse for us—and that really and truly. There must be a real exchange—and for Luther that was the point of the *communicatio idiomatum*. "Whatever sins I, you, and all of us have committed or may commit in the future, they are as much Christ's own as if he himself had committed them. In short, our sin must be Christ's own sin, or we shall perish eternally" (ibid., 278).

To be sure, Christ "in his own person" as the Son of God does not commit sins, but by entering into our place he takes them really and truly on himself. In our place, here on this earth among us, he no longer acts in his own person, but he is now a sinner and takes the sins committed by us "upon his own body" (ibid., 277).

> When the merciful Father saw that we were being oppressed through the Law, that we were being held under a curse, and that we should not be liberated from it by anything, He sent his Son into the world, heaped all the sins of all men upon him and said to him: "Be Peter the denier, Paul the persecutor, blasphemer and assaulter, David the adulterer; the sinner who ate the apple in Paradise; the thief on the cross. In short be the person of all men, the one who has committed the sins of all men. And see to it that you pay and make satisfaction for them" (ibid., 280).

One should note well: the merciful Father saw that we could not be liberated from the law by anything, so the Father sends the Son to be a sinner cursed by the law so as to pay and make satisfaction.

But how does such payment and satisfaction come about? How can he *be* a sinner? Luther uses concrete imagery indicating that it comes about because of Christ's entry into this place, our place, fully and totally, of his own will. He comes under the law. The curse of the law against everyone who hangs on a tree was obviously meant, Luther says, for criminals.

> Therefore this general Law of Moses included him, although he was innocent so far as his own person was concerned; for it found him among sinners and thieves. Thus a magistrate regards someone as a criminal and punishes him if he catches him among thieves, even though the man has never committed anything evil or worthy of death (ibid., 227-78).

7 / THE WORK OF CHRIST

One might protest that such is simply a miscarriage of justice—the magistrate punishes for guilt by association. The point, however, is that Jesus put himself there willingly. Before the judge he said nothing—other than that these criminals are his friends.

> Christ was not only *found* among sinners; but *of his own free will and by the will of the Father he wanted to be an associate of sinners and thieves* and those who were immersed in all sorts of sin. Therefore when the Law found him among thieves, it condemned and executed him as a thief" (ibid., 278; emphasis added).

And this occurs by full right. "Because he took upon himself our sins, not by compulsion but of his own free will, *it was right* for him to bear the punishment and the wrath of God—not for his own person, which was righteous and invincible and therefore could not become guilty, but for our person" (ibid., 284; emphasis added). His great love, one might say, got him in trouble, and he could not get out—for *he did not want to*. Or, as Luther put it, "Therefore Christ not only was crucified and died, but by divine love sin was laid upon him" (ibid., 279).

The payment or satisfaction takes place, however, not by some machinery of compensatory reckoning vis à vis God, but rather in that the law and sin attack him and damn him but cannot succeed and are in turn conquered by his invincible righteousness.

> The law . . . says: "I find him a sinner, who takes upon himself the sins of all men. I do not see any other sins than those in him. Therefore let him die on the cross!" And so it attacks him and kills him. By this deed the whole world is purged and expiated from all sins, and thus it is set free from death and from every evil. But when sin and death have been abolished by this one man, God does not want to see anything else in the whole world, especially if it were to believe, except sheer cleansing and righteousness" (ibid., 280).

But Luther can also speak in interesting fashion of *sin* attacking Christ:

> Not only my sins and yours, but the sins of the entire world, past, present and future, attack him, try to damn him, and do in fact damn him. But because in the same person, who is the highest, the greatest and *the only sinner*, there is also eternal and invincible righteousness, therefore these two converge: the highest, the greatest and the only sin; and the highest, the greatest, and the only righteousness. Here one of them must yield and be conquered, since they come together and collide with such a powerful impact. . . . Sin is a great and powerful god who devours the whole human race, all the learned, holy, powerful, wise, and unlearned men. He, I say, attacks Christ and wants to devour him as he has devoured all the rest" (ibid., 281, emphasis added).

Atonement takes place when Christ has absolutely entered our place and is attacked by the law, by sin, by death and the devil. Being found actually clothed in our sins, he is the object of the just and terrifying onslaught of the curse. He could not protest his own innocence. He was one of us. To claim his own innocence in any way would be to desert us and to leave us in our sins. But he came to be for us and so must enter into death and destruction.

The cry of dereliction from the cross is real. One cannot, for Luther, look on the cross as though it were simply the apex of a life of high moral purpose in which Jesus now remains true to the end and actively offers himself to God on our behalf. That would fit the picture of the heavenward traffic but not Luther's reversal of direction. The tradition pictured Christ's sacrifice as an active offering of self to God. Strictly speaking, the death of Christ was not necessary absolutely but only concomitantly, since it so pleased God.[16] Thus the tradition taught that Christ enjoyed the beatific vision at the moment of abandonment on the cross.[17] That is akin to more recent views that shy away from the cry of dereliction and speak of Jesus' perseverance in the face of tragedy. Not so Luther. Christ feels himself in his conscience to be cursed by God and really and truly enters into eternal damnation from God the Father for us.[18] Christ's death is not an active offering according to some available scheme of recompense. There *is* no such. His death can therefore only be a passive suffering, a "passion" in the strict sense of the word. There is nothing to do under wrath, death, and so on but to suffer it and to die. Christ, clothed in our sin, can only suffer himself to be attacked. The event must be a real one, and the outcome hangs in the balance.

This is the reason for the dramatic imagery and language in Luther. It is not a matter of imaginative embroidery or of using various pictures, where one conceptuality could just as well be substituted for another. It was, again, an attempt to say what a thing is, to speak of what is actually the case. The law, sin, death, and the curse over human existence attack Jesus. If there is to be any hope for humans, they must be defeated.

Thus also Luther's persistent use of the imagery of the devil as Leviathan who gets caught on the hook of the divinity. Luther recasts the image to fit his reversal. The tradition spoke of the humanity or the flesh as the bait that attracts the demon. Often the fishline was pictured as a chain of human beings from Adam down to Christ—to show Christ as "of the flesh" like us. Deceived by the flesh in seeking his ransom, the devil gets caught on the hook of the divinity. For Luther it is not simply the flesh or the humanity that is the bait; it is the *sinful* flesh that attracts Leviathan. The line is the chain of sinful beings for whom there is no hope: Adam who ate the apple, David the adulterer, Peter the denier, Paul the persecutor . . . and Jesus. The devil attacks with full right. There must be a battle, because only victory or defeat will settle the issue.[19] The point is that sin is the obstacle, not merely finitude or mortality. The devil can attack as accuser only through real powers:

7 / THE WORK OF CHRIST

the curse of the law. The attack is serious because it is right and we have no defense. Only deliverance from the curse can save.

In Christ, in his own body, the issue is joined, not on the level of God or divinity as such. It is a power struggle in the one who is attacked. The victory comes only because in him is also the power of life which triumphs. The duel is a real one. Just so is it marvelous. It is not simply a foregone conclusion. Christ could and did die; he suffered the pangs of death and abandonment. Yet in the resurrection the divine power overcomes even death, and thus conquers, kills, devours, destroys, buries, and abolishes death, sin, the curse, the law, and all the tyrants.

Luther expresses both the reality of Jesus' death and the invincibility of life in Christ by using formulas that set both against each other in Christ's person—formulas that are the christological basis for subsequent anthropological formulas, such as *simul iustus et peccator*:

> He was at once damned and blessed, at once living and dead, at once in sorrow and joy, in order to absorb all evil in himself and to give out all goodness.[20]

> Those who crucified Christ believed he was totally abandoned by God and damned . . . , or they held him to be merely human and thus for entirely dead, whereas he was at the same time quite alive in his entire person (*tota persona*).[21]

To say that Christ has conquered death and sin is at the same time to say that he is divine, for such works belong only to the divine power—indeed, that is what the divine power is. To conceive divinity in this fashion is for Luther part and parcel of his great reversal.

> For it belongs *exclusively* to the divine power to destroy sin and abolish death, to create righteousness and grant life. This divine power [the scholastics] have attributed to our own works, saying: "If you do this or that work, you will conquer sin, death and the wrath of God. In this way they have made us true God, by nature!"[22]

This is Luther's argument for the exclusive character of atonement in Christ. God gives of himself to defeat death and sin. Only the divine power can accomplish that.

The resurrection, one must see, now becomes a full, functional part of the atonement. Since Christ has been raised, there is no more sin, death, or curse, for those in faith are grasped by the resurrection.

> To the extent that you believe this, to that extent you have it. If you believe that sin, death, and the curse have been abolished, they have been abolished, because Christ conquered and overcame them in himself; and he wants us to believe that just as in his person there is no longer the mask of the sinner or any vestige of death, so this is no longer in our person, since he has done everything for us.[23]

The believer has everything from Him who has triumphed over death. But one must note well: The cross, the great reversal, must come home to us; it must be done "to us." We cannot stand by as idle spectators speculating about things beyond, wondering about how atonement works in heaven.[24] It works as the thing it is here on earth: the death of the Son of God for our sins. His death can work only as the death of the sinner who stands against him, for in the final analysis, to be a sinner is to be one *who will not receive from God*. The obstacle to reconciliation is unfaith: *sin*, not sins. Only when the sinner dies and the believer is raised up in faith does the wrath of God end, for only then is God, the boundless giver, placated. Then God is satisfied. That is why Luther could make the amazing statement that "the wrath of God is placated when sins are forgiven." God reaches the goal when he is allowed to be for us who he is: the creator and giver of every good. Then atonement is made.

Such a thought leads to the heart of the matter, the "for us." If the wrath of God, the curse over us, is to end and atonement be made, the cross must work on us and for us. We must be saved and made new by it.

> God's nature is that he makes something out of nothing. Therefore whoever is not yet nothing cannot be made into anything by God. Humans, however, always make something out of something else. But that is vain, fruitless work. Thus God raises up none but the rejected, makes none healthy but the sick, gives sight to none but the blind, makes none alive but the dead, none godly but the sinner, none wise but the foolish, in short, has mercy on none but the miserable and gives grace to none but those without it. Therefore the proud, holy, wise, or righteous cannot be God's material and God's work and make rather synthetic, pretentious, false, painted saints out of themselves, that is: fakes.[25]

There is no direct way to God or salvation under the old heavenward scheme of the law. God cannot be a God of love, a God who gives, under such a scheme. Wrath will simply never end in actuality. At best, Jesus will be only the giver of "help"—call it "grace" or whatever—in our attempts to still the wrath, or at worst he will be just an example. Atonement in any actual sense is an impossibility; the wrath will continue. That is what Luther means by saying that Jesus must die to end the wrath of God; he must die to give himself to us, *so* to end God's wrath over us.

But if God cannot be a God of love under such a scheme, and we will not surrender the scheme, the way can only be indirect: it can only pass through the cross. The wrath of God cannot be brushed aside or toned down. Indeed, it must be magnified against us to turn us from our ways. The cross is not a method for appealing to our sympathy or good will. The happy exchange is not a bargain for the Old Adam. Therefore Luther says of that exchange:

> We must look at this image and take hold of it with a firm faith. He who does

7 / THE WORK OF CHRIST

> this has the innocence and the victory of Christ, no matter how great a sinner he is. *But this cannot be grasped by loving will; it can be grasped only by reason illumined by faith.* Therefore we are justified by faith alone, because faith alone grasps this victory of Christ.[26]

The faith which simply receives the Christ hanging on the cross illumines reason to understand the way things actually are. Such reason sees precisely that we can be justified only by faith, that God's wrath eternally closes every other way. Indeed, God must be a God of wrath to us before being for us a God of mercy. The horror of Golgotha is the only way to the kingdom.

> Grace seems externally to be pure wrath, so deeply does it lie hidden, covered with . . . thick furs or skins . . . and we . . . cannot feel otherwise in ourselves than Peter says (2 Pet. 1:19) rightly: The Word alone enlightens us as in a dark place. Yes indeed, a dark place. Thus God's faithfulness and truth must always first become a great lie before it can become the truth. Because before the world it is called a great heresy. So it seems also to us always that God will leave us and not keep his Word and become a liar in our hearts. In sum: God cannot be God unless he first becomes a devil, and we cannot get to heaven unless we have first been in hell, cannot be God's children unless we have first been the devil's children. . . .[27]

A reason illumined by faith in the Jesus on the cross must reckon with the *deus absconditus*. The wrath of God cannot be seen through. It is magnified to the point where to the world and the fallen creature, God and the devil are indistinguishable. This is so because the cross spells not only the death of Jesus but also the death of the sinner. Jesus' death is not a substitution for our death; it *is* our death. It is the death of the one who stands against God, the one who will not simply receive from God. A reason illumined by faith sees that there is no way around the cross; the only way is through it.

A reason illumined by such faith will also see—*a posteriori*—something of the necessity for the cross. It was necessary not because God needed it but because God wanted to rescue us from our bondage, our insistence on our own projects—our insistence on having a God of wrath. Luther put his finger squarely on the problem when he saw it as a question of who shall be God. When we refuse to recognize that it belongs exclusively to the divine power to destroy sin and death, and instead take it on ourselves and our works, we attribute divinity to ourselves. We then encounter the wrath of the God who wills solely to have mercy. Really to end the wrath, God gives the Son to die, thus to put us to death and make us new in him. From the point of view of a theologian of the cross there could be no other way. The theologian of glory might speculate that God could have done it otherwise, or say that the death was only concomitantly a part of Jesus' self-offering to God. But that is to look away from the horror of Golgotha and to avoid the way things actually are. If God could, in fact, have done it some other way, then there is *no* justification for doing it the way it was done. The horror of Golgotha, the terrible price, is too great. Thus Luther:

> Christ teaches . . . , that we are not lost, and sinners have eternal life, only because God had pity, indeed, that it cost him his own beloved child, whom he put into our misery, hell, and death. . . . Now if there were any other way to heaven, he would certainly have established it: Hence, there is no other.[28]

Therefore Luther's treatment points the way to overcome the old antitheses in atonement doctrine: satisfaction versus victory, objective versus subjective. The divine wrath against sin is satisfied when love wins the victory. When the divine self-giving in Jesus raises up the person of faith, the person who *receives*, God has reached his goal. Love conquers wrath for us and in us.

The reversal of direction in Luther's doctrine of atonement leads quite naturally therefore to an application—proclamation of the Word and giving of the sacraments—which does the deed to the hearers, to create faith. If the wrath of God is placated when sins are forgiven, when the body and blood of Christ are given "for us," atonement is done to us then. The reversal is carried to the end. "God was in Christ reconciling the world unto himself . . . and *he has entrusted us* with this ministry of reconciliation." Atonement is in the proclamation, in the giving of it. God's justification for being God, God's success at being God, if one can say that, consists precisely in God's ability to get through to us, to make reconciliation and still be God.

Luther's achievement points us in the proper direction. Its abiding merit is the great reversal: Atonement occurs when God succeeds, at the cost of the death of the Son, in getting through to us who live under wrath. God succeeds in giving himself to us in such a way as to bring a real end to existence under wrath, sin, and death. God's mercy wins the victory over wrath *for us.*

Particularly important is the manner in which Luther moves to strip the roses from the cross. Christ comes among us and dies a real death "wrapped in our sins." He is not paying God according to some celestial bookkeeping scheme. He is *dying*—suffering the punishment of being found "among thieves," because he willed it so. Nor is he a religious hero, demonstrating the potency of his God-consciousness or his faithfulness to his calling to the end, thus becoming the example for all our religious aspirations. He was dying: feeling in himself and in his conscience the agony of the ultimate separation. God is hidden in his death; indeed, God dies. What that means is that all the systems by which theology has sought to rescue Jesus from death, making a meaning of it which obscures the fact of it, are suddenly cut away. Our theological theories cannot save Jesus, just as they cannot save us. Only God, the God who creates *ex nihilo*, who is the power of life itself, can do that.

7 / THE WORK OF CHRIST

The resurrection alone saves from death. A cross without roses brings something new: it puts to death and it raises up.

CRITICAL ESTIMATES

Did Luther succeed? Criticism usually comes from the point of view of the tradition, for the most part from Roman Catholic scholars.[29] The criticisms can be reduced to two major ones. First, the radical opposition of love and wrath seems to fracture the unity of God, especially when it is said or implied that God battles against himself. Dualism threatens. Second, the saving activity in the God-man Jesus seems to be carried out exclusively by the divinity; the humanity plays no part. Jesus, in the "happy exchange," *takes away* our sinful nature in order to give us his sinless nature. The human, the critics maintain, is not active, but only passive. Luther's view results in a dualism in God and monergism in salvation which cuts out the human nature of Jesus. The trinitarian continuity of the traditional view threatens to collapse. God fights against God; the God in Jesus Christ fights to overcome sinful human nature. It is his exclusive work.

A full discussion of such criticism would take us beyond the confines of this locus. Perhaps the most apt and direct reply would be to say that the criticisms come, for the most part, from a traditional scheme that fails to take account of the radical reversal of direction. The charge on the christological level, about the passivity or noncooperation of the human nature of Christ in salvation, is virtually an exact parallel of the charge made on the anthropological level: that human effort does not cooperate in the salvation of human beings. When the human task is understood as ascent toward heaven via the law, the charge is serious. If, however, the direction is reversed, if the ascent via the law is precisely the curse, if the inescapable trap of fallen humanity is to think of itself and of God in terms of that scheme so that one is always parceling out bits of human activity and bits of divine, hoping it will add up to salvation—if that is the problem, then something much more radical is necessary. The Christ of such a scheme would not *save* God's good creation. He would only attempt to assist us in our escape from it on our heavenward way, and in Luther's terms make only fakes and hypocrites. Luther's point is precisely that one must die to all that in order to be saved. Christ is indeed opposed to the cooperation of such sinful human nature. He is out to eradicate it in order that the true human nature, that which trusts and loves God, may emerge from the tomb. Then one becomes again the creature God intended. Then one can say that God so loved the *world*, his own creation, that he gave his only Son. Then God has reconciled the world to himself in Christ.

It is surely a drastic mistake to say that a Christ who enters into the world under wrath and the curse "wrapped in our sins" is not accomplishing anything according to his human nature. He is suffering and dying! To be sure, he accomplishes nothing by the world's standards. But what was there to "do" before Pilate and the priests? The miracle, no doubt, was precisely that he did nothing. "Nevertheless, not my will but thine be done!" If there had been anything to do, his Father would have sent "legions of angels." But therein—precisely in the flesh, according to the human nature—he "accomplished all things"; he "overcame the world." He fulfilled the Father's will in the flesh. Luther no doubt saw this much more radically than the tradition. There has really to be a death before there can be life; and the death cannot simply be a sham. It cannot be turned into support for the old scheme. Theological cries for continuity can all too easily be attempts to escape death: "Let this cup pass from me. . . ."

By the same token the dichotomy between wrath and love cannot be avoided. There is no way to construct a theological continuity between the two, because wrath will then simply remain in force. Continuity here means that the old continues and wrath wins. Wrath can only be conquered; the scheme of law under which we have placed ourselves is indeed real and represents a terrible truth. If we insist on having God in this way, God will oblige—and it will be real enough. God *is* wrathful outside the promise. Wrath can be overcome only in a concrete historical event, and the God of love manifest in that event can only be *believed*, "from the heart." To be saved means precisely to be freed from wrath, freed from law, from having to do this or that. One can only believe that God is not divided, that God is one. God is not divided because in the actual revelation, the concrete event, God reveals himself as one whose sole aim is to be freely and truly trusted as a God of mercy. This God will not have it any other way. Luther's point is that we *can* be saved only by faith. Faith alone will give God's creation back to us together with our true human nature.

If Luther is to be criticized, it will have to be that he did not go, or perhaps was not able in his context to go, far enough. The weight of the tradition was still too heavy. The reversal of direction signaled by the idea of the "happy exchange" marks a great advance. Yet there are still vestiges of something quasi-physical about such an exchange. Natures and sins seem to be shifted around too much like quantities. Furthermore, the powers attacking the Christ "wrapped in our sins" seem still to have much too abstract and mythological a coloring for contemporary eyes. If anything, Luther's formulations still have too much of the traditional metaphysical and mythological freight. He has pointed us in the right direction, and often himself used formulations on which we can build. It remains the task of the final chapter to draw on this and to attempt some constructive proposals.

7 / THE WORK OF CHRIST

NOTES

1. Signaled, e.g., by Walther von Loewenich's classic study *Luther's Theology of the Cross*, trans. H. Bouman (1929; Minneapolis: Augsburg Publishing House, 1976); and E. Vogelsang, *Der Angefochtene Christus* (Berlin: Walter de Gruyter, 1932).

2. A claim similar to Aulén's had been made almost a century before by J. C. K. von Hofmann and had actually led to a similar debate among Lutherans. The debate was inconclusive, however, largely because they had not come so far as to discover the theology of the cross. Conservative Lutherans were too leery of liberal views, and vicarious satisfaction still seemed the only alternative. See Gerhard O. Forde, *The Law-Gospel Debate* (Minneapolis: Augsburg Publishing House, 1967).

3. Theobald Beer, *Der Fröhliche Wechsel und Streit* (Leipzig: St. Benno Verlag, 1974), p. 213 and passim.

4. Gustaf Aulén, *Christus Victor*, trans A. G. Hebert (New York: Macmillan Co., 1931), pp. 107–8.

5. Ibid., pp. 111ff.

6. Paul Althaus, *The Theology of Martin Luther*, trans. Robert C. Schultz (Philadelphia: Fortress Press, 1966), pp. 218–19. Tiililä is another objector. The roots of the objection often go back to the previous debate (n. 2, above) and base themselves on the work of Theodosius Harnack. Harnack's work is questionable both because of its polemical intent in the debate and because it was done before the critical edition of Luther's works.

7. Althaus, *Theology of Martin Luther*, p. 193.

8. Ibid., p. 202.

9. See the following passages: "All such [atonement] cannot happen for nothing or without satisfaction of [God's] righteousness . . . ; righteousness must first be satisfied to completest perfection" (*WA* 10 I/1:121, 16–19). "If God's wrath is to be taken from me and I am to receive grace and forgiveness, it must be earned from him by someone: for God cannot be kind and gracious to sin, not remove punishment and wrath, unless payment and satisfaction is made" (*WA* 21:259, 9–12). "For Christ is the Son of God, who gave himself out of sheer love to redeem me. In these words Paul gives a beautiful description of the Priesthood and work of Christ, which is to placate God (*placare Deum*)" (*LW* 26:177). "We should comfort ourselves with Christ's suffering and death as the complete payment and propitiation (*Versöhnung*) of God" (*WA* 52:643, 39).

10. *WA* 21:264, 27. Note that Luther is not interested in a one-time act but in the ongoing effect, the *new* thing brought about by the cross.

11. *WA* 51:487, 29. Cf. Carl F. Wislöff, *Abendmahl und Messe*, AGTL 22 (Berlin: Lutherisches Verlagshaus, 1969), pp. 97ff.

12. Aulén claims that whenever Luther uses "Latin" terminology he gives it a different meaning. Ragnar Bring says Luther uses Latin terminology as a way of expressing the *sola gratia* (See Vilmos Vajta, *Theologie des Gottesdienstes bei Luther* [Göttingen: Vandenhoeck & Ruprecht, 1959], p. 192). Others maintain that Luther uses the terminology only as a concession to the tradition and then abandons it when he wants to set forth his own view. There is probably some truth to all the opinions, but

if they do not reveal the basic reason behind the use or nonuse, they are of little help to us.

13. *LW* 31:40, theses 19–22.
14. *WA* 8:442, 30. (Emphasis added.)
15. *WA* 302:291, 34ff. (Emphasis added.)
16. Wislöff, *Abendmahl und Messe*, pp. 97ff.
17. Ibid., pp. 99–100.
18. *WA* 5:603, 34; *WA* 56:392, 8. Cf. Wislöff, *Abendmahl und Messe*, p. 99.
19. It seems to make little difference for Luther whether the assailant is the law, sin, death, the curse, or the devil. The law attacks Jesus and kills him (*LW* 26:280). Likewise, sin "attacks Christ and wants to devour him as he has devoured all the rest.... It is necessary for sin to be conquered and killed..." (ibid., 281). Or death: "The almighty empress of the entire world ... clashes against life with full force and is about to conquer it and swallow it; and what it attempts, it accomplishes. But because life was immortal, it emerged victorious" (ibid., 281). And the curse: "clashes with the blessing" (ibid., 281–82). All these assailants can be spoken of in virtually the same breath.
20. *WA* 3:426, 34–36.
21. *WA* 4:33, 33–37.
22. *LW* 26:283.
23. *LW* 26:284.
24. *LW* 26:287: "The speculation by which Christ is grasped is not the foolish imagination of the sophists and monks about marvelous things beyond them; it is a theological, faithful, and divine consideration of the serpent hanging from the pole, that is, of Christ hanging on the cross for my sins, for your sins, and for the sins of the entire world.... Hence it is evident that faith alone justifies."
25. *WA* 1:183, 39–84, 10 (1517).
26. *LW* 26:284. Emphasis added.
27. *WA* 31 I:249, 16–250, 1 (1530).
28. *WA* 10 III:162, 10. Cf. Wisløff, *Abendmahl und Messe*, p. 98, n. 47.
29. See Beer, *Der Fröhliche Wechsel und Streit*, pp. 264ff., for a good summary of such criticism; also Yves M. -J. Congar, *Chrétiens en Dialogue*, UnSa 50 (Paris: Editions du Cerf, 1964), pp. 453ff.

3
Reconciliation with God

Reconciliation with God can occur only through God's coming to us in Jesus to die and be raised. The necessity for the cross roots in God's decision to be a God of mercy in spite of our bondage and rejection. To be true to that decision, God must come to us and bear the rejection concretely and actually. God's wrath is the obverse side of God's mercy: God will not be known other than as a God of mercy. The cross is the price God, in mercy, pays to be concretely for us, to put to death the old and to raise up the new. When faith is created, God has reached the goal and is "satisfied."

CUR DEUS HOMO?

Why did God become a man—indeed, why did God do so in just the way he did? Why did God suffer and die a shameful and painful death on the cross?

Luther has pointed us in the right direction. Atonement theories have dealt too much with abstractions and have not paid enough careful attention to the way things are. It is time now to take the final step. The fact is that we simply cannot get on with God. We cannot reconcile ourselves to God. Why? Just because God is God. We cannot bear that. God is the almighty Creator of heaven and earth. God rules over all things, and God's will ultimately will be done. That is too much. Furthermore, according to the Scriptures, God is an electing God. God chooses. "I will have mercy on whom I will have mercy" is virtually God's name. The very thought of such a God is a threat to us.

Cur deus homo? Precisely because we cannot reconcile ourselves to God, precisely because God is an electing God, this God "for his own name's sake," must come to us to have mercy concretely, historically. The necessity for the atonement rests ultimately in the electing love of God in Jesus Christ.

Once again we may let Luther be our guide. The situation we have been describing and to which our discussion of atonement leads is exactly that described by Luther in *The Bondage of the Will*. When Luther says that we may use the term "free will"—if we must use it at all—to designate our disposal

7 / THE WORK OF CHRIST

over "things below us" but not over "things above us,"[1] he was once again not laying out a theory but attempting to describe the way things actually are. We are, obviously, free in relation to those things "below" us. I can, relatively speaking, arrange my affairs as I see fit, administer my possessions, come and go as I please, do this or that. I can even decide to be pious and religious, go to church, and so on, if I so please. God, it seems, does not interfere with such affairs—except as occasional "accidents" or "interruptions" put obstacles in my way.

When, however, I come to the question of God, of that which is "above" me, I am faced with a different sort of problem. Why? Just because God is above me and because I can do nothing about that. In fact, I am bound to react in a certain way. The bondage of the will is the inescapable reaction of the alienated sinner to the very idea of God. It is not, as we might think, a deduction from the doctrine of God or God's immutability. Such abstract deductions do not *actually* enslave anyone; but bondage is real. Bondage has to do, for Luther, with our affections, with our love, with the real direction of the will. "Bondage of the will" is for Luther a description, finally indeed, a confession of our disaffection, our recoil from God's "godness," from God's being above us.

God is a threat and a terror to the alienated. Faced with the threat of God and especially with the mere idea of God's election, I can only say, "No." In defiance of God and all the logic of the case, I must simply assert my own freedom so as to have some say about my own destiny.

So, I must take over God's role. I must say to God, in effect, "God, I do not know what you plan to do; I cannot trust you. Therefore I must take my destiny into my own hands because I believe I can better decide such things."

So the assertion of "free will" is a faith. It is a faith in myself in defiance of the only God I know. The very reaction, the recoil, is the bondage. And I must do it. I simply am not free vis à vis that which is above me. I can only do one thing. The very assertion of freedom—the only thing I can do—*is* the bondage. The bondage is not something I am forced into. It is a bondage of *the will*. I do what I want. That is just the problem. I *can* do only what *I* want. I cannot do anything else—because *I do not want to.* It is not that I have no will. Indeed, I do. I am not a puppet. The question is of the way things are: of what in fact I do will.

We simply cannot be reconciled to one who is above us. The assertion of our freedom is simply a mark of our skepticism, of our defense against an almighty God. A theology based on such premises, however pious in appearance, can only be an attempt to tailor God to fit our aspirations. Atonement *theories* put God in the role of rescuing our sagging religious enterprises, our heavenward traffic. Jesus pays our debts, or becomes our inspirational hero.[2]

We picture ourselves as aspirants for heaven, straining to achieve the prize—our only problem being that we have occasional lapses or that we are too weak and need help to a greater or lesser degree, depending on how conservative or liberal we are. It is all a sham. The one thing we cannot stand about God is that he is God. Luther was quite right: "The natural man cannot will God to be God. Rather he wants himself to be God, and God not to be."[3]

Cur deus homo? Why the terror of Golgotha and the empty tomb? Because God has *elected* to have mercy. God has decided not to be for us the God of wrath whom we are bound to have. God can be that God, and God's being so is quite real. But God has decided not to be that God. If there is anything the Scriptures tell us, it is just that. God elects: "I will have mercy on whom I will have mercy." The problem, however, is just that: how to have mercy and how not to be a God of wrath for a people who in their alienation are bound to have it so. To a people unreconciled to God, a people who cannot trust God, election is the most fearsome thing of all. "I will have mercy on whom I will have mercy," in the abstract, is not comfort, but terror. Thus, in order to be just who he has decided to be, it is *God* who must come. There is nothing God can do about wrath in the abstract. We cannot be saved by a better theology, a better *idea* of God. God must *come* to save us. The cross and the resurrection are the solution to God's problem: how to be exactly who God wants to be for us; how to be an electing God and still be a God of mercy for those who are bound; how to release the captives. God, it is to be expected, knows that he is a problem for us, and God has undertaken to solve the problem. "His right hand and his holy arm have gotten him the victory." *Cur deus homo?* To *be* merciful to us.

We must once and for all carry through the reversal of direction in our thinking about and preaching of atonement. God comes to us. God comes to break the bondage. There can be no pandering to the so-called free will and its attempts to go to God, for that is the mark of our disaffection, and under it God remains the God of wrath for us. There must rather be a case of battle in which God actually comes in Christ to break into the "house of the strong man armed," to enter into real contention for the heart, mind, and soul of the disaffected.

That is the point of a theology of the cross. God cannot come directly to people bound to their own illusions. God can only die at the hands of such piety. God can only be rejected. So it must be if God is to unmask the bondage for what it is. Hence Luther maintained that in Christ, God comes "under the form of opposites," under the opposite of what an aspiring free will wants or expects. God comes not as the great and glorious ruler but as the humble, suffering, despised, and rejected outcast who is beaten, spit on, and executed, as one quite superfluous to the way we must run things. "He came to his

7 / THE WORK OF CHRIST

own home, and his own people received him not" (John 1:11). So it had to be. There is no way to get through to the bound, disaffected will directly. Hence life comes only through death. To put it most bluntly, our so-called freedom cannot stop until it has done away with God altogether. Only when that happens, only when the blood is actually spilled, is there a chance that we might be saved.

Only if God comes—*actually*—will there be any help. Only the concrete and real historical lover can save those bound in the prison of their own loneliness. The historical event itself is the revelation; it is God's breaking through to say, "I love you." The historical event itself, the cross, the resurrection, and the preaching of it, *is* what God has elected, predestined, to do for us. God has elected to be a God of mercy, to come to us, to be for us. Nothing else can actually save us from God's wrath.

If one turns aside here to "work" on the doctrine of God so as to avoid offending "free will," one misses the entire point. One does not see that the concrete and actual coming itself alone is God's apology for being God, a God of mercy and thus of election. "God was in Christ reconciling the world unto himself." If one does not see that, one will turn the cross and the preaching of it into a general and trivial truth, the illustration of the fact that God is, in general, love. Instead of preaching, instead of saying God's concrete "I love you," one will lecture on the nature of God, on a God who supposedly loves everyone in general but never gets around to saying "I love you" to anyone at all.

The problem of the bound will, the disaffected lover, cannot be solved by lectures on the essence of God or by theories of atonement. Nothing, absolutely nothing, will save the alienated lover but the concrete word, the "I love you." The question of what God might or might not have willed in eternity can be answered only by what God does do in time, by God's coming and by the preaching of it and the doing of it in the sacraments. To say that God does not elect or predestine is simply to say that God does not come and that God does not do anything of any importance concretely in our time.

God, that is to say, has undertaken to solve the problem God poses for us by actually coming. God does not call off almightiness or election in so doing, but carries it *out* in such a manner as to save, to create believers.[4]

Cur deus homo? Because *we* are the enemy, we have sold out to the tyrants; because *Homo sapiens* is bound and cannot be reconciled by any other means. God has elected to be a God of mercy. To be a God of mercy to those who have sold out, God must come. Not only must God come, but God must die and be raised. The "must" here, of course, is not the abstract *a priori* "must" of a rational or legal scheme, but an *a posteriori* reflection of the mercy actually given. When one begins to glimpse the actual end of the wrath, one sees that it could not have been any other way: "There is no other name under heaven given among men by which we must be saved" (Acts 4:12).

THE NECESSITY FOR ATONEMENT

The necessity for atonement roots therefore in two things: our bondage and alienation, our unwillingness to be reconciled, and God's decision to be true to himself, to be a God of steadfast mercy nevertheless. The cross and the resurrection are God's own solution to the problem we have with God; they are the outcome of God's resolve. Here Emil Brunner's conclusion that, "rightly understood," atonement and special revelation are one receives its due. But one cannot divide the cross into an act of special revelation to us and a satisfaction offered to God at the same time, as Brunner tends to do. The cross is God's self-giving to us. Just so, it is revelation and atonement at once. It is the carrying out of God's election to be merciful.

Karl Barth is the most prominent recent theologian to have seen this. He made it the central tenet of his *Church Dogmatics*. The cross is not a juridically or ritually prescribed means for propitiating God, but the means whereby the grace of the electing God invades and manifests itself in our fallen world. God has determined first and foremost to be merciful to the world in Jesus Christ. The creation, the incarnation, the cross, and the resurrection are the carrying out of this decision to be merciful. The Son of God journeys into a far country to make the decision manifest. Accomplishing this against all opposition is precisely his victory. It brings restoration of communion with God. As such it is Christ's triumph over the powers of sin and death. There is thus a liberal use of "victory" language in Barth's doctrine. Jesus is victor over the powers of darkness, the "Redeemer from sin and death and the devil" (*Church Dogmatics*, 4/1:766).[5] Atonement can be spoken of as "God's triumph in antithesis, in the opposition of man to Himself" (ibid., 4/1:82). Jesus is the "victorious king" (ibid., 4/3a: 165ff.).

As with Luther, however, the victory is not fundamentally different from a death for our sins, even a satisfaction of the divine righteousness. That is because Barth sees clearly that sin is first and foremost enmity against God's grace, the refusal to be one who receives from God. The Son of God in his journey suffers for our sin. He must suffer under the wrath of God. "In this place He has not only borne man's enmity against God's grace, revealing it in all its depth. He has borne the far greater burden, the righteous wrath of God against those who are enemies of his grace, the wrath which must fall on us" (ibid., 2/1:152). Since Christ comes into our place and suffers this wrath, Barth can say that it is now taken away from us. Christ has intervened for us. The "resolve in which man as such stands against grace" has been "ex-

7 / THE WORK OF CHRIST

piated" (ibid., 2/1:152). Barth can speak of Christ as being "laden with our sin" and as one who "suffered punishment for our sin." All this, however, does not serve to change *God* as such. It serves to carry out God's resolve to be gracious. The enmity rejects everything not of grace. As the one in whom God has elected to be gracious to all creatures, Jesus must bear the rejection that must fall on all as enemies of grace. Jesus is the one in whom God elects to be gracious and just so must also bear the rejection that would frustrate that election. He is the elected and the rejected one. Only so, he can be *for us*. God's election would be a terror if God were not also the one who bears our rejection for us. Jesus "must" die to be truly *for* us.

Like Forsyth, Aulén, and others, Barth can thus say that atonement does not bring about a change in God, or simply a change of heart in the sinner, but rather a changed situation because of God's initiative. He can also speak in terms reminiscent of Luther's "happy exchange." God in Jesus condescends to the creature while the creature is taken up into the blessedness and unity of the life in Jesus. But Barth reverses the usual picture. Condescension and humiliation are associated with the divine nature of Christ, the exaltation with his human nature. In the self-giving of God we see the true divinity, and in the triumphant Jesus creatures are exalted to fellowship with God (ibid., 4:1–2). The exchange means that Barth, like Luther, sees that the vital aspect is God's self-giving, not God's receiving of payment. Jesus is not a substitute payment. His work is not something extraneous to us to which we then subsequently relate. He is the one through whom the work of God is done on us and in us. Since he is the one who in rejection and election carries out the decision of God, it is through him and in him that we die and are raised. The old person is destroyed and the new is raised up.[6] Only in this sense is Jesus our "substitute" or "representative." Barth uses the German term *Stellvertretung*, which is difficult to render directly in English. "Place-taker" would perhaps be most accurate if it were understood in an active and repletive sense: Jesus actively and fully takes up the place where we are and should be. We seek continually to escape that place. He stays to the end. Since Jesus dies for us, we suffer and die in him and with him.

Barth's view is similar to the view we have proposed. However, there is an aspect to Barth's thought which attempts to go further and thus reveals the peril of the line of thinking we have been developing. In his desire to overcome the anthropologism of the nineteenth century and its "subjective" atonement, Barth runs the risk of removing the atonement from the human sphere altogether. Following his own adaptation of Anselm's *fides quaerens intellectum*, Barth "reasons into" the event of revelation to find that the antinomies supposedly resolved by the life, death, and resurrection of Jesus have "already" or transcendently been posed and overcome in God. Everything is anticipated and established in God's decision to elect, to be known as a God of grace.

Creation, fall, and redemption are simply the spelling out in time of that decision. The result is that one is never quite sure whether the historical event of the cross is the actual victory or just the revelation or manifestation of God's eternal victory.

Barth apparently would like to avoid this either-or and wants somehow to say both. If God's decision is to make himself known as a God of grace, then the victory is already assured by that prior decision, but at the same time can only be implemented by the historical doing of it, by making the decision known in the historical victory of Jesus. The decision was to *do* it. The result is a kind of oscillation in Barth's doctrine, where first one and then the other is said.[7] Can one have it both ways? The difficulty is somewhat the same as we have noted throughout the tradition. The eternal or transcendent victory would make the historical one a sham. It would put roses on the cross.

On the other hand, it has become apparent through the development of the tradition, and especially with Luther, that a strictly historical victory through a cross without any roses puts tremendous pressure on the doctrine of God: The *deus nudus*, the *deus absconditus*, the God of wrath, has virtually to be overcome by the "clothed," revealed God of mercy in Jesus Christ. A fearful dualism threatens between the *deus ipse* who, as Luther says, "neither deplores nor takes away death, but works life, and death, and all in all; nor has he set bounds to himself by his Word, but has kept himself free over all things"[8] and the God revealed in Jesus Christ. Barth expressly wants to banish the *deus ipse* and remove the threat of a deity so unbounded. That is a worthy objective. Everyone would like to do it. But how? Luther, again, was not spinning theological theory when he wrote those words. What he meant was that no mere theological assertion as such can bring God to heel. Theological theory cannot tear the mask from the face of the hidden God. One cannot see through God's wrath. Like virtually everyone else, Barth seems to want to try this—perhaps circumspectly, but to try it nevertheless. Thus he wants to reason solely on the basis of faith to arrive at the God who has elected to be merciful in Jesus Christ. He wants theologically to remove the threat of the *deus ipse*.

That Barth's attempt is valiant and brilliant goes without saying. But does it succeed? Perhaps the quickest answer is the reception of Barth's theology. It has not been perceived, finally or generally, as the lifting of the burden of "God" from human backs. Indeed, in its insistence on "revelation alone" it seemed to most to make the burden more oppressive. Luther's contention that one cannot penetrate the mask is only borne out. Instead of banishing the *deus ipse*, one succeeds only in mixing him with the *deus revelatus* and makes matters worse. Only the historical, concrete, suffering, and dying Jesus can save us from the wrath of the *deus ipse*. Only the revealed God can save us from the hidden God. Theology cannot do it. It cannot be the task of

7 / THE WORK OF CHRIST

theology to assure us that there is no *deus ipse*, no wrath, no danger, and no antithesis really to be overcome in time.

Barth's attempt shows clearly that theology comes up against real limits vis à vis God. Its true task can only be to foster a preaching of Christ and the cross that creates faith, for only such faith saves us from wrath. The historical event *is* the victory. Anything which detracts from that—in theology or outside of it—must be resisted. For nothing can be done about the terror of the absent God, the "naked" abstraction, the "hidden" God; nothing but concrete presence for us can save.

God's coming to us to be for us in Jesus' death and resurrection is the overcoming, the end, the satisfaction of God's wrath. Proponents of the doctrine of vicarious satisfaction and/or punishment have rightly seen that the death of Jesus on the cross alone makes the reconciliation with God possible. God is not reconciled to us, nor we to God, without it. The mistake has been to claim that the event makes God merciful by vindicating God's honor, or providing payment to the demands of God's justice, or satisfying the bloodthirstiness of God's wrath, or some such construction. God is not changed in the sense of being *made* merciful by the historical event. The event takes place because God *is* merciful and desires to be so concretely *for us*, in spite of our opposition and bondage. God gives himself in Jesus because he will not be a God of wrath.

This points us toward a solution to the persistent dilemma of reflection on atonement: Is God merciful before the cross, or only after the cross? The dilemma can be solved if we can think in terms of "the way things are." The divine wrath cannot be theologized or talked away, especially not by platitudes about a God of love. By the same token, it cannot be theologized away by fictions about payment. Wrath is an actuality under which we live in our fallenness and bondage, our separation from God. Wrath cannot be ended unless the God of mercy comes in actuality. Even God can do nothing about his wrath except to give himself to us completely, in death and resurrection. Perhaps this is what those who have talked about the inviolable moral order and the holiness of the divine love have been pointing to. But they cheapened their insight by proposing that God could be bought off. Not even Jesus or God can do that. Wrath can be ended concretely only in God's self-giving to us. Something must indeed happen in our history. But it is not payment to God. It is a gift from God.

The wrath of God, perhaps we can say, is double-edged. On the one hand, it is the reality of God's absence from us, as the *deus absconditus*, the mask behind which we cannot see. But God cannot be absent in the sense of "not here" at all. Thus, on the other hand, the wrath of God is the inescapable reality of God's omnipresence as the God of law—God in nakedness (*deus nudus*), as Luther put it. The naked God is God as sheer timeless abstraction, as the bare idea of the almighty, the immutable judge of all things. In either case—as hiddenness or nakedness—it is the reality of alienation, of absence from us, that comes to expression. God is hidden to fallen creatures who will not have him as a God of mercy. By the same token, God is timeless and immutable abstraction, the *deus nudus*, to those who will not have God clothed in the concrete event—a sheer terrifying abstraction that merges indistinguishably into Satan, the accuser and destroyer. And one should make no mistake about it. That is the way God *is* outside of Jesus Christ. If one wants to have God so, he will oblige. Even God can do nothing about that.

Wrath, we can therefore say, is the obverse of God's mercy. It is God's refusal to be known finally as anything other than a God of mercy. It is God's burning jealousy for his own. God hides from any who will not have him as the God of steadfast love. Because God will be a God of mercy, God's wrath forbids every other approach: "I will have mercy on whom I will have mercy!"

This points the way toward resolution of the problem of the relationship between the divine wrath and the divine mercy. One must again attempt to think in terms of the way things are. Since the problem is absence from us, there is no solution but presence for us. Since the problem is the naked abstraction, there is no solution but God clothed in the concrete event. That is why nothing can be done about the divine wrath in the abstract, in our systems as such. We may protest loudly that God is love, as liberal theology did; we may rail against God's timelessness and seek to remove it by erasing it from our textbooks. We will accomplish nothing if all that such protest and railing do is obscure the actual event of the cross. Not even God can do anything about divine wrath but conquer and end it *for us* by *coming*. Nothing can be done about hiddenness but revelation *pro nobis*. Nothing can be done about the naked abstraction except it be concretely eclipsed by the clothed God: in the manger; at his mother's breasts; on the cross; appearing beyond the grave. God present for us is the only solution to the absent God. Faith in the present God alone will save. There is no other way.

Once we attempt to think in terms of the way things are, we can see how subtle the problem is. Dogmatic expression can easily falsify accounts. On the one hand, God is not wrathful in the sense that God has to be paid off before becoming merciful. Because God is merciful and insists on being so, the Son is sent to die for us. On the other hand, there is a very real sense in which God is not what he aims to be for us, until God actually succeeds in accomplishing that aim. God is not, in actuality, merciful for us until the reality of wrathful absence has been overcome. Thus Luther could say: "As you believe, so is he." The God who dies on the cross for our sins, to put to death the sinner and raise up the new being, *is* the end of the absent God.

7 / THE WORK OF CHRIST

In this sense it can be said with Luther that the death of Jesus satisfies God's wrath—the wrath of the God who will not be known other than as a God of mercy. Jesus fulfills the will of God; he realizes the promise. In him everything meant by the cipher "God" is actualized. The abstract becomes concrete; the hidden is revealed. God is placated because God's mercy accomplishes its aim. As Luther put it, God is placated when sins are forgiven—and we finally believe that.

> Since all have sinned and fall short of the glory of God, they are justified by his grace as a gift, through the redemption which is in Christ Jesus, whom God put forward as an expiation by his blood, to be received by faith. This was to show God's righteousness, because in his divine forbearance he had passed over former sins; it was to prove at the present time that he himself is righteous and that he justifies him who has faith in Jesus. (Rom. 3:23–26)

God vindicates God; God manifests his own righteousness in giving himself in Jesus to be received by faith.

We cannot conclude this section without underlining the fact that such atonement costs God. As Jürgen Moltmann has maintained, the ultimate mystery of atonement takes place between Jesus and God.[9] Even though God is not paid in order to become merciful, it costs God to carry out the resolve to *be* merciful for us in a fallen world. If the only way to overcome wrathful absence is concrete presence for us, then the suffering and the death on the cross is the cost to God. This is the kernel of truth in the old "objective" and "penal" theories. The cross is the price of mercy. It is not paid to God; however, it is paid *by* God.[10] God gave his divine Son, abandoned him to death for us. "God so loved the world that he gave his only Son . . ." (John 3:16). The cross is what it costs God to be who he will be for us, rather than the one we insist on.

One must even say that the cross changes God. God serves notice that he will not be any more the absent one, the hidden one, the naked God of wrath. In the cross God becomes "other," the God of mercy for us. God comes. God says no to being a God of wrath; God dies to that. One does not plumb the depths of the concrete historical event and its singular importance unless one sees it in that light—even driving it to the lengths of this apparent split in the doctrine of God. If the cross does not make just this actual separation between "God" and "God," between wrath and mercy for us, then it accomplishes nothing. Then it will be just another illustration of our immanent religious sensibilities. Theologians—especially more recently—often pay lip service to the idea of change in God, but usually blanch at real change and swallow it up in platitudes drawn from organic imagery. The hidden God, the naked God, the God who is just the counterpart of our religious aspirations—but for all that is real enough—that God dies. God becomes other. Something very real is at stake. If the cross is just another illustration of what we already knew, then God cannot be justified. If God does not become other for us, the price is too great.

That is also the kernel of truth in the doctrine that God is objectively changed by the cross. But it was wrongly put. The idea of a payment made to God's justice making mercy possible does not lead to any real change. God changes objectively only by dying to himself as a God of wrath, saying no to that forever for us. Only thus is there any change in the way things really are. Faith alone grasps the dying God, the concrete God, and *dies with that God* to be raised. Faith is a flight from God to God, from the God of wrath to the God of mercy.

Yet this faith believes that ultimately God remains the same, that God reveals his own innermost "heart" in the cross. The cross is what it costs God to remain true to himself, to remain a God of mercy. This God changes, one may say, to remain the same, to carry out the promise. In the cross this God becomes the God that is—who he is. He becomes reconciled.

Admittedly there is a discontinuity for thought: God changes; God remains the same; God dies; God comes alive in Jesus; God gets a new name in this event. The gap cannot be closed in thought. The reason is that the actual, historical event of the cross *is* the gap; it creates the fissure and stands forever in it. The cross cannot ever simply be woven into the seamless metaphysical or ideological tapestry of time. It is a tear in the fabric. There was darkness at noon, "the curtain of the temple was torn in two," and "the earth shook, and the rocks were split" (Matt. 27:45, 51). It is a wound that does not simply heal and leave no scar. The cry, "My God, my God, why have you forsaken me?" demands an answer, an historical answer, not metaphysical, theological, or exegetical anesthesia. The Scriptures tell us that Jesus refused the wine mixed with gall. Theologians must not attempt to give it again posthumously.

D. M. Mackinnon once remarked of current tendencies to exegete the cry of dereliction as an indication of the "growth of the influence of Psalm 22 on the passion narratives," and so on, in which one must not overlook the "happy ending" of the psalm, that modern scholars speak as though Jesus on the cross were meditating aloud, drawing on "the spiritual literature of his people" instead of crying out in agony and desolation. "One detects in certain quarters an eagerness to treat the words of Christ in his passion almost as if they were the solemn liturgical utterances of the celebrant of a great service. After all, what is being described or represented is not a rite, but a murder and a defeat."[11]

It is an insult to the cross to make it another illustration of general and universally known truths. If the cross is an event of actual historical import,

7 / THE WORK OF CHRIST

then it is just this permanent wound, this death, this scar in the body of historical humanity. The only answer to the cry of dereliction can be resurrection.

The gap cannot be closed for thought as such because thought will always turn the actual and the particular into the universal. It will turn the actual act of love into wrath. Faith alone takes flight from God to God. The gap arises because the shepherd leaves the ninety-nine and comes to get the one who is lost. It is a perilous journey, "and blessed is he who takes no offense." Faith is just to be grasped by the one who makes this journey from the hidden to the revealed, the abstraction to the concrete, wrath to love. Faith means precisely to be grasped by the almighty and immutable one in the despised and dying Jesus. Faith is to believe that it was *for me*. Faith is to be grasped by the actual decision of the electing God in the Word of Jesus preached *to me*.

Such faith is reconciliation with God. The faith created by the shepherd who actually comes to get the lost sheep can at last let God *be* God. The terror, the anxiety, the bondage created by the abstraction, by ignorance of what God may or may not have decided in heaven is erased by what God has in fact done on earth. Faith can then let God be precisely God. Faith has no need to remake or redo God. Indeed, its confidence is based precisely on the fact that it *is* God who has come in Jesus: actually the almighty God. A reason illumined by this faith will see that nothing can be done about God. Only God's coming saves. The "mystery hidden for ages in God who created all things" is now made known "through the church" (Eph. 3:9–10 and passim). God is satisfied when he is believed, trusted, as the one who has mercy.

Such faith is also our reconciliation with the world God created. Faith means to move from abstraction to the concrete, to become an historical being, a creature of God once again, of the God who creates *ex nihilo*. It is to trust the dying and rising Jesus, the one who cried, "My God, my God, why have you forsaken me?" It is to die with him and in him, to die to the law, to wrath, to all the abstractions, the tyrants, the accusers—to await the resurrection begun in Jesus. Faith is to wager that God is ultimately on the side of the man of sorrows, the one who came in the flesh, died, and rose: God was *in Christ* reconciling the world unto himself. Faith is to be reborn a creature of that God. To have faith is to become a part of the world—this world—God is reconciling unto himself. Then perhaps what Luther spoke of as the "happy exchange" will really occur: Jesus takes our place and gives us his. He becomes historical so that we too might become so and be saved by the God of history.

NOTES

1. Martin Luther, *The Bondage of the Will*, trans. J. I. Packer and O. R. Johnston (Westwood, N.J.: Fleming H. Revell Co., 1957), p. 107. Also, *LW* 33:70.

2. We may protest that without what we call free will we cannot be held responsible for our sins. That is a common move, but it is only a clever diversionary tactic. We use accountability for our peccadilloes as protection against having to confess to sin itself: the fact that we have taken God's place and will not give it up. "Scripture sets before us a man who is not only bound, wretched, captive, sick and dead, but who, through the operation of Satan his lord, adds to his other miseries that of blindness, so that he believes himself to be free, happy, possessed of liberty and ability, whole and alive" (Luther, *Bondage of the Will*, p. 162). To the degree we claim such freedom and will not confess to our bondage we are not responsible. We can be made so only by having our eyes opened. Responsibility is not something we *have* as fallen creatures. We *become* responsible when we are addressed by God in Christ and we begin to realize how lost we are.

3. Martin Luther, Disputation on Scholastic Theology, Thesis 17 in *LW* 31:10.

4. That is why Luther could make statements that have gotten him into trouble ever since, such as the following: "If then we are taught and believe that we ought to be ignorant of the necessitating foreknowledge of God and the necessity of events, Christian faith is utterly destroyed, and the promises of God and the whole gospel fall to the ground completely; for the Christian's chief and only comfort in every adversity lies in knowing that God does not lie, but brings all things to pass immutably, and that His will cannot be resisted, altered or impeded" (*Bondage of the Will*, p. 84). For Luther it is the promise of the gospel, the actual coming of God to us, that is destroyed by attacks on God's immutability and "necessitating foreknowledge." If God's will is not done in the preaching and the sacraments, then it may just be chance that I was baptized. *God* never comes, never acts. We only hear "ideas" about God. The wrath then never ends.

5. Karl Barth, *Church Dogmatics*, 5 vols. in 14 (Edinburgh: T. & T. Clark, 1936–77).

6. H. Berkouwer, *The Triumph of Grace in the Theology of Karl Barth* (Grand Rapids: Wm. B. Eerdmans, 1956), p. 317.

7. Cf. Robert W. Jenson, *God after God* (Indianapolis: Bobbs-Merrill, 1969).

8. Luther, *Bondage of the Will*, p. 170.

9. Jürgen Moltmann, *The Crucified God*, trans. R. A. Wilson and John Bowden (New York: Harper & Row, 1974), pp. 145–46.

10. See the classic statement in Luther's Small Catechism: "Jesus Christ . . . is my Lord . . . who has redeemed me, a lost and condemned creature . . . not with silver and gold but with his holy and precious blood and with his innocent sufferings and death, in order that I might be his . . ." (*BC* 345). Christ purchases and wins (redeems) *me* to be his own; he does not purchase God.

11. D. M. Mackinnon, "Subjective and Objective Conceptions of Atonement," in *Prospect for Theology: Essays in Honor of H. H. Farmer*, ed. F. G. Healey (London: James Nisbet & Co., 1966), p. 175.

4

Atonement as Actual Event

The cross and resurrection of Christ must be understood in more actual terms as his deed done *to us*. The roses must finally be stripped away. Jesus came and died because God is merciful, not to make God merciful. We killed him because he forgave sins, not to make forgiveness possible. Just so does he sacrifice himself for us. The universally rejected one is vindicated by God alone through resurrection. Therefore we are judged and made new by faith. Reconciliation is made between God, God's creatures, and God's creation when death and resurrection are done to us in Christ.

TOWARD A NEW UNDERSTANDING OF SACRIFICE

Throughout the history of the tradition, the scriptural account of Jesus' death and resurrection has been used largely as a mine for texts to support this or that theory. The hermeneutic, whether ancient or modern, has with few exceptions been allegory: The historical account is a code, a surface manifestation of a real meaning to be found on a different and transcendent level. The historical event must be translated into eternal truth about the satisfaction of God's honor, or elevated to a sublime example of dedication to whatever religious people are supposed to be dedicated to, or transcribed into a story about the deception of cosmic tyrants. None of that is evident from the event itself. It comes from the moral, mythological, and metaphysical baggage we carry with us. The hermeneutic is basically gnostic: "Knowledge of the eternal logos" is the model.

Whatever the truth is in these views, the hermeneutic is mistaken. Argument about which theory Scripture supports in such cases is inconclusive and mostly beside the point. Above all, a new hermeneutical approach is needed. Luther has pointed in the proper direction with his movement away from allegory toward an understanding of the Word as active, as doing something to us. Only then will the "knowledge of the eternal" model finally be broken.

7 / THE WORK OF CHRIST

The movement of the tradition has been toward understanding atonement as a concrete, actual event in our time. It cannot be a question of what the event or the words about it are supposed to signify on some transcendent level. If atonement is to be actual, it must be a question of what the event and the proclamation of it does to us, for us, in us, to save and reconcile to God. A dogmatic of and for the church today must recognize this and assist in the task: it must be so constructed as to foster the proper preaching of the Word of the cross. It is in this that the shepherd comes to get the one who is lost.

Dogmatic theology here faces a subtle and difficult task. This can be seen from the tradition. Dogmatics is itself a relatively abstract "second order" exercise and cannot deliver what it talks about. That can be done only in the preaching and the sacraments. But the theology must then be done in such a way that it fosters proper preaching. That means dogmatic theology must be aware of its own peculiar problem: that it can so construct itself as to inhibit or even become a substitute for preaching. Instead of fostering a preaching that actually does the deed in the present, it can offer an interpretation that allows the event to recede into the past. A theory about atonement becomes a substitute for and perhaps even protection against the one reason that matters: the cross occurred, so that it could happen to us in our present. A dogmatic theology that prevents the happening by providing its own reasons—however grand, impressive, and exegetically proper—has defeated its own purpose. The cross is obscured by the theological roses. The movement of the tradition shows that what is needed above all is to strip the petrified roses from the cross so as to foster a preaching that does atonement in the living present. Dogmatics must be so constructed as to point to atonement as an actual event.

How can this be done? We must learn to look at things as they are, to see what is before our very eyes. Jesus' death, the Scriptures and the tradition unanimously assert, was a sacrifice "for us." But in what sense? That is the point at which the argument usually starts. The disagreement has centered largely around the understanding of the sacrifice: its nature, its purpose, and its efficacy vis à vis God. The reason for the argument and disagreement, no doubt, is that this or that idea or theory of sacrifice has been used to interpret the death of Jesus in the attempt to give it universal meaning. Our investigation indicates that this surely must be the wrong way to proceed. One must start more concretely from the ways things are. The death of Jesus must interpret and fulfill the nature of sacrifice, not vice versa.

What actually happened? It is basically a simple story. Jesus came preaching the forgiveness of sins, doing signs and wonders, announcing the coming of the kingdom, and we killed him. We would not have it. "No one can forgive sins but God alone," we said (Mark 2:7 pars.). The fundamental charge was blasphemy. We are not above invoking even the name of God to protect our kingdom from invasion. Blasphemy against the fundamental order of things—religious, political, economic, social—that is the charge.

The issue is thus simple and straightforward: Either he represents God or we do, through our priests, scribes, lawyers, merchants, magistrates, and kings, all our protectors. It came to that in the end. Pilate, one of our "kings," asks Jesus, "Are you the King of the Jews?" He answers, "You have said so" (Mark 15:2). He is given kingly robes, crowned with thorns, and presented to his people. The fundamental decision is made: "Shall I crucify your King?" "We have no king but Caesar" (John 19:15). Some, it is said, wanted the charge altered to read, "This man *said*, I am King of the Jews," but Pilate insists: "What I have written I have written" (John 19:21–22). The drama plays itself to the bitter end: "Let the Christ, the King of Israel, come down now from the cross, that we may see and believe" (Mark 15:32). He dies hanging between two other offenders against the order of this age, crying out in agony and despair. But the tomb does not hold him. He appears to his followers beyond the grave.

What sort of sacrifice is this, and how is it "for us"? It is surely mistaken to say that his Father *needed* the sacrifice in order to be changed to a merciful God. The owner of the vineyard repeatedly sends his servants to claim what is his own, but the tenants kill them. At last they kill the son and heir, thinking to take all for themselves (Mark 12:1–12). Throughout the Gospels precisely the acts of mercy and compassion which Jesus performs in the name of his Father incite the keepers of the order of this age to kill him. Jesus has to die, precisely because God proposes to be merciful. God proposes to be merciful concretely and actually in Jesus. God proposes to come to us and say, "*Your* sins are forgiven." God proposes to open the eyes of the blind, to unstop the ears of the deaf, to make the lame walk, and to preach good news to the poor. We cannot let that happen here. Anyone who intends to carry out such a program must prepare to die. Where could anyone get the authority to do that? Forgiveness full and free with no strings attached is just as dangerous and criminal here as robbery and sedition. It cannot be allowed. It shatters all order. So he must die, just as the thief and the rebel. But he will not desist. "Jerusalem, Jerusalem, killing the prophets and stoning those who are sent to you! How often would I have gathered your children . . . , and you would not!" (Matt. 23:37). So comes about his sacrifice. He dies at our hand. Even in death he cries, "Father, forgive them; for they know not what they do" (Luke 23:34). And just so it is *for us*.

The liberals were right: God is love; God is merciful. They did not see, however, that God's decision to be so *concretely* in Jesus is just the problem, since it does not fit any of our immanent religious schemes. They did not see clearly enough that, because God is merciful, we had to kill God's Christ.

7 / THE WORK OF CHRIST

They strained toward the truth, but failed because they were not radical enough. They did not see clearly enough that Jesus' death spells the end for us, not the final ratification of our highest religious ideals. P. T. Forsyth, too, approached the truth. But Jesus does not confess the moral holiness of God among us. This is not why he was crucified. He had the audacity to forgive sins. He "did" the *mercy* of God to us. He bore witness to that. Hence he had to be crucified. In that sense, as the liberals said, he was faithful to his calling—but not as the hero of a religious system. He stuck to the utterly wild and insane notion that he could forgive sins in the name of his Father.

Jesus dies for us and not for God. There is not just a little perversity in the tendency to say that the sacrifice was demanded by God to placate the divine wrath. We attempt to exonerate ourselves from the terrible nature of the deed by blaming it on God. The theology of sacrifice becomes part of our defense mechanism. This must now cease. Nothing in the Scriptures warrants it. Jesus' sacrifice for us cannot be explained in that fashion. A new understanding of the nature of that sacrifice is demanded. This new understanding must arise from the event itself and not impose previously constructed theories on it.

Current thinking about sacrifice has moved steadily away from narrow ideas of propitiation. F. C. N. Hicks's *The Fulness of Sacrifice* and Frances M. Young's *Sacrifice and the Death of Christ* provide examples. Hicks developed the idea that the blood of the sacrificial victim is or represents its life. Thus it is a mistake to focus narrowly on the death of the victim and identify it as propitiatory. Rather, in the sacrifice, the shed blood represents the surrendering of the life of the one making the offering. Sacrifice is fulfilled in Christ, therefore, not by a supposedly propitiatory death, for sacrifice does not mean the end of life. Rather Jesus' life is surrendered in order to be accepted, and in being accepted to be raised beyond earthly limitations to full communion with God. Thus his "body and blood" (e.g., in the Eucharist) give us a share in the divine life.

> He enters into our own self. It is Life given, broken, and surrendered; so transformed as to be universally accessible; that can enter into any life that has caught His spirit, has surrendered itself, allowed itself by dedication to be transformed, and so entering can become a part of each life and the common possession of all.[1]

Frances Young also insists that sacrifice must not be identified with ideas of penal substitution and propitiation. Sacrificial imagery is central to the thinking of the church, she claims, and covers a whole range of possible ideas. It can mean God's act of expiating sin as well as humankind's act of propitiating God. It could also be used in connection with the victory motif, implying aversion of the evil powers.[2] Thus sacrificial imagery relates to all the theories of atonement and should be reinstated in atonement thinking.

The picture is not complete, however, with an application to atonement theory. One must, for Young, press on to the "subjective" aspect of the sacrifice.

> Evil in us is not met and conquered by an act external to us.
>
> The objective act . . . must effect a transformation in the believer.
>
> The sacrifice of Christ was itself more than an atoning sacrifice; it was a sacrifice of worship and obedience. There were two sides to his sacrificial act, the removal of evil and sin by God, and the offering of perfect homage by man.[3]

The sacrifice of Christ must therefore be participated in through sacrifice of the believer—especially in the context of the worshiping community. "Sacrifice is properly treated as cult-language, not the language of law-courts and judgments; in this context, Christ's act is seen as a sacrifice in which Christians have to partake in order to receive its benefits."[4] This act of self-sacrifice, one gets the definite impression, is really the apex of the whole for Young. It corresponds to the heavy investment she has made throughout the book in speaking of the "moralization" or "spiritualization" of sacrificial practice—that what is demanded is not an empty act supposedly capable of buying-off God but a real giving of self to God: "I desire mercy not sacrifice," "The sacrifices of God are a broken spirit," and so on.

Both Hicks and Young demonstrate a movement away from understanding sacrifice in narrowly propitiatory terms and an attempt to reclaim a wider meaning for the life and worship of the church. The objective is praiseworthy, but it is difficult to avoid detecting a subtle but definite inclination toward the more subjective understanding of sacrifice. The sacrifice of Christ becomes the model to be reenacted by the cult community. Where "the blood is the life," the act of self-giving is something that can "enter into" a life that "has caught his Spirit," "surrendered itself, allowed itself by dedication to be transformed," and so forth. Even when Young speaks with great appreciation of the idea of sacrifice as a self-propitiation on God's part, and tries to recover the objective aspect of it, the attempt is vitiated by the tendency to swallow the whole in the sea of cultic imagery, pictures, and anthropomorphic and mythological language. She has not been able to penetrate to the actuality. As in most books on the sacrifice of Christ, there is very little about what actually happened back there in Jerusalem and on Golgotha, but a great deal about how sacrifice in general is supposed to work. This is then read back onto the events—which means that what happened actually has no particular significance.

The result, for both Hicks and Young, is that they are not able to reverse the direction. Sacrifice remains a means of God-ward traffic. "Sacrifice," Young says, "properly understood, is integral to a religious response to the universe" (*sic!*).

7 / THE WORK OF CHRIST

There is, of course, a considerable difference between a primitive tribe sacrificing to mysterious powers around it in nature and the Christian worship of God conceived as the Creator and sovereign of the universe. But there is one thing in common: sacrifice, material or spiritual, is a reaction to the unseen power believed to be hidden in the world about us, and the different types of sacrifice can be seen as expressions of different reactions to the environment.[5]

The sacrifice of Christ apparently does nothing to change any of that. Sacrifice is a means for somehow appeasing the "hidden powers" of the universe. Under these presuppositions it is a questionable thing to dismantle the notion of *propitiatory* sacrifice, for if Christ does not propitiate such hidden powers, then *we* shall have to do it by our sacrifice. Willy-nilly everything will fall back on us. No doubt that is the reason for the persistence of ideas about propitiation by penal substitution. If the direction is never reversed, propitiation is the only hope.

The great mystery surrounding all discussion of sacrifice is that no one seems to know exactly what it is, where it comes from, or what it is supposed to mean. The Scriptures themselves provide no real theological explanation of sacrifice and are even ambiguous about the propriety of doing it at all (see the many prophetic railings against it). There are directions about how to do it and when, but little indication of just *why* it is supposed to work. The result is that scholars and exegetes scratch around in religious phenomenology and ethnology for theories that are then imposed on the biblical material. Such practice may help to explain some cultic practices of the Old Testament, but it can be fatal when used to provide the "meaning" for the cross. It seems unlikely that Jesus' sacrifice could accurately be spoken of as his "religious response to the universe" or his "reaction to the unseen power believed to be hidden in the world about us."

To arrive at a new understanding of the sacrifice of Christ, one must above all pay close attention to what actually happened and what the Scriptures say about it. What happened was a murder. It was a cruel, bitter, excruciatingly painful, and utterly shameful execution. The apostle Paul must be our guide here. His writings are permeated by a sense for the utter folly, offense, and humiliation of the actual event. The "word of the cross" means just that—not some theory *about* it. Paul does not have many—if any—theories about the cross; he simply holds the actual cross in its horror before his hearers, hearers who are always, it seems, tempted to go off on this or that theoretical detour around the cross. "We preach Christ crucified," Paul says (1 Cor. 1:23), and crucified must, in the first instance at least, mean just that: hung on a cross to die the cursed and shameful death of a slave and criminal. One must not yet hurry on to say "sacrificed" so as to obscure and purify the utter folly of it with theological incense. How else could it be "a stumbling block to Jews and a folly to the Gentiles"? Martin Hengel is certainly right. One must no longer "dissociate talk of the atoning death of Jesus or the blood of Jesus from this 'word of the cross.'" "For the foolishness of God is wiser than men, and the weakness of God is stronger than men" (1 Cor. 1:25).

If we take the actuality of Paul's "word of the cross" as foundation, the Epistle to the Hebrews offers counsel as to how we might proceed. Not only is it the most sustained treatise on the sacrifice of Christ, it is also perhaps the most misunderstood—no doubt because we use it to reinforce our theories rather than let it speak. The epistle has two basic points: first, that Jesus was real; second, that his sacrifice was real in contrast to all others. Jesus was real. He was not a fake. He was not protected, not a Greek "divine man." He was made perfect through suffering (Heb. 2:10ff.); he had to go *through* death.

> Since therefore the children share in flesh and blood, he himself likewise partook of the same nature, that through death he might destroy him who has the power of death, that is, the devil, and deliver all those who through fear of death were subject to lifelong bondage. For surely it is not with angels that he is concerned but with the descendants of Abraham. Therefore he had to be made like his brethren in every respect, so that he might become a merciful and faithful high priest in the service of God, to make expiation for the sins of the people. For because he himself has suffered and been tempted, he is able to help those who are tempted. (2:14–18)

One should note that he has to be "made like his brethren" to *become* "a merciful and faithful high priest in the service of God, to make expiation . . ." and to be "able to help. . . ." The mercy must be an actual event, an "I love you."

Second, because Jesus was real, his sacrifice was real in contrast to all others. Previous sacrifices had only been pale, ineffective shadows of the real thing. They had been, so to speak, only a series of dry runs. With the cultic machinery and the endless repetition of sacrifices, we had only been practicing for the real event. Now, in the cross, the cruel and actual cross, it had happened. It happened, furthermore, not in the temple but out in the streets where everyone could see. He entered "once for all" (9:12) into the real holy place (heaven itself, 9:24) through the real curtain, his own flesh (10:20). He was killed not as part of a pious ritual in church but out in the streets, in a place of execution. Indeed, the writer concludes by saying that it all took place outside the gate, outside those holy places reeking of incense and creaking under the weight of inviolable traditions and reasons for everything.

In what surely must be one of the most offensive images in Scripture, the author likens Jesus' suffering "outside the gate" to the burning of the flesh and offal of the animals whose blood was taken into the sanctuary by the high priest. The real sacrifice takes place "out there" not "in the tent."

7 / THE WORK OF CHRIST

> We have an altar from which those who serve the tent have no right to eat. For the bodies of those animals whose blood is brought into the sanctuary by the high priest as a sacrifice for sin are burned outside the camp. So Jesus also suffered outside the gate in order to sanctify the people through his own blood. Therefore let us go forth to him outside the camp and bear the abuse he endured. For here we have no lasting city, but we seek the city which is to come. (13:10–14)

Such passages jolt attempts to construct a neat theory of sacrifice from the epistle. Jesus' death is compared not to the sacrifices in the temple and the ritual purification for sin but to the burning outside the camp of so much impure refuse. That ought to give us pause in a day when the phenomenology of religion and anthropology has supposedly unlocked for us the meaning of sacrifice and has looked to ritual and cultic practice from which to draw our meanings and theories.

The Epistle to the Hebrews, of course, presents no clear or consistent theory of sacrifice. The reason, surely, is that the writer does not start from some theory of sacrifice as such, but from the actuality of the death of Jesus on the cross, and by means of a contrapuntal comparison shows that the old practices have been completely eclipsed. The point is that the ritual was limited, bound up in itself, and never made it out into the real world where it could be universally for everyone, for all time. A change in the law (7:12) has come about in Jesus. His priesthood does not depend on tribal descent, but he is a priest "forever" "by the power of an indestructible life" (7:16). The blood sprinkled in the sanctuary may suffice for ritual purification for the priests, but not for the world. Jesus, however, suffered "outside the gate in order to sanctify the people through his own blood" (13:12). The sprinkling of defiled people with the blood of goats and bulls may suffice for ritual purification of the flesh, but "how much more shall the blood of Christ, who through the eternal Spirit offered himself without blemish to God, *purify your conscience from dead works to serve the living God*" (9:14). The contrast could hardly be more sharp. The sacrificial ritual was only "fleshly" and concerned itself with "dead works." The actual death of Jesus, however, the true sacrifice, penetrates through to the conscience to purify it from all that so one will serve the *living* God. Thus the author can conclude, "We have an altar from which those who serve the tent have no right to eat," and we are exhorted to "go forth to him outside the camp and bear the abuse he endured. For here we have no lasting city, but we seek the city which is to come" (13:10, 13, 14).

The Epistle to the Hebrews gives us a starting point. When atonement has slipped back into mere theological theory or pious ritual, it is time once again to go forth to him "outside the camp," to the real altar. The death of Jesus makes it clear that the cultic apparatus was only a rehearsal: We have been practicing for this one thing from time immemorial; now it has happened. We cannot go back to our rehearsals again.

The insistence on the reality of the sacrifice receives interesting confirmation from the work of René Girard, *Violence and the Sacred*.[6] Girard insists that we must look for a real origin for the practice of sacrifice, not just a psychological, cultic, or mythological one. Sacrifice, he maintains, performed the very real function of keeping violence outside the community. It has its origin in the actual murder of a surrogate victim. The estranged parties in the community, threatened by the destructive power of disorder, of unrestrained and unrevenged violence, descend on a surrogate victim who in some fashion or other is looked on as being responsible for the crisis. The surrogate victim is killed and the violence is averted. The sacrifice thus becomes the basis for a new order and harmony in the community. The surrogate victim "bears away the violence" in an actual sense. To say that the victim bears our sins is to say the same thing. Sacrifice as a real event averting violence is, according to Girard, the foundation of order and community. The surrogate victim is thus also the benefactor of the new order. The sacrifice as a real event both averts violence and unites the estranged parties possessed by its power.

Perhaps equally significant for our purposes is Girard's view of ritual or cultic sacrifice. Ritual sacrifice is an attempt to repeat and channel the benefit of the first and real sacrifice. It seeks to "extract from the original violence some technique of cathartic appeasement."[7] It seeks thus to reduce sacrifice to a formula, to remove all elements of chance. The aspects that were beyond human control—the time, the place, the selection of the victim, the procedure—are now premeditated and fixed by the ritual. Ritual sacrifice is founded on a double substitution: a ritually prescribed victim is now substituted for the original surrogate victim.[8] Most telling of all, however, is that such ritual sacrifice involves a certain obscuring of its own factual and real basis. That is because the ritual takes place within, subsequent to, the order already established by the original sacrifice and has as its aim the preservation of that order. It is preventive, not creative. The myths it tells about the sacrifice obscure the truth in attempting to point to it. Thus it is said, perhaps, that the sacrifice is necessary to appease "the gods" who are "wrathful." The cathartic violence is repeated on a substitute who will not evoke further revenge and prolong the violence. A lesser violence is "proffered as a bulwark against a far more virulent violence."[9] There is a transformation of the real into the unreal which is "part of the process by which man conceals from himself the human origin of his own violence, by attributing it to the gods."[10] "A delusion concerning its own factual basis—*not* the absence of that basis"—is, according to Girard, the trouble from which religion suffers.[11]

7 / THE WORK OF CHRIST

Girard's thesis provides significant background for the necessity of movement toward actuality and reality in speaking of atonement. One of our tasks must be removal of the delusion to arrive at the truth. The cross of Christ must be seen in that light.

THE ACCIDENT

We need a new, perhaps even a noncultic and nonreligious idea of sacrifice. This is certainly what the writer of Hebrews was suggesting with his invitation to go forth "outside the camp." At the risk of committing the very sin constantly railed at here—multiplying images—we might try, as a kind of project in thought, a more common and everyday use of the term "sacrifice" and a different conceptuality, that of "accident." The idea suggests itself for several reasons. It picks up Lessing's challenge about "accidental truths of history." Perhaps it is the very accidental character that is of the essence. Accidents just happen, and there is nothing to do but rearrange everything according to what happened. Accidents are opaque. One cannot see through them. Yet they raise most directly and in the most crucial way the question of God for us. Sometimes we call them acts of God! In an accident, one does not even have time to ask whether what occurs is relevant to one's life or not. It just happens, and there it is. An accident is just that tear in the fabric of time we noted at the close of the last chapter.

No doubt the image could be developed in many different ways, but perhaps we can say it like this: A child is playing in the street. A truck is bearing down on the child. A man casts himself in the path of the truck, saves the child, but is himself killed in the process. It is an accident.

The development of such an image can help us see what is at stake. The accidental death of the man who saved the child could be called a sacrifice, indeed, even a vicarious sacrifice. He gave his life for another. And the point is that this is all one needs to say. It is not a ritual or cultic sacrifice—not a substitution—but a real sacrifice, an actual one.

When the sacrifice is actual, certain questions immediately become irrelevant or beside the point. One would hardly waste much time arguing about "to whom" the man sacrificed his life. Yet this is what theologians have done. The reason, no doubt, is that they have too often been thinking about a cultic rehearsal where nothing actually happens, and have attempted subsequently to endow the empty event with universal meaning via this or that theory. Since nothing is accomplished by the sacrifice, one must shore it up with much cultic and metaphysical underpinning.

The man in our story gave his life *for* someone. The question "To whom?" is unnecessary. To whom could he have given it? To the truck? Hardly. To the child? Not really. To God? At best only in the indirect sense that he was faithful to the divine mandate to love at whatever the cost, but certainly not to pay God. If the sacrifice is real, one says all there is to say when one says it was *for* the other.

So also the New Testament. Jesus died *for* us; on our behalf, he gave his life as a ransom for many. The New Testament shows no interest whatever in the question of *to* whom his sacrifice might have been made. One has said all there is to say when one has said "for us all."

But in what sense is the sacrifice for us? In terms of our story, it would be all too easy to identify ourselves with the more or less innocent child playing in the street and look on the sacrifice as that which averts death. Were we to do that, however, we would remain with something akin to a superficial victory motif and with a tendency to overlook human sin. To make the story work properly, we must say that we are not the child playing in the street, but the driver of the truck. If anything, the child is our neighbor, not us. Suddenly there is the someone who throws himself in our unheeding way and is splattered against the front of our machine. If atonement is to be seen as an actual event, the cross should have that kind of direct, shattering impact. The roses must be stripped away once and for all. The cross cannot be brought back "within the camp." It remains outside, a permanent offense.

When we say that we drive the truck, we add a dimension strangely and conspicuously missing in most theories of the atonement: *we* did it. The theories usually gloss over this lightly or tend to place the blame abstractly, as though Jesus were crucified in a vacuum and the judgment and crowd scenes in the passion narratives had no point. "His blood be on us and on our children!" (Matt. 27:25). "Do not weep for me, but weep for yourselves and for your children" (Luke 23:28). Looking at atonement theory, one would think such words had not been written. Perhaps René Girard is right: our theories tend to transform the real into the unreal in order to conceal from ourselves the human origin of our violence, attributing it to God. In a day when there is much debate about "who did it," we must not fail to give the right answer at last: we did.

Blaming the Jews for the crucifixion has been a terrible sin, a particular Christian attempt to conceal the truth which has had tragic results. Faced with the cross, we can only confess, "We have done it." If we cannot say that, he did not die for us. The hymnody of the church has recognized this even if dogmatics has not:

>Who was the guilty?
>Who brought this upon thee?
>Alas, my treason,
>Jesus, hath undone thee.

7 / THE WORK OF CHRIST

> 'Twas I, Lord Jesus,
> I it was denied thee.
> I crucified thee.
> —Johann Crüger

At this point we must do some demythologizing of the classic view and take what Luther said even further. The cosmic enemies in the classic view—sin, death, law, the devil—must be seen as operating *through us* in our bondage, however we may regard their objective existence. The cross is the place where the actual battle against us and thus ultimately for us is joined. Jesus throws himself in our path. As such, the cross is not in the first instance a revelation of the love or mercy of God. It is rather the climactic manifestation of God's wrath against sin, God's attack against a humanity that will believe neither in God nor in God's creation. It is the expression of God's jealousy against a world that will not have this God as a God of mercy. The cross makes it plain that "all have sinned and fall short of the glory of God" (Rom. 3:23). Jesus, the one bearing forgiveness from God, puts himself in our path. The demons recognize him and speak for us: "What have you to do with us, Jesus of Nazareth? Have you come to destroy us? I know who you are, the Holy One of God" (Mark 1:24). And in the end we kill him.

Just so does he "bear our sins in his body on the tree" (1 Pet. 2:21–24). We must remove the last abstraction from Luther's talk of the "happy exchange" and all the dogmatic language about Jesus' bearing our sin. We cannot speak as though that were a matter of bearing some quantum or other, somehow equivalent to the sins of the whole world. That Jesus bears our sins in his body is no abstract affair, no strange metaphysical transference; it is actual and public fact. We beat him, spit on him, mock him as a "king," crown him with thorns, torture him, forsake him, kill him. He bears our sins in his body—actually. The real event occurs. It is not a rehearsal or a cultic substitution.

Here we must look, too, at the particular way in which Jesus died: on a cross. "He humbled himself and became obedient unto death, even death on a cross" (Phil. 2:8). He bore the curse: "Christ redeemed us from the curse of the law, having become a curse for us—for it is written, 'Cursed be every one who hangs on a tree' " (Gal. 3:13). Why that? It was the most degrading, shameful, despicable form of execution, the most terrible way to dispatch criminals and offenders against the established order, the most conspicuous and awesome manifestation of human justice. We cannot set up proofs or establish proof-texts for just why it had to be a cross, but we can see, perhaps, a certain inevitability in it all. He had to be executed as an offender against our order, under our justice. In that sense he had to bear the ultimate curse: the curse of the law. It had to be quite legal and proper. We must be clear about this. He was not crucified because of our peccadilloes against the order;

ATONEMENT AS ACTUAL EVENT

he was crucified by the order itself, so to bring a new order. He was a sacrifice for original sin as well as actual sins. Just so does he bear our sin in his body—the sin of an order alienated from the God of mercy, and setting itself up against that God. Just so also is he "made to be sin for us" though he "knew no sin" (2 Cor. 5:17–21). He could be nothing other than a criminal, an offender, even though he is innocent. René Girard says that the system of justice has superseded sacrifice in modern society.[12] No doubt that is a reason for the shift to legal concepts in postpatristic atonement theory. The cross is the end of law.

Nowhere is God's utter rejection of our sin more apparent than at the cross. Nowhere is the truth of our sin more exposed to the light of God's judgment. God rejects it and judges it precisely by refusing to have anything to do with it. God will have nothing to do with our violence, our claim to be free, our drives to dominate. There is nothing God can or will do but die at our hands: bear our sins. If there had been anything else to do, Jesus' Father could have sent "legions of angels" (Matt. 26:53). But then the Scriptures would not be fulfilled, "that it must be so" (Matt. 26:54). God remains true to himself: "I will have mercy on whom I will have mercy."

But how could such an event have universal significance? If we reduce it to this actuality, is it not just an isolated historical event? Is it not just an accident? Driving our truck down the street, innocently going about our business, how could we be held guilty? Or could we not also say, "Someone else did it"—way back there? How can it be "once, for all"? The theories have attempted to answer the question by fitting atonement into cultic, juridical, and moral structures that are supposed to be universally valid. But that is to freeze it, to turn it into an idea, and so to transform it into just that wrath from which we need to be saved. It is to make the cross serve the status quo, take it captive to the already existing order. It becomes merely preventative, not curative or creative. When the writer of the Epistle to the Hebrews invites us to "go forth to meet him outside the camp," he bids us turn our back on all that. "For," he says, "here we have no lasting city, but we seek the city which is to come" (Heb. 13:14).

What must be recognized finally is that Jesus' death has universal significance "for us" because he was universally rejected and yet raised from the dead. "This Jesus God raised up, and of that we are all witnesses. . . . Let all the house of Israel therefore know assuredly that God has made him both Lord and Christ, this Jesus whom you crucified" (Acts 2:32, 36). When they heard this, we are told, "They were cut to the heart," and said, "What shall we do?" Having died once, Jesus dies no more. Jesus' death has universal significance for us because God raised him from the dead. He, the universally rejected one, is vindicated by *God*. He is not a hero for our systems. He is not vindicated by us. He is vindicated by God. The one splattered against

7 / THE WORK OF CHRIST

the front of our truck comes back to say "Shalom." There is no strange transaction that takes place somewhere in celestial bookkeeping halls to make it universal. The one we killed, the one no one wanted, is raised from the dead. That is all. The stone the builders rejected has become the chief cornerstone.

Jesus had to die because God is forgiving and because God insists on being so. Jesus died precisely because he said, "I forgive you in God's name." He died because we would not have it. The resurrection is his vindication against us. Therefore, it is vindication against death, the power of death resident in our legalism (see 2 Cor. 3). It is the proof that he was right and we are wrong. God has made him Lord. God has now said what he has to say. God has at last "spoken to us by a Son" (Heb. 1:2).

This is precisely the difference between the Old and the New Testaments. The argument about whether there was grace or forgiveness in the Old Testament is beside the point. Everyone knows that God is gracious and forgiving. As Voltaire said, "C'est son métier" (that's his business). But left like that, forgiveness too is an abstract characteristic like any other. In Jesus, God actually comes to say "to you" what he was preparing to say all along. To say that it can be said to you means that it is now universal and must be said to all the yous in the world in the preaching of the church. If it can be said "to you," it can be said to all. It knows no bounds; it is unconditional. God, who is always gracious, was preparing, promising, to say it actually, concretely, in our time by first choosing a concrete people. This meant at first a restriction, a particularization. As such it means even a legalization, for a particular people must be shaped by law in this age. The peril of saying it precisely among his own is thus magnified to the utmost. "His own received him not" (John 1:11). To get it said precisely as forgiveness and not another law, Jesus must die and shatter all opposition even among his own. He must negate the law, the particularization, concretely, so that forgiveness can be said universally to all. Just so did he die for us. He died and was vindicated in the resurrection so that the "I forgive you" could actually be said. In that sense he won forgiveness for us. He won the right for it to be said. That is the New Testament. The testament or will that was prepared and promised is now actually given because the testator has actually died (Heb. 9:15ff.). Luther once put the matter succinctly: The sole difference between the Old and the New Testaments is that the Old said, "You must have Christ and his spirit," while the New says, "Here it is."[13] It is the "I now give it to you" that characterizes the *New* Testament. It can now be said to everyone. It is universal.

We should say something at this point about the question of universalism and its relative, cosmic salvation. Universalism, the idea that God must eventually save everyone, is an abstraction that like all such abstractions which try to prompt God does little real good and has no basis in Scripture. What Jesus won for us on the cross is precisely the right to say the saving word of forgiveness to all universally, and he commissioned his followers to *do* so. The will of God is revealed in the saying and doing. The task of dogmatics is to foster that concrete saying and doing in the confidence that it alone will save from all abstraction, law, and wrath. Universalism as an abstraction can add nothing to that, and it can harm the proclamation if it is taken to mean that there is no need to say the concrete word. If it functions to obviate the preaching, it is another abstraction that destroys the concrete and actual. Declaring people to be anonymous Christians or to be somehow universally saved can be like declaring the poor to be anonymous rich people. That is hardly a kindness. The abstraction is never completely kind or unambiguous. Only "he who comes" can save. Of course, the abstraction may serve other purposes. It may also function as a hope arising from having heard the concrete word—the hope that the God who has managed so to speak in Jesus will so speak to all, and use us to that end. In that sense it may function to remind us that we can have no vested interest in insisting that hell be populated. That is God's affair. It can also function to remind us that the authority we have is to preach the *good* news, to speak the word of forgiveness to all the yous concretely and that we do not have the authority to damn people—to say, "You are lost eternally." The universality given is the universality of the gospel. That cannot be withheld from anyone. It stops before no boundary. The eventual outcome of such speaking of the gospel is in God's hands. Theology cannot force God's hand.

The idea of a cosmic salvation also seems to have little basis in the Scripture, if taken to mean that through Jesus' death, resurrection, and exaltation the present empirical cosmos has undergone or is undergoing some mysterious change. The Scripture does not support a demythologizing that reduces salvation to a purely personal inwardness or existential self-understanding. There is indeed a cosmic dimension to the rule of the crucified and resurrected One. But for the time being that is hidden—the seed growing secretly. It will be manifest in the end-times, in the eschaton. Now Christ is "ruling from the tree." "The cosmos is penetrated by Christ, not because his exaltation has rendered redemption and existing reality one and the same, but rather because his Church, participant in the event of his cross and his instrument in its humiliation, its bodily dying, is extended and expanded over the earth."[14] The cosmic dimension is *eschatological*. The crucified and risen one must reign until he has put all enemies under his feet. Then the kingdom is handed over to God, who will be all in all (1 Cor. 15:28).

It must be recognized that unconditional and universal forgiveness is a dangerous and seditious thing in our world, in this age. It simply cannot be done. In this sense, too, the crucifixion had to be. Forgiveness is not safe unless it is creative, unless it actually brings a new world, a new age. So forgiveness can be given only in Jesus' name, in his name who was killed by us and was

7 / THE WORK OF CHRIST

vindicated. In him forgiveness can be given because he ushers us through death to life in his kingdom. "Here we have no lasting city . . ." (Heb. 13:14).

> "Are you the King . . . ?" . . . Jesus answered, "My kingship is not of this world; if my kingship were of this world, my servants would fight. . . ." Pilate said to him, "So you are a king?" Jesus answered, "You say that I am a king. For this I was born, and for this I have come into the world, to bear witness to the truth. Every one who is of the truth hears my voice." (John 18:33–37)

The resurrection of the universally rejected one means that the accident both judges and saves us. It is a faith-creating and faith-demanding event. We are judged. If the one smashed against the front of our machine is raised, the entire enterprise in which we are engaged is judged. "It was an accident," we might say. "How can we be held guilty if someone just ran out in front of us? There was nothing we could do." Of course. Just as with Pilate, the priests, the people. "Of course, we didn't intend to kill the Son of God, but how were we to know? It was an accident." Indeed. But God vindicates him. The truth is revealed. Not the peccadilloes, not the little misdeeds or mistakes, but the entire enterprise is called into question. Not just the moment of the accident, but all that leads to our being there at all is called into question: the grim inertia of all our religious, economic, social, juridical, and political systems which will not and cannot swerve aside no matter who gets in the way. "Accidents will happen." "Sometimes the innocent, unfortunately, get crushed." But this innocent one is raised. Then we are judged in the sight of God, the God who raises the dead and cares about the innocent. The world, of course, goes on. The truck pauses only momentarily. The world will pronounce the death accidental, absolve the driver, and leave time to heal the wounds. But if the one killed is raised, something else happens: ultimate judgment, a full stop, and grace. "But to all who received him, who believed in his name, he gave power to become children of God; who were born, not of blood nor of the will of the flesh nor of the will of man, but of God" (John 1:12–13).

The resurrection of the rejected one judges and saves at once. Faith will grasp the accident as the revelation of God and believe that it was "no accident," that God placed him in our path. The cross and the resurrection are the specific way God wants to get through to us and reveal who God actually is. God's innermost being comes to expression here. God slips into our world just in the little crack of the accident, softly and lightly, but with the ultimate authority of absolute grace. God does not come in the palace of kings, the halls of justice, or the temples of the priests. Just an accident in time. There God can be truly for us. There is no room elsewhere.

But what does this add up to *for us*? Atonement as an actual event means that through the word of the cross and the resurrection something is done to us. Atonement is done to us. The resurrection of the crucified One means death and life for us. If the event, the accident, happens to us, breaks into our lives with the impact we have been trying to describe, then it will involve a full stop and a new beginning: a death of the old and the resurrection of the new in faith. The word of the cross must be a word that does the cross to us, not one that directs attention elsewhere so as to enable us to avoid it. That is the kind of hermeneutic needed today.

Dogmatic theology cannot take the path of Hegel and his followers in attempting to assimilate the death and resurrection of Jesus to an immanent rational scheme: infinite Spirit going out from itself and returning to itself, understood as the necessary unfolding of its own nature. As Bonhoeffer put it, this is the "ultimate deceit" and "final strength" of the human *logos* or reason. It forestalls the claim of the *logos* of the cross by "negating itself and at the same time asserts that this negation is a necessary unfolding of its own nature."[15] The death and resurrection of Jesus cannot thus be assimilated to an immanent rational scheme and turned into a "speculative Good Friday." If Jesus is the one who comes to us through just that accident of which we have been speaking, we are suddenly thrown out of all immanent rational schemes, all those projects, ideas, and ideals that are supposedly to carry us to our planned and preconceived destinations, and thrown entirely on him, the one whom we, in our plans, killed and who yet rose. We cannot take him into our schemes; he takes us into his concrete life. "For to me to live is Christ, and to die is gain," says Paul (Phil. 1:21).

Full discussion of the meaning of death and new life for us must await the later *locus* on the Christian life. Here we shall give only brief indication of its significance. The idea of death and new life takes us into the area which has, in the tradition, been termed the "subjective" dimension of atonement. Resisting all along as we have the idea of an objective change in God might open our treatment to the charge of subjectivism. It should be obvious, however, that such a charge cannot hold. The reason is precisely that the cross means death and new life. The old subject is not just given an example to follow, or inspiration to encourage its flagging religious ambitions. The old subject dies and a new one is called into being in Jesus by faith. When faith in the unconditional mercy of God is created, a new subject begins to emerge.

This means that atonement is intensely subjective, in the sense that it has a profound effect on the subject. But the subject-object dichotomy is not at all apt to designate what happens if actual "at-one-ment" is to occur. Since it is a matter of death and new life coming from the actual event, it is entirely objective in the sense that it comes totally from without. The subject has nothing to do with it. The subject is put to death. Indeed, one could argue that the so-called objectivity of theories positing a change in God is really only apparent. God changes, but I remain the same. God has to be

7 / THE WORK OF CHRIST

"satisfied" to allow my system of legalistic thinking to remain intact. God is made to fit my picture. At bottom that is a very subjective stance. There is, ultimately, little to choose between so-called objective and subjective atonement theories. Both leave the subject more or less intact. The only argument between them is the degree of help needed.

If, however, atonement is the actual event, the accident that happens to us from without, it affects us profoundly subjectively. It ends the old life and begins a new one. It means death and resurrection. The old subjective views were partially right. They simply were not radical enough. They thought of a modification of the subject, not of its death and resurrection.

No doubt the claim that his death *is* our death is difficult for us to grasp. Again we are tricked by our tendency to get lost in abstraction. We think that something incredibly difficult or strange is being demanded of us. Living up to the law was difficult enough, but now we are told that we have to die. But the point is that his death is our death; he has died for us. Paul could put it quite simply: "We are convinced that one has died for all; therefore all have died" (2 Cor. 5:14). What is that death? It is simply the death administered through the word authorized by the cross and resurrection. When the word of forgiveness comes to a world bent on its own survival systems, that world is suddenly robbed of its whole reason for being. The death is suddenly having nothing to do. If Jesus lives after we have killed him, then we have died. To die means to be reduced to nothing, to be able to do nothing but wait. When the accident occurs, we are suddenly helpless. We can only wait for help. We are thrown out of the stream that usually protects us. If Jesus lives, then we as old beings are through.

We fear such talk of death and resurrection because we fear the loss of continuity. Is there not a continuity between the old and the new person? Is there not something to carry us across? It is a real and serious question. But it is of the same sort one should address to the cross. What was that death into which Jesus entered? Was he assured of continuity? The question is of the sort one must ask about forgiveness. Will I survive forgiveness? I may take it, perhaps, as old Adam and abuse it, use it as license, presume upon it, preserving myself, my continuity. Forgiveness will itself turn to poison if it does not bring that death and resurrection. It cannot be mixed with such continuity. Such talk of continuity may be used just to protect us from death. But we need have no fear. He has died for us. To believe that means to believe that my continuity is now entirely in him. We have already heard the author of the Epistle to the Hebrews say it: "He himself likewise partook of the same nature, that through death he might destroy him who has the power of death, that is, the devil, and deliver all those who *through fear of death* were subject to lifelong bondage" (2:14–15). Forth from the cross and the resurrection goes the absolutely unconditional word: it is all over; there is nothing to be done. Our death and resurrection are simply in the nothing. Faith is the death and resurrection. He has died for us in a double sense: died in the place we must die and died so as finally to get us, to claim us. To be finally grasped by the event itself, to have the accident happen, *is* to die and to be made new. It is to die to the old, to the abstractions, the universal truths of reason that are supposed to protect us from death, to the law, to sin, that is, to unbelief in God, in God's grace and creation. It is to die to all that so as to become oneself an historical being, not an abstraction. It is to be found in him who died accidentally so that one might be raised in him. It is to wait, to live by hope in the God who raised Jesus, the preacher of forgiveness, from the dead. To die thus and to await the resurrection is to be reconciled with the God who created this world.

Faith born of death and resurrection means that the believer counts on a new future, a new age, for the world God has created. Jesus' death for us must be taken also in that sense. He died to give us a new future, a new kingdom. If he is our death and resurrection, he is also our example. There is no difficulty in saying that when the event is actual. If his death for us opens a new future, then he is the pioneer, the one whom we follow. The kingdom he brought, the message of forgiveness, finds no room in this age. But we follow him. We may recall here the words from 1 Peter:

> For to this you have been called, because Christ also suffered for you, leaving you an example, that you should follow in his steps. He committed no sin; no guile was found on his lips. When he was reviled, he did not revile in return; when he suffered, he did not threaten; but he trusted to him who judges justly. He himself bore our sins in his body on the tree, that we might die to sin and live to righteousness. By his wounds you have been healed. (2:21-24)

Forgiveness does not work here, but we pray, "Forgive us our sins, as we forgive those who sin against us." For we look for the city to come. The significance of that must be spelled out at greater length in the *locus* on the Christian life.

Atonement understood as dying and rising in Christ in faith can also approach and be assimilated to the older patristic language of *theopoiesis*—of being "divinized" or "immortalized" through participation in the victorious and eternal divine life of Christ. There is always a danger that one may construe such divinization as an escape from death, as a detour around the actual death of Jesus. That would be the case if one maintained that because Jesus was divine he was protected from the death, and that one now participates in just that protection. One is not always certain whether the fathers avoid this danger successfully. If one is quite clear that the "divine life" we are participating in is that of the triune God who has gone through death in

7 / THE WORK OF CHRIST

his Son, and that our participation means going through death, by faith, then one can indeed speak of and celebrate such *theopoiesis*. That would be the point and conclusion of Luther's language of the "happy exchange." He takes *our* life, our place, in order to give us *his*. The exchange must be an actual event, however. He must take our place, our death, if we are to have his life. In that sense, Luther can speak expressly in words akin to those of the fathers: "Therefore God becomes man in order that man may become God. Likewise strength becomes weak in order that weakness may become strength. He put on our form and figure, image and likeness, in order to clothe us in his image, form and likeness. . . ."[16]

Atonement conceived as an actual event thus does justice to the concerns of all the various theories. It is objective; it comes from without entirely. God's wrath is satisfied in the sense that God's resolve to have mercy breaks through the abstractions, the bondage in which we are implicated, to create faith. Just so, is it also intensely "subjective." When faith is created, a new subject emerges, the historical being who, as a member of the body of Christ, the crucified and resurrected one, has become an historical being who waits, follows, and hopes. What Schleiermacher and Ritschl wanted can be seen to come to fruition: The divine love establishes an actual historical community. But this is the body of believers who have died and who look to the resurrection, who bear that stamp, who follow Christ, not a community of religious or moral idealists. Actual atonement is also the divine victory. The victory, however, is not abstract or mythological. Sin, death, the law, the devil—all the powers—are defeated in us. The new covenant is established.

> I will put my law within them, and I will write it upon their hearts; and I will be their God, and they shall be my people. And no longer shall each man teach his neighbor and each his brother saying, "Know the Lord," for they shall all know me, from the least of them to the greatest, says the Lord; for I will forgive their iniquity, and I will remember their sin no more. (Jer. 31:33–34)

> For God has done what the law, weakened by the flesh, could not do: sending his own Son in the likeness of sinful flesh and for sin, he condemned sin in the flesh, in order that the just requirement of the law might be fulfilled *in* us, who walk not according to the flesh but according to the Spirit. (Rom. 8:3–4)

NOTES

1. F. C. N. Hicks, *The Fulness of Sacrifice*, 3d ed. (London: SPCK, 1946), p. 26.
2. Frances M. Young, *Sacrifice and the Death of Christ* (Philadelphia: Westminster Press, 1975), p. 91.
3. Ibid., p. 95.

4. Ibid., p. 96.
5. Ibid., p. 111.
6. René Girard, *Violence and the Sacred*, trans. Patrick Gregory (Baltimore: Johns Hopkins University Press, 1977).
7. Ibid., p. 102.
8. Ibid.
9. Ibid., p. 103.
10. Ibid., p. 161.
11. Ibid., pp. 103-4.
12. Ibid., pp. 15ff.
13. Martin Luther, *Lectures on Romans*, trans. and ed. W. Pauck, LCC 15 (London: SCM Press, 1961), p. 199.
14. Roy A. Harrisville, "The New Testament Witness to the Cosmic Christ," in *The Gospel and Human Destiny*, ed. Vilmos Vajta (Minneapolis: Augsburg Publishing House, 1971), p. 57.
15. Dietrich Bonhoeffer, *Christ the Center*, trans. E. H. Robertson (New York: Harper & Row, 1978), p. 29.
16. *WA* 1, 28, 25-32.

EIGHTH LOCUS

The Holy Spirit

ROBERT W. JENSON

THE HOLY SPIRIT

Introduction

1. The Spirit That Spoke by the Prophets
   The Hebrew Scriptures
   The New Testament
   The Creedal Tradition

2. Pneumatological Soteriology
   The Doctrine of Grace
   Justification by Faith
   Predestination

3. Spirit-Discourse as the Church's Self-interpretation
   Ecclesial Christology
   The Spirit and God
   The Spirit and the Letter
   The Spirit and the Word
   The Spirit and History

4. Cosmic Spirit
   The Logic of Cosmic Pneumatology
   The Freedom of History
   The Spontaneity of Natural Process
   The Beauty of All Things

Introduction

The phenomenon we call "spirit" is both universal in human experience and universally remarked.[1] Thus, in uncommon agreement, Hebrew *ruach* and Greek *pneuma*, with their synonyms and related words, have identical backgrounds and usage.[2] Both initially meant "wind" and "breath," and neither ever fully lost this sense or reduced it to pure metaphor. In the uses that concern us, both evoke the liveliness of life, as the elusive and ever-moving breath, the wind that blows where it will to set still things in motion. In the world, the wind is both the dynamism in and of the world and, in its untraceable origin and destination, beyond the world. In us, the breath is both the motion of our own life and drawn in from and breathed out uncontrollably into the alien world beyond. Thus spirit is self-transcendence; the liveliness of each life is precisely its origin and end beyond itself. Moreover, spirit is both life in its openness to dynamism beyond itself, and the dynamism that comes on it; any Greek could have said with the Yahwist, "God . . . breathed into his nostrils the breath of life; and man became a living being" (Gen. 2:7). The Delphic oracle and the Hebrew prophets were equally "inspired," that is, blown through. Spirit, we may say, is personal being, not as "mind," knowing and leaving the other as what he or she is, but as creative, participatory, present to and in the other.

Nor does our use of such philosophically laden words as "transcendence," "personal," or "mind" create any great distance from biblical speech or, indeed, from similar speech in many cultures and religions. The Western philosophical tradition is here very straightforwardly taught by the Bible; such teachings as Hegel's doctrine of "spirit" as personal self-recognition in the other make a current in Western philosophy that is indebted to the Christian tradition in a remarkably uncomplicated way, whatever may happen in other currents or in the eddies between them and this one. In this *locus*, we can go back and forth between biblical and some philosophical language with a freedom that elsewhere might be disastrous.

Humanity is spirit; there is no mode of human life so tradition-bound or torpid that we are not a wind breathed to and by ourselves, to elude our own grasp, and that we do not experience this in ourselves. Just so, God, if God

8 / THE HOLY SPIRIT

of the living and not of the dead, must so surely be spirit that where this is fully grasped all other spirits are, over against this God, not-spirit, "flesh" (e.g., Isa. 31:3). Not only in Christian theology, the notion of spirit is a crossing place of anthropology, theology, and even cosmology.

The ways in which we, and perhaps other creatures, are spirit, and the relation between our spiritness and God's, are a concern of this *locus* in two connections; others are discussed in other *loci*. Of those to be discussed in this *locus*, one is the matter of Chapter 3; the other will be discussed in one section of Chapter 2, but perhaps should be touched on already at this point.

That we too are spirits is the possibility of God's presence to us as a spirit. Or rather, the triune God, being the mutual creative and participatory presence of Father and Son, is antecedently Spirit; and in that the triune God becomes present also to us, we too are spirit. Our reality as spirits, and our relation to God as the Spirit, is a chief concern of the Fourth *Locus*; here we introduce the matter only to warn against a prevalent perversion thereof, which misidentifies the subject of this *locus*.

That God and we are both spirits can, given a certain religious motivation, be taken to mean that "spirit" names a kind of being—perhaps an invisible kind over against the material kind—which God and we share. Religion unreformed by the gospel, outside or inside the church, regularly seeks to blur the difference between God and the human self, in order to alleviate the burden of our created distinctness and its responsibilities. In the notion of "spirit" as a common essence of God and human selves, such religion finds opportunity. Both in high mysticism and in Sunday-supplement self-help, being "spiritual" can mean melting into a just so equally indistinct and undemanding God. This temptation is an undercurrent of many of the problems we will discuss in this *locus*. And in the modern period, it has emerged in a way that has made the whole doctrine of the Spirit problematic.

In much idealist thought and in theology influenced by it, the self-transcendence, the spirit, of the creature *is* God, and conversely, the self-transcendence of God is itself the act of our creation.[3] There is historical irony here, for Western philosophy learned such profound understanding of spirit from the Scriptures and from the tradition of theology. Yet where this understanding's dialectics work in this idealist way, the biblical speech about God's Spirit is no longer comprehensible. It is fundamental in Scripture that God would be God were there no other spirits at all, and that this God's reality as Spirit precisely constitutes this independence.

The idealist dialectic has not remained the property of philosophers. Popular American religion has followed it in both theory and practice. The ideas and diction of those who now read Carlos Castenada or Alan Watts differ little from those who once read Ralph Waldo Emerson or Mary Baker Eddy, except

INTRODUCTION

that the percentage of sheer blather has risen. Speaking to a congregational group about God, one will sooner or later be asked why one does not make more of "the Spirit," and on probing will discover that what is in fact wanted is an analysis of religious experience, in itself a perfectly legitimate and necessary enterprise.

At the very beginning of our discussion, we must therefore lay it down bluntly: The *concept* of "spirit," of life's self-transcendence, indeed applies to God, the gods, and us, and whatever is spirit is just thereby involved with all else that is spirit. But the particular *reality* the New Testament calls "the Spirit" is the distinct and independent "Spirit of Yahweh," the particular Spirit of Jesus and his Father, distinct from us as we are from each other. And the mode of this Spirit's presence to other spirits is always that of Creator to creatures.

There is no kind of being called "spirit." What there is, is Jones, Smith, and God, each of whom is in his own way self-transcendingly lively. The paradigmatic uses of "spirit" are and must remain those in phrases with the pattern "the spirit of. . . ." There is "the spirit of Lincoln" or "the spirit of St. Luke's Congregation" or "the Spirit of God." Spirit is precisely the person or group as not immediately identical with itself; the genitive phrase marks the nonidentity. The self with whom the person as spirit is not identical is the "body"; just so, we also speak of "the body of. . . ." If we then use "spirit" as an ontological classification, as in "Humanity is spirit," it is simply to say that human beings are marked by this self-transcendence. And if we speak of "a spirit," this is a way of referring either to an individual of such sort or to the self-transcendence, the spirit of, such an individual. There is—we here assert in advance—no spirit-reality as a kind of thing; spirit is always *of* some individual or individual group.

The division of this *locus* appears to us not narrowly determined by the matter. We isolate four contexts in which the Christian tradition speaks of the Spirit of God and discuss them in something like an order of decreasing immediacy, beginning with the context which seems both most immediate and historically originating. But if someone thinks another division would have been more helpful, or disputes the historical judgment just made, we do not think that many material assertions of our discussion would be affected.

According to this division, Christian experience of and teaching about the Spirit are partly claimed fulfillment of Israel's experience of the Spirit, and so a mode of the gospel-proclamation itself (Chapter 1); partly a mode of soteriology corresponding to such proclamation (Chapter 2); partly the appropriate self-interpretation of the church, in which all the main recurrent problems of the church's life have to be fought out (Chapter 3); and partly speculative interpretation of the created world (Chapter 4). All four bodies

8 / THE HOLY SPIRIT

of experience and discourse are continuous with one another, both systematically and historically.

NOTES

1. For our purposes, we need not concern ourselves with the history-of-religions background of the biblical use of "Spirit," since the same notion appears generally, so that where it comes from in a particular case is of purely historical interest.

2. For the Greek, a compendious presentation of the historical-linguistic facts is by Hermann Kleinknecht, in *TDNT* 6:332–59. For the Hebrew, anyone may check the passages in just the one book of Genesis: 1:2; 6:3, 17; 7:15, 22; 8:1; 26:35; 41:38; 45:17.

3. The classic study, which made clear that idealist pneumatology is a perversion, is Erich Schaeder, *Das Geistproblem in der Theologie* (Leipzig: Deichert, 1924). Schaeder remained, however, methodologically within idealism, as he himself insisted; see, e.g., ibid., pp. 1–3. A complete break with idealism was first made by Karl Barth in his writings in the 1920s. The most prominent recent work within the idealist tradition (but attempting not very successfully to reckon with biblical critique) is Paul Tillich, *Systematic Theology*, 3 vols. (Chicago: University of Chicago Press, 1951–63), 3:11–30, 111–61.

1
The Spirit That Spoke by the Prophets

Israel's experience of and testimony to "the Spirit" are fulfilled in the prophetic message and experience of the church, by the strictly christological content of the message. The motifs of this biblical pneumatology are dogmatized in the third articles of the creeds.

THE HEBREW SCRIPTURES

To understand the Christian experience of and teaching about the Spirit, the compendious starting point is the New Testament account of Pentecost—not the story of wind and flames and a linguistic miracle, but the biblical interpretation that follows and for the sake of which Luke tells the story:

> This is what was spoken by the prophet Joel: "And in the last days it shall be, God declares, that I will pour out my Spirit upon all flesh, and your sons and your daughters shall prophesy . . . , your young men . . . , and your old men; . . . yea . . . , my menservants and my maidservants . . . shall prophesy. And I will show wonders in the heaven above and signs on the earth beneath . . . , before the day of the Lord comes. . . . And it shall be that whoever calls on the name of the Lord shall be saved." Men of Israel, hear these words: Jesus of Nazareth, a man attested to you by God with mighty works and wonders and signs . . . , you crucified and killed. . . . This Jesus God raised up. . . . Being therefore exalted at the right hand of God, and having received from the Father the promise of the Holy Spirit, he has poured out this which you see and hear. (Acts 2:16-33)

In the primal church, the religious phenomena that the gatherings of the newly risen Lord's disciples displayed were interpreted as the fulfillment of a fundamental motif of Israel's life: the coming of the Spirit of Yahweh to make prophets.

During and after the exile, Israel's faith became ever more exclusively expectation;[1] in that context, prophecy could be seen not merely as one phenomenon within Israel's religious life, but also as itself the normative form

8 / THE HOLY SPIRIT

of faithful life. Just so, the *content* of Israel's expectation could become liberation of prophetic existence from its exceptionality. Of the signs and wonders that are to accompany the fulfillment of God's word, the most material then can become that *all* God's people shall be speakers and not only hearers of that word. Such a complex of expectations appears, among a very few other places, in the book of Joel cited by Luke (Joel 2:28–32). The primal church said: In the fact of our existence, that is, in the bursting forth of the message that a crucified one is risen and in the manifestations accompanying this proclamation, Joel's prediction is fulfilled. Moreover, it was the reappearance in the Christian community, as one such manifestation, of the specific phenomenon of prophecy itself which gave occasion for this interpretation, that is, initiated Christian language about "the Spirit."[2] It is, therefore, the Hebrew Scriptures' talk of "the Spirit of Yahweh," and especially its connection with prophecy, which we must first and fundamentally examine.

Through the whole Hebrew Scriptures, "*ruach* Yahweh" maintains its primal impact. The Spirit is experienced as moving transcendent force, to create or throw down, whether in nature or society; this is especially true in the direct documents of religious life (e.g., Ps. 18:5; 104:29–30). At the very heart of Israel's faith, its confession of the exodus, Israel can say that the breath of Yahweh freed them from Egypt, in that Yahweh's *ruach* blasted the Egyptians and drove back the waters (Exod. 15:8–10). Above all, therefore, God's Spirit creates life: "The spirit of God has made me, and the breath of the Almighty gives me life" (Job 33:4). In one branch of Wisdom teaching and literature,[3] there developed an explicit doctrine of the *Creator Spirit*: "By his power he stilled the sea; by his understanding he smote Rahab. By his wind [Spirit] the heavens were made fair . . ." (Job 26:12–13). But the Spirit is also the *ruach* of judgment, especially in the prophets: "a spirit of judgment and . . . a spirit of burning" (Isa. 4:4; see also 27:8; 30:27–28). For "All flesh is grass. . . . The grass withers . . . when the *ruach* Yahweh blows upon it . . ." (Isa. 40:6–7). Both the spirit that is human life (Gen. 6:3; see also Job 27:3; 32:8; 34:14ff.) and the evil spirit in which humans carry out judgment on themselves (1 Sam. 16:14) can simply be called *God's* Spirit.

In Israel's narrative tradition, the Spirit is above all God's power on and through the charismatic leadership of Israel: Moses, the judges, the early kings, and the prophets who appear around these. Their activity belongs to God's creating, here of Israel: to God's throwing down what is and bringing forth what is to be. Thus in the stories of the judges, both the call to leadership and the release of particular actions are described with "And the Spirit of Yahweh fell upon . . ." (Judg. 3:10; 6:34; 11:29; 13:25). Each time this happens, history gives a lurch.

Decisive for us is the regular juxtaposition of the coming of the Spirit to evoke political action with the coming of the Spirit to evoke prophecy. The

THE SPIRIT THAT SPOKE BY THE PROPHETS

correlation is especially striking in the stories of Moses, who is made the archetype of both political leadership and prophecy, and of Saul, the last judge and first king. It was the Spirit that was "on" Moses, that enabled him to fulfill his public role. But when he was forced to share his responsibilities, so that "some of" his Spirit had to be given to others, the immediate result was that they "prophesied" (Num. 11:17-30). Of Saul, we repeatedly read that the Spirit "rushed upon" him, sometimes with the result that he undertook political action, sometimes with the result that he "prophesied" (1 Sam. 10:10-11; 11:6-7; etc.). But also the dynastic monarchy of the southern kingdom initially legitimated itself by the claimed initiative of the Spirit (2 Sam. 23:1-7): when David was anointed, the Spirit left Saul and "came upon" David (1 Sam. 16:13). The monarch thus took over the whole activity of the judges. This obviously meant military and political leadership, but at least the dynastic founder, David, had to be also a prophet (2 Sam. 23:2).

We know little concretely about this archaic prophesying by assault of the Spirit. Clearly it involved a complex of visible, indeed obtrusive and unmistakable, special behavior (e.g., Num. 11:17-30); thus of Saul we read: "And he too stripped off his clothes, and he too prophesied before Samuel, and lay naked all that day and all that night" (1 Sam. 19:24). It was often a communal phenomenon (e.g., 1 Sam. 10:10-11; 19:20ff.). It could happen either to permanent prophets or unexpectedly to anyone at all (e.g., 1 Sam. 19:20ff.; 1 Chron. 12:18). It was uncontrollable, and sometimes even unavoidably catching (1 Sam. 19:20-24). It could involve rapture, either physical or in vision (1 Kings 18:12; 2 Kings 2:11-16) and apparently other shamanistic capacities also (2 Kings 2:13-14).

But however different such Spirit-filled shamanistic prophesying may have been from the activity of the later classical prophets, one factor points to them and is decisive for archaic prophecy: the identity of the Spirit with freedom to speak on God's behalf, indeed, specifically to speak *promises* on God's behalf. What ancient evidence there is, is unanimous.[4] In an oracle legitimating the Davidic dynasty, perhaps reaching back to David himself,[5] David presents himself as one with promises to speak for God: "His word is upon my tongue. The God of Israel has spoken, the Rock of Israel has said to me: When one rules justly. . . ." And this claim is equated with the claim: "The *ruach* Yahweh speaks by me . . . " (2 Sam. 23:1-7). Only two stories actually describe a Spirit-filled prophesying with all archaic features. One, the Micaiah story, is about the making of true and false predictions about the outcome of battle; in this story, the question which prophet speaks truly is the same as the question which has the Spirit (1 Kings 22:5-28). The other, the Balaam story, depicts a shaman who despite himself speaks true promises instead of false curses; this is explained "And the Spirit of God came upon him" (Num. 22:41—24:25).

8 / THE HOLY SPIRIT

The attribution of prophetic speech to the Spirit is uncommon in the classical preexilic prophets, though it perhaps never died out (Hos. 9:7; Mic. 3:8); reasons can only be conjectured.[6] It is the more remarkable that the conception returns in full force in the exilic and postexilic prophets, that is, as Israel's hope becomes increasingly eschatological. Second Isaiah presents only the locution "And now the Lord God has sent me and his Spirit" (Isa. 48:16). But Ezekiel's entire self-conception repristinates that of archaic prophesying: the Spirit "falls upon" (Ezek. 11:5) and enters (Ezek. 2:2; 3:24) Ezekiel, enraptures him (e.g., Ezek. 3:12, 14; 8:3), and tells him what to say (Ezek. 2:2–3; 3:24–27; 11:5). Finally, in postexilic prophecy not only does this conception continue (Isa. 61:1), but there is a full-fledged doctrine of prophetic inspiration, as the agent of all revelation in Israel: all the law and the writings were "sent by his Spirit through the former prophets" (Zech. 7:12). Indeed, the whole work of God can now be identified with the presence of God's Spirit (Isa. 63:10–11). It is undoubtedly this late-prophetic impulse which accounts for the appearance in the last great history-work, that of the Chronicler, of Spirit-worked prophetic intervention as a standard event in the political history of monarchical Israel (2 Chron. 15:1–2; 20:14–15; 24:20). In any case, the Chronicler too has a total Spirit-theology of revelation: "Thou gavest thy good Spirit to instruct them . . . and didst warn them by thy Spirit through the prophets" (Neh. 9:20, 30).

It expresses the same connection of the Spirit with the word that also *wisdom* is understood as Spirit-worked, in both early and late texts. Joseph's wisdom is that the Spirit of God is in him (Gen. 41:38). Even the artisans of the desert sanctuary have their skill by the Spirit (Exod. 28:3; 31:3). And Daniel, the survivor by wisdom, is one in whom is "the spirit of the holy god(s)" (e.g., Dan. 4:8, 9, 18). The book of Job draws the point: "But it is the *ruach* in a man, the breath of the Almighty, that makes him understand" (Job 32:8).

We will understand the import of the correlation of Spirit and word only if we remind ourselves of a decisive characteristic of the prophetic word itself: it is not merely a word about the future, but a word that *creates* the future.[7] "By the word of the Lord the heavens were made" (Ps. 33:6), and here "the word of the Lord" is *terminus technicus* for the prophetic word.[8] Thus the kings feared the archaic prophets because their oracles not only predicted victory or defeat but also caused it to happen (e.g., 1 Kings 22:5–28). And centuries later, at the high point of self-conscious but still primally vigorous prophecy, we have the famous passage of Second Isaiah: "For as the rain and the snow come down from heaven, and return not thither but water the earth, making it bring forth and sprout . . . , so shall my word be that goes forth from my mouth; it shall not return to me empty, but it shall accomplish that which I purpose" (Isa. 55:10–11). That God creates by word and that God creates by the Spirit are alternative descriptions of the same event. In either description, the work of the prophets—and other word- and spirit-bearers—is God's continuing creative work, to throw down what is old and call forth the true Israel that is to be. Putting the two descriptions together: The Spirit is freedom for, and the power of, the word that opens the future.

In later Israel, the coming and presence of the Spirit, from characterizing the *speakers* of promise, became also a *content* of promise. This requires no further initial explanation than the basic notion of spirit. Since the Spirit is God's power as the life of Israel, a promise of new life for Israel must be a promise of a new coming of the Spirit. But such promise will not be spoken until it is new life that must be promised, until Israel's hope has become not merely hope for this or that historical good fortune but hope for rescue from death. That is, it will not happen until Israel has confronted its own death, until Israel's hope has had to become eschatological. Thus the promise of the Spirit first appears in Isaiah, but there gloriously: "Until *ruach* is poured upon us from on high, and the wilderness becomes a fruitful field. . . . Then justice will dwell . . ." (Isa. 32:15–16). When there is universal peace among all creatures, it will be because "the mouth of the Lord has commanded, and his Spirit has gathered them" (Isa. 34:16).[9]

The Spirit, as the dynamism of God's life and the life God gives us, is at the heart of Ezekiel's hope, right to the spirit in the chariot wheels (Ezek. 1:4, 17, 20–21). Above all, there is the vision of the valley of dry bones. Here the Spirit is at once life, breath, and wind, all as God's Spirit (Ezek. 37:1–14). And all this archaic imagery is eschatological promise of resurrection, of God's final triumph over Israel's separation from its life in God (Ezek. 37:13–14; 39:29).

Finally, in postexilic prophecy the connections in principle are stated. There must be eschatological hope just *because* God is the giver of Spirit and therefore the God of life and not of death: "nor will I always be angry; for from me proceeds *ruach*, and I have made the breath of life" (Isa. 57:16). And the presence of the Spirit is the union of the promises made by God's past acts with their final triumph: "Yet now take courage . . . ; for I am with you . . . , according to the promise that I made you when you came out of Egypt. My Spirit abides among you; fear not. . . . Once again, in a little while, I will shake the heavens and the earth" (Hag. 2:4–8). The Spirit is the—in both senses—present reality of God's eschatological power. The Spirit is at once the guarantee and the object of final hope.

Given how definitely, through the whole tradition of Israel, the Spirit is the Spirit of prophecy and wisdom, Israel's experience and interpretation of the Spirit could fulfill itself only in some union of that experienced prophetic Spirit with the hoped-for eschatologically outpoured Spirit just described. In

8 / THE HOLY SPIRIT

Ezekiel, there is a natural resonance between Ezekiel's pneumatic self-understanding and his promise of new Spirit, but there is no conceptual synthesis. Two syntheses were possible; both were made.

One synthesis is messianic: at the last, there will be triumphant life because God's people will be gathered by and around a last prophet (and king and wiseman), a final Spirit-bearer. So the great Messianic promise of Isaiah: "And the Spirit of the Lord shall rest upon him, the spirit of wisdom and understanding" that brings universal peace (Isa. 11:2-9). This line is continued by Second Isaiah, who describes "the servant of Yahweh": "I have put my Spirit upon him, he will bring forth justice to the nations" (Isa. 42:1). Since the servant is a prophetic figure, if not only that,[10] there is here a perfect union of eschatological hope with prophetic self-understanding.

The other synthesis is communal: at the last, death will be overcome because *all* God's people will be prophets, bearers of life. Hope for the coming of a nation of prophets emerges late and seldom in Israel's history, but then in full force. The main instance is the Joel passage already cited: "And it shall come to pass afterward, that I will pour out my Spirit on all flesh; your sons and your daughters shall prophesy, your old men shall dream dreams, and your young men shall see visions. Even upon the menservants and maidservants in those days, I will pour out my spirit" (Joel 2:28ff.). But there is also the remarkable if somewhat obscure oracle in Second Isaiah: "This is my covenant with them . . . : my spirit which is upon you, and my words which I have put in your mouth, shall not depart out of your mouth, or out of the mouth . . . of your children's children . . . from this time forth and for evermore" (Isa. 59:21).[11]

It is plain that the dialectics of Israel's knowledge of the Spirit will be completed only by yet one more step: hope for a people that is a community of prophets, and therefore is possessed of unquenchable life, because it is gathered by the final Prophet, hope for a people all of whom have the Spirit because among them is a Spirit-*bearer* whose prophetic mission is precisely to be the Spirit-*giver*. This step is not taken in the Hebrew Scriptures, unless in entirely transcendent-predictive fashion by Second Isaiah's "servant songs."[12]

THE NEW TESTAMENT

The traditions deposited in the synoptic Gospels continue the Hebrew Scriptures' use of "the [Holy] Spirit." Also in the synoptic Gospels, "the Holy Spirit" usually just means the Spirit of prophecy: "said in the Holy Spirit" can stand for "prophesied" (Mark 12:36 par.), and "will be filled with the Holy Spirit" can stand for "will be a prophet" (Luke 1:15-17). The Spirit inspires utterance (Matt. 10:20 par.; Mark 13:11 par.) and works rapture (Mark 1:12 par.; Luke 2:27). But also the life-creating reality of the Spirit appears in the Gospels' use, though notably only in contexts closely tied to the prophetic work of the Spirit.

This traditional language is used with almost complete concentration of reference to the person of Jesus. There are three great centers of Spirit-language in the evangelical narrative. First and perhaps most ancient, Jesus' *baptism* is unanimously in all four Gospels a descent of the Spirit. (Mark 1:9–11 par.). This descent is described as the descent of the Spirit to make a prophet: it inaugurates Jesus' preaching mission (Mark 1:12–15), issues immediately in rapture to another place (Mark 1:12 par.), and was at least initially described as a call-vision.[13]

It is of the first importance that the account of Jesus' baptism is introduced, unanimously in the tradition, with John the Baptizer's testimony: "I have baptized you with water; but he will baptize you with the Holy Spirit (and with fire)" (Mark 1:7–8 par.).[14] The prophet Jesus does not bear the Spirit only for his own empowerment; he bears him in order to give him,[15] and this gift is eschatological, a baptism with the fire of judgment. Thus is taken the final step in Israel's knowledge of the Spirit which was not taken in the Hebrew Scriptures, and it is taken apparently without laborious reflection. The entire New Testament doctrine of the Spirit is therewith achieved in principle.

Second, there is a general connection of the Spirit with Jesus' birth. God directly creates this child as a completely new thing. The connection is ancient, as shown by its appearance in both Matthew and Luke despite the disparity of their birth legends (Matt. 1:18–20; Luke 1:35). In Matthew, Mary's pregnancy is "in the Holy Spirit." In Luke, the Spirit will "come upon" Mary, exactly in the fashion of archaic prophetic seizure, to create the child: Mary will bring forth the child the way the prophets brought forth their words. Just so this child is God's eschatological new creation, called forth by "the Power of the Highest." The identity of the Spirit who creates Jesus with the prophetic Spirit is made inescapable in Luke, who depicts a positive epidemic of Spirit-filled prophecy in the vicinity of the birth (Luke 1:41, 67; 2:25ff.).

Third, Jesus' works, but especially his life-giving healings, are "in the Spirit of God" (Matt. 12:28; Mark 3:29–30). This power is explicitly equated with the approach of "the kingdom of God" (Matt. 12:28 par.); in Luke's version it is "the finger of God" (Luke 11:20). In Jesus' mission, the personal endowment of the prophet and the eschatologically life-giving power of God are indistinguishable.

It remains only to note that in Luke these apprehensions of the primal community are elaborated into a theology. Luke takes advantage of a Markan reference to a sermon of Jesus to give its supposed content (Luke 4:16–30): an interpretation of the Spirit-filled prophet of Isa. 6:1–4 as the promised last prophet of other Isaianic passages, and a claim that Jesus is he. Also, the final prophet's gift of the Spirit to his people, posited contextually in the

8 / THE HOLY SPIRIT

baptism narratives, is made explicit: Luke specifies that the "good things" Q said Jesus' disciples will be given are "the Holy Spirit" (Luke 11:13 par.). It is consistent with this Lukan reflection that Luke introduces prophetic rapture where Matthew and Mark have only travel (Luke 9:14), and has the only synoptic reference to inspired speech by Jesus (Luke 10:21:24).

The Spirit-interpretation of major parts of the evangelical narrative did not occur in a vacuum.[16] An experience and a self-conception in perceived continuity with those of archaic and late Israelite prophecy were a vital part of the life of the primal church and may indeed have dominated in some areas. The integral phenomenon of prophecy reappeared and played an important role in establishing the gospel and its tradition,[17] while people at least *called* "prophets," whose actual activities are hard to describe certainly, were evangelists and liturgical leaders in many communities.[18] There perhaps were even places where bands of ecstatics made the real congregation, surrounded by an outer group of postulants and hangers-on[19]—this may be part of the background for the expectation that appears in Luke, that manifest prophetic seizure is the normal sufficient condition or consequence of baptism (Acts 8:14–18; 11:15–17; 19:2–6). Most important, evangelists and leaders of all institutional types (apostles, teachers, or whatever) understood their own work and were understood by others in the terms of Spirit-filled prophecy and in direct continuity with Hebrew prophecy.[20] "Then Peter, filled with the Holy Spirit, said . . ." (Acts 4:8) states an archetype. Paul himself is one from whom we have direct testimony,[21] while from quite other parts of the church the traditions preserved in Acts stereotypically depict the work of the church's heroes as Spirit-given[22] and attribute to them both shamanistic acts and direct instruction by the Spirit's voice.[23]

Two constant further characters of this prophetic Spirit are decisive. First, this Spirit continues to be the breath of life, the *Spiritus Creator* who raises the dead, and can even animate a statue (Rev. 11:11; 13:15). The Spirit is the ontological opposite of death;[24] both Christ and we die by "the flesh" but rise "by the Spirit" (1 Pet. 3:18; 4:6). In a traditional formula given by Paul, the Holy Spirit is the reality-sphere of resurrection (Rom. 1:4).

Second, inspiration by this Spirit is invariably understood christologically. The risen Jesus has a spirit as any living person does; and this "Spirit of Jesus" simply *is* the Spirit of prophecy (Acts 17:1). When prophecy appears in the Christian gatherings, it is the risen Christ who sends the Spirit to create it (Acts 2:33). Indeed, even the Hebrew prophets were held to have been inspired by "the Spirit of Christ" (1 Pet. 1:11). The most drastic expression of this christological doctrine of inspiration is in a prophetic word, the truly remarkable saying: "For the testimony of Jesus is the spirit of prophecy" (Rev. 19:10). In this saying the Spirit is not an enabling or energizing power adventitious to mere speaking about Jesus. Gospel-telling does not need to become something more to be Spirit-filled; where the witness to Jesus occurs, there is the Spirit, and vice versa. With that, we are back with the Pentecost text from which we began: "This Jesus God raised up. . . . Being therefore exalted at the right hand of God . . . , he has poured out this which you see and hear."

Prophetic inspiration is the one great anchor of New Testament Spirit-theology. Baptism is the other. Baptism is the church's initiation rite.[25] In the missionary situation, it was therefore necessarily seen as the gate to a promised future: "Be baptized, and you *shall* receive . . ." (Acts 2:38). And therefore, further, within understanding shaped by the Hebrew Scriptures, baptism was merely thereby inevitably proclaimed and experienced as a rite of the Spirit, of the power of God's promises: ". . . shall receive the Holy Spirit." It is possible that in some places baptism's connection with the Spirit only meant incorporation into a community in which there were Spirit-filled people. But for the traditions that actually appear in the new Testament, initiation into the believing community is identical with the gift of the Spirit for all neophytes.[26] And therefore, generally in the New Testament, all believers are Spirit-bearers.[27]

The conviction that all the baptized have the Spirit must mean either that all members of the congregation are explicitly prophets or that the experience and understanding of Spirit-bearing include phenomena other than manifest prophecy. The former may have been the case in some regions, but predominantly in the New Testament and most explicitly in Paul, the latter is assumed or asserted to be the case.

Paul makes two steps. First, he in effect if not deliberately separates the constituents of prophetic activity into distinct "gifts," so that there is at least one gift for every believer, even the least ecstatic (1 Cor. 12:1–13, 27–31; Rom. 12:6–8). Second, he identifies the common feature that qualifies all these as gifts of the Spirit, as contribution to "the common good" (1 Cor. 12:7), as "the building up" of the community and its unity (1 Cor. 14:3ff.). The charism in the charisms is therefore love (Rom. 12:9ff.; 1 Cor. 12:31ff.), the final manifestations of the Spirit's presence not religious phenomena but "love, joy, peace, patience, kindness, goodness, faithfulness, gentleness, self-control" (Gal. 5:22–23). This does not mean the Spirit loses his character as Spirit of prophecy. As given for the building of community, the gifts are all communication-acts, most of them straightforwardly verbal; and on the lists of gifts, prophecy is again chief.[28]

If the church were a standing religious society of the present world, Paul's theology of the Spirit, in which contributing funds can be a Spirit-given act, would bowdlerize the Spirit's eschatological reality. But the church does not so understand itself anywhere in the New Testament; the church is the anticipating community. Paul therefore does not merely accommodate the other

8 / THE HOLY SPIRIT

great side of New Testament testimony to the Spirit, that the Spirit gives eschatological life; he is the chief witness.[29]

In one great passage (Rom. 8:1–27), Paul brings together all these sides of the New Testament's apprehension of the Spirit and nearly exhausts their dialectics in one magnificent sweep of argument and rhetoric. This argument's exposition can conclude our biblical discussion.[30] The passage is initiated when over against analysis of the old pre-Christ human situation Paul asserts a decisive eschatological change: There is "now no condemnation" for those in Christ Jesus. Contrary to how it has always been, there is now no fear that our life will have been, at the end, without value. The reason is that the standard of judgment[31] has changed. Once we were judged in a way that convicted of sin and sentenced to death and by which, therefore, sin and death maintained their control;[32] now we are judged in a way that frees for life and by which, therefore, the *Spirit* rules,[33] the opposite of death and bondage. This change in standards of judgment has been worked by the incarnation (vv. 3–4).

The penultimate outcome[34] of God's act in Christ is thus the existence of two kinds of people, those still in the situation before the great change and those in the new situation, those who live "according to flesh" and those who live "according to Spirit." "The flesh" is neutrally the creature as other than God, pejoratively the creature curved in on its otherness from God;[35] life "according to flesh" is life of the second sort, life that holds its breath, that tries to be purpose and energy for itself. Life "according to Spirit" is life that rejoices in being moved and inspired by God, to be just so itself spirit. In that we lived without Spirit lay the necessity of God's new act;[36] that we now live by the Spirit is the new fact worked by God's act.

We cannot here trace Paul's analysis of *how* the incarnation works the shift from the old situation to the new, except to note one point vital for our purpose: The argument functions by positing a double opposite to "Spirit": "flesh" and "the law."[37] The "law of sin and death" turns out to be "the Law" absolutely, in respect of the latter's failure. But "the Law" is a mode of God's *word*. Thus "Spirit" in this argument includes what Paul elsewhere calls "promise" or "the gospel";[39] Spirit here is the Power of the promises brought by the message about Christ. Thus also in Paul's opposition of "flesh" and "Spirit," the Spirit is the Spirit of prophecy, the Power of an utterance that creates the future.

Accordingly, Paul must now shift from third-person argument to second-person gospel-speaking, to the actual making of such a powerful utterance: "And you *are* 'in Spirit,' not 'in flesh' " (v. 9a). The Romans may be sure of their inclusion precisely because the Spirit of God is the same as the Spirit of Christ, that is, as the Spirit of the gospel which they know they have in fact heard and into which they know they have been baptized (v. 9b–d). And

THE SPIRIT THAT SPOKE BY THE PROPHETS

so Paul is free for unfettered proclamation of the Spirit-aspect of the absence of condemnation: the resurrection of the dead (vv. 10–11). "He who raised Christ Jesus from the dead will make alive also your mortal bodies, through his Spirit that dwells among you" (v. 11).[39] The word about Christ, the word which contains no condemnation, is just so Spirit; those who have heard it may therefore know that they are already in the power of eschatological life.

Just so, since believers are *now* in the grip of life, Paul turns briefly to exhortation: believers must not anachronistically live according to flesh (vv. 12–13). But on this occasion he is himself too inspirited to remain with exhortation. If we cling to the old ways, it is only out of fear. But—and now Paul is back with proclamation—fear is unnecessary. The Spirit from God might indeed have been an enslaving power; but in fact, as Christ's Spirit, he establishes us in Christ's own relation to God; he is a "Spirit of adoption" (vv. 14–15a). We have no more to fear than does the resurrected Christ himself! And the reality of this confidence is specifically Christian *prayer*, in which we address God as "Father"—as Christ did and does (v. 15b). Such prayer is itself legitimate only as prophetic utterance (v. 16); it is inspired by the Spirit (v. 15b).[40] "You have received the spirit of adoption, in whom we say, 'Abba,' that is, 'Father.' The Spirit himself bears witness, together with our spirit, that we are indeed *children* of God" (vv. 15b–16).

Wherewith the eschatological power of the Spirit breaks through all argument: "And if children, then heirs . . . fellow heirs with Christ" (v. 17). All creation is a mere present from God for the Child and children (vv. 17–18). Therefore it waits—or rather, cannot wait—precisely for us. Though we cannot understand it, this waiting too is verbal (vv. 19–22). The prayers of creation, perhaps the only true and necessary "speaking in tongues" are—it will appear further on (vv. 22, 26b)—the Spirit's, that is, they too are prophecy.

What it can mean to be inheritors of the universe we cannot say; we can only join the dumb creation in cries only God understands (v. 23).[41] Such a promise transforms all life into hope (vv. 23–25) and puts the true object of our prayer beyond our praying for it (v. 26). But life that is pure hope is itself prophetic ecstasy;[42] and the prayers we cannot conceive we may let the Spirit pray for us (v. 26). And just so, emptied of all that is not future to it, our life becomes even now true life: we have "the beginning of the Spirit (v. 23).[43]

THE CREEDAL TRADITION

The ancient church was perhaps more straightforwardly, and unimaginatively, biblical in its witness to the Spirit than in any other part of its theology. This was doubtless because Hellenic conceptions in this area, being both

8 / THE HOLY SPIRIT

undeveloped and in their basis very similar to the biblical, were both less challenging and less alienating than in other fields. We may, in pedestrian fashion, summarize what we have found in the New Testament so: (1) The Holy Spirit is the Spirit of the creating word, both of the Hebrew prophets and of the church; (2) the Holy Spirit is poured out in baptism, to make a prophetic community; (3) the Holy Spirit is the bond of this community; (4) the Holy Spirit is the power of the resurrection both now and eternally; and (5) the Holy Spirit is all these things because he is the Spirit of Christ. Precisely these points are the stock of patristic discourse about the Spirit. Moreover, the locations of patristic pneumatology are also the same as in the New Testament: prophecy and baptism.[44]

So long as the fathers' pneumatology remained within the sphere just defined, it was, if not overly creative, clear and unanimous.[45] The kind of alienation which in other matters both made confusion and elicited new insight appeared here only by attraction from another *locus*: In the pre-Nicene theology, the Spirit became implicated in the Logos-theology's interpretation of Christ as a mediating mid-being between God and creatures. Since the very notion of the Spirit is of God's active presence to us, this theology threatened to make the Spirit otiose and to create a binitarian, and paganized, interpretation of deity. Conversely, baptismal confession of the Spirit was the chief hindrance to the complete triumph of this theology, and the achieving of a theology with room for confession of the Spirit was identical with the achieving of true trinitarianism. But all this belongs to the Second *Locus*.

Since in the area covered here all the fathers said much the same things, a few early examples will suffice. Ignatius of Antioch described himself as a prophet, a "God-bearer."[46] He is so as a witness to Christ, and therein is in direct succession of the Hebrew prophets, who were "disciples" of Christ "in the Spirit," (*To the Magnesians*, ix,2), teachers in advance of the Christian congregations (*To the Philadelphians*, v,1–2). For the Spirit is Christ's Spirit (ibid., introd.); what the Spirit communicates is what Christ is and does (*To the Ephesians*, xvii,11), and Christ's will is done in the church through the Spirit (*To the Philadelphians*, introd.). At the same time, all in the congregation are God-bearers (*To the Magnesians*, introd., 7), indeed, "full of God" (ibid., xiv). Just so, the Spirit is the bond of divine unity among the congregation, identical with the presence of Christ (ibid., xv). The Spirit *is* love (*To the Trallians*, vi,1).

A key figure in the period of patristic pneumatology's crystallization was Irenaeus, bishop of Lyons.[47] He decisively identifies the Spirit that is experienced in the church as the *prophetic* Spirit, in confrontation both with wild prophecy and with some who reacted by denying the reality of churchly prophecy (e.g., *Against Heresies*, iii,11,9; 12,1; 19,1–2). This Spirit was given to Christ by the Father, that he may give him again: "The Lord, receiving the gift from the Father, himself gave the gift again to those who participate in him, sending the Spirit into all the earth" (ibid., iii,17,2). The effect of the Spirit's presence, thus given, is the "mingling and mixing" of God's Spirit with the creature, to restore the creature to God's image (*Demonstration of the Apostolic Preaching*, 97), the end of the old life and the beginning of a new (*Against Heresies*, iii,17,2).

The chief site of patristic pneumatology is the developing creedal tradition, both as repository and as lively authority.[48] The structure of our three-article creeds seems to have resulted from the threefold baptismal name of God drawing to itself material from summaries of doctrine and evangelical narrative used in catechetical preparation for baptism. To the naming of the Spirit, creeds through the creed-making period, from the middle of the second century to the end of the fourth and from all parts of the church, constantly attached one or more of the following items:[49] inspiration of the prophets, baptism,[50] the church,[51] resurrection, and eternal life. These may simply have been items of urgent confession in the time of early catholicism's self-definition against gnosticism and the sects, attached to "Spirit" because they logically fit there. Or they may have belonged to catechetical lists of vital theology divided among the three parts of the name, landing with "Spirit" because they were the concluding items. There was a logical fit, because the last items of a theological confession ordered on a history-of-salvation principle must occupy exactly the temporal slot, on the boundary of present and future, that is the Spirit's.

Whatever the precise formative history of the third article, the composite result is an adequate summary of New Testament witness. The Spirit inspires the word, creates the church, is given at baptism, overcomes death, and is an anticipation of final life. Only explicit stipulation of the Spirit as *Jesus'* spirit is missing; but there was no need for this, since the three-article creeds are but an expansion of the triune baptismal name of God, by which that relation is antecedently established. Dogma is often characterized as summary of Scripture; in most cases, it is not. But of the dogma established about the Spirit in the creedal third articles, the characterization is precise.

NOTES

1. See, e.g., Sigmund Mowinckel, *He That Cometh*, trans. G. Anderson (Oxford: Basil Blackwell, 1956).
2. Heinrich Kraft, "Die Anfänge des geistlichen Amts," *ThLz* 100 (1975): 81–98.
3. Job 33:4; 34:14; Ps. 104:29–30.
4. We will mention only passages where the Spirit is explicitly named, to avoid

8 / THE HOLY SPIRIT

all possible false extrapolations. This also enables us to avoid the dispute over the origin of archaic prophecy—on which see, for the bibliography and the position least favorable to our enterprise, Hans-Christoph Schmidt, "Prophetie und Tradition," *ZThK* 74 (1977): 255-72.

5. Gerhard von Rad, *Old Testament Theology*, trans. D. M. G. Stalker, 2 vols. (New York: Harper & Row, 1962-65), 1:310-11.

6. Ibid., 2:86-87.

7. E.g., ibid., 2:84-162. The extent to which primeval magical conceptions of the word's power are still alive in Mark is beside the point.

8. Ibid., 2:91-92.

9. Also Isa. 11:1-19; 28:5-6.

10. See Claus Westermann, *Isaiah 40-66*, trans. D. M. G. Stalker (Philadelphia: Westminster Press, 1969), ad loc. "Servant Songs."

11. How seriously one should take the words of Moses in Num. 11:29 is difficult to judge: "Would that all the Lord's people were prophets, that the Lord would put his Spirit upon them."

12. The obvious conclusion of Westermann's exegesis in *Isaiah 40-66*, which Westermann will not draw, is that the servant is a prophet whose personal memory encompasses the whole history of prophecy (i.e., in patristic language, in whom the logos is incarnate) and who dies and rises again.

13. At least in Mark; see, e.g., Kraft, "Die Anfänge des geistlichen Amts," cols. 91ff.

14. The point we make here is independent of what John may have meant.

15. This is the unanimous exegesis of the fathers, and a foundation of their ecclesiology.

16. For a quick survey of the New Testament, see Ernst Käsemann, in *RGG*[3] 2:1272-79.

17. E.g., Acts 11:27-28. On their importance, see Ernst Käsemann, "Sentences of Holy Law in the New Testament," in *New Testament Questions of Today*, trans. W. Montague (Philadelphia: Fortress Press, 1969), pp. 61-81.

18. Robert W. Jenson, *Visible Words* (Philadelphia: Fortress Press, 1978), pp. 191-94; there literature.

19. Georg Kretschmar, *Die Geschichte des Taufgottesdienstes in der Alten Kirche*, in *Leiturgia*, ed. K. F. Mueller and W. Blankenberg, vol. 4 (Kassel: Stauda, 1954).

20. 1 Pet. 1:11-12; Acts 7:51-52; Heb. 3:9; 9:8; 10:15; Acts 28:25; 2 Pet. 1:21.

21. Rom. 9:1; 15:18-19; 1 Cor. 2:4; 7:40; Phil. 1:19; 1 Thess. 1:5.

22. Acts 4:31; 5:32; 6:3, 5, 10; 7:55-56; 13:4; 15:28; 19:21; 20:22-23.

23. Acts 8:29; 10:19-20; 11:12; 13:2, 4; 16:6-7; 21:4.

24. See, above all, the great Pauline argument, Rom. 8:1-27, exegeted below.

25. On the following, see Jenson, *Visible Words*, pp. 126-51; there literature and citations.

26. E.g., from various branches of the church, Heb. 6:4; Acts 2:38; 19:2-6; 1 Cor. 6:11; 12:13; 1 Pet. 3:18-21; Titus 3:5.

27. Throughout the Pauline corpus and John. Elsewhere, e.g., 1 Pet. 1:2; Heb. 6:4; Rev. 19:10-11; Eph. 1:13; 2:2.

28. See the order of the lists in 1 Corinthians and Romans, and the whole of 1

THE SPIRIT THAT SPOKE BY THE PROPHETS

Corinthians 14, esp. v. 39. Paul can even return to simple identification of Spirit and prophecy; 2 Thess. 5:19-20.

29. On Paul's pneumatology in general, see Kurt Stalder, *Das Werk des Geistes in der Heiligung bei Paulus* (Zurich: Erziehungsverein, 1962), pp. 19-69.

30. The themes of this argument are by no means found only here in Paul. Practically the whole of it could be put together from other writings: 2 Cor. 1:22; 3:6, 8, 17-18; 5:5; Gal. 3:2-5; 4:6-7; 5:5, 16-25; 6:8. On the exegesis of this passage, see ibid., pp. 387-487.

31. This is clearly what *nomos* means here; v. 2.

32. ... *Apo tou nomou tes hamartias kai tou thanatou* ... is subjective *and* objective genitive; v. 2.

33. *Ho* ... *nomos tou pneumatos tes zoes* ... *eleutherosen* ... is the same construction; v. 2.

34. *Hina* carries over both this immediately following clause and the subordinated phrase; v. 4.

35. Eduard Schweizer, in *TDNT* 7:124-44.

36. Note the string of sentences with *gar* from v. 3 through v. 8.

37. For the same opposition: Rom. 7:6; 2 Cor. 3:6.

38. Thus in Gal. 3:2-3, "hearing with faith" and "beginning with the Spirit" are the same.

39. *Dia tou enoikountes autou pneumatos en hymin.*

40. *En ho.*

41. *Stenazomen.*

42. *Hosautos.*

43. *Ten aparchen tou pneumatos.*

44. On this paragraph, see Hans-Jochen Jaschke, *Der Heilige Geist im Bekenntnis der Kirche* (Münster: Aschendorff, 1976), pp. 8-147.

45. G. W. H. Lampe's naiveté about his own mild-Platonist presuppositions makes his *God as Spirit* (Oxford: At the Clarendon Press, 1977) historically useless.

46. Ignatius, *To the Philadelphians,* viii; *To the Smyrneans,* introd.; x,2; *To the Ephesians,* xviii,1; *To the Magnesians,* introd.

47. On Irenaeus in general, see Gustaf Wingren, *Man and the Incarnation,* trans. Ross Mackenzie (Philadelphia: Fortress Press; Edinburgh: T. & T. Clark, 1959). There is now a monograph on Irenaeus' pneumatology and its historical location; Jaschke, *Der Heilige Geist,* which see on the following.

48. The opinion of some earlier scholarship that the third articles are merely composites of original third, fourth, fifth, etc., articles consolidated to fit the later trinitarian dogma is untenable; e.g. Jaschke, *Der Heilige Geist,* pp. 135ff.

49. The fourth-century but pre-Constantinople creed of Jerusalem, e.g., had exactly this set; text in J. N. D. Kelly, *Early Christian Creeds* (New York and London: Longmans, Green & Co., 1960), pp. 183-84, which see on this whole paragraph: pp. 82-94, 111-13, 155-66, 188-96. The epithets of the "Nicene," actually the Constantinopolitan, Creed, "the Lord, the giver of life," do not belong to this history. They were inserted by the fathers of Constantinople as functional equivalents for Nicaea's "of one being" of the Son, and belong to the dialectics of trinitarian theology, with "proceeds from the

8 / THE HOLY SPIRIT

Father" and "with the Father the Son is worshiped and glorified."

50. In the Apostles' Creed "the forgiveness of sin" means the same as, e.g., "one baptism for the forgiveness of sins" in the "Nicene" Creed; ibid., pp. 160-61.

51. In the Apostles' Creed "communion of saints" is disputed, but probably means fellowship with past heroes of faith; thus it specifies that the extension of the church, just confessed, is not only in space ("catholic") but also in time; ibid., pp. 388-97.

2
Pneumatological Soteriology

Western Christianity's attention to the practical power of the gospel must be translated from causal language about grace to hermeneutical language about proclamation if it is fully to achieve its own truth. This translation is done by the Reformation doctrine of justification and issues in a new doctrine of predestination.

THE DOCTRINE OF GRACE

If we rehearse again the items of christological faith appropriated to the Spirit in the creedal third articles, we note that this is where *we* come into the creeds: Here appear faith, baptism, church, and eternal life. What is sketched in a third article is our life as it is, because reality is as the creeds otherwise describe it. The Spirit is, as we have seen in the New Testament, the creative and transforming power of that gospel address of which the three-article creeds are content summaries; the Spirit is precisely the fact that the gospel makes changes in us.

In the Western church, analysis of this impact of God in Christ on our actual lives, through proclamation and the sacraments, has been the continuing chief theological interest. It is salvation, justification, sacramental grace, faith, predestination, and so on, that have fascinated Western thinkers, not so much divine triunity or hypostatic union. That is, Western theological work has been directed mainly to the third article.

From its inception, the Latin church was practical in its concerns. Initially, this practicality of Latin Christianity amounted to a decidedly subevangelical works-righteousness. Tertullian was only unusually blunt: quoting at random, "Every man must satisfy God in the same matter in which he has offended."[1] It was when Augustine joined the practical concerns of the Latin church with the doctrine developed in the East, of God and his transforming works, that Western Christianity as we know it was created, in which the central concern is precisely the practical effect of God's living reality in our lives.

Prior to the Reformation, however, this theological enterprise was handled not as a doctrine of the Spirit but as a doctrine of "grace" (*gratia*). In part, this is merely a terminological crotchet, which will cause no trouble so long

8 / THE HOLY SPIRIT

as we remember it. If we want to find the medieval or Tridentine Roman Catholic equivalents for biblical, Eastern-patristic, or Reformation discussions of the work and nature of the Spirit, we must look under the heading "grace." It is Augustine's usage that shaped pre-Reformation Western theological terminology so,[2] and his usage had a basis in that of the New Testament, especially of Paul.[3] Behind the usage choice, however, there is a material theology that is deeply problematic.

The doctrine of the Trinity worked out by the Greek fathers conceptualized the creative relation of God to his faithful people in a specifically biblical way. As we have seen, the creedal statements about the Spirit merely summarized the Bible's witness; then the specific trinitarian dogma insisted that this preaching, community-gathering, and vivifying were no less than God's own reality among us. But Augustine's particular adaptation of trinitarian doctrine obscured this function of the doctrine. For Augustine, the three "persons," over against us, are functionally indistinguishable. Thus Augustine could no longer conceptualize the saving relation between God and creatures by saying that the Father and the Son are transformingly present in the Spirit, as the Greek originators of trinitarianism had done.

With the specifically Christian understanding of the relation between God and the faithful thus blocked, Augustine was left with the standard position of Western culture-religion: on the one hand there is God, conceived as a supernatural entity who acts causally on us; and on the other hand there are the results among us of this causality. In the subsequent Latin tradition, God and the objects of God's causality are then both interpreted accordingly: they are "substances," fundamentally self-sustaining and self-contained entities, who "act" over against each other, the result of which action is in us a *habitus*, an acquired disposition to behave and react in ways obedient to the will of God.[4]

That Augustine then pored over Paul for his material descriptions of God's action and our consequent "habits,"[5] is the great blessing of the Latin church; until recently, even the most alienated Western Christian showed more understanding of the great issues raised by Paul than do leading theologians of the Eastern churches. But that Paul's assertions were pressed into this utterly unsuited framework has been the Western church's great theological disaster.

The Augustinian framework of the doctrine of grace has been a difficulty, moreover, precisely over against the very dogma which is the fruit of Augustine's and the Augustinians' study of Paul: the declaration of the Council of Orange that all spiritual life is the work of grace in us and that "free choice [is] so weakened that . . . no one is able rightly to love or believe in God . . . , except by the prior initiative of the grace of God's mercy."[6] Perhaps the simplest way to see the difficulty is to note that whereas Paul can call fornication, enmity, and so on, "works," so that the *negative* phenomena of human life can indeed be fitted into a causal understanding of our relation to exterior influence, such things as love are precisely not effects but "fruits" (Gal. 5:19–23), which supposes a very different relation between God, whose fruits they are, and us, in whom they appear. More particularly, the difficulty appears historically in two ways.

First, Paul used the word "grace" (*charis*) and its derivatives both for the quality of God's behavior in Christ and for the gifts of the Spirit that are the fruits among us thereof.[7] Following his lead, Augustine used "grace" for both God's saving causality and the effects on our side, for both God's love to us and the love to God which God creates in us.[8] The terminology could have been a mere variant on Paul's, except for the conceptual framework in which it functioned. In that framework, the "grace" that is our love to God necessarily becomes an "habitual" quality[9] of the substance faithful-human, over against the "grace" that is a quality of the substance God. So Thomas Aquinas: "Grace may be understood in two ways: in one way as the divine aid that moves us to will and act well, in the other way as a divinely given dispositional quality (*habituale donum*) . . ."[10] (*Summa Theologica*, i–ii,111,2). Since both substances in question are personal, existing as mind and will (grace as a gift is a "habit" of *willing* the good), this ineluctably sets the problem of the cooperation between the graceful God and the—supposedly in *this* fashion—graced creature. The problem has been the crux of all Western theology.

The nature, profundity, and ultimate insolubility of the cooperation problem can all be displayed at once by citing the best solution yet offered, that of Aquinas. Grace, as a quality of God and as a quality of the faithful *taken together*, is divided by a crossing distinction

> according to the one who operates and the one who cooperates. The operation of any effect is not attributed to the one who is moved but to the one who moves. In that . . . our soul is only a moved reality and not a mover, only God being the mover, operation is attributed to God; in this respect, it is called "operating grace." But in that . . . our mind moves as well as being moved, operation is not solely attributed to God but also to the soul; in this respect, it is called "co-operating grace." (Ibid.)

When Aquinas' problem is the problem set, one must surely speak exactly as Aquinas does: God is the sole agent of salvation, but there is no way a *will* can be authentically "moved" except by itself co-willing. The difficulty is in pastoral practice. "Our grace-renewed souls cooperate with God's grace." "Must I cooperate?" "Yes." "All right, what do I have to do?" To the last question, at the end of that sequence, all answers are equally destructive of faith—even the biblical answer to an only superficially similar question: "Believe and be baptized."

8 / THE HOLY SPIRIT

Second, when the saving relation between God and believers is understood as the causality of one substance on another, salvation is necessarily understood as a *process*, in Aquinas' formulation, a "movement (*motus*) by which the human mind is moved by God from a state of sin to a state of righteousness" (ibid., i–ii,113,5). That is, grace is understood as the primary cause of a sequence of events, each of which must occur for the next to be possible. Thus, for example, early scholasticism defined a sequence with the following steps: first, impact of the church's mission, then appropriate response (*meritum de congruo*), sacramental infusion of love, "justification," authentically altered life (*meritum de condigno*), eternal reward.[11] Or, for another instance, pietist Puritan divines specified a sequence of modes of experience, each of which must occur before the next can: consciousness of sin, and struggle for righteousness in the terms of the law, defeat in this endeavor and acknowledgment that only God can save, a period of waiting for grace, experience of the goodness of God.[12]

Whatever may be the virtues of such descriptions as phenomenology of religion, they are theological catastrophes. For if salvation is thus understood as a stepped process between two agents, then unless I am to be a mere spectator of my own life, there must be points in the process when the move is up to me and where the next stage will not occur unless I make the move. It is in the transfer from third-person description to first-person and second-person teaching and preaching that this reveals itself as an evil. Thus, for example, in the Puritan scheme, when the preacher—with descriptive truth—says, "God freely forgives those who sincerely repent," I must then discover in myself whether I do indeed sincerely repent to know if God's forgiveness intends me in particular; and then it is my work of repentance and not the gospel which is the experientially decisive condition of my hope.

Indeed, it is in general the third-person descriptive modality of the doctrine of grace that is its flaw. For one thing, it may well be doubted that there is any vantage from which thus to observe the entities God and creature, so as to be able to describe the process between them. And be that as it may, the attempt to think from such a vantage has created in Western theology an alienation of the third article, a transformation of the biblical discourse about God's Spirit into a stipulation of method for our spirituality. That is, the traditional doctrine of "grace" is a works-righteous *structure* lodged at the heart of the chief theological concern and achievement of the Western church.

JUSTIFICATION BY FAITH

It was precisely this perversion that necessitated the Reformation. We will understand little about the Reformation if we understand it only as a protest against specific abuses or as a theological quarrel adjustable by dialectical reconciliation of opposed formulations.[13] The Reformation was a protest against a whole way of thinking about and proclaiming the faith, and against corresponding structures of the medieval Western liturgies of penance and the Supper—which came first, the theology or the liturgy, we need not settle here. There are two ways in which the reform occurred theologically.

It is a cliché that Luther radicalized the Western desire for the grace of God into desire for the graceful God. He was concerned no longer for God's effect on us but for God's own presence among us. Rather, he was concerned for God as *God's* effect on us—that is, precisely for God the Spirit. Thus an immediate consequence of Luther's insight was recovery of the biblical and pre-Augustinian discourse about the Spirit, an almost uncanny ability simply to speak and write biblical and patristic Spirit-language.[14]

Merely to talk of "the work of the Holy Spirit"[15] instead of "grace," as the theologians who followed Luther then regularly did, is not, however, a guarantee that the ancient perversion has been overcome. The Lutheran theologians of the sixteenth and seventeenth centuries conducted a careful analysis of the biblical testimony to the Spirit's work, taking Luther's catechetical "calls, gathers, enlightens, sanctifies, and preserves" as a model. As the later among them systematized the analysis, the Spirit "calls, illumines, convicts, justifies, renovates, unites with Christ, and sanctifies.[16] They called the sequence "the order of salvation," meaning a *logical* order; the Spirit does not, they thought, perform a mere collection of works in our lives, but one structured work. Each of the verbs—"calls," "illumines," and so on—represented a whole field for analysis of God's one act, within which the concern of these theologians was always the same: to display the nature and character of spiritual life precisely under the rule that we do *not* "cooperate" with God's grace. But this did not prevent Lutheran pietism, without formal contradiction of any individual item of orthodox Lutheran teaching, from turning the analysis into a traditional stipulation of a normal sequence of Christian experience.

Already the great Johann Arndt, starting with the descriptively orthodox proposition that only to "unfeigned repentance" is the "imputation of Christ's righteousness" promised (*True Christianity*, i,iv,13), established a sequence: "Remission of sins immediately follows true repentance" (ibid., viii,24). Whereupon he is promptly lost in advice for how to discover whether such true repentance is indeed present (ibid., xvi,49; iii; xviii,410) and maxims for promoting it (ibid., iii; vi,382; xvi,408). The disaster is then complete with someone like August Hermann Francke,[17] who for all his proper Lutheran insistence that the gospel is always decisive, nevertheless flatly stipulated that until the "repentance struggle" is over, the gospel simply cannot be heard, and made the completion of the struggle depend on the sincerity and per-

8 / THE HOLY SPIRIT

sistence of the penitent. Around this essential step Francke then constructed the same experience order we saw in the Puritans—which is no accident, since continental pietists and English Puritans made one network.

What is needed over against the whole traditional doctrine of grace is a complete shift of pneumatological discourse from this third-person vantage, from attempted description of a process between God and creature, to a location *within* the carrying-out of first- and second-person proclamation and teaching. Precisely as a doctrine of the work of the *Spirit*—of which work "calls, illumines, converts, justifies, renovates, unites with Christ, and sanctifies" is a perfectly good list—theology must be done from the location of the preacher, liturgical president, and adviser, and the recipient of these ministrations. To use recent jargon, pneumatology must become hermeneutical reflection, reflection about Christian discourse done in the course thereof, as part of that discourse's accomplishment, reflection about how to speak the gospel done internally to the speaking—which brings us to the Reformation's second theological mode: the proposed dogma of "justification by faith alone."

The Reformation doctrine of justification is not a new attempted description of a process of grace—and when it has been taken for such, sometimes also by would-be champions, the difference between the Reformation and the standard tradition has always promptly become obscure. The doctrine is rather an *hermeneutical instruction* to preachers, teachers, and confessors: so speak of Christ and of the life of your community that the justification for that life which your words open is the kind grasped by faith rather than the kind constituted in works.

That this is the character of the Reformation's dogmatic proposal can perhaps best be seen from the first, and for many Protestants the dogmatically authoritative, commentary on the proposal, Article IV of Melanchthon's Apology of the Augsburg Confession. Article IV of the Augsburg Confession itself said: "Furthermore it is taught, that we cannot obtain forgiveness and righteousness before God by our own power, merit, or works, but rather that we are justified by grace for Christ's sake, through faith." The papal response, the Papal Confutation,[18] was a flat contradiction: For example, "That . . . they attribute justification to faith alone is directly opposite to evangelical truth. . . . However much one may believe, if he does not do good, he is no friend of God" (Confutation, 6); when it is said "of good works that they do not merit the remission of sins . . . , this is . . . disapproved" (ibid., 20).

Melanchthon's Apology is mostly a long defense of the Augsburg Confession's fourth article, against this rejection. At the start of Article IV, he specifies the difference between the Reformers and their "adversaries" as that between "two kinds of teaching," two modes of churchly proclamation and practice, with the theories that sustain them. Of each, he proposes to discover and state the generating starting point (Apology IV, 4). He formulates the starting point of reforming teaching: "The whole Scripture can be sorted into two principal modes of discourse, law and promises" (ibid., 5). Thus the starting point of reforming teaching is hermeneutical: a conviction about the duality of ways in which churchly discourse functions or ought to function. The starting point of the adversaries' teaching is thus also an hermeneutical conviction, or rather the lack of this one: a failure to practice the distinction of law and promise (ibid., 7). The adversaries themselves would not distinguish the two theologies in these terms but just that is the difference between them and the reformers.

Melanchthon proceeds to exposition of the reformers' hermeneutic, with a metalinguistic description of "promise" (ibid., 7). The biblical promise has narrative content; it is "about Christ." This discourse about Christ, as a live act of communication, has a triply statable existential function: it "promises remission of sins, justification, and eternal life." As becomes apparent throughout the treatise (ibid., e.g., 44, 120, 292-93), the promise of remission of sins is not a statement that hearers will in the future be forgiven; the promise is rather a grant of forgiveness, an absolution, and is promise as absolution itself is promise, namely, of the restored life that ensues. Neither is justification promised as only future; it is rather the restoration just named (ibid., e.g., 40, 117, 161). The future content of the promise is eternal life, the content of blessing won by Christ. How narrative about Christ can have this existential function, Melanchthon does not say in the Apology. An answer to that question would be a doctrine of atonement, beyond the scope of the Apology and this *locus*.

To describe the *law* hermeneutically, Melanchthon needs two antithetical specifications of function, reflecting in their dialectic the ambiguity of fallen human life. In its own terms, the existential character of "law" discourse is precisely that it does not penetrate to the heart, that it works at the level of our mutual relations without engaging the original fear and hope by which these are for each of us *our* relations, or, what is the same thing, without engaging our relation to God (ibid., 214-17). The law's immediate sphere is "external and civil works," the "second table" of the decalogue (ibid., 34). And the level of judgment and motivation at which law operates is "reason" (ibid., e.g., 7, 34), by which Melanchthon does not understand a neutral "faculty" of the soul, but the entire activity of humanity's effort to order our own life, in its historical reality and continuity, insofar as this activity has not been effected by the gospel: "Nor does reason see another justice than the justice of law understood as civil order. Therefore there will always be those in the world who teach only a carnal justice, the justice of faith having been repressed" (ibid., 394). Reason's judgment is simply the judgment "of the world" (ibid., 212); "the righteousness of reason" and "civil works" are synonyms (ibid., e.g., 9, 288).

8 / THE HOLY SPIRIT

But law, since it is God's law, does speak *about* matters of the heart: "For the decalogue requires not only external and civil works . . . , but works located far beyond the power of reason, such as truly to fear God" (ibid., 8). Therefore it can gain access to the heart; and when it does, it has an existential function that is the opposite of promise. Those who hear the law in their hearts find that "law always accuses" (ibid., e.g., 38, 285), that is, it pronounces guilt instead of remission, creates enmity instead of justice, and promises hell instead of heaven (ibid., e.g., 36–38, 117, 128, 295).

We should not have difficulty with Melanchthon's concept of law. "Law" is human discourse as we daily and ordinarily practice and understand it: as a means of transferring information, as a regulation of common or opposing needs and interests—and with the potential of suddenly breaking all these quotidianities open, at which point the gospel must be at hand as pure promise, or all is lost.

The starting point of the adversaries is (from this point of view) that they assimilate these two modes of discourse to one (from their own point of view, of course, that they refuse to impose a dubious distinction) and determine the existential functions of the amalgam by the characteristics proper to "law." "From these, the adversaries take law . . . , and then seek by law remission of sins and justification" (ibid., 7). Remission and justification are still sought and Christ spoken of, because this intends, after all, to be Christian teaching (ibid., 17). But remission and justification now enter the church's discourse *as if* they were matters of controllable conditions and rewards, *as if* they were "external and civil works" (ibid., e.g., 9, 22–23, 34, 130–31). The conditions are then those named by biblical law as God's will for the saints (ibid., 122ff.): love of God, and so on. "Truly, works stick in humankind's eye. Human reason is naturally impressed with them; and since it only perceives works, and not faith . . . , supposes that these works must . . . justify" (ibid., 265). And discourse about Christ, when assimilated to the logic of law, becomes merely "historical" speech about him, lacking existential power of any peculiar sort (ibid., 7), a transfer from one head to another of the sort of information about Christ possessed also by devils and the damned (ibid., e.g., 48, 249, 303).

When Melanchthon is pressed to the minimum of his complaint about the dominant theology and its practice, it is always a simple lack he adduces (ibid., e.g., 121, 377). Given what we have seen, the issue is the sheer presence or absence, in what claims to be church, of "promise," of that radical proclamation of Christ that by its *non*legal character, by its *un*conditional bestowing of forgiveness and *un*conditional assuring of final salvation, is itself God's act to make all humanity right.

Melanchthon's demand for the doctrine of faith is both a demand that promise in fact occur in the church and a demand that the church's theological enterprise be the reflective support of the occurrence. There is a kind of theology that must occur in the church if promise—at least in the long run—is to occur: a reflection that takes the actual proclamation, and the logical and existential situation of the speaker and the hearer, as both its object and its reflective location. Where those committed to the Lutheran reform proposal see only other modes of theological reflection, perhaps the third-person process-describing that Melanchthon called "scholastic," there they must be pessimistic about prospects for unconditional proclamation. Where the *sort* of thinking we find in the Apology is absent, there we must eventually expect promise to be absent also.

We have called the Reformation doctrine of justification a "dogmatic proposal."[19] Were we to describe the Augsburg Confession's central contention, justification by faith alone, simply as dogma, we would thereby read out of the true church the bulk of Western Christendom, which has not accepted the contention. This neither the confessors at Augsburg nor we have wished to do.[20] Yet the contention of the Augsburg Confession was clearly proposed as a regulation of teaching that is decisive for the authenticity of the gospel, that must be binding on the whole church, and that is definitely potentially divisive of the church.[21] Thus "dogmatic proposal" is the precise description of the Reformation justification-doctrine's status to date. As we have noted, the papal representatives at Augsburg rejected justification by faith alone. And subsequent apparent rapprochement in the Committee of Fourteen was illusory.[22] But the action of the papal delegates was confirmed by no higher papal authority, and it is now generally agreed that the condemnations pronounced at Trent, though aimed at the Lutheran doctrine, do not in fact touch it.[23] The doctrine of Trent itself, to be sure, represents the traditional doctrine of grace at its most dubious.[24]

Within a hermeneutical mode of description, the classical descriptions of the Spirit's work (that the Spirit "calls," "illumines," and so on) will function very differently than in pietism or in standard contemporary Protestantism, which descends from the pietists. First the negative. None of these terms rightly names an experience or a modification of the habits of a substance, "the soul." All descriptions of how "conversion" (for example) works or feels are equally false, since conversion is not a process and has no feelings. This is not to say that processes and feelings in plenty do not fill believers' lives, only that no set of them is the Spirit's work of converting—and similarly for the other verbs on the traditional lists.

Rather, verbs specifying the Spirit's work must be understood as instructions to preachers, liturgical leaders, teachers, and advisers. For example, "The Spirit illumines" should mean "So speak of Christ and the lives of your hearers, that our lives' meaning in Christ is made visible." Nor do these instructions stipulate an experience or process in the hearer, which gospel-speaking is to strive to *produce*. We are not to exhort to or describe or even promise illumination. We are verbally to illumine—illumination is a work of the prophetic Spirit, that is, it is an aspect of the spiritedness of the preacher's words.

Returning to our first example, the instruction is not to induce, or manipulate, conversion by our discourse; the hearers' conversion is to be accomplished as the act of gospel-speaking itself. Conversion is a change in the communication situation within which every person lives; a proper sermon or baptism liturgy or penance liturgy just *is* that change. Using penance as the simplest paradigm, when the confessor says, "You have confessed cheating and coveting. Now I forgive all your sins, in Jesus' name," these words do not seek to stimulate conversion as an event external to their being said. Rather, this utterance *is* a conversion of the penitent's life, from a situation in which the word he or she hears and must live by is "You are a cheat and a coveter," to one in which the word he or she hears and must live by is "You are Jesus' beloved."

PREDESTINATION

Once the hermeneutic character of pneumatology is firmly established, we can flip back again to more direct discussion of God and God's work. When we do, we are in the doctrine of predestination. Predestination is simply the doctrine of justification stated in the active voice.[25] If we change "We are justified by God alone" from passive to active we get "God alone justifies us." That God's promise to us is unconditional or that God's will for us is final and externally unmotivated obviously come to the same thing. The need thus to consider the doctrine of justification in the active voice is given with the circumstance that we are dealing with the reality of God and the Spirit and must remind ourselves that God is indeed *God* the Spirit, lest even yet all turn into a fascination with our own spirituality. Conversely, we must remember that the doctrine of predestination is then itself hermeneutic, that it is instruction to speakers of the gospel, and not an attempt at third-person description of God's ways with humanity.

That the logic thus leads us to the Spirit as the predestining God[26] is untraditional and somewhat surprising. Predestination, like creation, redemption, and so on, is of course a work of the one triune God, in traditional trinitarian theory a "work directed externally" and therefore not to be parceled out to the identities. But the very word "*pre*destination" suggests, as what traditional trinitarianism called an "appropriation," a reference to the Father, to God as the prior given to all history. And this appropriation has worked out in the context in which traditional theology has set discussion of predestination: a context determined by the notions of prevenience and origin. Thus Aquinas defined predestination as "a division of providence,"[27] of God's total antecedent effective intention for all creatures. Calvinist theologians located the matter no differently: the decrees of general providence and predestination are one event in pretemporal eternity, differing only as this one divine decision determines, generally, the history of all creatures and, more narrowly, the history of intelligent creatures, in the ways appropriate to each sort.[28] For the modern period, Schleiermacher merely assimilated predestination and providence more simply even than before.[29]

Location of predestination doctrine primarily in the context of God's general rule of creation—crudely, in the first article of a standard creed—fits the general way the traditional doctrine of grace understands divine effectiveness among us, as supernatural causality. Readers will perceive that a shift of this location is proposed. Predestination discourse is fundamentally just assertion of the gospel's character as pure and unconditional promise. The assertion of predestination is fundamentally: "Since God says your life will be fulfilled with Christ for Christ's sake, it will be—because God says it, come or be what else may." Thus the primary location of predestination doctrine should be the second or third creedal article, and this must come out in the language and logic of the doctrine.

But there was a reason for the doctrine's traditional casting in the language of prevenience and origin, and the *problem* of the doctrine appears only when we reckon with this reason. The absoluteness of God's will, primarily asserted of God's will as proclaimed in the gospel, must be interpreted as universal, and it has been to that end that predestination has been coordinated to creation. For if the gospel promise of our ultimate fulfillment is indeed unconditional, the will that acts in this promising must encompass all events whatsoever. If God's will is not determining at any moment of reality's history, there will sometimes be valid responses to the gospel that begin "Yes but." It is a strict corollary of the Reformation doctrine of justification: All things happen by God's will.[30]

Our practical atheism finds such propositions mortally offensive. We can at most tolerate God as a supernatural helper for occasions when we autonomously decide our powers do not suffice. That we should be truly and pervasively dependent, that our destiny should not be in our final control, we take as a denigration. And indeed, the doctrine of predestination does set us down from self-vaunting as gods or beasts, to our precise status as human creatures.[31] For if we interpret God as indeed God, so that we are not God, we thereby posit some mode of predestination. The word "God," after all, marks the point where the metaphysical buck stops. Any serious religious interpretation of reality will therefore display some analogue of the biblical notion of predestination; and if, with the Bible, we apprehend reality temporally and historically, the metaphysical buck stops with a last *word*, a decisive *choice*, that is, with the precise notion of pre*destination*.[32]

Thus no even distantly Christian thought can avoid a doctrine of predestina-

8 / THE HOLY SPIRIT

tion. Fear of the doctrine is merely—or profoundly—fear of God. Nor can this fear validly argue, as it regularly does, that it is human freedom that must be defended against the notion of a truly final God. For the absoluteness of God's will is in no way inconsistent with the reality of our freedom. On the contrary, if we think of God and ourselves as competitors for control of our mutual affairs, so that to whatever extent God determines my destiny I do not, then increased assignment of determination to God must indeed mean lessened freedom for me. But the very point of the doctrine of predestination is to deny any such competition, any such appearance of God and creatures on the same level of decision. Precisely because God is absolute, we are in no competition with God's freedom to choose—and just so God's absolute freedom does not diminish our creaturely freedom. Medieval theologians worked this point out with beautiful precision and subtlety. Whatever God wills, they said, must indeed happen, and exactly as God wills it. Thus, if God wills some things to happen as acts of free choice, they will happen, and happen in that way.[33]

If there is the God of the Bible, there can be no such thing as the free will (*liberum arbitrium*) of traditional discussion.[34] But this classical posit of free will is much more than the simple posit that human acts are—some more, some less—freely done. The posit of free will is a metaphysical claim that this practical freedom manifests a core of indetermination over against all external choices. The free will most theology has worried about does not denote the actual freedom of our actions; it *explains* them, by a pseudodivine capacity that is supposed to belong to human substantiality.[35] This claim is inconsistent with the reality of the God of the unconditional gospel, who is in person, the explanation of our freedom. And it has no necessary relation to the actual freedom or unfreedom of our actions.

But while assertion of the unconditionality of God's will is not the problem of determinism versus freedom that it is often taken to be, there is a grave theological problem that opens just when one sees this. If all things happen within the choice of God, then the will of God becomes morally dubious, precisely by the light of that gospel for the sake of which we posited the absoluteness of God's will in the first place. If God wills all things, God in *some* way wills Auschwitz and the torture of the child in Ivan Karamazov's fable, and the damnation of the damned if God chooses. How is that to be reconciled with the revelation of God's will in the gospel as a "fountain of sheer love?"

Two absolute wills of God appear in our reflection, not easily interpreted as the same. Indeed, the two are absolute in different ways. The will of God proclaimed in the gospel is absolute by the immutability of its known content: God's gospel-affirmation of us is independent of all conditions. The

PNEUMATOLOGICAL SOTERIOLOGY

will of God posited as the prius of all events, on the other hand, is absolute precisely by the absence of known content: whatever happens, God wills it.

It is this threatening split in our image of God which is the true religious occasion of theological history's many attempts to mitigate the assertion of predestination. These run from the semi-Pelagianism with which Augustine's first powerful analysis of the doctrine was promptly met,[36] through such devices as the teaching (shared by Jesuits and most Lutherans from 1600 on) that God eternally preordains to salvation those who God foresees will by free choice believe the gospel when it is preached to them,[37] through Arminian Calvinism, to current benign neglect in hope that the whole question—and any real God with it—will go away.

Instead of such evasions, what is needed is the insight that God's general rule of creation is not the appropriate primary context in which to interpret the particular absoluteness of the gospel's God. The necessary step from the dominant tradition is recognition that our predestination is not the act of a God-the-Father abstracted from the triune relations, sorting fates in a pretemporal eternity. It occurs rather as the act in time of Christ's death and resurrection and of the proclamation of the gospel. When someone speaks to me the promises made by Christ's resurrection, that event *is* the event of God's choice about me.[41] Such a christological and hermeneutic understanding of predestination first emerged in early Lutheranism,[38] but it was carried to systematic reflection only by Karl Barth: "Precisely Jesus Christ is himself God's act of election, and therefore God's word, decision and beginning." Since Jesus Christ is a personal reality, it is only an alternate formulation: "Jesus Christ is the electing God."[39]

Although a christological interpretation of election is the first necessary step from the traditional position, it cannot be the last one. The logic that led to the traditional position remains and must be dealt with: God not only absolutely ordains my salvation in the christological word to me; God as Creator absolutely ordains all events. The early Lutherans tried merely to evade this logic;[40] the result was that also their new insight slipped away from them. Barth moved more drastically.[41] He reversed the traditional pattern altogether, incorporating God's general rule of creation *within* his choice of grace. This move set the structure of Barth's entire systematic theology. Barth's system is "supralapsarian": in all eternity, God has chosen to join the divine self to fallen creatures in Christ; therefore God chose that there should be creatures and to permit them to fall. And Barth's system has as its heart his notorious doctrine of the preexistence of the man Jesus Christ: the event in which there is God *and* something other than God is the life of Jesus Christ, and all temporal history is the consequence of this event. But Barth's systematics will not quite suffice.

8 / THE HOLY SPIRIT

Barth unites God's rule in Christ and God's rule of all history by making the Christ-event itself to be the reality of eternity, and he does this by bringing the trinitarian dialectic to new life. These are indeed what must be done. But Barth unites the two wills of God by the relation of only the Father and the Son. Correspondingly, the eternity that Christ fills is defined as pretemporality, thus remaining within the traditional interpretation. This creates the peculiar ambiguity that pervades Barth's theology: Has the abstract, pretemporally eternal, divine choosing come down to time to be Jesus' choice about us? Or has Jesus himself been taken from us into pretemporal distance? One can read Barth either way. The christological reality of predestination is not, after all, unambiguous in Barth's doctrine.

It can be no secret where we are heading. We will be able rightly to interpret the unity of God's absolute will only if we make *Spirit*-discourse—rather than Father-discourse or Son-discourse—the primary *locus* of our interpretation. It is indeed the human Christ's temporal address to us that is the event of God's eternal choosing about us, as the Lutherans and Barth have said. But the eternity of this moment must be established not by the prefix "pre-" but by the prefix "post-": it is in that the man Christ *will* be the agent and center of the final community, that his will for us is the eternal determination of our lives. The trinitarian dialectics can be the appropriate conceptual scheme of predestination only if the whole scheme—of Father, Son, *and* Spirit—is used and only if the Spirit's metaphysical priority ("God is Spirit") is affirmed. The speaking of the gospel is the event of predestination in that the gospel gives what it speaks about, but this eschatological efficacy of the gospel is the Spirit.[42] We must parody Barth: the Holy Spirit is the choosing God.

The deep offense posed by all legitimately predestinarian reflection is the split between God revealed in the gospel as absolute love and God revealed in all history as merely absolute. So long as only the first two articles are the context of our reflection, we must seek the unity of God in the past and present, and then we must seek a conceptual synthesis of the two images of God, a grasp of how they now are one. We must seek to *explain* how the God revealed in the gospel can consistently choose as God does in history; we must create a theodicy. But if we interpret predestination as the work of the Spirit, the Power of the future, we will leave off such synthesis. How the God of the gospel and the Will behind all events can be one is—we will say—the one truth about God reserved for the End, when we shall see God face to face. Luther, as always, is blunt:

> Faith is "of things that do not appear." Therefore in order that there be room for faith, whatever is believed must be hidden. . . . Thus [God] hides his eternal mercy . . . under eternal wrath, his justice under inequity. This is true faith,

to believe that he is merciful who saves so few and damns so many, who indeed makes us damnable by his own choice; so that he seems . . . to delight in the tortures of the wretched and to be more worthy of hate than of love. If therefore we could by any reasoning comprehend how that God is merciful and just who displays such wrath and inequity, there would be no need of faith.[43]

If we thus abandon the attempt now to know how God's will is one, how indeed God is one God, faith becomes what it is in Reformation discourse—a desperate conflict within an encompassing hope: "For Christ's sake, I trust the God who rules *this* world." From a third-person viewpoint, there is, in the case of any believer, no guarantee that the conflict will not burst the hope, that the hiddenness of God's goodness, which makes room for faith, will not also one day defeat faith. But for faith and proclamation themselves, recognition of the Spirit as the postdestining God does provide an appropriate conceptuality with which to carry on the struggle. As seen in the gospel, God's will is absolute because it is immutably determined, as love; as seen in the total course of events, God's will is absolute in that it is absolutely undetermined—whatever happens, God has willed. Precisely the synthesis of these two determinations is the notion of spirit: a determinate reality that just by the actual character of its particular determination is utterly free. The Holy Spirit is the freedom of Jesus' future to transform and renew all previous events whatever. Short of the end, we cannot conceive how Auschwitz can fit into the will of Jesus' Father, but we can conceive—in hope against hope—that triune structure of God's reality by which this unimaginable transformation will be accomplished. An isolated "God the Father" would have no such structure; of this God's goodness, Auschwitz is conclusive refutation.

To return to the main point, "God alone ordains your salvation" is a necessary form of the gospel, and "God alone ordains all" is a necessary corollary of it. Rightly understood as pneumatological statements, these are assurances and solicitations from the last future, promises of the encompassing sovereignty of the transformation to come: the winds that sweep through history and your life are but eddies and currents of the breath of new creation.

NOTES

1. Tertullian, *On Penitence*, 6,4.
2. Conveniently, E. Kahler in *RGG*³ 3:1639–40; there literature.
3. Above all in the antitheses of Rom. 3–5 and in the charism-doctrine.
4. That this correlative use of the language of substantiality and causality to both God and creatures is, as the scholastics said, by "analogy" does not affect the present point.
5. Conveniently, R. Lorenz in *RGG*³ 1:743–48.

8 / THE HOLY SPIRIT

6. In *Sacrorum conciliorum nova et amplissima collectio*, ed. J. D. Mansi (Venice, 1759ff.), 8:712ff., appended affirmations.

7. The *locus classicus* is Rom. 5:15–21. On the exegesis of this passage, and on Paul's general use of *charis, charisma,* and *dorea tou charitos*, see Kurt Stalder, *Das Werk des Geistes in der Heiligung bei Paulus* (Zurich: Erziehungsverein, 1962), pp. 363–87.

8. Gotthard Nygren, *The Augustinian Conception of Grace, TU* 64 (1957): 257–69; Étienne Gilson, *The Christian Philosophy of Saint Augustine*, trans. S. Lynch (New York: Random House, 1960), pp. 143–64.

9. Aquinas, *Summa Theologica,* i–ii,110,3: "And so the gift of grace is a certain *quality*."

10. The late-scholastic doctrine of "uncreated grace" and "created grace" is both the faithful formulation of this standard Western teaching and its *reductio ad heresiam*.

11. Johann Auer, *Die Entwicklung der Gnadenlehre in der Hochscholastik* (Freiburg, 1942–51), vol. 1.

12. An illuminating document of this conception is a work interesting and important in itself: Jonathan Edwards, "A Faithful Narrative of the Surprising Work of God" in Jonathan Edwards, *Works*, 6 vols. to date, ed. John Smith (New Haven: Yale University Press, 1957–), 4:144–211.

13. More fully, Robert W. Jenson, "On Recognizing the Augsburg Confession," in *The Role of the Augsburg Confession*, ed. Joseph A. Burgess (Philadelphia: Fortress Press, 1980), pp. 151–66.

14. The classic study is Regin Prenter, *Spiritus Creator*, trans. J. Jensen (Philadelphia: Fortress [Muhlenberg] Press, 1953).

15. From Quenstedt on, Lutheran dogmaticians have a major section with some such heading.

16. Pending the completion of more critical compendia, see Heinrich Schmid, *The Doctrinal Theology of the Evangelical Lutheran Church*, trans. Charles A. Hay and Henry E. Jacobs (Philadelphia: Lutheran Publication Society, 1889), pp. 413ff.

17. On the following, Erhard Peschke, *Studien zur Theologie August Hermann Franckes* (Berlin: Evangelical Press, 1964), pp. 28–42, 61–78.

18. Available in English translation in *The Augsburg Confession: A Collection of Sources*, ed. J. M. Reu (St. Louis: Concordia Seminary Press, n.d.), pp. 348ff. The Latin text is in *CR*, ed. C. C. Bretschneider (Braunschweig, 1859), 28:92–95.

19. For fuller discussion of this notion, see Eric Gritsch and Robert W. Jenson, *Lutheranism* (Philadelphia: Fortress Press, 1976), esp. pp. 2–7.

20. Indeed, the confessors asked only that the bishops "tolerate" them; Augsburg Confession, XVI, 2.

21. Against recent doubts on this score, see Jenson, "On Recognizing the Augsburg Confession."

22. For this and other viewpoints, see *The Role of the Augsburg Confession*, ed. Burgess; there also literature.

23. Vinzenz Pfnür, "Zur Verurteilung der reformatorischen Rechtfertigungslehre auf dem Konzil von Trient," *AHC* 8 (1976): 407–28.

24. E.g., *Canons and Decrees of the Council of Trent*, ninth session, V and VI, where we read such statements as that the grace of God works on sinners "so that

they . . . may be disposed by [God's] energizing and helping grace to convert themselves to their own justification, freely assenting to and co-operating with that grace."

25. See, e.g., the scope set for the doctrine of predestination by the Lutheran Formula of Concord, Solid Declaration, XI, 13: The entire doctrine is to be considered as "the counsel, decision and determination of God in Christ Jesus, who is the real 'book of life,' is revealed to us through the Word."

26. That it does so was pointed out to the author by Jonathan Jenkins, research assistant in this work.

27. Aquinas, *Summa Theologica*, i,23,1.

28. Heinrich Heppe, ed., *Reformed Dogmatics Set Out and Illustrated from the Sources*, rev. ed., trans. G. Thomson (London: George Allen & Unwin, 1950), vii,14.

29. Friedrich Schleiermacher, *The Christian Faith* (1830), ed. H. R. Mackintosh and J. S. Stewart (Edinburgh: T. & T. Clark, 1928), pp. 116–20.

30. Martin Luther, *On the Bondage of the Will*, WA 18:619: "For if you doubt . . . that God foreknows and wills all things, not contingently but necessarily and immutably, how will you be able . . . to rely on his promises?"

31. Ibid., p. 632: "Two things mandate the preaching of predestination; the first is the humiliation of our pride and the recognition of God's grace."

32. On the Hebrew Scriptures, in convenient summary, see Walther Zimmerli, *Old Testament Theology in Outline*, trans. D. E. Green (Atlanta: John Knox Press, 1978), pp. 21–58. The big notion is "covenant," which never means a "mutual" arrangement between Yahweh and Israel; see *THAT*, s.v. On the New Testament, see Erich Dinkler in *RGG*³ 5:481–83.

33. Aquinas' analysis is summarized, with all necessary references, by Harry J. McSorley, *Luther: Right or Wrong?* (New York: Newman Press, 1969), pp. 148–54.

34. Aquinas, *Summa Theologica*, i,83,1, defines the notion: "Free will is a cause of its own process (*motus*), in that man by free will moves (*movet*) himself to action." That Aquinas then tries to make this cause theologically harmless by making it inefficacious without God's grace helps not at all, for either, at the level of actual preaching and liturgy, this qualification is meaningless, or the posit of free will becomes itself meaningless, as Luther remarks in *Bondage of the Will*, WA 18:636: "What is an 'inefficacious' *power* except simply no power?"

35. Aquinas, *Summa Theologica*, i,83,1: "Although 'free will' can characterize an act . . . , according to its standard use it devotes rather a principle of the act, that by which man chooses freely. The principle of an act in us is a potentiality and a habit."

36. Karl Rahner, "Augustin und der Semipelagianismus," *ZKTh* 62 (1938): 171–96.

37. This is the doctrine of *intuitu fidei* or *praevisa fide*. John Gerhard, *Loci communes theologici* (1610), ii,ix,14: "We say, therefore, that those are elected by God from eternity for salvation; whom . . . he foresees will truly believe and persevere in faith to the end of life." See Hans Emil Weber, *Reformation, Orthodoxie und Rationalismus* (Gütersloh: Gerd Mohn, 1940), 1/2:93–104; 2:166–75.

38. E.g., Formula of Concord, Solid Declaration, XI. See Werner Elert, *The Structure of Lutheranism*, trans. Walter A. Hansen, 2 vols. (St. Louis: Concordia Publishing House, 1962), 1:10–11.

39. Karl Barth, *Kirchliche Dogmatik* (Zurich: Zollikon, 1932–67), 2/2:1–563, which

8 / THE HOLY SPIRIT

is cited here from this German original (pp. 102, 111) because the English translation is unreliable. On Barth's doctrine of election, see Robert W. Jenson, *Alpha and Omega* (New York: Thomas Nelson & Sons, 1963).

40. See the logically doomed struggles of the Formula of Concord, Solid Declaration, IX, 41ff.

41. On the following, see Jenson, *Alpha and Omega*; there references.

42. Also this is anticipated in the Formula of Concord, Solid Declaration, XI, 29–30, 73–75.

43. Luther, *Bondage of the Will*, WA 18:633.

3
Spirit-Discourse as the Church's Self-interpretation

The Spirit is the presence of the risen Christ. Since the church is essentially Christ's community, the church interprets the problems of its own life by doctrine about the Spirit. The problems of community arise in all communities; what is distinctive to the church is not the problems, but the answers imposed by the church community's specific character, that is, by the gospel.

ECCLESIAL CHRISTOLOGY

The church's self-understanding is intrinsically, and to a great extent historically, accomplished as pneumatology, which here functions as a sort of ecclesial christology.[1] Our first task in this chapter is to trace this logic.

Every community has spirit. To whatever extent you and I share a common life, to that extent you pose human possibilities that are new to me, simply by the ways in which you differ from what I already am. If these possibilities are at once surprising and fulfilling, that is, if they are liberating, you are present in my life as spirit. And just so my life also is itself spirit. If the possibilities you pose to me are in no way liberating, if you are not spirit in my life, we make no community, for the group we are has thus no space of freedom in which to conduct a moral life of its own.

Indeed, every community has *a* spirit. For nothing in the previous paragraph changes if the "you" in it is plural; the described event is not additive. If you are two, to make with me a community of three, it is still *one* spirit as which I encounter you and to which I respond as spirit. And it is the *same* spirit to which each of you responds, when the other of you and I are the two. It is *we* who are spirit for each of us. These last assertions would perhaps be impossible to prove, but they must be assumed, for if they are false, if we are so shut into individuality that each of us, necessarily facing a different set of people than any other of us, thereby encounters a different spirit, there

8 / THE HOLY SPIRIT

can be no community at all—which is the dismal analysis of many. "The spirit of America," "the team spirit," "the spirit of our family" are—we will therefore assume—individual realities.

Moreover, it is not strange for the spirit of a community to be identifiable also as the spirit of an individual, in case the existence of the community depends on the presence of the individual. Thus the spirit of an academic seminar that has so developed as to make a community will not be identifiably separable from the spirit of its teacher; in earlier times no one would have been embarrassed to speak of "a master and his disciples" in such a case.

We may therefore go some way in understanding the church's "possession" of Jesus' spirit without saying anything esoteric. The church, like any community, has a spirit. The risen Jesus, like any living person, has a spirit. And since the church simply *is* Jesus' disciples, its spirit and Jesus' spirit are identical.

But now, Jesus' community and the reality of its spirit differ in one decisive structure from that of other communities of master and disciples: to state the church's situation we had to insert "risen." The individual whose presence makes the church is not present in the church as its other members are. He has died; and though he nevertheless lives, by his liveliness to create the community of the church, it belongs to the very point of the proclamation "He is risen" that he is not merely resuscitated, that he has not returned to die again, that is, that he is not now an item of this age as his disciples still are.

The endings of all three synoptic Gospels (taking Mark's long ending), as well as Acts' preliminary repetition of the ascension story, show the paradox (Matt. 28:16–20; Mark 16:9–20; Luke 24:44–53; Acts 1:4–14). In Luke's ascension stories and in Mark, Jesus explicitly leaves this age, to be with God elsewhere; but also Matthew's concluding story is definitely of a farewell manifestation. The gloriously blunt Markan description must be quoted: "Then the Lord Jesus . . . was taken up into heaven, and sat down at the right hand of God" (Mark 16:19). The risen Lord is not present in the gatherings of the church as are the other members thereof; we cannot look about and discover, "Oh. *There* he is." Yet precisely the motif of presence is a chief point of all these accounts; classically in Matthew: "And lo, I am with you always" (Matt. 28:20). And in all four accounts, precisely at the crux of this paradox, the coming of the Spirit is promised, materially in the power and signs language of Matthew and Mark, explicitly by Luke. It is this complex—nobody's invention but simply given in the actual situation of the primal church—of which John finally makes a whole theological scene and discourse (John 16:5–15).

It is definitive of the church that we are Jesus' community. Therefore, as the church encounters decisions and problems that make it reflect on its own purpose and character, it must reflect christologically, it must interpret itself

SPIRIT-DISCOURSE AS THE CHURCH'S SELF-INTERPRETATION

by the fact and identity of the risen Jesus; the church necessarily develops a sort of ecclesial christology. But the risen Jesus is not an item of our age and so is not in the community as others are.

When we speak of the risen Christ simply as such, we rightly use the whole complex of whatever language we have for discourse about living people. But when we speak of the risen Christ as the *church's* determining person, we cannot but reckon with the oddity of his churchly personhood. Given the "spirit" phenomenon and language, it is this language that will inevitably and rightly serve the purpose.

Paul could write to the Corinthians: "For though absent in body I am present in spirit" (1 Cor. 5:3), describing a situation in which the Corinthians had to reckon with Paul's initiative and freedom, even though when they in turn intended him they had to do so at a distance, intending a person located somewhere else. In such a situation, as opposed to when Paul is "in body" present in Corinth preaching and advising, it is not that first Paul is personally present to the Corinthians and that then his being spirit is the future-opening aspect and reality of his presence; that he challenges and surprises them is in this case the whole evidence and truth of his being present. The Corinthians do not in this instance first discover Paul among them and second experience that he is spirit; they first encounter future-creating spirit, in being addressed by Paul's letter, and so, having also by way of the letter identified this spirit as Paul's, can say, "Paul is among us." This time Paul present simply is the spirit of his presence. But after the end of the resurrection appearances, Jesus' presence *always* has this structure. Therefore Paul says, "The Lord is the Spirit" (2 Cor. 3:17).

The analogy between Paul's presence from a distance and the risen Jesus' presence from a distance is not perfect; the kinds of distances are not the same. If a Corinthian journeyed to find Paul "in body," he could; not so with Jesus. But just this difference gives the notion that Jesus is spiritually present in the church great ontological weight, such as the notion of our spiritual presence to one another cannot have. Jesus is someplace else from the church, not because he is in another place but because he is of the coming eon. He must *come* to us not merely incidentally to spatial separation but because coming, advent, is in this age his proper mode of being. But that is to say that spirit is his mode of being. And so, while for Paul presence "in spirit" is a deficient mode, lacking presence "in the body," Jesus' spiritual presence is intensified presence—which can in appropriate contexts even be described as more unavoidably embodied than Paul or we ever are.[2]

We can now introduce the following material sections of this chapter. There are certain problems that arise in the life of every community simply because it is a community. Thus these problems arise, in appropriately particular form, also in the church. If a community is self-conscious about its spiritedness,

8 / THE HOLY SPIRIT

its effort to deal with such problems will occur as discourse about its spirit. Such effort by the church occurs, therefore, as pneumatology. Each of the following sections discusses one such problem in the church's pneumatological self-understanding. Each section first introduces a pneumatological choice that every community must make, then states the decision incumbent on the church, by criteria developed in the previous chapters, and finally analyzes a sample of historical instances in which this choice has, or has not, been carried out. The four choices posed do not make a system; they rather display the choices posited in the chief pneumatological problems that have become historically important for the church.

THE SPIRIT AND GOD

Every community has spirit, indeed *a* spirit. And every community has some god. The community's god may be the one *whose* spirit the community has. But more usually a community's god is its defense *against* its own spirit, for the normal function of religion is to provide stability. Conversely, a community's spirit is either the spirit of its god, or threatening and uncanny—perhaps demonic—dynamism.

The communal reality of spirit itself demands the posit of God or the gods in one of these ways or the other, for life in a spirit transcends the merely ethical. The status quo that the spirit challenges will not always be only our inadequate obedience to the values by which our community now coheres. In actual fallen history, a community's spirit will sometimes challenge the community's own legitimacy over against some or all of those values. Then the new creation toward which its spirit moves will include new value. When it is not merely my behavior that is challenged by the community's commitments, but the adequacy of the communal commitment itself, moral *creativity* is required.

When, for example, Americans in the last decades increasingly have come to the point of doubting that casting a ballot between the offerings of two manifestly conniving parties is a good thing, since we have been taught precisely by the ideology of representative government that casting a ballot between two slates submitted by one party is an evil, fervent reiteration of republican ideology will not halt political alienation. Only drastic institutional innovation will restore governmental legitimacy, and that innovation will involve the discovery of new value. Many, for example, now think that representative democracy in the nation can be saved only if it is paired with new institutions of direct democracy in the localities, and if these institutions have powers of decision encompassing much of what the representative government now decides. But to say such things involves affirming values that are not unprecedented but do not now belong to our communal commitment.

SPIRIT-DISCOURSE AS THE CHURCH'S SELF-INTERPRETATION

When a community must thus posit new good, we enter a space of freedom that we cannot independently inhabit. We turn dizzily in our own not-yet-being. When a community is called to posit new good, more must be present than the imperative that we should carry on, for it is the sense of "should" and "on" that is then undone. Thus the community confronts transcendence, and transcendence will appear either as the community's defense against the spirit that thus disorients it or as the very disorientation.

The first is the more likely event, and it has many forms. A community may freeze, exclude the moral challenge that brought it to crisis, and live by willingly unexamined tradition indefinitely—as America may go on voting more and more and meaning it less and less. A community may commit spiritual suicide, violating its own commitments—as a newly self-aware urban neighborhood may deny ethnic encroachers the very justice in the campaign for which it organized itself. In the modern West a fully nihilist relativity of all values may yet be achieved, in a public sphere ruled by a completely mechanist state and a private sphere lived only in the present tense. And if any of this is done, religious practices and institutions will be the main bulwark against the future, and God or the gods will be the status quo's chief justification; the transcendence of God's presumed timeless eternity will be set *against* the transcendence of spirit.

Or challenging spirit may be recognized as the spirit *of* God, as threat to what is, made by what more encompassingly and surely is. It is in a community's knowledge that good will come to pass despite all, because the future is God's, that the community can risk the vertigo of freedom, can allow its moral life to lead where we fear to go. It is in the knowledge of what surely will be that a community may be at once open and confident about what should be.

Only if, somehow, there is freedom not merely in the community, but also for the community from beyond it, is community a tolerable venture over the long run. Only if promises are made and relied on whose guarantor is none of the community's members or any combination of them can ethical community be sustained. In the kingdom of God, love will doubtless be greater than faith and hope (1 Cor. 13:13); in the meantime, love (i.e., the acceptance of strange possibility) is utterly dependent on faith and hope.

In Israel, the decision between positing God as defense against spirit and identifying spirit as God's own was made clearly and was a main event and determinant of its history. There are historical traces of a demonic experience of spirit. But the outcome of Israel's history is unequivocal identification of the breath of Israel's future with God.

The church claims to be established as a community by fulfillment of Israel's final hope for the Spirit. Thus the identity of God and Spirit is mandated also for the church. Only one further determinant must be recalled: in the

8 / THE HOLY SPIRIT

church there is a middle term. The Spirit is the Spirit of Jesus; the Father is the Father of Jesus; and *so* the Father and the Spirit are one God. The unity of God and Spirit is trinitarian. In the church, the Father is the *givenness* of God and the Spirit the *futurity* of God; and these stand against each other only by the different ways in which each is the one and the same God.

While the entire catholic tradition agrees in the above, a particular Western attempt to emphasize it has occasioned a great deal of dogmatic controversy.[3] In Western trinitarian teaching, Augustine made it customary to speak of the Spirit's procession from the Father "and the Son," emphasizing both the Spirit's immediacy to the Father, the "source of deity,"[4] and the christological determination of the Spirit. Eastern tradition uses a variety of expressions, perhaps best represented by the second council of Nicaea's "from the Father through the Son"; none has creedal status. From the fifth century, the practice of inserting "and the Son" into the Nicene-Constantinopolitan Creed grew in the West, with Charlemagne giving the decisive impetus, and Pope Benedict VIII, in 1014, finally stipulating it for the text to be said at mass. The insertion caused continual great offense in the East, partly on the strong ground that insertions should not unilaterally be made into conciliar creeds, and partly on the ground that there is a substantive theological difference between "and the Son" and "through the Son"—a much more dubious contention, which either chops logic very fine or betrays a residual hankering to arrange the three trinitarian identities in an Arian-style descending hierarchy of deity. Despite recurrent agreement that the difference, if any, between "and . . ." and "through . . ." should not be church-divisive, most notably at the Council of Florence in 1439, the *filioque* remains an offense between the Eastern and Western branches of the church. On the theology, the West is surely right; on the proper creedal text, the East is right.

Returning to the point itself, there can be in the church no transcendence and therefore, for example, no final authority, that is other than Spirit: the church's God *is* its Spirit. This norm has wide application in the church's life: this section's earlier discussion of representative polity can be directly applied. We will mention two matters in which the application has been actually struggled for. In the first, the historical struggle achieved enduring dogmatic significance.

The tension between leadership as office and leadership as gift of the Spirit is permanent in the church, as in every living community.[5] It is the very function of offices to be institutions of continuity and stability, to guard against disruption of a community's self-identity through time. Spirit, on the other hand, is the impetus of transformation given with the lead each of us has in some however tiny human possibility over the rest of us, and which will obviously blow more strongly from some than from others, whether these hold office or not. In the church, just *because* its spirit is God's Spirit, so that charismatic leadership is seen as divinely given, official leadership and charismatic leadership can never legitimately be more than dialectically opposed.

The church's initial chief ministry, the apostolate, was the perfect union of office and charism. As witnesses of the resurrection, the apostles embodied continuity with the church's beginning. As proclaimers of the gospel, they had pneumatic immediacy that could not be challenged; what they proclaimed was the right gospel just because they proclaimed it. And each of these authorities depended on the other. When the apostles died, the only ministry fully appropriate to the church ceased. Since then the imperative unity of office and charism must always be reachieved, and it has found its chief reality not so much in institutional characteristics of particular forms of leadership as in a sacrament of such unity: ordination.

Ordination claims to install in an office and grant a charism, by the same act.[6] It is the necessary audible and visible word of the gospel to those caught in the impossible tension of postapostolic ministry: the promise of the Spirit "for the work of a minister in the church of God," given not by uncontrollable experience but by institutionalized succession and procedure.

The unity of office and charism can never, after the apostles, be taken as settled; it is and must be repeatedly fought for. But one classic struggle established dogmatic principle. The North African church was disturbed from the closing decades of the second century through the whole of the fourth by pneumatological-ecclesiological controversy, which went through several periods but always involved a coherent complex of issues. Several of these issues will occupy us in this chapter. Our present concern is with the pair of issues agitated after the Decianic persecutions of 250–251, and in the Donatist controversy of the following century.

After the Decianic persecution,[7] charismatic authority clashed with the official authority of the bishops, over control of readmission to fellowship of those who had denied the faith under pressure. On the one hand, the continuation of an older charismatic movement, the "new prophecy" of the turn of the century, opposed all readmission of the lapsed, to maintain the church's eschatological rigor; on the other hand, heroes of the persecution claimed unchallengeable charismatic freedom to readmit. Against both, Bishop Cyprian of Carthage claimed that there is indeed a charismatic freedom over discipline, and that it belongs to the office of bishop. At synods in Carthage and Rome, Cyprian's position became the standard of the Western church.

In the subsequent Donatist controversy,[8] the converse question was posed: whether such charism of office depends on other charisms that are not granted by office, that is, whether the ministrations of an otherwise religiously unworthy bishop or priest can nevertheless be relied on. The anti-Donatist doctrine that the reliability of ministry does not depend on other spiritual gifts

8 / THE HOLY SPIRIT

in the minister was finally established, though not so much by particular councils or synods as by the founding significance for all Western Christianity of the theology of Augustine, the chief anti-Donatist polemicist.[9]

This historical preemption of charismatic ministry by "ordained" ministry carries an explosive consequence for the ordained.[10] Over against whatever other official leadership the church may from time to time have, and even more over against the commitment to the status quo given with their own official position, ordained ministers must be responsible to the free Spirit that they claim. The very *office* of the ordained ministry is to speak and enact the gospel with *charismatic* immediacy, without worrying about its possible alarming effects on the institution, for example, about whether conventional members—whose contributions and influence are needed—will be offended, or about whether the unconditionality of the gospel will lead to laxity in well-doing. The church must worry also about such things, and there may be officials charged to do it, but ordination is the grant of freedom not to.

We will discuss a second consequence of the church's spirit-deity coincidence yet more briefly, though it is not less important. As an existing community, the church will usually live in situations where it weighs on other communities to which its members also belong, most notably the political community. To the extent, usually great, to which a political community separates spirit and deity, its permanent chief political division will be between the demand for permanence and the demand for change, and the church will be a factor in this conflict. Calls for the church to keep out of politics are always but dissimulating attempts to enroll it on the side of permanence. Since Constantine first recognized that the church had acquired political potential, the church has had over and over to choose. No choice has yet been so principled as to acquire dogmatic authority for following generations; perhaps we are now being compelled to choose principle.

Over against the polity's permanent conflict between change and the status quo, the church must refuse to accept that stability and change are in fact incompatible: the Father and the Spirit are one God. But this very identity must put the church decisively on the side of the future, which in a world that separates deity and spirit means that the church must expect often to favor change. Since the church's inevitable interpretation by society as a religious group means that the church will be expected—also by its own uninstructed members—to be a support of the status quo, the openness of the church to change will itself be a fundamental choice by the church and a political act in the polity.

Also, current "theology of liberation" may sometimes betray the Spirit's creativity, by making of exodus and resurrection a timeless idea which we endlessly imitate[11]—and which, moreover, can be as comfortingly imitated by Afrikaner "freedom-fighters" as by the blacks they in turn oppress. What,

SPIRIT-DISCOURSE AS THE CHURCH'S SELF-INTERPRETATION

after all, did not Israel do to the Canaanites? But that the church's message and demeanor, in its christological specificity (to which we will come), may and must be at all times *liberation*[12] is something of which no part of the church should ever have needed to be reminded. The status quo does in fact sometimes need defending; and if the church, as an available group of pious people, is then used by Providence for that purpose, well and good. But *as* the church, as the community of the Spirit that is God, the church can never acknowledge a status quo as norm. For the church, encompassing reality is yet to come, and it is the Wind of the future that expresses the Creator.

THE SPIRIT AND THE LETTER

For any community, identification of its spirit over against other spirits is a continuing necessity. The American nation has an entire sovereign presbytery, the Supreme Court, continuously deciding what is in the spirit of the national community and what is not. On the most notable occasion when they and others similarly charged manifestly failed, only a civil war could settle the matter.

In the primal church, the problem appeared with urgent simplicity. In the daily governance and liturgy of the congregations, interventions claiming to be by the Spirit, and manifestly agitated by some spirit or other, clashed. Since, for example, the advice "Listen to Paul" and the advice "Ignore Paul" could not be of the same spirit, how could one tell which opened the community's true future? Said Paul, "I want you to understand that . . . no one can say 'Jesus is Lord' except by the Holy Spirit" (1 Cor. 12:3). That is, he provided a means of identification, which every community must have.

In a community for which its spirit is the Spirit of God, the identification of its spirit and the identification of God go together. Israel's identification of God is clear. Asked "Who or which do you mean, 'God'?" Israel answered, "Whoever got us out of Egypt." But while this identification was in itself straightforward, its strictly past tense had to make it ambiguous for the future-laden Spirit; the ambiguity appeared as the persistent problem of discerning true prophecy from false prophecy.[13] One could, of course, say that true prophecy had to be appropriate to exodus, for example, "liberating." But quandaries had still to appear.

Within the span of the Hebrew Scriptures, the problem became more pressing as Israel's faith became more decisively eschatological. What finally happened was that the problem dialectically became its own solution. The exilic and postexilic prophets joined free future to established past by prophesying as content of the future the past's decisive repetition. When the Spirit in which the prophets opened Israel's future came to be evoked as itself the eschatological gift of that future, then the exodus or the deliverance by David, appropriateness to which is the self-identity of the prophet's Spirit, became itself the promised future: there will be a "new exodus" (e.g., Isa. 40:3–5), a "new" exodic "covenant" (e.g., Jer. 31:31–34), a new David (e.g., Zech. 9:9–10).

"New exodus" and the rest are, of course, metaphors. But that classification gets us only a little way. In the "new exodus" and its like, history is decisively to repeat itself. Merely as such, the repetition of saving events is the main intuition of all mythic religion, but there its function is precisely to keep history from being decisive, to anchor possessed blessings in an eternal beginning.[14] The prophetic promise of *decisive* repetition, in contrast, does not mean reiteration of a timeless archetype, but faithfulness to a task begun and now to be finished. And it was as "faithfulness" that Israel conceived her God's eternity. But now we must note the kind of language we have just been compelled to use: the historical continuity posited by exilic prophecy is that of a personal life. The problem of true and false prophecy can finally be mastered only if the unity of Spirit-opened future and God-identifying past history is the historical self-identity of a person.

That is, the Spirit can be identifiable only if we can speak of him as the Spirit of so-and-so. Nor will it do merely to say he is the Spirit of God, and then characterize God as "personal," nor yet to say he is Israel's Spirit, and "personify" Israel, for both moves would be vacuously circular. The Spirit can only be identified as the Spirit "of" a person *otherwise* identified. The church's identification of the Spirit as the Spirit of Jesus is the dialectically necessary next step—though it is also contingent and possibly false.

The church's prophecy—"the gospel"—is "Jesus will triumph." The word "Jesus" identifies a single person, by his particular life and particular death, as does any proper name. The future, says the gospel prophecy, is *his*. The spirit of the church is identifiable as the spirit of this historically identified man; yet since this man nevertheless lives, the Spirit is not thereby inappropriately pinned to a merely past event or its historical deposit.

What is the true spirit of the church-community? That which can also be identified as the spirit of Jesus. This answer by itself does not solve a single practical problem. The church has still to labor as mightily as ever the Supreme Court. But identification of the Spirit by Jesus does shape the labor and eliminate certain possibilities.

If the Spirit is identifiable by Jesus, he is identifiable by an historical figure and so by the means of historical memory; that is, the identification of the Spirit is an *hermeneutical* labor. We thus come to Scripture. All the church is agreed that the self-identity of the gospel through its history, and therefore the identifiability of the Spirit, depend on Scripture.[15] In the Spirit, we can speak only the same message—in some sense of "same"—as the apostles, and are thus, after their death, dependent on the documents of their proclamation: on their texts (the Hebrew Scriptures) and on the sparse relics (the New Testament) of their actual activity. That is, we are dependent for the gospel's self-identity on recorded words. But how can such identify the Spirit? Are we not back with Israel's old problem? The whole history of the church could be written under the rubric of so many controversies "on the Spirit and the letter."[16]

Again and again we have so attempted to identify the Spirit by the letter of Scripture that little Spirit has been left. All doctrines of inerrancy and so forth fall under this verdict, and so, ironically, does what is usually now meant by "the inspiration of Scripture." If by this we meant that these texts belong to and have a special and necessary role in the Spirit's impelling of the church toward the End, the doctrine would be biblical. But what is nearly always meant is the opposite: an attempt to deify the letter. Nor yet does anything change in principle if Scripture is conceived as the document of a great religious movement or teacher and leader, and authority of some sort is attributed to the movement or leader, or if we make Scripture a field for the detection of subtextual primal archetypes. So long as we in any way deal with Scripture as a document of the past, from which we by some method or ideology have to extract a contemporary significance, we are dealing by the letter against the Spirit.

It is arguable that the church has survived at all only by the outbursts which so dead a hand of the past had to provoke: Montanism, various medieval movements, the Reformation-era spiritists, current theology that begins and ends in "the theologian's" freed-up experience, and so on. Nevertheless, such outbursts for the Spirit against the letter are if anything even less appropriate to the church's mission than the letter-bondage they react to. We come to the excluded possibilities customarily lumped together as "enthusiasm." The historically classic struggle was that between Martin Luther and those he called the *Schwärmer*. Luther's position was dogmatically asserted by the Augsburg Confession: "We condemn the anabaptists and others, who think that the Holy Spirit comes to us without the external speaking of the gospel."[17]

The spirit that is independent of the letter by which the Lord is identified is not in the church identifiable at all. And when the church becomes a field for the sweep and clash of unidentifiable spirit, the wise will depart. In such a church, we may by chance be called to the now so much admired peasant revolution, or to the splendid works and austerities of some early English spiritist movements. But we may equally be called to slaughter the innocents: When an outburst of "spiritual freedom" swept a medieval district, it was time for the Jews to seek refuge in the castles of the no more friendly, but letter-obeying, bishops.[18]

The great second- and third-century struggle with Montanism[19] displayed all the factors of the many subsequent such struggles, and its resolution has

8 / THE HOLY SPIRIT

been authoritative ever after. "Montanism" is a later name for the extreme form of a widespread reaction against the cooling of eschatological expectation in the second century, and with it of prophecy and ethical rigor—against, that is, a church which had acknowledged that the Lord's return would not necessarily be chronologically soon and that it had to settle in for a longer haul. Montanus and his two prophetesses announced the imminent time and place of the millennium and dictated rules of church discipline far harsher than any previously contemplated. On the readmission of the lapsed, they decreed: "The church *can* indeed remit guilt; but I will not do it, lest they commit more sin."[20] That neither such eschatological information nor such disciplinary rigor could be supported by apostolic witness did not bother the prophets, since they spoke directly for God. The spirit speaking through them said, "Neither an angel nor an elder, but I, the Lord, God the Father have come."[21] The prophecy of the "Paraclete" was a new and therefore higher revelation than that of the earlier prophets or of the evangelists and apostles.[22]

The Montanist movement was quickly expelled from the just then rapidly organizing church. In its home territory of Asia Minor, the church's very first synods were to combat it; in its second great territory, North Africa, the break was already sealed in 207 by a synod at Carthage. The chief point of separation was precisely the claim of a revelation by the Spirit that was not subject to control by the biblical witness to Christ; conversely, the anti-Montanist reaction was a chief impetus to the development of a definite New Testament canon.[23] Somehow the church's Spirit must be subject to the letter *about* Christ, and just so be the free Spirit *of* Christ. Understanding and practicing this dialectic is a chief and permanent pneumatological task of the church.

THE SPIRIT AND THE WORD

Israel's and the church's identification of God and Spirit and of Christ and Spirit is simultaneous with and dependent on identification of word and Spirit. This brings us to a third area.

The life of any community is above all shaped by whether in it word and spirit are one or two. Not to cast unnecessarily far afield for an extrachurchly example, the American community is now being perturbed precisely by confusion at this point. Democratic theory, which settlement of a new continent unexpectedly allowed to be put into practice, harbored two incompatible doctrines of communal spirit. America has tried to follow both.

One, in the line of Rousseau,[24] locates the community's spirit in prelinguistic shared impulse, in a "common will" that antecedes all joint attempts to reach consensus, which may be better divined by one inspired leader than by the assembled community. This theory has justified all modernity's totalitarian democracies, from Robespierre on; the leader is the one who "just knows"

SPIRIT-DISCOURSE AS THE CHURCH'S SELF-INTERPRETATION

what the people want. But it also justified the American Constitution, Mr. Madison's Newtonian machine-polity of representation and balances.[25] For, as Madison well knew and made plainer than we have since admitted, it is only interests, never moral convictions, that can be represented, or checked and balanced as if they were masses in motion. What our constitutional machinery is designed to produce is not a consensus about what is believed to be good, but a balance of what is premorally wanted. This balance can then be presented as the common good only on Rousseau's principle, only because the community's grasp of its own future good is presumed to subsist with or without joint moral reflection, that is, discussion and argument, and to express itself best in sheer joint want.

The other theory of democracy, given in Puritan theology of covenant, locates the community's spirit in face-to-face moral discourse.[26] The community's spirit is not just there, to be discovered by whatever means of divination; it comes into being by actual common discourse about the future of the community. In that we *argue* our common good, there is one spirit.

It is the polity of such discourse that Madison called "democracy" and rejected, because of its alarming spiritedness and because of its limitation, under the technology of the time, to small communities. But although the spirit of the word was thus shut out from our state machinery, it persisted, so long as Puritanism persisted, in a second informal public sphere.[27] In Athenaeums and Chautauquas, in the congregations of great preachers, in societies and clubs for one reform after another, there occurred the actual American ethical community, which civilized the frontier, established our education, fought slavery, campaigned for women's suffrage and industrial justice, promoted just wars and opposed unjust ones, and tried to outlaw liquor.

So long as both public spheres lived, our nation flourished as a community. For whenever matters become serious, Mr. Madison's mechanistic polity could call on the informal Puritan ethical community for spiritual succor. But in the ethical community's isolation from the state, it was unable to assimilate the great nineteenth-century immigrations of people who came for reasons of necessity rather than of religious or political conviction, and it never tried to recruit the great existing spirit of the black community. It was thus too weak to counter the post–Civil War rise of corporate capitalism, which creates a collective that depends not at all on discourse and demands that moral individuals merely set themselves over against this collective. The very existence of an American community is now threatened thereby.

Where there is community, there is communication. And the word is either itself spirit, or resistance to spirit; conversely, spirit is either word or subverts word. If we detach spirit from the word, it will attach itself instead to the world, and turn reactionary. The word is in any case the reality of our relation to each other and so to the future; it is by language that we have a world,

8 / THE HOLY SPIRIT

so as possibly to come together in it. Just so, we have the world as an interpreted world, and therefore as an interpretable world, as a world that might have been and so might be different. The question is, do we *open* possibility by our mutual addresses, so that our mutual presence in the word is spirit, or do we by our addresses *close* possibility, so that spirit is driven off to become a prerelational collective self?

In Israel, it is settled: There is no spirit that is not word, and there is to be no word that is not spirit. The word in any case is power; in the church and the rest of Israel, because of the content of its word, that power is spirit.

Most of the church's problems and controversies about its mission to the world, on the one hand, and about its internal liturgical life, on the other hand, have been and are centered on the relation of its word to the Spirit. There is a plain scriptural direction: the Spirit *is* the spirit of the Word about Christ. That this direction has historically often had little effect may be attributed to the extreme difficulty of holding on to it in daily churchly practice.

Sent into the world as a conspiracy on behalf of the world's own future, as the community of the spirit that is God the Spirit, how is the church to discern God's future? The question here is not of the criterion, as in the previous section, but of the nature of the activity of discerning. Throughout the church's history, many have turned from discourse as the way of such discernment, to one or another sort of divination or, in the modern world, to one or another ecclesiastical-bureaucratic analogue of Madison's need-averaging machine.

Often these two errors now combine, by virtue of their common basis. For example, "situation ethics," however qualified by scholarly advocates, have in churchly practice usually meant that the church—because it is so loving—just *knows* what in each situation has to be done. Argument is no longer required, or even tolerated. Install such diviners in a bureaucracy, as those that now administer "social concern," and what the church then *divines* always turns out to be what the world, years before, has discovered it *wants*: for example, most Protestant bodies' capitulation to abortion by free choice.

We are neither merely to accept the world's hopes as the world interprets them, nor merely to cast a contrary vision from the church population's own given impulses. The church's mission can be discovered only in an act of language, of interpretation. The one pole of interpretation is the church's constant claim that Jesus is risen, so that his particular human intention, defined by his particular life and death, must finally triumph. The other is the antecedent hopes and fears by which the people of a time and place are somehow related to the future. The outcome of such interpretation is on the one hand an eschatological metaphor, and on the other hand a founded ethic—the interpreting itself is the actuality of the Spirit.

SPIRIT-DISCOURSE AS THE CHURCH'S SELF-INTERPRETATION

For instance—an instance chosen for its reciprocal relevance to the principle under discussion—it is already a banality that Americans feel shut out from their governing. If we ask our fellow citizens, "What do you want?" they answer, "We want some say about our lives." This need can interpret and be interpreted by the assertion of Jesus' resurrection. As the claim of Jesus' liveliness is interpreted by the hope for participation, we will say, "In that Jesus lived wholly by his hope for his fellows, and in that he will triumph, there *will be* a polity in which none is excluded from final decision. In the kingdom, the last will be first." Thus appears an eschatological vision. As the hope for participation is interpreted by the claims of Jesus' aliveness, we will say, "What will happen can happen. Therefore a mutual polity is not a human impossibility; it is worth working for. And your hope for participation, since it is a look forward to Jesus' triumph, need not elbow your neighbor aside. In fact, your neighbor's sovereignty and yours can only grow together." Thus appears a founded ethic.

Turning to the church's inward life, all the great and trivial liturgical disputes that have torn the church have been about the relation of Spirit and word. Is it possible so to receive the Spirit, feathers and all, as to need no external verbal authority? If the recitation of the words of institution consecrates, do we need a subsequent epiclesis of the Spirit? Can I receive "water baptism" and still lack "Spirit baptism"? If baptized infants have the Spirit, can they be made to wait for first communion?

From the welter of cases in point, we choose one that is now actual in much of the church and seems likely to continue for some time: speaking in tongues.[28] Modern glossolalia can be described so: It is articulated speech that lacks one kind of articulation, that by which sounds and sequences of sounds are correlated to items of the world. It is articulated speech; it has rhetoric, melody, and, at least sometimes, rudimentary syntax.[29] But it does not have semantic articulation; rules correlating speech to the world's items and structures. Why would someone want to speak so? Precisely in order to speak without having to judge and shape one's utterance to the world and its ways.

But if one no longer speaks about the world, why speak at all? And why especially attribute such speech to the Spirit? As we have seen, all believing discourse, whether proclamation or prayer, has a quality of prophecy. Prophecy is the word that opens the future. But integral prophecy does so precisely in responsibility to the world that already is: It is the children of Abraham, in all their historical specificity, that will inherit the land, an historical figure, Jesus, who will judge all people in love. Glossolalia is prophecy that has cast off this bond to be nothing but sheer experience of how the prophetic word frees us from the way things are, sheer evocation of the possibility of transformation.

8 / THE HOLY SPIRIT

But just there is the difficulty. For Christ is an item of the world, and the Holy Spirit is his Spirit and the Spirit of the word that specifically tells about him, that is, of a word that does have the kinds of articulation that let it be about things in the world. The problem with tongue-speaking is the same as the problem with purely instrumental music in the services of the church. Music is undoubtedly the most powerful speech we have, except that it does not by itself say anything specific, whereas the gospel is specific. One could well say that instrumental music is the sophisticated church's equivalent of speaking in tongues. And that suggests the discrimination and test we need: It has long been understood that the proper churchly function of instrumental music is to release and vivify texts; a proper organ piece is a hymn prelude or an accompaniment of the gospel procession, or the like. Just so, proper glossolalia would release and vivify the prayers and proclamations in mundane language. If glossolalia is the natural and appropriate accompaniment and vivification of what others in the congregation are saying mundanely, and is recognized by them as such, it is a good thing. If not, it may not be permitted in the congregation at all, for then the spirit that moves is not the Holy Spirit, be it ever so religious and comforting to those who experience it. This spirit is again a dumb spirit, an urge from the premoral, precommunal needs of the mere collective group.

Finally in this line, one more phenomenon of the contemporary church must be mentioned, to avoid misunderstanding of the foregoing and for its own sake. Language and gestures can be used, not for communication, not for the word, but for the sort of exchange that is currently called "sharing." The *word* is discussion, argument, and proclamation and distinct affirmation or rejection; communication creates a common objective world and consensual purposes in it. "Sharing" refrains from all this; it is the mutual display and cosseting of preexisting individual needs and attitudes. That is, "sharing" is an actualization of Rousseauean premoral collectivity. All affirmations in this section are about the word; none are to be taken of "sharing."

"Sharing" can only occur between relatively few people at one time, since emotional intensity—real or fictive—is its necessary medium. The word, on the other hand, can occur between "two or three" or between two or three thousand. Thus "sharing" has a natural affinity for small groups. The point that must be made is: Where it is supposed that the Spirit blows more freely in small groups than in larger liturgical or deliberative groups, there the church's mandated identity of Spirit and word has been betrayed. The error here noted is now pervasive in the church, appearing impartially among charismatics, "facilitators," social activists, devotees of touching-and-feeling, and the soberest of the faithful. Wherever it appears, it is destructive of faith.

SPIRIT-DISCOURSE AS THE CHURCH'S SELF-INTERPRETATION

THE SPIRIT AND HISTORY

It is decisive for every community whether it understands possession of its spirit as a free event in the life of the community or its members, or as a natural endowment. The case that both makes the issue utterly clear and shows its importance is that of Nazi Germany, where the possession of true German *Geist* was exclusively a matter of "blood and soil," of genetics and geography. That Jews were some of the greatest adepts of German art, philosophy, literature, and communal tradition could not qualify them.

Our example shows where we think the danger of the one choice lies, but it should not be supposed that we think the spirit of no community should be given by nature. The choice discussed in this section differs from those of previous sections in that the same choice would not be best for all communities. The family is an obvious case of a community whose spirit must and should be given by blood. Moreover, there are a variety of combinations that may be right for various communities. The spirit of a community may be given naturally to some members and historically to some, as in a family with adopted members, or given naturally but liable to be lost historically, and so forth.

Insofar as the spirit of a community is a natural endowment, the community will display a characteristic important for our concern: Since any natural endowment varies quantitatively between individuals, and since this variation is only within limits alterable by history, such a community will have some who simply *are* more endowed with its spirit than others. Doubtless the classic extreme and self-conscious case was the gnostic[30] religious communities of late antiquity. In consequence of the transcendental history by which, according to gnostic lore, the world came into existence, there are three immutable human kinds: "matter-persons," incapable of virtue or religion; "soul-persons," capable only of culture and virtue; and "spirit-persons," whose culture and virtue are turned into saving religious knowledge by predetermined inner openness to transformation from beyond the world. If the middle, "soul-person" group is at all admitted to the community, then leadership is the sole prerogative of the pneumatics.

The church's choice can be in no doubt. One does not enter the church or receive its spirit save by baptism,[31] that is, historically, by an event *in* one's life. Even the practice of infant baptism does not change this; it only recognizes that birth into a home already under the church's discipline can be a claim on initiation. But just thereby birth into a disciplined home is itself conceived in historical categories, so that the claim it constitutes is not valid apart from the promise of the parents to teach the child and their tested ability to fulfill the promise.

8 / THE HOLY SPIRIT

A vital consequence of the church's mandated decision is that in the church there can be no spiritual aristocracy. This fundamental point was established in the church's first great struggle against alienation, the struggle in which the institution we call "church" was created. We need not here decide the much controverted question whether gnosticism was a movement that invaded or originated within the nascent Christian movement. Whichever, it was the most comprehensive threat of alienation that Christianity has yet experienced.[32] And one decisive point of the church's achievement of self-awareness in difference from the gnostics was over against the gnostic conception of spirit as natural endowment, with its aristocratic consequences.

The key antignostic polemicist was Irenaeus.[33] And the basis of his polemic, against both naturalism and aristocracy, is a strictly christological understanding of pneumatic endowment: "[God] promised to pour out [the Spirit] in the last days. . . . Therefore the Spirit descended on the Son of God who had become a son of man, with him becoming accustomed to dwell in the human race . . . and renewing humans . . . into the newness of Christ."[34] The Spirit is for all believers; just so, his coming depends on God's free choice and so is not given by nature.

But although the church overcame the explicit gnostic temptation, a closely related naturalistic conception was, nearly contemporaneously, accepted into the conceptual structure of standard theology, so that the church has ever since been ill-defended against misunderstandings analogous to gnosticism. Spirit is life, insofar as life is elusive and unpredictable. As patristic theology adopted modes of interpretation provided by the tradition of Greek reflection, it analyzed spirit's elusiveness in terms of certain characteristics of some realities, by which these realities evade our perception: invisibility, intangibility, inaudibility, and so on. The result is a version of the classic Greek two-level ontology, with a new Christian name, "spirit,"[35] for the upper level: There are "material" beings possessed of characteristics by which they are subject to our sense-bound apprehension; and there are "spiritual" beings, defined by the negation of all such characteristics. In Aquinas' definition, "a spirit is an invisible entity . . . ; thus we attribute this name to all immaterial and invisible substances."[36]

If we once accept that such terms as "immateriality," "invisibility," and the like define a kind of being, it is difficult to deny that these terms have some natural application to human being and that therefore human being must, at least in part, be of this kind; it is this that has led to the idea of "the soul." Therefore this metaphysics makes the Spirit a natural endowment of our race, however theology that works with this metaphysics may maneuver to deny the consequence. Thus there has been a tendency given in the conceptual structure of traditional theology which, in our view, runs counter to the pneumatological decisions of Scripture. It is our proposal to eliminate this item of metaphysics from theology; indeed, that has been an agenda item of this whole *locus*.

The first great theologian to break decisively with the identification of spirit with an incorporeal kind of being was Martin Luther. This break was the true crux of his controversy with the sacramentarians, and even of the sacramental and christological differences between him and John Calvin.

It is clear that the spirit/matter ontology must make the central gospel-assertion about the sacraments, of Christ's authentic and complete human presence in the Supper and in the church's life generally, into a conceptually difficult problem. For by such an ontology, the Lord who "*is* the Spirit" among us will just therefore *not* be a body among us. Thus the classical Western formulation of the Lord's bodily presence in the Supper, the doctrine of transubstantiation, accepting the spirit/matter opposition, can affirm the presence of Christ in the body only as the occurrence of a conceptual impossibility brought to pass by God's sheer omnipotence.[37] So Aquinas: the presence of the body of Christ cannot be discussed in terms of location, since a body can be only one place at a time (*Summa Theologica*, iii,75,1–2); therefore the presence of the body of Christ can come to pass only by a "conversion of the bread's substance into it," which is a sheer miracle, "wholly supernatural" (ibid., 4). But if the Supper is to function as sacrament, this miracle must be predictable: We must be able to know that at particular occasions of eating bread and wine it in fact happens. That is, there must be authorized secondary agents of the miracle. So Aquinas: the "power of consecration" resides in a formula of consecration, "This is my body," and in ordination's authorization to certain people to speak the formula truly (e.g., ibid., 82,1). Therewith at a stroke the medieval doctrine of priesthood and, built up around this, of the church.

But what if, as by all the Reformers, such institutionalized miracle-working is denied? Then there are but two possible outcomes. One is that the support is simply removed from under the ancient affirmations of Christ's bodily presence in the Supper, that the spirit/matter ontology is freed to produce its natural consequences. The presence of Christ in the Supper will then be understood as Spirit—which can be anyway presence-at-a-distance and causes no problem—and just so as not-body. Then the bread and the cup, which are manifestly bodies, can be presented not as the presence of Christ but only as means—reminders, symbols, or whatever—of an event that itself occurs in the realm of immateriality. Thus Calvin begins by defining: "Flesh must therefore be flesh and spirit spirit, each in the rule and condition in which God created it. And this is the condition of flesh, that it holds to its one particular place, and to its dimensions and its shape" (*Institutes* [1536], 123). Consequently, the presence of Christ's body in the sacrament must be construed as the gift to faith of the benefits Christ won in the body (ibid.), the function of the bread and cup being to remind us of Christ's body and its benefits (ibid., 120); insofar as the elements fulfill this function, they lead us away from their own reality as bodily objects "to spiritual realities" (ibid., 120), for "the sacrament is a spiritual thing, by which God feeds our souls, not our bellies" (ibid., 121).

The other possible outcome is that the spirit/matter ontology is broken through, and "spirit" recaptured for its biblical uses. This is what happened with Luther. He mocked the "enthusiasts" for supposing that "spirit is nothing more than a substance that has no flesh and blood." On the contrary, Christ's "very flesh . . . is sheer spirit [because it is] holiness and purity. For what can holiness and purity and innocence be except spirit, sheer spirit?"[38] Thus Luther's doctrine of Christ's presence in the Supper is created by abandoning the opposition of "body" and "spirit" as ontological kinds and relating them instead as moral—what we now call existential—categories. Luther is able to maintain the classic affirmations about Christ's reality in the Supper, without resting them on the medieval doctrine of the ministry, by locating them in a conceptuality utterly different from the standard Western metaphysics.

Further development of this matter would take us beyond this *locus*. It will be seen that our agreement, on the precise point, is with Luther. The objective, however, cannot now be to adjudicate the old controversy, but rather to carry on the conceptual revolution inaugurated by Luther, in the hope that thereby possibilities of interpretation will emerge in which Calvinists and Lutherans and Roman Catholics can join. In any case and in the meantime, one Lutheran affirmation must stand: "spirit" is not a kind of being specifiable by its differences from "matter."

The Spirit is Jesus' unlimited, resurrection-liberated freedom. What people do in their freedom is history. So also with Jesus: The Spirit is Jesus' freedom to effect historical reality. The Spirit is the very opposite of a liberation from history, or of a realm of being beyond history. The Spirit is precisely Jesus' freedom to be bread and wine, to live in our historically actual congregations.

NOTES

1. The epochal presentation of pneumatology as ecclesial christology is Schleiermacher's, exhaustively presented and criticized by Wilfried Brandt, *Der Heilige Geist und die Kirche bei Schleiermacher* (Zurich: Zwingli, 1968).

2. 1 Cor. 11:27. The point, if developed, would make the *locus* on the sacraments.

3. On the following history of the *filioque* ("and from the Son") controversy, see Dietrich Ritschl, "The History of the Filioque Controversy," in *Conflicts about the Holy Spirit*, ed. Hans Küng and Jürgen Moltmann (New York: Seabury Press, 1979), pp. 3–14; on the Eastern tradition, see Werner Jaeger, *Gregor von Nyssa's Lehre vom*

Heiligen Geist (Leiden: E. J. Brill, 1966), pp. 122-53; in Augustine, who initiated the Western tradition, see esp. *On the Trinity*, xv,17, 27-29.

4. If this point is not apparent, note the alternative below.

5. The standard history of the formative years of the struggle is Hans von Campenhausen, *Ecclesiastical Authority and Spiritual Power in the Church of the First Three Centuries*, trans. J. Baker (London: A. & C. Black, 1969). For a more complete statement of the author's analysis, see Robert W. Jenson, *Visible Words* (Philadelphia: Fortress Press, 1978), pp. 188-97. The clash of charisma and office goes back to the church's very beginning, if the interpretation of Matt. 7:22-23 and 23:8-10 offered by Käsemann is correct; Ernst Käsemann, "Die Anfänge christlicher Theologie, "*ZThK* 57 (1960): 163-71.

6. On the following, see Jenson, *Visible Words*, pp. 197ff.

7. On the following history, see Bernhard Poschman, *Busse und Letzte Ölung*, vol. 4, fasc. 3 of *HDG*.

8. W. H. C. Frend, *The Donatist Church* (Oxford: At the Clarendon Press, 1971).

9. Esp. Augustine, *On Baptism against the Donatists*. See James Breckenridge, "Augustine and the Donatists," *Foundation* 19 (1976): 69-77.

10. The charismatic claims for the official ministry appear as soon as the latter itself appears; Ignatius, *To the Smyrneans*, viii.

11. Roy J. Enquist, "Afrikaner Religion as a Model of Liberation Theology," *Dialog* 17 (1978): 207-11.

12. E.g., Robert McAfee Brown, *Theology in a New Key* (Philadelphia: Westminster Press, 1978).

13. Briefly, Walther Zimmerli, *Old Testament Theology in Outline*, trans. D. E. Green (Atlanta: John Knox Press, 1978), pp. 105ff.

14. Classically, Mircea Eliade, *Cosmos and History*, trans. W. R. Trask (New York: Harper & Row, 1959).

15. E.g., *The Thirty-Nine Articles of Religion*, VI: "Holy Scripture containeth all things necessary to salvation: so that whatsoever is not read therein, nor may be proved thereby, is not to be required of any man, that it should be believed as an article of the Faith . . . ;" *The Formula of Concord*, Solid Declaration, "On . . . the Norm," 3: the "prophetic and apostolic writings" are "the pure and limpid fountain of Israel and the sole true measure, by which all teachers and teachings are to be judged."

16. The title of Augustine's study of hermeneutics.

17. *Augsburg Confession*, V, 4. On the bases of Luther's opposition to enthusiasm and on its dogmatization in this confessional article, see Inge Lönning, "The Reformation and the Enthusiasts," in *Conflicts about the Holy Spirit*, pp. 3-14.

18. Robert L. Tuveson, *Millennium and Utopia* (Berkeley: University of California, 1949).

19. On the following, see Kurt Aland, "Bemerkungen zum Montanismus und zur frühchristlichen Eschatologie," in *Kirchengeschichtliche Entwürfe* (Gütersloh: Gerd Mohn, 1960), pp. 105-48; here the Montanist oracles are edited and collected. See also Douglas Powell, "Tertullian and the Cataphrygians," *VigChr* 29 (1975): 33-54; Jaroslav Pelikan, *The Christian Tradition: A History of the Development of Doctrine*, Vol. 1, *The Emergence of the Catholic Tradition (100-600)* (Chicago: University of Chicago Press, 1971), pp. 98ff., 106ff.

8 / THE HOLY SPIRIT

20. In Aland, "Bemerkungen," p. 114.
21. Ibid.
22. Ibid., pp. 132–33.
23. Hans von Campenhausen, *Die Entstehung der christlichen Bibel* (Tübingen: J. C. B. Mohr [Paul Siebeck], 1968), pp. 256–70.
24. Jean-Jacques Rousseau, *The Social Contract;* see esp., ii,3.
25. See Ralph E. Stavins, "Political Ethics," in *Religion and the Dilemma of Nationhood,* ed. Sydney E. Ahlstrom (Minneapolis: Lutheran Church in America, 1976), pp. 30–42.
26. Perry Miller, *The New England Mind* (Cambridge, Mass.: Harvard University Press, 1939–53).
27. On the history, see Sydney E. Ahlstrom, *A Religious History of the American People* (New Haven: Yale University Press, 1972), pp. 385–428, 637–47, 749–804, 842–94.
28. On the history, see Walter Hollenweger, *Enthusiastisches Christentum* (Zurich: Zollikon, 1969).
29. William Savarin, *Tongues of Men and Angels* (New York: Macmillan Co., 1972).
30. See, still, Hans Jonas, *Gnosis und spätantiker Geist,* 2d ed., 2 vols. (Göttingen: Vandenhoeck and Ruprecht, 1954), vol. I, pp. 178–90, 199–214, 243–83.
31. See Jenson, *Visible Words,* pp. 126–43.
32. Every few years somebody rediscovers the gnostics and proclaims them the "real" Christians. Anybody who wants to be a gnostic may, and there is no way to register "Christian" as a trademark. But someone who cannot tell that the New Testament documents one faith and, for example, the interesting Nag Hammadi texts another, is clearly not to be trusted out alone in the world.
33. On this paragraph, see Hans-Jochen Jaschke, *Der Heilige Geist im Bekenntnis der Kirche* (Münster: Aschendorff, 1976), pp. 181–86, 277–82, 299–303.
34. Irenaeus, *Demonstration of the Apostolic Preaching,* vii,xvii,1.
35. The Greek tradition itself did not call its upper ontological level *pneuma;* H. Kleinknecht, in *TDNT,* s.v.
36. Aquinas, *Summa Theologica,* i,36,1.
37. On the whole history of scholastic difficulty at this point, through Luther's radical innovations, see Hartmut Hilgenfeld, *Mittelalterlich-traditionelle Elemente in Luthers Abendmahlsschriften* (Zurich: Theologischer Verlag, 1971), pp. 183–232.
38. Martin Luther, *Confession of the Lord's Supper* (1528), *WA* 26:352.

4
Cosmic Spirit

Despite the perils of the enterprise, the Hebrew Scriptures and the doctrine of the Trinity compel us to describe a cosmic reality and work of the Spirit. In the often esoteric tradition, we find cosmic Spirit identified as the freedom of history, the spontaneity of nature, and the beauty of all things. The dogmatic task is to reclaim these insights by discovering what it must mean that this Spirit is the specific Spirit of Jesus and his Father.

THE LOGIC OF COSMIC PNEUMATOLOGY

In the previous two chapters, we have discussed the work of the Spirit mostly as a work only within the believing community. That is as it should be; it is the Spirit of Israel's particular God and of Jesus and of the church that is our object. Yet we cannot entirely confine ourselves to this analysis, for Israel's God is creator of all things. Thus if the Holy Spirit is God, this Spirit's wind must blow on and through all things. In the New Testament, the creator Spirit is almost exclusively proclaimed as the creator of the new life of God's particular people; but the very meaningfulness of this New Testament discourse depends on the Hebrew Scriptures, which evoke the Spirit as a universal creativity.

The enterprise of cosmic pneumatology is thus necessary; indeed, it is dogmatically mandated by the Trinity doctrine's assertion of the unity of Father and Spirit. But the enterprise is also perilous, for it must be the particular Spirit of Jesus and of the church to whom we attribute cosmic efficacy; that is, we must assert the universal potency of events in one little religious group. Such an assertion strains the Western intellectual tradition to breaking. As we will see, those who have ventured cosmic pneumatology have not always been able to avoid producing nonsense or myth. And conversely, the enterprise exposes theology to powerful temptation: to mitigate the offense by relaxing the restriction by "of Jesus and the church" a little, to fudge the particularity of the Spirit.

8 / THE HOLY SPIRIT

If a cosmic pneumatology faithful to the gospel is possible, its function will be double, and exactly match with respect to creation the function of the previous chapter's analyses with respect to community. First, we hope by interpreting the gospel's proclamation and invocation of the Spirit over against the world—as before over against the church-community—to display part of the sense of this proclamation and invocation, and so further their vitality and accuracy. Second, we hope to obtain true statements about the world, which are valuable for their own sake, just as we hope that the previous chapter is valuable truth about the church-community.

There are two great differences between analyzing the pneumatic reality of community and analyzing that of the world. First, there are not merely in possibility but in fact many communities, each with its spirit and its different pneumatic structure; thus our method could be to analyze the abstract pneumatic choices before "any community," and then state the church-community's proper actual decisions. But there is only one world; therefore our cosmic pneumatology must be concrete and specific from the start. Second, the church, whose Spirit we are discussing, is already a community but is not yet the world. Therefore in cosmic pneumatology we are one eschatological step back from the previous chapter, which is doubtless the prime cause of the undertaking's difficulty and peril.

We will derive our proposals by a simple device. We will note powerful cosmic pneumatologies from the tradition, and then try to save their insights by restoring whatever they may have lost of the offensive claim that it is *Jesus'* individual spirit of whom the insights are true. In the tradition, there seem to be three themes: the Spirit is the freedom of universal history; the Spirit is the spontaneity of natural process; the Spirit is the beauty of creation. We will consider each. In the very first cosmic pneumatologists, Theophilus of Antioch and Irenaeus, all three themes are already present.

Theophilus of Antioch was eccentric among the mid-second-century apologists in that he appropriated the biblical predicate and figure of "Wisdom" to the Spirit rather than to the Son (*To Autolycus*, ii,15);[1] this characteristic will recur in later cosmic pneumatologists.[2] It is then consistent with the biblical traditions about Wisdom that knowledge of creation is attributed to inspiration by this Spirit-Wisdom (ibid., ii,9) and that the Spirit-Wisdom is seen determinative in creation. The Spirit is God's "breath," by which he "begets life" in and "nourishes" all things (ibid., i,7; ii,3). Nor is the activity of the Spirit only exterior to creation; but just here, Theophilus can make his point only by reviving the crudest kind of myth: the Spirit of Genesis 1:2 "nourishes" the waters and then together they nourish creation (ibid., ii,3); creation is "surrounded" by the Spirit, and these together are surrounded by God's hand (ibid., i,5).

This Spirit-Wisdom tradition, with its attribution of the biblical Wisdom's cosmic function to the Spirit, was continued by Irenaeus[3] on a less mythic basis[4] and with greater specification of the Spirit's role. By the Word, God grants sheer existence; by the Spirit, he makes what exists a "cosmos," an ordered whole whose order is fundamentally one of mutual appropriateness and adaptation:[5]

> Since God is "logical," by his Logos he created all that is created; and since he is spiritual, by his Spirit he made a cosmos of all things. . . . Since then the Logos . . . grants the fact of being, and the Spirit grants order and shape . . . , the Logos is rightly . . . called God's Son and the Spirit God's Wisdom.[6]

It is Plato's aesthetic cosmology that Irenaeus draws on: the world is one and is God's world in that it is internally harmonious. This cosmology will in later theologians become a chief structure of theology, and in that role prove a doubtful blessing, but this story belongs in another *locus*, and in Irenaeus we are anyway dealing with a less principled adaptation. In that the Spirit has thus wisely shaped creation, the Spirit is able also to reshape it from within, "mingling . . . with the creature shaped by God that man might be in the image of God."[7]

THE FREEDOM OF HISTORY

In the Western tradition, one thinker above all others has taken the biblical evocation of the Spirit as a key to reality: Georg W. F. Hegel.[8] It is, in Hegel's interpretation, a central insight of the Western tradition that reality is at its heart conscious. All our knowledge of reality is just that—knowledge; and this tautology itself is both the chief puzzle posed by and to our attempt at knowledge and the chief clue to the puzzle. The puzzle: How *can* we know anything? What bridges the disjunction of knowing subject and to-be-known object? The clue: Perhaps *to be* anything at all, and so to be a possible object, is intrinsically *to be known*, so that there is no gap. The world is not first a mere given, and then subsequently and mysteriously the object of a consciousness, yours or mine; it is a given in that and only in that it is the object of a universal Consciousness. Reality is thus Consciousness-with that object that is given with itself.

But here a disjunction appears. In our self-consciousness, we know consciousness sometimes as *mind*, registering and leaving the object as it is, and sometimes as *spirit*, grasping the object precisely by intruding transformingly on it. Which experience shall we let lead our interpretation of universal Consciousness?

The Greeks said: "God is Mind—or something more like Mind than any mind is."[9] Hegel made the opposite, philosophically revolutionary choice: universal Consciousness is Spirit.[10] If the world subsisted as the object of Mind,

8 / THE HOLY SPIRIT

of Consciousness that leaves its object as it is, then the world would always remain as it is. Then the world would best be understood with the Greeks as a cosmos, a changeless structure encompassing the processes of history as a machine encompasses its own workings without itself being changed thereby. But it was exactly the sheer reality of historical change—the French Revolution—that burdened Hegel and that he needed to explain, not explain away, and therefore he instead interpreted universal Consciousness by the biblical intuition of consciousness as primarily spirit. The world subsists in that it is transformed, by a God who is—far from static Mind—lively Spirit.

Therefore historical change does not have its sense only in something else, the structure of a changeless cosmos within which it occurs. Historical change has its *own* kind of sense, the sense that spirit finds in its object: the sense of a community's lively debate or of creative process in the arts or of lifelong love.

Hegel formalized the logic of this sense by his famous three-step dialectic. Precisely what seems to prohibit that history make sense, the frequent occurrence of historic conflict so extreme that when conceptualized it amounts to contradiction, is the very location of historical meaning. Every historic reality sooner or later acquires, or rather evokes, its own negation; history is made of "thesis" and "antithesis." Thus, for example, the French revolutionary posit of "liberty, equality, and fraternity" evoked the Terror. History makes sense in that precisely from such contradiction a new thesis emerges, a "synthesis" embracing the contradiction in a larger meaning, as does the resolution of a good play's dramatic conflict. Thus Napoleon synthesized the Revolution and the Terror to create Europe's first popular state.

In that the world has *this* sort of sense for the Consciousness as whose object it subsists, neither can the world and this Consciousness merely lie over against each other; their relation too must have the three-step dialectic. Universal Consciousness evokes the world, the mere unconscious object, as its own opposite. But just so Consciousness finds its own Meaning—and meaning is the very self of consciousness—in this object, by this transforming action to fulfill itself as Spirit and not mere Mind, and to fulfill the world as history and not mere cosmos. Thus the Spirit not only creates but involves the world; the Spirit is the freedom *of* universal history. The Spirit is the act in which God as Consciousness overcomes history's apparently static standoffs, by creative discovery of the meaning of the contradictions. The Spirit is the freedom of whatever merely is, and just so is involved in some contradiction, for the new synthesis that will come of that conflict.

This reflection's debt to the gospel is obvious, but so is its alienation therefrom. The quickest stipulation of the alienation is dogmatic: The last paragraph's doctrine of God is clearly and intentionally trinitarian, but with the world where Christ ought to be, as the Object in whom the Father finds himself. To reclaim Hegel's truth for the gospel, we need only a small but drastic amendment: Absolute Consciousness finds its own meaning and self in the *one* historical object, Jesus, and *so* posits Jesus' fellows as its fellows and Jesus' world as its world. What we thereby provide a theory for is the assertion of the risen Jesus' universal lordship.

If the risen Jesus is Lord, not only is he Lord of the church, but his will determines the history not only of believers but also of all nations (e.g., Eph. 1:20–23).[11] Theology has had great difficulty stating so brash a claim, and when it has dared, it has regularly emptied it in the very attempt, disingenuously making Jesus Lord of the world by baptizing whatever the world anyway wants, as "really" Jesus' will. Throughout the theological recent past, we have been exhorted to let "the world determine the agenda," to "listen to what Christ is saying from outside the church," and so on. The exhortation is in fact nearly as old as the church; noting that its greatest triumph was the now decried "Constantinian era" may suggest how dubious it is. We must make the exact opposite move: we know who the Freedom of history is, because he is Jesus' Spirit and we know Jesus historically; and we thus can and must proclaim the world's agenda to it.

The Spirit of Jesus is the freedom in which universal history occurs. Here is our thesis. We will unpack it both ways, as an interpretation of the Spirit of Jesus and as an interpretation of history.

The specific Lordship of Christ outside the church occurs when and where the miracle of Hegelian "synthetic" creativity actually occurs. We must speak of "miracle" because that is what Hegel in fact described, whether or not he adequately so conceptualized it. Hegel, his vision guided by Christian proclamation, doubtless saw history at least insofar rightly: its process has meaning only in the free appearance of reconciliation between antithetical historical powers. We need not here decide the controverted question[12] whether or not Hegel's own system allows this reconciliation to be truly free transformation—to be eschatological—or compels it to be what we more usually mean by "synthesis," mere result, mere product. We will unambiguously posit the former, by identifying historical synthesis as *Jesus'* action, as what is possible only to a resurrected one.

We do not by this identification acquire criteria by which to look through history, identifying true reconciliations in order then to attribute these events especially to Christ. We do state a hope: living in the actuality of historical contradiction, we recognize therein the very sort of situation appropriate to the action of one whose freedom is that he is risen from the dead. In an historical confrontation, where we might otherwise see hopeless impasse, we therefore perceive instead the possibility of a new initiative of Jesus' love. And

8 / THE HOLY SPIRIT

we do also acquire the right to an after-the-fact application of this hope: the believer's ineradicable penchant to look back and say, "The situation was hopeless; but then the Lord. . . ."

Conversely, when Hegelian synthesis truly occurs, when new love freely appears out of historic contradiction, there some pieces of history are gathered for the kingdom of God. At the End, all history will be harvested as an inexhaustible complex of opportunity for the love of Christ. But if that were all that could be said, if there were no penultimate gatherings *in* history, then all temporal events would be equivalently grist for the End, and then all temporal events would lack point, since it would not matter what happens before the End. The assertion that Christ's Spirit is the very inner-historical freedom of history, that where events unpredictably triumph over impasse this is the act of his lordship, says instead that history is available to the final triumph of Christ's love by its own structure—recurring to Hegel, by the recurrent miracle of freedom at the juncture of synthesis with thesis-antithesis.

We must give at least one example. For all that it is now fashionable to deride an earlier American understanding of the appearance of this new nation as a creative act of God, and for all the harm such American self-consciousness doubtless has done, might not the proposition yet be true?[13] The antithesis of the Enlightenment to pietist Christianity, of "life, liberty, and the pursuit of happiness" to eschatological vision and commitment to the brothers and sisters, was synthesized in the local institutions equally of Massachusetts or Virginia and in the thought of someone like John Adams. May we not regard this as an act of Christ's Lordship? That this new thesis soon provoked a new contradiction, which perhaps still awaits its synthesis, need not inhibit our praise for what has been given.

THE SPONTANEITY OF NATURAL PROCESS

If the sort of biblical apprehension exploited by Hegel is true, all reality is historic and the traditional disjunction of "history" and "nature" is only preliminary. But, as preliminary, the distinction doubtless marks a real difference: between the uniqueness and final unpredictability of some events, those we call history, and the regularity and predictability of natural processes. Has the Spirit any role in the latter?

The most theologically influential of modern Anglo-American philosophies, "process" philosophy, has taken natural process as its paradigm of reality, and Christian theologians among the process-thinkers have devoted some attention to the role of Spirit in reality so conceived. According to process-thinkers, reality is composed not of things but of events, or, as they prefer to say, of "actual occasions." An enduring entity, a thing, is but a chain of such occasions, linked by shared characteristics and certain kinds of causal relations.

Each actual occasion is what it is as an integration of its antecedent occasions; for example, a speech is an integration of the experience of the speaker, the events that led up to the assembly addressed and the choice of speaker, and so forth. If each actual occasion's character were without remainder determined by the antecedent occasions it integrates, there would be no novelty in temporal process. But this does not seem to be the case. Anyway, assert process-thinkers, that integration occurs cannot itself be determined by the antecedent occasions; thus temporal process necessarily involves a factor of "event-spontaneity." And sometimes this event-spontaneity does seem to bring with it also a "character-spontaneity," so that the new actual occasion displays novel characteristics not explicable by its antecedents. The suggestion of some process-thinkers is that this spontaneity of temporal process is the referent of Christianity's discourse about the Spirit.[14]

There are several problems with this process-pneumatology.[15] The very choice of natural process as the paradigm of reality, so that history is understood merely as a subclass of process in general, surely prohibits complete faithfulness to the biblical witness to the free Spirit. And by making the spontaneity of cosmic process the chief validation of discourse about the Spirit, process-theology shares Hegel's trinitarian alienation; also in this thinking, the world is the trinitarian Son.

Yet here too there is a claim we cannot abandon. Insofar as natural process is, even penultimately, distinguishable from history, it must not by that distinction be made a realm in which Jesus' Spirit is ineffective. Our task is the same as throughout this chapter: here to reclaim natural spiritedness as *Jesus'* Spirit. And it must be a spontaneity of natural process in which we have to locate a natural reality of the Spirit. Our thesis must be: The Spirit of Jesus is the spontaneity of natural process.

But is there any spontaneity in natural process? The attitude toward nature usually fostered by the scientific enterprise is still a cause-and-effect determinism: we suppose that if we knew the total state of the world at any moment, we could predict its entire future. We are here doing dogmatics, not apologetics; this is not the place for a full-scale attack on determinism. But so much must and may be said: If we knew all there is to be known about the world at any moment, we could still not predict the future behavior of all parts of the world, because of an essential character of knowledge about the world.

All scientific knowledge, it now seems, is fundamentally statistical.[16] Its hypotheses about the world's behavior apply to populations—of gas molecules in a space, neutrons released by a fusion, planets in a galaxy, people in a

8 / THE HOLY SPIRIT

theater, or whatever—and have the form "Of this population, x% will do f under conditions F, G. . . ." Interpreted of individual molecules, neutrons, or theater-goers, such hypotheses become statement of odds: "It is x to y, that any one member of this population will do f under conditions F, G. . . ." And here it is vital to remember what every gambler must, that odds exert no pressure on individual events: when we know the odds are 10 to 1 against, say, filling a particular poker hand with two draws, this knowledge enables no prediction about the actual event other than repetition of the odds. It must therefore be said that there is a factor in natural process which can be interpreted as spontaneous and that it is the one process-thinkers point to, the actual individual occasion. Whether we should so interpret is another matter and does not seem determinable by the content or nature of our scientific knowledge. Believing that the Spirit is the freedom of all realms of created reality, we so interpret.

So to our thesis. Its consequences are shocking. First, if nature's spontaneity is Jesus' Spirit, nature does not subsist apart from personality. Apprehending an actual occasion, we confront someone's communicative freedom, we are in someone's intrusive presence. And we know that someone; the Gospels tell of him. Apprehending any actual occasion, we are involved in conversation with Christ and so in his conversation with his Father.

Our side of this conversation is prayer. If the freedom of natural process is someone's spirit, that someone can be addressed. We can meaningfully and reasonably ask, "Make it rain," because the rain will or will not occur in freedom that is someone's freedom. And if the spirit of natural process is the Spirit of Jesus and his Father, he can be addressed in trust and joy, by petition and praise.

Natural process is usually still understood as a network of causal determinism. Then prayer, if taken seriously, must be understood as appeal to an agent exterior to this network, to intervene in it. Prayer so understood is vulnerable to the old rationalist question: What kind of God would in the first place have made a world which that God has then constantly to adjust? In the contemporary church, such questions have extensively undone the practice of prayer, which is interpreted and phrased not as actual conversation with someone who can and does act but as self-help and self-exhortation: "Lord, make us feel right about the poor," instead of "Lord, feed the poor." Nor is it only petitionary prayer that succumbs. If God can do nothing about the crops or an election, for example, neither *has* God done anything about such matters, and there is also no basis for praise.

In fact, however, the one to whom we pray is not an agent merely exterior to natural process. All actual occasions occur not mechanistically determined but in freedom, and this freedom is the freedom not of mere chance but of a spirit. It is the freedom of the risen Lord's freedom, of the Holy Spirit, of the very Spirit we address in both petition and praise. The arrow of time is Jesus' breath.

Petition and praise are response to challenge and blessing. These then are what all occasions say to us. By every actual occasion, the risen Lord says: "There are possibilities. Ask" and "There are marvels. Praise." That believers are able to hear these addresses, that we are able so to interpret natural spontaneity, depends on the gospel, on our knowledge of the risen Christ. Thus the foregoing propositions about natural spontaneity provide no basis for an independent natural theology. Yet neither is there any reason Christ should not make himself heard in natural spontaneity also by unbelievers. Their ability to hear must then depend on guides other than the gospel—but if they hear, they hear.

On the present line, one other matter must be mentioned, and within this *locus* only mentioned. If the spontaneity of natural process is by a spirit, natural process has not merely a direction but a goal. And since we know whose spirit it is—that it is Jesus'—we know the goal: unconditional love. That is, we know the tendency of cosmic evolution: toward a world apt for love. With this assertion, we touch a long tradition of Christian speculation, of which Teilhard de Chardin[17] is the most recent notable representative. Consideration of the achievements and dangers of this tradition belongs in other parts of this work.

THE BEAUTY OF ALL THINGS

Readers will have noted how skimpy the previous two sections are compared to other discussions in this *locus*, and how often we have to say that full treatment of some matter would transgress the bounds of dogmatics. Perhaps this has been merely evasive of problems. But there is another preferable explanation: Insofar as the universal role of the Spirit is describable in books, these should be books of faithful speculation, making no strong claim to be the teaching of the churches. The dogmatic substance of what must here be said belongs not so much in books as in liturgies.

All liturgy is sacramental, for merely by its communal character and by the formalization of discourse this imposes, the gospel in liturgy becomes a visible and not merely audible word, elements of the natural world (gestures, cups, books, etc.) are made to speak. And Jewish and Christian liturgy brings also history out of its sheer dumb givenness and makes it speak. Does it say anything to us that, for example, some Aramaean tribes escaped oppression in Egypt and founded a little state in Canaan? Outside liturgy, it can become extremely doubtful that it does; the past can lapse into silent brute fact. But in liturgy the exodus says liberation and unconditional love. In liturgy, nature

8 / THE HOLY SPIRIT

and history are brought into the proclamation of the gospel and into answering prayer and praise. That is, liturgy says with manifest sense that nature and history belong to the community in which Jesus' Spirit lives.

At the great thanksgiving of the eucharist, the great traditional orders are not content that only those gathered around a particular table should thank God for his divine works. That departed saints and absent saints join is almost obvious. But then even in restrained Western orders appear "angels and archangels." And more exuberant orders, as that of the Apostolic Constitution,[18] go on from the angels and archangels to catalogs of natural phenomena and historic events, not quite making these subjects who directly sing the praises, but also not quite leaving them as only occasions of our praising. In liturgy, natural and historical events appear with spirit; and this seems—there—to make sense.

What about liturgy enables such discourse to have a sense that it would not have as mere propositions on a page? The suggestion emerges from bits of the tradition and from experience of liturgy: it is in that liturgy is *art* that angels and archangels and streams and stars are spirited in it. Sung, "with angels and archangels," seems perfectly natural. Even in a said service, if the language of the great thanksgiving has poetic dignity, all is well. But when liturgical experimenters have tried to make the prayers relevant by reducing them to prose, the presiding minister feels foolish at such passages.

That beauty is thus a third cosmic reality of the Spirit perhaps gains some plausibility from the circumstance that this claim can be interpreted as a Hegelian synthesis of the two previous. On the one hand, beauty is obviously in some sense in the eye of the perceiver; it is a phenomenon of the life of people which we here have called history. Yet not only the products of our eyes, works of art, are beautiful, but also occasions of nature. And their beauty cannot be plausibly interpreted as merely subjective in us; it is somehow a real character of the beautiful occasions. Without solving the great philosophical problem thereby posed,[19] we simply observe what all have observed who have seriously pondered the matter: Beauty at once is a real character of certain objects, whether only natural or also historic, and is in those objects only for personal subjects. Beauty is not only both natural and historic; it transcends the distinction.

Identification of beauty as a cosmic reality of the Spirit appears already in Irenaeus, but thereafter it is a decidedly esoteric tradition. Perhaps the most noteworthy more recent instance of this tradition is the sophiology of Sergius Bulgakov.[20] As a Russian, Bulgakov was heir of the Palamitic-sophiological tradition of Russian-Byzantine thought;[21] but he was greatly influenced by German idealism and spent most of his career in Western Europe.

According to Bulgakov, the Spirit lives in the cosmos as an aspect of *Sophia*,[22] the divine Wisdom by which the Lord created all things according to Prov.

3:19. Divine Wisdom is the nature of God, insofar as this nature is love, and so must be also outside itself, to be an *object* of love, insofar, that is, as it is God's nature to reveal himself. Creation is an act of sacrifice by God, in that God by creation gives up self-sufficiency; and just so creation is an act of love, a revelation of God's nature, an actuality of Wisdom. And in that God loves the created cosmos—which God must, since it exists only for love— God sacrifices also his exclusive possession of Wisdom, so that she is not only God's Wisdom but the creature's, a created Wisdom that is the immanent meaning of the cosmos. Thus Wisdom is both the nature of God and the meaning of the creature.

Since Wisdom is God's self-revelation, the Son and the Spirit—the "persons" who in trinitarian theology reveal the Father—are in this scheme, at least with respect to creation, mere aspects of Wisdom. The Son, as God's rationality, is the content of Wisdom; within created Wisdom, he is the abstract plan of the cosmos. The Spirit is the life of Wisdom; in created Wisdom; the Spirit is the actual appearing and triumph of the cosmos' purpose, the joy of the cosmos—in a word, its beauty. "Through the Third hypostasis, God not only knows himself as the Truth . . . , but *lives* the Truth, *senses* the Truth. And the reality of sensed truth is beauty."[23]

To understand fully the Sophia-Spirit's association with beauty, we must know that Sophia is not primarily an intellectual construct but an *image* of visionary and iconic experience. She (and in the accounts it is "she"[24]) *appears*, as the Wisdom figure of the Proverbs, to those seeking the knowledge of God in visionary experience. In Western Europe, the chief tradition of such appearances is in German mysticism, where the vision also produced intellectual constructions strikingly like Bulgakov's.[25] In Russia, much of the impulse for Wisdom speculation is an esoteric iconographic tradition, in which Wisdom and the Mother of God blend.[26]

The alienation of this sort of experience and construction from the gospel is obvious. Sophia is a myth on the verge either of nonsense or of polytheism. And Sophia—not a trinitarian hypostasis—has explicitly reduced the Son and the Spirit to aspects of herself, meanwhile acquiring exactly the role attributed by pre-Nicene theology to its "Logos"; thus the Nicene achievement is undone. In this system, we are introduced to the world's Beauty not by an experience of the gospel about Christ, but by private vision. Where claims then follow about this Beauty such as those made by sophiology, this is surely an actual heresy. Yet once again this alienation may be that of an authentic Christian insight come loose from its proper object. We will again make our reclamation experiment.

Insofar as a proposition can here function as our thesis, it must be: The beauty of the world, natural or historic, is the cosmic actuality of *Jesus'* Spirit, is the world's occurring openness to the final triumph of his love. But the

8 / THE HOLY SPIRIT

meaningfulness of such a proposition is clearly fragile: What can one do with it? The proposition could perhaps achieve reliable form in a speculative analysis of beauty, but that cannot be our task here. Dogmatically, we suggest, the reclamation of the world's beauty for Jesus' particular Spirit can be asserted only liturgically; the propositional form of our thesis is only an instruction to do this.

The Beauty we here wish to acknowledge, the one that Jesus' Spirit is, does not introduce herself in private visionary or aesthetic experience. She introduces herself through the public liturgy of the congregation, where the gospel about Jesus is communally spoken, and just so necessarily spoken dramatically and by formalized and therefore heightened audible and visible words. The claim that the world's beauty is Christ's Spirit is thus appropriately made only by celebrating christological liturgy beautifully.

A liturgy is in any case a work of art, and a liturgical order (the rubrics and texts for liturgy which can appear in books and pamphlets) is instructions for works of art, like a musical score or a playbook. Liturgical experimenters of the sort who suppose that "relevance" or "communication" is achieved by imposing the language, tunes, and ceremonies of "everyday" do not succeed in making liturgies that are not works of art; they make only bad works of art, dispirited works of art, prisons for Jesus' Beauty. Therefore the beauty of a liturgy is not, as generally supposed in the contemporary church, a nice extra, adventitious to the essential function of the liturgy. By its beauty, liturgy says one of the things it must say to be an event of the gospel. By its beauty, liturgy reveals Jesus' Spirit as Beauty, and so as a wind blowing through all the world to open it to final transformation.

If we thus by liturgical beauty claim the world's beauty for Jesus' Spirit, much follows for the world's beauty. We will close by naming two areas of such consequences.

Ethically, Christians may not regard the world's beauty as a secondary value. In our bureaucratic capitalist and socialist societies, it is generally acknowledged that beauty is a good thing. But in the crunch, if, for example, conventional techniques will not allow a new apartment building to be both profitable and in appropriate scale with its neighbors, neither will there be much question which value is to be sacrificed, nor will much effort be invested in seeking new techniques. Believers may not share this attitude. For it would be the new building's appropriate scale that would be the building's present openness to the final human Habitation.

Aesthetically, identification of the world's beauty as Jesus' Spirit provides the axiom of a specific Christian aesthetic: The world is beautiful in that it will be Jesus' stage, in that it will make a "unitive work of all arts"[27] of liturgical praise to the one "that sits on the throne and the Lamb." We here have space to suggest the character of such an aesthetic by only one example: Since beauty is the Spirit of the Crucified and Risen One, mere suffering is never beautiful (e.g., the "theater of cruelty" is perverse), but neither is any suffering irredeemable (e.g., there are no limits to the suffering that the theater may appropriately embody and transform).

One closing remark to the whole *locus*: An entire theology could, as Karl Barth once observed,[28] be done as doctrine about the Spirit. Readers will have noted how each chapter of this *locus* approaches some other *locus* or *loci* of this work and must restrain itself lest approach become trespass. As "grace," the Spirit has been the chief theological impetus of the Latin church; as a trinitarian identity, the Spirit's reality has been the chief theological impetus of the trinitarian and christological dogmatics of the Greek church. The Spirit is in fact discussed throughout dogmatics. Our decision to make "The Holy Spirit" a *locus* of its own, contrary to the tradition, was more a decision to explicate a point of view than a decision to explicate a subject matter.

As to the particularity of this point of view, readers will by now perhaps not be put off if we say the particularity is hermeneutic. Pneumatology is the attempt to explicate the whole work of God as a communal reality among *us*. Pneumatology is the attempt to make Luther's insistence on "for *us*," as the condition of all meaningful discourse about God, be itself the vantage of that discourse. Whether this attempt can succeed, we must judge together—as a decision by the Spirit!

NOTES

1. This identification may have been facilitated by the general fluidity of Theophilus' distinction between the Logos and the Spirit; e.g., *To Autolycus*, 1,7; ii,22.

2. There apparently is Jewish tradition behind this. The identification of Wisdom and Spirit persists even through Tertullian, Eustathius of Antioch, and Origen. See Georg Kretschmar, *Studien zur frühchristlichen Trinitätstheologie* (Tübingen: J. C. B. Mohr [Paul Siebeck], 1956), pp. 40–61.

3. Irenaeus, *Against All Heresies,* iv,vii,4.

4. Hans-Jochen Jaschke, *Der Heilige Geist im Bekenntnis der Kirche* (Münster: Aschendorff, 1976), pp. 257–59.

5. Ibid., pp. 261ff.

6. Irenaeus, *Demonstration of the Apostolic Preaching*, 5.

7. Ibid., 97.

8. On Hegel in general, see Charles Taylor, *Hegel* (Cambridge: At the University Press, 1975).

9. Aristotelian fragment 46, 1483a,24–28: "*ho theos e nous estin e epekeina ti tou nou.*" The motionlessness of Mind *is* its deity; see Aristotle, *Metaphysics*, xiii,7–9.

10. Especially on the following, see Georg W. F. Hegel, *Phenomenology of Mind* ("mind" is a bad translation of "Geist"), trans. J. Baillie, 2d ed. (London: George

8 / THE HOLY SPIRIT

Allen & Unwin, 1931); *Lectures on the Philosophy of History*, trans. J. Sibree (London: H. G. Bohn, 1861), introd.

11. The writer's insistence is on "but also in that which is to come," but we note that "not only in this age, but" is also there.

12. On the profound ambiguity of Hegel's system at all such points, see, e.g., Hans Küng, *Menschwerdung Gottes* (Freiburg: Herder Verlag, 1970).

13. On this paragraph, see Robert W. Jenson, "The Kingdom of America's God," in *Religion and the Dilemma of Nationhood*, ed. Sydney E. Ahlstrom (Minneapolis: Lutheran Church in America, 1976), pp. 6–14.

14. E.g., Lewis S. Ford, *The Lure of God* (Philadelphia: Fortress Press, 1978), pp. 29–44, 99–112; G. Palmer Pardington III, "The Holy Ghost Is Dead—The Holy Spirit Lives," in *Religious Experience and Process Theology*, ed. Harry J. Cargas and Bernard Lee (New York: Paulist Press, 1976), pp. 121–38.

15. For the author's principle objections to process-theology, see his review of John Cobb's *Christ in a Pluralistic Age*, in *Interp.* 31 (1977): 307–11.

16. For a precise statement at the heart of the matter, see Hans Reichenbach, *Philosophic Foundations of Quantum Mechanics* (Berkeley: University of California, 1944), pp. 1–44.

17. E.g., Pierre Teilhard de Chardin, *The Future of Man*, trans. N. Denny (New York: Harper & Row, 1964).

18. Text in *Prex Eucharistica*, ed. A. Hänggi and J. Pahl (Freiburg: University of Freiburg, 1968), pp. 82–100.

19. Classically by Immanuel Kant, *Critique of Judgment*.

20. For the following, see, on our particular concern, Serge Boulgakof, *Le Paraclet*, trans. from the Russian by C. Andrioni (Paris: Aubier, 1946), pp. 171–219; a general description, concentrating on our range of topics and with all possible documentation, is given by Charles Graves, *The Holy Spirit in the Theology of Sergius Bulgakov* (Geneva: World Council of Churches, 1972).

21. John Meyendorff, *A Study of Gregory Palamas*, trans. G. Lawrence (Leighton Buzzard, Eng.: Faith Press, 1964); Vladimir Lossky, *The Vision of God*, trans. A. Moorhouse (Clayton, Wis.: American Orthodox Press, 1963), pp. 124–37; Leon Zander, "Die Weisheit Gottes im russischen Glauben und Denken," in *KuD* 2 (1956): 29–53.

22. On the following, Graves, *Holy Spirit*, pp. 7–29.

23. Boulgakof, *Le Paraclet*, p. 176.

24. Indeed, ibid., p. 179: "These masculine and feminine principles [from Gen. 1:27], where there is impressed the image of divine Wisdom, of prototypical humanity, are the translation into created language of the distinction and unity of the Logos and the Holy Spirit, in Wisdom."

25. Ernst Benz, "Sophia-Visionen des Westens," in *The Ecumenical World of Orthodox Civilization*, ed. Andrew Blane (The Hague: Mouton, 1974), pp. 121–38.

26. Zander, "Die Weisheit Gottes."

27. Wagner's ideal.

28. Karl Barth, *Die protestantische Theologie im 19. Jahrhundert*, 2d ed. (Zurich: Zollikon, 1952), pp. 411–12.

NINTH LOCUS

The Church

PHILIP HEFNER

THE CHURCH

Introduction

1. The Doctrine of the Church—Focus and Challenges
   The Trinitarian Context for the Doctrine of the Church
   Challenges Growing Out of the Church's Embodiment
   The Challenge to Correlate the Faith of the Church and Our
      Experience of the Church
   The Impossibility of Doctrinal Finality

2. The Being of the Church
   The Church's Own Testimony: One, Holy, Catholic, and Apostolic
   Significant Images from the Tradition: People of God and Body of Christ
   Models That Summarize the Theological Tradition: Institution,
      Mystical Communion, Sacrament, Herald, Servant
   The Being of the Church in Light of Its Origins

3. Basic Elements of the Church's Life
   Marks of the Church
   Ministry
   Liturgy and Sacraments
   Preaching and Teaching
   Community of Love and Care of Souls
   Mission
   Church Order or Organization
   The Church's Concreteness as Source of Theological Truth
   The Concept of Adiaphora

4. The Church and the Kingdom of God
   Possibilities for Relating Church and Kingdom of God
   The Church Transparent to the Kingdom

Introduction

The doctrine of the church aims at making a foundational statement about the church which qualifies as a genuinely theological statement. To qualify as such, the doctrine must speak about what the church is, in the light of what we believe about God. From a slightly different angle, the doctrine must single out the understanding of the church consistent with the Christian faith in God. The doctrine goes on to illumine the implications of that understanding.

So conceived, it becomes clear what the doctrine does not intend. The doctrine is not concerned primarily to speak about the church from perspectives other than those of Christian faith in God. Such other perspectives abound, because the church is a concrete, empirical community in the world of other earthly communities and organizations. There are thus as many perspectives on the church as there are angles of perception on earthly communities in general: sociological, social-psychological, economic, historical, philosophical, and so on. These perspectives are often of high interest, because they relate the theological understanding of the church to other worldly concerns, often in surprising ways.

The nontheological perspectives are necessary for the church's well-being in that they temper the arrogance and preoccupation with self that too often afflict us when we immerse ourselves totally in theological reflection on the church. After all, there are more angles to the church and its existence than the theological. The church's relationship to God is an embodied relationship, and this embodiment includes various dimensions—social, psychological, economic, political, physical—that form the basis for entire worlds of discourse about the church, that are themselves very largely not oriented on the church's existence before God.

Further, nontheological perspectives exercise a criticism that is salutary for the church. Peter Berger has referred to this critique as the "experience of alternation," "negative thinking," or debunking.[1] This experience derives from awareness that a society is not always or exclusively what it professes to be. Members of the society called the church are not exempt from this experience. Some of the most important prophetic insights into the church in our era,

9 / THE CHURCH

as well as significant impulses for reform, have had their origin in non-theological analyses of the church.

The doctrine of the church must be informed by sociological, psychological, political, and historical perspectives. The community on which the theologian reflects is the same community the sociologist observes. Furthermore, it is this community, sociologically and historically described, which is related to God, and not another. If the church that is described by doctrine does not bear an intimate resemblance to the church that is seen from other angles, doctrine will be unconvincing and deceptive.

Having observed both the fascination and the contribution of the non-theological perspectives, we must insist that the criteria for understanding and assessing the doctrinal discussion of the church are different from those that apply to the other discussions. Among the illicit expectations that might be laid on doctrinal discussion of the church is that it solve many concrete problems that have arisen in the church. The doctrine of the church will not disclose which rendition of the liturgy ought to be implemented now, nor which organizational form is optimum for a projected merger of churches, nor which method of missionary evangelizing is best for a given time and place. Rather, the doctrine will serve to inform the process by which such judgments are made; it is the foundation from which the judgments proceed and the basis on which they must be justified or rejected. Doctrine forms the rationale for dealing with concrete problems and practice. There is no direct transition from doctrine to practice, precisely because theology views the church above all in its relationship to God, a relationship that is capable of many different embodiments, whereas practice is anchored in one particular embodied form.

It is not altogether clear just where within a theological system the doctrine of the church belongs. It is possible, for example, to begin with *christology*, inasmuch as the church is often said to be an extension of Christ in the world and to have been founded by Christ. When this position is adopted, the church's Christ-identity and Christ-status are emphasized.

The *doctrine of the Holy Spirit* may be the framework within which the church is brought on the doctrinal stage. Pentecost, the festival of the Spirit, is often considered to be the day of the church's origin. Others, like Luther in his Small Catechism and like the Augsburg Confession and its Apology, emphasize that the church consists of the believers and saints who have been "called, gathered, and enlightened" by the Holy Spirit. This approach emphasizes the freedom of the Spirit to move within the church and to move the church in unexpected ways, as the will of God requires.

The *doctrine of the Word* has received prominence in the last fifty years as the proper context for considering the church. The Word of God is in this case held to be the foundation of the church. In the service of the Word—its

INTRODUCTION

promulgation and its power to achieve God's will—the church finds its purpose and the rationale for its practice.

Still other theologians have begun their theological discussion of the church with the *means of grace*. Heinrich Schmid presents the ecclesiology of the orthodox Lutheran dogmaticians of the sixteenth and seventeenth centuries in this context.[2] The church consists most genuinely of believers and saints who have been gathered by the Spirit through the means of grace. The chief emphasis, therefore, is on the form this community should take, in order to be a fit vehicle of the means of grace. The criteria for judging such a community and for ensuring the purity of the means of grace form the content of the doctrine.

Each of these options presents important grounds for locating the doctrine of the church within the theological system. In this *locus*, however, still another route is followed: the *doctrine of the Trinity*. This doctrine is chosen as the one which properly locates the church, because it is *the* Christian doctrine of God and as such is the point of orientation for all genuinely *theo*logical discourse, and because it incorporates all the basic thrusts of the four other options.

NOTES

1. Peter Berger, *The Precarious Vision* (Garden City, N.Y.: Doubleday & Co., 1961), chaps. 1–2. See also James M. Gustafson, *Treasure in Earthen Vessels: The Church as a Human Community* (New York: Harper & Row, 1961).

2. Heinrich Schmid, *The Doctrinal Theology of the Evangelical Lutheran Church*, trans. Charles A. Hay and Henry E. Jacobs (1875; reprint ed., Minneapolis: Augsburg Publishing House, 1961).

1

The Doctrine of the Church— Focus and Challenges

The church is best understood within the context of the doctrine of the Trinity. That doctrine places the church within the work of God's Spirit in this world, to embody the meanings and rationale that God wishes to actualize for creation. Since those meanings are focused in the Logos, incarnate in Jesus Christ, the church is thoroughly christocentric in its nature.

THE TRINITARIAN CONTEXT FOR THE DOCTRINE OF THE CHURCH

To set the proper doctrinal context for our consideration of the church, it is helpful to remind ourselves of the basic structure of the trinitarian vision of God and state the way we mean to employ it. The trinitarian dogma is at once the normative Christian understanding of God and the basic vision of the world and its relation to God. The dogma speaks directly of God, while by implication it sets forth what Christians hold the world to be as a consequence of their vision of God.

The first person of the Trinity symbolizes the numinous mystery of God, what Rudolf Otto spoke of as the *mysterium tremendum et fascinosum*, the God of such power that no one can look on this God and live.[1] In the religious traditions of humankind, including those of Judaism and Christianity, it is not clear whether this powerful Mystery is beneficent or hostile. It is not clear what God's purposes are, nor indeed whether God is purposeful at all.

The second person, known as the Logos, is precisely the revelation and articulation of the purpose and meaning (the *ratio*) of this God. Thus it can be said that this Logos is the principle of intelligibility (*ordo intelligendi*) of God and hence of all reality.[2] The stoic philosophers spoke of the Logos embedded in the world's process, the World Mind, which accounted for the order of the world and for the correlation between the order and the human

9 / THE CHURCH

mind. Christian philosophers and theologians made a monumental contribution to and modification of classical philosophy by asserting that this Logos is Jesus Christ. As God's activity of articulating the divine rationale, the Logos can be said to be *homoousios*, of the same substance, with God. Indeed, this Logos is best understood *as* God.

The third person is the ordering principle of the realm of nature and history. This realm is referred to in classical philosophy as the *ordo vivendi* (order of life). The rationale of this *ordo vivendi* is one and the same as that which was revealed and articulated in the Logos. The third person is the embodiment, the actualization of God's meaning within the realm of natural and historical processes. Christians have identified this actualizing power with the Holy Spirit. As such they can affirm that this power too is truly God, as God is intrinsically involved in actualizing God's purposes. They also point to the sense in which the Spirit unifies the Godhead, bringing God's primordial being and purpose together in natural and historical actualization. These affirmations are central to the Christian faith, even though the faithful are fully aware that nature and history are shot through with evil.

Each of the "persons" in the trinitarian view of God is ultimate reality, what classically was known as *archē*, "first principle." That is to say, it is not the case that one of the persons is primary while the others are subordinate to that one, nor that one or two are elaborations or explications of a primary *archē*. Rather, all three are primary, foundational, and as such they constitute the basic structure and dynamic of all of reality.

This has several important implications. First, there is a certain finality or necessity in this threefold process, because it represents the process of God's being God. The three persons, or the three ways of God's being God, are the unfolding of God's own nature or being.[3] Intrinsic to the primordial being of the *mysterium*-God (First Person) is the articulation of the rationale of the Godhead (Second Person), and the actualization of God's own purposes in concreteness (Third Person). Second, the unfolding of God's being in the trinitarian framework thus belongs both to the fundamental character of reality and to the historical development of that reality. In classical terms, we say that this triune character of God is both ontological and revelational or "economic." Third, since the creating, sustaining, and consummating of the world is part both of the articulation of God's meanings and of the actualization of those meanings, this vision of God becomes a vision of the world as well. Creation and its fulfillment in the eschaton are associated with and taken up into both the second and third persons, and as such the basic character of nature and history is formed by the divine career itself. It is of the nature of God that he creates and that he actualizes himself in sustaining and perfecting what he created. It is therefore essential to the created order of nature and history that it be created and that it be sustained and perfected by the same power that created it in the first place. This constitutes a thoroughly theological understanding of the world, inasmuch as its being and development are perceived only under the aspect of God and God's being. It is not an exalted understanding of the world that drives us to the trinitarian view of God. Rather, the trinitarian vision of God compels us to an understanding of the world that places it within God's own career of being God.

The third of these implications is of great importance for understanding the church in theological perspective. The church is a concrete entity within the created order. Its existence, therefore, occurs within the realm of the third *archē*, the realm of nature and history and of the Holy Spirit. *This means that what happens in the church is best located and assessed when we say that it belongs to God's actualizing of the divine purposes in the concrete realm of nature and history.* The church is an instance of God's actualizing his rationale, in coexistence with the rest of the world which he has created and which he sustains and will finally bring to perfection.

The content that God actualizes is the rationale articulated in the Logos, Jesus Christ. The realm of the Spirit, that of nature and history, is itself also inscrutable; it may appear either beneficent or wrathful, arbitrary or absurd. It is only the actualization within the processes of nature and history of the divine meaning that gives confidence that the world is ultimately a part of our fulfillment rather than our devastation. The church is part of this substantive content that is actualized in the world. Its rationale is consistent with the rationale set forth in Christ.

With this latter insight we come near to the distinctiveness of the church. The church is the community that is explicitly centered on the articulation and revelation of God's purposes in Jesus Christ. This centeredness is the decisive dimension of the church's identity, life, and meaning. Consequently it holds itself accountable to the articulation of the divine rationale in Christ and draws its life from that source. The *locus* of the church's existence is the processes that actualize the divine rationale; this it shares with all its coexistents in the created order. What is distinctive to the church is not that it is caught up in that actualizing, nor that the Christ-rationale is actualized in its life; these belong equally to all created entities, according to the trinitarian view. What is distinctive to the church is that it intentionally takes as its raison d'être the explicit witness to the Christ-rationale as the key to understanding the entire process of nature and history.

With this we have arrived at a genuinely theological understanding of the church: Within the process of God's unfolding his being and purposes in concrete actuality, the church is that community whose very essence consists of the explicit witness to God's being and purposes as they have been articulated in Jesus Christ. This understanding of the church follows from what we believe about God, as that belief is set forth in the trinitarian dogma. Everything

9 / THE CHURCH

we say about the church in what follows is to be assessed by this primary theological affirmation. This affirmation, it must be remembered, is not an empirical description of the church, although it shares some elements with a possible empirical description, chiefly when it speaks about the content of the church's witness to Christ. Similarly, our basic affirmation is not an attempt to glorify the church in the face of the manifest discrepancy between our affirmations about the church and its actual existence. Rather, we affirm the theological concept of the church, which applies to the church despite the blemishes and ambiguities that are obvious.

Against the background of our primary theological affirmation, we can understand two other traditional affirmations, of the preexistence and the eternity of the church. If the church is what we have said, within the trinitarian framework, then God must have always intended the church, and in this sense the church is preexistent. God can never not have been God. God can never have been without the essential being which moves toward the actualization of his own articulated *ratio*.

Similarly, the rationale of God can never perish or disappear, even with the consummation of the creation which has served both the articulation and the actualization of God's being and meaning. The church therefore can never disappear, if it is constituted by witness to what and who God is within the process of his self-actualization. Neither of these statements should be interpreted except as theological affirmations. They do not mean that any concrete congregation, agency, or entire church body is preexistent or eternal. Since these affirmations are theological, they become finally statements about God: God is consistent with God; God has never not been God, nor will his final work with the world cease to be utterly expressive of the divine being and purpose. That the theological statements about the church collapse on themselves does not distress us, because that is precisely what genuinely *theo*logical assertions always do, become finally transparent to the one God.

Jürgen Moltmann is one of the few theologians who utilizes the trinitarian doctrine as the context for theological consideration of the church. Although his discussion follows the same formal lines as ours, he puts material content into the Christ-*ratio*: "The meaning of his giving himself to death on the cross is the liberation of the sinner from the burden of sin by virtue of reconciliation; and his liberation from the power of sin by virtue of substitution."[4] This liberation theme is certainly not uncongenial to the position we affirm, but we choose to state matters formally, so the theological character of the church is clear regardless of how one interprets the Christ-rationale.

Furthermore, Moltmann puts eschatological content into the processes of nature and history in a vivid manner.[5] Eschatology is basic to the view we have set forth, in that we speak of God's unfolding toward the consummation of the creation in accordance with God's fulfillment of his being. The

THE DOCTRINE OF THE CHURCH—FOCUS AND CHALLENGES

concepts of "unfolding," "consummation of creation," and the fulfillment of God's being through them are eschatological thrusts, which conceive of the final fulfillment as the decisive category for church and world. Therefore, we can agree with Moltmann's final statement:

> The church as the community of justified sinners, the fellowship of those liberated by Christ, who experience salvation and live in thanksgiving, is on the way to fulfilling the meaning of the history of Christ. With its eyes fixed on Christ, it lives in the Holy Spirit and thus is itself the beginning and earnest of the future of the new creation.[6]

We recall, however, that fixing on Christ itself takes place within the trinitarian framework of God's articulating activity in Christ. Further, it is important to recognize that nature is a dimension of history, so that the historical emphasis does not lose its cosmic dimensions.

CHALLENGES GROWING OUT OF THE CHURCH'S EMBODIMENT

There are challenges in each epoch of history in the face of which doctrine must offer theological resources that can be usefully appropriated. The church as an entity in the life of God may be eternal, but no doctrinal conceptualization or formulation is. The shape of the terrain in which the church exists in any given epoch contributes its contours to the actual form that the doctrine of the church takes in that period and to the way the doctrine is understood. The four following challenges grow out of the present epochal terrain and exert pressures on the doctrine. There may be several ways in which doctrine may respond to these challenges; but respond it must if it is to take root.

Ecclesia semper reformanda est has been a watchword of the Reformation tradition. It states the church's need for continual renewal and the fact that in a dynamic world, informed by God's lively word and presence, the church is never static and cannot make permanent the forms that prove effective in any particular time and place. Pope John XXIII said that the Second Vatican Council was convoked to open the church's windows and let in some fresh air. This image is appropriate to a time when the world is undergoing massive transitions that point to a new epoch whose lineaments are only dimly perceived by even the most serious and experienced observers. The image is fitting as well to a church that in many parts of the world is on the brink of new forms and insights, weary under centuries-old forms and assumptions that have grown ineffective at best and more often perverse. In other parts of the globe, younger churches find the ground moving so rapidly under their feet that they are not so much weary of existing forms as they are struggling

9 / THE CHURCH

first to find indigenous forms. In any case, the reform of the church is very much to the fore throughout Christianity. Where there is resistance to reform, laity groan, participation lags, and the church isolates itself in its own ghetto of ethnic and sectarian indulgence.

If the church is located in God's actualizing of his being and purposes, then reform is built into the church's nature. God's unfolding is irresistible and scornful of every superficiality, of every sentimental attachment for its own sake to what is old and familiar, of every attempt to grasp at permanence when the tide of God's unfolding demands another sort of obedience. The church's task is not so much to preserve the old as to be prepared to be obedient wherever God's unmanipulable and surprising ways lead. A doctrine of the church that does not embrace reform as central to the church's life cannot hope to be adequate.

The church today is literally a global church, a church "on six continents." Only in the last fifty years has this become true. In previous times, even though the language of universality and of outreach to the ends of the earth was used, the church was far from being worldwide in the literal sense. Even in the early twentieth century, when there was a church in every region, the churches were sometimes little more than outposts of foreign agencies. A number of important implications derive from the actual global nature of the church in our time.

First. The worldwide character of the church intensifies the sense that the church has a mission to press beyond all societal and cultural boundaries into new areas, geographically and culturally, that the church *is* mission. Churches that bear the mark of different cultures and societies rub shoulders in a way that keeps the missionary dimension of the church always before us. At the same time, our perception of the mission is considerably modified. It is increasingly recognized that no church is so strong, well-established, and pure that it might not need to become the recipient of the mission activity of some other church. Similarly, churches in formerly colonial areas of the world are no longer puppets of northern-hemisphere churches; they can undertake their own mission outside their lands. The worldwide character of the church demonstrates that the mission which constitutes the church is a relationship of reciprocity; mission is a two-way street.

Second. The mission of the church is now most likely to be the mission of a church to its own culture and society. If a church reaches out beyond its own cultural borders, it is to assist other churches in their own mission, not to do that mission in their stead. This means that nearly every culture of the world is now, in many areas for the first time, experiencing the impact of an indigenous church. The obverse of this is that *the* church is now constituted by churches that are indigenous to every culture of the world. *The* church is a blend of cultures, even though it professes one faith.

Third. The encounter of Christianity with the world's other religions is important in the new era. The encounter is no longer simply between those religions and the Christianity of Westerners who have no real personal stake in any religion except their own. Rather, the encounter is now with Christians whose own culture is an authentic meeting place of more than one religion. Indeed, for Asian and African Christians it is instead the case that their own culture, the culture that has shaped them and their social environment, is profoundly informed by a religion other than Christianity. In such cases, the culture to which Christianity seeks to become indigenous is not religiously neutral; it is molded by another great religion.

Fourth. In the efforts of the churches to penetrate their own cultures and be faithful to their own mission, they have in recent decades become aware that that mission calls for world-renewing activity as much as for evangelizing as such. In the 1960s and 1970s this experience gave rise to the debate over evangelization versus humanization. In the late 1970s and the 1980s, the same experience is raising the question whether the church ought not to participate in overt social and political activity which seems necessary for the well-being of their societies. Teilhard de Chardin developed a broad theological foundation for "building the world" as the most urgent and authentic activity Christians ought to engage in.[7]

The debate today is whether such a view is consistent with the faith. Those who object to the church's being involved in such world-renewing activities argue that the faith of the church is transcendent vis-à-vis all societies and all epochal situations; if the church fails to keep that faith in its transcendent purity, it has betrayed its most fundamental mission. On the other side it is argued that faithful witness to God's revelation in Christ in our time cannot be made if that witness does not participate in the renewal or re-creation of situations in which life is rendered marginal by poverty, hunger, injustice, oppression, and the like. The trinitarian framework helps us understand that the former position represents the wholesome desire to concentrate on the Christ-rationale in all circumstances, and that the latter position embraces the reality of God's unfolding the divine purposes within the concrete structures of nature and history. We respect both, although the overall direction of our discussion is toward responsible world-renewing activity as the way in which the church participates in God's own unfolding.[8]

Fifth. Mission to penetrate culture brings the church up against the phenomenon of secularization. The modern era has seen the irreversible secularization of most aspects of Western life. Such designations of our period as "the post-Christian era" serve to register the awareness that we tend no longer to need a religious "code" by which to account for our experience and understand it well enough for everyday living. Sickness, the weather, interpersonal relationships, development of the personality, and many other signifi-

9 / THE CHURCH

cant elements of everyday life can be taken at their face value and interpreted by reference to immanent causes rather than by supernatural processes.

Secularization does not mean that basic realities which people have experienced in their religious life are suddenly false or even incredible. The graciousness of life, the ability to endure under hardship, the experience of unmerited love from others—these realities, all central to religious perception, are as significant as ever. Nor has belief in God been suddenly disproved. One may still live with faith in the God who creates and sustains, and flourish in the midst of secularization.

The basic challenge of secularization to religious faith is to assert, proclaim, clarify, and conceptualize religious realities in the terms and thought forms of secularized social consciousness. Unless the faith is translated into such terms, the world in its secularized phase will find the faith unavailable. How is transcendence to be formulated in a world dominated by immanent causes? How is *sola gratia* to be understood by a self-consciousness which understands that human beings do in significant ways "make themselves" in their social and technological achievements? How does the church demonstrate its faith when its action in obedience to the command to show love and make things new can be made effective only in programs that appear to be thoroughly secular in their conception, procedures, and outcome?

Dietrich Bonhoeffer spoke of "worldly Christianity." He was often misinterpreted, as if he were putting aside religious faith, life, and churchly existence. On the contrary, he maintained these elements in his own life and called for us to probe the possibilities of talking about them in ways consistent with the secularized consciousness of the self and the world.[9]

It is essential that the doctrine of the church be able to address credibly these considerations of mission, world renewal, and secularization. The doctrine must speak relevantly of the church's being within the context of these elements. The challenges all emerge from the church's interaction with its social and cultural world and from the attempt to penetrate that world in accordance with the mission that is given to the church. The substance of the challenges is that the world which the church seeks to penetrate makes an impact on the church in the most intimate manner. The world becomes a part of the church in nearly every respect. Our placement of the church within the process of God's own actualizing of his being and purposes enables us to perceive that within the Third-Person realm all worldly phenomena are somehow caught up in God's own unity of meaning and direction. What the church means, therefore, occurs only within the network of its actual relationships to its natural and historical coexistents, within the Third-Person realm. Since all these entities are part of God's processes, the church can expect that it will not find its coexistents totally alien. This insight forms the ground for the church's experience that its cultural environment actually shapes and determines the church's understanding of and witness to the gospel. The doctrine of the church must provide the capability for understanding this reciprocal interaction between church and world.[10]

The burgeoning of the *ecumenical movement* in our century has brought us to the point where the oneness of the church is not only a value which we honor but a vivid image which we cannot avoid. Only the most sectarian groups can entertain the notion publicly and theologically that the authentic church is coterminous with any particular church or assembly of churches. The movement within the World Council of Churches and between communions, like Roman Catholicism, who are outside the council has been from openness to learn from others, through tolerance of diversity, to a kind of conciliarism which insists that diversity should not be a hindrance to unity. Dialogue has been established and authenticated. Now the call is to go beyond dialogue, even though the parties are not clear what the "beyond" includes. It becomes clearer every year that the life of the various churches is so intertwined that what happens in one affects the entire ecumenical body. Such a state of affairs is wholesome for the church, because it liberates it from sectarianism, even as it opens up a richer variety of ecclesial expressions, enhancing thereby the life of the whole and of each individual church.

The ecumenical movement challenges the very ground on which the individual churches judge what is "the church" and thereby liberates the churches from their own judgment and narrowness. Roman Catholicism's criterion that authenticity depends on obedience given to the Holy See; Anglicanism's criterion of tradition; Lutheranism's insistence on doctrinal consensus; the Free Churches' insistence that conscience or the stance of the free mind serves as criterion—all are simultaneously affirmed, but none is allowed to rule as sole arbiter. The *being* of the churches is allowed, and their perdurance gives us pause when we consider what this plurality means for our fundamental understanding of the church.

Finally on this line, we must consider the church as a political entity. The church, precisely because its explicit self-awareness is so firmly rooted in so powerful a frame of meaning as the Christ-rationale, has over the centuries taken its own authenticity for granted. Because its center of meaning is so powerful and so unselfishly good, the church has for the most part acted on the premise that, whatever it says and does, its intentions and actions are without further ado expressive of the meaning articulated in Christ. Even when it admits that its perceptions and actions are mistaken or sinful, it interprets the error exclusively within the framework of an interior wrestling, within the church community itself, with the question of how Christ's meaning is to be perceived and acted on. The church tends to insist that its actions be interpreted solely as part of its own religious pilgrimage.

Slowly but surely, the rise of what is now called "critical" thinking has taken

9 / THE CHURCH

away the privilege of the church, or of any other group or institution, to interpret itself so naively. This mode of thinking calls attention to the fact that every person, group, or institution consciously or unconsciously finds a niche in its world which aids its survival. This is natural and is required for survival. Survival requires, however, that certain features of life in that niche be cared for, maintained, and developed, so that the group itself can endure. These features of the niche may or may not be intimately related to the central meanings of the group or institution that exists there. Since, however, they are necessary for survival, they are sustained even if they otherwise are not related to the raison d'être of the surviving institution.[11]

When the church pours energy and time into the effort to survive in its niche, it finds that the features of the niche become intrinsic elements of its own shape. Furthermore, it finds itself adjusting its priorities to maintain the niche. All this is part of what it means for the church to be *embodied* in its world, and the processes of survival that we describe here are unavoidable.

The church finds itself, within the framework we have just noted, serving unavoidably interests other than that of the Christ-rationale to which it professes its explicit devotion. Its support of these interests has a social and political impact that may or may not be commensurate with the church's stated intentions. So, for example, when the niche that the world offered the church in the fourth century was that of *institution*, survival required the church to assume the institutional style and expend energy to keep the institutional structure alive and well. Thus the church, whatever its stated aims and wishes, made an impact on the world that was institutional in form. Again, in the Reformation, the Lutheran church found its niche as an institution within certain German provinces, playing a role that was desirable in the eyes of the rulers and that the latter therefore supported. Without this niche, so it seemed, the Lutheran movement would not have survived. Despite the fortissimo proclamation of "Christ alone" "Grace alone" and "Scripture alone" Lutherans also had the impact on the world of a politically favored institution and were inwardly shaped in that form. Finally, we point to the niche in the nineteenth century in Europe, which pressed the church to take the antirevolutionary stance in nearly every revolutionary situation. The consequence, contrary to what the church explicitly preached, was an inevitable bias for the favored ruling classes and groups, accompanied by a tilt against the working and peasant classes.

Critical reflection does not allow us to forget this political character of the church. Nearly every item of belief and practice that makes life possible for the church in this world becomes also an occasion for it to serve an interest not directly subservient to the gospel. The task of the church now is to distinguish between its obedience to the Christ-rationale and the concrete forms of its faith and action, not because the concrete forms are a matter of indifference but rather in order to be critical in directing those forms in a manner consistent with the church's aims. The church, like other groups, *can* redirect its own existence in a way that seems more appropriate to the gospel it represents.[12]

Several trends in theology today aim at pressing the church to be critical in the manner we are speaking of, and they offer assistance to this end. "Political theology" reminds the church that it can never evade the social-political realm. This school of theology urges the church to be aware of its political embeddedness, to perceive how the gospel is mediated to the church and by the church through the forms of the niche, forms that may be biased themselves, and to criticize those forms. "Liberation theology" presses the church to take action that will counter the interests foreign to the gospel, supporting counterbalancing or compensatory forms. For example, as an institution in Latin America the church is naturally inclined toward the dominant classes who are agents of injustice and oppression. Liberation theology argues that that institutional form may be turned to the benefit of the struggling classes who seek justice and equity. If that turnaround does not take place, the church should consider forsaking its institutional form and assume a less forceful one. When the forms of the niche are abandoned, the church faces disruption, even extinction. It must quickly find another niche, with alternative opportunities for developing strategies for survival and embodiment of the Christ-rationale.

Such reflection suggests to us that the embodiments of the church in its niches are the medium both of the church's receiving the revelatory message of its purpose and also of its communicating that message to the world. The embodiment cannot be avoided or taken for granted. It can, however, be critically assessed, and alterations can be reflectively undertaken. The doctrine of the church must render intelligible this phenomenon of the niche. It is incumbent on the doctrine of the church to facilitate this critical process rather than hinder it. Further, the doctrine must offer criteria for assessing old forms and projecting new ones.

THE CHALLENGE TO CORRELATE THE FAITH OF THE CHURCH AND OUR EXPERIENCE OF THE CHURCH

The embodiment of the Christ-rationale in this world of nature and history has always caused a certain puzzlement and embarrassment to the church. At times this embarrassment is due to the manifest error and even sinfulness of the church, which stand at variance with the aims and faith of the church. In such instances, the church does not want to be defined as synonymous with these unfaithful manifestations. At other times, the church is more aware

9 / THE CHURCH

of its incompleteness and longs for the time when, in God's fulfillment, it renders its fullest glory and praise to God. At still other times, the church is puzzled when it discovers Godlikeness or churchly traits in individuals and groups outside its precincts. In Mark 9:38-40, we read of the disciples encountering a man who cast out devils in Jesus' name, even though he was not of their number. Jesus' response to their puzzlement is reported: "Do not forbid him . . . for he that is not against us is for us." With these considerations we touch on what is perhaps the thorniest issue for the doctrine of the church: There is an inevitable and irremediable tension between what our faith tells us about the church and what we do in fact experience of the church. On the one hand, the church is inevitably an *embodied* community, while on the other hand, no set of embodiments adequately expresses what the church believes about itself.

The tradition of the church's reflection on its embarrassment has provided an extensive terminology with which to understand such phenomena. The most prominent is perhaps the distinction between the *visible* and the *invisible* church. The Lutheran tradition has relied considerably on this distinction. Leonhard Hutter writes:

> If you consider the outward fellowship of signs and rites of the Church, the Church Militant is said to be *visible*, and embraces all those who are within the assembly of the called, whether they be godly or ungodly, whether they be elect or reprobate. But if you consider the Church in so far as it is a fellowship of faith and of the Spirit dwelling in the hearts of believers, it is said to be *invisible*, and is peculiar to the elect.[13]

The Lutherans were caught up in the effort to explain the church of the sixteenth century—as well as in the following centuries—which was an established church that encompassed the entire population with the exception of the Jews. The *corpus christianum* still existed as a dominant notion at the time of the Reformation, and the principle *cuius regio, cuius religio* (whose rule, his religion) did not alter its force in the everyday life of a region. Everyone was a member of the church, by birth and by social custom. It was therefore perfectly clear that not everyone in the church was motivated by pure devotion to the faith. Furthermore, flagrant immorality was present in the church in such a situation and had to be accounted for.

The visible/invisible category made some sense out of such an experience of the church. The intention was never to bifurcate the church, as if visible and invisible referred to two churches that existed side by side. John Gerhard wrote:

> We do not affirm that there are two churches, the one true and internal, and the other nominal and external; but we say that the Church is one and the same,

viz., the entire assembly of the called considered in a twofold manner, namely, from within and from without. . . . In the former manner and respect we grant that even hypocrites and those who are not saints belong to the Church; but in the latter manner and respect we contend that only true believers and saints belong to it.[14]

This was an acknowledgment that we cannot see into people's hearts and discern their motivations and commitments. The parable of the wheat and the tares provided biblical warrant. God permits both good and evil to grow together in the same community until God is ready to separate them. In this worldly life, we are to permit both to flourish. Augustine had made the same point with the same terminology in the controversy with the Donatists, in which he argued that the church is a "mixed body," a *corpus permixtum*. This doctrine has become an essential part of orthodox Christian theology. It exercises an antipuritanical, antirigoristic influence.[15]

The polarity between *ecclesia late et stricta dicta* (the church broadly and strictly spoken of) treats the same problem. The *ecclesia late* referred to the entire body of church adherents. *Ecclesia stricta* designated only the believers and the saints, the elect who are the genuine church.

In contemporary theology, Paul Tillich has explored the polarity to which the classical terms refer, distinguishing the *sociological* and the *theological* aspects of the church. He introduces his distinction: "The paradox of the churches is the fact that they participate, on the one hand, in the ambiguities of life in general and of the religious life in particular and, on the other hand, in the unambiguous life of the Spiritual Community."[16]

Tillich's term "spiritual community" refers to the essential character of the church as the body of Christ. This essential reality is not visible, nor is it a separate entity alongside existing communities. Rather, it is the "power and the structure inherent and effective" in religious communities, enabling them to be the Body of Christ, whether they are Christian churches or not.[17] The sociological aspect of the churches is the acknowledgment that the religious community is subject to the same ambiguities and dynamics of social groups that all other social entities are. The theological aspect refuses to accept the sociological as being the sole and exclusive truth, although it does not deny the sociological character of the church.

These terms operate to clarify how it is that the church can fall below its own best goals and self-understanding. The terms *latent/manifest* and *ecclesia militans/ecclesia triumphans* (church militant/church triumphant) speak to the sense in which the church feels itself incomplete but moving toward fullness. Tillich has used the former polarity, latent/manifest, to great effect. He uses it to distinguish between a group's life *before* it encounters the power

9 / THE CHURCH

of God in a decisive manner, and a group that has had such an encounter. The latent groups are secular associations that have not come to terms with the revelation of Christ but that participate in God's power of unfolding his being in the world. These groups are not complete in their knowledge of God and hence, although they play a significant role in prodding and criticizing the church, they are open to profanization and demonization, because they will not come clean on their affirmation of the creator of Jesus Christ. These groups are *incomplete* churches, in the sense that they are not yet church, even though they participate in the power of God.[18]

The categories of church "militant" and "triumphant" speak to the church's awareness about itself, that it is in the midst of struggle that is the result of its imperfection. In the realm of eternal blessedness the church can live fully. Here on earth it must wait and work.

The doctrine of the church cannot be framed in such a way as to overcome the tension between our faith in the church and our experience of it. Nor can the doctrine be effortlessly incarnated in practice. The doctrine must, however, enable us to understand the tension, how and why it is intrinsic to the church, and how it fits into God's unfolding.

THE IMPOSSIBILITY OF DOCTRINAL FINALITY

The final challenge here discussed is that of intrinsic incompleteness in the church's process of defining itself. The church cannot attain doctrinal finality in describing itself, because it never stops growing and because there is no one set of criteria, images, or models of the church which can preserve all the church wishes to preserve.

Avery Dulles, in *Models of the Church*, has given us a full description of that mystery of the church which will not allow it to be exhausted in one final doctrine or image.[19] He sets forth five basic models, which cover all the major images of the church that have arisen over the centuries: institutional, mystical communion, sacrament, herald, and servant. After comparing them and concluding that all are true renditions of some aspect of the church, he writes:

> Without asserting that the five models studied in this book are the only possible ones, I would be skeptical of the possibility of finding any one model that would be truly adequate. . . . *We are therefore condemned to work with models that are inadequate to the reality to which they point.*[20]

Dulles has already insisted that images and models are more suitable for dealing with the mystery of the church than are propositions and doctrines as such. Therefore his conclusion is a challenge to theology to be alert to its own intrinsic inadequacy for dealing with the doctrine of the church, even when it works at the level of basic images.

Dulles does suggest that the various models can be blended "in such a way that their differences become complementary rather than mutually repugnant."[21] This includes the resolve to refrain "from so affirming any one of the models as to deny, even implicitly, what the others affirm." Dulles's axiom is enormously important. Since the models of the church refer back to actual concrete understandings of the church—understandings held by real people and ecclesial groupings—the injunction to blend the models is a call to bring these actual groupings into dialogue and interaction. The call to refrain from excluding any single model means that the legitimacy of all the groupings, so far as their conceptual understanding of church is concerned, is accepted. This is the same conclusion we drew earlier from the challenge of ecumenism. One can never hope to achieve a doctrine that can comprehend the whole. Rather, one hopes to bring all the various conceptions of the church into a harmony that will create a whole but not destroy any of the models.

Dulles's conclusion does not surprise us. We would expect, if the church is located in the unfolding of God in this world, that it would defy easy conceptual theological comprehension. Yet the unity of the models is necessary, since they witness to the unfolding *ratio* of the same one God. A doctrine of the church must explain how Dulles's conclusion is possible, while at the same time providing the basis for speaking of one church under one God.

NOTES

1. Rudolf Otto, *The Idea of the Holy* (1923; New York and London: Oxford University Press, 1958).

2. Charles Norris Cochrane, *Christianity and Classical Culture* (London: Oxford University Press, 1944), esp. chap. 11.

3. R. P. C. Hanson, *God: Creator, Saviour, Spirit* (London: SCM Press, 1960).

4. Jürgen Moltmann, *The Church in the Power of the Spirit: A Contribution to Messianic Eschatology*, trans. M. Kohl (New York: Harper & Row, 1977), p. 30.

5. Ibid., pp. 37–50 and passim.

6. Ibid., p. 33.

7. Pierre Teilhard de Chardin, *Building the Earth* (Wilkes-Barre, Pa.: Dimension Books, 1965).

8. Carl E. Braaten, *The Flaming Center* (Philadelphia: Fortress Press, 1978).

9. Dietrich Bonhoeffer, *Letters and Papers from Prison*, ed. E. Bethge, trans. R. H. Fuller (New York: Macmillan Co., 1972).

10. Philip Hefner, "Ecological Perspectives on Communicating the Gospel," *Lutheran World* 16 (1969): 322–38.

11. Jürgen Habermas, *Knowledge and Human Interests* (London: William Heinemann, 1972).

12. Moltmann, *Church in the Power of the Spirit*, esp. chap. 2.
13. Leonhard Hutter, *Loci*, 194, in Heinrich Schmid, *The Doctrinal Theology of the Evangelical Lutheran Church*, trans. Charles A. Hay and Henry E. Jacobs (Minneapolis: Augsburg Publishing House, 1961), pp. 592–93.
14. John Gerhard, *Confessio Catholica*, in Schmid, *Doctrinal Theology*, p. 592.
15. Augustine, *Contra Litteras Petiliani*, chaps. 94, 174, and passim; in *NPNF* 4, "St. Augustine Against the Manichaeans and the Donatists."
16. Paul Tillich, *Systematic Theology*, 3 vols. (Chicago: University of Chicago Press, 1951–63), 3:165.
17. Ibid., p. 162.
18. Ibid., pp. 153–61.
19. Avery Dulles, *Models of the Church* (Dublin: Gill & Macmillan, 1976).
20. Ibid., pp. 184–85. Emphasis added.
21. Ibid., p. 185.

2

The Being of the Church

The church is constituted by the activity of proclaiming and embodying the redemptive intentions of the One God in all places and times, touching all sorts and conditions of people. This calling brings with it the call to holiness, obedience, and faithfulness. The church's Christ-centeredness brings with it an essentially apostolic character that puts it in touch with all previous generations of Christians.

THE CHURCH'S OWN TESTIMONY: ONE, HOLY, CATHOLIC, AND APOSTOLIC

One of the most important sources for understanding what the church believes about itself is the fourfold affirmation of the "Nicene" Creed: "I believe in the One, Holy, Catholic, and Apostolic Church." In these four adjectives, much of the church's self-understanding is contained. Furthermore, here we are dealing with that to which the church itself, of its own free will, holds itself accountable. Each of these four affirmations exists under the ambiguities discussed earlier, as the tension between what our faith tells us about the church and what the church actually embodies in its life. That to which the church holds itself accountable is one thing; the way in which it actually embodies that accountability is another. Each of these poles of the tension must be considered in its integrity. In the dialectic between them, we see the earthly existence of the church played out as an embodied witness to God's intentions. The doctrinal affirmations made about the church are the product of considerable reflection and have emerged from the church's struggle to maintain itself as a community and an institution, with all that such a struggle implies about the dominant place of self-interest. Nevertheless, what the church says normatively about itself is clearly rooted in the primitive experience of the Christians, as that experience is reported to us in the New Testament.[1]

The affirmation of the church's *unity* is no exception to this basic rule. Oneness is professed in the New Testament witnesses as a basic characteristic

9 / THE CHURCH

of the community. Matthew 23:8–11 has Christ say: "You are not to be called rabbi, for you have one teacher, and you are all brethren." Nor are the disciples to forget that they have one Father and one Master, and from this single character of God the unity of the group derives. John 10 argues that the church is one flock, because it has one shepherd. A similar argument lies behind the "high-priestly prayer" of John 17, "that they may be one, even as we are one," and the image of the vine and the branches (John 15). Paul speaks regularly of the unity of the church following from the Lordship of the one Christ (Eph. 2, 4; Gal. 3). The great diversity of the church's members (1 Cor. 12), manifested in the various gifts of the Spirit, is unified by their all existing within Christ's one body.

What we see in the biblical record is a profoundly theological grounding of the unity of the church. The church's characteristic of oneness rests ultimately on the nature of God and the church's correlative relationship to God—indeed, there is no other cogent ground for asserting the oneness of the church. Such an assertion is thoroughly consistent with the basic theological affirmation outlined in the previous chapter, that the church is located theologically within the process of God's actualizing the divine purpose in the realm of nature and history. It would be incongruous if the church, thus placed theologically, were to contradict in its self-understanding the very nature of the God to whose purposes it witnesses. One could go even a step further and suggest that the radical monotheism for which both Judaism and Christianity are renowned requires as a correlate the unity of the religious community.

Unity, like all other attributes of the church, stands under the tensions that attend the discrepancy between what our faith tells us about the church and what we see actually embodied in its empirical life. The actual life of the church does not give us an unambiguous image of its unity. The concrete life of the church reveals that unity is both an indicative and an imperative for the church. The indicative stands at the heart of the church's being. Its one God, its one Lord Jesus Christ, its one common history in Jesus and its common remembrance of him in Scripture and creed—all these unitive elements stand at the origin of the church, quite beyond the church's contemporary decision or petition. Since the basic oneness of its existence is rooted in the being of God and God's action in Christ, the church has no option but to acknowledge that oneness is at the heart of its being.

In the church's concrete life, diversity and disunity are vividly actual. This diversity can be conceived and understood in two ways. On the one hand, it may be considered a scandal to the oneness that stands as God's gift to the church. Unity is very much an imperative from this point of view, something that must be striven for in face of the great odds posed by the natural stubbornness and sinfulness of the people and groups that make up the church. Since this diversity often follows the lines of ethnic, national, racial, social, and economic divisions, it has frequently been observed that the churches have permitted natural distinctions to dominate God-given unity. It is not uncommon to have such divisions termed "nontheological" factors of church disunity.[2]

On the other hand, the diversity of the church can be viewed in more positive terms, as a necessary part of the church's penetration of human existence. The church must become indigenous to the various cultures and mores that comprise individual and social existence. When the church's diversity is comprehended from this perspective, the unity of the church is no less an imperative, but diversity is not considered so much reprehensible as part of the challenge of bringing unity to the complexity and diversity of human being in this world.[3] Such reflection is consistent with Pauline usage. There Paul sees the *one* church present in the total universal church, comprised of all Christians (Rom. 16:4; 1 Cor. 7:17), but he also sees that church present in every local group of Christians (1 Cor. 1:2; 2 Cor. 1:1).[4] The unity of the church is not identical to organizational oneness. It can be manifested in the separate particularities of different churchly communities.

Both these perspectives on the church's diversity make legitimate points. The one reminds us forcefully that individual and group self-interest always threatens to manipulate the church for its own ends. The other testifies that there can be no unity in the church except as a unity of the natural diversity that characterizes the human race. A monolithic unity that suppresses or violates the life-giving multiplicities of humanity is as unsatisfactory in the church as the sectarianism that elevates natural interests in a manner blasphemous to the oneness of God's nature and will.

The form which unity should take has been an item of controversy throughout the church's history. The arguments range from those that require the most tangible visible unity conceivable, to those that propose a unity of "spirit" and attitude, even though churches remain outwardly quite separated. Among the former are the claims that organizational unity is desirable, or that full agreement on theological articles is necessary, or that obedience to a common church authority is prerequisite to unity. The ecumenical movement of the twentieth century has moved through several phases, learning from each and often becoming unrealistically optimistic or pessimistic because of its experience. One might suggest that the diversity of the churches is itself a gift of God, one which makes it possible for all sorts and conditions of people and groups to gather around Christ in the church, and that therefore any form of unity which trivializes or represses this diversity is to be avoided. On the other hand, the unity of the church is too important to be dealt with indifferently. If there is not unity in the Eucharist and ministry or in works of love for the world, one may reasonably ask whether a basic article of the church's faith and life has not been abandoned.

9 / THE CHURCH

The church's *holiness* is also rooted in the New Testament witness. The call to spiritual and moral earnestness rings in the opening of Mark's Gospel, in the message of John the Baptist (Mark 1:1–8, 14), just as it permeates the Sermon on the Mount (Matt. 5). The famous "therefore" rhetoric of Ephesians makes the point clearly: "I therefore, a prisoner for the Lord, beg you to lead a life worthy of the calling to which you have been called.... Therefore, putting away falsehood, let every one speak the truth.... Therefore be imitators of God, as beloved children" (Eph. 4:1, 25; 5:1). The demands grow intrinsically out of the action of God in Christ. The First Letter of Peter echoes Ephesians: "As obedient children, do not be conformed to the passions of your former ignorance, but as he who called you is holy, be holy yourselves in all your conduct; since it is written, 'You shall be holy, for I am holy' " (1 Pet. 1:14–16). The royal priesthood image intensifies this theme: "But you are a chosen race, a royal priesthood, a holy nation, God's own people, that you may declare the wonderful deeds of him who called you out of darkness into his marvelous light" (1 Pet. 2:9).

The church's attribute of holiness has been an item of grave controversy. Judaizers in the first and second centuries, Montanists in the second century, Donatists in the fourth century, Anabaptists in the sixteenth century, and various sects throughout the history of the church have protested the church's moral laxity, its lack of holiness. Each movement ultimately was judged sectarian, if not schismatic and heretical.

Holiness is often misunderstood, as it was by the sectarian groups. In the Old Testament, holiness is an attribute of God, first and foremost. Holiness pertains to God and to that which belongs to God. The ark of the covenant is holy (e.g., 2 Chron. 35:3) because it is God's and represents God's power. The land is holy, as are the very people of Israel (Exod. 19:6) for the same reason, that they belong to God: "And I will take you for my people, and I will be your God" (Exod. 6:7). The holiness of things in this world, of people, and of the church derive from God and God's holy being. To belong to God is to be holy; to be the recipient of God's power is to be holy. The church is holy because it is God's creation, the recipient of God's covenant of faithfulness and election, because it is the group of people that acknowledges that it belongs to God.

The call to holiness of conduct is a call to complete the unity with God that is ours by nature, a call to submit to God's transforming power as the ground of our being in this world. Holiness is not first of all a matter of morals: but it does include a moral aspect. Moral purity belongs to holiness because belonging to God transforms life. What sectarian and heretical groups have not understood is that moral purity is a fruit of belonging to God and not its cause. Holiness is not first of all something that human beings, whether inside or outside the church, do. Holy people do not make the church holy.

People do holy actions because they belong to God and acknowledge that fact about themselves. Election by God makes the church holy. The heretical and schismatic groups recognized that life in the church was characterized by holiness, but they erred in making it a human achievement rather than a divine gift. The church through the centuries has accepted impurity among its members and forgiven them if they showed that they were repentant; it has resisted the temptation to be rigoristic and to refuse forgiveness even for grave sins.

The indicative and imperative aspects of holiness are clear within the foregoing framework. The church has already been chosen; it already belongs to God, because God has acted preveniently in our behalf. Therefore, holiness as indicative is at the heart of churchly existence. It is also an imperative, a challenge to be fulfilled, because the church has not responded to the call of God as it ought and its life does not mirror its election.

As with the other creedal attributes of the church, holiness is not only an inner-churchly concern. In setting up the ideal of holiness, the church points to the fulfillment of all humanity. The call to holiness is a summons for all people to live in a manner that is worthy of humanity and commensurate with humanity's allegiance to the source of its life. Similarly, in its exercise of the "power of the keys," for judgment and forgiveness, the church prefigures the final vision of all humans, that although the call to holiness of life is unalterable and never to be amended, it also includes forgiveness. Imperfection does not rule out fulfillment. It is God's nature to be gracious to all people.

The attribute of *catholicity* is one of the most misunderstood of the church's creedal affirmations about itself. On the Roman Catholic side, the term has too often been treated as if it referred to the church whose shape is coterminous with the empirical Roman church. Protestants, on the other hand, have also associated the term with Roman Catholicism—an attitude reinforced by the Reformers' translation of the creedal word "catholic" with "Christian."

Catholicity has been better defined as "universality plus identity," as "universality plus continuity."[5] Both formulas refer to the same phenomenon: catholicity as the church's ongoing activity of actualizing itself universally in concrete forms and instances, in a manner that brings the fullness of its identity and heritage to bear within those actualizations, whether these are statements of doctrine, liturgical forms, organizational structures, decisions concerning ministry, or whatever. Catholicity is the church's conviction that it can actualize its identity in every dimension of life and that such actualizations can embody the fullness of its identity.

The experience of catholicity is discernible in the New Testament. The picture of Jesus himself becoming the center of a missionary religious community

9 / THE CHURCH

points to catholicity. Jesus was by all standards a provincial. He was a rural or small-town person; he did not travel any great distances. He was bound to one culture, language, nation, and race. We are not certain that he was literate or even very knowledgeable. Yet his own attitude toward people was catholic, as he reached out to people across the boundaries of his provincialism, to Romans and Samaritans, rich and poor, men and women. The first Christian missionaries, whether moving east to Syria or west toward the Mediterranean, were able to focus their efforts within the framework of Jesus' name and what they believed to be his message and intention. The Pentecost story is the narrative of the first Christians proclaiming Jesus of Nazareth to an international crowd. In all these settings, the universal and the particular are inextricably interwoven. The specific rituals of the Jews must be laid to rest before Paul can move freely into the gentile world, and when he does move it is as a Roman citizen, but one who is marked by his Jewish strangeness. Peter could not envision any conversion to Christ apart from Jewish circumcision, yet his name becomes associated with the see of Rome. Matthew 8:11 has Jesus say to the centurion, "I tell you, many will come from east and west and sit at table with Abraham, Isaac, and Jacob in the kingdom of heaven." The Epistles to the Colossians and the Ephesians both identify Jesus of Nazareth with the cosmic Christ who has existed before all time and holds all things together. Clearly, the Christian self-awareness reflected in the New Testament did not consider itself to exist in a backwater of particularities, but rather conceived of a broad significance that could permeate all dimensions of life.

The catholic aspect of the church can thus be said to have a twofold thrust. The first thrust is intensive. The intensive thrust aims at fullness in the church's reception and appropriation of the divine revelation that gives it identity. Under this aspect, the church immerses itself as completely as possible in the totality of what is and has been Christian, and it seeks to recapitulate within itself that fullness. The church is continually probing Scripture, recalling and interpreting Christian history, opening itself to the whole of the liturgical tradition and to the traditions of doctrine, piety, ethics, and church organization. The church recognizes that if it is at any single moment to be successful in actualizing the fullness of authentic Christian identity, it is desirable to have touched as much of the tradition of Christianness as is possible. The tradition is not approached uncritically, yet it is perceived as the family history, the history of the brothers and the sisters in faith, to be appropriated in a critical manner. Critical appropriation does not mean that some parts are accepted and others rejected, but rather that it is all accepted as *our* history, *our* identity, under the judgment that critical integrity demands.

The second thrust of catholicity is extensive, as the church reaches out to all people at all times in all places. This extensive outreach includes *spatial universality*, which encompasses what we commonly call "mission." Geographical outreach and evangelization are dimensions of catholicity: the church cannot be content with national, racial, cultural, or territorial boundaries, because the revelation that constitutes the church is universal in its relevance and design.

Temporal universality is also an aspect of the extensive thrust. The church's universality cuts across epochs, to include all times and generations in its purview. Each generation of the church seeks to be itself and to fulfill its responsibilities before God faithfully; but it does not despise previous epochs, and even though it must criticize them, the church does not attempt to slough them away as a snake sheds its skin.

Cultural universality is still another dimension of extensive outreach. The church recognizes that its existence is relevant to all aspects of a culture. It seeks to permeate a culture thoroughly: its art and philosophy, its prevailing view of personhood, its vision of what society should be. No aspect of culture is alien to the Christian revelation. The church likewise seeks to relate to all sorts and conditions within a given culture and society. All social and economic classes are to be touched, all age-groups, both sexes, all occupations, every social situation. Cultural universality comprehends intellectual challenges to the faith, as well as social and ethical tasks and the task of pastoral care.[6]

All that the church is able to recapitulate within itself in its intensive thrust is brought to bear on the totality of the extensive thrust. In every instance and place within the extensive thrust, intensive recapitulation seeks to actualize authentic Christianness, in whatever form is required. Catholicity is achieved when the fullness of the Christian revelation is so brought to bear as to express in a contemporary way the Christian identity. Catholicity combines openness to relevance in any time or place with richness of traditional Christian meaning.

Catholicity is an indicative in that the fullness of Christian revelation is given to us and the church is not content unless it is immersing itself in its traditions. Similarly, the church knows that it cannot be at peace unless it reaches out. Even in times of apostasy and doldrums this outreach is only dormant, waiting to burst forth.

On the other hand, catholicity is an imperative. What any particular time or place demands as authentic Christian response is never unambiguously clear. The church is perennially engaged in debate and critical self-appraisal when it considers how it should express itself concretely. By what strategy is a societal situation to be addressed? Which, if any, of the current philosophies is best suited for theology? What liturgical rendering of the eucharist is most edifying for the church in these times? These are all questions of catholicity. On the one hand, catholicity is never fully achieved; on the other hand, the church is always tempted to turn its back on the fullness of Christian tradition in

9 / THE CHURCH

favor of superficial relevance or a preferred provincialism. One facet of the Christian revelation is seized on as "ours," as if its truth justified indifference to other authentic dimensions of Christian meaning. One form of outreach is cherished, while others are ignored. The church goes through history misshapen, neither fully Christian in its own existence nor fully universal in outreach.

Later in this chapter we shall draw attention to some decisive implications of the church's *apostolicity*. Here it is enough to recall briefly what the attribute means. The biblical record does contain recollections of the centrality of the apostles in the early community. However, these are not among the most primitive traditions, and they could therefore be themselves tendentious passages, contemporary with the church's later reflection on apostolicity. The apostles and prophets are affirmed as the foundation of the church, the ones to whom alone the revelation of Christ was made (Eph. 2:20; 3:5). Matthew 16 and 18 describe the Lord's mandate to Peter and the promise of the power of the keys. In the "farewell discourses," the Gospel of John has the departing Jesus reiterate that the Spirit will keep the apostles in remembrance of all that Jesus has done and what he has told them about himself and about the Father (John 14:26; 15:26; 16:13ff.). Acts 1:21–22 records Peter's words that the successor to Judas should be one who has shared the experience of the original apostles.

The question of the church being apostolic did not arise in force until the apostles and other eyewitnesses to Jesus had died. After those deaths, the church had to ask at a deep level how it could be certain that its course of action and preaching was right, how it could judge adequately in situations of controversy and schism. The church's formal response to itself and its foes was that it held itself accountable to the *apostolic* witness concerning Jesus.

Two considerations must be kept in mind when we reflect on the church's affirmation that it is apostolic. First, the affirmation points to the fundamental dependence of the church on the heritage bestowed from the past. The church has received something that it could not in any age subsequent to the first century provide for itself: description of and witness to Jesus of Nazareth as the Messiah, the Christ. Since Jesus is identified with the Logos, the one who reveals the nature and intentions of God for creation, the church has no alternative but to declare its dependence on the most reliable testimony available concerning Jesus. This testimony has at its center the eyewitness legacy of the apostles. Even where the church later wishes to modify or even criticize the apostolic testimony, it can do so only by thoroughly assimilating and understanding that testimony. The eyewitness testimony is the chief source for critique of all utterance concerning Christ, including the eyewitness utterance itself. The creedal affirmation of apostolicity is the church's

THE BEING OF THE CHURCH

acknowledgment that it lives by what it has received and it is accountable to what it has received.

The first consideration suggests how apostolicity is indicative in the church's life. The church has no choice but to live out of the apostolic era; it lives off what it has received, not what it provides for itself. A second consideration, however, points to a way in which apostolicity is always to be achieved, always to be validated by the church's own activity. The church is not a passive recipient of its apostolic heritage. Although the church has from the beginning been dependent on the eyewitnesses for its memory of Jesus Christ and thus for understanding its own meaning as Christ's church, the church has had to take responsibility for defining the proper understanding and most important aspects of the apostolic testimony.

The idea of apostolic witness has to some extent functioned as ideology for the church, in that it has served to paint a picture of a pure, unambiguous, perfected knowledge of revelation at the origin of the church's life, which the church was called to preserve against all foes, heretics, and alteration or innovation. This is the view which Robert Wilken terms "the Eusebian hypothesis," after its most impressive propounder, the fourth-century bishop and church historian, Eusebius of Caesarea.[7] Since the time of Walter Bauer in the nineteenth century, who argued that before there was orthodoxy there was diversity of Christian opinion,[8] it has become a commonplace of informed opinion to acknowledge that the Eusebian hypothesis is itself a strategy to fight heresy more than it is an accurate historical judgment.

The church has, against the background of its dependence on the heritage of eyewitnesses, always had to decide what is correct opinion in matters of life and faith. It has not hesitated to take up this responsibility, believing that it is strengthened by God's Spirit in the undertaking. In so doing, the church acknowledges that it is seeking always to be faithful to the Christ of the first century, the Christ who, as the revealer of God, is at the center of the church's being and who is proclaimed by the apostles. Ideology enters when the church denies or covers up the fact that it has participated fully and actively in determining what that apostolic proclamation is and how it pertains to the issues in question at any given time. When the church announces in its traditional form, "It seems good to the Holy Spirit and to us" to do or say thus-and-such, it must be remembered that the Holy Spirit cannot become the scapegoat for "and to us." The church has received an apostolic gift; that is indicative. The church is beholden to that gift. The church is always defining what the gift is and what its implications are; that is imperative, always unfinished, always humanly touched with ambiguity and incompleteness.

The creedal affirmations are not simply adjectives from a venerable past

9 / THE CHURCH

that serve to describe the church. They are *canonical* affirmations, derived from creeds which are themselves received as normative within the church's tradition of self-understanding. They are not so much discrete adjectives as parts of the unified witness of the church concerning itself; and they are to be interpreted accordingly. As part of this witness, they must be set within the basic theological understanding of the church affirmed in Chapter 1: that the church is the community whose raison d'être is explicit witness to God's actualizing of his purposes concretely in nature and history.

Within this large theological context, the affirmations take on the seriousness they deserve. They become pointers or clues to what the life of the community called church tells us about God's purposes in the world. Apostolicity tells us that what God intends in his self-unfolding is embedded in the witness of the apostles to Jesus of Nazareth as the Christ. Holiness affirms that the community that centers on the Christ of the apostolic witness is cherished by God as God's own possession, and that to belong to God is to accept the pursuit of holiness as a given of life. Just as the presence of God in the world is attended by the reality of holiness, so also it is transparent to God's oneness. The world is one, its purposes and processes are one, because its creator God is one. The community in the world that seeks to be luminous with the witness to God is similarly to be one. The creator God, with the redemptive intention as set forth in Christ, cannot allow the divine presence to be confined in any way or possessed by any single group. This God's presence is unbounded, permeating all creation with the divine will. Nothing less than catholicity can signal such a powerful divine intention. When the affirmations are viewed in this light, it is clear why the church is indicatively one, holy, catholic, and apostolic; and it is just as clear why, finite as the church is, it must always strive after the four attributes. Finally, it is plain why the church is the church only when it *is* one, holy, catholic, and apostolic.

SIGNIFICANT IMAGES
FROM THE TRADITION:
PEOPLE OF GOD AND BODY OF CHRIST

We are speaking of the being of the church on the basis of the church's own interior sense of who and what it is. The creedal affirmations are freely chosen descriptions of the church's being, placed in a public context for regular reiteration. There are other symbols of the church's self-understanding, most of them in Scripture, that have nourished the church's reflection on itself. Here we briefly consider only two of the most important: people of God and body of Christ.

In acknowledging the image of the *people of God* as pertinent to its own

THE BEING OF THE CHURCH

being, the church affirms its links to the Old Testament and places itself in immediate relation to Israel and the Jews.[9] Most immediately, the church recalls the chain of symbols that cluster around the ideas of election and covenant. The church places itself in the position of the people whom God has chosen and to whom God has made promises: "I shall be your God, and you shall be my people." The image is of a people who follows the destiny to which God has called them, confident of God's faithfulness to guard and preserve them. The history of the people follows the contours of the situation. Whatever the environing world presents to the people, they must deal with.

Freedom marks the relationship between the people and God. God has freely chosen the people; they cannot claim to have forged their own status as people of God. For their part, they have chosen freely as well. So long as they are willing to take the consequences, they may turn their backs on the covenant—as, to be sure, they do at times. The elements of disobedience and failure are also factors that this image can take into account. The history of the people is not a straight line of progress in obedience and in effectively discharging God's will. Disobedience does not break the covenant relationship; God does not withdraw because people have failed in their calling. A remarkable give-and-take between God and people is evident, precisely because the people comprise a human community that is sensitive to its situation, sometimes to the point where human interests in that situation lead away from clear devotion to God's calling.

As the people of the promises of God, the church lives for the kingdom of God. The people have no greater goal than to follow God's leading through the history God has laid out and which God will bring to consummation. This awareness makes "people of God" an eschatological image. God consummates history in the establishment, according to God's free decision, of the kingdom of God. Since the people of God have the calling to obey God's will in history and to be the agents of that will, the people attend to the kingdom, pray for it, attempt to discern its outlines, and shape their own action so as to be commensurate here and now with the kingdom that has not yet arrived.

The "people of God" image is not as clear a symbol as one might wish to convey the concrete identity of the church, nor does it speak of the new situation in which the church finds itself as the people of the New Covenant. The "body of Christ" image supplements it at these two points.[10] Rooted especially in the Pauline literature, this image clearly identifies the church: it is the extension, the continuation of Christ in this world. Christ is the head of the body, into whom it grows. The church's mandate, growing out of its very nature, is to be Christ's presence in the world, in obedience to the Christ who governs as the head controls the body.

9 / THE CHURCH

Reinforcing the Christ-identity, the sacraments play a leading role in the church identified by this image. Baptism is initiation into the body. In the Eucharist we are joined to Christ through the reception of his body and blood. In this sacramental union, he dwells in us and we in him. If "people of God" speaks of the place of free will and decision in the relationship between God and the church, "body of Christ" lends itself rather to ideas of mystical participation in Christ. The image has fostered such attitudes since the time of the apostle Paul himself, who could speak of filling up in his own body what was lacking in Christ's sufferings and of being a new man "in Christ," just as Christ was "in him." The analogy is physical and biological, which naturally leads to further images that differ markedly from the analogy of volition and obedience that stands at the heart of the "people of God" image. It is important to accept the testimony of both images, allowing each to give insight into the nature of the church, just as each exercises a certain critique on the other.

The greatest weakness of the "body of Christ" image is its inability to speak of the weakness and failure of the church. The notion of the prolongation of Christ in the world through the church may suggest too often that the church is sinless like Christ. Indeed, this image may have been a favorite for so long with the institutional church precisely because it lends a mystical aura to the institution and plays down the critique of the church. "Body of Christ," with its sacramental emphasis, also underscores the newness of the New Covenant established by Christ. Intimate union with this Christ is union with that covenant. The people of the new Covenant may too quickly transfer the attributes of their Christ to themselves. This is one reason why the image of the people of God should be kept in closest touch with the image of the body of Christ.

MODELS THAT SUMMARIZE THE THEOLOGICAL TRADITION: INSTITUTION, MYSTICAL COMMUNION, SACRAMENT, HERALD, SERVANT

It is not possible in this *locus* to survey the length and breadth of the tradition of reflection on the church. Avery Dulles has, however, in a classic study, demonstrated that the tradition can be creatively recapitulated under five basic images, which also serve as "models" of the church.[11] A brief survey of these five models will show the breadth of the theological reflection.

The model of an *institution* defines the church "primarily in terms of its visible structures, especially the rights and powers of its officers."[12] It speaks of the church as a society that is centered in its hierarchical structure and whose main functions are to teach, sanctify, and govern. The church's chief purpose is to ensure eternal life to its members, and its members are clearly identified as those who give explicit allegiance to the institution. The institutional model flourished from the late Middle Ages, gaining strength during the Counter-Reformation, and it was clearly represented in the documents of the First Vatican Council. It has not been totally absent from Protestant views of the church, although it stands as the stereotyped position of Roman Catholicism. The stereotype is not altogether fair, since the model was sharply criticized at the Second Vatican Council as being guilty of, in Bishop De Smedt's terms, "clericalism, juridicism, and triumphalism." The church is paralleled by this model to the secular state; the model's externalism gives the church many of the state's characteristics.

A communitarian model of the church as a *mystical communion* has been increasingly in favor among Catholics and Protestants in the twentieth century. Since Pius XII gave this model papal approval in his encyclical of 1943, entitled *Mystici Corporis*, a host of theologians has supported a communitarian view. On the Catholic side, we count Yves Congar, Jerome Hamer, and Arnold Rademacher; Protestants include Emil Brunner, Dietrich Bonhoeffer, and Rudolf Sohm. These thinkers emphasize the communion of Christians with one another and with God in Christ, in sharp contrast with the institutional model. Externalism recedes, as the church aims at leading people, who may not always be legally validated members of the organized society, into communion with God through spiritual deepening and the bonds formed by the interior gifts of the Holy Spirit. The personal and the interpersonal are highlighted. This model can invoke considerable traditional support, since it assimilates into itself the images of the body of Christ and the people of God, which are largely community images. Protestant pietism, with its conventicle orientation, also validates this type of thinking about the church.

Ancient tradition, going back as far as Cyprian and Augustine and including Aquinas, justifies speaking of the church as the *sacramental* representation of Christ on earth. In Henri de Lubac's terms, the church "really makes Christ present. She not only carries on his work, but she is his very continuation."[13] A host of contemporary Roman Catholic theologians, including Karl Rahner and Edward Schillebeeckx, have made the sacramental model central to their thinking. In its dogmatic constitution on the church, *Lumen Gentium*, Vatican II endorsed it. The constitution refers, for example, to the church in these terms: "Christ sent His life-giving Spirit upon His disciples and through this Spirit has established His body, the Church, as the universal sacrament of salvation."[14] Elsewhere it speaks of the church as the "sacrament of the saving unity" of all humankind. Relatively few Protestant theologians or church documents have used the model.

9 / THE CHURCH

The sacramental model can bridge the tension between the institutional and communitarian models, since the external forms are essential and significant to a sacrament. The thinking behind the image is that Christ is God's sacrament, in that in his visible form God's grace is signified and conferred. However, as an individual, Christ is incomplete. In order to awaken the response of all humankind, Christ needs the church as an historically tangible extension of his presence in the world. Such a view gives great honor and purpose to the church, even as it provides a basis for criticizing the church and holding it accountable. As sacrament, the church's purpose extends to all who behold it, not just to Christians and church members, to purify and intensify the response of people to Christ's grace.

Protestants have seized on the model of *herald*, no doubt because it is centered in the Word of God and proclamation. As herald, the purpose of the church is to proclaim the gospel message, to present to the world the powerful gospel of Christ, to be appropriated existentially in faith. Building on classical Reformation traditions, Karl Barth, Rudolf Bultmann, Gerhard Ebeling, and the Roman Catholic Hans Küng have elaborated this ecclesiological motif. The orientation of this model lends itself to the Reformation concern for the clarity of the church's witness to grace, with relatively little interest in the structure of the church.

In the attempt to take secularization seriously, recent ecclesiology has often sought to describe the church as *servant* of the world. The previous four models all place the church in a privileged position with respect to the world, whereas the servant model emphasizes dialogue with the world. The transition from the First to the Second Vatican Council demonstrates this movement from privilege to service dramatically. *Lumen Gentium* speaks of the church as a pilgrim in this world, suffering in travail with all of creation. Several World Council of Churches documents have utilized servant themes, as have Catholic documents associated with liberation theology.[15]

All these models, together with their supporting motifs, can find some support in Scripture and tradition. Simply recounting them indicates the breadth of reflection on the essential nature of the church. Some of these models are commensurate with each other; some are irreconcilable with others. The models present diverse understandings of the chief purpose of the church, and in this diversity serious weaknesses, along with great strengths, are to be noted. Finally, whereas certain models bear an ecumenical witness, others are nearly restricted to either Catholics or Protestants. The diversity of the models is a welcome and wholesome testimony to the riches and honesty of the tradition of the church in thinking about its own essential being. At the same time, the very richness of the tradition reminds us that we must make distinctions: we must choose some aspects of the tradition over others, and we must justify our choices in a theologically responsible manner.

THE BEING OF THE CHURCH
IN LIGHT OF ITS ORIGINS

The being of the church is fundamentally conditioned by the circumstances of its origin. This is a basic axiom and merits close attention. By "the circumstances of its origin," we refer to the period between Jesus' first appearance as a public figure and the emergence of the church as a discernible entity, with characteristics that can be grasped and identified. We are speaking of what is often called "primitive" Christianity, the church in the time before it emerged as the catholic church, perhaps at the end of the first quarter of the second century. This period can, with considerable imprecision, be termed the "apostolic" period, in that it comprises the time in which the apostles lived and worked as well as the time when the subsequent generation made the decisions that validated the apostles and assured the preservation of their traditions.

The basis for the axiom that this period fundamentally conditions the being of the church is not that the period is superior to other eras. We cannot argue that this century gathered people who were intellectually, spiritually, or morally preeminent over all subsequent generations. Nor can it be said that early generations were more open and receptive to Christ and his teaching than later ones. There is no qualitative superiority attached to the apostolic period and experience. The grounds for the axiom are three. First, it is the period that stands closest to Jesus, and the period in whose configurations of language, culture, mores, images, expectations, and sensibilities Jesus Christ came on the scene. Second, this period stands as our only means of access to Jesus. This point is not the same as the first. If Jesus had left written documents, it would be possible for later generations to make new manuscript discoveries and score new triumphs of interpretation. As Jesus was, however, he has no access to us except through the witness left by the apostolic generation. All our insight into Jesus, all our criteria for judging what is authentically a part of the man and his message, are derived from what we learn from the earliest generations. Third, since the church emerged under the impact of Jesus, the configurations of the first century have become the foundations of the church and the primal norm of the church's life and faith. Since Jesus is inseparable in our knowledge and experience from the apostolic period, the church has no alternative to acknowledging the constitutive role of that period in its own life. It is not the case that the church cannot change from the circumstances of its origins; it can and has. Nor is it true that the church's period of origin is necessarily its best time; one can argue that several later epochs were better. However, whatever changes there have been have been alterations of the church that was originally formed out of the apostolic configuration, and they are judged good or bad according to discernment educated by that configura-

9 / THE CHURCH

tion. For this reason, it is proper to say that the apostolic configuration is the primal norm for the church.

We must understand this process in more detail if we are to comprehend adequately the being of the church. The church crystallized from the total experience of the apostolic generations, as that experience stood under the impact of Jesus. The wholeness of this experience must be acknowledged. Since there are no criteria for validating Jesus, or even for recognizing him, except those on which the apostolic generations bestowed authority, it must be said that Jesus' appearance as a human being, his distinction as a special person, his powerful attracting force, which gathered a community around himself, and finally his being acclaimed as Messiah and God, all transpired within apostolic experience, was crystallized into meaning within that experience, and was found normative within that experience. Jesus is not the fabrication of apostolic experience, but there is no external compulsion to recognize and accept Jesus as Messiah and God except that which apostolic experience validated from within its own structures.

The complexity of the apostolic experience defies adequate analysis, but some general lines need to be set down. What we have termed "apostolic experience" is the total life-experience of the apostolic generations, not just their ideas, ethical precepts, cultic forms, feelings, or any other segment of their life. These generations perceived and received Jesus as whole people, and their whole configuration of experience became the vessel in which his identity and impact were conveyed to the next generations, down to our own time.

This total configuration of experience contains many elements, corresponding to the various facets of experience, each of which has become in some way, to a greater or a lesser extent, constitutive and authoritative for the church. The apostolic configuration embraces a cultic dimension, an intellectual component, organizational thrusts, activities of preaching, teaching, evangelizing, as well as the oral and written preservation of the memory about Jesus and the turning of that memory to useful ends in the apostolic generations' activities of internal edification and external outreach. The cultic dimension of apostolic life developed into the liturgy of the church, in its "catholic" phase in the second century. The intellectual component became creed and dogma; the organizational thrust, the episcopal structure; traditions of preaching and teaching were passed on as such; attempts to preserve the memory about Jesus became the Scripture. Other elements of the apostolic experience could be listed: patterns of ethics, prayer, and the like.

The point is that each of these elements takes its place within a totality of lived experience among individuals and groups; none of the elements is properly understood when isolated from the total configuration. Furthermore,

THE BEING OF THE CHURCH

the inspirational and revelational character of apostolic experience pertains to the experience as such, in which the revelation of Christ was perceived, acknowledged, and declared authoritative, and not to any isolated discrete entity within that experience. It is the apostolic as such that is authoritative and canonical for the church. The configuration of experience out of which New Testament Scripture emerged is the inspired normative element as well as the finished Scripture, because it is that experience which made the Scripture possible.

We do not accept all apostolic phenomena as equally normative and binding. Scripture and creed have the greatest authority for later generations of the church, liturgy and episcopacy somewhat less, especially among Protestants. The authority granted an element of apostolic tradition depends on how closely it is related to Christ and whether it is necessary in order for later generations of Christians to have access to Christ. An element of the tradition does not become normative if it cannot become universal, over and beyond the particularities of its origin, and thus helpful to later Christians who do not share those particularities. The moral behavior of the first Christians, therefore, can never be authoritative in the way that Scripture or the creed is. Nevertheless, it is still part of the "canonical" experience of the apostolic generation, and as such it is a vessel of the reality and power of Christ which came to the apostolic generations. We are free to accept or reject any segment of the apostolic tradition; nevertheless, no segment of that tradition can be gainsaid as a vessel of Christ's presence, and we are accountable to the Christ-revelation conveyed therein. A generation of twentieth-century Protestants may choose to repudiate the apostolic liturgy, for example, but they are never free to ignore the witness to Christ conveyed in that liturgy, nor are they encouraged to separate themselves from what that witness may contribute to their larger knowledge of Christ. Although there may be good reasons for rejecting segments of the apostolic tradition, the church in any generation must find ways to convey these traditions to its successors, even though it does not cherish them in its own time.

The being of the church *is* apostolic, even when apostolic forms have been changed almost beyond recognition, because the apostolic configuration of experience made the changing forms possible in the first place. If the church should lose the sense of the pivotal character of the apostolic experience in its totality, we would have every reason to ask in what sense it really is in continuity with Jesus of Nazareth, the Christ.

What we have said about the origins of the church has several clear implications.

First. The church is a product of the crystallization of a generation's total experience, that of the first Christians. It is not possible to say with any cer-

9 / THE CHURCH

tainty that Jesus or any other figure "founded" the church intentionally or put together its forms. It is very clear that the church emerged out of the apostolic experience of Jesus.

Second. Since this apostolic era is constitutive for the church, the church continually probes it. The church is always caught up in an historical quest for a truer understanding of Jesus and the apostolic witness which gives us our knowledge of Jesus. This is true even though our faith cannot be based on historical research and even though historical certainty is never possible, because the norms for what the church does decide about faith and about itself are derived ultimately nowhere else than in the apostolic witness to Jesus Christ.

Third. Since a certain historical epoch's experience is constitutive for the church, the church will always share in the particularity of that epoch, despite the great distance it may have traveled from apostolic times in Palestine and the Mediterranean basin. It is not a mark of spiritual totalitarianism that every generation of the church in every place is asked to become once again apostolic. Rather, it is an inevitable consequence of our being formed by the configuration of apostolic experience.

What have we said, finally, about the *being* of the church? Nothing has been asserted in this chapter that was not implicit already in our fundamental theological axiom about the church, that the church exists to witness to the Christ-rationale, which is the rationale of God's self-actualizing in nature and history. We have focused on substantial traditional utterances. What emerges is that the church is animated by and held accountable to the activity which corresponds to what the revelation of Jesus Christ affirms about the nature of God. The church is constituted by the activity of proclaiming and embodying the redemptive intentions of the One God in all places and circumstances and times, touching all sorts and conditions of people with its embodied proclamation. The church's calling brings with it the call to holiness, obedience, and faithfulness. The Christ-centeredness of the church brings with it an essentially apostolic character: that the particularities of the apostolic generations are inevitably and inextricably also constitutive for what the church is in any subsequent generation.

NOTES

1. Certain aspects of our discussion of the creedal affirmations are indebted to Jaroslav Pelikan, whose thinking was conveyed both in conversation and in his series of lectures on the history of the doctrine of the church. See the pertinent sections of his *The Christian Tradition: A History of the Development of Doctrine*, vol. 1, *The*

Emergence of the Catholic Tradition (100-600) (Chicago: University of Chicago Press, 1971).

2. See H. Richard Niebuhr, *The Social Sources of Denominationalism* (New York: Living Age Books, 1957).

3. Hans Küng, *The Church*, trans. R. and R. Ockender (New York and London: Sheed & Ward, 1967), pp. 269-76.

4. Karl L. Schmidt, *The Church* (London: A. & C. Black, 1950).

5. Pelikan, *Emergence of the Catholic Tradition*. Also Gustaf Aulén, *Reformation and Catholicity* (Philadelphia: Fortress [Muhlenberg] Press, 1961).

6. See the discussion by Paul Tillich, *Systematic Theology*, 3 vols. (Chicago: University of Chicago Press, 1963), vol. 3, pp. 246-66.

7. See Robert Wilken, *The Myth of Christian Beginnings* (Notre Dame: University of Notre Dame, 1980).

8. Walter Bauer, *Orthodoxy and Heresy in Earliest Christianity*, ed. Robert Kraft and Gerhard Krodel (Philadelphia: Fortress Press, 1971).

9. Yves Congar, "The Church: The People of God," in *The Church and Mankind*, ed. Edward Schillebeeckx (New York: Paulist Press, 1965), pp. 11-38; in the same volume, Rudolph Schnackenburg and Jacques Dupont, "The Church as the People of God," pp. 117-30. See also Küng, *The Church*, pp. 107-49.

10. See Congar, "The Church," and Schnackenburg and Dupont, "The Church as the People of God." See also Küng, *The Church*, pp. 203-63.

11. Avery Dulles, *Models of the Church* (Dublin: Gill & Macmillan, 1976), pp. 1-96.

12. Ibid., p. 31.

13. Henri de Lubac, *Catholicism* (London: Burns, Oates & Washburn, 1950), p. 29, cited in ibid., p. 58.

14. *Lumen Gentium*, par. 48.

15. Dulles, *Models of the Church*, cites the Protestant documents as the Presbyterian Confession of 1967 and the Uppsala Report of the World Council of Churches of 1968.

3
Basic Elements of the Church's Life

The historical career of the church has led it to adopt certain concrete forms that are not in themselves theologically necessary. However, because these forms have become empirically necessary for the church's life and mission, they must be interpreted theologically. Traditionally they have been called "marks" of the church, and they include ministry, liturgy and sacraments, preaching and teaching, care of souls, mission, and church order.

MARKS OF THE CHURCH

In this chapter, we move to another level of theological discussion of the church. Here we discuss elements that, although they do not pertain to the eternal being of the church, are basic to the historical life of the church as it has thus far evolved. The considerations discussed in Chapter 2 originated in our strictly theological understanding of the church, as a moment in the unfolding of God's being. The elements of the church's life examined here must be related to that divine unfolding, but they have originated in the empirical course of the church's history. Empirically, they have proven to be necessary to the church's life, even though from a theological point of view they are not necessary. They must, however, be related to what we have insisted is the necessary theological nature of the church; and it is one of the main tasks of the doctrine of the church to identify and clarify that relationship.

Traditionally, the elements we discuss here have been called *notae ecclesiae*, "marks of the church." Luther writes that the marks of the church answer the question "But how can a poor, erring man know where this Christian, holy people in the world is?"[1] He lists seven marks, whose substance is included in the following discussion, under categories different from his. Luther's marks are: the Word, baptism, the Lord's Supper, the keys, the ministry, prayer, suffering, and "others." He considered these marks so important that he suggested calling them all sacraments. Recognizing that this usage would not be implemented, he called them "simply seven chief means of Christian sanctification, or seven holy possessions."[2] The term "sanctification" is important, because it indicates that through these basic elements the church lives out its life of faith and holiness in the world. These elements or marks enable the church to be truly the church.

MINISTRY

"Ministry" has both a broader and a narrower meaning. In its broader meaning it refers to the total activity of the church, as that activity fulfills the church's primary purpose. The church's purpose, in conformity with what we understand the church to be, is to witness explicitly to what Jesus Christ reveals to be the rationale and purpose of the world within the unfolding of God's being and purpose. Consequently, the ministry in this sense belongs first to God; it is God's purposes that are carried out within the church's ministry.[3] Without this sense of God's ministry as the undergirding of the church's ministry, no adequate substance or critique can be supplied for the activity of the church.

In this broader meaning, ministry refers to what the entire church, lay and ordained, does within the context of God's own ministry. There is no distinction between ordained and laity when viewed from this broader meaning. Both groups aim at the same divine purposes in their activity; both stand on the resources and under the judgment of the divine purposes. We may summarize briefly the witness of Christ to the rationale and purpose of the world within God's unfolding: God is in the process of bringing creation to the consummation God has planned for it; God is, consequently, a loving God who desires the fulfillment and not the destruction of that creation; the appropriate action for people who wish to glorify God and be obedient to God's purposes is to live a life that gives itself unto death, if need be, for the world, that the world may come to know its destiny at the hands of a loving God and let that destiny govern it. This summary becomes the statement of the church's purpose and a description of the primary goal of its ministry. Insofar as the activities of laity and clergy conform to that ministry, they can be interpreted as facets of that appropriate action which gives itself unstintingly that the world might know and fulfill its God-given destiny.

The *ordained ministry* serves a specific role within this larger ministry, which belongs to God and which forms the substance of the church's ministry.[4] That specific role is to ensure that the church does not forget who it is and what its purpose is. The ordained ministry exists for the purpose of reminding the church in an explicit manner of its nature, goals, and mission. This involves the ordained ministry, first, in teaching, preaching, and presiding over sacramental life; second, in maintenance and governance; and third, in the

BASIC ELEMENTS OF THE CHURCH'S LIFE

actual work of caring for people within the church (Seelesorge) and strengthening them in faith and body so that they can share in the church's ministry. The ordained minister has the task of *telling* the members of the church about their ministry and also of *doing* that ministry among them.

The ordained ministry's specific role is essential to the church for its larger ministry, even though the ordained often are not active in the front-line ministry of the church to the world. The ordained ministry is preeminent in that it speaks directly and explicitly about the core of the faith and acts on it. It is subordinate in that its task is to serve the entire church and ensure that the laity are informed about their ministry and strengthened for it. The ordained ministry is most intimately in touch with the theological and cultic center of the church, which accounts for its authority and dignity. It is also responsible for the maintenance of the church, the custodial work that is necessary if the church is to be faithful to its task of *never* failing to leave a clear witness to what the church is essentially about.

In the ancient church, the theological undergirding of the ordained ministry, as set forth by Cyprian, bishop of Carthage in North Africa, during the years A.D. 249–51, and carried on by Augustine, was the fundamental unity of the church.[5] The Christians were those who gathered in faith around Christ and the redemption that he offered and who lived lives of purity and good works commensurate with faith in Christ. In the early centuries, plagued by discord and schism, both Cyprian and Augustine were keenly aware that the one Christ and the one true faith required a community that was also one. They saw a profound illogic in the existence of separate and contrasting communities, each professing to be the true community of faith in Christ and commitment to the life of holiness.

The key to the unity of the church was the clergy.[6] There must be one bishop for each community—the office of bishop was related to a parish before it was related to a "diocese"—with clergy and people in communion with and loyal to the bishop. It was the bishop and the other clergy who preached and taught the faith around which the people gathered, who presided over the liturgy and the sacraments that nourished the people, and who disciplined the people so as to keep the community's witness pure. The church could not be the church without the clergy and the unity between people and clergy. Hence, the famous dictum, "Where the bishop is, there is the church."

The Reformation of the sixteenth century saw the church's life threatened not so much by schism as by the clouding and perversion of the faith around which believers gather. Consequently, for the reformers, clear testimony to the faith forms the theological undergirding of the ordained ministry. The Augsburg Confession puts this in classic form. Articles I, II, III, and IV recite the essentials of the faith—God, original sin, the Son of God, and justifica-

9 / THE CHURCH

tion. Article V follows immediately with its opening words, "In order that we may obtain this faith, the ministry of teaching the Gospel and administering the sacraments was instituted" (*BC* 31).

If we take properly into account the differences in historical setting between the reformers and Cyprian and Augustine, we can discern a basic similarity of the underlying theological emphases. Both positions emphasize the public and external witness which the ordained are to make within the church. For the ancients, threatened by dissolution, external witness to the truth of Christ provides a focal point for visible unity among those who profess Christ. For the reformers, explicit witness to the gospel of grace provides an objective standard of the church's identity. For the earlier period, the external witness stands as a rebuke and an alternative to the schismatics, who put their own interests over the rigorous demands of the faith. For the reformers, the external proclamation of the Word puts to flight the subjective misinterpretations and perversions of the gospel that leave the church uncertain as to the center of its identity.

Although each of these ways of undergirding the ordained ministry theologically is bound to its own time and place, they all exhibit an understanding of that ministry which is universally valid in any situation. The ordained ministry is monitor, herald, preacher, and proclaimer of the church's identity. The dignity and necessity of such a ministry are beyond question, even though such a ministry cannot exist for its own sake but serves the purpose of enabling all the faithful to carry out the ministry of God in the world.

This understanding of the ministry clarifies the basic logic of developments in the first and second centuries, which lifted one particular office, that of the "overseers" (*episkopoi*), above the many others that then existed in the church ("prophets," "teachers," charismatic ministries). The *episkopoi*, in their overseeing activity, provide the institutional framework within which the other ministries can function, while at the same time making a public recital of the faith that provides both substance and critique of those ministries. The aim of the overseers is not autocratic governance, however, but service (*diakonia*) to the entire body of believers. The ascendancy of the *episkopoi* was in a sense inevitable, since the church required as its chief ministers people who filled an office that had both the function of proclaiming the church's faith and of performing the tasks that hold the community together.

Certain elements of ordained ministry are rooted in the theological assumptions just described: preaching, liturgical and sacramental presidency, the "office of the keys." All are functions that set forth the faith of the church, the message and actuality of God's grace. Hearing confession, and the power of the keys to absolve or not, do in a compact manner embody all that the ordained ministry is about; hence their perennial significance in the history of the church. They contain the message of grace, bring it to bear on a specific

BASIC ELEMENTS OF THE CHURCH'S LIFE

situation and person, and demonstrate the focal place of the ordained ministerial functions in the existence of the community.

Although the theological undergirding for the ordained ministry is clear, the actual setting apart of those who are to serve in that ministry is fraught with ambiguity and some controversy. We will consider the call and ordination to ordained ministry under three polarities.

The first polarity is between ordained ministry and the "priesthood of all believers." Within Christendom as a whole and even within certain specific communions, there are differences of opinion between those who elevate the priesthood to an ontological status that pertains to the very person of the ordained minister, and those who insist that the office of the ordained is a creature of the laity and acquires whatever status it has by delegation from the communities of laity in which the ordained minister serves.[7] The concept of "the priesthood of all believers" is sometimes invoked as sanction for the view that the ordained ministry is a derived and conferred ministry: "You are a chosen race, a royal priesthood" (1 Pet. 2:9). The priesthood of all believers is seen as an antithesis to the ordained ministry, on the grounds that it asserts that every believer is a priest.

The concept of the priesthood of believers in fact affirms the need for ordained ministry, while at the same time putting that ministry in proper relationship to the laity. The concept does not assert, first of all, that every believer is a priest, but rather that whatever priesthood does exist belongs to and functions in behalf of all believers. The entire people, according to 1 Pet. 2:9, is and possesses the priesthood. The two significant implications of this are: first, that ordained priests are necessary in order to carry out the priesthood of all, and second, that those priests do not themselves possess or control the priesthood, but discharge it in behalf of the whole people of God.

A regularly called and regulated priestly group is required so that individual believers do not usurp or assume arbitrarily the priesthood that belongs to all. If any believer claims a priesthood to himself or herself by some intrinsic value, apart from selection by the whole, that believer is violating the claim of all other believers to the priesthood which is just as surely theirs. To establish an orderly process of setting apart priests and regulating their activity is to preserve the claims and rights to priesthood which belong to the whole people, and it is to preserve the eligibility of each believer to enter into that priestly group. The ordained ministry is not in opposition to the priesthood of all believers, but rather, properly conceived, implements that priesthood. The classical emphasis, in both Reformation and pre-Reformation church history, on "good order" (*vocatus rite*) in the calling and ordaining of ministers is an attempt to protect the reality of the priesthood belonging to all the believers and to prohibit priestly violations of that truth.

The ordained, however, cannot claim to control or possess the priesthood.

9 / THE CHURCH

They do not select their fellow priests, nor does the priesthood belong to the totality of the ordained. Whatever they do is in behalf of the whole people. This basic truth is violated by those traditions that assume the church belongs to the bishops and priests. Such an assumption is expressed whenever church practice allows the clergy to take possession of the policy-making process in the church or to treat the liturgy and preaching of the church as if it were their own possession.

This polarity is often a Protestant/Catholic tension. The former often do not exhibit a proper appreciation of the sacrality of the ordained ministry, while the latter manifest in their church practice a clerical domination that belies a genuinely catholic theology of the priesthood of all believers. Both groups are trying to escape these traditional perversions, but without great success.

A second polarity is between charisma and office. The "call" is the mandate that a believer receives to take up the ordained ministry, whereas ordination is a public act by which a person's call is acknowledged by the church, and that person is entrusted with the ministry of preaching, teaching, and presiding over sacramental life, maintenance, and governance. "Call" and "ordination" refer to a complex process in which the church aims at matching people who receive the charisma for ministry from God with specific responsibilities within the organized structure of the church. This tension between charisma and office is perennial and has dogged the church's life since the beginning.[8]

The very term "call" points to the perennial tension between the concept of the ministry of all believers and the ordained ministry. Luther and his Reformation colleagues emphasized that the "call," *vocatio*, first refers to the vocation or calling that comes to every Christian to live out the faith in the world.[9] This is in marked contrast to Roman Catholic usage, in which *vocatio* refers almost exclusively to the call to the priesthood. This difference in usage is also reflected in the respective understandings of Christian perfection. The Roman Catholic definition of perfection has traditionally been closely patterned after the life of the ordained, particularly the monastics. Protestants, on the contrary, tend to follow the suggestion of the Augsburg Confession (Article XXVII) in defining Christian perfection in terms of the grace that sustains daily life in the world, to which every Christian is called.[10]

The call to every Christian is from God. It may or may not be mediated through the institutionalized church, and it does not necessarily need the acknowledgment of the church to be carried out. Also, the call to ordained ministry derives from God, but it is mediated through the church universal as well as through the concrete community of Christians among whom the priest ministers; and this call must be acknowledged publicly by the church. It is because the call to the ordained ministry is a call to a public office, belonging to and representing the entire body of Christians, that this mediation and acknowledgment are required. The ordained minister receives an office and an officially assigned task; that is what distinguishes the call to ordination formally from the call which every Christian receives.

The tension between charisma and office in the ordained ministry parallels a third tension: that between the *ontology* of that ministry and its *function*. The ontological emphasis speaks of the "person" of the minister and the "indelible character" (*character indelibilis*) that ordination bestows, whereas the functional view speaks of what the minister does. The former validates the minister by a character of his or her being; the latter, by activities that are carried out. Reformation Christians, except for Anglicans, have emphasized the functional approach, and Roman Catholics and Orthodox have emphasized the ontological approach.

The two must be kept together. The ontological emphasis rightly calls attention to the fact that the functions of the ordained ministry require a person who can sustain those functions. Such a character of being comes only with God's gracious, that is, charismatic, preparation and sustaining action. The functional concern recognizes that the ordained ministry exists to serve purposes beyond and even sometimes quite apart from the person of the minister. The people who are ministers cannot claim any permanent possession of the charismata for ministry, except by God's grace. Furthermore, God can perform the divine ministry, with laity or ordained people, through even the most unfit, and often has.

It is not an easy thing to correlate in every case a call that comes from God, with the numinous dimensions that entails, with the structures of service that obtain within an organization, and with the processes of community affirmation and acknowledgment that are operative within that organization. The goal of the church's process of selecting ordained ministers is to bestow its ministerial office on those who receive the divine charisma for the office. This goal conforms to Paul's thinking in 1 Corinthians 12, to recognize the diversity of charismatic gifts by incorporating them into a variety of ordained ministries in the church. In this context, ordination by the church serves both to acknowledge the charisma that God bestows and over which the church has no control, and to bestow the privileges and responsibilities of the office, over which the church has been given custody, on the ordinand.

The church's ordination, which both acknowledges charisma and bestows office, is by tradition the prerogative of the bishop—or, in most Protestant churches, the bishop's equivalent—since the bishop represents the church universal. Whether explicitly or implicitly, the call of the local community of believers, among whom the priest will minister, also plays a necessary role in ordination. Whether the call of the local community is assumed in the bishop's acknowledgment, or whether ordination is made contingent on receipt

9 / THE CHURCH

of a formal local call, the theology of ordination implies service to a concrete community. Those groups that make ordination solely a function of the local community represent a fragmented theology in that they deny the place of the church universal.

The role of the bishop brings theories of apostolic succession to bear on ordination. The succession of the apostles became a matter of concrete urgency in the gnostic controversy of the late second century. Irenaeus and Tertullian laid the theological foundation for the doctrine. Since the gnostics could claim both Scripture and bishops to support their schism, it was necessary to demonstrate the apostolic authenticity of the orthodox bishops. Such authenticity had to include both apostolicity of faith and a continuous line of governing authority. The apostles were said to have had handed down their faith and authority over the churches, and neither element—faith or authority—could stand on its own without the other if the gnostic challenge were to be withstood.

There would be no reason to deviate from this classical formula of faith and governing authority in the tangible succession of the apostles, except for two facts: first, it is a matter of record that not all the bishops who have held the authority in direct succession have been orthodox in faith, and second, since the Reformation of the sixteenth century, most Protestants have been unable to claim direct linkage with apostolic governing authority, even though in some geographical areas they are the church for believers who have withdrawn from Roman Catholic jurisdiction in overwhelming numbers or who were never under that jurisdiction.

The basic strategy of the Reformation churches in the face of the judgment of history has been to assert that the apostolic succession of faith is preeminent over succession in the rite of ordination. On this basis, they have justified their own existence and criticized Roman Catholics for deviation from the faith. In response, Roman Catholics have over the centuries simply reasserted the position of Irenaeus and Tertullian, and thus disposed of the Protestants as schismatic and heretical. In recent years, since the Second Vatican Council, the Roman church has accepted that Protestant churches do manifest the signs of the Spirit and may be termed ecclesial communities. On the Reformation side, at least Anglicans and Lutherans, in dialogues with Roman Catholics, have acknowledged the primacy of Peter among the apostles and his preeminent role in the early church. Lutherans have acknowledged the significance of the papal office as a sign of unity and apostolic authenticity, insisting, however, that the "superiority over the bishops" which the pope possesses is "by human law" and not "divine" (*de jure humano*, not *de jure divino*), as Philip Melanchthon himself said in his subscription to the Smalcald Articles in 1537. Along with this qualified acceptance of the papacy, Lutherans acknowledge the primary role of Peter among the apostles and the continued efficacy of his primacy in the "Petrine function" within the church.[11] This function refers to the symbol of embodied unity in the church, that is, a teaching office freely accepted by the churches as their rallying point in the world.

The controversies over ordination, faith and governing authority constitute the major obstacles to church unity and intercommunion today between Roman Catholic and Eastern Orthodox bodies on the one side and Protestant bodies on the other. Regardless of their affirmation of faith, Protestant ordinations are not recognized by Catholics and Orthodox because they do not take place within the context of the apostolic succession of governing authority and do not include obedience to the bishops, and ultimately the pope, who stand in that succession. Since the Eucharist requires a validly ordained presider, and since the communicants profess their unity with the bishops through the presider, Roman Catholic and Orthodox authorities insist that it is improper for Roman Catholics and Orthodox to receive Communion from Protestant priests.[12]

As long as these controversies over ministry continue, Protestants have no option but to insist that succession in the faith of the apostles is primary and to follow that insistence with faithful attempts to be true to that faith, to repossess the catholicity that the Reformation events disrupted, and to follow the guidance of the Holy Spirit in their church life, including efforts to achieve unity in the universal church.

LITURGY AND SACRAMENTS

The liturgy, by which we mean the classical mass that has come down from apostolic times, is the church's full ordinary public act of prayer, praise, and devotion. In its context, the sacraments take place. We speak here of the sacraments on which there is widespread ecumenical agreement—baptism, Holy Communion, and penance.

The liturgy and sacraments are basic elements of the church's life because they embody for the church, in a fully embodied form, the heart of the church's faith and bring the believer into the fullest possible communion with the faith. Consequently, they constitute an epitome of the faith, its compact and full demonstration. The liturgy is a lucid, relatively unambiguous, and full expression within the church's own community of the faith that animates the church, that gives life to the church and to which the church is called to witness in the world. To refer back to our basic theological affirmations about the church, the liturgy and sacraments embody within the church that revelation of God's unfolding and God's purposes for the world which is manifest in Christ and to which the church is called to bear explicit testimony.

The liturgy and sacraments are constituted by symbolic actions and by words,

9 / THE CHURCH

participation in which enables people to receive God's revelation and respond in praise and gratitude to it. Consequently, the liturgy bears a compact, intense embodiment of God's loving assessment of the created order and God's intentions to bring that creation, despite its defects and sin, into intimate reconciliation with God and his purposes. The liturgy is therefore thoroughly centered in Jesus Christ. It bears to the believer the presence of Christ and invites full sharing in Christ. The celebration of the liturgy takes place within the context of the liturgical year, which is a reenactment of Jesus' life, death, resurrection, and teaching.

The first part of the mass, that of the catechumens, or "synaxis," consists of readings from Scripture that present Jesus' life and work and commentary on it, songs of praise and contemplation of that life and work, prayers in Christ's name, and preaching that relates Christ to contemporary life. The eucharistic portion of the liturgy is comprised of the most explicit and intense presentation of Christ: hymns celebrating his salvific work (Benedictus, Agnus Dei) and the prayer of thanksgiving, which ranks as a creedal recitation of Jesus' life and work, closing, in the epiclesis, with a plea that the Holy Spirit might incorporate the lives and activity of the worshipers into the work of Christ and its redemptive efficacy. The kiss of peace, the eating and drinking, and the final prayers involve the mind and body of each worshiper. The kiss involves a tangible expression of love and unity with fellow Christians, while the eating and drinking, together with the epiclesis and the later prayers that ask for full participation in the sacrifice of Christ, bring such a rich and intense encounter with God's work in Christ that it can scarcely be analyzed discursively.

Baptism, the rite of initiation into the community of believers, roots the life of the neophyte in the prevenient covenant love of God. The election of the believer is associated with the ritual cleansing, thereby providing a vivid symbol of the powerful blessing which God's election brings to all people.

The reality of divine grace—of God's intention to redeem creation—comes through strongly in all the forms of the liturgy. We call these forms an epitome of God's gracious intentions, because they are so lucid and because they involve the worshipers at several levels of their existence. Because the liturgical celebrations are contrived, they do not share the ambiguity that Christian life in the world must confront. That unambiguous clarity is precisely the proprium of the cultus, in contrast to other aspects of Christian life.

The liturgical forms present an epitome of the faithful human response to God as surely as they present God's gracious overture to the creation. The appropriate response is to receive above all, and then to receive gratefully and joyfully. This reception is fully embodied; its paradigm of intimacy is the eating and drinking, being fed by Christ's own body and blood, as these are caught up in Christ's supreme act of obedience unto death. Reception takes place within a community; it is not solitary. The reception involves intimate appropriation by the individual of Christ's benefits, but it also involves intimate horizontal love for and sharing with fellow human beings. Both the reception of grace and the expression of that grace in the life of love and service are thoroughly enfleshed, embodied, earthly. The cultus is the most explicitly material expression of the faith imaginable. In this too it is the epitome of what the faith entails outside the confines of the cultus.

When we properly understand the role of liturgy and sacraments, as the visible epitome or paradigm of the faith that animates the church, then we can discern the reasons they have traditionally been associated with ordained priests and bishops. The leadership of the priest and the priest's mandated activity of making clear what the church is about can hardly be separated from the priest's place in the liturgical and sacramental life of the church. The traditional prohibition, except in unusual circumstances, against anyone but an ordained minister presiding over these public acts of the church is a continuation of the minister's responsibility as watchman and herald to the community.

We can also appreciate anew why the reformers placed Word and sacrament at the center of the ministry and the life of the church, and why they insisted that Word and sacrament must be in conformity with the gospel of grace. Precisely because liturgy and sacraments convey so powerfully what the church and its faith are, their witness must be as clear and pure as possible. Article VII of the Augsburg Confession designates the gospel-purity of Word and sacrament as the touchstone for determining whether churches are or can be in unity. Article VII's famous *satis est* pertains to this: "For it is sufficient for the true unity of the Christian church that the Gospel be preached in conformity with a pure understanding of it and that the sacraments be administered in accordance with the divine word" (*BC* 32). Calvin echoes this sentiment in his *Institutes*.[13] This view is nothing but the judgment that the most adequate test for determining church unity is what a group tells itself is the center of the faith and the essence of the church. This is itself an expression of grace, since it raises up as test not that a church embody perfectly the faith in its life, and thereby be tested by works, but rather that a church adequately proclaim to itself the message of God's grace by which alone the church can live. Contrariwise, if such proclamation is present, all manner of other details can be overlooked; and such details dare not be made into a cause of disunion.

PREACHING AND TEACHING

The place of preaching and teaching in the church is easily deduced from what has already been said about ministry and liturgy. Preaching and teaching

9 / THE CHURCH

are essential to the life of the church because they are powerful instruments for communicating the gospel that stands at the heart of the church's life and for rendering that gospel actual within the church. Preaching and teaching can be considered together, since the terms are interchangeable in much of the church's tradition. Article VII of the Augsburg Confession, in describing the importance of a faithful communication of the Word of God in the church, uses "preach" in the German version and "teach" in the Latin. The centrality of preaching is stated forcefully by Luther. In his presentation of the marks of the church, he places "The Word" first; by that term he means preaching:

> This Christian, holy people is to be known by this, that it has God's Word. . . . We speak of the external Word orally preached by men like you and me. For Christ left this behind Him as an outward sign whereby His Church, His Christian, holy people in the world, was to be recognized. We speak, too, of this oral Word as it is earnestly believed and publicly confessed before the world, as He says, "He that confesseth me before men, him will I confess before my Father and His angels.". . . Wherever, therefore, you hear or see this Word preached, believed, confessed, and acted on, there do not doubt that there must be a true *ecclesia sancta catholica*.[14]

COMMUNITY OF LOVE AND CARE OF SOULS

Much of our description of the ministry, lay and ordained, has emphasized the activities of preaching, teaching, and reminding in the internal life of the church and in the church's witness to the outside world. This emphasis, however important, is defective to the extent that it overlooks the actualization of the life of grace, even if imperfect, in the church. This actualization of grace takes the form of mutual love and what classically was referred to as "care of souls": the building up of the people in the church through attention to their spiritual growth and development. There has been much talk in recent decades of the church as a model or paradigm community in the world, and a good part of this paradigmatic character has been thought of as taking the form of the loving and mutually encouraging community. This mark of the church finds a scriptural basis in 1 John: "We know that we have passed out of death into life, because we love the brethren. He who does not love remains in death. . . . By this we know love, that he laid down his life for us; and we ought to lay down our lives for the brethren" (1 John 3:14–16). This dimension of the church's life has its own intrinsic worth, according to the example and message of Jesus, but it also has instrumental value in strengthening the believers for their ministry in the world. To this we turn next.

MISSION

God sent Jesus Christ to save the world, not to found and sustain a church. The first part of this statement echoes John 3:16, while the second part voices an all-too-frequent criticism of the church, that it has often forgotten why it exists and concentrates instead on its own institutional maintenance. Our initial theological proposition about the church was that God made sure there would be a witness to what God is doing in the world, and that this witness is explicit in the church. Such a proposition shows the necessity of the church, but it also clarifies why the church must direct its gaze and effort primarily outward to the world and not inward to itself. The church's very essence is witness to what God is doing in the world.

Such considerations have prompted some theologians to say that the church *is* mission; it *is* outreach into the world.[15] H. Richard Niebuhr pictured the church as a "social pioneer," a community of the avant-garde, actualizing what God intended for the world in advance of the rest of the world.[16] In Chapter 1 we rehearsed the debates between those who consider mission to be evangelization that increases the church and those who consider it to be world renewal. Certainly mission means both, but just as certainly the stronger emphasis should be on the activity that witnesses to what God is doing, on world renewal. Furthermore, where evangelization wins new members to the church, the aim of that work is not to increase the church's size but to enable it to penetrate the world more successfully with the message and actuality of God's own ministry to the world.

Our assertion that the ministry of the church is first of all God's own ministry to creation reinforces the notion that the church's ministry is mission. This mission is given content by its transparency to God's nature as loving creator and redeemer, to God's will to bring the creation into full reconciliation with God, and to God's activity to consummate that will with regard to the creation. Such a view will not permit the church to leave mission far down in its priorities, and it will not allow the church to define its mission in institutionally self-serving terms.

Luther does not include mission among his seven marks of the church, but he does speak of other matters that imply it. "Suffering" is his seventh mark, and this suffering is elicited when the church faithfully witnesses to Christ in the world. Under the heading "other outward signs," Luther speaks of the sanctified life according to the "second table of Moses." This sanctified life consists largely of actions toward fellow humans in the course of daily life in the world. These comments remind us of the Lutheran doctrines of vocation and Christian perfection. Luther's situation was one in which the concept of the *corpus christianum* was viable for interpreting the world; all society was

9 / THE CHURCH

Christian. Hence the church's outreach could hardly be to evangelize non-Christians! Rather, it was for individual Christians to penetrate their daily situations with sanctified life, interpreted not only as the life of faithfulness to secular callings, but also as the turning of those callings into instruments for serving fellow human beings, glorifying God, and living out God's grace. Such living always entails suffering, living by faith, and good works.

In any case, whether the inclusion can be justified by reference to Luther and the other reformers or not, any list of the marks of the church today must include mission. In the current global situation, that mission must further be interpreted as actualizing in the life of the world a witness to the intentions and power of God to work the fulfillment of the creation according to God's will.

CHURCH ORDER OR ORGANIZATION

In our discussion of the ministry, we observed that the Roman Catholic and Orthodox bodies consider the episcopal organization of the church essential. We traced this view at least back to Cyprian, in whose time visible unity around an orthodox bishop was a matter of great urgency for the church's survival. This organization and unity imply obedience and allegiance to the bishop. For Roman Catholics, this obedience and unity extend to the bishop of Rome, the pope. Anglicans also approve the episcopal organization of the church as very nearly essential to its existence. They have argued that if the episcopacy is not of the church's *esse* (being), it is at least of its *bene esse* (well-being), or the *plene esse* (full being). Other bodies, such as the Church of Scotland, the COCU (Church of Christ Uniting) bodies in the United States, and the Church of South India, have considered a certain order to be essential to the life of the church; for most of them, the episcopal order is the norm.

Lutherans have never considered a specific church order necessary. They have defined the essence of Christianity in terms of proper understanding of the gospel of grace, rather than in terms of community structures. As we noted, Lutherans have increasingly come to accept the possibility of episcopal organization, so long as it is considered to be a matter of human law and not of divine law. Such a view is open to episcopal order but denies that it is of the *esse* of the church.

Lutherans recognize that they are a minority within Christendom in their attitude toward church order. Their position is consistent with their theological insistence that grace alone is the rule of Christian existence before God and the world. Such an insistence rejects any notion that a specific empirical form of behavior or organization is necessary for the church, or that it would make the church "better" in any theologically significant way. Lutherans are bound by the fact that their understanding of the *satis est*, that is, of what is necessary for church unity, puts the proclamation of grace at the center. Consequently, although they have no difficulty accepting various church orders for the sake of harmony, by human decision, they can scarcely resist the temptation to judge other bodies' insistence on specific organizational forms as an implicit denial of the primacy of grace. Such a judgment is patently unfair and misguided in many cases, and the fact that it is so provides the challenge for Lutherans, not only to goad other churches into a clearer sense for the implications of a theology of grace, but also to be more sensitive themselves as to how their insistence on grace can be ecumenically constructive and foster a proper church unity.

THE CHURCH'S CONCRETENESS AS SOURCE OF THEOLOGICAL TRUTH

There is now considerable discussion of the claim that perception of perennial theological truths emerges only in and from the concrete, particular life of the churches. The discussion is located chiefly in Latin America, and it is commonly known as "liberation theology." The theologians who belong to this movement are largely though not exclusively Roman Catholic and have devoted a great deal of attention to the doctrine of the church. For the theologians of this movement, the concrete life of the church cannot be ignored in discussing its universality and unity. That concrete life in Latin America is greatly diverse and sharply divided along lines of economic and social class. This fact of life demands that the church bring its theological self-understanding into intimate dialogue with social reality. When it does so, it recognizes that overcoming social-class distinction and exploitation cannot be excluded from concepts of mission and church order. Camilo Torres went so far as to say that class antagonism rendered the eucharistic unity of the church impossible; until that antagonism was overcome, the church could not profess to be one even in its symbolic life. Lutherans in South Africa have come to similar conclusions. Gustavo Gutierrez writes:

> It is undeniable that class struggle poses problems to the universality of Christian love and the unity of the church. But any consideration of this subject must start from two elemental points: the class struggle is a fact, and neutrality in this matter is impossible.[17]

Gutierrez brings the concrete social and organizational form of the church into direct theological significance. The mission of the church must include opposition to social evil, and so long as the church allows an evil social structure to mold its own organization and life, it fails to be a community that is one and loving. Methodologically, one cannot say that unity is an attribute of the church if social forces of oppressive division dominate the concrete life of the church. The essence of the church's unity is to be understood only in the process of observing the church's particularity and seeking to alter the shape of that particularity.

Benoit Dumas insists that the process of actualization must be understood eschatologically. Since the church is caught up in human alienation, the eschatological process of "dealienation" must in future mark the concrete historical shape of the church's life.[18] Dumas's and Gutierrez's view is dialectical: it relates eschatology and reality so as to challenge the church to work toward overcoming oppressive particularities. Hugo Assmann, on the contrary, holds that the essential thrust of the church is tenable only within a thoroughly historical and relative framework; the church always opposes the defective situation in which it lives and never deludes itself that it can be in this world what it essentially is.[19]

Juan Luis Segundo attempts to hold these contrasting positions together. Starting from the assumption that the "church is essentially described by the very fact of its incarnation in history," he builds on Teilhard de Chardin's vision of the church embodying a thrust that is exceptional and against the stream, yet it represents the power of the future.[20] The church is the community of "those who already know," and this "already knowing" brings them into dialogue with the world through action that embodies the future under the conditions of present life.[21] Embodying, as it does, a fundamental thrust of time, the church is concerned primarily with the world, not with the church. In its living dialogue with the world, the church aims at embodying the truth of the world's future.

The concrete consequences of the Latin American ecclesiology have included the so-called basic communities, communities that are committed to fashioning new social realities. These communities have become the seedbeds for reflection of many types—sociology, pedagogy, and theology. The concern for critical, eschatological embodiment in the church's life renders this Latin American ecclesiology an important voice in the search to understand both the existence and the essence of the church and a resource for linking them.

THE CONCEPT OF ADIAPHORA

The considerations we have just described, concerning the concrete life of the church, bring into our purview the concept of "adiaphora." Adiaphora are "those ceremonies or church usages which are neither commanded nor forbidden in the Word of God but have been introduced into the church in the interest of good order and the general welfare."[22] These are matters on which there can be disagreement and diversity without disturbing the unity of the church. The Formula of Concord professes:

BASIC ELEMENTS OF THE CHURCH'S LIFE

> We believe, teach, and confess that no church should condemn another because it has fewer or more external ceremonies not commanded by God, as long as there is mutual agreement in doctrine and in all its articles as well as in the right use of the holy sacraments, according to the familiar axiom, "Disagreement in fasting does not destroy agreement in faith."[23]

The Lutheran stance on church organization stems from the conviction that the matter is an adiaphoron. Similarly, Lutherans consider specific forms of liturgy, discipline, and the like to be matters on which there can be diversity and disagreement. Their opponents on the question of church order deny that it is in this category. For them, Lutherans define the substance of the faith too meagerly. If the parties disagree on whether a matter is an adiaphoron, they are likely to talk past each other, even if, as in the case of episcopacy, they share large areas of agreement.

The danger into which Lutherans and others like them may fall on the adiaphora question, is that they may consider adiaphora to be unimportant or unworthy of serious reflection. That a matter is an adiaphoron does not mean it is unimportant. External forms are mediators of grace and must be dealt with properly. Church order and liturgy, for example, may be dealt with quite wrongly and perpetrate great harm in the church if they are not made the object of responsible reflection. Decisions concerning adiaphora must be made on the basis of our fundamental theological principle: according to whether they convey adequately the truth of what God intends for creation, as set forth in Jesus Christ.

There is a hierarchy of values among the adiaphora. Some forms are more important than others. For example, it is obviously more important to consider carefully just how the bread and wine will be distributed in Holy Communion than whether the bread is white or dark. Some actions, even if their forms are adiaphoral, are themselves indispensable, for example, preaching. Other actions (e.g., incense in the liturgy) may be omitted altogether. Luther's discussion of the marks of the church takes sharp issue with discussions prominent in his day, because he insisted that a great many items were adiaphora and thus could not be considered true marks.

In considering the adiaphora, there is always a tension between the earthly form and the divine substance to be communicated. The forms are never adequately transparent to convey the truth about God's intentions, and thus they are always earthen vessels, as Paul writes.

Our attitude toward adiaphora should never be legalistic. The Formula of Concord resolved "adiaphoristic" controversies in the sixteenth century with the judgment that while we may decide to accept differing practices and forms, as Melanchthon was willing to accept the papacy, it is a violation of faith to

9 / THE CHURCH

insist that adiaphora be accepted as a condition of unity. Consequently a proper understanding of the adiaphora would never permit a legalistic attitude or practice.

NOTES

1. Martin Luther, "On the Council and the Church," in *Works of Martin Luther*, vol. 5 (Philadelphia: A. J. Holman, 1931), p. 270.
2. Ibid., p. 287.
3. T. W. Manson, *The Church's Ministry* (London: Hodder & Stroughton, 1948), esp. chap. 1.
4. Bernard Cooke, *Ministry to Word and Sacraments* (Philadelphia: Fortress Press, 1976).
5. Cyprian, "The Unity of the Church," in *The Fathers of the Church*, vol. 36, ed. Roy J. Defferrari (New York: Fathers of the Church, Inc., 1958), pp. 91–124.
6. Cyprian, "Letter to the People," in *The Fathers of the Church*, vol. 51, ed. (Rose Bernard Donna (New York and Washington, D.C.: Catholic University of America Press, 1964), p. 109.
7. Cyril Eastwood, *The Priesthood of All Believers* (Minneapolis: Augsburg Publishing House, 1962).
8. Hans von Campenhausen, *Ecclesiastical Authority and Spiritual Power in the Church of the First Three Centuries*, trans. J. Baker (Stanford: Stanford University Press; London: A. & C. Black, 1969).
9. Gustaf Wingren, *Luther on Vocation* (Philadelphia: Fortress [Muhlenberg] Press, 1957). Donald Heiges, *The Christian's Calling* (Philadelphia: Board of Publication of the ULCA, 1958).
10. See Albrecht Ritschl, "Introduction to the History of Pietism," in *Three Essays* (Philadelphia: Fortress Press, 1973), pp. 51–149.
11. See Paul C. Empie and T. Austin Murphy, eds., *Papal Primacy and the Universal Church* (Minneapolis: Augsburg Publishing House, 1974). Also Paul C. Empie, T. Austin Murphy, and Joseph A. Burgess, eds., *Teaching Authority and Infallibility in the Church* (Minneapolis: Augsburg Publishing House, 1978).
12. Paul C. Empie and T. Austin Murphy, eds., *Eucharist and Ministry* (New York: U.S.A. National Committee of the Lutheran World Federation, 1970).
13. *Calvin: Institutes of the Christian Religion*, ed. John T. McNeill (Philadelphia: Westminster Press, 1960), bk. 4, chap. 1, par. 9, pp. 1023–24.
14. Luther, "On the Councils and the Church," pp. 270–72.
15. Colin Williams, *What in the World?* (New York: National Council of Churches, 1964). Also *Where in the World? Changing Forms of the Church's Witness* (New York: National Council of Churches, 1963).
16. H. Richard Niebuhr, "The Responsibility of the Church for Society," in *The Gospel, the Church, and the World*, ed. K. S. Latourette (New York: Harper & Brothers, 1946).

17. Gustavo Gutierrez, *A Theology of Liberation* (Maryknoll, N.Y.: Orbis Books, 1973), p. 273. I am indebted to V. Westhelle for these references and those that follow in notes 18–21.

18. Benoit Dumas, *Los dos rostros alienados de la iglesia una* (Buenos Aires: Latinoamerica, 1971).

19. Hugo Assmann, *Teología desde la praxis de la liberación*, 2d ed. (Salamanca: Sigueme, 1976), p. 169.

20. Juan Luis Segundo, *The Hidden Motives of Pastoral Action* (Maryknoll, N.Y.: Orbis Books, 1978); and also his *De la sociedad a la teología* (Buenos Aires: Carlos Lohle, 1970), pp. 159–65.

21. Juan Luis Segundo, *The Community Called Church* (Maryknoll, N.Y.: Orbis Books, 1978), pp. 11ff., 126.

22. Formula of Concord, Epitome, Article X; *BC* 492.

23. Ibid., Article X, Affirmative Theses, 5; *BC* 493–94.

4

The Church and the Kingdom of God

The church stands in intimate and important relationship to the kingdom of God. The term we use to denote the relationship is "transparency." To be transparent to the kingdom means that the church proclaims that there is a kingdom of God, that the kingdom is redemption, and that the life of the church should be congruent with the kingdom.

POSSIBILITIES FOR RELATING CHURCH AND KINGDOM OF GOD

In this age, the church is *"ecclesia militans,"* the *"militant* church." The church provides a framework for its members, in which they can carry on the struggle for meaning and peace. It provides structures of organization, sacramental actions, kerygmatic presentations of God's grace, and a network of personal caring. This concrete environment is basic to the church's historical existence. The really pressing question, however, the question that is decisive for the church, is its relationship to God and God's fundamental purposes for creation. This question points us back to the fundamental theological assertion with which we began, that the church's essential role is determined by the recognition that it is a witness to the purpose that God has set for the created world.

This question of the church's relation to God's ultimate purposes is the question of its relation to the kingdom of God. The *ecclesia militans* stands in relation to the *ecclesia triumphans* (triumphant church), a comparable phrase that speaks of the church's nature and destiny as a participant in God's final consummation. "Kingdom of God" is a central biblical and theological representation of God's own final purposes for creation. The kingdom of God includes the dimension of the *actual accomplishment* of those purposes, hence the close association of kingdom and *consummation*.

There are basically three ways to conceive of the kingdom of God: as only future, as thoroughly realized here and now, or as a dialectical joining of the

9 / THE CHURCH

future and the realized. Practically all Christians hold to some form of the third, dialectical view.[1] It is almost impossible to hold to a thoroughly futurist view, since the Christian faith intrinsically holds that Christ brought redemption sufficient to the human situation. On the other hand, Christianity just as intrinsically believes that God's full consummation has not yet been accomplished.

Theology has nearly always tried to develop some form of the dialectical view of the relation between church and kingdom. Perhaps only those conceptions gathered under the "institutional" model of the church, dominant from the High Middle Ages until Vatican II, break the dialectic completely.[2] Such conceptions picture the church as a terrestrial entity that brings believers directly to the brink of God's consummation at the point of their death. They then enter directly into the vision of God. The church is simply a means of grace that transports to the heavenly precincts.

All other ecclesiologies concentrate on the tension between kingdom and church; they recognize that the two are not the same thing, but they do have a relationship. Avery Dulles summarizes the relation:

> From the second model [mystical communion], I would take over the idea that the Church is not a mere means of grace, but a place where grace is realized and lived even here on earth. The community of grace is an anticipation of the final Kingdom. From the third model [sacrament], I would adopt the view that the Church is to be, here on earth, a sign or representative of the salvation to which we look forward—a sign that is admittedly somewhat ambiguous in this earthly life, but one that promises to become clear and unequivocal when the final Kingdom arrives. From the fourth model [herald], I would derive the ideas that the Church proclaims the coming of the Kingdom in Christ, and that the proclamation itself is an eschatological event, in which God's saving and judging power is already at work. From the fifth model [servant], finally, I would accept the thesis that the Church has the task of introducing the values of the Kingdom into the whole of human society, and thus of preparing the world, insofar as human effort can, for the final transformation when God will establish the new heavens and the new earth.[3]

In Dulles's terms, then, we may say that the church is the anticipation, sign, proclamation, and actual preparation of the kingdom.

The understanding of the church as the anticipation of the kingdom has received great emphasis in the documents of Vatican II, in ecumenical statements of the World Council of Churches, and in a number of important contemporary theologians. *Lumen gentium*, for example, says:

> The Church "like a pilgrim in a foreign land, presses forward amid the persecutions of the world and the consolations of God," announcing the cross and death of the Lord until He comes. By the power of the risen Lord, she is given strength

to overcome patiently and lovingly the afflictions and hardships which assail her from within and without, and to show forth in the world the mystery of the Lord in a faithful though shadowed way, until at last it will be revealed in total splendor.[4]

Wolfhart Pannenberg presents an ecclesiology that is grounded in the kingdom of God.[5] The kingdom symbolizes God's future for the whole world; the church is an eschatological community, in that it is an anticipation of the "new humanity," the condition that God is preparing for the world to attain; the kingdom of God, consequently, clarifies why the church is important because it is an "honest institution" that brings humanity into touch with its ultimate destiny, and in doing so it brings them into touch with the proleptic kingdom of God. The church is not to be identified with the kingdom, nor is it the present form of the future kingdom. Rather its relation to the kingdom is that it has a "vocation" for the kingdom. This vocation is elaborated: "The Church in a secular society provides the individual with an opportunity to participate now in the ultimate destiny of human life. This is the Church's mandate and, if she is faithful to it, her special contribution."[6]

Or again, Hans Küng writes:

> The church is not a preliminary stage, but an *anticipatory sign* of the definitive reign of God: a sign of the reality of the reign of God already present in Jesus Christ, a sign of the coming completion of the reign of God. The meaning of the Church does not reside in itself, in what it is, but in what it is moving towards. It is the reign of God which the Church hopes for, bears witness to, proclaims. It is not the bringer or the bearer of the reign of God which is to come and is at the same time present, but its voice, its announcer, its *herald*. God alone can bring his reign; the Church is devoted entirely to its service.[7]

Küng links the church and the kingdom through the *preaching* of Jesus about the kingdom. Thus, the elements of Jesus' original preaching about the kingdom become later "ecclesiological imperatives." The church extends that preaching to the world but also preaches it to itself. The goal is that an encounter with the church's preaching about the kingdom should have the effect of Jesus' own preaching.[8]

THE CHURCH TRANSPARENT TO THE KINGDOM

The church, in the scheme that we have set forth in this *locus*, is the decisive temporal and spatial corporate symbolic manifestation of the meanings which God has actualized in creation and which God will consummate at the final

9 / THE CHURCH

day. To say this is to say that the church is the symbolic manifestation of the meaning of God for creation. It follows from this concept of the church that it must stand in intimate relationship to the kingdom of God. The best way to express this relationship is: The church is transparent to the kingdom of God.

The concept of transparency enables us to apprehend the complexity of the relationship between church and kingdom. First, it helps us preserve the superordinate position of the kingdom without minimizing the church. God establishes the kingdom, not humans, not even humans in the church. The church is not the object of God's redemptive intention; it is the world that God wills to redeem. We preserve these insights when we say that the church points beyond itself to God's meanings for the world. The kingdom embodies these meanings, in actualized form, so it is only natural that the church is transparent to the kingdom and not the converse. It is the world that God wills to redeem, and the concept of transparency makes it clear that the church's business is to be a means for communicating that intention for the world.

Second, the role of the human and human activity, in contrast to God and God's activity, is frequently misunderstood in reference to church and kingdom. It has been said often in recent theology that the church is human whereas the kingdom pertains to God. It is also often asserted that human action cannot bring in the kingdom, whereas the church abounds with human activity. The concept of transparency throws light on how these concerns may be expressed without vitiating the relation of church to kingdom. It is improper to say that the church is without remainder human, because the church says of itself that it intends to be transparent to the meanings that God holds for the world. Conversely, it is not correct to deny a human dimension to the kingdom, because God's final consummation of creation includes human being as a significant element. Although the kingdom is neither initiated nor perfected by human activity, the consummation is the consummation of human activity, the activity of the creatures that have been ordained by God as co-creators.

Third, by insisting on the symbolic character of the church, we enable a strong emphasis on the significance of the church without rendering it identical to, or a univocal expression of, God's final consummation. No aspect of the church's life is an end in itself. Its liturgy is symbolic of the Christian's stance in the world outside the church; its community of pastoral care and sharing exists to strengthen Christians for their life outside the church; its organization exists only to enable it to extend God's ministry to the world more effectively; its social ministry cannot accomplish the reform of the world, but it does signal the sort of reform and caring that should always be exercised by all human agents.

When we say that the church is transparent to the kingdom of God, we mean that among earthly institutions and communities it stands as the one that explicitly holds itself accountable to embody signals of what God is about in the world. This in turn means that the church is dedicated to the life that proclaims to the world that there is a kingdom of God, a final purpose for the world, that proclaims through word and deed that that final purpose is redemptive, and that seeks to ensure that all its words and deeds are consistent with the meanings of the kingdom.

The idea that the church is transparent to the kingdom of God provides a strong declaration of what the church essentially is, as well as a prescription of what the church must become. God's greatest gift to the church is that which provides its essential nature—the traditions of meaning that point to God. In its attempt to be faithful to this gift, the church finds its mandate and its judgment. Its structures, its message, its liturgy and communal life, and its outreach must always be reformed toward greater conformity with the intentions of God for the world. As the church focuses on these divine intentions and meanings, it renews its ties to the source of its life. The hope of the church points to the day when it will indeed not pass away but will be transfigured in God's own work of consummation.

NOTES

1. Avery Dulles, *Models of the Church* (Dublin: Gill & Macmillan, 1976), p. 103.
2. Ibid., pp. 103–4.
3. Ibid., pp. 113–14.
4. *Lumen Gentium*, art. 8.
5. Wolfhart Pannenberg, *Theology and the Kingdom of God* (Philadelphia: Westminster Press, 1969), pp. 73ff.
6. Ibid., p. 86.
7. Hans Küng, *The Church*, trans. R. and R. Ockender (New York and London: Sheed & Ward, 1967), p. 96.
8. Ibid., pp. 47–54, 96–104.

TENTH LOCUS

The Means of Grace

PART ONE: THE WORD
HANS SCHWARZ

PART TWO: THE SACRAMENTS
ROBERT W. JENSON

THE MEANS OF GRACE

Introduction

Part One: The Word

1. The Biblical Understanding of the Word of God
   The Word as the Means of God's Self-disclosure
   The History-Making Power of God's Word
   Jesus Christ as God's Final Word

2. The Dynamics of God's Word
   The Judging and Liberating Word: Law and Gospel
   The Word as Guidance: "Third Use" and Penance
   The Dialogical Word: Prayer and Liturgy
   The Empirical Word: Miracles

Part Two: The Sacraments

3. Sacraments of the Word
   Commands
   Promises
   Visible Words
   Fact and Meaning
   Actual Liturgy

4. Baptism
   The Command
   The Promises
   Regeneration
   The Integrity of Baptism
   The Uses of Baptism

5. The Supper
   The Command

CONTENTS

    The Authenticity of the Supper
    The Promises
    Eucharist
    Ego Berengarius . . .

6. The Return to Baptism
    Rites of the Spirit
    Penance
    Ordination
    Healing
    Marriage

Introduction

The means of grace comprise "the word" and "the sacraments" and are an intrinsic part of the Christian life.[1] But they raise many questions. How is it possible that grace can be communicated through words and objects? Should we understand this in a magical way or in a symbolic, spiritual way? Most religions employ means of grace similar to those in the Christian faith, be it in the form of sacred writings, ritual meals, initiation rites, propitiatory sacrifices, or prescribed washings and anointings. To what extent is the Christian understanding of the means of grace shared with the religious milieu out of which the Christian faith originated? The issue is further complicated in that the means of grace are intimately connected with the experiential side of humanity. The question then arises to what extent these means can be empirically described in their cause and effect. Can it be demonstrated that grace comes from God, or does it simply arise from within the emotional life of the individual? And is there a way to ascertain that these means are effective for the recipient? The judgment of Friedrich Nietzsche that Christians should look much more redeemed if there is any truth to the Christian faith cannot be ignored.

While we dare not suppress these issues, we must first investigate the nature of the Christian sacraments. The means of grace are central to the church. The Roman Catholic church is a predominately sacramental institution, intent on assuring its members that it administers the means of grace. By contrast, the main-line Protestant churches are often called the churches of "word *and* sacrament."

The term "means of grace" is not a biblical one, but the term "word" (*logos* or *rhēma*) is attested in the New Testament, while the term "sacrament" is missing. We learn in the book of Acts that the Christian community in Jerusalem "day by day, attending the temple together and breaking bread in their homes, . . . partook of food with glad and generous hearts" (Acts 2:46). This passage depicts a very early stage in the life of the Christian community. In addition to hearing the word of God in the temple, they also had their own gatherings around word and sacrament. Thus we read in Acts 2:42: "And they devoted themselves to the apostles' teaching and fellowship, to the breaking of bread and the prayers." We see here that the life of the Chris-

253

tians revolves around the word (Scripture and catechetical instruction) and sacrament (eucharistic fellowship). Both terms, "word" and "sacrament," need considerable clarification, especially with regard to the relation to the Jewish community out of which the Christian church emerged and with regard to Jesus Christ, the founder of the Christian church.

NOTES

1. For comprehensive studies on the subject of this *locus*, consult Bernard J. Cooke, *Ministry to Word and Sacraments* (Philadelphia: Fortress Press, 1976); and Robert W. Jenson, *Visible Words: The Interpretation and Practice of Christian Sacraments* (Philadelphia: Fortress Press, 1978). We must also note the results of bilateral denominational conversations, such as *One Baptism for the Remission of Sins* (1966), *Eucharist and Ministry* (1967), and *Eucharist as Sacrifice* (1970), resulting from the Lutheran–Roman Catholic dialogues in the United States.

PART ONE: THE WORD

1
The Biblical Understanding of the Word of God

Though appropriated by human conceptuality, the word of God is not a word about God but a word from God and thereby a word through which God discloses himself to us. Since it enacts history, God's word is not separable from God's actions. Jesus Christ is God's final word both as God's ultimate self-disclosure and as bringing history to completion through God's redemptive word and work. The incarnation of God's word in Jesus Christ opens for us full access to God.

THE WORD AS THE MEANS OF GOD'S SELF-DISCLOSURE

When we reflect on "the word of God," the question emerges whether we mean a word *about* God or *from* God. In his incisive essay "What Does It Mean to Speak of God?" (1925), Rudolf Bultmann attempted to clear the issue: "If 'speaking of God' is understood as *'speaking about God,'* then such speaking has no meaning whatever, for its subject, God, is lost in the very moment it takes place."[1] If God is the reality determining all else, speaking about God would be a contradiction, since it presupposes a standpoint external to what is being talked about. Since there can be no standpoint external to God, it is not legitimate to speak *about* God in general statements that presume to be valid without reference to the concrete, existential position of the speaker.

Karl Barth sensed a similar difficulty when he stated: "As ministers we ought to speak of God. We are human, however, and so cannot speak of God. We ought therefore to recognize both, our obligation and our inability *and* by that very recognition give God the Glory."[2] But Bultmann does not abandon the difficult task of proclaiming the word of God, and neither does Barth. Bultmann continues, "We can speak of him [God] only in so far as we are speaking of his Word spoken to us, of his act done to us. 'Of God we can only tell what he does to us,'" he concludes, quoting Wilhelm Herrmann.[3] Since we are on earth, we cannot speak of God in the true sense. But unless we want to recede into mystical silence, we must speak about God, though knowing that any speech about God is necessarily inadequate.

We conclude from these considerations, informed by Søren Kierkegaard's insistence on the infinite qualitative difference between God and humanity, that any word about God cannot be a word that has humanity as its initiator. To be of any significance in "describing God," it must be a word that describes us as we understand ourselves addressed by God. A word *about* God is a reflection of God's word to us. A word about God cannot be a descriptive statement about God, but it can be an approximation of how God acts with us.

Paul Tillich captured this situation well when he stated, "Everything religion has to say about God, including his qualities, actions, manifestations, has a symbolic character and . . . the meaning of 'God' is completely missed if one takes the symbolic language literally." Asking whether a nonsymbolic statement about God is possible, Tillich concludes: "There is a point at which a nonsymbolic assertion about God must be made . . . , namely, the statement that everything we say about God is symbolic."[4] Any word about God has at best symbolic character, but this does not mean it is of no value.

Tillich distinguishes between "sign" and "symbol," saying, "While the sign bears no necessary relation to that to which it points, the symbol participates in the reality of that for which it stands."[5] A religious symbol not only points to the divine; if it is a true symbol, it also participates in the power of the divine. Reviewing the abundant literature about God, one wonders, however, whether the symbols advocated actually disclosed much about God, since there seems to be little consensus about them. Wolfgang Trillhaas characterized the situation aptly: "Each dogmatician, especially among the modern ones, decrees the attributes [of God] differently than another, so that one cannot refute the impression that this process is governed by a certain arbitrary speculation which is nourished by the richness of biblical and at the same time philosophical tradition."[6]

Friedrich Schleiermacher sensed this subjective and speculative tendency when he noted that after the age of scholasticism, metaphysics was treated separately from Christian doctrine, in the philosophical discipline called natural theology. Yet he asserted that we should not forget that the representations of the divine attributes are of religious origin, not of philosophical origin. "All attributes which we ascribe to God are to be taken as denoting not something special in God, but only something special in the manner in which the feeling of absolute dependence is to be related to Him."[7] The adjectives we attribute to God are not descriptive of God, nor do they originate from human fantasy. They are an attempt to express how we experience God's

THE BIBLICAL UNDERSTANDING OF THE WORD OF GOD

relationship to us. To talk about God and God's likeness is different from speaking in a raised voice about ourselves. If these concepts truly express how we experience God's relationship to us, they indeed disclose some modality of God to us. Or, to use Tillich's terminology, they are true symbols and participate in the power of the divine to which they point.

It should be clear, however, that these concepts do not disclose God in the divine essence, that is, apart from God's self-disclosure. Luther appropriately stated this restriction when he said,

> It is therefore insane to argue about God and the divine nature without the Word or any covering. . . . Whoever desires to be saved and to be safe when he deals with such great matters, let him simply hold on to the form, the signs, and the coverings of the Godhead, such as His Word and His works. For in His Word and in His works He shows Himself to us.[8]

On another occasion Luther warned:

> Through their speculations some ascend into heaven and speculate about God the creator, etc. Do not get mixed up with this God. Whoever wishes to be saved should move away from God in his majesty, for He and the human creature are enemies. Rather grasp that God whom David also grasps. He is the God who is clothed in his promises. . . . Such a God one must have. . . . We know no other God than the one who is clothed in his promises. If he would talk to me in his majesty I would run away like the Jews did. But when he is clothed in the voice of man and accommodates himself to our capacity to understand, I can approach him.[9]

It is interesting to speculate about such things as the omnipotence or the aseity of God. Yet the only directive we have in our desire to talk theologically about God is the God-disclosive history that culminated in Jesus Christ. This does not mean that philosophical concepts of God's being are without validity. Biblical reflection on God's self-disclosure is itself not written in an original "Bible language." The Bible shows on every page that its conceptuality is borrowed from many different sources. But all conceptual tools must be judged, transformed, or verified by the degree to which they support the coming into language of the One who is disclosed in this history. Since the whole disclosive history culminated in God's final self-disclosure in Jesus Christ, we might also say that the meaning and truth attributed to all philosophical and religious experiences and concepts must be determined by reference to Jesus the Christ.

Wolfhart Pannenberg, in his "Dogmatic Theses on the Doctrine of Revelation," stated in his first thesis, "The self-revelation of God in the biblical witnesses is not of a direct type in the sense of a theophany, but is indirect and brought about by means of the historical acts of God."[10] The word of God is not a direct propositional statement, saying that God is this and that

10 / THE MEANS OF GRACE

way or that God demands this or that. God's word does not provide a self-descriptive analysis of God, but is a word that will not return empty. It refers us to what God is doing and to what we experience as God's doing. This does not imply a subjective and existential understanding of God's word. Pannenberg says that God's self-disclosive history came to its climax in Jesus of Nazareth "insofar as the end of all events is anticipated in his fate."[11] God in Christ Jesus becomes the interpretative tool for all our present encounters with God's word.

We are reminded here of Luther's principle "Whatever communicates Christ is true and acceptable." Luther said, "Whatever does not teach Christ is certainly not apostolic even though St. Peter or St. Paul teach it. Again, whatever preaches Christ is apostolic even though Judas, Annas, Pilate, or Herod might say it."[12] Any claim to represent the word of God must be judged by comparing it to Jesus Christ and his ultimate word. The finality of Jesus as God's disclosive or verbal history is again indicated in the statement "In many and various ways God spoke of old to our fathers by the prophets; but in these last days he has spoken to us by a Son. . . . He reflects the glory of God and bears the very stamp of his nature" (Heb. 1:1–3). In Jesus' words and actions, God is reflected. Yet in attempting to describe the word of God, we cannot confine ourselves to Jesus, since Jesus himself cannot be properly understood without the Jewish background out of which he emerged. Talking about "the Word of God," we must first investigate the phrase's biblical origin and usage.

THE HISTORY-MAKING POWER OF GOD'S WORD

In the biblical writings, three terms are especially important for word: the Hebrew *dabar*, and the Greek *logos* and *rhēma*. In the Septuagint the Hebrew *dabar* is usually translated as *logos* or *rhēma*. In Hellenism, *logos* has great significance as the world-reason, the world-law, as the *logos spermatikos*, the active principle in the world. Some of this usage may not be unrelated to the Hebrew understanding of "the word," since the founder of the Stoics, Zeno of Citium, was of Semitic (Phoenician) origin and especially emphasized the significance of the *logos*.

The term *dabar* gains special theological prominence in the Old Testament prophecy. A prophet does not speak on his own; as we hear of David, "The Spirit of the Lord speaks by me, his word is upon my tongue" (2 Sam. 23:2). The Spirit of God speaks through the person, using him or her as a medium for self-disclosure. The reception of God's word through a prophet is a Spirit-worked event. Yet in the Old Testament the connection between *pneuma* (Spirit) and word is not as evident as it is in the New Testament. The spiritual dimension is contained in every assertion concerning God's self-disclosure,

THE BIBLICAL UNDERSTANDING OF THE WORD OF GOD

and a prophet such as Hosea calls himself a "man of the Spirit" (Hos. 9:7).

Initially, in Israel, revelation occurred mainly through *signs* in which the word was expressed, such as the oracles of Balaam (Num. 24:2ff.). Eventually the word itself was the medium of God's self-disclosure. In the writings of the Old Testament prophets we then find the frequent opening: "The word of God that came to . . ." (Hos. 1:1; Mic.1:1). The word of God is present from the beginning of a prophetic existence. For instance, Isaiah introduces his discourse with "the word which Isaiah the son of Amoz saw concerning Judah and Jerusalem" (Isa. 2:1). We also notice a close connection between "word" and "Torah." In Isa. 1:10 we encounter the prophet's appeal: "Hear the word [*dabar*] of the Lord, you rulers of Sodom! Give ear to the teaching [*torah*] of our God, you people of Gomorrah!" In Jeremiah we observe that the law belongs to the priest, while the word is associated with the prophet (Jer. 18:18). For Jeremiah the law is already present in written form, and he remarks that "the false pen of the scribes has made it into a lie" (Jer. 8:8). The main concern of the prophet, however, is not with the Torah, but with the word. He knows he has been set apart as a prophet before he was born, and he is sure that the Lord puts his words into the prophet's mouth (Jer. 1:5, 9).

Jeremiah further distinguishes between *prophecy* and the prophet who proclaims *God's* word: "Let the prophet who has a dream tell the dream, but let him who has my word speak my word faithfully. What has the straw in common with wheat? says the Lord" (Jer. 23:28). There is a difference between normal prophecy—in which truth can also be disclosed—and the proclamation of God's word. The word of God is an irresistible force, like fire in which the chaff is consumed or like a hammer that breaks the rock (Jer. 23:29). Jeremiah wrestles with the word of God in terms of his own destiny as a prophet and realizes that the word of God transcends his personal limitations.

Second Isaiah perceives God's word as an historical force, and God's self-disclosure is seen as worked out in events. "The grass withers, the flower fades; but the word of our God will stand for ever" (Isa. 40:8). The word of God is a powerful agent that will bring results with the same certainty as the forces of nature (Isa. 55:10–11). It is a divine power that creatively accomplishes God's work on earth. It executes God's will, and does what it sets out to do.

The word is the medium of God's self-disclosure. The word discloses God and God's will. This is true for the prophetic word and for the word of law. The law is God's word and underlies the divine covenant (Exod. 24:7–8; 34:27–28). This word is a forceful agent. God pledges to the chosen people to sustain and guide them, but if they do not live up to the covenant, this means ruin for them. Thus God's word encounters the Israelites in a twofold way: as promise and as threat. The divine word or God's commandment is

10 / THE MEANS OF GRACE

not beyond the people's grasp. It is neither spatially nor geographically removed from them. In Deuteronomy we read, "The word is very near you; it is in your mouth and in your heart, so that you can do it" (Deut. 30:14). God's commanding word is not uttered in a distant land or in an esoteric language. It is accessible to everyone, so there is no excuse for not listening to it.

The word of God is not simply an instrument; it carries with it the power to bless or to condemn. If people follow it, God will bless them and their land, but if they turn away, they will perish, and the land they possess will be taken away from them (Deut. 30:16–20). The Israelites are admonished: "I have set before you life and death, blessing and curse; therefore choose life, that you and your descendants may live, loving the Lord your God, obeying his voice, and cleaving to him; for that means life to you and length of days" (Deut. 30:19–20). God's word is accusing and condemning as well as promising and freeing. Yet in both cases it is an active and powerful word. It affects the life of the people and communicates God's will.

Moreover, God's word is not confined to the sphere of the individual or of nations; it also affects nature. God's word is the agent through which the *world* is created and sustained. The first chapter of Genesis features the ease with which everything is created through God's word. "God said . . . and there was" is the continuous assertion of the Priestly account of creation. The emphasis on the creative word of God is continued by Second Isaiah when he asserts that God calls everything by its name, that is, that God has power over all things (Isa. 40:26); God brings forth the dry land when he tells the deep to dry up (Isa. 44:27).

God's word is creative of both history and nature. God directs the forces of nature to the ends decreed, and God guides history according to the divine will. God says of Cyrus, " 'He is my shepherd, and he shall fulfil all my purpose'; saying of Jerusalem, 'She shall be built,' and of the temple, 'Your foundation shall be laid' " (Isa. 44:28). Similarly, we hear in the Psalms how God creates and directs the world and its history with the divine word: "He sends forth his command to the earth; his word runs swiftly" and "He declares his word to Jacob, his statutes and ordinances to Israel" (Ps. 147:15, 19). God's word, being active in human history and nature, creates, directs, and sustains the world. It also pronounces judgment and announces forgiveness. This understanding of God's word is continued in the New Testament.

JESUS CHRIST AS GOD'S FINAL WORD

"The emphasis which the whole of the New Testament places on hearing . . . presupposes a preceding speaking."[13] Jesus occupies a prominent place in relation to the word because of his proclamation and his demand that the

THE BIBLICAL UNDERSTANDING OF THE WORD OF GOD

people listen to him. The work and word of Jesus do not function independently of each other; his word is a working and active word. It is an integral part of his mission. In the story of the healing of the paralytic, he first announces to the man that his sins are forgiven. Only then does Jesus heal him, to demonstrate that "the Son of man has authority on earth to forgive sins" (Mark 2:10). This sequence seems to indicate the flow of Jesus' activity. He never does something without using it as an illustration for his proclamation.

Occasionally we read in the New Testament that people call Jesus a prophet. But can he justifiably be called a prophet? He himself never refers to the word of God or to a word that was given for him to reveal. Neither at his baptism nor in the story of the transfiguration do we hear that God's word comes to Jesus, as we could assume if there existed an affinity to the Old Testament prophets. It would have been only natural that someone who did as much preaching and teaching as Jesus would also have a special word from God. Yet at baptism he is not commissioned to a specific ministry of the word, but he is accredited as God's Son. Gerhard Kittel rightly concludes: "There can be only one reason why the idea of a detailed Word of God imparted to Jesus Himself has not found its way into the record. This is that such an idea was felt to be inappropriate and inadequate to describe the relationship of Jesus with God."[14]

According to Matthew, Jesus confesses, "All things have been delivered to me by my Father; . . . and no one knows the Father except the Son and any one to whom the Son chooses to reveal him" (Matt. 11:27). This shows a much more intimate relationship between Jesus and God than could be expected to exist between God and a prophet. Jesus does not just bring a word from God; he brings the whole word and the total God. The closeness between God and Jesus is also expressed in that there is no discernible distinction in the New Testament between the terms "the word of God," "the word of the Lord," and "the word." They are simply used alongside each other, with the "word of God" being used thirty times, the "word of the Lord" eight times, and "the word" forty times. This lack of distinction between the word of God and the word of the Lord again seems to have its origin in Jesus. Ernst Fuchs has convincingly pointed out that Jesus spoke of the will of God as only someone who stood in God's place could do.[15] For instance, in his parables Jesus did not simply tell his audience how God acts, but he told them that God acts the way Jesus acts. We see this especially well in the parable of the lost sheep (Luke 15:3–7). When the Pharisees and scribes remarked, "This man receives sinners and eats with them" (Luke 15:2), Jesus told them in parables of God's concern for the lost and the sinful, implying that God acts like Jesus. The identification of Jesus and God can also be seen in Jesus' use of the term *ego eimi* (I am) and in his use of the term *abba*.[16]

The identification of Jesus with the word and with God was continued in

10 / THE MEANS OF GRACE

the first Christian community. There was an awareness that proclaiming the Word meant proclaiming what had taken place in the person of Jesus and that reception of the word implied faith in Jesus. We hear from Paul,

> I became a minister according to the divine office which was given to me for you, to make the word of God fully known, the mystery hidden for ages and generations but now made manifest to his saints. To them God chose to make known how great among the Gentiles are the riches of the glory of this mystery, which is Christ in you, the hope of glory. (Col. 1:25-27)

We are not provided with a theory of the word but are told that the word that is the center of Paul's ministry arises from the event of Jesus. Similarly, we hear that it is essential for the twelve to preach the word of God and, what is synonymous, to devote themselves to prayer and to "the ministry of the word" (Acts 6:2, 4). When the ranks of the twelve were replenished, it was only natural that a candidate should be "one of the men who have accompanied us during all the time that the Lord Jesus went in and out among us, beginning from the baptism of John until the day when he was taken from us—one of these men must become with us a witness to his resurrection" (Acts 1:21-22). In serving the word of God, the twelve were eyewitnesses of Jesus, the incarnation of God's word.

We should also note at this point that the original New Testament designation for the gospel tradition was *logos* or *logos theou* and not *euangelion* which denoted the missionary appeal.[17] These terms corresponded with the names then current in Judaism for Holy Scripture. The life and words of Jesus were understood in analogy to the Old Testament writings as the word of God for the new covenant community. The identification of Jesus with the *logos* is most prominent in the Gospel of John. Especially in the prologue we find emphasis on the historical and spatio-temporal concreteness of the *logos*. The word was not just something to be heard with the ear. It was also not just mediated through the speaking and teaching of Jesus. Jesus Christ was the word in person. There is no speculation about the *logos* in terms of personification or of identifying it with the Torah. All considerations of the *logos* focus on the statement that the *logos* became incarnate in the historical person of Jesus, or, more precisely, that the historical figure of Jesus was the *logos* through whom God had spoken in the Old Testament. God's word was conveyed not only by certain people in the Old Testament; now he spoke personally in Jesus of Nazareth. Consequently Jesus could claim of himself: "I do nothing on my own authority but speak thus as the Father taught me" (John 8:28).

The identification between God and Jesus is not restricted to the Johannine corpus. For instance, in Luke 10:16 we read in connection with the sending of the seventy: "He who hears you hears me, and he who rejects you rejects me, and he who rejects me rejects him who sent me." The identification with God is extended here even to the disciples. The word does not stop with Jesus but is continued in those whom Jesus sent. The continuity between sender (God), medium (Jesus), and proclamation (the disciples) is especially well expressed in the opening of the First Letter of John:

> That which was from the beginning, which we have heard, which we have seen with our eyes, which we have looked upon and touched with our hands, concerning the word of life—the life was made manifest, and we saw it, and testify to it, and proclaim to you the eternal life which was with the Father and was made manifest to us—that which we have seen and heard we proclaim also to you. (1 John 1:1-3)

The word of life made manifest is the content of the Christian proclamation and of God's word. Jesus is the bringer of life and of God's word. The person who hears the word and believes in the God who sent him "has eternal life; he does not come into judgment, but has passed from death to life" (John 5:24).

God's word is not information about something, but communication with God's will, which is fundamentally the announcement of new life. But John leaves no doubt that not everyone will accept Jesus and the word. By rejecting Jesus and God's word, one rejects God as the source of life and chooses death. As we have seen in the Old Testament, the word of God is an active word in those who encounter and accept it. Though judgment is an intrinsic part of the encounter with God's word, John does not understand the word as a judging word. The judgment is rather brought on the people by themselves. In the synoptic Gospels, however, the notion of the judgment day at which the faithful will be separated from the faithless is so prevalent that we get the impression that the word of God brings blessing or doom. The word does not leave anybody in a neutral corner, but necessitates a response that results either in acceptance and life or in rejection of God's word and death.

God's word is not confined to the strictly personal sphere. In the prologue of the Gospel of John, Jesus is identified with the word of the divine Creator. He is preexistent, being before the beginning of the world; and he is also the one through whom the whole world was created. The word of God is not an impersonal word, as we might conclude from Genesis 1, but a personal word, incarnate as Jesus Christ. The Gospel of John begins not with speculation about the process of creation but with the person of Jesus Christ in whom the creative word of God became flesh. Of course, the prologue bears analogies to Jewish thought, such as the role of wisdom as the divine agent of creation, and these may have influenced the discourse. There also may be some parallels between the prologue and Hellenistic speculations about the *logos*, as we can see in the gnostic literature of Nag Hammadi. Yet in John the main emphasis

10 / THE MEANS OF GRACE

is on Jesus' relation to the Father, which is expressed by identifying him with God's word. In sharp contrast to gnostic or Hellenistic thought, there is no speculation in John about the word apart from its historic incarnation.

The inclusion of nature into the domain of the word is also displayed in the synoptic material and in Paul. After Jesus calmed the sea, the people responded with awe and asked: "Who then is this, that even wind and sea obey him?" (Mark 4:41). The people rightly sensed the presence of the divine power when Jesus calmed the waves. The creative aspect of the word is also prominent in Paul's interpretation of the sacraments. Being drawn into the destiny of Jesus Christ, the word incarnate, the believers become new beings through baptism so that they "might walk in newness of life" (Rom. 6:4). Whoever is in Christ is a new creation, we hear Paul exclaim, emphasizing the creative benefits of Christ and the efficacy of his being God's word.

In the New Testament there is not so much emphasis as in the Old Testament on the promissory aspect of God's blessings. Part of the promise has been realized through the coming of Christ. Those "who have heard the word of truth, the gospel of your salvation, and have believed in him, were sealed with the promised Holy Spirit, which is the guarantee of our inheritance until we acquire possession of it" (Eph. 1:13–14). Something is already given to us through the coming of Christ. The situation has been changed from the hoping community of the Old Testament to the fulfillment in anticipation in the New Testament. The word of God has not returned empty; it has shown us a new avenue of life in Jesus Christ. Thus Christ becomes the center of hope and the focus of the Christian proclamation.

Since the Lutheran church has often been called the church of the word, it is not surprising that the man whose name it bears had much appreciation for the word. Luther was convinced that Christ could be found nowhere except in the word, that is, the proclamation of the church. But the church cannot communicate Christ without reference to the biblical word. While this word is not mystical or internal, the word proclaimed by the church and centered in the Bible is not strictly external either, restricted to a language event. It is at the same time an internal word which touches our hearts and which we believe. But without the external word, God does not give us the Spirit through whom we believe. The Spirit is not given in addition to the word. The Spirit works in and through the word. With his insistence on the external word, Luther wanted to counteract any spiritualistic and overly enthusiastic inclinations that might emphasize the internal word to the near exclusion of its external aspect.

Since God addressed us throughout the history of the chosen people, culminating in the life and destiny of Jesus Christ, there is no other way open to us to hear God but through the avenue of history. Luther asserted: "We must not, as the sectarians do, imagine that God comforts us immediately, without his Word. Comfort does not come to us without the Word, which the Holy Spirit effectively calls to mind and enkindles in our hearts, even though it has not been heard for ten years."[18] The word has divine power and convinces us that it is actually from God. The word does not need an external authorization, such as a teaching office, the Holy Spirit, or our intellect, to convince us of its truthfulness. The word itself, through the Spirit working in it, has convincing power "where and when" it chooses (Augsburg Confession, Article V). The word is an independent entity that cannot be manipulated to yield desired results, so that we could produce our own or someone else's conversion. Luther insisted, "God comes to me without any preparation or help on my part."[19] Nevertheless, Luther insists that we should preach, hear, and read the word. The reason for this is not that we could contribute anything to God's activity but that God does not want to act apart from external means. God is active through the preached, heard, and read word. The means of grace, word and sacrament, are vital for God's communicating himself to us. While Luther emphasizes that God's word does everything, he implicitly acknowledges our cooperation by insisting on external mediation. Yet he maintains the primacy of God's action, since our doing does not necessitate that God act. God has decided to act before we ever hear the word or ask God for forgiveness.

God's word appropriates to us God's self-disclosure in Jesus Christ. It is a word of promise, announcing for us participation in the new life in Christ and restoration as God's children. Since God does not confine divine activity to the life of Christians or Judeo-Christian history, the rest of creation also witnesses to God's creative, directive, and sustaining activity. This means that, in principle, God's word and will are known in places in which God's name is not adequately confessed. Of course, Luther is quick to admit that such knowledge of God and the word is not complete enough, because of our sinfulness and our wrong perception of the word, to ensure our salvation. For instance, Luther admits, "Reason knows that there is a God. But who or what it is that is a true God, reason does not know."[20] Furthermore, God wants to be sought or found not in sublime things but in the cradle and on the cross. Only the incarnation of God's word in Jesus Christ opens for us full access to God. This access, characterized as God's salvific action, encounters us not just as promise and grace; it also contains the potential of threat. Consequently, God's word has often been described as "law" and "gospel."

NOTES

1. Rudolf Bultmann, *Faith and Understanding*, ed. Robert W. Funk, trans. L. P. Smith (London: SCM Press, 1969), p. 53.
2. Karl Barth, "The Word of God and the Task of Ministry" (1922), in *The Word*

10 / THE MEANS OF GRACE

of God and the Word of Man, trans. D. Horton (New York: Harper & Row, 1957), p. 186. The German original reads "theologians" instead of "ministers." See *Anfänge der dialektischen Theologie*, vol. 1, ed. Jürgen Moltmann (Munich: Chr. Kaiser, 1966), p. 199.

3. Bultmann, *Faith and Understanding*, p. 63.
4. Paul Tillich, *Systematic Theology* (Chicago: University of Chicago Press, 1957), 2:9.
5. Ibid., 1 (1951): 239.
6. Wolfgang Trillhaas, *Dogmatik* (Berlin: Alfred Töpelmann, 1962), p. 121.
7. Friedrich Schleiermacher, *The Christian Faith*, ed. H. R. Mackintosh and J. S. Stewart (Edinburgh: T. & T. Clark, 1960), pp. 194-95.
8. Martin Luther, *Lectures on Genesis, Chapters 1-5*, *LW* 1:13, in his comments on Gen. 1:2.
9. Martin Luther, *Enarratio Psalmi LI* (1538), *WA* 40 II:329, 8-12, and 330, 1-7, in his exegesis of Ps. 51:3.
10. Wolfhart Pannenberg, "Dogmatic Theses on the Doctrine of Revelation," in *Revelation as History*, ed. W. Pannenberg, trans. D. Granskou (New York: Macmillan Co., 1968), p. 125.
11. Ibid., p. 139 (thesis 4).
12. Martin Luther, *Vorrede auf die Epistel S. Jacobi und Jude* (1546), *WA* DB 7:384, 29-32.
13. Gerhard Kittel, "*Legō* (Word and Speech in the New Testament)," *TDNT* 4:100.
14. Ibid., p. 114.
15. Cf. Ernst Fuchs, *Studies of the Historical Jesus*, trans. A. Scobie (Naperville, Ill.: Alec R. Allenson, 1964), pp. 154-55.
16. For the use of *ego eimi*, see Hans Schwarz, *On the Way to the Future*, rev. ed. (Minneapolis: Augsburg Publishing House, 1979), pp. 58ff.; for *abba*, see Joachim Jeremias, *New Testament Theology*, vol. 1, *The Proclamation of Jesus*, trans. J. Bowden (London: SCM Press, 1971).
17. Harald Riesenfeld, *The Gospel Tradition*, trans. E. M. Rowley and R. A. Kraft (Philadelphia: Fortress Press, 1970), p. 20.
18. Martin Luther, "The Beautiful Confitemini," *LW* 14:62, in his exegesis of Ps. 118:6.
19. Luther, *WA* 12:497, 2-3, in a sermon of April 6, 1523.
20. Luther, *Der Prophet Jona ausgelegt* (1526), *WA* 19:206, 32-33, in his exegesis of Jonah 1:5.

2
The Dynamics of God's Word

The same word of God meets us either as "law" or as "gospel." The proper distinction between those terms is intrinsic to a full understanding of God's word. God's word does not vanish for the justified ones; they encounter it both as guidance to new life and as the promise of acceptance. Since God's word asks for our response, prayer and liturgy are its proper verbal expression. In prayer we engage in free but responsible dialogue with God; liturgy is formalized dialogue in which some of God's actions are dramatized. The efficacy of God's word is particularly manifest in miracles. Though not proofs of God's activity, miracles remind us that God will bring all divine promises to fulfillment.

THE JUDGING AND LIBERATING WORD: LAW AND GOSPEL

One might at first wonder whether such typically Lutheran terms as "law" and "gospel" are adequate to characterize the dynamics of God's word. Yet we noticed in our biblical survey that God's word is not just promise and grace, that it can also be judgment and condemnation. Nevertheless, many systematicians avoid the terms "law" and "gospel" altogether. Even Luther confessed that terms are not important, that only the content is decisive. Yet it facilitates the description of God's word when we classify its different receptions by distinct terms.

God's word as preserved in the Christian community, encountered in the church's doctrine and proclamation, can assume one of three functions. If we rely on God's word, it is (1) a liberating and freeing word (gospel) and at the same time (2) a guiding and protecting word (*parenesis*). But if we assert ourselves and reject God's word, it will encounter us (3) as judgment and condemnation (law). Since the functional character of God's word is emphasized by these distinctions, the functional distinction between law and gospel is not identical with the difference between the Mosaic Law and the gospel of Jesus Christ. The distinction of law and gospel is historically derived from Jesus' opposition to the pious legalism of his own people and from Paul's struggle with Judaizing tendencies in early Christianity. It is founded in a diametrically opposed function and perception of the same word of God.

The tendency to collapse the law into the gospel is an ever-present danger among Christians. Since God is loving and caring, we might think there should be no threat connected with God's word. As a result of this kind of reasoning, one often advocates love without cost, and grace without consequences. Dietrich Bonhoeffer rightly protested against this "cheap grace," and in the same vein H. Richard Niebuhr warned against the attempt to preach a Christ without a cross, salvation without wrath, and a kingdom of our own desires. Especially proponents of "process" theology have advocated that if God is to win the world, it must be done with love and not with force.

While God's grace rules supreme, a negative reaction to that grace does not remain without consequences. Roman Catholic theologians too insist that the distinction between law and gospel "is regarded as the distinctive feature of the Christian faith, as contrasted not only with Judaism but also with all pagan religions, with philosophy, ethics, and the like."[1] The distinction between law and gospel is moreover necessary because the impact of the law is felt also outside the Christian realm.

The law has basically a twofold foundation. In its "civil use" it preserves the creation and guards it against destruction and chaos, while in its "proper and theological use" it serves to convict sinners of their transgression against the lord. In its civil use it is concomitant with God's preserving activity and should be known by all creation. The universal knowledge of the law has been asserted by the natural-law tradition, especially by Roman Catholic theologians but also by more conservative Protestants. Recently it has received renewed attention by ethologists who argue that there are basic norms of moral behavior common to all societies, human and nonhuman. Such common knowledge also seems to be advocated by the New Testament. For instance, Paul claims:

> When Gentiles who have not the law do by nature what the law requires, they are a law to themselves, even though they do not have the law. They show that what the law requires is written on their hearts, while their conscience also bears witness and their conflicting thoughts accuse or perhaps excuse them on that day when, according to my gospel, God judges the secrets of men by Christ Jesus. (Rom. 2:14ff.)

Paul does not claim that pagans know the law given to the Jews at Mount Sinai, but that they have something analogous, to which they must be as responsive and responsible as the Jews are to their Torah. The divine will is inscribed in their hearts; therefore they should know what to do.

Martin Luther inferred from Rom. 2:14 that if God had never given the written law through Moses, our human spirit would still know by nature that we should worship God and love our neighbor. In his disputes with the Antinomians, Luther argued that from the beginning of the world the decalogue has been inscribed in the human mind.

> Therefore, there is one law which runs through all ages, is known to all men, is written in the hearts of all people, and leaves no one from beginning to end with an excuse, although for the Jews ceremonies were added and the other nations had their laws, which were not binding upon the whole world, but only this one, which the Holy Spirit dictates unceasingly in the hearts of all.[2]

The natural law largely coincides with the law of Moses, but must be distinguished from the positive law of any society and also from the Jewish ceremonial law. Luther does not simply equate the Mosaic law with the natural law, since he is convinced that Moses interprets and clarifies the latter. Luther therefore states that the natural law "is clearly and well summarized at Mount Sinai and in a better way than by the philosophers."[3]

For Luther and the New Testament tradition on which he based his thinking, the law inscribed in the hearts of all people is not just law in its civil use. It also fulfills a "theological" function since it expresses God's will and since all people are by nature religious. As Rom. 2:14ff. tells us, God's eternal will is present in the human conscience to remind us of our alienation from God and show us that we do not live as we ought. Because of our alienation from God, this second, theological and convicting use of the law is often obliterated even within the Judeo-Christian tradition. Nevertheless, all of us have the possibility of knowing God's will, and thus we have no excuse for not living up to it.

When Paul says that "law came in, to increase the trespass" (Rom. 5:20), we might at first wonder why God would give the law in order to evoke sin and to let it develop all its power. But would it make sense to assume that humanity was sinless until it was explicitly confronted with the law? As much of the patriarchal history shows, humanity lived in sin long before the law was given on Mount Sinai. But as Jesus said in the Sermon on the Mount, often transgressions against the law were not understood as such, and the realization of our sinful nature lay dormant. When God gave the law, sin was exposed and set free so that it could be perceived as what it actually was—revolt against God. In this sense, sin is increased and sharpened through the law. The more conscientiously we attempt to fulfill God's will, the more we realize our shortcomings and discover our immense sinfulness. God's will, originally a sign of God's love and care, has now been turned into a sign of despair and of God's wrath.

The law sharpens our conscience and shows us that we are in a hopeless predicament. Luther said that the law always accuses us; it delivers us to God's wrath, to judgment, and to eternal death. Preoccupation with the law leads to condemnation instead of salvation. Yet Luther also saw that without the preaching of the law we do not hear God's truth. The law does not only show us our shortcomings and condemn us; it also moves us to seek God's grace. This is also the opinion of John Calvin in *The Institutes of the Christian Religion*, in which he shows this twofold movement of the law, toward judgment and toward grace, by adducing many quotations from Augustine.

In Rom. 5:20-21, Paul continues his statement that law came to increase sinfulness by adding: "But where sin increased, grace abounded all the more, so that, as sin reigned in death, grace also might reign through righteousness to eternal life through Jesus Christ our Lord." In his letter to the Galatians, Paul even contends that "Christ redeemed us from the curse of the law, having become a curse for us" (Gal. 3:13). The law leads and urges us toward Christ, and it is "our custodian until Christ came" (Gal. 3:24). The law was our tutor or custodian and kept us under its tutelage and yoke until we were released into freedom through Christ. Christ shows us that the law is not God's final word and the whole content of the Christian proclamation.

Though the gospel stands alongside the law, each has an entirely different function. The gospel proclaims that God's will has already been met in Christ. It shows us a gracious God who meets us in Christ and forgives us our sins. Paul expresses this eloquently when he says, "But now the righteousness of God has been manifested apart from the law, although the law and the prophets bear witness to it" (Rom. 3:21). God's righteousness has been met substitutionally in the life and destiny of Jesus the Christ. It is now evident that God wants the redemption of all people, not their destruction.

It would be wrong to assume that the gospel of redemption is confined to the Christ-event. The righteousness of God has its prehistory in the law and the prophets, as Paul reminds us when he says that "the law and the prophets bear witness to it." The Old Testament already testifies to the gracious love of God which culminates in the life and destiny of Christ. Karl Barth has picked up this insight in his famous paper of 1935 "Gospel and Law." He assures us that he does not intend to change the traditional order of law and gospel, but by reversing their sequence he wants to point out that "the law is in the Gospel, comes from the Gospel and is directed to the Gospel."[4] If we want to understand the law, we must first know about the gospel.

Barth agrees that God's word contains both law and gospel. Since the law is identical with God's will, we have access to it only in Jesus Christ, in whom God's word comes loudly and audibly to us. "When we see here the will of God being done, when, that is, we see His grace in action, the law is manifested to us."[5] When we perceive God's grace, we realize what the law actually demands. "The law, then, is in the Gospel as the tables of Sinai were in the ark of the covenant."[6] Barth can even say that "the law is nothing else than the necessary form of the Gospel, whose content is grace." We are reminded here somewhat of Augustine's style of argument, when Augustine defined evil both as a deficiency of the good and as a necessary contrast to help us perceive the good. But Barth reverses Augustine's argument by claiming that the goodness of the *gospel* makes us realize our depravity and sinfulness, so that we cling to the gospel. Barth defines the law as a form of the gospel since it bears witness to the gospel. He claims that the sequence of law first and then gospel is legitimate only if we first look at Christ, who reveals himself through the law as our Savior. Knowing that Christ affirms God's valid but misused law, we perceive our shortcomings and flee to God's grace, revealed in Christ who fulfills the demands of the law. For Barth, the proper sequence is gospel-law-gospel instead of law-gospel.

Karl Barth has certainly shown that we gain a clear vision of the law only if we preach God's word as law *and* gospel. The traditional sequence, of law first and then gospel, that Barth attacks is not foolproof, since it might leave the impression that it is synonymous with the succession of Old and New Testaments. Yet Barth's own preference of gospel-law-gospel is even more misleading, since it envelops the law with the gospel and obscures the fact that law and gospel are the same word of God. One cannot divide God's word into the words of law and the words of gospel. Whether we encounter law or gospel depends on how God's word meets us, as condemnation or as confirmation. If we would envelop God's demand in God's grace, the word of God would lose its seriousness, and we would be in danger of offering cheap grace. Luther rightly stated that the proclamation of the law is the indispensable and necessary presupposition for preaching the gospel. Without the law we would not recognize our own sinfulness but remain secure and proud of our moral capacity. In this way the law is God's "alien work" which allows us to appreciate the gospel as God's "proper work." While they function quite differently, law and gospel are certainly the same word of God.

We have seen that the distinction between law and gospel is not identical with that between the Pentateuch or the Old Testament, on the one hand, and the proclamation of Jesus or the New Testament kerygma, on the other hand. Yet "the law" can certainly denote the Pentateuch or even the whole Israelite system of law. At Jesus' time, some sorts of Judaism had turned God's word into a code of human regulations to assure their righteousness before God. The law had evolved into a self-assertive, legalistic, human system interposing itself between God and humanity and leading to a wrong understanding of human righteousness. Jesus addressed this situation in the Sermon on the Mount and other discourses. Today the attitude of many people is similar. They lead ethically virtuous lives and assume that their lives, though short of perfection, will ultimately be met with divine approval. Goethe summed up this popular sentiment in his dramatic poem *Faust* when he declared: "Who e'er aspiring, struggles on, for him there is salvation."[7] Yet such an understanding of the law will not lead to freedom. It will ultimately enslave people, since it suggests that they are righteous even though they are not. People will devote themselves to impersonal ethical principles, such as "the greatest good for the greatest number," instead of responding to God's personal will. Often these self-righteous attempts result in new barriers of injustice and inequality. Law divorced from the gospel can easily turn into a self-serving and self-justifying philosophy. We exchange the living will of God for ethical norms which we attempt to fulfill to justify our behavior.

Since we sin by turning our attention to the law instead of to God, we must remind ourselves that we thereby actually avoid God. We must be brought to repentance through God's word, which encounters us as God's accusing law and not as our self-designed plan. According to Luther, this demanding and accusing word of God can meet us anywhere, in such different items as, for instance, the rustling leaves of a tree or the Lord's Prayer. Each of the petitions in the Lord's Prayer can be perceived as a demand that reminds us of our imperfection. But the same word of God can also encounter us as gospel. Luther assures us that there is much gospel contained in the first commandment, since there God promises faithfulness. We also remember that the so-called Old Testament law originally served as gospel, as the pledge of God's faithfulness to which the Israelites were asked to respond. Only through failure to respond does the law assume an accusing function.

God's same word can meet us as law or gospel, as demand or as promise. But there is an irreversible movement from law to gospel. If we grasp the gospel in faith, we know about God's acceptance, and the condemning and accusing function of the law vanishes. The gospel has replaced the law, and we recognize God in an entirely different light. God appears to us no longer as a righteous God who demands compliance with the divine will, but as a gracious God who forgives us our trespasses for Christ's sake. If the gospel makes such a difference in our perception of God's word, the question emerges whether law still has any validity for the Christian.

THE WORD AS GUIDANCE: "THIRD USE" AND PENANCE

If it is true that Christ is the end of the law, as Paul claims, then the law should no longer be of any concern for us. Yet such quick discarding of the law would conflict with Jesus' claim that he did not come to abolish the law but to fulfill it. Indeed, it was the conviction of the New Testament writers that Christ fulfilled God's will substitutionally. This did not mean that the law has lost its validity for us as God's guiding will or as God's accusing law.

If it had, we would either live in the immediacy of God and have no need of any mediated guidance, or be totally sinless without need for repentance and renewal. Since we still live in this world and succumb to its sinfulness, we need guidance and repentance. Thus God's law meets us in its "third use," the use for the reborn; and it also meets us in the "office of the keys," that is, in penance.

The third use of the law has occasionally been disputed, especially by Lutherans, since Luther himself did not explicitly mention such a use. But it was evident to most reformers and even to Luther himself that the law is not without significance for the Christian. The emphasis on the third use is particularly strong in the Reformed tradition. Calvin claimed, "The third and principal use, which pertains more closely to the proper purpose of the law, finds its place among believers in whose hearts the Spirit of God already lives and reigns."[8] A similar line of thought was pursued by Philip Melanchthon, the Lutheran *Book of Concord*, and the theologians of Lutheran orthodoxy. It is interesting that Calvin introduces the third use of the law primarily with quotations from the Old Testament. For instance, he quotes the psalmist: "Thy word is a lamp to my feet and a light to my path" (Ps. 119:105) and "The law of the Lord is perfect, reviving the soul" (Ps. 19:7).

Christians certainly need moral directives and guidelines; they need to hear God's will to order their lives. Yet once we are confronted with the gospel and understand the full implications of God's gracious will, our response does not come from the pressure of the law. Christians live up to the law, not because of certain demands but because they love God and appreciate God's righteousness. Yet not even the Old Testament law can be properly interpreted in its own intention as a coaxing or urging institution. The Ten Commandments are not introduced with the assertion "This is what God demands." They are introduced with the reminder "This is what God has done for you." "I am the Lord your God, who brought you out of the land of Egypt, out of the house of bondage" (Exod. 20:2). The commandment to love one's neighbor is introduced in a similar way: "You shall love your neighbor as yourself: I am the Lord" (Lev. 19:18). Because God is gracious to us, we are called to transfer God's love to our neighbor. In the Old Testament, God's word was originally gospel and not a prescribing or condemning word. It was to show us the kind of God we have and to evoke our response, a response freely given. Being justified children of God, we do the will of God and want what God wants. Of course, such response to God's will is not without guidance.

We acknowledge the existence of commandments in the Bible that serve as guiding moral directives. It would be misleading, however, to regard them as "law" in the same way as the "civil" or even "convicting" uses. They depict an evangelical use in the original sense of the divine command. They do not express a demanding commandment in the sense of "You shall . . . ," but invite us, "You may because. . . ." They serve as guidelines in our attempt to meet the will of God, and they are not set as legal devices that might assure a righteous life. Christians are no longer oriented toward the law, but they do show an oscillating existence. They do not suddenly find themselves in the state of the redeemed beyond the possibility of sinning. Paul frequently used imperatives to show that the Christian existence is still marked by temptation and sin. Luther described the same situation when he characterized a Christian as "sinner and justified at the same time."

Being a Christian justified before God does not induce an ontological change, but it is indicative of a new relationship with God. This relationship is always subject to change and must be continually regained. We sit on the edge of a sword, always tempted to fall to one side or the other. Admittedly, Christians lapse into sin. Then God's word turns into law to drive them back to the gospel. Even in the Christian community it is not sufficient to proclaim the gospel alone. Because of our sinful behavior, it must be supplemented by preaching the law. As justified Christians we live without the law; but as sinners we live under it, and it drives us back to the gracious God.

Since God still remains with us through the law, the severing of our relationship with God is never bilateral. Even as lapsed ones we remain Christians. The promise of the gospel does not become void once we turn our backs to God. God's gracious Word continues to stand, and we always have the opportunity of returning to God. We do not live under the thumb of God, but are called to freedom as God's sons and daughters. While this freedom is not without limits, it would be inappropriate to call these limits "law." We should rather call them orders and guidelines that allow us to live responsibly. In their sinfulness Christians are confronted with a "convicting use" of the law. In their daily lives they attempt to fulfill the "civil use." But as new people of God they respond freely to God's will and no longer live under compulsion and pressure. The guidance provided to channel their response should perhaps not be called "law" but, as Paul Althaus suggested, "divine command."[9] In this category, we could also classify the New Testament exhortations concerning the Christian life (*Haustafeln*).

The distinction between law and gospel assumes a peculiar form in the office of the keys, or the practice of confession and absolution. The Roman Catholic tradition considers penance a sacrament, which includes the office of the keys. In the Augsburg Confession, penance is discussed after baptism and Holy Communion, and in Luther's Small Catechism it is placed after baptism and before the Lord's Supper. In his Apology of the Augsburg Confession, Philip Melanchthon makes penance one of the sacraments. But this suggestion has not been picked up by other Protestants. The Calvinist tradition refuses to consider confession and absolution a sacrament. Here we cannot pursue the question of what constitutes a sacrament. At this point it suffices to say that Protestants see that confession and absolution are intimately connected with the proclamation of law and gospel as the one word of God.

When we briefly survey the main passages in the New Testament that elucidate the function of the office of the keys, we notice a significant development. We hear Jesus' words to Peter: "I will give you the keys of the kingdom of heaven, and whatever you bind on earth shall be bound in heaven, and whatever you loose on earth shall be loosed in heaven" (Matt. 16:19). Peter is entrusted here with binding and loosing people on earth; this means with excluding and accepting them into the Christian community. In the Gospel of John, this function is extended to all the disciples and is understood more theologically as remission of sins. So we hear Jesus say to his disciples: "Receive the Holy Spirit. If you forgive the sins of any, they are forgiven; if you retain the sins of any, they are retained" (John 20:22–23). The Christian community, or at least the twelve, understood themselves to succeed Peter in the office of the keys. This is already obvious from Matt. 18:18, where the exercise of this office is no longer restricted to Peter. There Jesus says to his disciples: "Truly, I say to you, whatever you bind on earth shall be bound in heaven, and whatever you loose on earth shall be loosed in heaven."

The office of the keys is intimately connected with the proclamation of God's word. There is a parallel between listening to God's word and receiving forgiveness of sins. When Jesus sent out the disciples he admonished them: "And if any one will not receive you or listen to your words, shake off the dust from your feet as you leave that house or town. Truly, I say to you, it shall be more tolerable on the day of judgment for the land of Sodom and Gomorrah than for that town" (Matt. 10:14–15). The reception of God's word decides about life and death, and those who are charged with its proclamation shall symbolize this by shaking off the dust from their feet as a sign that they have separated themselves from those who rejected God's word. The ultimate consequence of the proclamation of God's word is to be made known to its listeners. The office of the keys is based on the pronouncement of law and gospel as the one word of God. Our response to this word has definite consequences, and those who pronounce the word are empowered to make known these consequences to the listeners by absolving them or leaving them in their sins. Since penance is inextricably connected with God's word, the public proclamation of this word and the use of penance are administered by the same people.

The office of the keys should never be considered in purely administrative terms. It is exercised on behalf of God and intends that the sinner be saved

10 / THE MEANS OF GRACE

and not perish. It is not a convenient means of enforcing authoritarian decisions. Those who handle penance do this on behalf of the Lord of the church and not in the name of human authorities.

Since proclamation and penance are inseparable, the church has realized that the one-time remission of sins through baptism cannot be the end of the penitential process. We are in need of continuous forgiveness. Martin Luther said in his Small Catechism: "The old Adam in us, together with all sins and evil lusts, should be drowned by daily sorrow and repentance and be put to death, and . . . the new man should come forth daily and rise up, cleansed and righteous, to live forever in God's presence."[10] Confession and absolution is a daily process and cannot be confined to special occasions when one has committed especially grave sin. Luther's Ninety-five Theses claimed at the outset: "When our Lord and Master Jesus Christ said, 'Repent' [Matt. 4:17], he willed the entire life of believers to be one of repentance."[11]

There is a controversy surrounding penitence which is similar to the one we have seen concerning the third use of the law. In the Roman Catholic tradition, there are three parts to the penitential process: contrition, confession, and satisfaction. But the Reformation tradition sees contrition and confession as sufficient (Augsburg Confession, Articles XI and XII). While Luther, in his Ninety-five Theses, rejected the imposition of satisfaction as administered by the clergy, he insisted that "inner repentance is worthless unless it produces various outward mortifications of the flesh." There is no law that can spell out the kind of restitution to be made in each case. Yet even if there were, we can never completely undo a sinful act since we are unable to reverse history. Only God who sets history in motion and has it under divine control can effect restitution in the true sense. This does not mean we should lean back and do nothing. Once we receive forgiveness, we need ethical guidance, showing us how to respond to the grace freely received. Satisfaction is not a new law or a demand, but an opportunity to restore that part of God's creation which we willfully impair through our sinful activities. If this opportunity is not grasped, Luther is right that even the most convincing "inner repentance is worthless."

God's freeing and forgiving word cannot be taken lightly. It asks for our response as new beings, a response expressive of our newly found union with God. If such a response is not forthcoming, as far as we can ascertain, it may be necessary that churchly sanctions be imposed on the unrepentant sinner. These sanctions, for instance, exclusion from certain offices or activities in the Christian community, should always be administered to the benefit of the punished. The movement from law to grace must always prevail. Though they should never be administered too quickly, church sanctions are not relics of medieval authoritarianism. They are an offer of grace through the administration of the law. Since God is a God of grace, sinners are punished not that they may perish but that they may amend their lives and live.

THE DIALOGICAL WORD: PRAYER AND LITURGY

God's Word invites our response. We are not confronted with God in an impersonal way, as we are by the laws of nature or by a merciless fate. God wants and establishes a dialogue with us, as shown in the New Testament by the many exhortations to pray. We hear: "Ask, and it will be given you; seek, and you will find; knock, and it will be opened to you" (Matt. 7:7). This dialogue is expressed primarily in two ways, in a more formalized and ritualized way in liturgy and in a less formal and often spontaneous manner in prayer.

We can distinguish many different kinds of prayer: corporate and individual, free and formalized, intercessory and doxological. The fundamental presupposition of prayer is that God engages in dialogue with us. It is further presupposed that there is a realm of freedom in which prayer can unfold its activity. If these presuppositions were not met, prayer would be nothing but an attempt to calm our nerves or to obtain self-control, the approach of Eastern meditation exercises.

Since God is our partner in prayer, we should not pray in a carefree, casual attitude. We also should not pray in a boasting attitude, convinced that God has no choice but to agree with the contents of our prayers (Matt. 6:5-7). A prayer should be precise and to the point, but offered in humility. Such is the Lord's Prayer, which Jesus taught his disciples; it begins with an affirmation of God's holiness and concludes with a doxology (Matt. 6:9-13). The emphasis on God's holiness informs our attitude in prayer as well as its content. When we hear Jesus say, "Whatever you ask the Father in my name, he may give it to you" (John 15:16), this does not mean that God will give us everything for which we ask. Dietrich Bonhoeffer elucidated the meaning of this often misunderstood passage when he wrote: "God does not give us everything we want, but he does fulfill all his promises."[12]

Prayer is not a frivolous attempt to discover how far-reaching God's power is—whether God can suspend the law of gravity or reverse the sequence of day and night. It is rather the reliance for Christ's sake on the promise expressed in the Psalms: "Call upon me in the day of trouble; I will deliver you, and you shall glorify me" (Ps. 50:15). Christ has overcome the destructive and anti-Godly powers, and we, as his followers, are encouraged to step to his side and call on God to deliver us and others from the impact of these powers. Through our prayers we are on God's side, cooperating and conversing with him about the future of the world. Martin Luther was right when

10 / THE MEANS OF GRACE

he called God's command and the prayers of the Christians the two pillars that support the entire world and without which the world would disintegrate.[13]

Prayer can have many contents. The most appropriate approach to God as the "wholly other" is that of adoration and praise. We should not only call on God as a security blanket or as a genie in a bottle. We should thank God for divine help and protection, acknowledge God's continual support, and praise God as our creator, sustainer, and redeemer. If we cease to pray, our life is no longer in tune with the source of life; we cut ourselves off from God and assume we are self-sufficient. Prayer as adoration and praise makes us recall the one from whom we have everything. We acknowledge our dependency and do not take anything for granted, such as good health, good weather, a job, our family. In his explanation of the first article of the Apostles' Creed in the Small Catechism, Martin Luther provided us with an interesting catalog of items that he attributed to God and for which we should thank God.

Most prayers are not primarily adoration but petition and intercession. Since God has invited us to a dialogue, it is only proper that we bring before God all our anxieties and personal afflictions: sickness, economic and family problems, and even our sinful aversions from God. There is no need to suppress any petitions, whether they envision eternal goals or temporal goals. But petitional prayers are more than presenting God with a shopping list. An essential part of Christian prayer is to seek God's forgiveness for past and present sins and to find hope for the future. If we do not include in our prayers the plea for forgiveness of sins, our dialogue with God will be tarnished by estrangement. The quest for forgiveness will also include reference to one's petitions and intercessions to discern whether they result from our own sinful and selfish interests or whether they were done to conform with God's will. Often prayers are only the result of piously disguised selfishness attempting to impose our desires on God's work. Thus petitions must first be concerned with renewal and inner strength. But petitional prayers include more than forgiveness. We will ask for inner peace and tranquillity in times of conflict, clarity of outlook, new strength at moments of fatigue, and power to cope with the daily demands of life.

We might ask why we should expect God to answer our prayers or to help us in times of need. Here the life and destiny of Jesus serve as the great paradigm of God's action. Since God has acted benevolently toward us in Christ, we can expect that God will again act so toward us. God cared about us insignificant beings so much that God came to us in the human form of Jesus Christ. As we hear in the Magnificat, "He has put down the mighty from their thrones, and exalted those of low degree" (Luke 1:52).

Among petitionary prayers, petitions for physical health and healing from disease are often most frequent. We must caution, however, against the idea that prayers work like magic and can substitute for adequate medical care or ward off undesirable events. But appropriate care and prayer are not mutually exclusive. Prayer (dialogue with God) and action (a result of that dialogue) are appropriate ways in which we can engage in the affairs of the world.

When we consider petitions concerning events in nature, we will usually affirm the protective orders of God and will not ask God frivolously to reverse the sequences of the seasons or to bring about other strange constellations. Yet it is part of our task as God's dialogue partners to remind God of those who are especially exposed to the dangers of nature, such as travelers, sailors, pilots, and miners. Again, prayers are intended not to replace protective measures but to accompany and perhaps enhance them. In a similar way, it is our prerogative and duty to pray for good harvest and to remind God of adverse conditions, such as floods, storms, and other disasters in nature, so that their impact may be softened or even averted.

Since prayer should not be a selfish action, we will keep in mind the well-being of others. The same adoration, praise, and petitions that we extend on our behalf we extend on behalf of others. Since prayers take the hope of fulfillment from the way God acted in Jesus Christ, their limits too should come from Jesus Christ. They should always conclude with the express or tacit admission with which the evangelist tells us that Jesus concluded his prayer in Gethsemane: "Nevertheless, not as I will, but as thou wilt" (Matt. 26:39). A Christian prayer is not a demand for God's surrender, but the prerogative and duty of dialogue with the one who formed the earth and the whole universe and who has been our dwelling place in all generations (Ps. 90:1–2).

When we consider the church's liturgy, we notice at once that it is formalized dialogue. Intrinsic to liturgy are prayers, usually at least the Lord's Prayer, and readings from the New and Old Testaments. Liturgy is, moreover, reenactment of God's saving action, especially such high points as the exodus from Egypt, the passion history, or the rescue of Noah. Through this reenactment of history, people are initiated into and reminded of God's activities, including fundamental divine promises. Liturgy also involves the people in the reenactment by ritual actions, such as the sacraments, through which the faithful participate in God's promises and through which these promises are remembered and appropriated.

Since liturgy is intimately connected with God's word and action, it remembers God's deeds, witnesses to God's presence, and expects God's coming to redeem God's promises. Liturgy flows out of God's word and action and symbolizes them realistically through word and action. In the liturgy we are drawn into the dialogue between God and the worshiping community. We explain our predicament and implore God's help, and God shows us what God has done, will do, and is doing. Since God is acting through the liturgical

10 / THE MEANS OF GRACE

process, liturgy has sacramental and miraculous aspects. While liturgy is formalized miracle, in which God's miraculous actions are dramatized, miracles can never be completely ritualized. Not only are they extraordinary, they are also outside the expected realm.

THE EMPIRICAL WORD: MIRACLES

Nowhere are word and action more closely intertwined than in miracles. While forgiveness and judgment also imply immediate action, the empirical side of these actions (forgiveness of sins or condemning someone) are usually removed from empirical investigation. Even the gospels admit this, as shown in the story of the paralytic (Mark 2:1–12). When Jesus announced to him that his sins were forgiven, immediately the factuality of this deed was questioned. Then Jesus countered: "Which is easier, to say to the paralytic, 'Your sins are forgiven,' or to say, 'Rise, take up your pallet and walk'? But that you may know that the Son of man has authority on earth to forgive sins . . . , I say to you, 'Rise, take up your pallet and go home'" (Mark 2:9–11).

A miracle shows immediately the empirical consequences of the word. Yet people are not always convinced that a miracle has happened and that its author is definitely disclosed. Some believed that Jesus had performed miracles through God's power; others accused him of being connected with the devil; and a third group remained totally indifferent to his deeds. A miracle is not like a magic act that demonstrates the power of the magician. Magic is often a ready-made device, but miracles always contain the moment of surprise. Jesus did not announce so-called healing services; his healings were spontaneous and not staged in advance. Miracles are also not demonstrations of God's power to convince onlookers who is in control.

According to the biblical witnesses, miracles are intrinsically related to the work of salvation. At the high points of God's salvation-history, we are confronted with miracles: the parting of the Red Sea, the virginal conception of Jesus, his resurrection as the Christ. Of course, one could object that miracles are literary devices to underscore the reality of God's salvational activity. Thus there might be no historical reality that pertains to them. Yet today even the severest critics of the New Testament sources admit that Jesus did indeed perform acts that his contemporaries regarded as miraculous and that we still consider highly unusual.

Jesus' miracles are not without analogies. Miracles are reported of contemporaries that show great similarity to those of Jesus. Most prominent are those of Apollonius of Tyana, an itinerant Neo-Pythagorean teacher who is supposed to have raised people from the dead and healed many who were sick. In antiquity miracles may have been attributed to certain people simply to emphasize their significance. But it is impossible to conclude on historical or literary grounds that none of the miracles attributed to Jesus took place. Even the similarity in structure between the miracle stories in the Gospels and in other ancient sources does not disprove their factuality. If one wants to convey a miracle, there are not many possible approaches. We must concede the possibility that miracles may have been attributed to people simply to enhance their status, that is, their special relationship to the gods. Each claim to truth must be carefully analyzed, and it should not be excluded *a priori* that some of the miracles attributed to Jesus may have no historical basis and serve only to emphasize his exceptional status. It should also be noted that the New Testament witnesses do not seem threatened by other miracle stories and are even convinced that performing miracles was not the exclusive prerogative of Jesus. Jesus himself warned of false Christs and of prophets at the end-time who would perform great signs and wonders (Mark 13:22). The apostles, too, knew of people who used sorcery to perform miraculous deeds (cf. Acts 8:9).

Since Jesus' miracles are closely tied to his mission, it is not sufficient to interpret them exclusively in the light of Near Eastern or Greco-Roman thought. We must understand them primarily from the goal of Jesus' life and destiny. It was his stated goal to announce and to bring about the kingdom of God; his miracles were signs and proleptic anticipations of the kingdom. Miracles were signs to illustrate his message, but not means to demonstrate his power and to legitimate him (cf. Matt. 12:38–39). They show that God is actively involved in the creative process and is not a distant God. He does not confirm the present course of affairs but is willing to give it a new and unexpected turn.

This involvement results in a decisive confrontation with the powers that want to destroy the creation. We read in the New Testament that Jesus was authorized by God to fight and overcome the destructive powers and that his victories became visible in miracles. The evangelists even tell us that these destructive powers recognized Jesus and exclaimed in anguish: "What have you to do with us, Jesus of Nazareth? Have you come to destroy us?" (Mark 1:24). Through Jesus' miracles, God overcame the powers and initiated a new order. The destructive and anti-Godly powers are not merely kept in check, but at one specific point, at which the miracle is performed, are forced to retreat. As the sick are returned to health, the dead are brought back to life, biologically impairing phenomena such as hunger are overcome, and physically limiting phenomena such as space and gravity are eliminated, we obtain glimpses of an entirely new creation. Miracles are signs of the coming kingdom and the reign of God. The seer in the book of Revelation, envisioning the eschatological perfection, says, "Death shall be no more, neither shall there be mourning nor crying nor pain any more, for the former things have passed away" (Rev. 21:4).

10 / THE MEANS OF GRACE

Jesus' miracles, however, were only temporary points of victory over the anti-Godly powers. The people he healed were again afflicted by diseases, those brought back to life died again, and those he fed became hungry again. Jesus was not essentially so helpless against the present structure of reality that he could provide only temporary help against the evils of this world. Rather, his miracles indicate that the present reality will be transformed into a new, undistorted reality, the new creation. The confidence for this assertion is derived from the resurrection of Jesus Christ. When God resurrected Jesus as the Christ through the power of the Spirit, Jesus never died again. In Jesus' resurrection, death was permanently, though proleptically, overcome through a new form of life (1 Cor. 15:55ff.). In Jesus the promised and hoped-for transformation of the whole cosmos has commenced. Jesus' resurrection was not a resuscitation, but the showing forth and anticipation of a new cosmos. Since the inauguration of a new reality happened in and with Jesus, its consequences extend far beyond the person of Jesus. God vindicated Jesus as the one whom God said he was, the bringer of a new life and the Messiah. This means that Jesus' resurrection gave his proclamation new credibility. We can now accept his proclamation, his miracles, and the miracles still being performed in his name as signposts foreshadowing and depicting a new world to come.

Miracles have eschatological quality. They point to a promised eschaton and anticipate proleptically the new world order that they introduce. They indicate that our present world is not endowed with permanence but is on its course to a new world. The present order will give way to a new order of perfection. Our world has only penultimate quality and will be changed into the new order that these miracles indicate. The unexpected character of the miracles also shows us that there is no developmental continuity between the present state of affairs and the new world to come. Salvation is neither continuation of the fallen creation on a higher level nor development toward the promised goal. Only something unprecedented and new, as it is foreshadowed in the miracles, can bring about the desired goal. This does not mean a discarding of the present and complete discontinuity, but there will be a total restructuring that will eliminate such distortions as pain, alienation, and decay and will allow for new life in the immediacy of God.

When we assign such importance to the resurrection of Christ, we must caution that none of the miracles, the resurrection included, is an empirical verification of God's activity. Though it is proper to conclude that God is indeed the actor in Christ's miracles, there is no necessity to do so. For instance, Matthew tells us that nobody could deny that the tomb in which Jesus had been laid was again empty. But this fact led to opposite conclusions. While the disciples proclaimed that Jesus had risen, other people said that his disciples had stolen his corpse by night (Matt. 28:13). Even when Jesus appeared personally to his disciples as the resurrected one, some doubted (Matt. 28:17) and some thought they saw a ghost (Luke 24:37). Though one can ascertain the state prior to a miracle and the state after a miracle has occurred, the miraculous act itself is inaccessible to investigation. It is never unambiguously clear whether a miracle is endowed by God with eschatological significance, whether we are confronted with an actual miracle worker or a fraud, or whether it is a seductive act of the anti-Godly powers intended to pull us away from God.

Since a miracle is not an empirical proof of the veracity of God's word, but the proclamation of God's word in sign language, it is susceptible to manipulation and rejection. The scribes and Pharisees did not change their minds when they were confronted with Jesus' miracles. They heard the miraculous message of the commencement of salvation and rejected it together with its signs. Jesus rightly reminded us: "If they do not hear Moses and the prophets, neither will they be convinced if some one should rise from the dead" (Luke 16:31).

This discussion of miracles would be obsolete if there were no scientific possibility of such occurrences. Before we side with those who reject miracles as contrary to the laws of nature or with those who assert that God can always interrupt the causal nexus, we should first define what we understand by "miracle." Often the term is used very loosely, as in the miracle of modern medicine. But a miracle should denote neither something astounding nor something highly complicated. For Christians, a miracle is an act of God which runs counter to our usual sense of experience and which becomes visible in the objective world. A miracle is an exception; something that occurs every day we would not call a miracle. The problem posed by a miracle, however, is not its exceptional character but that it becomes visible in the empirical world.

A miracle is a *mixtum compositum*. As an act of God it pertains to the metaphysical or supernatural dimension, but as something visible it belongs to the natural world. As the natural sciences increased in stature, a more and more stringent distinction was made between the natural (i.e., the object of the natural sciences) and the supernatural realm of God. If God is the agent of a miracle, it is commonly argued, God will proceed in a supernatural manner and not in a natural one. With this dichotomy between the natural and the supernatural, the potential for conflict was laid between those who claim that the natural context is so all-encompassing that it does not allow for "supernatural" exceptions and others who claim that God can interrupt the natural flow of events whenever God wants. At this point it is interesting to consult Augustine for a definition of "miracle." Augustine objects to the common notion that miracles are contrary to nature, since both nature and miracle are by the will of God and God's will is certainly not self-contradictory. He

10 / THE MEANS OF GRACE

then asserts, "A portent, therefore, happens not contrary to nature, but contrary to what we know as nature."[14] This means that for Augustine the dichotomy between the natural and the supernatural did not yet exist. He still saw the world as a unity governed by God's will in which some things simply occurred more frequently than others.

Not until the ninth century did the term "supernatural" make its appearance in Western theology. Especially from the thirteenth century onward, through the help of Thomas Aquinas, the term "supernatural" became standard theological vocabulary. For Aquinas, a miracle was defined as something difficult and unusual that surpassed the capabilities of nature and the expectations of those who surveyed its course. The first part of this assertion stayed within the definition of Augustine, while the second was prone to cause trouble for those asserting the factuality of miracles. It could imply that for normal action nature alone sufficed, whereas for miraculous activities both God and nature were necessary. One might then conclude that God was involved only in supernatural occurrences but not in those of every day. Unintentionally, the course was laid for divorcing God more and more from the natural realm and for relegating God completely to the supernatural sphere.

While Roman Catholic scholars never admitted that God had nothing to do with the natural world, they nevertheless followed the definition of Aquinas. For them a miracle had happened if a certain phenomenon (e.g., the healing of a paralyzed person) could not be sufficiently explained by assuming natural causes alone. This means that in a miracle God works separately from or at least in addition to other, natural, causes. Such an argument involves the danger of assuming that there are certain cause-and-effect sequences that run by themselves, independently of God, while for others God's immediate involvement is needed. Since our scientific knowledge of nature is continuously progressing, often something that has been declared scientifically impossible today is declared possible tomorrow. The occasions for divine intervention will then recede at the same rate as our scientific knowledge of the world increases. This becomes evident as we read the reports of miracles officially admitted by the Roman Catholic church and notice how their frequency decreases over the years. In the face of an ever-expanding knowledge of nature, God is in danger of being edged out of the world.

But the Protestant approach to miracles was not much more promising than the Roman Catholic approach. Johann Salomo Semler, for instance, advanced the theory of accommodation, suggesting that Jesus accommodated himself to the beliefs and views of his contemporaries, though he himself did not necessarily hold them. Thus he performed what in the eyes of pious Jews were exorcisms and miracles, knowing full well that these actions had natural causes. Especially during the era of the Enlightenment many "natural" explanations of the New Testament miracles were advanced. Most well known is the attempt to explain Jesus' walking on water as a natural deception in the morning mist as he waded in the shallow water, while his disciples believed he had actually walked on water. Similarly, the feeding of the five thousand was to be the result of his fascinating preaching when his audience completely forgot about food and thought that Jesus had indeed fed them. Some even went so far as to discard miracles altogether as deliberate deceptions introduced by the disciples to advocate Jesus as the true Messiah. How much at odds our scientific world view had at one time become with the accounts of the Bible is reflected in Rudolf Bultmann's famous verdict: "It is impossible to use electric light and the wireless and to avail ourselves of modern medical and surgical discoveries, and at the same time to believe in the New Testament world of daemons and spirits."[15]

In recent years, however, scientists discovered more and more that nature is not ruled by ironclad laws that it must obey. Nearly two hundred years ago Immanuel Kant argued that space and time are not given *a priori* but are conceptual tools that we need to discern objects in relation to one another. More than a century later, Albert Einstein showed that space, time, and matter are not absolute but are relative to each other depending on the velocity of the object. This means that space, time, matter, and the object denoted by these coordinates are inextricably related and relative to each other. Werner Heisenberg questioned the reality of the object even further, stating that one can never determine at the same time all the facets of an object and that we also cannot ascertain what happened with an object between one measurement and the next. In other words, the whole cause-and-effect sequence, which hitherto had remained unquestioned, suddenly became suspect. Hand in hand with the collapse of a strict determinism came a new understanding of the laws of nature. It was no longer tenable to perceive them as laws according to which events must occur; we should perceive them instead as laws derived from our experience of the way events generally happen. This means that laws are not determinative of events; conversely, events determine the laws according to which we expect further events of like nature to occur.

Some might want to rejoice that our present scientific understanding of nature once again allows for the miraculous intervention of God. Yet such an idea would violate the spirit of science, which assumes that even the most unusual occurrence has a this-worldly origin. It would also contradict the biblical understanding of God's activity. Neither the Old nor the New Testament conceived of God's working as contrary to or superimposed on nature. Nor was it assumed that there were ironclad laws that God must break to perform miracles. For the biblical witnesses, the whole world process was totally God's doing; miracles were only new and surprising ways of God's working. God's miraculous activity occurs within and through the present structure of nature. A miracle becomes visible in the natural context insofar as we observe something that runs counter to our usual sense of experience, the consequences of which allow it to be perceived as possessing saving significance. At times the miracle may just be an unusual constellation of causes, conforming to the laws of nature and occurring at the right time. For instance, according to Exod. 14:21, a strong wind began to blow just when the Israelites tried to cross the sea, and ceased when the Egyptians took the same route. As scientists, we will not resort to God but only to natural causes to establish causal relationships. Yet our faith that God is involved in all facets of life will not be satisfied with completely "natural" explanations. It will perceive that some totally natural events are quite "supernatural."

The natural context of cause and effect that is connected in an unusual way, and God's presence that allows for this connection, must be seen together to perceive the whole of reality. If we regard events *simply* as natural occurrences, this will lead to a truncation of the whole of reality. While the presence of God in any event, whether miraculous or not, is not scientifically demonstrable, such seeing together of God and nature brings into focus the whole of reality.

NOTES

1. Walter Kasper, "Law and Gospel," in *Sacramentum Mundi* 3:297.
2. Martin Luther, *Lectures on Galatians* (1519), *LW* 27:355, in his exegesis of Gal. 5:14.
3. Luther, *WA* 49:2, 1–2, in a sermon of January 1, 1540.
4. Karl Barth, "Gospel and Law," in *God, Grace, and Gospel*, trans. J. S. McNab (Edinburgh: Oliver & Boyd, 1959), p. 3.
5. Ibid., p. 8.
6. For this and the following quote, see ibid., p. 10.
7. Johann Wolfgang von Goethe, *Faust* ii/v, 7, 11936–37.
8. John Calvin, *Institutes of the Christian Religion* (2.7), ed. John T. McNeill, trans. F. L. Battles (Philadelphia: Westminster Press, 1960), 1:360.
9. Paul Althaus, *The Divine Command*, trans. F. Sherman (Philadelphia: Fortress Press, 1966).
10. *BC* 349.
11. For this and the following quotation, see Martin Luther, *Ninety-five Theses*, *LW* 31:25.
12. Dietrich Bonhoeffer, *Letters and Papers from Prison*, ed. Eberhard Bethge, trans. R. Fuller (New York: Macmillan Co., 1967), p. 213.
13. Martin Luther, *Sermon on the Gospel of St. John* (1537), *LW* 24:81, in his exposition of John 14:12.
14. Augustine, *The City of God*, trans. M. Dods (New York: Random House, 1950), 21.8, p. 776.
15. Rudolf Bultmann, "New Testament and Mythology," in *Kerygma and Myth*, ed. Hans W. Bartsch, trans. R. H. Fuller (London: SPCK, 1953), p. 5.

PART TWO: THE SACRAMENTS

3

Sacraments of the Word

Sacraments are external actions to which, according to a maxim of Augustine, the word comes so that the actions become themselves "visible words" of the gospel. The word comes to the action as the command that it be done; and the word comes to the action as a promise of the gospel made about and by the action. Just so, the mandated and promise-bearing rite itself speaks, and speaks in a way essential to the gospel, as the gospel's necessary externality. The great problem of sacramentology has been and is to grasp what sacraments say and what sacraments do as a unity.

COMMANDS

Conjunction with the word is posited in the very notion of "sacraments." Every religion has various rites, responding to its particular communal needs. Christianity is no exception. The theological notion of "sacraments" was created by Augustine's interpretation of Christianity's rites as *forms of the word*.

Augustine's famous maxim must be cited at the beginning of any treatise on sacraments: "The word comes to the element; and so there is a sacrament, that is, a sort of visible word."[1] The gospel, God's self-revelation in the words of human messengers, does not remain purely verbal but picks up actions and things ("elements") of the objective ("visible") world and addresses us with and by these to be also a more-than-verbal communication. It is this event, said Augustine, that is fundamentally afoot in the ritual life of the church. Augustine's maxim has been so universally used as the first premise by Western sacramental theology that it must be regarded as primary sacramental dogma of the Western church.[2]

With this interpretation, a common factor was discovered in a variety of rites, and a word was specified for them in respect of that factor. The word itself, *sacramentum*, had been adapted by Tertullian, two centuries before Augustine, from the standard religious terminology of Roman antiquity, where it meant any publicly binding religious act. Tertullian had baptism and the

Supper mostly in mind, but the word could be and for centuries was applied to any public rite that resembled baptism and the Supper in attachment to the gospel. The Eastern church never created such a term. What the West calls a sacrament the East calls a mystery, but it has never restricted "mystery" to this use.[3]

The connection of the word "sacrament" to the rites has several aspects, which will be discussed serially in this and the following two sections. We begin in this section with the simplest aspect: Sacraments are commanded.

Sacraments may be initially characterized simply as actions,[4] which together with more purely verbal preaching and teaching make up the life of the church. That the gospel would have had to embody itself somehow, we will argue later. Now we make a more primal observation: The church initiates its neophytes by washing them, celebrates meals of bread and loving-cup, and performs a variety of other actions because it apprehends authoritative commands to do these things. Moreover, the church has always been aware of this connection; the notion of divine mandate in some form or other has been a constant of the theology of the sacraments, perhaps especially emphasized by the Reformed tradition.[5]

The church itself, in its own self-conception, was created by the risen Lord's missionary command: "Go . . . , make disciples . . ." (Matt. 28:19–20). Or we may say the church is created by the obligation to bring the world a certain message, the "gospel," to proclaim abroad: "this Jesus . . . God raised up" (Acts 2:23). The church knows itself to be a community under command, a community with a mission.

The mandated mission-action is first a verbal action: "Go . . . , make disciples . . . , teaching. . . ." The gospel is precisely a specific message, something to be uttered. But it is an observable fact about the mission mandate, both at the beginning and thereafter, that it regularly involves commands of more-than-verbal actions. The passage in Matthew reads more fully: "Go . . . , make disciples . . . , *baptizing* . . . and teaching. . . ." Thus it belonged to what Paul "received" as the gospel, that the Lord had taken bread, given thanks, and said, "*Do* this . . ." (1 Cor. 11:23–25). And the connection has continued, mandating actions great and trivial. In the Epistle of James we read: "Is any among you sick? Let him call for the elders of the church, and let them pray over him, anointing him with oil . . ." (James 5:14).

Some such mandates of more-than-verbal action are only for a moment. Others are intended to accompany the mission mandate through the church's future, so that there will be a repeated and recognizable more-than-verbal rite of the gospel. Here we may introduce a standard term of sacramental theology and call these latter mandates "institutions." Some would-be institutions of gospel rites do carry the church's future with them and some do not. Thus the tradition of the gospel bears a changing deposit of instituted rites of the gospel ranging in authority and importance from baptism to the direction of the eyes during prayer. The simplest and primary use of the word "sacraments" is just a label for all these.

The same questions must be asked about all such actions mandated somewhere in the tradition as about verbal utterances that someone proposes to be the gospel. First, is such-and-such a rite *proper* for the gospel? Is it legitimately mandated? A good deal of winnowing is likely to occur at this point. For example, there are voices in the tradition that command "Promote indulgences" or "Meditate transcendentally" which must not be obeyed. In this way a second, narrower use of the word "sacrament" arises, which applies it only to those rites, mandated somewhere in the tradition, which are *legitimate*. Using the word so, there will still be many "sacraments"; Hugo of St. Victor, in the thirteenth century, counted thirty-two.[6]

We ask, second: Of rightly instituted rites of the gospel, which are mandated with greater authority? Are there some that are not voluntary or optional, that we *must* perform? Clearly, those commanded in the canonical fixations of the initiating mission mandate itself have such authority, for there is no way to omit them without disobeying the word that summons the church into being. Are there others with equal authority? Other entirely legitimate rites surely are optional, carrying little more authority than our own judgment of current suitability. Are there still other rites somewhere in between? Can we make a scale for these?

A third, even more narrow, use of the word "sacrament" results from such questioning, reserving the word for those rightly instituted rites whose superior authority we wish to commend. This is the most common medieval and modern use. The tendency has been to reserve "sacrament" for those rites with the highest authority, those we think we dare not omit. It is thus that lists of "*the* sacraments" are made and that specifying their number (seven, four, two, or whatever) begins to seem important.

This latter tendency is natural but perilous. When differing concerns move the question "What must we not omit?" different lists result. The medieval list of seven sacraments resulted from asking "Which rites are *necessary* to the church's saving mission?"[7] The Reformation lists of two or three or four sacraments resulted from a similar but not identical question: "Which rites have strictly canonical authority, so that their necessity is *undebatable*?"[8] Thus differences between lists of "the sacraments" do not necessarily mark material disagreement about what the church must do in any actual circumstance; for example, the Roman and Reformation bodies agree that the church must ordain, and their scholars agree that this necessity is not entirely beyond biblical dispute. But by the time lists harden, it is usually too late for such discrimination. Thus the Council of Trent disastrously decreed: "If any one says that . . . there are more or less than seven . . . , let him be anathema."[9]

10 / THE MEANS OF GRACE

The question "How many sacraments are there really?" is meaningless. There are as many "sacraments" as we narrow or broaden the word's use to cover.[10] There is only one rational procedure here, and there is now ecumenical near-consensus in it: About each legitimately instituted rite, we should inquire into the specific complex of scriptural, dogmatic, or other authority with which it is instituted, determine to obey appropriately, and let it go at that. This will be our method in the following chapters. For such examination, it is in the Western church appropriate to take the seven of the later medieval list. As for the words "the sacraments" it will hereinafter, except when within quotation marks, refer to all legitimate rites of the gospel, of unspecified number.

We must here note a difficulty—or what is regularly taken for a difficulty. Especially in the Western tradition, it was until recently supposed that where "sacrament" is used in the third sense above the mandator must be Christ, that is, it must be his direct authority that makes "the" seven (or four or two) strictly necessary.[11] Thus Aquinas, noting that Scripture does not record the institutions of all seven by Christ, posits extrascriptural tradition as guarantee that all were nevertheless so instituted;[12] Luther, noting the same circumstance but denying final authority to churchly tradition, can (at least in one mood) allow strictly "sacramental" status only to the two sacramental actions of which Scripture does record a dominical institution.[13]

Since the emergence of historical-critical biblical exegesis, it has been impossible to maintain this traditional criterion. Given the state of the texts, we cannot be certain that Jesus mandated any continuing rites for his followers. However the particular scholarly questions are regarded, dominical institution cannot be used dogmatically as it used to be, even for baptism and the Supper. As for the others on the medieval list, the notion of an extrabiblical tradition preserving dogmatically significant *material* tradition from the historical Christ has been almost universally abandoned.

We have therefore avoided the notion of dominical institution in the preceding discussion, substituting that of canonical institution. The authority that can mandate gospel rites whose necessity is past debate is the authority that mandates the gospel itself, the apostolic witness. The justification of this shift must be the general doctrine of Scripture and lies beyond this *locus*.

PROMISES

The Christian faith does not command rites for no reason. Thus the effective tradition of rites is carried by institutions that not only say "Do this" but also say what good will come of it. The instituting words are not only commands but also, to use the biblical and traditional word, "promises": they stipulate actions and attach some blessing to their doing, for example, "Repent, and be baptized . . . , and you shall receive the gift of the Holy Spirit" (Acts 2:38). It is especially the Lutheran tradition, guided by its general determination decisively to distinguish "law" from "gospel" or "promise," that has given this observation theological weight.[14] Throughout the following chapters, interpretation of each sacrament will be based on attention to what precisely is in each case commanded, what precisely is promised, and how command and promise work together.

The promise attached to a mandated rite may be and usually is unspecific. Every serious mandate of a rite is accompanied by this promise: Do this, and the life and mission of the church will be furthered. But some rites are instituted by far more specific promises. The most drastic instance is the Supper: Do this, and the bread and cup used will be my body among you. Here is another motive for distinguishing between "sacraments" and other rites: the supposition that a "sacrament" must be a rite of the sort that thus brings some *special* form of "grace."[15] And the rites on the traditional list, with which we will work, are all of this sort.

The question of authority arises not only about the commands that institute rites but also the promises. The authority carried by the mandates demands obedience; that carried by the promises demands faith. With most institutions of rites, this is not a problem. When voices from the tradition tell me to sign myself with the cross and promise that this will be an appropriate mode of testimony or prayer (i.e., that God will make it a blessing), no special mode of faith is proposed. If I believe, if I am indeed given to testimony and prayer, I can judge myself whether signing with the cross is an appropriate rite; and however I, in a particular situation, may judge, this does not define my faith. But when the instituting promise is "This is my body," there presents itself an object of faith which, if believed, makes faith itself different from what it would otherwise have been. It is not sacrilegious to say that the first reaction to such an extraordinary promise must be "Who says so?" Faith in such a promise will be right only if the promisor is equal and appropriate to the weight and particular quality of the promise.

It is perhaps this factor above all that led to reduction of the number of "sacraments" in the Reformation bodies. Thus Luther's objection to calling anointing, for example, a "sacrament" was not to the rite but to the demand that faith attach itself to this rite in any way different from other rites of the church. Immediately after articles on baptism, the Supper, penance, and ecclesial order, the Augsburg Confession, typically for Reformation confessions, states: "They [the Lutheran congregations] teach concerning churchly rites, that those are to be maintained that can be maintained without sin and that serve the peace and good order of the church. . . . But at the same time they instruct the people; so that consciences are not burdened, as if such rites were needed for salvation."[16] Behind the dispute about the number of "sacraments"

10 / THE MEANS OF GRACE

was at least one real question, that about the relation between churchly authority and faith.

In the present ecumenical situation, and with the benefit of hindsight, it is right to prescind from the old, hardened positions also in this connection. For reasons of convenience, we will group together all rites whose instituting promises do not specially modulate faith, and discuss them as "liturgy." We will be individually concerned about those rites whose instituting promises do modulate faith. The point is not to draw one line between rites with instituting promises that can make "sacraments" and those without. Instead we will examine each rite on our inherited list for what precisely is promised to it, on whose authority, and for what these circumstances may mean for faith and practice.

Finally among matters to be considered in this section, there is a major ecumenical-theological issue we can begin to untangle. The institution of a sacrament is a command to *do* something, for God's sake. That is, it is a command of "works," in the very sense in which "works" have been a matter of controversy throughout the history of the Western church. To these works, the institution of a sacrament then promises blessing, for example, the bodily presence of Christ or the gift of the Spirit. Does this not stipulate a work, by the performance of which we may claim God's grace? The Council of Trent decreed that the seven sacraments are "necessary to salvation,"[17] and as we have just seen, the Augsburg Confession (as other Reformation confessions) differs only as to the number of rites of which this is true.[18] But does this not mean that we "must do" these works "to be saved?" The suggestion is anyway so near that the sacraments have always been the chief objects of the continuing Western controversy about faith and works. Thus the Ninety-five Theses that triggered the Reformation were mostly about penance, and the great initial reforming tracts were mostly about penance and the Supper. Since the Reformation was the most decisive battle of the conflict about works, we must look briefly at the Reformation positions.

Few Roman Catholic scholars would now deny that the medieval church interpreted believers' participation in the sacraments as works by which we do "our part" in the process of sanctification, thus violating dogma held at least since the second Council of Orange (529), that God's grace is the sole active agent of our righteousness.[19] The language of "merits," so central to medieval and Tridentine piety, pushes almost irresistibly in this direction.[20] And it is fair to say that this remains the special Catholic temptation.

The Protestant temptation is the reverse. Article XXIV of the Augsburg Confession protests: "We are falsely accused of abolishing the mass." This was the concern of the most acute among the papal polemicists. Since, they worried, the Supper is clearly a work, must not "justification without works" include justification without the Supper[21] or indeed, without baptism, ac-

SACRAMENTS OF THE WORD

tual verbal teaching and preaching, or any other external event? Is not the necessary outcome of Reformation teaching a purely inward mystical communion with God, such as was promoted on the sectarian fringes of the Reformation?

It is obvious what the Reformation reply must be: that the Supper is not our work but God's.[22] But clearly the bread and cup do not materialize on the table directly from God's transcendence; the celebrant and not a voice from heaven speaks the promises attached to them; and *we* finally eat and drink. Throughout the Supper we are hard at work, as we are at all rites and preachings. Thus the papal theologians had a strong point, and one that went to the heart of the Reformers' contentions.

Moreover, history has shown that the papal theologians perceived an actual and not merely abstract possibility. Through the history of Protestantism, there have always been those who tried to obey the doctrine that we are justified without works by cutting down on works, at least those works that are interwoven with the events of God's grace, as at the sacraments. Thus there is visible throughout Protestant history a tendency to reduce the role of rites, "the sacraments" included, and within sacramental celebrations to eliminate as much of "our" action as possible, such as the congregational offering of the Supper's bread and wine or the prayer in which the narrative of the Supper's institution is traditionally embedded. That is, through the history of Protestantism there has been a tendency to "abolish the mass."

The beginning of alleviating insight into this tangle is, we suggest, to notice a peculiarity of the promises attached to sacraments: they are not promises of a grace to be found elsewhere than in themselves. "This is my body" or "Receive the Holy Spirit" are themselves the gospel, good words that faith receives, and what they specifically promise about bread and cup or washing with water is thus precisely that these rites are in specific ways more-than-verbal carriers of that same gospel of which the promises are verbal events. Thus the promises that institute rites of the gospel do not merely say something about the rites and then fall silent. They come first to the elements and then come to *us*, carried by the elements. They are promises not about the rites only but first and last about and to us and in between about the elements. Or as Augustine said, when the word comes to the elements, the elements themselves become visible words, of the same message the words bring.

Thus it is the next section, in which we will discuss sacraments as words, that supplies the final solution to our present problem. But already we can say that the works to which sacramental promises attach God's blessing are no other work than that of speaking the gospel. The "necessity for salvation" of our doing the sacraments is simply that of speaking the gospel itself. It is merely a tautology: If the saving gospel is not spoken, then it is of course not spoken. And if it is not spoken, for example, in the form of baptism,

10 / THE MEANS OF GRACE

then it is not spoken in the form of baptism. Or we may understand the matter so: The works we must do that the sacramental blessings may be achieved are not on our own behalf but on behalf of those to whom the mission sends us, also when that is (as in the case of the Supper) mutually one another. Thus if Reformation Christians understood their own position, they would give no occasion for Catholic fears about "abolishing the mass"; and if Catholics understood the gospel character of sacramental promises, they would not take sacraments as "works" of the sort "without" which justification is to be found.

A particularly pervasive, subtle, and ecumenical temptation to treat our sacramental actions as works by doing which we become righteous arises from the necessity to consider the possibility of disobedience to sacramental mandates. Having recognized the authority of a mandate, we may still not fulfill it, because of misunderstanding or lacking will. For example, a group of Christians may acknowledge the biblical command to "baptize," and still perform nothing resembling a cleansing bath, because they do not know what "baptize" means or even because they do not finally care. Thus the church has always had to consider what would constitute obedience to each acknowledged sacramental mandate and what would not. The chief historical case is the ancient church's lengthy effort to discriminate, among allegedly baptized people entering the catholic church from the chaos of sects, between those who had in fact been baptized and could be received as already members of the church and those who had undergone some other, if similar, rite. It was decided, and is catholic dogma, that a decent quantity of water, the triune name, and the public intention of those participating to obey the biblical command are necessary, but that for example, running water, particular ways of using the triune name, or right piety or theology of the baptizers are not.[23]

So far, so good. Such questions and decisions are unavoidable. And so long as we stick to the instituting *commands*, the question we ask is straightforward: How may we best obey? Moreover, it is clear that if we do not obey a particular sacramental mandate, that form of the gospel does not occur, and if the mandate was right and our disobedience deliberate, we do great sin. But if at this point we think simultaneously of the *promises*, a far from straightforward, indeed crassly works-righteous, question results: What must we do for the promise of grace to be fulfilled for us? To all *such* questions the only right answer is "Nothing," which in this context comes out to be "If that is why you would obey the command, do not obey it." Insofar as this last kind of question has become embedded in the tradition, often under the heading of questions about the "validity" of sacraments, it is an abundant source of perverse theology and practice.

Not least among perversities so occasioned has been the Western church's reductive attitude toward sacramental practice. When we ask "What *must* we do, for grace to be given?" the very question inclines us to do as little as possible. Under the heading of inquiring about "validity," the Western church has regularly asked, "Could we not leave————out, and still make————work?" The most melancholy chapter of this history has been baptism's steady reduction from the third century's great drama of renunciation and new beginning to our present perfunctory moistening.[24] There is also the reduction of the really "necessary" part of the Supper's great thanksgiving to incantation of the words of institution, a reduction completed theologically by the fifteenth-century Council of Florence's "Decree for the Armenians"[25] and carried into regular practice mostly by Protestants.

Here the Reformation's distinction of law and gospel must be observed. When the question is about what we are to do, only the mandate is our business; the promise is God's business. The only questions we may faithfully and meaningfully ask are two: First, How may we best and most obligingly obey the command? For example, what does the command "Baptize" now set before us as possibilities of eager obedience? Second, in the instance where the borderline is important (as when we must decide whether someone has in fact been baptized) we may ask, Is such-and-such a rite obedience to the mandate? What we may not do is substitute the second question for the first, and we certainly must not mix the mandate and the promise to make the question "What must we do to make this sacrament work for us?"

VISIBLE WORDS

The last part of Augustine's maxim is the theologically most penetrating: In that commands and promises of God "come to" actions and objects of the external world, these become themselves words of the gospel, they *speak* the gospel in a particular, "visible," way. In the next section, we will take up some problems in the way Augustine carried this insight through; here we wish only to appropriate it.

That our communication is never purely linguistic, that the words by which we address one another are partly what we ordinarily call "words" and partly gestures, found objects, artifacts, is both an obvious fact and one regularly noted. Augustine's category of "visible words" was not initially theological but was applied by him to social gestures, patriotic symbols, and so on;[26] recently it was popular to speak of "nonverbal" or "body language" communication. That *God's* word to us is of such a character is not, however, so widely accepted, since outside the faith of the Bible it is not generally supposed that God's self-revelation to us is actual discourse between humans; wordless inner communion is the more normal religious event. Augustine's maxim is a major self-differentiation of Christian faith from the generality of religion.

Augustine's sacramental theology embraced both ordinary and "visible"

10 / THE MEANS OF GRACE

words in one hermeneutic category: "signs." According to Augustine, "signs" are material objects regarded not for what they are in themselves but for their use to point to other realities.[27] Augustine's word for *what* a sign signifies is *res*, a word that will be used throughout this *locus*, since no translation ("reality," "thing") quite works. If the *res* in question is God and God's immediate works, all signs, those ordinarily called "words" and "visible" signs, are alike "visible" signs of "invisible" reality;[28] "sacrament" is then a word for the *doubly* visible sort of signs.[29] Thus, over against God and God's immediate works, all other reality is fundamentally one in its capacity to be signs: Verbal utterances are also sensory phenomena, and cups and bathtubs can speak. The reason words of language (e.g., "This is my body") must come to the gestures and objects for them to be "visible" words is only that words of language are "among humans" the "chief" signs that control the use of other sorts of signs.[30] Fundamentally, all the church's verbal and visible activity is one great sign set by God to speak of himself. Indeed, Augustine's final vision is that the entire evangelical history, precisely as a sequence of actual occurrences, is one great speech of God to us.[31] Thus: "The things our Lord did . . . are simultaneously works and words: works because they happened, words because they are signs."[32]

Augustine continued the tradition of the second- and third-century Greek-speaking theologians, whose central systematic concept was that of "the Word," God's eternally one and temporally persevering self-revelation and who interpreted all Christian life as aspects of this Word. Thus, archetypically, Irenaeus of the Supper: Christians "eat and drink God's Word."[33] In other connections, the Logos theology was a doubtful blessing, but in the present connection we may correctly see it simply as determination to interpret the church's foundation and reality comprehensively as God's self-communication. God "teaches" of God, and it is this event of which preaching, Scripture, baptism, episcopacy, and all the rest are but aspects.

Two questions arise here. First, What is the difference between what we ordinarily call "words" and speaking gestures or objects? Does not the distinction of "word and sacrament" collapse? Second, Why does God's word need "visible words" at all? Why do we need sacraments? In the major theological tradition both questions have been answered by means of the standard Western metaphysical division of reality into two great kinds: spiritual and material. In the next section, we will see that this metaphysics has been a chief hindrance to full development of sacramental understanding and practice. Therefore we must here begin the attempt to overcome the hindrance.

Traditionally, it has been said that language is more intimate to the "spiritual" realm of souls and meanings, that sacramental and similar signs are more intimate to the "material" realm, and that this is the important difference between them. So Aquinas: The human person is "composed of soul and body," "to whom the sacramental medicine is proportioned, that through a visible thing touches the body and through a word is believed by the soul."[36] If we presuppose the metaphysical division of "spiritual" and "material," this analysis is surely right; but the phenomenological observations[35] that support it can be stated without the metaphysics.

By a "word" in such formulations as Aquinas' is meant, we suggest, a communication in *language*, in a system of signs that has and works by rules of grammar. A language is constituted of semantic rules that regulate our use of its signs by the things about which we use them, and by syntactic rules that stipulate signs' relations to one another. For our present purposes, the vital consequent characteristic of the signs of language is their adaptability and, the obverse, their evanescence. By playing language's rules, we can instantly create new signs for each precise new intended meaning—as this paragraph is an absolutely new sign created to say what had never quite been said before. But just so any linguistic sign is also replaceable. By playing the rules or by stipulating additional rules, any sentence or word can be translated into others that share none of its native characteristics as a sound or mark. For example, "That is a horse" can be replaced by "¡ziv" if we stipulate that we will use "¡" for indefinite reference and that "ziv" is to be equivalent to "is a horse."

Thus there is an affinity of language to *spirit* in the biblical sense by two decisive determinants of the biblical use of "spirit." First, utterances in language are the location of living persons' capacity to meet the surprising future and that future's appearance in other persons' novelty and unexpectedness. Second, utterances in language can be learned (i.e., appropriated to the subject): The mind, which translates the meaning of one set of linguistic signs into quite another, can just so entertain that meaning indifferently to any one set of signs, and so "in" itself, without recourse to the external world where all signs are located. These two notes, of subjectivity and of openness to the other and his or her future, define the biblical reference of "spirit." It must be clearly noted that this biblical use of "spirit" is *not* the same as the metaphysical notion of "spiritual reality."

In contrast, a "visible" sign is one of the many signs that do not belong to a language, that are not fully ruled by grammar. Such are the signs of sign systems with no syntax, as the hand gestures of social converse; others are the wholly individual signs we call works of art. The particular incapacity and capacity of all such signs, for our present purpose, are their unadaptability and irreplaceability. Goya's *Family of Charles IV* once created, there is no way to make another picture that will "say the same thing," for there are no rules by which to instruct the making of the replacement or to test the equivalency. The bread and cup of the Supper once instituted, we cannot decide to say the same thing with popcorn and kisses, for there is no way to say what it *is* that the bread and cup say, except by the bread and cup.³⁶ And so the meaning of the bread and cup is not separable from their native actuality, from their mass and shape and ordinary use as objects in the world, as is not the case of the objects that linguistic signs are. Perhaps, thinking back a paragraph, the simplest way to note the difference between signs of language and visible signs is to note that when I have learned a sentence it is the sentence itself that is in my mind, whereas after studying the *Family of Charles IV*, there will be much in my mind, but not the picture itself.

Traditional terms are now easily justified, for given our actual evolutionary history, given the particular sensorium we have, sounds are for us the natural material of language, by virtue of the unlimited variety in which we freely produce them, and sights make the most common and most obvious sorts of nonlinguistic signs. Thus it is natural to call the words of language "audible" words and works of art, conventional or instituted gestures, and the like "visible" words, even when the work of art is a piece of music or a recited poem. We will use this traditional language.

We come to the second question: Why does the gospel need visible words? Again the traditional answer is cast in the traditional metaphysics. This time let us cite Calvin: "Thus the merciful God so tempers himself to our condition . . . , that since we are caught in the flesh and so do not think spiritually . . . , he leads us to himself by . . . fleshly elements, making what is spirit be seen in . . . flesh."³⁷ Given the dichotomy of spirit and matter, visible words necessarily appear as adaptations to an intrinsically regrettable situation; Calvin in this passage calls it our "imbecility."

There is undoubtedly some truth hidden behind this part of the traditional account, but here its inadequacy amounts to actual error. The distinction between audible and visible signs is only relative: sounds are also material, only more malleable than sights.³⁸ Thus a consistent application of the traditional principles must finally regard *all* God's word to us as a regrettably necessary accommodation. But this cannot be true of the biblical God, of whom John could say that God *is* his Word, explicitly meaning his Word to *us* (John 1:1ff.). One of the chief contributions of the specifically Lutheran Reformation is that it used the reforming doctrine of justification by faith to create a new and superior explanation of the gospel's need for visible words. We give that explanation here in our own terms.

The gospel is a message of our "justification" or "righteousness," our sufficient reason for life, which locates that righteousness not inside us but outside us. That is the point of "by faith, not by works": The excuse for my being is not anything I do or am, but what Christ has done and is. My righteousness is an "external" righteousness, to use the word that is the key to all Reformation theology. Just so, the gospel itself, the word that tells me of this righteousness, must be an external word, a message from outside me, of events

SACRAMENTS OF THE WORD

beyond my subjectivity. But no exhaustively *learnable* message can be such a word, which is why the gospel cannot be an audible word only.

If, for example, "Your sins are forgiven" were only an audible word, then (once having been told it) it could become something I had learned, and so a truth that within my self I could bring forth to tell myself, and so precisely not the gospel. If hearing the gospel justifies me, then if the gospel can become something I tell myself, I can justify myself—which is exactly what the gospel is to dispense me from doing. It is to defeat my attempt to make all truth *my* truth, the property of my subjectivity, that (to continue the example) "Your sins are forgiven" is spoken to me not as this audible word only but as an audible word "with" a visible word, the bath of baptism. For although I can take the sentence into my head, I cannot there accommodate the bathtub, and just so "Your sins are forgiven" is the justifying message of an external righteousness. If a sheerly linguistic version of the gospel could be concocted, it would merely so be no longer the gospel. In the Lutheran Reformation's understanding, which we believe in this matter to be correct, the sacraments make the *inalienable externality* of the gospel message and therefore are necessary to the authenticity of that message.[39]

Thus the distinction of "word and sacraments" does in a certain way collapse. It is a relative distinction only,[40] for there can be no purely nonverbal sacrament. But also, given what we have just noted, there can be no purely "audible" words of the gospel either; thus the import of a sermon is shaped by the appearance of the preacher, the architecture of the space, and so on. We attain clarity about sacraments only when we see that Augustine's maxim is intrinsically reversible: We can say that preaching, teaching, and so forth are "audible sacraments" as well as we can say that baptism, anointing, and so on are "visible words."

A sacrament is a total action that speaks the gospel audibly and visibly. The audible word comes to a mandated visible action and brings it to speech. Generally this meeting is not arbitrary. Washing with water can be brought to mean repentance because of the significance washing has as otherwise a function in life. Sometimes it is the more abstractly dramatic possibilities of an action that sacramental institution appropriates, as the laying-on of hands is appropriated to mean communal reception and empowerment.

Such appropriateness does not itself institute a sacrament. Washing does not constitute itself a sacrament by its symbolic possibilities; it is constituted a sacrament by the historically contingent command "Wash, for repentance and initiation."[41] Thus if we were to find ourselves without water and were then to look about for some other action than washing that had "the same" symbolic potential, we would not be perpetuating the same sacrament by other means; we would be abandoning baptism and instituting a new rite. Whether this proceeding would be legitimate depends on whether the historically actual mandate in the case (here of baptism) has only such authority as our momentary needs and judgment can override, or has an authority superior to such judgments.

In this connection, there is a vital and regularly unnoticed methodological point that can now be made for the remainder of the *locus*. Theology (at least by Reformation understanding) is fundamentally instruction to would-be speakers of the gospel: "Say such-and-such, rather than such-and-such, to be communicating the gospel." With respect to the audible word, theology thus takes the form of ideology, stipulation of concepts usefully to be employed and propositions truly to be maintained in and by the Christian community. It is this we usually think of as "theology." But with respect to the visible word, the fundamental form of theology must be stipulation of acts to be performed, that is, rubrics.

It is another evil consequence of the traditional metaphysics' prejudice in favor of the "inward" and "immaterial" that the theological role of liturgical rubrics is usually ignored and that theologians assume our ratiocinations about visible words are directly related to them in the same way as our ratiocinations about audible words are directly related to them. Since rubrics are the primary level of theology of visible words and are the link between visible words and reflection about them (which must be concepts and sentences), this usual presumption actually disconnects theology and sacramental practice, leaving each to go its own way. Protestants cultivate correct—or more usually now, satisfying—opinion about rites they rarely or carelessly perform, and Catholics excuse large accretions of superstitious or works-righteous sacramental practice on the grounds that such is not what the church "really" teaches. Both parties must learn that with respect to the *visible* proclamation of the gospel, orthodoxy or heresy are not right or wrong opinion but right or wrong stipulated practice.

There is one final matter to note in this section: To provide appropriate interpretation of the sacraments of the *gospel*, all these last points must be understood christologically. To do that, we must make a further phenomenological observation, to pair with that made earlier about "spirit": As audible words are the reality of personal spirit, so visible words are the reality of personal *body*—whereupon we must again hasten to prevent the misunderstanding that visible words are more "material" than audible words. My body is *myself*, in my address and presence to you, insofar as I am available to you, locatable by you, there for you, addressable in turn by you. And it is the visibility of my address to you that constitutes such reciprocity.

The christological point can then be stated. God's Word to us is Jesus Christ. Or, what is the same thing, the gospel is this Christ's self-presentation to us, his personal intrusion into our lives. Therefore, insofar as the gospel is spoken "audibly," this speaking is Christ's presence as spirit, as free subject over against us. Insofar as the gospel is spoken "visibly," this speaking is Christ's presence as body, as our object, available to us and reciprocally addressable by us. And in that the gospel is spoken both audibly and visibly, it is Christ's self-presentation in our lives as the one risen and living person—spirit from one side and body from the other, as are all living persons—that he in fact is.

FACT AND MEANING

The Western catholic tradition has insisted above all on two propositions about sacraments. First, sacraments are signs; they *mean* something, and that something is the gospel. This proposition has been established above all by the dicta of Augustine. Second, sacraments are events of grace; they *accomplish* something, and that something is the new reality of which the gospel speaks. The great support of this proposition has always been the immediate conviction of believers, from Scripture and liturgical experience. Both propositions are laid down, with utmost concision, by the Council of Trent, in terminology already long traditional: sacraments "contain the grace which they signify."[42]

Surely the catholic insistence is well supported by Scripture. We may take Paul's discussion of baptism, in Romans 6, as a central case. Plainly, we were not in mere fact "buried with" Jesus when we were baptized (Rom. 6:4). Rather, baptism *means* burial, a meaning that the act carries by virtue of the interplay between the act itself, with its symbolic possibilities, and the content of the audible word that comes to it. And yet Paul claims that the baptized are liberated from a bondage that had previously held us despite our intentions (Rom. 6:5-7). Moreover, also our future is factually otherwise than it would have been: "For if we have died with Christ, we believe that we shall also live with him" (Rom. 6:8). Or, staying with Paul, there is his discussion of the Supper in 1 Corinthians. The one loaf, shared by the many believers, *means* their unity as the one body of Christ (1 Cor. 10:16-17). Yet so actual is the unity thus achieved, that violation of it can lead to physical illness (Rom. 11:29-30).

It is, however, equally clear from the same passages that "Sacraments mean" and that "Sacraments create facts" should not be treated as independent propositions. The most noteworthy feature of Paul's arguments is the way in which his interpretations of sacramental meanings and his assertions of sacramental facts intertwine. And as is clear from all the foregoing, it is the trend of churchly sacramentology to make the two catholic rules one.[43] Thus, for example, we will have rightly understood the Supper only when we can state how the Supper's being a sign of Christ's self-giving to us and the fact of his sacramental presence in the Supper are one event.

Over against the gospel and its sacraments, the question about what a rite says and the question about what a rite is and does should solicit only one

10 / THE MEANS OF GRACE

answer. This roots in the deepest metaphysical insistence of the faith, that God *is* his Word with himself and to us, so that predicated of God, "says" and "is" are two words for the same thing. For the *triune* God, to be is to be in conversation, and by the being of God all being is defined. What this must mean for reality as a whole is beyond the scope of this *locus*, but it is clear that at least with the sacraments, since these belong to this God's word to us and are facts of his reality for us, meaning and fact may not be separated.

Right reflection on the sacraments, therefore, must describe what happens in a sacrament, including God's actual creating presence in it, precisely by analyzing its character and structure as a word, a "sign," an event of communication. What a sacrament says to us is what it is for us. And this rule does not in any way diminish the actuality of what happens; it is precisely this last point that sacramental theology must grasp.

It is hard to think that serious theologians would explicitly dispute these last paragraphs. Moreover, Augustine's inclusion of words and sacramental events under one category of *signs*, and his location of all signs at the same ontological level over against God, seem to be directly on the way to fulfilling their demands. Yet the tradition has had great difficulty grasping sacramental facts and meanings as one. And the first great failure was Augustine himself.[44]

There is no doubt that Augustine, especially in his later work, intended fully to affirm the common Christian traditions of, for example, Christ's "real presence" in the Supper. But his analytical work always pulled him in another direction. One indication of this is his answer to a question that was to become decisive at several points in later history: Do unbelievers or the lapsed, if they nevertheless commune, receive Christ's body? Augustine said they do not.[45] According to him, sharing the sacramental signs is one thing and sharing the *res* they signify is another, which may or may not accompany the sacramental sharing. Therewith the sacramental conception is quite undone.

It is clear what hindered Augustine: the metaphysical interpretation of spirit and matter as two kinds of reality. Since the *res* of a sacrament is always somehow God's reality, it is "spiritual" and just therefore *not* "material," even if called "Christ's body and blood."[46] Thus the material signs can point to their *res* only by pointing *away* from themselves, and it is finally only the soul and not the body that can participate in the sacramental fact. "One thing is seen, another is known. What is seen has a corporeal appearance, what is known has spiritual fruit."[47]

Augustine left his irresolutions to the Western church, and they have remained the framework of our struggles about the sacraments. The famous ninth-century controversy over the Supper between Paschasius Radbertus and

Ratramnus of Corbie became a paradigm for subsequent history and can function so also for us.[48]

The issues between Radbertus and Ratramnus cannot better be stated than by Charles the Bald's original request for advice: "Is that which in the church is eaten by the . . . faithful, the body and blood of Christ, there in a mystery or in fact (*in veritate*) . . . ? And is it the same body that was born from Mary?" Radbertus answered the first question "Symbolically and in fact" and the second "Yes." Ratramnus answered the first question "Symbolically and not in fact" and the second "No." The conflict was crudely stated but clear. Its official resolution was the victory of Radbertus' proposition that "figure" and "actuality" are the same in the sacraments. But how this could be so did not appear.

Thus Augustine's final bequest to Western sacramentology was an inherently unstable balance between sacramental meanings and sacramental facts, which nearly every theological movement has tipped one way or the other, weighting fact to the detriment of meaning or meaning to the detriment of fact. For traditionalists, the outcome of the controversy just described fixed the balance in the first position. But when a reform movement has somewhat relaxed the bonds of tradition, Western theology's basic Augustinianism has regularly tipped the balance to the other and equally deleterious position.

Protestant polemics have seen the first form of error best represented by the scholastic slogan that the sacramental realities are established *ex opere operato* by virtue simply of the fact that the sacramental signs are performed.[49] And undoubtedly there is something in Protestant alarm at the phrase. But it is difficult to be sure just what the controverted assertion is. Is it that the sacramental facts are established independently of the subjective state of the sacramental ministers? Then it only affirms the ancient decision against the Donatists, with which the main-line Reformation agreed.[50] Is it that what the sacramental signs *say*, also about those realities that occur as the sacramental acts themselves, is *true* independently of the subjective reception of the sacramental recipients? Then again Reformation theology must agree. As Luther said of baptism, "It is not our first concern, whether the one baptized believes or not, for that cannot make the baptism false; everything depends rather on God's word and command."[51] Is it that sacraments achieve their *purpose* independently of believing reception? But nobody ever said that.[52] Or, finally, is it that the realities that are to occur as the sacramental acts occur independently also of the *possibility* of faith, that is, of whether the sacramental signs actually speak and speak the gospel? That also *silenced* rites can be actual sacraments? *This* assertion must be rejected.

It will be best to locate the error by pointing to actual *practices* that suppose a sacramental actuality of silenced rites. And there have been many such:

10 / THE MEANS OF GRACE

private masses, where there is no congregation for the visible word to address; the transformation of anointing the sick for their recovery into a rite for the dying or already dead; "emergency" baptism; or votive celebrations whose sacramental benefits are to accrue to the absent. Against all such, the Reformation polemic is appropriate.[53]

The opposite inclination has appeared most influentially in the sacramental theories and practice of the Swiss and "radical" Reformations. We may again cite Calvin himself: "We must be led, by a certain analogy, from the corporeal realities that are proferred in sacraments to spiritual realities. . . . Thus the sacrament does not make Christ to be the bread of life; but insofar as it recalls to our memory that he is made that bread, with which we so eagerly nourish ourselves, it sets before us that bread's delight and savour."[54] It is a common factor of the otherwise diverse sacramental theories of standard Protestantism that the actual events to which the sacramental signs point are said to happen elsewhere. So, on baptism, the confession shared by most American Baptists: "Baptism is . . . ordained . . . to be unto the party baptized a sign of his fellowship with [Christ] in his death and resurrection; of his being engrafted into him; of remission of sins; and of his giving up unto God."[55]

It is clear what is needed to end this oscillation and to fulfill the biblical pattern. First, we must adopt firm methodological rules: that we have not grasped what *happens* in a sacrament until we have grasped it by analysis of that sacrament as communication, and that we have not grasped what a sacrament *means* until we see it refer precisely to its own actuality. Second, we must be far more willing than theology has been to revise our traditional grasp of reality in order to obey these rules. Within the limits of this *locus*, these tasks will best be undertaken mostly in consideration of particular sacraments.[56] But there is one general point that can be made here.

The distinction between "word" and "sacraments" is relative; there are no words without some visible aspect and no sacraments that are purely nonverbal. Thus what is to be said about the power and reality of God in the sacraments begins as what can be said about the power and reality of God in his Word as such. There is a basic alternative: Does God's Word to us speak of a presence and creativity of God that occurs elsewhere—in pious exercises or mystic experience or in the occurrence of sacraments even when silenced? Or *is* God's Word itself God's creating presence? We have earlier discussed the necessary, and indeed biblically obvious, answer. God's word to us is God's self-presentation; as I am present to you in that I address you, so is God to us. God's word to us is the very word by which God creates history and history's world. And the word in question is no esoteric or inward word; it is the law and the gospel, the story about Christ, the word that is "near you, on your lips and in your heart (that is, the word of faith which we preach)" (Rom.

10:8). Also of the visible word (and the word always is somehow visible) all this is true. The sacraments *are* God's visible self-presentation to us, in God's own full reality and to be our Creator.

Through the gap between sacramental fact and sacramental meaning, perverse or foolish sacramental practice often enters the church's life. For we have assured ourselves that however false or inane what is audibly or visibly said may be, the sacramental facts (whatever they may be) are given. Many Protestants have the worst of both sides here, expecting little to happen sacramentally but expecting also that whatever does happen will occur whether or not it is audibly or visibly spoken. Sacramentology must gather the courage to say that such assurances are simply false.

The last assertion in no way affirms the common Protestant position earlier rejected. But sacramental fact is precisely the *truth* of sacramental meaning, the truth of those promises made about and by a rite. "This is the body of Christ," the celebrant says; and if we believe this is rightly said, we take the bread and cup as in fact Christ's body. If a liturgical leader says something else, or says this about some object of which he or she is not bidden by adequate authority to say it, we suppose no sacramental happening. Just so, if the liturgy of the Supper audibly and visibly confirms participants' private religiosities, we must not expect the solidarity of the congregation as Christ's one body to be silently established.

Ultimately, only a consistently christological interpretation, as was begun at the end of the previous section, can heal the division of sacramental fact from sacramental meaning. When the gospel is indeed spoken, however obscurely or lethargically, this speaking is Christ's own presence. And the future outcome of Christ's presence is neither manageable nor predictable by us; the blessed consequences of a botched sacramental celebration may be greater than those of the most authentic ministration. But Christ's *presence* and *present* action *in* any sacramental act is his address to us as spirit and his availability to us as body, and these are the audible words we then hear and the visible words we see. There is no presence and present action of Christ behind the back of this his true spirit and body.

ACTUAL LITURGY

An abstraction we have so far allowed ourselves must now be removed. We have proceeded as though a sacrament could be the visibility of only God's word to us and not also and simultaneously of our word to God. Or, if one prefers to retain the word "sacrament" for the one direction of the conversation between God and his people, we have proceeded as though a rite could be purely sacramental and not simultaneously—we must now introduce the controversial word—sacrificial. This supposition is manifestly contrary to fact.

10 / THE MEANS OF GRACE

It is doubtful that hearing can itself ever be an essentially nonverbal act. To apprehend an address *is* (one might well argue) to complete the double movement from registering through reflection to new words—which latter may be spoken only to myself. And however that may be, *God's* word definitely cannot be heard without confession, petition, and praise: "For man believes with his heart and so is justified, and he confesses with his lips and so is saved" (Rom. 10:10). Responding to God's law and gospel is not a separate work added to hearing them; it is their natural correlate. Thus every actual sacrament is an audible and visible *conversation*. Or, if one prefers, every actual rite is simultaneously sacramental and sacrificial.

As every rite of the gospel is a conversation, God's address and our response, so every proper rite of the gospel is, like every proper conversation, a complex exchange. Since the one side of the conversation is a "we," the lines of communication are multiple and crossing; Christian rites are antiphonal. Since the other partner of the conversation is the *triune* God, the same can be said of that side. And most important, these complications of God's address and ours mean that God does not appear to address us as a supernatural entity; God's word and the human speakers' word are the same. It is our word for God that is God's word to us. Thus the final complexity of Christian rites is that most utterances within them are addressed, by their created speakers, simultaneously to God and to the other believers present; insofar as these utterances are visible, they are both sacrament and sacrifice. Such, for example, are nearly all the psalms, the very paradigm of Christian prayer.

We have used the word "sacrifice." The Reformation polemic against "the sacrifice of the mass" (which we will consider in its place) has made Protestants allergic to the word. It is time to get over this prejudice. In every context but the Reformation polemic, "sacrifice" has a wide use: In the Bible, in religious language generally, and in phenomenological study of religion, a "sacrifice" is any address to God, insofar as it is more than merely verbal. In Christian rites, not only does God's word to us become visible, but so do our words to God: we adopt postures during prayer; we march around during some hymns or root ourselves in our places; we take up an offering of money or kind; we raise the cup and loaf. All that is what "sacrifice" denotes, and if we refuse to use the word, we merely cripple our vocabulary.

Protestants have wanted Christian rites not to be "sacrifices" because they think of sacrifices as "works" designed to obtain God's grace; that is, they narrow the word to mean what is in fact only one possible kind of sacrifice, "propitiation." Not calling our rites "sacrifices" and avoiding those ritual features we associate with the term will anyway not save Protestant rites from works-righteousness, if that is otherwise their content. If the congregation is regularly exhorted to contribute funds out of obligation to "stewardship," the Sunday collection is a propitiatory rite whether it is solemnly presented at the altar or not. The true principle is that prayers and praises become works-righteous by their *content*, however dominantly or minimally these are done visibly, that is, however much or little they are phenomenologically sacrifices. The Pharisee's prayer, "God, I thank thee that I am not like other men . . ." (Luke 18:11), was a wrong prayer verbally and would have been made no worse by becoming more visible in a thank-offering of turtledoves.

With this abstraction out of the way, we are in position to discuss briefly the comprehensive object of this *locus*: the liturgy. The total Christian liturgy is the total reality of believers' audible and visible discourse, for God and to God, made up of those audible and visible words that are so regularly repeated as to be rites and of those that are for the moment only, and among rites of those that by some narrowed usage are "sacraments" and of those that are not. Believers come repeatedly together to *do* something. What they do on each such occasion is *a* liturgy, a complex event of audible and visible communication. It is such events that are the actual referents of all statements in this *locus*. Here we have four general propositions to make about them, which can be quickly stated because they follow directly from the preceding.

First, we must attend to what now can be seen as a tautology: Every liturgy is a communication event. Insofar as liturgy is silenced, audibly or visibly, it goes wrong. This does not mean that silence has no place within the liturgy. But liturgical action that proceeds *opere operato* in the last sense described is false.

Second, since a liturgy speaks, we must ask what it says. Every liturgy in the church is to be the gospel to us and right prayer to God—this is another tautology. A *liturgical hermeneutics* must be practiced in the church, an examination of actual and proposed rubrics, both for continuing orders and for single liturgies, by the same norms that hold for all teaching and preaching. We must always ask, Is what by these rubrics would get said indeed the gospel? It is as disastrous for the one Christ to be "distributed" to the congregation by individualized disks and glasses as it would be for the preacher to say verbally, "You are not one body in Christ." Or if what the people see regularly enacted before them, as "baptism," is in fact a patently harmless moistening, and one with no moral or social consequences, it will be useless for verbal instruction to maintain that we "die with Christ."

Third, every whole liturgy is *one* utterance. A succession of silent actions may be performed in close proximity without cohering, but the law of context prevents this from happening with actions that speak. If I speak two sentences to you that are separated by no clear break, either they make sense together or neither does. Thus everything that happens at any one liturgy, especially including those items that are commonly regarded as not belonging to "the liturgy," such as a sermon or the hymns, either makes one communication event, one coherent conversation, or is silenced also in its several parts.

Fourth, we can specify the nature of the coherence just demanded. A liturgy is to be a word of the gospel; the gospel is primally a story. Putting the two characterizations together, a liturgy is dialogic narrative. That is, a liturgy is a *drama*: Its coherence is of the sort possessed by a play or an opera. Whether a particular liturgy is a brief kiss of peace between two believers parting or a papal mass at a eucharistic congress, its coherence is dramatic in character. Insofar as we are responsible for liturgies, we will attend to the same matters of pace and sequence and transition with which theatrical directors work. Here too is the primary reason for liturgy's ineradicable penchant for heightened language, music, costume, choreography, and decoration, a penchant it shares with all drama.

It is time to move to discussion of particular sacraments. There is no area of theology where false abstraction is more misleading. And the very notion of "*the* sacraments" is very abstract. We have worked with it as long as we dare.

NOTES

1. Augustine, *Commentary on John*, 80,3.
2. So, e.g., Martin Luther, Large Catechism, "Baptism," 18.
3. Friedrich Kattenbusch, *Das apostolische Symbol* (Leipzig: Hinrichs, 1894–1900), 2:84ff.
4. So also the standard Lutheran dogmaticians, e.g., John Gerhard, *Loci theologici*, xviii,24.
5. Thus it is typical of English-language Reformed confessions to treat sacraments under the general heading of "ordinances"; e.g., Westminster Confession, XXV, 4. But see also the Lutheran Formula of Concord, Solid Declaration, Article VII, 83–84.
6. Hugo of St. Victor, *On Sacraments*, ii.
7. E.g., Thomas Aquinas, *Summa Theologica*, iii,65,4.
8. So Luther in *On the Babylonian Captivity of the Church*, WA 6, 484–573.
9. Council of Trent, "Decree on Sacraments," canon 1.
10. This contention has dogmatic status for Lutherans. So the Apology of the Augsburg Confession, Article XIII, 17: "For no sensible person will quarrel much about the number of sacraments or the use of the term, if only those things are actually kept in the church that have the mandate of God and the promises of the gospel."
11. So Council of Trent, "Decree on Sacraments," canon 1: "If anyone says the sacraments of the new law were not all instituted by Christ . . . , let him be anathema."
12. Aquinas, *Summa Theologica*, iii,65,2.
13. E.g., Luther, *Babylonian Captivity of the Church*.
14. We cite the standard dogmatician, Gerhard, *Loci theologici*, xviii,11: "By 'the

word' is to be understood: first a mandate . . . and second a promise, and indeed the gospel itself."

15. So, e.g., Aquinas, *Summa Theologica*, iii,72,1.

16. Augsburg Confession, Article XV.

17. Council of Trent, "Decree on Sacraments," canon 4.

18. Luther himself is as always blunt. On baptism, Large Catechism, "Baptism," 6: "We must have ourselves baptized or we will not be saved."

19. For a typical contemporary Roman Catholic view, Harry J. McSorley, *Luther: Right or Wrong?* (New York: Newman Press, 1965), pp. 111–27.

20. This can be seen even in intended assertions of the monergism of grace, such as those of the Council of Orange itself, e.g., canon 18. The classic statement is that of the Council of Trent, "Decree on Justification," canon 24: "Justice once accepted . . . is conserved and augmented before God by good works."

21. There is now a compendious and splendid monograph on this history: Vinzenz Pfnür, *Einig in der Rechtfertigungslehre?* (Wiesbaden: Steiner, 1970).

22. E.g., Luther, Large Catechism, "Baptism," 35: "Answer: yes, our works indeed contribute nothing to salvation, but baptism is not our work but God's."

23. E.g., Council of Arles (314), canon 8; Council of Nicaea, canons 8, 19.

24. Robert W. Jenson, *Visible Words* (Philadelphia: Fortress Press, 1978), pp. 152–65; there literature.

25. Council of Florence, "Decree for the Armenians": "Forma huius sacramenti sunt verba Salvatoris . . . : sacerdos enim in persona Christi loquens hoc confecit sacramentum."

26. Augustine, *On Christian Doctrine*, iii,3.

27. Ibid., ii. On Augustine's hermeneutic in general, see Gerhard Strauss, *Schriftgebrauch, Schriftauslegung, und Schriftbeweis bei Augustin* (Tübingen: J. C. B. Mohr [Paul Siebeck], 1959); Ragnar Holte, *Béatitude et Sagesse* (Paris: Études Augustiniennes, 1962), pp. 335–60. On the place of sacraments in the scheme, see Johannes Betz, *Eucharistie in der Schrift und Patristik*, vol. 4, fasc. 4a of *HDG* (1979), pp. 150ff.

28. Augustine, *On the Catechizing of the Uninstructed*, 50, speaking of *words*: "Signacula quidem rerum divinarum esse visibilia, sed res ipsas invisibiles in eis honorari."

29. Augustine, *Epistle 138*, 7: "Cum [signa] ad res divinas pertinen, sacramenta appellantur."

30. Augustine, *On Christian Doctrine*, ii,3.

31. Strauss, *Schriftgebrauch*, pp. 109ff.

32. Augustine, *Commentary on John*, 44,1.

33. Irenaeus, *Against All Heresies*, iv,38,1.

34. Aquinas, *Summa Theologica*, iii,60,6.

35. The following observations are more fully developed in Jenson, *Visible Words*, pp. 12–25.

36. Augustine is wrong when he says, "I could express the meaning of all [visible] signs . . . in words, but I could not make the meaning of words clear by [visible] signs" (*On Christian Doctrine*, ii,3). This manifest error is determined by his adherence to the spiritual/material ontology.

10 / THE MEANS OF GRACE

37. John Calvin, *Institutes of Christian Religion* (1536), iv,102.
38. Augustine had this clearly in view; *On Christian Doctrine*, iii,4.
39. Luther, Large Catechism, "Baptism," 29–30: "Faith must have something that it believes. . . . So faith hangs here on the water. . . . [The 'enthusiasts'] are so foolish that they separate faith and the thing to which faith clings . . . , however outward it is. Indeed, it must and shall be outward . . . , as indeed the whole gospel is an outward oral preaching. . . . Whatever God does and works in us, he wants to work through such an outward arrangement."
40. Also, finally, according to Catholic theology; e.g., Aquinas, *Summa Theologica*, iii,60,6–7.
41. Beautifully stated and argued by Aquinas, ibid., iii,60,5.
42. The Council of Trent, "Decree on Sacraments in General," canon 6.
43. This intention is clear in the first great scholastic treatise on sacraments; Hugo of St. Victor, *On Sacraments*, ii,6. And it is a chief goal of modern Roman Catholic sacramentology: see Edward Schillebeeckx, "Transubstantiation, Transfinalization, Transignification," *Worship*, 40(1966): 324–38.
44. On the following, see Bernard Neuenheuser, *Taufe und Firmung*, vol. 4, fasc. 2 of *HDG* (1956), pp. 51ff.; Betz, *Eucharistie*, pp. 150ff.
45. E.g., Augustine, *City of God*, xxi,25.
46. The dilemma posed for interpretation of Christian sacraments by this conceptuality appears systematically in the continuing difficulty in specifying what is "sign" and what is *res*. The *res* signaled by all sacraments is the grace of God. In the Supper, for example, the signs are bread and cup. So where do the body and blood of Christ fit? The standard scholastic solution is that they are *res* signified by the bread and wine, but also signs of the ultimate *res*. (Peter Lombard, *Sentences*, iv,8,7). The "characters" supposed to be imprinted by some other sacraments (baptism, confirmation, and ordination) have the same middle position (Aquinas, *Summa Theologica*, iii,66,1).
47. Augustine, *Sermon*, 172.
48. On the following, see Neuenheuser, *Eucharistie* pp. 15–34.
49. The phrase first appears with dogmatic status in the decrees of the Council of Trent, "Décree on Sacraments," canon 8. The Protestant polemic is classically stated by the Apology of the Augsburg Confession, Article XII, 12. On the history, see Friedrich Loofs, *Leitfaden zum Studium der Dogmengeschichte*, 5th ed. (Halle: Niemeyer 1953), 2:471ff.
50. E.g., Augsburg Confession, Article VIII, 3; Thirty-nine Articles of the Church of England, Article XXVI.
51. Martin Luther, Large Catechism, "Baptism," 52–53.
52. Peter Lombard's *Sentences*, the textbook of all scholasticism, go so far as to say, "Whoever comes forward without faith . . . , receives the sacrament but not its reality" (iv,4,2).
53. Classically, Martin Luther, *On the Abomination of the Secret Mass*, WA 18:22–36.
54. Calvin, *Institutes*, "On Sacraments," 119–20.
55. The Philadelphia Confession, "Of Baptism," 1.
56. For the author's more direct attempt, see Jenson, *Visible Words*, pp. 12–60.

4

Baptism

We are canonically commanded to initiate into the church those whom the mission proclamation brings to penitence, by washing them in the triune name. To those who have been thus initiated, baptism promises the forgiveness of sins and the gift of the Spirit. The task of baptismal theology is to understand how baptism can be regeneration, that is, at once an audible and visible word that promises these gifts and the past fact to which such promises can appeal. The task of the church at the present moment is to recover the integrity of baptism. The task of believers is always to *use* their baptism.

THE COMMAND

For any missionary community, initiation must be the chief rite, and Christianity has always retained enough missionary self-consciousness to regard baptism as the chief sacrament, or at least as the gateway to other sacraments.[1] Moreover, baptism is the only sacrament confessed in the ecumenical creeds.

The primal church apprehended a command to baptize, directed to themselves and to their successors, as a direct command of the risen Lord and as integral to the church's founding mandate. It is time to cite in full the passage in which this apprehension appears most explicitly: "Go therefore and make disciples of all nations, baptizing them in the name of the Father and of the Son and of the Holy Spirit, teaching them to observe all that I have commanded you" (Matt. 28:19-20). The pseudo-Markan parallel is close (Mark 16:15-16).[2] Exegetes often regard these passages as retrojections of the church's self-consciousness, but if there were indeed appearances of the risen Lord, there is no reason the giving of this mandate cannot have been among their incidents.

In any case, the New Testament would mandate baptism also without recording these particular resurrection appearances. In all strands and strata of the New Testament witness, no distinction is conceived or conceivable between the church's doing its mission and people being baptized. Paul assumes that

10 / THE MEANS OF GRACE

all believers come into the fellowship by baptism, including himself (Rom. 6:1–9; 1 Cor. 1:11–17; 10:1–12; 12:13). In Acts the very syntax is controlled by the supposition that to be converted, to enter the church, and to be baptized are all the same thing.[3] And the same supposition is apparent wherever else in the New Testament the matter comes up (e.g., 1 John 2:18–27; Titus 3:5). We are commanded to baptize merely in that we take the mission command as directed also to us. This logic was established by the circumstances in which the primal church made "baptizing" its practice, which circumstances we must now briefly describe.

What, after all, does "baptize" mean? The New Testament texts simply assume that all readers know what rite is referred to, and indeed in a way we do, insofar as the rite has been practiced continuously from then to now. But for exegesis of the texts, we need also more historical confirmation. Beyond reasonable doubt, the primal church adapted baptism from the practice of John the Baptist.[4] John preached repentance, renewing the prophetic proclamation of God's coming triumph with such immediacy that those convicted by him had only one remaining possibility: instant self-abandonment to the judgment of God. For such penitents, John provided a rite: he *washed* them, exploiting the act's obvious symbolic possibilities. That he immersed them is not certain,[5] and that baptism must be by immersion is nowhere said in the New Testament.

Jesus himself and probably some of his disciples had submitted to John's baptism. When Jesus' resurrection and the pentecostal experience of the Spirit launched the mission of the gospel, those granted faith by the apostolic proclamation became penitents exactly in John's sense, though that was not all they became. The apostles welcomed these penitents with the same rite by which they (or some of them) had themselves repented. Thereby baptism became what it had not been for John: an initiation.

The Christian community is a missionary community; and every such community, drawing people from outside itself into itself, accomplishes the transfer with some rite of passage. More specifically, the character of the gospel message is such that those who believe it are merely thereby recruited to be its messengers, drafted into the company from whom they have heard it. But those who believe the gospel are made penitents, for whom the apostles stipulated John's rite; since they are simultaneously also neophytes of the resurrection community, this baptism becomes their initiation. It is this logic that basically establishes and determines the rite.

Thus the canonical command is, so far: Initiate into the church those whom the gospel calls to repentance, by washing them. One element remains: This is to be done "into the name 'Father, Son, and Holy Spirit.'" The import of this phrase has been disputed, but for the purpose of this section it is clear enough: As the apostles healed by saying, "In Jesus' name, be well," so we initiate by saying, "In the name of the Father, Son, and Holy Spirit, be baptized."[6] We are to invoke by name the God at whose command the act is done and whose agency accomplishes its effect.

Here the dogmatic tradition has been faithful to Scripture. The dogmatic development concluded with the rule of the Council of Florence: "The matter of this sacrament is real, plain water: it does not matter whether cold or warm. The form is, 'I baptize you in the name of the Father and the Son and the Holy Spirit'—though we do not deny that baptism is truly accomplished also by other wordings."[7] The reference simply to "water" should be interpreted by the proposition of Thomas Aquinas, who introduced the terminology in which the decree is cast: "The sacrament is not, of course, accomplished in the water itself, but in . . . the washing."[8] The reference to other wordings is to the Eastern formula, "N. is baptized in the name . . ." and doubtless covers also the interrogatory formula most anciently used in Rome, "Do you believe in. . . ."

If the dogmatic tradition is biblical, widespread practice is not. Straightforward attention to the canonical mandate of baptism clearly would never lead to "baptism" by dribbling or dabbing, as if the water were an ointment. The command is remarkably simple: to *wash*. Therefore whatever practices are perceived *as* washing in a given culture or group (from the ancient nude immersion to a laving of head and hands in very inhibited congregations) are obedient, and practices not so perceived are disobedient. Through most Christian history, baptism has normally been by immersion.[9] And there has been remarkable ecumenical consensus in the material point. Thomas Aquinas and Martin Luther both taught that immersion, though not strictly mandated, is the most desirable practice because it most plainly *says* one great thing that baptism *is*, burial and new emergence.[10]

Thus the instituting rubrics of baptism do not closely specify the rite; there are many ways we might obey a command to "baptize" in the triune name. The liturgy of baptism has consequently mostly been shaped not by baptism's instituting command but by its theological interpretation, that is, by the promises of its benefits, and will therefore be discussed in the next section. Two further questions must be touched on in this section: who is to baptize and who is to be baptized.

Matthew and Mark took the command to baptize as addressed simply to the disciples, to the Christian community. This understanding has been maintained, except in the Reformed tradition.[11] Despite powerful clericalizing forces in the ancient and medieval church, the dogmatic development kept the ministry of baptism open, if grudgingly. Again the Council of Florence: "The minister of this sacrament is a priest. . . . But in case of need not only a priest

10 / THE MEANS OF GRACE

or deacon, but a layman or a woman can baptize—or even a pagan or heretic . . . ," if the latter will publicly act as the church's agent.[12] Classical Reformed theology, however, insisted that baptisms done by the unordained, with special mention of women, must be done over again.

As to whom we are to baptize, the biblical command is in itself unambiguous. We are to baptize those whom the gospel mission brings to repentance and into the church. But this stipulation adjudicates only if those brought to repentance and those entering the church are the same group. In the missionary situation they are, and baptism is in its origins a rite for adult converts. But when the world unexpectedly lasted beyond the church's founding generation, it became a regular event that people entered the life of the Christian community not by repentance but by being born into it; then the biblical stipulation of whom to baptize became a problem rather than a guide.

Whether the apostolic church baptized infants (i.e., people too young to repent) and if at all, under what circumstances, we simply do not know, despite centuries of scholarly effort.[13] Nor do we know by what events and arguments the catholic practice of opening baptism to infants born to certain parents came about, that is, of permitting baptisms that are rites of initiation but not rites of repentance. By the time for which the baptismal practices of the church are first known to us, the turn of the second and third centuries, infant baptism had been established.[14] So long as the mission continued to bring in large numbers of converts (in Mediterranean territories, until the end of the fourth century), baptism was not dominated by infants, and the rite itself could be and was continued as an adult rite of repentance.

It is important to note that the ancient decision was not that the children of Christian parents *should* be baptized as infants, only that they *could* be. Many pastors of the ancient church recommended postponement, and many parents postponed.[15] It is also important to see that *either* decision, to baptize infants or not to baptize them, empties one side of the biblical stipulation, for if we delay baptism of infants born to practicing Christians in order that it may be for them a rite of repentance, they are meanwhile growing up in the church, and their baptism when it comes will not be their initiation.[16] Therefore the arguments for or against infant baptism cannot be drawn directly from baptism's mandate, but depend on interpretation of what is promised as the purpose and outcome of baptism. This much must here be emphasized: The question about baptism does not come up about infants at all except in the cases of those infants not clearly excluded by the canonical mandate, that is, those born to parents who live so explicitly as disciples that if their children are ever to be initiated it must be done soon. About these, the church is indeed compelled to ask, "Can we not baptize them? Is baptism the sort of rite that *can* be done for them?"

THE PROMISES

What New Testament witness promises to baptism precisely responds to the two sides of baptism's mandate. Both aspects are concisely stated in the baptismal kerygma Luke attributes to Peter: "Repent, and be baptized . . . for the forgiveness of your sins; and you shall receive the gift of the Holy Spirit" (Acts 2:38). On the one hand, baptism forgives the sins of the penitents who submit to it; on the other, it gives the blessings of the community into which it initiates.[17]

In characterizing baptism as "for the forgiveness of . . . sins," Peter's formula is exactly that with which the synoptic Gospels describe John the Baptist's rite (Mark 1:4 par.). The identification of baptism with forgiveness is so close in Acts that the mere phrase "forgiveness of sins" seems normally to denote baptism (Acts 5:31; 10:43; 13:38; 26:18). In the remainder of the New Testament, the phraseology itself is not common, though, as we shall see in a moment, the matter is central. In the earliest postbiblical tradition, the terminology of Acts is standard,[18] and this characterization of baptism then enters various versions of the "rule of faith" and finally the three-article creeds, as that of "Nicaea," which confesses "one baptism for the forgiveness of sins," or that of "the Apostles," where "the forgiveness of sins" again simply means baptism.[19] The Council of Florence once more: "The effect of this sacrament is the remission of all original and actual guilt, and of all penalty."[20]

On the other side, as an initiation rite, baptism obviously must grant "all rights and privileges" of the body into which it initiates. The remarkable gifts said by the New Testament to be given by baptism are simply the privileges claimed by a remarkable community. In that the church is the community of the "justified" and "sanctified," baptism justifies and sanctifies (1 Cor. 1:26-31; 6:8-11). In that the church fulfills the prophecies of a kingdom of priests or of a nation of prophets, baptism appears as the requisite anointings (Heb. 10:22; 1 John 2:18-27). In that the church is persecuted and raised above the persecutors, baptism "saves" (1 Pet. 1:3-21). In that the church is the bride of Christ, baptism is the bride's toilette (Eph. 5:25-27). What predications of this sort actually appear in the New Testament are clearly a matter of rhetorical chance.

All these ecclesial metaphors for baptism are eschatological. The church's privileges are particular anticipations of the life of the kingdom of God. Just so, they can all be evoked together as "the gift of the Holy Spirit," for the Spirit *is* the advance payment on the eschaton, the life of a community whose life is specific and founded hope for the fulfillment of God's promises (2 Cor. 1:22; 5:5; Eph. 1:14). The decisive New Testament characterization of all this side of baptism is therefore that it is the gift of the Spirit.[21] The difference between John's baptism and Christian baptism is that the latter bestows the Spirit (Mark 1:8 par.; Acts 19:1–7). Jesus' own baptism is depicted as anointing with the Spirit for his prophetic mission[22] (Mark 1:9–13 par.). In Ephesians, baptism "seals" with the Spirit (Eph. 1:13; 4:30), in Hebrews it makes "partakers of the Spirit" (Heb. 6:4). According to Paul, in 1 Corinthians, baptism initiates into "one Spirit" as a pair to the "one body," and the justification that baptism effects is "in the Spirit" (1 Cor. 12:13; 6:11).

That baptism grants the Spirit is somewhat ambiguously attested in the later churchly tradition. It is the chief theme of the Eastern church's baptismal theology and liturgy and richly developed in this way also in the West.[23] But it has entered the dogmatic tradition only in one way, though that the most powerful possible: by inclusion of baptism in the creedal articles devoted to the Spirit and his works.

To conclude our consideration of baptism's instituting promises, we must consider the New Testament's two great baptismal passages. Romans 6:1–11 and John 3:1–8 are witnesses to baptism both as repentance and as gift of the Spirit, and theologically conceptualize the duality.

The argument of Rom. 6:1–11 responds to the question "Why not continue to enjoy sin, if we will be forgiven anyway?"[24] Paul's answer is that such a question, in the mouths of the baptized, is meaningless babble. The choice between sin and obedience to God is no longer in their subjective competence because of what has happened to them. By being baptized "into" Christ, they have come to be included in the reality of Jesus' death; and therefore that relation of want and possible satisfaction no longer subsists between Christians and the world, to which the question "Why shouldn't I . . . ?" could meaningfully refer. Righteousness is now the Romans' only real possibility. In this theology the two aspects of baptism, freedom from the past and new possibility, come together.

John 3:1–8 brings the two together in another way.[25] There are, in the ontological scheme of John's theology, two kinds of people, those who are "flesh" and those who are "spirit," so constituted in each case by *origin* "from" flesh or spirit. (John 3:6). Since all begin as flesh, the beginning from and as spirit is a beginning "again" (John 3:3)—as the theological tradition will appropriate John's theology, it is "rebirth," "regeneration." At some point in the history by which the canonical text came about, the new birth from the Spirit was qualified as birth "of *water and* the Spirit" (John 3:5). Thereby two points were made. First, the regenerating work of the Spirit, who in himself blows unpredictably (John 3:8), is made biographically locatable: The baptized can say, "*Then* it happened to me." And second, the baptism in water for repentance that John the Baptist had practiced and the baptism in the Spirit that he had promised (John 1:33) became one event, which thus points in both temporal directions, to be precisely *re*birth.

The two great baptismal passages just cited make a final and essential observation unavoidable, which once made is seen to apply to the whole New Testament: The past tense of baptism is an essential point of biblical witness to baptism. Since the New Testament is written for believers, it is of course written to the already baptized. But this does not remain incidental when baptism becomes thematic; rather, it is seized on as the very reason for bringing up baptism at all. Thus it is the heart of Paul's argument to the Romans that they *have been* baptized, that this event is irrevocably a part of their pasts and that *therefore* a kind of life is closed to them that would otherwise have been open and inevitable. Again, it is the pivot of John's proclamation that baptism is a once-only new *beginning*. Or, to mention some of the minor passages, that the Hebrews must look *back* to baptism (Heb. 6:4) or that believers *are* prophets, *having been* anointed (1 John 2:18–27) are the very reasons the authors mention baptism. Here also is the basic reason why infants can be baptized: Faith's use of baptism is in any case after the fact.

At last we may look at the actual rite, which throughout the church's history has been a dramatic enactment of the promises just stated,[26] as these were at any time and place appropriated. Our knowledge of baptismal liturgy before A.D. 200 is sparse and conjectural.[27] By the third and fourth centuries, about which we do have detailed knowledge and which have some claim to be thought of as the classic age of baptism,[28] baptism had become a great three-act drama.[29] Orders varied between East and West and between localities, but the plot was the same throughout the church,[30] and it is this to which we will most attend.

The first act of baptism enacted separation from the old life. For months or years, unless there was an emergency, converts were submitted to the discipline of the catechumenate, a school for believers which instructed in theology but was more concerned with training for the religious and moral shock of entry into the church's radically different life. The catechumenate was a time of disciplined prayer, of supervised good works, of public examination in the faith, of blessing by the laying on of hands, of feeding with salt, the ancient world's means of purification and so the "sacrament of the catechumens," and of exorcism, the rite of effective prayer for the catechumen's detachment from the gods and habits of the old world.[31] At last, normally in the vigil of Easter night, intensified exorcisms and other exercises ended with the journey to the place of baptism.

The second act, of several scenes, enacted the rebirth itself. First came the epiclesis over the font, an invocation of the Spirit on the waters that they might be waters of new birth. To invoke the Spirit, the epiclesis narrates the biblical events by which baptism is instituted, and so it is also a parallel to the Supper's narrative of "the night in which Jesus was betrayed." Then the candidates were stripped; this was to be no partial washing, and the neophytes were to carry nothing but themselves through the waters from the old life into the new.

The great transfer itself followed quickly. The candidate renounced the ruler of the old age and all his ceremonies and moralities. In the East, this was a direct address, facing west: "I renounce you Satan, and all your rites and all your works." The last exorcism followed, then confession of faith in the new Lord, in the East done as a precise pair to the renunciation of Satan: a creedal recitation, or an address facing east, "I believe and I bow down to you, O Father, Son, and Holy Spirit," or both. Here also might come the first anointing, for the bath was (before, after, or both) accompanied always by liberal use of consecrated oils, which had become, by processes not well known to us, the chief sign of the Spirit and which were in any case a necessary and cherished part of bathing in Mediterranean antiquity.[32] The washing was a bath by immersion with invocation of the triune name, in the West by the neophyte's confession of faith in response to the three questions, "Do you believe in God the Father Almighty, Creator . . . ? / . . . in Jesus Christ, his only Son . . . ? / . . . in the Holy Spirit . . . ?" and in the East by the more explicit formula "N. is baptized in the name of the Father, Son, and Holy Spirit."

The third act of baptism was again in several scenes. It enacted the beginning of new life, by the Spirit in the church.[33] The neophytes emerged, washed and oiled, and were clothed in new garments. They were then led to where the congregation was holding the vigil, where they "must originally have halted the . . . vigil . . . , in a huge surge of sentiment . . . as the neophytes—still damp, oily, fragrant, and dressed in new garments—were presented to the church by its bishop."[34] Then the bishop conducted the specific rite of the Spirit, a prayer, with laying on of hands, marking with oil, or both, with a text such as this from late second-century Rome: "Lord God, who have made them worthy to obtain the remission of sins by the bath of new birth, make them worthy to be filled with the Holy Spirit, and send them your grace, that they may serve you. . . ."[35] Finally the neophytes, of whatever age, joined the congregation for the Supper, receiving extra chalices of water and of milk and honey, the food of infants and of the promised land.

We have called this rite classic. The description is justified, for the subsequent history of baptism is the history not of new ritual or interpretations but of the dismantling of these. The necessary condition of the dissolution was the dominance of infant baptism; we will therefore reserve the further history for the section entitled "The Integrity of Baptism."

REGENERATION

We do not choose to be born, nor do we choose our parents or our nationality or the time we are born. Yet just those circumstances, utterly unyielding in their sheer factuality, are the most existentially decisive of our lives. Such realities make "new birth," "regeneration," precise for the ontological statement of baptism's claims. And through much modern theological history, "baptismal regeneration" has been the conventional label for what is affirmed or denied by those who say baptism is or is not an event *of* grace and not only a word *about* grace.

Such claims provoke Martin Luther's famous catechetical question "How can water do such great things?" How can all that was said in the previous section be true? Luther's answer is ecumenical: "Water as such indeed does not do it, but the word of God with and accompanying the water."[36] But this answer, while true, only poses the theological problem and does not solve it, for how are the word and the water "with" each other and how *can* they be?

Baptism is an audible and visible word of forgiveness and hope which appeals for our interpretation and our faith. And baptism is, as water-bath, an external event, irrevocable in the past, a given *to* which the word of forgiveness and hope appeals, if need be *against* our interpretations and unbelief. In this reality, it lets Paul say, "I know you would like to indulge yourselves, and use the gospel as your justification. But, willy-nilly, it is too late for that." How can baptism be both? That is the question with which baptismal theology has struggled. The question has its operational cash value in baptism's unrepeatability and in the possibility of infant baptism. We cannot here recount the whole history, but only describe the key positions and offer our own solution.

The most impressive baptismal theology yet created is perhaps that of the Greek fathers.[37] They explicated the specific reality of baptism by the central concept of all late-antique religiosity, Christian or pagan: "image."[38]

An image, such as a statue or painting or dramatic figure, is not identical with that of which it is the image, but neither is it any other thing. Late-antique philosophy and theosophy seized on this middle status in being to bridge the increasingly experienced gap between God and our world. So the Christian image-theologies of the apologists and of Origen make Christ the temporal and visible image of the supposedly timeless and invisible deity, through whom this deity can be present and at work in the temporal world and in whom we can see him. Moreover, once it is posited that there is this mediating mode of being, there need not be just one level of mediating images between God and us. As many may be supposed as seem needed to account for the experienced situation.

As, then, the death and resurrection of Christ are the image of God's loving being, so our baptism can be the image of Christ's death and resurrection,[39] and that is precisely what the fathers found in Romans 6. The drama of our descent into the water and new and cleansed emergence is the image-reality through which Christ's death and resurrection become present to involve us,

10 / THE MEANS OF GRACE

and in which we can see and know him as the one so at work. This participation is real because an image is its own kind of reality. Moreover, as the Spirit is God's emanating power, the Spirit can be understood as an immanence of Christ in the water which obtains in that the washing is Christ's image. This union of the Spirit with the water is then the great theme of Eastern baptismal liturgy and instruction.

Within its metaphysical scheme, this theology is profound and true. But it may be doubted that the scheme itself is finally compatible with the gospel, though that cannot be argued here.[40] And however that may be, the scheme has never fully seized the mind of the Western church. In the Western theological development[41] that culminated in high scholasticism, baptism was interpreted in less mystically heated terms: of God's *action* as agent and of God's *effects* on us on the particular occasion of baptism, both action and effect being denoted by the same word, "grace." We will sketch this theology as it appears in the thought of its perfecter, Aquinas.

As God works in creation by using creatures as means, so God chooses to use the bath and the proclamation of the triune name as together one instrument of grace.[42] The transformation God works by this instrument is *justification*.[43] Since the Pauline connection of faith and justification is maintained, baptism is "the sacrament of faith."[44] Here, however, the problem begins. Since faith is a free act, it is not invariably present at baptism, but when and until faith is present, the *res* of baptism is not given; thus faith becomes the *condition* of baptism's efficacy.[45]

But what then of the factuality of the sacramental event? If there is no faith, does nothing happen? And if nothing happens, what of the baptized unbeliever who later comes to faith? Must not that person be baptized again? Aquinas' solution became standard for scholastic theology and was taken into the dogmatic tradition by the Council of Florence:[46] Baptism in any case grants a "permanent character."

Aquinas defines a "character" as a personal potentiality, that is, the right to engage in some act and to do so with basis in reality for the achievement of the action.[47] The particular character granted by baptism is the potentiality of participating in the church's ministry, of hearing and speaking the gospel audibly and visibly.[48] That is, the "character" permanently granted by baptism is exactly what the Reformation would later call "the priesthood of all believers," responsible membership in the church as a decisive event also in reality under God. As for the permanence of the character, this is simply the permanence of Christ's priesthood in which the baptized participate.[49]

Since this is the baptismal theology of the medieval church at its best, it is not surprising that there was no controversy specifically about baptism between the pedobaptist reformers and their papal opponents—though there was controversy about every concept used in stating the scholastic doctrine:

"justification," "faith," "grace," and "sin." Yet the Reformation movement did have baptismal theologies different from that of scholasticism and closely related to the Reformation contention.

The Calvinist move was simple.[50] The structure of scholastic teaching was maintained, minus the doctrine of the "character." This left a doctrine at the one extreme of Western theology's Augustinian/realist pendulum. Calvin laid down the rule: "Nor [is] . . . water an instrument of our forgiveness, regeneration and renewal . . . , it is only the knowledge and certitude of such gifts that are found in the sacrament."[51]

Infant baptism was thus left without foundation, and modern "baptist" movements have always claimed to fulfill the true tendency of Reformed teaching.[52] Classical Calvinism provided a substitute for the "character": interpretation of the *res* of baptism as a "covenant" of grace, which as a social contract can and according to Scripture does include the children of believing parents.[53] Few exegetes would now support this exegesis. The doctrine itself was given its functional test by New England Puritanism; the debacle of the "halfway covenant" surely reveals that other paths must be attempted.[54]

Luther's baptismal theology, which became part of the Lutheran dogmatic tradition in the catechisms, is related more complexly to the scholastic inheritance. The technical doctrine of "character" is again missing, yet all of its purposes are vigorously asserted.[55] One first wonders how this is done. The other departure from scholastic doctrine provides the explanation: the very different role of faith. In scholastic teaching, faith is condition and goal of baptism. The catechisms teach rather that the word and bath of baptism are together a necessary *object* of faith: "Faith must have something that it believes, that is, to which it can cling and on which it can stand. So here faith clings to the water. . . . They are indeed foolish who separate faith and the thing it clings and is bound to, however outward it is. Indeed, it *must* be outward."[56]

As soon as so drastic a thing is said, the irrevocability of both baptism and infant baptism cease to be problematic. And the need for the "character," or any replacement, disappears. For the external fact of baptism remains fixed as an item of my past, and if *it* is the object of faith, then it is always there to be believed, to enable precisely justifying faith. "One must use baptism . . . , so that when sin or conscience afflict us, we say, 'I am nevertheless baptized, and if I am baptized, I am promised that I shall be made blessed.'"[57] For the baptized who did not then believe or those baptized in infancy who doubt whether infants can believe, Luther's counsel is brief: "If you did not believe then, believe now."[58] With such teaching, the essential *past tense* of biblical baptismal teaching is for the first time appropriated into the dogmatic tradition.

But is it not so that only God can be an object of faith? Especially according to Martin Luther? Precisely, and that leads us to the heart of Luther's new understanding. One passage brings all the motifs together: "So here faith clings to the water and believes that in baptism is sheer blessedness and life, not because of the water as such . . . , but because the water is embodied with God's Word and command and because God's name cleaves to it. When I believe this, what do I believe except in God? Who has put his word into baptism and planted it there, and proposes this outward thing to us, that we may grasp the treasure in it?"[59] In the embodiment with the triune name and baptismal mandate and promises, the plain unchanged water is nevertheless "divine, blessed, fruitful and grace-filled water,"[60] for to cling to this word-embodied-with-water and to believe in God is one act.

If what Luther claims is true, its truth must be interpreted christologically, and the christological flavor of Luther's own language is unmistakable. It is always God in Christ who is the object of faith. Therewith we come to the systematic proposal of this section. Finally, baptism must be understood also as it belongs to the life and presence to us of the risen Christ. As is true of all living people, Christ lives and is present to us as spirit and body. He is a subject who addresses us, in the word of the gospel, and he is our reciprocal object, available to us and our response, in the sacramental visibility of the gospel. What specific event is baptism in this spirited and embodied life of the risen Lord?

If I am truly present to you, it belongs essentially to the body side of my presence that there was a first event in your biography to which you can point and say, "Then and there we were introduced and shook hands" or "I first saw him then and there." To be more abstract, *temporal locatability* essentially belongs to the body presence of any person. Baptism is the risen Lord's temporal locatability. If indeed Christ is risen, and if indeed the promises of baptism are true, then baptism is what the risen Lord does to me that locates him temporally for me, without which location he would be no body and no presence to me. This proposition, we propose, is the necessary interpretation of the nearly ecumenical[61] doctrine that it is God-in-Christ who baptizes, and that *therefore* water can do such great things.

THE INTEGRITY OF BAPTISM

The problems of baptismal practice that plague the contemporary church result from the dismantling of the ancient rite. The various parts of the first and third acts of the classic rite have disappeared or been separated from the whole, leaving us with both sacramental vacancies and floating purposeless rites. The development began with the legitimation of infant baptism, but this would not by itself have sufficed to shape the history as it has been shaped. Other necessary conditions have been the coming to *dominance* of infant baptism and (as is always the case) a series of sheer historical accidents.

The dogmatic legitimation of infant baptism would not by itself have made baptism of infants the dominant practice. Baptism in infancy is legitimate as one possibility for children of people whose own way of life is such as to make it, by careful though of course fallible judgment, probable that the children will never need to be converted but will be raised from birth in the discipline of the faith. It is neither likely nor suggested by Scripture that such people will ever be many. If catechumenal testing were maintained for adult applicants, and if it were remembered that children of parents who do not live as disciples are not candidates for baptism in infancy, we would have to expect that there would in every community always be plenty of people outside the church from whom adult converts might come. But the establishment of Christianity as the official religion of the Roman Empire both produced a flood of dubiously committed "converts" and made their catechumenal testing or their later serious examination as parents impossible, since standards of church membership could not now be very different from those of general social acceptability. A few generations of this necessarily created a situation in which nearly all baptisms were of infants, and that situation, with equal necessity, has perpetuated itself even though the civil status of Christianity has been crumbling for centuries.

When baptisms are mostly of infants, the original catechumenate must disappear.[62] Historically, instruction and testing first fell into abeyance, leaving a dubiously meaningful ritual (salt, exorcisms, etc.) and then this ritual was undone by the "validity" question, "What can we leave out?" In Rome the first stage was reached by the sixth century; the second stage was only recently concluded. The bath was thus left without a prior rite, and baptism as a whole was left without discipline. It would not have been or now be difficult to devise new rites and new disciplines specifically for infant baptism. There could well be a sort of catechumenate for parents of to-be-initiated children, accompanied by the understanding that if parents chose not to undergo it, their children would later be welcome under their own profession and testing. But the same established relation to society that made infant baptism the norm also did not suggest efforts on such lines.

There are now several, not just two, possible policies, and the choice among them depends on several factors. "Baptist" solutions straightforwardly enable restoration of the catechumenate, and at the start of the various modern Baptist movements this has always been a goal, whether stated in such terms or not. Baptist solutions doubt the value of baptism in infancy, admit only penitents to the church (at least in theory), and demand the baptism of all these, whether they have been baptized before or not. Typically, Baptist positions result from

10 / THE MEANS OF GRACE

the confluence of a radically Augustinian understanding of sacraments with the conviction that the church must withdraw from its Constantinian amalgamation with civil society.[63] At the other extreme, some pedobaptist positions take baptism as necessary to salvation in a way that overrides all other considerations and compels baptism of all who can be obtained. If the positions otherwise stated in this chapter are more or less right, neither of these is an appropriate solution. Right doctrine, we propose, recognizes baptism of infants as legitimate where mandated (but as not always mandated) and sees that some sort of baptismal discipline is necessary. Then the choice of forms of baptismal discipline, and the occasions and balance of infant and adult baptisms, will depend on our general understanding of the right relation of the church to surrounding society and of our estimate of what is at the historical moment needed in that relation. Thus our final choices will depend on matters not to be discussed in this *locus*.

The third act of baptism was dismantled in a different fashion, by the detaching of its two chief events, the rite of the Spirit and first communion, to become separate rites. In this process, historical accident was decisive.

In the ancient church, the usual minister of baptism was the bishop, that is, the pastor of the town congregation.[64] As the church moved from the Mediterranean into more sparsely settled northern territories, dioceses became too large for the bishop's baptismal role to be generally maintained. For the bath itself, this carried no problem; it was understood that at need presbyters (or indeed anyone) could baptize. But a closer association had developed between the bishop and the rite of the Spirit, and the bishops of the West (unlike those of the East) refused to surrender this prerogative. The northern churches appear to have initially solved this problem by practicing a rite of baptism with no "confirmation" at all (we must now introduce this fatal medieval label for the rite of the Spirit). But later, under pressure from the Carolingian empire's drive for liturgical uniformity, they agreed to follow the Roman baptismal order, but only with the proviso that confirmation should be a separate episcopal rite, performed shortly *after* baptism. The interval once established, two forces steadily widened it through the medieval centuries: first, parental fears about infants' salvation and high infant mortality, which by the high Middle Ages had led to the rule of baptizing all infants within days of birth and had destroyed the old baptismal festivals, and second, the difficulty of producing a rationale for confirmation once it had been postponed, which led parents and priests to say, "The child is baptized—what is the hurry?"

After the separation was once made, theologians had to rationalize it.[65] The task was onerous, since every distinct blessing attributed to the new separate "sacrament" of confirmation had to be subtracted from baptism, without admitting that this was being done. Conversely, once it was argued that confirmation was "a sacrament" with its own "character" distinct from baptism's and therefore appropriately performed on some occasion other than baptism, some role in life had to be found for it. Through the centuries, among Catholics and Protestants,[66] detached confirmation has been drafted as a puberty rite, a second try after distrusted infant baptism, a graduation ceremony for church school, an ordination to lay ministry, a programmed conversion, a repeatable reaffirmation of baptismal promises, and who knows what else. And again conversely, theological rationales have been produced for each such role. Now the gifts of the Spirit are many, and the church may well need rites for all these functions, it is not of the first importance what we call them. But the integrity of baptism *is* important: If prayer for the coming to individuals of the Spirit simply *as such*, with laying on of hands, anointing, or some other profound gesture, is offered otherwise than as the conclusion of baptism, either this prayer is not meant seriously or baptism is effectively repudiated. The liturgical movement in all denominations has struggled since its beginning for the elimination of separately celebrated confirmation and for rites of baptism with a clear rite of the Spirit. Scripture and dogma are unambiguously behind the effort.

Nor would first communion have been uprooted merely by the dominance of infant baptism. That the concluding event of classic baptism is first communion was determined by biblical theology, especially by Paul: What baptism initiates into is the church as the one body of Christ (Rom. 6:1–11), and the sacramental reality of this oneness is the sharing of the one loaf (1 Cor. 10:17). That people should be initiated by washing and that this not be initiation into the Supper would be a severe biblical anomaly.[67] When baptismal groups became mostly or all infants, nobody for centuries supposed that should make any difference at this point. The whole church communed infants at baptism into the twelfth century,[68] and all provinces of the church not determined by the medieval Roman development still do.

The separation of first communion from baptism in the Roman West was caused by increasing scrupulosity about profanation of the consecrated elements and, backhandedly, about the requirement of private confession before communing. By the early twelfth century, fear that unweaned infants would refuse to swallow the bread had led to the custom of communing them with wine only. But then even greater clerical worry about spilling the wine led to reservation of the cup for priests only. Thereby infants were left with neither. At the same time, the opinion was growing that individual exercises of repentance were the necessary preparation for communing, and this doctrine was used to validate the already accomplished exclusion of infants. Since infants were almost the only neophytes, first communion was thereby set adrift from baptism, to be celebrated at some later age; this age has since floated up and down, in response to changing pedagogical and pietist opinions.

It is important to note that all theological reasons for postponing first com-

10 / THE MEANS OF GRACE

munion to some age of reason or the like are after the fact. None was perceived until it became necessary to justify steps already taken. They may nevertheless be satisfactory, but to suffice, they must sustain a heavy burden of proof: of present ecumenical rejection of the scrupulosity that once evoked them, of so sharp a break with the ecumenical tradition, including the major and original part of the Roman tradition, and most important, of the clash of biblical understandings of baptism and the church with lengthy exclusion of baptized people from the Supper.

It may fairly be said that the various arguments for separating infant baptism and first communion are denominational and historical variants of one argument: Since the Supper is a visible word, and since the preparations thought necessary are also verbal activities (as, e.g., confession or "self-examination"), people should not commune until they are sufficiently verbal.[69] Judgment of the matter therefore depends on the following considerations. First, does the Supper so differ from baptism in respect of its verbality and relation to other verbal acts that we must exclude people from the one and not the other?[70] If there are sufficient reasons, we must precisely define them and then enforce them wherever they apply, also with adults. If there are not, baptism and first communion must be reintegrated, at whatever age. Second, what is empirically known about the induction of infants into the verbal life of the community? And in this connection, what does "sufficiently" mean?

Looking back through this section, the questions the church faces about its initiatory practices are various. They are also peculiarly intractable, since changes here are changes in deeply rooted responses and expectations. Moreover, not all the clashing arguments are easily adjudicated. Yet so much at least can be said with the clear support of Scripture and dogma: The practices created by the mere scattering of the church's erstwhile baptismal rite are not tolerable. It is centuries more than time for the church to attempt reform ecumenically.

THE USES OF BAPTISM

It is essential to what baptism means and is that it is in believers' *past*. Therefore believers' main question about baptism is "What are we to do with it?" Since it was Luther who most decisively appropriated the import of baptism's past tense, it is not strange that the Small Catechism presents the most famous and decisive dogmatic statement of baptism's use: "[Baptism] means that the old Adam in us shall be drowned and killed by daily contrition and penitence, with all his sins and lusts, and that a new man shall daily emerge and rise, to live in righteousness and purity eternally before God."[71]

The statement is built around Paul's description of the baptismal event. It interprets Christian life in a way new in Western theological history. The problem has always seemed to be: After baptism, what do we go on to do next? Answers are generally advanced with a bad conscience, since the eschatological nature of the gifts biblically ascribed to baptism, if they are taken seriously, plainly leaves no space for progress or development in faith or holiness themselves. Luther finally said what had to be said: We do not go on to anything at all; rather, Christian life has as its one essential content that we "daily" "return" to baptism.[72]

We will not further exegete Luther's particular theology. We will try rather to unpack the return to baptism in concepts suggested by our chapter so far. We have two propositions.

First, baptism enables the freedom of faith. Baptism is for the forgiveness of sins; it justifies. That is, baptism breaks the power of the past to close and pervert the future. I ask, "Am I justified?" That is, is there, despite all that has been, a justification for my living, a sufficient reason to go on? If I am baptized, all basis for any answer but yes has been destroyed, for I can now say no only by quite objectively accusing God of lying—by which, of course, the no is made implausible. I may and shall always say, "I am nevertheless baptized."

My baptism broke the bond of the past on the future, and this concluded *event* just so *speaks* always: "You are justified." And baptism is a promise that my life will be concluded and fulfilled in the eschatological fellowship of Christ and his saints; this *promise* of a sufficient reason for my life has been made irrevocable as a concluded *event*. The dialectic can work whichever way history and my life need; either way, baptism allows faith to be sure. The chief modern heresy is that faith confuses itself with modernity's intensified subjectivity, so that "justified by faith" comes to mean "justified by sincerity," which is always (and indeed in principle) unsure and therefore binding. There have been few modes of human existence so unfree as the contemporary anxiety for self-realization. Baptism is to prevent all this.

Second, baptism enables righteousness. The new birth of baptism, as an *eschatological* birth, is not (as we have just noted) a new start from which we go on to other things. The only life left to the baptized is the dying and freedom that is the content of baptism; all else is now, for them, mere illusion. Now we must specifically remind ourselves that the freedom of baptism is not the freedom to do what I want, what I would otherwise have done. It is precisely *not* the freedom opened by the typical pseudoevangelical sermon: "Never mind, Jesus loves you anyway." Throughout the New Testament, baptism is adduced precisely as the impossibility of such empty freedom.

The gospel promise of new life, of the kingdom of God, is precisely of new *life* in a final *community*. Therefore it has moral content, and that content is the will of God for the community of all creatures, as shown through Israel's history and all history. Christians have at this point with one accord commended the Ten Commandments as a compendious statement of the life God seeks for us.[73] The freedom of the baptized is, on the one hand, the endless possibility of mutual love and creativity opened in God's stated will for us, and, on the other hand, release from all that makes this will oppressive and unattainable. To borrow another expression from Luther, believers' freedom is precisely "desire and love for all God's commands."[74]

The audible and visible word of baptism is the word whose hearing is eschatological birth. It is thus the last word, the last judgment, an unconditional declaring and establishing of the value of neophytes' lives. It comes after all else is said and done. After baptism, it is too late for promises to do better, too late for "getting myself together," too late for guilt to be of use. The baptized have their lives to live *after* the effective and specific hearing of the final judgment. Therefore their moral life is the common life of those who are past having anything to lose or gain in their relation to their fellows. It is the common life of those for whom ulterior motivations and mitigations, while psychologically operative, are nevertheless morally irrelevant. It is, in short, the liberated life of those for whom it is too late for the will of God and the good of the neighbor to have any reward but themselves, since they have already been made sure of their own reward. This insight belongs to the Reformation's dogmatic proposal; Article VI of the Augsburg Confession says, "It is taught among us that we must do good works of all sorts as God commands them for his sake" and says nothing more on the subject.

With these last reflections we have not left the sacraments. The daily return to baptism is no merely inward or mental-emotional event. It too has and must have rites, traditionally those discussed in the last chapter of this *locus*, and especially penance. This was true also for the Reformation: the Large Catechism's plea for daily drowning of the old Adam, that the new person may emerge, continues directly with "An Exhortation to Confession," for which the Small Catechism at this point provides an order.

Finally in this section, there is one sort of good work so especially enabled by baptism, according to the New Testament and decisive parts of the theological tradition, that it must be separately noted. Baptism is recruitment to the church's gospel mission to the world. To use language now unavoidable though somewhat skewed, baptism is the rite of lay ministry.

The community into which baptism initiates has many great claims for its own life, but it is not *defined* by those claims, it is defined by its mission.[75] The double foundation of the church is Jesus' resurrection appearances, which were simultaneously commissionings of witnesses, and the pentecostal coming of the Spirit, the immediate consequent of which was the inauguration of the mission preaching. It is no accident that the theology of Acts, which nearly identifies the presence of the Spirit with the prosecution of the mission (Acts 1:8), also makes so much of the connection between baptism and the Spirit (e.g., Acts 9:17-18; 10:44-47).

In the Reformation bodies it is customary to define the church's ministry, the service it performs by God's will, as the "ministry of the word,"[76] and Roman Catholics do not disagree in principle.[77] Insofar as this definition refers to the ministry the word *does*, the service performed for the world by the audible and visible proclamation of the gospel, this mission is entrusted simply to the Church as such. *All* the baptized are commissioned to speak the gospel in and to the world. The doctrine of the priesthood of all believers is often thought of as a specialty of Luther's theology, and in some of its less measured expressions it is.[78] But in its substance, it is ecumenically affirmed.[79] Whether or not we should say with Luther in his earlier days that "Whoever comes out of the water of baptism can boast that he is already consecrated priest, bishop and pope,"[80] Aquinas teaches that the baptized are indeed consecrated to responsibility for the church's verbal and sacramental mission—that is the very "character" of baptism. Whatever we later find true about the particular ministry to which some are ordained, it must not be so interpreted as to obscure this ministry of all the baptized.

NOTES

1. E.g., Council of Florence, "Decree for the Armenians."
2. There has been disagreement about *when* baptism was initiated—at Jesus' baptism, by this command, on some unrecorded occasion in between, or at Pentecost. If command and promise are distinguished, the problem is eased, since there need not then be any one instituting event; for Luther it is obvious that the Matthean commission is the command that established baptism; Small Catechism, "Holy Baptism," 4. Thomas Aquinas made roughly the same distinction with the same result. According to Aquinas, insofar as baptism has efficacy, it acquires it from Jesus' baptism, but insofar as the institution is the command to *do* this efficacious thing, the Matthean commissioning is the institution; *Summa Theologica*, iii,66,2.
3. E.g., Acts 8:12; 9:18; 18:8. See G. R. Beasley-Murray, *Baptism in the New Testament* (Grand Rapids: Wm. B. Eerdmans, 1962), pp. 104-20.
4. On this and the following paragraphs, see Robert W. Jenson, *Visible Words* (Philadelphia: Fortress Press, 1978), pp. 126ff. There fuller presentation and bibliography.
5. Heinrich Kraft, "Die Anfänge des geistlichen Amts," *ThLz* 100 (1975): 82-98.
6. On this further, see Jenson, *Visible Words*, pp. 129-30. Whether there was in the apostolic church a development from use of Jesus' name only to the full trinitarian formula, we do not know. The passages in Acts that describe baptism as "in Jesus' name" (e.g., 2:36; 8:16) are theological descriptions, not rubrics. See Georg Kretschmar, *Studien zur frühchristlichen Trinitätstheologie* (Tübingen: J. C. B. Mohr [Paul Siebeck], 1956), pp. 196-216.

10 / THE MEANS OF GRACE

7. Council of Florence, "Decree for the Armenians."
8. Aquinas, *Summa Theologica*, iii,66,1.
9. For the West, see Aidan Kavanaugh, *The Shape of Baptism* (New York: Pueblo Publishing Co., 1978), p. 62.
10. Aquinas, *Summa Theologica*, iii,66,7. Luther, Large Catechism, "Baptism," 64–65.
11. Heinrich Heppe, ed., *Reformed Dogmatics*, rev. ed., trans. G. Thompson (London: George Allen & Unwin, 1950), pp. 612–13.
12. Council of Florence, "Decree for the Armenians."
13. This effort reached its end for our purposes in the controversy between Joachim Jeremias, *Infant Baptism in the First Four Centuries*, trans. D. Cairns (Philadelphia: Westminster Press, 1962); and Kurt Aland, *Did the Early Church Baptize Infants?* trans. G. R. Beasley-Murray (Philadelphia: Westminster Press, 1963).
14. Georg Kretschmar, "Die Geschichte des Taufgottesdienstes in der alten Kirche," in *Leiturgia*, ed. K. F. Mueller and W. Blankenberg, vol. 4 (Kassel: Stauda, 1954), pp. 81–86.
15. A notable case is Augustine himself; Augustine, *Confessions*, i,11.
16. The American Puritan experience is revelatory here. Horace Bushnell's comments are final: "What is the use of a fold, if the lambs are to be kept outside til it is seen whether they can stand the weather?" *Christian Nurture* (reprint ed., New Haven: Yale University Press, 1947), p. 265.
17. The biblical faithfulness of the tradition at this central point is gratifying, e.g., Aquinas' definition of baptism's work, *Summa Theologica*, iii,62,2: "homo moritur vitiis et fit membrum Christi."
18. *Epistle of Barnabas*, vi,11, xi,1, xvi,8; *The Shepherd of Hermas*, Mandate iv,3,1–3.
19. J. N. D. Kelly, *Early Christian Creeds* (New York and London: Longmans, Green & Co., 1950), passim.
20. Council of Florence, "Decree for the Armenians."
21. Eduard Lohse, "Taufe und Rechtfertigung bei Paulus," *KuD* 11 (1965): 308–21, 311ff.; Werner Kümmel, *The Theology of the New Testament*, trans. J. E. Steely (Nashville: Abingdon Press, 1973), pp. 131ff.
22. Jenson, *Visible Words*, pp. 127–28.
23. Burkhard Neuenheuser, *Taufe und Firmung*, vol. 6, fasc. 2 of *HDG* (1956), pp. 47–59, 87–93.
24. For greater detail and literature, see Kümmel, *Theology*, pp. 137ff.
25. Rudolf Bultmann, *The Gospel of John*, trans. G. R. Beasley-Murray, (Philadelphia: Westminster Press, 1971), pp. 131ff.
26. On the following, see Kretschmar, *Taufgottesdienst*.
27. What can be known, or guessed, is neatly presented by Kavanaugh, *Shape of Baptism*, pp. 16–54.
28. Frank Senn, "The Shape and Content of Christian Initiation," *Dialog*, 14 (1976): 97–107.
29. Hugh M. Riley, *Christian Initiation* (Washington, D.C.: Catholic University of America Press, 1974).

30. Except in the churches of the farther Near East, whose rite became no part of the continuing tradition; Gabriele Winkler, "The Original Meaning of the Prebaptismal Anointing and Its Implications," *Worship* 52 (1978): 24–45.
31. On the theology of exorcism, see Jenson, *Visible Words*, pp. 153–54.
32. Kavanaugh, *Shape of Baptism*, pp. 25–31; Jenson, *Visible Words*, p. 156.
33. Kavanaugh, *Shape of Baptism*, p. 47: "The newly baptized are received into full communion . . . by a series of hospitable acts."
34. Ibid., p. 65.
35. Hippolytus, *Apostolic Tradition*, 21.
36. Luther, Small Catechism, "Holy Baptism," 9–10.
37. Neuenheuser, "Taufe und Firmung," pp. 59–70.
38. On this, see Robert W. Jenson, *The Knowledge of Things Hoped For* (New York: Oxford University Press, 1969), pp. 24–57.
39. On the following, see Neuenheuser, "Taufe und Firmung," pp. 59–70.
40. For such an argument, see Jenson, *Knowledge*, pp. 90–98.
41. Neuenheuser, "Taufe und Firmung," pp. 47–59, 79–96.
42. Aquinas, *Summa Theologica*, iii,62, 64.
43. Ibid., 66,1–2. Ibid., 66,1: ". . . interioris justificationis. Quae est res tantum huius sacramenti."
44. Ibid., 68,4.
45. Ibid., 68,8.
46. Ibid.: "Alio modo requiritur aliquid ex necessitate ad baptismum, sine quo character baptismi imprimi non potest. Et sic recta fides baptizati non requiritur." Council of Florence, "Decree for the Armenians."
47. Aquinas, *Summa Theologica*, iii,63,4.
48. Ibid., 63,1–3; Neuenheuser, "Taufe und Firmung," pp. 88ff.
49. Aquinas, *Summa Theologica*, 63,5.
50. On this subject, we may trust Heppe, *Reformed Dogmatics*, pp. 611–26, for a reasonable summary and selection of sources.
51. John Calvin, *Institutes of the Christian Religion* (1536), 110.
52. Also Karl Barth, *The Teaching of the Church Regarding Baptism*, trans. E. A. Payne (London: SCM Press, 1948).
53. Calvin himself began the development of this doctrine; *Institutes*, 118.
54. Sydney E. Ahlstrom, *A Religious History of the American People* (New Haven: Yale University Press, 1972), pp. 158ff.
55. Luther, Large Catechism, "Baptism," 53: "If the word is with the water, the baptism is right, even if faith is not added; for my faith does not make baptism but receives it." Ibid., 54: "For there is the water and God's word even if it is not received as it should be, *just as* the unworthy who come to the Supper receive the true sacrament" (emphasis added).
56. Ibid., 29–30.
57. Ibid., 43.
58. Ibid., 55–56.
59. Ibid., 29.

10 / THE MEANS OF GRACE

60. Ibid., 26.
61. Aquinas, *Summa Theologica*, iii,64, 66,6; Luther, Large Catechism, "Baptism," 10.
62. On the history, see Kavanaugh, *Shape of Baptism*, pp. 54–86.
63. Ahlstrom, *History*, passim. The stated characteristics fit also the position of Barth, *Teaching*.
64. On the following history, see Nathan Mitchell, "Dissolution of the Rite of Christian Initiation," in *Made, Not Born*, ed. Murphy Center for Liturgical Research (Notre Dame, Ind.: Notre Dame University Press, 1976); J. D. C. Fisher, *Christian Initiation: Baptism in the Medieval West* (London: SPCK, 1965), passim.
65. For a summary of early efforts, see Mitchell, "Dissolution." The best effort is by Aquinas, *Summa Theologica*, iii,72; his desperation is apparent in every sentence.
66. Both Calvin and Luther rejected separate confirmation. It was reintroduced, and retained in England, as graduation from a postbaptismal catechumenate. Leonel L. Mitchell, "Christian Initiation: The Reformation Period," *Made, Not Born*, pp. 83–93.
67. This is maintained in theory by the theological tradition; Aquinas, *Summa Theologica*, iii,80,6.
68. There can be no doubt about this. The massive documentary record of sacramentaries, synodical decrees, letters, and so on is painstakingly reported by Fisher, *Christian Initiation*, pp. 1–108. See Fisher also for the following history.
69. Aquinas' reasons (*Summa Theologica*, iii,80,9) may be taken as typical for Catholics and Protestants alike, early and late, both in content and in complete ignorance of the history.
70. A good example of the problem is the Large Catechism of Luther, which presumes continuation of the medieval practice, yet with respect to the need for understanding and faith says exactly the same things about baptism and the Supper; "Baptism," 32–34; "Lord's Supper," 33–36, 61.
71. Luther, Small Catechism, "Holy Baptism," 10.
72. E.g., Luther, Large Catechism, "Baptism," 78.
73. So even Luther, hardly to be suspected of legalism, made the Ten Commandments the first item of Christian instruction and said that if it were not for sin they would (in that they include the first commandment's mandate of faith) constitute the complete statement of God's revelation; ibid., "The Creed," 1–2.
74. Ibid., 68–69. The German reads "Lust und Liebe." On this whole side of Luther, see Albrecht Peters, *Glaube und Werk: Luthers Rechtfertigungslehre im Lichte der Heiligen Schrift* (Berlin: Lutherisches Verlagshaus, 1967), pp. 59–112.
75. On the specific missionary self-consciousness of the primal church, see Ferdinand Hahn, *Das Verständnis der Mission im Neuen Testament* (Neukirchen-Vluyn: Erziehungsverein, 1962).
76. So the first and foundational Augsburg Confession, Article V.
77. Not even at the time of the Reformation; see the Papal Confutation, Article V.
78. Luther, *Address to the German Nobility*, LW 44: 123–217.
79. So Vatican II, "Dogmatic Constitution on the Church," 10.
80. Luther, *Address to the German Nobility*, p. 129.

5
The Supper

We are canonically commanded to give thanks to God for God's saving works in Christ, joining the thanksgiving by sharing bread and a cup of wine. In the Western dogmatic and liturgical tradition, this command has been badly understood and obeyed, especially by a too-abstract concentration on the "sacrament" as against the "sacrifice." In themselves, of course, the sacramental promises are indeed "the chief thing" in the Supper, which by them is qualified as an anticipation of the messianic Supper, brought to pass by the risen Christ's availability as the bread and cup. The great Western controversy about "the sacrifice of the mass" can be resolved if Protestants can overcome their prejudices and Catholics can acknowledge the need and legitimacy of the Reformation's critical doctrine of justification. The controversy about the mode of Christ's bodily presence can be resolved only by fundamental metaphysical and ecclesiological new reflection.

THE COMMAND

From the beginning, Christians have celebrated their special meal, "breaking bread . . . with glad and generous hearts" (Acts 2:46), obeying a command to "do this" and passing on the command. That this mandate has apostolic authority is documented directly: Paul explicitly includes it in what he "received" and in what his congregations must obey (1 Cor. 11:23–26).[1] The same tradition appears in two versions in the synoptic Gospels, where the texts' character as instituting rubrics is apparent (Mark 14:22–25; Matt. 26:26–29; Luke 22:15–20).[2] To see the mandate's content, we may conflate the texts: Jesus took bread, gave thanks, broke it, gave it to his disciples, and said "Take [Mark, Matthew]. Eat [Matthew]. This is. . . . Do this for my remembrance [Paul, Luke]. Likewise, after supper, he took the cup, gave thanks, gave it to them, and said "All of you drink from it [Matthew]. This is. . . . Do this, whenever you drink it, for my remembrance [Paul]."

"Do this." What is "this"? There are two exegetical possibilities. "Do this" should perhaps be read as a gloss emphasizing the rubrical character of the

10 / THE MEANS OF GRACE

entire text.[3] In that case it is all the actions listed that are mandated. Or perhaps "Do this" in Paul's and Luke's texts should be read for what it would have meant as an "instituting" utterance of Jesus. Then there is in the texts only one possible referent of "this": the "thanksgiving" Jesus has just performed.[4] It is, one fears, worth pointing out that the referent of the explicit "Do this" cannot be the eating and drinking, since only the Pauline and Lukan texts have "Do this" and in them there is no mention of eating and drinking. Fortunately for our purposes, either exegetical possibility yields the same mandate, for in the structure of a formal Jewish meal of Jesus' time, a first "thanksgiving" was shared by sharing bread, and another, after the regular meal, was shared by the cup,[5] so that "give thanks" in fact includes all the listed acts. It thus also becomes apparent that even on the first possibility the listed actions are not an unstructured set. The bread and cup are there as means by which the company shares the thanksgiving offered by the leader, as visible words of the company's communion in praise of God.[6]

What, then, was such a table-thanksgiving?[7] The root exclamation is "Blessed—the Lord God!" It is addressed both to God and to the gathering: "Bless thee, God!" and "God is blessed" at once. God is praised for his saving works, in creation and the history of all people; thus the doxology is simultaneously a narrative *remembering*. So, for example, in the extremest brevity, the *birkat ha-mazon*: "Blessed art thou, O Lord our God, King of the universe, who nourishest all the world in goodness, benevolence and mercy. Blessed art thou, Nourisher of the universe. We give thee thanks, O Lord our God, because thou hast given us the inheritance of a goodly land."[8]

Such commemoration of God's past acts must, within the structure of Israel's faith, terminate in *invocation* of the fulfillment of the promises contained in them. So the remainder of the *birkat ha-mazon*: "Have mercy, O Lord our God, on Israel thy people and Jerusalem thy city and Zion the place of thy glory. . . . Blessed art thou, O Lord, who wilt build Jerusalem." In such invocation, the remembering of God's acts becomes a *reminding* of God about God's promises. It is fundamental in Israel that God's new saving acts are God's remembering of what must follow from previous acts: "And God heard their groanings and God remembered his covenant . . . " (Exod. 2:24). Therefore all petition in Israel is reminding: "Remember thy congregation . . ." (Ps. 74:2).

It is such table-thanksgiving that we are canonically commanded to perform, with two christological modifications, one explicit in the mandate and the other inevitable materially. First, in the narrative of God's saving acts, we are centrally to include Jesus. We may paraphrase the Pauline-Lukan command: "Give thanks to God, for *my* remembrance."[9] This is to be a reminding of God; the construction with "for" has final sense, "to bring me to mind." Second, the eschatological invocation with which thanksgiving concludes must in the Christian context become invocation of the Spirit, and in the actual prayers of the church it quickly does so.

Let us draw together all elements of the mandate that creates the Supper. We are to praise God by narrative, transitive remembering of God's saving acts, centered in what happens with Jesus, and by prayer for their fulfillment. And we are to participate in this thanksgiving by sharing bread and a cup.

Over against much of the church's past and present practice, two points must be explicitly made at this point. First, we may not ask, over against the previous paragraph, "But could we not do such-and-such different or less and still get the blessing?" And second, it is the *rite* just described that is biblically commanded. In connection with the *mandate*, the biblical texts say nothing whatever about bread and wine simply as substances; they speak about a specified ritual *use* of bread and a cup of wine. The command is not to take in some minimal quantity of the two substances; it is to join in the praise of God by sharing bread and a loving-cup.

When the church's thanksgiving becomes historically ascertainable, we see that it was exactly what obedience to this command would require. And indeed the Christian prayers seem to have developed directly from existing Jewish prayers.[10] If the prayers of the *Didache* were, as seems likely, at least originally eucharistic,[11] they carry us back to the apostolic church—not to "the" apostolic thanksgiving, but to prayers used in some strand of the developing tradition. With the bread: "We give thanks to thee, our Father, for the life and knowledge which thou hast revealed through Jesus, thy son. To thee be glory forever! As this bread was strewn over the hills and is now gathered into one, gather thy church from the ends of the earth into thy Kingdom." With the cup(?): "We give thanks to thee holy Father, for thy holy Name that thou hast made dwell in our hearts, and for knowledge and faith and immortality which thou hast revealed through Jesus the Son. To thee be glory forever! Thou, Lord Almighty, hast created all things for the sake of thy name, and hast given food and drink to human creatures, that they might thank thee, and to us thou hast given spiritual food and drink unto eternal life through Jesus your son. To thee be glory forever! Remember, Lord, thy church, to defend it from all evil and perfect it in thy love. Gather it, sanctified, from the four winds into the kingdom prepared for it. For thine is the power and the glory forever. Amen."[12] In these prayers the Spirit is not yet explicitly named. But Justin Martyr, around the year 150, says that the thanksgiving is "to the Creator of all, through the name of the Son and the Spirit,"[13] and the next available actual text, that of Hippolytus' *Apostolic Tradition*, from the end of the second century, has a full-blown invocation: "And we pray, send the Holy Spirit upon the offering of thy holy church, uniting all who share the holy gifts and filling them with the Holy Spirit."[14]

Christians from the beginning have given thanks to the Father, remember-

10 / THE MEANS OF GRACE

ing the saving works by the Son and invoking their fulfillment in the Spirit. This trinitarian structure results simply from obedience to the patterns of Jewish table-thanksgiving, within a christological context. It is worked out, with great variety but with faithfulness, in all the liturgies of the ancient church, and after the emergence of explicit trinitarian dogma becomes the deliberate pattern of the fourth-century orders that have been the basis of all development since.[15]

There is no reason the church's thanksgiving must always follow the pattern of fourth-century prayers, but they have the authority of ecumenical consent and classic form, and it is proper to describe them briefly.[16] There is an opening dialogue, incorporating the standard opening of Jewish table-prayer. Then the narrative Doxology begins, of God's great works from creation through the whole history of salvation. It is broken by two short biblical hymns, the Sanctus and Benedictus, and terminated either by the narrative of institution, the narrative of the particular act of God by virtue of which we dare to do the Supper, or by an epiclesis, an invocation of the Spirit to sanctify the gifts and the congregation. The anamnesis, which either begins before the narrative and incorporates it or more usually immediately follows it, is the direct fulfillment of the mandate that all be done for *Jesus'* remembrance; beginning with some such address as Hippolytus' "Remembering, therefore . . . ," it has the general content of the second article of a three-article creed. Then comes the (sometimes the second) epiclesis, so that the order established is precisely that of the creeds. Finally, the thanksgiving ends with a last burst of doxology. Intercessory prayer has appeared at places that vary from order to order.

We must remind ourselves that the Christian thanksgiving is not an act in and for itself. It was mandated as the table-thanksgiving of a meal. Initially, as supposed by Paul's text, there was a thanksgiving with bread before a regular meal and a thanksgiving with the cup afterward. But in Paul's Corinth we see that the first blessing has migrated to join the second, making a special thanksgiving-meal after the regular meal;[17] this order is supposed by the Markan text.[18] Next the two meals became distinct observances, and the two thanksgivings of the thanksgiving-meal were joined into one; we do not know quite when or how these things happened,[19] but they had already occurred in Justin Martyr's congregation by the year 150.[20] Finally, the vacated place before the thanksgiving-meal was filled by a synagogue-type service of Scripture and prayer, such as the Christians had to provide independently after separation from the synagogues; this too is attested by Justin. Thus was created the Christian "liturgy" or "mass," the central act of Christian worship, in which the Supper is the second part of a powerful two-act structure.

The development just described need not be lamented, but it has tended to obscure the meal-character of the Supper, or perhaps we should say the meal-thanksgiving character of Christian thanksgiving. The bread and cup now carry a heavy burden. Not only are they the ceremonial thanksgiving-courses, they are also themselves the whole meal. There is no reason this cannot work, but strict attention must be paid to what might be called the gustatory reality of the bread and wine. They must not be mere symbols of food and drink but bread and wine that can nourish and cheer, partaken by real breaking, drinking, tasting, chewing, and swallowing.[21]

Finally, as to who is to share the bread and cup, and who is to preside at the thanksgiving, the situation is at once simple and complex. Taking the matter of the communicants first, it seems plain that since baptism is initiation into the community whose sacramental actuality is the Supper, proper communicants are the baptized. And it is indeed ecumenical consensus that all and only the baptized are to be communed, unless there is powerful reason to exclude some of them. But there is no unanimity about what reasons may suffice for exclusion. For Roman Catholicism, it has traditionally been "mortal sin" or lack of mental capacity;[22] for the Reformed tradition, lack of "true faith";[23] and for the Lutheran tradition, the claim to satisfy either of these criteria.[24] The disagreement results from different opinions about the relation of sin and grace and about the nature of the church, and therefore its resolution lies outside this *locus*.

On the question of the proper minister of this sacrament, the New Testament gives us no direct guidance at all. Nevertheless, there is ecumenical consensus that only the ordained should preside.[25] But there is no agreement about the justification or exact nature of the restriction, the discussion of which therefore belongs in the section on ordination in the next chapter.

THE AUTHENTICITY OF THE SUPPER

If the ancient ecumenical liturgical tradition was faithful to the biblical mandate, the later Western liturgical tradition and the relevant dogmatic tradition have not been. The Supper's fidelity to its founding mandate has been deeply compromised. This is not our discovery; the desires stated in the following are in large part only urgent established goals of the liturgical movement in all denominations.

Much of our difficulty, ironically and somewhat surprisingly, has come from the exclusivity with which the Western church has attended to the Supper as "sacrament" rather than as "sacrifice." It is, after all, a sacrifice, an audible and visible act of prayer, that is directly commanded by Scripture. This act becomes then the "element" of a "sacrament" by the promises made to it, which we have yet to discuss. The medieval dogmatic development forgot this entirely. If we turn to the Council of Florence, we read: "The matter is wheaten bread and grape wine. . . . The form . . . is the words of the Savior, by which he created this sacrament; for the priest speaking in the person of Christ makes the sacrament."[26] The direct content of the biblical command, the act of thanksgiving, is omitted altogether from this list of items necessary to a valid sacrament. In its place appears the priest's recital of the words of institution, an act that can be *no* part of what the biblical "Do this" commands.

We do not know at what point the biblical institution-account, in a harmonized version, became part of the thanksgiving; in Hippolytus it is already in its familiar place. The reasons are anyway compelling: The liturgical narrative of institution is the "haggadah" or cult-legend of the Supper, telling why we do this thing, and just so is a convenient way of bringing the promises attached to the Supper to verbal expression, which would have to be done somehow. But while the inclusion of the narrative of institution in the thanksgiving is appropriate, it is also plain that a rite consisting merely of its recitation over bread and wine, followed or not followed by their consumption, is not obedient to the Supper's institution.

The doctrine represented by the Council of Florence came about as part of a general and profound transformation in the understanding and practice of the Supper. From being a dramatic *action of* the congregation, it came to be and be understood as a dramatic *spectacle for* the congregation, an allegorical enactment of Jesus' death and resurrection, a "pure sacrament" of an ocular sort. The shift began in the patristic period and was fully carried out in the Carolingian church.[27] In this spectacle, clearly the priest had to be seen as playing the role of Christ, and with this notion came an inevitable concentration on the only part of his script that provides actual words of Christ. Already Jerome laid it down, in a vastly influential saying: "By what words is the consecration effected . . . ? The words of the Lord Jesus. All else that is said are the words of the priest. . . . But when the time comes to make the sacrament, the priest used not his words but the words of Christ."[28] As soon as the fatal question of minimum action for "validity" is posed to this understanding, the doctrine of Florence results.

It belongs to the same development that the Latin West ceased to understand even the terminology of the biblical command. The Greek verbs for "give thanks" are *eucharistein* (in all texts) and *eulogein* (in Mark and Matthew for the thanksgiving with the bread), used synonymously and with *eucharistein* the clearer and dominating term. In the biblical texts the object of these verbs is of course God; *God* is "thanked." But from very early the Greek-speaking church also spoke of "eucharistizing" the bread and cup to be the body and blood of Christ.[29] This theology, which derives the sacramental reality of the elements from their use in the thanksgiving, is profound and right, so long as the sense of "give thanks" is remembered. The Latin-speaking West did not long remember it.[30]

Thus the Latin translation of *eulogein*, "*benedicere*," which was also the standard word for "blessing" someone or something, made it possible to stretch the texts of Matthew and Mark to say that Jesus' decisive utterance had the *elements* as its object, so that he made the sacrament by blessing the bread and cup, that he did this with the words "This is my body. This is my blood," and that *this* is what the priest is to do "in the person of Christ."[31] The tremendous conceptual distortion involved here, which to this day involves Catholics and Protestants equally, is not our present concern, only the total misunderstanding of the Supper's instituting mandate. We must reiterate: The presiding minister is not to bless the *elements*; he is to bless God, *using* the elements, and just so there happens whatever happens to the elements.[32]

Whether or not the historical developments are connected, it belongs in effect to the same misfortune, that the medieval thanksgiving of the Western church, the "Roman canon" imposed on all the west by Carolingian centralizing, is an ecumenical oddity, the one relatively ancient territorial prayer that is phenomenologically not clearly a thanksgiving. The history by which this came about [33] is conjectural and not our concern. Analysis discovers that the canon has the same abstract structure as the ancient orders, but where the narrative doxology of God, and even the invocation of the Spirit, should be, there is in the canon no longer anything of the sort. Instead there are *petitions* for the acceptance of our sacrifice. The theological problem with these petitions themselves will be discussed in a following section; here our concern is that thanksgiving is largely missing. Neither was this affliction cured by the Reformation, for when in the controversy over sacrifice the main-line reformers eliminated the petitions, they usually put nothing in their place, not knowing that anything belonged there.

It is ironic that those most thoroughly entrapped by these peculiarly medieval and clericalist developments have been Protestants. In practice, only they have made orders actually prescribing the Florentine minimum, consisting of incantation of the words of institution and consumption. And the attempt that appears throughout Protestant history to devise a Supper that at the center is to be only sacrament and not simultaneously sacrifice depends on the medieval disappearance of the sacrifice of thanksgiving both from the dogmatically stated essentials of the Supper and from the Supper as actually celebrated.

We must note two further disasters to the Supper's authenticity. First is the Supper's administration "under one species," the withholding of one element (historically, almost always the cup) from some segment of the congregation.[34] There is now widespread ecumenical agreement that such practices are contrary to the command of both Scripture and the ancient tradition. Withholding the cup is not limited to the medieval church or Tridentine Catholicism. Whether the cup is kept from most of the congregation by the clergy's metaphysical scrupulosity or by the laity's own hygienic scrupulosity, the result is the same. Substitution of small quantities of wine distributed in little glasses helps not at all; it is precisely sharing a cup that is the mandated action.[35] Nor are theories of concomitance to the point;[36] it is not what is or is not in the bread that is here at issue but what is commanded to be done. Anticipating the promises of the Supper, if Christ gives himself over to us in the bread and cup, then crumbs and spills are part of the humiliation he assumes, and if he makes us brothers and sisters in the cup, then sharing one another's human messiness belongs to the humiliation *we* thereby assume.

The second disaster to the Supper's authenticity is the development and proliferation of private masses, celebrations of the Supper as the act of a priest only.[37] If the understanding of the Supper's institution presented here is even slightly correct, this practice is intolerable. It is also dying out, and would scarcely need to be mentioned here were it not for its decisive role in the development of the liturgical habits and interpretations that the Reformation attacked as "the sacrifice of the mass," which we must discuss in its place.

THE PROMISES

Aquinas defined the *res* of the Supper as "the mystical body" of Christ, the eternal and vivifying unity of Christ with believers and so of believers also with one another.[38] We are unlikely to improve on this definition. The Reformed tradition did not try; for example, according to the *Leiden Synopsis* what is signified is "that most close union or *koinonia* by which we are united with Christ our Head."[39] Luther agreed: What the Supper signifies and effects is "the fellowship of all the saints." He then emphasized, characteristically but by no means innovatively, "This fellowship consists in this, that all the spiritual possessions of Christ and his saints are shared with . . . him who receives this sacrament."[40] The total Supper, Luther said, is the "testament" of such sharing; the narrative of institution is this testament's audibility, saying as it does that Christ gives himself to us as the one who died for the forgiveness of our sin.[41]

It is with relief that we register such ecumenical consensus, and so with hope that we turn again also to Scripture. What are the Supper's instituting promises? For the sake of understanding, we must briefly state what currently seems known about the Supper's origin.[42] The origin of the Supper was probably not one event but several.[43] First was Jesus' meal-fellowship with his closest followers.[44] This fellowship was the visibility of Jesus' message: It was open to the final fellowship of the kingdom (Luke 12:8) and offensively included "publicans and sinners" (Mark 2:15 par.; Matt. 11:19 par.; Luke 15:1). The fellowship, apparently terminated by the crucifixion, was necessarily reinitiated by the resurrection (Luke 24:15–35).

Then there was a special event of this fellowship "in the night in which he was betrayed."[45] Little can be said about that night with any certainty. We do not know for sure whether it was a Passover meal, or how much of the institution narrative is an actual report of events at that meal. What is certain is that the supper was indeed a *last* supper. It was therefore remembered as a farewell supper, as the disciples' participation in the crucifixion. And when the meal-fellowship was resumed, this memory interpreted the fellowship: "Remember, our fellowship is with the one who has died to be with us!" One may say that the Supper as known by Paul and the Synoptics was created by interpretation of the renewed meal-fellowship by the theology of the cross.

Third was the series of resurrection appearances that were appearances *at* the meal-fellowship.[46] Thus the kerygmatic summary of Acts 10:38ff. simply identifies the witnesses of the resurrection as those "who ate and drank with him after he rose from the dead." It is in Acts that we hear of eschatological joy at the meals (Acts 2:46); the meal appearances of the risen one made the meals anticipations of the Lord's final coming. The great cry "Come, Lord" was kept in the Jerusalem congregation's Aramaic, "Maranatha," also by Greek-speaking congregations.[47]

The period of these developments was an historical moment; by the time Paul wrote to Corinth it was over, and the rite specified by the apostolic rubrics was in practice. Our historical knowledge of origins has as its sole theological purpose understanding the promises attached to this rite.

The most obtrusive sayings have been historically least appropriated. Mark 14:25 (par.) reads: "I say to you, I shall not drink again of the fruit of the vine until that day when I drink it new in the kingdom of God." Luke 22:16 reads: "I tell you I shall not eat it [Passover] until it is fulfilled in the kingdom of God." Whatever may have been the original context of these sayings, or their historical relation to each other,[48] their sense in the present context is the same. On the one hand, Jesus' oath is fulfilled in the church's Supper; somehow, each celebration is an event "in" the kingdom, in that Jesus joins it. But on the other hand, the kingdom itself is not yet come so long as Jesus' words still need to be remembered. A popular term of much recent exegesis irresistibly suggests itself to state both aspects at once: Each celebration of the Supper is an *anticipation* of the last and fulfilling fellowship of Christ and his people.

Anticipation is visible prophecy, when the prophecy is promise and not merely prophetic denunciation. Thus there are true and false prophets, since anyone can make predictions. That we come together to assure one another of the kingdom's fellowship, enacting it and not only speaking of it, does not bring the kingdom or establish our citizenship therein—unless God makes it so. That God indeed does so is the content of faith in the sacrament; the

10 / THE MEANS OF GRACE

object of this faith is the coming of the risen Christ to join the fellowship and make it indeed be an eschatological fellowship.

Thus we are led to the other promises of the institution texts: "This is my body. This cup is the new covenant." But before a direct attempt on these crosses of the exegetes, we will turn to the other chief New Testament passages about the Supper. What we learn from them may help when we return to these words of institution.

That John 6:51–59 is a gloss on the preceding discourse is apparent—whether the gloss is by "John" or a later editor. John 6:35–50, the "bread of life" passage, evokes the revelation in Jesus as the true bread that nourishes eternal life.[49] But the true bread comes from heaven, and Jesus is a man whose father and mother his hearers know; thus the assertion of their identity necessarily causes offense. But just that necessity is the possibility of faith, which consists in the transcending—by God's predestination—of offense.

But John's readers do not confront Jesus and do not know his parents. How then can they be offended—or believe? It is this question to which verses 51–59 respond. The readers' situation is not different from that of Jesus' hearers, for in the Supper they are confronted with bread and wine, whose provenance they know, as the body and blood of Jesus, and therefore as literally the true bread and drink of revelation. This is as offensive a situation as that of Jesus' hearers. Indeed, John's central claim is that the offense is the same offense. If the offense is overcome, the act of faith is precisely (and now quite literally) the act of the Supper's eating and drinking; hence John's blunt insistence on these acts.

First Corinthians 10:14–22 is one of several attempts by Paul to deal with continuous social pressure on Christians to share pagan sacrificial meals.[50] Two things about Paul's position are worth noting. First, to him it is obvious that the Supper and pagan sacrificial feasts are species of the same genus. Second, what differentiates the Supper is the different *community* whose visible word it is. The bread and cup are a "communion" with Christ, and just so make the partakers "one body" also among themselves.

Third and last, there is the text in which Paul's version of the narrative of institution appears, 1 Cor. 11:17–34.[51] Paul accuses the Corinthians of failing to "discern" the body, in that they eat and drink unworthily. It is the relation between the two parts of the charge that releases the passage's splendid dialectics. "The body" to which the Corinthians insufficiently attend and which they insufficiently distinguish from other bodies is plainly the body given as the bread and cup; otherwise it could not be the narrative of institution that established the gravity of the offense. But the "unworthy" behavior is the Corinthians' uncomradely behavior to each other;[52] that is the problem of the whole chapter. We may summarize the sacramental situation as Paul grasps it: In that the bread and cup are given, there is a body present that is Jesus, and there is a body present that is the community, and a person's relation to the one is not distinguishable from that person's relation to the other.

Now we must turn to the words of institution, that is, those interpretations of the rite that are built into the canonical instructions for it. We begin with a statement of an exegetical rule. Much historic difficulty will be overcome if we have it always clearly in mind: So long as we are exegeting for dogmatic—rather than historical or perhaps homiletic—purposes, our concern is primarily not with what these sentences might have meant as utterances of the historical Jesus,[53] but with what they mean as interpretations, canonically authoritative, of the church's rite, the very rite whose origins we have sketched and which Paul and John discuss. However the institution narratives may have come into being, and whatever relation to the events of Jesus' Last Supper they may have, it is as rubrics and interpretation of the church's Supper that we have them. *Within* the narrative structure of the accounts, it is decisive for the meaning of the sayings that they appear in the mouth of Jesus.

We have three interpreting sayings to exegete: the cup saying of Paul, the bread saying of Paul and Luke, and the double bread/cup saying of Mark and Matthew. We will begin with the Pauline cup-saying, because it is simplest.

"This cup is the new covenant in my blood."[54] The saying presents few obscurities. A thanksgiving cup simply *is* a "covenant"; sharing one always establishes some community. What is asserted by the saying is, first, that the covenant established by *this* cup is the new one, that is, the final communal bond among God and his people, promised by the prophets. The promise that here "comes to the element" is nothing less than the entire eschatology of the Hebrew Scriptures; all the hopes of Israel are at once to be proclaimed and fulfilled by the cup. Asserted second is that the new covenant is "in" Jesus' blood. Covenants are always in someone's blood;[55] community means death, as was known to the early church from Scripture and is anyway shown by all experience. The cup can be what it is, because of Jesus' death.

"This is my body which is for you" is not in Paul half of a double saying with "This is my blood," as it is in Mark and Matthew. The Pauline saying must be read by itself,[56] and "body" must therefore be taken with its usual Pauline sense:[57] The body is simply the person, *as an object* of other persons— and through them of himself—as an available, addressable, vulnerable presence. Against the background of other New Testament discussions of the rite, it should not be difficult to grasp the interpretation this saying makes of the rite; how the saying can be *true* is another matter, the matter of the section below entitled "*Ego Berengarius*. . . ." The community of believers exists and is open to the eschaton in that it is community with the risen Jesus. The risen Jesus is a real person, and if he is actually present he is an object among us: We can locate him, turn to him, even affect him. We may

10 / THE MEANS OF GRACE

paraphrase the saying: "In your meal-fellowship, the object to which you may turn to be turning to me is the thanksgiving bread."

Two further determinants must be added promptly. First, "This is my body" appears set into the rubrical sequence; it is the taking, giving thanks, and eating that are the permitted *turning to* this object as to Christ. Second, the body is "for" us, or as Luke has it (in the longer text), "given for" us. This is sacrificial terminology: Jesus' objective self, objective for us as the bread, is a sacrificed self; death between us and God belongs to its givenness.

The institution texts of Mark and Matthew correspond to a celebration that has both thanksgiving courses together, after the regular meal. In such celebrations, the interpreting sayings for bread and cup necessarily came to be heard as paired and so to be assimilated together as one double saying. If the cup is paired to the bread, then the pair to "body" must be "blood," which was already there in the earlier form. Now we have "This is my body. This is my blood." The promise of the new covenant, formerly the direct content of the cup saying, now appears in a subordinate phrase: The blood is "blood of the covenant." That the blood is "poured out for many for the forgiveness of sins" is special Matthean tradition for the sacrificial motif that has appeared in all versions.

In Mark and Matthew, "This is my body" and "This is my blood" say together what "This is my body" says in Paul; in a celebration interpreted by this double saying, the bread and cup come to say visibly together what the bread says by itself in a "Pauline" celebration. This undoubtedly enriches the symbolic structure of the visibility that is the Lord's visibility, but the gain is purchased by partial loss of the cup's independent eschatological meaning. The right policy, both theologically and liturgically, is surely to reckon with and exploit both traditions of interpretation.

The great question that now presents itself is How can this modest table-fellowship be such great things? We have repeatedly encountered the biblical answer: Because the Lord is there as bread and cup. But this answer, while religiously complete, is conceptually a difficult puzzle for all heirs of the spiritual/material metaphysics. Indeed, the puzzle has so dominated Western theology of the Supper that we must discuss it for itself, at length and after all else is in place; it is anyway a close parallel to the question about baptismal regeneration. Meanwhile one other question must be dealt with.

We have interpreted "This is my body" so: We may attend to the bread and cup as to the object as which the risen Christ is available to us. But within the christological interpretation we have offered for the church's total ritual life, have we thereby said anything about the bread and cup that we do not say about all parts of the gospel's visibility? It was in part to keep this question from arising that scholastic theology avoided a general christological interpretation of the sacraments, referring to grace made possible *by* Christ, and so on, rather than to his person.⁵⁸ The tactic belongs to a general complex of thought that we have denounced, but if we eschew it, we are left with the present question.

We propose the following. It is always vital to ask what a particular audible and visible sacramental sign specifically says, even knowing that any linguistic paraphrase must be a distortion. The bread and the cup, accompanied by their interpretive sayings or some equivalent, specifically say, "There *is* Jesus' body among you." "This is my body" does not, after all, presuppose that *something* is Jesus' present body and pick out "this" candidate as the true one over against "that" mere pretender. It is precisely "is my body" that is the surprising news.

That the present risen Christ is not a disembodied "pure spirit," that he is spirit and body among us, is itself a vital promise of the gospel—1 John 4:1–3. If it were not so, every gospel address would, as we have seen, be false. To be saying the gospel, part of what the church must say, in the name of Christ, is "Lo, I—the actual I, who can be your object as well as make you mine—am with you always." And here there is a logical twist: If this word were not *itself* embodied it would simply be false—and with it the gospel would be false and all forms of Christ's presence illusions. The bread and cup are its contingent embodiment, the visible word by which the gospel's visibility proclaims itself. And in all parts of the church in which the Supper is no longer the dominating service, Christ has in fact come to be thought of as a disembodied spirit and, insofar as this conception then controls preaching and teaching, the gospel is not heard.

EUCHARIST

The ancient church did not much worry about the specific problems (of real presence, propitiatory sacrifice, and so on) on which the later Western tradition has spent so much thought.⁵⁹ It reflected on the Supper as one whole event, and its theology of the Supper was the unpacking and meditation of the dialectical determinants of its one name for the event, "eucharist," "thanksgiving." Moreover, this reflection mainly took place in the development of liturgy itself and secondarily in catechetical exposition thereof.

As the classic prayers of thanksgiving developed, it is in the anamnesis that the liturgical orders' self-understanding appears most clearly. In Hippolytus' anamnesis there is a tight cluster of mutually defining verbs that reappear in the same general configuration in the later more developed orders: "*Remembering* therefore his death and resurrection, we *offer* to thee this bread and cup, *giving thanks*. . . ."⁶⁰ Remembering, sacrificing, and thanks-giving are but aspects of one act and must be understood by one another.

That the act here being performed is a sacrifice ("we offer") is understood;

10 / THE MEANS OF GRACE

that is simply the category for actions of this sort, at hand so soon as there is enough self-consciousness about the act to require one. In the *Didache*, the Sunday Eucharist is believers' "sacrifice,"[61] and when Clement writes from Rome before the end of the first century, regulating the services means above all regulating "the oblations."[62] The Christians were well aware of the similarity between the Supper and the rites of the religions around them; when they needed to differentiate their sacrifices from others, they did this by its spirituality and place in the history of salvation. In argument with a Jewish thinker who advanced the Greek Enlightenment thesis that true sacrifice is spiritual and needs no material offerings, Justin Martyr wrote: "That prayers and thanksgivings . . . are the only perfect sacrifices . . . , I too assert. But only the Christians have in fact undertaken to do this, and that in the memorial made by their food and drink."[63]

The same quotation from Justin makes all the connections as well. The thanksgiving *is* the sacrifice; indeed, by eliminating everything extraneous to thanksgiving the Christian sacrifice is what all other sacrifices, by the testimony of their own analysts and advocates, would like to be. But we can equally well say that the memorial is the sacrifice. And it is because a memorial is the sacrifice that the sacrifice is pure, consisting only of thanksgiving. And yet the sacrifice is a real sacrifice and not merely mental, because the memorial is the food and drink. And finally, the thanksgiving-sacrifice is by its content the mandated memorial of Jesus.

One further conceptual determinant of the classic prayer must be drawn in: the epiclesis. So Hippolytus immediately follows the complex just described with the petition "And we pray that thou wouldst send thy Spirit. . . ."[64] The epiclesis is the liturgical reality of what has been called "the eucharistic incarnation-principle."[65] The prayer as a whole and in this special part is an invocation of the Logos and of the Spirit, and it is by the analogy of this coming of the Logos and the Spirit to flesh with their coming to flesh in the incarnation that the presence of Christ in the Eucharist is understood. Thus, according to Irenaeus, the elements "receive the epiclesis of God," to become the "body and blood of the Logos."[66]

In the great theologies of the fourth century,[67] all this is drawn together by the same conceptuality we noted in the chapter on baptism. The thanksgiving offering is the *image* of Christ's offering, so that, as Gregory of Nazianzus put it, our participation in the thanksgiving offering is a "communion" of Christ's offering.[68] The power and reality of this communion are the Spirit and the Word implored by the thanksgiving as epiclesis. And the object-presence of Christ as the elements occurs within and as a factor of this dramatic and dynamic presence of Christ in the whole eucharistic action.

Again we may doubt that this integral vision is transferable without distortion into the medieval and modern Western world. Such a unified practice and understanding of Eucharist is nowhere to be met in medieval or later Western liturgy or theology, not even in the great thinkers and churchmen of high scholasticism or the Reformation. That the mass is a sacrifice continued to be the understanding of both practice and interpretation through the Middle Ages. But whether the fault lay in shortcomings of the Western adaptation or in the original patristic vision of Eucharist or elsewhere, what had in the ancient church been Christianity's unifying presumption was suddenly to become a chief occasion of the controversy that divided the Western church. Article XXIV of the Augsburg Confession stated that the mass is precisely *not* a sacrifice, and the entire Reformation movement immediately assented. It was one of the few permanently agreed positions of all the Reformation's branches that, as the Church of England's Article XXXI put it, "the sacrifices of Masses, in the which it was commonly said that the Priests did offer Christ for the quick and the dead . . . were blasphemous fables."

The remainder of this section must be devoted to the controversy about the "sacrifice of the mass." An article published in the reports of the Lutheran/Catholic dialogue convincingly argues that "there is a substantial identity of view between Luther and Roman Catholicism on the understanding of the mass as sacrifice." This leaves the article with the task of considering how it was possible for Lutherans and Roman Catholics "to engage in polemics over a point on which they are agreed."[69] It is indeed a question, and one on which the article is perhaps not so convincing. Its position is fairly typical of recent study, and this suggests that the chief task is to discover precisely what the Reformation controversy was about, which has not been easy.

We will adopt a strategy which will carry through the next section also and which requires some apology: We will make Martin Luther's teaching the pivot of analysis, for Luther's thought first created the solid front against "the sacrifice of the mass" (also in England),[70] and it was Luther whose reassertion of the Catholic doctrine of Christ's presence created a second line of conflict that bisected the first.

In the work that launched his polemic against "the sacrifice of the mass," the *Sermon on the New Testament, that is, the Holy Mass* (1520), Luther analyzed the senses in which one *should*, by his understanding, call the mass a "sacrifice." First, the offertory would be an appropriately sacrificial act if it were an actual presentation of the people's gifts, as Luther knew it once had been. Second, as prayer and thanksgiving, the mass is a proper "spiritual" sacrifice, offered by the gathered people, and such prayer is "more precious, more appropriate, stronger, and more acceptable" because the people bring it together. Third, we dare not bring this sacrifice to God by ourselves, but "lay it on Christ" whose eternal priesthood it is to bring it to God. Fourth, it is therefore not we who offer Christ but Christ who offers us. Finally, and most surprising, Luther can say in view of the last point, "It is acceptable

10 / THE MEANS OF GRACE

and even beneficial to call the mass a sacrifice, not on its own account, but that we with Christ may offer ourselves, that is, lay ourselves on him. . . ."[71]

So far Luther affirmatively on the mass as sacrifice. Does Catholic teaching demand more? Some Roman Catholic theologians have said not.[72] But it seems that two points of essential conflict still may remain.

First, it is certainly Catholic teaching that our eucharistic sacrifice is a work done by us "for the benefit of the living and the dead."[73] Around this language much Protestant-Catholic polemics have circled, and the scheme within which it has functioned is a necessary object of Reformation critique. But that the assertion itself is false is not so evident. If prayer is heard, then intercessory prayer is indeed a work done for others. The doctrine of justification without works certainly does not mean that no works for others, including the work of prayer, are to be done. And there is no apparent reason why the thanksgiving of the mass (supposing, as is practically *not* the case with the Roman canon, that there is one) should not also be intercessory. Whether these intercessions can be for the dead as well as for the living depends on whether prayer generally can be for the dead, a matter outside the scope of this *locus*.

Second, it is certainly catholic (and not merely Roman) teaching and liturgical tradition, that the eucharistic sacrifice is offered not only with words but also with the consecrated bread and cup.[74] So Hippolytus: "We offer to you this bread and cup, giving thanks. . . ." Again, there is from the viewpoint of the Reformation doctrine of justification clearly some problem here. And yet the assertion itself is impeccable, for the Supper's thanksgiving must and will have some visibility, as all words do, and it is as the visible words of the thanksgiving that bread and cup enter this event in the first place. Moreover, if this means that Christ is the offering as well as the priest, in that those objects that are his body for us are the visible word of the offering, why should this in itself not be so?

If we add these two conclusions to Luther's own list, we arrive at a doctrine of eucharistic sacrifice that should be acceptable to Roman Catholicism. It is idle to speculate whether Luther would accept the additions, but there is nothing materially in his thought to prevent it. But what then has the controversy been about?

Here two points must be made that have not always been sufficiently noted. First, in the Reformation polemics themselves, the attack on the sacrifice of the mass was an immediate function of the doctrine of justification by faith.[75] Second, this doctrine of justification was and is a critical doctrine.[76] It does not primarily invite comparison with other doctrines; it provides a particular norm for the reform of the church's actual proclamation. Its critique of "the sacrifice of the mass" is thus not primarily a proposal about the doctrine of eucharistic sacrifice; it is an examination of the event then conventionally referred to by the phrase "the sacrifice of the mass." If, therefore, we are doubtful about what Luther meant by "Down with the sacrifice of the mass," what we must see is what he did to the mass when he had opportunity. We will find four main changes.

First, Luther drastically cut the Roman canon. Moreover, he tells us precisely why.[77] He had only one reason: He rejected the *texts*.[78] Consider only the "*Te igitur* . . .": "Therefore, O most merciful Father, we beseech thee . . . , that thou wouldst find these gifts, these offerings, these holy sacrifices acceptable and bless them, which we offer first for thy holy catholic church. . . ." The sacrifice is here the elements as precisely something *other* than the thanksgiving *with* the elements; the prayer is *about* the sacrifice and its acceptability—and anyway no thanksgiving is offered, these very texts having replaced it. The prayer is neither thanksgiving for God's accomplished grace nor petition for its particular exercise; it is precisely petition that God *be* graceful, that God find us and our offering "acceptable." It is the mass that *so* describes itself as sacrifice that is the "sacrifice of the mass" Luther attacked.

Second, Luther abolished private masses.[79] At a private mass there is no common meal at all, nor anyone to hear and apprehend the sacrament. The elements are thus robbed of their eucharistic and sacramental meaning, and any sacrifice now offered with them cannot be the eucharistic sacrifice but must be whatever sort of sacrifice we choose to make.[80] Just so it cannot be a right sacrifice. The alleged sacrifice of Jesus' body and blood, *detached* from Eucharist, is the "sacrifice of the mass" Luther refused to countenance.

Third, Luther demanded that the promises of the Supper again be spoken audibly.[81] The objection is much the same as it was for the private mass. A silenced sacrament is no sacrament at all, and a sacrifice that is no sacrament cannot be a thanksgiving but must be the works-righteous prayer Christians are not to make. Whether the Supper is silenced as a visible word, by suppression of the meal, or as an audible word, by suppression of the verbal promises, the result is finally the unacceptable same.

Fourth and finally, Luther denounced the customary catechetical and pastoral exhortations with respect to the mass[82] which commended it as an excellent item of our part of the cooperative process of salvation;[83] such exhortation is not uncommon also in Protestant circles. In this context we must consider an historically chief point of strictly theological controversy. The Augsburg Confession's Article XXIV denounces as a decisively influential "theological opinion" "that Christ by his passion made satisfaction for original sin and instituted the Mass in which an oblation was to be made for daily sins." Roman Catholics have always denied that any responsible medieval or Tridentine theologian taught that Christ's passion did not suffice also for "daily" sins. But Protestants have continued the accusation. The history of charges and

10 / THE MEANS OF GRACE

countercharges has been complicated and at some ecumenical junctures important.[84]

What is remarkable is that producing the texts[85] does not seem to help. To Protestants, they seem clearly to teach the heresy, to Roman Catholics they seem equally clearly not to. It depends on the framework. Medieval and Tridentine theology and pastoral practice think of salvation as a process leading by ordered steps from the state of sin to the state of holiness. In the process, original sin is wiped away by baptism, enabling a clean start. In the continuing process thereafter, the grace available is all won by Christ, but its renewed application depends at each step on our doing our part. Now, if the whole scheme does not diminish Christ's work, this is not more diminished when it is specified that participation in the sacrifice of the mass is chief among the works demanded. But it is precisely the scheme that the Reformation protested.

Where then does the great Western controversy stand? The argument about the theology of eucharistic sacrifice can be resolved and indeed perhaps is already resolved. Protestants must acknowledge the linguistic prejudices which deprive them of much that is legitimate to the faith, which indeed, in their extreme liturgical consequences, sometimes create a celebration of the Supper most dubiously obedient to the biblical mandate. Then we are left with what was there at the beginning: the Reformation's critique of the church's perennial attempt to make God's gifts into our means of religious success. The critique found certain targets in the sixteenth century and will find at least as many now, some of them the same ones, on all sides of all denominational lines. The ecumenical question here is whether we can agree together that such critique is appropriate and needed.

EGO BERENGARIUS . . .

In the year 1079, a Roman synod compelled the famed but suspect theologian Berengar of Tours to subscribe the following profession: "I Berengar from the heart believe and with the mouth confess, that the bread and wine which are placed on the altar are in substance changed, by the mystery of holy prayer and the words of our Redeemer, into the true, proper and vivifying flesh and blood of Jesus Christ our Lord; and that after the consecration they are the true body of Christ that was born of the Virgin, offered on the cross for the salvation of the world, and sits at the right hand of the Father, and the true blood of Christ that poured from his side, and that they are these not only through a sign and through sacramental efficacy but in the proper reality of their nature and in the truth of their substance. . . ."[86] This is the earliest official statement of the classic Western doctrine of real presence to have imposed itself on later theology.[87] Whatever we may think about some of its language, it remains the dogmatic claim we have either to accept and understand or reject and refute.[88]

It is again the *truth* of a sacrament's promises that we must consider here. How can the Supper be at once an audible and visible word of the gospel, and a sheer reality to which this word refers? And it will by now be apparent that all the promises made biblically about the Supper, and made by the Supper to us, depend for their truth on the presence of Christ as bread and cup. The concentration of Western scholastic and Reformation-era theology on the fact and mode of the presence has been one-sided but by no means intrinsically inappropriate. To assert that the bread and the cup are in fact the body of Christ, and to assert that the Supper's promises are true, are the same thing.

Nobody has denied that the bread and cup are Christ's bodily presence, except groups for whom the sacramentality of the gospel, and so its character as gospel, is entirely forgotten. The historic disputes have only been about *how* Christ's body is this bread and this cup. But the disputes themselves have not therefore been trivial, nor is their present quiescence necessarily a good sign. As we shall see, their operational cash-value is nothing less than decision about the place of the church-institution, on the one hand, and faith's final vision of reality, on the other hand.

Berengar's confession has two parts: that the *consecration* is an effective change of the elements and that the consecrated *elements* are the body and blood of Christ not merely as sacramental signs are what they signify but by continuity of identity with the historical and ascended Christ. The specific doctrine of transubstantiation is not taught here, though later councils and theologians regularly supposed it was, reading their own meanings back into its language.[89] The matters of consecration and real presence are intertwined in the theological history and must be so discussed in the following.

The serious doctrines of real presence are those of Roman Catholicism, the Calvinist Reformed, and the Lutherans. We will discuss them in that sequence. Catholic theology will be described in its classic form, Aquinas' doctrine of transubstantiation, and in the work of a chief modern theoretician, Edward Schillebeeckx.

Aquinas' initial solution for the problem of sacramental truth in the Supper is that Christ's body and blood occupy the same middle position held in baptism by the "character": they are at once sign and *res*.[90] Clearly, they are the *res* signified by the bread and wine, but they are also signs. That is, like the bread and cup, they *mean* our communion with God and are simply *there* to be apprehended in this meaning, whether or not they find faith. But Christ's body is not there apparently; it is present only as *its* sign, as the bread and cup. Thus the bread and cup must mean Christ's body in some

10 / THE MEANS OF GRACE

way that transcends the otherwise universal separability of signs from what they signify.[91] It is this relation that the doctrine of transubstantiation is to explain.

Boundary conditions of Aquinas' explanation are set by the standard Western metaphysics, according to which a true human body, also the risen Christ's body, necessarily has a spatial location and can acquire another location only by leaving its present location. The risen Christ's location is heaven, which he does not leave; therefore he does *not* come to be located on the altars of earthly churches.[92] But if he does not *move* there, how is he there? Aquinas' solution is that the "substance" of the bread and wine is "converted" into the "substance" of Christ's body, the "accidents" of bread and wine nevertheless remaining.[93] For us, this explanation requires some explanation itself.

The "accidents" of any real thing are its entire empirical reality, all the characteristics by which it is available to experience. The "substance" of any real thing is the "this chair" or "John Jones" or "Christ's body" that the *mind* grasps *in* experience, and which it then knows in a way that transcends all possible experience.[94] If we ask wherein this transcendence consists, we are in the deepest thicket of metaphysics. For our present purposes we can say that it consists in the *purposiveness* of any real thing, never apparent to the senses yet nevertheless known by the mind. A thing's substance is what it is by virtue of what it is for, which is what it *really* is within a universe that is structurally teleological because created by God.[95] That the bread and wine are substantially the body of Christ means that being the body of Christ is what they are for, and "for" in that way by which everything they empirically are is decided and sustained, including their being on the altar, being nourishment and cheering drink, and so on.

One may well ask how, precisely within this metaphysics, substance and accidents can be separated in this fashion. According to Aquinas, it can happen only by a miracle, a new miracle at each mass.[96] But if this miracle is to enable a sacrament, it cannot happen as the Spirit blows. It must be a predictable miracle; we must know where to find it. This is guaranteed by the existence of the church. Summarizing Aquinas' position: God grants to the church, through its own sacramental structure, the authority to invoke the miracle, to say "This is my body" and have it become true.[97] It is this posit of a new miracle at each mass that makes the notion of consecration by a blessing addressed *to* the elements attractive, at least initially, to Catholic doctrine.

If we now turn to a prominent modern Catholic sacramentologist, Schillebeeckx, we are struck first by the thoroughness of his adaptation of modern modes of thought and of modern biblical studies. His understanding of all sacraments is personalist: They are the necessary historical and so embodied aspect of our personal encounter with God in Christ.[98] It is comprehensively christological, fulfilling many of the desiderata of this *locus*: All the sacraments are means by which the ascended Christ maintains personal communion with us.[99] And it is eschatological, thus reflecting modern biblical study: The *res* is the eschaton, and sacramental signs are needed precisely because Christ is already glorified and we are not yet.[100]

But even more striking is the continuity of certain conceptual structures. First, the boundary conditions supposed by Aquinas are also supposed by Schillebeeckx: The ascended Christ, in his "own" embodiment, is precisely absent. Thus our sacramental encounter with him is bodily in our experience, but in itself only "quasi-bodily":[101] "We encounter Christ, though he be bodily absent, in a . . . bodily way."[102] Second, this bodily encounter with an absent body is thoroughly Thomistically accounted for by the way in which "substance" is *meaning*; in the metaphysically interpreted universe a change of meaning is an ontological transformation, so that if bread and cup come in the full metaphysical sense to mean Christ's body, that is a change sufficient to the dogma.[103] Third and finally, the *truth* of the miracle is guaranteed by the supernatural faith and ministry of the church.[104]

Reformation dissent from this Catholic pattern was begun by the Swiss reformers. It is the more remarkable that Calvinist Reformed sacramentology, seemingly so removed from Catholicism, is structurally very close to it.[105] The traditional boundary conditions are unchallenged, even emphasized. Thus Calvin himself: "For this is the hope of our resurrection and ascension into heaven, that Christ rose and ascended. . . . And this is the eternal truth of any body, that it is contained in its place."[106] Calvinist insistence on what the elements and actions *mean* reminds us especially of the modern forms of Catholic teaching,[107] though Calvinism's positions on the third point of Catholic structure gives that insistence a very different outcome. As to that third point, it is alarmingly aphoristic, but in fact precise, to say that the Calvinist position is created simply by removing the supernatural authority of the ordered church from its key position and then making necessary adjustments.

That the existence of the church must not be supposed to guarantee the truth of the word of promise is indeed a fundamental Reformation insight; rather, the word is the guarantor of the church and all its rites. Calvinism's way of removing the church from its untenable place was functionally to substitute the faith of individuals, worked by the Spirit, for the faith and authority of the church. We will drastically summarize the archetypical teaching of Théodore de Bèze.[108] The Supper's elements and action have, by natural analogy to the *res* of the Supper, the power to bring them before the mind, perfectly supplementing the word's different way of doing the same. The Spirit uses the word and the visible sign together, miraculously to gain access to the soul and thus to create faith. And by faith, to which local separa-

10 / THE MEANS OF GRACE

tion means no more than to the Spirit who creates it, the believer is joined to the whole Christ in heaven, in a spiritual-bodily communion as intimate and complete as any Catholic or Lutheran could wish.

This is surely a plausible account of real presence. It does, however, have consequences. Whereas the existence of the believing church can be thought to guarantee the presence of Christ's body independently of the faith or unfaith of the communing individual, the individual's own faith obviously cannot make that guarantee. Therefore the classic Reformed theologians taught that for the unbelieving communicant Christ is simply absent.[109] Thus there is also a structural shift: Christ's body and blood are *res* only and not also sign.[110] There is, by the Calvinist account, nothing in the Supper that is both *res* and sign. As for *consecration*, the only action to which the old notion could apply is Christ's own thanksgiving at the Last Supper; what we do now is by our whole eucharistic action identify for the congregation the present bread and cup as within the scope of Christ's action.

When Swiss reformers began in the 1520s to develop this sort of doctrine, they thought they were only carrying on the intention of Luther. It was he, after all, who had insisted that the *word* is the chief thing always. And the Lutheran stipulation that Christ's presence is coterminous with the performance of the visible word, that "outside" the mandated rite there "is no sacrament,"[111] certainly seemed to point in the same direction.

But Luther vehemently repudiated them, opening a second conflict about the Supper which so divided the Reformation as repeatedly to expose it to military repression. That Luther broke with Zwingli and his followers is not surprising; they taught no presence of Christ in the Supper other than his general spiritual presence in the church[112] and so missed the primal Reformation concern for externality. But also between the Lutherans and Calvin's followers the break proved insuperable and lasting. What can have been so vitally at stake?

We suggest that a new vision of reality was at stake, an interpretation of how the mere word of the gospel, without help from either church-worked miracles or subjective faith, could carry the burden laid on it by the doctrine of justification.[113] In Reformed doctrine, the Supper's visible promise of bodily communion with Christ is not *true* when addressed to an unworthy recipient and so is, by Luther's view, no gospel promise at all, which only the unworthy need. It is the structure that led to such consequences that Luther broke.

We may begin with the kind of analysis we made before. For Luther, as for the scholastics, Christ's body is both *res*, over against the bread and cup that signify it, and itself a sign, present in any case to point to the communion of Christ and his saints.[114] Nor does Luther condemn transubstantiation as an explanation of how this can be so; he merely sees no need for *any* explanation.[115] But that is itself the remarkable feature of this doctrine. Luther's lack of need for explanation, where all others had seen sacramental theology's greatest problem, can be unpacked from two sides.

On the one side, Luther dropped the boundary assumption that had shaped all previous Western doctrines of Christ's presence. For Luther, Christ's risen body has no location (or other spatial characteristics) of its own, distinct from its location (and other characteristics) on the altars. He therefore has no need to overcome a spatial separation between Christ's body in heaven and the bread and cup on the altar, whether by the power of the church or by the power of faith. In the 1528 *Confession of Christ's Supper*, he adopted a standard late-scholastic distinction.[116] By this distinction, there are three ways in which something can be present somewhere. Something may be in a place by occupying the dimensions that define that place; this is the way in which "material" entities were and are thought to be located. In this way, says Luther, God is not present anywhere—nor is the risen Christ. Or a *person* may be in a place as a subject: the place is the place that person apprehends and addresses, the place *before* that person. In this way, says Luther, all the universe is but one place for God, to which God is present, and is one place also for the bodily risen Christ, whose location is precisely God's right hand of omnipresence. Or a person may be somewhere in that he or she is *available* there, intendable and addressable there. In this way, says Luther, Christ's body is where the bread and cup are, and this place can be any place, in that all places are one to Christ.

As Luther interprets, the bodily risen Christ in fact has no other body than the embodiment of the gospel, including and self-proclaimed by the bread and cup, for his "location" at God's omnipresent right hand is simply his sharing in God's possibility of making himself available where he wills.[117] The conception of a quasi-local heaven, to contain Christ's "proper" body, is simply abolished.[118] Thus Christ's presence as the bodies, bread and cup, is no problem and requires no miracles, whether of transubstantiation or of faith—once the miracle of the resurrection and the ascension is posited. This drastic solution reworks the notion of "body,"[119] detaching it from definitions by "materiality" and defining it instead phenomenologically: Whatever makes a person available to and intendable by other people *is* that person's body.

We have already been using this interpretation of embodiment, anticipating discussion of Luther but also following the lead of modern biblical studies and existential reflection. In the present context we must add one point to the phenomenology already laid down: Whatever makes a person available to others is *truly* that person's body if it does the same for him or her, that is, if it also lets the person see who and what he or she is.

On the other side, Lutherans needed no metaphysical explanation of why the bread and cup could with equal truth be called signs of Christ's body and simply Christ's body, because at this point they pressed the identity of

10 / THE MEANS OF GRACE

meaning and being, operative through the whole tradition, to its outcome by making communication *constitutive* of reality. We can see this already in the first Lutheran response to the Swiss initiative, the *Suevian Syngramma*,[120] written by Luther's most speculative young follower, Johannes Brenz, with Luther's enthusiastic approval.

The bread and cup, Brenz says, are by themselves effective symbols of Christ's body, but they are also simply Christ's body itself, *in that* they are not by themselves but "have with them" the word of Christ's promise.[121] Again, there is no more difficulty with Christ's presence as body than with his presence as the Spirit, since the same "vehicle," the word, carries both.[122] Here the word is understood not as a mere sign of reality, pointing to reality that stays where it is, but as the *bearer* of reality. One drastic passage makes the point: "When Christ said 'My body given for you . . . ,' does he not comprehend his body . . . in the word . . . ? So that whoever grasps this word grasps the true body of Christ . . . ? But since the mere word has such power that it bears Christ's actual body to us *whenever* we hear it . . . , why should it not retain that power when it 'comes to' the bread and cup of the Supper . . . ? The whole miracle is the miracle of the word."[123]

By the common Western metaphysics, words are signals that leave the reality of which they speak where and as it was, however powerfully they may affect those who hear them. The doctrine is merely an application of the matter/spirit ontology. Brenz, and Luther, rejected the doctrine. They refused to subject sacramental reality, in which words bear realities and bread and wine speak, to an alien interpretation. Instead, they let the sacramental events, taken in their overt reality, define the characteristics of being.

It cannot be claimed that Lutheranism has fully or successfully worked out the metaphysical revolution contained in the Lutheran understanding of Christ's eucharistic presence.[124] Nor is this the place to undertake it. We will, however, attempt one systematic development within the new metaphysical boundary-conditions set by Luther: a doctrine of eucharistic consecration which obeys the norm of the section above on the authenticity of the Supper, that whatever change the elements undergo is effected by their being taken and used as visible words of the thanksgiving, and which does not posit any miracle worked at that moment.

The consecration need not be one single act. Bread and cup are the signs we are concerned with only in that they are presented to us in a verbal context that lets them visibly say what can be true only if they are indeed the bodily self-presentation of Christ. The establishing of this context, however it is done, surely belongs to the consecration. There are many verbal contexts that can in this sense consecrate; the recitation of the narrative of institution is but one possibility, though an obvious one.

There remains the question of the *truth* of this presentation.[125] Here we must think of the word of thanksgiving, insofar as this is a memorial offering. The thanksgiving praises God for past acts and prays for fulfillment of the promises made by them. It is remembrance also in the sense that it reminds *God* of his commitments. But we offer the bread and the cup as the memorial. That is, we offer them to God as objects in which God may recognize his own intentions; we offer them as God's body. If God accepts this offering, if God acknowledges the past that the bread and the cup make visible as his past and the promises they make visible as his commitment, the bread and cup are truly God's body, that is, the body of Christ. And God does accept the offering; the promises that the Supper itself speaks are God's act of acceptance. No further explanation of real presence is needed, beyond this analysis of the eucharistic word.

The conceptual revolution begun by Luther offers a way beyond the ancient ecumenical impasses. Ecumenical theological labor along its lines might find a way of affirming Christ's bodily presence that would answer Catholic concern for its independence over against communicants' faith or unfaith, but that also would not depend on the kind of church-controlled miracle the Reformed have protested, while yet not individualizing faith or devaluing the church. And such labor might also find a way of understanding ritual consecration which would honor the reality and efficacy of the church's eucharistic act while not perpetuating historic misunderstanding of Scripture.

Meanwhile we must still ask, Should the differences between the three great Western interpretations of Christ's embodied presence prohibit eucharistic fellowship? We must register our judgment that in themselves they should not. If they are not to, one rule must be ecumenically adopted: Each group must restrain itself from practices that can be conceptually legitimated by its theoretical position but are offensive to the other groups. The bare mention of the chief of them will conclude our chapter. Catholics must curb the cult of the elements outside the Eucharist[126] (e.g., the Corpus Christi procession, the benediction of the Blessed Sacrament), even though its legitimacy follows from Catholics' present understanding of consecration and presence. Conversely, Lutherans must adopt ceremonially respectful ways either of preserving remaining elements for the next celebration or of finishing them all within one celebration, even though by Lutheran present understanding of consecration and presence there are only bread and wine outside the eucharistic action proper. And Calvinists must cease to inflict on Catholic and Lutheran visitors formulas of thanksgiving and distribution that suggest the absence of Christ's body, even though these may be the fullest liturgical formulas for what Calvinists now think to be the case.

10 / THE MEANS OF GRACE

NOTES

1. For the present state of exegesis of these texts, see Ferdinand Hahn, "Zum Stand der Erforschung des urchristlichen Herrenmahls," *EvTh* 35 (1975): 553–63.
2. E.g., Günther Bornkamm, *Early Christian Experience*, trans. P. Hammer (New York: Harper & Row, 1963), pp. 138–41.
3. Hans Conzelmann, *I Corinthians*, trans. J. W. Leitch (Philadelphia: Fortress Press, 1975), p. 198.
4. Joachim Jeremias, *The Eucharistic Words of Jesus*, trans. N. Perrin (Philadelphia: Fortress Press, 1977), pp. 249–50, 174–78.
5. Ibid., pp. 35, 108–10, 173–78, 232–33.
6. Ibid., Ferdinand Hahn, "Die alttestamentlichen Motive in der urchristlichen Abendmahlsüberlieferung," *EvTh* 27 (1967): 338ff.
7. J. P. Audet, "Literary Forms and Contents of a Normal *Eucharistia* in the First Century," *TU* 73 (1959):643–62; Louis Bouyer, *Eucharist*, trans. C. U. Quinn (Notre Dame, Ind.: Notre Dame University Press, 1968), passim. Texts in Anton Hänggi and Irmgard Pahl, eds., *Prex Eucharistica* (Freiburg: Editions Universitaires, 1968), pp. 5–57.
8. Here in reconstruction of Finkelstein, cited from Hänggi and Pahl, *Prex Eucharistica*, p. 10.
9. Bornkamm, *Early Christian Experience*, pp. 141–42. There has been a good deal of debate about what additional conceptual freight is carried by "remembrance" in this passage. The position is summarized and bibliography given by Robert W. Jenson, *Visible Words* (Philadelphia: Fortress Press, 1978), pp. 71ff. What is remarkable is how little difference the argument makes for the sense of the mandate.
10. Bouyer, *Eucharist*, pp. 91–226, 309–10.
11. Johannes Betz, *Eucharistie in der Schrift und Patristik*, vol. 4, fasc. 4a of *HDG* (1979), pp. 28ff.
12. *Didache*, ix,3–4, x,1–5.
13. Justin Martyr, *Apology I*, 65,3.
14. Hippolytus, *Apostolic Tradition* (B. Botte, ed., *Sources Chrétiennes* [Paris: Editions du Cerf, 1968], p. 52).
15. Bouyer, *Eucharist*, pp. 244–82.
16. An excellent survey is in *A Dictionary of Liturgy and Worship*, s.v. "Anaphora," by W. Jardin Brisbrook. Texts are in Hänggi and Pahl, *Prex Eucharistica*, pp. 101–460.
17. Jeremias, *Eucharistic Words*, pp. 115–22.
18. Some scholars think that Mark already supposes the next step; Willi Marxsen, *The Beginnings of Christology: A Study in Its Problems*, trans. Paul Achtemeier and L. Nieting (Philadelphia: Fortress Press, 1979), pp. 88–122.
19. *RGG*[3], s.v. "Abendmahl" by G. Kretschmar.
20. Justin Martyr, *Apology I*, 65.
21. The Reformed tradition was initially refreshingly clear on this point; Heinrich Heppe, *Reformed Dogmatics*, rev. ed. trans. G. Thomson (London: Allen & Unwin, 1950), p. 630.
22. Thomas Aquinas, *Summa Theologica*, iii,80,4–9.
23. Heppe, *Reformed Dogmatics*, p. 629.

24. Martin Luther, Large Catechism, "The Sacrament of the Altar," 39ff.
25. The Reformed tradition was most vehement; Heppe, *Reformed Dogmatics*, p. 629.
26. Council of Florence, "Decree for the Armenians."
27. Nathan Mitchell, *Cult and Controversy* (New York: Pueblo Publishing Co., 1982), pp. 44-65.
28. Ambrose, *On the Sacraments*, iv,14.
29. Betz, *Eucharistie*, pp. 27-28.
30. Not even by such as Aquinas; see *Summa Theologica*, iii,78,1; 83,4.
31. Ibid., 78,1 ad 1.
32. The classic Reformed theologians saw clearly the impossibility of the medieval exegesis and much of what the correct exegesis would be. Though they too did not know what "thanksgiving" was, they were at least aware of the lack. Heppe, *Reformed Dogmatics*, pp. 632-33.
33. Bouyer, *Eucharist*, pp. 187-243.
34. For the medieval history of such practices, see W. H. Freestone, *The Sacrament Reserved* (London: Mowbray, 1917).
35. Matt. 26:27, "All of you, drink from it"; 1 Cor. 11:25, "This cup is the new covenant. . . ."
36. Mitchell, *Cult and Controversy*, pp. 157-63.
37. Theodor Klauser, *A Short History of the Western Liturgy*, trans. J. Halliburton (New York and London: Oxford University Press, 1969), pp. 94-112.
38. Aquinas, *Summa Theologica*, iii,73,1; 79,4.
39. *Leiden Synopsis*, xlv,6.
40. Martin Luther, *The Blessed Sacrament of the Holy and True Body of Christ* (1519), *WA* 2:743.
41. Martin Luther, "Sermon on the New Testament"(1520), *WA* 6:353ff.
42. Hahn, "Zum Stand," pp. 553-63.
43. Ibid., pp. 553ff.
44. Ernst Lohmeyer, "Das Abendmahl in der Urgemeinde," *JBL* 56 (1937): 217-52; Jeremias, *Eucharistic Words*, pp. 66-67, 205.
45. For a full statement of the following and literature, see Jenson, *Visible Words*, pp. 63ff.
46. Oscar Cullmann, *Early Christian Worship*, trans. S. Todd and J. B. Torrance (London: SCM Press, 1953), pp. 14-18.
47. See 1 Cor. 16:23; *Didache* x,6; Rev. 22:20.
48. Hahn, "Die alttestamentliche Motive," pp. 356-57; Hahn, "Zum Stand," pp. 555-56; J. B. Higgins, *The Lord's Supper in the New Testament* (London: SCM Press, 1952), pp. 41ff.
49. On this text, see Eduard Schweizer, "Das johanneische Zeugnis vom Herrenmahl," *EvTh* 7 (1948): 263ff. Hahn, "Zum Stand," pp. 561-62.
50. Bornkamm, *Early Christian Experience*, pp. 123ff., 143-54; Ernst Käsemann, *Essays on New Testament Themes*, trans. W. J. Montague (London: SCM Press, 1964), pp. 108ff.
51. Ibid., pp. 119ff.

10 / THE MEANS OF GRACE

52. Against the long and plainly erroneous churchly traditions that locate it in insufficient self-examination or wrong opinion about the elements. But see the exegesis of Marxsen, *Beginnings of Christology*, p. 93.

53. Jeremias' *Eucharistic Words* is a treasure of historical information, but its exegesis is vitiated for our purposes by false method just at this point.

54. Oswald Bayer, "Tod Gottes und Herrenmahl," *ZThK* 70 (1973): 355ff.; Günther Bornkamm, "Die Eucharistische Rede im Johannes-Evangelium," *ZNT* 47 (1956): 166–69.

55. Hahn, "Die alttestamentlichen Motive," pp. 358–73.

56. For more detailed argument, see Jenson, *Visible Words*, pp. 80ff.

57. Hahn, "Zum Stand," pp. 558–59.

58. Edward Schillebeeckx, *Christ the Sacrament of the Encounter with God* (New York and London: Sheed & Ward, 1963), p. 60, continues this way of making the distinction.

59. On the following, see Betz, *Eucharistie*, pp. 26–112.

60. Hippolytus, *Apostolic Tradition*, 52.

61. *Didache*, xiv,1.

62. Clement of Rome, *To the Corinthians*, xl,2.

63. Justin Martyr, *Dialogue with Trypho*, cxvii,2–3.

64. Hippolytus, *Apostolic Trdition*, 52.

65. Betz, *Eucharistie*, p. 43.

66. Irenaeus, *Against All Heresies*, iv,18,4; v,2,3.

67. Betz, *Eucharistie*, pp. 68–77.

68. Gregory of Nazianzus, *Oration IV*, 52.

69. James F. McCue, "Luther and Roman Catholicism on the Mass as Sacrifice," in *Lutherans and Catholics in Dialogue III: The Eucharist as Sacrifice* (New York and Washington, D.C.: U.S.A. National Committee for the Lutheran World Federation and Bishops' Conference for Ecumenical and Interreligious Affairs, 1967), p. 46.

70. Francis Clark, *Eucharistic Sacrifice and the Reformation* (London: Darton, Longman & Todd, 1960), pp. 99–176.

71. Luther, *Sermon on the New Testament*, 365–66, 368–69.

72. E.g., the Roman Catholic delegation to the American Lutheran/Catholic dialogue; *Lutherans and Catholics in Dialogue III*, pp. 187ff.

73. The Council of Trent is insistent on this; "Decree on the Sacrifice of the Mass," canon 3.

74. Clark, *Eucharistic Sacrifice*, pp. 73–98.

75. E.g., Luther, *Smalcald Articles*, ii,a–b.

76. Robert W. Jenson, "On Recognizing the Augsburg Confession," in *The Role of the Augsburg Confession*, ed. Joseph A. Burgess (Philadelphia: Fortress Press, 1980), pp. 151–66.

77. In the work in which he did the surgery, the *Formula Missae* (1523), *WA* 12:205–20, 207–8, and in a work devoted to the precise matter, *On the Abomination of the Secret Mass*, *WA* 18:291–334.

78. Devotees of the truncated anaphora Luther thus produced sometimes claim that he did it so that the narrative of institution should not be incorporated in a prayer, but there is no documentary hint or trace of such a motive.

79. On this point Luther informs us fully in *On the Misuse of the Mass*, *WA* 8:513–517.
80. Luther is clear on this point; *WA* 8:514.
81. E.g., Martin Luther, *On the Babylonian Captivity of the Church*, *WA* 5:497–573, 516.
82. Martin Luther, *On Abrogating the Private Mass*, *WA* 8.
83. With dogmatic claims by the Council of Trent, "Decree on the Sacrifice of the Mass," chap. 2: "This sacrifice is propitiatory, and . . . by its means it is effected that we obtain mercy and find grace . . . , if we draw near to God contrite and penitent. . . . For the Lord, placated by its oblation and conceding the grace and gift of penitence, forgives. . . ."
84. On the history, see Clark, *Eucharistic Sacrifice*, pp. 469–503.
85. Collected in ibid., passim.
86. Council of Rome II, "Confession for Berengar."
87. For the history, see James F. McCue, "The Doctrine of Transubstantiation from Bérenger through the Council of Trent," *Lutherans and Catholics in Dialogue III*, pp. 89–124.
88. Thus it is affirmed by the Council of Trent, "Decree on the Eucharist," canons 1–2 (on which see McCue, "Transubstantiation," pp. 113–122) and by the Augsburg Confession, Article X, and its Apology, Article X.
89. McCue, "Transubstantiation," pp. 89–101.
90. Aquinas, *Summa Theologica*, iii,73,1.
91. Ibid., 75,1.
92. Ibid., 75,1 ad 3; 75,2; 76,2–4.
93. Ibid., 75,2–4.
94. Ibid., 75,5 ad 2.
95. Klaus Kremer, *Die Neuplatonische Seinsphilosophie und ihre Einwirkung auf Thomas von Aquin* (Leiden: E. J. Brill, 1966), pp. 351–474.
96. Aquinas, *Summa Theologica*, iii,75,4: "Est omnino supernaturalis, sola Dei virtute effecta."
97. Ibid., 78,4–5; 82,1–3.
98. E.g., Edward Schillebeeckx, "The Sacraments: An Encounter with God," in *Edward Schillebeeckx OP*, ed. M. Redefern (New York and London: Sheed & Ward, 1972), pp. 11–24.
99. Schillebeeckx, *Christ the Sacrament*, pp. 54–65.
100. Schillebeeckx, "The Sacraments," pp. 22–25.
101. Ibid., p. 23.
102. Ibid., p. 25.
103. Edward Schillebeeckx, "Transsubstantiation, Transfinalization, Transsignification," *Worship* 40 (1966): 334ff.
104. Schillebeeckx, "The Sacraments," pp. 37–45.
105. This is now noted by scholars; so the fine interpretation *in bonam Catholicam partem* by Jill Raitt, *The Eucharistic Theology of Theodore Beza* (Chambersburg, Pa.: American Academy of Religion, 1972).
106. John Calvin, *Institutes of the Christian Religion* (1536), iv,122.
107. Heppe, *Reformed Dogmatics*, pp. 636–44.

10 / THE MEANS OF GRACE

108. Drawn from Raitt, *Eucharistic Theology*.
109. Heppe, *Reformed Dogmatics*, pp. 650ff.
110. Ibid., pp. 636ff.
111. This became confessional; *Formula of Concord*, Solid Declaration, Article VII, 73.
112. *RGG*³, s.v. "Zwingli," by G. W. Locher.
113. On the following in greater detail, see Robert W. Jenson, "Of Another Spirit," *Lutheran Theological Seminary Review* 62 (1982): 3–14.
114. E.g., Luther, *Sermon on the New Testament*, 359.
115. McCue, "Transubstantiation," pp. 105ff.
116. Martin Luther, *Confession of Christ's Supper* (1528), *WA* 26:261–509, 327ff.
117. This is at least the interpretation of Luther's move made by Martin Chemnitz, *The Two Natures in Christ* (1578), trans. J. A. O. Preus (St. Louis: Concordia Publishing House, 1971) and enshrined in Lutheran scholasticism.
118. The Lutherans had great demythologizing sport with this. Johannes Brenz, *Von der Majestät unsers lieben Herrn und einigen Heilands Jesu Christi* (Tübingen, 1562), 100ff., asks if Jesus takes little walks up there; and, putting his finger on the precise dogmatic point, inquires (31a): "During the time after Christ's resurrection, before he visibly ascended to heaven—friend, tell me: When he was not appearing to his disciples, where *was* he? Or, when in his visible ascension the cloud received him—friend: Where had he got to?" Thus the Lutherans were the one great confessional group for whom Copernicus was simply no problem.
119. It was this that so outraged Calvin and his followers; Calvin, *Institutes*, xv,121: "Quis enim dubitet corpus Christi phantasticum fuisse, si ea conditione fuit?"
120. A response on behalf of the young reforming pastors of Suevia to their own former teacher, Oecolampadius; Johannes Brenz, *Syngramma Suevicum*, *Werke*, ed. M. Brecht and G. Schäfer (Tübingen, 1970), 1/1:222–78.
121. Ibid., p. 244.
122. Ibid., p. 275.
123. Ibid., p. 242.
124. But see the work of the seventeenth-century Lutheran metaphysicians; Walter Sparn, *Wiederkehr der Metaphysik* (Stuttgart: Calwer, 1976).
125. For fuller presentation of the following, see Jenson, *Visible Words*, pp. 34–38, 45–50.
126. On the history, see Mitchell, *Cult and Controversy*.

6

The Return to Baptism

If baptized life is return to baptism, it must be itself sacramental. Rites of the return to baptism grant the Spirit, since this is baptism's content. By only *penance*, the rite of the Spirit's return, does the Spirit grant himself as such after baptism. Other rites bestow the Spirit for some juncture or task of baptized life. Four such rites have been so continuous and prominent as to appear on the traditional list. Of these, *confirmation* has already been discussed. The others are *ordination, healing,* and *marriage*.

RITES OF THE SPIRIT

If the content of baptized life is indeed *return* to baptism and not a development of baptism or a progression from it, baptized life must be as sacramental an event as baptism itself.[1] The Supper, moreover, will not by itself suffice; we need rites whose visible and audible communication is specifically "Back to baptism." The church has had five such rites of enough persistence and prominence to appear on the medieval list of seven. One of these, confirmation, should never have become a *return* to baptism and has been discussed in its proper place as a part of baptism.

Rites of return to baptism must be rites that bestow the Spirit, either as such or in respect of particular gifts or charisms, for the Spirit is the whole positive content of baptism. A rite by which after baptism the Spirit *as such* bestows himself can only be a kind of "repetition" of baptism, following the Spirit's "withdrawal" and involving a fresh "repentance" and forgiveness of sins—the quotation marks already indicate the main dogmatic problems of *penance*. Otherwise, the Spirit bestows specific gifts for specific crises and tasks of life in the church. Thus there are, or should be, innumerable churchly invocations of the Spirit. Identifiable rites develop at regular and prominent junctures. There should be, and in fact are, many such rites; that only three, *ordination, healing,* and *marriage*, appear on the traditional list of "sacraments" is partly an historic narrowing and partly the result of the New Testament's concerns.

The total events of penance, ordination, healing, and marriage (and of whatever other such rites may appear) are each complex and unique. But the central act of bestowal is similar in all: prayer with imposition of hands, anointing, or both. Thus the rites of return to baptism in effect repeat that part of baptism that can be repeated, though we must not presuppose that intention to do this always shaped their historical origin. Nor is this accidental; the last act of baptism and the sacraments we now consider all depend on the biblical association of the Spirit with this ritual pattern.

Imposition of hands, on other people or on objects, is so obvious a gesture of acceptance and interpersonal empowerment that its religious use is almost universal.[2] It was variously practiced in Israel and early Judaism, notably in the latter at the ordination of rabbis.[3] From the first, it was clear to Christians that true religious community and power is the Spirit, so that in one way or another a communion of the Spirit was always what they said by their use of the universal religious gesture. In the New Testament, imposition of hands appears as (1) a healing act of Jesus (e.g., Mark 5:23 par.) and of the apostles (e.g., Acts 28:8), (2) the gift of the Holy Spirit associated one way or another with baptism (Acts 8:14ff.; 19:5–6; Heb. 6:2), and (3) as creation of "apostles," "deacons," and "presbyters" (Acts 6:6; 13:3; 1 Tim. 4:14; 2 Tim. 1:6).

In the Near East and the Mediterranean littora, anointing with oil was a necessity of life, a refreshment, and often the only possible medical treatment. Therefore it too became a widely practiced religious gesture of many applications also in Israel.[4] The only sacramental anointing mentioned in the New Testament is for healing; one passage commands the practice as a rule (James 5:14). The much wider use of anointing in the ancient church probably depends partly on the New Testament's use of the *metaphor* of anointing for decisive Christian realities (1 John 2:20; 2 Cor. 1:21).

PENANCE

No specific rite of penance is mandated by Scripture,[5] nor any specific procedure. But the New Testament does unambiguously enforce that the church must have *some* procedure and rite to deal with the sins of its members. The New Testament also makes promises of God's grace to such a procedure and its rite. That the traditional rite is prayer and blessing with imposition of hands is a decision of the ancient church, with compelling biblical reasons.

Both the necessity and problematic of penance are set by central features of the New Testament understanding of sin. First, if the *baptized* disobey God's good will for his people, this cannot be regarded as mere moral imperfection, to be dealt with pedagogically or ethically, for the baptized are past such judgments. In the decisive witness, Rom. 6:1–11, Paul says that violations of God's law are not allowed to the baptized precisely because they are impossible for the baptized. Yet that the baptized nevertheless do sin is presupposed even by Paul's strange exhortation not to and is taken for granted throughout the New Testament (Matt. 18:21–22). But if moral lapses must be seen as ontological anomalies, they can be dealt with only sacramentally.

Moreover, it is the *community* that must somehow deal with the sins of the baptized, for, second, the necessary self-discipline of the church cannot be separated from concern for the righteousness of its members. Every living community can maintain its identity only by policing its borders according to the norm of its purposes; a political party cannot allow people who regularly campaign for opposition candidates to vote in its caucuses. But the spirit of *this* community, the church community, is the Spirit of love, kindness, faithfulness, and so on, to which immorality, idolatry, anger, and so forth, are simply opposites (Gal. 5:16–26). Nor have these moral claims anything to do with self-satisfaction; it is precisely as it is sent into the world for the mission of the kingdom of God that the church must care for the authenticity of its representation of the kingdom. When people so live as to disprove the church's claim to the Spirit, the community must eventually separate itself from them.[6] And in fact, throughout the church's history, where and when the church has kept no discipline it has also lost its mission.

Third, neither can the disciplinary judgments of the church be separated from the disciplinary judgments of God. If the church finds itself obliged to exclude a member, this reverses what baptism did—but it is God who acts in baptism. Just so, if the church readmits an excluded member, this must somehow be a new baptismal act of God. Matthew's community cited the Lord: "Whatever you bind on earth shall be bound in heaven, and whatever you loose on earth shall be loosed in heaven" (Matt. 18:18). In the New Testament's various catalogs of sins, those that exclude from the church and those that exclude from the kingdom turn out to be the same.[7] It is above all the interpretation and practice of this identity between the church's disciplinary act and God's that has agitated the history of penance.

Just so, fourth, we see that the church's care for members' sin cannot be restricted to cases arising from its own strictly disciplinary necessities. For sin itself, whether disciplined by the church or not, must be a lapse from baptism, and the sinner so be in need of God's new baptismal act, which God gives the congregation to perform. The church must "loose" also where it has not itself "bound." The point can be reached more directly: If the baptized, despite what might seem to follow from baptism, also need to hear the gospel of forgiveness, the gospel, as an essentially external word, must also in this instance be spoken by the community.

This brings us to the fifth and last of these considerations: the priority of "loosing," for the content of baptism is precisely forgiveness, and the Spirit is the spirit of love. Therefore, to what would seem the necessary disciplinary question, "How often shall we forgive?" the answer is, "seventy times seven,"

10 / THE MEANS OF GRACE

as often as it takes (Matt. 18:22). This is perhaps *the* hard demand on the church's practice.

Throughout its history, the church has struggled to satisfy all these mandates, at once, or to evade them.[8] The assignment is perhaps manageable only for times and places. The history begins in the New Testament church.

Without suggesting that any uniform practice is described in the New Testament, we note the following. There were many possibilities of mutual correction which did not proceed immediately to exclusion (e.g., 2 Cor. 2:5-11; Gal. 5:19—6:3; James 5:19; 1 John 5:16-17). With many sorts of fault, matters never went so far; "there is sin which is not mortal" (1 John 5:17). But with—to take one catalog—immorality, greed, idolatry, slander, drunkenness, and theft (1 Cor. 5:11), it clearly could go so far; even then it was perhaps refusal to accept corrections that actually brought about exclusion. As for forgiveness, it was seventy times seven at hand.[9]

From Matthew's part of the church we have an actual rule of congregational procedure.[10] First the offended person is to reprove the sinner alone; then a delegation is to visit the sinner; then the congregation meets, "and if he refuses to listen even to the church, let him be to you as a Gentile and a tax collector" (Matt. 18:15-17). The great theological proposition about binding and loosing, which has with much reason traditionally been read as penance's institution, follows (Matt. 18:18). "Binding and loosing" was standard terminology for a rabbi's disciplinary authority in the synagogue;[11] here it is applied to the congregation's authority over its members. Of this authority, Matthew's rule says nothing less than that God promises eschatologically to ratify the congregation's decisions.

The saying is affixed to the rule of procedure as a dogmatic statement. The responsibility it promises the congregation is indeed frightening. But "promises" is the right word, for Matthew takes both the rule and the saying into a composition, making the whole of the chapter, whose unitary sense is the absolute command for brothers, "seventy times seven," to forgive brothers "from the heart" (Matt. 18:35).[12] It is the eschatological power of forgiving and restoring to fellowship that Matthew teaches, although this is meaningful only if binding and excluding are also actual. And he provides the christological basis of this authority in the verses immediately following his assertion of it: The congregation's act of restoration and forgiveness is an act of prayer that God must grant, for when the congregation gathers for prayer in Jesus' name, Jesus himself is one of the prayers (Matt. 18:19-20). The entire local congregation is empowered so awesomely to invoke the gospel; Matthew has carefully excluded references to "the twelve" that were in his sources.[13]

In the church's postbiblical history, two great systems of penance have appeared. The first, referred to in Catholic terminology as "canonical penance," was the penitential system of the ancient church. The history of its formation is conjectural.[14] It appears fully formed in the measures taken following the Decianic persecution (249–251) to deal with a flood of repentant apostates.

The formal procedure of penance was for "mortal" sins: criminality, apostasy, and sexual misconduct.[15] Voluntarily or at the behest of the bishop, the sinner confessed his or her acts. It was then the bishop's responsibility to judge whether the case required exclusion from full fellowship (i.e., from the Eucharist) and whether the sinner could be "admitted to penitence," for the latter was by no means automatic. Because the sinner had already by the act of sin excluded himself or herself from Christ's mystical body, exclusion from the Eucharist was understood not as punishment but as an act of pastoral care. Admission to the status of "penitent" was by public confession of sins and prayer with imposition of hands. Penitents were assigned a special place in the service and allowed only partial participation, were the object of regular prayer by the congregation, and were obligated to such works of penance as fasting, sexual abstinence, and much prayer. The bishop was to judge the time of penitence and could assign periods from a few days to the whole life. Readmission was again by prayer and imposition of hands.

Such penance was in effect a second catechumenate, on more rigorous terms in view of demonstrated failure, with a rite of reception that was a liturgical parallel to baptism, without the unrepeatable bath. And so the ancient church understood the matter.[16] A special consequence of the parallel with baptism was the unrepeatability of penance: As baptism could be done only once, so penance. A "third repentance" would have had to be another rite altogether. What would that be?

There was in the ancient church no uniform interpretation of penance other than what is immediately involved in the parallel with baptism.[17] It was taught that "mortal" sin, which excluded from the church, of course required primarily the forgiveness of God, and that the church's penance was that forgiveness of God. It was understood also that mortal sin was incompatible with the indwelling of the Spirit, so that the reconciliation was a new self-giving of the Spirit. But the relationships were, perhaps wisely, not clearly defined, and certain points were later to be fateful. In that the "works of penitence" were done to show to the church that trust once betrayed could with confidence be restored, their imposition was reasonable; and it was then reasonable to say that the works achieved the reconciliation. But did they also achieve the reconciliation with God? In fact, it was usually said that they did,[18] that it was the penitence and not directly the rite of reconciliation that brought God's forgiveness. And what of "venial" sins, which the church disciplined only informally? The analogy made it easy to think that "satisfaction" for them was simply made by pious acts, even though here only God's forgiveness was in question and not at all that of the church.

The ancient form of penance was overwhelmed by the Constantinian settlement's flood of doubtful converts.¹⁹ Faced with whole congregations of "mortal" sinners, the bishops at first reacted with ever more punitive periods and tasks of penance. They succeeded only in frightening sinners into postponing their penitence (which, after all, could not be repeated) until in the sixth century penance had become a final preparation for death or was simply evaded. Thereby a vacuum was created in the actual life of the church—much like that which has long existed in Protestantism—which had to be filled somehow and was in fact filled by a new system of penance, created in Ireland and carried across Europe by the seventh- and eighth-century rechristianizing mission of the Irish and Scottish monks.[20]

The forms of Irish church life were developed in considerable independence from the general Western church, and after canonical penance was in decline. A system of penance was created around narrowly pastoral considerations. The system applied to all sins, "mortal" or not, was available when and as often as conscience or pastoral oversight required, involved no exclusion from the Eucharist, and imposed works of penitence, "satisfactions," in doses adapted to the misdeeds committed. The history of interaction in the Carolingian and early medieval church between "Irish penance" and the remains of the older system is complicated. It is the outcome that concerns us: the system of "private" penance, a perilous synthesis of the practices of the Irish monks and the ideology of canonical penance.

Penance is by this system done as often as needed and in any case as preparation for Communion; so much remains of the old connection between penance and exclusion from the Supper. Sin is confessed to the confessor only and in detail. Since there is no exclusion from the congregation, it was quickly seen that there is no need to wait to perform the rite of reconciliation; this now follows immediately after the confession. Appropriately to the now strictly interpersonal situation, the reconciliation has not only prayer but an indicative declaration: "I absolve you. . . ." Works of satisfaction are then imposed, to be done later.

This order has momentous consequences, in which the millennially postponed problems of penance become unavoidable and demand solution. The rite's function in communal discipline has been so attenuated that in fact the rite is what the church never before had, a sacrament sheerly of God's forgiveness and the believer's sin, as such and in direct confrontation.[21] Now the question cannot be avoided:[21] *What* achieves reconciliation with God? The tradition of ancient penance imposed the answer: the works of penitence. But in this procedure the only work of penitence sinners bring to the absolution is their subjective and verbal confession itself. Thus it came to be taught that it is *contrition* as such that achieves reconciliation with God.[22]

No Christian theologian could tolerate such a doctrine of salvation by works as medieval penance thus seems to carry, and the scholastics found here a principal task. From Augustine they inherited and emphasized the doctrine that if in fact I come to contrition, this is itself an interior work of God's grace, for which God must be praised. But at least in the new situation this doctrine by itself will leave sinners defenseless before the question "Does God in fact grant me contrition? Am I *really* contrite?" And it is in danger of making the actual rite unnecessary: What then is the *absolution* for?[23]

No two scholastics had exactly the same answer to these questions, but it is possible to construct a skeletal common doctrine.[24] The sacramental sign is composed of apparent contrition, confession, and satisfaction, as the penitent's act, and absolution as the minister's act.[25] Within this complex, absolution, by virtue of God's grant of the "keys," the power to bind and loose, is an efficient cause of the reconciliation.[26] This doctrine is reconciled with the patristic doctrine that true contrition obtains forgiveness, by saying that true inner contrition is what is in this sacrament both sign and *res*, and so the direct effect of the sacramental sign.[27] If then the sinner comes to confession already truly contrite, essentially included in this contrition is desire precisely for absolution; if the sinner comes imperfectly contrite (i.e., out of servile fear or egocentric desire for salvation), it is the effect of the absolution to turn such "attrition" into "contrition."[28] This doctrine, bent toward its more legalistic possibilities and without the key theological explanation, was then given dogmatic claims by the councils of Florence and Trent.[29]

Do these theological moves work? It seems to depend on the viewpoint. As textbook propositions, they evidently describe the situation between God, the penitent, and the confessor accurately and subtly. But if we think from the situation of the living penitent, the scholastic assurances may dissolve. What may I, seeking forgiveness in penance, *rely* on? As in the Supper I rely on Christ's body and blood? Here the equivalent to Christ's body and blood is supposed to be my own true repentance. I may look to the sacramental sign to make my repentance true, but the very act of then looking back to my state of repentance, to find in *it* the sure gift of the sacrament, is a new spiritual act that for all I know may be egocentrically or fearfully done and so undo my repentance. The uncontrollable variability of interior repentance and the limitation of absolution's effectiveness to absolution's moment are in fact heavily emphasized by the scholastics.[30] Finally, my true interior repentance is simultaneously condition and effect of grace, which is undoubtedly descriptively true but leaves me existentially exactly where I was.

If I am alive to the dialectics of my own subjectivity (as medieval penance will train me to be), I may find that my actual situation is still that posed before the scholastic efforts were made: If I truly repent, and so have forgiveness, I may praise God for the gift of repentance, but to know *that* I truly repent and so *that* I am forgiven, I either have to look to my act of repentance, and so become works-righteous in the standard religious way, or look to God's sheer, sacramentally unsecured gift of repentance, and so open myself to the endless and destructive terror of the question "But does God grant *me* true repentance?"

The reformers programmatically located their reflection at the place of the penitent and came to see in the medieval practice and interpretation of penance the paradigm case of what ailed the church's proclamation of the gospel.[31] It is all very well that Western theology since Augustine has located the final agent of my spiritual progress in God's utterly free act on me. But if in my actual apprehension of the church's message the gospel's promises are regularly made conditional on my in fact making one or another step of that progress, the Augustinian codicil either has no living meaning, leaving me to make the step and to determine if I have made it, and so leaving me with my works for my spiritual assurance, or it acquires existential meaning, leaving me at the mercy of an arbitrary God. That the reformers were correct in their diagnosis was then confirmed by the Council of Trent, which decreed, "No one can know with the certainty of faith . . . that he has attained the grace of God."[32]

From this common diagnosis, the main-line reformers took opposite ways. Those in the line of Zwingli and Calvin dissolved the specific rite of penance back into the general preaching of the gospel and the general pastoral activity of the church.[33] The Lutherans took the opposite step, which in our judgment the entire history of penance and its biblical foundation demand. They dogmatically mandated the rite, within the list of "sacraments,"[34] and provided an order.[35] And they defined the *absolution* as such as "the sacrament,"[36] "by divine right,"[37] itself directly the medium of God's forgiveness, explicitly *without* detour by way of the penitent's contrition.[38] Absolution is defined as "the very voice of the gospel,"[39] more particularly and formally, as "the word of God, which the power of the keys pronounces for individual cases."[40] Thus the sinner's side of penance can have as its "parts" not contrition, confession, and satisfaction, but only "contrition and faith,"[41] corresponding to the law which brings him or her to confession and the gospel the sinner there apprehends.[42]

The reformers' hopes for an evangelical penance were defeated by the same Constantinian secularization that had undone ancient penance and by the moral individualism and relativism of the modern world. And we must record that the medieval system of private penance is now collapsing also in the Roman Catholic church,[43] following promptly the Second Vatican Council's opening to modernity. In both quarters the vacuum has most recently been filled by "pastoral counseling." Some of this has been excellent and pastoral, more has been a poor imitation of secular therapies, directed to a relativistic society's goal of personal self-fulfillment rather than to the church's goal of righteousness. None, without an audible and visible rite, reaches to the level where the sin of the baptized is. Where in the world church or in smaller sectarian communities the consciousness of mission is alive, there also discipline is maintained, and with it some form of disciplinary penance. But in the established Western church there is little discipline of any sort.

Nevertheless, we must conclude by proposing what order of penance the church *should* in the foreseeable future have, in fidelity to Scripture. There should be one rite of absolution, with prayer for and unconditional pronouncing of forgiveness. The sacramental heart of the matter is the word of the minister: "At the command of our Lord Jesus Christ, I forgive your sins. . . ."[44] The visibility of this address should be the imposition of hands.[45] The rite should have two uses. Whom the church has bound, the church must reconcile to itself, and here the setting of conditions is appropriate. Also in this use, the absolution itself is unconditional. When the church has not bound, and the penitents come of their own accord or by pastoral request, no further requirements are allowed; this use of the rite is merely a sacrament of the gospel.[46]

Reinstitution of mandated church discipline in the Western bodies must undoubtedly await Providence's further destruction of the church's Western establishment and secularization. Until there is discipline, a true rite of private penance will also be established only here and there and by great pastoral effort. The effort, however, is not optional and is with promise.

HEALING

That Christians pray for recovery of their sick and proclaim to them God's healing will is itself too natural to require justification. The New Testament, moreover, sets sickness and recovery in a specific context. Bodily disaster, as the one unavoidable reminder of death, is understood as a central fact and a betraying signal of creation's bondage to evil. Jesus' proclamation of the imminence of God's victory, a proclamation so urgent as itself already to liberate from evil, therefore became visible especially as healing (Mark 5–6). Mark's capsule scene of Jesus' mission, Mark 2:1-12, shows him as Lord over sin and sickness; the difference is that healing is visible and forgiveness is not. Thus Jesus' healings were very precisely *sacraments* of the coming kingdom. When the twelve were sent out as extensions of Jesus' mission, their commission was to replicate Jesus' proclamation also in this respect (Mark 6:6b-13 pars.). And in that the apostolic mission itself renewed the mission of the twelve,[47] we see the apostles healing in the same style and context (e.g., Acts 3:1-10).

The New Testament records a rite that the twelve used: "They . . . anointed with oil many that were sick and healed them" (Mark 6:13). And much later, in the second-generation church, we find a rite in use that is derived from that of the twelve; this is mandated for the congregations addressed by "James": "Is any among you sick? Let him call for the elders of the church, and let them pray over him, anointing him with oil in the name of the Lord; and the prayer of faith will save the sick man, and the Lord will raise him up; and if he has committed sins, he will be forgiven" (James 5:14–15). Moreover, substantial gospel promises are here attached to the rite.

Does all this make the canonically binding mandate of a rite? Both the older Catholic exegesis, which simply said that it does, and main-line Reformation exegesis, which said that it does not, argued unhistorically. We cannot take mission instructions to the apostles, or the urging of a rule for one group of early congregations, as directly addressed to our bishops or presbyters.[48] Nor can we simply say that healing was a special grant to the first apostles for their situation only, as both Luther and Calvin did,[49] for as a more historical exegesis has made plain, the fact of a postapostolic generation is itself an anomaly for the gospel; we have not simply proceeded from the apostolic situation to something else.

Surely what we find, for our situation, in the New Testament is *permission* to do what we anyway want to do: pray for the recovery of our sick and assure them of the efficacy of such prayer, and do both in the specific context of the church's mission against creation's bondage, in which illness is more than misfortune and healing is a sign of the gospel's future triumph.[50] To such prayer and assurance the New Testament attaches the promise of healing, in that total sense which encompasses physical recovery as its visible aspect.

Penance and healing have traditionally been linked as the inner and outer aspects of the gospel's one victory over the evil of this age;[51] the linkage appears explicitly in the text from James. The connection is the clearest way to see how healing is a return to baptism. Healing is located on the hinge between the old age, our continuing subjection to which is marked most decisively by physical evil, and the freedom of the coming kingdom, which is ours in hope. That is, healing is located precisely where baptism locates us.

The chief theological problem about healing is simply the general problem with specific petitionary prayer. We can here address that problem only peremptorily: We are in fact bidden by the Lord to address God as "Father," bringing also our suggestions for God's governance of the universe, with the assurance that God will hear our requests as a true parent hears the requests of maturing children, not always assenting to but never ignoring them. If we have a conception of reality that does not allow God to govern creation freely, it is our conception of reality that must be reworked. And if we have a conception of God that does not allow God genuinely to hearken to us as children, it is our conception of God that must be changed. In order to make each prayer for healing with glad confidence, we need not expect every prayer to be granted.

THE RETURN TO BAPTISM

If we speak such prayer and assurance, it must, in the deep theological context in which Scripture locates it, seek specific visibility. And the New Testament does offer a rite, which the church practiced for eight centuries as something entirely obvious and uncontroversial.[52] Surely the counsel of James, that the presbyters of the church should pray for the sick person in his or her presence, and anoint the sick person with invocation of Jesus' name, may be followed in the absence of any strong reason not to.

It is likely that there would have been no controversy about anointing of the sick, or break in its practice, except for two circumstances. One was emergence of a list of "*the* sacraments" and medieval insistence that healing belonged on the list. Even in anointing's form as "extreme unction" (which we will mention next), Luther was willing to include it "among the sacraments that *we*—that is the church through its history—institute," which do indeed "give remission and peace."[53] But admonished by the Council of Trent that they must accept the then existing rite as "instituted by Christ . . . and promulgated by . . . James,"[54] Protestants refused, and the entire practice fell into disuse among them.

The other was the Carolingian transformation of anointing the sick for their recovery into "extreme unction" to speed the evidently dying.[55] As Luther and Calvin alike noted,[56] this was church history's most bizarre example of sacramental arbitrariness—from which it does not follow that no rite for the dying is needed. It would have seemed that the Council of Trent had fixed the medieval usage on Roman Catholics. But the Second Vatican Council in substance reversed Trent (however that is now to be rationalized), and instructions for a rite of anointing were given which may well command ecumenical concurrence.[57]

The council's reformation of Catholic practice has been widely effective, and an initial revival of rites of healing, often with anointing, is occurring among Protestants. Both developments are dogmatically right.

ORDINATION

In this section we are not going to be concerned with every rite that might be used to grant some office established in the order of the church, and so in some sense to "ordain." We are going to focus on a specific rite, the historical referent of the term "ordination," about whose institution and force we will inquire as we did about baptism and the Supper. This procedure is justified for there is one historically continuous and identifiable rite called "ordination," the practice of which transcends conflict about its meaning, just as there are such rites called "baptism" and "the Supper" and as there is no such rite of penance or healing. The rite that is our topic is that described in the pastoral Epistles of the New Testament and perhaps in the book of Acts[58]

10 / THE MEANS OF GRACE

and continuously practiced in that the church has deliberately followed these descriptions as rubrics.

The pastoral Epistles were directed to the self-understanding and discipline of the third generation of Christian leaders (i.e., to those who were no longer either apostles or assistants of apostles) in the form of pseudonymous letters from "Paul" to "Timothy" and "Titus," the latter appearing as links between the apostolic generation of leaders and later generations and as archetypes of Christian official leadership.[59] The exegesis of the pastoral Epistles and especially of their understanding of ministry and ordination is controversial, but the ordination texts have recently been subjected to an analysis of unprecedented detail and care, which allows at least the following to be said with some confidence.[60]

In the congregations to which the pastoral Epistles are addressed, there is a well-established structure of official leadership, that is, of offices that precede and survive their occupants. There are "bishops," "presbyters," "deacons," and "widows." The model of the congregation is the ancient world's household; though the father is God, the bishops and/or presbyters exercise a "householder's" leadership. So far as can be ascertained, the rite we are concerned with was for these latter offices only.[61] The rite is most powerfully evoked in two of the several passages that refer to it.[62] "Do not neglect the gift you have [literally, "the charism that is in you"], which was given you by prophetic utterance when the council of elders ["presbyters"] laid their hands on you" (1 Tim. 4:14). "Hence I remind you to rekindle the gift [again, "charism"] of God that is within you through the laying on of my hands" (2 Tim. 1:6).

As this ordination can be reconstructed from the total evidence of the letters, it involved (1) the bestowal of a charism, jointly accomplished by a Spirit-filled invocation ("prophecy") and by the imposition of hands and (2) the verbal commission of the deposit of apostolic faith, with the charge to preserve and pass it on. The rite was public; indeed, it involved formal witnesses.[63]

How then does "Paul" understand the rite's purpose? A charism is here, as in the historical Paul's understanding, a particular and personally determining concretion of the Spirit's presence; here, however, the particularizing factor is not as in Paul individual circumstance and the unpredictable choice of the Spirit, but the office.[64] As in the original Pauline understanding, a charism is the unity of Spirit-constituted *authority* and *ability*, for some service to the congregation; the difference is that here the service is defined by an impersonally established role.[65] Thus ordination in these congregations is simultaneously a personal liberation and empowerment and a legal act.[66]

It is also reasonably clear what the episcopal/presbyteral task was, for which ordination spiritually qualified. It was, to be sure, a general "householding" of the congregations, but its central and defining task was determined by the wrenching situation of the third-generation church. The delay of the Lord's coming and the death of the apostles imposed (if these were not to be taken as refutations of the faith) one need above all: ascertainable historical continuity with the apostolic preaching of the gospel. Timothy and Titus are above all to care for the true *teaching* they have received from Paul and ordain bishops and presbyters fit for the same task.[67] And since there can in Christianity be no final separation between truth and persons, ordination also establishes a continuity of succession in the office; it is precisely as the first links from Paul that Timothy and Titus are decisive, and part of the charism granted by ordination is the power not to "pass on" the charism but indeed to ordain others in turn.[68]

Finally, insofar as the pastoral Epistles contain a theological interpretation of all this, it is the parallel with baptism.[69] One aspect of the parallel is decisive for our purposes: precisely as the historical Paul used the *past tense* of his readers' baptisms to close and open the possibilities of their lives, so the "Paul" of these writings used the past tense of "Timothy's" and "Titus' " ordinations to establish his assurances and exhortations.[70]

There is the rite and its meaning. The question is, must we practice it? Biblical mention and discussion of a rite practiced only at some periods and in (so far, at least as we know) some parts of the New Testament church does not by itself constitute a peremptory command to us. If there is a binding mandate to ordain, *argument* plays a larger role in ascertaining this than it does in the cases of baptism or the Supper. As it seems to us, the argument is, in its starkest simplicity: (1) If the church is to continue past the first generation—that is, if our own baptisms are divinely mandated—then there must be in the church just such an office as the pastoral letters are concerned with, but (2) such an office can, in the church, be established only by some such rite as ordination, and (3) if that is the case, then the canonical status of the pastoral Epistles must successfully urge ordination as the appropriate rite against all but the weightiest objections. We must now briefly support the first two steps of the argument.

The church was *never*, and that by divine right, an undifferentiated collection of people subsequently compelled for order's sake to establish offices, for the same events—the resurrection appearances and the outpouring of the Spirit—established both the church and its first authoritative office, the apostolate.[71] The church is the community of those who have heard and believe the message "Christ is risen"; the apostles were those who initiated the message. Thus the apostolate was an office—that is, a location of continuing authority at least partly independent of the personal qualities of its occupants—intrinsic to the very existence of the primal church.[72]

No community can exist through even the briefest stretch of time without offices, for as community requires various relationships of mutual authority, continuous community requires continuously identifiable positions of authority. In the case of the church, which identifies itself by the One in whom it believes, the one essentially required office is an office of historical memory, for the existence of the church is essentially determined by the fact that the One in whom it believes is ascended, and must therefore be remembered to be known. With the question "But did the Lord . . . ?" we must have some place to turn. The apostles were by definition those who had met the risen Lord and who could answer the question.

At the same time the *content* of apostolic memory was an odd one, for what we are principally to remember about Christ is that he is *risen*, that is, that he is no more a mere item of the remembered past but is rather the essentially future one. Thus true speech about Jesus can be given only by the Spirit, by the guarantor of the eschaton (2 Cor. 5:1–10). Paul's dogma is precise: "No one speaking by the Spirit . . . ever says 'Jesus be cursed!' and no one can say 'Jesus is Lord' except by the Holy Spirit" (1 Cor. 12:1–3). It is a criterion of the Spirit's initiative that the past Jesus is *not* put behind us; but to assert of this Jesus what must be asserted is given only by the Power of the End. Thus all true speech for Jesus is prophecy, a gift of the Spirit.[73]

With the apostles themselves these considerations mark no difficulty. The same circumstance that constituted their *office*, the appearance to them of the risen Lord, constituted also the *charismatic* immediacy of their message. They had the message by no human authorization, but from the Lord alone; what they proclaimed as the gospel *was* the gospel just because they proclaimed it, for "the gospel" is by definition the message of their own meeting with the Resurrected (Gal. 1:1–17). Their entire self-understanding was thus modeled on the prophets of Israel.[74] With them office and charism were identical.

What then, when the apostles died without the Lord's return? Unless this is to mean that the church ceases, new provision must be made for the church's essential office. That is, there must be a successor *office of charismatic historical memory*—precisely the sort of office we see in the pastoral Epistles. That the particular office in the pastorals is episcopal/presbyteral is the contingent outcome of a sorting process from the numerous offices and momentary ministries that had existed under the apostolic leadership.[75] The question of the necessity of a threefold structure of this office (of bishops, presbyters, and deacons) is separate from the question of this section; our present point is only that the emergence of *some* such office is a condition of the church's continuance as other than a memorial society or a gnostic coven.

But how is a *charismatic office*, and one for historical continuity at that, to come about? It should be clear that the apostolic identity of office and charism cannot be replicated. Only a sacrament might fill the gap, a rite that sets in the office precisely *by* bestowing the charism, and that so can as a past biographical fact fill the place the resurrection appearances had for the apostles.

Can we by a rite grant a charism? Yes. Baptism even grants the charism of charisms, the priesthood of all believers. Are we authorized to? We are if God means us to carry on with the church, that is, if our baptisms and the commission they lay on us are true.

It is, then, mandated with absolute authority that there be in the church a rite with precisely the structure, purpose, and meanings of the pastoral Epistles' "ordination." And the canonical position of the Pastorals surely means that ordination should in fact be the rite, unless in a particular situation overwhelming dogmatic objections appear. Finally, the foregoing establishes nothing about what other offices and unofficial ministries there should always or from time to time be in the church, or about what rites these should involve; it establishes only the necessity at all times of one office and of one rite.

Both the office and the rite have been maintained in the church through all vicissitudes. There is no room to trace the history, which anyway is not in this matter decisive. We report only the earliest preserved postbiblical rubrics, again from Hippolytus: "When a presbyter is ordained, let the bishop put a hand on his head and let the presbyters also touch him and let the bishop pray: 'God and Father of our Lord Jesus Christ, regard this your servant and grant him the Spirit of such grace and wise judgment as belongs to presbyters, that he may uphold and govern your people with a pure heart.' "[76] The great Western division is decisive for our present dogmatic situation here also. And again there are three serious doctrines of ordination.

With respect to the visible sign, the Catholic tradition has not been so clear as might have been expected. In the Carolingian centuries,[77] further symbolism was added to the imposition of hands: the "delivery of instruments," that is, in the case of presbyters, the ceremonial giving of a chalice, and anointing. Such can be the church's short memory, that the Council of Florence, following Aquinas, made the delivery of instruments the sacramental sign and that the Council of Trent mentioned only anointing as "required."[78] But since an "apostolic constitution" of 1948,[79] and the new Roman liturgy of 1968,[80] it is definite also for Catholics that the essential sign is imposition of hands. With ordination, the "character" is the chief thing[81] in that what is "*res only*" is the edification of the mystical body of Christ, which lies beyond the one being ordained. In this scholastic terminology, to which we shall for present purposes adhere, the biblical notion of *charism* is divided between the notion of the "character" and the notion of a "grace" given by the Spirit that accompanies the character to equip presbyters to minister "worthily."[82] The character is permanent,[83] for the same reason that of baptism is permanent.

It was the *content* of the "character" that divided the church. The Council of Trent neatly summarized the medieval tradition: Ordination grants "the power to consecrate and offer the true body and blood of the Lord, and to remit and retain sin."[84] The reformers denied that anyone had or should have the power to offer "the sacrifice of the mass." They further denied that ordained priests possess a unique power to bring the sacramental reality to pass, as the Council of Florence had put it, to "make" the sacrament. And they found in the claim of such power the key to the unevangelical authority of the medieval church.[85]

The Augsburg Confession and its Apology are in this connection the basic Reformation dogmatic documents.[86] What they in effect do is replace the medieval understanding of the purpose of ordination, leaving the rest of the traditional understanding in its place as noncontroversial. If, the Apology teaches, the priesthood is understood as the Augsburg confession's Article V defines it, as the "ministry of preaching the gospel and providing the sacraments," rather than as a sacrificial priesthood, "then we gladly call ordination a sacrament," precisely in its ritual character as imposition of hands, because the church is commanded to provide ministers and has the promise of God that God will bless and be at work in that ministry.[87] Thus the Augsburg Confession's article on this ministry of word and sacrament (Article V) explains the necessity of a public office by its part in the necessary externality of the gospel and says that God establishes the office; in its article on ecclesial order (Article XIV), it stipulates that no one should exercise this public office until ordained.[88]

The Augsburg Confession said all that it needed to say for its own purpose as a reforming manifesto within a not-yet-divided Catholic church. But its appropriate silence on many points became a misfortune for denominational Lutheranism, for insofar as Lutheranism has, unhistorically, come to treat the Augsburg Confession as a compendium of basic theology, as though one could construct on any topic a complete doctrine from its statements, it has been possible to derive a doctrine of ordained ministry missing many biblically essential Catholic elements. Consequently, the history of Lutheranism has been a confused and debilitating conflict between more Catholic understandings of ordination and those that see ordination simply as installation in a function.

The Reformed tradition went on to create a more precise doctrine of ordination. The office is defined, with the whole Reformation, as "ministry of the word of God." In specifying how people enter this office, Reformed theology drew mostly from the legal side of the tradition: A person becomes a minister of the word when and in that the church, acting by whatever instruments are established by its law for the purpose, *elects* that person to it. The rite of ordination, normally the imposition of hands by predecessors in the office, is a public confirmation, *after* the fact, of the granting of office and does not bestow a charism.[89]

At present the understanding of ministry is in considerable flux in all three groups. It appears to be possible so to understand the Catholic tradition that the Reformation attack loses much of its occasion, and for Lutherans to hold and practice a doctrine of ordination satisfactory to Catholic norms.[90] Even the Reformation substitution of "word and sacrament" for "sacrifice" is evidently not a final barrier. Nor is there any apparent reason why Reformed understanding should not draw on what it says elsewhere about the Spirit's use of signs, to develop its teaching about ordination toward confluence with other traditions. It would appear that the key to reconciliation is the understanding of the term "power" in propositions to which Roman Catholicism is committed. If only ordination gives the power to consecrate or to bind and loose, does this mean that only ordained people *can* do these things, or that only they *should,* or is yet some third sense intended?[91]

The operational test of ecumenical mutual acceptability is a matter we have several times touched and must now make thematic: ordination's unrepeatability. A doctrine is correct, we suggest, only if it makes clear why ordination cannot and need not be repeated—whether the effect of the rite is conceptualized as "character," "office," "effective sign" or whatever. For the heart of the matter is that ordination recapitulates baptism in respect of a particular gift in and for the congregation, a gift that requires this recapitulation for its bestowing. Baptism is always there in the past of the believer, to enable him or her in doubt and temptation to say, "Nevertheless, I am baptized!" Just so it is the very grace of ordination that it is an external event in the ordained person's past that does not go away but enables him or her, in the impossible tension between official position and prophetic charism, to say, "Nevertheless, I am ordained!"

MARRIAGE

In view of the general variability of the notion of sacrament, it is appropriate to end the discussion of the traditional list with the oddest of the seven, marriage.[92] Marriage is and has been consistently taught by the church to be a reality of creation, conducted by families, individuals, and communities and equally actual among Christians, Jews, and pagans.[93] Christian marriage is simply marriage among the baptized, for whom this aspect of their life is transformed by baptism, as are all other aspects. Medieval churchly control of marriage grew out of historical needs and never changed the fundamental doctrinal understanding. How then is marriage a sacrament?

Christian rites of marriage grew in the early centuries out of the natural participation of pastors in familial ceremonies.[94] Their sense is quite simply that the church prays and proclaims the good will of God for the new union. The ceremonies themselves began eclectically. In the Western church, the main ceremony was for a long time the priest's veiling of the bride and partially of the groom, surviving still, in more Catholic rites, as the placing of the priest's stole over their hands. This originated as a parallel to the veiling of women

10 / THE MEANS OF GRACE

entering orders, to make clear the church's insistence that marriage too is a holy vocation and a new relationship with Christ.[95] In the East, the main ceremony is the garlanding of the couple, a straightforward adoption of antecedent familial festivity.[96] The ring was once a legal betrothal token.

Once the participation of the church in the event of marriage is established, there is good reason for the wish to single it out among the myriad of churchly events—which, in the vocabulary of the late-antique and medieval church, was likely to be done by finding reason to call it "a sacrament." From the one side, marriage is the fundamental anthropological event, the occurring coincidence of communal need and individual destiny. As every anthropologist knows, marriage is the basic unit of society. Thus the sanctification of marriage by baptism is the sanctification of no ordinary event. And from the other side, the unique intimacy and permanency of the marriage union makes it the only possible created image of the union with Christ established in baptism (Eph. 5:21–33). When the baptized marry, they cannot entirely separate the two relations. It will not be possible actually to live a relation which the gospel makes its way of talking about the relation created by baptism, without both relations being determined thereby.[97]

When the scholastics then set out to fit this "sacrament" into their general sacramentology,[98] the first question was: What here is the sign? What one wanted to say was that marriage itself was the sign, especially since in the Ephesians passage it is marriage as such that is an image of Christ and the church. But it was still clearly understood that it is not the church's rite but the personal, familial, and societal consent to intercourse that creates a marriage.[99] Thus the Western church arrived at the remarkable result that "sacrament," a particular term for Christianity's *rites*, is applied to an act that is not a rite at all, that an event is called a "visible Word" of the gospel that has no christological content, being speakable also by those who have never heard of Christ. The conceptual development is a splendid instance of the illicit conversion that happens often enough in theological history, that what is originally a mere *description* of something concrete acquires a life of its own. Here, that a sacrament is a sign of grace which grants what it signifies was once a true theological statement about Christian rites; then it came to be thought that whatever is somehow a sign of grace and grants what it signifies must be a sacrament.[100]

The reformers rejected this doctrine with derision,[101] and indeed it will not do. If we wish to elevate marriage above other rites of the church (as there is good reason to do), we must recognize that in this instance it is the unique importance and relation to baptism of the *object* of the rite that justifies the emphasis, but that it is still the rite that is a sacrament. That is, we should follow the general path of the Eastern churches, which never followed the

THE RETURN TO BAPTISM

scholastic development and so always saw marriage much more in the same light as other churchly rites.[102]

The content of the rite is therewith also specified. Needed is prayer for the gifts of the Spirit for the unique opportunities and obligations that faith must find in the marriage of the baptized, as all orders provide it. And the ceremonial gestures should be imposition of hands (as many orders in fact provide) or similar gestures. What is here "sign and *res*" is the public association of the couple's faithfulness to each other with their faithfulness to Christ.

NOTES

1. This is a decisive explanation of the need for further sacraments after baptism. Where the notion creeps in that baptism only initiates a process, a decisive explanation is not possible, and metaphorical explanations appear, which are homiletically effective but dogmatically shaky. The most usual is that the other sacraments "nourish" the life baptism begins.
2. *RGG*[3], s.v. "Handauflegung," by S. Morenz.
3. Ibid., s.v. "Handauflegung," by H.-D. Wendland.
4. Ibid., s.v. "Salbung," by E. Kutsch.
5. Although there was a traditional rite in at least part of the New Testament church, if, as seems likely, "the laying on of hands" in 1 Tim. 5:22 refers to reconciliation; Martin Dibelius and Hans Conzelmann, *The Pastoral Epistles*, trans. P. Buttolph and A. Yarbro (Philadelphia: Fortress Press, 1972), ad loc.
6. See 1 Cor. 5:9–11; 2 John 11. On the first, see Hans von Campenhausen, *Ecclesiastical Authority and Spiritual Power in the Church of the First Three Centuries*, trans. J. Baker (Stanford: Stanford University Press; London: A. & C. Black, 1969), pp. 134–35.
7. The lists are worked out by Herbert Vorgrimler, *Busse und Krankensalbung*, vol. 4, fasc. 3 of *HDG* (1978), pp. 6–10.
8. Of the entire history there is now a satisfactory account; see ibid. A brief account is provided by Nathan Mitchell, "The Many Ways to Reconciliation," in *The Rite of Penance: Commentaries III*, ed. N. Mitchell (Washington, D.C.: Liturgical Conference, 1978), pp 20–37.
9. Vorgrimler, *Busse und Krankensalbung*, pp. 9–10, 23–27.
10. On this passage, see Günther Bornkamm, *Geschichte und Glaube*, vol. 2 (Munich: Chr. Kaiser, 1971), pp. 37–50; von Campenhausen, *Ecclesiastical Authority*, pp. 137ff.
11. For its different sense in the Petrine passage, Matt. 16:18–19, see Bornkamm, *Geschichte und Glaube*, pp. 45ff.
12. Analyzed in ibid., pp. 40–42.
13. Ibid., pp. 40–41.
14. Vorgrimler, *Busse und Krankensalbung*, pp. 28–69.

10 / THE MEANS OF GRACE

15. On the following, see ibid., pp. 43–47.
16. E.g., Tertullian, *On Penitence*, VII:10ff.; 12:9; Cyprian, *Epistle LV*, 22.
17. On this and the following, see Vorgrimler, *Busse und Krankensalbung*, pp. 43–68, 82–85.
18. Not by Augustine; see ibid., pp. 84–85.
19. Ibid., pp. 74–82, 89–92.
20. On the following, see ibid., pp. 93–113.
21. So Thomas Aquinas, *Summa Theologica*, iii,84,2–3: the final matter of the sacrament is the penitent's sin; the form is the absolution.
22. Vorgrimler, *Busse und Krankensalbung*, pp. 104–31. This was also the teaching of Aquinas, *Summa Theologica*, iii,86,2–6.
23. Vorgrimler, *Busse und Krankensalbung*, pp. 129–30.
24. The following is drawn from Aquinas; for the relation of his teaching to that of other scholastics, see ibid., pp. 129–38.
25. Aquinas, *Summa Theologica*, iii,84,1–2; Council of Florence, "Decree for the Armenians."
26. Aquinas, *Summa Theologica*, iii,84,3: "Cum dicit, 'Ego te absolvo,' ostendit hominum absolutum non solum significatione sed etiam effective."
27. Ibid, 1.
28. Vorgrimler, *Busse und Krankensalbung*, pp. 131–35.
29. Council of Trent, "Decree on the Holy Sacraments of Penitence and Extreme Unction," canons 4–10.
30. Vorgrimler, *Busse und Krankensalbung*, pp. 129–53.
31. The classic exposition of this is the Apology of the Augsburg Confession, Article IV and Article XII, 1–43.
32. Council of Trent, "Decree on Justification," chap. 9.
33. E.g., The Second Helvetic Confession, XIV.
34. Augsburg Confession, Article XI.
35. Martin Luther, Small Catechism, "The Sacrament of Holy Baptism," 21–29.
36. Apology of the Augsburg Confession, Article XII, 4; XIII, 4.
37. Ibid., XII, 12.
38. Ibid., 6, 20.
39. Ibid., 39.
40. Ibid., 99.
41. Augsburg Confession, Article XII, 4–5.
42. Apology, Article XII, 29, 35, 39.
43. Vorgrimler, *Busse und Krankensalbung*, pp. 196–202.
44. Martin Luther's order; Small Catechism, "The Sacrament of Holy Baptism," 28.
45. Among Roman Catholics restored after late-medieval attenuation.
46. Apology, Article XII, 98ff.
47. Ferdinand Hahn, *Das Verständnis der Mission im Neuen Testament* (Neukirchen-Vluyn: Erziehungsverein, 1962), pp. 32–39.
48. As the Council of Trent, "Decree on the Sacrament of Extreme Unction," chaps. 1, 3.
49. So Martin Luther, *On the Babylonian Captivity of the Church*, WA 6:497–673, 570–71; John Calvin, *Institutes of the Christian Religion* (1536), 178.

THE RETURN TO BAPTISM

50. There is a beautiful rumination on this by Karl Rahner, *Meditations on the Sacraments* (New York: Seabury Press, 1977), pp. 79-93.

51. So by the Council of Trent, "Decree on the Sacraments of Penitence and Extreme Unction," chap. 1.

52. Vorgrimler, *Busse und Krankensalbung*, pp. 218-20.

53. Luther, *Babylonian Captivity*, WA 6:570.

54. Council of Trent, "Decree on the Sacraments of Penitence and Extreme Unction," canons. 1-4.

55. On the history and theories, see Vorgrimler, *Busse und Krankensalbung*, pp. 220-25.

56. Luther, *On the Babylonian Captivity*, WA 6:570: "Therefore I do not condemn this 'sacrament' of extreme unction itself; but I will always deny that it was mandated by the apostle James, since his rite corresponds to ours neither in form nor in power nor in purpose." Calvin, *Institutes*, 177-78.

57. Second Vatican Council, "Constitution on the Sacred Liturgy," 73-75.

58. In Acts 6:1-6 "deacons" (by this account the first) are created in that "the apostles" "prayed and laid their hands on them." In Acts 13:1-4 "prophets and teachers" of the congregation at Antioch "set apart" two of their number as missionaries by imposition of hands following fasting and prayer. The instruction to do this latter was a prophetic utterance in the group.

59. Herman von Lips, *Glaube-Gemeinde-Amt* (Göttingen: Vandenhoeck & Ruprecht, 1979), pp. 106-8.

60. Ibid.

61. Ibid., pp. 106-50.

62. The others are 1 Tim. 1:18; 5:22; 2 Tim. 1:13; 2:1-2; Titus 1:5.

63. Von Lips, *Glaube-Gemeinde-Amt*, pp. 240-65.

64. Ibid., pp. 184-223.

65. Ibid., pp. 221-23.

66. Ibid., pp. 264-65.

67. Ibid., pp. 106-61.

68. Ibid., pp. 220-78.

69. Ibid., pp. 211-15, 260-63.

70. Ibid., pp. 161-82.

71. Von Campenhausen, *Ecclesiastical Authority*, 13-14.

72. Friedrich Hahn, "Der Apostolat in Urchristentum," *KuD* 20 (1974): 54-77; Hans von Campenhausen, "Der urchristliche Apostelbegriff," *Studia Theologica* (Lund) 1 (1948): 96ff.

73. On charismatic ministry in the primal church, see von Campenhausen, *Ecclesiastical Authority*, pp. 67-70; *RGG*³, s.v. "Geistesgaben," by E. Käsemann.

74. Von Campenhausen, *Ecclesiastical Authority*, pp. 62ff., 182-90.

75. Robert W. Jenson, *Visible Words* (Philadelphia: Fortress Press, 1978), pp. 190-97; there the literature.

76. H. B. Foster, *The Ordination Prayers of the Ancient Western Church* (London: SPCK, 1967), pp. 1-11; see there also the classic Roman prayers, pp. 24-29.

77. *A Dictionary of Liturgy and Worship*, s.v. "Ordination," by J. D. Crichton.

78. Council of Florence, "Decree for the Armenians;" Aquinas, *Summa Theologica*,

Sup., 34,5; Council of Trent, "Decree on the Sacrament of Ordination," canon 5.

79. Pious XII, *Sacramentum Ordinis.*

80. *The Rites of the Catholic Church*, 2d series (New York: Pueblo Publishing Co., 1980), pp. 60–69.

81. Aquinas, *Summa Theologica*, Sup., 34,2 ad 1; Council of Trent, "Decree on the Sacrament of Ordination," canon 4.

82. E.g., Council of Florence, "Decree for the Armenians: "Augmentum gratiae, ut quis sit idoneus minister."

83. Council of Trent, "Decree on the Sacrament of Ordination," canon 4.

84. Ibid., canon 1.

85. All that was to be said in the first reforming tract on the matter: Martin Luther, Babylonian Captivity, 560–67. Luther wrapped up his polemic: "The church of Christ knows nothing of this sacrament; it was invented by the church of the pope." He went on to a more historical and theologically reasonable position, but since it is a matter of great scholarly controversy what that position was, we will in this section refer not to Luther but to the Lutheran confessions, whose sense is clear. The two opposed positions about Luther are represented by Wilhelm Brunotte, *Das Geistliche Amt bei Luther* (Berlin: Lutherisches Verlagshaus, 1959), and Helmut Lieberg, *Amt und Ordination bei Luther und Melanchthon* (Göttingen: Vandenhoeck & Ruprecht, 1962), pp. 19–242.

86. A precise analysis of the total position of the Lutheran Confessions is by George A. Lindbeck, "The Lutheran Doctrine of the Ministry: Catholic and Reformed," *TS* 30 (1969): 586–612.

87. Apology of the Augsburg Confession, Article XIII, 7–13.

88. That this is what *rite vocatus* means is clear both from the vocabulary of Melanchthon's theology (on which see Lieberg, *Amt und Ordination*, pp. 330–39) and from the subsequent discussion in the *Confutatio Pontifica*, XIV, and the Apology, Article XIV.

89. John Calvin, *Institutes*, 183–91; Heinrich Heppe, ed., *Reformed Dogmatics*, rev. ed., trans. G. T. Thomson (London: George Allen & Unwin, 1950), pp. 677–83.

90. *Lutherans and Catholics in Dialogue IV: Eucharist and Ministry* (New York and Washington, D.C.: U.S.A. National Committee of the Lutheran World Federation and the Bishops' Committee for Ecumenical and Interreligious Affairs, 1970).

91. Ibid., pp. 120–37, 227–82, and passim.

92. For all historical information in the following, see the compendious history of marriage provided by Edward Schillebeeckx, *Marriage: Human Reality and Saving Mystery* (New York and London: Sheed & Ward, 1965), pp. 225–380.

93. This is ecumenically agreed; the secularity of marriage was the very basis of the reformers' attack on Roman practice.

94. Schillebeeckx, *Marriage*, pp. 244–56.

95. Ibid., pp. 260ff., 302–9.

96. Ibid., pp. 345ff.

97. Ibid., pp. 280–314.

98. Ibid., pp. 327–43.

99. Council of Florence, "Decree for the Armenians": "Causa efficiens matrimonii regulariter est mutuus consensus per verba de praesenti expressus."

100. So the argument of the Council of Trent, "Decree on the Sacrament of Matrimony."
101. E.g., Calvin, *Institutes*, 193–95.
102. Schillebeeckx, *Marriage*, pp. 344–56.

ELEVENTH LOCUS

Christian Life

GERHARD O. FORDE

CHRISTIAN LIFE

Introduction

1. Justification
   Justification by Grace
   Justification by Faith
   Law, Gospel, and Conscience

2. Justification and Sanctification
   The Separation of Sanctification from Justification
   The Unity of Justification and Sanctification

3. Justification and This World
   Justification and the Law
   The Self as God's Creature
   This World as God's Creation

4. Justification Today
   The Question of Relevance
   Relevance: The Life of the Individual
   Relevance: The World Vision

Introduction

A *locus* on the Christian life is potentially the most dangerous in dogmatics. It is concerned with giving an account of how the act of God in Christ impinges on, effects, and affects the lives we live. Such an account is potentially dangerous because, as the tradition shows all too patently, the rhetoric has a way of running away with itself and becoming inflated and oppressive. In the anxiety to demonstrate that the Christian life is different, vital, relevant, abundant, and obviously superior to every other kind of life, the encomiums pile up, often fired by enthusiasm and hubris rather than by reality.

The danger is at least threefold. In the first place, Christians are enticed into playing the world's game, into going everyone one better. The Christian life is measured by the world's yardstick. It is pictured as the unqualified fulfillment of all the old Adam's dreams, particularly the most pious and religious. Then the battle is lost. Christianity succumbs to moralism. Second, inflated rhetoric leads either to hypocrisy or to despair. One deludes oneself that one has succeeded (at least as well as the next person) in measuring up to it, or one despairs because one cannot. The former is perhaps most common. Third, the danger is that the rhetoric will float above reality, living a life of its own in dogmatic texts and sermons with little or no relation to what Christians or others actually think or do. It becomes a fiction that may entertain those who still have a taste for it on Sundays but has no vital function in their lives.

One of the first tasks of a dogmatic *locus* on the Christian life is to bring the rhetoric to heel so that it can perform its proper function. The rhetoric must be true to what the Christian life really is and should be. Dogmatics should attempt to foster a proper use of language so that the preaching of the Christian message actually is productive of a Christian life in the true sense and is not false or empty. We certainly want to claim that the Christian message fosters a life that is better, relevant, true, vital, and so on, but dogmatics must do this in a manner consonant with the Christian hope itself, not succumbing to the world's measurements.

We are concerned, that is to say, with the *Christian* life, the specific kind of life lived in the light of God's act in Jesus Christ, and not with just any kind of religious life or whatever the world may deem so or aspire to. The basic assumption is that if God has indeed acted to save us, without our aid

11 / CHRISTIAN LIFE

or counsel, in Jesus Christ, then the *Christian* life will be quite other than those schemes where no such redemption is believed or hoped for—and other, moreover, in a manner consonant with the redemption itself, not with the world's conceptions of otherness.

It is important, therefore, to put the right question, lest we set off in the wrong direction at the outset. The basic question cannot be the direct one about what the Christian life is or what makes it different. The basic question must be one which arises from within, from the startling nature of the message of grace itself. The Christian life is one which results from grace already given; it is not a life somehow dedicated to achieving grace. In putting the question *about* the Christian life, one must be careful not so to call the Christian life into question as to kill it and put it back on the rhetorical treadmill. The Christian life should be good news, not law and drudgery. The question with which we deal must itself reflect the good news.

The apostle Paul set the basic question for us in just this fashion. "Are we to continue in sin that grace may abound?" (Rom. 6:1). That is the basic question for the Christian life. It is the only question left to ask if one attends to the Christian message with any care and discernment. If God has done it all for us, then the real question is *whether and why there is anything left to do at all*. But are not the assumptions behind such a question and the question itself dangerous? Of course they are. But salvation by grace, proclaimed unconditionally, *is* a dangerous thing. Nevertheless, God has taken the risk and we must follow God in it. It cost God the cross. It cost a death. Paul says that for us too it is only through that death that we will find what the Christian life is: "We were buried therefore with him by baptism into death, so that as Christ was raised from the dead by the glory of the Father, we too might walk in newness of life" (Rom. 6:4). The Christian life is life from the dead. Therefore its basic question is one which must be put with a smile, with joy irrepressible: "*Is* there anything left to do?" Nothing must quench that joy.

A dogmatic chapter on the Christian life is dangerous because it has to do with death and life. We can see the danger in the question whether we should sin the more that grace may abound. If it is not properly answered, everything is lost. If we answer with a shocked No and piously turn our backs to return to our petty moralisms, as if it were not a serious question, we shall have to go our way to our own death. If on the other hand, in premature enthusiasm, we answer Yes and take the question as occasion for gratification of the flesh, it will turn to poison. Unless we catch something of the vision, we are in a precarious position. "To him who has will more be given; and from him who has not, even what he has will be taken away" (Mark 4:25). That is the ultimate danger.

Paul's answer is the only answer: "How can we who died to sin still live

INTRODUCTION

in it?" (Rom. 6:2). One must note the past tense: We *died*. We have to do with "the newness of life" out of death. Explicating that must be the concern of the *locus* on the Christian life.

Traditional Protestant dogmatics has done this by dealing with the question of justification, the basic saving act, and its relationship to sanctification, the fruit of the saving act in the believer's life, and how this affects the believer's relationship to church and world. In spite of protest that might be made against narrowing the matter down to such ancient formulations, we shall honor the tradition, believing it to be no random or time-conditioned caprice that led to stating the problem of Christian life in these terms. Justification by faith is, after all, *the* dogma of the Protestant Reformation, and the only dogma about the Christian life yet proposed. Dogmatics must discuss with the tradition such things as justification, sanctification, law and gospel, the "order" of salvation, the two kingdoms, the world, and freedom, because only through such discussion with the tradition can we arrive at responsible formulations today.

The question of the adequacy and relevance of the traditional conceptualizations will, of course, have to concern us. Every interpretation is a reinterpretation, which at least covertly addresses the question of relevance. No doubt that will be equally true here. The question of relevance will concern us more directly in our final section.

A dogmatic *locus* on the Christian life is not immediately concerned with ethics as such, with specific counsel about actions to be taken in concrete situations, or about how to live amid the ambiguities, pressures, and boredoms of modern industrial society. We are concerned rather with the foundation for ethics, with the tree and its roots rather than the fruit, to use the biblical image. This too is apparent from our question "Shall we sin the more that grace may abound?" The answer to that question lays bare what the Scriptures call the "heart." The way one answers it reveals one's "soul." This is difficult to express in any one concept. It has to do with one's *vision*, with what one ultimately sees and hopes for, with one's answer to the question "Why go on?" It has to do with one's basic hold on life itself, with one's faith. This does not mean that the question of the "fruit," the question of ethics, is at all unimportant. The good tree will bear good fruit. But we are concerned here with what makes the tree good so that it *can* bear fruit. The Christian life must be seen as a faith, a vision, a hope, a basic hold on life effected by God's act in Jesus Christ, which leads subsequently to attitudes and actions in the world for others.

On the deepest level the question of relevance has to do with this faith, vision, and hope. The question is whether this vision today has power to claim people in the face of alternative visions: Marxism, atheism, existentialist "absurdity," nihilism, tragic despair (tinged, perhaps, by religious or "Christian"

11 / CHRISTIAN LIFE

ideas), or whatever. The question is not merely about the relevance of this or that particular formulation—whether, for instance, modern people still suffer from guilt or are afflicted with an "introspective conscience"—but whether the Christian vision can be presented with power to claim allegiance. The question is whether there is such power in the Christian view itself and whether it can be expressed without distortion. One might be tempted, of course, to make Christianity relevant by borrowing from or accommodating "the spirit of the times." That would be to sell one's soul to gain the world. This *locus* is written under the conviction that such strategy is neither honest nor wise. The power to claim people today must arise from the Christian message itself. Only thus can its relevance be established.

1
Justification

The death of the old and the resurrection of the new, by the word of justification in proclamation and sacrament, are the basis of the Christian life. Justification by faith in the divine word cannot readily be synthesized with thinking in terms of law, process, and progress, but must be seen as an eschatological event, as new life from death, in which the depth of human sin is unmasked at the same time as righteousness is granted. Law is ended as "the way," driven out of the conscience by Christ, and given its proper function in exposing sin, unbelief, and mistrust. To foster the Christian life, the proclamation of the church must do this, not just describe it.

JUSTIFICATION BY GRACE

"You, therefore, must be perfect, as your heavenly Father is perfect" (Matt. 5:48). "It is written, 'You shall be holy, for I am holy'" (1 Pet. 1:16). "A new commandment I give to you, that you love one another; even as I have loved you" (John 13:34). Such passages set in no uncertain terms the goal of the Christian life: perfection, holiness, and love. One could no doubt add others. But what do the exhortations mean?

The second part of each statement is the catch: "as your heavenly Father is perfect," "for I am holy," and "as I have loved you." We could find (and have found) it easy enough to set up schemes to realize in our own fashion the first part: the perfection, the holiness, the love. It is questionable, however, whether such schemes reach the goal set in the second part. Human schemes of perfection, holiness, and love are substituted for God's own perfection, holiness, and love. God's perfection, holiness, and love are *given* in God's action *for us* in Jesus Christ. To be perfect as God is perfect, holy as God is holy, to love as God loves, poses therefore a different problem than that to which our schemes are directed. God's perfection, holiness, and love pass ours by, going in the opposite direction. God and the sinner are truly and tragically like two ships that pass in the night. Therewith the problem of explicating the *Christian* life is exposed. Can these ships ever meet?

The problem comes sharply into focus around the idea of justification. The

11 / CHRISTIAN LIFE

very term suggests a legal or moral process. It implies a standard, a law, according to which the justice in question is to be measured. The natural and inevitable human tendency is to think of the relationship to God in terms of such schemes and standards. There is a "way" to God: to perfection, to holiness, to righteousness and justice. If the way could be traversed successfully, we would arrive at the goal and be "saved." The sinner, though fallen, has a conscience, a *synteresis*, a voice or remnant of the moral law within that impels along the way. Perhaps the conscience is weak or damaged by the fall, but it is there and in need only of proper education and sensitizing. Law conceived as the way, as the eternal standard of justice, holiness, and righteousness, reinforced by the demands of the conscience, provides the basic logical and structural framework of the relationship to God.

Throughout this *locus* "law" is to be taken in a functional rather than a material sense. "The law" in this sense is demand, that voice which "accuses," as the reformers put it, arising from anywhere and everywhere, insisting that we do our duty and fulfill our being. Anything which does that exercises the function or "office" of the law. Law is not a specifiable set of propositions, but is one way communication functions when we are alienated, estranged, and bound. This understanding of law transcends the usual kind of argument, as when, for instance, it is maintained that "law" should be understood as "Torah," a gracious gift in the covenant rather than a harsh imposition, or when it is said that Paul misunderstood the law. Such exegetical considerations, important in their own right, are not decisive for the question at hand. It makes no difference at the outset, therefore, whether "the law" involved is biblical, the natural law, the law of being, the law of Christ, or the faces of starving children on the television screen. It is the way the communication functions, its "use," that matters. The assumption we fallen humans make is that the law is the way, that we can be saved by response to a demand, by "the works of the law." We assume we can end the voice by acceding to its demands.

The question about justification meets this universal human assumption head-on. No doubt that is one reason discussion of justification is central in the dogmatic treatment of Christian life. Here the issue is joined in the clearest fashion. How are we justified? How are we made just? How does the voice end? What does God's act in Christ have to do with it? Taken literally according to common meaning, the term "justification" would mean "make just" (*iustum facere*) according to the law or standard in question. The natural assumption is that justification is some sort of movement from the state of being unjust to the state of being just, from the state of sin or guilt to the state of righteousness. Taking the law as the way leads to interpreting justification as change, progress, process.

JUSTIFICATION

The New Testament, however, throws up insurmountable roadblocks along such a way. Taken as a whole, the New Testament is a sustained polemic against "the righteous." It is impossible to avoid that fact. It is not simply Paul who conducts the polemic, even if he brings it to its sharpest and most penetrating focus. Everywhere the idea that we are justified by our efforts under the law is attacked. The attack apparently stems from Jesus himself. He came to call not the righteous but sinners. The publican, not the Pharisee, was justified. Virtually everything Jesus did was (rightly) interpreted by the "righteous" as polemic against them, who thought of the law as a way to God. It is indeed true that only the righteous can enjoy fellowship with God. But, according to the New Testament, the righteousness available before God can never be reached by the law, by responding to the demand. Paul was only bringing into sharp focus the entire New Testament message when he declared justification to be by faith in God's act in Christ. Justification is solely God's doing.

> But now the righteousness of God has been manifested apart from the law, although the law and the prophets bear witness to it, the righteousness of God through faith in Jesus Christ for all who believe. For there is no distinction; since all have sinned and fall short of the glory of God, they are justified by his grace as a gift, through the redemption which is in Christ Jesus, whom God put forward as an expiation by his blood, to be received by faith. This was to show God's righteousness, because in his divine forbearance he had passed over former sins; it was to prove at the present time that he himself is righteous and that he justifies him who has faith in Jesus. (Rom. 3:21–26)

Exegetes may argue that Paul's statements on the matter are the most extreme and radical in the New Testament and that one can find milder ones elsewhere. Such speculation may be of exegetical interest but cannot be determinative for dogmatics. Dogmatics must be able to cope with the most sharply focused and radical statements. If Paul is the most radical, then dogmatics must cope with Paul and cannot search for milder forms merely to soothe its tastes; the so-called plurality of the New Testament message cannot be used dogmatically to escape the offense of its most radical formulations. Justification comes entirely apart from the law. Everyone is in exactly the same situation: *All* have sinned and fallen short of the glory of God. God shows *God's own* righteousness in justifying those who have faith in the crucified and risen Jesus. Justification is by such faith alone.

What does such justification mean, and what is its impact on our lives? It is immediately apparent that its proclamation is a severe challenge to our natural assumptions about justification as a "making just" according to our schemes of justice. It radically questions our ideas of progress and process. Paul was blunt about it. Justification by faith in Jesus means death and resur-

11 / CHRISTIAN LIFE

rection. It means death to the sinner, the old being "under the law," and life and freedom to the new. The being who thinks in terms of law dies in order that the believer might arise.

> For I through the law died to the law, that I might live to God. I have been crucified with Christ; it is no longer I who live, but Christ who lives in me; and the life I now live in the flesh I live by faith in the Son of God, who loved me and gave himself for me. I do not nullify the grace of God; for if justification were through the law, then Christ died to no purpose. (Gal. 2:19–21)

Such death and newness of life are Paul's answer also to the faint of heart who fear that radical leave-taking from law and its schemes will lead to immorality and license.

> Are we to continue in sin that grace may abound? By no means! How can we who died to sin still live in it? Do you not know that all of us who have been baptized into Christ Jesus were baptized into his death? We were buried therefore with him by baptism into death, so that as Christ was raised from the dead by the glory of the Father, we too might walk in newness of life. (Rom. 6:1–4)

The Christian life begins with baptism, with dying in Christ to the old life under law so that we might walk in newness of life, the life of faith. Paul knows that justification by faith raises the most radical questions. He puts the questions in the most radical form himself: Is the law bad? Shall we sin that grace may abound? Paul knows that unless the question is raised, we have not yet glimpsed what justification by faith is about and have not yet broken from the law. Paul also knows that one *cannot* answer the question by a return to the law. Shall we sin that grace may abound? One cannot say, "No, of course not, because there is still, after all, the law. . . ." One can only go straight ahead: You have died. How can you still manage to sin? Justification by faith means death and newness of life, a break with the past and a new beginning.

The history of the tradition shows that the church has had difficulty coping with the radicality of its own message at this point. It is fair to say, by way of generalization, that there were two attempts prior to the Reformation. One, found in the Greek fathers and in Eastern Christianity, works with the idea of divinization (*theōsis*): the elevation of the human into the sphere of the divine union with God. The other, characteristic of the Latin fathers and Western Christianity, works with ideas of law, satisfaction, and justice: becoming righteous with the aid of divine grace. In many ways the first, the idea of divinization bears the most promise and is closer to the views that eventually surfaced in the sixteenth-century Reformation. This is so because such a view stresses the radical newness that comes through participation in the divine, the creative "energies" unleashed for salvation in the resurrection of the crucified one. The human person is assumed into the internal life of God.[1] We are new beings in Christ by participation in the power of his life, apart from the law, and not so much by becoming good through our own efforts.

However, there are indications that even with such formulations the radicality of the New Testament message can be obscured and betrayed. It is not always clear in the Greek fathers whether the God in whom one participates is actually the *triune* God of the Scriptures rather than the God of, say, Plato or Plotinus. The human subject to be divinized seems to be a continuously existing substance who does not die to be raised in the incarnate, dying, and rising Son but is rather rescued *from* death to be gradually divinized. Thus divinization can all too easily come to be looked on as another process of gradual transformation, according to an ontological scheme not seriously interrupted by the *death* of Christ and the consequent *death* of the sinner, the Old Being. Where that is the case, the God in whom we participate is not the triune God but the God of the philosophers.

The manner in which the theology of divinization can then simply become another theology of works becomes evident when it is confronted with questions of morality and ethics—the perennial test case where bad conscience forces true colors into view. The following can suffice to say what happens:

> It is important to note that according to the Eastern Christian theology, the Incarnation means an ontological (i.e., physical and appropriate to human nature and being) superelevation, which, however, must also express itself ethically. Therefore good deeds of man are a *conditio sine qua non* of divinization. Thus a moral life and divinization are the two inseparable poles of Redemption. If one of them is given up, the whole structure necessarily collapses. Thus divinization entails very many existential, moral, ontological and inter-Personal implications, as well as inseparable unity of ontology and ethics.[2]

If such is the case, the theology of divinization is not decisively different from similar systems that developed in the West. Where the incursion of the divine into the human does not mean the actual death of the old and the resurrection of the new, the tendency is to set up a way of salvation that is simply a synthesis with human religious ambition.

In the West, with its concern for law, righteousness, and justice, the problems of coping with the radicality of the New Testament message have been more overt only because the theology was less subtle. The basic presupposition has been that the law is the eternal standard according to which justice, righteousness, and salvation are measured and gained. Yet the task of squaring

11 / CHRISTIAN LIFE

this presupposition with justification by faith, by grace alone, has caused continuous uneasiness. From the beginning, the tradition has wavered between rigorism and laxness, asceticism and indulgence. Unable to dislodge the law as the way, the Western tradition has attempted the impossible: to combine justification by faith with moral progress according to law. Instead of being a justification *apart* from the law, God's act is reinterpreted as a justification *according* to the law. God's act in Christ is looked on as providing "grace" to enable one to do the law and, at least in some respect, acquire merit toward salvation. Grace becomes a thing of some sort—even if of a very "spiritual" sort—a power or virtue or habit that is infused to enable those who avail themselves of it to go the way demanded in the law. Since this kind of combination of law and grace has been dominant in the West, we shall concern ourselves predominantly with it in the remainder of our treatment.

The movement toward combination reaches its finest expression in the great medieval syntheses like that of Thomas Aquinas. Justification is described as a *movement* from a *terminus a quo* (starting point) to a *terminus ad quem* (goal), that is, as a process. The movement is comprised of (a) the infusion of grace, (b) the movement of the free will toward God in faith, (c) a movement of the free will in recoil from sin, and (d) the remission of guilt.[3] The difficulty in defining justification as such a process is apparent from the scheme itself. Where does justification occur? With the infusion of grace or with the remission of sins? Aquinas tries to escape the difficulty by saying that the movement "could be called" justification because every movement takes its character from its end, the *terminus ad quem*. Furthermore, the movement is to be understood as instantaneous temporally. Nevertheless, it can be understood only as indeed a movement, a change in the moral subject from sin to righteousness, effected by the infusion of grace.[4]

The dogmatic distinctions only thinly veil the systematic problem involved in attempts to combine justification by grace with the idea of moral movement or process. In its simplest form the problem may be stated thus: If justification conceived as forgiveness comes at the beginning of the process, the process is superfluous (why undertake the process if one already has been given what is expected?); if, on the other hand, justification comes at the end of the process, justification is superfluous (why the need to be made or declared just if one has become so?). Both the divine act of justification and the human process of becoming just according to law cannot simultaneously be real. The attempt to put them together in the same scheme can only have the effect of rendering one of them superfluous or fictional. Given the entrenchment of law, conscience, and process, we need not waste time guessing which. History has relieved us of the necessity to speculate in any case. Law has remained the reality, the structural and determining factor for the Christian life; grace has become more or less fictional, a matter of pious talk whose relevance is eventually questionable.

The outcome of the attempted synthesis has been disastrous for the Christian life. Grace functions only as an anti-Pelagian codicil to make the scheme verbally Christian.[5] Our work and "cooperation" are the essential thing, even though we cover our tracks by *saying*, "Of course, it is all by grace." Every Christian dogmatic claims to hold justification by faith. Even Pelagius did so. It is, after all, a biblical doctrine, and one can hardly afford to deny it. But it is effectively reduced to a mere verbalism. Pelagius was more honest than the subsequent tradition when he denied the idea of a supernatural "substantial" grace altogether and equated grace with natural endowment and teaching.

Further, the attempt to synthesize justification by faith with the scheme of law and process can only mean that grace so conceived will tend to undercut and militate against works. Again, Pelagius was the one to see this clearly and to move against such grace. The church, of course, could not follow Pelagius since that would have meant the demise of grace altogether. The result is a Christian life suspended between grace *and* works, not knowing which way to turn. The church has vacillated between rigorism and laxness, legalism and liberty, asceticism and eudaemonism, self-denial and self-indulgence. The problem was apparent already in the early enthusiasts and gnostics. One could go either way. If law is the way, being Christian could mean that everything the law demanded was given—that the "resurrected life" or gnostic "spirituality" was already achieved—so that one could henceforth do as one pleased. Grace then makes works unnecessary. Indeed, one might further one's cause by a kind of negative asceticism: wearing out "the flesh" by profligate living, a kind of moral suicide practiced, apparently, by some gnostics. On the other hand, being Christian could mean just the opposite. Grace cannot displace the legal process. Grace is at best a help to fulfill the law; judgment is still outstanding. An ascetic life is the best insurance. One purges the flesh to rescue the spirit. One may attribute whatever success one has to "grace," but the works are primary. Grace becomes a verbalism, a fiction.

The vacillation has been apparent from the early schisms—Novatianism, Donatism, Montanism—to the present day.[6] The church knows it is commissioned to preach forgiveness and justification, but seems never able to have a clear conscience in doing so. Rigorist schismatics and "holiness" movements incarnate the bad conscience created when "too much" forgiveness or grace vitiates the resolve under law. So the church opts, willy-nilly, for a place in between. It pronounces forgiveness but demands penance. It forgives the eternal aspect of sin, but not the temporal. It places itself in the position of having to dole out grace in portions that it deems will not be harmful to the legalistic process. It becomes the administrator *over* grace, dispensing merits from its treasury to the deserving. The rhetoric about the Christian life piles up—often in innocent and well-meaning ways—to ensure the process against failure.

JUSTIFICATION BY FAITH

The attempt to synthesize justification and the legal process works only as long as it is not seriously questioned, that is, as long as the conscience it awakens is not too honest. The Christian life it fosters can be all too much like the emperor's new clothes in Hans Christian Andersen's tale. Its righteousness exists largely in the imagination of subjects afraid to question the authorities and risk exposing their own failure or inability to play the game. When someone naive or honest enough to speak the truth appears, the charade is over. This is what happens when reformation, most often under the influence of the radical New Testament gospel, occurs in the church. Reformation has happened and must happen again and again. Since the Reformation of the sixteenth century affords the classic example, we shall use that as the starting point for dismantling the synthesis between justification and law, suggesting "justification by faith" as an alternative basis for the Christian life.

Martin Luther experienced the failure of the synthesis in his own conscience. He applied himself to every resource to get the grace necessary to improve, but found in all honesty that nothing worked. The rhetoric just did not match the reality. When grace is a thing, a "virtue" supposedly available by prescribed channels, and when one is supposed to be justified (improved) by such grace, one is then simply excluded if one is honest enough to admit that the improvement has not, in fact, occurred. One can come to either of two conclusions, and perhaps to a bit of both. Either one has not turned the key to the channels of grace (one has not worked hard enough, applied oneself enough) or, more serious yet, God, the giver, the electing one, has simply decided not to give it. The "terrors of predestination" are the ultimate outcome of the attempt to synthesize God's act of justification with human progress under law. Unable to verify progress, one can only conclude that God has turned thumbs down.

The system turns against the seeker precisely at the point of greatest need. When justification means improvement and grace is the power to improve, "justification by grace" is potentially and finally very bad news for sinners. Regardless of the degree to which the rhetoric stresses the primacy of grace, one is thrown back on one's own resources. "Cooperation" and improvement under the system means that *everything* eventually depends on the human contribution. One can say that grace goes before, during, and after the action. One can say that grace provides 99.44 percent or even 100 percent of the power. It makes no difference. Everything will hinge on what the sinner is supposed to do. The synthesis is useless when it is needed most. A grace rendered fictional cannot help. That is what Luther discovered.

The assertion of "justification *by faith*" in the sixteenth-century Reformation can be understood only if it is clearly seen as a complete break with "justification *by grace*," viewed according to the synthesis we have been describing, as a complete break with the attempt to view justification as a movement according to a given standard or law, either natural or revealed. For the reformers, justification is "solely" a divine act. It is a divine judgment. It is an imputation. It is unconditional. All legal and moral schemes are shattered. Such justification comes neither at the beginning nor at the end of a movement; rather, it establishes an entirely new situation. Since righteousness comes by imputation only, it is absolutely not a movement on our part, either with or without the aid of what was previously termed "grace." The judgment can be heard and grasped only by faith. Indeed, the judgment creates and calls forth the faith that hears and grasps it. One will mistake the reformation point if one does not see that justification "by faith" is in the first instance precisely a polemic *against* justification "*by grace*" according to the medieval scheme. Grace would have to be completely redefined before the word could be safely used in a reformation sense.[7]

Justification by divine imputation is grace for sinners. Indeed, we can be candidates for such righteousness only if we are sinners—and completely so. For Luther that meant that in place of all human schemes of movement from sin to righteousness we must put the absolute simultaneity of sin and righteousness. Imputed righteousness as a divine act brings with it the *simul iustus et peccator* (simultaneously justified and a sinner) as a simultaneity of total states. We must take care in grasping what is being said here. The *simul iustus et peccator* is not a conclusion drawn from a bad conscience under the legal system; it is not resignation to the fact that no matter how hard we try we never quite make it. That would put us back in the same scheme as before. The confession that we are sinners at the same time as we are justified is a conclusion drawn from the divine action, the divine imputation and forgiveness. The simultaneity of sin and righteousness as total states is the *actual* situation revealed by the divine act of justification. The divine act itself shatters all human presumption about progress and process. God has something else in mind.

This is readily apparent from a look at Luther's lectures on Romans, where the *simul iustus et peccator* is first set forth. Commenting on Rom. 4:1–7, Luther maintains that imputation of righteousness to Abraham and its equation with forgiveness of sins can be understood only in terms of the

11 / CHRISTIAN LIFE

simultaneity of sin and righteousness.[8] If God *imputes* righteousness, if God simply *forgives* sin, then we *must* be sinners. It would make no sense for God to impute righteousness if we were partially or wholly righteous already. God would be wasting breath. Thus in order for *God* to be "justified when he speaks and true when he judges" we must be sinners *at the same time* as God's speaking makes us righteous. One is justified by hearing and believing God's judgment, and such hearing and believing lead to the realization and confession that we *are* sinners. We are unmasked by the overpowering divine judgment. The love given reveals, at the same time, how unlovely we are. Only on the strength of the love given could we see and face the truth simultaneously.

Luther's understanding of the *simul* is a radical attack on human ideas of progress according to the law. At the outset in the commentary on Romans he suggests a major revision of the fundamental scheme. "The exodus of the people of Israel has for a long time been interpreted to signify the transition from vice to virtue. But one should, rather, interpret it as the way from virtue to the grace of Christ." The Christian life is not an exodus from vice *to* virtue, but *from* virtue, to the grace of Christ! "Because," Luther continues, "virtues are often the greater and worse faults the less they are regarded as such and the more powerfully they subject to themselves all human affections beyond all other goods."[9] The more the pursuit of virtue succeeds in absorbing all desires and affections, the more dangerous it becomes.

Thus, for Luther the most vital enemy of the righteousness of God is not so much the "godless sinner" as the "righteous" who are absorbed in their own ideas of law and moral progress. Such theologians think, Luther says, "*ad modum Aristotelis*" (after the fashion of Aristotle), where the gaining of righteousness means acquiring virtue and removing sin.[10] For such thinking, imputation could only be a kind of legal fiction or manner of speaking, due to the incompleteness of the process or "in view of its end." Imputation is a kind of temporary loan until righteousness is *really* earned. Against this pattern, Luther sets an entirely different sort of thinking: a thinking "*ad modum scripturae*" (in the scriptural mode), in which the divine imputation is the creative reality which by the very fact of imputation unmasks its opposition, the reality and totality of sin, *at the same time*. If God is to be justified when he speaks, all thinking, speaking, and judging *ad modum Aristotelis* must be banished from theology. Before the divine tribunal no saints, only sinners, appear.[11] Justification by divine imputation creating faith is a complete break with the exodus from vice to virtue because the divine imputation is fully as opposed to human righteousness as it is to unrighteousness.

The divine imputation *makes* us sinners at the same time as it declares us righteous. Luther was insistent that at the outset these be understood as total states. This requires a radical reorientation in thinking about the Christian life. It destroys our usual notions of moral progress. The point is that we *can* be saved *only* by listening to and believing God and God's judgment. We can be saved only by faith in what God says about us and our final destiny. Viewed *coram deo* (before God), our virtues are no better than our vices. The difference is only a matter of taste. Some like vice and some like virtue; both do what *they* like. And virtue may be the more dangerous precisely because it gains everyone's approval. Sin is revealed by the absolutely unconditional nature of the divine action. Sin is revealed as a totality, not a partiality: of our virtues as well as our vices. We begin to see that the attempt to gain virtue was fully as reprehensible as the pursuit of vice. One attempt is no more inspired by the love of God than the other. When we begin to believe God and God's judgment, sin is unmasked simultaneously. When God says, "I forgive you. I declare you just for Jesus' sake," sin is unmasked and attacked at once. To be justified by faith is to believe *God's* word, God's judgment, and to begin to realize that only that word will save. The divine judgment, the divine word, is a totality, complete, unconditional, creative in and of itself. It unmasks and attacks its opposite. When one recognizes by the power of the divine judgment that one is *simul iustus et peccator*, the real battle for the Christian life can begin. Sin as a total state can be fought only by faith in total imputed righteousness. Anything less would lead to hypocrisy or despair.

Justification by faith always appears dangerous, because of our incurable tendency to think in terms of law, virtue, and moral progress. Church people, religious people and their teachers, are especially inclined to think that way. Hence justification by faith generally has most difficulty precisely in the church. It is more apparent there than elsewhere, perhaps, that we live "under" the law. Hence the church always seems to stumble when it comes to this doctrine. It fails to realize that this incurable disease is precisely what we have to be saved *from*.

Nevertheless, the sentiment that justification by faith is dangerous is, in a way other than expected, quite right. That is because justification by divine unconditional decree spells death to the old being. Like the demons who recognized Jesus, the "old Adam" rightly senses that in justification the end breaks in—the end to the pursuit either of vice or virtue. That is precisely why it is so feared. Resistance takes all sorts of guises. Justification by faith is said to be "too cheap," to lead to moral laxity and ethical quietism, to erode human responsibility. Justification is only for people with morbid and introspective consciences, not for the healthy and robust. The ruses are all quite true, of course, as long as one accepts the old Adam's premises and tries to subordinate grace to law. But in essence they are nothing but attempts to stave off the death of the old. They are defense mechanisms against the

11 / CHRISTIAN LIFE

grace of the One who died and rose for us, defense mechanisms against justification for his sake. Justification is dangerous indeed. It spells death to the old. But only then will there be newness of life.

Somehow the church has rarely realized the radical nature and power of this message of justification. It has trembled on the brink of freedom and then turned back. The reason must lie in our incurable tendency to think in terms of "something to do." If "doing the law" is hard enough, how can we die? Language about death and new life is *terra incognita* left largely to ascetics and mystics. Death of the old comes to be looked on as a particularly strenuous exercise in "self-denial" and "purgation of the flesh," the ultimate in spiritual exercises, preparatory to final "mystical vision." But that is simply to turn death into another law. Spirituality becomes the art of getting as close to suicide as one dares.

The failure has been to realize that the divine pronouncement of justification for Jesus' sake *is* the death and the new life. To believe the message of justification *is* to die and be raised to newness of life. Justification as imputation for Jesus' sake declares precisely that there is nothing to do. It is unconditional. To die is to be put in the situation of being able to do nothing, to be absolutely passive, to wait for the word: "Awake, O sleeper, and arise from the dead, and Christ shall give you light" (Eph. 5:14). The word of justification is precisely that kind of word. It kills the old exactly because it pronounces that there is nothing to do. Faith is to believe that and to be raised from the destruction of all our schemes, to something new. Faith is to be delivered, to participate in the exodus from virtue to the grace of God.

Therefore faith that believes the justifying act of God *is* death and resurrection. It is to be delivered from life under the law to something utterly new. Paul does not present death as one more thing to do. He simply announces the accomplished fact:

> We are convinced that one has died for all; therefore all have died. (2 Cor. 5:14)

> We were buried therefore with him by baptism into death, so that as Christ was raised from the dead by the glory of the Father, we too might walk in newness of life. (Rom. 6:4)

> I through the law died to the law, that I might live to God. I have been crucified with Christ; it is no longer I who live, but Christ who lives in me; and the life I now live in the flesh I live by faith in the Son of God, who loved me and gave himself for me. (Gal. 2:19–20)

The divine judgment flowing from the death and resurrection of Jesus, the word of forgiveness and justification pronounced for his sake, *is* the doing of death and resurrection to us. The faith created by that word *is* the death and resurrection. Luther knew it too:

> "I am crucified with Christ." Paul adds this word because he wants to explain how the law is devoured by the law [Christ]. If Christ is crucified to the law, so also am I. How? *Through faith*. I am crucified to the law; I have nothing more to do with it, because I am crucified to it and vice versa, because I have died with Christ *through grace itself and faith (per ipsam gratiam et fidem)*. . . . *If you believe in Christ then you are co-crucified through faith spiritually*, just as he is dead to the law, to death, etc. Paul is not speaking here of the *imitatio*, which means to *become* co-crucified. That happens in the flesh, as Peter (1 Pet. 2:21) says: "Christ suffered for you and left you an example that you should follow in his steps." Here Paul does not speak of that crucifixion, but of the primary co-crucifixion by which the devil and death are crucified. Where? In Christ, not in me. That crucifixion by which I die to the law is resurrection, because Christ has killed my death and bound up my law. *And I believe that*.[12]

To believe in Christ *is* precisely to die to the old and be raised to the new. It is not an action, an "imitating" (though that comes later "in the flesh"), but simply an "undergoing," a being slain and raised up by the word. It must not be looked on, however, as figurative or symbolic. The death inflicted by the word of justification which reduces us to nothing is the real death, the true spiritual death. It is so because it is the death of sin, the death of all defiance against the God who will have mercy. It is the death of death, because the believer survives in Christ. "It is no longer I who live, but Christ who lives in me." Indeed, Luther can say that the only thing to which the word "death" really and truly applies is sin. Because of Christ, sin will die and never return. Only of sin can that be said.[13] The other death, the physical death we must die, Luther calls *das Todlein* (the little death).[14] The spiritual death encountered in the word of justification is the real death. To survive that is to be raised to newness of life. Rejection of it, refusal of the totality and the reality of it, is to allow the old Adam to continue his own way to whatever death awaits him. We *can* be justified only by faith.

If justification thus conceived brings death and newness of life, it is basically an eschatological act. The breakup of the legal scheme and accompanying ideas of human progress means that a new reality is introduced: the eschatological kingdom, the new being in Christ.

> That realm of judgment in which the situation of our being as sinner is so totally depotentiated is nothing other than the kingdom of the last things. In the final analysis it is this and the coming aeon that stand opposed to each other in the *simul iustus et peccator*. The person in Christ is the person of the new age. The judgment of God which proclaims this person as established over against the opposing earthly situation is likewise the anticipatory proclamation of the new world. The faith which receives and grasps that new status in Christ is an eschatological event; it is ever and anew the step out of this world of the visible,

tangible, given reality, the world in which the *totus peccator* is the reality, into the eschaton.¹⁵

Justification as death and resurrection, as an eschatological event, means that the question about the Christian life must be posed anew, from a radically different vantage point. If we are robbed of our plans and ideals under the law, we seem suddenly to have lost our reason for being. The ground has been cut out from under our feet. If justification means suddenly being told there is nothing we have to do, if we come up against just that death, what are we to do? We must see that this is a real question. It is possible that we might not survive such an act of justification. It could ruin us. It is from this vantage point that Paul's question, *the* question about the Christian life, is launched: Shall we sin the more that grace may abound? What shall we then do? What is the way forward from here? We shall have to take up these questions in our subsequent chapters. Before we do, we must begin to ask about the place of law in the light of this gospel of justification.

LAW, GOSPEL, AND CONSCIENCE

Justification by faith "apart from the works of the law" is a radical questioning of the place of law in the dogmatic system. Law is disenfranchised as a way of salvation.

> The righteousness of God has been manifested apart from law, although the law and the prophets bear witness to it, the righteousness of God through faith in Jesus Christ for all who believe. (Rom. 3:21-22)
>
> For Christ is the end of the law, that every one who has faith may be justified. (Rom. 10:4)
>
> If a law had been given which could make alive, then righteousness would indeed be by the law. (Gal. 3:21)
>
> Now before faith came, we were confined under law, kept under restraint until faith should be revealed. . . . But now that faith has come, we are no longer under a custodian; for in Christ Jesus you are all sons of God, through faith. (Gal. 3:23, 25)¹⁶

Grasped by the gospel, one sees immediately that the law is not the way and that no synthesis is possible. There is an end and a new beginning. The slave has become a son and heir (Gal. 4:1-7). A death has occurred, so that the wife is no longer bound by law to the husband but is free to remarry without being charged with adultery. "Likewise, my brethren, you have died to the law through the body of Christ so that you may belong to another, to him who has been raised from the dead. . . . We are discharged from the law, dead to that which held us captive" (Rom. 7:1–6).

Such an eschatological gospel raises shattering questions about law, about the basic structures and presuppositions of life "in this age." It is important to see that it is the unconditional, eschatological nature of the gospel itself that does this. The particular makeup and problems of individuals and their conscience—of a Paul, an Augustine, a Luther, or whomever—have nothing to do with the matter. The new marks the end of the old. One cannot put new wine in old skins. Anyone grasped by the gospel will have to put the questions. Paul put them himself with a radicality and seriousness hardly surpassable. "What then shall we say? That the law is sin?" (Rom. 7:7). "Is the law then against the promises of God?" (Gal. 3:21). "Do we then overthrow the law by this faith?" (Rom. 3:31).

Paul answers his own questions in each instance with a resounding negative: "By no means!" "On the contrary, we uphold the law" (Rom. 3:31). Paul can answer with that resounding negative, however, only because in the light of the gospel the place and function of the law are fundamentally redefined and because in the redefinition the law is actually strengthened and established. The law was "added because of transgressions, till the offspring should come to whom the promise had been made" (Gal. 3:19). It is not the way itself; that is precisely why it is not against the promises. The promises are the way; they alone "make alive"; they alone are intended to do so. "If a law had been given which could make alive, then righteousness would indeed be by the law" (Gal. 3:21). Then indeed the law and the promises would be diametrically opposed, and the promise would destroy law or vice versa. "If justification were through the law, then Christ died to no purpose" (Gal. 2:21).

The law has a function quite other than the promise. The law was given to make apparent the trespass, to reveal and convict of sin, to expose the fundamental lostness and incompleteness of life without promise, life without God, without future. "Before faith came, we were confined under the law, kept under restraint until faith should be revealed. So that the law was our custodian until Christ came, that we might be justified by faith" (Gal. 3:23–24). The law makes apparent our incompleteness; it "confines," shuts in, does the work of the custodian, making plain that the goal has not been reached. The law makes sin apparent. "If it had not been for the law, I should not have known sin" (Rom. 7:7).

This functional description of the law must not be understood in a psychologizing sense, as though it were merely a matter of an overly sensitive "introspective conscience" being afflicted and convicted by the law so that one is convinced that one needs salvation. That would mean only that the

11 / CHRISTIAN LIFE

system based on law and conscience remained intact: One is convicted of one's vices and misdeeds under the law and driven to despair over the inability to be virtuous so that one cries for the help of grace in one's *own* quest. In all that the old Adam remains quite intact—shaken, perhaps even "despairing," but still intact. The cry of the conscience-stricken old Adam is still just the last grasp at the self and its quest for virtue. If one cannot make it on one's own, perhaps one can commandeer "help" by being sorry enough. Repentance is looked on as an act—the last attempt of the old Adam to rescue itself from shipwreck. Consequently, such repentance may well be only for the morbid and overly sensitive failures of the system, not for the robust.

Such psychologizing does not get at the question of *sin*. It may reveal a few sins; but they are mostly peccadilloes, the little vices or hindrances that frustrate our quests for virtue. Righteousness is still by the law, and Christ still died to no purpose. When Paul, and all serious reformers in the church, said that without the law sin would be unknown, something much more radical was meant. The claim must be seen *theologically* precisely within the context of the argument about justification by faith. When Paul, for instance, in Rom. 7:7ff., uses the law "You shall not covet" as an example, claiming that the very law awakened "all kinds of covetousness" in him, that is not to be understood merely in the psychological sense that prohibition feeds the fires of lust and desire for forbidden fruit. That hardly explains Paul's meaning when he goes on to say that sin, "finding opportunity in the commandment, wrought in me all kinds of covetousness" and that "apart from the law sin lies dead." Paul can hardly mean that without the law he would not lust after this or that and that such sin comes into being only when the law forbids it. The point rather is that the law, the prohibition of vice, even when heeded, leads only to the pursuit of virtue *apart from the promise*, in defiance of the gift of mercy. I am not cured of covetousness by the law at all. Now I covet virtue; I embark on the path of self-righteousness, self-salvation. Sin as refusal of God's mercy, of God's justification for Jesus' sake, is awakened precisely by the law. The law tempts me to go it by myself.

The law, therefore, exposes *sin*, not just sins. Not just our little failures over which we might despair in our covetousness of virtue are uncovered, but sin itself: the quest of self-salvation and whatever success we may think we have achieved. What is revealed is that sin dwells in us, that we are "sold" to it, and cannot escape. Our failures as well as our successes are only different kinds of covetousness. That is why Paul can say, "Apart from the law sin lies dead" and "I was once alive apart from the law, but when the commandment came, *sin* revived and I died; the very commandment which promised life proved to be death to me. For *sin*, finding opportunity in the commandment, deceived me and by it killed me" (Rom. 7:8-11). The law, given the fact of sin, could, even though it is holy, just, and good, do nothing but awaken more sin. And this is the function of the law, "in order that sin might be shown to be sin, and through the commandment might become sinful beyond measure." What is revealed thereby is not that the law is sin but precisely that the law is good and "spiritual" and that "I am carnal, sold under sin." I can will what is right and good, perhaps, but I simply cannot do it. For "under the law" I cannot escape being a covetous being. Sin dwells in me. Encounter with the law makes that plain. I can hear and approve, thus acknowledging the goodness of the law; but I can in no way do it. Thus, I do what I do not want, so "it is no longer I that do it, but sin which dwells within me"—the point being not that I am thereby exonerated, but that I am condemned because I see that the law is good while I am sold under sin.

Precisely in this manner the law is upheld and established. Once its function is seen in the light of the message of justification by faith, it stands forth in pristine clarity and beauty. Only when one tries to mix law and gospel, only when one thinks that righteousness comes by the law, will the law be disestablished. Then the law will have to be reduced to manageable proportions. One will have to indulge in casuistry to make it applicable to this or that case. One cannot let it sound. Instead of letting it function to reveal sin, it is used to mask sin. Thus it is watered down, tamed, neutralized.

The Reformation's insistence on justification by faith as an eschatological event brought with it a reassertion of the functional understanding of law. Luther especially insisted that law must be clearly distinguished from gospel and the proper "uses" of the law carefully explained. The distinction between law and gospel and the doctrine of the uses of law are of primary importance because they contain the key to virtually everything we want to say subsequently about the Christian life.

The basic distinction between law and gospel should be clear, since we have been talking about it all along. The law is not the way of salvation, and the gospel is something quite other than law. What good then is the law? Paul has provided an answer: The law functions to unmask sin. The sixteenth-century reformers started from this and extended it to a more formal doctrine of the "uses of the law." Since the first formulations, there has been debate about whether there are two or three uses of the law. Luther, it seems, generally spoke explicitly only of two,[17] whereas Melanchthon and later reformers spoke of three. They are, in chronological order rather than order of importance, (1) the political use (to restrain evil and preserve order), (2) the theological use (to expose and convict of sin), and (3) the use in the life of the reborn (to guide Christian living). Here we shall treat only the theological use (the most important for the Lutheran reformers), since that follows directly from our argument, reserving discussion of the others for subsequent chapters of our locus.

For Luther, as for Paul, justification by faith means complete reassessment

11 / CHRISTIAN LIFE

of the place of the law. If law and gospel were both ways of salvation, one or the other of them would have to give way. Since, however, gospel is the way, law must be seen in an entirely different light. Only thus will it be truly established. Its use is not to provide a way of salvation. It is not an eternal ontological structure providing a way to final reward, ratified and legitimated in the individual conscience. Its use is to reveal, unmask, and convict of sin. It says, "No exit!" It makes absolutely final the fact that we can be saved only by faith in the justifying word which comes quite apart from the law. *Lex semper accusat* (the law always accuses).[18]

Once again, this is not to be understood in a psychologizing way. Perhaps the most convenient way to get at the issue is to approach it in terms of the question of conscience. Invariably, in a world turned in on itself, talk about the accusing function of the law is psychologized in terms of the modern understanding of the introspective conscience. Karl Holl, the father of much modern Luther research, added to the difficulty by characterizing Luther's religion as a *Gewissensreligion* (religion of conscience).[19] Talk about the accusing function of the law was thereby drawn into the Kantian and Freudian trap. The picture is that conscience sets up a certain order, a "categorical imperative" perhaps, an unimpeachable "ought" under which we stand. This "ought" is then taken as the voice of God—or at least as an echo, however faint, thereof. When this voice awakens feelings of guilt, one is supposed to turn to Christ for relief. The accusing function of the law ostensibly fits this scheme. It produces the guilt by appealing to the conscience, so that one will turn to Christ. If Christ does not salve the conscience, one will then have to turn elsewhere: to the psychiatrist's couch, or to some other stratagem, to Nietzsche's posit of the "superman," to denial of "god" altogether, to nihilism, or whatever. Holl was wrong, however, as is every tendency to treat the issues involved here in this internalizing way. Christ becomes a mere "help" to make the system work. But then we only become further mired in the quicksands of conscience. That is the sad tale of the modern world.

The accusing function of law vis-à-vis the conscience must be seen in the light of what we have discovered about the gospel of justification by faith. The sin which the law reveals and convicts of is precisely the sin of the system proposed by "conscience": the idea that there *is* a way of virtue by which the accusing voice could be stilled. That such virtue is to be gotten with the aid of Christ makes little difference. The scheme is simply another variation of the attempt to synthesize law and gospel. A Christ who is supposed to help the system of virtue set up by conscience will never cease to accuse. Such a Christ will soon have to be brushed aside. This too the modern world knows well. The law which accuses in the true sense is a reflection of justification by faith. What it reveals is that there is no way, no system of virtue by which the voice of conscience can be stilled. Not even Christ or "grace" can help one acquire enough virtue to do that. The law reveals that not only our vices but also the very quest for virtue condemn us; for also the quest is a denial of the God who justifies by faith. The law accuses *finally*, so that there can be an end and a new beginning.

Conscience must be seen in the light of faith. As Luther put it, *Christ* must reign in the conscience. Law does not belong there at all. We can be saved only by simply believing the promise of God. One must just be still and listen. "Conscience" and the "stern voice of duty" will insist that this is "too cheap," "too easy," and a thousand other things, and summon us back to the battle for virtue. But that is just the problem. To succumb to that voice is precisely to lose: to lose Christ and return to the self. The law returns to the conscience. Sin finds its opportunity in the very goodness of the commandment, as Paul put it. One can be saved from sin for good works, *only* by faith. Christ and his unconditional grace must reign in the conscience. There *is* no other way. Everything must begin and end by simply trusting that word which says, "You are mine and I will never let you go."

The point, therefore, is that the law must be expelled from the conscience by Christ and kept out in faith. The law may have its legitimate place in ruling "the flesh"—that will be the subject of a later chapter—but only Christ belongs in the conscience. The person God intends is the person of faith who is one person, "one cake," with Christ.[20] One is delivered over to conscience in the moment one desires to be a personality in and of oneself. The helplessness of the sinner over against conscience is grounded in this insistence on being-for-oneself, in the modern conception of the personality as that which stands on and lives out of itself and its own internality. Left to oneself, one is at the mercy of conscience and its fickleness and unpredictability. Who knows when and in what form, however preposterous, it will attack? Conscience is in that sense indeed a reality, but a reality to which one is delivered only in separation from God. It is like the thirst of the alcoholic or the desire of the addict. It was meant for good, but since it has lost its good, it is arbitrary and insatiable and drives only to death.[21]

Conscience is not therefore just an "introspective" affair in which one is convicted by the inviolable voice of the law within and its eternal order. Conscience does not reflect order and constancy. It is insatiable, fickle, and arbitrary. It does not represent God's presence within us, it represents his absence, that we are left to ourselves. Conscience can unpredictably make mockery of any presumed freedom and emancipation. Who knows when some long-forgotten past indiscretion will return to haunt? When tragedy strikes or death draws near, what preposterous associations will not conscience make to answer our agonized and tormented "Why?" One may take steps to still the voice, usually by "works." But the voice is insatiable, especially in the face of death. "The world," Luther says, "becomes too small"[22] because of the conscience.

11 / CHRISTIAN LIFE

It is not just moral law within that afflicts because of conscience. The world, all of nature without, can close in on us. A favorite of Luther's which crops up again and again is the "rustling leaf" of Lev. 26:36.

> There is nothing smaller and more ignored than a dry leaf lying on the ground crawled on by worms and unable to protect itself from the dust. . . . But when the *moment* comes, horse, rider, lance, armor, king, princes, all the strength of the army and all power is frightened by its rustling. Are we not fine people? We have no fear of God's wrath and stand proudly, but yet are terrified and flee before the wrath of an impotent dry leaf. And such rustling of the leaf makes the world too small and becomes our wrathful God, whom we otherwise poo-poo and defy in heaven and on earth.[23]

Modern Protestantism and psychologism have denaturalized and moralized conscience so that it has nothing to do with the external world. That was not the case in Paul or the reformers. For Paul, to be under the law means to be trapped by "the elemental spirits of the universe" (Gal. 4:3). For Luther the rustling leaf strikes terror, because being cut off from God we do not have life in ourselves and something out there can take it from us. Cut off from God and delivered into the grip of conscience, we cannot dispose over our lives. The conscience thus reveals to us our "being-in" the world, a world which becomes too narrow for us. Conscience makes us refugees and exiles with no place to rest. Cut off from God, conscience drives us ultimately to wish that there were no God. Apart from Christ, atheism is finally the only hope.

It is in this light that one must see the accusing function of law. To recognize that law always accuses is precisely to assign it its proper use, to fix its limit and establish it. The law must not be admitted into unholy alliance with the conscience. It must not be confused with gospel. To do so is absolutely fatal. Between the work of the law and the promise of the gospel stand the cross and the resurrection, as the absolute dividing line. The law kills the old so that the new can be raised up. One is not cajoled by law and conscience into being a better person. One is put to death as the seeker after virtue, so that one may be raised to newness of life.

This eschatological vision marks the ultimate distinction between law and gospel. Law and its function are limited to the old age. Gospel is the coming of the new. Christ takes up his place in the conscience. Law is driven out to perform its proper work elsewhere.[24]

The functional understanding of law arises therefore from the eschatological nature of the gospel. Justification by faith apart from the works of the law means a fundamentally new view of reality. For the fallen world, the law represents reality, possibility, and opportunity, the only future the world knows or can conceive of, the only known scheme that works. That is why the world

JUSTIFICATION

clings to it so desperately. Justification by faith, however, proposes something else: the power of the in-breaking of God's kingdom in the midst of our time. The gospel, the sheer goodness and favor of God in Christ, God's complete unconditional mercy, gives possibility, not the law. The law was added "because of the trespass," the failure to see. The law accuses and kills. It reminds the world that it has fallen from its true destiny.

The law is not just "laws"; it is the voice arising from anywhere and everywhere, the whole creation "groaning in travail" waiting for the sons and daughters of God to appear (Rom. 8:19ff.). It is the "letter," the empty shell of a world that has lost the Spirit. It is like having to command someone to make love who has forgotten or never knew how. It is the darkness of a world that can no longer see and must have rules instead. It is the rustling of a leaf on a dark night which strikes terror and cries, "Where are you, Adam?" The very existence of law means that what it demands, what it points to, is gone; and no amount of law-preaching will bring it back. Insofar as law brings knowledge, it does not bring knowledge of the good, but knowledge of sin:

> ... not knowledge of that which should happen, but knowledge of that which has already happened; not knowledge of open, but of excluded and lost possibilities.... Whether one is a Jew, or a sinner, or heathen; whether pious or godless; every mode of existence is like others in spite of all difference in that it is existence under the law. Every religion or world view, even the atheistic—also a Christianity which has been perverted from faith to an ideology—has the common structure of law. They are all against faith. For "lex est negatio Christi" (law is the negation of Christ).[25]

The understanding of law ultimately has its roots deep in the hermeneutical problem of "letter and spirit," as it is reflected in the 2 Cor. 3:6 passage: "[God] has made us competent to be ministers of a new covenant, not in a written code [letter] but in the Spirit; for the written code [letter] kills, but the Spirit gives life." Previous tradition took this passage in a Platonizing sense, to mean that the letter was only an inadequate sign, an allegory of a deeper spiritual truth. To pass from letter to spirit was the way because to remain on the level of the letter would be to die in the land of mere "appearances," where all is decay and death.

Allegorical exegesis is built on this presupposition. The mere "literal" history must be translated into "spiritual truth," into eternal verities, doctrines, and laws (above all, laws). That "the letter kills" means that the letter is inadequate, partial, a secret code to a deeper meaning. To be saved one must find the "spiritual truth." The spiritual truth, however, is only whatever form of law the spirit of the times suggests. It is the quicksands of conscience. With few exceptions the hermeneutic has remained the same to modern times. The

11 / CHRISTIAN LIFE

characters may change, but the plot remains the same. Law is taken in a material and ontological sense as providing the way of salvation. That is the "secret" of the allegory, the moral of the story.

The functional understanding of law roots in a fundamentally different hermeneutic, which takes the 2 Corinthians passage at face value. The letter, the written code, the literal account kills; and the Spirit alone gives life. The letter is no secret code for the old Adam to solve, so as to find the way to life. The letter, the whole history of God with his people, leads to the cross and spells one thing for the old Adam: *death*. Only then will it mean new life in the Spirit, new life in the Second Adam. The whole text of Scripture, indeed the whole of history and creation, which becomes "too small," works in the first instance as the letter, the *opera literalia dei* (literal works of God), the "masks" of God which accuse and destroy the old Adam. The letter kills. It makes apparent that there is no way out.[26]

"Do we then overthrow the law by this faith? By no means! On the contrary, we uphold the law" (Rom. 3:31). To uphold the law means first to let it sound in its unrelenting, pristine majesty, without any "veil" (2 Cor. 3), to allow it to do its work as letter which kills. This upholding is possible, however, only because there is something else: The Spirit gives life—the Holy Spirit of God, not the spirit of the times. Indeed, the letter kills *so that* the Spirit can give life. In this way the exodus from virtue to the grace of God occurs. We pass through the waters of baptism, through death to life by the grace of God.

Justification by faith gives possibility; law does not. God's eschatological kingdom is humanity's tomorrow. The law must function first and foremost to cut off every other possibility. Only thus will we be reborn into the world God creates. The "letter," the story of God's struggle with his people, our story under law, must work to end every attempt to escape, every form of self-justification according to our own schemes and projects, in order to place us before the God of time to wait and to hope. The killing function of the law makes us historical beings. It cuts off every form of escape: metaphysical, religious, or psychological. That is its chief "use." Only when that happens will other uses open up as well, for only when the law kills in that fashion will we receive this world back as a gift. Only when we cease to use law as an escape for the self will we begin to see what law is for here as well. The possibility of a *Christian* life opens up.

We cannot conclude this already lengthy chapter without at least some preliminary words about the relevance and primacy of the doctrine of justification by faith in the discussion of the Christian life. It has become virtually a platitude today that justification language is hardly appealing to "contemporary" religious sentiment, and that biblically speaking and otherwise there is a host of other "images" (e.g., life, light, love, meaning, truth, overcoming alienation, liberation) that might serve better. No doubt such considerations must be taken into account when one is concerned with the task of communication and preaching. Dogmatically speaking, however, one cannot avoid dealing with the relationship to God and God's work toward us in terms of the doctrine of justification. This is true for several reasons. The first is the historical reason: The dogma was formulated in those terms, and dogmatics can no more avoid discussion of them than it can avoid discussion of "substance," "essence," "nature," and so on in dealing with the Trinity and christology. One may want to go on and redefine, but one must start with the dogma and attempt to understand it in its own terms.

Second, discussion of justification is necessary because it deals directly with the basic structural components of the biblical and dogmatic systems: the concepts of law and justice. These are not simply a Pauline obsession, nor the preoccupation of those with afflicted consciences. Throughout the Scriptures, it is a fact of prime importance that God is the final judge. Justification deals directly with the ultimate judgment of God. Furthermore, justification by faith deals directly with the root human sin under the law: the sin of the self-made person, the sin of self-righteousness. Justification by faith is not a sop for those of afflicted conscience; it is an attack as well on the secure. No other image makes the point as directly and clearly as the doctrine of justification. It is no coincidence that Paul uses the doctrine precisely in such instances: against the "Judaizers" and against the "enthusiasts" who think already to have made it. One could well argue that the doctrine of justification by faith is most needed precisely when people sense the least need for it!

Finally, justification-language is crucial precisely *because* of the communication problem. The basic question is what we are supposed to do in communicating the word of God to others. Justification language tells us straight out: We are to *justify*, to *pronounce* just, and *deliver* the judgment. The reason for the primacy of justification and related concepts of imputation, reckoning, forgiveness of sins, and so on is that speech shaped by and around these concepts is a quite particular use of language: It does what it says. Justification decides the issue it talks about. It does not merely talk about or describe what salvation might be like, it actually gives it. It simply says: "I pronounce you just for Jesus' sake." The deed is done.

Justification and forgiveness of sins are dogmatically primary precisely because they stipulate directly what sort of communication is supposed to take place in the church. There are indeed other images in Scripture and elsewhere. They tend, however, to remain just that: images. They describe and illumine the relationship to God in enlightening, helpful, and often inspiring ways. But they do not establish it. Description in the indicative mood, no matter how enticing, can all too easily lapse back into law. I am left wondering what is the matter with me, that I do not experience such marvelous things.

When it was said that the article on justification is the "article by which the church stands or falls," it was this kind of communication that was at stake. Here is the point of the "proper distinction between law and gospel." The church is to pronounce, to *do* the imputation, unconditionally. Particular preoccupation with or dependence on the legal metaphor or the problems of conscience is not the reason, dogmatically speaking, for the primacy of the doctrine of justification. The reason is to show clearly and unmistakably the kind of communication that must go on in the church. If the church forgets to speak the kind of language demanded by justification, a language that actually does what it talks about, then the church will "fall" and lose its reason for being. The sixteenth-century reformers saw the whole of Scripture agreeing on justification, and insisted that all doctrine be judged in the light of justification precisely for this reason. The point is to deliver the goods.

Robert Jenson and Eric Gritsch have made this point by characterizing justification by faith as a dogmatic proposal to the church catholic which is "metalinguistic," that is "not a particular proposed *content* of the church's proclamation, along with other contents" but "stipulation of what kind of talking—about whatever contents—can properly be proclamation and word of the church." It is "an attempt to state minimal identifying characteristics of the language activity we call 'gospel.'"[27] Justification means being addressed by an absolutely unconditional affirmation and promise, an end and a new beginning, a death and resurrection. If this is in any way compromised and flattened out into a mere description, it becomes a report *about* Christianity instead of the deed which *makes* Christians. Then it is no longer the gospel.

NOTES

1. Petro B. T. Bilaniuk, "The Mystery of *Theosis* or Divinization," in *The Heritage of the Early Church: Essays in Honor of Georges Florovsky*, ed. David Neiman and Margaret Schatkin, Orientalia Christiana Analecta 195 (Rome: Pontifical Institute, 1973), p. 352.

2. Ibid., p. 355, n. 62.

3. Thomas Aquinas, *Summa Theologica*, 1, 2ae, q. 113, art. 6., in *Nature and Grace*, ed. A. M. Fairweather, LCC 11 (Philadelphia: Westminster Press, 1954), pp. 192–93.

4. Ibid.

5. Eric W. Gritsch and Robert W. Jenson, *Lutheranism: The Theological Movement and Its Confessional Writings* (Philadelphia: Fortress Press, 1976), p. 39.

6. Novatian provoked a schism (251) because the church was ready to forgive "mortal" sins. The Donatists (fourth century) rebelled against the validity of sacramental acts done by priests guilty of mortal sins. Montanists, like most "spiritualists," became essentially a "holiness" sect after the enthusiasm wore off.

7. The recent penchant for combining grace and faith into the formula "justification by grace through faith" is perhaps understandable given certain modern developments, but (in spite of words suggesting such a formula in the Augsburg Confession IV) it is strictly speaking at best redundant and at worst compounding a felony. When one misses the complete interdependence of grace and faith (grace *is* the gift of faith; faith alone lets grace *be* grace), one turns faith into a "subjective response" and can then only cover one's tracks by saying, "Of course, it comes by grace!" *Faith* then simply takes the place once occupied by "works" or "merit" in the medieval system and all the problems repeat themselves. Given such misunderstanding it is clear that one cannot use the formula "justification by faith" today without careful work of reclamation.

8. Martin Luther, *Lectures on Romans*, trans. and ed. W. Pauck, *LCC* 15 (Philadelphia: Westminster Press, 1961), pp. 124, 125. Cited hereafter as Luther, *Romans*. Also *LW* 25:257ff.

9. Ibid., p. 4.

10. Ibid., p. 128.

11. For an excellent recent treatment of this, see Leif Grane, *Modus Loquendi Theologicus: Luthers Kampf um die Erneuerung der Theologie (1515-1518)*, trans. E. Groetzinger (Leiden: E. J. Brill, 1975).

12. *WA* 40¹: 280, 3–6; 280, 9–281, 4, 11–13. Translation and emphasis mine. *LW* 26:165ff.

13. Luther, *Romans*, p. 179. *LW* 25: 310.

14. Hans Joachim Iwand, *Nachgelassene Werke*, vol. 5, *Luthers Theologie*, ed. J. Haar (Munich: Chr. Kaiser, 1974), p. 197.

15. Wilfried Joest, *Gesetz und Freiheit*, 2d ed. (Göttingen: Vandenhoeck & Ruprecht, 1956), p. 59.

16. Exegetes who maintain that Paul had a distorted or jaundiced view of the law mostly fail to understand the radical nature of the eschatological gospel that had grasped Paul and its effect on the law. Whether Paul was influenced by late rabbinic "distortions" of authentic "Torah" has little or nothing to do with the matter. Precisely the *gospel* determines Paul's attitude toward the law, not the rabbis or his own "conscience" or psyche—exactly as he himself says (Phil. 3:6ff.). The new sets off and determines what is *old*. Though "blameless" under the law, Paul says, "For [Christ's] sake I have suffered the loss of all things, and count them as *skubala* (dung) in order that I may gain Christ and be found in him, not having a righteousness of my own, based on the law, but that which is through faith in Christ."

17. The literature is extensive. See, e.g., Ragnar Bring, *Gesetz und Evangelium und der dritte Gebrauch des Gesetzes in der lutherischen Theologie*, Zur Theologie Luthers: Aus der Arbeit der Luther-Agricola Gesellschaft in Finnland 1 (Helsinki, 1943); Lauri Haikola, *Usus Legis*, UUA (Uppsala: Lundquistska Bokhandeln, 1958); Werner Elert, *Zwischen Gnade und Ungnade* (Munich: Ev. Pressverband, 1948).

18. Apology of the Augsburg Confession, Article IV, 38, *BC* 112.

19. Karl Holl, *Gesammelte Aufsätze,* vol. 1, 2d and 3d ed. (Tübingen: J. C. B. Mohr [Paul Siebeck], 1923), pp. 35ff. Cf. Iwand, *Luthers Theologie*, pp. 176ff.

20. *WA* 40 I:285, 5. *LW* 26:168.

11 / CHRISTIAN LIFE

21. This accounts for Luther's seemingly ambiguous stand on *synteresis* and conscience. It is there, but in and of itself it does no good—now. Cf. Iwand, *Luthers Theologie*, p. 187.

22. Iwand, *Luthers Theologie*, 129, WA 24:140, 21ff.

23. WA 19:126, 16ff.

24. Does one appeal to "conscience" in preaching? No doubt, as Luther often said, one would preach in vain if there were no conscience. But one must preach, perhaps we can say, as though conscience were the empty house of Jesus' parable, now occupied by seven more demons. One must not preach in such fashion as to solidify their tenure in the house. One assumes indeed that people live and suffer "under the law," but that what they are suffering from is the *misuse* of the law, the assumption that law, in conjunction with conscience, *is* the way. Many today like to say that we do not need, therefore, to preach "the law," but only the gospel. That is a mistake. The "law" that must be preached is the absolute offense of the unconditional gospel, the "letter" which kills, so the spirit can make new—the kind of law which destroys the illusions about law as the way and thus drives the demons from the house.

25. Gerhard Ebeling, "Erwägung zur Lehre vom Gesetz," in *Wort und Glaube* (Tübingen: J. C. B. Mohr [Paul Siebeck], 1960), p. 291 (translation mine). The Luther quotation is from WA 40 II:18, 4ff.

26. This is the reason one cannot, as Barth would have it, preach gospel before law. The word addresses us always as letter which kills first, and through that the Spirit makes alive.

27. Gritsch and Jenson, *Lutheranism,* pp. 42, 43.

2
Justification and Sanctification

Justification and sanctification must be grasped as a dynamic unity in the light of God's eschatological act that brings new life from death. "Progress" in sanctification is not immanent moral progress but the coming of the kingdom of God among us through the power of unconditional justification. Growth is growth in grace. Sanctification cannot be separated from, or more than, justification. Sanctification occurs when unconditional justification begins to take the person away from sin, not just to take sin away from the person. There is death to the old, and rebirth to the new in heart, mind, and soul. Justification *sola gratia* sets free from works and just so inspires spontaneity and naturalness in doing truly *good* works.

THE SEPARATION OF SANCTIFICATION FROM JUSTIFICATION

"Are we to continue to sin that grace may abound?" The question obviously makes people nervous. To that degree also the answer is likely not to be grasped: "By no means! How can we who died to sin still live in it?" (Rom. 6:1–2). Justification means the end of law and of thinking according to law. It means the death of the old and the resurrection of the new in faith.

> We know that our old self was crucified with him so that the sinful body might be destroyed, and we might no longer be enslaved to sin. For he who has died is freed from sin. But if we have died with Christ, we believe that we shall also live with him. For we know that Christ being raised from the dead will never die again; death no longer has dominion over him. The death he died he died to sin, once for all, but the life he lives he lives to God. So you also must consider yourselves dead to sin and alive to God in Christ Jesus. . . .
>
> But thanks be to God, that you who were once slaves of sin have become obedient from the heart to the standard of teaching to which you were committed, and, having been set free from sin, have become slaves of righteousness. I am speaking in human terms, because of your natural limitations. For just as you

11 / CHRISTIAN LIFE

once yielded your members to impurity and to greater and greater iniquity, so now yield your members to righteousness for sanctification. (Rom. 6:6–11, 17–19)

If we are unable fully to grasp the identification of justification by faith with death and resurrection, we will encounter nothing but difficulty in relating justification and sanctification. We will always be struggling and tinkering with the system of law, trying to make it work by all sorts of theological fine tuning.

Something of that sort seems to have occurred after the Reformation. Justification by faith as imputed righteousness was accepted and became the talisman of the new movement, but death and resurrection, the end of the law, was not. We need not tarry here to ask why.[1] Broadly, what happened was that after the Reformation, Protestants again attempted just what could not be done: to synthesize justification by faith with thinking "after the fashion of Aristotle," with thinking according to the scheme of progress under the law. What resulted was a theology which carries within itself a profound inner contradiction.[2] Again, either one or the other (the righteousness which comes by faith or thinking "after the fashion of Aristotle") has to give way. Again, history shows the former to be most often the loser. The law once again takes its place as the structural backbone of the dogmatic system.[3]

Once that occurs, two things immediately follow for dogmatics which try nevertheless to be Protestant and evangelical. First, justification must be defined as an absolutely forensic declaration. Second, it must be antiseptically removed from all contamination by the subsequently necessary idea of progress in sanctification on the other. Justification must be understood as absolutely forensic, that is, as a sheer decree acquitting the guilty party. Thus the following:

> "Justification denotes that act by which the sinner, who is responsible for guilt and liable to punishment . . . , but who believes in Christ, is pronounced just by God the judge." This act occurs at the instant in which the merit of Christ is appropriated by faith, and can properly be designated a *forensic* or *judicial* act, since God in it, as if in a civil court, pronounces a judgment upon man, which assigns to him an entirely different position, and entirely different rights. By justification we are, therefore, by no means to understand a moral condition existing in man, or a moral change which he has experienced, but only a judgment pronounced upon man, by which his relation to God is reversed, and indeed in such a manner, that a man can now consider himself one whose sins are blotted out, who is no longer responsible for them before God, who, on the other hand, appears before God as accepted and righteous, in whom God finds nothing more to punish, with whom He has no longer any occasion to be displeased.[4]

From this summary by Heinrich Schmid, one can sense something of the beauty and objectivity of Lutheran orthodoxy, but also something of the anxiety involved in holding the position. Justification is stated boldly. It is a forensic act, a purely legal judgment, made by God for Christ's sake, as distinguished from a physical act, a judgment made on the basis of or entailing some empirically verifiable characteristic or action in the person judged. And indeed, the forensic nature of the judgment, taken just as such, is not the problem. That is orthodoxy's finest achievement. The problem lies rather in the presupposition of the system: that the law is the eternal standard according to which the judgment is made. Thus arises the anxiety. In order to keep the forensic judgment pure, one has absolutely to separate justification from a "moral condition" or "moral change." Given the presuppositions, one can maintain the comfort of justification only by separating it absolutely from its effect.

But then it becomes difficult to say exactly why sanctification and good works must (may? will?) follow. One lands willy-nilly back in the same systematic problem encountered all along. Either forensic justification makes the process unnecessary, or the process makes justification as a forensic act unnecessary and fictitious, again a mere "anti-Pelagian codicil." It is not strange, therefore, that dispute should have broken out over the necessity of "good works." If forensic justification fully saves, how necessary are good works? Shall we not sin the more that grace may abound? When the eschatological nature of the justifying event is lost, when it is no longer a matter of death and new life, when the old subject simply remains under the law, justification threatens to become mere justification of the status quo. Then one must come down hard on the necessity of good works in order to forestall moral laxity. But then the dynamic, the spontaneity and *hilaritas*, of faith is lost. One answers the question "Shall we sin the more that grace may abound?" by saying, "By no means! Because good works are necessary too, for salvation, you know!"[5] Then the battle is lost.

The increasing isolation of forensic justification as an "objective" sheer judgment could mean only that Protestant divines were faced with the question of mediation all over again. How does the subject appropriate something so objective and pure without contaminating it? How can this be conceived without confusing it with a subjective process? The question, of course, masks the real problem: How can the subject appropriate such justification without dying and being made new, that is, how can the subject survive intact? The answer, of course, for anyone who takes the New Testament seriously, is that the subject cannot. Justification involves death of the old and rebirth of the new. Given the presuppositions of the orthodox Protestant scheme, however, a way must be found to avoid such death. A way must be found to make the subjective appropriation of the objective fact conceivable as an order, a process. One has to provide a theological shuttle service between the objec-

11 / CHRISTIAN LIFE

tive and the subjective. The Reformation's *propter Christum et per fidem* (because of Christ through faith) becomes a succession, a progress, in which the *propter Christum* is the objective truth and the *per fidem* the subjective appropriation. Wilhelm Dantine states the point:

> The merit of Christ waits before the closed door of the heart like an immovable object, even though it carries in it the entire salvation of mankind. Only some action from within the heart can open the door and permit the salvation treasure to enter the existence of man. Even if one seriously takes into account the fact that faith was correctly evaluated as a gift of the Holy Spirit, did it not nevertheless lead to an understanding of faith as an independent means, and, finally, as the merit of pious inwardness? . . . One can also diminish the merit of Christ by appealing to the Holy Spirit, especially if one reduces this merit to a dead, heavenly "thing" no longer capable of action as Lutheran Orthodoxy has already done. . . .
>
> The so-called objective fact of salvation thus really forms only something like a common foundation. It represents a basis on which the so-called subjective fact is only then able to begin the really decisive action. It almost seems as if God had to be reconciled anew through faith.[6]

The split between the subjective and the objective could only mean that the theologians would have to busy themselves with the question of order once again. The result was the so-called *ordo salutis* (order of salvation). The first steps were taken already by Melanchthon in speaking of three steps of *notitia*, *assensus*, and *fiducia* (knowledge, assent, and trust), by which one moves from knowledge of the objective fact to assent under the weight of certain "proofs" and finally to trust under the influence of the Holy Spirit.[7] Such an initial analysis cannot but invite further refinement, especially at the last step of trust. How does such trust come about? Later dogmaticians developed the *ordo salutis* to deal with the problem, involving such steps as the call (*vocatio*), illumination, conversion, regeneration, mystical union, and renovation. In doing this, according to Heinrich Schmid, they "seek to collect under one general topic, all that is to be said concerning what God or more accurately the Holy Ghost, does, in order to induce fallen man to accept of salvation through Christ, and what takes place in order to bring about the designed change in man."[8] No doubt such a collection could be helpful, were it looked on simply as an attempt to spell out with fullness what justification by faith means. The attempt to set it forth as an "order," however, is disastrous. Even Schmid, whose love for the orthodox fathers is evident, is constrained to remark, "The introduction of an independent development of these conceptions led to an arrangement of the entire doctrine which we cannot call a happy one."[9] Among other things, it led to a fundamental distinction between the means of salvation on the part of God (word and sacraments)

JUSTIFICATION AND SANCTIFICATION

and the means of salvation on the part of man (faith and good works). Faith becomes the subjective condition for salvation.

The attempt analytically to describe the *ordo salutis* was a tricky task, and the dogmaticians could not agree on the correct order. Justification, forensic or otherwise, tended to get lost in the dogmatic woods. Dantine observes:

> Its limitation to the territory of applied grace took increasing effect . . . and perhaps one will even have to conclude that here the old truth has again proved itself, according to which the greatest radiance is always followed by the deepest misery. . . .
>
> A contributing factor to this decline was, without a doubt, the particular development of the *ordo salutis* . . . , into the scheme of which justification was squeezed as into a bed of Procrustes, there to lose its essential center and strength. . . . The Spirit, in Himself free and sovereign, was transformed into a front-rank man at attention, as it were, and the only consolation about this iron chain of interlinked divine operations was now that almost every dogmatician had a different notion of which order of march the living God should follow. At least a little freedom was left for the Holy Ghost, albeit only through the disunity of the dogmaticians! Later, a more and more penetrating interest in the proceedings and occurrences in the human realm was all that was needed to make a chain of religious occurrences in the human soul out of acts of a Spirit squeezed into a human scheme. Finally the whole order of salvation was transformed into a human process of development.[10]

The attempt to spell out the order only leads back to where it all began. Of course, one could say that discerning the order was a purely analytical task for dogmatic purposes and that such "order" was to be conceived as "instantaneous" and not a temporal succession. But Thomas Aquinas had said the same about his doctrine. And once the step is taken it seems inevitably to return to a temporal scheme.

The separation of justification from sanctification in this manner thus leads only in one direction: The process of sanctification becomes the primary reality; justification fades into the background as something everyone presupposes or takes for granted, but which possesses no real dynamic. Justification becomes a kind of frozen idea. Once that happens the way is open to further temporalizing and psychologizing of the "order." This is what happens in at least some forms of pietism. A "dead" orthodoxy could be vitalized only in the same way as an "arid" scholasticism (by mysticism, for instance): turn it into a "way" with a certain series of "steps" (awakening, conversion, etc.) in the religious progress of the individual subject.

Therewith the fate of justification as an objective truth, as an eschatological act from without, is sealed. The subject and its religion occupy the center of the stage. A psychologized *ordo salutis* can readily be recast as the "pure

11 / CHRISTIAN LIFE

practical religion" of the subject, shorn of all "objective" and "theoretical" elements (Kant), or as a religion of "pious feelings" (Schleiermacher), or even stretched out into a "history-of-salvation" (von Hofmann and others) and finally universalized into a "history of spirit" (the Hegelians). History as such becomes the process in which the divine realizes itself in time in the subject. Time itself becomes a process of "sanctification." Justification as an eschatological act is lost altogether. Eschatology is absorbed into immanent teleology.

THE UNITY OF JUSTIFICATION AND SANCTIFICATION

Justification cannot be synthesized with the idea of progress according to law. We saw that in our chapter on justification by faith. Now we have also seen that justification cannot be separated as a purely forensic act and hermetically sealed from sanctification conceived as progress according to the law. Justification then becomes irrelevant. Only one way remains open: to grasp justification and sanctification as a dynamic unity in the light of the eschatological nature of the divine action. Justification by faith means the death of the old and the resurrection of the new. Sanctification is what results when that is done to us. "How can you who have died to sin still live in it?" That is the only way our question can be answered. If there is progress or growth involved—and no doubt there is—it must be conceived quite differently from the progress according to law, from the quest to become a virtuous person. The aim of this section is to grasp the unity of justification and sanctification, and the kind of growth involved.

Since later developments in Protestantism precluded proper grasp of the relation between justification and sanctification, it is necessary to return *ad fontes* (to the sources) for help. We have to discover whether the Reformation is of moment dogmatically at all, for if what developed out of the Reformation is to be taken as its entirely legitimate offspring, there is not a great deal to choose between it and previous dogmatics. At best the Reformation's dogma would be a minor adjustment or complementary truth to the older systems, in which the issues were stated usually in more comprehensive terms. We must return to the original sources to discover whether this is the best Protestant dogmatics can do.

We can best attack the problem by asking whether in Luther, for instance, who posits the *simul iustus et peccator* with such vigor, it is possible to discover any distinctive ideas about sanctification or Christian growth. The *simul*, it is to be recalled, was posited precisely to counter the idea that justification is to be synthesized with ideas of progress according to law. The justifying act unmasks and exposes all our pretense about becoming virtuous persons, by the very fact that it is an unconditional divine imputation to be received only by faith. To be justified by God's act means to become a sinner at the same time. The totality of justification unmasks the totality of being a sinner. Thus the *simul iustus et peccator* as total states would seem to militate against any talk of progress in sanctification.

There are many utterances of Luther's which reject all ideas of progress.[11] Sanctification must simply be included in justification because the latter is a *total* state. Sanctification is simply to believe the divine imputation and with it the *totus peccator.* Where can there be more sanctification than where God is revered as the only Holy One? God is revered as such only where the sinner, the real and total sinner, stands still at the place where God enters the scene. Like Moses before the burning bush, or Isaiah in the temple, or Saul on the Damascus road. That place is the place where the sinner must realize that his or her own way is at an end. Only those who stand still and hear, who know that they are sinners and that Christ alone is their hope, only they give God the glory. Only they are then sanctified—by God and God's holiness. All human holiness is simply consumed by the divine fire.

From this point of view the way of the sinner in sanctification, if it is a movement at all, is a movement from nothing to all, from that which one has and is in oneself to that which one has and is in Christ. Such a movement can never be completed this side of the grave. Nor could it be a continuous movement through increasing degrees of approximation. Rather each moment, each encounter with the shock of divine holiness, could only be at once both beginning and end, start and finish. The Christian could never presume to have reached a certain stage in sanctification, which then is to form the basis for the next stage. Anyone who has ever been overwhelmed by the magnitude of the divine imputation knows that it is always a matter of beginning again. Thus Luther would say: "To achieve is always to begin again."[12] Encounter with the divine holiness soon disabuses one of all idle dreams of progress.

By the same token, however, the light of the gospel begins to shine through the mists of our dreams. The imputation means that the Christian never has an endless process of sanctification ahead which must be traversed in order to arrive at holiness. Those who have the imputed righteousness may know that they have arrived. The ultimate goal has been given. Such people would know, of course, that this is not a goal one has attained but one always granted anew for the sake of Christ.

According to this initial reading of the imputation and the *simul*, the movement of the Christian life is not a continuous or steady progress, but rather something more like an oscillation or resonance, in which beginning and end are always equally near. In attempting a diagram (admittedly a risky venture!)

11 / CHRISTIAN LIFE

Wilfried Joest suggests the following:[13]

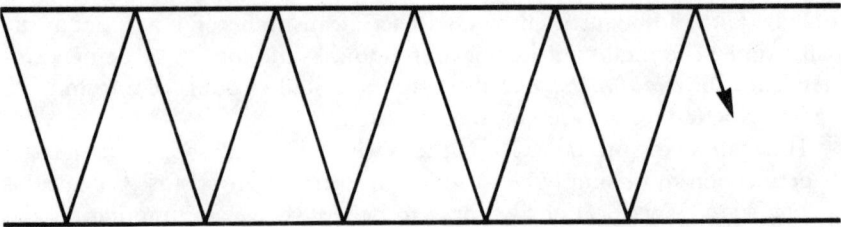

The bottom line represents the person as total sinner in and of himself or herself, while the top line represents the person as totally just in Christ. The zigzag line represents the oscillation, the *transitus* of the Christian life.

While this view of the Christian life resulting from the divine act of justification is foundational, it does not give the whole picture. In many instances Luther himself does speak of a kind of progress or growth. He can even speak in surprising fashion of the Christian as one who is "*partly* just, *partly* a sinner" (*partim iustus, partim peccator*). In this vein he can speak of faith as a beginning, but not yet the whole. Faith is not a perfect fulfillment of the law but only the beginning of fulfillment. Indeed, what is still lacking will not be imputed for Christ's sake. The imperfection of our actual attempts to fulfill the law stands under the protective mantle of nonimputation. In such instances, Luther speaks of faith in the imputed righteousness as the "first fruits of the Spirit" (*primitias spiritus*) which is not yet the whole. Such faith is the beginning because it is the beginning of the actual hatred of sin and its expulsion and the doing of good works. In faith the law is fulfilled *imputatively*, but thereafter it is to be fulfilled *expurgatively* (by driving out sin), for when the Spirit is given one begins *ex animo*, from heart and soul, to hate all those things that offend the Spirit. Indeed, one begins not only to hate the things but also to hate one's very *self* as sinner (the *odium sui* so odious to more fragile theologies) and to hope and long for the day when such will no longer be the case. Luther can even say we are to do good works in order finally to become externally righteous. To have sins remitted by grace is not enough; they are eventually to be totally abolished.[14]

What have we here? Is this a contradiction of all we have found so far? Has Luther simply gone back on everything said about the *simul iustus et peccator* as total states? What is especially remarkable is that the champion of justification by faith can speak of the expurgation and abolition of sin in terms which even the most enthusiastic exponent of moral progress would find shocking. How is this possible? Some say that in the heat of later battles and in disappointment with the moral laxity of the young Reformation, Luther like Melanchthon had to change his tune somewhat. But statements of the sort in question are present from the very beginning. They are to be found, for instance, precisely in the same context where the *simul iustus et peccator* was first formulated: in the lectures on Romans, to chapter 4:1-7. Not knowing what to make of this, some scholars think that Luther had not yet rid himself of remnants of the medieval tradition or Augustinian humility-piety. When this kind of material is found, Luther is suspected either of not ridding himself completely of medieval piety or of compromising his principles in the face of practical exigencies. Since it is found both early and late, however, it is more reasonable to assume that it belongs to the substance of Luther's Reformation theology, and to suspect that once again he has simply not been understood very well.

It is necessary, therefore, to look more carefully to discover what is meant. Here we can perhaps do no better than to look at the section in the lectures on Romans, since that is the place where the *simul* was first propounded and has also been the object of much of the controversy. After setting forth the *simul iustus et peccator* as the result of the divine imputation, Luther moves immediately to a discussion about concupiscence. He castigates the scholastic theologians for thinking "after the fashion of Aristotle" that the sinfulness of concupiscence is actually removed by what they call "grace," and that what remains is only the "seeds" of sin. He says that he was entirely led astray by this, "because I did not know that though forgiveness is indeed real, sin is not taken away *except in hope*, that is *in the process of being taken away* by the gift of grace which starts this removal, so that it is only not reckoned as sin." And a bit later he expands this:

> Yet this concupiscence is always in us; therefore, the love of God is never in us, except insofar as grace has given us a beginning of it. We have the love of God only insofar as the rest of concupiscence, which still must be cured and by virtue of which we do not yet "love God with our whole heart" (Luke 10:27), is by mercy not reckoned as sin. We shall love God only at the end, when it will all be taken away and the perfect love of God will be given to those who believe and who with perseverance always yearn for it and seek it.[15]

Thinking "in the fashion of Aristotle" according to human notions of progress leads to an entirely false notion of sanctification. The human notion of progress it presupposes always remains intact. The question then is how much one can accomplish according to the scheme either with or without what was called "infused grace": how far up the ladder of progress one could get. When, in order to exalt the supposed power of such grace, it was simply *asserted* that concupiscence is removed in some fashion or other, the discourse tended to lapse into fiction and lose touch with the way things are. In this scheme, grace becomes a theological abstraction added only to make the scheme "Christian," merely an added help in the scheme of what human powers properly

11 / CHRISTIAN LIFE

should accomplish. But that is just pious sublimation of natural desire, the sanctified self-centeredness which Luther knew all too well did not lead to actual love of God. The scheme leads only to hypocrisy or despair. One either deceives oneself into thinking concupiscence is actually gone or despairs if one is honest enough to admit it is not.

Faith, however, born of the imputation of total righteousness, begets the beginnings of honesty as well. Such faith sees the truth of the human condition, the reality and totality of human sin, and has no need to indulge in fictions. It will see that concupiscence indeed remains and that it is *sin* but that God nevertheless does business with sinners. Such faith will see the fantastic magnitude of the divine act and thereby *begin* to hope that one day concupiscence will be gone. Such faith will begin, at least, to love the God who comes all the way to die for sinners. Such faith will begin to hate sin and to hope for that righteousness it knows it can never attain by any human power with or without "infused grace." Only imputed righteousness grasped by faith leads to such beginnings. Faith which in the light of imputed righteousness sees the truth about sin, will cry to God "out of the depths": "Wretched man that I am, who will deliver me . . . ," and actually begin to "hunger and thirst after righteousness."

When Luther speaks in this vein, he speaks of *actual affections* (love, hope, hatred of sin, etc.) and not about theological abstractions. The unconditional nature of the divine imputation which sets the *totus iustus* over against the *totus peccator* kindles the first beginnings of actual hope and love for God and God's righteousness; whereas before there had been only hypocrisy or despair. There is no contradiction for Luther between the *simul* and the *partim*, once the divine imputation has destroyed all thinking "after the fashion of Aristotle." If justification is unconditional and total, it explodes into love and good works. If not, it simply leaves the self to contend with its own righteousness and despair.

What sort of progress or growth is here envisaged? Is the *transitus* in the life of the Christian no longer simply an oscillation between two wholes? Under the impulse of the imputed righteousness, does one gradually improve, so that "nonimputation" covers what is left? Does one not, after all, return to point zero every time one begins again? Could one perhaps apply the popular slogan "Become what you already are" and see the Christian life as a gradual process of catching up to the *totus iustus*? Does one set of accomplishments form the basis for the next—as with the steps of the mystical way? Does one attain a certain approximation of the goal?

Such a scheme might suggest itself on first glance. But many go wrong here. If there were growth of that sort, progressive sanctification would mean progressive emancipation from the divine imputation. The more one progresses, the less grace one would need. Such thinking would lead to Karl Holl's idea that justification is an "analytical" rather than a "synthetic" judgment, that is, a judgment made by God on the basis of God's analysis of the whole process and its successful completion (one is declared just because God knows one will *become* so), rather than a judgment which by its sheer unconditionality and liberality makes (synthesizes) what it declares.[16] If there were such a process and justification were an analytical judgment, we would be back at square one. Imputed righteousness would be a temporary loan given to cover lack of capital until one earned enough oneself. The more one acquired, the more the imputation could recede into the background. The picture would be something like this:

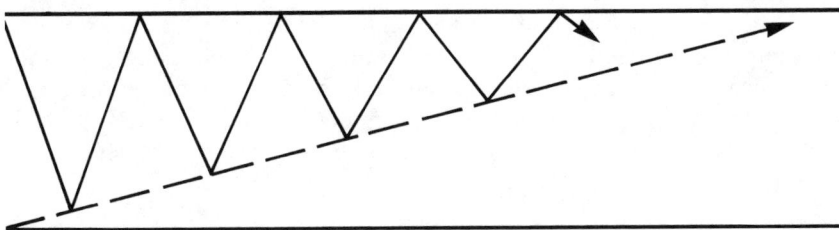

One gradually leaves the line of the *totus peccator* and by the power of grace ascends to the line of the *totus iustus*.[17]

But this would be a serious misunderstanding of Luther's point. Imputed righteousness is not a mere starting point, a temporary loan, and it cannot be allowed to recede into the background. It is the perpetual fountain and constant power of whatever we may accomplish. To look on it as something we gradually need less of would be to deny it altogether. Imputed righteousness, precisely because it is synthetic, unconditional, pure, makes its own way and creates its own justice.

We cannot understand what Luther means by growth or progress in sanctification unless all ordinary human perceptions of progress are reversed, are stood on their heads.[18] The progress Luther has in mind is not our movement toward the goal but the goal's movement in on us. Imputed righteousness is *eschatological* in character; a battle is joined in which the *totus iustus* moves against the *totus peccator*. The "progress" is the coming of the kingdom of God among us. That is why complete sanctification is always the same as justification and cannot be something more added to it or separated from it. Complete sanctification is not the goal but the source of all good works. The way is not from the partial to the whole, but from the whole to the partial. Good works do not make a person good, but a good person does good works—as the famous maxim has it. Imputed righteousness is not a legal fiction but the "power of God unto salvation" which attacks sin as a total state and will eventually reduce it to nothing. It is always as a *whole* that it attacks,

11 / CHRISTIAN LIFE

as unconditional, freely given, absolute gift. It attacks its opposite in the form of both hypocrisy and despair. The good works that result are not building blocks in the progress of the Christian; they are the fruit of the whole, the "good tree."

Expulsion of sin is therefore quite the opposite of a morally conceivable process of sanctification. In the latter process the person remains more or less constant, and only the properties are changed. The person is the "substance" in scholastic terms, whose "accidents" are altered. One supposedly "puts off sin" as though one were peeling paint from a wall or taking heat from water.[19] The entire picture must be reversed: The person is taken away from sin. The heart, mind, soul, affections—that which constitutes the person in the biblical sense—are taken away from the lust either for vice or for becoming a virtuous self. Imputed righteousness, precisely because it is unconditional, does not offer a new paint job. It does not merely "take sin away" and leave the moral person intact. It begins to take the person away from sin. There is a death and new life involved, which proceeds according to no immanent moral scheme.

> Human righteousness . . . seeks first of all to remove and to change the sins and to keep man intact; this is why it is not righteousness but hypocrisy. Hence *as long as there is life in man and as long as he is not taken by renewing grace to be changed, no efforts of his can prevent him from being subject to sin and the law.*[20]

Sanctification always comes from the whole, from the penetration of the eschaton into time, and thus involves the death of the old and rebirth of the new. One never does leave the "always beginning anew" behind, for the beginning is the first fruits of the resurrection.

The movement, the growth, envisaged by Luther is thus a reversal of this-worldly conceptions.

> Where he is concerned to describe sanctification, he very often grasps at formulations which stand the natural-rational picture exactly on its head. For our question the following is the result: The progress of the sanctified Christian life for Luther is unconditionally a procedure *sui generis*. It can be compared to no immanent moral movement, with no continuous psychological development in the realm of the identity of the ethical subject with itself. Furthermore: Wherever that progress takes place—whether in the beginning or farther on—it always happens as a whole. If it takes place extensively only in little steps, or in isolated actions against particular sins, intensively the whole is always there; the total crisis, the entire transformation of the person, dying and becoming new, is wholly present.[21]

Joest suggests the following diagram (again in spite of the risk involved in such attempts):[22]

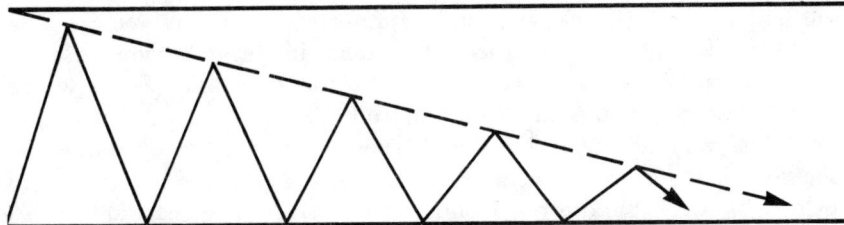

The way does not lead from below, the *totus peccator*, upward; rather, the totality of righteousness imputed to faith descends toward the lower reality. The difference and opposition between the two is not increasingly overcome from below by the ascent of the sinner, but rather from above, by the descent of the totality of grace. The movement does drive toward fulfillment, however, when by the power of the coming reality the *totus peccator* shall finally die completely and by grace alone be turned totally to love the God who gives it. *Then* we shall love as we are loved. In the end we shall realize that if we are to be saved, it will have to be by such grace "only." The growth envisaged is growth in grace and just so is it growth in truth about ourselves vis-à-vis God and God's righteousness.

In this view, justification and sanctification are a dynamic unity. Sanctification is what happens when the unconditional and eschatological event of justification breaks into one's life. Sanctification is what happens when one acts out of faith in the gift of total and complete righteousness, when one simply takes God at God's word. Faith issues in good works—that is, neither in laxity and vice, nor in rigorism and the lust to be a virtuous person—done for the sake of the other.

This opens up a new view of the Christian life. The movement is always from faith to works. One cannot measure Christian existence by works, concluding back from the works to one's status before God. Every attempt to do that is a mistake. Not only does it lead to hypocrisy or despair for the individual, it also destroys all possibility of seeing the goodness of our works. It is the devil's art, Luther says, to spoil precisely the goodness of our works. This happens when one puts works *before* faith, or concludes from works to the status of the Christian. For then "under the law" we will only come to the conclusion that we have not done much, that absolutes are too hard to reach, and that everything is in vain. Trying to base one's life on works, one will lose even them.

Being Christian means to find one's being in faith, in simply hearing the unconditional proclamation of the righteousness that is not in works. Such a position will be attacked by both the vicious and the virtuous, by the sub-

11 / CHRISTIAN LIFE

Christian and the super-Christian. But if one is going to be saved from both vice and virtue, there is no other way. Hearing the divine declaration alone will set free over against works. And we must be free. The movement from faith to works must be a movement of freedom. If not, we become prisoners of our works. We look at *them* to find our being, our status. We are walled in by our deeds like prisoners in a dungeon. "When you look to what you have done you have already lost the name of Christian. It is indeed true that one should do good works, help others, advise, and give, but no one is called a Christian for that and is not a Christian for that."[23] The quest to be a virtuous or pious person is *not* a Christian quest.

> Making pious people is not the business of the gospel but only making Christians. It is more a matter of being Christian than being pious. Someone may well be pious but not a Christian. A Christian does not know how to say anything about his piety, he doesn't find anything good or pious in it; should he desire to become pious he will have to look to some other and foreign piousness.[24]

A proper dogmatic view of the Christian life does not, therefore, identify with the old ideals of piety and the quest to be a virtuous person. Being holy or saintly in that sense cannot be identified with being Christian. The Reformation means a complete break with such thinking.

> Here it finally dawns on one why Reformation comes about, because here it is not merely mistakes and shortcomings that are repaired, but here the *ideal* that shaped the entire life of the Middle Ages is rejected: "Therefore one is not called a Christian because one accomplishes much; something higher is here. Rather it is because one takes something from, draws from, Christ, and simply lets oneself be given to. When one no longer takes from Christ, then one is no longer a Christian. The name Christian stays only in the taking and not in the giving or the doing, and that one takes from no one except from Christ. When you begin to regard what you have done then you have already lost the name of Christian."[25]

Such a view is preposterous for the world and the old Adam, but this is exactly what it means to die to the old and be born again to the new. One must simply be still and listen where God enters the scene—and believe, for only such faith will save.

This rejection of the ancient ideal of piety and sanctity is what lies behind Luther's shocking advice to Melanchthon: "Be a sinner and sin boldly, but believe even more boldly and rejoice in Christ, who is victor over sin, death, and the world."[26] The point is that when one begins to be grasped by the overwhelming gift of grace, when one is beginning to die to the old, the temptation (*Anfechtung*) will always sound: "Is it not dangerous?" "Are you not going too far?" "Is not the grace too cheap?" "If you lose your 'virtue,' what will protect you then?" Luther's advice in such situations was: "Be a sinner and sin boldly, but believe even more boldly." The point is not to go out and find some sins to commit. The point is rather not to be deceived by the glitter of ideals, of sanctity and piety, by the quest for the Holy Grail. Christ and Christ alone has dealt with sin and saves sinners. It is impossible for there to be any sin which is not removed by him and by him alone. "Be a sinner and sin boldly, but believe more boldly" is simply the stance of a faith which knows that Christ alone saves sinners.

Out of such faith *good* works come. Sanctification happens. The good works come out of the spontaneity, the freedom, the "*hilaritas*" of faith. They come out of the love and the hope that begin to dawn when one realizes the unconditionality of grace, when the old self dies. The good works come out of the beginning of the "always beginning again." They come from the *good* tree. They come from faith.

> Faith is a divine work in us which changes us and births us anew out of God (John 1:13), and kills the old Adam, makes us into entirely different people from the heart, soul, mind, and all powers, and brings the Holy Spirit with it. Oh, it is a living, busy, active, mighty thing, this faith, so it is impossible that it should not do good. It does not ask if good works should be done, but before one asks, has done them and is always active. Whoever, though, does not do such work is a faithless person, peeking and poking about for faith and good works not knowing what either faith or good works are, who putters and patters many words about faith and good works.[27]

Luther spoke of "*quellende Liebe*" to designate the spontaneity and freedom with which works flow forth from faith.[28] The phrase is difficult to translate into English; it means a love "bubbling over," "springing forth" as from a spring. The point is that the love bubbles forth from itself because of faith and is not dependent on the attraction of its object.

But here again caution must be exercised. There is a long tradition in modern Protestant ethics which attaches itself to this kind of statement and uses it to maintain that Protestant ethics, in distinction from Roman Catholic ethics, is "spontaneous" rather than legalistically forced. This became the basis for what was called an "ethics of disposition" or "motivation" (*Gesinnungsethik*). Inspired mostly by nineteenth-century idealism, the idea is that genuine ethical action must flow spontaneously from within rather than be forced from without. The problem, however, is what this "within" is. For most of modern Protestantism, this "within" is "the voice of conscience," the "moral law within," or the "human moral autonomy" of Kantianism. It is a mistake to identify what is being said by Luther and the other reformers with this *Gesinnungsethik* of modern Protestantism. The "spring" of the "bubbling-over love" is not "the moral law within" or the supposed "autonomy" it fosters. The "spring" is the word of God, the justification given

11 / CHRISTIAN LIFE

for Jesus' sake. That "spring" alone purifies the heart from the lust for either vice or virtue so that good works will flow forth.

The word is spoken; faith hears. From that good works flow. We hear every day anew. We begin again. Sanctification comes to us from God's eschatological word and kingdom. It is the spontaneity of life in the Spirit. Surely such a view at least more nearly approaches what we find in the New Testament than do more traditional views. Synthesizing justification with sanctification under the aegis of a legal scheme has as little to do with the New Testament message as does a stringent separation of the two; because the New Testament does not see the two as different enough either to synthesize or to separate. The reason is the eschatological vision. The entire question of one's being as Christian is bound up with one's stance vis-à-vis the eschatological kingdom breaking in Jesus. All distinctions, sinner/righteous, Jew/gentile, slave/free, male/female, and so on, are simply wiped out insofar as they are supposed to be determinative for one's being before God. What matters is one's *faith*, *love*, and *hope*.

This is what stands behind the sayings, teachings, and parables of Jesus as well as the injunctions of the epistles. The kingdom of heaven is like treasure hidden in a field which, when a man found it, he went and sold all he had to possess (Matt. 13:44 and par.). The joy at stumbling onto something entirely unexpected changes everything—like a precious pearl so long sought and finally discovered, or a lost coin, or a lost sheep. Nothing really matters but that. Not to see that is to be blind, according to the Gospels.

Two types of people are set over against each other: the type whose being is determined by works, and the type whose being is determined by faith and hope, who have caught the vision. When the Gospels must decide between the two, always that which gives praise to and lives in the light of God's grace is commended and chosen, regardless of status or achievement. The publican is justified rather than the Pharisee (Luke 18:9ff). The prodigal who wastes his life but yet returns gladdens the Father's heart, while the son who remains in the house does not see (Luke 15:11ff.). Simon the Pharisee simply cannot understand Jesus' acceptance of the "woman of the city" who washes his feet with her hair. Only faith can grasp that scene. The woman is the truly sanctified one. That is the shocking thing. She acts out of faith and hope and therefore knows what to do. Her sins are forgiven "for she loved much; but he who is forgiven little, loves little" (Luke 7:36ff.). From the usual human perspective the logic of that statement is hopelessly garbled. From the eschatological perspective the statement makes perfect sense. The forgiveness and the love are part of the same package.

The teachings of Jesus and the injunctions in the Epistles must be viewed in the same light. They are posed from the eschatological perspective. They have to do with what one who is slain and made alive by the eschatological

JUSTIFICATION AND SANCTIFICATION

word does and is to do. One cannot expect that such teachings will be generally understood or approved by the children "of this age." That is not because Christians are so much the paragons of virtue that the world scoffs at their strictness and rigor—that Christians try to be perfect examples of that virtue which the world generally approves but does not want to be "too serious" about. It is rather because the Christian life will be *hidden* from this world and inexplicable to it. Sometimes—perhaps most of the time—the Christian life will appear to follow quite ordinary, unspectacular courses no doubt *too* ordinary for the world. But sometimes it will appear to go quite contrary to what the world would deem wise, prudent, or even ethical. Why should costly ointment be wasted on Jesus? Would it not be better to sell it and give to the poor? Should not Jesus' disciples fast like everyone else? Why should one prefer the company of whores and sinners to polite and virtuous society? Why should a Christian participate in an assassination plot? The Christian life is tuned to the eschatological vision, not to the virtues and heroics of this world.

It has become something of a platitude among religious people that the Sermon on the Mount sets forth the sort of ideal life the world might aspire to and admire. On the contrary, the Sermon on the Mount is one of the most antireligious documents ever written, because of its eschatological perspective. The people it calls "blessed" would hardly qualify as members of virtuous and religious society: the poor in spirit, the mourners, the meek, those who hunger and thirst for righteousness (not those who *have* it!), the merciful, the pure in heart, the peacemakers, the persecuted for righteousness sake, the reviled. The religious and the virtuous are not on the list and in all likelihood would not wish to be. Indeed, the attempt to break the hiddenness is precisely the dangerous thing: "Beware of practicing your piety before men in order to be seen by them; for then you will have no reward from your Father who is in heaven" (Matt. 6:1). Those who wish to be vindicated in their piety before this world, who wish to be praised by other people, *have* their reward: "Thus, when you give alms, sound no trumpet before you, as the hypocrites do in the synagogues and in the streets, that they may be praised by men. Truly, I say to you, they have received their reward" (Matt. 6:2). The goodness or the Christianness of one's life should be hidden even from oneself: "But when you give alms, do not let your left hand know what your right hand is doing, so that your alms may be in secret; and your Father who sees in secret will reward you" (Matt. 6:3).

Good works, that is, come as spontaneously and unspectacularly and naturally as fruit from the good tree. Good works should be as natural, say, as running to pick up and comfort a hurt child. No one would think to call that a good work. It is just natural. But that is exactly the point. One would not, attending to the child, bother to let the left hand know what the right hand is doing. One would not be practicing one's piety before others to be

11 / CHRISTIAN LIFE

seen by them. One would be caught up in concern for the child. And when it was over, it would be forgotten. The truly good works, no doubt, are all those we and the world have forgotten. But the Father sees "in secret." His eschatological kingdom will come. The hidden will be revealed.

But how is that possible—such naturalness, such spontaneity? Do not these descriptions remove the Christian life from the realm of the humanly possible? Of course. That is just what it means to say that the eschatological word as law, as letter, reveals sin—reveals just how lost we are at the same time as the Spirit gives life. That is what it means to say that we can be saved only by God's grace in Jesus. We can be saved only by listening to his word of justification and believing it. That alone will begin the cure, even if it is a matter of always beginning again. The world may perhaps suggest a thousand better ways that appeal to our ambition and pride or self-reliance. But they will not work. They will lead neither to sanctification nor to good works. "No one who puts his hand to the plow and looks back is fit for the kingdom of God" (Luke 9:62). One who is justified by faith is sanctified by being drawn into its eschatological vision and hope. One who catches that vision will be sanctified by it; one who does not is blind. "For to him who has will more be given; and from him who has not, even what he has will be taken away" (Mark 4:25).

NOTES

1. Perhaps it was too radical for the young movement to absorb. The threat of moral chaos no doubt made it difficult to make clear what was involved. But something of that sort seems always to be the fate of Christian eschatology. It is sacrificed for the sake of expediency and continuity, with the result that the gospel gets buried. Moral chaos we always have with us—maybe just because we bury the gospel!

2. Hans J. Iwand, *Um den rechten Glauben*, Gesammelte Aufsätze, ed. K. G. Steck (Munich: Chr. Kaiser, 1959), pp. 17ff.

3. Lauri Haikola, *Studien zu Luther und zum Luthertum*, UUA (Uppsala: Lundequistska Bokhandeln, 1958), pp. 9ff.

4. Heinrich Schmid, *The Doctrinal Theology of the Evangelical Lutheran Church*, 3d ed., trans. Charles A. Hay and Henry E. Jacobs (Minneapolis: Augsburg Publishing House, n.d.), pp. 424–25.

5. One brave but bumbling soul, Nicholas von Amsdorf, had the temerity to suggest that good works were detrimental to salvation. Taken at face value, the statement is of course preposterous. Yet in his own way, on the practical level fostered by centuries of timid semigospel preaching, Amsdorf was right. Much of the good work done by church people, the little bit one has defined as necessary, *is* detrimental to salvation. The good works resulting from preaching their necessity turn out to be mere tokens, a pittance that insulates and excuses from deeper involvement. All the attempts to mediate between those who held out for necessity and those who claimed good

JUSTIFICATION AND SANCTIFICATION

works detrimental resulted mostly in much tinkering with the language (see Formula of Concord, Article IV), which only masks the real problem: Forensic justification simply will not fit with the traditional scheme. Afraid that such justification goes too far, one takes back with the other hand what one has given with the one and gets mired in the question of the necessity of doing good works "too."

6. Wilhelm Dantine, *Justification of the Ungodly*, trans. Eric and Ruth Gritsch (St. Louis: Concordia Publishing House, 1969), pp. 32–33.

7. Cf. Jaroslav Pelikan, "The Origins of the Subject-Object Antithesis in Lutheran Theology," *CTM* 21 (1950): 94–104.

8. Schmid, *Doctrinal Theology*, p. 407.

9. Ibid., p. 408.

10. Dantine, *Justification*, p. 18.

11. Wilfried Joest, *Gesetz und Freiheit*, 2d ed. (Göttingen: Vandenhoeck & Ruprecht, 1956), pp. 60ff.

12. "Proficere, hoc est semper a novo incipere." *WA* 56:486, 7.

13. Joest, *Gesetz und Freiheit*, p. 62.

14. *WA* 40²:351, 27ff.

15. Martin Luther, *Lectures on Romans*, trans. and ed. W. Pauck, LCC 15 (Philadelphia: Westminster Press, 1961), p. 129. *LW* 25:262.

16. Karl Holl, largely on the basis of his interpretation of the famous illustration of the patient believing the promise of the doctor and like images used in the lectures on Romans, came to the judgment that justification for Luther was "analytic." The passage is important enough to bear repeating: "It is similar to the case of a sick man who believes the doctor who promises him a sure recovery and in the meantime obeys the doctor's orders in the hope of the promised recovery. He abstains from those things which have been forbidden him, so that he may in no way hinder the promised return to health or increase his sickness until the doctor can fulfill his promise to him. Now is this sick man well? The fact is that he is both sick and well at the same time. He is sick in fact, but is well because of the sure promise of the doctor, whom he trusts and who has reckoned him as already cured, because he is sure that he will cure him; for he has already begun to cure him and no longer reckons to him a sickness unto death" (*LW* 25:260). Careful reading reveals that Holl misses the point. Everything hinges on the patient's belief and trust in the doctor and his promise. The promise makes the patient well (already cured, "just") at the *same time* as he is sick ("sinner"). The doctor's promise *is* the cure which takes the patient away from the sickness unto death and produces a different way of life. F. Brunstäd was right in opposing Holl by insisting on a *synthetic* justification. Cf. Karl Holl, *Gesammelte Aufsätze*, vol. 1, 7th ed. (Tübingen: J. C. B. Mohr [Paul Siebeck], 1948), pp. 119, 125; vol. 3, p. 532; F. Brunstäd, *Theologie der lutherischen Bekenntnisschriften* (Gütersloh: Bertelsmann, 1951), p. 76.

17. Joest, *Gesetz und Freiheit*, p. 70.

18. Ibid., p. 93.

19. Luther, *Romans*, p. 194.

20. Ibid.

21. Joest, *Gesetz und Freiheit*, p. 93.

22. Ibid., p. 98.

11 / CHRISTIAN LIFE

23. *WA* 10¹ 2:431, 6ff.
24. Ibid., 430:30ff.
25. Hans Joachim Iwand, *Nachgelassene Werke*, vol. 5, *Luthers Theologie*, ed. J. Haar (Munich: Chr. Kaiser, 1974), p. 137. The quote is from *WA* 10¹ 2:431, 1ff.
26. *WA* Br 2:372, 83ff.
27. *WA* DB 7, 8:30ff.; *LW* 35:370–71 (Preface to Romans).
28. Cf. Iwand, *Luthers Theologie*, pp. 141ff.; *WA* 36:360, 22ff.

3
Justification and This World

Justification as an unconditional act does not abolish the law, but upholds it in all its stringency, obviating both antinomianism and the "third use of the law." Justification by faith fosters a new understanding of the life of the Christian "under the law" in this age. Because the end and goal are given to faith, the law is now to be incarnated "in the flesh." To be "saved" means to be "reborn" into *this* world. God's commandments take the Christian into this world, not on a quest for another or for one's own holiness. A distinction between the "two kingdoms" (this age and the next) must indeed be maintained for the sake of the unconditional gospel, but this must not mean either synthesis or separation. The unconditionality of the eschatological kingdom prevents synthesis at the same time as it prohibits separation or premature escape from this world to the next. Thus this world is given back to the believer as God's good creation for the time being as a place for service.

JUSTIFICATION AND THE LAW

Justification as an unconditional eschatological act apart from law and its works demands reassessment of our ideas about the law. Paul put the question for us: "Do we then overthrow the law by this faith?" Does justification make us antinomians, enemies of the law? So it might seem at first glance, and especially in light of the persistent polemic against thinking in terms of law, moral progress, the quest for virtue, found in the earlier pages of this *locus*. The answer Paul gives is therefore likely to be puzzling: "By no means! On the contrary, we uphold the law" (Rom. 3:31). How is the law upheld precisely by maintaining we are justified entirely apart from it? Attempting an answer to that question is the task of this section. It is important because it is one of the building blocks in constructing an understanding of the relationship between eschatological justification and life in this world. Living under the law is a determinative factor for life in this world, this "age." If a positive

11 / CHRISTIAN LIFE

relationship to it is not established, eschatology will lead only to abandoning this world—a temptation all too prevalent in Christian circles.

How does justification by faith uphold the law? We have already seen the beginning of the answer in the treatment of the functional understanding of law. In the light of the unconditional nature of justification, the law functions first and foremost to reveal sin, to reveal that apart from justification by faith there is no hope for us. Precisely justification as an unconditional gift, therefore, insists that law be established in its absolute clarity, stringency, and strength. Precisely justification will insist that there be no loopholes in the law, no watering down, no casuistic amelioration. "I testify again to every man who receives circumcision that he is bound to keep the whole law" (Gal. 5:3). To break one commandment is to break them all. One cannot comfort oneself with the platitude that one is at least as good as the next person, or congratulate oneself on being a champion of the law even if one does not exactly keep it.

> But if you call yourself a Jew and rely upon the law and boast of your relation to God and know his will and approve what is excellent, because you are instructed in the law, and if you are sure that you are a guide to the blind, a light to those who are in darkness, a corrector of the foolish, a teacher of children, having in the law the embodiment of knowledge and truth—you then who teach others, will you not teach yourself? (Rom. 2:17–21)

Precisely from the point of view of the eschatological breaking in of the kingdom in Jesus, no relaxation of the law is envisaged. Indeed, the law is restated in all its vigor.

> Think not that I have come to abolish the law and the prophets; I have come not to abolish them but to fulfill them. For truly, I say to you, till heaven and earth pass away, not an iota, not a dot, will pass from the law until all is accomplished. Whoever then relaxes one of the least of these commandments and teaches men so, shall be called least in the kingdom of heaven; but he who does them and teaches them shall be called great in the kingdom of heaven. For I tell you, unless your righteousness exceeds that of the scribes and Pharisees, you will never enter the kingdom of heaven. (Matt. 5:17–20)

Only one who knows about the end and telos of the law will be able to accept that. Indeed, only from the point of view of unconditional justification will one be able to put Matthew together with Paul. Precisely because imputed righteousness is an absolute gift, which is the end and the telos of the law given to faith, it upholds the absolute demand of the law as its counterpart. When the end and the goal are not *given*, the law becomes endless, insatiable, and threatens to devour everything and destroy everyone. It becomes the irresistible weapon in the hand of the accuser, Satan, the attorney for the prosecution. Then *we* must take steps to end it: We must water it down, apply it casuistically, comfort ourselves moralistically with whatever "dole of vanity can serve the human soul for daily bread," or call our analyst to cure us of our hang-ups. That is the secret of antinomianism of every sort, overt and covert—and most antinomianism, as we shall see, is covert, parading in the guise of championing the law. "Christ is the end of the law, that every one who has faith may be justified" (Rom. 10:4). Wherever that is not realized, there is trouble and people are, quite literally, destroyed.

Unable to rhyme Matt. 5:17–18 with Rom. 10:4, the dogmatic tradition has experienced nothing but trouble over the law. When one does not see that "heaven and earth" *do* "pass away" in the eschatological fulfillment anticipated and grasped by faith, and that just such fulfillment *is* the end and the goal, Paul and Matthew are at irreconcilable odds. Unable to grasp this fulfillment as end, the tradition for the most part had to indulge in what was strictly forbidden by both Matthew and Paul: tampering with the content of the law to arrive at a compromise. The result was the idea that in Christ the ceremonial laws of the Old Testament were abrogated (thus throwing a sop to Paul's claim that Christ was the "end" of the law) while the "moral" law was not (thus supposedly satisfying Matthew's claim that not one iota or dot would pass away until "the end"). But that is patent nonsense which only confuses the issue further and completely obscures the eschatology involved. Neither Testament makes that kind of distinction between ceremonial and moral law. Indeed, it seems that in most instances, ruptures of the ceremonial law are more serious than those of the moral law. Furthermore, the tradition was left with the problem of deciding just what was moral and what was ceremonial. Are the first three commandments, for instance, moral or ceremonial? One might, of course, as happened most generally, try to settle on the decalogue as the moral law. But there is a good deal in the Old Testament and the New outside the decalogue which might also qualify as moral and ethical material of the highest quality. Who is to decide?

The outcome of such confusion was, in general, that natural law became the arbiter. Natural law decides what is moral and what is not. But therewith the fate of the church's understanding of law was sealed, as well as of its eschatological outlook. Natural law became the structural backbone of the theological system, displacing eschatology. Without eschatology, however, the church had to take over administration of the law and reduce it to manageable proportions, distinguishing "mortal" and "venial" transgressions of law, applying it casuistically to this or that case, separating what ought to be done by everyone from what might be done by the more serious and dedicated. In short, under the guise of being for the law the church tended to become

11 / CHRISTIAN LIFE

covertly antinomian. As a result, the question of law never ceased to bother, and outbreaks of reformation in the name of the gospel became the recurring fate of the church.[1]

Where the gospel of justification by faith is not comprehended in its full eschatological sense, as bringing end and new beginning, death and new life, there will be trouble with the law. Where the gospel is not grasped, the law will not be grasped either. The important point is faith: that Christ is the end of the law so that everyone who has *faith* may be justified—faith experienced as new life from death.

Where Christ is not the end of the law—its goal and fulfillment—then we with our theology must take steps to bring it to heel. That is the root cause of all antinomianism in the church. Antinomianism is a curious and interesting phenomenon dogmatically because it is the attempt to remedy one mistake by another. It is the attempt to remedy the mistake of nomism by the mistake of antinomism. Once the eschatological outlook has been displaced by an eternal order of law, antinomianism is the attempt to remedy the situation with a false and realized eschatology. It is the attempt to end the law by a theological *tour de force*. Antinomianism wants to solve the problem of law by removing it or relaxing or changing it.

This is demonstrated by the antinomian controversies following the Reformation. Once justification by faith had again been reasserted in radical fashion, it was natural that heavy pressure would be brought to bear on the received understanding of law. John Agricola rightly sensed that justification by faith could not simply be combined with the older idea of law as an eternal order, still evident in some of Philip Melanchthon's theological constructions.[2] Agricola tried to solve the matter by positing a temporal (and perhaps spatial) end to the law. Since Christ is the end of the law, the law must be banished from the church. The law belongs in city hall; only the gospel is to be preached in the church. True repentance comes from the preaching of the New Testament message about Christ, not (as Melanchthon is supposed to have held) from the Old Testament and the law. The nomism that results from loss of eschatology is countered by an antinomism, by false eschatology.

Nomism is ill-equipped to counter antinomianism with evangelical weapons, because it has already compromised the eschatological gospel. Hence it can fight only from the position of law and charge its opponent with the sin and heresy of antinomianism. The victory of nomism over antinomianism in the church is therefore hardly cause for celebration. True opposition can be launched only from the position of a faith which has been grasped by the eschatological justification. If justification exposes sin and upholds the law against sin at the same time as it grants fulfillment, one cannot speak of a temporal or spatial end to law in *this* age. The end is eschatological: anticipated in faith and given in full only at the parousia. The remedy for antinomianism is not nomistic but eschatological. From the perspective of one who knows that Christ is the end of the law *to faith*, antinomianism is not so much a heresy as an impossibility. One cannot get rid of law by theological erasure. The end does not come because theological textbooks say it has. The law must and will remain "on account of sin," until the final end of the sinner and the complete appearance of the new being. Law cannot be banished by theologians. Any attempt to do so will lead only to its return in worse form. Agricola, for instance, wished to banish the Old Testament law, but turned right around and made a law of the New Testament. Only Christ is the end of the law. The end is an eschatological event. Faith is grasped by that and thus, *knowing the end*, upholds the law. One who is grasped by the eschatological vision waits for the day when law will be no more because what it demands and points to will be given in full.

The debate about the "third use" of the law shifts the argument to the other pole of the eschatological dialectic. If the former controversy was about the use of law *before* faith, this latter is about use of the law *after* the eschatological event. The question is whether one can or should speak of a "third" use of the law in addition to the political use (to restrain evil) and the theological use (to convict of sin): a use of the law by the reborn Christian *as* Christian, in which law functions as a "guide to the Christian life." One can see immediately that the issue is still the eschatological one: What difference does the eschatological event make vis-à-vis the law? Does "the Christian" still need the law after believing the word of justification? Some say yes, some say no. The Protestant tradition has had, and continues to have, representatives on both sides of the issue.

The confusion results, once again, from failure to argue consistently from an eschatological perspective. Thus there is most often a good deal of terminological ambiguity. What does one mean by "the reborn Christian" who now, supposedly, "uses" the law in a "third" way? Is it because one is a Christian that one now uses the law in a third way? Or is it because one is not yet completely a Christian that one still needs the law as a guide? The classical definition would seem to be that it is the former. Because one is a "reborn Christian," one may now use the law in a way different from others: not to convict of sin or to restrain evil but simply as a guide to what one should do as a Christian.

If that is what is meant by the "third use," it is clear that anyone grasped by the eschatological perspective must resist it, for the sake of the radical newness of eschatological hope. Law cannot be reintroduced *after* the end, for the end means perfect fulfillment. A perfect lover would not need laws about what to do. A perfect Christian would not need to be told what was right or wrong. One must hold out for that vision lest law conquer all. The day when all will be "written on our hearts" is the center of the biblical prom-

11 / CHRISTIAN LIFE

ise. To surrender that is to surrender biblical eschatology. Luther, it seems, argued consistently from this point of view and is thus generally regarded as opposing a "third use" of the law.[3]

From the eschatological perspective the legitimate concerns badly expressed in the idea of a third use of the law can be sorted out. First, one who has been grasped by the eschatological vision looks on law differently from one who has not. But that is not to say that one sees a "third" use. What one sees is precisely the difference between law and gospel, so that law can be established in its *first* two uses this side of the eschaton. Before that vision or when it fades, law is misused as a way of salvation, a means of escape. One does not know the difference between law and gospel.

Second, one grasped by the eschatological vision will recognize the continuing need for the law. But this too does not mean a third use. Rather, just because of "rebirth" in faith, one will see how much one is a sinner and will be until the end. One will see that one is not yet a "Christian." One will see precisely that one has no particular advantages over those who are not yet reborn. One will see one's solidarity with the rest of the human race and wait in hope until the end, leaving the heroics and pretensions to spiritual athletes.

The idea of a third use of the law after rebirth thus obscures the eschatological nature of that event and consequently mistakes our relationship to this world. "Rebirth" does not mean premature translation in time into a state different from that of the rest of humankind, in which one is now privileged to use the law differently. That would be a false eschatology. Rebirth, since it leads to the understanding of self as *simul iustus et peccator*, simply cannot share such an idea of conversion. One is never converted in that sense, because one must be converted anew each day. Until the end, therefore, one grasped by the eschatological vision will know that he or she needs the law in precisely the same way that the rest of humankind needs it: to restrain evil and convict of sin.

The idea of a third use furthermore contains a certain amount of hubris. It seems to assume that humans are the users of the law, so that one can now speak of the Christian as "using" the law in a third way. But that cannot ultimately be the case. God is the author of the law; God, not we, is the user of the law. We cannot preside over the law's use in order to speak of a third use which neither restrains evil nor convicts of sin.

Ultimately it must be asked whether the idea of the third use does not entail a covert antinomianism. Antinomianism, we have said, roots in the fact that when the eschatological end of law is missed, theology must step in to alter and tame that law. What are we to say of a law that has become a more or less harmless guide? What is actually proposed is an alteration in the view of law to fit the view of the Christian life as immanent moral progress. Because one does not want to die, one disarms the law and makes it relatively harmless. Law is changed to accommodate sin.

The eschatological perspective cannot abide such a view of law. "Whoever then relaxes one of the least of these commandments and teaches men so, shall be called least in the kingdom of heaven." If one is seriously to maintain imputed righteousness as the eschatological power of new life out of death, one can speak neither of a temporal end to the law nor of its transformation into a third thing, a more or less neutral guide. The law is not to be changed; the *sinner* is to be changed. For Luther the sinner as the *totus peccator* is attacked by law unto death, until the new being arises who actually begins to love that law, that will of God. There are only two possibilities vis-à-vis law as the expression of the will of God. It is either an enemy or a friend, but never a neutral guide. It impinges on us either as the letter which kills or as the Spirit which gives life, but never as something in between.[4]

Exegetes who think they are doing the Old Testament a favor by making its view of law akin to the "third use" may therefore simply be covertly antinomian. Thinking to construct an apology for the Old Testament and its law, they succeed only in robbing it of its majesty and power—what the reformers called its "office." For the reformers there was nothing pejorative in speaking of the Old Testament as *law*, in majestic and even terrifying glory. Just so, the Old Testament gained a status and "office" worthy of and pointing to its counterpart in the New. Only tender antinomians have to find ways to apologize for it.

The same kind of interpretation would apply to the New Testament paraenetic materials. It can hardly be maintained that the exhortations of the New Testament, taken literally, in any degree attenuate the will of God or God's law. If anything, the stakes are raised precisely because of the gospel. We are even exhorted to arise from the dead. How shall we do that? The exhortations are either bad news or good news—between which our actual life as *simul iustus et peccator* resonates until the day when Christ shall be all in all. But they are *not* something in between.

To be true to a view of the Christian life rooted in justification by faith, one must arrive at a different understanding of the relationship between life and law. We cannot look on life as ascent into the rarified air of what the world calls spiritual. That is always the world's substitute for eschatology. Rather, life is a descent, an "incarnation" in the world in service and love. Luther tried to get at that with his formula *"conscientia in evangelio, caro in lege"* (the conscience in the gospel, the flesh in the law).[5] The conscience is ruled and captivated by the gospel, by the eschatological vision. The "flesh" however, the empirical life I live in this age, remains "in the law," and in a double sense: The law attacks "the flesh," which is inimical to the will of God, and under the impulse of the spontaneity and joy fostered by the gospel

11 / CHRISTIAN LIFE

this empirical life is to become the fulfillment of the will of God. Because of the gospel in the conscience, the Christian is free so that the true battle can be joined in the flesh.

The greatest danger for the eschatological view that speaks of the death of the old and the resurrection of the new is that the idea of the "new person" can all too easily become a mystical theologoumenon without substance, something the theologian calls on to solve all dogmatic problems. That, no doubt, is what those who insisted on the "third use" of the law were most afraid of: the "reborn" Christian who does not know what to do and is cast on his or her own feelings or autonomy. The new being, however, is to be incarnated in down-to-earth fashion in the concrete calling of the Christian in this world. In that battle—in the calling in this world, in the flesh—the law of God is ultimately not an enemy or an emasculated guide but a true and loved friend. For one should make no mistake about it: *The law of God is to be and will be fulfilled*. It will not be fulfilled, however, by our powers, but only by the power of the righteousness of God given to faith.

THE SELF AS GOD'S CREATURE

When justification by faith is grasped as an eschatological event that puts the old to death and raises up the new, we receive ourselves and the world back again as God's good creation. If Christ is the end and goal of the law, he is also the end, goal, and existential limit of our lives in this age. "For to me to live is Christ, and to die is gain" (Phil. 1:21). Where that is not the case, we shall have to depend on our efforts under the law to carry us to whatever "beyond" awaits. The law then becomes endless and we its eternal slaves. Furthermore, the law is then "used" by us (not by God, its author) as a preparation for eternity, an escape hatchway from this world. It is not used *for* this world as was intended; it is used for the next. It is a preparation for eternity, a means by which I supposedly can shape my own destiny—which is to say, extend my selfishness into eternity, if I can manage it.

Where the eschatological nature of justification is not grasped, self and world as God's good creation are also lost. Being a creature of God is not good enough. We are always on our way somewhere else, using the law as our instrument and even piously attempting to enlist the aid of Christ and his grace in our quest. We then have no time for this world or for others. We are preparing for eternity. "God, I thank thee that I am not like other men, extortioners, unjust, adulterers, or even like this tax collector. I fast twice a week, I give tithes of all that I get" (Luke 18:11–12).

But here once again the "eschato-logic" proves itself: "From him who has not, even what he has will be taken away" (Mark 4:25) and "Whoever would save his life will lose it" (Mark 8:35). The attempt to combine justification with such self-understanding under the law leads only to loss of the goodness of creation. If we think to exalt grace as the source of strength to make our escape, this can be done only by denigrating our created, natural strength. To give glory to grace we have to take it away from creation. Thus we end by turning grace into a blasphemy against creation. "Total depravity" in this context means a total annihilation of natural goodness. We lose the very life we had thought to save. Once again, the impossibility of combining salvation by works with grace demonstrates itself.

We can receive the self back as God's good creation only when we begin to view our lives from the perspective of eschatological faith. Christ is the end of the law to faith. The eschatological kingdom is God's unconditional gift. It comes by God's grace and power alone, in God's good time. That is the end and goal of our lives, our personal existential limit. When this is grasped in faith, we begin to see at last that our corruption and depravity consists not in falling from some moral and spiritual height, but precisely in aspiring to such heights on our own strength and virtue. We succumb to the temptation "You shall not die, you shall be as gods, knowing good from evil." Our depravity consists not in what we have lost of our created goodness, but in what we have added to it: precisely the attempt to "be as gods," to escape from creation. The totality of our depravity consists in the blindness: We do not even see that our virtues are as sinful as our vices. Both under the guise of being virtuous and religious and in addiction to self-serving vices, we are bent on escaping from creaturehood and creation. Creation is not good enough for us.

Justification as an eschatological event gives unconditionally the end and goal of life, to faith "for the time being." They are given to faith, not to sight. It must be done so, for justification must create freedom. It must truly heal and save the disaffected heart, soul, and mind. This can be done only if all is done in complete freedom and spontaneity. The goal of life cannot be forced on us. Therefore it comes in hidden form, *sub contrario*, given to *faith*. By such faith the end and goal are given, and we can begin to believe in the goodness of being a creature, to wait "for the time being" for the coming of the kingdom in its fullness. We are given back the self as a good creation; we are given time for this world, for this creation.

That is what being saved means. To be reborn means to be born again into the world God created, to become a member of the truly human race. To die to the old means to die to both the viciousness and the heaven-storming pretentions of the religious old Adam and to walk in the newness of *created* life. What was lost in the fall was *faith*, in God and God's creation. To be saved, healed, is to receive creation back again as God's gift, to again receive

11 / CHRISTIAN LIFE

time for it, to get room to live, to rejoice and give praise to the Creator. It is to have one's lips unsealed so that the mouth will "show forth his praise." This happens when the end and the goal are given in Christ.

What then does one do when one is saved? One lives in this world as God's creature "for the time being." What does that mean? It means that—as Luther's catechism has it—we should "fear, love, and trust in God above all things," and do what God has commanded us to do—in "the flesh." With the conscience claimed by the eschatological promise, the "flesh" lives in this world in the law of God. The point in saying that is not, now, to reinstate what was called the third use of the law. The "flesh" in *this* world "for the time being" is to do the commandments of God not in some third way but as its entry into this world where the rest of humankind lives.

One can best see what the Reformation originally meant by this by looking at a writing like "The Judgment of Martin Luther on Monastic Vows" (1521).[6] The point is simply that following God's commandments will take us into the world of the neighbor in service and love, not into the world of self-chosen and self-serving "religious" works. The point is not that Luther sought to relax the ideals or to polemicize against communal life as a possible base for service to the world, or to reduce everything to the lowest common denominator of what is attainable in daily life. The point is rather that in the context of the penitential system the monastic vows lead to self-chosen holiness which is not commanded by God. God, for instance, does not command poverty as some sort of ideal for everyone who wishes to be truly holy. Such vows do proceed not from faith or from the commandment of God but rather from one's own lust for holiness. And whoever has this lust for holiness will never be satisfied with the commandments of God, because the commandments of God take one away from self into the world of the other.

Living by the commandments of God "in the flesh" is the opposite of one's own quest for holiness. It means incarnating what God has commanded in and for the world. The law is to be used in that way, as its author intended. The rejection of monastic vows, and with them the quest for one's own holiness, meant for Luther a new understanding of and love for God's commandments. What God commands takes us into the natural, created world. Here the proper place of "natural law" is to be found. By natural law most seem to mean "supernatural" law, a law built into the universe which, if followed, leads to eternal bliss, a kind of built-in permanent escape mechanism. Revealed law is then something like the completion, the clarification of what has been dimmed by the fall, the final extension of the escape ladder. That is not what Luther meant by it, even when he compared and often identified the commandments of God with "natural law." He meant precisely *natural* and not supernatural law. The commandments of God do not command anything contrary to life, anything supernatural or superhuman, but rather what anyone who properly consults his or her reason would have to acknowledge as good and right—exemplified, say, by the golden rule. Following the commandments of God and the natural law will hardly serve one's inflated and grandiose quests for holiness, but it might lead to good works in this world. It will not lead to the isolation of pole-sitting "holy men," but it might make Christians who are involved in giving themselves to this world. When the conscience is captivated by the gospel, "the flesh" living in the law does *good* works: It does what God wants.

Once again it is seen that such obedience is not spectacular in the world's eyes. It is quite ordinary most of the time. God's commandments do not lead to spiritual heroics: just honor your parents, do not kill, steal, commit adultery, covet, and so on. But this is just the sort of life about which one might say, "Yes, we all ought to live naturally and peacefully like that." At bottom the good work to which God's command leads is something so self-evident, so unspectacular, so plain, that it speaks a language everyone should understand.[7] The eschatological end given to faith gives us back the gift of life, of created life in this world. It *saves* us. It makes us human beings again.

THIS WORLD AS GOD'S CREATION

The relationship between justification and the world as we know it brings us to the much discussed and disputed doctrine of the two "kingdoms" or "realms." So much ink has been spilled over this matter that it is not possible for us here to follow all the arguments. Perhaps, however, in light of what we have already said, the issues can briefly be sorted out. If justification is an eschatological event that creates the faith we have spoken of, then through such an event faith receives the world back again as God's good creation. The understanding of the world as God's good creation is the result of eschatological faith, not of speculation about how it all began. When the world's end and goal are given to faith, it begins to appear, to faith alone, as the world God intends.

Since the eschatological kingdom is promised only to faith and not yet to sight, there is for the time being a duality; there are two "ages," two sorts of "rule" or sovereignty. This is the basis for any doctrine of "two kingdoms," and it must be maintained in spite of the distortions and ill use the doctrine has suffered through the centuries. The distinction between this age with its kind of rule and the coming age with its rule must be made for the sake of the eschatological and unconditional nature of the gospel. Where the distinction is blurred or lost, the gospel will be drawn into various compromises with the workings of this age, made conditional, and eventually be lost. "My kingship," Jesus said before Pilate, "is not of this world; if my kingship were of this world, my servants would fight, that I might not be handed over to

11 / CHRISTIAN LIFE

the Jews; but my kingship is not from the world" (John 18:36). Nothing one can do with the resources of this world can avail to bring in or establish Jesus' kingship. The distinction at that point is absolute, and must be so, or there is no gospel.[8]

Problems with the doctrine of the two kingdoms arise not because two such sorts of rule are distinguished but because the doctrine comes into a world that already possesses its own doctrines of two kingdoms. The doctrine comes into a world which in its fallen state is already split: material versus spiritual, sensible versus intelligible, real versus ideal, secular versus sacred, and so on endlessly.[9] Since the territory is already occupied by various "two kingdoms" doctrines, the eschatological doctrine is usually mixed with one or the other of them. The world already has its laws, its ways to heaven; and the inevitable tendency is always to enlist the gospel in one cause or another and so lose it.

The question therefore is not whether "two kingdoms" or types of rule or kingship should be distinguished (that cannot be avoided), but how they can and should be related. The question of the relationship of the two kingdoms is really the macrocosm of what we have already seen in the microcosm of the relationships between law and gospel, and between justification and sanctification. The attempt to synthesize law with gospel is disastrous. Likewise the attempt to synthesize the rule or kingship of Christ with that of this age and its ambitions will be disastrous and ultimately destructive. In the microcosm of individual piety it produces either despair or presumption. It drives to self-destruction: either despair over self and failure or pride in the ability of the self to deny itself and come as close as possible to suicide without actually committing it. In the macrocosm it produces tyranny, oppression, imperialism, genocide, and murder. One or another of the world's false eschatologies is enforced and sanctified with the name of Christ and the gospel. Like the "flesh" which in the microcosm is to be shucked off for the sake of the "spirit," in the macrocosm the "masses," the "non-Aryans," the "unbelievers," the "minorities," all who do not fit the plan, become expendable.

Faced with such attempts at synthesis, a "two kingdoms" doctrine inspired by the gospel will always say no. The gospel of Jesus Christ simply cannot be synthesized with the causes of this age, however grand or just. The eschatological kingdom comes as an unconditional gift. God puts to death the old and raises up the new *in Christ*. Where that is not held absolutely, humans take up stones, cudgels, and arms to kill, supposedly to complete the job left unfinished by Christ. The result is self-destruction in the microcosm and destruction of others in the macrocosm. God gave the Son to save the world, *this* world. He has died for us. One cannot bring in the kingdom by discipline, tyranny, or by exterminating its enemies. By such means, one only realizes the kingdom of the adversary.

JUSTIFICATION AND THIS WORLD

The second error would be separation of the two kingdoms. In the microcosm of individual piety, this occurs in the absolute separation of justification from sanctification. One tries to combat the premature synthesis of justification and sanctification by leaving the scheme of law intact, by making justification a forensic sheer declaration and separating sanctification as a subsequent process under the "third use" of the law. The result is a false eschatology. One prematurely escapes from the world into an isolated realm—perhaps the church—where one is separated from the rest of the world with one's own special use of the law. The rule or kingdom of Christ has been identified or confused with one of the world's idealisms.

In the macrocosm, this error identifies the eschatological kingdom of Christ with the church; and the church, understood as a species of ideal religious community according to the world's models, is separated from the mundane and profane affairs of this world. Religion is separated from the state, and from politics, economics, and so on. But the result of such separation is again that the world is abandoned to the adversary. Where vestigial remains of humanistic tradition persist, justice will prevail to some extent, but probably not for long. A world that has forgotten what law is for will easily find ways to justify human avarice and malice, most often under the form of high-sounding ideals and the promises of false eschatologies.

Both the synthesis of the two kingdoms and their separation result from false eschatology. Synthesis thinks it possible to combine Christ's kingdom with this-worldly projects; separation thinks it possible prematurely to escape into an eschatological vestibule apart from the world. Neither is possible for a faith born of unconditional justification. Justification is the end and goal; it is death and resurrection. As such it is the believer's absolute personal and existential limit, which makes possible a turning to this world, a receiving back of this world as God's creation. We shall receive the world, this world, as God's good creation, as the place to which we turn to serve, only to the extent that we believe unconditional justification as our true eschatological limit and goal. The gift of the eschatological kingdom is the only thing which opens up for us *this* world as also God's kingdom. The creaturehood of this world is a belief and hope, granted to faith.

To faith, neither synthesis nor separation is possible. The distinction is absolute: God's eschatological kingdom comes solely and unconditionally by God's power, inaugurated by the death and resurrection of Christ, carried to faith by the proclamation, and empowered by the Spirit. And precisely because the distinction is absolute, we are given back this world as God's creation in which to serve and carry out God's will in anticipation of God's ultimate triumph. Thus we pray: "Thy kingdom come, thy will be done, on earth as it is in heaven." Because the distinction is absolute, there is only one place, one kingdom for the time being, in which we can live, work, and serve: this

11 / CHRISTIAN LIFE

world. No escape is possible. We must wait, serve, and hope, until the kingdom of this world is become the kingdom of our God and of Christ. It is perhaps curious: Only where the kingdoms are thus distinguished will there be functionally one kingdom. Whenever the distinction is not absolute, the eschatological kingdom will be confused with one of the world's religious kingdoms, and all will be lost. The world's doctrines, no matter how much they *claim* to be "one kingdom" doctrines, always *function* as two; this world, the present world, is always sacrificed for the sake of some other ideal world.

The world is given back to us as a place in which to serve—indeed, as the only place in which we can serve. To die and to be raised to newness of life by faith is to die to all escapism—either of the "fleshly" sort or the "spiritual," and to be reborn a creature in God's creation. To die and be raised to newness of life is to die to all individualism and to become a member of Christ's body, the church, to worship, pray, and praise. The church is that body which believes and bears witness to the coming of God's kingdom by the power of God's unconditional grace. Precisely in that light the church engages in its activity in and for this world. Perhaps one can say, the church is the macrocosm of Luther's formula: "Conscience in the gospel, flesh in the law." Knowing the unconditional gospel, the church bears witness to and incarnates the proper use of the law in the world. This is the basis for its political activity. The law and politics are for taking care of people. "The sabbath was made for man, not man for the sabbath" (Mark 2:27). In the light of unconditional grace, the church cannot separate itself from political concerns, but must look on itself as the witness to the proper use of God's creation and God's law, in taking care of God's creatures.

How does the church which has heard decide what to do? It uses its head and its heart in the concrete situation, to attempt to incarnate the commandment of God. In this task the church can and must utilize all the wisdom of its own tradition and experience as well as the wisdom of the world. In seeking answers in concrete situations to the question "What should we do?" the church can draw on the work of the wise of all ages, the specialists who can help in seeking to apply the commandment of God to take care of the earth and the neighbor in complex and changing situations.

From this vantage point, we can also make better sense of Paul's injunction to "be subject to the governing authorities" (Rom. 13) and of the Reformation's derivation of respect for civil authority from the fourth commandment ("Honor your father and mother that it may be well with you and you may live long upon this earth"). Because of the promise given to faith, we are sent into this world with respect for the authority God has established there under the law. The point of the injunction is not to make Christians into reactionary conservatives or subservient slaves to the status quo. It would hardly have occurred to Paul (or to Luther and the reformers) that anyone grasped by the power of the eschatological promise would be such. Only centuries of attempted synthesis between "eternal law" and the gospel have eroded the eschatological vision and turned Christians into reactionaries. The point of the injunctions is quite the opposite. Christians are likely to be impatient enthusiasts, who think the gospel gives them the right to rebel against and flaunt all existing order. The injunctions remind that this is not so. God is still God—in this world as well. Redemption is not against creation. If Christians are not reactionary conservatives protecting the status quo, neither are they in principle revolutionaries thinking to bring in the eschaton by force. Their concern is for the proper use of law and authority to care for human beings and to foster truly human existence and just societies. The Christian aim is to support causes, laws, and authorities that give promise of justice, whatever form (conservative, liberal, or even revolutionary) these may take at a given time, always remembering that God's kingdom comes by God's power alone in God's good time.

The gospel as the unconditional promise of the kingdom humanizes and naturalizes the law. No doubt we can say even that it "contextualizes" the law—as long as we realize that the gospel does this and not just the passage of time or historical expediency. The distinction between the two kingdoms or kinds of rule is made precisely to foster such humanization. God's rule in the gospel is the rule of unconditional grace, and as such is the limit and ultimate goal of the rule of this age, which is a conditional rule of law. The tendency is always to project the rule of law into God's eternity and thus tyrannize people rather than care for them. The distinction between the rules is made both to give the rule of law its proper place and to protect the world from the tyranny of the religions which have become a substitute for eschatology (which is what most political ideologies have been and are, including the Marxist dream of the "withering away of the state"). The distinction must be made also (and perhaps especially) for biblical and Christian religions that have succumbed to a false eschatology. The criticism must begin at home. Before rashly plunging into political adventure, we must get our eschatology straight, lest we just add to the tyranny. Centuries of church history do not breed confidence that Christians are immune from destructive religious ideologies.

Separation of church and state, of religion and politics, is an impossible move from the eschatological standpoint. The church as a sociological organization is not an eschatological vestibule into which one can prematurely escape from politics. The distinction makes that clear. Such separation is therefore not to be identified with necessary "two kingdoms" teaching. But church people and theologians should not forget that the actual separation we now have is a political expedient necessitated by bad theology: The world had to take steps to protect itself from false eschatology and its tyranny. If the political

11 / CHRISTIAN LIFE

and social activity of the church just means imposing bad eschatology, the world is no doubt better off without us. The political activity of the church will be properly executed when the church acts in the faith that God's kingdom comes by God's unconditional grace and that for the time being we are to care for God's creatures and God's creation.

NOTES

1. Cf. Martin Werner, *Die Entstehung des christlichen Dogmas*, 2d ed. (Bern: Verlag Paul Haupt, 1941), pp. 197ff.

2. The controversy started over the tricky issue of whether law preaching or gospel preaching leads to "true" repentance.

3. Formula of Concord (Article VI) vacillates on the issue. On the one hand, it speaks of a third use of the law to be applied to the regenerate, but then it goes on to say it is necessary because regeneration is incomplete in this life. It is an attempt to have it both ways and thus threatens only to obscure the issue.

4. Wilfried Joest, *Gesetz und Freiheit*, 2d ed. (Göttingen: Vandenhoeck & Ruprecht, 1956), pp. 190ff.

5. See ibid., pp. 76ff., 998–99.

6. *LW* 44, 243ff. See Hans Joachim Iwand, *Nachgelassene Werke*, vol. 5, *Luthers Theologie*, ed. J. Haar (Munich: Chr. Kaiser, 1974), pp. 147ff.

7. Iwand, *Luthers Theologie*, 150.

8. Cf. Gerhard Ebeling, "Die Notwendigkeit der Lehre von den zwei Reichen," in *Wort und Glaube* (Tübingen: J. C. B. Mohr [Paul Siebeck], 1960), pp. 407ff.

9. See ibid., esp. pp. 420ff.

4
Justification Today

The doctrine of justification is always and everywhere relevant because it speaks of God's judgment on our existence and drives to the direct declaration of that judgment itself. For that reason justification language is dogmatically primary and is the plumb line for the church's proclamation: the article by which the church stands or falls. Its relevance for individual life is that it delivers from the prison all construct for themselves in the fear and denial of death. Its larger relevance for the life of the world derives from the vision it inspires, in contrast to competing visions. It directs our vision beyond absolutism and relativism to the hope that God's will be done "on earth as in heaven."

THE QUESTION OF RELEVANCE

Is what we have said about justification "relevant" today? Arguments about relevance are somehow always elusive, mostly depressingly dull and finally inconclusive. Probing for the "modern" person, to whom one is supposed to be relevant, has become more and more like shooting at a moving target. As Karl Barth put it, one seems always to be running after the train that has just left. Perhaps part of the problem is that we mistake relevance for topicality. The topical is peculiar to a particular *topos*, a restricted time and place, as are styles which come and go, or "topics" of current interest expatiated on in television talk shows. The topical is here today, gone tomorrow. To be *relevant*, the matter in question must be lifted above the merely topical to the status of that which always and everywhere applies. It is thus redundant to inquire about the relevance of something "today." If it is relevant at all, it is always so.

To be precise we should therefore put our question thus: Is justification by faith as we have described it relevant, or was it only of topical interest? Is it always and everywhere applicable, or does it answer only to certain restricted states and needs of the human psyche? More specifically, Does talk of justification carry credence only for those afflicted by a guilty conscience produced by excessive legalism and penitential practice? Does justification

11 / CHRISTIAN LIFE

language depend too much on metaphors drawn from legal and juridical spheres?

Arguing for the relevance of justification by faith is perhaps like making an apology for marriage in a brothel. Those who have some inkling of what is involved will not need to be convinced, and those who do not will hardly be convinced by such an exercise. But there is utility in such argument nevertheless, since dogmatics is intended as aid and instruction to teachers and preachers. Thus we can make a beginning by reiterating some of the points made in the note at the end of the first chapter of this *locus*. Speaking in terms of justification is dogmatically necessary and relevant (always and everywhere), because such speech deals directly with God's judgment on our existence. It deals directly with the concrete structures of law and justice under which we live. It is a mistake to say that such language is restricted to Paul, Augustine, Luther, and a few others who had some problem with "the law." Everywhere in scripture God is the judge, the ultimate judge over human existence. The "last judgment," the ultimate sentence, is certainly of some relevance. Justification deals directly and conclusively with that judgment. It says what the judgment *is*: You are justified for Jesus' sake.

No doubt there are other metaphors, other pictures and images, for our relationship to God which are important and enlightening and instructive for our communication of the gospel: love, light, truth, meaning, reconciliation, redemption, and so on. They lack the dogmatic importance accorded to justification language, however, because they tend to remain just metaphors, describing the relationship rather than creating it. "Justification" and related concepts like "imputation," "reckoning," and "forgiveness of sins" maintain their relevance because they point to a quite specific use of language, a use consonant with the eschatological character of the event: *doing* the deed, *delivering* the judgment. Justification language, when properly spoken, does not just talk *about* the relationship to God, it decides the issue. It speaks simply and directly: "I forgive you all your sins for Jesus' sake," "I pronounce you just by virtue of Christ's righteousness." It tells us, in effect, why the apology for marriage is not likely to work in the brothel: One cannot merely describe the marriage, one has to give the bridegroom.

Dogmatically speaking, the reason for the priority and abiding relevance of justification language lies just here: It stipulates what kind of communication is supposed to take place in the proclamation of the church. If justification is an unconditional eschatological pronouncement, then it has simply to be pronounced. There may no doubt be all sorts of ways to do that without using the actual terminology of "justification," but this language remains the dogmatic plumb line for the church's proclamation. Thus the article on justification is that by which the church stands or falls. When the church forgets this use of language it has lost its reason for being.

The question whether justification appeals to this or that state of the human psyche or answers to this or that need or consciousness of guilt is dogmatically secondary. Indeed, one can well ask whether justification by faith is strictly speaking relevant to the old Adam at all. It spells the *end* of the old Adam. In that sense it does not cater to our needs as old beings at all; it makes *new* beings. It puts to death and raises up. The relevance of the justification proclamation therefore does not depend on guilt feelings or the "introspective conscience." These may, no doubt, be one "point of contact"—a more persistent one than many moderns think—but there are others. The justification proclamation is an attack on the old being, on whatever folly it happens to be engaged in. It attacks the proud, the secure, the super-religious, as much as it attacks and attends to despair. Indeed, Paul seems to apply the message more to secure super-Christians and Judaizers than to the despairing. Justification as unconditional gift is relevant always and everywhere because it means the end of whatever selfish folly we have gotten ourselves into, be it despair, pride, plain boredom, sloth, or the attempt to stave off thoughts of tomorrow by filling our barns today. Justification for Jesus' sake is good news for all. It grants newness of life, life in the Spirit.

RELEVANCE:
THE LIFE OF THE INDIVIDUAL

The Epistle to the Hebrews sets forth for all time a basic statement about the relevance of the Christian message in what we have called the microcosm of the life of the individual: Jesus partook of our nature, "that through death he might destroy him who has the power of death, that is, the devil, and deliver all those who through fear of death were subject to lifelong bondage" (Heb. 2:14-15). Ernest Becker's recent study, *The Denial of Death*, can explicate for us what this means in contemporary terms.[1] Unlike other animals, we, as human beings, know we are going to die, and we cannot bear it. We cannot bear our finitude. Our life project is the denial of death. As the serpent whispered, "You shall not die, you shall be as gods!" We embark on our own cause (*causa sui*) and build our own defenses against death—and necessarily so. We need protection against death; thus we build the lie—the vital lie—of character and maturity. Exactly as we have been saying, this quest is to be a person of substance and virtue, who will supposedly survive death. But the very project we are engaged in becomes our prison. We are trapped by our own lie. Becker says:

> The defenses that form a person's character support a grand illusion, and when we grasp this we can understand the full drivenness of man. He is driven away from himself, from self-knowledge, self-reflection. He is driven toward things

11 / CHRISTIAN LIFE

that support the lie of his character, his automatic equanimity. But he is also drawn precisely toward those things that make him anxious, as a way of skirting them masterfully, testing himself against them, controlling them by defying them. As Kierkegaard taught us, anxiety lures us on, becomes the spur to much of our energetic activity: We flirt with our own growth, but also dishonestly. This explains much of the friction in our lives, we enter symbiotic relationships in order to get the security we need, in order to get relief from our anxieties, our aloneness and helplessness; but these relationships also bind us, they enslave us even further because they support the lie we have fashioned. So we strain against them in order to be more free. The irony is that we do this straining uncritically, in a struggle within our own armor, as it were; and so we increase our drivenness, the second-hand quality of our struggle for freedom. Even in our flirtation with anxiety we are unconscious of our motives. We seek stress, we push our own limits, but we do it with our *screen against despair* and not with despair itself. We do it with the stock market, with sports cars, with atomic missiles, with the success ladder in the corporation or the competition in the university. We do it in the prison of a dialogue with our own little family, by marrying against their wishes or choosing a way of life because they frown on it, and so on. Hence the complicated and second-hand quality of our entire drivenness. Even in our passions we are nursery children playing with toys that represent the real world. Even when these toys crash and cost us our lives or our sanity, we are cheated of the consolation that we were in the real world instead of the playpen of our fantasies. We still did not meet our doom on our own manly terms, in contest with objective reality. It is fateful and ironic how the lie we need in order to live dooms us to a life that is never really ours.[2]

That is an almost perfect modern statement about "all those who through fear of death were subject to life-long bondage." Becker's quote from Otto Rank sums up the matter "once and for all, for all future psychoanalysts and students of man: 'Every human being is . . . equally unfree, that is *we . . . create* out of freedom, a prison.' "[3]

The story of Howard Hughes is a modern parallel to the parable of the rich fool in this vein. He was so afraid of death that it killed him! He retreated into seclusion with his hoards of wealth, fearing all who might make some claim on him or "contaminate" him with their touch. He would not even wear clothes and sat alone in darkened rooms watching movies. In the end, when help was needed the self-made prison was too secure. Extreme, no doubt, but parabolic of the prison we all construct. Parabolic also of a world so bent on self-preservation that it is choking on its own refuse.

The proclamation of justification—of daily renewal in the unconditional promise—is relevant always and everywhere because just by its very unconditionality it is the "death of death." Justification brings the death which we fear so much forward to meet us, and through it grants new life, and thus deliverance from bondage. It is relevant always and everywhere because bondage to the fear of death is universal. It is relevant because its unconditionality absolutely forestalls and rejects categorically any attempt to synthesize or connect it with the self-made prisons, with the projects we set up in our futile attempts to deny finitude and death. It is relevant because it gives us back our lives as God's creatures and sets us free. "For *freedom* Christ has set us free; stand fast therefore, and do not submit again to a yoke of slavery" (Gal. 5:1).

From this vantage point, the perennial protests against unconditional justification must be seen as protests put from within the prison of our *causa sui* projects. As old beings we fear the death such justification brings. The cries, questions, and protests are the death rattle of the old being, who knows that the prison wall has been breached and that the end of all his pet projects draws near. "But don't we have to do *something*?" "Is not *unconditional* grace dangerous?" "Who will be good if *nothing* is demanded?" "Is not such grace 'cheap'?" and so on and so on. The old being can hope to rescue something from the threatening disaster to its *causa sui* projects only by claiming some little bit to do or by casting doubts on the wisdom or propriety of an unconditional gift. The questions are designed to put anyone who proclaims justification by faith alone on the defensive. And most generally, alas, the strategy succeeds. One says, "Well, yes, now that you mention it, there *is* a little something. . . ." Or one tries to forestall the danger by hedging grace about with certain minimal conditions, raising the price just a little—perhaps at least to the level of the bargain basement. Thus, though the prison has been broken into, we stay in our cells.

When that occurs, when the death rattle of the old being frightens us onto the defensive, the battle for relevance is lost. Then justification indeed becomes of merely topical interest, to those prisoners who perhaps can make use of it in further sealing themselves in. If justification by faith is to be relevant at all, one cannot go on the defensive. The questions must be met squarely and offensively. Is not such grace "cheap?" No, it is not cheap; it is priceless; it is *free*. "Is not unconditional grace dangerous?" Of course. God takes a great risk to get what he wants. "To him who has, more will be given; from him who has not, even that which he has shall be taken away." One can take offense at the unconditional gift and lose everything. But God, apparently, does not want just a little something. He is out to get everything: all the heart, soul, mind, strength, and love of others. "But don't we have to do *something*?" How like us in our last extremity piously to hold out for a little "something"! It demonstrates our true intent: That is all we had ever planned to do. "Don't we have to do something?" No. Simply be still for once and listen. Faith, Luther insisted, arises out of the absolute passivity of listening to God's justifying word. Out of that death, that passivity, life comes, life born by the divine Spirit.

11 / CHRISTIAN LIFE

The question must then be put in an entirely different way. Paul put it, "Shall we sin the more that grace may abound?" That is the only question left to ask. "What are you going to do now that there is nothing you *have to* do?" "What's the matter? Don't you *want* to do good?" "How can you who died to sin still live in it?" Paul's question reflects incredulity: How can you manage sin once you have heard the unconditional word? Put this way, the questions often bring the shock of surprise and sometimes even a smile to the lips. That smile is just the point. In it is hidden the entire relevance of the doctrine of justification.

RELEVANCE: THE WORLD VISION

The wider relevance of justification by faith, in the macrocosm, the world and its future, consists in the kind of vision, the basic hope in life, that it inspires. What we have already said in the previous sections has laid the foundation and needs only to be explicated more pointedly.

Justification by faith fosters a hope that "endures all things" in unreserved service of this world, because of the unconditional promise of eschatological fulfillment. It fosters a hold on life which believes that the world will progress most surely toward its appointed goal precisely when it believes that the goal will be granted by God alone in God's good time. The world will progress most surely, that is, when it ceases building its own prisons in its denial of death and begins to behave as though God justifies sinners. The doctrine promotes a vision that does not, therefore, "abolish the law," but hopes for the ultimate fulfillment of God's will, the ultimate doing of God's commandments—indeed, the inscription of God's law in the heart. It believes that the will of God is the ultimate good of truly human existence—that the sabbath, the final eschatological rest, was made for man, and not man for the sabbath. Thus it does not find it necessary to alter one iota of the law, but looks to the day when the law will end because what it points to will be realized. Having a foretaste of things to come in justification by faith, the believer hopes and serves in this world.

It is important to say this because the vision will be quite different when justification is not understood as bringing an end and new beginning into our present by faith. The church will then falter—as it does today—between a legalistic absolutism on the one hand and an accommodating relativism on the other. In the past, the most common failing has no doubt been legalistic absolutism (though not without casuistic accommodation where necessary). Where justification is not the end and telos, law becomes absolute and eternal. Man is made for the sabbath. People become expendable for the sake of the absolute (usually identified with the status quo or the desires of the rulers). Pretensions to political power, tyranny, and inquisition in the history of the church testify to the evil outcome of such a vision.

Instructive in this regard is the Jansenist movement in seventeenth-century France, perhaps one of the last attempts to reassert a kind of pristine theological and legalistic absolutism in the face of casuistic compromise with the modern world. For many Jansenists such absolutism simply meant denial of and retreat from the world. For someone like Pascal, however, escape was impossible. There is no place here where one can escape to achieve the absolute. Humans are caught between the "grandeur and the misery" of created existence. Held by the absolute and yet knowing it is unattainable leads to a "tragic vision."[4] Nowhere can one escape the demanding voice and searching eye of God. One can only remain in the world and try one's strength, even though one knows the task is hopeless. "Christ will be suffering the torments of death to the very end of the world; for all that time we must not sleep."[5] Such tragic vision imagines no further change or transformation. The absolute is given and is unattainable, and one cannot go back to the world of compromise. Jesus is on the cross to the end of time.

> In this eternal and intemporal moment which lasts to the very end of the world, tragic man remains alone, doomed to be misunderstood by sleeping men and exposed to the anger of a hidden and absent God. But he finds, in his very loneliness and suffering, the only values which he can still have and which will be enough to make him great: the absolute and rigourous nature of his own awareness and his own ethical demands, his quest for absolute justice and absolute truth, and his refusal to accept any illusions or compromise.[6]

The tragic vision is, perhaps one can say, a disappointed absolutism. The absolute is not surrendered, but the hold on life is tenuous. Perhaps one could say that an atheistic existentialism is the secular counterpart to that vision. The tragic vision holds onto God but finds life a tragedy; the existentialist surrenders God, and finds life absurd. Both are disappointed or disillusioned absolutists.

The predominant modern replacement for the absolutism of the past has been relativism, the idea that truth (or, in our case, law) is relative to its historical context. As a protest against absolutism there is some right in the assertion, but a theology based on justification must raise questions about the antinomianism and ultimate destructiveness of the vision. Dogmatic theology must pay attention to the manner in which this vision evolves and the effect it has on the world today.

Relativism is a human attempt to domesticate the law. Where law has no eschatological end, this is perhaps the only recourse. Relativism evolved out of the failure of theology to assert the eschatological vision of the end and goal, death and resurrection. Kant took the absolute out of its metaphysical

11 / CHRISTIAN LIFE

heaven and placed it within the pious heart, to protect and ensure the autonomy of the individual vis-à-vis the law. Hegel found even "the law within" too "heteronomous" and dissolved it in the dialectic of history: the "concept" by which the present is grasped only to be challenged by the new antithesis and taken up into a higher synthesis. The "law" is constantly negated to be taken up in "higher" synthesis, and is thus entirely relative to its place in the dialectical movement of history. Marxism takes the dialectic and uses it to change the course of history, not merely to understand it. But the result of the relativism is that right and wrong can then be evaluated entirely in terms of our own vision. Human beings can be sacrificed quite easily for the sake of the cause.

From the point of view of a theology of justification, the significant thing in this development is that it involves a kind of eschatology, a doctrine about the end, carried by the idea of negation. But what is false is that it is always *the law* that is negated, not the old Adam. The old Adam escapes unscathed and appears on the stage of history as the one who embodies, understands, and eventually carries out the negation. Unnegated themselves, old beings appear now in the role of arch-negators, revolutionaries, the arbiters over the lives and deaths of other beings. The truth, the law, is relative to their vision. Human beings are expendable. The result is, if anything, worse than absolutism. If the absolutist was a wolf, the relativist is a wolf in sheep's clothing. Who knows when or where the knife of the relativist will strike?

Today a relativism that pronounces a benediction on all our vices seems to be threatening. A theology of justification must consider carefully what it means by the claim to uphold the law in the light of its hope. Threatened by relativisms and puzzled by "liberation" movements, the church seems to halt, if not to incline toward reversion to old absolutisms. The church seems unable to handle either the relativism or the egoism and narcissism in many liberation movements, not being able to put its finger on what is wrong. As protests against the tyranny of past absolutisms, the liberation movements are most often quite justifiable. But the difficulty is that like Marxists, liberationists are too often revolutionaries who have taken the right to negation into their own hands, presiding over questions of life and death. Absolutist tyranny and injustice must be resisted, but it is no gain for the church if it simply falls prey to a relativism that once again justifies arbitrary destruction of human life—whatever the age, creed, sex, or color. Neither absolutist nomism nor relativist antinomianism will save or liberate us. Neither circumcision nor uncircumcision matters, but a new creation and "faith working through love" (Gal. 6:15; 5:6).

The vision and the hope inspired by justification can help us find our way between the tyranny of yesterday's absolutisms and today's relativisms. The vision is not absolutist: The sabbath was made for man, not man for the sabbath. Nor is the vision the "tragic vision" of the disillusioned absolutist. Christ is not on the cross until the end of time. Having died once to sin, he dies no more. He is risen and is the end of the law to all who believe. The "revolutionary" move to put the world on the cross until the dawn of its secular vision is no better. *Christ* has died for us, once for all, that the law of God might be fulfilled in us, "who walk not according to the flesh but according to the Spirit" (Rom. 8:4). The Christian vision leads into the world, to suffering for and with others in the expectation of God's will being done on earth as it is in heaven. The aim is not to gain one's own holiness or to bring in the kingdom by force or tyranny, but to care for God's creatures and God's creation. "The creation waits with eager longing for the revealing of the sons of God" (Rom. 8:19).

NOTES

1. Ernest Becker, *The Denial of Death* (New York: The Free Press, 1973).
2. Ibid., p. 56.
3. Ibid., p. 62.
4. Lucien Goldmann, *The Hidden God: A Study of Tragic Vision in the Pensées of Pascal and the Tragedies of Racine*, trans. Philip Thody (London: Routledge & Kegan Paul, 1964), esp. pp. 62ff.
5. Quoted in ibid., p. 80.
6. Ibid., p. 81.
7. The Hegelian idea of the "cunning of reason," according to which even the worst of wrongs are used in the progressive self-realization of Spirit in the dialectic of history, is one of the most dangerous and destructive of modern ideas. The fall becomes a blessed event and everything is potentially justifiable—from the murder of millions of Jews to abortion on demand and Afghanistan. One's own vision of tomorrow justifies whatever murder, killing, and tyranny one might see fit to inflict today, all in the name of "justice." The church cannot accept such antinomianism—however subtly disguised.

TWELFTH LOCUS

Eschatology

HANS SCHWARZ

ESCHATOLOGY

Introduction

1. The Biblical View of the Future
   A Definition
   The Nascent Eschatology of the Old Testament
   The Eschatological Horizon of the New Testament

2. Continuing Tensions in the History of Eschatology
   The Gradual Transformation
   The Enthusiastic Fervor

3. Major Currents in Christian Eschatology
   The Tension between Promise and Fulfillment
   Emphasis on the Individual Person
   Emphasis on the Corporate Dimension
   The Cosmic Aspect of Eschatology

4. Secular Options
   Secular Existentialism
   Marxist Communism
   Secular Humanism

5. The Content of Christian Hope
   Ground Rules
   The Starting Point of Christian Eschatology
   Death and Resurrection
   The Last Judgment
   Parousia and the Kingdom of God

Introduction

Eschatology, or the doctrine of the last things, has long been regarded as a dubious enterprise.[1] Martin Luther claimed that as little as a child knows in the mother's womb about this life, so little do we know about life eternal. Yet Luther himself and most of his contemporaries did not doubt the heavenly reality. The story was different during the Enlightenment. Hermann Samuel Reimarus, in particular, became famous when he denounced the resurrection of Jesus as a deliberate fraud designed by the disciples. This alleged fabrication enabled them to proclaim Jesus as Savior and to become his apostles instead of returning on his death to their drudgery as fishermen.

When a generation later Immanuel Kant in his *Critique of Practical Reason* called the immortality of the soul a postulate of pure, practical reason, he did not endow the doctrine of an afterlife with new credibility. It was simply necessary to his metaphysical system to ensure that at least in eternity we could fulfill the highest good, which he thought was demanded from us. It also enabled him to discern a resolution of the tension between the direction of our existence (attaining the highest good) and the actual content of our existence (not completely attaining the highest good).

Before Reimarus, Herbert of Cherbury had claimed in his book *De veritate* (1624) that the notion of reward and punishment after this life is both reasonable and consonant with the biblical teachings. This twofold foundation of an afterlife on reason and revelation bore the seeds of potential conflict, reason eventually gaining the upper hand. Thus frequently, only that part of eschatology has been asserted that is defensible by reason. The death blow to eschatology, however, came in the nineteenth century when Karl Marx, a student of the German philosopher Ludwig Feuerbach, claimed that the hope in a better hereafter only serves to suppress the desire for change of the economic conditions of this world. He advocated a dissolution of the belief in the hereafter in order successfully to tackle the problems of this life.

Theologians too became more and more hesitant to portray the Christian hope in otherworldly imagery. In the late nineteenth century, Albrecht Ritschl depicted the kingdom of God mainly in social categories, as did Walter Rauschenbusch, the main representative of the social-gospel movement at the dawn of the twentieth century. Though Rauschenbusch did not renounce belief

12 / ESCHATOLOGY

in the hereafter, much more important for him was the social and communal dimension of the Christian faith. Adolf von Harnack, in his famous lectures *What is Christianity?* (1899/1900), told his audience that Jesus shared with his contemporaries the idea of the coming of the kingdom with outward signs but that the distinctive center of Jesus' proclamation was not the final apocalyptic battle that this idea implied. It consisted rather in the Fatherhood of God and the infinite value of the human soul. The trend indicated in Harnack's position was clear. All speculations about heaven, hell, or an afterlife were suspect in an age governed by reason and nascent technology.

A change occurred when Albert Schweitzer published his small booklet *The Mystery of the Kingdom of God: The Secret of Jesus' Messiahship and Passion* (1901). Schweitzer rejected the liberal alternative that had reigned supreme in the latter part of the nineteenth century, that Jesus was to be praised as the moral teacher of the Sermon on the Mount, while the eschatological world view he espoused had to be rejected. Schweitzer proposed that Jesus' message and world view had to be understood either in totally eschatological terms or in totally noneschatological terms. Schweitzer himself opted for a completely eschatological picture. According to Schweitzer, Jesus realized at his baptism that he had to work as the unknown and hidden Messiah until the messianic age appeared. Though Jesus put much effort into preaching, there were only meager results, which made him realize that the coming of the kingdom would be delayed. Then Jesus discovered that John the Baptist was Elijah reincarnate. When John was beheaded and the kingdom did not come, Jesus faced the prospect that he too had to suffer a violent death. He finally went to Jerusalem with his disciples, determined to bring about the kingdom of God. When he entered the city claiming to be the Messiah, the Jewish authorities accused him of blasphemy and put him to death. He died, but nothing happened.

Though Schweitzer presented a unified picture of Jesus, interpreting him in a thoroughly eschatological context, he was still confined to a basically liberal outlook. This became evident in his second book, still a standard reference, *The Quest of the Historical Jesus* (1906). He declared Jesus' ethics to be "interim ethics," aimed at preparation for the coming kingdom of God. Since the kingdom did not come when Jesus expected it, our ethics cannot be derived from Jesus' ethics, contrary to the claim of liberal theology. Yet, similarly to liberal theology, Schweitzer was not willing to discard Jesus completely. He found validity in Jesus' demand of world denial and perfection of personality. Jesus' enthusiasm and heroism are important for us too, because they are derived from his decision for the kingdom of God and from a faith in that kingdom which was only strengthened by his encounter with obstacles. Schweitzer then proposed that we need more people like Jesus. He summed up his assessment of Jesus, saying:

INTRODUCTION

> In the knowledge that He is the coming Son of Man He [Jesus] lays hold of the wheel of the world to set it moving on that last revolution which is to bring our ordinary history to a close. It refuses to turn, and He throws himself upon it. Then it does turn; and crushes Him. Instead of bringing in the eschatological conditions, He has destroyed them. The wheel rolls onward, and the mangled body of the one immeasurably great Man, who was strong enough to think of Himself as the spiritual ruler of mankind and to bend history to His purpose, is hanging upon it still. That is His victory and His reign.[2]

While Schweitzer himself actually claimed that Jesus was deceived in his eschatological expectations, he demonstrated that the biblical message is indeed thoroughly imbued with and imbedded in eschatological thought. The New Testament scholar Ernst Käsemann posed the issue slightly differently when he stated, "Apocalyptic is the mother of Christian theology." This means that apocalyptic, or the notion that history has a definite transworldly goal toward which it is rapidly moving, is the context out of which the Christian faith arose. While not many in the twentieth century have followed Schweitzer's so-called "consistent eschatological" approach, the debate continues on how to interpret the biblical eschatological message for our day.

In our time the reappropriation of the biblical eschatological message has been facilitated by an amazing change in human self-understanding. The self-assured posture characteristic of the first phase of the Enlightenment is rapidly vanishing. In his essay "Answer to the Question: What Is Enlightenment?" (1783), Immanuel Kant could still claim:

> Enlightenment is man's release from his self-incurred tutelage. Tutelage is man's inability to make use of his understanding without direction from another. Self-inflicted is this tutelage when its cause lies not in lack of reason but in lack of resolution and courage to use it without direction from another. *Sapere aude!* "Have courage to use your own reason!"—that is the motto of enlightenment.[3]

Kant was here asserting the dominance of the human intellect and the ability of reason to control all external forces. Any dependence on someone or something else was labeled immaturity. Humanity was still confident of its capacity to master its own destiny.

This idea of humanity's unlimited creative potential was especially fostered in the nineteenth century by the theory of evolution. The door now seemed to be open for new and unprecedented human progress. In the same century the door was pushed wide open for millions of European immigrants to explore, cultivate, and settle the New World, America. More than any other writer, Herbert Spencer shaped the outlook of North America in the second half of the nineteenth century by converting Darwin's theory of evolution into an instrument of unbridled optimism. On his visit to North America, Spencer was hailed as a prophet, since he had proclaimed that humanity was in control of its own destiny. It could determine its own progress and advance to new and unprecedented heights. "Progress," "prosperity," and "hope" have never been alien words in the New World. Utopian communities have seriously attempted to return to the communal life they sensed to have existed in early Christianity; others have attempted to bring about the very kingdom of God.

The Calvinistic strains of piety that dominated this nation from the very beginning had at the center of their hope the kingdom of God. In popular understanding, one was predestined at birth either to be received into heaven after life on earth or to be condemned to eternal damnation. Of course, one wanted to find out as early as possible what one's destiny would be. And it was often thought that the fact of election could be seen in earthly success. Thus Calvinists worked tirelessly to prove to themselves and to others that they were on the right side. Yet the results of this work could not be enjoyed, but had to be added to the continuous increase of employed capital. This Calvinistic work-ethic was facilitated in its implementation by a largely unexplored continent, the riches of which invited exploitation. It was aided further by the large number of pietistic immigrants who had fled their respective state churches to escape oppression and often outright persecution. The otherworldliness of most pietistic groups necessarily entailed the responsible use of time here on earth. Time was not to be spent in worldly joy and amusement but in self-crucifying work.

These religious convictions often led to splendid industrial success for their grandchildren, many of whom long ago discarded the religious premises of their ancestors. The name "Bethlehem Steel" still reminds us of hardworking Moravians who settled in the forest of Pennsylvania, but the steel company is now an armament enterprise. As H. Richard Niebuhr in his classic *The Kingdom of God in America* (1937) has convincingly pointed out, the pietistic and Calvinistic groups finally favored a heaven of their own earthly design. The belief that one could be virtuous enough to acquire heaven issued in a radical transformation of life on earth and so undermined, in the long run, the expectation of heavenly bliss. Through hard work, conditions on earth become attractive enough, in the "new world," to make achievers forget life in heaven.

The progressive and expansive drive of humanity, especially in the United States, continued well into the twentieth century. After its brief participation in World War I, the United States emerged as a stronger political and economic power than ever before, conscious that its forces had given the final blow to militaristic Germany. Though the depression caused misery for millions, a "new deal" restored prosperity, and soon afterward the United States became the haven for refugees from Nazi Germany. Again, it was a matter of conscience to enter the war to defeat Nazi Germany. Though smaller wars continued after World War II, the United States and most of the industrialized

INTRODUCTION

world entered a phase of unprecedented prosperity. Nothing was too good or too far away for most of the people: from the two- and three-car family to the conquest of the moon.

Within less than a decade sentiment had completely changed. While in the 1960s some theologians successfully picked up the nineteenth-century slogan of Friedrich Nietzsche and Jean Paul that God is dead and that the world is devoid of metaphysical guidance, the late 1960s already witnessed a plethora of new religious movements, mainly influenced by the religions from the East and by the occult. In the 1970s we saw a return to traditional values and to a more conservative kind of religiosity. How should we explain this amazing change in self-understanding?

On the one hand, we have experienced an increasing ambiguity of progress. Certainly the material well-being of most of us has increased tremendously. But at the same time we have sensed an atrophy of feeling and belonging. We have been so much on the road of progress, rushing from one achievement to another, that we have lost the meaning of our rushing. Thus we have created a world of high material standards without deeper meaning, and of goods for consumption without ultimate value. The "throw away" society has degraded the individual human being to a productive and consuming element that is discarded as soon as it is no longer profitable to maintain. Thus, the individual human being has decreased in value at the same time as the values we created have increased. Amid external splendor, this kind of progress leads to increasing meaninglessness, and to questioning the propriety of the worship of progress.

The ambiguity of progress manifests itself in yet another way. While we have achieved feats undreamed of a century ago, scientific and technological progress has introduced new and frightening prospects. As we have managed to harness the energy of the atom, we have become threatened by an atomic war. While chemicals are used to kill weeds and pests and to eradicate many diseases, the widespread use of certain chemicals has threatened the survival of many species. Even humanity has become subject to more and more chemical pollution with already evident deleterious effects. This increasing ambiguity of progress indicates that we are discovering limits to technological progress beyond which the benefits to society no longer clearly outweigh the risks and hazards. Thus progress and human ingenuity, once celebrated, are no longer accepted with unqualified endorsement. As the pace of progress falters, we are confronted with its most severe limitation, the limited and finite earth we inhabit. Unlimited potential creativity has proven to be wishful thinking. The question is no longer "How much better shall we live than our ancestors?" but rather "Is there any meaningful future to live for?"

We have become painfully aware that we cannot shape the future so freely as we thought in the naive exuberance of the dawning Enlightenment. As the future becomes less and less predictable in regard to natural resources, political constellations, and personal security, the fundamental question has become one of meaningful survival. Willy-nilly, our own time has become ominously similar to the age when Christianity made its first daring steps. We remember that this was the time when the Roman Empire had reached its greatest expansion, when traditional values began to crumble, when the first serious cracks in the Roman culture presaged its demise, and when the yearning for salvation became more intense. We also remember that this was the time of apocalypticism, when religious seers sensed the onrushing end close at hand, and when the ultimate future was seen in transnational and transworldly terms. To elucidate the biblical hope for our own future, we shall thus return to our roots and investigate first the Old and then the New Testament message of hope.

NOTES

1. The most thorough treatment of Christian eschatology remains Paul Althaus's *Die letzten Dinge: Lehrbuch der Eschatologie*, 7th ed. (Gütersloh: Bertelsmann, 1957); a more recent work on eschatology that had considerable impact is Jürgen Moltmann, *Theology of Hope: On the Ground and the Implications of a Christian Eschatology*, trans. James W. Leitch (New York: Harper & Row, 1967). For an extensive treatment of my own approach, see Hans Schwarz, *On the Way to the Future: A Christian View of Eschatology in the Light of Current Trends in Religion, Philosophy, and Science*, rev. ed. (Minneapolis: Augsburg Publishing House, 1979). A noteworthy book that adduces also a considerable amount of material from outside the Judeo-Christian tradition is John Hick's *Death and Eternal Life* (New York: Harper & Row, 1976).

2. Albert Schweitzer, *The Quest of the Historical Jesus: A Critical Study of Its Progress from Reimarus to Wrede*, trans. W. Montgomery (New York: Macmillan Co., 1966), pp. 370–71.

3. Immanuel Kant, "What Is Enlightenment?" in *Foundations of the Metaphysics of Morals and What Is Enlightenment?* trans. L. W. Beck (Indianapolis: Bobbs-Merrill, 1959), p. 85.

1
The Biblical View of the Future

The biblical experience of God is constitutive of the Christian hope. The Old Testament does not reflect a tradition of failure. It shows in its progression the necessity for the Judeo-Christian tradition to include in eschatological reflection more than the corporate existence of a people or of all nations. The proleptic anticipation of the End and the still outstanding fulfillment, including that of the individual human destiny, are main emphases of New Testament eschatology.

A DEFINITION

If we want to attain an accurate assessment of eschatology, we should first attempt a definition of it. The *eschata* as the subject matter of eschatology include all concepts connected with life beyond death. Heaven and hell, a final judgment, immortality and resurrection, and even reincarnation, purgatory, and the concept of a soul can be subsumed under this term. But eschatology is not confined to those things that stand at the end. As Jürgen Moltmann, in *Theology of Hope*, has reminded us, the doctrine of the Christian hope embraces both the object hoped for and the hope inspired by it.

Eschatology does not just mean discourse about the so-called "last things," that which happens in the end. It must consider everything that is related to this end. Though the various movements toward the end do not constitute a unidirectional process, certain causes will undoubtedly urge more toward some ends than others. The indifference toward the body exhibited in many Far Eastern religions will lead to a desire for extinguishing all of life. An emphasis on God the creator will be congenial to the hope in the resurrection, while a separation of creation from redemption will be open to the concept of the immortality of the soul. Conversely, our conceptualization of the final end will exert an immense influence on our attitude toward the present life. A reliance on God's final grace will lead toward a more detached attitude toward life here, while an emphasis on human self-reliance in attaining the final goal will engender an attitude of craving for the present.

12 / ESCHATOLOGY

Eschatology influences the conduct of our present life, contemplates the outcome beyond this life, and investigates the way that leads to that outcome.

Often the eschaton, as that which stands at the end, is not regarded as the goal of a linear progression. It can be the cessation of all life cycles, as in the notion of reincarnation or of the return to the beginning, to the garden which humanity once inhabited and to which the blessed will regain access. Even Paul can compare the new creation and Christ, the new Adam, with the old creation and the first Adam. But for Paul there was a clearly progressive movement from the first Adam and the first creation to the new Adam and the new creation. Many other religions, however, advocate a cyclic or periodic movement, either in terms of new life cycles or in analogy to the seasons of the year. In this context it is not without significance that Thanksgiving, or the harvest festival, is the only quasi-religious holiday in the United States that is publicly sanctioned. Each year our thoughts return to the first Thanksgiving of the Pilgrim Fathers and extend forward to the continued prosperity promised—by the President—for the future. There has even been some speculation that all of Israel's eschatology had its origin in an annual enthronement festival of Yahweh at which Yahweh assumed power and assured the arrival of the rainy season. Though there were enthronement psalms in the Israelite psalter (e.g., Ps. 47:93; Ps. 96), the seasonal or cyclic cult of a god who dies and rises to assure a good harvest and natural fertility was certainly not at the center of Old Testament piety, if it ever existed in Israel. There were other motifs that were much more central, such as the coming of the anointed one or the advent of the day of the Lord.

THE NASCENT ESCHATOLOGY OF THE OLD TESTAMENT

The history traceable in the Old Testament spans roughly a millennium, while that of the New Testament covers barely a century. Thus the development of eschatology is much more perceptible in the Old Testament than in the New. Theodore Vriezen distinguishes four stages of Old Testament eschatological thought, with one period partly overlapping another or even running parallel to it: (1) There was the pre-eschatological period (before the classical prophets), when the future was largely perceived in the light of the past, that is, the idealized age of David. Israel's hopes were then mainly political and national. (2) There was a proto-eschatological period (Isaiah and his contemporaries), in which the vision of a new people and a new kingdom emerged. There was a hope for a kingdom that would embrace the whole world and rest on spiritual forces that sprang from God. (3) There was the actual eschatological period (Second Isaiah and his contemporaries), in which the kingdom of God that would change the world was not only *seen* as coming, in visions, but was also *experienced* as coming, in hope. (4) Finally, there was the transcendental eschatological period of apocalyptic. Salvation was expected to come not in this world but either spiritually in heaven or after cosmic catastrophe in a new world. Even if we were to devise a scheme different from Vriezen's, we would note that from the very beginning the relation between the individual and the corporate existence of the people was a chief and problematic topic.

As for all other known peoples, it was clear for the Israelites that death was the end only of our present state of individual being. They envisioned a shadowy existence beyond death in Sheol. Yet they did not yet envision a life beyond death in the full sense. "Sheol cannot thank thee [O Lord], death cannot praise thee; those who go down to the pit cannot hope for thy faithfulness" (Isa. 38:18), as King Hezekiah eloquently expressed. God is the God of life, and therefore death is not his abode. No thanks to God emerge from the dead. When "pit" is set in parallel to "Sheol," it indicates a metaphoric use of "pit" to mean the world beyond death. Literally, it refers to the pit in which the remains of a decayed corpse were preserved when the "beds" in the stone-hewn tombs were used over again. Even Hezekiah's use of the term "Sheol" must be understood in a metaphorical sense, expressing the anguish about the sickness with which he is afflicted. Thus "Sheol" denotes not just the shadowy existence beyond death but, by metaphoric extension, all hostile and threatening powers and the anxiety they produce.

Hope was largely this-worldly and was centered in the continued existence of the community. Vision of the end did not leave untouched the Israelites' understanding of life on this side of death. Life was seen as a precious gift, and the ultimate blessing was to die like Abraham at a ripe age (Gen. 25:8) or like Jacob surrounded by his sons (Gen. 49:33). The sons would carry on one's name; therefore they were bearers of hope. It was especially devastating to die without a male heir. Early and premature death could thus be understood as a punishment for godlessness (1 Sam. 2:32). In contrast to the view of Greek mythology, death was not perceived as a fate over which God had no ultimate control. Surely, the Israelites knew that sooner or later everyone had to die. But both death and life were directed and destined by Yahweh, who alone would not grow old and weary. Even Moses had to die, although God buried him so that nobody could find his tomb (Deut. 34:5–6). In the narrative of Moses' death we also note that the dead did not occupy an exceptional status through which they could exert power over or in behalf of the living. Faith in Yahweh did not allow an ancestor cult or prayers to the dead. Even the few instances where someone was translated from this life directly into the eternal presence of Yahweh did not engender a cult connected with these people. We simply hear that God took Enoch (Gen. 5:24) and that Elijah went up by a whirlwind into heaven (2 Kings 2:11). The Israelites, however,

12 / ESCHATOLOGY

were not stymied by the prospect of death. Their emphasis was on this life and its pleasure, and on obedience to the decrees of Yahweh so that Yahweh might lengthen one's days.

But eventually the understanding emerged that there must be more to life than what we encounter here on earth. At the close of the Old Testament we hear about a resurrection with a twofold outcome: "And many of those who sleep in the dust of the earth shall awake, some to everlasting life, and some to shame and everlasting contempt" (Dan. 12:2). Even earlier, we hear in Isa. 26:19: "Thy dead shall live, their bodies shall rise. O dwellers in the dust, awake and sing for joy!" Other passages that are frequently quoted in this context as evidence for an Old Testament understanding of resurrection of the dead, such as Job 19:25-26 ("I know that my Redeemer lives . . .") or Ps. 73:24 ("Thou dost guide me with thy counsel, and afterward thou wilt receive me to glory"), do not apply here. The first points to an expectancy that lies strictly within this life (redemption from the accusations of Job's friends) and the other renders an ambiguous Hebrew text.

It is nearly impossible to answer with certainty the question of why the Israelites refrained so long from trusting in an afterlife, especially since most neighboring religions had rather elaborate concepts of an afterlife. Perhaps it was their neighbors' fear of death and of haunting spirits that made Israel eschew all undue speculations about death and invocations of the deceased. Israel's strong sense of corporate identity under the leadership of Yahweh may also have made elaborate concepts of an afterlife less necessary. Especially during the collapse of the Israelite nation and the Babylonian captivity, however, the notion of fulfillment in a corporate life waned. When the Israelites, therefore, came in contact with Zoroastrian ideas of an afterlife, these concepts found open ears among many Israelites.

Parsiism or Zoroastrianism, as the Iranian religion is called, dates back to the prophet Zarathustra (or Zoroaster according to Greek transcription), who seems to have lived among the peasants of eastern Iran in the sixth century B.C. He taught a strict monotheism analogous to that of the Israelite religion. Yet this monotheism is modified by a definite dualism between Ahura Mazda, the almighty, and Angra Mainyu or Ahriman, the manifestation of everything evil. Characteristic of Zoroaster's teaching is the notion of the twofold outcome of history: the good will be allotted an eternity of bliss beyond the grave, while evil people will experience an eternity of woe.

After death the soul of the deceased must cross the Chinvat bridge, which stretches over hell, an abyss of molten metal and fire. For the good the bridge grows broader and broader for easier transit and ascent into heaven, while for the wicked it grows narrower until it is like a razor-thin sword, from which the soul falls into the abyss of hell where it will be eternally tormented. The Zoroastrian religion also teaches a judgment and completion of the whole world. Three thousand years after Zoroaster a savior will come and bring the present world to its end. The dead will be resurrected, and both the good and the wicked will have to pass through a flood of molten metal. The good will pass through without harm and enter the new world, while the wicked will be either purified or burned. After this universal purification Ahura Mazda's sovereignty will be complete, and together with him the good will enjoy a new heaven and a new earth.

It is difficult to claim with certainty a definite causal relationship between concepts in Iranian religion and Israelite faith. But one cannot but be struck by parallel between the Iranian religion on the one hand and Judaism and Christianity on the other. Especially regarding eternal life, an ultimate judgment, and the notion of heaven and hell, catalytic influences cannot be denied. When the Jews abandoned the idea of Sheol as a shadowy and impersonal existence that will be conferred on all regardless of how they have lived on earth, there evolved among them an understanding of afterlife which was similar to Zoroaster's teachings. It can hardly be mere coincidence that Daniel, the reputed secretary of Darius, king of the Medes and Persians, explicitly mentioned everlasting life and eternal punishment: "And many of those who sleep in the dust of the earth shall awake, some to everlasting life, and some to shame and everlasting contempt" (Dan. 12:2). It is also worth noting that the prophets, who vehemently opposed most "syncretistic" attempts, seemed to have no objections when these "Persian" notions of an afterlife were introduced into Jewish faith.

The reason for the relatively easy reception might be twofold. During the fifth and sixth centuries B.C. the whole Near East seemed to wrestle with the destiny of the individual and of the world at large. Soteriological and eschatological systems were eventually developed in Hellenistic gnosticism, apocalyptic Judaism, and finally in Christianity. The time seems to have been ripe for such concepts. But there may be a more significant reason why the Jewish people adopted a more elaborate understanding of an afterlife. The strictly this-worldly corporate fulfillment of life proved to be untenable in the long run. The advance of history brought too many obstacles to such fulfillment. Thus the notion of Sheol had to be deepened to allow for differentiation between the final destiny of the faithful and the godless. Also the notion of existence in Sheol had to assume more lifelike features. We may then conclude that the Israelite notion of Sheol bore no intrinsic obstacles to the catalytic influences exercised by Persian ideas. As the attitude of the Sadducees shows, however, not everybody went along with these new developments. At the time of Jesus we still encounter purists who rejected the notion of a resurrection.

The *universal* scope of salvation stands not at the beginning but at the end of Israel's history. For instance, whenever God's judgment is mentioned, it

12 / ESCHATOLOGY

is understood as occurring during one's lifetime on earth. God declares, "Vengeance is mine, and recompense for the time when their foot shall slip" (Deut. 32:35). God is faithful; God sticks to the divine orders and promises and wants us to be like-minded. The trustworthiness and faithfulness of Yahweh are revealed in the covenant Yahweh makes with Israel. But Yahweh keeps divine obligations and promises, while the people do not live up to their part. Then Yahweh becomes the judge of the Israelites. Since other gods are considered to be inferior to Yahweh, divine judgment eventually extends beyond the boundaries of Israel. As early as Amos, it is announced that other nations are included in Yahweh's judgment, and even earlier Egypt's pharaoh has to acknowledge Yahweh's superiority and let the people of Israel go. Toward the close of the Old Testament the mighty foreign empires are compared with wild and ferocious animals that will have to accede to the final victory of God when God's kingdom is erected. We notice that the cause for God's judgment is usually arrogance, pride (Isa. 16:6–7), and disobedience (Mic. 5:15).

As early as the eighth century, the judgment day of the Lord was a familiar object of Israel's expectations. Often this day was thought to be a day of salvation for Israel as, for instance, in Isa. 2:2–4:

> And it shall come to pass in the latter days that the mountain of the house of the Lord shall be established as the highest of the mountains, and shall be raised above the hills; and all the nations shall flow to it, and many peoples shall come, and say: "Come, let us go up to the mountain of the Lord, to the house of the God of Jacob; that he may teach us his ways and that we may walk in his paths." For out of Zion shall go forth the law, and the word of the Lord from Jerusalem. He shall judge between the nations, and shall decide for many peoples; and they shall beat their swords into plowshares, and their spears into pruning hooks; nations shall not lift up sword against nation, neither shall they learn war any more.

The prophets, however, turned these nationalistic expectations into a pronouncement of calamity and disaster. Amos especially said that it would be a day of darkness with no light in it, with one calamity striking after another (Amos 5:18–20). It would be a day of sword, hunger, and pestilence, a day of great sorrow (Isa. 30:25), and of fright and anxiety. God would destroy the whole world (Isa. 13:5), and great changes would occur in nature, such as earthquakes, darkness, drought, and fire. The judgment day of the Lord, one of the main themes in the prophetic proclamation, does not just result in a national vindication, but neither is it mere gloom and darkness. Granted, the prophets emphasized more and more that Israel would stand under judgment too. But in analogy to the growing understanding of the destiny of the individual, the corporate vindication and redemption of Israel were also eventually conceived as coming not simply in this life. The vision of the valley of dry bones promises that the Lord will bring the people of Israel out of

THE BIBLICAL VIEW OF THE FUTURE

their graves and place them in their own land (Ezek. 37:13-14). Only through absolute defeat and destruction could a new creation and full salvation be obtained. Moreover, Yahweh assures the prophet that Yahweh's Spirit will enter into these people so that they shall live. But the this-worldly aspect of God's promise is never totally abolished. After long and dire predictions of Israel's destruction, Amos concedes, "It may be that the Lord, the God of hosts, will be gracious to the remnant of Joseph" (Amos 5:15).

What will be the goal of Yahweh's judgment, the goal that is envisioned in a new creation and the erection of Yahweh's kingdom? Toward the end of the book of Amos we read that the fallen tabernacle of David will again be raised up and that the wasted cities will be rebuilt and inhabited. There will be plenty to eat and drink, and it will be "as in the days of old" (Amos 9:11). Salvation is still seen as essentially connected with Israel. Yet especially in Isaiah it is not confined to Israel. Granted, Mount Zion will tower over all other nations and all nations shall flock to it, but it is the mountain of the Lord and not of Israel to which they will come (Isa. 2:3). There will be peace between people and in nature; everyone will have plenty to eat and will enjoy a long life (see Isa. 7:21-25; 11:6-9). Since this picture is expanded to include all nations and all nature, Isaiah is rightly called the first prophet of eschatological expectation.[1]

The prophets after Isaiah continued to pursue this vision, yet Israel's gradually more hopeless struggle for national survival made it clear that only a radical action of God could change the situation. Human depravity in Israel was perceived to be of such magnitude that God would have to put a new spirit within them, remove their stony heart, and give them one of flesh (Ezek. 11:19). But God has not abandoned Israel. God reemphasizes the divine intention: "They shall be my people, and I will be their God" (Ezek. 11:20). Since Ezekiel speaks at a time when Israel has collapsed as a nation, he even resorts to the metaphor of the resurrection of the dead to stress the miraculous aspect of God's new creation (Ezek. 37:1-14).

When we come to Second Isaiah, the destruction of Jerusalem is history. But he, too, does not give up on the salvation promised by God. On the contrary, it is in the immediate future that the prophet envisions salvation. Again parallels are drawn between the days of old and the impending salvation. The prophet uses the term *bara* (to create), in analogy to Genesis 1, to indicate that God will start a new creation with Israel and the world. "The ransomed of the Lord shall return, and come to Zion with singing; everlasting joy shall be upon their heads" (Isa. 51:11). Since God is steadfast in divine promises, Israel will be a light to the nations and the covenant of the people (Isa. 42:6). There will be a royal highway for the Lord, with the valleys being elevated and the mountains being planed (Isa. 40:3-4). In picturesque language the prophet describes how the Lord has protected the chosen people.

12 / ESCHATOLOGY

Even the creation of heaven and earth has its sole purpose in Israel (Isa. 51:16). But this picture has been painted in colors too strong for the captives in Babylonia to accept, so they complain instead that their Lord has forgotten them (Isa. 49:14) and that their ways are hidden to the Lord (Isa. 40:27).

The prophet recognizes the stubborn and rebellious character of the people (Isa. 48:8) and finally concludes that someone must vicariously suffer for the sinful people so that they can be cleansed from their sins. The servant of the Lord, whom the prophet now introduces, "will not fail or be discouraged till he has established justice in the earth" (Isa. 42:4). He will be a light to the nations that salvation may reach the end of the earth (Isa. 49:6). Even about this unselfish servant the prophet confesses: "He was despised and rejected by men; a man of sorrows, and acquainted with grief." Then, however, he continues: "Surely he has borne our griefs and carried our sorrows; yet we esteemed him stricken and smitten by God, and afflicted. But he was wounded for our transgressions, he was bruised for our iniquities; upon him was the chastisement that made us whole, and with his stripes we are healed" (Isa. 53:3ff.).

Who might this servant of Yahweh be? It is unlikely that the prophet would think of the rebellious and stubborn Israelite nation as such a gentle and self-sacrificing servant. It is also unlikely that he would describe his own death in identifying himself with this servant. Certainly, it is not impossible that he and his message faced ultimate rejection by the exiles. Perhaps we will be unable to arrive at an answer to the question of the servant's identity unless we consider that figure which over the centuries receives increasing prominence in Israel, namely, the Messiah.

Messianic figures that usher in a new age or that promise to provide salvation are known in many religions, the Israelite religion being no exception. But initially the concept of a Messiah was of very modest scope. "Messiah," or "anointed one," usually denoted the king of Israel (2 Sam. 1:16), who was anointed when he was designated king of Israel, but could also refer to the high priest (Lev. 4:5). Yet the expected king of the end-time was not called the Messiah.[2] The only exception is Isaiah 45:1, where we read, "Thus says the Lord to his anointed, to Cyrus, whose right hand I have grasped to subdue nations before him." To call the Persian King Cyrus "Messiah" evidently reflects the high expectations connected with his edict that allowed the Israelite exiles to return to Jerusalem. Since the eschatological fulfillment of history is intimately connected with God as its actor, the Old Testament does not know of a person, called Messiah, who is to bring about the eschatological salvation. Yet in the Old Testament the hope is already present for a God-provided figure who will usher in the eschaton. This figure seems to have originated in a retrospective glorification of David and the promise that was given to him through Nathan (2 Sam. 7:12–15).

THE BIBLICAL VIEW OF THE FUTURE

In the promissory history of Israel the messianic figure who is expected to bring about eschatological salvation is mostly associated with the house of David. The blessing of Jacob over Judah (Gen. 49:8–12) can be considered the oldest of the messianic expectations: The scepter shall not depart from Judah until the promised one comes who will usher in an age of paradisial fruitfulness. He will bind his foal to the vine, and he will wash his garments in wine. The oracle of Balaam (Num. 24:15–19) announces that a star shall come forth out of Jacob and have dominion over the neighboring nations. The restoration of "the fallen booth of David" in the book of Amos points in a similar direction (Amos 9:11–15). When Israel is restored to its glory as in the "days of old" (Amos 9:11), it will have dominion over all the nations. The messianic time will be one of prosperity and peace when "the mountains shall drip sweet wine . . . my people Israel . . . shall rebuild the ruined cities and inhabit them" (Amos 9:13ff.).

In Isaiah the messianic references are expanded beyond the scope of the immediate national and historical reality. While many exegetes hesitate to consider Isa. 7:10–17 a messianic reference, two other announcements, Isa. 9:1–6 and 11:1–8, have clearly messianic character. In the midst of the darkness of destruction a great light is shining (Isa. 9:1–6), and the anointed one will be called "Wonderful Counselor, Mighty God, Everlasting Father, Prince of Peace." In Isa. 11:1–8 the messianic peace gains even more prominence when the "Spirit of the Lord" will rest on the Messiah, whose reign will include all nature. Finally Micah proclaims that from Bethlehem, the village of David, will come forth the one "who is to be ruler in Israel, whose origin is from of old" (Mic. 5:1ff.). Again this promise presupposes the return of the Israelites to their homes and emphasizes messianic peace and the greatness of the kingdom.

Toward the end of the Old Testament era, Haggai and Zechariah realized that neither the destruction of Israel nor its return from the exile had ushered in the messianic kingdom. But they remembered that God once was present in the temple in Jerusalem, and so they emphasized the importance of rebuilding the temple as a prerequisite for the coming of Yahweh and Yahweh's kingdom (Hag. 1:7–8; Zech. 4:9). Both prophets thought they stood at the beginning of the time of salvation initiated by the rebuilt temple. Now messianic prosperity would start (Hag. 2:19) and everybody would enjoy messianic peace (Zech. 8:12). They considered Zerubbabel, the royal heir of David's throne, to be the anointed of the Lord and the coming Messiah (Hag. 2:20–23; Zech. 4:6–10). But to their disappointment, Zerubbabel was never enthroned, and the hope for the fulfillment of the Davidic promise needed another revision. One generation before Zechariah, Second Isaiah had judged the situation much more realistically in the songs of the servant of Yahweh, claiming that true deliverance and fulfillment of salvation could be brought about only

12 / ESCHATOLOGY

through the vicarious suffering of the servant. Though the messianic element of the victorious king is not lacking in Second Isaiah's description of the suffering servant, the prophet did not dare to identify him with an historic figure.

In the apocalyptic literature of the intertestamental period, it is more clearly advanced that the bringer of salvation could not be identified with a figure of past or present history, but would be acting in and through history. In the apocalyptic visions of Daniel, *God* is still understood to be the ruler of the world who brings about cosmic and political changes and causes the eschatological time of salvation to commence. But in 1 Enoch, 2 Ezra, and 2 Baruch, the Messiah enjoys a more independent position. He is the one who destroys the enemies and brings about the salvation of Israel. There is also increasing emphasis on the Messiah's preexistence: He who existed before all the worlds comes from heaven in the end-time to initiate salvation. To some degree this independent status is already prefigured in the "son of man" imagery of Daniel 7 where, be the son a corporate or an individual figure, he signalizes the final victory of God's power and greatness and, at the appointed time, ushers in the final triumph of God's people and kingdom.

While the prophets think of the political enemies of Israel as God's enemies who will be converted or destroyed during the end-time, in apocalyptic writings all anti-Godly powers are included. If God shall have dominion over the world, all powers have to succumb. While God's kingdom is still to be established on this earth, according to 1 Enoch, the main tendency is to idealize the kingdom. At its center is a new Jerusalem that is either a purification of the old one (2 Enoch 6–36) or its replacement (1 Enoch 83–90). In the Similitudes of Enoch the kingdom is to be established not only on a transformed earth but also in a transformed heaven. In the Assumption of Moses, a book that probably originated when Jesus was still a youth, this vision is expanded further. The eschatological events no longer at all occur on a nationalistic or this-worldly plane. They are supramundane, and the kingdom is viewed as a kingdom of *heaven*.

The transnationalistic and supraworldly view of God's reign was possible because the apocalyptists viewed history as a unity. The unity of history, engendered by a monotheistic faith in the one God who shapes and destines the world to the divine purpose, had been part of the Israelite heritage long before the intertestamental period. But now the apocalyptists believed that they stood at the brink of the end and were therefore able to look back at the whole of history and interpret its meaning in terms of the divine purpose. Present and future were presented in one continuous progression preordained by God. All evil tendencies would grow until they completely dominated the political powers of this world. Then the end of this age would be near. But the visible symptoms of the coming end, utmost evil, unrest and wars, and disturbance in nature and especially in the stellar course, were

THE BIBLICAL VIEW OF THE FUTURE

at the same time the travails indicating the birth of a new eon. The new eon would be completely juxtaposed to the old one. It would be the unlimited dominion of the kingdom of God.

This theocentrically developed and highly deterministic concept of history included all powers and all nations. Apocalyptic thought transcended the nationalistic eschatological expectations of Israel and opened the dimension of a new hope for the whole universe. This is the context in which Jesus of Nazareth came to stand; the apocalyptic dimension of the kingdom of God was the center of his eschatological message.

THE ESCHATOLOGICAL HORIZON OF THE NEW TESTAMENT

The eschatological outlook of the New Testament is not just a continuation of that of the Old Testament, though it cannot be explained without it. The continuity has to be seen at least in theological and ethnic terms: Yahweh, the God of Abraham, Isaac, and Jacob, is the father of Jesus of Nazareth, and Jesus was a Jew. While we agree with Rudolf Bultmann that the proclamation of Jesus is the presupposition of New Testament theology as it now stands, we cannot dispense with considering Jesus' understanding of eschatology, lest we lose the ground on which the New Testament eschatology, rightly or wrongly, rests.

We must agree with Albert Schweitzer that it is impossible to write a biography of Jesus in the strict sense. But such books as Norman Perrin's *Rediscovering the Teachings of Jesus*[3] and Joachim Jeremias's *New Testament Theology*, Volume 1, *The Proclamation of Jesus*,[4] indicate that at least the main features of Jesus' proclamation and self-understanding can be ascertained. In Jesus' own proclamation and self-understanding, we find clues that he is of truly eschatological significance. For he engendered a peculiar eschatological outlook in his followers and considered himself an eschatological figure.

While Jesus' proclamation was totally eschatological, he did not indoctrinate his listeners with certain eschatological ideas. He rather confronted them with a radical decision for or against God, which was pronounced in such a way that it was at the same time a decision for or against Jesus. "Follow me, and leave the dead to bury their own dead" (Matt. 8:22), "No one who puts his hand to the plow and looks back is fit for the kingdom of God" (Luke 9:62), and "Blessed is he who takes no offense at me" (Matt. 11:6) are some of the passages that indicate the urgency of an immediate decision here and now. Contrary to apocalyptic thought or to the promissory history of the Old Testament, the present has replaced the future by becoming the decisive point of history.

The decisiveness of the present is enlightened through Jesus' own actions.

12 / ESCHATOLOGY

When John the Baptist sent two of his disciples to ask Jesus whether he were the promised one or they should wait for someone else, Jesus responded by referring to his actions and quoting the Old Testament promises of the messianic age (Isa. 35:5–6): "The blind receive their sight, the lame can walk, lepers are cleansed, and the deaf hear, the dead are raised up, the poor have good news preached to them" (Luke 7:22). And when Jesus turned water into wine at the wedding in Cana (John 2:1ff.), we must understand this epiphanic miracle in the light of the Old Testament understanding of wine as the symbol of the time of salvation. Jesus demonstrated that with his own actions the age of salvation had commenced. He talked about the new wine that should not be poured into old wineskins (Matt. 9:17). The time of the old eon is past, and the time of salvation has been initiated. With Jesus the kingdom of God has started (Luke 11:20). The centuries-old hopes that have been projected into the future or into the present for so long have become real in Jesus. He is the realization of the future and therefore the goal of history.

Jesus emphasized the decisive character of his own person and of the present time. But he did not proclaim an impending end of the world, except to reinforce the urgency of an immediate decision for or against God. The synoptic source Q, which contains many sayings of Jesus, does not indicate that Jesus was concerned about the immediately approaching end of the world. Neither his Jewish contemporaries nor their polemics after his death accused him of having falsely announced an immediate end of the world. Surely they would have exploited such false prophecy had it been uttered. Jesus did not side with John the Baptist, who fervently proclaimed the immediate coming of the end.

Jesus did not proclaim a new doctrine of the last things or a definitive doctrine of Christ (Christ being the Greek translation of Messiah, "the anointed one"). An analysis of the New Testament shows that he probably refused the title "Messiah" whenever it was conferred on him. Perhaps he was suspicious of the political and nationalistic aspirations connected with the coming of the Messiah and did not want to be taken for a political liberator. During his ministry he was never accused of conspiring against the Roman occupation or wanting to revolt against it. Though he was finally charged with political crimes, he clearly denied them. He was different from Judas Maccabaeus or Bar Cochba or the many other messianic liberators before or after him.

Yet it is unlikely that Jesus never used a title when he spoke about himself. His parabolic style of speech would also at least suggest that he may have used titles. And there was indeed a title untainted by political or nationalistic colors, which Jesus seems to have used: "Son of Man." Unlike "Messiah," it is almost exclusive to the gospel tradition, and there it appears mostly in sayings of Jesus and only seldom when people are addressing Jesus. In Judaism the term "Son of Man" arose from an apocalyptic context, and the main eschatological function of the Son of Man was that of presiding over the final judgment. Jesus, however, expanded and modified the concept of the Son of Man by joining it with the image of the suffering servant. He who judges the world in the name of the Lord also suffers vicariously for it and reconciles it with God. Jesus expressed this when he said: "For the Son of man also came not to be served but to serve, and to give his life as a ransom for many" (Mark 10:45).

The deepest self-understanding of Jesus, however, cannot be expressed with a title. He is a strictly singular phenomenon, since he is God's final self-disclosure, in whose destiny the end of all history occurred in proleptic anticipation. Jesus' confession that he was this direct and final self-disclosure of God led to his conviction as a heretic. If we want to understand the full implications of his self-understanding, we must again return to the Old Testament. In Second Isaiah and other postexilic writings, the phrase "I am" or "I am he" is used in an absolute sense, that is, with no object following (Isa. 41:4). And we find Yahweh's self-introductions with this phrase, asserting that Yahweh was the Lord of history. Very likely this phrase was also used in temple worship announcing the presence of the Lord. As the Septuagint shows, the Greek translation of "I am" or "I am he" is *ego eimi*. This is different from the *ego eimi* formulas in the Gospel of John which have an object following, for example, "I am the bread of life."

At a few decisive places in the Gospels, Jesus uses *ego eimi* analogously to Yahweh's divine self-predication in the Old Testament. For instance, Jesus says in Mark 13:6: "Many will come in my name, saying, 'I am he!' and they will lead many astray." In Matthew this self-predication of the Lord is no longer understood as such and is replaced by the christological statement "I am the Christ" (Matt. 24:5). Most important, when the high priest asked Jesus in the trial, "Are you the Christ, the Son of the Blessed?" Jesus replied, according to Mark 14:62, "I am; and you will see the Son of man sitting at the right hand of Power, and coming with the clouds of heaven." Jesus did not admit that he was the Messiah but confronted the court with this theophanic self-predication. Small wonder that the trial was soon over. By revealing himself as God's self-disclosure and therefore as God, Jesus had committed the worst crime possible in the eyes of the Sanhedrin. His answer was clearly blasphemy in their sight and rendered any further investigation unnecessary. Again the other evangelists interpreted the answer of Jesus differently. In Matthew the theophanic self-predication was changed to a simple affirmative reply. Jesus supposedly replied, "You have said so. But I tell you, hereafter you will see the Son of man seated at the right hand of Power, and coming on the clouds of heaven" (Matt. 26:64). On the other side, Luke retained the original

12 / ESCHATOLOGY

response, but by adding "You say that I am" (Luke 22:70), he too showed that he lacked genuine understanding of what had happened.

A similarly misunderstood theophanic self-predication occurred in Jesus' dialogue with the Samaritan woman. When she spoke words of the traditional messianic expectation, "I know that Messiah is coming . . . ; when he comes, he will show us all things," Jesus corrected her by saying, "I who speak to you am he" (John 4:25–26). With this response Jesus revealed himself as the full self-disclosure of God. But the woman was too much caught up in traditional messianic ideas to understand the full meaning of his words.

Since Jesus perceived himself to be the decisive factor in history—God's coming into our own sphere—any speculation about the final end of the world was clearly secondary (Mark 13:32). He saw no need to comfort the criminal on the cross with promises about the future, but assured him, "Today you will be with me in Paradise" (Luke 23:43). Jesus' person, proclamation, and action demanded an immediate decision which in turn implied an immediate reward. This does not mean that the future was unimportant for Jesus. On the contrary, because of the present that he inaugurated the future again becomes significant. It becomes predictable, because it has received its future-directedness from the life and destiny of Jesus Christ. In this way Jesus determined the future. But very few understood this. In line with popular messianic hopes and expectations, most were quite disappointed with Jesus. They had expected that he would be the political messianic leader who would liberate Israel from its political and military oppressors. Even some of the disciples confessed after Jesus' death that they "had hoped that he was the one to redeem Israel" (Luke 24:21).

After Jesus' resurrection, the big question for the Gospel writers was how to respond to his person and destiny. They could have interpreted his resurrection as the first act of the final eschatological drama and intensified the apocalyptic expectations of the end of the world. Since the Gospels were written several decades after Jesus' death and resurrection, they also could have admitted that the end had not come so soon as many had hoped, and then concentrated on a biographical sketch of the Lord. But they did neither. Amid their individual diversity, the Gospel writers wanted to convey the same conviction: The life, destiny, and resurrection of Jesus are God's final self-disclosure; we live in an interim between this self-disclosure and the universal transformation of the world. Therefore all history, past, present, and future, must be interpreted in the light of what happened in and with Jesus. The evangelists differed considerably from each other, however, in interpreting the interim period.

Mark, the earliest Gospel, reflects more than the others the debate among Christians about how one should respond to popular apocalyptic expectations connected with Jesus. Many people had expected that Jesus would bring about the end of the world and were then disappointed when the final events did not occur so quickly. Mark saw one way of countering these vain hopes by asserting that Jesus wanted no outsider to understand fully the secret of God's kingdom and Jesus' messiahship. This reserved to the apostles, coming from the Easter event, the authority to interpret correctly the life, destiny, and proclamation of Jesus (Mark 4:11–12). Moreover, Mark asserted that before Christ would finally return in glory the gospel must be preached to all nations (Mark 13:10). This means that the interim period between the resurrection of Jesus and his final coming is the time of world mission.

In Matthew's Gospel we encounter a much more elaborate understanding of the interim. This Gospel wants to show that Jesus had not come to abolish the law and the prophets but to fulfill them (Matt. 5:17–18). He fulfilled the Emmanuel promise (Isa. 7:14; Matt. 1:22–23), the Galilee promise (Isa. 9:1; Matt. 4:12–15), the Bethlehem promise (Mic. 5:2; Matt. 2:5–6), and the servant of the Lord promise (Isa. 53:4; Matt. 8:17). Since the Old Testament promises found their fulfillment in him, the people conferred on him many of the Old Testament eschatological titles. He was the Messiah, the son of David, the king of Israel, the Son of God, and the Son of Man, to name just a few. Jesus is depicted as the bringer of the eschaton, but more important, as standing in true continuity with the Old Testament.

The continuity between the Old Testament and Jesus is crucial for Matthew's interpretation of the interim. Since historical Israel had neglected and lost its commission to be the light of the nations, Jesus founded the church as the true Israel (Matt. 16:18). The church has now replaced Israel and exists in continuity with the Israel of promise. But the church has no permanence. While it has specific orders and structures (Matt. 18:15ff.), it is only an interim community. The church is also a mixed group of "believers," and only in the final judgment will the just be separated from the unjust (Matt. 13). The church waits for and points to the final judgment, when Christ will return in glory to select the chosen ones. The tenor of the notion of the coming judgment is important for Matthew, and many passages, such as the Sermon on the Mount (chaps. 5–7), the sending out of the twelve (chap. 10), and the apocalypse (chap. 24), remind us that the judgment is *the* coming event.

Luke finally abandons the strict idea of an interim between Jesus' death and his parousia by interpreting history in the light of God's history of salvation which had culminated in Jesus. This becomes evident in the opening chapters of his Gospel, when he places Jesus in the context of world history (Luke 2:1–4 and 1:5–6). History is then divided into three epochs: (1) the time of Israel; (2) the time of Jesus, the central part of history; and (3) the time of the church. All history receives its proper valuation through its focal point, Jesus of Nazareth. When Luke introduces John the Baptist as the last prophet—instead of as Jesus' forerunner (Luke 16:16)—he wants to make clear

12 / ESCHATOLOGY

that Jesus was without precedent. The law and the prophets covered the first period, and then suddenly Jesus appeared as the center of time.

Luke does not want his readers to bother with impending eschatology. "When you hear of wars and tumults, do not be terrified; for this must first take place, but the end will not be at once" (Luke 21:9) is his reassuring note. The decisive event has happened. Jesus has come, and some day he will bring about the final end. But the end will add nothing essentially new to salvation. In analogy to his ascension, Christ will return as the exalted Lord. Luke's view of history and eschatology radiates confidence and not resignation or pessimism. God has provided the interim as the time of the church, but how long it will last and when the end will come are of no interest, since Jesus has announced the end and the coming of his kingdom. There is no reason to doubt Jesus, since his proclamation was validated through his miracles, his resurrection, and his ascension. Nor are Christians alone in a hostile world. The exalted Christ in heaven is active through his word, proclaimed throughout the *oikoumenē*. His people work in "his name" and "his spirit," carrying the gospel to ever new shores as the church expands and thrives. Without fear or wild expectations, Christians live confidently in this world, since they know that their Lord will bring about the final end of all history. To instill this posture is the main concern of Luke, both in his Gospel and in the Acts of the Apostles.

The Gospel of John not only replaces the eschatological vocabulary of the Synoptics with its own terminology, but also has no specific apocalyptic passages (cf. Mark 13; Matt. 24; Luke 17; 21). Though Jesus says he "will come again" (John 14:3), a phrase which is not used in the other Gospels, he also assures believers that they have eternal life now (John 5:24). When Martha says to Jesus about her dead brother, "I know that he will rise again in the resurrection at the last day," he replies, "I am the resurrection and the life; he who believes in me, though he die, yet shall he live, and whoever lives and believes in me shall never die" (John 11:24ff.). John's heavy emphasis on the present as the time of salvation does not eliminate the hope for future fulfillment. By actualizing the future hope, John wants to demonstrate that in Jesus Christ the former dichotomy between present and future is bridged. Through the incarnation Jesus brought our world and the beyond, present and future, together. The oppositions between life and death, time and eternity, present, past, and future, are only relative. Through the coming of the divine into the sphere of the created, the main task of salvation has been accomplished; the ruler of this world has been judged (John 16:11).

But Jesus was not the kind of Messiah whom everybody expected. He came to his own, but his people did not receive him. (John 1:11). The Gospel of John convincingly shows that the unbelievers constantly misunderstood Jesus, since they could not grasp his true salvific significance. They excluded themselves from participation in the real future, because only believers were able to discern that Jesus opened that future for them. Believers have the promise of the Comforter or Holy Spirit (John 14:15ff., 25–26; 16:4b–11, 12–15), whom Jesus Christ will send to guide them into all truth. The comforter bridges the gulf between the historical Jesus and the proclamation of the gospel and legitimizes the existence of believers as a waiting existence. Believers participate in a salvation that has been brought about proleptically but that is not accessible without faith in Jesus as the Christ.

The Gospel of John encourages a faithful eschatological existence of proleptic fulfillment and yet of expectation. "But these are written that you may believe that Jesus is the Christ, the Son of God, and that believing you may have life in his name" (John 20:31). This characterizes the intention of the gospel: to give witness to the eschatological significance of Jesus and to bridge the gulf between Jesus' redemptive act and his second coming. In its basic description of the tension in the Christian's existence the Gospel of John is very close to Paul.

Paul was neither a disciple nor a follower of Jesus during his life on earth, yet we will notice that he understood very well how to incorporate the life, destiny, and resurrection of Jesus Christ into his own eschatological outlook. Although Paul's writings are the earliest documents we have in the New Testament, he represents the most reflected eschatological perspective within the New Testament. It is only proper to present him as the conclusion of the New Testament.

A key to Paul's eschatological message is his own self-understanding. When Paul introduced himself to the Roman congregation he said:

> Paul, a servant of Jesus Christ, called to be an apostle, set apart for the gospel of God which he promised beforehand through his prophets in the holy scriptures, the gospel concerning his Son, who was descended from David according to the flesh and designated Son of God in power according to the Spirit of holiness by his resurrection from the dead, Jesus Christ our Lord, through whom we have received grace and apostleship to bring about the obedience of faith for the sake of his name among all the nations, including yourselves who were called to belong to Jesus Christ. (Rom. 1:1–6)

Paul introduced himself as an apostle who had been appointed to a proper place and a peculiar task in the series of events to be accomplished in the final days of this world. These events have as their central figure the Messiah, Christ Jesus, crucified, risen, and returning to judgment and salvation. Since Jesus Christ is the fulfillment of the Old Testament prophecies, there is continuity between Paul's proclamation and the Old Testament faith. Through his resurrection Jesus of Nazareth was exalted as our Lord Jesus Christ and designated Son of God.

12 / ESCHATOLOGY

According to the Old Testament's expectations and promises, the series of final events must now have started. The decisive point, the death and resurrection of the Messiah, has been passed, and Jesus Christ has taken his place at the right hand of his Father in heaven. "What remained was his *parousia* and the coming of the kingdom of heaven in power and glory."[5] Jesus, formerly the Messiah of the Jews, had been enthroned as Lord and Savior of the whole world. He is the Lord of the universe (Phil. 2:9ff.): All cosmic powers and the whole universe belong to him, and through faith in him people of all nations and races now have access to his kingdom and to salvation. This good news constitutes the gospel for non-Jews, and Paul was chosen to proclaim it to them in the interval between the resurrection of Jesus Christ and his coming in power.

Paul perceived the life of Christians as extending between two eons. The old eon has passed away and the Messiah has come, but the new eon is not fully here because the Messiah is not yet here in power. Yet we live in the final era, and history will conclude its course according to the preordained plan of God that is leading up to the definite goal, the destruction of the old world and the creation of the new and eternal eon. The decisive events, the resurrection of the dead and the surprising advent of the day of the Lord (1 Thess. 5:2), are now made possible and initiated through Christ's resurrection (1 Cor. 15). We live in a transitional period of faith (2 Cor. 5:7) and waiting (Rom. 8:23ff.). But the coming eschaton is not totally outstanding, since salvation is active in us now. We participate in the gifts of grace, in faith, love, and hope (1 Cor. 13) and are not like those who have no hope. We have died with Christ in our baptism, and we live in Christ and Christ in us (Gal. 2:20). Christian existence is a dialectical existence. It is lived in the world, but not of the world. The power of existence is given us from beyond, the beyond which will come to us in the eschaton.

While Paul knew of the dialectical character of existence between actualization in anticipation and still outstanding fulfillment, he was occasionally affected by the eschatological fever of impending eschatology. For instance, he was convinced that since his conversion the coming of the eschaton had already made progress (Rom. 13:11); he was sure that the Lord was close at hand (Phil. 4:5); and he assured the people in Thessalonica that the Lord would still return in his lifetime (1 Thess. 4:15). But an impending eschatology was not intrinsic to his faith. His hope was bound not to a fixed date but to the gospel that pronounced the fulfillment of the Old Testament promises and called for trusting existence.

Paul preserved Christian eschatology from two major threats: unhistorical spiritualism and overanxious disappointment. In his argument with gnostics in Corinth, he emphasized the proleptic and preliminary eschatological character of Christian existence. The interim is not yet the time of fulfillment. It is the time of the proclamation of the gospel, when we can and shall realize the ethical teachings of Christ. But for those who were on the brink of disappointment because the eschaton had not yet arrived, Paul emphasized that the eschatological fulfillment is a future event affecting our earth. Jesus' resurrection has validated the apocalyptic idea of the resurrection of the dead and by anticipating it through his own resurrection has provided us with a foundation for hope. While Jesus pictured the present as the time of decision, Paul described it as a time of faithful and active waiting to enter into the fulfillment of the new creation. Paul incorporated the Christ-event into the kerygma and proclaimed it in a Christian era, for the decisive turning point of history had already occurred.

NOTES

1. Theodore G. Vriezen, *An Outline of Old Testament Theology* (Newton, Mass.: Charles T. Bradford, 1958), p. 360.

2. See A. S. van der Woude, "Messias," in *BHH* 2:1197. For the following see also Hugo Gressman, *Der Messias* (Göttingen: Vandenhoeck & Ruprecht, 1929), p. 1. Though the king was understood as viceroy and mandatory of Yahweh himself, as expressed in the royal psalms, the office of the king did not seem to have much influence on the development of the idea of the Messiah. See Gerhard von Rad, *Old Testament Theology*, trans. D. M. G. Stalker (New York: Harper & Row, 1962), 1:318ff.

3. Norman Perrin, *Rediscovering the Teachings of Jesus* (New York: Harper & Row, 1967).

4. Joachim Jeremias, *New Testament Theology*, trans. John Bowden (Charles Scribner's Sons, 1971–).

5. Anton Fridrichsen, *The Apostle and His Message*, UUA (Uppsala: Lundequistska Bokhandeln, 1947), p. 4.

2
Continuing Tensions in the History of Eschatology

The initial hope for an early return of Christ gradually gave way to a hope for eternal bliss in heaven. The Christian faith, having become a majority religion, established itself firmly on this earth through its sacraments, liturgy, and dogma. This increasing acculturation was rejected by enthusiastic reform movements, which continually forced the church to reconsider its own self-understanding as an interim institution. The church never made one eschatological concern its exclusive preoccupation, yet it has never abandoned the hope for the conclusion of this earthly history and the resurrection of all at the last day.

THE GRADUAL TRANSFORMATION

Initially the hope for the end of the world and the early coming of the kingdom were vibrant parts of the faith of the Christian community. An influential recent school of theology, initiated by Albert Schweitzer, has claimed that the decisive crisis in the earliest period of Christianity came when these hopes and expectations were disappointed. In *The Mysticism of Paul the Apostle*,[1] Schweitzer claimed that this apostle initiated a profound reinterpretation of the old expectations when he replaced the *coming* of Christ with *being* in Christ. The Gospel according to John served the same purpose by saying that salvation is already a present phenomenon.

Martin Werner, a student of Albert Schweitzer, attempted to show that the whole dogma of the early church resulted from this adjustment to the delay of the parousia.[2] The de-eschatologization went parallel to the creation of the sacraments, which were tied to the death of Jesus. Where these new teachings were not accepted, as among the gnostics, the saving work of Christ had to be explained without reference to Jesus' death and resurrection. Consequently Jesus was understood mainly as a teacher or as the guide to the heavenly abode. Werner argues that a tremendous crisis happened in the early church. The end did not occur with Jesus' death and resurrection, as many

12 / ESCHATOLOGY

had expected. These reacted by rejecting not only the idea of the imminent end but also the whole belief in the return of Christ. This uncertainty is already reflected at the fringes of the New Testament, for instance in 2 Pet. 3:3–4: "First of all you must understand this, that scoffers will come in the last days with scoffing, following their own passions and saying, 'Where is the promise of his coming? For ever since the fathers fell asleep, all things have continued as they were from the beginning of creation.'" Then the "delay" is explained with the words "But do not ignore this one fact, beloved, that with the Lord one day is as a thousand years, and a thousand years as one day" (2 Pet. 3:8). Werner contends that the warning against doubts is seen everywhere, in James, in 1 and 2 Clement, in the *Didache* and in Hermas. Elsewhere we hear that many defect from the Christian faith.

When we attempt to evaluate the thesis of a tremendous crisis of faith in the early church, as proposed by Werner and others, we cannot but notice the scant evidence. Admittedly, many defected from the church once full-scale persecution of the Christians took place. Yet defections under such pressure were understandable, for many had joined the church for the wrong reasons. Then there were certainly people who were disappointed that there was not more visible progress of the kingdom. As we will see later, impatience with the eschatological progression has plagued the church from its beginning until now. Yet any large-scale disappointment would have been reflected much more extensively in the literary documents. It is simply wrong to claim that the original framework of faith collapsed within a short time and had to be replaced by a new one.[3] Indeed, a change took place, as more and more history emerged on the horizon and receded into the past. But the change came slowly and very likely was not even perceived as such by most. A radical and exclusive future orientation of the faith, as Schweitzer and Werner assume, never existed in reality.

The present-oriented approach to eschatology began not with Paul and John but with Jesus himself. He was convinced that the kingdom had arrived with him and that through him its power was already at work, in the midst of the people, giving life through his words and deeds (Luke 11:20). But as we have seen in our survey of Jesus' message, with the focus on the present there was also the emphasis on the future dimension of eschatology: the time of complete fulfillment was imminent. In the later life of the church, gradually and in many ways imperceptibly, the bipolar structure of eschatology, of present fulfillment and imminent completion, was changed into a structure in which the imminent completion received less emphasis. The eschaton was not entirely forgotten; intense external pressure, as occurred in the persecution of the Christians, could rekindle the hope for an early advent of the Lord.

Almost simultaneously, the hellenization process by which Christianity adopted many Greek thought patterns, led in a different direction, as the eschatological hope came to be expressed in Hellenistic categories. The faithful now hoped that just as God saved their souls, so God would save their bodies amid all trials and persecutions, and in the same way as God saved the body, God would also save the church. Irenaeus concluded his *Against Heresies* with the hope that "his offspring, the First-begotten Word, should descend to the creature, that is, to what has been moulded, and that it should be contained by Him; and, on the other hand, the creature should contain the Word, and ascend to Him, passing beyond the angels, and be made after the image and likeness of God."[4] The Spirit of God who has given life to the soul continues its work with humanity by giving life to the body at the resurrection.

In one sense, the resurrection is thus understood as a completion of salvation. The last judgment is seen in the same light. What had commenced with Christ, the acceptance or rejection of salvation, is brought to completion at the last day. Again Irenaeus: "It is manifest that the souls of His disciples also, upon whose account the Lord underwent these things, shall go away in the invisible place allotted to them by God, and there remain until the resurrection, awaiting that event; then receiving their bodies, and rising in their entirety, that is bodily, just as the Lord arose, they shall come thus into the presence of God."[5]

Irenaeus' statement contains the concept of an abode or purgatory in which the soul of the dead remains until the universal resurrection. We should not denounce this as a deviation from biblical teaching, since the point of the assertion is antignostic. Irenaeus wanted to reject the gnostic idea that at the end of this earthly life the soul immediately ascends to its heavenly abode. As the early fathers fought the pagan idea that a part of the human person is simply immortal, it was important for them to assert that there is no rectilinear ascent to God. Once we die, life is over. And against the devaluation of the body, the fathers also wanted to affirm the resurrection of the whole body and not merely of the soul. To be sure, Irenaeus, though quoting extensively from the Scriptures, went beyond the biblical documents. For instance, he suggested that there is a "gradation and arrangement of those who are saved." Some will be taken up into the heavens, some will dwell in paradise, and some will inhabit the city.[6] He attempted to document his conclusions with numerous biblical quotations, but the biblical witnesses do not dwell on such details.

In contrast to those at the fringes of Christianity, the fathers maintained a sober judgment. They did not succumb to utopian speculation in predicting the parousia for the immediate future, nor did they reject all eschatological discussion. The church maintained at the center of its hope the coming fulfillment of both individual and corporate destiny. Tertullian summed this up very eloquently: "We are a body knit together as such by a common religious profession, by unity of discipline, and by the bond of a common hope."[7] Yet

12 / ESCHATOLOGY

he also adds that we pray "for the delay of the final consummation." The church had not abandoned its Christian hope. But as it became more and more established it did not ask for its own premature dissolution, since much of the then known world was still unevangelized. Nevertheless, the zeal for the completion of the kingdom was still present. Tertullian rhetorically asked: "If the *manifestation* of the Lord's kingdom pertains unto the will of God and unto our anxious expectation, how do some pray for some protraction of the age, when the kingdom of God, which we pray may arrive, tends unto the consummation of the age?"[8] Yet the motivation for this zeal was not just the triumph of God, but the end of servitude and of domination by pagan powers.

Undoubtedly, the biblical witness was heard, but gradually the idea of an established church and of the kingdom on this earth received more and more attention. We see this perhaps best in Augustine. The church, in which many godless are mixed, compares to the kingdom in two stages of its development. The church is the pilgrim church on earth and will be the heavenly church at the completion. Since the latter is identical with the kingdom of God and is also one with the church on earth, some day the present church will become the kingdom. Particularly in *The City of God*, Augustine advanced the notion of two cities, the earthly city and the heavenly city. Part of the latter sojourns on earth and is at present a captive or a stranger within the earthly city, but it has already received the promise of redemption and the gift of the Spirit. Thus the heavenly city, through the part with which it sojourns on earth, calls citizens out of all nations, and gathers together a society of pilgrims of all languages.[9] Of course, the kingdom on earth is still a mixed company of saints and sinners. "Where both classes exist, it is the Church as it now is, but where only the one shall exist, it is the church as it is destined to be when no wicked person shall be in her. Therefore the Church even now is the kingdom of Christ, and the kingdom of heaven. Accordingly, even now His saints reign with Him, though otherwise than they shall reign hereafter."[10]

While Jesus also emphasized the presence of the kingdom, with Augustine the emphasis has changed. The saints—and this means also those in public functions in the church—already rule in the kingdom. Though Augustine still looked forward to the final completion and the visible return of Christ, as most Christians have done through the centuries, he trusted in the gradual progress of the kingdom. This trust was also supported through the idea of the millennium, that the saints would reign with Christ during a thousand years. The final completion, though not forgotten, could recede into the background.

During the Middle Ages the doctrine of the last things was mainly left to popular piety and to those outside the main stream of theology. Certainly it is not just accidental that Thomas Aquinas died before he could write the treatise of eschatology for his great *Summa Theologica*. The fervent hope for the coming of the Lord was gradually replaced by the sacrament of penance, through which one was assured of entrance into heaven, and by an increasingly elaborated system of purgatory. Once people passed through this vale of tears, they would enter eternal bliss, since the church as the visible representative of the heavenly city mediated their salvation. Salvation as the end of world history was exchanged in favor of salvation at the end of individual history. The cosmic dimension of eschatology receded and the existential component gained.

The same attitude is also inherent in mysticism, which in the latter Middle Ages had widespread appeal among many for whom the institutional ways of salvation had become too restrictive. Again the attempt was made to attain union with the divine through immediate communion. This urge for immediacy, for communion with God without outward manifestations, can assume revolutionary forms whenever it captures the imagination of the masses. The ecclesiastical apparatus, which tries to institutionalize all emotions and forms of devotion, is then perceived as an obstacle to free access to God. Similarly, politico-social structures which were designed to uphold ecclesiastical domination become targets of the discontent.

Martin Luther, the most prominent representative of the Reformation, joined the mainstream of the church in rejecting millennial ideas.[11] Yet in contrast to the church of his time, he rediscovered the necessary tension between our present state and hope for the future, and the urgency of its resolution. Contrary to the Roman triumphalism, he emphasized the servanthood of the church, the reign of Satan on earth, and the hiddenness of the church of God. Thus he hoped for the last day and the final defeat of Satan.

The medieval church too awaited the coming of the Lord, yet emphasis was primarily on the individual's ability to pass unharmed through the last judgment. The posture of the church as the institution that could guide the individual to salvation through liberal use of the sacramental benefits supported this attitude. Though the interest in the goal of history and of the world was not abandoned, the emphasis was clearly on the individual. Hence Luther's own initial vexing question: How do I obtain a gracious God? Yet Luther broke through this eschatological individualism. Important for this development was his decision that the papacy was the Antichrist. Popular imagination depicted the Antichrist in all his evils and tried to guess the time of his advent. Since Luther finally concluded that the Antichrist had already come in the form of the papacy, which had set itself above God's word, Luther expected the end soon and anxiously awaited its coming. The last day was for him no longer a day of wrath but an eagerly awaited day that would end the rule of Antichrist and all evil powers. Like the first Christian community, Luther expected the "dear, last day."[12]

12 / ESCHATOLOGY

Most other reformers picked up Luther's realism. The faithful realized that they were in a mighty battle between God and Satan and they awaited its final conclusion. A century later this intense hope was diminished. A privatization of piety again occurred, and the goal was again the heavenly bliss, but not the last day and the coming of Christ. Only some pietistic circles maintained the lively biblical hope for a final resolution.

In the eighteenth and nineteenth centuries we encounter a general spiritualizing of eschatology. Either eschatology was eliminated as a relic of a past world view (this was the trend of rationalism) or it was made to provide a frame for sociopolitical transformation of the world. Albrecht Ritschl made redemption consist of being freed from the world and ruling over it in a spiritual way. In realizing that God governs the world, we receive from his hands everything, both good and evil. Salvation is totally present; wherever there is forgiveness of sin there is life and bliss. Though Ritschl claimed Luther for his view, the contrast between the two is significant. Though Luther emphasized the present occurrence of salvation, he did not neglect its future dimension. The general mood of the nineteenth century with its liberal and speculative eschatology can be summarized by Otto Pfleiderer, professor in Jena and later in Berlin:

> The primitive Christian faith in the return of Christ and the establishment of his Kingdom on earth embodied the ideal of an earthly realization of the Kingdom of God. It set up the extensive and intensive penetration of humanity by the Christian spirit as the aim and task of history. The victorious coming and kingly rule of Christ on earth is achieved by the organization of all mankind in a fellowship of children of God, and by the continuous ethical transformation of all society through the power of Christian spirit. But since this takes place within the historic life of nations, the process is bound to human conditions and limits.[13]

The recovery of the historical and corporate dimension therefore came at the expense of the metaphysical aspect of eschatology. There is no longer a divine catastrophe that will usher in the eschaton; as Walter Rauschenbusch said, "This change from catastrophe to development is the most essential step to enable modern men to appreciate the Christian hope."[14] Yet today that optimism about human advancement is widely disappearing. Perhaps a more biblically oriented eschatology may have a new chance.

THE ENTHUSIASTIC FERVOR

The first attack on the acculturation of eschatology came already in the middle of the second century, by the Phrygian self-proclaimed prophet Montanus and his followers. Studying the Johannine writings, they came to the conviction that a final and highest level of revelation was to be attained through them, that the time of the Paraclete (Comforter) had commenced. The Paraclete was supposed to speak through Montanus. The heavenly Jerusalem was soon to descend from heaven. In the expectation of the near end, Christians should fast, dissolve their marriages, and assemble in Pepuza in Asia Minor to await the end.

The enthusiastic movement soon spread to Rome and North Africa, where one of the most eloquent theologians of the early church, Tertullian, joined the Montanist cause. Though the end did not occur as predicted, the enthusiastic movement persisted for some time. Important for the movement were the utterances of the prophets, which were collected as new sacred writings, and a high estimate of the *charismata* (gifts of the Spirit). Their ethical rigorism, strict fasting, charismatic enthusiasm, and so on, proved attractive to many. They valued martyrdom and believed that deadly sins could be expiated only through martyrdom.

Initially the church did not know how to react to the Montanists. Theologically the Montanists were rather orthodox and were opposed to gnosticism. Moreover, the end of the world was attested in Scripture, the gifts of the Spirit were necessary for the church, and the church considered itself a pilgrim on earth. But eventually the church realized that its own teachings were more biblically sound than the enthusiasm of the Montanists. Besides, many Christians did not accept the idea of the "thousand-years dominion."[15] So one remembered the scriptural admonition that in the end false prophets would arise and mislead many. This prediction was applied to the Montanists; soon they were persecuted by the church. Yet their eschatological fervor was to be rekindled many times through the history of the church.

Prominent theologians of the early church, such as Irenaeus and Hippolytus of Rome, were millennialists, looking toward a visible progress and triumph of the kingdom before the final end. The peak of this hope's popularity, and at the same time its domestication, came after Christianity had attained the status of an official state religion. In particular, Eusebius of Caesarea, in his *Ecclesiastical History*, interpreted the victory of the church during the reign of Constantine as the beginning of the "millennium." Barely a generation after Eusebius, Augustine achieved the most lasting interpretation of the millennium, as far as the official church was concerned, when he equated the institutional church with the present kingdom of God.[16] Augustine did not consider the millennium a period in the future, but a period in the history of the institutional church of our own time. Even the "chaining of Satan," expected by millennial thought, occurs in our history. Jesus has already chained Satan, and any nation that has entered the sphere of the Christian church is saved from his power. While Satan can still lead individuals astray, he can no longer do so with entire such nations. The divine powers of the future

12 / ESCHATOLOGY

kingdom of God manifest themselves through the kingdom here and now, the salvation of nations is realized by the church. Though the present age is doomed to perdition, in the church the future redemption is at work.

The victory of the church over its pagan environment notwithstanding, expectation of the early end of time reemerged repeatedly in the medieval church. Around the year 1000 such hopes were especially high, because many followed the idea that a millennium would elapse between Christ's first bodily appearance and his parousia. Many medieval sects also kept alive the expectation of the imminent end of time.

Millennialism gained its most lasting prominence through Joachim of Fiore (ca. 1145–1202), a prophetic abbot and founder of the Cistercian monastery San Giovanni in Fiore, a village on the heights of the rugged Sila Mountains in Calabria, Italy.[17] Like Montanus, Joachim proclaimed the advent of the age of redemption through the coming of the Holy Spirit. In his commentary on the book of Revelation, Joachim argued that a new "third age" was soon to begin. From a supposed exact correspondence of the Old and the New Testaments, and from the equality of the persons in the Trinity, he concluded that there would be three successive periods of revelation in which the three persons of the Trinity would be revealed. The first epoch was that of the revelation of the Father, characterized by law and fear. The second, the time from the coming of Christ to 1260, was the period of the Son and was characterized by grace and faith. The third and final period was inaugurated by Saint Benedict and is the period of the Spirit, dominated by love and the Spirit. The first period, resting on the Father, is an order of the married; the second, resting on the Son, is an order of the priests; the third, resting on the Spirit, is an order of the monks. Each of these periods overlaps the next somewhat, and through an accurate recapitulation of the former period on a higher level one is able to make certain general predictions concerning the future. In the first period learning prevails; in the second, wisdom; in the third, the fullness of knowledge.

Joachim thought of himself as still belonging to the second stage and he did not draw revolutionary conclusions from his historical and theological constructions. Though announcing the advent of a messianic leader, he did not even criticize the church of his time. Later followers were less patient. The Franciscan "Spirituals" of the thirteenth and fourteenth centuries thought of themselves as leaders of the new order, with Saint Francis as their new messianic head. Since knowledge of God could now be obtained immediately through contemplation, they rejected sacraments and preaching. They even rejected the clerical hierarchy, including the pope. The Scriptures and theology were replaced by the order of Saint Francis. When we hear that they also denounced the Emperor Frederick II as the Antichrist, we are not surprised that their revolt did not last, and that church and state authorities persecuted them.

CONTINUING TENSIONS IN THE HISTORY OF ESCHATOLOGY

The fire once kindled, however, it could not be easily extinguished. Ernst Bloch calls Joachim the most influential social utopian of the Middle Ages, because there were to be no class distinctions in the third age.[18] It was to be an age of monks, of universal monastic communism. Bloch sees the fundamental principle of Joachimism in the presumption that revelation is open-ended. He appreciates the active fight of Joachimism against the social principles of a Christianity that had associated itself with class-conscious society and had compromised its message a thousand times over.

For centuries Joachim's writings were propagated, and pamphlets written in his spirit and under his name. Even Thomas Müntzer, the opponent of Luther and apocalyptic utopian and "new Daniel" who wanted to enforce God's will rigorously in this eschatological end-time, refers to Joachim.[19] In a letter attached to his discourse *Von dem gedichteten Glauben* (Concerning the Invented Faith) he mentions Joachim's eternal gospel against which the "carnal scribes" extol themselves in mockery.[20] The Lutherans rejected categorically any such utopian ideas, in the Augsburg Confession of 1530: "Rejected, too, are certain Jewish opinions which are even now making an appearance and which teach that, before the resurrection of the dead, saints and godly men will possess a worldly kingdom and annihilate all the godless."[21]

Despite this rejection the fire of utopian dreams was not extinguished. Gotthold Lessing, one of the spiritual leaders of the Enlightenment in Germany, shows a familiarity with a trinitarian periodization of history and refers to the third age as an age of "a new eternal gospel."[22] It is of more far-reaching consequence that even Engels, Marx's collaborator in the Communist Manifesto, declared in 1842: "The self-consciousness of mankind, the new Grail, around whose throne the nations joyfully assemble, that is our profession, that we become knights of this Grail, to put the sword around our waists and joyfully venture our life in the last holy war after which the thousand years empire of freedom will emerge."[23]

In the context of such secularized versions of millennialism we must also mention the idea of the kingdom of God in America, a country which has been called the New World not merely because it was discovered relatively late. And we must also mention the attempt in Germanic Europe to establish a thousand-year *Reich* or a Third Reign. The messianic consciousness of this attempt can be seen in the fact that Adolf Hitler was greeted by the millions with "*Heil!*"[24] It can only be considered as one of the bizarre tragedies of history that this "messianic" leader, as one of his main goals, sought to exterminate the same Jewish nation in whose midst these chiliastic ideas originated.

Today millennial thought is mainly advocated by sects, such as Jehovah's Witnesses or Seventh-day Adventists, and by fundamentalist groups who have as their main concern the pronouncement of immediate doom on the world

12 / ESCHATOLOGY

and rescue of the faithful. We would be too hasty if we assumed that millennial and enthusiastic groups have contributed nothing to the Christian faith. At least they are a constant reminder to the church, that all its involvement in the affairs of the day and its attempts to win the world for Christ must be prefaced with the eschatological proviso "until he comes." Of course, the hope for the return of Christ was never abandoned in the church. Yet it was often relegated to secondary status. Here groups on the fringes of the church have rendered valuable service by forcing the church to sharpen its vision.

NOTES

1. Albert Schweitzer, *The Mysticism of Paul, the Apostle*, trans. William Montgomery (New York: H. Holt, 1931).
2. Martin Werner, *The Formation of Christian Dogma: An Historical Study of Its Problem*, trans. S. G. F. Brandon (Naperville, Ill.: Alec R. Allenson, 1957).
3. So, rightly, Ernst Benz, *Evolution and Christian Hope: Man's Concept of the Future, from the Early Fathers to Teilhard de Chardin*, trans. H. G. Frank (Garden City, N.Y.: Doubleday & Co., 1968), p. 24, in his insightful study.
4. Irenaeus, *Against Heresies* (5.36.3), in *The Ante-Nicene Fathers*, ed. Alexander Roberts and James Donaldson (Grand Rapids: Wm. B. Eerdmans, 1979), 1:567.
5. Ibid., (5.31.2), 1:560.
6. Ibid., (5.36.2), 1:567.
7. For this and the following quote, see Tertullian, *Apology* (39), in *Ante-Nicene Fathers*, 3:46.
8. Tertullian, *On Prayer* (5), in *Ante-Nicene Fathers*, 3:683.
9. Cf. Augustine, *City of God* (19.17), in *The Nicene and Post-Nicene Fathers*, first series, ed. Philip Schaff (Grand Rapids: Wm. B. Eerdmans, 1979), 2:412.
10. Ibid., (20.9), 2:430.
11. For a good summary of Luther's eschatology, especially as it contrasts with medieval thought, see Paul Althaus, *The Theology of Martin Luther*, trans. Robert C. Schultz (Philadelphia: Fortress Press, 1966), pp. 417ff.
12. See Paul Althaus, ibid., pp. 420-21, in his excellent treatment of Luther's eschatology.
13. Otto Pfleiderer, *Grundriss der christlichen Glaubenslehre*, par. 177, as quoted in Walter Rauschenbusch, *A Theology for the Social Gospel* (Nashville: Abingdon Press, 1945), pp. 225-26, n. 1.
14. Rauschenbusch, *Theology for the Social Gospel*, p. 225.
15. Justin Martyr, *Dialogue with Trypho* (80), in *Ante-Nicene Fathers*, 1:239.
16. So, rightly, Benz, *Evolution and Christian Hope*, p. 26.
17. For the following see Hans Schwarz, *On the Way to the Future*, rev. ed. (Minneapolis: Augsburg Publishing House, 1979), pp. 183ff.
18. For the following, see Ernst Bloch, *Das Prinzip Hoffnung* (Frankfurt am Main: Suhrkamp, 1959), 2:590, 592, 597, 596.

19. See the extensive biography by Walter Elliger, *Thomas Müntzer: Leben und Werk*, 3d ed. (Göttingen: Vandenhoeck & Ruprecht, 1976), pp. 444–45.

20. See Letter of "Müntzer an den Schösser Hans Zeiss, Allstedt, 1523 Dez. 2," in Thomas Müntzer, *Schriften und Briefe: Kritische Gesamtausgabe*, ed. Günther Franz and Paul Kirn (Gütersloh: Gerd Mohn, 1968), p. 398. See also Bloch, *Das Prinzip Hoffnung*, pp. 593ff. When Müntzer mentions here that he has read Joachim's Commentary on Jeremiah, it is based on a misunderstanding. The Commentary on Jeremiah was a pseudo-Joachimite document, printed in Venice in 1516 (cf. Müntzer, *Schriften und Briefe*, p. 398, n. 6). This shows what popularity Joachim enjoyed in the sixteenth century.

21. Augsburg Confession (Article XVII), in *BC* 38–39.

22. Gotthold Ephraim Lessing, *The Education of the Human Race* (86–89), in *Lessing's Theological Writings*, trans. Henry Chadwick (Stanford: Stanford University Press, 1967), pp. 96–97. Though not mentioning Joachim explicitly, he refers to some of the enthusiasts of the thirteenth and fourteenth centuries, who, according to Lessing, have perhaps caught a glimpse of this "new eternal gospel" and erred only in predicting its arrival as so near to their own time.

23. Karl Marx and Friedrich Engels, *Historisch-Kritische Gesamtausgabe* (Frankfurt am Main: Marx-Engels-Archiv, 1927), 1/2:225–26, as quoted in Bloch, *Das Prinzip Hoffnung*, p. 598.

24. It seems strange that, in describing Joachim and his idea of the Third Reich, Bloch passes over Hitler and his utopian dreams with silence. Should this indicate that Hitler's program cannot be integrated into a "principle of hope"?

3
Major Currents in Christian Eschatology

In our century, biblical eschatology has been at the center of Christian theology. The New Testament tension between promise and fulfillment is reflected in contemporary theology. Christian eschatology must also keep in tension the emphasis on the individual person with that on corporate structures. The cosmic aspect of eschatology places this doctrine into the arena of historical responsibility, and it is there that Christian eschatology becomes for many a source of hope and an inspiration for the future.

THE TENSION BETWEEN PROMISE AND FULFILLMENT

Biblical eschatology has dominated twentieth-century theology more than any other topic. At first glance the debate appears confusing. Except for the common agreement that the New Testament provides a thoroughly eschatological outlook, there is hardly any conceivable standpoint or opinion that has not been advocated by at least one respectable scholar within this century. While we cannot delineate all options, we want to mention four matters that deserve our attention. The first of these is the basic tension between promise and fulfillment; the second is the emphasis on the individual person; the third is the emphasis on the corporate scope of eschatology; the fourth and last is the issue of a cosmic eschatology.

The *tension between promise and fulfillment* originates from the fact that the parousia, the advent of the Lord in glory, did not come as early as some had expected. Yet this delay did not cause so radical a reorientation in eschatological thought as has occasionally been claimed. Joachim Jeremias has rightly stated:

> In the matter of the eschatological expectation there is no difference between Jesus and the early Church; they both expected that the first stage of the eschatological crises would be marked by the sudden irruption of the time of

tribulation and the revelation of the satanic power over the whole earth, and they both—Jesus and the early Church—were certain that this last tribulation would end with the triumph of God, the *Parousia*.[1]

But Jesus and the early church soon found themselves at opposite points. While Jesus pointed to the sudden irruption of tribulation, the attention of the early church was directed to the end of the tribulation and the messianic parousia. There were several reasons for the church to assume that it had moved beyond the mere expectation of the end. Jesus and the early church found the key to the meaning of his passion and death in Isaiah 53, and both understood it as a voluntary sacrifice by which he atoned for the sins of the world. Moreover, his disciples and the early church experienced Christ as the resurrected one, who confirmed for them the special significance of his death. But this also opened their eyes to the fact that a new world was dawning. Though Jesus was only provisionally enthroned as the Lord of the universe, there was no doubt in their minds that his definite enthronement in glory was soon to follow. For instance, Paul calls those who are baptized in Christ's name and accept his atoning death and resurrection a "new creation." They are no longer part of this corrupt generation. Thus "a real experience of the dawning of God's new world stood at the beginning of the history of the church."[2] Yet we must also remember Paul's caution that the parousia is not yet here in fullness. There is still an eschatological proviso. The tension between promise and fulfillment, characteristic of the Christian existence in general, must also mark our approach to eschatology.

In dialogue with his Basel colleagues and representatives of consequent eschatology, Fritz Buri and Martin Werner, especially Oscar Cullmann has devoted his energy to the issue of the New Testament understanding of time. Cullmann starts with the assumption that the New Testament indeed knows about a delay of the parousia.[3] The issue of a delay is touched on in Matthew and is implicit in Luke-Acts (Acts 1:6). We notice a change in Paul's own mind from saying that the parousia will come in the readers' lifetime to a much more tenuous answer later in his life (1 Thess. 4:15; Phil. 1:23). Especially instructive is 2 Peter, where the author concedes that scoffers will come saying, "Where is the promise of his coming? For ever since the fathers fell asleep, all things have continued as they were from the beginning of creation" (2 Pet. 3:4). Then he assures his readers that for the Lord, one day is as a thousand years and a thousand years as one day, implying that the parousia may still be long outstanding.

Cullmann notes that the evangelists recognized that the parousia had been delayed. Yet they still preserved sayings of Jesus that promised the coming of the kingdom within the lifetime of Jesus' audience (Mark 9:1). Cullmann then asks why the New Testament hope was thus untouched by the delay of the parousia. He points out that for Jesus as well as the New Testament the expectation of the imminent parousia is not the starting point of faith but a consequence of faith derived from what has already occurred. The lame walking, the blind regaining their sight, and the dead being resurrected to life are events interpreted by Jesus as signaling the onrushing eschaton. The conviction that the main event has already occurred is thus not an evasive answer resulting from the delay of the parousia, but the foundation for hope in the immediacy of the end.

In the biblical understanding of history, Cullmann finds a threefold division of time: before creation, from creation to parousia, and after the parousia. This threefold division is overlaid by a twofold division: the present age and the coming age. The decisive midpoint of the two-part time line is the coming of the Messiah, the messianic time of salvation, and its miracles.[4] In Judaism the dividing midpoint still lies in the future. But not so for Christianity. The Christians reflecting on Christ's death and resurrection realize that they are participating in a new age. The Messiah has come, salvation is present, and history has been advanced to a new age. According to the threefold division of time, Christians still live between creation and parousia. But according to the twofold division they are already beyond the midpoint, belonging to the new age. Thus Jesus is the center of time.

Cullmann contends that the idea of an *immediately* coming eschaton resulted from the tension between already-occurred salvation in Jesus Christ and not-yet-occurred final realization of this salvific act. Since salvation is *already* actually present, it guarantees that the *not yet* of its own final realization will soon be changed; thus the hope for an immediately coming eschaton can emerge. Later the unknown extent of the interim became more pronounced. But the idea was not abandoned that we live in the last time. Since the expectation of the future eschatological events is founded in already-occurred salvation, the "already" prevails over the "not yet."

Jesus' own ministry reflects the tension between the "already" and the "not yet." He proclaimed the coming of the kingdom of God as a future event and anticipated it in his person in a proleptic way. The combination of parallelism and mutual interdependence of the "already" and the "not yet" is the essence of Jesus' eschatological outlook. The "already" and the "not yet" depend on each other and presuppose each other; assertions about the present point toward the coming fulfillment, while claims concerning the future are grounded in their present anticipation and initiation.

Cullmann's approach seems to be very close to the New Testament witnesses, and he emphatically asserts the present and future dimensions of eschatology. Though we still wait for a new heaven and a new earth and for the resurrection of the dead, we live now in the period of salvation leading up to a universal transformation. But we wonder whether we can say as easily as Cullmann that it does not really matter that Christians have been waiting for nearly two thou-

12 / ESCHATOLOGY

sand years for the coming of the eschaton. Perhaps we must concede more realism to those who claim that the expectation of the end of the world soon to come was part of Jesus' outdated world view and is therefore no longer tenable.

While Cullmann attempts to understand eschatology by considering the biblical notion of *time*, the German systematician Wolfhart Pannenberg is mainly concerned with the concept of *history*. In his widely discussed "Dogmatic Theses on the Doctrine of Revelation" (1961), he claims, "Revelation is not comprehended completely in the beginning, but at the end of the revealing history" (thesis 2).[5] History discloses its full meaning as God's history only at its end. The individual acts are not in themselves so transparent that we can discern God in them; they reveal God only if placed in the universal historical context. In the Old Testament the meaning ascribed to various historical events had to be continuously revised and expanded as history progressed. Pannenberg goes even further to claim that "the universal revelation of the deity of God is not yet realized in the history of Israel." It found its fulfillment "in the destiny of Jesus of Nazareth, insofar as the end of all events is anticipated in his destiny" (thesis 4).[6] With this argument Pannenberg counters the claim of Albert Schweitzer that Jesus believed his life or at least his death would bring about the end of the world, a belief that was never fulfilled. Pannenberg attempts to show that in Jesus the end of the world has indeed occurred in proleptic anticipation. In apocalyptic Judaism, the end and fulfillment of all history had been understood to be connected with the resurrection of the dead, an event which happened in a proleptic way in and with Jesus. Since history finds its conclusion in the life, death, and resurrection of Jesus, his destiny is the key to unlocking the meaning of history. Since God manifested himself in the Christ-event, Jesus has a truly eschatological character. At the end of the world there will occur on a cosmic scale what happened in and with Jesus on an individual scale.

We wonder why Pannenberg attributes such significance to Jesus' resurrection. Could it really establish for us that in Jesus the end of history occurred in proleptic anticipation? Pannenberg would respond that we must perceive it in its proper context, namely, the relationship between history and resurrection as understood in the intertestamental period. In the context of apocalyptic the resurrection was perceived as foreshadowing the eschaton. It thus validated Jesus' claim that he stood in God's stead and that in his destiny the End had commenced. Jesus is therefore the focal point for our understanding of eschatology. In him our own future has been paradigmatically anticipated. He also inspires and enables us to live toward the future. Since we know about God's caring action in Jesus, the final coming of the kingdom should not cause any anxiety.

Yet we should not simply wait for history to run its course. Since Jesus proleptically anticipated the promised future, we, as his followers, are also able to participate proleptically in this future. But the values of past and present are still with us. Pannenberg reminds us that Jesus was only the forerunner and herald of the still imminent kingdom: "The history of modern revolutions illustrates the fatal flaw in living so exclusively for the future that all cherishing and celebrating of the present are precluded."[7] To pursue mere futurism is unrealistic, since the ultimate fulfillment of the coming kingdom is beyond our human power to effect. Yet we are not condemned to inactivity. Jesus and his future inspire us to prepare the present for the future to come. Thus we can make our present conditions more attuned to the promised future and we can open ourselves and our world to the future of God's kingdom. In contrast to many other proposals, Wolfhart Pannenberg has succeeded in showing that biblical eschatology has significance beyond the existential now. He directs our attention again to the relation of eschatology and history and shows the necessity of integrating nature and existence.

EMPHASIS ON
THE INDIVIDUAL PERSON

When we now direct our attention to approaches that place primary emphasis on the individual person, we notice, to our initial surprise, that we must deal with two almost totally unrelated groups. The first is mostly influenced by existential philosophy or by a transcendental bifurcation of history, while the second represents a literalistic interpretation of Scripture, supposedly unencumbered by cultural and philosophical concepts and values. The first group gained prominence through such eminent scholars as Rudolf Bultmann and C. H. Dodd, while the latter has its most prominent representative in the evangelist Hal Lindsey.

When we deal with Rudolf Bultmann's approach to eschatology, we notice at once that for him this is a central category. He characterizes Jesus' message as an eschatological message, standing in the historical context of Jewish expectations about the end of the world and God's new future. Jesus points to the signs of the time and proclaims that God's reign is dawning; at the same time, he *is* "the sign of the time." As the bearer of the word, he demands from his audience a decision for or against him which is simultaneously a decision for or against God and therefore implies a christology. The singular character of Jesus was then explicated by the early church when it understood "Jesus as the one whom God by the resurrection has made Messiah," and so "awaited him as the coming Son of Man."[8] Bultmann characterizes the early church as an eschatological community. When the earliest church proclaimed Jesus as the coming Messiah or the Son of Man, it stayed within the frame of Jewish eschatological expectations.

12 / ESCHATOLOGY

Since God raised Jesus from the dead and made him Messiah, exalting him to be "the Son of Man who is to come on the clouds of heaven to hold judgment and to bring in salvation of God's reign . . . , the indefinite mythological figure, Messiah, has become concrete and visible."[9] Jesus' coming, cross, and resurrection had the meaning of an eschatological occurrence, and therefore the earliest church regarded itself as a community of the end of days. For Bultmann it is clear that Jesus and the New Testament writers believed in a future eschaton. They thought that the end of history and of the world was about to commence. Yet the problem for us today is "that the parousia of Christ never took place as the New Testament expected. History did not come to an end, and, as every schoolboy knows, it will continue to run its course."[10] Since the hoped-for parousia did not occur, Christians eventually doubted the immediate coming of the end. The early church still kept the hope for a future eschaton alive. But it expected the end of the world in a more and more distant and unknown future. Bultmann therefore asserts that eschatology in the sense of a universal change in nature and history must be discarded, because it is part of a past mythical world-view. The surprising fact, according to Bultmann, is that the mythical world-view of the New Testament does not lend itself to a strictly cosmological interpretation. To obtain its real meaning, it must be interpreted in anthropological or existential terms. Instead of taking the apocalyptic imagery literally, we should ask for its existential meaning.

In the New Testament a distinction is already made between the expected end and the goal of history. While in Jewish apocalyptic, history is still interpreted in the context of eschatology, for Paul history is dissolved into eschatology. The latter has lost its meaning as the goal of history and is now understood as the goal of the individual human being. What really matters is not world history but the history of the individual and the encounter with Christ, because in confrontation with this eschatological event the individual is enabled to exist truly historically. Again Bultmann finds support in New Testament writers. Paul emphasizes that the turn of the eons has occurred and that in Christ the realization of the future has become a present possibility. Judgment and resurrection are happening now, when we die and rise with Christ in our baptism, and the believer who is in Christ becomes a new creation. Our existence is no longer tied to the past. The future is open to us in the dialectic of indicative and imperative, an existence according to flesh or according to spirit. Though Paul still describes the eschatological judgment in apocalyptic terms as a future event, decisive is what now happens to our own existence. Neither is it necessary, therefore, for us today to understand the goal of history as some apocalyptic cataclysm. Even Paul's hope that the great drama of eschatological events might occur during his lifetime is labeled by Bultmann an unimportant sideline in Paul's actual eschatological outlook.

In his endeavor to demonstrate that New Testament eschatology should be interpreted in existential categories, Rudolf Bultmann refers extensively to the Johannine writings. While Paul is indebted to Jewish apocalyptic terminology, John uses gnostic terms to convey an eschatological gospel. John employs the gnostic dualisms between light and darkness, truth and lie, above and below, and freedom and bondage—a dualism usually understood cosmologically as denoting certain "localities"—to communicate the gospel. Again Bultmann contends that John transposes this cosmological dualism into *"a dualism of decision."*[11] Confronted with Jesus, humanity must decide for light or darkness, for God or against God. Thus Jesus' coming is the judgment, and our reaction to revelation becomes decisive. Salvation becomes a present occurrence: Whoever accepts Jesus as God's revelation *has* eternal life and has passed through judgment.

The Gospel of John, in its emphasis on the present as the time of salvation, is seen by Bultmann as a protest against the traditional, dramatic, and primitive eschatology. Yet he cannot avoid noting that some passages in John do nevertheless point to a future eschaton (John 6:44; 6:54). But Bultmann assumes that a later editor interpolated these references. While the actual existence of such a later churchly editor is not uncontested by other scholars, Bultmann's own hypothesis would attest to the fact that, contrary to his claim, Christian theology cannot exist in the long run without a future goal of history. If the original writer of the Gospel of John indeed omitted the hope for a future fulfillment and completion of nature and history, a later generation found it necessary to reintroduce the future dimension of history.

Evaluating Bultmann's approach, we agree that the present-oriented aspect of eschatology needs to be emphasized. Eschatology cannot be concerned only with the so-called "last things," but is essentially connected with the present. Yet Bultmann forgets that the present aspect of eschatology is but a foreshadowing of its future dimension. The future element cannot be eliminated from the New Testament in favor of an exclusive emphasis on the existential without rendering the present unintelligible. We also wonder whether Bultmann's highly individualistic approach allows for a significant involvement with the ethical and social issues of our time.

Yet Bultmann does pose a very serious question for us: How can we, at the end of the twentieth century, still accept a future eschaton entailing God's provision of a new world and a total transformation of the present, without asserting at the same time that this is to be accomplished by us? We seem to know the laws of this world too well to be open to such a total surprise.

The British New Testament scholar C. H. Dodd is another influential

12 / ESCHATOLOGY

theologian who emphasizes the existential impact of eschatology. Dodd is bothered not by the apparent disparity between our twentieth-century world view and that of antiquity but by the unresolved question posed by Albert Schweitzer: How was it possible that the false hope for an early return of Christ in glory could not affect the substance of Christian hope?

Dodd assumes that the first Christians expected the last judgment and Christ's coming almost any day. "During the first century events occurred from time to time which raised hopes that it was at hand; but they were always disappointed, as similar hopes have been disappointed many times since."[12] Though their hopes for an early return of Jesus Christ proved wrong, the center of their hope remained unchanged, since they gradually realized that the decisive event had happened: Christ had indeed come. While they were hoping for a second coming, they derived the strength to continue hoping amid disappointment from the fact that Christ had already come. In Jesus, God had confronted the Jewish people in his kingdom, power, and glory. It was the hour of decision, because in Jesus the eternal had entered history. In the coming of the kingdom of God the eschaton had become reality.

Dodd finds backing for this concept of "realized eschatology" in the proclamation of Jesus. Jesus made use of traditional apocalyptic symbolism to illustrate the radically different and absolute character of the kingdom of God; he proclaimed in parables the idea that the kingdom had already come. The advent of God's kingdom also implied judgment; those who rebuked Jesus for his actions and teachings pronounced judgment on themselves and excluded themselves from the kingdom. Jesus announced threatening catastrophes resulting in a final triumph. He would rise from the dead, the kingdom of God would come with power, and the Son of Man would descend on the clouds of heaven. For Dodd, all those events attest to the same fact: "Immediate victory out of apparent defeat." Jesus rose to a new life after his death, gathered his frightened followers, empowered them with his Holy Spirit, and sent them as his evangelists into the world. Through his resurrection Christ was invested with power and glory and became the invisible king of humanity. So started the kingdom of Christ on earth; it was to keep the church growing and alive throughout the centuries.

> The Church prays, "Thy Kingdom Come"; "Come, Lord Jesus." As it prays, it remembers that the Lord did come, and with Him came the Kingdom of God. Uniting memory with aspiration, it discovers that He comes. He comes in His Cross and Passion; He comes in the glory of His Father with the holy angels. Each Communion is not a stage in process by which His coming draws gradually nearer, or a milestone on the road by which we slowly approach the distant goal of the Kingdom of God on earth. It is a reliving of the decisive moment at which He came.
>
> The preaching of the Church is directed towards reconstituting in the experience

of individuals the hour of decision which Jesus brought. . . . It assumes that history in the individual life is of the same stuff as history at large; that is, it is significant so far as it serves to bring men face to face with God in His Kingdom, power and glory.[13]

When the early Christians gradually became aware that Christ had won the victory and that they already shared in it, they readjusted their thinking accordingly and escaped a disastrous disappointment. But strange as it may seem, they did not discard the hope for another coming of Christ. The reason for this, Dodd contends, was their awareness that the tension still had to be resolved between the realization of God's achieved victory and the experience of their daily difficulties in this world.

Dodd also realizes that some passages in the New Testament mention a breakdown of the physical universe before Christ's coming, thus reinforcing the notion of a second coming. While Dodd does not want to take the imagery of falling stars and darkening sun literally, he knows that the most elegant symbolic interpretation cannot do justice to the reality contained in that imagery. Yet Dodd claims that the final coming of Christ will not be another coming in history, because he already came once in history, in his resurrection. It will be an event *beyond* history and not at the conclusion of history. This means that it is not tied to a particular point of the historic progression of time. Since Christ comes beyond space and time, Dodd asserts that John is not mistaken when he claims in his Gospel that *now* is the judgment of this world. Whenever people now believe that the Lord is near and that judgment is come, neither are they mistaken. The eschaton is not connected with a particular period of history. The blessings of God's kingdom may be enjoyed both in the present and the future, since they are "never exhausted in any experience that falls within the bounds of space and time."[14] At one point, however, all history will be taken up into the larger whole of God's eternal purpose. Christ will come that last time, and everything will reach its fulfillment, so that we shall see our lives as God sees them.

Dodd presents an impressive interpretation of eschatology. He wants to escape from a seemingly antiquated cosmology without falling into the trap of projecting an earthly utopia as the goal of history. But Dodd's transcendentalistic approach that asserts an eschaton beyond history rests on too many disconnected peculiarities of history to provide justified hope for the future. Eschatology thus becomes an individual experience with a universalistic tinge. But a twofold outcome of history—not one beyond history—is too firmly embedded in the New Testament to be changed into a universal homecoming of the individual, without substantially changing the Christian message.

While scholars such as Bultmann and Dodd excite the theological world, popular attention goes to people like Hal Lindsey, who gear their writings to the great and widespread interest in eschatology among the laity. Within

12 / ESCHATOLOGY

the last few years, articles on eschatology have appeared in secular weeklies such as *Time* and *Newsweek* and in virtually all religious magazines, and bumper stickers still warn "When the Rapture comes, this car will be driverless." Contrary to views voiced just a decade ago, people are now more ready than ever to accept that the return of the Lord is near.

Hal Lindsey does not simply want to satisfy curiosity about the future. He realizes that there are many modern-day prophets whose predictions about the future enjoy the greatest revival since the days of ancient Babylon. To counteract these misleading and false prophecies, of both the religious and the secular variety, he seeks to give new credibility to the biblical prophecies. He rightly admits that prophecy is not unique to the Bible. Yet, endowed with a keen sense of biblical realism, he claims that what is unique to the Bible "is that it has been 100 per cent accurate in *every* prophecy fulfilled to date."[15] "The events leading up to the coming of the Messiah-Jesus are strewn throughout the Old and New Testament prophets like pieces of a great jigsaw puzzle."[16] Jesus himself gave us a list of signs to look for in order to prepare us for his coming and for the end of the age: People will arise calling themselves Messiah; there will be wars and rumors of wars; a great outbreak of worldwide famine will occur on a scale never before known to humanity; plagues will sweep the world; there will be a great increase in lawlessness and inhumanity; and earthquakes will increase in intensity and frequency. Yet one of the most important keys to the puzzle was the return of Israel to its ancient homeland and its reestablishment as a nation in 1948. Since then, all the important political alignments that lead up to the final battle at Armageddon have occurred. Lindsey, however, comforts us: "As black as this picture looks, the future was never brighter because as things get tougher in this old world, it only means that Messiah-Jesus' coming is that much nearer!"[17]

Lindsey maps with precision the timetable for the final events. But, he concedes, the Bible tells us that people will remain unconcerned about God and the prophetic warnings about God's coming judgment upon sin. But "those who have believed in him [Jesus] as savior, then becoming true children of God, will be taken out of the world and great judgment will fall on those left."[18] During the following seven years of pretribulation on earth, God will still attempt to convince people to accept his Lordship. At the end of this period, however, the Messiah will come in glory and there will be a terrible outpouring of God's wrath on sinful and God-rejecting people.

Yet if we believe in God as Lord, we need not be afraid. We need not even wait for God until the kingdom comes to earth. For already God graciously holds out the promise that God will personally come into our lives through our wills if we but do the inviting. Hal Lindsey assures us that "we can experience the peace and inner joy of his kingdom in our hearts while we wait the coming of the king."[19] But Lindsey leaves no doubt that present corporate structures will not support us in our Christian way of life. The world is the devil's, and the church is led into ever greater apostasy from its Lord. The great religious system of the time of the tribulation will be powerful, we hear Lindsey say, but it will also be godless.[20] The church is compared with a harlot; it is worshiping through a false religious system; the ecumenical movement is a mania that leads to apostasy. But, Lindsey assures us, faithful Christians will escape through the rapture and consequently "should be living like persons who don't expect to be around much longer."[21]

In this apocalyptic situation we should accept Jesus as Lord and Savior. He will bring new purpose for life, peace of mind, stability in spite of circumstances, and true fulfillment to our personality, as well as eternal life. God does not even want us to try to reform our lives. God instead wants us to be available to the Spirit, who now lives personally within us. Christ will work in us a life of true righteousness characterized by unselfish love for God and for others. We will also want to share the good news of salvation with others whom God will lead to us. While on the one hand we should plan our lives as if we will remain on earth for our full life expectancy, we should live as if Christ were coming today, Lindsey assures us in conclusion.[22]

We admire Hal Lindsey for his stated intention to lead us back to a biblical and apocalyptic realism. Like some at the time of Jesus, he emphasizes the imminence of the parousia. We also note that he is not exclusively future-oriented, but strives to maintain a proper balance between the future we hope for and the present we already enjoy in anticipation. Yet Lindsey's view of the world in which we live is almost gnostic: There is no good in it. He could hardly agree with Luther's explanation of the first article of the creed that God has created and sustained "us and *all* that exists together with our house, home, family, and property." Though Lindsey urges us to show the love of Christ to others and to witness to them, he regards the world as beyond repair, the domain of the devil, and rightly bound for hell. Any social responsibility or engagement beyond the private sphere seems to be missing. That state and government are good arrangements of God instituted to preserve peace and order (Rom. 13) is completely neglected; they are perceived only as the apocalyptic beast (Rev. 13). Thus a retreat to the private sphere is coupled with an otherworldly eschatology that does not transform our world but destroys it.

EMPHASIS ON THE CORPORATE DIMENSION

Turning to approaches that emphasize primarily the corporate dimension of eschatology, we at once note an immense interest in the affairs of the day and a questioning of the extent to which these affairs are conducted in a way

12 / ESCHATOLOGY

commensurate with what God has intended or at least promised for us. Thus social structures gain primary attention in this attempt to relate the biblical message to today's issues. One is somewhat reminded here of the experience of the pioneer of the social gospel, Walter Rauschenbusch, who confessed that he was unable to fill the hearts with heavenly hope as long as the stomachs remained empty.

The this-worldly implications of eschatological thought have been vigorously emphasized by the German systematician, Jürgen Moltmann. In his incisive work *Theology of Hope: On the Ground and the Implications of a Christian Eschatology*,[23] he claimed at the outset that Christian eschatology is not just the doctrine of the so-called "last things" that will occur in the End, but it embraces both the object hoped for and the hope inspired by it. Christian eschatology also deals with practical implications, with church life and burning political and social issues, such as social justice, world peace, and personal freedom and responsibility. The appearance of his *Theology of Hope* therefore marks another breakthrough in recent reflection on eschatology. Backed by the earlier thesis of Ernst Käsemann that apocalyptic is the mother of Christian theology, he claims that Christianity in its totality is eschatological; nothing that pertains to it is exempted from its impact.

Moltmann contrasts the Israelite religion of promise and the static epiphanic religions in the environment of Israel. After Israel had conquered the promised land, Yahweh was still conceived as a God who pointed to a new future. This meant that the Old Testament promises were constantly being modified and expanded. Of course, some were also realized in history. To these "fulfilled" promises Israel owes its existence, since amid all the trials of history they provided the continuity in which Israel was able to recognize the faithfulness of its God. Yet the promises were never completely fulfilled, and there remained continuous overspill that again pointed to the future. The tension between promise and fulfillment continued through the whole of Israel's history and was a strong incentive for its own historic progression.

According to Moltmann, the same is true in the New Testament, because the revelation in Christ is at the same time good news and promise. The Old Testament history of promise does not simply find its fulfillment in the gospel of Jesus Christ and get superseded; it finds its future in the gospel. The gospel is promise, and as such it is a down payment on the promised future. In this context the centrality of Christ's resurrection becomes apparent, because it is a "history-making event in the light of which all other history is illumined, called into question and transformed."[24] Again the resurrection stories point beyond themselves. Moltmann perceives them in the line of prophetic and apocalyptic hopes and expectations of that which is bound to come according to God's promise. Cross and resurrection lead us to a new future in promising life as a result of the resurrection from the dead, and the kingdom of

MAJOR CURRENTS IN CHRISTIAN ESCHATOLOGY

God in a new creation. Again the forward thrust becomes noticeable when Moltmann understands the encounters with the resurrected one as "call" appearances. In them the recognition of Christ coincides with recognition of his mission and his future.

For Moltmann the reality of the world becomes historic, inasmuch as it is the mission of theology to perceive the world as the field of missionary endeavor, examining it for possibilities of world-transforming missionary hope. "The call to obedient moulding of the world would have no object, if this world were immutable," he declares.[25] Thus Moltmann does not reject the revolutionary progressiveness of the modern age. But he reminds us to incorporate the open horizons of modern history into the true eschatological horizon of the resurrection, and thereby to "disclose to modern history its true historic character."[26] To live up to this task, the church cannot just be the conservative factor and caring agency for individual people that society wants. The church's task and mission is rather determined by its own peculiar horizon of the eschatological expectation of the coming kingdom of God, by the coming peace and righteousness, and by the coming human freedom and dignity. Salvation for Moltmann means not just "salvation of the soul, individual rescue from the evil world, comfort for the troubled conscience, but also the realization of the eschatological *hope of justice*, the *humanizing* of man, the *socializing* of humanity, *peace* for all creation."[27]

In more recent writings, Moltmann pursues the topic of eschatology from other angles. For instance, in *The Crucified God* he declares at the outset, "The cross is not and cannot be loved. Yet only the crucified Christ can bring the freedom which changes the world because it is no longer afraid of death."[28] In developing a theology of the cross, he then concludes that since the rejected Son of Man was raised up in the freedom of God, "faith in the resurrection becomes faith that raises up, wherever it transforms psychological and social systems, so that instead of being oriented on death they are oriented on life."[29] Thus the theology of the cross urges us to psychological and political liberation of humanity.

And in his ecclesiology, *The Church in the Power of the Spirit*, we read:

> The prayer for the Spirit makes people watchful and sensitive. It makes them vulnerable and stimulates all the powers of the imagination to perceive the coming of God in the liberation of man and to move in accord with it. Thus prayer therefore leads to political watchfulness and political watchfulness leads to prayer.[30]

According to Moltmann, eschatology urges us toward political and economic liberation, human solidarity, solidarity with nature, and struggle for the realization of hope.

Moltmann rightly reminds us that eschatology leads to action instead of complacent passivity or resignation. He awakens the church to the fact that

12 / ESCHATOLOGY

in the past it has left the earthly-eschatological anticipation of God's kingdom too readily in the hands of enthusiasts and utopians. In reacting against this manifest neglect, Moltmann draws the future-directedness of eschatology so much into the reach of human possibilities that autonomous humanity will have trouble understanding that all its work has only an anticipatory character. His almost exclusively sociopolitical emphasis bears so much resemblance to the Calvinistic idea of establishing a theocracy on earth that we hesitate to agree with it without first expressing a loud and clear eschatological caveat to all such too-human endeavors.

Examining another branch of eschatological thought that emphasizes the corporate dimension, it becomes clear at once that its horizon is not as comprehensive as in Moltmann's approach. The reason for this is evident. The authors of this particular strain of theology are deeply moved by their own geographic and socioeconomic conditions, which are in either Latin America or black North America.

James H. Cone, professor of theology at Union Theological Seminary in New York, puts the issue well when he claims that as long as this country is divided on the basis of color, "it is the task of the Christian theologian to do theology in the light of the concreteness of human oppression as expressed in color, and interpret for the oppressed the meaning of God's liberation in their community."[31] Thus the content of one's own socioeconomic experience becomes normative for reflection on what eschatology means. Again Cone provides a thoroughgoing eschatological approach when he states: "Christian theology is a theology of liberation. It is a *rational study of the being of God in the light of the existential situation of an oppressed community, relating the forces of liberation to the essence of the gospel, which is Jesus Christ.*"[32] Understandably, from his socioeconomic perspective, Cone emphasizes the present aspect of eschatology. For example, he claims that the black revolution is God's kingdom becoming a reality in America. Cone finds backing for this assertion in the New Testament, because there too the kingdom is an historical event. But it is not an attainment of material security, nor is it mystical communion with the divine. It rather has something to do with the quality of one's existence, when one discovers that people are more important than property. Yet Cone does not agree with the idea that the kingdom will be achieved by black people. While he insists that the kingdom is God's doing, he also asserts that it is something happening today. For instance, it erupts when black people live as if the values of this world have no significance. In principle the kingdom is accessible to everyone and will have far-reaching effects not only on the black community but on the white community as well. But black theology is an attempt by the black community "to see salvation in the light of their own earthly liberation."[33]

While Cone assures us that salvation as liberation from oppression and bondage is consistent with the Bible, he refers mainly to the Old Testament. His assurance that the New Testament continues this trend is tenuous. For instance, freedom from slavery is understood in the New Testament mainly in reference to slavery to sin and therefore to one's own evil inclinations, not in reference to bondage to other people. But Cone is certainly correct when he asserts that an eschatological perspective is inadequate if it does not challenge the present order. Unless the hoped for future can become present, thereby forcing us to make changes in this world, eschatology hardly has any significance for black people. But despite the white corruption of the future, black theology cannot forfeit the future. "Black Theology," we read, "cannot reject the future reality of life after death—grounded in Christ's resurrection—simply because white people have distorted it for their own selfish purposes."[34] If God is truly the God of the oppressed, Cone declares, God will vindicate us, and the future must mean that our fight for freedom has not been in vain. Thus the struggle for liberation is grounded in the past and present reality of God. Cone concludes that "to hope for the future of God is to know that those who die for freedom have not died in vain; they will see the kingdom of God. This is precisely the meaning of our Lord's resurrection, and why we can fight against overwhelming odds."[35]

Though Cone rejects elaborate speculation about the End, about white robes and celestial choirs, he does not reject the end altogether. He even claims that precisely the future of God allows us to strive toward its proleptic realization in the present. Yet, we might ask, why should we strive so hard, even to the point of self-sacrifice, if God will bring about the future anyhow? Perhaps we should remember that the notion of liberation as portrayed in the Old Testament ultimately proved insufficient. We should take the primary cues for liberation not from the Old Testament, as Cone does, but from Paul. There we would see our existence described as a new creation under the disguise of the old one, and we would be cautioned by a strong dose of the eschatological proviso in our attempts to bring about the kingdom with might.

When we now refer to one Latin American representative of liberation theology, he must stand for a great number of other theologians of that region, such as Paulo Freire, Hugo Assmann, Denis Goulet, or Juan Luis Segundo. Gustavo Gutiérrez, professor of theology and social sciences at the University of Lima, Peru, whose position we briefly want to sketch, has provided us with the most comprehensive theology of liberation.

Recognizing the thin layer of a privileged upper class that provides the veneer for a continent of poverty and widespread exploitation, we are not surprised that Latin American theologians have become leaders and teachers in the theology of liberation. At the center of their concern is not so much doctrine and thought as strategy for alleviating human wrongs. This is also evident when Gutiérrez characterizes the theology of liberation as theology of salvation incarnated in the concrete historical and political conditions of today. Writing from a context of oppression, he calls for a revolutionary transformation of the very basis of a dehumanizing society. Though "liberation theologians" often use Marxist categories, Gutiérrez confesses that there is no panacea that would guarantee the desired transformation. Christians involved in the process of liberation proceed by trial and error in their attempt to shape a different social order and a new way of being human.

While hope is central to a theology of liberation, there is no euphoria. The joy of the resurrection presupposes the death of the cross. Yet one dare not lose sight of the final goal. "It is important," Gutiérrez reminds us, "that beyond—or rather through—the struggle against misery, injustice, and exploitation the goal is the *creation of a new man.*"[36] The Old Testament shows us that God is a history-making God and that salvation means a re-creation of history. In the New Testament the theme of a new creation is reiterated. Creation and salvation therefore belong together, since God makes the cosmos from chaos and leads from alienation to liberation. Gutiérrez reminds us that we are also invited to participate in this process. By engaging ourselves in the work of creation through our own labor, we take part in the all-embracing salvific process. Through our struggle against misery and exploitation, we can transform this world, and in our attempt to build a just society we become part of God's saving action which moves toward fulfillment. Salvation is not a return to the beginning but a striving forward to something new and unprecedented.

This vision of salvation and new creation would lack momentum without the eschatological promises that permeate the Bible. Gutiérrez reminds us, however, that there is a difference between the various promises made by God throughout history and the Promise that unfolds and becomes richer and more definite in the succession of the individual promises. "The Promise is not exhausted by these promises nor by their fulfillment; it goes beyond them, explains them, and gives them their ultimate meaning. But at the same time the Promise is announced and is partially and progressively fulfilled in them."[37] Gradually the Promise is disclosed in all its implications and proleptically fulfilled in historical events. It incessantly projects itself into the future and creates an unrest and a mobility toward the future. Gutiérrez knows that in order properly to correlate the Promise and history, both the present and the future of the Promise must be equally emphasized. The Promise, which occupies a central place in the thought of Gutiérrez, is the efficacious self-disclosure of God's love and is synonymous with God's self-communication. Being both self-disclosure and good news, the Promise is the heart of the Bible and enters into a decisive stage in the incarnation of the Son and the sending of the Spirit.

Since the Promise is intimately connected with the eschatological fulfillment, Gutiérrez discovers in eschatology "the driving force of salvific history radically oriented toward the future. Eschatology is thus not just one more element of Christianity, but the very key to understanding the Christian faith."[38] But the intrinsic eschatological structure of the Christian faith must not be spiritualized. For example, when the prophets announce the kingdom of peace, this implies the establishment of justice on earth. Similarly, the coming of the kingdom and the parousia necessarily involve historical, social, and material realities. We must not forget the human consequences of the eschatological promises and their power to transform unjust social structures. Gutiérrez therefore emphasizes that elimination of misery and exploitation can be understood as a sign of the coming kingdom. As the Scriptures indicate, eschatological promises are being fulfilled to some extent throughout history. Yet Gutiérrez is quick to add that they cannot be clearly and completely identified with one or another social reality. There is always a promissory overspill that eventually asks for resolution in the eschaton. But Gutiérrez again reminds us, "The complete encounter with the Lord will mark the end of history, but it will take place in history."[39]

Gutiérrez wants to make sure that historical conditions are not neglected while we hope for an eschatological resolution. But does he not overstate his case? If the complete encounter with the Lord were to take place in history, as Gutiérrez asserts, it would only be another point in history. Yet we are not hoping for such a continuation even on a more just scale, but for a totally new creation that receives history and transforms it into a larger whole. While we appreciate the balanced approach of Gutiérrez that neither neglects the present nor is oblivious to the future and that appeals to the individual person and still pays careful attention to social structures, we nevertheless wonder whether he does not favor some kind of evolutionary approach to eschatology, albeit with Christ at its center. The immense depravity of humanity not only causes the conditions that cry out for liberation but also prevents liberation from becoming an historical event. Therefore salvation is not simply perfection or fulfillment; it is inaugurated by a totally new creation.

THE COSMIC ASPECT OF ESCHATOLOGY

Emphasis on the corporate dimension of eschatology often implies a steadily progressing line of history, sometimes even to such an extent that eschatology is almost totally drawn into the horizon of history. While the modern notion of progress originated initially from within the Judeo-Christian tradition, this does not automatically mean that the future to which progress points is endowed with reality. In an age dominated by technology and science, we must also consider what kind of future is allowed for by the prognosis attained from these fields. Once this question is answered, we must ask further whether

12 / ESCHATOLOGY

such a future would allow for an eschaton provided by God *or* by us. We remember the verdict of Rudolf Bultmann, that the expected end of the world has not come and that all of us know that an eschatology affecting the whole cosmos is wishful thinking. Other theologians, however, have not been so ready to abandon the cosmic sphere. More than anyone else, Pierre Teilhard de Chardin devoted special attention to the cosmic dimension of Christian eschatology.

The French Jesuit paleontologist, Pierre Teilhard de Chardin, held a unique position, since he combined profound scientific erudition with an imaginative theological perspective. He conceived of humanity as part of a universal evolutionary process moving from alpha to omega (Rev. 1:8). Cosmosphere (the inanimate world), biosphere (the animate world), noosphere (the human world), and christosphere (the realm of Christ) are the main stages of the universal, upward-slanting evolutionary process. Through hominization, humans become human, making the transition from the animal world to the noosphere. Through christification, the evolutionary process will come to its fulfillment, and everything will be received into Christ. The universe, and within it humanity, has a definite destiny and future.

Life is not an absurdity, as held by Jean-Paul Sartre, and human existence is not suspended over nothingness, as Martin Heidegger had projected. Even totalitarian trends in modern technology and bureaucratic government are but a temporary aberration in the movement toward unity. Teilhard assures us that there will be a further and consistent complexification of the noosphere due to the increase of knowledge about the universe at large and the psychosocial pressure on our planet's surface. But Teilhard does not despair over our planet becoming too small for an ever-growing population. The intense psychosocial pressure will unify humanity, its society, and its culture, and in the end will lead toward personalization, increased differentiation, and a richer fulfillment of the individual. Manifold trials and errors notwithstanding, evolution is always an ascent to increased consciousness.

Teilhard conceives of evolution not as a never-ending process but as having a definite goal in christification. Under intense psychosocial pressure the evolutionary process will suddenly erupt, and everything will be received into and end in Christ. But Teilhard dismisses the notion of a final catastrophe as the end of our present world. Such a sidereal disaster could lead only to the extinction of part of our universe, rather than to the fulfillment of the whole universe. Teilhard does not have a naive and blind trust in the future, since a "worldly faith is not enough in itself to move the earth forward."[40]

Christogenesis, when everything will be received and end in Christ, is not a natural phenomenon or a product of evolution. There is an ascending anthropogenesis, humanity becoming human, and a descending permeation of christogenesis, the world being drawn into Christ. "Natural" evolution toward humanity and "supernatural" descent in the incarnation are joined in salvation-history. The unifying movement of the human family (upward-slanting and forward-moving) and the activity of Christ in salvation-history (from above and permeating the whole reality of humanity) are fused in the christogenesis. Thus hominization only prepares the way for the parousia.

Though the genesis of humanity is constitutive for the genesis of Christ through his church in the human family, it is the descent of Christ that superanimates humanity. The crowding of the human family does not warm the human heart, but union through love and in love unites individuals. In Christianity, Teilhard claims, we have witnessed the birth of love. Only through organic unification of all people in God can human individuals perfect themselves or exist in fullness.

The universal upward evolutionary and metaphysical movement toward the future does not imply a neglect of the individual person. Rather, the personal and universal future of Christ at the summit of evolution endows our own individual and corporeal existence with meaning and direction. Teilhard asserts that in Christianity alone faith in a personal and personalizing center of the universe is alive and has a chance of surviving. In Christianity eschatological hope is kept alive, growing, and set to work, so that one day

> the tension gradually accumulating between humanity and God will touch the limits prescribed by the possibilities of the world. And then will come the end. Then the presence of Christ, which has been silently accruing in things, will suddenly be revealed—like a flash of light from pole to pole. Breaking through all the barriers within which the veil of matter and the watertightness of souls have seemingly kept it confined, it will invade the face of the earth. And, under the finally liberated action of the true affinities of being, the spiritual atoms of the world will be borne along by a force generated by the powers of cohesion proper to the universe itself and will occupy, whether within Christ or without Christ (but always under the influence of Christ), the place of happiness or pain designated for them by the living structure of the Pleroma.[41]

The whole evolutionary process is directed toward and finds its fulfillment in the parousia of Christ, in the creation of a new heaven and a new earth.

We may wonder whether Teilhard's view of the evolutionary process is not too optimistic when he judges, for instance, that humanity will not submit to resignation in the face of adversities but will continue to struggle. We may also question whether Teilhard does not perceive the evolution of humanity and the kingdom of God (or salvation in and through Christ) too easily as aspects of the same homogeneous process. But then we should remember that the first creation and the new creation are both brought about by God. Last, we may ask whether Teilhard does not grossly overestimate human resourcefulness in the face of our growing population and our rapidly diminishing natural resources. Though none of these questions can be ignored, we must

12 / ESCHATOLOGY

thank Teilhard for reminding us in an impressively christocentric manner that the eschatological goal of salvation is of cosmic dimension. It is a gift provided by God's grace and not the result of human achievement.

There is one other strain of theology that is deeply influenced by our scientific world view and that deliberately attempts to relate the Christian message to the world in which we live. This kind of theology draws heavily on the thought of the Anglo-American mathematician and philosopher Alfred North Whitehead. It has often been claimed that this theology gives us a chance to see how world and faith belong together in a way that most other Christian thought forms find hard to accomplish. Yet the representatives of process theology are as diverse as any group of theologians might be. For instance, David Griffin categorically states, "The belief that we will have further occasions of experience beyond bodily death, along with the related belief in the resurrection of Jesus . . . should be regarded as an optional dimension of the Christian faith."[42]

John B. Cobb, the most influential American representative of process theology, goes a great deal further than Griffin when he declares that inherent in the structure of our Christian existence is a tension and incompleteness beyond which we are unable to go. Christ is the ground for our hope that what we experience now is not the final possibility for humanity. In Jesus the tension between the reality of the self and the call to the new was overcome, so that in him a new structure of existence emerged. Cobb even goes so far as to say that "apart from Christ there is no hope for a better future."[43] Yet he checks this exclusivistic-sounding assertion immediately, saying, "Whenever hope is present in history, Christ is present, whether recognized or not. But apart from the history of Jesus, hope is distorted, and Christ's effective presence is blocked."[44] This means that Christ is present beyond the "Christian confines" and transforms the world by persuading it toward relevant novelty. Cobb concretizes creative transformation through Christ under the headings "the city of God," "the perfection of love," "the kingdom of heaven," and "the resurrection of the dead."

Cobb cites Italian-American architect Paolo Soleri's organic city as a primary example of how to unite the human community into a new community of love. Though Soleri does not mention Christ, he sees himself as the bearer of the energies of creative transformation. Cobb concedes, however, that such transformation will not take place voluntarily, but only under pressure, perhaps even necessitating a collapse of our present way of living.

In his discussion of the perfection of love, Cobb notes that this also ought to include an interiorization of pluralism, so that our understanding and existence may be transformed and moved toward a new spiritual unity. Here he especially cites Buddhism and Christianity as two opposing ways to conceive of the goal of salvation. He hopes that both could be transformed by internalizing each other and could move toward a future unity. In making this move, Cobb hopes that the West could free itself from its attachment to individualized existence as a final goal, a vision that has often caused human misery and threat to human survival. Cobb is calling for a radical kind of love which could carry us into a postpersonal form of Christian existence.

When Cobb investigates the significance of the kingdom of heaven, he is conscious that to do this properly we must move beyond purely worldly hopes. But again he offers a this-worldly analogy to the kingdom of heaven encountered in Christian proclamation, namely the kingdom of heaven interpreted by Whitehead. Though Cobb is not oblivious to the differences between the two concepts, he notes that in both cases there is a relationship of continuity and completion between what will be and what is, rather than one of discontinuous reward or punishment. Though neither Jesus nor Whitehead identifies the kingdom of heaven with specific sociopolitical programs, both undergird the importance of forming appropriate and relevant images of the kingdom and acting on them. Yet both find the unambiguous good that sustains hope in the face of historical ambiguity to be beyond history.[45] Both realize that historical action can have significance only if it is grounded outside of history. Thus Cobb comes to the conclusion that ultimately Whitehead's notion of the kingdom, the principle of creative transformation, was not his own invention but was engendered by Christ.

Finally, Cobb analyzes the meaning of the resurrection of the dead. He recognizes the New Testament image of resurrection as a powerful element of hope. Yet he wants us to reflect not just on one's own personal end but on the death of others and finally the death of all. This endeavor gains special momentum when he attempts to merge the concepts of kingdom and resurrection. Cobb claims that resurrection conceived of in the narrow confines of the self would lead to individualism. In the notion of the kingdom, however, everything exists from and for God, and there takes place a transformation of the structure of existence by summing up all history and completing it in God. According to Cobb, this means that the line between the transcendent kingdom of heaven and history is not as strict as it might seem, for "the vision of the City of God to be realized in history participates in the nature of the kingdom that is already being realized in heaven."[46] Yet it also implies that we will no longer be exclusively preoccupied with ourselves. We will participate in the destiny of the biosphere and in that of our fellow creatures as they participate in ours. "The one Christ who transforms events in history also transforms the events of history by the resurrection into the Kingdom of heaven."[47] Cobb therefore makes the Christian images of hope, kingdom, resurrection, city of God, and perfection of love converge by pointing toward

12 / ESCHATOLOGY

a transcending of our separate individuality in a fuller community with other people and with all things. In this community the tensions between self and Christ decline and will disappear in the final consummation.

Reflecting on John Cobb's approach, we note the immense concern for eschatology as affecting both the human existence and the whole web of life. Human destiny is inseparable from the destiny of the whole world. Yet Cobb's organismic approach is applied not only to the objects of the Christian hope (living world, humanity, and cosmos) but also to its content. Its different images are seen not as complementary, illuminating different facets of hope but as virtually identical, as pointing to the same hope. Since these different facets originated from distinct and separate but not unrelated concerns, a leveling of hope to one object hardly meets the original intentions. Though they are not necessarily conflicting, they do significantly supplement each other and are not just expressive of the same hope. After listening to Cobb, we wonder whether the most persuasive voice for him is not that of Plato and his notion of recollection instead of Christ and the notion of creative newness. We should remember here that under the impact of history, Israel realized that there could be no continuity between the present age and the age to come. Jesus, too, emphasized the need to die in order to live again. While we laud Cobb's emphasis on unity, it must be paired with Teilhard's recognition that unity does not exclude individuality and diversity but rather enhances it.

In his noteworthy book, *A House for Hope*, William A. Beardslee, another representative of process theology, seems to provide an option that is closer to the Christian hope when he first cautions that the resurrection could not mean a resurrection to biological existence unless it would involve the limitations we experience in this life. Yet, he continues, "little as we can imagine it, eternal life as renewal of the soul after death is a valid hope in our time and one which can and will reinforce the more short-range hope that is so essential for human survival."[48]

John Cobb has reminded us that our destiny is inseparably connected with that of the rest of the world. But Teilhard told us that even a sidereal disaster would not bring about the eschaton. The finitude of our environment, however, becomes an ever more pressing issue, and any consideration of eschatology would lack persuasiveness unless it could show that our historical existence does not preclude hope.

Our rapid technological advancements have increased the possibilities for good and bad to such a Promethean dimension that none of us can any longer escape from the ethical implications of the technological process. Though our self-confidence is severely shaken, the notion is still widely held that humanity is mature and can solve its problems without reference to God. Yet Langdon Gilkey warned us that the myth "of man come of age through an increase in his knowledge is not merely an inaccurate myth theologically. Even more, it is a dangerous myth in applied science."[49] Where we have become our own ultimate reference point in the decision-making process, development and use of technology do not emerge as true servants but contribute to our bondage in sinful egotism. They are used for the purpose of exerting technocratic tyranny (socialist countries) or of stimulating our sinful and greedy impulses, for example, the profit motive, national pride, and national, ethnic, generic, or class paranoia (Western capitalism). As a consequence, we encounter mutual exploitation, misuse of our environment, and depletion of our natural resources. Misuse of technological progress has taken on such huge and global dimensions that the day of reckoning has already begun.

Onrushing doom has taken on such apocalyptic features that the eschatological dimension of ecology cannot be overstated. We may illustrate this with three examples:

First, the greenhouse effect. Through the rapid increase in the use of carbon-base fuels (coal, oil, gas), we are releasing so much carbon dioxide into the earth's atmosphere that nature is no longer able to balance this by absorbing it in the oceans or by using up carbon dioxide in plants and setting free a corresponding amount of oxygen. The dilemma is aggravated by our plundering the last extensive forest covers of the earth in the Amazon basin and in equatorial Africa. Carbon dioxide, moreover, might easily act in our atmosphere similar to the glass roofs in a greenhouse. Being colorless and too heavy to escape the atmosphere, it would let the sun's rays permeate but prevent the heat from escaping. This would increase the average surface temperature on the earth, shift the climatic zones by several hundred miles toward the poles, melt Arctic ice, and raise the sea level by several hundred feet. The results of such a worldwide flood can be easily visualized when we remember that most of the Netherlands is already below sea level and shielded through dikes, and that most of the East Coast and the Gulf Coast, including Florida, is only a few hundred feet in elevation.

Other experts, however, predict that atmospheric pollution caused by agricultural dust and chemicals might easily act as a "protective" cover that would lower the surface temperature of the earth. Today nearly one-third of the earth's surface is already shielded from sun rays by a low cloud cover. If this cloud cover were to increase by just 5 percent, it would lower the earth's temperature by four degrees Celsius. This would nearly suffice to usher in a new ice age, a situation that would drastically compound our problem of feeding a rapidly increasing population. We notice from these conflicting expert opinions that even the threats we face have become ambiguous.

The second example is pleonexia, or our insatiable desire to accumulate more and more disposable material goods. The demand for energy needed to manufacture and service these goods will continue to put a severe strain

12 / ESCHATOLOGY

on our finite national and global carbon-base fuel resources and will add more and more natural resources to the scarcity list. Though there is the possibility that we could rejuvenate our energy supply system if we succeeded in taming the powers released by the nuclear fusion of deuterium and tritium into helium, the picture looks less promising for other natural resources. Many ore deposits are being rapidly depleted, and the costly search for minerals and ores on the bottom of the sea and in other barely accessible locations demonstrates the immediacy of our dilemma.

The third example of the eschatological dimension of ecology is overpopulation. Modern hygiene and advancements in medical technology have enabled us greatly to reduce premature death and assure procreation for most people once they reach sexual maturity. But on a global scale we have not reduced our rate of procreation correspondingly. Therefore, we have disturbed the natural equilibrium between birth and death and caused an actual population explosion, increasing the world population in this century by nearly 250 percent. But our ecosphere is finite and can support only a limited number of people, roughly between 6 to 8 billion. Beyond this number, pollution, malnutrition, and depletion of natural resources will increase so dramatically that catastrophes will result. Yet all present trends considered, we will already be pushing against this ceiling by the turn of the century.

These examples demonstrate that we live in an apocalyptic age in which the end of life as we know it is threateningly close at hand. We must take immediate and drastic steps to avoid a global disaster. Most alert people agree with this conclusion. But there is considerable disagreement about outlining strategies for the future. Confronted with conflicting proposals of how to remedy our precarious situation, we must remember that we live in an apocalyptic age. If we want to be true to our Judeo-Christian tradition, we will realize that hope in an apocalyptic age can come only from perceiving apocalyptic thinking in the broader context of eschatology. Faced with our possible doom and differing claims of how to escape, a reliable directive and strong enough incentive for action can be found in the Judeo-Christian tradition from which modern progress has sprung, along with its innate potential for misuse.

The Christian understanding of eschatology provides the proper context for assessing the apocalyptic dimension of technological progress. It can give us both the incentive and the ability to stop the exploitation of our environment and prevent our own self-destruction. The Christian gospel reminds us that we already participate in a proleptic way in the new creation which was initiated through Christ's resurrection. Thus human reason no longer needs to remain totally estranged from God. It can produce new tools and insights for providing a better world. It can design and implement agricultural reform and social and economic legislation; it can reassess the validity of our family structures. Even the necessary reorientation of human progress from an accumulation of more and more material goods to a development of inner values lies within the possibilities of human reason. Our task is not to exploit and abuse God's creation but to cherish and guard it against destruction. To accomplish this goal God has endowed us with a discerning mind, and he has given us his self-disclosure in Jesus Christ to remind us of this task.

The eschatological promise as proclaimed by the Judeo-Christian tradition allows us to perceive the goals and limitations of all our actions, including our involvement in the ecological crisis. Painful as it may be, it shows us that our world is transitory and devoid of lasting value. But the interim character of our world does not necessitate a deterioration of present conditions and should not elicit our resignation. On the contrary, a new creation has already started in Jesus Christ, and we are invited to participate now in this new creation in a proleptic way. This means that the transitoriness of our present situation may be a transition toward the better. Since the present is clearly marked as interim, we cannot expect perfection now. Yet by proleptically anticipating the future we may envision a state approaching perfection. To transcend this limitation would result in the utopian attempt to replace the God-provided eschaton with an eschaton of our own making. But an eschaton resulting from our own actions would be analogous to our present crisis situation because the present crisis has resulted precisely from our neglect of God's promise to provide the eschatological fulfillment.

As Eugen Rosenstock-Huessy rightly asserted, "Christianity is the founder and trustee of the future, the very process of finding and securing it, and without the Christian spirit there is no real future for man."[50] The Christian faith knows about Jesus Christ, the first perfect human being, who made the transition from fragmentariness to completeness. Moreover, it proclaims this transition as a possibility for all of us. To find the appropriate attitude in our present situation, we must look to Jesus of Nazareth, the perfecter of the old life and the initiator of a new life. By imitating him, we discover that we should live in this world as God-responsive and God-responsible beings. This posture would exclude an understanding of progress as an accumulation of material goods. It would also mitigate against relinquishing our responsibility to a technocratic elite or neglecting this responsibility in a carefree laissez-faire attitude. Instead, it would ask us to refrain from accepting the overabundance of goods that technological civilization offers by emphasizing the inner quality of life and finding fulfillment in living with and for others.

Since the final realization of our life's goal can be attained only in the eschaton, ultimate and lasting hope can come only from the expectation of Jesus Christ as Lord of all and from the new creation that he initiated. But the correlation between the imitation of Jesus and the expectation of Jesus Christ can aid us in the evaluation of our present ecological crisis and can

12 / ESCHATOLOGY

help us to attain a proper attitude. It shows us that we live in an apocalyptic age and that there is need for faithful action and not for despair.

NOTES

1. Joachim Jeremias, *The Parables of Jesus*, trans. S. H. Hooke (New York: Charles Scribner's Sons, 1955), p. 51.
2. Joachim Jeremias, *New Testament Theology*, vol. 1, *The Proclamation of Jesus* (New York: Charles Scribner's Sons, 1971), p. 311.
3. On the following, see Oscar Cullmann: *Vorträge und Aufsätze, 1925-1962*, ed. Karlfried Fröhlich (Tübingen: J. C. B. Mohr [Paul Siebeck], 1966), pp. 414ff.
4. Oscar Cullmann, *Christ and Time: The Primitive Christian Conception of Time and History*, trans. F. V. Filson (London: SCM Press, 1962), p. 81.
5. Wolfhart Pannenberg, "Dogmatic Theses on the Doctrine of Revelation," in *Revelation as History*, trans. D. Granskou (New York: Macmillan Co., 1968), p. 131.
6. Ibid., p. 139.
7. Wolfhart Pannenberg, *Theology and the Kingdom of God* (Philadelphia: Westminster Press, 1969), p. 126.
8. Rudolf Bultmann, *Theology of the New Testament*, 2 vols., trans. Kendrick Grobel (New York: Charles Scribner's Sons, 1951-55), 1:43-44.
9. Ibid., 1:34.
10. Rudolf Bultmann, "New Testament and Mythology," in *Kerygma and Myth: A Theological Debate*, ed. Hans W. Bartsch, trans. R. H. Fuller, 2 vols. (London: SPCK, 1953-62), 1:5.
11. Bultmann, *Theology of the New Testament*, 2:21.
12. C. H. Dodd, *The Coming of Christ: Four Broadcast Addresses for the Season of Advent* (Cambridge: Cambridge University Press, 1954), p. 6.
13. C. H. Dodd, *The Parables of the Kingdom* (New York: Charles Scribner's Sons, 1961), pp. 164-65.
14. Ibid., p. 169. See also Dodd, *Coming of Christ*, pp. 14-25.
15. Hal Lindsey, *The Promise* (Irvine, Calif.: Harvest House, 1974), chap. 1 (unpaginated).
16. Ibid., next to last chapter.
17. Ibid.
18. Ibid., last chapter.
19. Ibid., last sentence of book.
20. Hal Lindsey, *The Late Great Planet Earth*, with C. C. Carlson (Grand Rapids, Mich.: Zondervan Publishing House, 1973), p. 133.
21. Ibid., p. 145.
22. Ibid., p. 188.
23. Jürgen Moltmann, *Theology of Hope: On the Ground and the Implications of a Christian Eschatology*, trans. James W. Leitch (London: SCM Press, 1967).
24. Ibid., p. 180.
25. Ibid., p. 288.

26. Ibid., p. 303.
27. Ibid., p. 329.
28. Jürgen Moltmann, *The Crucified God: The Cross of Christ as the Foundation and Criticism of Christian Theology*, trans. R. A. Wilson and John Bowden (New York: Harper & Row; London: SCM Press, 1974), p. 1.
29. Ibid., p. 294.
30. Jürgen Moltmann, *The Church in the Power of the Spirit: A Contribution to Messianic Eschatology*, trans. M. Kohl (New York: Harper & Row, 1977), p. 287.
31. James H. Cone, *A Black Theology of Liberation* (Philadelphia: J. B. Lippincott Co., 1970), p. 12.
32. Ibid., p. 17.
33. Ibid., p. 220–25.
34. Ibid., p. 247.
35. Ibid., p. 249.
36. Gustavo Gutierrez, *A Theology of Liberation: History, Politics, and Salvation*, trans. and ed. Sister Caridad Inda and John Eagleson (Maryknoll, N.Y.: Orbis Books, 1973), p. 146.
37. Ibid., p. 161.
38. Ibid., p. 162.
39. Ibid., p. 168.
40. Pierre Teilhard de Chardin, *The Future of Man*, trans. N. Denny (New York: Harper & Row, 1964), p. 265.
41. Pierre Teilhard de Chardin, *The Divine Milieu: An Essay on the Interior Life* (New York: Harper & Row, 1960), pp. 133–34.
42. David Ray Griffin, *God, Power, and Evil: A Process Theodicy* (Philadelphia: Westminster Press, 1976), p. 312.
43. John B. Cobb, *Christ in a Pluralistic Age* (Philadelphia: Westminster Press, 1975), p. 186.
44. Ibid.
45. Ibid., p. 229.
46. Ibid., p. 255.
47. Ibid., p. 256.
48. William A. Beardslee, *A House for Hope: A Study in Process and Biblical Thought* (Philadelphia: Westminster Press, 1972), p. 149.
49. Langdon Brown Gilkey, *Religion and the Scientific Future: Reflections on Myth, Science, and Theology* (New York: Harper & Row, 1970), p. 95.
50. Eugen Rosenstock-Huessy, *The Christian Future, or, The Modern Mind Outrun* (New York: Charles Scribner's Sons, 1946), p. 61.

4

Secular Options

The Christian hope must be delineated in constant reference to secular varieties of hope. Insofar as secular options consciously acknowledge their limitation to finitude, they can provide an accurate analysis of the human condition and its potential for improvement. If they deny their limitation to finitude, they deny the eschatological proviso and provide an overly optimistic version of human hope. We will discuss three movements: secular existentialism, Marxism, and secular humanism.

SECULAR EXISTENTIALISM

Søren Kierkegaard, the spiritual ancestor of modern existentialism, considered life a venture in which we are sustained by our trust in a gracious God. Present-day existentialists, especially of the secular variety, have largely abandoned such a metaphysical reference point and view life simply within the limits of this world. This becomes immediately evident with Martin Heidegger, the most prominent representative of contemporary existentialism. In his history-making work, *Being and Time*,[1] Heidegger attempts to understand time as the possible horizon for our understanding of Being. Since Being-there (*Dasein*) means being in the world, and since Being-there is always temporal, there is undeniably a constant lack of totality that finds its end in death. Something is still missing and outstanding in our earthly existence. We are thrown into this world and are in danger of losing ourselves in the groundlessness and nullity of inauthentic existence. This everyday existence is characterized by idle talk that is shallow and does not get to the roots of things, by curiosity that jumps from one novelty to another, and by ambiguity that assumes it has solved everything. Heidegger claims that through this state of mind one is subject only to temptation, tranquilizing, alienation, and entanglement. Heidegger recognizes that we cannot escape from our everyday existence, but he urges us to opt for a different way of looking at our existence, a mode he calls authentic existence.

The reason for Heidegger's appeal to authentic existence is evident: "If existence is definitive for *Dasein*'s Being and if its essence is constituted in part by potentiality-for-Being, then, as long as *Dasein* exists, it must in each case, as such a potentiality, *not yet be* something."² Being-there, as we experience and conduct it, is therefore determined by inauthentic existence, inauthentic because it is always less than the whole. Thus only authentic existence brings into focus the totality of existence by considering *Dasein* as Being-toward-death. This can lead to inauthentic existence too if we speak in such abstract terms as "they die" or "one dies." For authentic Being-toward-death "*can not evade* its own most non-relational possibility, or *cover up* this possibility by thus fleeing from it, or *give a new explanation* for it to accord with the common sense of the 'they.' "³ Without fleeing it or covering it up, *we* must exist toward death as a distinctive possibility of *Dasein* itself. Heidegger does not want us to brood over the possibility of death, but to anticipate the possibility of the impossibility of any existence at all. Death is *Dasein*'s own possibility. Being towards this possibility discloses to Dasein its own potentiality-for-Being, in which its very Being is the issue."⁴

When Heidegger finally concludes that the existential-ontological constitution of *Dasein*'s totality is grounded in temporality, it becomes evident that Heidegger describes existence as appearing strictly within this world. We live in this world surrounded by the possibility of death, facing an end at which our very existence is threatened by annihilation. Heidegger even calls for authentic existence, by which he means not covering up the possibility of annihilation by relying on how others face it. Humanity is described as existing in solitude at the brink of its very destruction. While Heidegger leaves open the possibility of God and immortality, he makes no assertions about them. They do not come into focus for someone restricted to the analysis of this life. Heidegger, therefore, does not consider the possibility that our understanding of this life might be decisively shaped by God's promise of the completion of our life in the hereafter.

While Heidegger perceives the world that surrounds us in almost neutral colors, the picture has changed for the French existentialist, Jean-Paul Sartre. Sartre presented his main system in a book bearing the characteristic title *Being and Nothingness* (1943), in which, similar to Heidegger, he distinguishes Being-in-itself (nonconscious Being) from Being-for-itself (conscious Being). Again, any metaphysical reference point is excluded. We hear that "Being is without reason, without cause, and without necessity."⁵ Already in his introduction Sartre posits, "Being is. Being is in itself. Being is what it is."⁶

The nonconscious Being-in-itself is the Being of the phenomenon of which we can only say that it is. Being-for-itself is actually in opposition to and preferable to Being-in-itself. Yet both forms of Being are inseparable from each other, even while enjoying relative independence. By introducing the conscious self, Being-for-itself annihilates Being-in-itself and brings

SECULAR OPTIONS

Nothingness into the world so that it can stand for Being and judge other beings knowing what it is not. Nothingness comes between the self and the other so that Being-for-itself can stand out and assess the other. While Being-for-itself addresses and assesses the other, it stands in conflict with others by making an object of them, and vice versa. Sartre can even go so far as to say that the others are evil, as they desire to infringe on my freedom. One's own existence is especially vulnerable, since existence precedes essence. One cannot rely on one's essence because essence is only that which has been. So one must live Being-for-itself, forever choosing for oneself without relying on anything or anyone else. Small wonder that, for Sartre, freedom is viewed as being condemned to be free. Thus Sartre admonishes us that we must avoid bad faith, that is, escaping the responsible freedom of Being-for-itself and instead relying on the past, or oscillating between past and future, or synthesizing both. The world comes into being when we project ourselves toward the future without relying on the past or on any preestablished norms.

There is not much hope in this picture of solipsistic humanity projecting itself in anguish toward an unknown future, in perpetual conflict with others who also struggle along. Perhaps Régis Jolivet was right when he pondered, "You lose your breath, like Kierkegaard, floating on his 6,000 fathoms of water, solitary, without the dimmest star in the sky to reassure and guide him. How can man, incapable of motivating his conduct either metaphysically or morally, powerless to justify himself to his own reason, stand this conflict much longer without becoming a tortured neurotic."[7] Sartre indeed describes a hopeless situation out of which there is no escape, a situation that, if it should not end in despair, is absurd. While Sartre's approach perhaps adequately characterized the mood of the French resistance in the face of Hitler's occupation army, it may again become attractive as one hope after another collapses that Western materialism has projected. Yet Sartre's approach is at best only descriptive of our precarious situation. It does not show us a way out or give us any direction for meaningful living in the face of increasing uncertainty about the future.

Albert Camus attempts to move beyond the negativity of his fellow Frenchman, Jean-Paul Sartre. In *The Myth of Sisyphus*,[8] Camus concludes that there are no metaphysically guaranteed directives for conduct. Confronted with life's absurdity, Camus declares, however, that suicide is not a legitimate solution. It would conflict with human pride, since it would be an admission of human incapacity. But Camus continues to search for a way that leads beyond nihilism. Surely, the outcome of our fate is fatal, but that does not mean that everything else must be fatal too. There still remains a world "of which man is the sole master." Once we are aware of the fatality of life, we are able to plunge into it. Therefore, in the wake of revolt there comes freedom and diversity. But soon Camus recognizes that his conclusions are too optimistic to be true. In his later novel, *The Rebel* (1951), he acknowledges the dark sides of revolt and rebellion. "One might think," he declares, "that a period which, in the space of fifty years, uproots, enslaves, or kills seventy million beings should be condemned out of hand."[9] Yet Camus notes that its probability must still be understood. Thus he seeks to inquire concerning the attitudes, pretensions, and conquests of modern human rebellion. In spite of all our advances, our children still die unjustly even in a perfect society. The sum total of evil has not diminished in the world during the last twenty centuries. Once God was dethroned, people found themselves fighting one another, and once the kingdom of grace was conquered, the kingdom of justice began to crumble. Camus finds that evil is not simply a sociological phenomenon that might change, given improvement of socio-economic or political conditions. Revolution, forgetful of its own origins, becomes contaminated, denies life, and dashes toward destruction. "When revolution in the name of power and history becomes a murderous and immoderate mechanism, a new rebellion is consecrated in the name of moderation and of life."[10] Camus calls us to constant vigilance and contends that rebellion, without claiming to solve everything, can at least confront its problems. This means that humanity, being finite, cannot be deified or replace God.

But what, we might ask, is the prospect for humanity? In one of Camus's last stories, "The Growing Stone" (1957), he seems to provide an answer when in the plot the French engineer D'Arrast substitutes for the exhausted mulatto ship cook and picks up the stone to fulfill the cook's vow. Characteristically for Camus, however, the engineer does not carry the stone to the cathedral, the place where the cook vowed to place it. He carries it back to the small hut in which the cook lives, as if to indicate that help can come only from human solidarity in taking on ourselves one another's burdens. Through the warmth and friendship of simple people, our inner life may be restored.[11]

While Camus very perceptively describes our situation and our intrinsically evil nature, especially as we attempt to rid ourselves of all metaphysical restrictions, two questions emerge: (1) If we are really as evil as Camus describes us, how can our hearts be warmed by rediscovering our communal nature? Is not the modern state with all its care agencies becoming less and less personal and therefore colder instead of warmer? (2) Even if we could provide and sustain warmth and love for one another, as Camus demands and hopes, would not finitude and death eventually stare us in the face? We must accept the accurate description of the human situation that secular existentialism provides. But we are unable to perceive how it can lead us to a new future beyond the confines of uncertainty and finitude or how it can provide a hope for the future that will not waver in the face of adversity.

MARXIST COMMUNISM

Nearly a century older than secular existentialism, Marxist communism exhibits a drive and a hope for the future that has captured the imagination of millions of people around the world. So far it has painted the future in bright and promising tones, claiming that once the religious projections of human desires have been recognized as such and subsequently abandoned, humanity will be free to create a new world in place of this old one. Hundreds of millions of people, either voluntarily or involuntarily, have become captive to a "gospel" that projects one five-year plan after another and promises that it will meet all the needs of humanity. It is the most powerful pseudoreligious movement the world has seen.

In the *Manifesto of the Communist Party* (1847), Karl Marx and Friedrich Engels set the tone for their program when they declared that the history of all hitherto existing society is the history of class struggle. The Communists "openly declare that their ends can be attained only by the forcible overthrow of all existing social conditions. Let the ruling classes tremble at the communist revolution. The proletarians have nothing to lose but their chains. They have a world to win."[12] Indeed, this prospect for a new world has served as a mighty stimulus. In many countries the underprivileged have taken these words to heart and have attempted to achieve a revolution of the existing and quite often unjust and demeaning social order. But it is not just open rebellion or despair that should give the incentive for global revolution. Marx is convinced that only when religion as the illusory happiness is abolished can the issue of real happiness be addressed.

For Marx, religion projects an illusory and imaginary heaven to subdue the yearning for the real heaven, that is, new socioeconomic conditions on earth. He even calls religion the opiate of the people by which capitalists numb the senses of the people in order to continue their process of exploitation and oppression. There is certainly some truth in Marx's observations. Religion has often been used as an escape from earthly reality. This may be both legitimate and dangerous. Even if self-induced, we need dreams and visions of a brighter future to cope successfully with life when things on this earth look all too dark. In this way, a projection can serve as a stimulus to master adverse situations and perhaps ameliorate them somewhat. On the other hand, a projection can become a kind of primary reality that renders the world and its conditions secondary. Especially religious fanatics, even those of the pietistic and quietistic variety, can pursue this avenue. Marx certainly must have had the latter possibility in mind when he rejected religion as a dangerous projection.

Yet it is characteristic of the genuine Christian hope that the heavenly reality that is hoped for is transformed in an anticipatory and proleptic way into an

12 / ESCHATOLOGY

earthly reality. Thus the Pauline observation "You are a new creation" is not just a forensic declaration about a new state of being, but is at the same time coupled with the imperative to show forth this new quality. Unlike Marxists who want to create heaven on earth in its fullness, since there is no heavenly reality left for them, Paul is always cognizant that any anticipation can only be of preliminary character and is tarnished by the continuous relapse into the old state of being. Even Marxists seem to recognize this to some extent when they call for reeducation. But they also assume that once the conditions are right, the new humanity will indeed appear. This confident optimism is especially well expressed by the German neo-Marxist Ernst Bloch.

In his three-volume work, *Das Prinzip Hoffnung* (The Principle of Hope),[13] Ernst Bloch shows that the principle of hope is a universal characteristic of humanity. From the first cry of a helpless baby wanting to draw attention to its desires, to an adolescent eager to escape the confines of family and home town, to the exhausted senior citizen who is waiting for eternal bliss, human existence is characterized by hope and a movement toward the future.

In his interpretation of Marx, Bloch asserts that his most important point was that knowledge can be related not only to the past but also to that which is supposed to come. The world cannot be changed without envisioning its objective real possibilities. If we do not know what is actually possible, we will simply tread water. Once an event has occurred, it is not closed and finished; it is an advance on a world that is open to change. This kind of knowledge implies happiness, because it implies that through human transformation the world can become a home. Bloch is careful to show that he does not simply stay at the level of wishful thinking, since desires alone do not advance us. All dreams about the future must be oriented toward objective possibilities. According to Bloch, Marxism emphasizes the future and makes the future its main concern, since reason cannot flourish without hope, and hope cannot speak without reason. The anticipation of the future must be expressed in a variety of avenues, including art and poetry, but it must always be done in sobriety. Yet we dare not exclude enthusiasm, which is fantasy in action, since Marxism is opposed to the undialectic and unimaginative commonplace that asserts that humanity will always remain the same. If Marxism lives up to its claim as quartermaster of the future, sobriety and enthusiasm must dynamically complement each other and push toward exact anticipation and concrete utopia. Bloch assures us that Marxism takes seriously the fairy tales and dreams of the golden age.

Bloch delineates three categories of the dialectic process in which the world moves: frontier, novelty, and matter, all three presupposing hope. "Frontier" is that which will be determined next in history. "Novelty" is the real possibility of the not-yet-become which can be activated. "Matter" is not a static object but that which determines whatever can happen historically. Matter is moved being, the foundation and substance through which our future will be carried to term. Through us hope is determined, though its results still must be justified in the open-ended history and in the sphere of objective and real decisions. Bloch's engagement in the process of history-making becomes evident when he claims that the only optimism that can be justified is a militant optimism. Real being, we hear, is constituted in the future, since essence is not yet at hand; essence is that which pushes in the objects toward itself and which is expecting its genesis in the process. Teleology is not caused by a mythological power, Bloch claims, because the goal is not given but emerges from the active process and originates in it and is continuously enriched. We are not surprised that Bloch refers to Aristotle and his notion of causation in order to explain the creative process.

But what is the goal of all that striving? Bloch calls it happiness, freedom, nonalienation, Golden Age, land of milk and honey, and the eternal feminine. The direction of these paradigms is evident. We still live in a kind of prehistory in which the goal has not yet appeared, though it is vividly sensed. Therefore, the real genesis is not in the beginning but at the end. Once we have taken history by its roots and have founded our being without succumbing to alienation and self-denial, something emerges in the world which shines into our childhood and in which no one has yet been, our mother country.[14] Humanity is creating its own future, Bloch says, and once all the obstacles are overcome, we will enjoy paradise, a state of dreaming innocence.

The big challenge to such a history-making venture is the issue of death. Is this not the great barrier to which everything must succumb? Surprisingly, Ernst Bloch does not think so. Since our essence lies in the future and has not yet become, it is beyond becoming and perishing. Even if our essence had already become, death in its deadly and dying form would again be outside the province of the completeness of our existence.[15] Whenever existence comes close to its essence, then duration and not petrification commences, a state that implies novelty without transience and corruptibility. Without mentioning it, Bloch is talking here about what we usually call the Christian hope for life eternal. And that which according to him assures us that all becoming will not end in void is what Christian faith usually calls "God." This is the strange paradox in Bloch's system. On the one hand, he assures us that religion, God, and eternal life are no longer needed; on the other hand, he resorts to metaphors and a conceptional framework that, unless all this is only empty rhetoric, imply the realities he wants to discard.

Since Bloch is so insistent on exact anticipation, one should also ask what warrants we have in our present history that anticipation is already taking place. Unless the signs are misleading, the promised liberation that Marxism advances has not yet occurred, not even in a remotely anticipatory way. Thus the process of history seems to be the harshest critique of Bloch's hope for

12 / ESCHATOLOGY

the gradual realization of the mother country. In China, however, repeated claims have been made that such transformation is indeed happening.

During his lifetime, Mao Tse-Tung mobilized more people and called them to reexamine their ideas and their modes of operation than any other figure before him. By comparison, even the initial success of Karl Marx was modest. Even people outside the Communist sphere of influence have repeatedly claimed that a new kind of humanity is evolving in China. China has not only been considered a model for development in the Third World, it is also a unique phenomenon indicating the radical conversion of a feudalistic society.

It is indeed an unprecedented kind of transformation that Chairman Mao envisioned. He claimed that the world has reached an historic moment and that China is centrally involved. There is the possibility of complete removal of darkness in the world and a transformation into a new bright world. What distinguishes Mao from both Marx and Bloch is the fact that he did not only espouse certain goals and doctrines but, as the absolute ruler of roughly 800 million people, had the means to put them into reality. Since he opted for a permanent revolution in which no new hierarchies should be permanently established, he was able to abandon ideas that did not yield the desired results.

Mao knew well that the material basis of the world does not react to just any kind of pressure. Thus he called for thorough investigation into the objective laws of the world in order to transform it. Unlike most Marxists, Mao did not simply identify matter with spirit, but saw them in mutual interdependence. He affirmed that in the general development of history the material determines the mental, and social being determines social consciousness. But he also asserted that there is a reaction of mental on material things, of social consciousness on social being, and of the superstructure on the economic base. Thus Mao rejected the idea of a self-propelling and self-determining matter and acknowledged the emotive force of the spirit within the life process. Yet in contrast to Christian faith, he failed to see that the Spirit is also the life-giving power.

A similar affinity and contrast to Christian faith become apparent when we ask about the goals Mao envisioned and the means by which he wanted to achieve them. Mao wanted to ensure a better life for China's hundreds of millions and to develop his country into a prosperous and powerful one with a high level of culture. At the same time, Mao wanted to change the whole way people conduct themselves, insisting that

> at no time and in no circumstances should a Communist place his personal interest first; he should subordinate them to the interests of the nation and of the masses. Hence, selfishness, slacking, corruption, seeking the limelight, and so on, are most contemptible, while selflessness, working with all one's energy, wholehearted devotion to public duty, and quiet hard work will command respect.[16]

SECULAR OPTIONS

If people have made mistakes in their work, other Communists should persuade them to see their mistakes in order to help them to change and start afresh. They should not exclude them—unless they are incorrigible.[17]

When we ask to what extent these visions have been realized, we cannot but notice that the people of China are vigorously molding themselves and are being vigorously molded by internal forces derived from the messianic vision of a new society and a new world. Mao's principles of equality, frugality, diligence, and hard work have made China self-supporting and strong within an amazingly short time and have instilled certain virtues into the lives of many. Since we live, however, on a finite earth, in the long run there will be limits to growth even in China, and creativity and prosperity will encounter their most serious limitation in finitude.

Since the new regime after Mao's death is more open to the outside world, we now hear that the great proletarian cultural revolution of 1966 was only a limited success and induced more instability than is profitable for social and material progress. We also notice that China is discovering its own limitations and its dependence on foreign technology, capital investment, and markets for its products. And we discover that much of the education and reeducation was not voluntary and implied the relinquishing of personal freedom and security. This evidently was the price to be paid for undeniable achievements in common striving, in eradicating such social vices as prostitution, bribery, theft, and robbery, and in assuring that everyone has enough to eat and need not worry when sickness strikes or old age and retirement come.

When one reads the little red book *Mao Tse-tung's Quotations*, one cannot but be struck with the seemingly biblical rhetoric. We hear that we must have faith in the masses and faith in the Party, that of all things in the world people are most precious, that when we die for the people it is a worthy death, and that all people in the revolutionary ranks must care for each other and must love and help each other. Yet we also hear that we cannot love enemies, as we cannot love social evil, and that our aim is to destroy them. While we are astounded at Mao's genuine love for the people and his profound desire to do what is best for China, we cannot but note his immense rage at those who will not follow his way of virtue and diligence. Yet this is not simply a personal shortcoming of Mao. It is ultimately characteristic of all who strive to attain heaven on earth. Such ventures cannot tolerate less than perfect people. They cannot accept that people are always inclined to put themselves ahead of others.

While the inability to accept earthly imperfection can lead to actual advances in social behavior, as in the new China of Mao, it also bears the danger of brutality, as we see in the concentration camps of Stalin or in similar camps under Mao. Christians, however, mindful of the heavenly perfection promised as God's gift, are often oblivious to earthly progress and adopt a much

12 / ESCHATOLOGY

too relaxed posture in the face of God's realization of the promise. Thus, endeavors such as Mao's new China can become catalysts for Christians to make more real that in which they already share proleptically. But Mao's vision of the new society will ultimately fall short of its goal; it cannot replace the heavenly reality.

SECULAR HUMANISM

Until recently the West has enjoyed an unrestrained optimism, largely due to its immense technological and economic expansion. The first shocking experience for this kind of optimism was the gradual realization that fewer and fewer nations aspired to follow the Western way to the future. The alternative for many had become Marxist communism, which seemed to provide more instantaneous results. Yet there too a sobering occurred, since more and more people recognized that, instead of providing freedom and prosperity for everyone, Marxist communism often only replaced one form of dictatorship with another. In spite of ethnic and class revolts in many countries and occasional shortages of energy and raw materials, the overall picture in the West has still remained optimistic. This is nowhere characterized better than by the *Humanist Manifestos* signed in this century by respected scientists and representatives of the humanities.

The first *Humanist Manifesto* appeared in the United States in 1933, just a few months after the Nazis had gained power in Germany. The *Humanist Manifesto* wanted to establish a new attitude to religion, since our larger understanding of the universe, our scientific achievements, and a deeper appreciation of the human brotherhood had created a situation in which the old religious beliefs seemed to have lost their guiding values.

The signers of the *Humanist Manifesto I* were confident that we would learn to face the crises of life in terms of our knowledge of their naturalness and probability. They believed that humanism would assume the role of a social and mental hygiene, discouraging sentimental and unreal hopes and wishful thinking. Of course the notion of God was discarded, since humanists regarded the universe as self-existing and not created. They acknowledged no metaphysical powers that guarantee our values. Yet the hope was expressed that "reasonable and manly attitudes will be fostered by education and supported by customs."[18] This belief in the inherent goodness of humanity and its unlimited potential for self-improvement stood in stark contrast to the time in which it was spoken, the years prior to World War II. An edition of both manifestos now rightly admits that it has since been superseded by events and that it did not and could not address itself to future problems and needs.

In the preface of *Humanist Manifesto II* the tone is more subdued. It is now recognized that the events of history "make that earlier statement seem far too optimistic. Nazism has shown the depth of brutality of which humanity is capable. Other totalitarian regimes have suppressed human rights without ending poverty. Science has sometimes brought evil as well as good. Recent decades have shown that inhuman wars can be made in the name of peace."[19] But again, the belief in a caring God is rejected in the *Humanist Manifesto II* of 1973, almost at the same time that the Arabs were waging the Yom Kippur War and imposing the first oil embargo on the West. The humanists who signed the document believe that it is harmful to divert people with false hope in heaven hereafter. Though they explicitly acknowledge that the future is filled with dangers, they are still committed to the positive belief in the possibilities of human progress and to the values central to it. Since they reject any divine purpose or providence, they claim that we create meaningful life as we create and develop our futures. In Marxist fashion they assert that the promise of heaven or the threat of damnation is both illusory and harmful, since it distracts us from present concerns, from self-actualization, and from rectifying social wrongs. At the same time, they admit that reason must be tempered with humility, and they summon us to work jointly toward a human world. Thus they express hope that we can initiate new directions for humanity and that ancient rivalries can be superseded by broadly based, cooperative efforts. That we will survive and prosper only in a world of shared human values is their final point.

While we cannot but agree with the cautions that are here expressed, we wonder where the optimism that is retained receives its power. Naturally we agree with all the envisioned goals, especially since more than any other institution the church emphasizes the notion of a global family and the necessity for human solidarity. Yet can reason really achieve these goals if left to itself? We could refer to human depravity, to challenge any reaching for the stars, but we may be more convincing if we refer to the lesson we have learned from history.

Human progressiveness, as we have seen, originated out of the Judeo-Christian context. But, once the progressive spirit emancipated itself from the guiding context that gave it birth, it behaved in an autonomous and irresponsible fashion. How many atrocities have been committed in the name of progress in the last two centuries, starting from the genocide of the American Indians to the concentration camps in Nazi Germany? When reason became its own court of appeal, quite often it turned against its own master, humanity, and contributed to new dependency and renewed slavery. Here the insight of the *Humanist Manifesto II*, that reason must be paired with humility, should have been more radically applied. Ever since the building of the tower of Babel, human hubris has brought misery on the human race. Reason is too fragile an instrument to assure any future, even mere survival, unless it is guarded and guided by external safeguards. We should remember that

12 / ESCHATOLOGY

only humans pray, since only humans need God. If God as our restrictive and directive force is denied, the future will become more bleak than it was before.

It is exactly impending doom that is widely felt among secular humanists. Among the many that concern themselves with the future, we pick two that will stand for many more: futurologist Alvin Toffler, and economist Robert Heilbroner.

When Alvin Toffler wrote his best seller *Future Shock* (1970), his intention was not to frighten us. On the contrary, since the future would be better, Toffler wanted to help us come to terms with it and the massive changes it implied, on both a personal and a social level. If we develop the consciousness needed to undertake the control of change and if we make creative use of change to channel change, "we can not only spare ourselves the trauma of future shock, we can reach out and humanize distant tomorrows."[20]

Only five years later, when Toffler published the *Eco-Spasm Report*, his confident optimism was badly shattered. He is now convinced that a breakdown of our industrial civilization is occurring, in which we face the destruction of our energy base, our value systems, our sense of space and time, and our economy. He assures us that the years immediately ahead will be painful. But Toffler does not want to give up in resignation. On the contrary, he assures us: "The truth is that we are not helpless. The emerging future is not predestined; it is the outcome of decisions taken by us in the present. Even now we can take intelligent steps to regain control over our runaway fate."[21] Toffler's stand is symptomatic of many secular humanists. They see the writing on the wall, but are somehow convinced that we will pull through again as we have done many times before.

Robert Heilbroner is more cautious. In 1960, when most people were thinking in terms of an unlimited political and economical upswing, Heilbroner was challenging our naive optimism. He contended that optimism had misled us in two particulars. It caused us to overestimate the degree of freedom in history, and it gave us a simplistic idea of the forces of history so that we considered technological progress solely in terms of the enhancement of our productive powers without ever estimating its social impact. Thus he called for an assessment of what is historically possible and urged us to prepare for the often unexpected and unwelcome repercussions of the forces of history.[22] Later, the year before Toffler's *Eco-Spasm Report* appeared in print, Heilbroner again warned us:

> Today that sense of assurance and control has vanished, or is vanishing rapidly. We have become aware that rationality has its limits with regard to the engineering of social change, and that these limits are much narrower than we had thought; that many economic and social problems lie outside the scope of our accustomed

instrumentalities of social change; that growth does not bring about certain desired ends or arrest certain undesired trends.²³

Heilbroner does not want to paint a dark and threatening picture and then, nevertheless, conclude with a modified optimism. Though the prospect of the impending predicament is very unpleasant, he argues that we have become startlingly aware that the quality of life is already deteriorating and that the question of whether worse impends cannot be denied. The industrial growth process will be forced to slow down within a generation or two and will probably have to give way to a decline thereafter. Yet if we continue the present way of doing things that restricts our vision to a short-term future, Heilbroner warns us that we will be confronted with convulsive change, change forced on us by external events rather than by conscious choice, by catastrophe rather than by calculation.

But Heilbroner also does not want to evoke in us an attitude of passive resignation. He is convinced that our present industrial society has no future and will likely be replaced by a society that recovers some of the values of "primitive" cultures without reverting to their level of ignorance and cruel anxiety. The human prospect is not an irrevocable death sentence. Though the risk of enormous catastrophes exist, we will survive and are not headed toward an inevitable doomsday. The challenges of the future can and will be overcome. To prod us onto the right track, Heilbroner invokes the figure of Atlas from Greek mythology, who in endless perseverance bore the weight of the heavens on his shoulders. If we want to rescue life, Heilbroner contends, the spirit of conquest and aspiration will not suffice; it must be supplanted by the spirit of perseverance. If, however, the spirit of Atlas falters within us, then even Heilbroner is convinced that the determination to preserve humanity will perish.

In a more recent publication, Heilbroner is much less convinced that anyone can predict what the future has in store for us. He now concedes that we see more clearly than past generations that our present era cannot go on forever and "that in our own time we will have to live through periods of wrenching change even if the system [of capitalism] survives. What comes thereafter is still a closed book."²⁴ Beyond pointing to the limits of our finite earth, which we are discovering in increasingly painful fashion, Heilbroner also indicates that more and more people are unable to find satisfaction in our present civilization, in the plastic wealth and the impersonal employments that industrialization generates.

It is now time for us to conclude. By eliminating the religious dimension from our daily pursuits and secularizing the world, we are bringing earthly doom on ourselves. We have created an artificial world without direction and deeper meaning. At this point, where all our human pursuits falter, and where

12 / ESCHATOLOGY

we discover that we must reform our way of approaching the future, perhaps the biblical notion of eschatology can aid in our quest.

NOTES

1. Martin Heidegger, *Being and Time*, trans. J. Macquarrie and E. Robinson (London: SCM Press, 1962), p. 276.
2. Ibid., p. 276.
3. Ibid., pp. 304–5.
4. Ibid., p. 307.
5. Jean-Paul Sartre, *Being and Nothingness: An Essay of Phenomenological Ontology*, trans. H. E. Barnes (New York: Philosophical Library, 1956), p. 619.
6. Ibid., p. lxvi.
7. Régis Jolivet, *Sartre: The Theology of the Absurd*, trans. W. C. Piersol (Westminster, N.Y.: Newman Press, 1967), p. 106.
8. Albert Camus, *The Myth of Sisyphus and Other Essays*, trans. J. O'Brien (New York: Alfred A. Knopf, 1967), p. 117.
9. Albert Camus, *The Rebel: An Essay on Man in Revolt*, trans. A. Bower (New York: Alfred A. Knopf, 1971), p. 3.
10. Ibid., p. 305.
11. Albert Camus, "The Growing Stone," in *Exile and the Kingdom*, trans. J. O'Brien (New York: Alfred A. Knopf, 1958).
12. Harold J. Laski, *The Communist Manifesto of Marx and Engels: With the Original Text and Prefaces* (New York: Pantheon Books, 1967), p. 179.
13. Ernst Bloch, *Das Prinzip Hoffnung*, 3 vols. (Frankfurt am Main: Suhrkamp, 1969), 3:1619.
14. Ibid., 3:1628.
15. Ibid., 3:1390–91.
16. *Mao Tse-tung's Quotations: The Red Guard's Handbook,* intro. Steward Fraser (Nashville, Tenn.: International Center, George Peabody College for Teachers, 1967), p. 269.
17. Ibid., p. 275.
18. *Humanist Manifestos I and II* (Buffalo, N.Y.: Prometheus Books, 1973), p. 9.
19. Ibid., p. 13.
20. Alvin Toffler, *Future Shock* (New York: Random House, 1970), p. 487.
21. Alvin Toffler, *The Eco-Spasm Report* (New York: Bantam Books, 1975), p. 69.
22. Robert Heilbroner, *The Future as History* (New York: Harper & Row, 1968), pp. 179–80.
23. Robert Heilbroner, *An Inquiry into the Human Prospect* (New York: W. W. Norton & Co., 1974), p. 17.
24. Robert Heilbroner, *Beyond Boom and Crash* (New York: W. W. Norton & Co., 1978), p. 89.

5

The Content of Christian Hope

The resurrection of Jesus Christ is the ground and the limit of Christian hope. Without indulging in a travelog eschatology, we must bring to expression the hope contained in the Christ event. Christians are initiated in Christ's death and resurrection through baptism. They are asked to anticipate proleptically their new life in the present. Since Christ bore the judgment of the world, the judgment is an event of the past for those who bear his name.

GROUND RULES

Before we explicitly engage in discourse about the content of Christian hope, we must lay out some ground rules for that discourse. If faith is hope in that which is not yet seen, eschatology is central to the Christian faith. But what distinguishes Christian hope from credulity and from mere speculation? After all, the final end has not yet occurred. Since it is assumed that the end is in many ways discontinuous with the present, we cannot simply extrapolate present conditions and project them to some future point that we label "the eschaton." We must refrain from a travelog eschatology that claims it has a blueprint or slideshow of hoped-for fulfillment. Whether we talk about heaven or hell, judgment or eternal life, and resurrection, these concepts do not denote parts of the physical world that we can at least potentially touch and see. They are necessarily symbols. Like talk about God, they attempt to express something essentially unavailable.

Yet we dare not become completely speechless. When Paul talked about the new life of the resurrection, he used the *via negativa* (negative way) to juxtapose perishable with imperishable and mortal with immortal. This allowed him to express the utter difference between our way of experiencing things now and of our hope for the ultimate future (1 Cor. 15:53–54). Similarly, we could use the *via analogica* (analogous way) to show the continuity between the hoped-for goal and our present existence. We talk about a new creation in analogy to our present one and about a new life in analogy to the present life. Especially with this form of speech we must be cautious as not to degrade the hoped-for future into an extrapolation of the present. Finally, we could use the *via eminentia* (superlative way) showing the superiority of the eschaton. In contrast to our limited life, we can then talk about life eternal, and in contrast to our present trials and judgments we talk about the last or final judgment. It is interesting that these three ways are also classical ways of talking about God, showing the intimate connection between God-talk and eschaton-talk.

When we say that our concepts should be taken not descriptively but symbolically, we do not want to leave the impression that they lack concrete content. Paul Tillich rightly reminded us of what distinguishes sign and symbol. While a sign bears no necessary relation to that to which it points, a symbol participates in the reality for which it stands. Symbols are not the result of conjectures or wishful thinking. This becomes evident when we remember that Christian eschatology is grounded in the Christ-event. Since Christ proleptically anticipated through his death and resurrection the end we hope for, he becomes both the criterion for appropriate speech about the end and the verification that such end is indeed a distinct possibility for us. This does not mean that Christ is the scientific or empirical proof of the veracity of our own ultimate future. An empirical proof of the content of hope would be a contradiction in itself. Moreover, the future is always to some extent open and undetermined. But Christ is the essential ground and direction of the Christian hope.

We have been confronted with different and sometimes conflicting emphases in the interpretation of Christian echatology. We have become aware of the finitude of our historical potential. We have seen massive secular efforts to find alternatives to the Christian hope. We might wonder how much room is now left for a positive development of Christian eschatology. While assertions about eschatology gain credibility in the world only if they take into account the general empirical conditions to which they relate, eschatology is not the science of the material future of our world. It is the word of God that is related to these empirical facts by placing them into the larger context of the world's ultimate history. The starting point for Christian eschatology, therefore, cannot be the world and the possible future it might contain, but God who has opened a new and otherwise inaccessible future for the world in Jesus Christ.

THE STARTING POINT OF CHRISTIAN ESCHATOLOGY

Since the resurrection of Jesus Christ is the starting point of the Christian faith, it may also be assumed that it is the starting point of Christian

THE CONTENT OF CHRISTIAN HOPE

eschatology. When we say that the resurrection of Jesus Christ is the starting point of Christian eschatology, we do not mean that the resurrection simply shows us a new future as an otherworldly possibility. The hope for a new future also deeply affects the way we address our existence in this world. Eschatology, extending itself into the future, directs our attention to the way we live in the present.

The resurrection of Jesus is the decisive element for the formation of the Christian community. But no scientific experiment could remove the ambiguity left by Jesus' death on the cross. The resurrection is an event that in its full implication exceeds empirical verification. Even Paul could only refer to others who believed they had seen the resurrected one and to Scripture to "prove" the fact of the resurrection (1 Cor. 15). But the first Christian community did not just use "resurrection" as a metaphor to denote who Jesus was for them. They were convinced that something had in fact happened to him, for which they used the phrase "he was resurrected." That something drastic had happened to Jesus was also emphasized by their addressing him as *Kyrios* (Lord), a term that in the Septuagint was still reserved for God. The confession of Jesus as Lord was even seen as parallel to faith in his resurrection from the dead (Rom. 10:9). Becoming *the* Lord meant that all other powers and lords were now secondary in the experience of the faithful. Yet there was also another change in terminology. While Jesus had steadfastly refused to call himself "Messiah," the church now openly proclaimed him so. A fact that had been hidden and concealed had now been disclosed: Jesus is the Messiah.

There is another indication that Jesus' resurrection must be seen in a larger context. Quite frequently Scripture suggests that the salvific activity of God occurs in analogy to God's creative activity in the beginning. In Second Isaiah the same word (*bara*) is used to denote God's promised salvation as is used to signify God's creative activity at the beginning (cf. Gen. 1 and Isa. 42:5 et al.). The prologue of the Gospel of John resembles the opening of the creation story in Genesis, indicating the close connection—almost a repetition—between creation and salvation. Christ's coming to us must be seen in the perspective of God's creative activity. Paul goes a step further when he speaks of Christ as the second Adam: He is a life-giving being in contrast to the first Adam who was a living being. With Christ, new life has come into this world; world history has made a decisive turn; salvation is now a present possibility.

We must be careful not to perceive the resurrection as a return to an ideal past state. Paul indicates future-directed movement when he states that for Christ and in Christ all things were created (Col. 1:16). The "very good" that God pronounced over creation at the beginning does not imply an ideal condition to which we will one day return. In the church's attempt to find a primal gospel in the words of the curse (Gen. 3:15) or in the gospel writer's attempt

12 / ESCHATOLOGY

to trace Jesus' ancestry back to Adam and finally to God himself (Luke 3:38), the notion is expressed that there is an ascending line from the creation at the beginning to the new creation in Jesus Christ. Thus Paul can call Jesus a new creation or its firstborn (cf. 1 Cor. 15:20). What God has done in Christ's resurrection is not simply part of God's present creative activity. It is something new and unprecedented. This is also indicated by the epiphanies of the resurrected One.

Contrary to other "resurrection" stories in the Bible, Jesus is not perceived as having returned to this life. His resurrection was not a resuscitation, indicating that in certain exceptional instances people can be returned to their former state of life. Jesus went beyond this present life to a new state of being. Yet this new state of being was not completely discontinuous with his former state. Those to whom Jesus appeared could still recognize him as the one they had known. He was able to appear to them as a fully human being with the ability to speak, eat, drink, and be touched. At the same time, he was not confined to his former state. Our space-time continuum was no longer a limiting factor for him. He could suddenly appear or disappear in their midst, and he finally ascended to his Father. Thus Jesus Christ's resurrection is the indication of a new form of life, the beginning of a new creation.

We must note that the resurrection of Jesus did not simply verify the idea of the resurrection, an idea prevalent among many Jews of his day. If he were simply the first one to be resurrected, the odds would still be heavily against our experiencing a resurrection like this. Our hope in a resurrection beyond this life is built not simply on the fact of a resurrection but on *who* was resurrected. Jesus was not just another human being, although he was exceptionally gifted, as many had surmised during his lifetime. Only because he was recognized as the Messiah did his resurrection have special significance. According to apocalyptic thinking, it could have been expected that someone, perhaps a person called Jesus, would be the firstborn of the resurrected. But since Jesus was also the Christ, he could become the presupposition of our own resurrection. Paul emphasized this point when he claimed, "If Christ has not been raised, then our preaching is in vain and your faith is in vain" (1 Cor. 15:14). Within the horizon of apocalyptic hope, Jesus was recognized as ushering in the eschaton through his resurrection. In calling Jesus resurrected, the disciples had realized the eschatological significance of this event.

Since Jesus' resurrection was not the beginning of the resurrection for all the faithful, people realized that what happened in Jesus was an anticipation of what was to happen on a universal scale. Confidence for this faith came from the fact that his followers realized in the light of his resurrection that what he had done and said during his lifetime had actually been of messianic quality. In the destiny of Jesus as the Lord, the end had occurred in proleptic anticipation, and God was fully self-disclosed. The New Testament proclaims Jesus not only as "the first-born from the dead" (Col. 1:18), but also as the one in whom we shall be united "in a resurrection like his," so that we too "might walk in newness of life" (Rom. 6:4–5). Thus the resurrection of Jesus serves as a foundation of hope for our individual and corporate fulfillment in the eschaton.

We might initially assume that the resurrection of Jesus Christ directs our attention only to the future. But the first Christian community did not experience the resurrection only as their ground of hope for the future or as their stimulus to spread the gospel of Christ's redemptive action. Paul especially does not tire of reminding his readers that the dying and rising of Christ have immense implications for our present life. "We were buried therefore with him [Jesus Christ] by baptism into death, so that as Christ was raised from the dead by the glory of the Father, we too might walk in newness of life" (Rom. 6:4).

Baptism enables us to participate in Christ's death and resurrection and makes us not only members of the Christian community but members of the body of Christ and therefore new creatures. "If any one is in Christ, he is a new creation; the old has passed away, behold, the new has come" (2 Cor. 5:17). The new creation is a present reality and not merely a future possibility. We are already a new creation, participating in the benefits that Christ has achieved for us through his death and resurrection. Our relationship with God and Christ has become new and is reflected in the way we relate to other people. Nothing is more important for Paul than the fact of this new creation (Gal. 6:15). If we live according to the Spirit imparted to us in baptism, we have overcome all desires of the flesh and walk in a new life.

The frequent imperatives in the Pauline literature indicate that the new creation is not always actualized by us. But this interim state of participation in the new creation, in which we still succumb to the desires of the flesh, will not continue forever. There is a clear line of direction indicated. The goal of the new creation is its all-inclusive nature. It is the confident tone of the New Testament that when Christ, who is our life, appears, we will also appear with him in glory (Col. 3:4). Up to then, however, together with the whole creation we moan and groan as we wait for the redemption of our bodies and for the full disclosure of the new creation (Rom. 8:23).

While we can be confident that nothing can separate us from the love of God and the eschatological promise that this love entails, we should not simply sit and wait. Throughout his letters Paul admonishes his listeners that we are to give witness to the fact that we are already participating now in this new creation. Individually and through the church as their corporate structure, Christians are a living witness to the hope that is within them. They give account of this hope, not through some kind of lip service, but by molding themselves and being molded ever more radically to the demands of Christ.

For instance, the involvement of the church in acts of charity and in the struggle for justice, human rights, and access to the necessities of life, does not just indicate that the church is an extension of God's loving hand. With its limited resources, the church can at best provide limited help for the wounds of the hurting world; it can never fully heal them. Yet with its actions the church foreshadows a world free from anguish, suffering, and despair. Amid the strife and struggle of today's world, the church is a beacon of hope and a rallying point for the oppressed. It radiates signs of the new world order, when there will be justice and peace for all creation. The church does not just point to the future with its words and actions. It also anticipates the future proleptically when it engages itself in the struggle for the underprivileged, the rejected, and the exploited. Struggles for a better world are then anticipations of that which will come on a universal scale, when the new creation will encompass all creation.

The proleptic aspect of the Christian existence is nowhere better exhibited than in the church's liturgical actions. When the community gathers for the eucharistic meal, all distinctions of rank and class disappear. As individual members of the body of Christ, all are equal before God. Since there is no undifferentiated existence, members receive their peculiarities through their different functions, but they are not ontologically distinguished as being of higher or lower rank. The intimate communion between the believers and with their Lord foreshadows their new state in the heavenly city. Correspondingly, the twofold assertion in the words of the institution, "Do this in remembrance of me," does not just mean that we should remember Christ's sacrifice. It also implies that God should remember the sacrifice of his Son and speed up the coming and completion of his kingdom. Each time the Eucharist is celebrated, the community prays for the coming of the Lord, proclaims the beginning of the time of salvation, and anticipates the blessings of the parousia. The community reminds itself and God that it will celebrate the Eucharist until Christ comes in the parousia, when the eschatological promises will be fulfilled. Thus the church is an interim community, anticipating the eschatological fulfillment and attempting to inaugurate it in a proleptic way for itself and for the world, as a witness that one day this fulfillment will be all-encompassing and evident. In the intervening time, between Christ's resurrection and the parousia, we are still faced with finitude and with the brokenness of a life delimited by death. How death and the promise of the resurrection are related to each other will be our next point of reflection.

DEATH AND RESURRECTION

Death is the border of this life. It annihilates all the differentiations that we experience in this life. Yet what does it mean that we must die? It means,

THE CONTENT OF CHRISTIAN HOPE

first, that we are mortal. This distinguishes us from God, who does not grow old or die—even if his death has occasionally been announced. Yet we do not just discover our mortality in the act of death. As soon as the first hairs turn gray and our strides become slower, we realize that death will some day overtake us. We are in the process of letting things go: things that belong to our youth, to maturity, or even to old age. As Ernest Becker in his *Denial of Death* has told us, death is an ever-present phenomenon and companion of life. Thus death is both a demarcation and a process.

Death is a complex phenomenon and can assume many different features. It can mean the cessation of life, as in biological death or brain death. Then all vital functions cease irrevocably, and we are pronounced clinically dead. But often clinical death is pronounced long after we died. With modern medical equipment it is possible to continue certain vital functions almost indefinitely, even if they could never again be sustained by our own bodies. But we experience death not only at the end of life but as the very presupposition of life and its constant companion. Life can only be engendered and sustained if someone else dies. It may not always be as dramatically demonstrated as when a spider eats her male companion after she has been fertilized. Life is always dependent on something else to sustain itself. These food materials must lose their life so that other life can continue and grow. Even when we look at ourselves, we are continuously dying in order to live. Cells are being replaced to give way to new cells, and by the time we die, there is hardly anything original left. We have been completely replaced without noticing it.

The whole life stream shows signs of aging; humanity is no exception. Of course, Teilhard assumed that there is a continuous ascent to higher forms of life. Similarly, Henri Bergson claimed that there is a life force pervading nature that drives life to ever higher levels. Yet increasing differentiation in the tree of life reduces more and more species to obsolescence. In the struggle for existence only the fittest will survive in plenty, while others will be relegated to less desirable ecological niches or be exterminated. Our struggle is only indicative of our malaise. We are confronted with death and try desperately to escape from it. The evolutionary struggle may well attest to the fact that creation wants to escape from the all-embracing power of death.

All living beings have a death-awareness. Cattle in the slaughterhouse sense somehow the danger of imminent death; animals often become restless in the face of the destructive forces of imminent natural disasters. But we do not face death only as a terminal outcome of extreme situations. The troublesome fact is that we cannot control our awareness of death or postpone it to the end of life. Death-awareness is for us a continuously threatening phenomenon, and it may interrupt our most exciting this-worldly pursuits. We are reminded here of Buddha, who enjoyed all the pleasures of this life

12 / ESCHATOLOGY

and suddenly, having become aware of life's finitude, underwent such a change of outlook that he devoted the rest of his life to meditation and preaching. Knowing about death, we live our lives; knowing about the irrevocable, unconditional, and ultimate end of our individual lives, we face death. Yet this knowledge of our finitude need not lead to pessimism. The Old Testament reminds us that we can live a fulfilled and satisfied life and die "in a good old age, and full of years" (Gen. 25:8).

Death can assume many faces. It can be a friend that finally terminates life after our long struggle on earth with its ups and downs, its promises and failures. Or death can be the enemy that we battle at the prime of life. Again death can be the grim reaper that takes away a teenager through a fatal car accident. Consulting the Bible, we will see that death can show many faces.

First, we must recognize that death is a basic order in God's creation. Thus the psalmist reflects, "The years of our life are threescore and ten, or even by reason of strength, fourscore; yet their span is but toil and trouble; they are soon gone, and we fly away" (Ps. 90:10). Only God is immortal, and everyone else must die (1 Tim. 6:16). Even Christ became a life-giving being only through his death and resurrection. Death and finitude indicate the basic difference between the Creator and the created. Thus it is difficult to think that biological death is a result of sin and the fall.

Western theologians from Augustine onward taught that humanity was once in a pristine state when we had the possibility of not sinning and not dying. Today very few theologians speculate about a once sinless and hence deathless state. Paul himself stated that "the wages of sin is death" (Rom. 6:23) and that "sin came into the world through one man and death through sin, and so death spread to all men because all men sinned" (Rom. 5:12). But death was a much too threatening prospect for Paul for him simply to talk about an individual human being who introduced death to us through his sinful action. Rather Paul pointed to the emergence of the age of death (and of sin) that had its starting point in Adam and contrasted it with the age of life that commenced with Christ.

Fear of death in the Bible is not just fear of biological death but fear of the confrontation of our sinful existence with God. Death is God's inescapable "No" to the way we conduct our lives and to our alienation from God. Since God is on both sides of death, we cannot escape from God in death. We must face up to the fact of how we live our lives. Thus death gives each moment of our life its singularity and its irreversible character. The fear of death, of going down into the pit, is also fear of facing God, who will confront us with the way we have lived our lives.

Death is also beneficial for Christians. Paul reminds us, "We were buried therefore with him [Christ] by baptism into death, so that as Christ was raised from the dead by the glory of the Father, we too might walk in newness of

THE CONTENT OF CHRISTIAN HOPE

life" (Rom. 6:4). Death for the Christian means dying in our sinful self, taking over the death of Christ, and rising as new beings. But the Pauline imperatives indicate that this "baptismal death" only initiates the process of dying; it never comes to an end in this life. Resurrection from death is an eschatological occurrence. To emphasize the continuous need for dying, Martin Luther said in his Small Catechism that we must die "daily" in our old Adam and be daily resurrected to newness of life. Consequently, Luther distinguished a threefold death: First there is the biological death that we share with the rest of the animated world as the cessation of this life. Second is the spiritual or eternal death of those who are condemned. This death usually coincides with the biological death and applies to those who reject God's grace. Third, there is death as the end of our sinful self, a death that can commence at any point in this life and that will be finished by our biological death. Daily death, in the light of the gospel, is reaching out to the eschatological fulfillment, and manifesting something of this new life already today. Yet our daily dying reminds us also of the fragmentary character of all anticipation and points us to the final resolution of the discrepancy between the intentionality and actuality of our life. Death, therefore, is the precondition for new life and the other side of the resurrection.

That death is not the final answer to the human phenomenon is virtually universally accepted. While not everybody will agree with the Christian notion of the resurrection, most people will insist that somehow they will live on, either in their deeds, in their descendants, or in the community in which they worked. Thus the idea of *immortality* is a widespread phenomenon.

The idea of immortality is expressed in many different ways, from memorial plaques on college and seminary campuses, to halls of fame, to perpetual care in our cemeteries. But Christian circles informed by biblical exegesis often reject the idea of immortality. It is held that a human being forms a unity that cannot be dissected into a mortal body and an immortal soul. Indeed, we do not hear in the creation account that the first human being was created by God's infusing a soul into the lifeless body; rather God infused his breath or spirit and thus the human being became alive. It is God's Spirit, and not a soul, that makes the difference between life and death. This is expressed in the frequent petitions in the Old Testament that God should not take his Spirit from us, lest we become lifeless like those in Sheol.

There is an occultism that claims it has means of communicating with the deceased, that is, souls. The Bible tells us that in his despair over the future, King Saul asked a medium at Endor to let him talk with Samuel, who had died a few years before (1 Sam. 28). Thus the Bible does not deny the possibility of communicating with the deceased—though it warns not to indulge in these practices. Research in parapsychology has also shown that some occult phenomena cannot be doubted, such as farewells to people who are many miles removed at the time of death. There are reliable accounts of apparitions of the deceased at their time of death or of clocks that suddenly stopped without being run down, or of pictures that fell from the wall without apparent cause. There does seem to be a connection between such phenomena and the death of a loved one.

But paranormal phenomena only tell us that someone has died. They do not indicate what state the person assumes once he or she is dead. Similarly, appearances of people long since deceased do not give many clues to their whereabouts. Often these "spirits" tell us minute and exact details about past events, but are remarkably vague in assertions concerning their own state. These "spirits" could result animistically from the subconscious powers of the medium, thus being produced by them and not by the deceased, or they could actually be apparitions of the spirits of the deceased. Even the claim of hypnotic recall of past existences, often adduced as evidence for reincarnation, does not lead us further in our quest for a post-mortem existence. People have told about their so-called prior existence under hypnosis, giving evidence of linguistic knowledge and historical details of distant periods of which they could have had no conscious prior knowledge. Yet they had no idea where they had been between one incarnated existence and another.

More promising results are provided by recent investigations of so-called "near-death experiences," especially as they are related by Raymond A. Moody in *Life after Life* and *Reflections on Life after Life*.[1] Moody tells us that in extreme situations, or when people return to life after clinical death has been pronounced, many recall experiences that are remarkably similar. Usually the people interviewed relate several of the following experiences: hearing their doctors or other spectators pronounce them dead, extremely pleasant feelings and sensations during the early stages of their experiences, unusual and often extremely unpleasant auditory sensations at or near death, the sensation of being pulled very rapidly through a dark space of some kind, looking on one's own physical body from a point outside of it and floating in a weightless body, awareness of the presence of other "spiritual" beings in the vicinity, glimpses of other beings who seem trapped in an unfortunate state of being, encounter with a bright light that at first is dim and rapidly gets brighter until it reaches an unearthly brilliance and often is identified with Jesus Christ or an angel, rapid panoramic review of one's life presented to the dying person by the light(-being), a flash of universal knowledge and insight into the nature of things, a vision of a city of light, the approach to a border of some kind, and return to the physical body and initial regret.

Since Moody also reports that these experiences were not limited to people who were resuscitated, the issue is not whether they actually returned from death to life, but what kind of reality is reflected in their experiences. We might at first be tempted to say that in cases of extreme shock or anxiety some or all of these enumerated phenomena can be experienced. But we still would be unable to answer the questions of physicians, who simply cannot understand how patients could have described the things they did, for example, details about resuscitation efforts, unless they really were hovering just below the ceiling. The difficulty here is a fundamental anthropological one.

In the Judeo-Christian tradition a human being is understood as a unity. Though Israel was convinced that death did not mean dissolution, life in Sheol was a shadowy existence, not actual life. The New Testament adopted the Hellenistic distinction between body, soul, and mind, but continued to understand the human being as a unity. A human being was not understood as sinful according to the body and sinless according to the soul. Not just the soul of Jesus was resurrected, but the whole Jesus with body, soul, and mind. This was very different from what one would have expected in Hellenistic circles. According to Plato and Aristotle, the soul was what really mattered. Since the soul was thought to be invisible, immaterial, and indivisible, it was also believed to be immortal. Plato even conceived of the body as a prison of the soul, a limitation that never allowed the soul to attain its highest intentions. Thus one looked forward to redemption from the body and union with the divine. Yet the soul was essential for the bodily life process. It was the principle of all life and knew the eternal ideas of truth, goodness, and beauty. Since the soul did not attain its goal in one attempt, Plato thought of a cycle of rebirth and purifications until the soul was reunited with the godly. How dangerous the body-soul dichotomy can become was shown in gnosticism, when the creation and redemption of the world were attributed to two distinct and antagonistic powers. Thus gnostics thought that the redeemer came into an alien world, to rescue the divine sparks that were hidden in redeemable people and lead them through purification to their heavenly destiny.

With modifications, Christian theologians adopted the Greek body-soul dichotomy and taught the immortality of the soul. But during the Enlightenment serious questions were asked about how there could be something immortal in us. In his *Critique of Pure Reason*, Immanuel Kant showed that we cannot assert with certainty that there is something indivisible (e.g., soul) in our world. He also claimed that we can prove with certainty only what pertains to our space-time continuum. This would rule out a proof of the existence of an eternal, immaterial soul. At the same time, in his *Critique of Practical Reason*, Kant postulated the immortality of the soul on the grounds of practical reason. He argued that though we know about the highest good we can never fulfill it completely in this life. Thus the evident disparity between our willing and our achieving needs a resolution that can be attained only through the assumption of an infinite life beyond our present existence. These positions indicate how ingrained the notion of immortality is in our minds.

It is still official Roman Catholic doctrine that each person is endowed with

12 / ESCHATOLOGY

an immortal soul, and most Protestants also share belief in immortality, expressed in many of our favorite hymns. Even the reformers, such as Zwingli, Calvin, and to some extent, Luther, taught the immortality of the soul. In recent years, especially under the impact of a renewed listening to the biblical documents, the idea of an immortal soul has become increasingly suspect. A human being is again seen as a unity. Karl Barth perhaps overstated the case when he claimed that the notion of immortality is a typical thought engendered by fear. Karl Rahner puts the issue more correctly when he states that there is no rectilinear continuation of our empirical reality beyond death. "In this regard death puts an end to the *whole* man."[2]

Death is the end of our life, but it is not the end of our being. Paul expresses this in 2 Cor. 5:1–5 in contradistinction to gnostic thought: When we die, our earthly tent (i.e. our body) will be destroyed. But we do not look forward, as in gnosticism, to our soul's survival. On the contrary, we long to put on our heavenly dwelling so that we may not be found "naked." That which would *survive* is not sufficient by itself for life eternal; it must be further clothed so that our being attains completion. This was to some extent already the Old Testament hope. We remember that the Israelites feared that God might take the divine spirit from them, so that they would become like those in Sheol. But they came to hope that the Spirit would be poured out over all flesh at the end of time (Joel 2:28–29). The Spirit was poured out on the disciples at Pentecost, and the Spirit (of life) was imparted to us at baptism. It was the Spirit of God that raised Jesus from the dead, and this Spirit now dwells in us to give us new life (Rom. 8:11). Though there is no dissolution of the being, any immortality would at best be an immortality in analogy to the existence of Sheol, but not in analogy to real life.

Though in our present life, body and mind (or soul) are usually seen as coextensive, they can also seem incongruous. Parapsychology has shown for a long time that the mind (or soul) can extend itself far beyond the region occupied by our body. Near-death experiences seem to substantiate the same point. We may conclude that occasionally and in highly unusual situations our mind (soul) extends so far that we can obtain a glimpse of a larger whole of which we are part. In each instance, however, the mind (soul) is not totally disconnected from the body. Eventually the unity of body and mind (soul) is resumed. Such experiences do not prove that we are immortal.

While God's relationship with us is sustained and finalized in and through death, life is not a human prerogative. It is a gift of God that God will bestow on us in abundance as the new life. But as the Apostles' Creed expresses, this new life will neither be a shadow existence as in Sheol nor a spiritual existence as in Platonic or gnostic thought. It will entail a resurrection of the body.

Since we are endowed neither with divine qualities nor with an immortal

THE CONTENT OF CHRISTIAN HOPE

soul in the Platonic or gnostic sense, meaningful existence beyond death must be a resurrection of the dead. This hope is expressed in the Apostles' Creed, where we say that we believe "in the resurrection of the body." This does not mean a biological revivification, such as is found in the case of the young man in the village of Nain (Luke 7:15) or of Lazarus (John 11:44). Nor does it imply that we would have to fight for the elements of our own bodies, on finding that we share them with others. A resurrection in analogy to our own present bodily existence would only perpetuate the limitations and tensions to which we are subject now.

When the early church included the belief in the resurrection of the body in the Apostles' Creed, it was attempting to protect itself from the idea that the resurrection is only a spiritual event, in analogy to Greek or gnostic thought, in which only the soul or divine spark lives on in eternity. The Christian hope was thus expressed as a resurrection of the body, or of the "flesh" as the original Greek and Latin reads. In popular Greek, "flesh" (*sarx*) did not just mean flesh; it could also mean "body." A bodily existence was thus a real one, in contrast to what we might encounter in a dream or in art. Here lies for us today the importance of the belief in the resurrection of the body. Resurrection is not a paranormal occurrence in analogy to occult phenomena or to hallucinations, but a reality that pertains to our whole being.

Occasionally the question is raised whether there are different stages of the resurrection. Answers to this would border on speculation. The implications of our response to the gospel and the seriousness of the final judgment suggest that all will be resurrected to an immortal state, at which point our respective future will be finalized. Some Christians occasionally have advanced the apocalyptic idea that the dead will first be resurrected in an unchanged way, so that they can be recognized. Then those who will be condemned and those who will be accepted will be changed as they deserve (2 Bar. 50–51). This idea lies beyond the scope of the New Testament. When Paul suggested that the dead will be raised imperishable, whereas we shall be changed (1 Cor. 15:52), he expected still to be alive at Christ's return when he, together with other Christians, would be transformed to participate in the new creation.

But what can the faithful hope for in the resurrection of the body? Biblical passages such as "In the resurrection they neither marry nor are given in marriage, but are like angels in heaven" (Matt. 22:30) indicate that the resurrected state is not a continuation of our present life, not even on a different level. The "otherness" of the resurrection should caution us against the frequent desire for a travelog eschatology. When Paul talked about the resurrection, he did so by negating our present conditions. Perishable-imperishable, dishonor-glory, physical-spiritual, and mortal-immortal are the antitheses he used (1 Cor. 15:42–54). We will encounter a fundamental change.

If the change we encounter is so all-inclusive, we might wonder whether the "we" who will be resurrected will be discontinuous with the "we" who died. Indeed, the resurrection implies a radical change in identity and personality. We are resurrected to a *new* creation. But already now our personality undergoes tremendous changes when we advance through the stages of life, from childhood to adolescence, maturity, and old age. Though these changes may be painful, we always remain the same person. Similarly, we may expect that we shall remain ourselves once we are received into the fullness of new life.

Since death terminates our individual lives, and resurrection is our destination beyond death, the question frequently emerges as to what happens "between" death and resurrection. From our vantage point, not everybody dies at the same time. Therefore the universal resurrection we hope for does not seem to coincide with the death of individuals. Often the notion has been introduced of an elaborate intermediate state in which we will wait until all are assembled for the final resurrection and for judgment day. Paul also encountered uncertainty about the state between death and the final fulfillment when people asked him concerning the destiny of those who had died. In his response Paul did not elaborate ideas of immortality, reincarnation, or purgatory, concepts that were certainly known to the inquirers. He showed them that an intermediate state is of no interest to us, since our destiny will lie in our confrontation with the returning Lord (1 Thess. 4:15; 1 Cor. 15:25).

The notion of an intermediate state largely results from the "time discrepancy" we experience between death and the outstanding resurrection. We are usually inclined to view the hereafter or the beyond in analogy to our this-worldly experience. If people die at different times, we assume that they will either be resurrected at different times or stay somewhere until they are all resurrected together at the same time. Yet time is not an independent entity but is intimately connected with space and matter. Already Augustine observed that time is an indication of transitoriness and is inexplicably connected with this world. This means that unless we want to believe in a material hereafter that is subject to change and decay, we cannot use the concepts of time, extension, and matter if we talk about anything beyond this present world. But if life eternal is immaterial, timeless, and not extended, is it not meaningless? This would certainly be the case, if life eternal were unstructured. But neither does our life issue into a timeless void of undifferentiated being.

The goal beyond our earthly existence is usually described with the term "eternity," denoting the same quality of existence that is attributed to God. In talking about God, however, we realize that the category of time does not fit. While for us there is time and aging, for God there is no sooner or later, not even a too late. God has created the world in its transitoriness and temporal limitation, but God is not subject to time and change. But through Jesus and the Spirit, God was and continues to be present in space and time.

THE CONTENT OF CHRISTIAN HOPE

The eternity of God, into which we are received upon death, is often conceived of as "endless time." Again we must be careful not to equate it with time stretched out to such an extent that it does not have boundaries. Eternity is also not a state of eternal bliss from which all consciousness has been removed. It is neither nirvana nor an ideal state of which time is a copy, as in Platonic thought. God does not recall us to him; God moves creation to the goal God intended before the world was founded. Thus eternity is essentially perfection, perfection of time, space, and matter. The limiting qualities that cause the anxieties and hurts of this world are no longer present. Eternity, as the sphere of God into which we are received at death, is not above or beyond our time-bound world, and yet gives it its meaning and direction. Expressing the fulfillment of time, eternity is not monotony, but active, unrestrained, and unlimited participation in communion with the living God.

It is not without significance that the New Testament writers do not give a uniform answer to the question of when complete fulfillment of our present life will be reached. On the one hand, we hear that the dead are asleep until they will be resurrected on judgment day (1 Cor. 15:20; 2 Pet. 3:4). On the other hand, we learn that with death some kind of final destiny is already reached. In the parable of the rich man and Lazarus, Jesus implies that both found their preliminary destinations, Abraham's bosom and Hades, immediately after they died (Luke 16:19–31), and he also promised the one criminal on the cross: "Today you will be with me in Paradise" (Luke 23:43). To complicate the issue even further, according to the Gospel of John the tension between waiting and having arrived is overcome in statements such as "Truly, truly, I say to you, the hour is coming, and now is, when the dead will hear the voice of the Son of God, and those who hear will live" (John 5:25). We also remember Paul's comment "If any one is in Christ, he is a new creation" (2 Cor. 5:17), indicating that the expected fulfillment is not simply outstanding.

We must conclude here that the response to the confrontation by Jesus and his message determines the final outcome of our lives. It then also touches the understanding of our present life and its quality. But the New Testament writers were realistic enough to note that even those who lived their life in accordance with the incarnate Word of God had to die and did not enter into a visible heaven. Thus they attempted to maintain both that the incarnate Word of God enables the faithful to participate now proleptically in the new creation and that there is a transition between life and death which points to a fulfillment beyond death. The latter can be described as sleep, from our experience of a "time discrepancy," or as the final destiny, if we reflect on it from the perspective of God, who is on both sides of death. Since we put our hope not in a state between death and resurrection but "in the resurrection of the body and the life everlasting," the notion of an intermediate state of sleep until judgment day is at most an optional construct. To expand this into a belief in purgatory seems to go beyond what is warranted by Scripture. Here we might do well to remember Martin Luther's advice: "In a similar way as one does not know how it happens that one falls asleep, and suddenly morning approaches when one awakes, so we will suddenly be resurrected at the Last Day, not knowing how we have come into death and through death."[3]

Once we are completely engulfed by death, we have transcended the border of this life and of our space-time continuum. On its other side there is neither growing nor diminishing, but only God's eternal and immediate presence. Since we see people crossing the border of our space-time continuum at different times, we can legitimately use a New Testament image and say that the dead "sleep" until judgment day. In God, however, all the different times coincide. When using the term "sleep" we must remember that the distinction between past, present, and future exists only for us time-bound creatures and not for the Creator. When we cross the border of space and time, we encounter God's eternal presence and become coeternal with God and all the others who have gone before us. Regardless of when we cross the demarcation between this life and life eternal, we will appear at the "other side" at the "same moment" together with everyone else. Thus the confrontation with God in death will result in the eternal judgment.

We have noticed that we can talk about an intermediate state only in figurative approximations. Even in calling it a state of "bodiless sleep" we encounter an evident contradiction, since we cannot conceive of sleep without thinking about a body. Yet in our attempt to express the fact that death and resurrection, though intimately related, are not the same, and in trying to relate our present experiences to the future we hope for, we must resort to such necessarily inadequate concepts.

Since death confronts us immediately with God's eternity, the idea of a reincarnation or of a migration of the soul to another form of existence would be contradictory to reaching our goal. We would then be thrown back into this finite life with all its ambiguities. The intention of these common ideas and widespread concepts is evident, however. They want to express the concern that life as it manifests itself cannot be the sum total of our experience. At the same time, they give witness to the immense alienation between ourselves and the goal we intend to reach. Thus the fear emerges that to be immediately confronted with the eternal seems to leave no chance for our being accepted. What such fearful existence overlooks, however, is the immensity of God's grace. Though God certainly says no to our present life, and though death witnesses to our brokenness, God does not discard or reject us. He accepts us in infinite grace and goodness. Yet at the entrance to life eternal stands not only death but also God's judgment. While in generations past this prospect has caused many anxieties, we have now become so oblivious to the idea of judgment that it often seems to be a relic of a time long gone by.

THE LAST JUDGMENT

Though we usually assure each other that things are just fine, the plain facts of life tell us otherwise. We need only think of the frequent tensions and breakups in families, congregations, and labor and management relations, or the astoundingly high rate of all kinds of criminal activities. It makes a difference to us whether we admit our own shortcomings or whether somebody else judges us because of them. But ultimately, a truthful judgment is not an imposition from outside; it is rather a pronouncement of where we have stood all along. In Jesus' parable of the wheat and the weeds, we do not hear that at the end the Son of Man will turn some of the wheat into weeds. On the contrary, both grow up together and then are separated at the end of time. Thus judgment is also self-inflicted human judgment, and not just a phenomenon relegated to the end of history.

The claim made by Friedrich Schiller and others, that world *history* is world judgment, is too sweeping to be true. Popular sentiment was more cautious when it coined the saying that God's mills grind very slowly but grind exceedingly fine. If historical events were to find resolution in themselves, we would not need a goal of history that transcends history. But historical events are not just part of the larger context of world history. They point beyond themselves and have eschatological significance. Precisely in that dual structure, of being self-contained and also pointing beyond themselves, historical events become problematic. The question is, To what extent has an event eschatological significance, and to what extent is it self-contained? The New Testament writers are cognizant of this problem when they alert us to watch for the signs of the end, even while they steadfastly refuse to provide us with a timetable for discerning the things that will happen before the eschatological fulfillment (Matt. 24:32–33 and 36–37). At most we can say that at certain times historical events are living reminders of the end, speaking sometimes with clarity but quite often with utter ambiguity.

The fruits of our evil actions or the inflicted judgment can to some extent be experienced in this world. But to perceive world history or individual history only as God's judgment would often make us despair over God's justice, when we see that evil people are seemingly rewarded while good ones are not. At the same time, we should be happy that history does not coincide with God's judgment. The psalmist recognized our precarious predicament when confessing that it is only by God's grace that we are not all done with. Without God's compassion our lives and our works could not be sustained. With all

12 / ESCHATOLOGY

its imperfections, history cannot stand in God's sight unless God undeservedly sustains it and brings it to fulfillment. But history cannot be totally divorced from God's purposes either, unless we conceive it in gnostic or Manichean fashion as being intrinsically evil and of the devil.

History is the place where our aspirations can be lived out and tested. Thus history is at once the area in which we live our lives in allegiance to the destiny to which we aspire, the place at which our readiness for final fulfillment becomes discernible, and the location in which we experience our inability to attain the final destiny. In all these instances human freedom is presupposed. This means that history is always human history, lived out either in conformity to God's will or in opposition to it or, what amounts to the same, oblivious to it. Regardless of how history is executed, it is always related to God's will. Thus the manifestation of God's will compared to the actual history is what we call judgment. In many ways history anticipates divine judgment, either by inaugurating in a proleptic way something of the new life we hope for or by excluding such a vision from our daily pursuits. But since history is not concomitant with God's history, there can also be an appeal to grace and compassion before the judgment.

Since history is not concomitant with judgment, the latter cannot simply be a working out of history. Thus a judgment just according to "works" would contradict the differentiation between history and judgment. Since the divine judgment is not totally discontinuous with history, however, there must also be a judgment according to works. This notion is all-pervading in the New Testament.

The end of history is not an ultimate evolutionary ascent; it is the parousia of the Lord and the final judgment.

> For the Son of man is to come with his angels in the glory of his Father, and then he will repay every man for what he has done. (Matt. 16:27)

> When the Son of man comes in his glory, and all the angels with him, then he will sit on his glorious throne. Before him will be gathered all the nations, and he will separate them from one another as a shepherd separates the sheep from the goats. (Matt. 25:31-32)

> For the Lord himself will descend from heaven with a cry of command, with the archangel's call, and with the sound of the trumpet of God. (1 Thess. 4:16)

> We must all appear before the judgment seat of Christ, so that each one may receive good or evil, according to what he has done in the body. (2 Cor. 5:10)

> And I saw the dead, great and small, standing before the throne, and books were opened. Also another book was opened, which is the book of life. And the dead were judged by what was written in the books, by what they had done. (Rev. 20:12)

THE CONTENT OF CHRISTIAN HOPE

The New Testament insists on the seriousness of judgment. It contradicts the liberal idea of a God who persuades and will eventually accept everyone, since God's job is to forgive.

The New Testament stands in stark contrast to the idea that "a God without wrath brought man without sin into a kingdom without judgment through the ministrations of a Christ without a cross."[4] Yet it would be wrong to understand the final judgment as the great awards day. If we were simply to be judged on account of our own achievements, there would be no hope for us. As the psalmist noted, O Lord, who can stand before you and who can withstand your anger? But it is by your grace that we are not totally done with (cf. Ps. 90). Thus grace is the decisive element in the last judgment. Our response to God's grace will decide our final acceptance or rejection. Thus we hear, "Whatever a man sows, that he will also reap" (Gal. 6:7), and "Every one to whom much is given, of him will much be required; and of him to whom men commit much they will demand the more" (Luke 12:48). There is no impersonal neutral guideline according to which we will be judged. Our own historical limitations and possibilities will be taken into acount.

The notion of an eternal life in which we could make up for the deficiencies we experience here on earth, and the idea of a purgatory in which we will be cleansed so that we have a better chance of being accepted, miss the point of a final judgment. We need not be afraid of encountering God at the wrong moment so that our chances would be greatly diminished, or of encountering God somewhat prematurely so that we would not quite be ready with the response that is expected. All historical peculiarities of our existence will be considered and accounted for. Any growth or purification in an intermediate state beyond death would diminish our historic responsibility in this life. Since we will meet God immediately in and upon death, the last judgment will finalize our historic existence. It will judge it in an irrevocable, final, and binding manner. Since Christ will judge in the name of God, there is no higher court of appeal. We are held accountable for what we have done or left undone.

In all its seriousness, the final judgment has a comforting aspect. Since we are living in the interim between Christ's resurrection and his parousia and participate already in the new world through baptism, judgment implies the final disclosure of this new world without contamination and impairment. Judgment, therefore, is the entrance to the new world. Thus the cry *"Maranatha"* (Our Lord, come!) was familiar in the liturgy of the first Christian community (cf. 1 Cor. 16:22). Similarly, the book of Revelation closes with "Amen. Come, Lord Jesus!" (Rev. 22:20). For Christians, judgment day is not to be dreaded but to be expected with anticipation. Since Jesus Christ, our Lord, will be the judge, there is reason to look forward to this day with confidence. Since he redeemed us, he will certainly not condemn us now.

Judgment day will be the day of the glory of the Lord, since he who has been neglected and despised so frequently will finally return in glory and power and will assemble with him those who confess his name. Martin Luther rightly looked forward to this day when he said in many of his letters: "Come, dear, last day."[5]

We still might wonder whether the notion of an ultimate, universal judgment day is not as obsolete and antiquated as the imagery with which its advent is usually expressed. While we certainly must avoid travelog eschatology, we must find ways to express the finalization of our life. One of the immense difficulties theology has to cope with is our ability to talk only about things that are on our level, that is, items or relations that can be made visible within our space-time continuum. But God, the last judgment, and the eschaton are not part of our visible world. Yet, they also are not totally discontinuous with it. Thus we can use terms that usually denote things within our world to talk about "things" that are of eternal significance. But at the same time we must keep in mind that anything beyond this world can never be in strict analogy to things in this world. This means that the concepts we use to talk about eternal "things" are always somehow inadequate. We have a choice between mystical silence and inadequacy. Yet it is not totally arbitrary to go beyond silence.

Since God's self-disclosure in our visible world was in human form and since Jesus returned to God with a promise of coming again, the mystery himself has broken the silence, so that we have the immense privilege and arduous task of bringing into language that which is beyond all language. Yet the venture has to be made continuously, since God's self-disclosure must be related to our continuously changing history and our awareness of it. We cannot speak in ancient tongues but must interpret God's word for our time, a word which points to our own future.

In the light of these considerations, how should we then speak about God's ultimate judgment? We must first affirm that the ultimate goal of our life is our participation in God's eternity. If we could realize this goal, we would live at each moment in accordance with the eternity of God. But in our sinful self-centeredness we usually live according to our own ideas of right and wrong. With death our self-centered life will cease, and the extent of our participation in the eternity of God will become finalized and completed. The fragmentariness of our earthly life will become visible and irreversible in the face of its eternal destiny, and we will experience as God's final judgment the discrepancy between the possibility and the actuality of our earthly life. In actuality, we will have long since pronounced this judgment on ourselves through our earthly life. But when we are in accord with Jesus Christ, that is, God's eternal Word, we have the assurance that the distortion of our life will be overcome. Jesus Christ never allowed this discrepancy to develop in his own earthly life and he promised the same to his followers. Through alignment with him, our death will result in resurrection to judgment—and to eternal life.

It is evident in the New Testament that not everyone will claim Jesus to overcome the discrepancy between our life's goal and our actual attainment. Thus Jesus and the New Testament witnesses emphasize a twofold outcome of the final judgment. "The gate is wide and the way is easy, that leads to destruction, and those who enter by it are many. For the gate is narrow and the way is hard, that leads to life, and those who find it are few" (Matt. 7:13–14). In the Gospel of John we encounter the same prediction actualized in the present: "He who believes in the Son has eternal life; he who does not obey the Son shall not see life, but the wrath of God rests upon him" (John 3:36). And the book of Revelation says in typical apocalyptic fashion, "And the smoke of their torment goes up for ever and ever; and they have no rest, day or night" (Rev. 14:11).

But the New Testament also contains assertions that God wants all people to be saved. Thus the notion of a last judgment necessarily leads to reflection on the universal homecoming of all people to God.

The idea of humanity's universal homecoming rests on a narrow biblical basis. The Greek term for this idea, *apokatastasis pantōn*, "restitution of all," occurs only once in the New Testament (Acts 3:21), when Peter told his audience that heaven must receive Jesus "until the time for establishing all that God spoke by the mouth of his holy prophets from of old." Peter was referring to the fulfillment of the Old Testament promises and not to a universal homecoming. Other passages in the New Testament, such as 1 Cor. 15:22, where Paul said that as in Adam all die, so "in Christ shall all be made alive," and where the all-inclusiveness of Christ's redemptive act is emphasized, seem to provide a better basis for the idea of a universal homecoming. Yet the representatives of this idea are usually not much interested in founding it on biblical grounds.

The origin of the notion of a universal homecoming goes far beyond the Bible and seems to be anchored in a cyclic view of history. All people have the chance of an eventual purification, and after the destruction of the devil and his powers even hell will be purified. For instance, Plato holds that a person's soul can return from Hades, the place of the "underworld," after a certain period and be reincarnated. After death, the migration continues because the human soul is like water. First it comes down from heaven, then it ascends into heaven; and again it must go down to earth in eternal change. This cyclic view of history is reinforced by the astrology of antiquity, in which the term *apokatastasis* stands for the return of the stellar bodies to their initial starting point.

In the early church, Origen advocated a cyclic view of history when he said:

12 / ESCHATOLOGY

For the end is always like the beginning; as therefore there is one end of all things, so we must understand that there is one beginning of all things, and as there is one end of many things, so from one beginning arise many differences and varieties, which in their turn are restored, through God's goodness, through their subjection to Christ and their unity with the Holy Spirit, to one end, which is like the beginning.[6]

Origen believed that in the divine goodness God would restore through Christ the entire creation to one end, and that even God's enemies would be conquered and subdued. Through various methods of correction, by the instruction of angels and higher powers, and by the use of creatures' free will, everyone would be renewed and restored, having undergone various movements of progress. In the end there would be a complete destruction of the body, "for wherever bodies are, corruption follows immediately" and the end of all things will be incorporeal.[7] Even the devil would not be excluded from the final spiritual unity with God. This return to the beginning, however, was not understood as final goal or fulfillment, because it always included the possibility of a new fall and of new salvational cycles.

The idea of a universal homecoming has always attracted speculative minds. Yet the church has never granted it official sanction. As the Augsburg Confession shows, it has on occasion been necessary officially to reject such a dangerous idea. The idea of a universal homecoming is very closely connected with the notion, firmly rooted in Roman Catholic beliefs, that there is a purgatory. Again there is not much biblical backing for the notion of a purgatory apart from the intertestamental reference in 2 Macc. 12:44-45: "For if he [Judas] were not expecting that those who had fallen would rise again, it would have been superfluous and foolish to pray for the dead. But if he was looking to the splendid reward that is laid up for those who fall asleep in godliness, it was a holy and pious thought. Therefore he made atonement for the dead, that they might be delivered from their sin." The prayers for the dead that are mentioned here still comprise an essential part of Roman Catholic piety connected with the notion of purgatory. The Council of Trent was perhaps aware of the scant biblical basis for the notion of purgatory when it approved this doctrine with reference to the Bible *and* the ancient tradition of the fathers. Today most Roman Catholic theologians admit that the main proof for the existence of purgatory and the cleansing fire connected with it lies in the testimony of the fathers.

The church did not merely continue the Jewish custom of commemorative and intercessory prayer for the dead. Referring to 2 Maccabees 12, Augustine already named prayer, good works, giving of alms, and eucharistic sacrifice as means of intercession for the dead. On the threshold of the dawning Middle Ages, Pope Gregory the Great even claimed that the eucharistic sacrifice was not just a remembrance of Christ's suffering, as Augustine had taught, but a real repetition of Christ's sacrifice. Since Gregory also taught that some of the graver sins could be forgiven in purgatory, the Eucharist provided him with an effective means to change the lot of the souls of the deceased. Its sacrifice is so efficacious that it releases the souls from purgatory.

In the eleventh and twelfth centuries letters of indulgence for sins committed became popular, since through them inconvenient church sanctions could be changed into more convenient ones or even totally relinquished. It was soon asserted that indulgences could also be applied to the punishment in purgatory. The church now felt able to extend its power of absolution into purgatory. The indulgence became especially important for those who had not yet finished their preparation for death, because it gave the bereaved a tool to ameliorate the lot of their loved ones.

Because the Reformation had been ignited by a dispute over the practice of indulgences, the idea of purgatory was a sensitive topic for the Reformers and the Protestant churches. In his Ninety-five Theses of 1517, Martin Luther reacted strongly against the abuses of indulgences. At the same time he still naively assumed that "the pope neither would nor could forgive any punishments, except those imposed through the judgment of the canon law or through himself."[8] Initially he also held that there was indeed a purgatory. But since he could not find sound scriptural support for the idea, and since he discovered more and more misuses connected with it, he became very skeptical and finally wrote his *Rejection of Purgatory* (1530).

The notion of purgatory usually implies that we can exert some influence on human destiny beyond death. The popularized slogan of Johann Tetzel, seller of indulgences and contemporary of Martin Luther, "As soon as the gold in the casket resounds, the rescued soul to heaven bounds"[9] certainly does not convey appropriate Roman Catholic teaching. Indulgence and attribution of good deeds are thought possible only through intercession and not mechanically. But the idea of intercession for the deceased pictures the afterlife as analogous to this life, a thought foreign to the mainstream of New Testament tradition.

Though we are sympathetic to the basic human attempt to safeguard the destiny of our loved ones in the hereafter, the New Testament vehemently asserts that the life of the departed is not similar to life here on earth. The final judgment is not a surprise action. It only confirms and makes irreversible what has already shown in and through our present life. Thus, in the Gospel of John, Jesus affirms: "He who hears my word and believes him who sent me, has eternal life; he does not come into judgment" (John 5:24), and Paul attests to the same in saying, "Therefore, if any one is in Christ, he is a new creation; the old has passed away, behold, the new has come" (2 Cor. 5:17).

The concept of spiritual growth beyond death, implied in the notion of purgatory, expresses the insight that the power of God's grace does not cease once we die. But unless we conceive of God enacting our growth, in analogy to a puppeteer bringing about the movements of puppets, such growth would require our response to God's activity. Can we actually talk about "growth" beyond death? Most Roman Catholic theologians today admit that death is not just a transitional stage with a subsequent rectilinear continuance in analogy to life here on earth. Death is a rupture and a dimensional borderline beyond which there is something entirely different from what we face here on earth. Nevertheless, they still do not want to abandon the idea of a purgatory.

We have noted that a cyclic view of history often gives rise to the idea of a universal homecoming. We also have had problems with the ideas of a continued growth beyond death, and of an ability to influence the state of the deceased. But there is a legitimate interest in a universal homecoming, for the New Testament is convinced that God wants all people to be saved. In wrestling with the destiny of Israel, Paul expresses the sentiment "God has consigned all men to disobedience, that he may have mercy upon all (Rom. 11:32). In a similar way we hear that God our savior "desires all men to be saved and to come to the knowledge of the truth" (1 Tim. 2:4). Thus we are confronted with the seemingly conflicting insights that God's love wants all to be saved, but that God's justice requires all the disobedient to be punished.

We could attempt to solve the evident paradox between God's love and justice by asserting a pedagogical God who threatens with justice in order that we might flee to the divine love. But the anthropomorphic notion of a pedagogical God, who punishes in order to save, fails to realize that the judgment is a disclosure and finalization of our life and not of God's universal love. The New Testament that tells us about God's universal love does not teach a universal homecoming. On the contrary, it confronts us with a twofold outcome of human history, with acceptance and rejection. Jesus' parables of the five wise and the five foolish maidens (Matt. 25:1–13) and of the rich man and Lazarus (Luke 16:19–31) convey the prospect of a definite and irrevocable final judgment of rejection or acceptance. And a saying like that found in Mark 9:43, "If your hand causes you to sin, cut it off; it is better for you to enter life maimed than with two hands to go to hell, to the unquenchable fire," again demands from us a decision with ultimate consequences. Even Paul, though emphasizing salvation as the universal *intention* for everybody, does not mute Jesus' call for a decision; he only expands it by breaking through the ethnic barrier of the initial church.

Universalism contradicts the New Testament insistence that our response to the gospel determines for us the outcome of the final judgment. God grants us the privilege of choosing our own destiny and takes us seriously in our choice, even if we reject God. Contrary to the sentiment of some who advocate a universal homecoming, a twofold outcome at the last judgment would not impair God's authority. The God who now rules over the saved and the condemned will then be revealed as the victor over hell and all anti-Godly powers. This is the deepest meaning of God's being "all in all." Consequently, we must conclude that God invites everybody to attain the final goal, but that there is a "too late" for us.

It should make us wonder, however, that even conservative theologians find at least some merit in the idea of a universal homecoming. We should also not forget that at the fringes of the New Testament it is mentioned that Jesus Christ in the Spirit "went and preached to the spirits in prison" (1 Pet. 3:19), again implying a chance of salvation for those who did not have that chance while they were alive. Deliberations of such a nature may also have found their way into the Apostles' Creed in the phrase Christ "descended into hell" or, as it is now more adequately translated, "went to the dead."

Without circumventing the salvific power of Christ, the church evidently affirmed the hope that those also could be saved who had not encountered Christ during their lifetime on earth. Yet it never dared to declare that therefore everyone will eventually be saved, nor did it define how someone could be saved through Christ's descent. Our reflection today must show a similar restraint. While we fervently hope and pray that all humanity will be saved, we cannot take for granted that it will indeed be so or outline a way in which God will reach this goal. We know that the saved will be saved only for Christ's sake.

We know that we are confronted with Christ's decision-demanding word: Repent and follow me. The response to this call determines our life here and beyond. As we accept God's offer to direct our lives according to our eternal destiny, a universal homecoming is meaningless for our salvation, since we will be saved according to the promise of his redemptive word. Ultimately, the hope for the all-embracing love of God, expressed in the notion of a universal homecoming or purgatory, grows out of the concern for others. But with regard to the final destiny of those whom we cannot reach or who do not respond positively (as far as we can ever tell), we should not make their final destiny into a dogmatic issue. Even in our most fervent concerns for them we must acknowledge God's ultimate sovereignty, while at the same time praying that God's never-ending grace will finally prevail.

PAROUSIA AND THE KINGDOM OF GOD

Coming now to the final part of eschatology, the disclosure of God's kingdom, we must again assert that in many ways God's kingdom is already a present reality. This is expressed in the church's teaching that Christians are part of the new creation and also, though in an impatient way, in the idea of millennialism.

Christians do not simply wait and hope for some pie-in-the-sky phenomenon. The very fact that they are Christians allows them to participate proleptically in the new world to come. Of course, the tension has not always been maintained between expectation of the end to come and anticipation of that end in daily living. There has been both passive resignation and utopian fever. Before we discuss that aspect of the Christian hope which clearly pertains to the future, we must first direct our attention to its prolepsis in the Christian life. Thus the sacraments are intrinsically eschatological, pointing to the promised fulfillment and at the same time anticipating it proleptically.

The eschatological quality of Christian life is affirmed throughout the New Testament. The Gospel of John especially shows that the present is endowed with eschatological significance, since in it our response to the gospel decides between life and death. The eschaton is anticipated in our present confrontation with the word of God. We hear Jesus say: "He who hears my word and believes him who sent me, has eternal life; he does not come into judgment, but has passed from death into life" (John 5:24), or "He who does not believe is condemned already" (John 3:18). The present is decisive time, since it will determine our future. The future will thus not contain anything unexpected, but it will consolidate and clarify our response to God's offer of a new creation.

Also Paul emphasizes the anticipatory moment of the end. He devotes almost a whole chapter (Rom. 6) to showing that through Christ's death and resurrection we are now a new creation and are dying and rising with Christ. "Now is the acceptable time; behold, now is the day of salvation," he declares (2 Cor. 6:2). Such an emphasis runs counter to any attempts to comfort us with hope for a better hereafter. Jesus too, referring to his actions, tells his inquirers: "But if it is by the finger of God that I cast out demons, then the kingdom of God has come upon you" (Luke 11:20; Matt. 12:28). If the faithful would refrain from anticipating the future they hope for, this would modify not only their present existence but also their future one. Their present decisions and attitudes do not eliminate the final judgment; they determine it. The present is the decisive time for Christians, because the whole future is at stake. Of course, our present activities should not result from a works-righteous attitude with the expectation of compensatory awards at the final judgment. Our attempt to anticipate the end proleptically is possible only because Christ has anticipated the end of all history in his resurrection and invites us to share in it. Thus our attitude can only be one of response and not of initiative. Marxists are right in pointing out that, contrary to our own intentions, we have often not responded well to the eschatological situation.

THE CONTENT OF CHRISTIAN HOPE

But they, on the other hand, have fallen short by exclusively emphasizing humanity's own initiative.

Jürgen Moltmann has rightly reminded us that our response to Christ's eschatological message must consist of more than missionary proclamation of faith and hope. It must also include bodily obedience in day-to-day living. This response reflects a visible and active discipleship that results in productive obedience to Christ in the affairs of the world. "The expectation of the promised future of the kingdom of God which is coming to man and to the world to set them right and create life, makes us ready to expend ourselves unrestrainedly and unreservedly in love and in the work of reconciliation of the world with God and his future."[10] Creatively and faithfully, believers will be involved in anticipating the new world. But in our emphasis on the anticipatory character of eschatology, we dare not forget that it is only proleptic anticipation and not the provision of the end itself. The anticipatory character of our activities is enabled by and points to the future fulfillment. This attitude of proleptic anticipation is deeply ingrained in the New Testament, where the anticipated eschaton is depicted as pointing to and enabling the future fulfillment, and vice versa. Thus the coming of the end is a process, since it involves our action, and it is also a surprise, since its completion is beyond our possibilities.

Teilhard de Chardin has rightly claimed that the kingdom does not break into this world without preparation. The time has to be ripe for the coming of the Lord. This idea has two significant implications: There is a definite avenue that leads up to the final events, and the coming of the final events expects a certain preparedness on our part. Similarly, there are two moments to the coming of the eschaton in the New Testament: We are asked to watch for the signs of the times and we are summoned to be prepared.

The call to discern the signs of the times has often led people to design timetables for eschatological fulfillment. This is especially the case at times of crisis and major political change, such as the beginning of the Constantinian era, the time of the Reformation, and in our most recent period. Yet Jesus clearly denied that one could predict the beginning of the eschaton and the parousia of the returning Christ when he said: "Of that day and hour no one knows, not even the angels of heaven, nor the Son, but the Father only" (Matt. 24:36), and "it is not for you to know times or seasons which the Father has fixed by his own authority" (Acts 1:7). The endeavor to predict the coming of the eschaton is a vain attempt to control the future. If it were successful, it would allow us to calculate when to start preparing for the end. Christians should be characterized by an eschatological life-style, living as if each day were their last.

The eschaton is not something for the coming of which we can start preparing from a certain time onward. It is the God-provided goal that will emerge at a God-provided point and toward which our whole life should be directed with unceasing attention. Jesus drove this point home with the parable of the five wise and the five foolish maidens (Matt. 25:1–13). Those who had directed their whole life toward preparation for the coming kingdom were able to enter into the kingdom when it came, but those who thought they could start their preparation at a certain self-determined point were excluded. Thus the parable ends with the admonition "Watch therefore, for you know neither the day nor the hour." Nevertheless, the idea of being able to arrive at the date of the coming of the eschaton has remained amazingly attractive.

Amid recent political and economic uncertainties, interest in predictions of the End has risen dramatically, as can be seen by the flood of books published on that topic within the last ten years. Hal Lindsey especially has had an immense impact on many believers. While we acknowledge the biblical realism that underlies his endeavor to point to the immediacy of the eschaton, we question the appropriateness of the underlying hermeneutics. Every Old Testament prediction or promise that has not yet been fulfilled in exactly the way it was predicted is taken and transposed onto the contemporary scene with the claim that it will be fulfilled soon.

Two criticisms are in order here. First, Old Testament predictions and promises were continuously revised and expanded in their own time, as the promise of the Messiah paradigmatically shows. Thus to pinpoint the exact date when a certain promise was to be fulfilled was ill-advised even in biblical times. Second, the New Testament witness is deeply convinced that in the Christ-event all the Old Testament promises found their fulfillment and not just their continuation. In Jesus, God's self-disclosure occurred, and with his resurrection the first fruit of the new creation has been reaped. All further events are seen as contingent on the Christ-event. To go back to the Old Testament and look for signs and predictions that could be projected on the screen of the present or the future would dangerously relativize the Christ-event. Christ would be not the answer to the Old Testament hopes and aspirations but only a continuation of them. Thus zeal for predicting the End, instead of emphasizing preparedness, can easily lead to a circumvention of our trust in God and in Christ's efficacious work.

We should not go to the other extreme of becoming oblivious to the signs of the times. There are several major apocalyptic passages in each of the synoptic Gospels (Matt. 24; Mark 13; Luke 21) which state the signs of the end: emergence of false prophets, climactic wars, catastrophes in nature, famines, persecution of the Christians, and the proclamation of the gospel to all people (Mark 13:10). While the Gospel of John does not contain any longer apocalyptic passages, it is complemented by those in the book of Revelation (Rev. 6, 8, 13, 16). Yet the evangelists are emphatic that these signs do not provide a timetable according to which we can calculate the coming of the end.

THE CONTENT OF CHRISTIAN HOPE

Instead, the evangelists reemphasize Jesus' own message, which culminated in the demand for immediate readiness. Thus, the mention of signs leads not to calculations but to the call for preparedness in the face of the sudden approach of the eschaton. We hear Jesus say: "What I say to you I say to all: Watch" (Mark 13:37), and "For as the lightning comes from the east and shines as far as the west, so will be the coming of the Son of Man" (Matt. 24:27); and we hear him tell the parable of the five wise and the five foolish maidens (Matt. 25:1–13). Even Paul asserts, "The day of the Lord will come like a thief in the night" (1 Thess. 5:2). Immediate readiness does not necessarily express belief in the chronologically near return of the Lord, but shows that our present attitude is expressive of our ultimate future. The watchword of the Middle Ages, *"Memento mori"* (Be aware of your death), was closer to the New Testament than a traditional belief in the final end of history. *"Memento mori"* reminds us not just that we never know when we will die but that death will make our present life-attitude irreversible. This is why we are called to respond to the demand for immediate readiness with a life-attitude of preparing anticipation and not with a once-in-our-lifetime decision. Christians are asked to live their lives in active anticipation, as if each moment were their last.

Though Jesus told inquirers at his trial that his kingdom was not of this world, there is no doubt that his kingdom will drastically affect this world. Perhaps the situation is most vividly described in 2 Pet. 3:10, where we read: "But the day of the Lord will come like a thief, and then the heavens will pass away with a loud noise, and the elements will be dissolved with fire, and the earth and the works that are upon it will be burned up." While people sometimes have thought to identify this cosmic upheaval with an atomic war, we would miss the intention of such a text by such modernizations. The notion of a fire at the end of time does not just indicate destruction, but affirms that all uncleanliness and sinfulness must disappear when the Lord returns. Thus the world must be burned or cleansed to be presentable to its Lord. Paul expresses the same notion in less apocalyptically colored imagery when he insists, "The creation itself will be set free from its bondage to decay and obtain the glorious liberty of the children of God" (Rom. 8:21). Thus the coming and completion of the kingdom are not a spiritual event but have cosmic consequences. At their conclusion there will be a new heaven and a new earth.

Often the notion of a cosmic dimension of eschatology, and the passages in the New Testament that contain it, have been used to construct a timetable of these events. Terms frequently associated with such a timetable are "millennialism," from the Latin "one thousand years"; its synonym "chiliasm," from the Greek "one thousand"; "dispensationalism," the teaching that there are several distinct "dispensations," or periods, of God's action with the world;

12 / ESCHATOLOGY

"tribulationalism," the teaching that a great tribulation will occur prior to Christ's second advent (cf. Matt. 24:21); and "rapture," referring to the catching up of living Christians from this earth to meet Christ at his second coming (1 Thess. 4:17). The most widespread and oldest of these ideas is the notion of a millennium.

The main reference of millennialists is Rev. 20:1–15, where we read that the martyrs will be resurrected at the first resurrection and that Satan will be bound on this occasion for a thousand years, so that the martyrs can reign with Christ. Other biblical passages sometimes quoted to support millennial views do not mention the thousand years (e.g., 1 Cor. 15:23–38) or provide only remote analogies. The origin of millennialism, however, lies outside the New Testament in Jewish apocalyptic. We have noted that there were two main trends of apocalyptic expectation. There is a national hope for a messianic kingdom, according to which the Jewish people will rule with the Messiah over the nonbelievers after a final war, and there is a universalistic expectation of the salvation of the faithful beyond the destruction and recreation of the world. Though both ideas were often combined with each other and with non-Jewish eschatological thoughts, they differed sufficiently in that the national expectation survived as a separate idea of an interlude before the universal enthronement of the Messiah.

When we finally attempt to express the expected fulfillment of our hope with positive assertions, we are immediately confronted with the limit of language. While we cannot indulge in a cinematographic eschatology, we must also beware of undue restraint. Furthermore, the expected goal is not totally withdrawn from our experience, since Jesus and the New Testament invite us to put our trust in something we can already to some degree anticipate in present life. We also remember that the goal of all history has been anticipated proleptically in Jesus' life and destiny. The New Testament's portrayal of this future and its anticipation in the present seem to provide a possibility of positive assertions about the new world.

The kingdom of God, or the new world to come, has started with Christ's coming. It has also a future dimension, and admission into it necessitates a decision, for "not every one who says to me, 'Lord, Lord,' shall enter the kingdom of heaven" (Matt. 7:21). Though it may not always be evident now who will be able to enter the kingdom, at one point the decision will be manifest. Good and evil will be separated, and it will become evident who has entered the kingdom of God and who has not (cf. Matt. 13:30; 49ff.). But Jesus refused to separate the faithful Christians from the rest of the community in the present age. Instead he pointed to the future dimension of such perfection: "Let both grow together until the harvest; and at harvest time I will tell the reapers, Gather the weeds first and bind them in bundles to be burned, but gather the wheat into my barn" (Matt. 13:30). The kingdom's

THE CONTENT OF CHRISTIAN HOPE

future dimension will find its fulfillment in the final judgment, when already existing separation will become visible and irreversible. The kingdom of God, or the new world which will then be openly manifested, is usually denoted with the term "heaven," while the exclusion from this new world is often associated with "hell."

We may question whether in our rationally minded age humanity's final destiny can be called "heaven" or "hell." In many religions, heaven is understood as the abode of the gods, while hell is usually associated with the devil, demons, and other figments of a fantasy world. In the New Testament "heaven" is used about as frequently as "kingdom of God." At some places the phrases are even merged to form "kingdom of heaven" (cf., e.g., Matt. 3:2; 5:3). Yet to resort to the term "kingdom of God" would not provide a conceptual remedy, since for us kingdoms belong to a past age. "Kingdom" is usually associated with kings, queens, and princes and lives on only in fairy tales. We do not want to talk about heaven in terms of a pre-Copernican topography, but neither do we want to revert to a fairy-tale or feudalistic picture of the kingdom.

Admittedly, the Bible in its pre-Copernican world view often used "hell" and "heaven" in a local way. But already in the Old Testament "heaven" is not just used for cosmological topography. It also denotes in a theological sense the dimension of God and God's power, the source of salvation. In rabbinic literature, "heaven" can even become a paraphrase for "God." The theological understanding of heaven is clarified further in the New Testament. Heaven is the dimension of God, the source of salvation; it is the integrating focus for the present and future blessings of salvation in the new eon. A theological understanding of heaven had to move beyond the prevalent three-story world view of the Bible, as indicated in the exclamation of David, "Behold, heaven and the highest heaven cannot contain thee; how much less this house which I have built!" (1 Kings 8:27), and in the assertion of Paul, "He who descended is he who also ascended far above all the heavens, that he might fill all things" (Eph. 4:10).

We also notice a growing understanding of the concept of "hell" (*Sheol*). In the earlier parts of the Old Testament, *Sheol* indiscriminately denotes the shadowy existence of all who have died (cf. Ps. 89:48). But *Sheol* is also already interpreted as the dimension of alienation from God and the sphere of death. In postexilic times, perhaps through the influence of Parsiism, Sheol was a temporary dwelling place and was different for the righteous than for the godless. In the New Testament, *Gehenna* (hell) names the place where the "worm does not die, and the fire is not quenched" (Mark 9:48). While "hell" denotes an already present reality (Matt. 25:41), only after resurrection and judgment will hell be disclosed as the realm of eternal torment. In apocalyptic thinking, Gehenna was still associated with the Hinnom valley near

Jerusalem, but this kind of localization was abandoned in the New Testament. In contrast to apocalyptic, the New Testament does not paint the torments of hell in drastic colors, unless in attempting to awaken the conscience of listeners (cf. Matt. 10:28). Like heaven, hell has its peculiarity not from a cosmological locality but from its relationship with God. Only in the world of fairy tales and fantasy is hell the domain of the devil. According to the biblical witness even the anti-Godly powers are under God's control.

In talking about hell, we talk about something unknown to Christians. Allusions in the New Testament, such as "outer darkness," "weeping and gnashing of teeth" (Matt. 22:13), and "eternal fire" (Matt. 25:41), evoke hell in terms of pain, despair, and loneliness. They express the anguish of knowing what one has missed with no possibility of reaching it, and witness to a state of extreme despair without hope of recuperation. Such anguish and despair will not result from a local separation from God but must come from a dimensional separation from God and the faithful.

Faithful Christians, however, look forward to "the resurrection of the body and life everlasting." For them hell is of no existential concern. It serves only as an admonition to reach their eternal goal and to appreciate its undeserved character. Luther remarked, "As little as children know in their mother's womb about their birth, so little do we know about life everlasting."[11] Indeed, the New Testament imagery of the new Jerusalem, of a city of gold with walls of precious stones and with twelve gates, each made of one pearl (Rev. 21), describes more an attraction in Disneyland than the ultimate goal of our lives. Even the promise that we will see God "face to face" (1 Cor. 13:12) seems discontinuous with our present reality. Similarly, the prospect that God will dwell with the elect, "and they shall be his people, and God himself will be with them; he will wipe away every tear from their eyes, and death shall be no more, neither shall there be mourning nor crying nor pain any more, for the former things have passed away" (Rev. 21:3-4), so that "God will be everything to every one" (1 Cor. 15:28), is totally different from what we experience now.

Immediacy to God, abolition of anguish and sorrow, and enjoyment of permanent beauty and perfection are so contrary to our present life of fear and alienation, pain and suffering, transition and change, that we might be prone to discard these hopes as utopian dreams. Such a response would be justified if Jesus Christ had not shown us through his death and resurrection that this fulfillment is actually attainable. Because of Jesus Christ and the promise contained in the Christ-event, the hope for final realization of such a destiny is a realistic hope. Humanity is invited to come home to God. Its perpetual yearning for self-transcendence, deification, elimination of death, and progress toward perfection need not remain an utopian dream, but will find its fulfillment in life everlasting.

THE CONTENT OF CHRISTIAN HOPE

NOTES

1. Raymond A. Moody, Jr., *Life After Life* (New York: Bantam Books, 1976) and *Reflections on Life After Life* (New York: Bantam Books, 1978).
2. Karl Rahner, "The Life of the Dead," in *Theological Investigations*, vol. 4, *More Recent Writings*, trans. K. Smyth (Baltimore: Helicon, 1966), p. 347.
3. Martin Luther, *WA* 7²:235, 17–20.
4. H. Richard Niebuhr, *The Kingdom of God in America* (New York: Harper & Row, 1959), p. 193.
5. Paul Althaus, *The Theology of Martin Luther*, trans. R. C. Schultz (Philadelphia: Fortress Press, 1966), pp. 420–21.
6. Origen, *On First Principles: Being Koetschau's Text of De Principiis*, trans. G. W. Butterworth (New York: Harper & Row, 1966), p. 53.
7. Ibid., p. 247.
8. Martin Luther, *Disputation on the Declaration about the Virtue of Indulgences*, in *WA* 1:239, 18–19.
9. Roland H. Bainton, *Here I Stand* (Nashville: Abingdon Press, 1950), p. 78.
10. Jürgen Moltmann, *Theology of Hope: On the Ground and the Implications of a Christian Eschatology*, trans. James W. Leitch (New York: Harper & Row, 1967), p. 337.
11. Luther, *WA* TR 3:276, 26–27.

Indexes to Volumes One and Two

Index of Names

Persons cited or referred to are listed. In the case of medieval and Reformation era persons, no uniform rule has been imposed on the form of listing; each will be found by that name most commonly used as first identification.

Abelard, I: 33, 415; II: 6, 23, 24, 26, 47
Abraham, I: 88, 104, 121, 245, 281, 291, 451; II: 85, 157, 208, 407, 483, 491, 569
Adam, I: 121, 243, 279, 284, 328, 332, 335, 380 n.9, 385, 388, 394, 395, 399, 401, 403, 410, 411, 413–16, 420–23, 425–27, 434–36, 444 n.4, 448, 450, 451, 453, 455, 525, 564; II: 20, 25, 37, 40, 55, 57, 96, 395, 419, 420, 438, 558, 562, 575
Adams, E. M., I: 247 n.18
Adams, John, II: 170
Adorno, Theodor, I: 252
Aetius, I: 133 n.47
Agricola, John, II: 448, 449
Ahlstrom, Sidney, II: 164 n.27, 335 n.54, 336 n.63
Aland, Kurt, II: 163 n.19, 164 nn.20–22
Albert, Hans, I: 27 n.8
Alexander of Alexandria, I: 125, 126
Alexander, S. C., I: 351 n.4
Allan, George, I: 263 n.14
Alszegby, Zoltan, I: 428 n.5
Althaus, Paul, I: 50, 78 nn.7,14,15, 459, 506, 515 n.17, 549, 556 n.12; II: 48, 49, 62 nn.6,7,8, 276, 288 n.9, 480 n.1, 510 nn.11,12, 587 n.5
Altizer, Thomas, I: 42, 177 n.1, 471 n.6
Ambrose, I: 394, 405 n.29, 412, 413, 423, 424; II: 363 n.28
Ambrosiaster, I: 424
Ames, William, I: 191 nn.6,7
Amir, Yehoshua, I: 132 n.12
Amos, I: 282, 342; II: 486, 487, 489
Amsdorf, Nicholas von, 442 n.5
Anaximander, I: 116
Andersen, Hans Christian, II: 406
Anselm of Canterbury, I: 16, 34, 206, 215, 225 n.2, 236, 247 n.20, 415; II: 6, 14, 19–25, 37–39, 42 nn.15,17,18–20,24,26,28,29, 43 n.39, 47, 52, 70
Apollinarius, I: 502–3
Apollonius of Tyana, II: 282
Aquinas, Thomas, I: 10, 13, 14, 34, 35, 38, 61, 142, 143, 159 nn.22,24,39,40,41,42, 160 nn.43,44,45,47, 172, 173, 177 n.6, 178 n.27, 185, 190 n.2, 191 nn.6,7,21, 205, 206, 214–17, 225 n.2, 227 n.27, 238, 300, 303, 304, 311, 316, 319 nn.8,19, 331–33, 344, 345, 350, 352 n.10, 394, 415, 458, 537; II: 127, 128, 134, 140 n.9, 141 nn.27,33,34,35, 160, 161, 164 n.36, 215, 286, 294, 300, 301, 312 nn.7,12, 313 nn.15,34, 314 nn.40,41,46, 317, 324, 333, 333 n.2, 334 nn.7,10,17, 335 nn.42–49, 336 nn.61,65,67,69, 344, 355–57, 362 n.22, 363 nn.30,31,38, 365 nn.90–94, 96,97, 381, 386 nn.21,22,24–27, 388 n.81, 404, 422 nn.3,4, 429, 504
Aristotle, I: 10, 13, 34–36, 61, 116, 131 nn.4,6, 147, 150, 164, 165, 172, 177 n.4, 178 n.8, 185, 191 n.8, 215, 216, 229–31, 307, 333, 374; II: 177 n.9, 408, 426, 433, 434, 547, 565
Arius, I: 47, 125–29, 133 nn.45,46,48–54, 134 n.59, 144, 299, 501, 502, 545
Armstrong, A. H., I: 225 n.4
Arndt, Johann, II: 129
Arnobius, I: 334
Arnold, Matthew, I: 232, 233
Assmann, Hugo, I: 348, 352 n.29; II: 238, 241 n.19, 527
Asterius, I: 133 n.47
Athanasius, I: 31, 126–30, 133 nn.42,51, 134 n.62, 135, 142, 148, 158 n.3, 159 n.27, 299, 319 n.7, 502
Athenagoras, I: 132 nn.15,26
Audet, J. P., II: 362 n.7
Auer, Johann, II: 140 n.11
Augustine, I: 13, 32–34, 61, 141–45, 149–53, 156, 159 nn.20,23,24,25,28,31,36, 164, 170, 182, 205, 214–17, 309–11, 320 n.30, 331, 332, 335, 337, 338, 340 n.20, 343, 344, 379, 383 n.57, 387, 395, 397, 406 n.34,42, 410–15, 424–27, 428 n.9, 438, 457, 458; II: 46 n.92, 125–27, 137, 148, 150, 163 nn.3,9,16, 199, 202 n.15, 215, 225, 226, 272, 273, 285, 286, 288 n.14, 291, 297, 299, 300, 303, 305–7, 312 n.1, 313 nn.26–30,32,34,36, 314 nn.38,45,47, 334 n.15, 373, 374, 386 nn.18,19,20, 413, 462, 504, 507, 510 nn.9,10, 562, 568, 576

INDEXES

Aulén, Gustaf, I: xvii, 41, 57, 84, 86 n.3, 303, 319 n.17, 342, 454, 463 n.19; II: 6, 9 n.4, 36–41, 45 n.83, 46 nn.84,85,87–92,94,95,97, 47–49, 62 nn.2,4,5,12, 70
Austin, J. L., I: 224
Ayer, Alfred, I: 220, 227 n.18

Baier, Johann, I: 11, 37, 190 n.2
Baillie, John, I: 225 n.3
Bainton, Roland, II: 587 n.9
Baird, Robert, I: 248 n.33
Balaam, II: 261, 489
Balthasar, Hans von, I: 471 n.2
Baltzer, K., I: 97 n.7
Barbel, Johannes, I: 113 n.23
Barbour, Ian, I: 227 n.24, 320 n.29
Bardy, Gustave, I: 133 n.43, 134 n.59
Barnard, L. W., I: 132 nn.15,16
Barrett, C. K., I: 381 n.29
Barth, Karl, I: xvii, xviii, 6, 29, 41, 43 n.3, 48, 59 n.8, 73–75, 86 nn.1,2, 151, 153, 154, 158 n.17, 160 nn.64,66,67,68,69,70, 161 n.71, 166, 177, 178 nn.11,12,13,14, 210 n.3, 227 n.27, 277, 305, 331, 342, 347, 348, 351 n.2, 352 n.25, 406 nn.36,44, 435, 445 n.9, 469–71, 484, 506, 515 nn.18,22, 519, 537, 540, 542 n.16, 543 n.18, 546, 552, 556 n.4; II: 8, 69–72, 77 n.5, 108 n.3, 137, 138, 141 n.39, 142 n.39, 177, 178 n.28, 216, 257, 267 n.2, 273, 288 nn.4,5,6, 335 n.52, 424 n.26, 461, 566
Basil the Great, I: 97 n.23, 130, 158 nn.7,12, 331, 340 n.18
Basilides, II: 20
Bauer, Bruno, I: 517
Bauer, Walter, II: 211, 221 n.8
Baumgartner, Charles, I: 427
Baur, F. C., I: 72
Bayer, Oswald, II: 364 n.54
Beardslee, William, II: 534, 539 n.48
Beasley-Murray, G. R., II: 333 n.3, 334 n.13
Beauvoir, Simone de, I: 234, 240, 248 n.30
Beck, J. T., I: 68
Becker, Ernst, I: 406 n.49, 436, 445 n.18; II: 463, 464, 469 nn.1,2,3, 561
Beer, Theobald, II: 63 nn.3,29
Bellarmine, Robert, I: 38
Benedict of Nursia, II: 508
Bengel, J. A., I: 68
Benz, Ernst, II: 178 n.25, 510 nn.3,16
Berdyaev, Nicolas, I: 324, 328, 339 nn.2,7
Berengar of Tours, II: 354, 355
Berger, Peter, II: 183, 185 n.1
Bergson, Henri, II: 561
Berkouwer, G. C., I: 405 n.19, 526 n.3; II: 77 n.6
Bernard of Clairvaux, I: 418
Berry, Wanda, I: 374, 381 n.20, 382 nn.38,41, 430 n.41
Bethune-Baker, J. F., I: 43 n.3
Betz, Johannes, II: 313 n.27, 362 n.11, 363 n.29, 364 nn.59,65,67
Bilaniuk, Petro, II: 422 nn.1,2

Birch, L. Charles, I: 320 n.34
Blankhertz, H., I: 179 n.32
Bloch, Ernst, I: 14, 27 n.15, 443, 444, 486, 494 n.10; II: 509, 510 n.18, 511 nn.20,23,24, 546–48, 554 nn.12,13,14
Blondel, Maurice, I: 24
Boethius, I: 177 n.6
Bonaventura, I: 34, 86 n.2, 160 nn.45,46, 161 n.74, 205, 214
Bonhoeffer, Dietrich, I: 42, 380 n.9, 393, 401, 405 n.26, 407 n.52, 435, 445 n.13, 462 n.2; II: 95, 99 n.15, 194, 201 n.9, 215, 270, 279, 288 n.12
Boniface VIII, I: 557
Bornkamm, Günther, I: 97 n.18; II: 362 nn.2,9, 363 n.50, 364 n.54, 385 nn.10–13
Bornkamm, Heinrich, I: 160 n.54
Bouillard, Henri, I: 227 n.27
Bousset, Wilhelm, I: 112 n.14
Bouyer, Louis, II: 362 nn.7,10,15, 363 n.33
Braaten, Carl, I: 27 n.9, 495 n.11, 515 n.13; II: 201 n.8
Brace, G. Loring, I: 405 n.21
Braithwaite, R. B., I: 210 n.1
Brandt, Wilfried, II: 162 n.1
Braun, René, I: 132 nn.14,28, 133 nn.35–40, 158 n.5
Breckenridge, James, II: 163 n.9
Brenz, Johannes, I: 179 n.40, 509; II: 360, 366 nn.118,120–23
Bresnahan, James, I: 247 n.19
Bretschneider, C. C., II: 140 n.18
Bring, Ragnar, I: 62 n.12, 423 n.17
Brinktrine, Johannes, I: 319 n.8, 341, 351 n.1, 352 n.16
Brisbrook, W. Jardin, II: 362 n.16
Brophy, Brigid, I: 251, 262 n.6
Brown, Raymond, I: 556 n.8
Brown, Robert McAfee, II: 163 n.12
Brunner, Emil, I: xvii, 41, 48, 59 n.9, 60 n.10, 73, 276, 277, 294 n.3, 301, 303, 318 n.2, 319 nn.13,16, 328, 331, 334, 339 n.6, 340 n.23, 347, 393, 396, 405 n.27, 406 n.36, 421, 429 n.26, 484, 546, 556 n.3; II: 35, 36, 45 nn.78–82, 69, 215
Brunner, Peter, I: 166, 178 nn.10,26
Brunotte, Wilhelm, II: 388 n.85
Brunståd, F., II: 443 n.16
Buber, Martin, I: 48, 380 n.9
Buddha, I: 565
Bulgakov, Sergius, II: 174, 178 nn.20,23,24
Bultmann, Rudolf, I: xviii, 16, 21, 22, 27 n.14, 41, 60 n.11, 77, 347, 348, 380 n.11, 381 nn.18,27, 427, 431 n.49, 444 n.3, 484, 490, 494 nn.1,7, 495 n.17, 528, 529, 535, 542 n.3, 549, 556 n.9; II: 216, 257, 267 n.1, 268 n.3, 287, 288 n.15, 334 n.25, 491, 517-19, 521, 530, 538 nn.8-11
Buren, Paul van, I: 42, 471 n.6
Burgess, Joseph, I: 210 n.5, 264 n.27; II: 140 n.22, 240 n.11
Burhoe, Ralph, I: 357 n.3

592

INDEXES

Buri, Fritz, II: 514
Bushnell, Horace, II: 334 n.16
Butler, Cuthbert, I: 59 n.1
Butterfield, Herbert, I: 320 n.29

Caird, G. B., I: 294 n.17
Cairns, David, I: 406 nn.36,40, 429 n.26
Cajetan, I: 227 n.27
Calov, Abraham, I: 37, 346
Calvin, John, I: 36, 41, 63–65, 68, 73, 203, 207, 209, 211 n.12, 217, 226 n.15, 331, 387, 417, 418, 421, 429 n.21, 460; II: 161, 233, 240 n.13, 272, 275, 288 n.8, 302, 308, 314 nn.37,54, 335 nn.51,53, 336 n.66, 357, 358, 365 n.106, 366 n.119, 374, 376, 377, 387 n.49, 56, 388 n.89, 389 n.101, 566
Campbell, Donald, I: 357 n.3
Campbell, J. McLeod, II: 44 n.59, 45 n.67
Campenhausen, Hans von, I: 43 n.3, 97 n.14; II: 163 n.5, 164 n.23, 240 n.8, 385 nn.6,10, 387 n.71
Camus, Albert, I: 250, 325; II: 543, 544, 554 nn.7–10
Cassian, John, I: 414
Castenada, Carlos, II: 106
Cauthen, Kenneth, I: 405 n.16
Charles the Bald, II: 307
Chemnitz, Martin, I: 37, 64, 70, 78 n.16, 338, 339, 340 n.32, 509, 554; II: 366 n.117
Childs, James, I: 331, 340 nn.15–17, 395 n.11, 526 nn.8,11
Chubb, Thomas, I: 211 n.22
Clark, Francis, II: 364 n.70, 365 nn.84,85
Clement (pseudo), I: 109, 111 n.1, 112 nn.3,21
Clement of Alexandria, I: 13, 30, 31, 204, 205, 215, 231, 310, 400
Clement of Rome, I: 498; II: 350, 364 n.62
Cobb, John, I: 42, 178 n.15, 316, 317, 320 n.49, 321 n.50, 405 n.23; II: 178 n.15, 532–34, 539 nn.43–47
Coccejus, Johannes, I: 38, 68
Cochrane, Charles, II: 201 n.2
Collingwood, R. G., I: 231, 246 nn.5,6, 343, 351 nn.3,5, 354
Cone, James, I: 191 n.5; II: 526, 527, 539 nn.31–35
Congar, Yves, II: 63 n.29, 215, 221 nn.9,10
Constantine the Great, I: 10, 127, 128; II: 150, 507
Conzelmann, Hans, I: 372, 379, 381 n.28, 383 n.56, 427, 431 n.49, 445 n.14, 462 n.10, 464 n.30; II: 362 n.3, 385 n.5
Cooke, Bernard, II: 240 n.4, 254 n.1
Copernicus, II: 366 n.118
Cox, L. Hughes, I: 227 n.22
Crichton, J. D., II: 387 n.77
Cullman, Oscar, I: 41, 511, 513, 515 n.25, 535; II: 15, 363 n.46, 514–16, 538 nn.3,4
Cyprian, I: 32, 413, 557; II: 149, 215, 225, 226, 236, 240 nn.5,6, 386 n.16
Cyrus, II: 262, 488

Dale, Robert, II: 44 n.59
Dallmayr, Fred, I: 263 n.11
Dandekar, R. N., I: 244, 248 nn.41,44, 256, 263 nn.19,21,22
Daniel, II: 112, 485, 490
Daniélou, Jean, I: 108, 112 nn.8,20,22, 113 nn.23,27, 159 n.19, 404 n.13
Dantine, Wilhelm, II: 428, 443 nn.6,10
Darius, II: 485
Darwin, Charles, I: 354; II: 477
Davey, Noel, I: 519, 526 n.1
David, I: 281, 283, 287, 293, 342, 345; II: 53, 55, 111, 151, 152, 259, 260, 482, 487–89, 495, 497, 585
Davies, W. D., I: 406 n.37
Denney, James, II: 44 n.59
Descartes, René, I: 218, 247 n.20
Dewart, Leslie, I: 166, 178 n.9
Dewey, John, I: 231, 246 n.4
Dibelius, Martin, II: 385 n.5
Dilthey, Wilhelm, I: 21
Dinkler, Eric, II: 141 n.32
Diodore of Tarsus, I: 503
Dionysius (pseudo), I: 34
Dioscuros, I: 504
Dodd, C. H., II: 517, 519–21, 538 nn.12–14
Donatus, I: 32
Dostoevski, Feodor, I: 437, 445 n.20
Douglas, J. D., I: 569 n.9
Dowey, Edward, I: 211 n.12
Driver, Tom, I: 526 n.5
Dubarle, A. M., I: 383 n.52
Duchesne, Louis, I: 133 n.43, 134 nn.61,64
Dulles, Avery, II: 200, 201, 202 nn.19–21, 214, 221 nn.11–13,15, 244, 247 nn.1–3
Dumas, Benoit, II: 238, 241 n.18
Duns Scotus, John, I: 173, 206, 415, 416
Dupont, Jacques, II: 221 nn.9,10

Eastwood, Cyril, II: 240 n.7
Ebeling, Gerhard, I: 41, 381 n.23; II: 216, 424 n.25, 460 nn.8,9
Eckhart, Johannes (Meister Eckhart), I: 34
Eddy, Mary Baker, II: 106
Edwards, Jonathan, II: 140 n.12
Eichrodt, Walther, I: 210 n.4, 373, 374, 378, 380 nn.1,2, 381 n.21, 382 n.34, 383 n.52, 404 n.7, 430 n.30, 445 n.15
Einstein, Albert, II: 287
Elert, Werner, I: 50, 78 n.10, 158 n.18, 191 nn.17–19, 352 n.20, 380 n.12, 383 n.56, 542 n.7; II: 43 n.42, 141 n.38, 423 n.17
Eliade, Mircea, I: 112 n.4, 244, 248 n.40; II: 163 n.14
Elijah, I: 552; II: 476, 483
Elliger, Walter, II: 511 n.19
Emerson, Ralph Waldo, II: 106
Empie, Paul, I: 210 n.5, 264 n.27; II: 240 nn.11,12
Engels, Friedrich, II: 509, 511 n.23, 545
Enoch, II: 483, 490
Enquist, Roy, II: 163 n.11

593

INDEXES

Erasmus of Rotterdam, I: 46, 63, 417
Eunomius, I: 126, 133 n.55, 149, 215
Eusebius of Caesarea, I: 133 n.42; II: 211, 507
Eusebius of Nicomedia, I: 125, 127
Eutyches, I: 47, 504, 505
Evans, Robert, I: 335, 340 n.27
Ezekiel, I: 173, 378; II: 112 n.14, 487

Fagerberg, Holsten, I: 383 nn.54,60, 430 n.44, 464 n.26
Farrer, Austin, I: 223, 227 n.26
Ferguson, John, I: 211 n.13
Fernandez, Domiciano, I: 430 n.45
Festugiére, A. M. J., I: 132 n.9
Feuerbach, Ludwig, I: 24, 494 n.10, 540; II: 475
Fichte, Johann Gottlieb, I: 170, 171, 518
Flacius, Matthias, I: 418, 419
Flew, Antony, I: 220, 227 n.19, 297, 318 n.1
Flick, Maurizio, I: 428 n.5
Fisher, J. D. C., II: 336 nn.64,68
Ford, Ford Madox, I: 462
Ford, Lewis, I: 247 n.26; II: 178 n.14
Forde, Gerhard, I: 179 n.33, 227 n.28; II: 62 n.2
Forsyth, P. T., I: 536, 542 n.13; II: 31–36, 44 nn.60–66, 45 nn.67–75,77, 70, 82
Foster, H. B., II: 387 n.76
Foster, Michael, I: 320 n.29
Fox, J. R., I: 244, 248 n.37
Francis of Assisi, II: 508
Francke, August Hermann, II: 129, 130
Francoeur, Robert, I: 334, 340 nn.25,26
Frank, Erich, I: 307, 319 n.26
Frank, H. R. von, I: 510
Franks, R. S., II: 43 nn.30,31, 44 nn.43,44
Frederick II, II: 508
Freestone, W. H., II: 363 n.34
Freire, Paulo, II: 527
Frend, W. H. C., II: 163 n.8
Fridrichsen, Anton, II: 499 n.5
Fritz, K. von, I: 131 n.8
Fromm, Erich, I: 234, 247 n.16, 405 n.20
Fuchs, Ernst, I: 41; II: 263, 268 n.15

Gadamer, Hans-Georg, I: 15
Galileo Galilei, I: 61
Gallagher, William, I: 463 n.7
Galloway, Allan, I: 292, 294 n.19
Gerhard, Johann, I: 11, 37, 165, 177 n.6, 183, 184, 186, 187, 191 nn.6,9,11,13, 336, 340 n.30, 345, 352 n.13, 554; II: 43 nn.41,42, 141 n.37, 198, 202 n.14, 312 nn.4,14
Gerhart, Mary, I: 264 n.25
Gerrish, Brian, I: 209, 210 n.8, 211 n.11, 212 n.33, 226 n.12, 416, 417, 429 nn.14,15,19
Gess, Wolfgang, I: 510
Gewirth, Alan, I: 235, 247 n.18
Gilbert de la Porrée, I: 160 n.45
Gilkey, Langdon, I: 26 n.5, 203, 210 n.9, 269, 271, 273 nn.1,3, 299, 307, 318 n.3, 319 n.25, 320 n.28, 349, 350, 352 nn.24,31, 382 n.47, 388, 404 n.8, 463 n.13; II; 534, 539 n.49
Gilson, Etienne, I: 78 n.1, 211 nn.20,21,24, 216, 226 n.8; II: 140 n.8
Girard, Renée, II: 87–89, 91, 99 nn.6–8,10–12
Gloege, Gerhard, I: 43 n.3, 50
Goethe, Johann Wolfgang von, I: 350; II: 273, 288 n.7
Gogarten, Friedrich, I: 41, 42, 308, 320 n.29, 484
Goldmann, Lucien, II: 469 nn.4–6
Goulet, Denis, II: 527
Grane, Leif, II: 423 n.11
Grant, Robert, I: 212 n.35, 404 n.14
Graves, Charles, II: 178 nn.20,22
Gregory the Great, I: 415; II: 576, 577
Gregory of Nazianzus, I: 130, 140, 158 nn.9,11,14,16; II: 38, 350, 364 n.68
Gregory of Nyssa, I: 97 nn.23,24, 130, 133 n.55, 139–41, 158 nn.9,10,13,15, 168, 170, 329, 331–33, 337, 338, 339 nn.10,11, 340 n.19; II: 38, 46 n.93
Green, Michael, I: 542 n.1
Gressman, Hugo, II: 499 n.2
Griffin, David, I: 309, 319 nn.11,12, 320 n.31, 321 n.50, 556 n.9; II: 532, 539 n.42
Grillmeier, Aloys, I: 43 n.3, 112 n.22, 113 n.23, 132 n.20, 133 n.43, 134 n.60, 514 n.1, 515 n.9
Gritsch, Eric, II: 140 n.19, 422, 422 n.5, 424 n.27
Grundmann, Walter, I: 381 n.26, 382 n.45
Guggisberg, H. R., I: 160 n.54
Gunton, Colin, I: 160 n.64, 178 nn.14,16
Gustafson, James, I: 264 n.28, 449, 463 n.8, 464 n.29; II: 185 n.1
Gutierrez, Gustavo, I: 352 n.28, 380 n.13, 567; II: 237, 238, 241 n.17, 527–29, 539 nn.36–39

Habermas, Jürgen, II: 201 n.11
Haggai, II: 489
Hahn, Ferdinand, I: 112 n.16; II: 336 n.75, 362 nn.1,6, 363 nn.42,43,48,49, 364 nn.55,57, 386 n.47, 387 n.72
Haikola, Lauri, II: 43 n.34, 423 n.17, 442 n.3
Hall, Douglas, I: 365 n.1
Hamer, Jerome, II: 215
Hamerton-Kelly, R. G., I: 556 n.1
Hamilton, William, I: 42, 471 n.6
Hänggi, Anton, II: 178 n.18, 362 nn.7,8
Hanson, N. R., I: 221, 227 n.21
Hanson, R. P. C., II: 201 n.3
Häring, Bernard, I: 382 n.39
Harless, Adolf von, I: 346
Harnack, Adolf von, I: 30, 43 nn.2,3, 45–48, 59 nn.6,7, 73, 78 n.17, 404 n.14, 428 n.5, 485, 492, 494 n.8, 495 n.19, 512, 513, 514 n.2, 515 n.29, 527, 535, 559; II: 476
Harnack, Theodosius, I: 212 n.36; II: 62 n.6
Harrison, Jane, I: 131 n.1
Harrisville, Roy, II: 99 n.14
Hart, H. L. A., I: 235, 247 n.19
Hart, Ray, I: 526 n.10
Hartshorne, Charles, I: 14, 42, 167, 178 nn.17,18, 199, 210 n.2, 236, 237, 247 n.21, 315, 321 n.49, 386, 404 n.3
Harvey, Van, I: 464 n.32
Hasse, Friedrich, II: 42 n.8

594

Hefner, Philip, II: 201 n.10
Hegel, G. F. W., I: 14, 15, 40–42, 72, 147, 150, 152, 153, 160 nn.49,62, 170, 233, 246 n.9, 513, 518, 537, 540, 541; II: 95, 105, 167–71, 177 nn.8,10, 178 n.12, 468
Heidegger, Martin, I: 14, 15, 537; II: 530, 541, 542, 554 nn.1–3
Heiges, Donald, II: 240 n.9
Heilbroner, Robert, II: 552, 553, 554 nn.21–23
Heim, Karl, I: 404 n.7
Heinecken, Martin, I: 404 n.9
Heisenberg, Werner, II: 287
Heller, Agnes, I: 263 n.15
Hengel, Martin, I: 97 n.19, 112 n.14; II: 8, 9 n.9, 12, 17, 42 nn.1,7, 85
Hepburn, Ronald, I: 270, 273 n.2, 293
Heppe, Heinrich, II: 141 n.28, 334 n.11, 335 n.50, 362 nn.21,23, 363 nn.25,32, 365 n.107, 366 nn.109,110, 388 n.89
Herbert of Cherbury, II: 475
Herder, J. G., I: 68
Hermas, I: 109, 113 nn.28,29; II: 502
Herod the Great, II: 260
Herrmann, Wilhelm, I: 537; II: 258
Heschel, Abraham, I: 208, 212 n.30, 382 n.46, 463 n.16
Hesiod, I: 10
Hezekiah, II: 483
Hick, John, I: 211 n.15, 223, 227 n.31, 237, 238, 247 nn.21,22,25,27, 395, 396, 406 n.35, 428 n.5, 441, 445 nn.21,27, 470, 471 n.4, 481 n.3, 542 n.1, 558, 559, 568 nn.2,3; II: 480 n.1
Hicks, F. C. N., II: 82, 83, 98 n.1
Hiers, Richard, I: 395 n.11
Higgins, J. B., II: 363 n.48
Hilary of Poitiers, I: 414
Hilgenfeld, Hartmut, II: 164 n.37
Hippolytus, I: 110, 113 n.33, 519; II: 335 n.35, 339, 340, 342, 349, 350, 352, 362 n.14, 364 nn.60,64, 381, 507
Hirsch, Emanuel, I: 160 nn.52,56,60,62, 178 n.23
Hitler, Adolf, II: 509, 511 n.24, 543
Hodgson, Leonard, I: 84, 86 n.5
Hofmann, J. C. K. von, I: 17, 40, 68; II: 62 n.2
Holl, Karl, II: 416, 423 n.19, 434, 443 n.16
Hollaz, David, I: 11, 37, 64, 66, 345, 352 n.13, 554
Hollenweger, Walter, II: 164 n.28
Holte, Ragnar, II: 313 n.27
Homer, I: 10, 116, 141
Honorius I, I: 507
Hooker, Morna, II: 42 n.5
Hooykaas, R., I: 307, 320 nn.27,29
Horney, Karen, I: 382 n.43
Hosea, I: 225 n.4, 317, 342, 368, 376, 444; II: 261
Hoskyns, Edwyn, I: 519, 526 n.1
Howe, George, I: 320 nn.43,44
Hugo of St. Victor, II: 293, 312 n.6, 314 n.43
Hume, David, I: 234, 237, 239, 247 n.23, 248 n.28

Hume, R. E., I: 319 n.9
Hutter, Leonhard, I: 37; II: 43 n.37, 198, 202 n.13

Ignatius of Antioch, I: 97 n.12, 102, 111 n.2, 118, 337, 410, 555; II: 120, 123 n.46, 163 n.10
Ingram, Paul, I: 248 n.33
Irenaeus of Lyon, I: 31, 122, 132 nn.32,34, 299, 304–6, 310, 313, 319 n.4, 331, 397, 400, 411, 415, 519, 525, 526 n.9, 555; II: 20, 27, 37, 40, 120, 123 n.47, 160, 164 n.34, 166, 167, 174, 177 nn.3,6,7, 230, 313 n.33, 350, 364 n.66, 503, 507, 510 nn.4–6
Isaac, I: 88, 104, 121; II: 208, 491
Isaiah I, I: 101, 282; II: 114, 261, 431, 487
Isaiah II, III, I: 202, 285, 287, 292, 293, 300, 309, 342, 453; II: 112, 261, 262, 482, 487, 489, 490, 493, 557
Iwand, Hans-Joachim, II: 8, 9 nn.10,11, 44 nn.57,58, 423 nn.14,19, 424 nn.21,22, 442 n.2, 444 nn.25,28, 460 nn.6,7

Jacob, I: 88, 104, 121; II: 208, 262, 483, 486, 489, 491
Jaeger, Werner, I: 131 n.5, 230, 246 n.3; II: 162 n.3
James, I: 64; II: 292, 376, 377, 387 n.56, 502
James, Ralph, I: 178 n.15
Jaschke, Hans-Jochen, II: 123 n.44,47,48, 164 n.33, 177 nn.4,5
Jastrow, Robert, I: 357 n.1
Jenkins, Jonathan, II: 141 n.26
Jensen, Ole, I: 273 n.4
Jenson, Robert, I: 27 n.11, 97 n.21, 133 n.41, 160 nn.62,65, 178 n.14, 179 nn.34,35,38, 190 n.2, 191 n.4; II: 77 n.7, 122 nn.18,25, 140 nn.13,19,21, 142 nn.39,41, 163 nn.5,6, 164 n.31, 178 n.13, 254 n.1, 313 nn.24,35, 314 n.56, 333 nn.4,6, 334 n.22, 335 nn.31,32,38,40, 362 n.9, 363 n.45, 364 nn.56,76, 366 nn.113,125, 387 n.75, 422 n.5, 424 n.27
Jeremiah, II: 261
Jeremias, Joachim, I: 488, 494 n.9, 495 n.13; II: 268 n.16, 334 n.13, 362 nn.4–6,17, 363 n.44, 364 n.53, 491, 499 n.4, 513, 538 nn.1,2
Jerome, I: 63; II: 342
Joachim of Flores, I: 160 n.45; II: 508, 509, 511 nn.20,22,24
Job, I: 282, 285, 287, 293, 301, 309, 398, 405 n.15, 443, 444, 453; II: 112, 484
Joel, II: 109, 110, 114
Joest, Wilfried, II: 423 n.15, 432, 436, 443 nn.11,13,17,18,21, 460 nn.4,5
John the Baptist, I: 12, 460, 490, 561; II: 115, 206, 264, 316, 319–21, 476, 492, 495
John of Damascus, I: 31, 215, 507; II: 46 n.86
John the Evangelist, I: 29, 47, 56, 64, 72, 107, 120, 121, 225 n.4, 374, 377, 389, 410, 530, 545, 546, 553; II: 44 n.42, 122 nn.14,27, 144, 210, 265, 266, 277, 346, 347, 493, 496, 497,

INDEXES

501, 502, 519, 521, 557, 569, 575, 577, 580, 582
John Scotus Erigena, I: 34
John XXIII, II: 191
Jolivet, Régis, II: 543, 554 n.6
Jonas, Hans, I: 131 n.9, 132 n.9; II: 164 n.30
Joseph, II: 112, 487
Judah, II: 489
Judas Iscariot, II: 210, 260
Judas Maccabaeus, II: 492
Jüngel, Eberhard, I: 131 n.7, 154, 160 n.64, 161 nn.71,72, 179 n.33, 471 n.7
Jungmann, Josef, I; 97 n.11
Justinian, I: 189
Justin Martyr, I: 13, 30, 31, 118–21, 132 nn.15,23–27,29, 133 n.32, 205, 410, 555; II: 339, 340, 350, 362 nn.13,20, 364 n.63, 510 n.15

Kähler, E., II: 139 n.2
Kähler, Martin, I: 40, 481 n.1, 515 n.26, 519–21, 526 n.4
Kant, Immanuel, I: 14, 15, 39, 40, 77, 160 n.60, 172, 218, 233, 234, 236, 240, 246 nn.10–14, 247 n.20, 248 n.32, 272, 381 n.25, 383 n.56, 390, 403, 405 n.17, 518, 537; II: 30, 31, 34, 178 n.19, 287, 430, 467, 475, 477, 480 n.3, 565
Kantzenbach, F. W., I: 60 n.12
Käsemann, Ernst, I: 63, 78 n.5, 421, 429 n.25, 464 n.31, 535, 542 n.11; II: 122 nn.16,17, 163 n.5, 363 nn.50,51, 387 n.74, 477, 524
Kasper, Walter, I: 46, 53, 59 nn.2,3, 60 n.14; II: 288 n.1
Kattenbusch, Friedrich, II: 312 n.3
Kaufman, Gordon, I: 212 n.26, 300, 319 n.10, 381 n.30, 405 n.16
Kaufmann, Walter, I: 234, 247 n.16
Kavanaugh, Aidan, II: 334 nn.9,27,32–34, 336 n.62
Kelly, J. N. D., I: 97 n.15, 113 nn.30–32,34–36, 133 nn.43,44, 160 nn.50,51, 191 n.15, 290, 294 n.17, 428 nn.7–9, 514 nn.1,4,6, 515 n.7; II: 123 n.49, 334 n.19
Kenny, Anthony, I: 247 n.25
Kessler, Hans, II: 7, 9 n.8, 42 nn.2,8–14,16,21–24,27, 43 n.43
Kettler, F. H., I: 132 n.18
Kierkegaard, Søren, I: 16, 201, 202, 207, 209, 210 n.7, 212 nn.26,36, 226 n.16, 246 n.1, 258, 259, 261, 262, 264 nn.26,32,33, 370, 371, 374, 377, 381 nn.15,17,19,20, 382 nn.37,42,50, 394, 402, 403, 404 n.10, 406 n.31, 407 nn.54,55, 427, 428 n.1, 430 n.48; II: 258, 464, 541, 543
Kinder, Ernst, I: 430 n.46
King, Robert, I: 223, 227 n.29
Kitamori, Kazoh, I: 542 n.6
Kittel, Gerhard, I: 371, 381 nn.26,33, 404 n.15; II: 263, 268 nn.13,14
Klauser, Theodor, II: 363 n.37

Kleinknecht, Hermann, I: 132 n.21; II: 108 n.2, 164 n.35
Klotz, John, I: 320 n.42
Klubertanz, George, I: 190 n.2
Kluckhohn, Clyde, I: 240, 248 n.29
Knitter, Paul, I: 471 n.5, 559, 568 nn.4,5,7, 588 n.8
Koch, Hal, I: 132 n.10, 351 n.8
Koch, Klaus, I: 382 n.47
Koester, Helmut, I: 158 n.6
Konow, Sten, I: 178 n.22
Kraft, Heinrich, II: 121 n.2, 122 n.13, 333 n.5
Kraft, Heinz, I: 134 n.57
Kremer, Klaus, II: 365 n.95
Kretschmar, George, I: 97 nn.13,16,22, 112 n.22, 113 nn.24,25, 132 n.30; II: 122 n.19, 177 n.2, 333 n.6, 334 nn.14,26, 362 n.19
Kuhn, Thomas, I: 221, 227 n.21
Kümmel, Werner, I: 381 n.18, 495 n.12; II: 334 nn.21,24
Küng, Hans, I: 53, 543 n.19, 559; II: 178 n.12, 216, 221 nn.3,9,10, 245, 247 nn.7,8
Kutsch, E., II: 385 n.4

Lactantius, I: 334
Lampe, G. W. H., I: 150, 160 n.58, 291, 294 n.18; II: 123 n.45
Laski, Harold, II: 554 n.11
Lazareth, William, I: 459, 464 n.27
Lazarus, II: 567
Leeuw, Gerhardus van der, I: 179 n.36, 312, 313, 320 n.35
Leeuwen, H. van der, I: 320 n.29
Leibniz, Gottfried, I: 218
Leontius of Byzantium, I: 506
Leo X, I: 458
Lessing, Gotthold, II: 88, 509, 511 n.22
Levy-Bruhl, Lucien, I: 424
Lewis, C. S., I: 394, 406 n.32, 440, 441, 445 nn.23,24,28
Lewis, Edwin, I: 405 n.16
Lieberg, Helmut, II: 388 n.85
Lindbeck, George, II: 388 n.86
Lindsell, Harold, I: 569 n.10
Lindsey, Hal, II: 517, 521–23, 538 nn.15–22, 582
Lips, Herman von, II: 387 nn.59–61,63–70
Little, David, I: 248 n.29
Locher, G. W., II: 366 n.112
Locke, John, I: 149, 160 n.53
Loewenich, Walther von, I: 212 n.36; II: 62 n.1
Löfgren, David, I: 344, 352 nn.11,12
Lohmeyer, Ernst, II: 363 n.44
Lohse, Bernard, I: 226 n.10
Lohse, Eduard, II: 334 n.21
Loisy, Alfred, I: 492, 495 n.18
Lonergan, Bernard, I: 14, 42, 230, 246 n.2
Long, Charles, I: 277, 294 nn.6,7
Lönning, Inge, II: 163 n.17
Loofs, Friedrich, I: 515 n.12; II: 314 n.49
Loomer, Bernard, I: 319 n.6
Lorenz, R., II: 139 n.5
Lossky, Vladimir, II: 178 n.21

Lotze, Hermann, I: 40; II: 30
Löwith, Karl von, I: 351 n.3
Lubac, Henri de, II: 215, 221 n.13
Lucian of Antioch, I: 125, 133 n.43, 501
Lukacs, Georg, I: 252, 253, 262 n.10, 263 n.15
Luke, I: 72; II: 109, 110, 115, 116, 144, 319, 338, 347, 348, 493, 495, 496
Luther, Martin, I: xviii, 10, 11, 16, 26, 35, 36, 38–41, 46, 47, 49, 51, 52, 54, 59 n.4, 61–71, 73–77, 78 nn.3,4,12,13, 153, 173, 177, 179 nn.33,39,40, 182–84, 186–88, 190 n.1, 191 nn.12,14, 203–5, 207, 209, 210 n.8, 211 n.18, 212 nn.29,36, 216, 217, 224, 226 n.15, 302, 331, 332, 334, 337, 339, 340 nn.21,22, 344–46, 352 n.15, 371, 373, 380 nn.3,8, 382 n.48, 406 n.41, 417, 418, 421, 422, 429 nn.16,18, 436, 456–58, 460, 507, 508, 519, 522, 533, 534, 545, 552–54; II: 31, 36, 37, 43 n.39, 46 n.92, 47–61, 62 nn.6,10,12, 63 n.19, 65–67, 69, 71, 73, 74, 76, 77 nn.1–4,8,10, 79, 90, 92, 98, 99 n.13, 129, 138, 141 nn.30,31,34, 142 n.43, 153, 161, 162, 163 n.17, 164 nn.37,38, 177, 184, 228, 234, 235, 239, 240 nn.1,2,14, 259, 260, 266, 267, 268 nn.8,9,12,18–20, 269–80, 288 nn.2,3,11,13, 294, 295, 307, 312 nn.2,8,13, 313 n.18, 314 nn.39,51,53, 317, 323, 325, 326, 330–33, 333 n.2, 335 nn.36,55–59, 336 nn.60,66,70–74,78,80, 344, 351–53, 358–61, 363 nn.24,40,41, 364 nn.71,75,78, 365 nn.79–82, 366 nn.114,116,117, 376, 377, 386 nn.35,44,49, 387 nn.53,56, 388 n.85, 406–8, 410, 411, 413, 415–18, 423 nn.8–10,13, 424 nn.21,24,25, 430–39, 443 nn.15,16,19,20, 450, 451, 453, 458, 462, 465, 475, 505, 506, 509, 510 n.11, 523, 563, 566, 570, 574, 577, 586, 587 nn.3,8,11

McCue, James, II: 364 n.69, 365 nn.87–89, 366 n.115
McDermott, Brian, I: 428 n.5, 430 nn.45,47, 464 n.22
Macedonius, I: 47
McGill, Arthur, I: 445 n.22
McInerny, Ralph, I: 190 n.2
MacIntyre, Alisdair, I: 227 n.19
McIntyre, John, II: 42 n.25
MacKinnon, D. M., I: 297, 318 n.1; II: 75, 77 n.11
Macquarrie, John, I: 27 n.9, 84, 153, 160 n.63, 444 n.7
McSorley, Harry, II: 141 n.33, 313 n.19
Madden, Arthur, I: 225 nn.2,6
Madison, Gary, I: 264 n.25
Maier, Jean-Louis, I: 159 nn.24,35
Mann, Ulrich, I: 131 nn.1,2
Manson, T. W., II: 240 n.3
Mao Tse-tung, II: 548–50, 554 nn.15,16
Marcellus of Ancyra, I: 128, 134 n.60
Marcion, I: 277, 305, 499
Mark, II: 13, 116, 122 nn.7,13, 144, 206, 317, 343, 347, 348, 362 n.18, 375, 494, 495

Markus, R. A., I: 225 n.4
Martha of Bethany, II: 496
Martin-Achard, Robert, I: 444 n.4
Marx, Karl, I: 14, 15, 24, 42, 251–53, 262 nn.7–9, 263 n.15, 537, 540; II: 475, 509, 511 n.23, 545, 546, 548
Marx, Werner, I: 131 n.8, 158 n.6, 178 n.7, 190 n.3
Marxsen, Willi, I: 489, 490, 495 nn.15,16; II: 362 n.18, 364 n.52
Mary the Virgin, I: 504, 505, 522, 533, 534, 546, 547; II: 115, 307
Mascall, Eric, I: 247 n.25
Matthew the Evangelist, II: 115, 116, 144, 263, 284, 317, 343, 347, 348, 369, 370, 446, 447, 493, 495, 514
Maximus the Confessor, I: 412
Mayr, Franz, I: 161 n.75
Melanchthon, Philip, I: 36, 37, 63, 67, 149, 178 n.31, 418, 509, 536, 542 n.14; II: 130–33, 230, 239, 275, 276, 388 n.88, 415, 428, 432, 438, 448
Melito of Sardis, I: 132 nn.13,15, 188, 191 n.16
Menninger, Karl, I: 365 n.2
Merleau-Ponty, Maurice, I: 252, 263 n.13
Meslin, Michel, I: 134 nn.61,67
Metz, Johann Baptist, I: 42, 569 n.11
Meyendorff, John, I: 225 n.7, 406 n.44, 445 n.17; II: 178 n.21
Micah, II: 489
Michel, A., I: 159 n.37
Miller, Arthur, I: 325
Miller, Perry, II: 164 n.26
Mitchell, Basil, I: 221, 227 n.20
Mitchell, Leonel, II: 336 n.66
Mitchell, Nathan, II: 336 nn.64,65, 363 nn.27,36, 336 n.126, 385 n.8
Moberly, R. C., II: 44 n.59, 45 n.67
Moltmann, Jürgen, I: 24, 26 n.1, 17 n.16, 42, 313, 320 n.37, 336, 340 n.31, 382 n.48, 455, 463 n.16,18, 464 n.21, 494 n.6; II: 9 nn.10,11, 74, 77 n.9, 190, 191, 201 nn.4,5,6, 202 n.12, 268 n.2, 480 n.1, 481, 524–26, 538 nn.23,24,25, 539 nn.26,27,28,29,30, 581, 587 n.10
Monod, Jacques, I: 355
Montague, Ashley, I: 405 n.21
Montanus, II: 154, 506–8
Moody, Raymond, II: 564, 587 n.1
Moore, Edward Caldwell, I: 43 n.3
Morenz, S., II: 385 n.2
Moses, I: 88, 121, 205, 552, 565; II: 53, 110, 111, 122 n.11, 235, 271, 285, 431, 483, 490
Moule, C. F. D., I: 160 n.59, 489, 495 n.14
Mowinckel, Sigmund, II: 121 n.1
Muehlenberg, Ekkehard, I: 158 n.18, 418, 419, 429 nn.22,24
Münzer, Thomas, I: 461, 464 n.34; II: 509, 511 n.20
Murphy, T. Austin, I: 210 n.5, 264 n.27; II: 240 nn.11,12
Murray, John, I: 225 n.7

INDEXES

Nathan, II: 488
Neander, Augustus, I: 430 n.38
Negri, Antonio, I: 252, 263 n.12
Nestorius, I: 47, 503–5, 515 n.13
Neuenheuser, B., II: 314 nn.44,48, 334 n.23, 335 nn.37,39,41
Neve, J. L., I: 43 n.3
Neville, Robert, I: 304, 319 nn.5,20, 320 nn.33,46, 321 n.51
Nicholas of Cusa, I: 206
Niebuhr, H. Richard, I: 469, 471 n.1; II: 9 n.3, 221 n.2, 235, 240 n.16, 270, 478, 587 n.4
Niebuhr, Reinhold, I: 331, 368, 371, 379, 380 n.7, 383 nn.55,59, 406 n.49
Nielsen, Kai, I: 234, 246 n.15, 248 n.31
Niemöller, Martin, I: 567
Nietzsche, Friedrich, II: 253, 416, 479
Nilsson, Martin, I: 131 n.1, 132 n.10
Noah, I; 121, 382 n.49; II: 281
Nock, A. D., I: 211 n.19
Norris, R. A., Jr., I: 211 n.25, 535, 542 n.12
Novatian, I: 132 n.33; II: 422 n.6
Nygren, Anders, I: 41, 423, 429 n.29
Nygren, Gotthard, II: 140 n.8

Oberman, Heiko, I: 226 n.11, 416, 429 n.13
O'Connor, D. J., I: 247 n.19
Oecolampadius, II: 366 n.120
Ogden, Schubert, I: 42, 178 n.15, 308, 319 n.6
Origen, I: 13, 30, 31, 69, 109, 113 n.25, 122–26, 128, 130, 133 n.41, 134 n.58, 135, 137, 158 n.1, 215, 225 n.4, 305, 334, 343, 344, 391, 401, 407 n.53, 411, 412, 553, 555; II: 20, 177 n.2, 323, 575, 576, 587 nn.6,7
Ott, Heinrich, I: 388, 404 n.11
Otto, Rudolf, II: 34, 45 n.76, 187, 201 n.1
Outka, Gene, I: 264 n.31
Ownes, Joseph, I: 158 n.6

Pahl, Irmgard, II: 178 n.18, 362 nn.7,8
Pannenberg, Wolfhart, I: 14, 26 n.7, 27 nn.8,12, 42, 50, 60 nn.17,18, 78 n.11, 132 nn.12,17, 177 n.3, 178 n.20, 191 n.4, 201, 205, 210 nn.3,6, 211 n.17, 223, 225 n.4, 226 nn.10,13, 227 n.31, 261, 262 n.1, 264 n.30, 304, 319 n.20, 380 n.6, 392, 405 n.24, 481 nn.2,4, 542 n.4, 546, 549, 556 nn.5–7,11; II: 245, 247 nn.5,6, 259, 260, 268 nn.10,11, 516, 517, 538 nn.5–7
Pardington, G. Palmer, III, II: 178 n.14
Parmenides, I: 141
Pascal, Blaise, I: 369, 381 n.17, 428, 431 n.50. II: 467
Paul, I: 29, 47, 61, 64, 72, 73, 89, 92, 93, 106, 108, 112 n.17, 201, 242, 270, 289–93, 337, 338, 367, 369, 372, 374, 377, 381 n.18, 385, 388, 389, 427, 434, 437, 448, 450–52, 454, 455, 458, 460, 463 n.10, 525, 545, 546; II: 12, 14, 17–19, 53, 55, 62 n.9, 84, 85, 96, 116–19, 123 nn.28–30, 126, 127, 140 n.7, 145, 151, 204, 205, 208, 214, 229, 239, 260, 264, 266, 270–72, 274, 292, 305, 315, 320, 321,
323, 329, 337, 338, 340, 345–48, 368, 369, 378, 379, 380, 396, 400–402, 410–18, 423 n.16, 445–47, 458, 462, 463, 482, 497–99, 502, 514, 518, 519, 527, 546, 555, 557–59, 562, 566–69, 575, 577, 578, 580, 583, 585
Paul, Jean, II: 479
Paul, Robert, II: 44 n.59, 46 n.97
Paul of Samosata, I: 120, 500, 501
Peacocke, Arthur, I: 320 n.41, 355, 357 n.2
Pedersen, Johannes, I: 178 n.25
Pegis, Anton, I: 247 n.24
Pelagius, I: 32, 335, 413, 424, 436, 502; II: 405
Pelikan, Jaroslav, I: 43 n.3, 112 n.22, 132 nn.14,18, 191 n.20, 211 n.13, 226 n.7, 281, 294 n.11, 311, 320 n.34, 343, 351 n.7, 383 n.60, 411, 412, 414, 428 n.4, 429 n.10, 430 nn.35,37; II: 163 n.19, 220 n.1, 221 n.5, 443 n.7
Pellauer, David, I: 264 n.25
Penner, Hans, I: 248 n.33
Perrin, Norman, II: 491, 499 n.3
Peschke, Erhard, II: 140 n.17
Peter, I: 47, 64, 292, 473, 560, 562; II: 12, 53, 55, 58, 116, 206, 208, 210, 230, 260, 277, 319, 411, 575
Peter Lombard, I: 34, 86 n.2, 143–45, 159 n.24, 160 n.48, 477; II: 314 n.52
Peters, Albrecht, I: 380 n.8, 381 n.23, 382 n.48; II: 336 n.74
Peters, R. S., I: 235, 247 n.18
Peterson, Erik, I: 471 n.7
Pfleiderer, Otto, II: 506, 510 n.13
Pfnür, Vinzenz, II: 140 n.23, 313 n.21
Phipps, William, I: 526 n.5
Pilate, Pontius, I: 561; II: 40, 61, 81, 94, 260, 455
Pius XII, II: 215, 388 n.79
Plantinga, Alvin, I: 288 n.32
Plato, I: 10, 31, 128, 132 n.11, 147, 152, 165, 173, 177 n.2, 214, 215, 226 n.8, 300, 307, 309, 333; II: 167, 403, 534, 565, 575
Plotinus, I: 124, 216; II: 403
Polanyi, Michael, II: 212 n.31
Polycarp of Smyrna, I: 410
Popper, Karl, I: 250, 251, 262 n.4
Porter, J. R., I: 430 n.32
Poschman, Bernhard, II: 163 n.7
Powell, Douglas, II: 163 n.19
Praxeas, I: 122
Prenter, Regin, I: xvii, 50, 86 n.4, 204, 211 n.16, 303, 319 n.18, 346, 352 nn.21,23, 373, 381 n.32; II: 140 n.14
Prestige, G. L., I: 212 n.32
Prosper of Aquitaine, I: 414
Pummer, Richard, I: 248 n.35

Quell, Gottfried, I: 373, 381 n.33
Quenstedt, Johann, I: 11, 37, 345, 554; II: 43 n.38, 140 n.15

Radakrishnan, Servapali, I: 178 n.22, 245
Radbertus, Paschasius, II: 306, 307

INDEXES

Rademacher, Arnold, II: 215
Rahner, Karl, I: 14, 26 n.6, 42, 53, 60 n.20, 84, 86 n.5, 154, 161 n.72, 235, 247 n.19, 430 n.42, 515 n.31, 558, 559; II: 141 n.36, 215, 387 n.50, 566, 587 n.2
Raitt, Jill, II: 365 n.105, 366 n.108
Ramsey, I. T., I: 42
Rank, Otto, II: 464
Ranke, Leopold von, I: 20
Rashdall, Hastings, II: 44 n.59
Ratramnus of Corbie, II: 307
Ratschow, Carl Heinz, I: 43 n.3
Rauschenbusch, Walter, II: 475-76, 506, 510 nn.13,14, 524
Raven, Charles, I: 351 n.6, 515 n.10
Reese, William, I: 210 n.2, 321 n.49, 404 n.3
Reichenbach, Hans, II: 178 n.16
Reimarus, Hermann, I: 517; II: 475
Reinhard, Lukas, I: 29
Reu, J. M., II: 140 n.18
Reuchlin, Jacob, I: 63
Reumann, John, I: 275, 277, 294 nn.1,4,5,14
Rewak, W. J., I: 445 nn.10,16
Richardson, Cyril, I: 150, 160 n.57
Ricoeur, Paul, 263 n.25, 371, 373, 374, 379, 380 nn.1,14, 381 nn.15,16,25,32, 382 nn.35,45, 383 n.58, 385, 390, 391, 403, 404 n.2, 405 n.18, 406 n.49, 410, 424, 428 n.2, 430 nn.34,47, 439, 445 n.14, 453, 463 nn.15,17
Riesenfeld, Harald, II: 268 n.17
Riley, Hugh, II: 334 n.29
Ringgren, Helmer, I: 281, 294 n.12
Ritschl, Albrecht, I: 40, 73, 347, 350, 470, 483, 484, 535; II: 26, 28, 29-31, 33, 44 nn.47,48,50-54, 45 n.77, 98, 240 n.10, 475, 506
Ritschl, Dietrich, II: 162 n.3
Ritter, Adolf, I: 134 nn.57,63,65-68
Roberts, Preston, I: 325, 339 n.3
Robespierre, II: 154
Robinson, H. Wheeler, I: 423, 424, 430 n.31
Robinson, J. Armitage, I: 132 n.32, 308
Robinson, James, I: 494 n.5
Rodgers, John, II: 45 n.77
Rodgerson, J. W., I: 430 n.33
Rondet, Henri, I: 429 n.11
Rosenstock-Heussy, Eugen, II: 537, 539 n.50
Rouët, M. J. de Journal, I: 134 n.58
Rousseau, Jean-Jacques, II: 154, 155, 164 n.24
Roy, Olivier du, 159 nn.21,32,33
Ruether Rosemary, I: 425, 430 n.41
Ruiz, Jóse, I: 368
Russell, Bertrand, I: 250

Sabellius, I: 120, 500, 514 n.3
Sabourin, L., I: 383 n.60
Samuel, II: 111, 563
Santmire, H. Paul, I: 406 n.45, 444 n.7
Sartre, Jean-Paul, I: 250, 253, 263 n.14, 425, 430 n.39, II: 530, 542, 543, 554 nn.4,5
Saul, II: 111, 431, 563
Savarin, William, II: 164 n.29

Schaeder, Erich, II: 108 n.3
Schäfer, R., II: 44 nn.49,55,56
Schelling, Friedrich, I: 14, 41, 518, 537, 540
Schillebeeckx, Edward, II: 215, 314 n.43, 355-57, 364 n.58, 365 nn.98-104, 388 nn.92,94,95-98, 389 n.102
Schiller, Friedrich, I: 232, 246 n.7, 383 n.56; II: 571
Schimmel, Annemarie, I: 243, 248 nn.34,36, 263 nn.23,24
Schindler, Alfred, I: 159 nn.24,29,30
Schlatter, Adolf, I: 40
Schleiermacher, Friedrich, I: 11, 12, 15-17, 21, 26 nn.2,3, 39, 40, 43 n.4, 150-52, 160 n.61, 172, 178 n.28, 206, 211 n.23, 218, 253, 254, 263 nn.16,17, 303, 304, 310, 317, 319 nn.21-23, 331, 347, 382 n.43, 394, 400, 405 n.31, 406 n.47, 452, 463 n.14, 470, 483, 502, 504, 511-13, 514 n.3, 515 nn.9,27,28, 517, 518, 521, 536; II: 26-31, 44 nn.45,46, 45 n.77, 98, 135, 141 n.29, 162 n.1, 258, 268 n.7, 430
Schlette, H. R., I: 568 n.11
Schlier, Heinrich, I: 60 n.11
Schlink, Edmund, I: 50, 60 nn.15,16, 422, 429 nn.27,28, 542 n.10
Schmaus, Michael, I: 29, 59 n.2, 159 n.26
Schmid, Heinrich, I: 43 n.3, 78 nn.6,9, 346, 352 nn.13,14, 17-19, 405 n.19, 445 n.11, 515 n.20; II: 43 nn.35,36,40, 140 n.16, 185, 185 n.2, 426, 428, 442 n.4, 443 nn.8,9
Schmidt, Hans-Christoph, II: 122 n.4
Schmidt, Karl, II: 221 n.4
Schmidt, M., I: 160 n.55
Schmitals, Walter, I: 294 nn.15,16
Schmitz-Moorman, Karl, I: 455, 464 n.22
Schnackenburg, Rudolph, II: 221 nn.9,10
Schoonenberg, Piet, I: 425, 426, 430 nn.40,43
Schopenhauer, Arthur, I: 173, 178 n.30
Schrange, Wolfgang, II: 112 nn.10-13
Schultz, Robert, I: 406 n.41, 429 nn.20,23
Schwarz, Hans, II: 268 n.16, 480 n.1, 510 n.17
Schweitzer, Albert, I: 40, 72, 484, 494 n.3, 511, 513, 515 n.24, 518, 519; II: 476, 477, 480 n.2, 491, 501, 502, 510 n.1, 516, 520
Schweizer, Alexander, I: 517
Schweizer, Eduard, II: 123 n.35, 363 n.49
Scott, Nathan, Jr., I: 323, 339 n.1
Scroggs, Robin, I: 444 n.3
Searle, John, I: 234, 247 n.17
Seeberg, Reinhold, I: 43 n.3, 212 n.36
Segundo, Juan, I: 313, 320 n.38, 348, 352 n.30, 406 n.48; II: 238, 241 nn.20,21, 527
Selle, Eugene Te, I: 471 n.3
Sellers, R. V., I: 514 nn.1,5, 515 n.15
Semler, Johann, II: 286
Senn, Frank, II: 334 n.28
Servetus, Michael, I: 150
Shakespeare, William, I: 251
Sheehan, Thomas, I: 263 n.12
Sherry, Patrick, I: 221, 222, 227 nn.23,25
Siggins, Ian, I: 515 n.19, 526 nn.2,7, 542 nn.8,9, 556 n.2

599

INDEXES

Simon, II: 440
Sittler, Joseph, I: 292, 294 n.19
Smedt, Charles de, II: 215
Smith, John, I: 217, 226 n.14
Socinus, Faustus, II: 6, 43 n.31
Socrates, I: 118, 136, 144, 173, 209; II: 17
Soelle, Dorothee, I: 380 n.13, 382 n.40, 443, 444, 445 n.33, 461, 464 nn.33–35, 495 n.20, 567
Sohm, Rudolf, II: 215
Soleri, Paulo, II: 532
Solomon (king), I: 280, 293, 342, 345
Solomon (pseudo), I: 372, 405 n.15
Sophocles, I: 131 n.3
Sparn, Walter, II: 366 n.124
Spencer, Herbert, II: 477
Spinoza, Baruch, I: 218, 237, 247 n.20
Sponheim, Paul, I: 211 n.23, 320 nn.47,48
Stählin, Gustav, I: 374, 377, 382 nn.36,51
Stalder, Kurt, II: 123 nn.29,30, 140 n.7
Stavins, Ralph, II: 164 n.25
Steiner, George, I: 250, 251, 262 nn.2,3,5
Steininger, Hans, I: 248 n.38, 254, 263 n.18
Stendahl, Krister, I: 455, 464 n.20
Stephen, I: 20
Strauss, David Friedrich, I: 73, 517, 540
Strauss, Gerhard, II: 313 nn.27,31
Strawson, P. F., I: 178 n.19, 228 n.32
Strigel, Victor, I: 418, 419
Stuart, Moses, I: 514 n.3
Stuhlmacher, Peter, I: 97 n.8
Stuhlmüller, Carroll, I: 294 n.13
Suarez, Francisco, I: 227 n.27
Swinburne, Richard, I: 321 n.51

Tatian, I: 132 n.31
Taylor, Charles, II: 177 n.8
Teilhard de Chardin, Pierre, I: 42, 292, 294 n.19, 319 n.12, 326, 335, 339 n.5, 351 n.6, 392, 403, 405 n.22, 407 n.56; II: 173, 178 n.17, 193, 201 n.7, 238, 530–32, 534, 539 nn.40,41, 561, 581
Tennant, Frederick, I: 247 n.27, 382 n.43, 406 n.48, 410, 411, 413, 428 nn.3,6, 440, 445 nn.23,25,26, 463 n.11
Terrien, Samuel, I: 210 n.4
Tertullian, I: 13, 32, 122, 123, 128, 129, 132 n.19, 142, 161 n.73, 203, 204, 206, 211 n.13, 304, 310, 334, 412, 413, 425, 519; II: 37, 49, 125, 139 n.1, 177 n.2, 230, 291, 386 n.16, 503, 504, 507, 510 nn.7,8
Tetzel, Johann, II: 577
Theodore de Bèze, II: 357
Theodore of Mopsuestia, I: 503
Theodosius I, I: 130, 135
Theophilus of Antioch, I: 120, 132 nn.13,15,26, 310; II: 166, 177 n.1
Thielicke, Helmut, I: 86 n.4, 216, 226 n.9, 436, 445 n.15
Thomasius, Gottfried, I: 510
Tiililä, Osmo, II: 9 n.5, 43 n.32, 46 n.96, 62 n.6
Tillich, Paul, I: xvii, xviii, 6, 12, 14, 16, 20, 26 n.4, 27 nn.10,13, 41, 42, 43 n.3, 75, 78 n.18, 84, 153, 160 n.63, 178 n.24, 199, 203, 210 n.3, 211 n.10, 213–15, 219, 225 nn.1,3, 226 n.17, 228 n.34, 239, 293, 294 n.20, 306, 310, 313, 319 n.24, 320 nn.32,39,40, 328, 329, 331, 339 nn.8,9, 346, 347, 352 nn.22,26, 368, 371, 380 nn.8,10, 389, 391, 392, 397, 404 n.12, 405 n.24, 406 nn.38,46, 452, 463 n.14, 470, 512, 513, 515 n.30, 540, 542 nn.2,17, 558, 561, 562; II: 108 n.3, 199, 202 nn.16–18, 221 n.6, 258, 259, 268 nn.4,5, 556
Timothy, II: 378, 379
Tindal, Matthew, I: 211 n.2
Titus, II: 378, 379
Toffler, Alvin, II: 552, 554 nn.19,20
Toland, John, I: 211 n.22
Torrance, Thomas, I: 191 n.10, 304, 319 n.20
Torres, Camilo, II: 237
Toulmin, Stephen, I: 221, 227 n.21
Towner, W. Sibley, I: 382 n.47, 442, 443, 445 nn.30–32
Trible, Phyllis, I: 340 n.33
Trillhaas, Wolfgang, I: 43 n.1; II: 258, 268 n.6
Troeltsch, Ernst, I: 40
Troisfontaines, R., I: 434
Trooster, S., I: 444 nn.5,8
Tuveson, Robert, II: 163 nn.18

Underhill, Evelyn, I: 179 n.37

Vaihinger, Hans, I: 210 n.1
Vandervelde, G., I: 429 nn.11,12; 464 nn.25,26
Vanneste, Alfred, I: 428 n.5, 430 n.47
Virgil, I: 312
Voegelin, Eric, I: 245, 248 nn.42,43, 255, 263 n.20
Vogelsang, E., II: 62 n.1
Voltaire, Francoise-Marie, II: 92
Von Rad, Gerhard, I: 41, 96 n.2, 97 nn.4,6,20, 368, 376, 378, 380 nn.4,5,9, 382 nn.34,47,49, 383 n.53, 397, 405 nn.15,25, 406 nn.37,39, 407 nn.50,52, 433, 435, 444 nn.1,2, 445 nn.12,29, 448, 450, 461, 463 nn.3,9,12, 464 n.36; II: 122 nn.5–8, 499 n.2
Vööbus, Arthur, I: 335, 340 n.28
Vorgrimler, Herbert, II: 385 nn.7,14, 386 nn.15,17,22,23,28,30,43, 387 nn.52,55
Vriezen, Theodore, II: 482, 483, 499 n.1

Walker, Williston, I: 404 n.14
Wand, J. W. C., II: 7, 9 nn.6,7
Watt, A. J., I: 247 n.18
Watts, Alan, II: 106
Wayman, Alex, I: 244, 248 n.39
Weber, Hans, II: 43 nn.28,33,35, 44 n.44, 141 n.37
Weger, K. H., I: 430 n.42
Weigel, Gustave, I: 225 nn.2,6
Weiss, Johannes, I: 484, 494 nn.2,4
Weizsäcker, Carl von, I: 351 n.4
Welch, Claude, I: 84, 86 n.5, 515 n.23
Wendel, Francois, I: 212 n.27, 226 n.15, 429 n.21

Wendland, H. D., II: 385 n.3
Wengst, Klaus, I: 112 n.9
Werner, Martin, I: 113 nn.23,26; II: 460 n.1, 501, 502, 510 n.2, 514
Wesley, John, I: 460
Westermann, Claus, I: 211 n.14, 278, 279, 294 nn.2–10, 330–33, 337, 340 nn.12–14, 393, 395, 397, 401, 405 n.28, 406 nn.33,43, 407 n.51, 434, 444 n.6, 462 n.1, 463 n.4; II: 122 nn.10,12
Westhelle, Vitor, I: 352 n.27; II: 241 nn.17–21
White, Lynn, I: 339 n.4
Whitehead, Alfred, I: 14, 15, 42, 167, 227 n.30, 238, 247 n.26, 315–17, 319 n.6, 320 n.45, 449, 463 n.6, 537; II: 532, 533
Wilamowitz-Moellendorf, Ulrich von, I: 131 n.1
Wilken, Robert, I: 112 n.14, 568 n.1; II: 211, 221 n.7
William of Ockham, I: 34, 206
Williams, Colin, II: 240 n.15
Williams, George, I: 429 n.17, 464 n.24
Williams, N. P., I: 381 n.31, 400, 404 n.13, 406 n.46
Williams, Sam, II: 42 nn.2,3,4,6
Wingren, Gustaf, I: 212 n.28, 264 n.28, 273 n.4, 303, 319 n.17, 448, 459, 463 n.5, 464 n.28, 526 n.9; II: 123 n.47, 240 n.9
Winkler, Gabriele, II: 335 n.30
Wisløf, Carl, II: 62 n.11, 63 nn.16–18,28
Wittgenstein, Ludwig, I: 14, 15, 24, 42, 221, 224, 537
Wolff, Hans, I: 444 n.1, 445 n.19
Wolfson, Henry, I: 43 n.3, 97 n.14, 514 n.1, 515 nn.11,14,16
Woude, A. S. van der, II: 499 n.2
Wurthwein, E., I: 178 n.21

Yerkes, James, I: 542 n.15
Young, Francis, I: 404 n.4; II: 82, 83, 98 nn.2,3, 99 nn.4,5

Zander, Leon, II: 178 nn.21,28
Zechariah, II: 489
Zeno, II: 260
Zerubbabel, II: 489
Zimany, Roland, I: 211 n.11
Zimmerli, Walther, I: 97 nn.3,5, 112 nn.4–7; II: 141 n.32, 163 n.13
Zoroaster, II: 484, 485
Zosimus I, I: 435
Zwingli, Ulrich, I: 64, 65, 507, 553; II: 358, 374, 566

Index of Subjects

The particular unity and variety of this work prohibited attempts to make an index on strictly consistent principles. Some of the following entries list instances of terms or sets of terms; others are guides to subjects; and others mix these procedures. Choices of entries and of the principles of various entries were dictated mostly by the hope of practical utility. Moreover, readers should not depend only on the index, but should make the fullest use of the table of contents. Listings of whole *loci*, or chapters, appear in bold.

Absurd, absurdity, I: 42, 85, 87, 88, 171, 270, 271, 325; II: 189, 397, 467, 543
Accidents, I: 142, 419; II: 356, 436
Act, action, activity, **10**; I: 25, 54, 57, 87, 90, 92, 101, 120, 140, 152, 166, 173, 185, 199–205, 213, 215, 218, 223, 224, 229–31, 235, 236, 239, 243, 255, 257, 258, 269, 270, 272, 280, 281, 288, 293, 299, 300, 306, 307, 312, 313, 326–28, 333, 334, 343, 345–48, 350, 363, 365, 367, 371, 375, 376, 378, 379, 388, 391, 392, 398, 399, 436, 439, 440, 448, 453, 474, 479, 483, 486, 492, 524, 529, 534, 535, 538, 540, 550, 554, 568; II: 6, 11, 12, 15, 17, 27, 30, 33–37, 39, 41, 53, 60, 72 n.10, 79, 83, 110, 111, 117, 118, 126, 129, 131, 135, 136, 141 nn.34,35, 150, 156, 166, 168, 169, 170, 175, 191, 193, 195–97, 205, 206, 210, 211, 213, 220, 228, 229, 231–33, 235, 238, 246, 394, 395, 397, 399–401, 404, 407, 409, 410, 412, 414, 426, 427, 429–32, 434, 439, 445, 458, 488, 491, 492, 494, 525, 528, 531, 533, 537, 557, 558–60, 575, 578, 580
Adam, I: 121, 243, 279, 284, 291, 292, 328, 332, 335, 346, 365, 380 n.9, 385, 388, 394, 395, 399, 401, 403, 410, 411, 413, 414–16, 420–23, 425–27, 435, 436, 444 n.4, 448, 450, 451, 453, 455, 520, 525, 564; II: 20, 25, 37, 40, 55, 57, 96, 278, 330, 332, 395, 409, 411, 414, 419, 420, 438, 439, 453, 463, 468, 482, 557, 558, 562, 563, 575
Adiaphora, II: 238–40
Adoptionism, I: 501, 503, 506, 507, 514, 531, 546
Alexandria, School of, I: 13, 30, 77, 125, 128, 400, 501, 504, 508, 518
Alienation, I: 176, 199, 331, 374, 388, 548; II: 24, 35, 50, 66–69, 73, 91, 120, 128, 146, 160, 168, 171, 175, 238, 271, 280, 284, 400, 421, 528, 541, 547, 562, 570, 585, 586

Amyraldism, I: 37
Anabaptism, I: 417, 456; II: 153, 206
Analogy, I: 23, 94, 95, 118, 144, 145, 151, 182, 206, 214–17, 227 n.27, 239, 331, 343, 354, 520, 521, 533, 550, 551; II: 41, 139 n.4, 214, 264, 265, 285, 308, 350, 357, 371, 486, 487, 492, 496, 533, 555, 557, 566–68, 578
Angels, I: 33, 49, 65, 109, 112 n.15, 291, 344, 372, 394, 402, 563, 572, 575, 581; II: 21, 51, 61, 85, 91, 154, 174, 503, 520, 564, 567, 672, 575, 581
Anglicanism, II: 195, 230, 236, 351
Anhypostasia, I: 506
Antichrist, II: 505, 508
Anticipation, I: 19. 26, 46, 89, 104, 108, 165, 205, 566, 568; II: 70, 109, 110, 117, 244, 245, 260, 266, 283, 284, 319, 344, 345, 411, 447, 448, 457, 481, 493, 515, 516, 517, 523, 526, 545–47, 558, 560, 563, 573
Antinomianism, I: 305; II: 271, 445–51, 467, 468, 469 n.7
Antioch, School of, I: 412, 501, 503, 518; II: 20
Apocalypticism, I: 287, 288, 342, 443, 484, 487, 529; II: 13, 19
Apollinarianism, I: 502–4, 513
Apologetics, **1,1**; I: 120–23, 213, 221, 260–62, 316, 364, 479; II: 171
Apologists, I: 10, 12, 13, 119, 120, 122, 125, 141, 331; II: 20, 166, 323
Apology of the Augsburg Confession, I: 394, 430 n.44; II: 130, 131, 133, 184, 276, 312 n.10, 314 n.49, 382, 386 nn.31,36,37–40,42,46, 388 nn.87,88, 423 n.18
Apostles, apostolicity, I: 21, 23, 25, 31, 45, 50, 55, 62, 66, 75, 77, 469, 473, 476, 478, 480, 492, 521, 523, 527, 559, 566; II: 149, 152, 154, 203, 210–12, 217–20, 230, 231, 253, 260, 294, 316, 318, 333 n.6, 337, 339, 345, 368, 375, 376, 378–81

INDEXES

Apostles' Creed, I: 46, 110, 111, 363, 528, 529, 546, 548; II: 124 nn.50,51, 280, 319, 566, 567, 579
Apostolic Constitutions, II: 174
Arianism, I: 124, 126–30, 133 n.47, 148, 149, 151, 188, 299, 500–503, 513, 545; II: 148
Aristotelianism, I: 13, 14, 35, 38, 125, 128, 214, 216, 217, 536; II: 177 n.9
Arles, Council of, II: 313 n.23
Arminianism, I: 37; II: 137, 299
Ascension, I: 528, 529, 552, 553, 555, 564, 585; II: 144, 355, 357, 359, 366 n.118, 380, 496
Athanasian Creed, I: 71, 148, 149
Atheism, I: 42, 170, 203, 270, 369, 476, 567; II: 135, 397, 418, 419, 467
Atonement, **7**; I: 57, 197, 387, 434, 452–54, 548; II: 131, 576; theories of, I: 197, 452–54; II: 6, 7, 19–41, 47–50, 80–82, 88, 91, 95–98
Attributes of God, **2.6**; I: 67, 85, 86, 95, 103, 117–19, 125, 140, 142, 146–48, 157, 166, 237, 239, 301, 499, 501, 504, 507–10, 514, 530–36, 553, 554; II: 26, 28, 30, 32, 38, 48, 54, 92, 126, 160, 161, 204, 206, 210, 212, 214, 237, 258, 259
Augsburg Confession, I: xviii, 37, 62, 332, 380 n.3, 385, 404 n.1, 405 nn.16,30, 449; II: 5, 9 n.2, 130, 133, 140 n.21, 153, 163 n.17, 184, 225, 228, 233, 234, 267, 276, 278, 295, 296, 313 n.16, 314 n.50, 332, 336 n.76, 351, 353, 365 n.88, 382, 386 nn.34,41, 423 n.7, 509, 511 n.21, 576
Augustinianism, I: 35, 36, 63, 142, 147, 148, 215, 412–15, 419, 420, 422, 447; II: 24, 42 n.22, 126, 129, 307, 325, 328, 374, 433
Authority, I: 25, 26, 30, 35, 38, 45, 47, 48, 49, 51, 55, 61, 62, 64–70, 72, 74, 75, 89, 95, 96, 150, 367, 449, 477, 480, 555; II: 93, 94, 121, 130, 133, 148, 150, 154, 157, 161, 205, 218, 219, 225, 230, 231, 263, 264, 267, 278, 282, 283, 293–98, 304, 309, 337, 340, 347, 357, 370, 378–82, 406, 458, 459, 495, 508, 579, 581
Autonomy, I: 25, 303, 307, 393, 395, 396; II: 468

Baptism, **10.3–6**; I: 36, 58, 91–93, 95, 97 nn.17,23, 110, 111, 122, 123, 142, 177, 291, 379, 383 n.60, 385, 412, 413, 417, 430 n.36, 456–58, 461, 464 n.23, 546, 558; II: 115–18, 120, 121, 124 n.50, 125, 134, 157, 159, 214, 223, 231, 232, 263, 264, 266, 276, 278, 396, 402, 410, 420, 476, 498, 518, 555, 562, 563, 566, 573
Baptist, II: 308, 325, 327
Barmen Declaration, I: 52
Beauty, I: 13, 19, 203, 230, 231–33, 235, 263 n.15, 329, 331; II: 165, 166, 173–77, 415, 427, 565, 586
Being, **2.3–5**; I: 17–19, 34, 56, 57, 85, 101, 102, 107, 109, 184, 189, 214, 217, 219, 225 nn.4, 234, 241, 255, 312, 331, 370, 371, 393, 395, 402, 415, 435, 438, 447, 448, 450, 459,
463 n.4, 486, 487, 503, 512, 513, 523, 524, 525, 527, 528, 530, 531, 532, 534, 535, 539, 540, 541, 556, 560, 562; II: 6, 20, 27, 50, 55, 105–7, 123 n.49, 145, 160, 161, 167, 188–92, 194, 195, 200, 204–6, 212, 216–21, 223, 224, 229, 232, 236, 259, 266, 306, 323, 360, 402, 403, 409, 411, 417, 437, 449, 451, 452, 455, 459, 463, 464, 465, 468, 479, 526, 531, 537, 541–43, 546–48, 558, 561, 562, 564–66
Bible, I: 21, 22, 26, 30, 38, 41, 51, 56, 62–77, 95, 96, 101, 152, 156, 169, 172, 173, 176, 276, 277, 282, 292, 314, 315, 342, 393, 425, 475, 477, 484, 501, 518, 527, 532, 540, 563, 565; II: 6, 11, 19, 129, 136, 154, 162, 166, 167, 171, 258–60, 266, 269, 275, 282, 287, 298, 299, 301, 302, 308, 310, 318, 321, 325, 330, 341, 342, 354, 356, 357, 359, 368, 421, 475, 522, 527, 528, 558, 562, 563, 566, 575, 576, 585
Black theology, II: 526, 527
Body, I: 30, 94, 108, 174–77, 183, 215, 300, 309, 326, 333–38, 343, 344, 370, 379, 397, 402, 423, 425, 434, 503, 505, 507, 519, 523, 531, 552; II: 107, 119, 145, 161, 162, 232, 295–97, 300, 302, 304–6, 308, 309, 326, 343, 347, 348, 352, 356–59, 375, 425, 481, 503, 559, 561, 563, 565–70, 576, 586
Body of Christ, I: 23, 177, 379, 503, 505, 507, 519, 523, 531, 552, 554; II: 51, 56, 59, 90, 91, 97, 98, 162, 199, 204, 212–15, 225, 232, 235, 295, 300, 305–9, 311, 314 nn.46, 319, 320, 329, 342–44, 346, 352–61, 366 n.119, 373, 379, 381, 412, 458, 559, 560
Buddhism, I: 243, 244, 254, 565; II: 532, 561

Call (vocation), I: 324, 326, 330, 375, 395, 399, 421, 448, 449, 459, 525, 532, 534, 548; II: 29, 30, 129, 130, 133, 153, 199, 206, 207, 213, 224, 227–31, 236, 245, 262, 384, 428
Calvinism, I: 37, 67, 68, 149, 177, 245, 392, 405 n.19, 506–9; II: 134, 137, 162, 277, 325, 355, 357, 358, 361, 478, 526
Canon, of Scripture, I: 22, 56, 61, 63, 64, 69, 71, 275, 305; II: 154, 212, 219, 293, 294, 316–18, 320, 337, 347, 353, 370, 372, 376, 379, 381, 577
Cappadocia, School of, I: 31, 130, 135–37, 139, 156, 169, 215, 412
Carthage, Council of, I: 385, 414, 424, 430 n.36, 434, 435, 457; I: 149, 154
Catechetics, catechumenate, I: 83, 152; II: 121, 129, 321, 327, 349, 371
Catechisms, I: 52, 83, 152, 302, 373, 380 n.3, 456, 457; II: 184, 276, 278, 280, 313 nn.18,22, 214 n.29, 325, 330, 332, 333 n.2, 335 n.36,55, 336 nn.70–72, 353, 363 n.24, 386 nn.35,44, 454, 363
Categorical supremacy, I: 199–202, 208, 213, 219, 223, 231, 237, 239, 243, 245, 254, 255, 386, 433, 434, 447
Catholic, catholicity, I: 32, 55, 473, 557, 561, 566; II: 121, 148, 203, 207–9, 212, 217, 218,

228, 298, 305, 314 n.40, 318, 353, 382, 422
Chalcedon, Council and Creed of, I: 47, 131, 148, 188, 501, 505–7, 511–14, 515 n.15, 519, 527, 533, 535, 536
Character, as sacramental concept, II: 229, 324, 325, 328, 333, 355, 381, 383
Charism, charismatic, II: 110, 117–19, 121, 127, 139, 148–50, 158, 163 n.5, 226, 228, 229, 315, 319, 329, 367, 378–83, 385, 507
Christ, **6, 7**; I: 47, 48, 51, 71, 72, 74–78, 106, 108–11, 118, 120, 121, 126–29, 155, 168, 173, 177, 182, 184, 186, 188, 198, 201, 223, 255, 270, 275, 289–92, 294, 303–7, 331, 335, 338, 343, 349, 351, 365, 367, 379, 398, 413, 420, 421, 436, 444, 451, 452, 454–56, 458, 461, 462; II: 118–20, 125, 127, 130–33, 135, 137, 138, 141 n.25, 143, 145, 154, 156, 160–62, 170, 172, 173, 175–77, 184, 187–91, 195–97, 200, 204–6, 208, 210–12, 216, 219, 220, 224, 225, 226, 232–35, 244, 259, 260, 262, 264, 266, 267, 272–74, 279, 281, 282, 284, 294, 296, 302, 304–6, 308, 309, 311, 319, 323, 324, 326, 337, 342–44, 346, 348–58, 360, 377, 384, 385, 395, 399–404, 408, 410–14, 416–19, 423 n.16, 425–28, 431, 432, 438, 439, 447–49, 451, 453, 454, 456–58, 462, 465, 467, 469, 482, 492, 493, 496, 497, 499, 501–4, 506, 508, 510, 515, 518, 520, 521, 524, 525, 527, 529–31, 533, 556, 558–60, 562, 567, 572, 573, 575–77, 579, 581, 584
Christology, **6, 7**; I: 11, 31, 32, 57, 77, 107, 109, 120, 188, 277, 289, 292, 301, 305, 316, 317; II: 143, 145, 162 n.1, 184, 304, 309, 326, 338, 340, 348, 357, 370, 384, 421, 493, 517
Church, **8.3, 9**; I: viii, 6, 7, 9, 11, 22, 26, 29–37, 40, 43, 45–58, 61–65, 67, 69–72, 75–77, 83, 84, 91–93, 95, 96, 97 n.23, 99, 102, 103, 107–11, 113 n.26, 122, 124, 130, 131, 135, 140–42, 148–51, 157, 177, 181, 187, 200, 202, 203, 210 n.7, 221, 224, 259, 270, 287, 297, 298, 304, 335, 342–44, 378, 379, 396–98, 400, 404 n.14, 410–14, 421, 424, 434–36, 447, 451, 456, 457, 461, 464 n.23, 469, 473–77, 480, 481, 483, 487–94, 497–99, 502–5, 511–14, 527, 530, 534–37, 550–54, 558–61, 563–65, 568; II: 5, 6, 29, 32, 36, 46 n.97, 76, 80, 82, 83, 89, 92, 93, 106, 107, 109, 110, 116, 117, 119–21, 122 n.51, 125, 126, 128, 132, 133, 165, 169, 172, 173, 176, 177, 276, 278, 281, 291–96, 298, 299, 304, 306, 307, 309, 315–18, 321, 322, 324, 326–30, 332, 333, 339, 340–43, 347, 349, 351, 353, 354, 356–59, 361, 368–72, 374–77, 379–92, 384, 397, 399, 405, 406, 409, 410, 414, 422, 447, 448, 457–62, 466–68, 469 n.7, 478, 487, 490, 495, 496, 501–5, 507, 508, 510, 513, 514, 517, 518, 520, 522, 524, 525, 531, 559, 560, 567, 577–79
Circumcision, II: 208, 446, 468
Commandment, commandments, I: 302, 367–69, 435, 459, 479; II: 24, 113, 131, 132, 194, 238, 239, 261, 267, 271, 275, 276, 280,

291, 294–96, 298, 299, 303, 307, 312 n.10, 313 n.14, 315–19, 326, 328, 332, 333 n.2, 336 n.73, 337–44, 354, 368, 370, 375, 376, 379, 381, 382, 399, 414, 415, 417, 419, 445–47, 451, 454, 455, 458, 466
Communication of attributes, I: 499, 501, 507–11, 513, 514, 515 n.21, 530, 532, 533, 539, 541, 542, 552–55; I: 27, 53, 54, 300
Community, I: 23, 46, 49, 50, 51, 55, 57, 95, 106, 137, 155, 232, 235, 252, 269, 270, 280, 281, 286, 292, 298, 323, 364, 365 n.3, 395, 423, 426, 457, 473, 474, 478, 479, 491, 493, 497, 498; II: 11, 26–30, 33, 83, 87, 98, 110, 111, 114, 115, 117, 120, 124 n.51, 126, 138, 143–47, 150–52, 154–56, 158, 159, 165, 166, 168, 173, 174, 176, 183–85, 189, 191, 195, 198, 199, 203–5, 207, 210, 212–15, 218, 225–38, 244, 247, 253, 254, 264, 266, 269, 276–78, 281, 292, 304, 315–19, 327, 330–32, 344–47, 358, 368, 369, 375, 379, 380, 383, 454, 457, 478, 483, 495, 505, 517, 518, 526, 532, 534, 557, 559, 560, 573, 584
Concord, Book of, I: 37, 51, 53, 60 n.19, 65, 78 n.8, 110, 319 nn.14,15, 340 n.29, 419; II: 275
Concord, Formula of, I: 37, 62, 65, 78 n.2, 320 n.40, 336, 372, 418, 419, 459, 461, 506, 508, 509; II: 141 nn.25, 38, 142 nn.40,42, 163 n.15, 238, 239, 241 nn.22,23, 312, 366 n.111, 443 n.5, 460 n.3
Confessing Church, I: 52
Confession, I: 91, 111, 149, 213, 257, 365, 372, 471, 498, 519, 522, 527, 534–38, 553, 561, 562, 564; II: 14, 20, 33, 34, 66, 110, 121, 130, 226, 234, 239, 276–78, 308, 310, 322, 329, 332, 371–74, 407, 408, 557
Confessions, I: 22, 51–54, 65, 224, 363, 373, 402, 474, 505, 506, 519, 527, 534, 536–38, 553, 561, 562, 564; II: 296, 372, 388 nn.85,86
Confirmation, II: 322, 328, 329, 367, 382
Confucianism, I: 243, 244, 256
Conscience, I: 62, 203, 209, 374, 548; II: 17, 32, 33, 55, 59, 86, 195, 270, 271, 295, 325, 331, 373, 398–400, 403–7, 409, 413, 414, 416–19, 421, 422, 423 n.16, 424 nn.21,24, 439, 451, 452, 454, 455, 458, 461, 463, 478, 525, 586
Consciousness, I: 17, 23–25, 39, 49, 51, 76, 144, 145, 152, 163, 170, 171, 173, 206, 207, 218, 231, 251, 255, 304, 316, 335, 343, 371, 375, 392, 394, 400, 452, 505, 506, 510, 512, 518, 520, 522; II: 27, 28, 45 n.75, 59, 112, 128, 159, 167–70, 194, 315, 350, 463, 464, 509, 530, 542, 548, 552, 569
Constantinople, Councils of, I: 47, 111, 503, 506, 507, 533
Conversion, II: 133, 134, 161, 208, 267, 316, 327, 428, 429, 450, 498
Cooperation, I: 323, 325–28, 330, 337, 350; II: 60, 127–29, 141 n.24, 246, 267, 279, 353, 354, 405, 406
Cosmos, cosmology, I: 74, 120, 203, 214, 238,

INDEXES

241, 245, 255, 279, 281, 298, 356, 393, 510, 514, 529, 538, 541, 555; II: 34, 36, 40, 79, 90, 93, 165–68, 171, 173–75, 284, 498, 513, 516, 521, 528–39
Councils, I: 32, 47, 52, 54, 65; II: 148, 154, 355
Covenant, I: 105, 172, 200, 285, 346–48, 367, 398, 439, 448, 458; II: 13, 14, 26, 98, 114, 141 n.32, 152, 155, 206, 213, 214, 232, 261, 264, 272, 325, 338, 346–48, 363 n.35, 400, 419, 486, 487
Creation (New Creation), **4**; I: 10, 20, 34, 56–59, 75, 87, 104, 121, 142, 143, 154, 177, 182, 186, 190, 199, 200, 202, 203, 207, 224, 239, 244, 363, 369, 373, 380 n.9, 385–88, 390, 393–99, 401–3, 404 n.14, 409, 419, 433, 435, 437, 439, 442, 443, 447–49, 453, 455, 462 n.1, 463 n.4, 469, 494, 499, 501, 527, 531, 532, 541, 551, 554, 559, 563; II: 19, 21, 28, 32, 33, 36, 39, 60, 61, 69, 71, 79, 90, 97, 106, 112, 113, 115, 118, 119, 125, 134, 137, 139, 146, 150, 161, 166–70, 175, 187, 188, 190, 191, 206, 210, 212, 216, 224, 232, 235, 236, 239, 243, 245, 246, 261, 262, 265–67, 270, 278, 283, 284, 306, 308, 310, 324, 338, 340, 356, 375, 376, 383, 419, 420, 445, 452, 453, 455–69, 481, 482, 487, 488, 498, 499, 502, 514, 515, 518, 525, 527–29, 531, 536, 537, 546, 555, 557–63, 565–69, 575, 577, 580, 582, 583
Creation: continuing, I: 286, 303, 342, 344, 350; II: 129, 262; from nothing, I: 201–3, 270, 271, 278, 282, 286, 291, 292, 297, 303, 309–13, 316, 317, 321 n.51, 324, 328, 345, 350, 386, 391, 402, 520; II: 59, 76; orders of, I: 346, 347, 448, 449
Creationism, I: 297, 314, 315, 334, 392, 405 n.19, 425
Creator, I: 50, 56, 76, 96, 121, 124, 125, 129, 137, 173, 174, 181, 184, 185, 227 n.27, 238, 270, 272, 275, 276, 278, 281, 282, 284–93, 299–307, 310, 312, 315–18, 323, 324, 326, 327, 336, 338, 343–46, 355, 357, 364, 372, 386, 387, 389, 395, 401, 409, 410, 433, 436, 438, 443, 455, 459, 502, 527, 541; II: 21, 37, 57, 65, 84, 107, 110, 116, 137, 151, 165, 212, 235, 259, 265, 280, 309, 322, 339, 454, 481, 562, 570
Creature, I: 49, 121, 124–27, 129, 137, 144, 154, 171, 172, 179 n.31, 184, 189, 227 n.27, 275, 301, 307, 324, 327, 328, 335–37, 344–46, 354, 355, 364, 379, 385, 387, 388, 392–95, 397–401, 403, 409–22, 433, 435, 438, 455, 459, 501, 502, 510; II: 21, 22, 26, 29, 32, 33, 38, 39, 50, 58, 60, 70, 73, 76, 77 nn.2,10, 79, 106, 107, 112, 118, 120, 121, 126–28, 130, 134–37, 139 nn.4, 167, 175, 227, 246, 259, 324, 331, 339, 452, 460, 465, 469, 503, 533, 559, 576
Creeds, I: 22, 26, 47, 50, 51, 53, 54, 56, 65, 90, 110, 111, 122, 124, 127, 130, 131, 163, 188, 190, 289, 290, 302, 305, 474, 511–13,
519, 529, 530, 536; II: 109, 119–21, 123 n.49, 125, 135, 148, 204, 207, 211, 212, 218, 219, 319, 322, 340, 523
Cross, I: 102, 153, 154, 174, 182, 183, 188, 189, 205, 216, 257, 480, 483, 487, 489–94, 497, 498, 522–24, 529, 531, 533, 534, 541, 546–49, 551, 562, 564; II: 5, 6, 8, 9, 11–14, 16–23, 28, 30–33, 35, 36, 39–41, 50, 52, 54, 55, 57–60, 62 n.10, 63 n.24, 65, 67–69, 71–75, 79–81, 84–86, 88–91, 93–96, 110, 190, 244, 270, 295, 344, 345, 354, 396, 403, 411, 418, 420, 467, 469, 518, 520, 524, 525, 528, 557, 573; theology of the, **7.2**; I: 205, 212 n.36, 509, 510, 533; II: 67, 345, 525

Death, I: 72, 95, 100, 115, 140, 153, 183, 188–90, 209, 216, 250, 291, 332, 346, 353, 372, 373, 385, 389, 400, 410–12, 425, 433, 434–37, 439, 444 n.4, 447–63, 470, 475, 479, 480, 490–94, 497, 498, 523, 524–26, 531, 533, 534, 537, 538, 541, 547–52, 555, 562, 564, 565, 566; II: 7, 12–17, 19, 21–26, 28–30, 32–34, 36–40, 43 n.42, 48–61, 62 n.9, 63 n.19, 65, 68–72, 74, 76, 77 n.10, 79, 80, 82, 84–86, 88–98, 113, 114, 116, 118, 121, 137, 144, 152, 156, 190, 224, 232, 234, 244, 262, 265, 272, 277, 278, 283, 284, 308, 311, 320, 323, 331, 334 n.17, 342, 347–49, 372, 375, 377, 379, 396, 397, 399, 401–3, 409–12, 414, 417–20, 422, 425–27, 430, 436, 438, 440, 443 n.16, 448, 451–53, 456–58, 461, 463–68, 475, 476, 481, 483, 484, 488, 492, 494, 496, 498, 501, 503, 514–16, 520, 525, 527, 528, 534, 536, 541, 542, 544, 547, 549, 555–57, 559–71, 573, 575, 577, 578, 580, 585, 586
Death of God theology, I: 42, 470
Deism, I: 13, 68, 470
Deity of Christ, **2.3–4, 6.3, 6.5**; I: 90–95, 99–102, 105–10, 144, 545, 546, 554; II: 13, 39, 41, 48, 55, 56, 58, 60, 70, 97, 120, 125, 148, 150, 153, 188, 212, 258, 526, 551, 572
Demons, demonic, I: 372, 389, 441, 443, 455, 488, 498; II: 6, 7, 18, 19, 36–41, 47, 48, 61, 68, 146, 147, 200, 283, 287, 409, 418
Destiny, I: 62, 101, 251, 305, 323–30, 334, 335, 337, 338, 343, 356, 376, 399, 406 n.36, 434, 455, 524, 525, 532; II: 50, 135, 136, 243, 245, 261, 266, 272, 280, 283, 384, 409, 419, 452, 478, 485, 493–97, 503, 516, 530, 533, 534, 558, 565, 568, 569, 572, 574, 577, 579, 584, 558
Determinism, II: 171, 172, 287
Devil, I: 372, 373, 387, 389, 405 n.16, 417, 437, 439, 454, 458, 491, 494, 498, 548, 549, 555, 563; II: 20, 21, 37–40, 48–51, 55, 58, 63 n.19, 69, 85, 90, 96, 98, 132, 198, 411, 437, 463, 522, 572, 575, 576, 585, 586. *See also* Satan
Dialectical theology, I: 6, 14, 34, 41, 484, 512, 540, 541; II: 106, 118, 154, 168, 203, 238, 243, 244, 331, 498, 546
Divinization, I: 103, 109, 116, 118, 130, 307, 308, 368, 398, 510, 538; II: 97, 98, 402, 403

Docetism, I: 307, 308, 475, 499, 500, 503, 506, 510, 514, 518, 520, 521, 532, 546, 547; II: 27, 44 n.42
Dogma, I: 5, 22, 23, 26, 29–32, 35–38, 45–52, 55, 57, 58, 60 nn.11,12, 62, 71, 72, 77, 95, 115, 127, 129–31, 137, 141, 151, 163, 175, 181, 190, 207, 212 n.34, 329, 470, 475, 477, 478, 480, 497, 505, 506, 511–14, 517, 558–60, 566; II: 5, 19, 32, 121, 123 n.48, 126, 130, 133, 218, 291, 296, 298, 329, 330, 340, 357, 397, 421, 430, 501
Dogmatics, 1; I: 83–85, 151, 165, 242, 259, 262, 363, 403, 469, 470, 474, 476, 477, 502, 508, 512, 519, 546, 553; II: 6, 8, 9, 21, 25, 31, 39, 41, 50, 80, 89, 93, 133, 171, 173, 176, 177, 294, 317, 320, 324, 325, 327, 330, 332, 337, 341, 347, 355, 370, 395–97, 401, 421, 422, 426, 430, 447, 448, 452, 462
Donatism, I: 32, 61, 456; II: 149, 150, 199, 206, 307, 405, 422 n.6
Dort, Synod of, I: 37
Dualism, I: 32, 183, 271, 304–6, 310, 331, 333, 334, 369–71, 373, 385–87, 389, 402, 405 nn.15,16, 529; II: 36, 39, 40, 60, 71, 484, 519

Easter, I: 379, 455, 478, 480, 483, 487, 488, 492, 493, 522, 524, 527, 535, 550–52, 555, 560, 562, 563; II: 321
Eastern Orthodoxy, I: 31, 32, 62, 74, 126, 148, 507; II: 384, 402, 403
Ebionitism, I: 475, 479, 499, 500, 501, 503, 506, 514, 518, 531
Economy, of God, 122, 143, 144, 152, 154–56, 438, 470, 514, 541; II: 74, 106, 120, 121, 126, 134, 138, 148, 160, 172, 188–91, 193, 194, 200, 204, 231, 263
Ecumenical, ecumenicity, I: 43, 45, 52, 129, 131, 148, 470, 506, 507, 554; II: 195, 201, 205, 216, 231, 244, 294, 296, 298, 315, 317, 323, 326, 330, 340, 341, 343, 344, 354, 361, 377, 383, 523
Election. *See* Predestination
Emanation, I: 299, 300; II: 40
Embodiment, I: 15, 35, 59, 177, 186, 252, 473, 475, 517, 526, 561, 562; II: 39, 145, 177, 183, 184, 188, 191–98, 203, 204, 220, 231–33, 238, 246, 247, 292, 349, 356, 357, 359, 361, 446, 468
Empiricism, I: 18, 214–18, 222, 523; II: 253, 282, 285, 356, 451, 452, 556
Enhypostasia, I: 506
Enlightenment, age of, I: 9, 25, 33, 38–41, 68, 69, 71, 149, 150, 160 n.60, 207, 475, 492, 511, 517, 527, 546; II: 178, 286, 475, 477, 479, 509, 565
Enthusiasm, I: 69, 493; II: 18, 153, 161, 162, 163 n.17, 266, 308, 395, 396, 405, 421, 422 n.6, 459, 507, 546
Ephesus, Council of, I: 47, 414, 461
Epiclesis, II: 157, 232, 321, 338–40, 350
Episcopacy, I: 149, 153, 225, 226, 228–31, 233, 236, 239, 300, 322, 328, 333, 371, 372, 376, 378–81
Epistemology, I: 18, 19, 138, 205, 206, 210, 216–18, 230, 391, 403, 536
Eschatology, 12; I: 25, 42, 46, 76, 108, 183, 223, 226 n.13, 255, 286, 293, 336, 342, 348, 484, 485, 487, 488, 491, 494, 495 n.11, 517, 524, 529, 533, 538, 540, 551, 555–57, 563, 564, 566, 568; II: 13, 17–19, 31, 34–36, 93, 112–15, 117–19, 149, 151, 154, 156, 157, 166, 170, 190, 213, 238, 244, 283–85, 319, 331, 332, 338, 345–48, 357, 370, 399, 411–13, 415, 418, 420, 423 n.16, 425, 429, 430, 435, 437, 440–42, 442 n.1, 445–60, 462, 466, 467, 469; theology of, I: 14, 42, 313, 347, 348, 484, 537
Eschaton, 12; I: 46, 50, 101, 108, 167, 175, 176, 205, 226 n.13, 257, 258, 286, 313, 349, 441, 462, 484, 486, 488, 489, 491, 524, 538, 565, 566; II: 93, 121, 138, 139, 151, 153, 157, 170, 176, 188, 283, 284, 319, 345, 347, 357, 380, 412, 436, 445, 446, 450, 451, 452, 454, 468
Essence, I: 57, 146, 147, 185, 206, 237, 251, 308, 484, 501–3, 512, 532, 533, 536, 539, 556; II: 68, 106, 189, 233, 235, 236, 238, 259, 409, 421, 543, 547
Ethics, ethical, I: 12, 13, 25, 39, 108, 183, 231, 241, 244, 261, 262, 308, 326, 403, 460, 484–87, 495 n.11, 528, 555; II: 29, 30, 146, 147, 154–57, 176, 208, 218, 269–79, 368, 397, 403, 439, 441, 447, 467, 476, 478
Eucharist (Lord's Supper, mass), **10.3–6**; I: 36, 58, 92, 110, 177, 186, 458, 507, 508, 510, 553; II: 51, 82, 129, 157, 161, 162, 174, 205, 209, 214, 223, 231, 232, 239, 276, 560
Eutycheanism, I: 504, 505, 508, 512
Evangelicalism, I: 559, 563, 568
Eve, I: 328, 332, 448; II: 25
Event, 18, 46, 65, 91, 93, 101, 104, 140, 165–68, 171, 172, 175, 190, 224, 527, 530, 535, 539, 541, 545, 549, 551, 567; II: 6, 13, 26, 35, 55, 61, 68, 70, 71, 75, 79–99, 138, 159, 169–74, 176, 260, 261, 266, 281, 291, 297, 300, 302, 305, 306, 308, 311, 312, 320, 323, 324, 331, 345, 349, 352, 384, 412, 415, 437, 449, 455, 462, 516, 520, 521, 555–58, 571, 581, 582, 586
Evil, **5.4–5**; I: 19, 56, 57, 85, 234, 239, 248 n.32, 257, 271, 281, 284, 301, 304–6, 308, 311–13, 316, 318, 324, 331, 335–37, 351, 356, 363–65, 368, 370, 372–75, 380 n.9, 382 n.46, 386–91, 393, 400, 402, 404 n.7, 406 n.49, 410, 412, 416–18, 420, 422, 425, 427, 488, 491; II: 22, 23, 33, 34, 36, 37, 39, 45 n.75, 53–56, 82, 83, 110, 146, 188, 198, 237, 273, 278, 284, 339, 375, 376, 415, 449, 450, 453, 484, 490, 505, 506, 525, 527, 543, 544, 549, 551, 572, 584
Evolution, I: 14, 42, 252, 269, 271, 286, 314, 326, 334, 343, 345, 346, 354–56, 391, 392, 400, 434, 442, 455, 484; II: 173, 302, 477, 529–31, 572

607

INDEXES

Existence, existential, I: 13–15, 21, 22, 24, 26, 41, 84, 104, 138, 139, 199, 200, 206, 219, 220, 236–38, 240, 241, 254, 255, 272, 284, 288, 291, 301, 306, 310, 328, 333, 334, 342, 343, 359, 363, 377, 389, 301–93, 401, 404 n.14, 409, 426, 427, 438, 444 n.4, 445 n.29, 448, 449, 469, 476, 481, 485, 506, 510–13, 517, 521, 522, 524, 528–30, 533, 536, 538, 542, 547, 564, 565, 566; II: 28, 37, 55, 93, 118, 131–33, 159, 162, 167, 183, 189, 190, 194, 197, 203, 205, 209, 210, 225, 230, 236, 238, 243, 257, 260, 261, 275, 331, 357, 374, 380, 397, 419, 428, 437, 452, 453, 459, 461, 462, 466, 467, 475, 481, 483, 485, 497, 498, 517–20, 524, 526, 527, 530–34, 541–43, 546, 547, 555, 557, 560–62, 564–68, 570, 573, 580, 586

Existentialism, I: 14, 16, 41, 88, 139, 270, 373, 427, 485, 529, 536; II: 397, 467, 517, 541–50

Experience, I: 12, 15–17, 26, 34, 52, 55, 58, 62, 63, 70, 75, 76, 103, 106–8, 110, 115–17, 141, 183, 213, 215–18, 221, 222, 231, 232, 235, 255, 289, 290, 292, 304, 307, 310, 316–18, 324, 349, 354, 363, 364, 372, 373, 388, 392, 395, 396, 410, 413, 420, 422–24, 428, 436, 438–40, 450, 455, 459, 473, 479, 493, 520–22, 524, 527, 530, 533, 537, 538, 541, 547, 550, 563, 565; II: 26, 27, 29, 30, 41, 105, 107–9, 113, 116, 117, 128–30, 133, 145, 147, 153, 157, 167, 171, 174–76, 183, 191, 193, 194, 197–200, 203, 207, 210, 217–19, 220, 253, 287, 288, 305, 308, 316, 347, 356, 357, 395, 406, 422, 426, 448, 458, 479, 483, 514, 520, 521, 522, 526, 532, 542, 550, 557, 559, 561, 564–66, 568, 569, 570, 572–74, 584, 586

Exorcism, I: 91, 379, 488; II: 286, 321, 322, 327

Faith, **11**; I: 6, 9, 10–13, 15–18, 21–23, 25, 29–31, 33, 34, 36–42, 45, 46, 48–50, 52–55, 57, 58, 61, 62, 65, 67, 68, 70, 71, 74, 75, 77, 83, 84, 88, 95, 96, 111, 115, 130, 135, 165, 171, 173, 175, 197, 199, 201, 202, 204, 206–10, 214–16, 218, 221, 222, 224, 226 n.13, 230, 235, 236, 241, 242, 245, 255, 256, 260, 269–72, 275, 277, 290, 298, 302, 304, 306, 309–12, 315, 323, 324, 328, 336, 344, 349–51, 356, 363, 367, 369, 372, 376, 379, 385–92, 402, 403, 410–12, 414, 416, 417, 420, 421, 427, 442, 447–49, 451, 453, 456, 458, 460, 469–71, 473, 474, 476–80, 484, 487, 490, 493, 494, 498, 499, 512–14, 517, 519–21, 527, 528, 531, 533, 534, 536–38, 549, 550, 553, 554, 557, 558, 560–63; 566; II: 18, 22, 26, 27, 31, 35, 45 n.77, 51, 56–59, 61, 65, 66, 70–76, 77 n.4, 79, 94, 95, 97, 98, 109, 123 n.38, 124 n.51, 125, 127, 129, 130, 132, 138, 139, 141 n.37, 147, 151, 158, 161, 163 n.15, 188, 193, 194, 196–98, 200, 203–5, 208, 209, 211, 216, 217, 220, 224–25, 230, 231, 233, 236, 239, 244, 253, 264, 270, 274, 288, 294–97, 299, 302, 306–8, 314 nn.39,52, 316, 321, 324–27, 331, 335 nn.46,55, 336 n.70, 338, 339, 341, 345, 346, 354, 355, 357–59, 361, 374, 376, 378, 379, 385, 476, 477, 483, 497, 498, 501, 502, 508, 515, 525, 529, 537, 547, 548, 555, 556, 557, 581

Faithfulness of God, I: 102, 105, 116, 155, 170–72, 185, 377, 380, 436, 559; II: 29, 30, 32, 33, 58, 59, 117, 152, 171, 203, 206, 213, 220, 234, 236, 274, 369, 385, 486, 524

Fall, **5.2-3**; I: 24, 59, 284, 313, 323, 325, 328, 329, 332, 335, 336, 337, 350, 356, 444 n.4, 445 n.17, 447, 448, 522, 525, 539; II: 71, 137, 146, 400, 453, 454, 469 n.7, 562, 576

Father, God the, I: 73, 93–96, 100, 101, 106–8, 110, 111, 119, 120, 121, 123–30, 137, 140, 142–46, 148, 151, 155–57, 158 n.14, 164, 169, 171, 172, 174–76, 181, 185, 187, 189, 190, 205, 216, 277, 288, 289, 299, 302, 317, 373, 389, 400, 462, 469, 470, 495 n.19, 500–503, 505, 507, 521–23, 528, 531, 532, 536, 539, 547, 552, 564; II: 22, 26, 28, 30, 34, 53, 54, 61, 81, 82, 91, 105, 107, 109, 119–21, 124 n.49, 126, 137–39, 148, 150, 154, 165, 172, 175, 204, 210, 263–66, 279, 315, 317, 322, 339, 353, 354, 376, 381, 399, 402, 416, 440, 441, 442, 476, 491, 498, 508, 558, 559, 572, 581

Fathers of the Church, I: xvii, 26, 30, 33, 35, 47, 70, 141, 164, 186, 352 n.9, 387, 394, 411, 502, 505, 519, 530, 531, 555, 568; II: 38, 97, 98, 120, 121, 122 n.15, 123 n.49, 126, 129, 160, 323, 342, 351, 373, 402, 403, 428, 503, 576

Federal theology, I: 38, 68

Fideism, 24, 216

Flesh, I: 75, 111, 143, 155, 207, 257, 370, 379, 416, 418, 420, 424, 453, 457, 498, 523, 531, 553; II: 17, 27, 28, 94, 106, 109, 110, 114, 118, 119, 161, 162, 233, 278, 320, 350, 396, 405, 410, 411, 417, 445, 451, 452, 454–56, 458, 469, 487, 497, 518, 559, 561

Flesh of Christ, I: 502, 509, 510, 519, 523, 527, 530, 531, 533, 534, 553, 561, 562; II: 20, 39, 53, 55, 61, 76, 85, 98, 265

Florence, Council of, I: 159 n.38; II: 148, 299, 313 n.25, 317, 319, 324, 333 n.1, 334 nn.7,12,20, 341, 342, 363 n.26, 373, 381, 382, 387 n.78, 388 nn.82,99

Forgiveness, I: 39, 54, 91, 109, 284, 363, 437, 454, 457; II: 15, 17, 21, 23, 25, 26, 29, 33, 51, 57, 59, 62 n.9, 79–82, 92–94, 96, 97, 124 n.50, 128–32, 134, 207, 262, 263, 267, 277, 278, 280, 282, 302, 303, 308, 315, 319, 320, 322, 323, 331, 344, 348, 367, 369–77, 404, 405, 407, 408, 410, 421, 433, 440, 462, 577

Franciscanism, I: 415, 416

Free churches, II: 195

Freedom, I: 25, 51, 57, 61, 62, 105, 150, 154, 156, 166, 170, 174, 187, 203, 204, 208, 209, 218, 230, 233–35, 237, 241, 244, 256, 258, 263 n.15, 269, 298–302, 317, 323, 327, 329,

608

331, 336, 343, 344, 346, 349, 369, 372, 374, 376, 379, 385, 388, 390, 391–93, 398–403, 404 n.14, 410, 411, 422, 425–27, 433, 435, 437, 439–42, 453, 462, 510, 531, 534, 539, 541, 542, 554, 565; II: 11, 18, 23, 24, 33, 38, 43 n.31, 66, 68, 77 n.2, 111, 113, 126, 136, 137, 139, 143, 145, 147, 149, 150, 153, 162, 165–70, 172, 173, 184, 213, 272, 274, 276, 279, 320, 331, 332, 376, 397, 402, 410, 417, 429, 438, 439, 442, 453, 464, 509, 519, 524, 525, 527, 543, 547, 549, 550, 552, 572. *See also* Will, free

Fulfillment, I: 18, 101, 104, 105, 138, 156, 176, 275, 288, 293, 312, 313, 341, 343, 353, 356, 461, 488, 492–94, 497, 524–26, 537, 541, 545, 555, 556, 565, 567; II: 18, 50, 109, 110, 113–15, 135, 139, 157, 170, 176, 188–91, 198, 199, 207, 213, 234–47, 274, 279, 319, 338–40, 345, 347, 361, 380, 432, 437, 447–49, 452, 453, 466, 485, 498, 515–17, 528–31, 537, 555, 559, 560, 568, 569, 571, 576, 581, 585, 586

Fundamentalism, I: 64, 75, 174, 334; II: 475

Gender of God, I: 93–96, 157, 305; II: 175, 178 n.24

Genevan Confession, I: 65

Glory, I: 54, 302, 328, 421, 490, 491, 493, 494, 509, 528, 534, 535, 547, 548, 554, 556, 564; II: 257, 260, 264, 339, 357, 431, 514, 520

Glossolalia, II: 156–58

Gnosis, I: 29–31, 209, 568; II: 20

Gnosticism, I: 30, 31, 128, 209, 210, 304, 305, 334, 389, 404 n.14, 411, 494, 513, 519, 547; II: 20, 40, 53, 79, 121, 159, 160, 164 n.32, 230, 265, 266, 380, 405, 485, 498, 501, 503, 507, 519, 565–67, 572

Goal of world, history, I: 48, 101, 199, 202–8, 213, 219, 220, 222, 249–50, 254, 255, 258, 259, 262, 306, 334, 342, 348, 349, 393, 395, 399, 402, 515; II: 65, 199, 213, 229, 245, 284, 413, 431–35, 446–48, 452–59, 466, 467, 481, 482, 487, 492, 498, 505, 518–21, 528, 530, 532, 551, 555, 569–571, 574, 576, 579, 581, 584, 586

Good, 19, 138, 174, 190, 202, 213, 225 n.4, 234, 256, 257, 284, 302, 306, 307, 313, 317, 331, 332, 336, 346, 356, 364, 368, 370, 372, 373, 380 n.9, 385, 387, 390, 393, 399–403, 416, 417, 419, 427, 435, 438, 439, 443, 547; II: 22, 39, 57, 117, 128, 147, 155, 195, 199, 273, 274, 338, 414, 415, 417, 419, 437, 439, 441, 452, 453, 466, 475, 484, 506, 523, 533, 551, 565, 584

Gospel, 6, 11, 12, 25, 26, 29, 30–33, 35, 36, 41, 42, 45–55, 57, 60 n.12, 61–64, 66, 68–70, 73–75, 89, 90, 95, 96, 99–102, 110, 111, 118, 119, 126, 127, 129, 147, 154, 157, 173, 177, 181, 183, 184, 187, 188, 190, 200, 201, 206, 207, 209, 257, 260, 269, 270, 313, 343, 346, 411, 449, 453, 474, 492, 495 n.19, 502, 529, 531, 533, 545, 547–49, 551, 553, 557, 559, 561–63, 565–67; II: 18, 22, 26, 77 n.4, 93, 106, 107, 116–18, 125, 128–39, 143, 149, 150, 152, 153, 158, 161, 166, 168, 169, 173, 174, 195, 196, 216, 226, 233, 234, 264, 266, 267, 269–79, 291–95, 297–99, 302–5, 307–12, 312 n.10, 313 n.14, 314 n.39, 316, 318, 323, 326, 331–33, 348, 355, 358, 359, 369, 370, 374–76, 379, 380, 382, 384, 397, 406, 412, 413, 415, 416, 418, 419, 422, 423 n.16, 424 nn.24,26, 431, 438, 442 nn.1,5, 445, 448, 450–52, 455, 456, 458, 459, 460 n.2, 462, 492, 495–99, 509, 519, 524, 526, 536, 557, 559, 563, 567, 578, 580, 582

Gospels, I: 288, 483, 501, 519, 523, 530, 533, 554; II: 12–14, 16, 18, 33, 81, 114, 115, 144, 172, 206, 210, 265, 282, 283, 319, 337, 440, 493, 494, 496, 521

Grace, I: 6, 14, 19, 32–34, 37, 39, 53, 59, 61, 63, 66, 71, 92, 106, 108, 205, 216, 217, 256, 269, 270, 272, 291, 335, 346, 349, 350, 401, 410, 414–18, 420, 450, 451, 457, 458, 460, 461, 486, 498, 507, 510, 530, 536, 546; II: 18, 19, 27, 32, 35, 44 n.42, 49, 57, 58, 62 nn.9,12, 69–71, 92, 94, 97, 125–30, 133, 135, 137, 140 nn.9,10,24, 141 nn.24,31,34, 177, 185, 194, 196, 216, 226, 229, 232, 233, 234, 236, 237, 239, 243, 244, 253, 267, 269, 270, 272, 273, 276, 278, 279, 295–98, 205, 210, 313 n.20, 314 n.46, 323–26, 341, 348, 353, 354, 365 n.83, 368, 373, 381, 383, 384, 396, 397, 399, 401–17, 423 n.7, 425, 427, 432–34, 437–40, 442, 452, 453, 458–460, 465, 466, 481, 497, 498, 508, 532, 544, 563, 570–73, 578, 579; "alone," I: 53, 546; II: 62 n.12, 194, 196, 425

Ground, of world, history, I: 96, 199, 202–8, 213, 218–20, 222, 229–46, 257, 261, 262, 374; II: 532, 555, 556, 559

Guilt, 5; II: 7, 17, 29, 30, 40, 54, 132, 154, 319, 332, 398, 404, 416, 426, 461, 463

Habit (*habitus*), II: 126, 127, 141 n.35, 404

"Happy exchange," I: 534; II: 47, 52, 57, 60, 61, 70, 76, 90, 98

Healing, I: 91; II: 263, 280, 282–84, 286, 308, 316, 367, 368, 375–77

Heart, I: 16, 39, 302, 308, 449, 554, 564; II: 33, 34, 48, 70, 75, 98, 131, 132, 199, 204, 207, 234, 262, 267, 270, 271, 275, 308, 310, 381, 397, 425, 428, 432, 433, 436, 439, 440, 441, 449, 453, 458, 466, 468, 487, 531, 544

Heaven, I: 58, 177, 204, 241, 256, 257, 285, 292, 309, 344, 404 n.14, 437, 453, 462, 469, 499, 528, 529, 553, 554, 555, 557, 558, 563, 564; II: 57–60, 67, 76, 110, 132, 144, 259, 277, 297, 346, 356, 358, 359, 366 n.118, 369, 418, 428, 441, 446, 447, 451, 456, 457, 461, 468, 469, 476, 478, 481, 483, 485, 488, 490, 496, 498, 501, 504, 505, 507, 515, 518, 531, 533, 546, 549, 551, 555, 567, 569, 572, 575, 581, 583, 585, 586

609

INDEXES

Hegelianism, I: 13, 40, 317, 518, 537, 540, 541; II: 95, 105, 170, 174, 430, 469 n.7
Heidelberg Catechism, I: 37, 509
Heidelberg Disputation, I: 204, 210 n.8, 371, 381 n.24, 417
Hell, hades, damnation, I: 58, 256, 346, 372, 373, 404 n.14, 528, 548, 549, 559; II: 49, 55, 58, 59, 93, 132, 136, 139, 476, 481, 484, 485, 523, 555, 569, 575, 579, 585
Hellenism, I: 30, 31, 103, 111, 115–23, 135–54, 164, 166, 169, 175, 311, 343, 478, 487, 492, 498, 500, 512, 513, 527, 530, 532, 533, 536, 540; II: 14, 15, 119, 160, 167, 169, 265, 266, 300, 565
Helvetic Confession, Second, II: 486 n.33
Hermeneutic, hermeneutics, I: 15, 20–23, 41, 49, 53, 69, 71, 73, 77, 123, 479, 485, 492, 523, 529, 563; II: 79, 95, 125, 130, 131, 133, 137, 152, 156, 157, 163 n.16, 177, 311, 313 n.27, 419, 420, 451, 582
Hiddenness of God, I: 90, 124, 173, 174, 182, 183, 188, 201, 205, 209, 216, 231, 232, 234, 235, 369, 396, 493, 494, 497, 509, 534; II: 19, 39, 58, 59, 71–74, 138, 139, 417, 441, 453, 467, 505
Hinduism, I: 243, 244, 245, 255, 256, 300, 565
Historical-critical method, I: 11, 20, 21, 25, 39, 47, 50, 66, 71, 72, 74, 475, 476, 477, 518, 519, 527, 537, 550; II: 282, 294, 376
Historicism, I: 23–25, 474, 475, 523
History, I: 13, 15, 20, 21, 23, 25, 26, 37, 38, 40, 48, 50, 59, 71, 72, 74–77, 104, 116, 122, 123, 129, 137, 143, 152, 153, 167, 172, 184, 200, 217, 228 n.31, 250, 252, 253, 256, 262, 563 n.14, 269, 272, 278, 279, 281, 284, 288, 289, 293, 306, 313, 315, 328, 329, 341–44, 346–44, 346–51, 353, 355, 364, 388, 391, 393, 403, 404 n.14, 450, 461, 469, 470, 476, 478, 485, 492–94, 499, 500, 502, 504, 513, 514, 518, 523, 524, 527, 529–31, 533–36, 538–41, 547, 549–51, 553–55, 560–63, 567, 568; II: 19, 20, 22, 23, 27, 33, 37, 40, 72, 76, 110, 112, 114, 131, 132, 134, 135, 137–39, 146, 147, 152, 156, 157, 159–62, 165–71, 173–75, 188–91, 193, 194, 204–6, 208, 211–13, 220, 223, 226, 230, 238, 259, 260, 262, 266, 267, 278, 281, 297, 300, 302, 303, 308, 316, 331, 338, 343, 345, 355, 356, 369, 370, 380, 404, 419–21, 430, 459, 468, 469 n.7, 477, 484, 487, 490–96, 498, 499, 501, 505, 506, 515–21, 524, 525, 528, 529, 532, 533, 546–48, 552, 556, 557, 571, 572, 575, 578, 580, 583, 584
History of salvation, I: 31, 38, 40, 41, 56, 68, 141, 313, 347, 448, 546, 551, 552, 565; II: 28, 121, 282, 340, 350, 420, 430, 495, 531
Holiness, I: 116, 124, 222, 223, 336, 420, 430 n.32, 500, 501, 510; II: 7, 22, 31–36, 44 n.62, 45 nn.67,75,77, 72, 81, 162, 202, 206, 207, 212, 220, 224, 225, 279, 331, 354, 399, 400, 405, 422 n.6, 431, 438, 445, 454, 469, 497

Holy Spirit. *See* Spirit of God
Homoousia, I: 127–31, 134 nn.56,62, 137, 502, 503, 505, 506, 513, 519, 532, 539; II: 188
Hope, I: 14, 15, 23, 59, 102, 104, 105, 107, 138, 173, 183, 251, 253, 256, 263 n.15, 284, 292, 312, 313, 363, 447, 461, 484, 498, 524, 538, 555, 556, 564, 566, 568; II: 11, 21, 23, 51, 55, 84, 93, 97, 112–14, 119, 128, 131, 139, 147, 156, 157, 169, 170, 247, 280, 319, 323, 395, 397, 418, 420, 431, 433, 434, 439, 440, 442, 449, 457, 458, 461, 466, 468, 475, 478, 481, 483, 488, 491, 492, 496, 499, 501–4, 506, 510, 513–15, 518–21, 524, 525, 531–34, 536, 541, 543–47, 551, 555, 556, 558, 559, 560, 567, 568, 569, 573, 579, 580, 581, 586
Humanism, I: 250, 283, 523; II: 541, 550
Humanist manifestos, II: 550, 551, 554 nn.17,18
Humanity, human being, **4,3**; I: 6, 14, 18, 23, 26, 35, 53, 67, 75, 78, 89, 94, 116, 142, 198, 203, 204, 207, 208, 222, 230, 235, 242, 248 n.32, 249, 250, 253, 255, 257, 258, 263 n.15, 264, 269, 272, 275, 283, 284, 286, 291, 342–44, 346, 347, 353–56, 363, 365, 368, 369, 372, 373, 375, 378, 385, 387–403, 405 n.16, 410, 412, 414, 415, 417–26, 428, 434, 435, 437, 440, 442, 448, 450–52, 454, 455, 457–59, 476, 484, 486, 502, 504, 505, 514, 518, 521, 522, 524, 525, 528, 530, 532–34, 537, 539, 545, 549, 554, 556, 558–60, 564, 566; II: 18, 19, 22, 25, 28, 29, 32, 33, 36–39, 48, 51, 54, 55, 57, 60, 82, 107, 118, 127, 131, 132, 134, 160, 176, 178 n.24, 187, 205, 207, 215, 216, 235, 245, 253, 258, 271, 273, 400, 402, 403, 428, 431, 434, 440, 442, 450, 454, 456, 467, 478, 479, 482, 484, 506, 509, 522, 526, 529, 530–32, 534, 543–48, 550, 551, 553, 558, 562, 571, 575, 579, 580, 585, 586
Humiliation of Christ, I: 510, 542, 545, 547–49, 552; II: 17, 52–55, 70, 84, 279, 344
Hypostasis, I: 130, 134 n.56, 135–39, 141, 158 nn.2,5,6,7,13, 168, 176, 245, 306, 505, 506, 513, 530, 532; II: 125, 175. *See also* Identity, Person
Hypostatic union, I: 479–99, 502–14, 517, 521, 522, 524, 528, 532, 538, 539–42; II: 21, 39, 48, 56, 60, 125

Idealism, I: 14, 35, 39, 41, 147, 440, 540; II: 106, 108 n.3, 174, 439, 457, 458
Identity: of God, **2.1–4**; I: 56, 164, 165, 168, 171, 172, 174, 176, 181, 189, 190, 229, 230, 281, 285, 469–71, 513; II: 145, 147, 148, 150–54, 158, 161, 177, 208, 214, 263, 266; of Jesus, I: 100, 469, 473, 476, 478, 479, 481, 492, 498, 500, 505, 508, 522, 524, 534, 540, 541, 545, 557, 560–64, 566, 567; II: 169, 263
Idolatry, I: 368, 371, 498
Illuminationism, I: 214, 218, 222; II: 428
Image, 18, 19, 31, 56, 99, 107, 108, 144, 206, 214, 275, 286, 287, 291, 300, 301, 305, 317, 323–25, 327–33, 335–38, 355, 368, 376,

396–98, 400, 406 n.36, 412, 413, 415, 417, 421, 422, 428 n.9, 438, 459, 525, 526, 539, 545, 552, 560; II: 39, 41, 48, 55, 57, 74, 82, 85, 88, 98, 121, 137, 167, 175, 191, 195, 200, 212–14, 217, 323, 324, 350, 384, 421, 443 n.16, 503, 521, 533, 583, 586
Imagination, I: 18, 19, 21, 239, 246 n.4, 248 n.40, 251, 289, 306, 373, 389, 404 n.14, 520; II: 55, 266, 406, 505, 525, 530, 545
Imitation, II: 16, 17, 20, 23, 26, 29, 52, 206, 411
Immortality, I: 188–90, 255, 400, 412, 434, 524; II: 20, 40, 47, 55, 97, 339, 481, 503, 542, 561–63, 565–68
Immutability, impassibility, I: 105, 115–21, 141–44, 166, 188–89, 500, 501, 508, 530–33; II: 73, 136, 159
Incarnation, I: 32, 57, 142, 158 n.15, 206, 256, 343, 369, 453, 477, 500–6, 509–13, 515 n.21, 517, 518, 522, 525, 526 n.6, 527–30, 532, 533, 539–41, 545, 547; II: 20, 32, 37, 48, 52, 69, 118, 238, 257, 264, 266, 267, 350, 403, 451, 496, 528, 530
Initiation, I: 92, 95, 96, 458; II: 117, 159, 214, 232, 253, 281, 292, 303, 315, 316, 318, 319, 327, 329, 341, 515
Inspiration, I: 64, 66, 67, 69, 71, 74, 226 n.15; II: 112, 116, 117, 121, 153, 166, 219
Islam, I: 242, 243, 245, 254, 256, 257
Israel, I: 21, 45, 56, 61, 65, 76, 88–92, 94, 95, 99, 103–5, 112 n.4, 115, 118, 119, 245, 277, 280–88, 293, 368, 375, 376–78, 423, 435, 442, 450, 461, 469, 491, 531, 532, 552, 559; II: 12, 19, 81, 91, 107, 109–15, 141 n.32, 147, 151–54, 156, 163 n.15, 165, 206, 213, 261, 262, 273, 274, 288, 331, 338, 347, 368, 380, 408, 482–86, 488–91, 494, 495, 516, 522, 524, 534, 565, 567, 578

Jansenism, II: 467
Jehovah's Witnesses, II: 509
Jesus, I: 6, 17, 18, 21, 23, 25, 26, 29–31, 34, 40, 45, 46, 48–50, 56–59, 61, 62, 72–77, 89, 91–93, 95, 96, 97 n.19, 99–101, 103, 106–8, 110, 111, 111 n.2, 119, 121, 123, 128, 130, 131, 137–39, 144, 151, 153–56, 164, 167, 170–72, 174, 176, 184, 185, 187–90, 200, 202, 205, 207, 215, 216, 219, 223, 224, 226 n.13, 228 n.33, 249, 256–61, 276, 277, 288, 290, 291, 303, 336, 343, 347, 363, 365, 369, 420, 424, 439, 447, 451, 452, 454, 455, 457, 458, 459, 461, 462, 464 n.30, 469–71, 473–76, 478–81, 483–85, 487–93, 494 n.7, 495 nn.11,19, 497–514, 517–42, 545, 546, 548–64, 566, 568; II: 2, 5–8, 11–21, 23–31, 33, 35, 37, 40, 43, 43 n.42, 44 n.42, 47, 51, 54–60, 63 n.19, 65, 66, 69–76, 79–82, 84–86, 89–97, 107, 109, 115–17, 121, 134, 137–39, 144, 145, 148, 151, 152, 156, 157, 162, 165, 166, 169, 171–76, 187–89, 198, 204, 207, 208, 210–12, 218–20, 224, 232, 234, 235, 239, 245, 257, 259, 260, 262–67, 270, 272–74, 277–84, 286, 287, 294, 304, 305, 316, 320, 332, 333 n.2,6, 338, 339, 342–50, 366 n.118, 370, 375, 377, 380, 396, 399, 401, 409, 412, 414, 421, 424, 440, 441, 442, 446, 455, 456, 462, 463, 467, 475–77, 485, 490–99, 501, 502, 504, 507, 513–23, 526, 532, 533, 537, 555, 557–59, 564–66, 568, 571, 574, 575, 577–84, 586
Judaism, I: 72, 106, 107, 109, 254, 278, 290, 343, 493; II: 14, 204, 270, 271, 273, 286, 368, 485, 492, 515, 516
Judaizers, I: 61; II: 206, 270, 421, 463
Judgment, I: 6, 19, 58, 62, 69, 104, 109, 205, 255, 282, 288, 332, 372, 375, 376, 378, 421, 443, 486, 487, 490, 493, 498, 528, 529, 537, 538, 548, 553, 555, 556; II: 6, 11, 13, 18, 19, 24, 25, 32, 35, 36, 38, 39, 41, 45 n.67, 89, 91, 94, 110, 115, 118, 157, 207, 208, 233, 237, 239, 244, 247, 262, 265, 269, 270, 272, 282, 316, 332, 369, 371, 381, 405, 407–11, 421, 426, 427, 435, 461, 462, 484, 485–87, 493, 495, 497, 503, 505, 518–20, 522, 555, 556, 567–80, 585
Justice, I: 43, 187, 205, 256, 346, 415, 417, 420, 421, 424, 439, 443; II: 7, 14, 21–25, 31, 32, 39, 42 n.22, 54, 72, 75, 90, 91, 94, 114, 131, 132, 138, 147, 274, 313 n.20, 400, 402, 403, 421, 457, 459, 462, 469 n.7, 488, 524, 525, 529, 544, 560, 571, 578
Justification, 11; I: 36, 37, 41, 53, 58, 63, 64, 66, 84, 108, 207, 217, 258, 364, 369, 420, 421, 437, 455, 457, 461; II: 2, 5, 14, 24, 31, 32, 58 n.24, 59, 63, 74, 125, 128, 130–35, 141 n.24, 225, 296, 297, 302, 303, 313 n.20, 319, 320, 323–25, 331, 337, 352, 358, 397

Kairos, I; 52, 205–9, 217, 222, 223, 242, 249, 256–61
Kantianism, I: 13, 42, 388; II: 27, 28, 31, 35, 439
Kenosis, I: 509, 510, 541, 542, 547, 548
Kerygma, I: 14, 22, 49, 60 n.11, 111, 470, 477–81, 483, 491–93, 497, 498, 513, 527–29, 546, 559, 562, 566; II: 243, 273, 319, 345
Keys, Office of, II: 210, 223, 226, 275–77, 373, 374
Kingdom of God, I: 18, 23, 25, 46, 59, 61, 91, 106, 108, 183, 254, 347, 348, 367, 443, 447, 464 n.30, 469, 480, 483–94, 497, 498, 522, 524, 538–41, 548, 551, 564; II: 11, 27–30, 34, 58, 80, 93, 94, 97, 115, 147, 157, 170, 208, 213, 243–47, 270, 277, 283, 319, 331, 339, 344, 345, 369, 375, 376, 411, 419, 420, 425, 435, 440, 442, 446, 451, 455–60, 469, 475, 476, 478, 482, 486, 489, 490–92, 495, 496, 498, 501, 502, 504, 506–9, 515–17, 520–22, 524, 525, 527, 529, 531–33, 560, 573, 579–87
Kingship of Christ, I: 497; II: 12, 25, 69, 81, 90, 94, 114, 456, 520, 522
Knowledge, 9, 13, 17–19, 29, 30, 39, 48, 55, 124, 145, 153, 174, 182, 200, 202–4, 206–9, 214, 216, 218, 225 n.4, 230, 248 n.33, 257–59,

611

INDEXES

262, 315, 316, 324, 333, 337, 368, 396, 397, 400–402, 407 n.52, 411, 418, 450, 477, 514, 523, 538, 541, 561, 563; II: 20, 28, 29, 40, 79, 114, 115, 159, 166, 167, 171–73, 211, 217, 220, 270, 286, 339, 345, 419, 428, 446, 463, 508, 546, 564, 578

Knowledge of God, 3; I: 9, 10, 14–16, 18, 34, 39, 49, 56, 61, 85, 93, 100, 124, 141, 150, 298, 331, 332, 369, 371, 394, 447, 469, 470, 541; II: 28, 29, 35, 175, 267, 508

Language, I: 14, 15, 24, 41, 42, 48, 63, 67, 69, 73, 74, 84, 85, 94, 99, 103, 107, 108, 110, 118, 119, 143, 145, 148, 150, 152, 156, 157, 169, 172, 181, 186, 219, 220–22, 224, 225 n.3, 231, 234, 235, 241, 250, 264 n.25, 298, 392, 443, 487, 507, 509, 511, 512, 530, 534–36, 547, 553, 558, 563; II: 8, 38, 55, 83, 110, 115, 125, 129, 135, 144, 145, 152, 154–56, 158, 174, 176, 178 n.24, 258, 259, 262, 285, 300–303, 310, 312, 326, 332, 352, 354, 355, 395, 410, 421, 422, 455, 461, 462, 487, 574, 584

Language-analysis, I: 14, 536

Lateran Council, Fourth, I: 372, 416

Law, 23, 32, 33, 36, 39, 48, 56, 64, 157, 176, 197, 204, 205, 207, 235, 242, 245, 256, 261, 271, 284, 291, 303, 305, 325, 344, 346, 349, 350, 367, 369, 371, 374, 376, 377, 381 n.16, 424, 454, 459, 531, 556; II: 11, 13, 18, 22, 24, 25, 34, 35, 37, 38, 42 n.22, 44 nn.42,62, 47, 48, 50–57, 60, 61, 63 n.19, 72, 76, 86, 90, 92, 93, 96–98, 118, 128, 131, 132, 230, 236, 260, 261, 267, 269–79, 287, 288, 295, 299, 308, 310, 368, 374, 396, 397, 399–405, 407–22, 423 n.16, 424 nn.24,26, 425–27, 430, 432, 437, 442, 445–69, 495, 496, 508

Law, natural, I: 36, 204, 211 n.13, 235, 247 n.19, 459; II: 270, 271, 407, 447, 454, 455

Legalism, I: 48, 51, 61, 364; II: 18, 48, 92, 96, 132, 215, 270, 273, 276, 336 n.73, 373, 382, 400, 405, 406, 435, 439, 448, 449, 461, 462, 466–68

Liberalism, I: 20, 43, 51, 73, 206, 207, 347, 488, 489; II: 6, 26, 31, 32, 34, 36, 75, 81, 82, 476, 573

Liberation, I: 25, 183, 348, 566, 567; II: 143, 151, 162, 173, 190, 195, 262, 269, 278, 332, 378, 421, 494, 525–29, 547, 583

Liberation theology, I: 14, 24, 42, 313, 347, 348, 368, 369, 375, 537; II: 150, 197, 216, 236–38, 468, 527, 528

Life, I: 23, 59, 62, 71, 75, 76, 78, 87, 88, 99, 100, 106, 108, 140, 229–31, 233–35, 242, 243, 245, 249, 251–53, 257–59, 262, 269, 270, 276, 291, 292, 301, 325, 332, 333, 337, 339, 346, 353, 368, 375, 376, 389–91, 394, 410, 411, 414, 428, 433–37, 441, 442, 447–49, 456, 460, 462, 462 n.1, 463 n.4, 493, 494, 498, 517, 524, 528, 531, 534, 538, 539, 541, 545, 546, 549–51, 555, 558, 565, 566; II: 13, 14, 16, 18–20, 22, 24, 25, 27–30, 33, 38, 40,

43 n.42, 56, 59, 61, 67, 68, 70, 71, 82, 83, 86, 88, 94–98, 105, 107, 110, 113, 114, 116, 118, 119, 121, 123 n.49, 125, 126, 128, 129, 131, 135, 141 n.37, 143, 152, 156, 159, 160, 165, 166, 174, 175, 191, 192, 194, 199, 204–8, 211, 215, 217, 218, 223, 224, 228, 231–34, 236, 237, 243, 246, 247, 253, 262, 264–67, 269, 272, 276, 277, 280, 283, 285, 295, 300, 302, 308, 321, 322, 326, 330–32, 339, 346, 367, 395, 475, 481–83, 485, 487, 493–97, 503, 516, 520, 521, 523, 525, 527, 534, 536, 537, 541, 543, 544, 547, 553, 555, 556–70, 573–75, 577–81, 584, 586

Liturgy, I: 23, 83, 92, 93, 96, 124, 176, 188–90, 286, 304, 498, 501, 519, 535; II: 35, 75, 116, 129, 130, 133, 134, 141 n.34, 151, 156–58, 173, 174, 176, 184, 207–9, 218, 219, 223, 225, 228, 231–33, 239, 246, 247, 269, 279–82, 296, 304, 305, 309–12, 317, 320, 321, 324, 328, 329, 337, 340–42, 344, 348–52, 354, 381, 501, 560, 573

Logos, I: 9, 10, 13, 18, 30, 31, 96, 111 n.2, 120, 121, 123–26, 131, 132 n.33, 133 n.54, 144, 155, 158 n.15, 171, 188, 203–9, 211 n.13, 217, 219, 222, 223, 229, 235, 256–61, 306, 343, 351, 356, 397, 473, 501–3, 505, 508–10, 521, 522, 530, 531, 533, 538, 545, 560, 567; II: 18–20, 26, 79, 95, 120, 122 n.12, 167, 175, 177 n.1, 178, 187–89, 210, 260, 264, 265, 350

Lord, I: 26, 76, 91–93, 96 n.1, 106–8, 121, 181, 183, 187, 257, 285, 286, 288, 299, 369, 377, 379, 387, 436, 452, 455, 462, 475, 476, 480, 483, 489, 498, 499, 505, 514, 523, 524, 535, 538, 549, 550, 553–55, 558–62, 564, 567, 568; II: 8, 24, 154, 161, 169, 170, 173, 174, 206, 210, 244, 245, 261–64, 270, 272, 275, 278, 292, 300, 315, 322, 339, 342, 345, 369, 375, 376, 379–81, 483, 486–89, 493, 496, 503, 505, 514, 522, 523, 527, 529, 537, 557, 558, 560, 572–74, 581, 583

Lord's Supper. See Eucharist

Love, I: 15, 16, 32, 33, 41, 92, 100–102, 105, 127, 145, 153, 166, 167, 170, 173, 174, 256, 258, 259, 269, 291, 303, 325, 331, 337, 346, 349, 355, 356, 376, 382 n.46, 387, 388, 395, 397, 398, 414, 441, 453, 459, 483, 487, 498, 504, 510, 530, 532, 534, 535, 538, 539, 541, 556; II: 6, 11, 18, 24, 25, 26, 28–36, 38, 44 n.62, 48, 51, 54, 57, 59–61, 62 n.9, 65, 66, 72, 73, 76, 81, 89, 90, 98, 117, 120, 127, 128, 134, 136, 138, 139, 147, 156, 157, 168, 170, 173, 175, 194, 205, 232, 234, 236, 270, 271, 275, 332, 339, 369, 399, 408, 409, 420, 433, 434, 437, 439, 440, 451, 454, 462, 465, 468, 498, 508, 523, 528, 531–33, 549, 559, 578, 579, 581

Lucian, Creed of, I: 158 n.4

Lucianists, I: 125, 128, 129, 133 n.43

Lumen Gentium, II: 210, 221, 244, 247 n.4

Lundensian theology, I: 41, 303

Lutheranism, I: xvii, xviii, xix, 36, 37, 51, 52, 64–66, 68, 149, 166, 177, 186, 200, 228 n.33,

612

260, 302, 320 n.40, 336, 337, 344, 373, 392, 405 n.19, 418, 422, 435, 447, 450, 455, 456, 458, 460, 506–10, 548; II: 62 n.2, 129, 133, 137, 138, 162, 185, 195, 196, 198, 230, 235, 236, 239, 254, 266, 269, 277, 295, 302, 303, 312 n.10, 325, 341, 351, 355, 358, 359, 361, 364 n.72, 366 nn.117,118,124, 374, 382, 388 nn.85,86, 415, 509

Manicheism, I: 304, 361; II: 572
Maoism, I: 565
Marks of the Church, II: 223–36, 239
Marriage, I: 338, 339, 389, 449; II: 367, 383–85, 462, 464, 507, 508
Martyrdom, I: 29, 68, 125; II: 15, 20, 507, 584
Marxism, I: 252, 253, 271, 476, 565; II: 397, 459, 468, 509, 541, 545–51, 580
Mary, I: 500, 504, 505, 533, 546, 547
Mass, II: 22, 148, 231, 232, 296–98, 308, 310, 312, 337, 340, 344, 351, 352, 353, 356, 382.
  See also Eucharist
Materialism, I: 13; II: 543
Matter, I: 238, 307, 308, 313, 333–35, 339, 343, 345, 356, 440, 499, 530, 531; II: 159–62, 287, 300–302, 304, 306, 313 n.36, 348, 359, 360, 456, 531, 546, 548, 568, 569
Memory, remembrance, I: 26, 89, 93, 115, 145, 397, 403, 521; II: 152, 211, 218, 308, 337–40, 345, 349, 350, 361, 362 n.9, 380
Mercy, I: 187, 256, 285, 344, 421, 522, 523, 556; II: 6, 21–23, 25, 26, 33, 35, 49, 53, 57–59, 61, 65, 66, 68, 69, 71–76, 79, 81–83, 85, 90, 91, 95, 98, 138, 139, 302, 338, 353, 365 n.83, 374, 411, 414, 417, 419, 433, 441, 578
Merit, I: 217, 415, 416, 434, 546; II: 7, 130, 296, 404, 406, 423 n.7, 426, 428
Messiah, I: 489–93, 500, 522, 559, 560; II: 8, 11, 114, 210, 218, 284, 287, 476, 488–90, 492–98, 499 n.2, 515, 517, 518, 522, 549, 557, 558, 582, 584
Metaphysics, metaphysical, I: 14, 18, 39–42, 83, 147, 163–67, 202, 217, 220, 230, 231, 233, 262, 264 n.25, 315, 316, 363, 364, 389, 433–46, 470, 471, 475, 478, 500, 510, 517, 522, 530–33, 536–38, 540; II: 16, 28, 30, 31, 39, 52, 61, 75, 79, 88, 135, 160–62, 258, 300–302, 304, 306, 344, 348, 356, 357, 360, 420, 479, 541, 543, 544
Millennium, II: 154, 504, 505, 507–10, 580, 583, 584
Mind, I: 18, 19, 34, 35, 39, 117, 124, 143, 145, 152, 153, 172–74, 215, 228 n.32, 236, 238, 309, 332, 334, 370, 397, 402, 424, 524, 550, 562; II: 105, 127, 128, 167, 168, 177 nn.9,10, 187, 267, 271, 301, 302, 356, 357, 425, 436, 439, 453, 465, 537, 565, 566
Ministry, I: xviii, 9, 61, 72, 74, 207, 490, 493, 498, 554, 555; II: 5, 11, 59, 149, 150, 162, 163 n.10, 205, 207, 223–31, 233–36, 246, 263, 264, 317, 324, 333, 357, 378, 380, 382, 492, 515

Miracles, I: 13, 24, 68, 73, 222, 288, 344, 440, 441, 483, 484, 486, 488, 489, 528, 538; II: 30, 61, 109, 161, 169, 170, 269, 282–88, 356–61, 492, 496, 515
Mission, 5, 6, 26, 55, 58, 109, 115, 118, 155, 254, 257, 260, 262, 481, 512, 522, 535, 553, 559, 568; II: 114, 115, 117, 128, 153, 156, 192–94, 207–9, 223, 224, 235–37, 263, 264, 283, 292, 293, 295, 298, 315, 316, 318, 320, 332, 333, 369, 371, 375, 376, 495, 525
Modalism, I: 119, 120, 122, 123, 126, 128, 130, 134 n.60, 150, 151, 154, 500, 532
Monarchianism, I: 122, 281, 283, 500, 501
Monenergism, I: 509
Monergism, II: 60
Monism, I: 271, 300, 307, 310, 331, 333, 334, 369, 387
Monophysitism, I: 504–7, 514, 532
Monotheism, I: 56, 76, 243, 470, 471, 500; II: 28, 204, 484, 490
Monotheletism, I: 507
Montanism, I: 304; II: 153, 154, 163 n.19, 206, 405, 422 n.6, 507
Moral, morality, I: 39, 40, 47, 61, 70, 73, 74, 202, 204, 218, 223, 230, 234, 235, 240–45, 254, 306, 313, 314, 331, 335, 336, 363, 365, 367, 369, 374, 386, 411, 412, 417, 433, 437, 438, 447, 455, 471, 475, 483, 484, 488, 501, 504, 510, 511, 518, 537; II: 6, 16, 17, 19, 31–34, 36, 40, 45 n.77, 47, 72, 79, 82, 83, 98, 136, 143, 146, 147, 155, 158, 162, 206, 217, 219, 270, 273, 275, 311, 321, 322, 331, 332, 368, 369, 374, 395, 396, 400, 402–5, 407–9, 418, 420, 425–27, 432, 436, 439, 442 n.1, 445, 447, 450, 453, 476, 543
Mother of God, I: 504, 533
Mystery, I: 18, 30, 31, 46, 58, 74, 108, 116, 138, 183, 200, 209, 355, 385, 428, 455, 474, 486, 487, 498, 505, 506, 522, 533, 535, 553, 564; II: 7, 8, 41, 74, 76, 84, 187, 200, 245, 264, 292, 307, 354, 574
Mystical, mysticism, I: 34, 39, 202, 210, 216, 219, 398, 471, 487, 512, 554; II: 106, 175, 266, 299, 308, 410, 429, 434, 452, 505, 574
Mystical communion, II: 200, 214, 215, 244, 297, 344, 371, 381, 428, 526
Myth, I: 10, 14, 18, 19, 77, 104, 116, 118, 168, 171, 172, 263 n.15, 277, 278, 312, 328, 329, 335, 337, 356, 373, 385, 386, 389, 390, 391, 400, 405 n.25, 439, 462 n.1, 470, 475, 513, 524, 527–30, 532, 540, 545, 547–49, 551–53; II: 40, 61, 79, 83, 87, 98, 165–67, 175, 483, 518, 534

Nag Hammadi, II: 164 n.32; II: 265
Name, I: 15, 56, 87–93, 95, 96, 96 n.1. 99, 110, 346, 371, 470, 497, 498, 553, 557, 560, 563; II: 69, 81, 82, 93, 121, 134, 198, 208, 298, 315, 316, 322, 339, 456
Naturalism, I: 13, 20, 24, 25, 68, 73, 254, 271, 344, 350; II: 159, 160, 171, 174, 175, 285,

INDEXES

286, 288, 405, 425, 434, 436, 441, 442, 453, 455, 482, 530, 561
Natural theology, I: 10–12, 14, 15, 35, 38, 39, 56, 141, 150, 151, 153, 182, 203, 205, 206, 216, 230, 233, 242, 298, 348, 534; II: 29, 31, 35, 173, 258
Nature, natures, I: 13–15, 18, 23, 24, 33, 34, 40, 68, 84, 146, 216, 217, 222, 233, 234, 230, 239, 244, 254, 269, 270, 271, 284, 287, 288, 298, 304, 307, 308, 313, 318, 328, 329, 335, 336, 342, 343, 350, 351, 354, 355, 391, 392, 400, 403, 404 n.14, 405 n.16, 410, 412–15, 417–19, 420, 425, 434, 440, 469, 494, 499, 504–8, 511, 512, 514, 520, 521, 522, 525, 528, 531, 532, 534–36, 539, 541, 546, 550, 551, 554, 561; II: 28–30, 38, 44 n.62, 52, 56, 57, 60, 61, 84, 85, 95, 110, 129, 160, 165, 170–75, 188–94, 204, 205, 212, 220, 224, 235, 243, 247, 253, 259–62, 266, 270, 271, 279, 281, 285–87, 354, 403, 421, 446, 463, 467, 486, 487, 489, 490, 517–19, 525, 533, 561, 582
Negative theology, I: 117, 119, 137, 206, 215, 227 n.27, 541, 548; II: 95, 468, 555
Neo-orthodoxy, I: 42, 301, 348; II: 35
Neoplatonism, I: 32, 34, 300, 307
Nestorianism, I: 504, 505, 507, 508, 513, 533
Nicea, Council of, I: 47, 111, 127, 135, 502, 514, 533; II: 148, 313 n.23
Nicene, Nicene-Constantinopolitan Creeds, I: 57, 71, 110, 129–31, 502; II: 123 n.49, 148, 203, 319
Nihilism, I: 83; II: 147, 397, 416, 543
Ninety-five Theses, II: 278, 296, 577
Nominalism, I: 35, 173, 216, 217, 226 n.11, 416, 560
Norm, criterion, I: 22, 25, 26, 45, 47, 49, 51, 55, 56, 61–66, 74, 95, 110, 111, 148, 277, 364, 451, 469, 470, 475, 477, 492, 507, 523, 566; II: 119–21, 146, 148, 151, 154, 163 n.5, 173, 176, 187, 203, 208, 212, 217–20, 230, 233, 236, 260, 291, 293, 294, 306, 319, 327, 352, 360, 369, 379, 382, 383, 526
Novatianism, II: 405

Obedience, I: 48, 67, 155, 157, 189, 208, 400, 447, 459, 525; II: 21, 25, 26, 32–34, 45 nn.67,77, 48, 83, 126, 192, 194–96, 203, 205, 206, 213, 214, 220, 231, 232, 236, 262, 294, 295, 297–99, 317, 320, 337, 339, 340, 342, 425, 455, 484, 497
Object, objective, I: 174, 530; II: 6, 34, 36, 37, 74, 83, 95, 96, 174, 175, 226, 285, 300, 302, 305, 325, 326, 343, 347–50, 352, 361, 368, 371, 384, 427, 428, 430, 464, 546
Ockhamism, I: 35
Office, II: 26, 43 n.42, 148–50, 163 n.5, 226–31, 264, 267, 377–83, 451
Ontology, ontological, I: 34, 117, 130, 136, 140, 147, 152, 163–79, 290, 294, 299, 304, 306, 309, 313, 331, 363, 369, 386–88, 390, 391, 394, 399, 439, 500, 511, 528, 530–36,

539–41, 545; II: 107, 115, 145, 160–62, 188, 227, 229, 276, 306, 308, 313 n.36, 320, 323, 324, 357, 369, 403, 416, 420, 542
Orange, Second Council of, I: 387, 414, 420, 434, 457; II: 126, 296, 313 n.20
Order, I: 30, 103, 203, 238, 357, 301, 308, 317, 318, 355, 448, 456; II: 21, 22, 24, 32–34, 36, 38, 72, 81, 87, 90, 91, 130, 131, 167, 188, 189, 223, 227, 232, 236–39, 276, 284, 340, 343, 374, 384, 397, 415, 417, 428, 429, 448, 459, 495, 523, 545, 560, 562
Order of Salvation, II: 128–30, 428, 429
Ordination, II: 149, 150, 161, 224–31, 233, 318, 329, 341, 468, 377–83
Origenism, I: 124, 125, 129, 135

Pantheism, I: 34, 300, 307, 310, 476
Papacy, II: 133, 230, 231, 236, 333, 388 n.85, 508, 577
Papal Confutation, II: 130, 336 n.77
Parable, I: 219, 223, 225, 443, 486, 489, 538; II: 199, 263, 440, 520, 571, 578, 582, 583
Parapsychology, II: 563, 566
Parousia, I: 493, 499; II: 448, 495, 498, 501, 503, 508, 513–15, 518, 523, 529, 531, 560, 572, 573, 579–87, 581
Patripassionism, I: 189, 532
Peace, I: 43, 486, 564, 565; II: 117, 243, 377, 441, 455, 489, 522, 523, 525, 529, 551, 560
Pelagianism, I: 32, 36, 61, 414, 502; II: 137, 405, 427
Penance, II: 37, 49, 51, 129, 130, 134, 231, 274–78, 295, 316, 327, 367–77, 405, 454, 461, 505
Pentecost, I: 476, 551; II: 117, 316, 332, 333 n.2
Person, I: 23, 57, 73, 75, 105, 122, 123, 135, 136, 139, 143, 144, 146–48, 150, 158 n.5, 165, 169–73, 175, 224, 333–35, 364, 370, 387, 392, 395–97, 400–402, 406 n.41, 412, 414, 416, 422–24, 426, 430 n.32, 475, 502, 504, 506, 511–13, 521, 526, 527, 530, 538, 539; II: 5, 7, 56, 96, 105, 106, 126, 127, 145, 152, 159, 172, 175, 188, 209, 226, 229, 243, 260, 264, 265, 300, 301, 305, 342, 347, 349, 356, 357, 359, 378, 379, 403, 411, 417, 421, 425, 427, 431, 432, 437, 438, 452, 453, 461, 463, 478, 492, 494, 503, 508, 513, 517, 523, 530, 531, 540, 564, 568, 573
Pharisees, I: 486, 488; II: 263, 285, 311, 401, 440, 446
Philosophy, philosophical, I: 10, 30, 31, 35, 38, 40–42, 72, 73, 87, 117, 147, 167, 181, 203–5, 231, 239, 253, 271, 306, 311, 316, 343, 512, 530, 531, 536, 538; II: 105, 106, 174, 188, 209, 258, 259, 271, 274, 323
Pietism, I: 5, 16, 34, 38, 39, 51, 68, 149, 347; II: 128, 129, 133, 170, 215, 429, 478, 506
Platonism, I: 13, 35, 125, 144, 200, 216, 218, 225 n.4, 230, 306, 411, 503, 536; II: 123 n.45
Pluralism, I: 37, 43, 45, 558; II: 8, 532
Pneumatology, I: 58, 109; II: 108 n.3, 109, 120, 121, 123 nn.29,47, 130, 134, 143, 146, 149,

154, 159, 162 n.1, 165, 166, 171, 177
Political theology, I: 10, 24, 461; II: 197, 458–60, 525–29
Polytheism, I: 56, 127, 243; II: 175
Positivism, I: 53, 221, 252
Power, powers, I: 61, 67, 101, 106, 115, 173, 185, 203, 237, 275, 278, 281, 285, 288, 293, 299, 301, 303, 312, 329, 371, 387, 433, 474, 484, 485, 498, 514, 524, 531, 534, 538, 541, 542, 546, 549, 553, 554, 564, 565, 566; II: 24, 26–28, 38, 40, 56, 84, 85, 87, 94, 188, 195, 199, 200, 206, 216, 226, 233, 238, 244, 258–62, 266, 267, 282, 283, 303, 308, 324, 360, 368, 370, 378, 380, 382, 383, 398, 404, 406–8, 419, 433, 435, 437, 452, 453, 457, 483, 493, 502, 507, 520, 529, 551, 578
Pragmatism, I: 24, 25
Praxis, I: 7, 14, 24, 25, 30, 263 n.14; II: 486, 487, 491
Prayer, I: 50, 54, 88, 90, 92, 93, 95, 106, 108, 110, 149, 155, 172, 176, 177, 218, 439, 460, 524, 534; II: 119, 157, 158, 172, 174, 204, 218, 223, 231, 232, 253, 264, 269, 274, 279–92, 295, 297, 310, 311, 321, 322, 329, 339, 340, 341, 343, 349–53, 361, 364 n.78, 368, 370–72, 375–77, 383, 385, 387 nn.58,76, 483, 525, 552, 576, 579
Preaching, proclamation, I: 7, 22, 31, 39, 49, 54, 74, 75, 77, 91, 110, 111, 149, 152, 176, 177, 297, 357, 474, 476–78, 481, 483–85, 492, 498, 513, 517, 519, 523, 524, 527, 536, 538, 548–50, 552, 557, 572; II: 17, 18, 59, 68, 72, 77 n.4, 80, 92, 93, 110, 115, 117, 119, 125, 126, 128, 130, 133, 137, 139, 141 nn.3,4, 144, 157, 158, 169, 208, 210, 216, 218, 220, 223–26, 228, 232–34, 239, 244, 245, 257, 261, 263–67, 269, 272, 273, 276–78, 284, 285, 287, 292, 297, 300, 303, 304, 311, 312, 316, 332, 333, 349, 352, 374, 382, 395, 396, 399, 401, 405, 410, 419, 421, 422, 424 n.24, 437, 442 n.5, 448, 457, 460 n.2, 461–64, 476, 491, 494, 497, 508, 520, 562
Predestination (election), I: 37, 38, 108, 205, 209, 291, 387, 391, 414, 415, 420, 421, 451, 453, 461; II: 31, 65–70, 77, 125, 134–39, 141 nn.25,29,31,37, 142, 160, 198, 199, 206, 207, 213, 232, 267, 374
Presbyter, II: 328, 376–81
Presbyterian Confession of 1967, II: 221 n.15
Presence of God, I: 185, 200, 216, 286, 290, 341, 342, 367, 376, 396, 474, 475, 497, 501, 507, 509, 534, 535, 538, 540, 547, 550, 552, 553, 560, 561; II: 73, 74, 105, 106, 112, 113, 117, 120, 121, 126, 129, 144, 145, 161, 162, 172, 191, 212, 216, 232, 243, 266, 281, 296, 304–6, 308, 309, 323, 326, 347, 349–51, 354, 355, 358–61, 378, 417, 483, 568
Priest, priesthood, I: 283; II: 94, 161, 206, 227–29, 233, 261, 317, 319, 324, 329, 333, 342, 343, 351, 352, 382, 383, 488, 493, 508
Priesthood of all believers, II: 227, 228, 324, 333, 381

Priesthood of Christ, II: 25, 26, 85–88, 204
Priestly document, I: 276, 280, 286, 287, 382 n.49, 393, 398, 421, 448; II: 262
Process, I: 152, 245, 255, 271, 300, 342, 343, 347, 350, 353, 532, 564; II: 7, 128, 130, 133, 166, 168–73, 188–90, 194, 200, 204, 227–29, 265, 287, 353, 354, 400, 403, 404, 406–8, 427, 429, 430–42, 506, 528, 530, 531, 535, 546–48, 553, 561, 581
Procession of the Spirit from the Son, I: 57; II: 148, 162 n.3
Processions, I: 57, 137, 138, 142–44, 146–48, 155, 156, 299; II: 148
Process theology, I: 14, 42, 167, 210 n.3, 315–18; II: 170–72, 178 n.15, 270, 532
Progress, II: 213, 367, 374, 400, 401, 414, 426, 428, 430–42, 450, 479, 482, 529, 535, 536, 537, 549, 551, 576, 586
Promise, I: 26, 46, 49, 64, 76, 88, 89, 104, 105, 171–73, 199, 224, 285, 434, 437, 443, 456, 457, 461, 484, 488, 492, 524, 528, 554, 565; II: 61, 74, 75, 77 n.4, 92, 109, 111, 113, 114, 117–19, 131–35, 137, 139, 141 n.30, 147, 149, 152, 159, 210, 213, 259, 261, 262, 266, 267, 269, 274, 276, 279, 281, 284, 291, 294–99, 309, 312 n.10, 313 n.14, 315, 319–22, 326, 329, 331, 333 n.2, 337, 338, 341, 342, 344–49, 353, 355, 357, 358, 360, 361, 368, 370, 374–76, 392, 413, 414, 417, 418, 422, 443 n.16, 449, 454, 458, 459, 464, 466, 486–89, 492, 494, 495, 497, 498, 502, 504, 513, 514, 517, 522, 524, 528, 529, 537, 542, 549–51, 557, 559, 560, 574, 575, 579, 582, 586
Prophet, prophecy, I: 13, 66, 68, 87, 103, 168, 219, 222, 223, 225, 252, 256, 281, 282, 286, 367, 368, 374, 377, 378, 423, 443, 450, 473, 505; II: 12, 19, 44 n.42, 105, 109–20, 122 nn.4,11,12, 123 n.28, 134, 149, 151, 152, 154, 157, 210, 226, 260, 261, 263, 272, 283, 285, 319–21, 345, 347, 378, 380, 383, 387 n.58, 401, 412, 446, 482, 485–90, 492, 495–97, 507, 522, 529, 575, 582
Prophethood of Christ, II: 25, 26, 43 n.42, 263
Protestantism, I: 12, 20, 22, 23, 29, 32, 33, 36, 41, 45–48, 54, 62, 66, 67, 70, 71, 73, 75, 77, 84, 217, 427, 519; II: 25, 133, 207, 215, 216, 219, 229, 230, 253, 270, 277, 286, 296, 297, 304, 307–10, 329, 337, 343, 352–54, 372, 377, 397, 418, 426, 427, 430, 439, 449, 566, 577
Protestant orthodoxy, I: 11, 13, 34, 36–39, 43, 51, 54, 64, 66–68, 305, 342, 477, 503, 514, 519, 532; II: 6, 19, 24, 25, 43 n.39, 211, 229–31, 236, 427–29
Providence, I: 24, 65, 67, 277, 293, 303, 313, 341–51, 531; II: 134, 135, 151, 375, 551
Punishment, I: 376, 423; II: 6, 21, 24–26, 29, 32, 35, 43 n.39, 52, 54, 59, 62 n.9, 70, 72, 371, 426, 475, 483, 485, 533, 577
Purgatory, I: 548; II: 481, 503, 505, 568, 570, 573, 576–79

615

INDEXES

Puritanism, I: 308; II: 128, 130, 155, 325, 334 n.16
Purpose, plan, I: 234, 238, 270, 271, 285, 287, 292, 293, 301, 305, 306, 312-14, 317, 318, 324, 326, 327, 336, 354, 392, 442, 448, 455, 456, 459, 545, 555-57; II: 112, 118, 188, 189, 192-94, 197, 204, 212, 216, 224, 229, 231, 232, 243, 247, 262, 266, 413, 490, 521, 523, 545, 551, 555-57

Q source, II: 12, 116, 492

Rationalism, I: 13, 18, 24, 25, 39, 72, 518
Realism, I: 216, 217, 415, 416, 424; II: 325, 522, 523, 582
Reality, I: 15, 17-19, 83, 85, 93, 101, 108, 116, 123, 126, 136, 142, 146, 152, 165, 199, 202, 204, 208, 209, 213, 215, 218, 223, 224, 231, 235, 236, 238, 239, 241, 242, 244, 249, 252, 255, 258, 261, 278, 281, 293, 300, 307-9, 313, 364, 365, 368, 370, 373, 375, 377, 385, 386, 390, 393, 396, 401, 403, 409, 423, 435, 439, 441, 442, 470, 485, 490, 493, 498, 502, 513, 523, 525, 527, 529, 530, 533, 536-38, 540, 541, 546, 551, 560, 561, 565; II: 35, 40, 56, 73, 87, 107, 114, 125-27, 131, 135, 136, 144, 149, 162, 166-68, 170-72, 174, 177, 187, 188, 193, 194, 199, 212, 237, 238, 245, 257, 258, 282, 284, 287, 288, 300, 301, 305-9, 323, 324, 329, 350, 354-56, 358, 360, 376, 395, 404, 406, 411, 412, 417, 418, 437, 464, 475, 521, 525, 529, 531, 545, 546, 556, 559, 564, 579, 586
Reason, I: 9, 10, 11, 12, 16, 17, 18, 24, 34, 36, 39, 47, 62, 68, 71, 120, 150, 152, 182, 203, 205, 206, 214, 217, 226 n.13, 230, 233, 234, 270, 306, 311, 316, 331, 365 n.3, 369, 370, 392, 395, 397, 416, 417, 418, 419, 424, 479, 484, 524, 537, 538, 549, 550; II: 30, 31, 58, 70, 76, 95, 97, 131, 132, 173, 187, 190, 219, 260, 263, 267, 330, 341, 371, 377, 421, 455, 462, 469 n.7, 475-77, 496, 536, 537, 542, 547, 551, 565
Recapitulation, I: 305, 525; II: 20, 21, 37, 40, 208, 209, 214, 508
Reconciliation, I: 25, 530, 541, 568; II: 5, 6, 9, 20, 24, 29, 30, 31, 32, 33, 36, 50, 51, 57, 59, 65, 72, 76, 79, 169, 190, 232, 235, 371, 372, 373, 385 n.5, 462, 581
Redemption, 7; I: 30, 40, 56, 96, 199, 209, 224, 252, 269, 272, 276, 285, 288, 290, 291, 292, 304-6, 313, 335, 341, 342, 348-50, 373, 411, 444, 447-49, 455, 459, 469, 499, 536, 548, 562; II: 134, 225, 232, 235, 243, 244, 246, 247, 272, 280, 304, 396, 401, 403, 459, 462, 481, 484, 486, 504, 506, 508, 559, 565, 573
Reformation, I: xviii, 13, 32, 34, 35, 36, 38, 39, 41, 46, 50, 51, 53, 56, 57, 58, 62, 63, 67, 68, 70, 73, 74, 75, 76, 77, 110, 148, 149, 157, 216, 224, 335, 336, 342, 345, 346, 389, 397, 405 n.16, 412, 417, 419, 457, 507, 511; II: 5, 20, 24, 31, 41, 47, 49, 125, 126, 128, 129, 130, 133, 135, 139, 191, 196, 198, 215, 216, 225, 227-31, 278, 293, 295-99, 302, 303, 304, 307, 308, 310, 324, 325, 332, 333, 337, 343, 344, 351, 352, 354, 355, 357, 358, 376, 382, 383, 402, 406, 407, 415, 426, 428, 430, 432, 433, 438, 448, 454, 458, 505, 577, 581
Reformed theology, I: 37, 51, 65, 66, 507, 508, 548; II: 275, 292, 312 n.5, 317, 318, 325, 341, 344, 355, 357, 358, 361, 361 n.21, 363 nn.25,32, 382, 383
Reformers, I: xvii, 33, 38, 69, 217, 334, 378, 383 n.54, 417, 421; II: 130, 131, 161, 207, 225, 226, 233, 275, 297, 324, 343, 374, 381, 384, 388 n.93, 400, 407, 414, 415, 418, 422, 439, 451, 458, 506, 566, 577
Regeneration, I: 419; II: 45 n.75, 315, 321, 322-25, 331, 332, 348, 425, 427, 428, 445, 449, 450, 452, 453, 460 n.3
Reincarnation, II: 481, 482, 564, 568, 570
Relations: trinitarian, I: 91, 96, 107, 123, 126, 127, 137, 140, 142-44, 146-48, 155-57, 160 n.45, 169, 171, 189, 288, 535, 541; II: 137
Relationship, I: 17, 39, 142, 144, 200, 203, 204, 205, 208, 209, 218, 224, 239, 251, 254, 255, 257, 269, 270, 272, 279, 298, 299, 302, 304, 307, 310, 311, 315, 324, 327, 331, 332, 334, 335, 337, 338, 341, 344, 345, 367-69, 374, 378, 382 n.35, 391, 394-401, 405 n.16, 406 n.41, 409, 417, 418, 422, 427, 429 n.20, 435, 436, 442, 448, 449, 450, 459, 461, 462, 474, 513, 539, 554; II: 22, 23, 27, 30, 33, 37, 119, 126-28, 131, 183, 184, 187, 204, 213, 214, 243, 246, 259, 263, 276, 384, 400, 421, 446, 462, 464, 566, 586
Religion, I: 5, 6, 10, 12, 16, 20, 30, 31, 39, 40, 57, 65, 72, 73, 83, 85, 87, 88, 94, 100, 103, 105, 112 n.4, 116, 117, 127, 163, 164, 169, 172, 175, 198, 199, 206, 211 n.12, 221, 231, 239, 240, 242-45, 248 n.40, 251, 252, 254, 257, 260, 263 n.15, 272, 277, 284, 307, 311, 392, 470, 476, 487, 492, 512, 524, 527, 538, 558, 559, 561, 562, 564-68; II: 27-31, 86, 106, 126, 146, 147, 152, 159, 193, 253, 258, 270, 299, 309, 310, 321, 327, 350, 409, 416, 420, 429, 430, 441, 453, 454, 457-59, 462, 479, 481, 482, 484, 485, 488, 501, 503, 524, 545, 547, 550, 553, 585
Repentance, I: 54, 261, 453, 487, 490; II: 11, 33, 128, 129, 274, 275, 278, 303, 316, 318, 319, 320, 329, 367, 371, 373, 374, 414, 448, 460 n.2
Representation, I: 567; II: 33, 70, 148, 244, 258
Resurrection, I: 58, 100, 101, 105, 106, 107, 111, 119, 140, 153, 183, 184, 185, 189, 205, 226 n.13, 255, 291, 292, 346, 436, 455, 461, 470, 475, 479, 480, 487, 491-94, 497-99, 517, 522-25, 528, 529, 537, 538, 546, 548, 549, 550, 551, 552, 562, 564, 566, 567; II: 9, 11, 13, 17-19, 24, 26, 28, 30, 31, 34, 36, 37-40, 52, 56, 60, 67-70, 72, 76, 79, 81, 91-98, 110, 113, 116, 120, 121, 137, 144, 145, 149, 150, 156, 157, 162, 169, 232, 264, 282,

616

284, 285, 308, 315, 316, 323, 326, 332, 342, 344, 345, 349, 357, 359, 366 n.118, 379, 380, 396, 399, 401, 403, 410, 411, 412, 418, 422, 425, 426, 430, 436, 440, 451, 452, 456, 457, 458, 462, 467, 469, 475, 481, 484, 485, 487, 494–99, 501, 503, 509, 514–18, 520, 521, 524, 525, 527, 528, 532–34, 536, 555–71, 575, 580, 582, 584–86
Revelation, I: 6, 9, 10, 13, 14, 15, 16, 17, 18, 23, 24, 30, 31, 34, 35, 45, 46, 47, 49, 50, 54–56, 61, 66, 67, 74, 108, 121, 123, 129, 141, 150, 151, 153, 154, 178 n.24, 182, 199–212, 213–28, 270, 278, 311, 316, 348, 349, 355, 369, 450, 452, 469, 470, 529, 530, 533, 534, 538, 540, 541, 552–56, 559; II: 8, 35, 36, 61, 68–71, 73, 90, 94, 112, 136, 154, 175, 187, 189, 193, 197, 200, 208–11, 219, 220, 231, 232, 257–60, 261, 263, 267, 291, 299, 300, 336 n.73, 346, 475, 507, 508, 509, 514, 516, 519, 524, 574
Revivalism, I: 6
Revolution, I: 42, 486, 488, 489, 491, 565; II: 40, 153, 162, 167, 168, 196, 361, 459, 468, 517
Righteousness, 11; I: 90, 106, 285, 336, 394, 395, 416, 420, 422, 449, 450, 459, 460, 485, 534; II: 5, 14, 16, 24, 30, 38, 48, 49, 54, 56, 62 n.9, 69, 74, 97, 128, 129, 130, 272–76, 296, 302, 303, 310, 311, 320, 326, 331, 369, 374, 395–469, 423 n.16, 523, 525
Rite, I: 70, 93, 95, 244, 293, 374; II: 14, 19, 69, 75, 86–88, 117, 198, 208, 230, 232, 253, 291–99, 303, 304, 307–9, 311, 315–18, 319, 321, 322, 326–30, 332, 339, 342, 345, 350, 358, 361, 367, 371–81, 383–85
Roman Catholicism, I: 12, 14, 29, 33, 35, 37, 38, 42, 45–48, 53, 54, 56, 57, 62, 66–68, 70, 74, 77, 110, 149, 166, 200, 260, 383 n.53, 392, 397, 417, 419, 426, 427, 456, 457, 559; II: 25, 60, 125, 137, 162, 195, 207, 215, 216, 228–31, 236, 237, 253, 254, 270, 276, 278, 286, 293, 296–98, 304, 313 n.19, 314 n.43, 329, 330, 333, 341, 343, 351–58, 361, 364 n.72, 370, 374, 376, 377, 381, 387, 386 n.45, 439, 565, 576–78
Romanticism, I: 33, 39
Rome, Council of, II: 149, 365 n.86

Sabellianism, I: 151, 503, 532
Sacrament, 10; I: 6, 10, 23, 32, 33, 52, 58, 91, 93, 177, 216, 456, 458, 469, 552, 554; II: 59, 68, 77 n.4, 80, 125, 149, 161, 162, 162 n.2, 173, 200, 214–16, 223, 225, 226, 228, 231–33, 239, 244, 253–389, 399, 428, 501, 505, 508, 580
Sacrifice, I: 57, 90, 261, 436, 492, 548; II: 5, 7, 13, 14, 16, 17, 19, 20, 22, 25, 28, 29, 33, 35, 37, 48, 55, 79–91, 175, 232, 253, 309–11, 337, 341, 343, 344, 346, 348, 349, 350, 352, 353, 354, 365 n.83, 382, 383, 514, 560, 576, 577

Salvation, I: 29, 30, 31, 33, 36, 49, 57, 58, 65, 67, 71, 74–76, 89, 95, 104, 108, 129, 149, 175, 200, 206, 209, 232, 233, 260, 329, 342, 372, 376, 406 n.41, 416, 420, 452, 458, 470, 487, 493, 497, 498, 501–5, 513, 514, 520, 521, 533, 534, 538, 545, 547, 549, 557–62, 564, 565, 566, 568, 569 n.11; II: 6, 9, 13, 16, 21, 24, 25, 36, 40, 57, 60, 92, 93, 125, 127–29, 132, 137, 139, 141 n.37, 163 n.15, 191, 215, 232, 244, 266, 267, 270, 272, 274, 282, 284, 285, 295, 296, 297, 310, 313 n.22, 319, 328, 339, 340, 353, 354, 372, 373, 397, 403, 404, 412–16, 420, 421, 427–29, 435, 442 n.5, 450, 453, 480, 483, 485, 486–90, 492, 496–98, 501, 503, 505, 506, 508, 515, 518, 519, 525, 526, 528, 529, 531–33, 557, 560, 578–80, 584, 585
Sanctification, I: 96, 124, 365 n.3, 461; II: 34, 45 n.75, 49, 86, 130, 224, 235, 236, 296, 319, 330, 339, 340, 384, 425–42, 456, 457
Satan, I: 364, 372, 387, 389, 403, 410, 473, 485, 498, 522, 548; II: 21, 34, 73, 77 n.2, 322, 447, 505, 506, 507, 584. *See also* Devil
Satisfaction, vicarious satisfaction, I: 548; II: 6, 7, 14–16, 19–27, 29 nn.39,43, 31–33, 35–38, 45 n.75, 48–54, 57, 59, 62 n.9, 69, 72, 76, 79, 88, 96, 253, 278, 310, 311, 353, 365 n.83, 371, 372, 373, 402
Savior, I: 54, 476, 521, 523, 560, 561, 563, 564, 567; II: 273, 341, 475, 485, 498, 522, 523, 578
Scholasticism, I: 10, 11, 33, 34, 36–40, 51, 144, 147, 171, 173, 174, 185, 186, 205, 217, 303, 345, 347, 394, 415, 477, 507, 508, 552; II: 19, 52, 56, 128, 133, 139, 140 n.10, 164 n.37, 258, 307, 314 n.52, 324, 325, 348, 351, 354, 358, 359, 366 n.117, 373, 381, 384, 385, 429, 433, 436
Science, I: 9, 12, 13, 15, 16–20, 23, 39, 40, 42, 74, 76, 208, 221, 222, 230, 231, 233, 262, 271, 272, 297, 308, 314, 315, 316, 318, 324, 343, 354, 386, 392, 403, 475, 476, 477, 546, 551; II: 171, 172, 285, 286, 287, 288, 479, 529, 530, 532, 551, 556, 557
Scotism, I: 35, 173, 206, 415, 416, 451
Scots Confession, I: 65
Scripture, I: 6, 10, 11, 21–23, 25, 26, 29, 34, 36, 41, 45, 46, 47, 48, 50, 52, 53, 55, 56, 61–78, 87, 90, 92, 99, 102, 103, 105, 108, 123–25, 143, 145, 155, 170, 174, 185, 200, 201, 210 n.7, 224, 226 n.15, 276, 280, 293, 305, 394, 458, 460, 477, 492, 508, 538; II: 9, 13, 15, 19, 37, 65, 67, 75, 77 n.2, 79, 80, 82, 84, 85, 91–93, 106, 114, 115, 117, 121, 131, 141 n.32, 151–53, 160, 163 n.15, 165, 204, 208, 212, 216, 218, 219, 230, 232, 254, 264, 294, 300, 305, 317, 325, 327, 329, 330, 341, 343, 344, 347, 361, 368, 375, 377, 379, 397, 403, 420, 421, 422, 451, 462, 497, 503, 507, 517, 529, 557, 570
Scripture alone (*sola scriptura*), I: 36, 47, 50, 51, 53, 62, 65, 196

INDEXES

Sects, sectarianism, I: 23; II: 192, 195, 205, 206, 266, 297, 298, 375, 509
Secularism, I: 308, 309
Secularization, I: 12, 42, 283, 297, 308, 309; II: 193, 194, 216, 374, 375, 469
Self, I: 147, 173, 189, 202, 213–16, 218, 219, 220, 221, 223, 224, 225, 230, 234, 235, 240, 243, 254, 331, 334, 364, 368, 370, 371, 373, 374, 375, 377, 378, 381 n.20, 398, 401, 409, 410, 424–28, 452, 460; II: 27, 32, 38, 106, 114, 137, 156, 167, 169, 183, 194, 274, 348, 414, 417, 420, 421, 432, 434, 439, 442, 450, 452–55, 456, 532–34, 542, 543, 551, 586
Senses, I: 71, 231, 240
Sermon on the Mount, I: 483; II: 206, 271, 273, 441, 476, 495
Servant, service, I: 531, 534; II: 114, 200, 216, 226, 244, 378, 451, 454, 455, 457, 458, 488, 489, 490, 495, 497
Seventh-day Adventistism, II: 509
Sexuality, I: 94, 95, 308, 334, 338, 339, 398, 412, 448, 449, 520, 522; II: 371
Shintoism, I: 565
Sign, I: 175, 483, 486, 487, 491, 546; II: 110, 144, 230, 244, 245, 258, 259, 261, 271, 283, 285, 300–302, 305–8, 313 n.28,29,36, 314 n.46, 322, 349, 354–58, 359, 360, 373, 375, 381, 383–85, 419, 476, 517, 522, 529, 547, 556, 560, 571, 581–83
Simul iustus et peccator, I: 54, 334, 458; II: 56, 276, 407–9, 411, 430–35, 450, 451
Sin, **5**; I: 24, 32, 33, 36, 56, 57, 59, 95, 109, 145, 198, 204, 208, 209, 217, 226 n.12, 257, 258, 262, 269, 284, 291, 324, 328, 332, 335, 336, 338, 343, 344, 349, 356, 363–463, 365 n.3, 381 n.16, 382 nn.34,35,48, 383 n.54, 405 n.16, 406 n.41, 430 n.32, 444 n.4, 445 n.29, 480, 491, 493, 494, 498, 505, 520–22, 525, 528, 534, 548, 555, 563, 564; II: 5–7, 11–16, 19, 21–24, 27, 29–34, 37–41, 45 n.67, 48, 49, 51–57, 59, 61, 62 n.9, 63 n.19, 63 n.24, 69, 70, 73, 74, 77 n.2, 79, 80, 81, 82, 83, 85–91, 97, 98, 118, 124 n.50, 128, 131, 132, 134, 154, 190, 204, 207, 225, 232, 263, 267, 270–78, 280, 282, 295, 298, 302, 308, 315, 319, 320, 325, 331, 334 n.17, 336 n.73, 341, 344, 353, 354, 368, 369–76, 381, 396, 399, 400–402, 404, 405, 407–9, 411–17, 419, 425, 427, 430–36, 438–40, 442, 446, 448, 449, 450, 451, 453, 466, 469, 488, 514, 522, 527, 562, 573, 576, 577
Smalcald Articles, I: 405 n.16; II: 9 n.1, 230
Socinianism, I: 37, 150; II: 24, 25, 26, 42 n.28
Son, I: 73, 93, 106, 110, 111, 120, 121, 123–30, 136, 137, 140, 142–46, 148, 151, 153, 155, 156, 158 n.14, 169–75, 185, 188, 205, 289, 291, 470, 479, 480, 489, 490, 492, 495 n.19, 499–502, 505, 507, 510, 511, 515 n.21, 521–23, 525, 527–36, 538, 539, 545–48, 552, 553, 557–62, 564; II: 22, 23, 25, 35, 38, 53, 57, 59, 60, 62 n.9, 69, 73, 74, 92, 94, 98, 105, 123 n.49, 124 n.49, 126, 138, 148, 160, 162 n.3, 166, 167, 171, 175, 225, 260, 263, 315, 317, 322, 339, 340, 402, 403, 410, 456, 495, 497, 508, 528, 560, 569, 575, 581
Son of Man, I: 443, 489, 490, 507; II: 13, 15, 160, 263, 282, 477, 490, 492, 493, 495, 517, 518, 520, 525, 571, 572, 583
Sophiology, II: 174, 175
Sophists, I: 418; II: 52, 63 n.24
Soteriology, I: 36, 94, 188, 205, 272, 293, 377, 386, 411, 451, 452, 499, 519, 534, 545; II: 13, 14, 19, 20, 25, 26, 42 n.22, 107, 485
Soul, I: 30, 32, 141, 144, 145, 172, 203, 206, 211 n.12, 214, 215, 220, 333–36, 344, 388, 392, 401, 412, 413, 416, 418, 420, 425, 484, 503, 505, 519, 522, 523, 531; II: 32, 127, 131, 133, 159, 160, 162, 223, 234, 301, 306, 357, 397, 425, 429, 432, 436, 439, 447, 453, 465, 475, 476, 481, 484, 503, 525, 531, 534, 562, 563, 565, 566, 567, 570, 575, 577
Space, I: 186, 200, 232, 396, 528, 529, 530, 541, 550, 552; II: 208, 262, 264, 287, 303, 356, 357, 359, 448, 521, 552, 558, 565, 568, 569, 570, 574
Spinozism, I: 300
Spirit, **8**; I: 15, 40, 48, 101, 147, 151, 152, 153, 156, 157, 165, 168, 172–75, 285, 305, 333–35, 339, 343, 356, 368, 416, 418, 420, 503, 531, 548, 558; II: 19, 27, 28, 29, 30, 82, 92, 95, 105–78, 187–91, 205, 271, 301, 302, 304, 305, 306, 309, 320, 326, 349, 369, 398, 405, 420, 430, 441, 456, 487, 518, 537, 548, 551, 563, 564, 566, 579
Spirit of God (Holy Spirit) **8**; I: 6, 17, 23, 24, 51, 57, 58, 64, 66–71, 75, 92, 93, 96, 101, 102, 106–11, 112 n.19, 121–31, 133 n.33, 136, 137, 140, 142, 143, 145, 148–53, 155–57, 169, 171, 173, 174, 185, 187, 189, 190, 200, 217, 226 n.15, 272, 344, 367, 416, 418, 419, 420, 474, 479, 487, 494, 501, 522, 537, 538, 546, 551–54, 562; II: 18, 27, 37, 82, 86, 92, 98, 105–78, 184, 187, 194, 198, 204, 210, 211, 215, 230, 231, 232, 260, 261, 265, 267, 271, 275, 277, 284, 295, 296, 297, 309, 315, 316, 317, 319, 320–22, 328, 329, 332, 333, 339, 340, 343, 350, 356, 358, 360, 367–69, 371, 379–81, 385, 419, 420, 424 n.24,26, 428, 429, 432, 439, 440, 442, 451, 457, 463, 465, 469, 469 n.7, 487, 489, 496, 497, 503, 504, 507, 508, 520, 523, 548, 559, 563, 566, 568, 576, 579
Spiritual, spirituality, I: 106, 150, 206, 224, 500, 501; II: 29, 30, 84, 126, 134, 145, 149, 160, 162, 167, 199, 217, 220, 234, 253, 260, 266, 300, 301, 308, 313 n.36, 339, 348, 350, 351, 358, 360, 373, 374, 405, 411, 415, 419, 450, 451, 453, 456, 458, 482, 506, 508, 564
Spiritualists, I: 69
Stoicism, I: 13, 32, 289, 300, 306, 307, 343, 425; II: 187, 260
Subject, subjectivism, I: 16, 17, 197, 217, 452, 475, 530, 537, 538, 540; II: 6, 7, 34, 36, 47, 70, 83, 95, 96, 98, 174, 226, 257, 258, 260

618

301, 303, 307, 320, 326, 359, 372, 373, 403, 404, 423 n.7, 427, 428, 429, 430, 436
Subject/object, I: 152, 153, 168, 170, 174, 176, 182, 186, 187, 188, 189; II: 35, 95, 167, 168, 169, 171
Subordinationism, I: 119–24, 125–28, 130, 131, 149, 150, 151, 154, 156; II: 188
Substance, I: 122, 123, 128, 135, 136, 141, 143, 145–48, 165–68, 177 n.6, 231, 300, 307, 417, 419, 502–4, 512, 536, 540; II: 126–28, 133, 136, 160–62, 173, 188, 239, 339, 354, 356, 403, 417, 421, 433, 436, 463
Substitution, II: 15, 24, 25, 29, 33, 52, 58, 70, 82, 84, 88, 190, 272
Suffering, I: 101, 171, 182, 183, 188, 189, 209, 216, 259, 346, 364, 382 n.46, 437–44, 447, 453, 455, 460, 461, 475, 488, 493, 494, 522, 531–33, 541, 547, 548; II: 13–16, 19, 24, 25, 29, 32, 33, 38, 49, 52, 53, 55 61, 62 n.9, 67, 71, 74, 77 n.10, 85, 177, 214, 223, 235, 236, 467, 469, 488, 490, 493, 560, 576, 586
Supernatural, supernaturalism, I: 20, 23, 68, 73, 141, 150, 215, 244, 344; II: 126, 135, 194, 285, 286, 288, 310, 357, 365 n.96, 405, 454, 530
Supralapsarianism, II: 137
Symbol, I: 6, 15, 19, 26, 31, 40, 57, 58, 72, 77, 175, 248 n.40, 324, 354, 373, 375, 424, 453, 478, 492, 505, 522, 524, 529, 540, 545, 546, 547, 548, 549, 551–55, 560, 561, 563; II: 12, 161, 212, 213, 231, 232, 237, 246, 253, 258, 259, 299, 303, 305, 307, 316, 341, 348, 360, 381, 411, 520, 521, 555, 556

Taoism, I: 244, 254
Teaching, I: 10, 11, 13, 39, 45–47, 49, 52, 55, 62, 70, 72, 77, 85, 110, 342, 435, 477, 485, 489; II: 59, 112, 120, 130, 131, 133, 173, 215, 217, 218, 223, 224, 226, 228, 231–34, 239, 253, 261, 263, 264, 267, 292, 297, 300, 303, 304, 311, 321, 324, 325, 327, 349, 352, 357, 379, 387 n.58, 405, 425, 440, 441, 459, 462, 579, 583
Technology, I: 272, 356, 401; II: 155, 476, 479, 529, 530, 549
Telos, teleology, II: 13, 28, 29, 356, 430, 446, 466, 547
Theodicy, I: 221, 318, 351, 364, 387; II: 138
Theology, I: 1–78, 99, 102, 103, 115, 117–19, 121, 123, 129, 137, 141, 143–45, 147, 149, 151, 153, 166, 169, 179 n.31, 189, 285, 290, 292, 298, 313, 318, 330, 336, 343, 345, 348, 353, 416, 419–21, 438, 443, 447, 461, 470, 484, 509, 510, 528, 533, 534, 546; II: 29, 31, 34, 39, 59, 66, 67, 71–73, 80, 82, 93, 95, 105, 115, 120, 121, 123 n.49, 127, 130, 132–34, 138, 148, 160, 161, 184, 196, 238, 244, 286, 292, 298–300, 304, 307, 324, 348, 351, 354, 355, 403, 459, 468, 476
Theopaschitism, I: 188–90, 191 n.19
Thirty-nine Articles of the Church of England, I: 420; II: 163 n.15, 314 n.50

Thomism, I: 14, 35, 38, 42, 214, 215, 217, 227 n.27, 237, 299, 334
Time, I: 101, 102, 105, 115–17, 119–21, 126, 142, 151, 154, 155, 157, 163, 164, 168, 172, 175, 184, 185, 200, 205–9, 217, 222, 224, 232, 250, 256–61, 501, 528–30, 534, 541, 550, 553, 561, 564, 565, 568; II: 27, 34, 68, 73, 75, 80, 121, 150, 152, 209, 218, 226, 264, 287, 326, 370, 419, 420, 429, 430, 448, 451, 453, 457, 459–61, 466, 478, 495, 496, 513, 516, 519, 521, 541, 552, 558, 565, 568–70, 574, 580–83
Torah, I: 90, 459; II: 261, 264, 270, 400, 423 n.16
Tradition, I: 10, 20–23, 25, 26, 33, 34, 40, 43, 46, 49, 54, 58, 70, 74, 150, 157, 165, 183, 185, 186, 189, 237, 260, 277–79, 283, 285, 286, 289, 290, 293, 300, 304, 307, 313, 317, 318, 332, 335, 336, 338, 349, 356, 371, 386, 387, 393, 396, 399, 403, 421, 428, 436, 481, 488, 525, 533, 540, 551, 557, 559–63, 567; II: 2–46, 55, 60, 61, 62 n.12, 71, 79, 80, 95, 105–7, 115, 116, 126, 130, 137, 148, 160, 166, 167, 173, 174, 177, 208, 209, 212, 214, 216, 219, 229, 234, 264, 278, 293, 294, 295, 298, 300, 303, 305, 306, 317, 319, 320, 324, 325, 330, 332, 337, 339, 341, 343, 352, 360, 382, 395, 397, 402, 404, 405, 447, 458, 536, 537
Traducianism, I: 334, 392, 405 n.19, 412, 413, 425
Transcendence, I: 15, 42, 87, 101, 155, 190, 203, 208, 215, 231, 233, 250, 253, 269, 307, 355, 367, 368, 388, 389, 485, 500, 529, 530, 566; II: 8, 20, 29, 79, 80, 105–7, 110, 114, 147, 148, 159, 194, 261, 297, 346, 356, 383, 517, 534, 537, 570, 571, 586
Transubstantiation, II: 161, 355–57, 361
Trent, Council of, I: 37, 38, 70, 412, 419, 420, 424, 430 n.36, 435, 456–58; II: 20, 126, 133, 293, 296, 305, 312 nn.9,11, 313 nn.17,20, 314 nn.42,49, 353, 354, 365 nn.83,88, 373, 374, 377, 381, 386 nn.32,48, 387 nn.51,54, 388 nn.81,83,84, 389 n.100, 403, 412, 420, 457, 576
Trinity, **2**; I: 11, 31, 56, 71, 75, 200, 206, 210 n.3, 243, 261, 290, 291, 294, 299, 397, 406, 438, 470, 471, 471 n.1, 477, 497, 502, 503, 512, 524 n.3, 517, 530, 532, 535, 539–41; II: 5, 97, 105, 106, 120, 123 n.49, 125, 126, 138, 139, 148, 165, 168, 171, 175, 177, 185, 187, 191, 193, 298, 306, 317, 322, 340, 403, 421
Truth, I: 12–13, 19, 23–26, 29–33, 37, 45–48, 50, 52, 54, 55, 88, 105, 141, 147, 170, 181, 187, 198, 205, 210, 214, 224, 228 n.31, 255, 261, 332, 356, 385, 462, 469, 474, 478, 493, 520, 521, 523, 527, 530, 536, 539, 540, 541, 546, 548, 550, 559, 563; II: 7, 26, 28, 35, 40, 41, 44 n.42, 58, 68, 79, 82, 89, 92, 94, 125, 128, 130, 138, 145, 166, 169, 175, 199, 206, 226–28, 237–39, 259, 261, 266, 267,

INDEXES

272, 302, 303, 309, 355, 357, 358, 360, 361, 379, 406, 408, 419, 420, 428–30, 434, 446, 462, 467, 468, 565
Two-kingdoms doctrine, I: 461, 554, 555; II: 397, 445, 455–60
Two-natures doctrine, I: 47, 57, 477, 478, 497–542; II: 20, 70

Ubiquity, I: 507–9, 552
Understanding, I: 12, 16, 18, 21, 201, 206, 209, 259, 365, 365 n.3, 367, 372, 385, 410, 412, 418, 433, 477, 484, 547; II: 58, 93, 106, 110, 114, 126, 146, 170, 189, 195, 199, 201, 210–12, 226, 228, 233, 253, 259, 260, 262, 269, 287, 303, 304, 326, 328, 330, 336 n.70, 342, 344, 349, 350, 355, 356, 361, 378, 380, 382, 415, 416, 418, 446, 453, 491, 516, 536, 569, 585
Unitarianism, I: 150, 272, 470, 497
Universalism, I: 305, 559, 563, 564, 568; II: 92, 93, 570, 578

Vatican I, I: 45; II: 20, 215, 216
Vatican II, I: 38, 45, 62, 191; II: 215, 216, 230, 244, 336 n.79, 374, 377, 387 n.57
Victory, I: 291, 312, 454, 498, 525, 548, 555, 564, 568; II: 7, 30, 34, 36–41, 48–50, 55, 56, 58, 59, 67, 69, 71, 72, 82, 89, 98, 113, 152, 156, 157, 175, 316, 375, 376, 477, 486, 490, 504, 507, 508, 520, 521
Virgin birth, I: 379, 383 n.60, 413, 424, 500, 522, 527, 528, 530, 546, 547, 556 n.8; II: 354
Vocation. *See* Call

Westminster Confession, I: 37, 65, 420; II: 312 n.5
Will, I: 39, 89, 104, 121, 143, 145, 172–74, 187, 199, 200, 202, 206–9, 218, 224, 229, 230, 240–42, 250, 255–57, 259, 284, 292, 299, 300, 303, 307, 312, 323, 326, 331, 332, 338, 341–43, 346, 347, 349, 363, 364, 365 n.3, 367, 369, 370 372–75, 378, 379, 381 n.20, 383, 387, 388, 390, 395, 397, 399, 401–3, 415–19, 421, 424, 426, 427, 436, 439, 448, 450, 452, 456, 462, 474, 504, 507, 512, 521, 522, 539, 540, 563, 564; II: 13, 26, 31, 32, 38, 53, 54, 58, 61, 65, 66, 68, 74, 77 n.4, 93, 94, 120, 126, 127, 132, 134–39, 141 n.30, 154, 169, 184, 185, 205, 212, 213, 235, 236, 246, 261, 263, 265, 267, 270–72, 274–76, 280, 285, 286, 331–33, 368, 375, 383, 446, 451, 452, 457, 461, 466, 469, 504, 572; bondage of the, **5.3**; I: 375–80, 450, 452, 461; II: 37, 65, 66, 69, 72, 90, 96, 136, 274, 305, 438, 464, 465; free, I: 32, 36, 206, 388, 390, 398, 402, 411, 412, 414, 417, 420, 440, 441; II: 65, 67, 68, 77 n.2, 136, 141 nn.34,35, 214, 404, 576
Wisdom, I: 29, 31, 106, 200, 204, 205, 230, 282, 284, 289, 292, 293, 306, 307, 331, 346, 371, 395, 401, 405 n.15, 442, 450, 453, 534, 539, 564; II: 110, 112–14, 166, 167, 174, 175, 177 nn.2,24, 265, 508

Witness, I: 23, 26, 45, 52, 54, 56, 67, 77, 91, 103, 207, 217, 275, 422, 423, 459, 474–77, 519, 524, 550, 551, 555, 567, 568; II: 5, 15, 32, 82, 117, 118, 120, 126, 154, 171, 190, 193, 195, 201, 203, 204, 210–12, 216, 219, 220, 226, 231, 234, 236, 243, 245, 259, 264, 267, 270, 272, 273, 281, 282, 319, 321, 378, 458, 497, 503, 523, 570, 586
Word, **10**; I: 6, 10, 18, 23, 30, 31, 32, 39, 48, 58, 65, 74, 143, 155, 172, 175–77, 204–9, 216, 217, 222, 223, 256–61, 276, 309, 331, 393, 421, 475, 499, 514, 527, 530, 538, 541, 552, 554; II: 42, 43, 58, 59, 71, 76, 79, 80, 97, 112, 113, 116, 119–21, 122 n.7, 130–35, 137, 141 n.25, 149, 153–58, 173, 176, 184, 253–389, 422, 428, 440–42, 466, 496, 514, 579
Word of God, **10**; I: 9–11, 13, 22, 31, 41, 42, 46–49, 52, 61, 62, 65–69, 73–76, 104, 143, 202, 205, 344, 418, 456, 506, 561; II: 110, 118, 137, 166, 184, 191, 216, 223, 226, 233, 234, 238, 253–389, 421, 439, 503, 505, 527, 556, 569, 574, 580
Works, I: 36, 37, 39, 57, 58, 61, 101, 108, 122, 140, 143, 202, 287, 288, 292, 332, 336, 341, 363, 389, 393, 416, 420, 447–62, 484, 507, 511, 546; II: 17, 56, 58, 60, 86, 116, 125–32, 134, 174, 190, 225, 232, 233, 236, 257, 259, 263, 273, 280, 296–300, 302, 304, 310, 313 nn.20,22 320, 332, 340, 352, 353, 371–74, 400, 403, 405, 414, 417, 420, 421, 423 n.7, 425, 427, 429, 432, 434–42, 442 n.5, 443, 445, 455, 501, 572, 576, 580
World, **4.2**; I: 6, 7, 13, 14, 18, 19, 23, 24, 31, 33–35, 54–56, 59, 78, 117, 121, 143, 149, 152, 153, 167, 168, 175, 182–84, 186–88, 198, 200, 204, 206, 215, 216, 218–23, 225, 226 n.11, 230, 233, 238, 239, 246 n.14, 254, 260, 263 n.15, 269, 270, 275, 276, 281, 282, 287, 289, 327, 329, 334, 335, 337, 341, 344, 346, 348–50, 353, 356, 365, 368, 372, 376, 385, 392, 398, 404 n.14, 410, 417, 425, 440, 441, 443, 449, 450, 454, 474, 484–87, 489, 493, 494, 498, 501, 502, 510, 512, 522, 527, 528, 530, 531, 534, 538, 539, 541, 545, 546, 550–57, 563–66, 568; II: 19, 23, 27, 30, 32, 33, 36, 37, 51, 54, 58, 63 n.24, 69, 74, 76, 86, 90, 92–94, 97, 105, 107, 131, 155–59, 166–69, 171, 172, 175, 183, 184, 187–89, 191, 193–95, 197, 200, 201, 205, 206, 208, 212, 213, 216, 224, 226, 228, 232, 234–36, 238, 243–46, 260, 262, 265, 270, 271, 275, 279–81, 284–87, 292, 299, 302, 308, 318, 319, 323, 333, 354, 369, 374, 395–98, 411, 412, 416, 418, 419, 438, 441, 442, 445–60, 464, 467, 475, 477, 479, 482, 483, 485–87, 490, 492–98, 501, 504, 506, 510, 514, 516–18, 523, 525, 527, 528, 530–32, 534, 536, 541–43, 545, 548, 549, 551, 555, 557, 560, 565, 568, 569, 573, 574, 580, 581, 583–85
World Council of Churches; II: 195, 216, 221 n.15, 244

INDEXES

Worship, I: 23, 71, 77, 88, 104, 126, 199, 259, 370, 427, 469, 498, 499, 501, 502, 524, 534, 535, 561; II: 12, 83, 84, 232, 271, 340, 458, 479, 523

Wrath of God, I: 346, 373, 375, 376, 421, 436, 452–54, 451, 548; II: 5, 6, 14, 22, 24, 25, 28, 30, 31, 34–37, 47–51, 54–61, 62 n.9, 65, 67–69, 71–76, 77 n.4, 77, 82, 90, 91, 93, 98, 138, 139, 270–72, 418, 522, 573, 575